GREEK LAUGHTER

This is the first book to offer an integrated reading of ancient Greek attitudes to laughter. Taking material from literature, myth, philosophy, religion and social mores, it analyses both the theory and the practice of laughter as a richly revealing expression of Greek values and mentalities. From the exuberantly laughing gods of Homeric epic to the condemnation of laughter by some early Church fathers, the subject provides a fascinating means of investigating complex features of cultural psychology. Greek society developed distinctive institutions (including the symposium and certain religious festivals) for the celebration of laughter as a capacity which could bridge the gap between humans and gods; but it also feared laughter for its power to expose individuals and groups to shame and even violence. Caught between ideas of pleasure and pain, friendship and enmity, play and seriousness, laughter became a theme of recurrent interest in various contexts. Employing a sophisticated model of cultural history, Stephen Halliwell traces elaborations of the theme in a series of important poetic and prose texts: ranging far beyond certain modern accounts of 'humour', he shows how perceptions of laughter helped to shape Greek conceptions of the body, the mind and the meaning of life.

STEPHEN HALLIWELL is Professor of Greek at the University of St Andrews. His most recent book, *The Aesthetics of Mimesis: Ancient Texts and Modern Problems* (2002), has been awarded an international prize, the 'Premio Europeo d'Estetica' for 2008.

D1521525

GREEK LAUGHTER

*A Study of Cultural Psychology from Homer
to Early Christianity*

STEPHEN HALLIWELL

CAMBRIDGE
UNIVERSITY PRESS

CAMBRIDGE UNIVERSITY PRESS
Cambridge, New York, Melbourne, Madrid, Cape Town, Singapore, São Paulo, Delhi

Cambridge University Press
The Edinburgh Building, Cambridge CB2 8RU, UK

Published in the United States of America by Cambridge University Press, New York

www.cambridge.org
Information on this title: www.cambridge.org/9780521889001

© Stephen Halliwell 2008

This publication is in copyright. Subject to statutory exception
and to the provisions of relevant collective licensing agreements,
no reproduction of any part may take place without
the written permission of Cambridge University Press.

First published 2008

Printed in the United Kingdom at the University Press, Cambridge

A catalogue record for this publication is available from the British Library

Library of Congress Cataloguing in Publication data
Halliwell, Stephen.
Greek laughter: a study of cultural psychology from Homer to early Christianity / Stephen Halliwell.
p.   cm.
Includes bibliographical references and index.
ISBN 978-0-521-88900-1 (hardback) – ISBN 978-0-521-71774-8 (pbk.)
1. Laughter – Greece – History – To 1500.   I. Title.

BF575.L3H35 2008
152.4′30938 – dc22   2008019386

ISBN 978-0-521-88900-1 hardback
ISBN 978-0-521-71774-8 paperback

Cambridge University Press has no responsibility for the persistence or
accuracy of URLs for external or third-party internet websites referred to
in this publication, and does not guarantee that any content on such
websites is, or will remain, accurate or appropriate.

Contents

v

Preface

In his characteristically bittersweet essay *Elogio degli uccelli*, 'A eulogy of birds', written in 1824, Giacomo Leopardi puts in the mouth of Amelius (a fictionalised version of Plotinus' student of that name) a set of meditations which, among other things, treat the singing of birds as a kind of laughter. This thought gives Amelius the cue for a digression on the nature of laughter itself, which he regards (in a perception so typical of Leopardi, and one which later influenced Nietzsche) as a paradoxical capacity of humans, 'the most tormented and miserable of creatures'. After pondering a number of laughter's qualities – including its strange connection with an awareness of the vanity of existence, its appearance as a sort of 'temporary madness', and its association with inebriation – Amelius gives a startling undertaking: 'but these matters I will deal with more fully in a history of laughter which I am thinking of producing . . .' ('Ma di queste cose tratterò più distesamente in una storia del riso, che ho in animo di fare . . .'), a history in which he promises to trace the intricate fortunes of the phenomenon from its 'birth' right up to the present.

This passage in Leopardi's wonderful essay is, as far as I am aware, the first place where anyone ever contemplated such a peculiar thing as a 'history of laughter'. Amelius' promise (and Leopardi's vision) is, for sure, not without irony, especially since he had earlier stated that the nature and principles of laughter can hardly be defined or explained. Yet the idea reappeared later in the nineteenth century when the Russian socialist Alexander Herzen (as quoted by Mikhail Bakhtin in his book on Rabelais) mused that 'it would be extremely interesting to write the history of laughter'. It was to be two other Russians who in the twentieth century took active steps towards converting the idea into practice. One was the folklorist Vladimir Propp, who sketched out his thoughts on laughter in more than one text and left a book on the subject unfinished at his death in 1970. The other was Bakhtin himself, who in the 1940s and later developed his now well-known (though controversial) model of carnival and the carnivalesque as a major test case of a 'culture of laughter' in which particular needs and mentalities were socially manifested. Whatever verdict might be reached on Bakhtin's specific model, it was his work more than anything else which established the possibility of addressing laughter as a fruitful topic of cultural history. And in recent decades the subject has indeed received an increasing amount of attention from historians of many periods between antiquity and the contemporary world. For all his irony, Amelius (or, rather, Leopardi) seems to have been prescient.

But what might it mean to pursue the history of one of the most familiar yet elusive of human behaviours? After all, the most influential of all approaches to laughter remains the one (itself partly of ancient ancestry) paradigmatically linked with both Bergson and Freud. This is an approach whose highest priority is the construction of general explanatory models (whether of 'humour', 'the comic' or some related category) to which history, it seems, is irrelevant. Henri Bergson's argument in *Le rire* (first published in book form in 1900) allows itself to refer to the 'essence' and 'laws' of the comic; yet despite its insistence that the 'natural environment' of laughter is the social world, it tells us virtually nothing about historical variations, shifts or tensions in the perception of what counts as 'laughable'. This absence of history, and its displacement by universalising theory, is equally a feature of Freud's 1905 book, *Der Witz und seine Beziehung zum Unbewussten* (*Jokes and their Relation to the Unconscious*). Freud, who cites Bergson's views with some approval, aspires to reduce jokes, and the pleasure they release in laughter, to a set of 'universal', 'essential' principles. (Freud was always, in part, a Platonist.) Even though sexual mores and social aggression are central to his theory, he never confronts the problem of historical variability in the operation of such factors of human behaviour. It would be ill-advised to deny that insight and stimulus can be found in the sometimes subtle observations of Bergson (for whom laughter and the comic are near-synonymous) and Freud (for whom they are not), as well as in the psychological theorising which has followed in their wake. But there is a price to be paid for dissociating psychology from history. And it is too high a price where laughter is concerned.

The present book is not, even so, exactly a 'history' of ancient Greek laughter. Like Leopardi's Amelius, I think a history of laughter is something worth imagining yet (ultimately) incapable of being written. But it is certainly vital to regard laughter as *having* a history and therefore as most rewardingly to be studied within wider investigation of cultural forms and values. Although in one respect a deeply instinctive gesture, laughter's psychological energy and vivid physical signals generate expressive protocols and habits with complex social ramifications. As regards Greek antiquity, my dominant aim in this book has been to explore both the *idea* and the *practice* of laughter, including some of its intricate entanglements with religion, ethics, philosophy, politics and other domains. It needs stressing that I have not attempted to formulate a conception of Greek 'humour', nor to analyse at length Greek theories of 'the comic', even if my arguments inevitably touch on such issues from time to time. Surprising though it may seem, comic drama in its own right plays a deliberately subordinate part in the enquiry. Even in those chapters (4, 5 and 8) where comedy does figure prominently, I offer not so much a reading of the genre *per se* as a sort of meta-reading of its relationship to broader Greek perceptions and experiences of laughter. I try to elucidate attitudes to and uses of laughter – as enacted behaviour, symbolic imagery and an object of reflective analysis – across a wide spectrum of Greek culture, from Homeric epic to the writings of Greek church fathers in the early centuries of Christianity. I am interested in Greek representations and evaluations of laughter above all where they impinge on the dialectic of cultural self-definition and conflict. Guided by such basic coordinates as pleasure and pain, friendship and enmity, honour and shame, Greeks themselves often took laughter very seriously; and we too should do so in order to enrich our understanding of their myths, their literature and their lives. And because no one has tackled the material in quite this way before, I have supplied extensive and detailed documentation, both primary and secondary, in the hope that it may enable others to assess the evidence closely for themselves.

Arguments developed in this book have been presented as papers over many years and in many places. I owe sincere thanks to hosts and audiences in Bari, Birmingham, Boston, Cambridge, Freiburg, Glasgow, Glenalmond, Grenoble, Harvard, Lecce, London, Manchester, Mannheim, New York, Nottingham, Oxford, Philadelphia, Rome, St Andrews and Syracuse for their interest, encouragement and criticism. In the later stages of the project it was a particular pleasure to share some of my ideas with the audiences of the Gaisford lecture in Oxford, May 2005 (see Halliwell (2005)), and the Roberts lecture at Dickinson College, September 2005: I am grateful to Chris Pelling and Marc Mastrangelo, respectively, for organising those events. At Dickinson, I was fortunate to have as a commentator Ralph Rosen, with whom I have enjoyed congenial exchanges on other occasions as well. Many individuals have generously sent me copies of their own, or sometimes others', work: my thanks to Mario Andreassi, Simone Beta, Bracht Branham, Christian Brockmann, Michael Clarke, Rossella Saetta Cottone, Angela Gigliola Drago, Anna Tiziana Drago, Steven Evans,

Olimpia Imperio, Melissa Lane, Dina Micalella, Jeffrey Rusten, Ineke Sluiter, Isolde Stark and Piero Totaro. The list of friends and colleagues who have helped me in various ways (including the most important of all, by challenging my ideas) is too long to present in full; but I would like to single out for warm appreciation Kai Brodersen, Herb Golder, Jon Hesk, Harry Hine, Jason König, Rosanna Lauriola, Sian Lewis, Anatoly Liberman, Nick Lowe, Giuseppe Mastromarco, Karla Pollmann, Michael Silk, Alan Sommerstein, Onofrio Vox, Peter Woodward and Bernhard Zimmermann. I am also indebted to the erstwhile Arts and Humanities Research Board (AHRB, now the AHRC) for facilitating my work on this project with a Research Leave Award in 2004. I benefited greatly at the penultimate stage of writing from encouraging comments on a complete draft from David Konstan, always a perceptive critic. Last but not least, Linda Woodward has saved me from errors with her meticulous copy-editing, and Michael Sharp at Cambridge University Press has been a supportive editor throughout.

Note to the reader

(1) Dates are BC unless otherwise indicated.

(2) The spelling of Greek names involves compromise, and therefore some inconsistency, between traditional Latinisation (which I usually prefer on grounds of familiarity) and the stricter principles of transliteration. I have tried to avoid forms that might puzzle non-specialists.

(3) The abbreviations of ancient authors' names and works for the most part follow those used in the *Oxford Classical Dictionary*; the Index of selected authors and works should also be consulted.

(4) All translations, from texts both ancient and modern, are my own unless otherwise indicated.

(5) All comic fragments are cited from *PCG* (see under Abbreviations below) unless stipulated otherwise, but '*PCG*' is normally added to fragment numbers only of minor playwrights.

(6) The names of modern scholars appearing after references to ancient texts indicate the specific editions used; this applies especially to minor authors or to texts which can be cited with different systems of numeration. The editions appear in the bibliography under the editors' names.

(7) Most miscellaneous abbreviations are self-evident, but note the following: BF = black-figure, RF = red-figure, Σ = scholia.

Abbreviations

ABV	J. D. Beazley, *Attic Black-Figure Vase-Painters* (Oxford, 1956)
ANRW	*Aufstieg und Niedergang der römischen Welt* (Berlin, 1972–)
ARV²	J. D. Beazley, *Attic Red-Figure Vase-Painters*, 2nd edn (Oxford, 1963)
CA	*Collectanea Alexandrina*, ed. J. U. Powell (Oxford, 1925)
CAG	*Commentaria in Aristotelem Graeca*, 23 vols. in 28 (Berlin, 1882–1909)
CEG	*Carmina Epigraphica Graeca*, ed. P. A. Hansen, 2 vols. (Berlin, 1983, 1989)
CPG	*Corpus Paroemiographorum Graecorum*, eds. E. L. Leutsch and F. G. Schneidewin, 2 vols. (Göttingen, 1839–51)
DGE	*Diccionario griego-español*, eds. F. R. Adrados and E. Gangutia, in progress (Madrid, 1980–)
DK	*Die Fragmente der Vorsokratiker*, eds. H. Diels and W. Kranz, 6th edn, 3 vols. (Berlin, 1952)
EGF	*Epicorum Graecorum Fragmenta*, ed. M. Davies (Göttingen, 1988)
FGrH	*Die Fragmente der griechischen Historiker*, ed. F. Jacoby (Berlin/Leiden, 1923–58)
FHG	*Fragmenta Historicorum Graecorum*, ed. C. Müller, 5 vols. (Paris, 1841–70)
GELNT	*A Greek-English Lexicon of the New Testament and other Early Christian Literature*, eds. W. F. Arndt and F. W. Gingrich, 2nd edn (Chicago, 1979)
IEG	*Iambi et Elegi Graeci*, ed. M. L. West, 2nd edn, 2 vols. (Oxford, 1989–92)
IG	*Inscriptiones Graecae* (Berlin, 1873–)
LfgrE	*Lexikon des frühgriechischen Epos*, eds. B. Snell *et al.* (Göttingen, 1955–)

LIMC	*Lexicon Iconographicum Mythologiae Classicae*, 16 vols. (Zurich, 1981–97)
LSJ	*A Greek–English Lexicon*, eds. H. G. Liddell and R. Scott, 9th edn (Oxford, 1940), with a revised supplement, ed. P. G. W. Glare (Oxford, 1996)
*OCD*³	*Oxford Classical Dictionary*, eds. S. Hornblower and A. Spawforth, 3rd edn (Oxford, 1996)
PCG	*Poetae Comici Graeci*, eds. R. Kassel and C. Austin, 9 vols. in 11 (Berlin, 1983–)
PETF	*Poetarum Elegiacorum Testimonia et Fragmenta*, eds. B. Gentili and C. Prato, vol. i, 2nd edn (Leipzig, 1988), vol. ii (Leipzig, 1985)
PG	*Patrologiae Cursus Completus. Series Graeca*, ed. J. P. Migne, 162 vols. (Paris, 1857–66)
PGL	*A Patristic Greek Lexicon*, ed. G. W. H. Lampe (Oxford, 1971)
PGM	*Papyri Graecae Magicae*, 2nd edn, eds. K. Preisendanz and A. Henrichs, 2 vols. (Stuttgart, 1973–4)
PLF	*Poetarum Lesbiorum Fragmenta*, eds. E. Lobel and D. Page (Oxford, 1955)
PMG	*Poetae Melici Graeci*, ed. D. L. Page (Oxford, 1962)
RE	*Paulys Realencyclopädie der classischen Altertumswissenschaft* (Stuttgart, 1893–1978)
SEG	*Supplementum Epigraphicum Graecum* (Leiden/Amsterdam, 1923–)
SH	*Supplementum Hellenisticum*, eds. H. Lloyd-Jones and P. Parsons (Berlin, 1983)
SIG	*Sylloge Inscriptionum Graecarum*, ed. W. Dittenberger, 3rd edn, 4 vols. (Leipzig, 1915–24)
SSR	*Socratis et Socraticorum Reliquiae*, ed. G. Giannantoni, 4 vols. (Naples, 1990)
SVF	*Stoicorum Veterum Fragmenta*, ed. H. von Arnim, 3 vols. (Leipzig, 1903–5), with index vol., ed. M. Adler (Leipzig, 1924)
ThesCRA	*Thesaurus Cultus et Rituum Antiquorum*, 5 vols. (Los Angeles, 2004–5)
TrGF	*Tragicorum Graecorum Fragmenta*, eds. B. Snell *et al.*, 5 vols. in 6 (Göttingen, 1971–2004)

CHAPTER I

Introduction: Greek laughter in theory and practice

Laughter . . . is a reflex that characterises man alone and has its own history . . . We do not laugh now as people once laughed . . . a definition [of the comic and of laughter] can be only historical.

Vladimir Propp

Men have been wise in many different modes, but they have always laughed the same way.

Samuel Johnson[1]

NATURE AND CULTURE, BODIES AND MINDS

When ancient Greeks laughed, did they take themselves to be yielding to an instinct rooted in their animal bodies or displaying a characteristic they shared with their gods? Might they have imagined, for that matter, that they were doing *both* those things at the same time?

In broaching such large, scene-setting questions, it is hard to avoid taking initial orientation from Aristotle's famous obiter dictum in the *Parts of Animals* that humans are the only living things capable of laughter. This proposition – sometimes replaced in antiquity, and even conflated (as it occasionally still is), with the logically distinct idea of laughter as part of the *essence* of humans – addresses an issue which has continued to provoke debate right up to the contemporary study of animal behaviour.[2] It would be

---

[1] First epigraph: Propp (1984) 127 (first published in Russian, 1939). Propp and Bakhtin (ch. 4, 204–6) were exact contemporaries: I am grateful to Anatoly Liberman for checking Propp's posthumously published book on laughter (see Liberman's introduction in Propp (1984) xvii) and confirming that it cites Bakhtin for the idea of unrestrained, 'Rabelaisian' laughter; I am not aware of references to Propp in Bakhtin's work. Second epigraph: Johnson, *Life of Cowley*, in Brady and Wimsatt (1977) 365; quoted slightly inaccurately in Halliwell (1991a) 279.

[2] For Aristotle's claim (*Part. An.* 3.10, 673a8) and its later history, see ch. 6, 315–16. Critchley (2002) 25, paraphrasing the tradition, slides from laughter as 'proper to' humans (i.e., in Aristotelian terms, an exclusive capacity of theirs) to laughter as 'essentially human'. Aristotle never asserts the latter, though he does regard laughter as belonging to a fully human life: ch. 6, 307–31.

unreasonable to expect Aristotle, for all his wide-ranging biological interests, to have anticipated the findings of the modern science of ethology, which claims to identify among other primates (and possibly elsewhere too) forms of behaviour that are physically and even socially analogous to laughter (and smiling) and that can help shed light on the evolution of these types of body language among humans.[3] But it is nevertheless surprising that Aristotle did not qualify his predication of human uniqueness in this respect. At a simple level of what might be called 'folk ethology', others in antiquity certainly reached divergent conclusions. It is true that the only direct denial of the Aristotelian tenet is found in the Christian Lactantius, writing in Latin in the early fourth century AD. But Lactantius' assertion that laughter can be observed not only in the appearance of the ears, mouths and eyes of certain animals (he is presumably thinking, in part at least, of dogs) but also in their capacity to play both with humans and among themselves, can hardly have been original with him.[4] In fact, even during Aristotle's own lifetime Xenophon, an aficionado of hunting with dogs (a favourite activity of many wealthy Greeks), has no difficulty in detecting 'smiles' on the faces of eager hounds. Nor does he feel any need to elaborate the point, which must therefore have been readily intelligible to his readership, even though it is only many centuries later, in the ornate didactic poetry of Oppian, that dogs are again depicted in such terms.[5] Aelian can similarly adduce the smiles of oxen in a way which suggests an uncontroversial perception that would probably have been familiar to farmers and others.[6] For the purposes of imaginative assimilation rather than literal description, it was easy to picture certain kinds of animal behaviour as redolent of laughter. The Philocleon of Aristophanes' *Wasps*, for instance, when prancing around scoffing drunkenly at his fellow-symposiasts, is compared to a frisky little ass. The accused in a fourth-century Athenian court case (to be considered

[3] For modern ethological literature, and some traces of 'folk ethology' in antiquity, see Appendix 1. The Aristotelian commentator David (c. AD 600), *In Isag.* 204.14–16, wrongly claims that Aristotle called the heron capable of laughter in *Hist. An.*

[4] Lactantius, *Div. Inst.* 3.10.2, arguing that the only uniquely human property is knowledge of god; but he assumes the familiarity of 'only humans laugh'.

[5] Xen. *Cyn.* 4.3, where the (rare) verb ἐμμειδιᾶν reinforces the adj. φαιδρός, 'bright', at 4.2 (cf. n. 33 below); the whole context, 4.2–4, posits expressive body language in animals (as does Ael. *NA* 5.25; cf. next note). See *ibid.* 5.4 for the kindred idea of animal *play* (hares frolicking in a full moon); cf. the 'bright' (γαληνές) face ascribed to fawning dogs at ps.-Arist. *Physiog.* 6.811b37–8, with Clarke (2005a) 43–4 for affinities with smiling. Oppian, *Cyn.* 1.507, 523, 4.363 uses καγχαλάω (ch. 2 n. 15) of the laughter-like excitement of hunting dogs; cf. the same verb of deer at *Cyn.* 2.237 (with 246 for a smile-like look). Oppian, *Hal.* 2.626 (different author?) has jackals 'laughing' over dead stags.

[6] Ael. *NA* 6.10. Aelian's ascription of scorn (*katagelan*) to the hare watching its pursuers, *ibid.* 13.14.32, is not directly facial but reads a mental state into body posture; cf. n. 91 below on owls.

in more detail later) is alleged to have displayed exultant derision for his battered enemy by performing a crowing cock song-and-dance around him. The epigrammatist Meleager makes a disturbed lover hear (with intense vexation) the early cock-crow itself as the bird's voicing of pleasurable laughter. And at least some people thought they heard laughter-like sounds in the neighing of horses.[7] To such images can be added the suggestive vignettes of Aesopic fables, in which laughter or smiles are commonly ascribed to animals. Does this convention of the genre depend only on anthropomorphising fantasy, or might it obliquely reflect habits of thinking which were more diffusely present in dealings with animals? Patchy though the overall evidence may be, not everyone was as confident as Aristotle of excluding laughter from the expressive repertoire of species other than humans.[8]

When we turn from animals to the other end of the spectrum, the situation is rather clearer. Aristotle himself, it is worth noting, held a larger world-view in which there was no room for belief in laughter as a trait of the divine.[9] For him, therefore, laughter was one of the things which helped define a peculiarly human position in the world, suspended between the domains of animals and gods. But most Greeks thought otherwise. The anthropomorphic traditions of Greek religion left no doubt that laughter (and smiles) had an important place in the divine realm; a deity incapable of laughter was the exception, not the rule.[10] The remarkable Homeric images,

---

[7] Philocleon: *Wasps* 1305–6; cf. n. 91 below, with ch. 4, 209–10, and the 'laughing' ass in the next note (Ar. *Wasps* 179 has the opposite, a comically 'weeping' donkey). Conon's cock-crowing dance: 34–5 below. Meleager: *Anth. Pal.* 12.137.4 (cf. n. 89 below). Horses: Eutecnius, *Para. Opp.* 12.28 Tüselmann (unknown date) describes a horse's neigh as 'like a laugh of shared pleasure in its rider' (οἷα δὴ προσγελῶν ἐκείνῳ καὶ συνηδόμενος); cf. Appendix 1 n. 24. Surprisingly, no ancient text ascribes laughter as such to monkeys/apes, despite their supposedly intrinsic risibility (ch. 6 n. 94; cf. 31, 41 below on Semonides' monkey woman), though Galen, *Usu part.* 1.22 (3.80 Kühn) pictures one as a playmate of children; in the Renaissance, by contrast, Erasmus ascribes laughter to dogs and monkeys: Screech (1997) 3. McDermott (1938) 181 (no. 123), 240–1 (no. 337), detects smiling apes in visual artefacts; cf. 180 (no. 119), 211 (no. 288). But a simian's curving mouth is no guarantee of a smile: see e.g. Robinson (1931) pl. 59.420A (with 99, no. 420).

[8] Laughter/smiles in animal fables: e.g. Aesop 39, 150, 226, 232 Perry, Babrius 94.6, 106.29, 107.9, 140.7; cf. the anthropomorphic laughter of donkey and ostrich in Job 39.8, 17. Akin to fable is occasional depiction of animal laughter in art: see Lissarrague (2000) 110 for a terracotta mirthful ass. On the other hand, Lucian's mockery of Peripatetic belief in the human uniqueness of laughter, *Vit. Auctio* 26, depends satirically on the *redundancy* of pointing out that an ass cannot laugh; cf. his play on this (and the equivalence of laughter and neighing/braying: n. 7 above) at *Asin.* 15. For a tangential link between laughter and camels, see Appendix 1 n. 14.

[9] Aristotle frames the divine in terms of contemplative blessedness, not practical activity (a conception of the gods he finds 'ridiculous'): *EN* 10.8, 1178b8–22.

[10] The goddess Adrasteia/Nemesis is *skuthrōpos*, 'grim-faced', in Men. fr. 226, therefore without smiles/laughter (cf. n. 101 below): this symbolises implacable vengefulness; but Lucian, *Apol.* 6

in both the *Iliad* and *Odyssey*, of collectively 'unquenchable' or irrepressible laughter among the Olympians – laughter, what's more, directed by gods against *other* gods – are the most concentrated testimony to the character of those traditions. But they were far from unique. In addition to other passages in the Homeric poems themselves, depictions of divine laughter appear in numerous texts and in all periods of Greek literature; they will figure frequently in subsequent chapters of this book. Nor is the idea of the laughter of gods exclusively 'literary'. As Chapter 4 will explain in detail, it informs a great deal of practical Greek religion, helping to explain the ethos of many of its festivals and rituals, not least those in honour of Demeter and Dionysus, deities both thought of as capable of laughter in rather distinctive ways. The very concept of religious festivity (ἑορτάζειν, the enactment of *heortai*) is closely entwined in Greek thought with notions of 'play', celebration and laughter; and it makes no sense to worship the gods in this way unless they themselves can somehow appreciate and share the spirit of laughter, as Homer and others had shown them doing. The grip of this religious mentality in the archaic and classical periods induced Plato, in a gesture of radical theological revisionism (and bodily puritanism), to argue the need specifically to repudiate belief in gods who were 'lovers of laughter' (*philogelōtes*) and who could be 'overcome' by it.[11] Some of Plato's later followers in turn resorted to allegorical readings of Homer to resolve what they saw as the problem. Yet the tenacity of the older model of the divine within Greek culture was such that Choricius of Gaza, a rhetorician working in the sixth century AD against a mixed background of pagan and Christian values, felt able to claim that laughter, alongside rationality (*logos*), was actually one of two features which humans shared with the divine and which separated them from 'irrational nature', i.e. from other animals.[12] So Choricius, as it happens, half agrees and half disagrees with Aristotle.

The uncertain, problematic relationships between human laughter and the behaviour of animals and gods supply useful preliminary illustrations of the kind of issues which must be faced in an attempt to construct a historically nuanced perspective on the status of laughter (and the distinct but closely kindred phenomenon of smiling) in ancient Greek culture. But they also provide an initial indication of how we can obtain a firmer handle on the elusiveness of laughter by situating it within larger frameworks

---

allows her vindictive derision (*katagelan*). Other instances of non-laughing deities, such as Hom. *Od.* 8.344 (ch. 2, 82–3), are exceptional.

[11] *Rep.* 3.388e–389a.

[12] Choric. *Apol. Mim.* 93–4 (Foerster), with Reich (1903) 204–30 on the work as a whole. A modern attempt to connect laughter and rationality can be found in Scruton (1983) 153–65.

of cultural meaning, value and symbolism. This entails accepting that laughter, though an evolved means of somatic expression with well entrenched, if complex, underpinnings in the brain, has its own history.[13] It is subject, in both its physical coding and its psychological implications, to the social, ethical, religious and other pressures of particular times and places. What makes laughter, and the patterns of body language in which it shapes itself, exceptionally challenging but also rewarding to study is its double-sided character. It exists at the interface, so to speak, between body and mind, between instinct and intention. Though by definition inarticulate (i.e. non-linguistic), it is nonetheless a means of communication (i.e. often *para*linguistic) and can be far-reaching in the attitudes and values it embodies. Though often resistant to cognitive understanding, it is woven into ordinary life in ways which entangle it with such fundamental concerns as sex, religion, ethnicity, politics, food and drink. Though typically fugacious in its vocal and facial manifestations, it can function as a highly charged medium of personal and social relationships. Though sometimes involuntary, it can be either encouraged or inhibited not just according to individual inclination but under the influence of education, mores and ideology. As the anthropologist Mary Douglas has maintained, while part of a 'universal language of bodily interruptions' laughter nonetheless becomes subject to varying cultural thresholds of tolerance.[14] And all this means that we can look for its historical traces and cultural significance even where its immediate sounds and appearances have vanished.

This book will attempt to demonstrate, then, that it is possible and worthwhile to write parts of the cultural history of ancient Greek laughter, *gelōs*, including its negative counterparts, agelastic and antigelastic conduct.[15] To do so involves charting the place of laughter within habits of

---

[13] Neurological research shows various brain pathways are involved in physical laughter *per se* and in its expressive accompaniment to cognitive/affective states; hence the possibility that the act and the states can come apart (cf. ch. 2, 93–6, for a Homeric case in point). Damasio (2004) 74–9, 307–8, Ramachandran (1998b) 199–211 offer brief accounts; more technical discussion in Arroyo *et al.* (1993), McCullagh *et al.* (1999), Wild *et al.* (2003). For the idea of laughter's 'history', see my Preface; cf. Pfister (2002a) v–ix.

[14] Douglas (1975) 86–8. The (in)voluntariness of laughter is a sliding scale, not an either/or distinction: cf. Ruch and Ekman (2001) 427–8; Winn (2001) 424 garbles the point. At one extreme stand pathological seizures *vel sim.*: Provine (2000) 165–71; cf. ch. 2 n. 105. Less extreme are barely controllable outbursts (cf. ch. 6 n. 138, with 8–10 below). At the opposite end lies conscious manipulation, e.g. 'forced' or sarcastic laughter. In between are many gradations. Smiling, except as pathological rictus, is usually more under (semi-conscious) control than laughter: see Provine (2000) 49–53; Kris (1964) 226–9 reads smiling psychoanalytically as a controlled (and potentially deceptive) substitute for laughter.

[15] In addition to employing 'gelastic' as a general adj. for laughter-related/arousing behaviour, I use 'agelastic' (with the noun 'agelast': see nn. 100–2 below) to denote 'non-laughing', 'avoiding laughter',

behaviour, forms of life, and systems of value. The enterprise is made more feasible by the fact that laughter happens to be a subject on which such eloquent and reflective types of ancient discourse as poetry, philosophy and rhetoric have important things to say and to show. It is an object of representation and evaluative scrutiny in a perhaps surprisingly large range of Greek texts, from Homer to late antiquity.[16] Laughter mattered to Greek minds and lives in multiple respects – stretching, as we have already glimpsed in rudimentary outline, from their views of the body to their conceptions of the divine. It is remarkable, for instance, that virtually every major school of Greek philosophy, and many of its individually most notable practitioners, took up an explicit stance towards the uses (and/or abuses) of laughter, something that could hardly be claimed about most modern philosophy and philosophers. Why this is so should be left to emerge gradually and cumulatively, not least in Chapters 6–7. But one can anticipate to the extent of saying that laughter seems to have a set of intricate connections with the broader schemes of value – of friendship and enmity, honour and shame, pleasure and self-discipline, freedom and servility – that structure the dominant modes of expression, as well as the underlying tensions, of Greek culture. Whether, when, at whom/what, and how to laugh (if at all) constitutes a cluster of questions whose repercussions spread out into many vital regions of Greek thought and action.

To clarify how I propose to bring such questions to bear on the representation of laughter in ancient texts, I should at once add two notes of caution, one of which will impose limitations on, while the other enlarges, the scope of the enquiry. The chief limitation is that this book is not centrally about ancient views or senses of 'humour', nor about ancient theories of 'the comic'. No hermetically sealed definition of humour is possible, especially in view of the historical evolution of the term and the difficulty of establishing a consistent lexicon of humour across languages, both ancient and modern. A relatively neutral approach to the subject might demarcate humour as above all the sphere of behaviour which aims self-consciously at arousing amusement in others 'for its own sake', which is not to deny that humour can also be used for further purposes such as persuasion, ingratiation, deception or the exercise of power. But much argument over the

---

and 'antigelastic' to characterise a stronger, principled antipathy. (There is no Greek precedent for this last usage; in its only occurrence, ἀντιγελᾶν means 'laugh back in retaliation': ch. 10 n. 16.) Note also the adj. *misogelōs*, laughter-hating, Alex. Aet. fr. 7.2 *CA*, *Vita Eur.* 5 (ch. 6 n. 16).

[16] My enquiry extends, selectively, down to the fourth century AD, with occasional glimpses beyond. For continuing/evolving traditions of laughter in medieval Byzantium, see the stimulating perspective of Magdalino (2007).

definition of humour in any case moves beyond the level of the descriptive to that of a *normative* understanding of preferred/prohibited means, (un)acceptable objects, and (in)appropriate contexts for the creation of amusement. If humour, on any standard account, typically includes joke-telling, banter, many forms of play-acting and playfulness, as well as the basic materials of comic performances (from, say, solo mimicry to fully staged comic drama), this book will certainly mention numerous ancient situations to which such categories of behaviour are relevant. My aim in doing so, however, will not be to pursue the concept of 'humour' *per se*, but to tackle the wider psychological, ethical and cultural concerns which such behaviour generates within ancient frameworks of perception. Even comedy itself, and the concomitant theorising of 'the comic' (or 'the laughable') in antiquity, does not lie at the centre of my interests. When I do discuss comic drama directly (particularly in Chapters 4, 5 and 8), my focus will be fixed on what it can help us discern about larger ancient evaluations of laughter as a set of social behaviours.[17]

If what has just been said underlines that the phenomena of laughter include much more than the phenomena of humour, it is equally important to stress that my investigation will not be narrowly confined to actual occurrences of physical laughter, or even to the physically distinct but behaviourally cognate phenomenon of smiling.[18] I shall also be persistently interested in metaphorical and metonymic laughter, a category which embraces all the ways in which gelastic vocabulary and symbolism can be drawn on to convey ethical and social judgements or to characterise states of mind. Whereas much 'humour' is incorporated in specific kinds of practice or marked language games (jokes, banter, anecdotes, mimicry, play-acting and so forth), metonymic laughter is a much more fluid factor in social behaviour. One immediate illustration of this is the notion of implicit or 'concealed' laughter as an index of superiority, contempt, or deception. Someone can be thought of as 'laughing at' another even when not manifesting any of the bodily signs of laughter. In special instances,

---

[17] Turk (1995), esp. 309–12, touches on the difference between the humorous/comic and a diffuse 'culture of laughter' (German *Lachkultur*), the latter a Bakhtinian notion; cf. Bausinger (1992). As early as 1725–6 Hutcheson distinguished between laughter and ridicule: Hutcheson (1997) 230 (with 235 for historical shifts in 'what is counted ridiculous'). A pithy case for taking a definition of humour to be impossible (because of the intrinsic uncertainty of 'when and where we might laugh') is made by Cohen (2001) 380. Cf. Liberman (1995): an interesting set of data, but insufficient to support his larger historical claims. On the Greek side, Rapp (1947–8) is mostly flimsy. Plebe (1956) attempts a broad correlation of Greek laughter in life and comedy.

[18] On the relationship between laughter and smiles, see Appendix 1. For economy of expression, I sometimes allow 'laughter' to cover laughter and/or smiling; but the distinction is always explicit where it matters.

laughter can be entirely 'in the mind', thus invisible on the face. A wonderfully emblematic case in point is the 'sardonic' smile of Odysseus, within the cunning secrecy of his *thumos* (his motivational 'heart'), in Book 20 of the *Odyssey*.[19] Metaphorical laughter can be a potent vector in various kinds of social interaction.

In both its literal and metaphorical forms, laughter can serve as an expression of individual and cultural mentalities. The material addressed in this book cuts across the fields of education, politics, law, religion, war, philosophy, sex, sport, drinking and more besides. It turns out, accordingly, that to ask questions about the causes, uses and consequences of laughter is always to engage with issues 'bigger' than laughter's strictly physiological dimensions. That is not to say, however, that the somatic basis of laughter is not significant in its own right. The fact that people laugh (to varying degrees) 'with' their bodies – in the tautening of facial muscles, the staccato rhythms of breathing-cum-vocalisation (χα χα χα being the Greek equivalent of 'ha ha ha'), and often in accompanying gestures of physical excitement (e.g. clapping)[20] – is a prominent consideration in many of the themes I shall be exploring in the following chapters, from the depiction of the violently derisive suitors of the *Odyssey* to early Christianity's imprinting of laughter with the sinfulness of corporeal (even diabolical) disorder and dissolution.

The strongest laughter, in fact, is a physically arresting occurrence. It possesses a convulsiveness which takes over the person and defies restraint; its force can be so intense that one may even die of it – literally, as well as metaphorically.[21] The physiology of laughter undoubtedly received some

---

[19] 20.301–2: see ch. 2, 93. Hidden laughter is recognised from a modern theoretical perspective by Zijderveld (1996) 42. On 'sardonic', see n. 21 below.

[20] χα χα χα: *PGM* XIII.162, 473 (*P. Leiden* J395: n. 32 below); cf. Arnould (1990) 144. Eur. *Cyc.* 157 is not, *pace* Eirez Lopez (2000) 16, a formal vocalisation of laughter, though an actor could easily have added one; Ar. *Peace* 1066 is a stylised annotation; Hdas. 3.93 is probably somewhat different (Headlam (1922) 160–1). Laughter accompanied by clapping: e.g. Ion Chi. *FGrH* 392 F6 (ch. 3, 108–9), the Tarentines' glee over an obscene insult at Dion Hal. *Ant. Rom.* 19.5.3, and Athanasius' image of sympotic mirth at *Ctr. Ar.* 1.4 (26.20 *PG*); cf. Pan at *Hom. Hymn* 19.37.

[21] Literal death by laughter is claimed for the painter Zeuxis (amused by his own depiction of an old woman) in the Roman grammarian Festus (from Verrius Flaccus) *s.v.* Pictor, Reinach (1921) 192, no. 211; for Rembrandt's possible reflection of this story in the late Cologne 'self-portrait', see Blankert (1973), Blankert (1997) 34–40, with Schwartz (1985) 354–7 for good ills.; cf. ch. 7 n. 23 for a different identification. Other reputed victims: the comic poet Philemon (test. 1, 5 *PCG*, with ch. 9 n. 24), a legend echoed in Rabelais *Gargantua* 1.20 (cf. Bakhtin (1968) 408–9); the mime-writer Philistion (*Suda s.v.* Φιλιστίων); the philosopher Chrysippus (ch. 6 n. 103). Baudelaire (1976) 155 recalls the latter (the editor's note, 1348, is confused). Cf. Joubert (1980) 61–2, 131–3 for Renaissance thoughts on the subject, Karle (1932/3) 876 for comparative material, and Provine (2000) 182–4 for modern cases. Different is 'laughter' as reflex of (fatal) chest wounds: ch. 6 n. 140. So too is dying with a 'sardonic' grimace (cf. ch. 2 n. 100) after eating poisonous herbs, e.g. Dio Chrys. 32.99, Paus.

close attention in the ancient world. The evidence for such enquiries is at least as old as the *Problemata* produced in Aristotle's Lyceum.[22] But as it happens the most elaborate remarks on the subject in the Greek tradition are preponderantly from late antiquity, and some of the most notable are formulated by those Christian writers whose antigelastic moral agenda will form the subject of my final chapter. In a passage of impressively scandalised fervour in one of his homilies on Ecclesiastes, Gregory of Nyssa rails against the 'madness' (*paranoia*) of laughter, which he says is 'neither a form of reason nor an act with any purpose', and which he proceeds to describe in a *tour de force* of distaste as involving 'an unseemly bodily loosening, agitated breathing, a shaking of the whole body, dilation of the cheeks, baring of teeth, gums and palate, stretching of the neck, and an abnormal breaking up of the voice as it is cut into by the fragmentation of the breath'.[23] Close (not to say fixated) observations such as these could coexist with more fanciful convictions about physiological mechanisms (in the intestines, chest and blood) underlying laughter. But there is a recurrent moralising emphasis on ideas of bodily loosening, opening and excitation.[24]

10.17.13, anon. *Anth. Pal.* 7.621, or the related notion of dying 'laughing' from a poisonous spider's bite at Strabo 11.4.6; Timaeus *FGrH* 566 F64 traces sardonic laughter to a different context of death (human sacrifice to Cronus on Sardinia). *Metaphorically* 'dying from laughter': Hom. *Od.* 18.100 (ch. 2 n. 94), Ar. *Clouds* 1436, Pl. *Euthd.* 303b (ch. 6, 290), Plut. *Mor.* 54d, Lucian, *Iup. Trag.* 31 (ch. 9, 429); cf. Aretaeus, *De causis* 1.7.8. Ar. *Frogs* 1089 is different (ch. 2 n. 5).

[22] Ps.-Arist. *Probl.* 11.13, 900a24, 11.15, 900b7–14; cf. ch. 6 n. 143. Cic. *De Or.* 2.235, with irony (ch. 7 n. 25), suggests that no progress had been made understanding laughter's physiology.

[23] Greg. Nys. *Hom. in Eccl.* 2 (44.645 PG): διάχυσις δὲ σώματος ἀπρεπὴς καὶ πνεύματος κλόνος καὶ βρασμὸς ὅλου τοῦ σώματος καὶ διαστολὴ παρειῶν καὶ γύμνωσις ὀδόντων τε καὶ οὔλων καὶ ὑπερῴας αὐχένος τε λυγισμὸς καὶ φωνῆς παράλογος θρύψις συνεπικοπτομένης τῇ κλάσει τοῦ πνεύματος. (The first phrase is printed as διάλυσις δὲ στόματος, 'opening of the mouth', in *PG*; but see text and apparatus in McDonough and Alexander (1962) 310.) For βρασμός (shaking/'boiling'), cf. ch. 10 n. 104. See next note for another passage from Gregory, with Baconsky (1996) 181–4 on both texts. Laughter later became a distinctive interest of Renaissance physiology/medicine: e.g. Joubert (1980) 47–62. For a summary of respiratory and other components of laughter, see Ruch and Ekman (2001) 432–3, 439–40.

[24] Simplic. *In Epict. Ench.* 41 (Hadot), calling laughter an 'overflow' (ὑπερέκχυσις) of exhilaration, mentions 'swollen' breathing and quasi-bubbling vocalisation. Heightened breathing is implied in laughing νειόθεν, i.e. from deep inside the chest (a 'belly laugh'), at Lucian, *Peregr.* 7 (ch. 9, 464), and 'holding back' laughter in the chest, Ap. Rhod. *Argon.* 4.1723 (ch. 6 n. 138); cf. laughter in/from the 'heart', ch. 2 n. 34. Other physiological references to laughter: Basil, *Reg. fus.* 17 (guffawing and over-excitation: 31.961 *PG*, with ch. 10, 514–15); Greg. Naz. *Carm.* 37.886.2–3 *PG* ('loosening' of the face), 37.953.11 *PG* (shaking cheeks, increased heartbeat); Greg. Nys. *Hom. opif.* 12 (44.160 *PG*; opening of bodily channels; agitation of intestines, esp. the liver); and the very late (seventh century AD?) Meletius med. *Nat. hom.* 44 Cramer (from intestines to face). Further Christian evidence in ch. 10 n. 104. For physiognomy's attention to laughter/smiles (nothing in the oldest text, ps.-Arist. *Physiogn.*), see ps.-Polemon, *Physiogn.* 19 Foerster (ὑπογελᾶν of a shifty look in the eyes; cf. ch. 6 n. 107), 20 (laughing eyes associated with deception/malice; smiling, watery eyes indicate justice, gentleness etc.), and the adaptation of Polemon in Adamantius, *Physiogn.* 1.4 (playful laughter-lovers, *philogelōtes*), 1.17 (distinguishing laughter in the eyes and on the whole face; cf. 1.20); for laughter

Even before the impingement of Christian values, the ethical traditions of Greek paganism placed so much weight on self-control and the capacity to resist (excessive) pleasure that the sheer physicality of laughter could create a presumption of moral danger.[25] It is no accident that Thersites, a symbolic figure of ridicule incarnate from Homer onwards, receives an exceptionally full physical description in the *Iliad* that seems to match up his ugliness with the subversive unruliness of his bent for mockery. And yet even in this domain ambiguity is always present. To take the other side of the Homeric coin, and to rephrase the questions posed at the start of the present chapter: if the gods themselves, with their special bodies, could give way to 'unquenchable laughter', how could such yielding be always or altogether bad? The physicality of laughter is never in itself the whole story and can only be judged when laughter is placed within contexts of social meaning.

The interpretation of laughter, then, requires attention to the close but not always transparent relationship between corporeal signals and the 'affective surges' which prompt and are conveyed by them.[26] Yet as soon as we (or the Greeks) ask what kind of affect or emotion laughter embodies, the complexity of its psychology, and hence the cultural complexity of its uses, demands to be acknowledged. Henri Bergson's claim that laughter is 'normally' accompanied by a *lack* of feeling or affect ('l'*insensibilité* qui accompagne d'ordinaire le rire') is at best a narrowing of focus to one kind of laughter, at worst a theoretical screening out of a mass of divergent evidence.[27] All attempts, indeed, to construct comprehensive theories of laughter, whether in direct relation to the explication of humour/comedy or within a wider frame of reference, are radically misconceived. There is no cogent reason to suppose that laughter erupts from, or is reducible

---

in the eyes, cf. Appendix 1 n. 29. See now the extensive reappraisal of the Polemonian tradition in Swain (2007). Differently, Anon. med. *Nat. hom.* 2.1–3.1 (Ideler) explains why some people enjoy laughing by reference to purity of blood: i.e., in humoral terms, they are 'sanguine'. Ps.-Hippoc. *Epist. Ptol. hom. fab.* p. 281 (Ermerins) similarly connects a predisposition to laughter with pure blood and good health (cf. n. 39 below).

[25] Goldhill (1995) 14–20 stresses a threat to self-control as an important strand in Greek concerns about laughter. The claim of Garland (1995) 76 that 'laughter in antiquity knew no moral boundaries' (*à propos* mockery of physical sufferings; cf. ch. 2 n. 30) occludes numerous considerations traced in this book.

[26] The psychological implications of laughter's physical forcefulness are central to Plessner (1941); cf. the reflection of his views in Critchley (2002) 7–9.

[27] Bergson (1975) 3 (his itals.); cf. *ibid.* 4: the comic involves 'une anesthésie momentanée du coeur' and is addressed solely to the intelligence. Translation in Sypher (1980) 63–4. Anthropological material which undermines Bergson's theory can be found in e.g. the Amazonian case study of Overing (2000); cf. the general perspective of Driessen (1997). De Sousa (1987) 287–95 offers philosophical objections to Bergson's view.

to, a single type of feeling, mood, or psychic state. Laughter, we might say (adapting a remark of Wittgenstein's on Freud's theory of jokes), 'has a rainbow of meanings'. Thus the 'canonical' modern triad of laughter theories (or, perhaps preferably, theories of humour) – those of superiority, incongruity and release – all fail as monolithic explanations of the full gamut of data to be accounted for, however illuminating they may be where subsets of the data are concerned.[28] They fail not only because of their unsustainably totalising ambition, but also because they isolate psychology from culture. No one in antiquity quite aspired to a grand theory of this kind, though some thinkers offered definitions of, or generalising observations on, 'the laughable' (τὸ γελοῖον).[29] Part of the interest of the mosaic of Greek testimony I put together in this book lies, I believe, in its demonstration of a widespread, frequently debated awareness of the difficulty of pinning down the volatile workings of laughter. Greek representations of laughter revolve around a sense of its unstable association with both positive (amiable, cooperative) and negative (hostile, antagonistic) emotions, with (innocent) 'play' and socially disruptive aggression, with the taking of pleasure and the giving of pain, with the affirmation of life and the fear of death (archetypally thought of as the kingdom of the '*un*smiling' and the laughter-*less*).[30] These polarities will be expounded further in various parts of this book. But even these powerfully dialectical contrasts, which offer a corrective to sometimes one-sided modern models of the relationship of

---

[28] Wittgenstein's remarks on Freud's theory: Moore (1959) 316–17. Lucid appraisals of the three main theories of laughter/humour in Lippitt (1994), (1995a), (1995b). Cf. e.g. Levinson (1998), Morreall (1983) 15–37, the latter's own theory (38–59) being a pragmatic synthesis of the other three; from a classical angle, see Robson (2006), esp. 76–94. The 'superiority' theory, though still thriving (Buckley (2003)), was dismantled as early as Hutcheson (1997; orig. 1725–6), esp. 226–31, but his own incongruity theory is overstated. Lloyd Morgan (1914) pithily objects to grand theories, recognising an intrinsic indeterminacy in laughter (803); cf. Cohen (1999) 43 ('Every general theory of jokes known to me is wrong'). Milner (1972) 1 warns against 'sweeping claims', then constructs yet another compendious theory of humour. Such theorising breeds fallacies: Greenfield (2000) 156, neglecting the difference between necessary and sufficient conditions, asserts that 'the unexpected in all cases [*sic*] cause[s] amusement'. The profusion of modern theories of laughter/humour, in several languages, can be traced through bibliography C in Mader (1977) 146–52 and the annotated bibliography in Zijderveld (1983) 60–100; cf. the chronological Bibliography A by Milanezi in Desclos (2000) 591–600. Historical overviews in Hügli (1980), (2001), Winkler (1998), Preisendanz (1976).

[29] Obvious cases are Pl. *Phlb.* 48a–50b (see ch. 6, 300–1) and Aristotle's definition at *Poet.* 5.1449a32–37 (ch. 6, 326–8). For surveys of ancient approaches to 'the laughable', see Grant (1924), Plebe (1952); Süss (1920) is brief but perceptive.

[30] See ch. 7 n. 89 for 'unsmiling' death, with 384–5 and ch. 9 *passim* for death itself as a paradoxical subject/location of laughter. Snell (1960) 41 comments in passing on a Greek association between laughter and vitality (and therefore the 'godlike'); cf. Reinach (1911) 588, Rudhardt (1992) 404, though none of these scholars notes laughter's contrasting connection with destructive, even death-related forces.

laughter to aggression, do not exhaust the compass of Greek thinking on the subject, let alone the numerous inflections which that thinking exhibits in specific cultural contexts.[31]

As a further component in this sketch of a preliminary perspective, it is worth advancing (but qualifying) the claim that at the base of Greek attitudes to laughter seems to lurk a perception of it as a kind of energy of nature, almost a life-force in its own right. Highly emblematic here is the symbolism of laughter – first grievously lost, then bountifully recovered – in the myth of Eleusinian Demeter, goddess of fertility, a myth which will receive close attention in Chapter 4. It is the exception not the rule, however, for Greeks to treat laughter as itself a divinity. If it is true that the Spartans did so (I shall return to this below), the likeliest explanation is that Laconian culture externalised a nervous respect for something it knew could undermine even rigorously disciplined bodies from within. On a larger scale of things, the intriguing motif of a causal role for laughter in cosmic creation, as found in more than one Near Eastern and oriental culture, does not show up directly in Greek texts until a late date and in a cluster of arcane settings, including those of so-called gnosticism, Hermetic writings, and certain strands of Neoplatonism. A Greco-Egyptian magical papyrus of the fourth century AD contains, amidst its collection of prayers and spells, an elaborate cosmogony in which a primal god laughs and guffaws seven times, thereby bringing into being other deities, light and the rest of the cosmos. Not altogether dissimilarly, we hear that the second-century gnostic-Christian sect of Valentinians believed that light itself had been generated from the laughter of Sophia ('Wisdom'), a primordial divine energy involved in the creation of the world. Hermetic and Neoplatonic texts offer other variations on the cryptic symbolism of laughter

---

[31] In modern ethology, laughter's relationship to aggression divides opinions. At one extreme stands e.g. Eibl-Eibesfeldt (1989) 381 ('laughing is primarily aggressive'; cf. 138, 'friendly aggressive behaviour', an odd formulation). At the other, Andrew, *apud* van Hooff (1972) 239, denies evidence for laughter's aggressive motivation. Lorenz (1966) 152, 253–4 takes a *via media*, accepting aggressive origins but seeing them 'redirected' into supple social functions. In popular thinking, laughter is now often dissociated, in very un-Greek fashion, from aggression: van Hooff (1972) 229–30 cites statistical evidence. In psychology, Freud's view of (unconscious) aggression in many jokes has been widely touted; cf. e.g. Koestler (1975) 51–97, who finds an element of 'aggressive-defensive' emotion behind *all* humour/laughter: see Mulkay (1988) 96–101 for a critique. *A priori* claims are surprisingly found in Bakhtin (1968) 90 (laughter's 'idiom is never used by violence and authority'), (1986) 134 ('violence does not know laughter'): brief but shrewd criticism of Bakhtin on this point in Averintsev (1993) 16–17; cf. n. 83 below. Bloom (2004) 183–4 concisely illustrates laughter's coupling with cruelty, though his larger argument about humour lacks focus. For some Greek instances, see 25–30 below; cf. a Roman case (Mark Antony guffawing at Cicero's mutilated corpse), Plut. *Ant.* 20.

as an aspect of divine or cosmic creativity.[32] In contrast to such esoteric systems of thought, when mainstream Greek paganism ascribes laughter to its gods, not least in their Homeric moments of 'unquenchable' laughter, it does so in ways that make the anthropomorphic impetus evident. Yet such depictions leave room for a sense that the natural energies of *gelōs* are not only magnified among the Olympians but also take on something of the incomplete intelligibility of everything associated with the gods: as we shall see in the next chapter, the laughter of Homer's gods both is and is not like that of humans. Most Greeks are unlikely to have rationalised what was involved in imagining gods capable of laughter. But in living with such images of the divine they seem to have been committed to the assumption that *gelōs* was not itself an independent deity, but something more like a force of nature that could show itself both inside and outside the human world.

That cultural premise helps to inform something else found as early as Homer. This is the application of gelastic vocabulary of laughter to large-scale effects of light, sound and even fragrance in the natural world. Etymology may provide a clue to what is happening here, but it is not the exclusive key to cultural sensibilities. It appears likely (though not certain) that the Greek *gel-* root (*gelōs*: 'laughter'; *gelan*: 'laugh') has an etymological connection with ideas of brightness, lustre, or gleaming light, as though the essence of laughter were a kind of vital radiance – an idea not without some observable physical basis.[33] But where an association between laughter and light is directly attested, especially in poetry, it is hard to separate it from a

---

[32] The magical papyrus is *P. Leiden* J395 (cf. n. 20 above), *PGM* XIII.163–92, 472–524, translation in Betz (1992) 176–8, 185–6: Smith (1986) ponders the murky religious background; on Hermetic/Orphic connections, cf. Copenhaver (1992) 97–8, West (1983) 255–6; a fictionalised reference in Eco (1984) 467. Valentinian gnostics: Iren. *Haer.* 1.1.7–8 Harvey (cf. Epiphan. *Pan.* 1 410 Holl); cf. ch. 10 n. 110. For Hermetic ideas, see the equation of the sun with laughter, both human and cosmic, in an astrological epigram at Stob. 1.5.14 (cf. Scott (1924) 532), the divine smile that creates nature at Stob. 1.49.44.72, and the emergence of gleaming ethereal matter as a kind of cosmic laughter at Stob. 1.49.44.94; Norden (1924) 65–7, also citing the sun's smile of theogonic creativity at Procl. *In Remp.* 1 128 (Kroll), moots Zoroastrian affinities. Proclus *ibid.* illustrates a Neoplatonist allegoresis of laughter as symbolic of the divine; cf. ch. 2 n. 27, and see Procl. *In Prm.* 1022–3 Cousin, with Radke (2006) 321–9. Gilhus (1997) 14–22 adduces germane Near-Eastern material. While Greek culture (with rare exceptions: n. 10 above) regarded laughter as a property of Olympian gods, this does not mean, *pace* Schefold (1992) 77, that laughter '*came from* the gods' (my itals.), still less that it was itself a divinity, as Fehrle (1930) 4 suggests (followed by Propp (1984) 134). On a Spartan cult of Gelos, see 44–5 below.

[33] Physiological factors in the 'brightness' of laughter (and smiles) are briefly mentioned by Ruch and Ekman (2001) 439. On the etymology of γέλως see Chantraine (1968) 214 (cf. 12, 208), Frisk (1960–70) 1 295, Stanford (1936) 114–17, Plebe (1956) 20–1, Arnould (1990) 138–9, Buck (1949) 1106–7: Plebe, Stanford (too doctrinaire: Appendix 1 n. 16) and Verdenius (1972) 243 wrongly deny the possibility of metaphorical transference from human laughter to nature. Contrast Allen *et al.* (1936) 220 ('smiling nature is personified'), West (1966) 170–1 ('metaphor'; note his parallel from

tendency to personify the natural world, to project quasi-human features (not least, emotions) onto its more-than-human forces. Most users of most languages – even the finest poets – are not actively conscious of etymology very much of the time. In other words, it is doubtful whether we should privilege the idea of human laughter as an etymological extension from the splendour of radiant light. At least equally important is the imaginative tendency to represent nature as metaphorically manifesting, on an enlarged scale, the surging energy or emotional flaring of 'laughter'. Such usage, in any case, extends along a spectrum of tones and nuances. When at *Iliad* 19.362 the whole earth is said to have 'laughed' with the gleaming bronze of the Greeks' armour (γέλασσε δὲ πᾶσα περὶ χθών), the description is of an entire landscape, so to speak, of intensely *shimmering* light. But the whole passage conveys a complex interpenetration of the human and natural. The earth reflects a kind of exhilarated atmosphere around the immensity of the army's bronze brilliance. At the same time the notion of 'laughter' in this setting carries an ironic twist, given the death-bringing menace of the troops, now led again by the vengeance-seeking Achilles. And that irony, if discerned, is fully in keeping with the ambiguities of some other Iliadic occurrences of laughter which we shall encounter in the next chapter.

Moreover, we can see from a passage such as Hesiod, *Theogony* 40, where Zeus's palace 'laughs', i.e. resounds joyfully, with the lovely voices of the singing Muses, that whatever is surmised about the origins of such usage, its scope extends to sense modalities other than sight.[34] Since human laughter is heard as well as seen, that is not entirely surprising. But the music of the Muses can hardly be imagined as sounding just *like* laughter. Rather, Hesiod prompts us to think of it as suffused with a tonal vibrancy which both

the *Rig Veda*), Miralles (1993) 53–4; cf. Arnould (1990) 139. Clarke (2005a) 39–43 (cf. 48) rightly sees semantic complexity in such usage (including 'ambiguities of personification', 41), but his discussion is marred by the undefended translation of γελᾶν as 'smile' (cf. Appendix 1). Etymology should not be confused with semantics (despite the interesting challenge in Clarke (2005b)): Olson (1998) 195 misleadingly states that 'γελάω is *properly* "shine"' (my itals.); similarly Richardson (1974) 146; cf. Appendix 1, 523. Comparable usage, independently of etymology, is found in many languages, including Latin: Glare (1982) 1653, *s.v. ridere* 3. Simon (1961) 646–7 stresses laughter's Greek association with divine 'radiance' in general; cf. now Clarke (2005a) 45–8. Relatedly, φαιδρός ('bright') and cognates, applied to face/eyes, often imply smiles (cf. English 'beaming'): e.g. Aesch. *Agam.* 520 (with Fraenkel (1950) II 265), 725, Soph. *OC* 319, Eur. *Medea* 1043, Xen. *Cyr.* 2.2.16, Lucian, *Dial. mort.* 6.3, Philostr. maj. *Imag.* 1.8.1, 2.7.5, Longus, *Daphnis* 4.22.4, Heliod. *Aeth.* 10.7.3; cf. the extension to witticisms at Lucian, *Sat.* 13; see LSJ 1912, *s.v.* φαιδρός, with Appendix 2, 534, 545. Γάνυμαι, lit. 'gleam', is occasionally comparable, though Clarke (2005a) 39 overstates in making 'smile' a standard translation: for (rare) links of γανοῦμαι/γάνυμαι with laughter (never explicitly with smiles), see Philo, *Ebr.* 62.2, Theodoret. *Comm. psalm.* 51.9 (80.1257 PG).

[34] This passage is commonly interpreted as a metaphor for (visual) 'brilliance': e.g. Arrighetti (2000) 148 = (2006) 105. But the connection with the Muses' voices (in the instrumental dative, 41), plus the echoing of Olympus, makes it preferable to take the metaphor as predominantly sonic.

expresses and causes pleasure: laughter is here evocative of the physical, even 'atmospheric' manifestation of divine pleasure (the top of Olympus is said to reverberate with the echoes of the singing).[35] A further variant on such imagistic resonance occurs in the *Homeric Hymn to Demeter*, where the whole of the sky, earth and sea are described as having 'laughed' (ἐγέλασσε, 14) in response to the preternatural bloom and odour of the narcissus, whose growth lures Persephone into a trap where Hades will abduct her. Since the narcissus's exceptional radiance and fragrance are here depicted as a deliberate trick on Gaia's part (as a favour to Zeus, 9), the reactions of sky, earth and sea are impossible to detach from a psychologising sense of divine mood or emotion. This is a factor which is sometimes wholly benign: for example, in Theognis' picture of how, when Leto gave birth to Apollo on Delos, the whole island was filled with the smell of ambrosia, 'the expansive earth (or Earth) laughed' (ἐγέλασσε δὲ γαῖα πελώρη), and the deep sea 'rejoiced' (γήθησεν).[36] But in Persephone's story there is a further layer. Just as the earth's exhilaration at *Iliad* 19.362 paradoxically precedes imminent bloodshed, so in the *Hymn to Demeter* the divine-cum-natural world's sensitivity to a luminous, fragrant flower is inescapably shaded by the dark events about to take place within this setting of beautiful fertility.[37] Feelings of celebration and lushness are combined with undertones of danger and deception. Even in the 'mythology' of laughter, it seems, there is room for irony and ambiguity to operate.

The language of laughter (and smiles) as projected onto the world of sea, sky, meadows, flowers, spring, grapes, and more besides, has a long history in ancient literature, especially poetry.[38] More could be said about

---

[35] Cf. *Hom. Hymn* 4.420, where Apollo's laughter is an instinctively joyous response to (and almost antiphonal echo of) the sound of the lyre.

[36] Theog. 8–10; cf. *Hom. Hymn* 3.118 (earth 'smiles' as Leto prepares to give birth). In addition to *Hom. Hymn* 2.14, the sea is 'laughing' at ps.-Aesch. *PV* 90 (adapted, with licence, by Nietzsche, *Gay Science* §1), adesp. trag. 336 (*TrGF* II 105), the latter emphasising the light effects of ripples (φρίκη): Jebb (1905) 279 wrongly infers that the 'primary' sense of γελᾶν was smile, not laugh (cf. Appendix 1, 523); Clarke (2005a) 40 too is misleading on this point (cf. n. 33 above). The Platonic pun at *Rep.* 5.473c evokes the *sound* of water (hence ἐκγελᾶν, 'laugh out loud'); sound is also relevant to the plashing waves at Oppian, *Hal.* 4.334, Heliod. *Aeth.* 5.1.2. Cf. the sea-like woman's happy laughter at Semon. 7.27–8 *IEG*. In the comparison of a deceptive woman to the sea at Babrius 22.15, προσγελᾶν (if the emendation is right) possibly means 'smile': Perry (1965) 34–5, with apparatus; cf. Appendix 1, 524–5.

[37] Although female fertility is crucial here, and likewise at Theog. 8–10, Miralles (1993) 8–14 overloads the feminine/procreative implications of laughter in general; cf. his own qualifications on 23. On Demeter's laughter of (rediscovered) fertility elsewhere in the *Hymn*, see ch. 4, 161–6.

[38] The figure of speech is rare in prose, though see Theophr. *Caus. plant.* 1.12.8, 4.5.1 (διαγελᾶν of temperate weather), ps.-Arist. *Probl.* 23.1, 931a35, 23.24, 934a25–6 (ἐπιγελᾶν of the sea's narrow ripples in shallows?). Later (mostly poetic) examples, with personification and/or emotional resonance, include Sosicrates fr. 2.1 *PCG*, Ap. Rhod. *Argon.* 4.1171, (various authors) *Anth. Pal.* 5.144, 147, 6.345,

its expressiveness as sensually emotive imagery. My sole concern here has been to draw attention to how the earliest passages in which the trope occurs bring into play both a sense of more-than-human fecundity *and*, sometimes simultaneously, a perception of the dangerously charged energies of (divinely controlled) nature. How far Greek poets and their audiences consciously correlated such feelings with their understanding of human laughter itself, we cannot now say with confidence. But it is symbolically suggestive that in this magnified form laughter represents a phenomenon of complex resonance. An irreducible complexity, as I shall argue throughout this book, inheres in Greek attitudes to what takes place when human beings themselves engage in laughter.

This complexity can to some extent be broken down, as already indicated, into a set of always potentially unstable contrasts between socially and psychologically positive/negative dynamics: between friendship and enmity; between superior beings (the gods) and 'inferior' beings (including women, children, slaves and occasionally animals too); between life-affirming or life-enhancing (harmonious, mutually gratifying, fertile) and life-denying (conflictual, destructive, death-related) connotations; between health (laughter as 'therapy') and madness (laughter as embodied disorder). Take, as an immediate illustration, the last of these dichotomies. Laughter as 'therapy' has become a fashionable idea in recent years; it may therefore surprise some to learn that it certainly existed in ancient Greece. One of the more intriguing works in the Hippocratic corpus, Book 4 of *On Regimen* (*De victus ratione*), probably written somewhere around 400, deals with dreams as symptoms of health and disease. At one point, as a cure for dreams which betray mental agitation and anxiety, its author prescribes a period of rest spent 'turning the mind above all to reflections that induce laughter' (πρὸς θεωρίας, μάλιστα μὲν πρὸς τὰς γελοίας . . .). Many centuries later, a treatise by Choricius in defence of laughter in the theatre contains an anecdote relating how a private performance by a jester (*gelōtopoios*) once cured an otherwise intractable disease. In more existential (and problematic) terms, the legendary Democritus' quasi-absurdist laughter at human existence is called 'therapy' in the pseudo-Hippocratic *Epistles*

7.668, 9.363.2/6, 791, 10.2, 4, 6, 11.48, Ael. *NA* 15.5, Quint. Smyrn. *Posthom.* 2.210, 6.3, Nonnus, *Dion.* 7.344, 22.7, 38.416, Oppian, *Cyn.* 1.15, 2.580, *Hal.* 1.459, Philostr. maj. *Imag.* 1.26.2 (a painted mountain with a 'smile like a human's'), Philo, *Mut. Nom.* 162, Heliod. *Aeth.* 5.1.2 (n. 36 above), Synesius, *Hymn* 8.36 (Christian-Neoplatonist symbolism, 'laughing' aether; for a Renaissance Neoplatonist parallel, cf. Gage (1993) 78), *Anacreontea* 48.10 (West). More banally, cf. the twinkling(?) shoe in Myrinus, *Anth. Pal.* 6.254.5, with Gow and Page (1968) II 320–1. In Latin, Lucr. *DRN* 5.1396 (cf. 1.8) juxtaposes 'smiling' weather with human laughter and joking (1389–1402). Gage (1993) 77–8, without noting ancient precedents, cites an association of laughter/smiles with light in Dante.

which tell his story: though the narrative context is special and paradoxical (the other Abderites think Democritus *mad*), the broader subtext is that laughter can be good for the mind, capable of helping it cope with the pressures of life. Such notions of laughter as an antidote to both psychological and even physical ailments may have exercised a wide appeal at the level of ancient 'folk psychology'. An association of laughter with health is attested in various contexts, from the legendary (Theopompus described a people called the Eusebeis, 'Pious', who supposedly led long disease-free lives and died laughing) to the pragmatically medico-religious. More than one text relating to Asclepius, god of healing, contains a gelastic element. In a fourth-century inscription from Epidaurus the god himself laughs before curing a boy, a motif which is parodied, and given a satirical twist, in Aristophanes' *Wealth*. In a much later hymn to Asclepius' son Telesphorus, from second-century AD Athens, father and son are pictured dancing with joy (the implication of the verb *paizein*, 'play', here) at every act of healing they effect, and at the same time they are said to bring exuberant laughter to the faces of their devotees.[39]

At the opposite end of the scale, however, laughter could count as a sign of nothing less than derangement. (We saw above how the two opposites confronted one another in the legend of Democritus.) Once again, the Hippocratic corpus provides us with relevant material. The *Epidemics* contains more than one documented case study in which 'laughter' is cited as a symptom of delirium, while other Hippocratic references to the subject include both a general acknowledgement of such symptoms and a remarkable passage, from the treatise *Glands*, in which the 'grimacing smiles' (σεσηρόσι μειδιήμασι), i.e. rictus, of those suffering from brain-disease are said to be combined with 'weird hallucinations' (ἀλλοκότοισι φαντάσμασιν). This last text reminds us of the earliest and most unforgettable of all ancient couplings of laughter and madness, the macabre episode in *Odyssey* Book 20 where Athena inflicts a temporary but death-prefiguring gelastic seizure on the suitors. Even at its extremes, it would appear, the mythical imagination can intersect with the medical particulars of real life. Later mythical cases of the theme of madness manifested in laughter include the violent

---

[39] Laughter as 'therapy' (modern views: Provine (2000) 189–207): the texts cited are Hippoc. *Vict.* 4.89 (cf. Lloyd (1987) 32–7 on the work), Choric. *Apol. Mim.* 101–2 (Foerster), ps.-Hippoc. *Epist.* 17.4, 10 (ch. 7, 360–1), Theopomp. *FGrH* 115 F75c (*apud* Ael. *VH* 3.18), *IG* iv² i.121.70–1 (the Epidaurian boy) = *SIG* iii no. 1168.71–2 (cf. Buck (1955) 291, Herzog (1931) 12–13), Ar. *Wealth* 723, and the second-century AD hymn at *IG* iii i.171, with Furley and Bremer (2001) i 268–71, ii 235–9 (no. 7.7.1, lines 15–17). By contrast, the Tirynthians' laughter at Athen. 6.261d–e is a disease (*pathos*) from which they seek a 'cure': ch. 4, 155–7. Cf. the Asclepian deity Hugieia ('Health'), called πραΰγελως, 'soft-laughing', in Licymnius 769.3 *PMG*.

hallucinations of the Sophoclean Ajax (roaring with derision as he imagines himself gloating in front of the army's commanders) and the comparable frenzy of Heracles (frothing at the mouth and laughing insanely as he prepares to kill his own children) in Euripides' *Hercules Furens*. In the historical realm, Herodotus depicts the Persian Cambyses laughing (in mockery of the Egyptian cult of Apis) as he slips into derangement; later on, the historian invokes the king's mockery of religion as a specific symptom of his mania. Plutarch has a description of how Cleomenes I of Sparta, who allegedly killed himself in a crazed fit of self-mutilation, died 'laughing and grimacing' (γελῶντα καὶ σεσηρότα). In more mundane and at least semi-metaphorical terms, one of Aristotle's students, in the *Problemata*, calls all laughter a sort of 'fit' or 'derangement' (παρακοπή), apparently with reference to its physically abrupt, uncontrollable character. Plutarch can speak, with a degree of hyperbole, of the 'manic, sardonic laughter' of atheists. And we saw earlier how a polemical Christian agelast, Gregory of Nyssa, could picture the whole physiology of laughter as an irrational corporeal eruption. Other evidence could be added, but the nature of the association in question, and the scope of its influence (from medicine to myth), should by now be clear.[40]

A promoter of health, then, or a symptom of madness. In its extreme form, that contrast accentuates the instability that often surfaces in Greek attitudes to laughter. This instability, with the social volatility that follows from it, is reflected most obviously in conflicting uses of the Greek terminology of laughter, which will be extensively documented in the course of this book. A convenient example is the verb *skōptein* (plus cognates, especially the noun *skōmma*), which often means 'mock' or 'deride' in an explicitly hostile sense, but can also, contrary to what is sometimes claimed, signify 'joke' or 'jest' non-maliciously (and usually intransitively); in this latter connection, it is pertinent that *skōptein* can sometimes mean 'pretend'.[41]

---

[40] Texts cited: Hippoc. *Epidem.* 1, case 2, *Epidem.* 3, 2nd series, case 15 (ch. 7 n. 66), *Aph.* 6.53 (cf. Galen, *Hipp. aph.* 18a.90 Kühn), *Gland.* 12, Hom. *Od.* 20.345–9 (ch. 2, 93–6), Soph. *Aj.* 303 (with Garvie (1998) 153–4), Eur. *HF* 935, Hdt. 3.29, 38 (with Lateiner (1977) 177–8), Plut. *Mor.* 223c, ps.-Arist. *Probl.* 35.6, 965a14, Plut. *Mor.* 169d, Greg. Nys. *Hom. in Eccl.* 2 (n. 23 above). Arnould (1990) 227–32 discusses the theme. On the medical side, Anon. med. *Morb. acut.* 1.2 (Garofalo) makes laughter a symptom of *phrenitis*, a term whose physiological reference (intestinal/cerebral) fluctuates but which denotes a cause of derangement: Pigeaud (1981) 71–100, van der Eijk (2005) 119–22. Excessive laughter stems from *phrenitis* also at Epiphan. *Pan.* 11 26–7 Holl (= Iren. *Haer.* 1.9.3 Harvey); cf. (metaphorically) Asterius of Amaseia, *Homil.* 4.1.2, and, in the Latin tradition, Celsus, *De med.* 3.18.3, Augustine, *Serm.* 99.7. Cf., tangentially, the link between diaphragm (*phrenes*) and laughter at Arist. *Part. An.* 3.10, 673a11, ps.-Arist. *Probl.* 35.6, 965a15. Aesch. fr. 290 *TrGF*, φρὴν ἀγέλαστος (metonymy for 'mind'), may indirectly allude to laughter's basis in the chest.

[41] Kindstrand (1976) 168 wrongly claims that *skōptein* is always 'ill-natured'; likewise Cope (1877) 11 24. Traces of a similarly normative slant in ancient lexicography at Ammonius, *Vocab. diff.* 443

Conversely, even a word-group like that of *charis*, which has strong associations with graceful, pleasing, even charming 'wit', can occasionally exhibit pejorative applications of undesirable 'facetiousness', as indeed, paradoxically, can the language of 'play'.[42] What underlies these and related features of the rich Greek vocabulary for gelastic behaviour is a recurrently ambiguous evaluation of the potential of laughter – of the permeable border, as it were, between 'to laugh' (*gelan*) and 'to laugh down' in scorn (*katagelan*). When, to select a vivid instance, a passage of Dio Chrysostom describes personified avarice as never laughing or smiling (ἀγέλαστος καὶ ἀμειδία-τος) yet, in the very same sentence, as 'laughing in scorn' (καταγελῶν) at all cultured education, the language invites us to imagine not only two different kinds of facial expression (and the ironic sense in which this face both does and does not 'laugh') but also, more importantly, two quite distinct correlations between the face and the mind.[43] Nuances of this kind will be adduced frequently in my later chapters. But in order to elucidate the gelastic ambiguities which give rise to them, I want now to probe the most basic tension that characterises Greek perceptions of laughter.

THE DIALECTIC OF PLAY AND SERIOUSNESS

A distinction between the playful and serious is probably available in all languages. But the contrast acquires culturally specific features in the language and thought of ancient Greece. The Greek verb *paizein*, 'play', together with its cognates (noun *paidia*, adjective *paidikos*, etc.), is derived from *pais*, 'child', and laughter is unsurprisingly thought of as part-and-parcel of

(Nickau). Surviving usage is more complex, as LSJ *s.v.* σκώπτω indicates. Benign/playful cases include: Hdt. 2.121e.4, Xen. *Cyr.* 1.3.8, 1.3.10, 5.2.18, *Symp.* 4.29, 6.1 (contrast *episkōptein* at 1.5, and also, but ironically, 8.4), Pl. *Meno* 77a, 80a, Arist. *EN* 4.8, 1128a25, *Rhet.* 2.4, 1381a33–6, adesp. el. 27.6 (ch. 3, 114–17), Aeschin. 1.126 (but rejecting Demosthenes' self-presentation: n. 113 below), Plut. *Mor.* 46d (n. 125 below), 629e, 634a. *Skōptein* signifies 'pretend' at Xen. *Symp.* 9.5; *episkōptein* likewise at 8.4; cf. children's manipulation of their father at Theophr. *Char.* 7.8. *Skōpt-/skōmm-*terms contrast with seriousness at e.g. Isoc. *Helen* 11 (cf. Zajonz (2002) 130–1), Hdt. 2.174 (Amasis). In probably its earliest surviving occurrence, *Hom. Hymn* 2.203, *skōptein* evokes simulated, ritualised abuse (ch. 4, 162–3). Cf. Schmidt (1876–86) II 451–3.

42 Pejorative *charis*: Eur. fr. 492 *TrGF* (χάριτας κερτόμους, 'jeering wit': ch. 3 n. 84), Ar. fr. 171 ('bomolochic' mockery: cf. n. 53 below), Dem. 18.138 (associated with abuse), Pl. *Apol.* 24c (cf. 27a, d). On the general link between *charis* and laughter, see ch. 3 n. 27, ch. 6, 312–13. Unfriendly 'play', equivalent to 'mockery', is cited by LSJ 1288, *s.v.* παίζω II 2, from Lucian, *Nigr.* 20, Agathias, *Anth. Pal.* 10.64.4 (both involving personified Fortune); cf. the compounds ἐμπαίζειν (ch. 10 n. 2), καταπαίζειν (esp. Ar. fr. 171: see above), προσπαίζειν (add e.g. Pl. *Laws* 10.885c to LSJ's entry), and n. 51 below on Theog. 1211. Differently, satyric 'play' is disparaged in Soph. fr. 314.354 *TrGF*; it reflects the satyrs' childishness (366) and 'stupid jokes' (μῶρα καὶ γελοῖα, 369): cf. Appendix 2 n. 62.

43 Dio Chrys. 4.91–2 (Diogenes the Cynic speaking); cf. n. 101 below, ch. 8 n. 20.

childhood, appearing first in the early months of life and then becoming so habitual that it is hard to suppress. An apocryphal but revealing anecdote from Theophrastus' work *On Comedy* relates how the people of Tiryns, when they needed to avoid laughter during a religious sacrifice, decided to exclude children, attempting thereby, perhaps, to restrain the child in themselves.[44] It is linguistically plausible that traces of the spirit of children or the young are present, at least faintly, in the extended application of the *paizein* word-group to adult modes of behaviour. But that connection is always marked by difference as well, since adult *paidia* implies conscious adoption of an alternative frame of mind: performing the spirit of childhood, so to speak, rather than being a child. This extended notion of *paidia* collects strong associations, even to the point of personification in visual art, with a cluster of activities that include music, song, dance, festivity, the relaxed intimacies of commensal friendship, and – at the heart of the cluster – laughter.[45] The common conjunction of laughter and 'play' is both socially and psychologically complex. It centres on behaviour that does not simply reproduce the 'first order' play of childhood but involves (ideally) a self-conscious suspension of the normal consequentiality of 'taking things seriously'.[46] Children's own play can, of course, be regarded (by adults) as serving a prospective purpose – a sort of mimetic rehearsal

---

[44] Theophr. fr. 124 Wimmer (*apud* Athen. 6.261d–e), fr. 709 Fortenbaugh (1992) II 554: see ch. 4, 155–7. Children's laughter (half their life, alternating with tears: Marcus Aur. *Med.* 5.33) is reflected in conventions of visual art: Appendix 2, 551. On the development of laughter and smiles in infancy, see ch. 6 n. 142. For a modern theory of the relation between 'the comic' and childhood, see Freud (1989) 207–11, Freud (1976) 286–92.

[45] The vocabulary of play and laughter combined: e.g. Theog. 1211 (but cf. n. 51 below), Hdt. 2.173, Ar. *Frogs* 374–5, 388–92, Hippoc. *Morb. Sacr.* 17, Xen. *Cyr.* 2.3.18, Pl. *Euphr.* 3e, *Crat.* 406b–c, *Rep.* 5.452e (the last two with φιλοπαίσμων: ch. 4 n. 1), *Laws* 7.816e, Isoc. 10.11, Arist. *Rhet.* 1.11, 1371b34, 2.3, 1380b3, *EN* 4.8, 1128a14, 10.6, 1177a4, Antiphanes fr. 217.4, adesp. el. 27.4 *IEG* (ch. 3, 114–17), *SEG* xv 517 A col. 11.31 (ch. 4 n. 61), Lucian, *Prom. es* 6 (comedy personified), *Alex.* 25, *Bis acc.* 10, Dio Chrys. 32.1, Plut. *Lyc.* 25.2, *Mor.* 1101e, Rufin. *Anth. Pal.* 5.61 (a real game plus erotic play: Page (1978) 92–3). *Paidia* is near-synonymous with laughter at Arist. *EN* 2.7, 1108a13, 23, as *EN* 4.8 confirms (ch. 6, 308–10). Play *vis-à-vis* song, dance, festivity (often implying laughter): e.g. Hom. *Od.* 8.251–3, 23.134, Hes. fr. 123.3 Merkelbach–West (Kouretes), ps.-Hes. *Scutum* 277, 282, 298, Hdt. 9.11.1, Ar. *Frogs* 333, 388, Pl. *Euthd.* 277d–e (with ch. 6, 288). 'Play' and dance: cf. Lonsdale (1993) 33–6, with Buck (1949) 1108–9, West (1997) 46 n. 195 for other languages. See Schmidt (1876–86) III 447–56, IV 205–8, Meerwaldt (1928) 160–5 for the semantics of the *paizein* word-group, Burkert (2003) 96–107 for broader reflections. 'Play' and commensality: ch. 3 n. 36. Personifications of Paidia appear on classical vases alongside Aphrodite, Dionysus, music, drama and dance: Shapiro (1993) 180–5, Kossatz-Deissmann (1994). The rare epithet παραπαίζων ('playing alongside') is applied to Dionysus in *IG* II² 4787 (an imperial Attic dedication), and probably to a deity in the Lemnian Kabeiroi cult (ch. 4 n. 14): Follet (1974) 32–4. For the nexus of laughter and dance, see nn. 89, 91 below.

[46] Cf. my distinction between 'playful' and 'consequential' laughter in Halliwell (1991a), esp. 280–7, treating the first as (ideally) self contained, game-like, 'harmless', the second as part of the field of social cause-and-effect. Cf. Socrates' collocation of jesting (*gelōtopoiein*) with board games at Xen. *Symp.* 3.9.9. A striking case of consequential laughter (whether literal or metonymic), is Thuc. 3.83.1: simplicity of character 'was derided and suppressed' (καταγελασθὲν ἠφανίσθη) by moral relativism;

for life, as Aristotle describes it.[47] But it is also supposedly enclosed in an innocently make-believe world, and thus provides a paradigm for the conception of adult 'play' as a kind of deflection from the pressures of social existence: a slackening of the tension of the taut 'bow' of life, in a long-lived sentiment that was interestingly ascribed to at least two non-Greek sources, king Amasis of Egypt and the philhellene Scythian Anacharsis.[48] That suggests the possibility of playful laughter as an expression of lightheartedness, an ideal which figures prominently in templates of symposiac exhilaration (see Chapter 3), where the heady action of wine is often represented as a (willed) 'forgetting' of worries and an immersion in the pleasures of the moment. Such a concept of play appears explicitly as a catchword of sympotic hedonism: 'let's drink, let's play', says the voice of the archetypal symposiast in an elegy by Ion of Chios; 'drink, play, for life comes to an end', says another, in a Middle Comedy by Amphis.[49]

We might characterise playful laughter provisionally, then, as a cooperative, reciprocally pleasurable form of behaviour: one which requires all parties to accept the rules of the game, above all the psychological and social presupposition of self-contained, 'safe', non-antagonistic exchange. Playful laughter is a badge and unifying agent of friendship; at a lower level of intensity, it is a component of eirenic sociability, which is one reason why the *receiver* or target, as well as the producer, of (would-be) playful laughter carries some responsibility for determining its impact. Knowing how to 'take', as well as make, a joke is understandably treated by Aristotle as an important facet of social adroitness, not only from the point of view of his own philosophical perspective but also in his sifting of general attitudes on friendship in the *Rhetoric*.[50] There is, however, a widespread Greek recognition of the difficulties of circumscribing laughter within the realms of the recognisably, safely playful. One person's 'play' may not always please another, and the vocabulary of 'play', as already mentioned, can even (in extreme cases) take on abrasive connotations.[51] The ideal conditions of

---

cf. Hornblower (1991) 487. At the other end of the spectrum, note the concession to make-believe 'play' even within the moralistic setting at Pl. *Rep.* 3.396e (cf. ch. 5, 226).

[47] *Pol.* 7.17, 1336a33–4; see Halliwell (2002b) 178–9. Something comparable is expressed at Pl. *Rep.* 7.536e–537a.

[48] Relaxation as 'slackened bow': Amasis at Hdt. 2.173; for Anacharsis in later sources, see Kindstrand (1981) 109 (A10A–D), 129–30, with Praechter (1912) for the wider trope. Germane is Aristotle's reference to Anacharsis as advocate of relaxing play at *EN* 10.6, 1176b33–4 (ch. 6, 268, 309).

[49] Ion Chi. 27.7 *IEG* (cf. 26.16), Amphis fr. 8: see ch. 3, 114–16.

[50] *Rhet.* 2.4, 1381a33–6; see ch. 6, 307–31, for Aristotle's own ethical perspective.

[51] A (woman's) mocking 'play', equated with abuse (δεννάζειν), is deprecated at Theog. 1211; cf. ch. 3 n. 36. On unfriendly 'play' cf. n. 42 above.

playful laughter can never be taken for granted. More than anything else, this is because the laughter of (putative) play is often *superficially* disrespect-ful, agonistic or aggressive. Much joking depends upon the appearance or pretence of insult, as Aristotle, again, was quick to appreciate (see below for his notion of 'educated *hubris*'). Accordingly, the dividing line between play and actual aggression – between the autonomous give-and-take of the former and the consequential animus of the latter – is thin. This line is often invisible within the ostensible content of gelastic behaviour and can only be discerned in contextual rules which are implicitly accepted or disrup-tively breached by participants. In Greek culture, the status of such rules is always delicate; they operate against the background of deeply rooted sensitivities to shame and dishonour. Yet it makes sense to suppose that the more ingrained such sensitivities are, the more a culture might *need* opportunities for playful laughter – and, simultaneously, the deeper will be the anxieties that become attached to the practice of such laughter. I contend that much of the material explored in this book is compatible with this double-sided hypothesis.

Even where children or the young themselves are concerned, laughter is a subject which raises ethical and educational problems for Greek ways of thinking. From one angle, for sure, the association between laughter and childhood is part of a life-affirming nexus of values to which I have already alluded. The avian chorus of Aristophanes' *Birds* emblematically promise the audience (including their 'children and their children's chil-dren') 'wealth-and-health, life, peace, youth, laughter, choruses, feasts and bird's milk' (729–34). That miniature catalogue places laughter at the centre of a continuum of pleasures in which the worlds of young and old merge into a utopian vision. But from a less wishfully celebratory standpoint the laughter of the young carries risks of irreverence and scurrility. 'The young', writes Aristotle, 'are lovers of laughter and therefore adept at wit' (φιλογέλωτες, διὸ καὶ εὐτράπελοι), before adding, in a shrewd oxymoron, that wittiness (*eutrapelia*) is 'educated *hubris*'.[52] With just a couple of brush-strokes, as it were, Aristotle acknowledges the need for the laughter of the young to be subjected to 'civilising' control, if it is not to become (especially during the transitions of adolescence) a destabilising vehicle for insults. In the *Clouds*, Aristophanes moulds the Just Argument into a caricature of the conservative educational moralist who laments the demise of the prac-tice of beating children for 'playing the buffoon' (*bōmolocheuesthai*), i.e. for

---

[52] *Rhet.* 2.12, 1389b10–12: cf. ch. 6, 323–5. On the association of *hubris* with laughter, insult and abuse, see 33–7 below; a good illustration at Dio Chrys. 65.7. Cf. Chadwick (1996) 294–5.

instinctively seeking the gratifications of laughter.[53] Two generations later, in the *Areopagiticus*, Isocrates confirms that such attitudes really existed and perpetuated themselves. Under a more rigorous educational regimen, he claims, Athenian children used to avoid buffoonery and related vices, such as answering back and abusing their elders. But these days they are actually praised for being witty (*eutrapeloi*, the same term as Aristotle's above) or good at cracking jokes (σκώπτειν δυναμένους). The Socrates of Plato's *Republic* goes a step further and suggests that under democracy not only do the young break free of adult control, but adults themselves constantly engage in wittiness (*eutrapelia*) and facetiousness (*charientismos*) in order to emulate the young and ingratiate themselves with them.[54] Democracy even affects the way people laugh. According to Socrates, it spawns a kind of gelastic 'youth culture'.

Anxieties of the kind just adumbrated, related as they are to the educational and social value of self-discipline (*sōphrosunē*), assume even larger proportions where adolescence and early manhood are concerned. The activities of groups of young men mockingly victimising people in the Athenian agora, for instance, conjure up a scene where laughter is separated from violence by a narrow boundary.[55] I shall shortly examine a forensic speech by Demosthenes in which the fraught nature of that boundary is dramatically brought to life. The central point here is conveniently highlighted by a verbal association between unconstrained laughter and the impudent tendencies of young men. To be *neanikos* ('typical of a young man') is,

---

[53] *Clouds* 969–72. Cf. *bōmolochos*, *ibid.* 910, and disapproval of 'giggling', κιχλίζειν, 983 (cf. ch. 10 n. 52); Aristophanes uses the latter of Crates' comedies in fr. 347.4, but for the text of *Clouds* 1073 see ch. 3 n. 31. Compare the Unjust Argument's view that well educated boys should blush when mocked (992; subtext: 'modern' children no longer think it shameful to be ridiculed). Contrast avoidance of *bōmolochia* by Spartan boys (n. 125 below), models of self-control (Xen. *Lac. resp.* 3.4–5), or the legend of Plato's laughter-shy boyhood (Diog. Laert. 3.26: ch. 6, 277). Aristophanes uses the *bōmolochos* word-group (ironically) to deprecate unsophisticated comedy (*Peace* 748, *Frogs* 358); likewise *phortikos*, 'crude' or 'vulgar' (*Clouds* 524, *Wasps* 66, cf. *Lys.* 1218): Edwards (1991), esp. 169–78, offers one approach (but over confident on authorial intentions). Arist. *EN* 4.8, 1128a4–5, also links *bōmolochos* and *phortikos* (ch. 6, 311, 322); cf. ch. 7 n. 122, with Hippoc. *De medico* 1 (the vulgar doctor who laughs too much). On *bōmolochos* see Wilkins (2000) 88–90, Beta (2004) 249–53.

[54] Isoc. 7.49 (cf. 15.284), Pl. *Rep.* 8.563a–b. Bremmer (1997) 18–21, positing a 'growing unacceptability of less refined humour' in the fourth century, exaggerates the sociological significance of mostly philosophical views. And Isocrates, if representative (dubious: his are conservative gripes), suggests the *reverse* of Bremmer's claim; cf. ch. 6 n. 135.

[55] See Phryn. fr. 3 for a comic but suggestive image (with *PCG*'s note on line 5), including the metaphor of 'stinging' or 'scratching' with mockery (implying obscene gestures? cf. Ar. *Ach.* 444, *Kn.* 1381, *Peace* 549, *Clouds* 651–5, for the verbs σκιμαλίζειν and καταδακτυλίζειν, with Taillardat (1965) 357–8). Ar. *Kn.* 1373 links adolescents to the agora, though the point is uncertain: see Chadwick (1996) 36, with the counter-image of respectable youths at Isoc. 7.48. More on the agora: ch. 5, 231–5. Cf. the much later vignette of scoffing youths (in the baths) at Eunap. *Vitae Soph.* 10.1.9.

in this sense (to which pejorative use of 'adolescent' in English approximates), often to be aggressively derisive of others: hence, for instance, the application of the term to the scoffing, hubristic antics of the comically rejuvenated Philocleon of Aristophanes' *Wasps*.[56] Plato goes so far as to call *neanikon* the behaviour of any spectator who, while nervous of a reputation for buffoonery (*bōmolochia*) in ordinary life, yields to the shameless pleasures of laughter in the comic theatre (a place where one might be aware of the hilarity of boys in the audience).[57] Comic theatre, so the Platonic argument runs, induces a sort of psychological regression, a lapse into 'younger' ways of laughing that overrun the defences of both body and mind.

If concerns about the insidious energies of laughter sometimes focus on the behaviour of children and adolescents, the difficulty of demarcating acceptably playful laughter becomes a greater challenge once we move into the fully adult realm. If the activities of 'play' can ideally be construed as freely chosen, mutually pleasing, bracketed from ordinary social consequences, and bound by agreed (if unwritten) rules, many kinds of laughter will fail these tests.[58] Although Greek draws a general contrast between things suitable for laughter (γελοῖα) and things that ought to be taken seriously (σπουδαῖα), the extent to which any particular use of laughter can count as playful is often uncertain. The problematic difference between playful and non-playful laughter cuts across the serious/laughable dichotomy and renders it asymmetrical. To be playful is, by definition, to step outside (or, at least, to suspend) 'seriousness'; but to laugh may or may not be a playful act. One insight into this point can be gained from a passage in Plato's *Laws*, a work which itself elsewhere emphatically affirms a serious/laughable dichotomy (7.816d–817a). In Book 11 (934e–936a) the Athenian formulates a prohibition on public insult and abuse (*blasphēmein*,

[56] See *Wasps* 1303–7 for a nexus of *hubris*, exuberance, mockery and *neanikos*; cf. *ibid.* 1362 (with ch. 4, 208–10). The superlative *neanikōtatos* describes the Sausage-Seller at Ar. *Kn.* 611 (Bowie (1993) 52–7 makes him an ephebe); cf. Halliwell (1991a) 285 and n. 19. Pl. *Rep.* 3.390a calls Achilles' Iliadic insults against Agamemnon νεανιεύματα, '[insolent] young man's talk'; Admetus is called νεανίας for hurling abuse at his father, Eur. *Alc.* 679. Cf. Dover (1974) 103. Parallel usage at Lucian, *Somn.* 5, γελάσιμα καὶ μειρακιώδη, 'ludicrous and adolescent'. A snapshot of abusive young men at Pl. *Charm.* 154a (in the competitive gymnasium: n. 82 below); cf. the (young's) unbridled laughter at Eur. fr. 362.22–3 *TrGF*. Fisher (1992) 97–9 documents the connection between youth and *hubris*. On the 'youthful' spirit of the symposium, see ch. 3 n. 31. Cf. the Latin verb *iuvenari* of satyrs, Hor. *Ars Po.* 246, with Brink (1971) 292.
[57] *Rep.* 10.606c; cf. ch. 5, 255–6. Ar. *Clouds* 539, *Peace* 766, Eup. fr. 261, Pl. *Laws* 2.658d, Theophr. *Char.* 9.4, 30.6, and (by implication) Arist. *Pol.* 7.15, 1336b20–1, variously indicate boys' attendance at comic theatre.
[58] Huizinga (1949) 7–13 offers a classic account of social play *qua* self-contained and rule governed; but cf. *ibid.* 5–6 for how play, though 'non-serious', can be taken seriously (as with, e.g., professional sport), thus carrying no necessary connection with laughter.

kakēgoria, *loidoria* are among the terms he uses) in the well-governed city. But this leads him to insist on a separation even in the case of stage-comedy between laughter that involves 'play' and is free of animus (ἄνευ θυμοῦ) and laughter which precisely entails animus (μετὰ θυμοῦ) and carries with it the risk of social harm. However difficult it may be to apply this distinction to comedy, the urgency of the distinction between playful (harmless) and 'consequential' (socially divisive) forms of laughter is evident.[59] Nor are we dealing here with exclusively Platonic moralism. The argument is rooted in preoccupations that had a general purchase on Greek ways of thinking. To put the point pithily, the need to know how (to try) to distinguish between insults and jokes, together with an awareness of how easily the latter might slip into or be mistaken for the former, was a matter for recurrent unease in a culture where the dynamics of maintaining or losing status (or impugning the status of others), of suffering or avoiding shame (or wielding its public power against others), were so fundamental.

Nothing bears out that observation more than the Greek tendency to regard mockery (especially *katagelan*, 'laughing down') not just as something that may accompany (or degenerate into) other, more physical forms of antagonism, but as an intrinsically aggressive, harmful act in its own right. Mockery is standardly classed as a species of *hubris* (malicious offensiveness), which makes Aristotle's definition of wit as 'educated *hubris*' (above) all the more revealing.[60] It was rare individuals and groups who were impervious to, or capable of resisting, this strongly sustained apprehension; such individuals, as we shall later see, were typically regarded as abnormal rather than admired. The fear of being mocked (with impunity) by one's enemies is an atavistic constituent of Greek cultural psychology. The fear is made more pressing by a proclivity to see the division between friends and enemies as an all-embracing categorisation of the social world. Thus, just as playful laughter is archetypally something to enjoy with friends, so the

---

[59] On *Laws* 11.934e–936a see Morrow (1993) 371–4, with Saunders (1972) 116–17 for the sequence of thought. No individual passage encapsulates a simple Platonic attitude to comedy: see ch. 6, 300–2, ch. 10, 485–7.

[60] The *hubris* of ridicule, taunts or insults: Soph. *Aj.* 196–8 (reading καγχαζόντων?), 955–61, *Ant.* 482–3, 838–40, *El.* 794, Eur. *El.* 902 (with 27–8 below), Thuc. 6.28 (n. 95 below), Ar. *Ach.* 479, 631, *Wasps* 1318–20, *Thesm.* 63, Pl. *Prot.* 355c, *Symp.* 219c (metaphorical laughter), Xen. *Cyr.* 5.2.18 (by negation), 8.1.33, Dem. 9.60, 22.63, Aeschin. 2.181–2 (with n. 64 below), Arist. *Top.* 6.6, 1444a5–8, *Rhet.* 2.2, 1379a29–30, 2.3, 1380a28–9. Mockery is commonly perceived as a potential cause of violence: e.g. Lys. 3.43 (including fights resulting from 'games', *paidiai*, if the alternative ms. reading is correct), Dem. 54.18–19 (with 37 below), Pl. *Laws* 11.934e–935b (with 24 above), Arist. *Metaph.* 5.24, 1023a30–1, Hyp. fr. 97 Jensen; see ch. 3 n. 22 for sympotic evidence. Cf. the juxtaposition of verbal and physical 'blows' at Ar. *Clouds* 1373–6. Feinberg (1985) 226–36 explores such issues from a modern legal standpoint.

laughter of contempt, superiority or triumph is a vital weapon in the definition and pursuit of enmity. The potency of hostile laughter is such that
Greek states sometimes passed laws against certain kinds of public abuse
(*loidoria*) or denigration (*kakēgoria*), though we are not well placed to know
how effective they were in practice.[61] Derision by one's foes, if not answered
in kind or with some other reassertion of one's honour, makes a person a
laughing-stock, *katagelastos*, literally 'laughed down' or 'defeated by laughter'. At the limits, derision can be felt as even worse, because more injurious
to reputation (as well as to one's self-image), than death itself – as Heracles'
wife Megara (a figure with a firm sense of the status she derives from her
heroic husband, but also with limited capacities to retaliate in his absence)
explicitly declares in Euripides' *Hercules Furens* (285–6). Worst of all (as
also implied in the passage just cited) is the thought of such humiliation
after one's death. Equally, however, such a situation can be viewed from
the reverse angle. Being able to inflict humiliating derision on others with
impunity brings with it an intense satisfaction. When the tables are turned
on Lycus, Megara's oppressor, in the *Hercules Furens*, Megara's father-in-law
Amphitryo rushes off to gloat over Lycus' corpse (731–3).

The frisson of triumphant mockery of the dead – a frisson of exhilaration
for its perpetrators, and (in a rather apt sense) mortification for those who
picture themselves or their kin as its victims – is attested across the whole
history of ancient Greek culture. The evidence stretches from, for example,
the vivid Homeric hypothesis of Trojans jumping with euphoric contempt
on the grave of Menelaus, to the lurid Lucianic scenario of the dead tyrant's
slave who copulates with his master's former mistress in the presence of his
corpse before directly insulting the latter in word and action (with blows and
spitting).[62] The fear of ignominy associated with hostile laughter, whether
before or after death, applies with special force in 'heroic' contexts, where
the stakes of honour and shame are highest. The motif is prominent in a
number of tragedies whose protagonists, including women (Medea one of
them), are especially susceptible to thoughts of posthumous dishonour at
the hands of their enemies.[63] But much that stands out in heroic patterns

[61] On Athenian legislation, see MacDowell (1978) 126–9, Halliwell (1991b) 49–51, with n. 71 below
(Solon). Arist. *EN* 4.8, 1128a30–1, Isoc. 11.40 imply widespread Greek practice; cf. the implications
of Xen. *Cyr.* 1.2.6. Arist. *EN* 5.2, 1131a19 categorises abuse and 'vilification' (προπηλακισμός) as kinds
of 'violence' alongside physical assaults (cf. *Pol.* 2.4, 1262a27); he proposes restrictions on indecent
speech (*aischrologia*) at *Pol.* 7.17, 1336b3–12 (ch. 5, 247).
[62] *Il.* 4.176–81, Lucian, *Cataplus* 12 (with ch. 9 n. 46).
[63] Such 'heroic'/tragic sensitivity to laughter is abundant: see Aesch. *Pers.* 1034, *Eum.* 789/819, Soph.
Ant. 839, *Aj.* 79 (endorsed by Athena), 196–9 (with Garvie (1998) 145–6), 367, 382, 958–62, *OT* 1422
(with n. 64 below), *El.* 1153, 1295, *Phil.* 1023, 1125, *OC* 902–3, 1338–9, Eur. *Medea* 383, 404, 797, etc.

of behaviour and feeling is a magnification (and reinforcement) of attitudes and values that were understood at all levels of Greek society. When Aeschines asked a democratic jury in 343 to acquit him on a charge of political bribery, he could assert, with the expectation that his audience would appreciate the sentiment: 'it is not death that is terrible, but outrageous treatment (*hubris*) at the point of death. Is it not pitiful to have to see an enemy scoffing in one's face (ἐπεγγελῶντος) and to hear his insults with one's own ears?' Aeschines may be alluding to a provision in Athenian law which in some cases allowed a victorious prosecutor to jeer at a condemned criminal immediately before execution.[64] Such provision must have had a long 'prehistory', whether in the domain of official justice or outside it: there are few Homeric moments, for instance, more difficult to forget than Eumaeus' gleeful taunting of Melanthius in *Odyssey* 22 as the goatherd hangs trussed in agony from a roof-beam awaiting 'execution' (which eventually takes the form of dismemberment and disembowelling).[65] Mockery of someone about to die later makes a historically momentous appearance in the gospels' description of the treatment of Jesus by Roman soldiers, a description that reflects wider familiarity with the laughter of sadism in ancient Mediterranean cultures. I shall return to that scene in the final chapter of this book.

We must take account, however, of a faultline in traditional Greek feelings about mockery of the dead. There is a misfit, as it were, between theory and practice: between a formal tendency to proscribe ridicule of the dead and, on the other hand, a discernible cultural impetus towards the pleasure of celebrating the death of one's enemies.[66] A chilling moment at the climax of Euripides' *Electra* enacts this tension with psychological acuteness. Electra, who had herself earlier contemplated with horror the thought of being abused by her enemies at the point of death (697–8, where the verb

---

(with Mastronarde (2002) 20), *Hec.* 1257–8, *Bacch.* 1032–40 (with opposing views). Discussion in Grossmann (1968) 75–83, Blundell (1989) 62–5, 148, 194, Arnould (1990) 36–42, Dillon (1991).

[64] Aeschin. 2.181–2: the crime concerned is unclear (Gernet (1968) 306 n. 18), but Dem. 23.69 cites the right of a successful prosecutor for murder to witness an execution; cf. Allen (2000) 203, and Griffin (1980) 184, who juxtaposes the Aeschines passage too readily with less vicious laughter. Cf. someone spitting (ch. 7 n. 104) in the condemned Phocion's face, Plut. *Mor.* 189a, *Phoc.* 36.2, and the Inlaw's (comically grotesque) fear of mockery while exposed to die on the 'plank' at Ar. *Thesm.* 941–2. Hdt. 1.129.1 records an egregious instance of face-to-face derision of a fallen enemy (Harpagus and Astyages). Thus Creon's significant *refusal* to mock at Soph. *OT* 1422.

[65] Taunts at *Od.* 22.194–9 (ἐπικερτομεῖν: cf. ch. 2 n. 50), death at 474–7: my point is unaffected by possible interpolations; see Fernández-Galiano in Heubeck *et al.* (1988–92) III 250–2, 304–5. Note that, in line with the sentiment at 22.411–12 (ch. 2 n. 88), Odysseus does not order the taunting (22.173–7).

[66] See Bond (1981) 254: 'a much-needed rule, normally disregarded'. Cf. the candid motive for a symposium in Alc. 332 *PLF*.

καθυβρίζειν carries clear connotations of mockery), is brought face to face
with Aegisthus' corpse. She feels compunction at the thought of insulting (*hubrizein*) her defeated enemy, but nonetheless *wants* to do so: 'I am
inhibited by shame, but I still want to say the words' (αἰσχύνομαι μέν,
βούλομαι δ' εἰπεῖν ὅμως, 900). Dismissing her fears of social resentment,
Orestes persuades her to yield to her impulse, which she duly does with
a tirade she reveals she has often mentally rehearsed in the past. Electra
is in no doubt that Aegisthus has received his just deserts. Her speech is
nonetheless an outlet, as she admits, for the *hubris* of triumphalist malice,
spiced with sexual taunts against the murdered usurper.[67] Electra's conduct
is a display of violent derision – something to which an actor might easily add appropriate vocalisation. No Greek would have any difficulty in
classifying it as an exercise in 'laughing down' an enemy, and all the more
potent, as well as disturbing, for being delivered over that enemy's bloody
corpse.

Awareness of a powerful drive to abuse one's dead enemies coexists
throughout Greek culture with an ethical imperative to restrain that drive.
But the balance between urge and restraint varies greatly with the social, ethical and psychological parameters of each situation. According to Penelope
in the *Odyssey*, 'everyone reviles a [harsh] person after his death' (τεθνεῶτί
γ' ἐφεψιόωνται ἅπαντες, 19.331). Her generalisation justifies itself implicitly in terms of communal consensus about a hated individual, but the same
verb (ἐφιάομαι and compounds: to ridicule and/or play) occurs elsewhere
in the *Odyssey* in descriptions of the debauched lifestyle of the suitors and
the scornful mockery those suitors target against Odysseus. It is also used
by Odysseus himself. On the very point of announcing his true identity,
he declares (in a premonition of the suitors' death, encoded in bitter irony)
that 'it is now time to prepare a meal in the daylight . . . then afterwards to
play in a different way with song and with lyre'.[68] Odysseus allows himself
an oblique hint at the pleasure of contemplating the death of his enemies.
The obliqueness makes all the difference. The *Odyssey*, as I shall show in
Chapter 2, makes a profound theme out of the whole issue of when it is
and is not right (or safe) to laugh at one's foes, living or dead. The poem,
one might say, breaks down Penelope's broad generalisation (19.331, above)

---

[67] Sexual taunts: Eur. *El.* 918–24, 945–51, with Cropp (1988) 160; on the *hubris* of the scene, and the
ethics of revenge, cf. Fisher (1992) 433–4.

[68] *Od.* 17.530 (suitors), 19.370–2 (maidservants), 21.429 (Odysseus' coded irony). On the semantics of
ridicule/play in ἐφιάομαι, see Chantraine (1968) 394, *s.v.* ἐφία, with Caggia (1972) 25–8; cf. Nagy
(1999) 256–7 (but overlooking *Od.* 17.530). The scepticism of Heubeck in Heubeck *et al.* (1988–92)
III 205 is unnecessary. Cf. ch. 2 n. 98, ch. 3 n. 6.

into a more complex set of perceptions. The suitors and maidservants are partly defined by their surrender to irresponsible group laughter, not least as manifested in mockery of the disguised Odysseus. For old Eurycleia – who observes the maidservants' treatment of the beggar with bitter distaste ('these bitches', she calls them, αἱ κύνες αἵδε, 19.372) – the sight of the slaughtered suitors, with blood-spattered Odysseus standing over them, will produce an instinctive shriek of ecstatically liberated celebration. Odysseus himself, a master in the suppression (and internalisation) of laughter, tells her to rejoice only in her heart: 'it is impious to celebrate over slain men' (22.411–12). But Eurycleia's laughter is only temporarily stifled. When, just afterwards, she runs to tell Penelope the news, she is said to cachinnate (καγχαλάω) with irresistible joy. And the shape of the narrative prompts us to see her earlier glee at the killing of the suitors as impulsively resurfacing in that moment of sheer delight, once she is away from Odysseus' restraining gaze.[69]

The derision of a fallen enemy fuses together, in a peculiarly taut form, what I earlier called the life-affirming and the death-related energies of laughter. Such derision affirms '*my*' life at the triumphant expense of '*your*' defeat and death. This highly charged state seems to be fuelled, on the one hand, by a sense that the finality of death marks an unarguable victory: 'a dead body revenges not injuries', as William Blake was to put it.[70] If that were the whole story, however, we would hardly be able to explain the antiquity and tenacity of injunctions *against* mockery of the dead. In addition to the Odyssean material cited above, we find such an injunction (as well as other antigelastic sentiments) ascribed to the Spartan Chilon, one of the Seven Sages; and to another of the seven, Solon, Athenian tradition even ascribed a law against 'denigrating the dead'.[71] The principle is also incisively enunciated – 'it is not good to jeer (*kertomein*) at dead men' – in a fragment of Archilochus, while a character in Cratinus (though the attribution is not certain) formulates the point in terms, similar to those at *Odyssey* 22.412, of not 'vaunting' over those one has killed.[72] The Cratinus fragment grounds the interdict in 'fear': principally, no doubt, fear of the hidden power of the dead to retaliate, a factor explicitly adduced by the sophist Hippias in Plato to explain why he does not ridicule his

---

[69] Cf. ch. 2, 57, 87.   [70] 'Proverbs of Hell': Keynes (1969) 151.

[71] On Chilon see ch. 6, 265–7. Solon's law: Dem. 20.104 (plus 40.49, Hyp. fr. 100 Jensen, both without Solon's name), Plut. *Solon* 21; cf. Halliwell (1991b) 49, with n. 61 above. Sommerstein (2004a) 207 notes a lack of evidence for enforcement of such a law.

[72] Archil. 134 *IEG* (cf. the general warning against exulting in victory, 128.4 *IEG*), Cratinus fr. 102 (with *PCG*'s note *ad loc.*); καυχᾶσθαι, in the latter, is associated with laughter (in a rather different context) at Athen. 2.39e.

predecessors;[73] but perhaps also fear of incurring the resentment of the gods. Athenian orators appeal, with the force of self-evidence, to a conviction that it is exceptionally shameful or shocking to deride the dead. Theophrastus depicts the slanderer, *kakologos*, as equally extreme for abusing his family and friends (behind their backs) and for speaking ill of the dead. Aristotle, in his lost dialogue *Eudemus*, suggested that it was impious to abuse the dead, because they had passed to a better world, but this is a philosophical justification of a principle clearly carrying with it a traditional sanction.[74] Yet it goes without saying that the frequency with which mockery of the dead is deprecated speaks itself for the strength of the perceived impulse (the pleasure of conclusive victory/revenge) to engage in such behaviour. Penelope's generalisation, quoted above, is reiterated by the Sophoclean Teucer ('everybody loves to stand over the dead and scoff at them', τοῖς θανοῦσί τοι | φιλοῦσι πάντες κειμένοις ἐπεγγελᾶν) in his anxiety to protect his brother's corpse. His anxiety is soon borne out by the contumely of Menelaus and Agamemnon, the latter prepared to encourage Odysseus to 'trample' on the dead man, a practice it is wishful thinking to regard as exclusively 'oriental'.[75] Finally, Old Comedy, here as elsewhere free to indulge in gelastic shamelessness (a subject I shall tackle in Chapter 5), can extract extra, self-conscious hilarity from directing satire at the dead. Witness the prologue of Aristophanes *Peace*, where a pretentious Ionian spectator imagines that the dung-beetle on stage is an allegory of Cleon, 'since *he*'s in Hades on a diet of liquid faeces!'[76]

If mockery of the dead was subject to nagging apprehension, fewer doubts troubled the more regular, down-to-earth forms of hostile laughter. Such laughter traded on the standard social currency of shame. Only outright moralists warn against mockery *tout court*. The culture at large fears it but recognises it as too potent (and gratifying) a medium of stigmatisation and revenge to forgo, when the opportunity presents itself.[77] 'To feel pain is the

---

[73] Pl. *Hp. Maj.* 282a: Hippias is responding to Socrates' suggestion that experts might laugh at the primitiveness of their predecessors.

[74] Orators: Isoc. 15.101, 16.22, Dem. 40.47–9; more obliquely, Isae. 2. 15, 47. Theophr. *Char.* 28.6: see ch. 5, 238–9. Arist. *Eud.* fr. 65 Gigon, 44 Rose (*apud* Plut. *Mor.* 115b–c), in the speech of Silenus (ch. 7, 339–40).

[75] Teucer's anxiety: Soph. *Aj.* 988–9. Agamemnon's contumely: *Aj.* 1348; for trampling a corpse, with accompanying laughter, cf. Soph. fr. 210.47–9 *TrGF*. On the latter, Carden (1974) 22–3 misguidedly follows the attempt of Fraenkel (1950) II 412 to regard trampling on fallen enemies as 'oriental': Fraenkel jumps from a motif in visual art to a wider inference about cultural mentalities; the end of his note is tendentious.

[76] *Peace* 47–8: σπατίλη is a medical term, used euphemistically by the Ionian; cf. Olson (1998) 77, Rosen (1984) 396. Other examples of Old Comedy's satire of the dead: Halliwell (1991b) 51.

[77] Pittacus *apud* Stob. 3.1.172 deprecates mockery of misfortune; see DK 1 64, with ch. 6, 265–8, for other early sages. A similar embargo at Men. fr. 860. On the pleasure (and legitimacy) of vengeance,

lot of humans, but for a free person to be derided is far more shameful,' says an unknown character in Menander, speaking with a sentious confidence few would have contradicted.[78] Fear of being a laughing-stock to one's neighbours, or of giving one's enemies the pleasure of exulting at one's suffering, are clichés of Greek literature. While such formulas must include the sniggering one might imagine taking place behind people's backs, they are also a reminder that mockery was something that had a special bite when it occurred in the street, market-place or other public spaces.[79] If derision tends to be associated in heroic contexts with a threat to posthumous reputation, in more mundane settings it is linked pragmatically to the shamefulness of *exposure*. The plaintiff in Lysias' third speech (3.9) explains that for a long time a sense of shame induced him to endure in silence his rough treatment at the hands of Simon, his rival for the sexual favours of a Plataean boy, rather than be exposed to the widespread derision which he knew would follow from the publicity of a court case. We do not have to believe all the circumstantial details of his story in order to see the plausibility of the psychological persona Lysias creates for his client. The plaintiff's motivation presupposes a social world (that of most Greek cities in antiquity) in which any individual perceived as vulnerable could easily be picked out and targeted by group ridicule.

Iambic poets, unsurprisingly, have reason to foreground this kind of vulnerability for their own satirical purposes. The speaker in Archilochus 172 *IEG* berates Lycambes for being out of his mind: 'you are plain for all the citizens to see as a great laughing-stock' (νῦν δὲ δὴ πολὺς | ἀστοῖσι φαίνεαι γέλως). This is not metaphor, even if Lycambes may well be a fictional figure; it pictures a person's exposure to ridicule in the streets of the city. Similarly, Semonides portrays the ugly type of 'ape' or 'monkey' woman who, as she walks through the streets, is a laughing-stock to everyone (εἶσιν δι' ἄστεος πᾶσιν ἀνθρώποις γέλως, 7.74 *IEG*), though as it happens she is too shameless to *care* (*ibid.* 79, a detail I shall return to). When, in a very different register of poetry, the Dionysus of Euripides' *Bacchae* announces his intention to lead the transvestite Pentheus through the streets of Thebes (in a kind of perverted *kōmos*, revel), so as to expose

including mockery, cf. Dover (1974) 182–3. Burckhardt (1977) II 331–7, translated in Burckhardt (1998) 72–7, registers the importance of mockery (though not other kinds of laughter) in Greek culture; but his treatment is marred by sweeping assertions (cf. ch. 5 nn. 54, 81).

[78] ἐλευθέρῳ τὸ καταγελᾶσθαι γὰρ πολὺ | αἴσχιόν ἐστι, τὸ δ' ὀδυνᾶσθ' ἀνθρώπινον: Men. *Epitr.* fr. 10 (Arnott/Sandbach).

[79] A laughing-stock to neighbours/enemies: Hes. *WD* 701 (with West (1978) 328), Archil. 196a.33–4 *IEG*, Theog. 1033, 1107, Semon. 7.110–11 *IEG*, Democ. fr. 293 DK (criticised: ch. 7, 351), Soph. *Ant.* 647, Ar. *Kn.* 319–21, Men. fr. 860 (deprecated).

him directly to the mockery of the people, he evokes a kind of behaviour which would have resonated with Euripides' first audiences.[80] Many classical Athenian sources, from comedy to oratory, agree on the possibility of being victimised by group laughter in the city's crowded public places, not least in the supposedly vulgar atmosphere of the bustling agora.[81] As we shall shortly see, it was readily accepted that the energies involved in derision could easily be channelled into physical aggression. The occasions of such exposure to ridicule were multiple. They extended from casual, spontaneous social baiting or friction (most intense, perhaps, in the intimate ambience of the gymnasium, where masculine bodies as well as egos were on display) to more 'orchestrated' incidents such as the quasi-ritual humiliation of unsuccessful athletes, the jeering of substandard performers (musicians, actors, rhapsodes) by watching crowds, the spotlighting of individuals in an audience by mocking choruses, and perhaps sometimes even charivari-type customs of 'folk justice' whereby people were cornered in the street for public denunciation and ignominy.[82] But the laughter of crowds was too compelling to be excluded even from more formal environments. Its frequent eruption in the major institutions of Athenian democracy (Assembly, Council and lawcourts, where official audiences were, moreover, often augmented by groups of onlookers), and its consequent manipulation by public speakers, is a germane phenomenon which I shall address in Chapter 5.

When not specifically invited or encouraged, and therefore in a sense controlled, by some kind of 'laughter-maker' (*gelōtopoios*) or comic performer,

---

[80] Eur. *Bacchae* 854–5: for the play's thematisation of laughter, see ch. 3, 133–9.

[81] See ch. 5, 231–5, for this view of the agora. Aristophanic images of public mockery include *Kn.* 319–20 (relatively innocuous), *Wasps* 542, 1287 (metaphorical – Aristophanes beaten up by Cleon! – but revealing), *Peace* 476 (symbolic), *Thesm.* 226, 940–2 (with n. 64 above). Cf. abusive wrangling and mockery in the streets at e.g. Theophr. *Char.* 6.7, Pl. *Rep.* 5.473e–474a (metaphorical), *Laws* 11.935a–c. For a real-life vignette, see *IG* IV² i.121.124 (= *SIG* III no. 1168.124: cf. Herzog (1931) 16–17, Buck (1955) 293), where the prematurely bald Heraieus is 'ashamed of being derided by others' (αἰσχυνόμενος . . . καταγελάμενος [*sic*: Aeolic] ὑπὸ τῶν ἄλλων).

[82] (1) Gymnasium (cf. n. 56 above): see the victimising group laughter in Plato's *Euthd.*, with ch. 6, 287–90; cf. ps.-Pl. *Amat.* 134b, where laughter adds to erotically charged antagonism, Lys. fr. 75 Thalheim (mockery leading to serious conflict), ps.-Pl. *Eryx.* 397d, Diog. Laert. 6.91. (2) Athletes as targets: see the slapping/jeering of a Panathenaic runner at Ar. *Frogs* 1089–98 (Dionysus' reaction is implicitly that of the watching crowd), with Σ on 1093 for local custom in the Ceramicus; cf. the imagery of Pl. *Rep.* 10.613b–d, and the subtext of Pind. *Pyth.* 8.86–7 (with *Ol.* 8.67–9), where Burton (1962) 189 detects 'athletic cliques' insulting defeated competitors. (3) Performers: Pl. *Ion* 535e for unsuccessful rhapsodes, with *Prot.* 323a for auletes etc.; cf. Epict. *Diss.* 2.16.9–10, Alciph. *Epist.* 3.35.3. Whistling actors off stage, if we believe Dem. 19.337, could go beyond jeering; cf. Dem. 21.226 (with n. 89 below) for whistling/hooting by theatre audiences against individual citizens. (4) Mocking choruses: e.g. the *phallophoroi* in Semus of Delos *FGrH* 396 F24 (ch. 4, 183). (5) Charivari folk-justice: ch. 4 n. 73.

the 'chorused' laughter of a group or crowd directed against one or more individuals is likely to be in some degree a vehicle of victimisation. It may tap something deep in the evolutionary origins of laughter itself.[83] What is exceptional about ancient Greek society in this respect is that it shows an unusually sustained, obsessive sensitivity to this and related forms of 'laughing down', as well as reflecting that sensitivity across the entire spectrum of its public discourse – from the life-and-death clashes of heroic myth all the way to the street-level abusiveness that was conventionally (and as early as Homer) ascribed to 'fish wives', inn-keepers, prostitutes and other socially 'low' types.[84]

It will be useful now to put more flesh on the claims already made, and at the same time guide us back round to the unstable relationship between playful and consequential uses of laughter, by focusing on a particular test case: the episode of acute enmity between individual Athenian citizens depicted in Demosthenes' speech *Against Conon* (54), written some time in the mid-fourth century. The speech is the prosecution case for a charge of assault, though it is pertinent that the plaintiff, Ariston, maintains that a graver charge of *hubris* would have been justified. Particularly germane is Ariston's allegation that the actions of Conon and his sons compounded physical injury with outrageous offensiveness, ἀσέλγεια, a term readily coupled with *hubris*, as here, and one which can encompass shameless derision.[85] Ariston's case includes a narrative of his first encounter, in

---

[83] Dunbar (2004) 130–1 speculates on laughter's origins in 'chorusing' primate behaviour, Donald (1991) 187 locates the 'mimetic' origins of group laughter in 'vocomotor' games of derision; cf. laughter's contagiousness: Provine (1996) 198–200, (2000) 129–51. But group laughter is relatively slow to develop in young children: Blurton Jones (1972) 280. Bergson (1975) 4–6 (transl. in Sypher (1980) 64–5) finds the roots of the comic in group laughter against individuals; cf. Eibl-Eibesfeldt (1989) 315–16, Lorenz (1966) 253, Pinker (1998) 546–7, 551, with Lloyd Morgan (1914) 803 on laughter's 'social chorus'. Bakhtin (1986) 135 notes 'the social, choral nature of laughter', though he bafflingly claims that 'laughter only unites; it cannot divide'; cf. n. 31 above. More aptly, Screech (1997) 17 observes: 'laughter is one of the ways in which crowds . . . may react to the sight of suffering'. Laughter's alignment with social groups is the basis of Röcke and Velten (2005). For Homeric images of group laughter, see ch. 2, 76–7 (Thersites), 81–3 (Hephaestus), 86–92 (suitors/maidservants as jeering gangs), 98–9 (*Iliad* 23). But group dynamics are not a *necessary* condition of laughter: Prusak (2004) 381–3, invoking Augustine's famous thoughts at *Conf.* 2.9, criticises Bergson and others in this respect.

[84] Hom. *Il.* 20.251–5 already has a stereotype of women swapping abuse in the street, an anti-image of heroes. Greek males displace onto (low) women the unseemliness of their own addiction to taunts and invective. The topos appears at Diog. Laert. 1.70 (Chilon), Ar. *Kn.* 1400–3, *Frogs* 857–8, *Lys.* 457–60, *Wealth* 426–8, Pl. *Rep.* 3.395d, *Laws* 11.934e–935a, Men. frs. 472, 887; it is dramatised at Ar. *Wasps* 1388–1414, *Frogs* 549–78. For comparative anthropological reflections on male attitudes to women's laughter, see Apte (1985) 67–81; but cf. Glenn (2003) 151–61 on the difficulty of identifying gender differences in conversational laughter.

[85] *Aselgeia* and *hubris*: 54.4, 13, 25; cf. Lys. 24.15, Isoc. 16.22–3, Dem. 21.1, 31, 24.143; cf. MacDowell (1990) 220. The former's relation to vulgar or licentious laughter is visible at Eup. frs. 172.15, 261.2,

a garrison camp in northwest Attica, with Conon's sons, who allegedly led a life of drunkenness, violence and abusive taunts against Ariston and his companions (54.3–6). The potency of ridicule as a social weapon is highlighted. After initially putting up with their truculence, Ariston claims that it was only when the sons engaged in ceaseless jeering (χλευάζειν)[86] at his group, compounding their drunken aggression (παροινεῖν) and foul-mouthed abuse (κακῶς λέγειν), that he and his friends decided to inform the general in charge of the camp; though even that did not stop the offensive behaviour. The interest of this text for my purposes is independent of its veracity. However selective and one-sided his story may be, Ariston offers the jury what Demosthenes must have crafted to be a persuasively disturbing image of how laughter could operate in a socially 'consequential' manner, running alongside and reinforcing physical antagonism.

The motif of such laughter is exploited again to striking effect later in the prosecution speech. In a remarkable account of what he claims was a brutal mugging by his enemies (8–9), Ariston describes how after being stripped, battered and kicked into the mud he heard his assailants produce a stream of foul insults against him – too foul to be repeated to the jury.[87] One detail he does recount, however, as proof of the depths of Conon's *hubris*: the latter 'sang' in crowing mimicry of a victorious fighting-cock, while his accomplices cheered him on by encouraging him to flap his elbows like bird's wings. Taunting a wounded or defeated enemy, sometimes standing over their body, was an old ritual of triumphalism, available on the (epic) battlefield but also, as we saw with Euripides' *Electra*, in other contexts too.[88] Moreover, the imagery of cock-fighting provided a ready-made symbolism of masculine prowess in a culture like Athens: the vocal and physical gestures ascribed to Conon are likely to have been a familiar type of ostentatious self-assertion, as the existence of the verb περικοκκύζειν ('to crow round') and related terminology tends to confirm.[89] But the

---

Ar. *Wasps* 61, Dem. 2.19, Isae. 3.13 (*kōmos*), Men. *Perik.* 383 (with ch. 8 n. 56), Plut. *Mor.* 552b, 854d, Diod. Sic. 16.87.2 (komastic excess). On *Against Conon* as evidence of social-cum-litigious feuding, see Cohen (1995) 119–30 (with 126, 128 on the motif of laughter).

[86] *Chleu-* terms denote strong, often *risqué*, derision: Arist. *Top.* 6.6, 144a5–8 defines χλευασία as a kind of *hubris*; see e.g. the contemptuous farting in Epicrates fr. 10.30 *PCG*; cf. ch. 4 n. 20.

[87] See ch. 5 n. 17 for this (rhetorical) refusal to repeat the words. The imagery of Pl. *Rep.* 5.473e–474a, though drolly metaphorical in context, mirrors the socially real risk of mockery-cum-violence.

[88] Battlefield gloating: e.g. Hom. *Il.* 8.161–6, 11.378–83 (at a distance, but jumping with joy: ch. 2, 56–7), 13.374–82 (brutal irony), 22.330–6 (Achilles over Hector), 22.371–5 (Greeks mutilating Hector's corpse), 21.427–33 (Athena's crowing over Ares and Aphrodite: ch. 2, 66, 68).

[89] περικοκκύζειν (or –κοκκάζειν?) denotes contemptuous 'crowing' at Ar. *Kn.* 697, accompanied by dance (Neil (1901) 101; cf. n. 91 below). Cf. ἐπικοκκάστρια, of quasi-mocking Echo, at *Thesm.* 1059, with Taillardat (1965) 176–7; crowing is boasting at Lycoph. *Alex.* 395. Meleager projects laughter

mimicry involved makes the behaviour, I suggest, intrinsically double-edged. Superimposed on gratuitous violence, as Ariston is adamant that it was, Conon's action might seem a shocking exhibition of sadistic derision, as well as arrogant contempt for the laws of the city. Yet pictured in its own terms, floating free from its alleged context of violence and *hubris*, Conon's mimetic crowing suggests nothing so much as the prancing of a comic actor, and supported by a comic chorus.[90] Conon, with rhythmic support from his friends, does a sort of song-and-dance routine, a routine both indicative of and calculated to arouse laughter (in some). In a dance culture like that of ancient Greece, mockery like everything else could be choreographed: the energy and expressiveness of rhythmic bodily movement (including manual gesture, *cheironomia*, an important element in Greek dance) intensify the communication of ridicule.[91] But to sing and frolic in mimicry of a bird (and when lubricated with alcohol, if we believe the prosecution: 7) looks like revelling lightheadedly in an impromptu little comedy. Could this really be the behaviour of a vicious thug?[92]

onto the cock itself (*Anth. Pal.* 12.137); so does Lucian, *Gall.* 14, but with full anthropomorphism. Note the bird sound κλώζειν (hoot, cluck) of jeering theatre crowds at Dem. 21.226, Alciph. *Epist.* 3.35.3, Hesych. *s.v.*, with the cognate noun at Philo, *Legat.* 368.1, Plut. *Mor.* 813f. Cockfighting symbolism: a (spurious?) tradition has Themistocles instituting an annual cockfight in the theatre to celebrate victory over Persia, Ael. *VH* 2.28; cf. Fisher (2004) 70–1, Csapo (1993) for the sport's masculinist ethos, but with the caution of Herman (2006) 283–5. Fighting-cocks are emblems on hoplite shields: e.g. the BF amphora (Munich 1408) in Vierneisel and Kaeser (1992) 110 (ill. 13.7).

90 Comic fighting-cocks are depicted on the 'Getty birds' RF vase (Getty Museum 82.AE.83) illustrated in e.g. Taplin (1993) pl. 24.28, Csapo (1997) pl. 5B: see Taplin *ibid.* 101–4, Csapo (1993) 2–7, 20–3 for the possibility that the vase records the first version of Ar. *Clouds*, in which the Arguments were probably costumed as cocks (Dover (1968) xc–xciii). For a general association between mimicry and joking, note the po-faced remarks of Isoc. 15.284.

91 Ar. *Kn.* 696–7 probably evokes an impudent dance (n. 89 above); cf. Philocleon's 'animal spirits' at *Wasps* 1305 (n. 7 above, with *Clouds* 1078, where dancing enacts contempt for morality). Hdt. 3.151 ascribes mocking dances (κατορχεῖσθαι, κατασκώπτειν) to Babylonians; cf. Aristion, similarly from the safety of walls, at Plut. *Sulla* 13.1. Ribald dancing is a metaphor for rhetorical indecency at Hyp. *Phil.* fr. 21.7 Jensen (ch. 5 n. 33). Pl. *Euthd.* 277d–278e pictures choreographed taunts within religious ritual (ch. 4, 288), Dion. Halic. *Ant. Rom.* 7.72.10–12 describes the *sikinnis*, performed in satyr costumes, as full of jeering and mockery (cf. ch. 4 n. 76); Ael. *NA* 15.28 links the *skōps* dance to owls' imitative mockery. Lucian, *Prom. es* 6 personifies Old Comedy in terms of play, laughter and dance. The verb ἐξορχεῖσθαι (lit. 'dance out') can mean 'deride': e.g. Plut. *Mor.* 1127b, with LSJ *s.v.*, III.2, *PGL s.v.*, 3–4. The rare verb ἀπασκαρίζειν (ἀσκαρίζειν is cognate with σκαίρειν and σκιρτᾶν, 'leap', 'frisk': cf. ch. 4 n. 151) probably denotes a gelastic jig in Men. fr. 881, perhaps in Cratinus fr. 27 too. For a striking Christian view of laughter as the *devil* dancing, see ch. 10, 507–8. Cf. ch. 2 n. 86.

92 Fisher (1992) 50–1 inadvertently highlights the issue: rightly stressing how the description of Conon imputes *hubris*, he nonetheless calls the behaviour 'absurd'. Cf. MacDowell (1978) 131–2, who overlooks the possible ambiguity (to hearers) of the crowing image. Herman (2006) 156–9, interestingly arguing for Athenian approval of not retaliating to provocation, does not take the jury's uncertain laughter into account.

We fortunately do not need to decide the facts of the case to be able to see how the ambiguities of laughter are activated in this judicial situation. Ariston himself allows us to imagine the conflicting lines of argument and evaluation that were played out in the courtroom. Anticipating the defence's strategy (and trying, of course, to preempt it), he opens a window on an intriguing set of possibilities. He purports to know that Conon 'will try to divert the case from his hubristic deeds, present it as a matter of innocent laughter and jokes (γέλωτα καὶ σκώμματα), and say that the city knows many sons of fine, respectable families who, in the playful way of young men (παίζοντες οἱ ἄνθρωποι νέοι), have devised ribald nicknames for themselves and call one group the 'Erect Phalluses' (*ithuphalloi*), another the 'Hold-your-own-Bottle' gang (*autolēkuthoi*) . . .'.[93] Ariston proceeds to ascribe proleptically to Conon the claim that these clubs are always getting involved in petty fights over courtesans (*hetairai*) and that these are just the routine escapades of young men. Later on, Ariston himself will suggest that the clubs have sexual (mock) initiatory rituals too indecent to describe, and will claim that the 'Triballoi' (the name taken from a Thracian tribe) to which Conon himself allegedly belonged in his youth stole sacred offerings to eat at their dinners.[94] Over and above the historical interest of these glimpses of well-to-do groups of young Athenians who initiate one another into a world of sexual adventure, casual violence and daring profanity – a world which, for us at least, carries some resonance of the notorious episode of the mutilation of the herms in 415[95] – we can see that what is at stake in this trial will require the jury to attempt to distinguish (psychologically, ethically and legally) between frivolous horseplay and antisocial violence. What one party alleges to be a case of vicious assault and *hubris*, the other will explain away as the innocuous capers of the young, a sort of late-adolescent 'play'

---

[93] Dem. 54.13–14. There has been much disagreement over whether *autolēkuthos*, '[carrying] one's own oil-bottle', is sexual slang: cf. 'wankers', Murray (1990a) 157. The debate, including related interpretation of Ar. *Frogs* 1200–47, can be traced in Borthwick (1993), Dover (1993) 337–9, Bain (1985), Sommerstein (1996) 263–5. As regards *ithuphalloi*, cf. the ritual performers cited in ch. 4, 183: the clubs' names may evoke such risqué theatrical traditions.

[94] 54.17, 39: see Sandys and Paley (1910) 226–7, Carey and Reid (1985) 100–1; on Athenian perceptions of Triballians, Dunbar (1995) 702, Arnott (1996) 683–4. Cf. the *Kakodaimonistai* ('Evil-Spirit Club'), Lys. fr. 53 Thalheim, with ch. 5 n. 76. Germane images of violence over courtesans at Lys. 3.43 (n. 60 above), Isae. 3.13 ('fights and *kōmoi*'), Theophr. *Char.* 27.9.

[95] À *propos* the Hermocopidae of 415, Thuc. 6.28.1 refers to comparable, earlier acts of young men's vandalism as 'drunken pranks' (μετὰ παιδιᾶς καὶ οἴνου), as well as private parodies of the Mysteries 'for scandalous mockery' (*hubris*): his terms, or those of the informants he is describing, display the same tension (between play and danger) that the Ariston-Conon clash revolves around. Whatever the political subtext in 415, the vandalism/profanation in question reflected a world of sympotic/komastic excesses. See Murray (1990a) 149–61, but his denial that the Mysteries were 'parodied' struggles with Thucydides' use of the term *hubris*; cf. Fisher (1992) 145.

(*paizein*). In the background lies a tension between different conceptions of the acceptability of exuberant behaviour fuelled by heavy drinking in the symposium.[96] Ariston's own narrative plots a trajectory that started with derision, deteriorated into violence, and was capped by hubristic taunting. The aim of the defence, it seems, was to write aggressive hostility out of the story, leaving nothing more than 'playful' laughter – in this case, a sort of decadent social comedy – at its beginning, middle and end.

In order to reach their decision, then, the dicasts must have had to reflect, among other things, on legitimate and illegitimate causes of laughter: on what they themselves might or might not find risible.[97] Ariston tries to sway them by addressing this point head-on. The law, he insists, imposes penalties on even minor offences such as abusive language (*loidoria*), so as to discourage the escalation of social enmities ('from abuse to blows, from blows to wounds, and from wounds to killings', 19). Given this, he continues with heavy sarcasm, 'if Conon says "we've formed a sort of club called 'Erect Phalluses', and when we're involved in pursuing our sexual desires we beat up and throttle anyone we like", will you then *laugh* at this and acquit him? I hardly think so. None of you would have laughed if you had happened to be present when I was being mauled, stripped, and violently assaulted . . .' He then adds a detail which pointedly tries to occlude laughter by evoking near-tragic circumstances, namely that when his mother and other female relatives saw his wounds, they screamed and wailed 'as if someone had died' (20). The issue between the two families is presented by Ariston as a matter not just about who insulted/hit whom first, but about where to draw the boundary between 'play' and scoffing contempt for both individuals and the laws. Implicated in the question of whether assault, or any other crime of violence, took place, is the more fluid issue of the attitudes and states of mind of the participants.

On one level, therefore, the trial itself – or, more precisely, the atmosphere in the court – must have been a contest between the arousal and blocking of laughter. Ariston himself, as we have seen, describes Conon's crowing cock 'dance' in order to adduce it as a damning sign of the defendant's hubristic spitefulness. But he thereby takes some risk that the jury will perceive the anecdote as simply ludicrous. Later, Ariston defies the jury to contemplate the possibility of laughing at/with Conon's account of events. Yet that alternative account, if Ariston's anticipation of it is accurate (and, in the

---

[96] The groups in question are dining-cum-drinking clubs: see esp. 39–40, with references to drinking/drunkenness at 3–4, 7, 14–16 (alleged against Ariston himself), and 33 (n.b. συμπόται).

[97] Unless otherwise indicated, I use 'risible' in the standard modern sense of 'meriting laughter', not its original Latin(ate) sense, 'capable of laughter'.

published version of the speech, that is likely to be so), clearly attempted to make the jury complicit in a sense of the 'playful', ludicrous antics of the clubs of young men involved. The situation thus beautifully illustrates Gorgias' maxim, endorsed by Aristotle, that orators should 'destroy their adversaries' seriousness with laughter, and their laughter with seriousness'. The rival speeches in this case must have engaged in an implicit dialectic about both the use and the significance of laughter. Not for the only time in an Athenian lawcourt (or political assembly), laughter became both a technique and a topic of rhetoric.[98]

TO LAUGH OR NOT TO LAUGH?

Laughter was a recurrent object of evaluative reflection in Greek culture. In the most general terms, it could be thought of, like most things, as conditional on the principle of *kairos*, the 'right time' or 'proper occasion', and therefore as something that could easily be out of place or '*untimely*' (*akairos*). Isocrates, in a passage of Polonius-like moral directives, provides a four-square formulation of this principle, correlating it with the seri-ousness/laughter dichotomy I have already discussed. 'Do not be serious when laughter is in order,' he writes, 'nor enjoy laughter when the context demands seriousness: everything untimely (*akairos*) causes pain.'[99] Such normative thinking coexisted, however, with a recognition that laughter was an impulse to which individuals and communities were disposed in variable degrees. For individuals, this variation can be plotted along two dimen-sions, which intersect at certain points: the active (whether/when/how one laughs), and the passive or receptive (whether/how one reacts *to* laughter, directed either towards oneself or at others). One extreme was represented by the 'agelast', the person who temperamentally avoids laughter altogether (and is therefore scarcely likely to 'take a joke' well).[100] From a popular point

---

[98] Gorgias' maxim: Arist. *Rhet*. 3.18, 1419b3–4 = Gorg. fr. 12 DK. Buchheim (1989) 80 gives further references, including Pl. *Grg*. 473e (ch. 6 n. 50); cf. [Anaxim.] *Rhet. Alex*. 35.19. See ch. 5, 227–37, for oratorical uses of laughter.

[99] μηδὲ παρὰ τὰ γελοῖα σπουδάζων, μηδὲ παρὰ τὰ σπουδαῖα τοῖς γελοίοις χαίρων· τὸ γὰρ ἄκαιρον πανταχοῦ λυπηρόν: Isoc. 1.31 (cf. anxiety about symposia at 1.32). The disjunction obscures the possibility of *mixing* seriousness and play, a long-lasting Greek notion: e.g. Pl. *Symp*. 197e, 216e, Xen. *Mem*. 1.3.8, adesp. el. 27 *IEG* (ch. 3, 114–17), Meleager, *Anth. Pal*. 7.421.9–10, Ach. Tat. *LC* 5.14.4, Philostr. *Vita Ap*. 4.11, with ch. 7, 372–4, on the 'seriocomic' (*spoud[ai]ogeloion*). On laughter and the 'right time', see Index *s.v. kairos*; cf. Choric. *Apol. Mim*. 60 (alluding to Isoc. 1.31, see above), 94 (Foerster).

[100] The adj. ἀγέλαστος has active and passive senses, 'not-laughing' and 'not-to-be-laughed-at': LSJ *s.v.* 3, Nuchelmans (1955); *DGE* I 19, *s.v.*, omits Hom. *Od*. 8.307 (ch. 2 n. 70). For sinister connotations of the former, see Aesch. *Agam*. 794 (a context of forced smiles); cf. Aesch. fr. 290 *TrGF*, n. 40

of view, such behaviour seemed a contradiction of ordinary human sociability, and still more of the intensified religio-social expectations of festivity
(see Chapter 4). The agelast was consequently associated with a solitary,
alienated existence, like that of the legendary misanthrope Timon. The
eponymous loner (*monotropos*) of an Old Comedy by Phrynichus describes
his own life as one without (among other things) marriage, company, laughter and conversation; and Diogenes the Cynic (a complicated connoisseur
of certain uses of laughter, as we shall see in Chapter 7), in one of Dio
Chrysostom's speeches, depicts the spirit of avarice as a figure who never
laughs or smiles and thinks festivals a sheer waste of expenditure.[101] But to
be *agelastos*, without laughter, could also be a vivid marker of a temporarily
desperate, grief-striken condition like that of the goddess Demeter (an icon
of life itself) after the loss of her daughter Persephone.[102]

There was a third possibility too, however. The agelast might be a person
who moved in society but held principles, or a view of life, which made
laughter inappropriate. We will see in later chapters that some important
figures were included in this category, in terms that may be a matter more
of folklore, legend or idealisation than historical record, but are no less
(perhaps all the more) revealing for that. It may seem unsurprising that
some of these figures were philosophers. Even so, we need specific not
merely stereotypical explanations for the image of the agelast in the cases
of Pythagoras, Heraclitus, Anaxagoras and (with qualifications) Plato. Not
only were not all agelasts philosophers (the class could also be thought to

above, with LSJ for cognate verb and adverb (ἀγελαστί: the form ἀγελαστεί at ps.-Herodian,
Part. 257.1 Boissonade is not attested elsewhere and is omitted by the lexica). French 'agelaste' was
coined by Rabelais, used three times in *Pantagruel*: Rabelais (1994) 519 (with 1483 n. 9), 703, 785;
discussion in Ménager (1995) 80–3; cf. Joubert (1980) 100, 104 for sixteenth-century usage.
'Agelast' was not used in English, it seems, till 1877, though *OED* records 'agelastic' (noun) as early
as 1626. See the Rabelais-influenced use of the word by Bakhtin (1968), e.g. 122 n. 65, 212, and its
revival by Kundera (2000) 159–65 as foil to his quasi-Bakhtinian view of the novel's liberating spirit
of laughter; cf. Kundera (2007) 106–8.

[101] Phryn. fr. 19 (cf. ch. 8, 396), Dio Chrys. 4.91–2 (19 above). Cf. the link between misanthropy
and sullenness at ps.-Arist. *Virt.* 7, 1251b15–16; contrast the paradoxical laughter of the solitary
Myson at Diog. Laert. 1.108 (ch. 6, 267–8). The person who never laughs at all is 'good for nothing' (φαῦλος) in Anon. med. *Physiogn.* 25 Foerster (cf. Appendix 1 n. 19). One kind of 'scowling'
(*skuthrōpazein*) is attacked as misanthropic at Dem. 45.68 (cf. Hesk (2000) 222–7); related sentiments, opposing *skuthrōp-* terms and laughter, occur at e.g. Eur. *Alc.* 774, 797 (cf. ch. 3, 131–2), Isoc.
1.15 (balanced by reservations about *outright* laughter), Choric. *Laud. Arat.* 63–4 (Foerster), where
agelastic Epaminondas is cited (n. 103 below), *Apol. Mim.* 61; note Aesch. *Cho.* 738 for hypocritical
manipulation of the contrast. Different is the 'straight face' (ἀγέλαστος . . . καὶ σκυθρωπός) with
which Cicero delivers witticisms at Plut. *Cic.* 38.2. On other uses of *skuthrōpos* see Index *s.v.*

[102] See *Hom. Hymn* 2.200, with ch. 4, 161–4. The same adj. (n. 100 above) connects with grief at Aesch.
Cho. 30. Cf. the laughter-less life of Byzantium during Justinian's closure of theatres, Procop. *Hist.
arc.* 26.11.

include the politicians Pericles and Phocion, and the playwright Euripides). It was just as feasible to find (or create) an individual philosopher, Democritus, who came to stand in popular legend as the *ne plus ultra* in the practice of laughter.[103] And beyond the level of individual reputations, there is no doubt, as we shall see in Chapter 6, that several schools of ancient philosophy – including Cynics, Epicureans and even, in certain respects, Stoics – learnt to practise and/or theorise certain types of laughter for their own purposes. But the persona of the (supposed) agelast, whether philosopher or otherwise, remained an arresting way of crystallising certain questions about human nature and experience. Most memorably and influentially of all, as I shall discuss in my final chapter, it was taken up and applied in the Greek-speaking Christianity of Basil of Caesarea and John Chrysostom to none other than Jesus. The distance between the laughing gods of Homer and the (allegedly) agelastic 'son of god' of early Christianity is the ultimate measure of the scale of cultural issues explored in this book.

The opposite extreme from the agelast was occupied by the inveterate buffoon (*bōmolochos*) or jester (*gelōtopoios*, literally 'laughter-maker'). This was the sort of person who might assume 'professional' form as an entertainer at a symposium or other celebration, but who 'in life' could easily be regarded as a flawed, unbalanced character. But how draw that distinction, between performance and life, with complete confidence? The Homeric figure of Thersites remained throughout antiquity an emblem of the problems of definition and demarcation in this area.[104] His description in the *Iliad* evokes a quasi-professional role as army jester, but his compulsion to engage in ridicule is presented as marring his judgement of the contexts and consequences of laughter.[105] Traces of the 'Thersites problem' can be found even where he is not mentioned directly. When Aristotle distinguishes an appropriate disposition for laughter from the opposing faults of excessive

---

[103] Supposed agelasts include Heraclitus (ch. 7, 344–6), Epaminondas (n. 101 above, with ch. 3 n. 48), Pythagoras, Anaxagoras, Pericles, Euripides, young Plato, and Aristoxenus (see ch. 6 nn. 15–17, 20–1, 24, 29 for the last six); for Phocion, see Plut. *Phoc.* 4.2, *Mor.* 187f, stressing general avoidance of emotional display (cf. *Phoc.* 5.1–3, including the term *skuthrōpos*: n. 101 above). Compare the Persian Aglaïtadas, Xen. *Cyr.* 2.2.11, 14–16 (cf. Demetr. *Eloc.* 134–5), though he manages a smile at his friends' mockery (16); Σ Tzetz. on Ar. *Frogs* 843 lists Telamon (father of Ajax?), Aglaïtadas, Pythagoras, and Pambo (fourth-century AD Egyptian desert monk) as proverbial agelasts. On 'laughing' Democritus, see ch. 7 *passim*.

[104] A vivid instance is (the legendary) Democritus' description of humanity at ps.-Hippoc. *Epist.* 17.5 (Smith (1990) 82): 'each and every one is a Thersites of life' (Θερσῖται δ' εἰσὶ τοῦ βίου πάντες); cf. ch. 7, 362.

[105] See ch. 2, 69–77. For the social ambiguity of a jester, cf. ch. 3, 143–4, on Philippus in Xen. *Symp.* But jesters could club together: thus the Athenian group, meeting at the temple of Diomeian Heracles (location uncertain: Travlos (1971) 340, but cf. Parker (2005) 472–3), mentioned by Athen. 6.260b, 14.614d–e, and perhaps alluded to at Ar. *Ach.* 605 (Storey (1995) 182–3).

indulgence and agelastic surliness, his depiction of the *bōmolochos* as a character under the control of laughter, not *in* control of it, and addicted to trying to arouse it at every turn, is unmistakably reminiscent of the Homeric Thersites.[106] Aristotle approaches the subject, of course, from his own philosophical angle, but his assumption that one can laugh too much as well as too little was widely shared. Even the Theophrastean flatterer, by stuffing his cloak into his mouth as he (supposedly) bursts with amusement at his patron's bad jokes, shows an awareness of a social code that deprecates excessive mirth.[107]

Variations (and instabilities) in the operations of laughter depend not just on its agents but also on its human objects or targets. This factor clearly has a bearing on whether or how far laughter is perceived as 'consequential' or otherwise. Two separate but complementary points of principle are visible here: first, the notion that hostile laughter calls (in terms of honour and shame) for reprisals; the second, that non-hostile laughter needs to be taken in the right way (ideally, as we saw, in a spirit of reciprocally amiable 'play') if it is not to be converted by the recipient into grounds for enmity. The consequentiality of laughter, as of other forms of social behaviour, depends at least as much on the reaction of the 'receiver' as on that of the agent or perpetrator. The advice ascribed to Cleobulus of Lindos, one of the canonical Seven Sages (who will receive some further attention in Chapter 6), 'not to join in laughing openly at those who are being mocked, as you will become an enemy of theirs', clearly presupposes that the victim in such a situation will seek opportunities for revenge.[108] This means that insouciance about being a target of ridicule actually constitutes a recognisable aberrancy, a symptom of a deficient sense of honour or self-worth. We have already glimpsed a case of this with the 'ape' or 'monkey' woman of Semonides 7.74–9 *IEG*: she is (for her ugliness) the butt of everyone's laughter in the streets, yet she could not care less. In addition to the risibility of her ape-like nature, the fact that this jibe is made (satirically) about a *female*, whose capacity to react might be thought limited (unless her honour is defended by male relatives), only strengthens the underlying norm of sensitivity to laughter.[109]

A range of other texts reinforce this point. 'To endure denigration without response, or watch this happening to one's relatives, is slavish,' writes Aristotle; and similar sentiments are voiced, as apophthegms of standard

[106] See ch. 6, 311.   [107] Theophr. *Char.* 2.4.
[108] Cleobulus *apud* Diog. Laert. 1.93: μὴ ἐπεγγελᾶν τοῖς σκωπτομένοις· ἀπεχθήσεσθαι γὰρ τούτοις. Slightly different wording at Stob. 3.1.172 (DK 1 63). Cf. ch. 6, 266.
[109] Cf. Lloyd-Jones (1975) 83–4, with 31 above. On the risibility of apes, cf. ch. 6 n. 94.

morality, in Menandrian comedy. A psychologically subtle vignette in Plato's *Republic* depicts a wife who feels anger (and arouses an intensified sense of honour in her observing son) at the 'unmanly' temperament of a husband who, among other things, accepts insults without retaliation. That same kind of non-retaliatory behaviour (carried to the extreme of laughing oneself, with unconcern, at denigration) is seen as characteristic of the 'dissembler', *eirōn*, in Theophrastus – a problematic characteristic precisely in virtue of the uncertainty and duplicity that it introduces into social relationships.[110] It is true that a litigant might claim, as Lysias' client does in *Against Theomnestus* (10) 2–3, that most denigration should be regarded as of no consequence and that it is 'illiberal' to go to law even where actionable slander is concerned. But this is part of a carefully calculated rhetorical strategy, designed to project an image of the individual's eirenic, non-litigious disposition; in any case, the speaker's remarks are a foil to the fact that he *has* brought a charge of slander against Theomnestus for allegedly calling him a parricide, a slur to which it would be shameful, he explains, not to retaliate. Perhaps only the (comic) parasite can afford to *boast* of his nonchalance about being mocked. It is the parasite's métier to live and die by laughter, as it were: he survives by abandoning many of the scruples that inform the social status of most people, including sensitivity to ridicule.[111] Such standards could sometimes be qualified by a principled disregard for vulgar abuse. A character in the comic poet Philemon articulates the idea that it is somehow 'more cultured' (μουσικώτερον) to ignore vilification; 'for the abuser, if the abused ignores him, abuses himself in the very act of abuse'.[112] But exceptions of this kind smack of philosophical detachment from widely shared values, and it is indeed individual philosophers, especially, though rather differently, Socrates and Diogenes the Cynic, who present the most conspicuous examples of (near) imperviousness to mockery – examples which will receive close attention in Chapters 6 and 7.

The reverse side of the expected resentment on the part of mockery's victims is the capacity to take well-intentioned laughter in the right spirit

---

[110] Arist. *EN* 4.5, 1126a7–8, Men. frs. 513, 837, Pl. *Rep.* 8.549d, Theophr. *Char.* 1.2, with Diggle (2004) 171–2. Theophr. *Char.* 6.2 may be pertinent, but see ch. 5 n. 58 for textual difficulties. An unknown character speaks of mockery (*skōptein*) washing over him ('like an ass in rain') in Cephisodorus fr. 1 *PCG*. For a mythological case of disregarded abuse involving, of all people, Heracles, see ch. 4, 186–7.

[111] Parasites welcoming laughter against themselves: Antiphanes frs. 80.9–10, 193.11–12, Nicolaus fr. 1.31–2 *PCG*; cf. Plut. *Mor.* 46c. Note Philippus at Xen. *Symp.* 1.11–16: *failure* to draw laughter is a disaster for him ('laughter has perished from mankind; I'm done for!': 1.15), though one ironically assimilated into his repertoire (ch. 3, 144–5).

[112] ὁ λοιδορῶν γάρ, ἂν ὁ λοιδορούμενος | μὴ προσποιῆται, λοιδορεῖται λοιδορῶν: Philemon fr. 23. Part of the fragment is endorsed at Plut. *Mor.* 35d.

and perhaps respond with reciprocally amiable laughter of one's own. I touched earlier on Aristotle's recognition that the dynamics of laughter within friendship depend on the symmetry of these 'active' and 'passive' roles. He speaks at *Rhetoric* 2.4, 1381a33–5, of friends who have the ability to play both roles, knowing how to tease (or poke fun, τωθάζειν) and be teased, to make but also take a well-judged joke. It is the symposium, as Chapter 3 will explain, which becomes the paradigmatic context in which such balanced, non-consequential exchanges of laughter can ideally be practised, though at the same time the heady intimacy of the drinking-party remains vulnerable to more aggressive, disruptive kinds of ridicule. A further extrapolation of the ability to accept friendly laughter in the right frame of mind is a willingness to laugh at oneself. But a prime piece of evidence for this idea, from Aeschines *Against Timarchus*, also attests the uncertainty that could attach to it. Aeschines sets up Demosthenes as ostensibly prepared to make a joke against himself (involving his nickname Bat(t)alos, meaning either 'stammerer' or, perhaps, 'soft arse') in order to appear 'pleasantly easy-going and happy to laugh about his own behaviour' (ὡς ἡδὺς ἀνὴρ καὶ περὶ τὰς ἰδίας διατριβὰς γελοῖος). But Aeschines' whole point is that this is a ruse designed to play down the sexually lubricious reputation of Demosthenes' associate Timarchus.[113] We do not need to unpick all the tangled political and legal issues of the speech to see that while Aeschines allows in principle that being able to laugh at oneself could count as an attractive trait, the readiness with which he can suggest that it might be feigned for ulterior motives is culturally symptomatic. As with the case of Theophrastus' dissembler, cited in my previous paragraph, Aeschines assumes that his audience will find it plausible to suspect of duplicity anyone who purports to be immune to the sting of public ridicule.[114]

To Greek ways of thinking, it is not only individuals who vary in their habits *vis-à-vis* laughter. Whole communities could also be perceived as displaying exceptional attachment to or aversion from laughter. I have already mentioned Theophrastus' story about the people of Tiryns and their (unsuccessful) attempt to exclude laughter from religious sacrifices. That story (itself a kind of joke) is meant to illustrate the pathological extremes of habitual laughter: it is precisely because they suffered from a gelastic addiction that the Tirynthians needed to seek divine help in the matter, though the upshot of the tale is a paradoxical reaffirmation of the power of laughter even in religious contexts.[115] The same section

---

[113] Aeschin. 1.126; see Fisher (2001) 265–7 for discussion of context.
[114] For other cases of laughing at oneself, see ch. 6 n. 101.   [115] See n. 39 above.

of Athenaeus which preserves that fragment of Theophrastus also testifies to the reputation of the Phaestians, in Crete, for practising witty banter and cultivating a heightened sense of the ridiculous/comic from childhood onwards: the pursuit of laughter, on this account, was a cultural peculiarity, noted as exceptional by other Cretans.[116] In a more sweeping vein, Dio Chrysostom criticises a fanaticism for theatrical shows and entertainments in imperial Alexandria as involving a kind of collective culture of endless laughter and frivolity, a social vice that was supposedly sapping the energies of the community for more sober, earnest purposes.[117]

It may seem initially counterintuitive that of all ancient Greek communities it should have been the Spartans, with their reputation for being the hardest, severest of peoples, among whom laughter – or perhaps one should write Laughter – was allegedly the object of religious cult, uniquely so within the mainstream public religion of Greek city-states.[118] According to Plutarch, this cult was marked by a small statue of the deity (Gelos) dedicated by the great Spartan culture-hero, Lycurgus. Plutarch relates this circumstance (which is perhaps the more credible for having been derived from the early Hellenistic Spartan historian Sosibius) by way of stressing that the Spartans, for all their toughness, did in fact make use of laughter in their dealings with one another. They did so, on his account, both to make more palatable the exchanges of personal criticism that were an integral part of their ideological 'consciousness raising', and, by Lycurgus' own design, as an occasional relief, at symposia and elsewhere, from the otherwise relentless toil of their austere way of life. This picture of Laconian mores suggests that laughter counted as something psychologically and socially necessary to the militarised regimen of the Spartiates, yet as a factor which existed in firmly controlled counterpoint to the harsh, uncompromising demands of that regimen. Elsewhere, in his life of *Cleomenes*, Plutarch tells us that the Spartans had shrines dedicated to 'fear, death, laughter and other such elemental experiences (*pathēmata*)', a formulation which *prima facie* makes laughter one of the basic coordinates (physical, psychological and social) of a rather darkly coloured map of existence.[119] In the case of fear, however,

---

[116] The claim comes from the Cretan historian Sosicrates (second-century), *FGrH* 461 F1, *apud* Athen. 6.261e.

[117] Dio Chrys. 32.1–5.

[118] The nearest parallel is the festival of laughter at Thessalian Hypatia posited (fictionally?) by Apul. *Met.* 2.31, 3.11: see Milanezi (1992), esp. 134–41. The painting of personified Gelos at Philostr. maj. *Imag.* 1.25.3 (quoted as epigraph to Ch. 3) is not testimony to religious practice: such a figure appears nowhere in regular Dionysiac cult.

[119] Spartan statue/shrine to Laughter: Plut. *Lyc.* 25.2 (Sosibius *FGrH* 595 F19, where Jacoby's commentary moots a misunderstanding of the face of an archaic statue), *Cleom.* 9; cf. Choric. *Apol.*

so Plutarch explains, this was because the Spartans actually recognised the communal value of something that might otherwise easily be framed in wholly negative terms. If that is right, then in the case of laughter we might conjecture that the Spartans had a nervous but canny reverence for an impulse which counted as a force of nature (manifesting itself, like fear, in keenly somatic form) and was deemed sufficiently dangerous to be treated as at least quasi-divine. Difficult though it is to penetrate into the Spartan mentality, the idea of its deification of Gelos makes best sense as the expression of an attempt neither to keep laughter at bay nor to encourage its unbridled celebration, but to harness its power to the cohesion of a scrupulously regulated society of equals.

There is evidence that already in the classical period some Athenians held (or were motivated to promote) an unsympathetic image of Spartans as dour and, by implication, averse to laughter. A passage of Demosthenes, for instance, uses the verb *skuthrōpazein*, to be 'po-faced', of the allegedly chosen demeanour of a group of Athenians 'who claim to be following Spartan mores (*lakōnizein*)'.[120] But any simple equation between Sparta and aversion to laughter was, at best, a convenient stereotype. The broader traditions about Spartan culture suggest that it was committed not to an agelastic, let alone antigelastic, code of conduct, but rather to a watchful, closely monitored ambivalence about the power of *gelōs*. One side of this ambivalence was visible in a prohibition on laughter-inducing behaviour in some contexts where many other Greeks revelled in it. In the first book of Plato's *Laws* (637a–b) the Spartan Megillus claims that his city forbids the over-indulgent scurrility of the symposium, the *kōmos* and the Dionysiac festival. As regards the latter, he specifies the ribald customs of (masked) 'men on wagons' who paraded through the streets mocking various people indecently; he contrasts Sparta in this respect not only with Athens but even with a Dorian colony like Taras.[121] Even after making allowances for an exaggerated portrait of Spartan puritanism (and the Athenian interlocutor gently hints at the possibility of hypocrisy, 1.637b–c), there is no

---

Mim. 91–2 (Foerster). For Spartan 'worship' of personified laughter, fear, etc., see Richer (1999) 92–7, 106–7, Richer (2005) 111–12. David (1989) provides an excellent survey of the whole subject of Spartan laughter; cf. Milanezi (1992) 127–31. The views ascribed to the Spartan Chilon should not be taken as peculiar to his culture: cf. 29 above, with ch. 6, 265–7.

[120] Dem. 54.34, describing Conon's associates (see 33–8 above); cf. n. 101 for *skuthrōp-* terms. The passage is complicated by a charge of hypocrisy: harsh public faces mask private excess. Cf. Plut. *Phoc.* 10.1, describing one of these same people (Archibiades) in similar terms. For an oblique hint (and contradiction) of stereotypically dour Spartans at Ar. *Lys.* 1226, see n. 123 below. On Athenian laconism in general, cf. Rawson (1969) 18–45.

[121] 'Men on wagons': ch. 4, 177–81, ch. 5, 228–9.

reason to doubt that certain (Dionysiac) forms of 'licensed' public laughter had no official place in Spartan society. On the other hand, Megillus may be telling us only one half of the story. It is certain that already in the archaic period Sparta had its own varieties of ritual-cum-comic performances. These included a local type of masked mime, acted by mummers called *d(e)ikēliktai* ('exhibitors'), which seems to have extracted gelastic potential from such components of Laconian culture as the use of training in theft to inculcate cunning in the young. Another species of spectacle, presented by figures called *brullichistai*, is obscure in its details but involved less than entirely decorous dances and the wearing of distorted female masks. It is tempting to connect the last detail with whatever practices lay behind the votive terracotta masks (or models of masks) found in the Spartan sanctuary of the goddess Ortheia (probably only later associated with Artemis) and dating from the later seventh and, predominantly, the first half of the sixth century. Some of these seem conspicuously 'grinning' (with open/curved mouth, teeth showing, and heightened cheeks); others may represent grimaces or even demonic ferocity *à la* Gorgoneion (and the Spartan finds also include Gorgon masks).[122] The classification and significance of these votives, including the vexed question of whether many of them depict female faces, remain insecure. But they certainly do not impede the general inference that a putative Spartan aversion to Dionysiac scurrility was counterbalanced by the performances of *brullichistai* and others in which laughter and religion were mixed together.

Furthermore, if Plato's Megillus, in the passage cited, seems to imply that 'symposia' fell into the category of prohibited occasions of laughter for Spartans, he should probably be taken to mean private, unregulated drinking parties (as opposed to the common 'messes' of the Laconian system) where heavy inebriation might lead to extreme loss of self-control. We have seen that Plutarch was quite happy to regard the symposium, in some sense, as a

---

[122] The main evidence for δ(ε)ικηλίκται/δ(ε)ικηλισταί is Athen. 14.621d–622d (Sosibius *FGrH* 595 F*7; cf. TI); cf. Plut. *Ages.* 21, Hesych. *s.vv.* δεικηλισταί, δίκηλον, Σ Ap. Rhod. *Argon.* 1.746. Βρυλλιχισταί: Hesych. *s.v.* (cf. *s.v.* βρυδαλίχα); Pollux *s.v.* βαρυλλικά may be related. See Pickard-Cambridge (1927) 228–32, 253–61 (with uneven conviction), including the hypothetical connection with votive masks (below). The attempt of Stark (2004) 34–40 to reconstruct the social status of Spartan comic performers outstrips the evidence. On the Ortheia masks (for spellings of the name see Davison (1968) 169–72), Dickins (1929) 167, 172–4 accepts a link with 'ritual dances'. Carter (1987) 356–7, with a different classification of the faces, rejects that link (though Carter (1988) offers her own speculative link with choral poetry, deriving the masks, via Phoenician influence, from NE models used in worship of a fertility goddess; she takes many of the masks to represent demons. Other views include David (1989) 11–12, Seeberg (1995) 10–11. On the masks' expressions, cf. e.g. Dickins (1929) 166, 179 ('grinning'), Carter (1987) 383 ('grimacing' plus 'jeer[ing]'). Cf. Appendix 2, 546.

Spartan institution, and one where the laughter of relaxation had 'Lycurgan' endorsement. This was not simply a post-classical perception. In the fifth century, Critias (uncle of Plato) referred in an elegiac poem to young men at Sparta drinking only enough to produce a lightened, cheerful mood that would conduce to 'moderate' or 'measured' (*metrios*) laughter and retention of self-discipline.[123] This reflects, in fact, a more widely held, if precarious, Greek ideal of the standards a good symposium should live up to; Chapter 3 will elaborate on this theme. So too do the comments of Xenophon in his *Constitution of the Lacedaemonians*, where we are told that drinking in the messes, in an atmosphere where older men educated their younger colleagues, was always free from aggressive offensiveness (*hubris*), drunken quarrelling (*paroinia*) and shameful or obscene talk (*aischrologia*).[124] Such a conception of Spartan restraint was not exclusive to staunch laconophiles like Critias and Xenophon. Aristotle's *Constitution of the Laconians* stated that Spartans learnt both to make and take jokes in a harmonious manner (Aristotle's own conception of the mean, in other words) from childhood onwards. This reciprocal capacity to practise and receive laughter in the best way remains a Spartan hallmark in Plutarch.[125]

These testimonies show that for certain admirers and intellectuals, at least, classical Sparta could be held up as a society where laughter was carefully supervised but permitted a measured outlet. Two further passages from Plutarch's *Lycurgus* confirm this impression. One is the description of festivals, watched by the kings, elders and entire citizen body, at which choruses of girls targeted individual young males with jibes that were simultaneously playful yet sufficiently 'biting' to serve as a public means of shaming and correction.[126] The other is a passing reference to how older Spartan men would frequently visit the exercise grounds to watch adolescents engaged in 'fighting and jesting with one another' (μαχομένοις καὶ σκώπτουσιν ἀλλήλους); the young, Plutarch explains, had a plethora of 'fathers and tutors' to control and rebuke them if they erred in any way. In this latter

---

[123] Critias 6 *IEG*: see ch. 3, 125–7. Note the comic image of Spartans as 'witty' (χαρίεντες) at a good symposium, Ar. *Lys.* 1226 (but with a hint of the speaker's surprise? cf. n. 120 above). On Spartan drinking: Fisher (1989), esp. 27–32, Murray (1991) 90–2.

[124] Xen. *Lac. resp.* 5.6; see Rebenich (1998) 107–13, Lipka (2002) 148–59 for Xenophon's treatment of Spartan dining/drinking.

[125] Aristotle's treatise was epitomised in the second century by Heracleides Lembos: see Arist. Titel 143,1, 2.13 Gigon (fr. 611.13 Rose), attributing harmonious exchanges of joking (ἐμμελῶς καὶ σκώπτειν καὶ σκώπτεσθαι) to Spartans; for *emmelōs*, 'harmoniously', cf. ch. 6 n. 121, with *Rhet.* 2.4, 1381a33–6 (21, 43 above). Taking jokes in the right spirit is a 'Spartan' quality at Plut. *Mor.* 46d, 631f (implausibly tame); cf. *Lyc.* 12.4, where ideal jesting (*skōptein*) avoids buffoonery, *bōmolochia*: contrast the Athenian images cited on 22–4 above.

[126] *Lyc.* 14.3: see ch. 4, 189.

case it is implicit, both in the conjunction with (mock) fighting and in the surveillance provided by older men, that the adolescents' laughter should be read not as casual childhood frivolity but as an exhibiton of that character-forming use of reciprocal joking noted just above.[127] Laughter here takes on the status of verbal sparring, matched symmetrically with physical sparring. What these two further passages have in common, therefore, is the idea of laughter as incorporated into a tightly regulated system of collective Spartan ideology. In both cases one might wonder whether what we are being offered is a *post hoc* justification, or even a fictional transposition, of phenomena that possess obvious affinities with more widespread types of Greek behaviour – the performance of mockery by festive groups (to be examined in detail in Chapter 4), and spontaneously competitive adolescent banter, respectively. We should accept, however, that there seems to have been a sharply focused Spartan upbringing in the lessons of group ridicule. And we do not need to imagine for ourselves what that could have meant when such laughter was channelled by the society against *others*. Xenophon, who had access to good information in the matter, reports a contemporary episode in which the Spartans publicly humiliated their own Mantinean allies, even though some of them had been killed in the fighting, for having run away from light-armed peltasts 'like children afraid of bogey-women'.[128] Mass jeering (ἐπισκώπτειν) and 'infantilisation' of one's allies in such circumstances is not a practice most Greek armies would have risked.

From *outside* then (our only available perspective), Spartan attitudes to laughter came to be considered as buttressing not relaxing the system's rigorous code of values. On the other hand, those attitudes might equally be regarded as a paradigmatic display of the measured balance that many non-Spartans thought a necesssary curb on a potentially disruptive element of human psychology and behaviour. As we have already observed, laughter is often associated in Greek culture with the unruliness of the young, the surging energy of bodily instincts, and the insolence, even subversiveness, of mockery. The threat that such things pose to a social system based on uncompromising militarism is not hard to discern. For any orthodox Spartan who knew the *Iliad*, the figure of Thersites must have seemed a token of the threatening irreverence of laughter within a military setting,

---

[127] Plut. *Lyc.* 17.1; cf. 25.2. David (1989) 4 plausibly connects such 'jesting contests' with the Spartans' reputation for apophthegmatic ('laconic') wit. The conclusion of Bremmer (1997) 22 that Spartan life 'made festivity and mockery intolerable' is exaggerated. For a suggestion that Spartans allowed themselves more aggressive, hubristic laughter against inferiors (helots etc.), see Fisher (1989) 43.

[128] ὥσπερ μορμόνας παιδάρια: Xen. *Hell.* 4.4.17; cf. ch. 6 n. 35 for the 'bogey-woman' motif.

though whether Spartans would have approved of the general laughter which greets Thersites' physical punishment by Odysseus is less easy to say. It would be naive to suppose that social control of laughter at Sparta could have been maintained without ambiguity and rupture.

As it happens, a story in Herodotus gives us something at least approximating to one glimpse of a real (at any rate credible) use of devastating laughter as a political weapon in late archaic Sparta. It concerns the occasion, in the late 490s, when Demaratus, deposed from the kingship on the grounds of doubts about his paternity and now the holder of a lesser magistracy, was publicly insulted by his royal successor Leotychidas. Herodotus narrates how the latter sent a slave to ask Demaratus in public, at the festival of the Gumnopaidiai, what it was like to be a mere magistrate after having been king. Leotychidas' motive, according to the historian, was to direct laughter and contempt against Demaratus.[129] The festival setting is intriguing: was Leotychidas ironically taking advantage of the more general conventions of festive mockery which later sources report (see on Plutarch above)? Demaratus is said to have attempted a barbed rejoinder (including a thinly veiled threat) before leaving the gathering in shame, with his head covered, and shortly afterwards defecting to Persia. But was Leotychidas' behaviour appropriate for a Spartan king? Whatever its historical credentials, the anecdote could be thought to send ambiguous signals. It shows laughter being employed in a manner which reflects a pent-up power perhaps indicative of Spartan psychology, while at the same time leaving one to wonder whether its calculated offensiveness conforms to or breaches Spartan protocols of self-discipline. The use of a slave to relay the question from king to ex-king nicely encapsulates the problem: it adds to the public humiliation while avoiding face-to-face ridicule. Leotychidas himself laughs, as it were, from a distance. It is not merely pedantic to point out that Herodotus' text does not tell us whether other Spartans, hearing the question put to Demaratus, actually laughed too. But the historian's own narrative does later recount how Leotychidas 'paid the price' for his treatment of Demaratus. He suffered his own ignominy and died in exile.

That is perhaps an aptly inconclusive note on which to end both these brief reflections on Sparta and my preliminary survey of the ambiguities of laughter in Greek culture. All in all, our evidence supports the inference

<hr/>

[129] ἐπὶ γέλωτί τε καὶ λάσθῃ: Hdt. 6.67, with hendiadys; λάσθη denotes pointed contumely, akin to *hubris* (cf. Ael. fr. 155 Hercher). See David (1989) 16, who thinks Herodotus transmits a version told by Spartan informants. Lateiner (1977) 178 stresses Leotychidas' eventual downfall (Hdt. 6.72); he also examines the Herodotean episodes in which Demaratus is the recipient of further ill-fated laughter (from the Persian Xerxes). Cf. Griffiths (1995) 41.

that Spartans manifested acute ambivalence about the power of laughter. If so, they were betraying in a locally heightened form a kind of uncertainty and anxiety which had wide currency in the Greek world. The chapters which follow will examine a series of texts and contexts in which the complications of Greek views of laughter can be seen at work, both in their own right as narrative and dramatic representations of the phenomenon, and in their relationship to many of the major preoccupations of the culture as a whole.

CHAPTER 2

Inside and outside morality: the laughter of Homeric gods and men

And on the assumption that gods too philosophise . . . I do not doubt
that they thereby also know how to laugh in a superhuman and new
way – and at the expense of all serious things!

Nietzsche[1]

BETWEEN PATHOS AND BLOODLUST: THE RANGE OF HOMERIC LAUGHTER

It is a far-reaching cultural fact that so much of the ancient Greek collective repertoire of behavioural paradigms and self-images (in religion, ethics, psychology, warfare, politics) was grounded in the songs of Homer. Yet it might seem surprising and counterintuitive to extend that thesis to, of all things, the manifestations of laughter. After all, there is at first sight not much opportunity for laughter, whether for characters or audiences, in the *Iliad* and *Odyssey*. But while in purely quantitative terms laughter does not bulk large in Homeric epic, its appearances in both poems are all highly charged with significance and contribute symbolically to narrative moments which were to remain powerfully resonant for later Greeks. In the *Iliad*, occurrences of laughing and smiling are distributed across more than half the books of the poem and divided almost equally between gods and humans. But a majority of the relevant passages are clustered in five main scenes: the gods on Olympus at the end of Book 1, the Thersites episode in Book 2, the Hector and Andromache encounter in Book 6, the fighting of the gods in Book 21, and the funeral games in Book 23. In the *Odyssey*, laughter is mentioned almost twice as often as in the *Iliad*, though smiles only half as often, but between them the two forms of behaviour contribute

---

[1] *Beyond Good and Evil* 294, Nietzsche (1988) v 236. ('Und gesetzt, daß auch Götter philosophieren . . . so zweifle ich nicht, daß sie dabei auch auf eine übermenschliche und neue Weise zu lachen wissen – und auf Unkosten aller ernsten Dinge!' German spelling modernised.)

to a tellingly clear-cut pattern. Apart from the remarkable (and problematic) laughter of the gods in Demodocus' song of Hephaestus' revenge against the adulterous Ares and Aphrodite, Odyssean laughter is overwhelmingly associated with the depraved suitors and their illicit feasting in the palace of Ithaca, while it plays only a subdued (though pregnantly anticipatory) role in the lives of Odysseus himself and his family. Smiling, on the other hand, is something the suitors never do, yet is represented as a subtle means of communication for the hero himself and those connected with him. This fits both with the independent consideration that smiling is more under the control of humans than laughter (and therefore capable of being consciously manipulated as a code of expression), and with the *Odyssey's* densely elaborated thematics of self-betrayal and self-concealment.[2]

There are multiple questions to be posed about Homeric laughter. Why is it that in both poems, though only once in each case, an outburst of collectively irrepressible ('unquenchable') laughter is attributed to the Olympian gods? (And why is the only occurrence of 'unquenchable' laughter among humans a case of momentary but unforgettably macabre madness?) Although the gods are portrayed as capable of laughing in several ways, from the affectionate to the bitterly caustic, from the conciliatory to the triumphalist, why is it that they *never* laugh at human beings (never, for sure, at the human condition), only at themselves? Why is it, furthermore, that in the *Iliad* Zeus and Hera are the only gods who smile (while Aphrodite *philommeidēs*, 'lover of smiles', never actually does so), and why do we hear specifically of Zeus laughing, but not Hera (with an ostensible but ironic exception at 15.101–2)?[3] In the human domain, why does Thersites, singled out as someone addicted to making others laugh, step into the limelight at a critical moment in *Iliad* 2, only to be reduced to tears of physical pain which turn him, paradoxically, into an object of laughter in his own right? Why does Ajax go into battle at *Iliad* 7.212 with a weird smile that echoes the look of a Gorgon? What, by sharp contrast, does it mean for Odysseus' 'heart' to laugh at *Odyssey* 9.413 or for him to smile 'sardonically', and again inwardly (in this *thumos*), at 20.301? Not all these questions will yield easy answers. But I shall try to integrate them, and others besides, into an investigation of how the Homeric poems employ

---

[2] Lateiner (1995) 75 wrongly makes the suitors smile; likewise Lateiner (1992) 450. Miralles (1993) 7, 19 mistakenly claims that γελᾶν and μειδ(ι)ᾶν in Homer are 'in principle' synonymous (ΣbT on *Il.* 7.212 denies this). Control of smiles and laughter: ch. 1 n. 14.

[3] Miralles (1993) 23, eliding the difference between laughter and smiles, claims that Hera 'laughs the most' in the *Iliad*: in fact, four of the relevant passages involve smiles. Zeus's two laughs, discussed in my text below, are at 21.389, 508.

both the actuality and the idea of laughter to cast sidelong but revealing illumination on divine and human existence (what connects them, what differentiates them) at moments of crisis and special intensity.

Homeric laughter spans a spectrum of feeling that includes both positive and negative emotions: from the most intimate shared delight to a terrifying bloodlust, from public celebration to concealed malevolence, from connotations of sensually life-enhancing brightness to those of violent menace. Yet it is an instructive generalisation that there is extremely little amiable laughter or smiling in either epic: when such things do occur, they carry the force of the pointedly exceptional. In the Iliadic world of war, it is hardly suprising that opportunities for lighthearted social pleasure are severely limited, though that in turn might prompt us to wonder why the poem contains quite as much laughter as it does. But even in the *Odyssey*, where such opportunities are greater, Menelaus' smile (to Telemachus) at 4.609 is arguably the only such gesture of pure affability in the whole work, whereas the prevailing association of laughter with the suitors' tainted lives creates a thematic current of suspicion about the body language of overt mirth. Far from reducing it to insignificance, however, the restricted scope of Homeric laughter places its occurrences in a complex motivic relationship to the darker zones of experience that dominate both poems.

Part of that complexity can be broached by considering two profoundly contrasting Iliadic instances. The first of these is the parental laughter of Hector and Andromache in response to their baby Astyanax's fright at his father's plumed helmet (6.471, ἐκ δ' ἐγέλασσε πατήρ τε φίλος καὶ πότνια μήτηρ: 'and his own father and queenly mother laughed out loud'). On one level, as critics since antiquity have often remarked, the moment has timeless pathos – a simple indication that the most instinctive affections can survive amidst the bloodshed and grief of war. The scholia on the passage comment that the poet has 'taken this from life', and represented it with consummate vividness (*enargeia*); they also note, with more psychological subtlety, that such parental laughter is naturally triggered by a 'small cause after so much pain'.[4] But it is not enough to observe this level of meaning without grasping that the laughter of 471 belongs to a cumulative set of images in the scene. It picks up Hector's loving smile at 404 (ἤτοι ὃ μὲν μείδησεν ἰδὼν ἐς παῖδα σιωπῇ, 'he smiled as he looked in silence at this child'), while at the same time it is superimposed on, yet without cancelling, Andromache's tears in that earlier passage (405).

---

[4] ΣbT on 467, 471. Line 471 falsifies the claim of Woodbury (1944) 115 that Paris is the only hero to laugh in the *Iliad*.

It prepares the way, in turn, for Andromache's own ambiguous laughter at 484 (see below). Moreover, the antithesis of the parents' eloquent laughter and the infant's instinctive fright, as it clings to its nurse, is shadowed by the brutal reality of war. Astyanax's recoil not only obliquely reminds us that warriors' helmets are objects of intended terror to those who behold them. It also reinforces the poignant subtext of the episode: the nearness of the deaths of both Hector and his son. The dramatic irony is, as it were, spelt out when Hector, having removed the helmet (a gesture that momentarily suspends his warrior identity) and kissed his child, proceeds to pray that the Trojans, including Andromache, may one day admire Astyanax himself as a successful warrior 'far better than his father', successful enough to bring home 'bloody spoils' of battle to his mother and thereby cause her to feel *joy* in her heart (476–81) – a troubling piece of psychological counterpoint to the mother's laughter at her baby in the present scene. Given the audience's knowledge of how appallingly different the actual upshot will be (the father's body mangled behind Achilles' chariot, the son's thrown from the city walls), the whole context assumes a bittersweet quality which suffuses the description of Andromache, after Hector passes the baby to her, as 'laughing through her tears' (484, δακρυόεν γελάσασα), a unique Homeric phrase.[5] The passage thus incorporates an intricate sequence of imagery (Hector's smile, Andromache's tears, the baby's cry, both parents' laughter, Hector's dream of the mother's future joy at her son's success in battle, Andromache's laughter-through-tears) which transforms the significance of laughter from the merely, sentimentally natural into the richly, disquietingly symbolic.[6] Andromache's state of mind is stamped at 484 with an unresolved ambivalence, transmitting a sense of the precariousness of tenderly shared laughter – ultimately, the laughter of love – in the

[5] The image should not be undertranslated as *smiling* through tears, e.g. Evans (1969) 61. See Arnould (1990) 93–9 for such symptoms of mixed emotions (adding Heliod. *Aeth.* 10.38.4 for an elaborate later case), with ch. 6 n. 41 for the noun *klausigelōs*, 'crying laughter'; note, differently, the erotic symbolism of baby Eros' laughing and crying at Meleager, *Anth. Pal.* 5.178.4. Cf. Blurton Jones (1972) 280–1 for modern theories that connect laughter and crying physiologically; Plessner (1941), (1970) offers a comparative philosophical psychology of the two behaviours. The explanation of Andromache's laughter as overflow of joy in Chrysip. *SVF* III 436, *apud* Philo, *De migr. Abrah.* 156–7, is wide of the mark; the mother's emotions are in turmoil. Cf. *Argon. Orph.* 447, δακρυόεν γελόων, where Peleus kisses the infant Achilles. Radically different is the combined laughter and weeping of the suitors at *Od.* 20.346–53; see 95 below. A purely physical explanation of tears of laughter is offered by ps.-Alex. Aphr. *Probl.* 1.31. Ar. *Frogs* 1089, overlooked by Sittl (1890) 9, implies 'I laughed till my tears [of hilarity] ran out': rightly Del Corno (1994) 222; *pace* Dover (1993) 328, Sommerstein (1996) 254, withering/shrivelling is beside the point. Rabelais, *Gargantua* 1 20 provides a memorable image of the tears of laughter.

[6] The point was partly registered by Eustath. *Comm. Il.* II 366–7 (van der Valk), noting the concentration of body language in the passage.

circumstances of deadly conflict. 'Excess of sorrow laughs', to borrow a piercing formulation from a later poet, seems an apt summary of the scene's many layers of meaning.[7]

Now set against this complexity a very different moment of compressed emotion which occurs just 250 lines later but belongs to the world which Hector reenters after putting his helmet back on and saying farewell to his wife. This is the point at which, now back on the battlefield, Hector is confronted by the massive Greek hero Ajax striding towards him 'with a smile across his gruesome face', μειδιόων βλοσυροῖσι προσώπασι (7.212). The ancient critics whose views are reflected in the scholia on this passage misinterpreted Ajax's smile as a sign of nobility of character, or the expression, more bizarrely, of a certain kind of 'gentleness' (ἥμερόν τι). Even their suggestion that, unlike a laugh (which would denote 'stupid recklessness'), it conveys a kind of heroic confidence that terrifies Hector but encourages the Greeks, is wide of the mark.[8] The first thing to be said about the description of Ajax's look is that it is pungently startling, a uniquely phrased oxymoron. A smile can certainly be enigmatic and even deceptive, as other passages in the *Iliad* itself attest, but its primary social significance is a gesture of reassurance or friendship.[9] A smile on the face of a man consumed with the desire to kill is supremely paradoxical, a chilling evocation of bloodlust. The adjective *blosuros* acquired various nuances in later Greek,

---

[7] 'Excess of sorrow laughs. Excess of joy weeps.' Blake, 'Proverbs of Hell', *The Marriage of Heaven and Hell*, in Keynes (1969) 151. Hegel (1975) I 159 thought 'smiling through tears' characteristic of Romantic art, though he did not integrate this point into his sense of the 'epic' qualities of the Hector–Andromache meeting (*ibid.* II 1083–4). To find even a trace of the 'heartless' in Hector and Andromache's laughter at their baby, with Rapp (1947–8) 277, is not only obtuse but symptomatic of a schematic theorising that has blighted much writing about laughter.

[8] ΣbT on *Il.* 7.212, endorsed by Levine (1982b) 104, Beck (1993) 85, detect gentleness and/or nobility; cf. the apparent echo of this reading at Plotin. *Enn.* 1.6.5.14. Ps.-Aeschines, *Socr. Epist.* 14.4, describing a *blosuron* smile ('mixed with laughter') on Socrates' face at his trial, may reflect a similar view (or does this echo the mock fierceness of *Phaedo* 117b? cf. ch. 6 n. 40). The supposed connection with nobility may stem from the usage of *blosuros* at Pl. *Rep.* 7.535b (and elsewhere); cf. Adam (1899), (1963) II 144. Similarly aberrant is the diagnosis of 'serenity', Plebe (1956) 24; cf. Miralles (1993) 28–31, following the misleading claim of Σ on 6.404 that strong laughter is not heroic and thereby undermining one of his own theses (see nn. 2, 13, 16). Most far-fetched is Clem. *Paed.* 2.5.47, taking *Il.* 7.212 as parallel to the Christian ideal of a face combining sobriety with the avoidance of severity; cf. ch. 10, 490. The bloodthirstiness of Ajax's look is correctly diagnosed by Kirk (1990) 262 ('savage joy in battle'); Pulleyn (2000) 272 detects a mixture of the 'terrible' and the quasi-divine; similarly, Malten (1961) 12. The tone of *Il.* 7.212 was well read by Philostr. min. *Imag.* 10.21, who finds/imagines the same look in a painting of blood-crazed Pyrrhus (βλοσυρὸν ὁρῶν μειδιᾷ); cf. Appendix 2, 532.

[9] In early Greek, smiling is a polyvalent expression; cf. Friedländer (1969) 9 ('Lächeln ist vieldeutig'). Apart from the eroticism of Aphrodite *philo(m)meidēs*, 'lover of smiles' (n. 35 below), it can signify conciliation (*Il.* 4.356), fondness (*Il.* 6.404, 8.38, *Od.* 4.609), reassurance (*Od.* 22.371), (mild) condescension (*Hom. Hymn* 3.531), malice (*Il.* 21.434, 491), the sinister (*Il.* 10.400) and the enigmatic (*Il.* 15.47, *Hom. Hymn* 7.14). The Homeric instances are all discussed in my text and notes below. Cf. Milanezi (1995) 239–41.

but its two uncompounded Homeric occurrences (the other describes Hector's eyebrows at *Iliad* 14.608) involve a semantics which encompasses both 'bristling' and 'terrifying'.[10] Its application to the Ajax of Book 7 is best elucidated by the description of the Gorgon as βλοσυρῶπις, 'fierce-eyed' (in origin maybe even 'vulture-eyed'), at *Iliad* 11.36. If that is right, however, we need to appreciate that since nowhere in antiquity do we find an explicit description of the Gorgon's bared-teeth grimace as an (ominous) 'smile', we may well be dealing at 7.212 with a unique Homeric fusion of ideas.[11] The transfixingly fearsome look on the face or in the eyes of a Gorgon is eerily glimpsed behind the aggressive advance of Ajax, who is compared to the god of war himself going into battle full of 'heart-devouring strife' (7.208–10). The addition of a smile converts the image into an unsettling emblem of pleasure precisely at the prospect of death-dealing combat. Instead of carrying a Gorgon emblazoned (in familiar Greek fashion) on his shield, Ajax *becomes* a human surrogate of Gorgonic menace. His gaze, while eliciting a frisson of delight from his fellow Greeks (214), strikes deep terror in the Trojans, including Hector (215–16).[12]

As the contrasting reactions of the two sides reveal, the significance of Ajax's appearance can only be immediately evaluated from the irreconcilable standpoints of his friends and his enemies. But what matters is that Ajax's smile conjures up a state of mind – and, equally, a state of body – which, in its deadly merging of pleasure and violence, is outside the bounds of stable ethical comprehension. Ajax's behaviour lies at the furthest reaches of the Iliadic concept of *charmē*, the exultation or joy in fighting which supposedly defines the mentality of battlefield combat in general. His weirdly smirking face gazes beyond the limits of morality; it might even be thought close to a kind of madness.[13] What confronts us here is something more

---

[10] The fullest discussion of *blosuros*, with a speculative theory of its origin, is Leumann (1950) 141–8; his treatment of *Il.* 7.212 is narrow (142, 148). Cf. Adam (1899). LSJ's entry on the adj. omits Callim. *Hymn Dem.* 52 (the eyes of an aggressive tigress, simile for violent Erysichthon); note the association with bloodshed at Aesch. *Eum.* 167–8. *Blosuros*, denoting sternness, is specifically contrasted with (benign) laughter at Procl. *In Crat.* 181 (Pasquali), with reference to divine images.

[11] Cf. Hainsworth (1993) 221–2 on Homeric Gorgons, though he misses the full force of the connection at 7.212. Clarke (2005a) 37–8 (read 'Ajax' for 'Ares') sees that connection clearly but too quickly assumes that the Gorgon grimace was generally perceived as a kind of smile/'grin': on this complex issue, see Appendix 2, 539–41.

[12] Hector himself is compared simultaneously to a Gorgon and to Ares at 8.349; for Homeric warriors and the Gorgon, cf. Vernant (1991) 116–18, but without mention of *Il.* 7.212. A different bloodthirsty 'grin' belongs to the knife-sharpening barbarian, preparing to flay Marsyas, at Philostr. min. *Imag.* 2.2 (the verb is σέσηρε: n. 100 below). On the gruesome laughter of soldiers, compare Wilfred Owen's 'Apologia Pro Poemate Meo' 5–8, a poem built around dark paradoxes of laughter and war/death: text in Stallworthy (1986) 101–2.

[13] Did *Il.* 7.212, together with the story of Ajax's later madness, help to produce the proverb Αἰάντειος γέλως, applied to the insane (e.g. *Suda s.v.*; cf. Men. *Perik.* fr. 10 Sandbach, Arnott (1979–2000) II

'primitive' than the gesture of triumph exhibited by Paris at *Iliad* 11.378, where, having shot Diomedes in the foot, he laughs spontaneously, leaps from his ambush, and crows about his strike.[14] As he advances remorselessly in *Iliad* 7, Ajax is raw bloodlust incarnate. Even in the brutal world of the *Iliad* such an extreme symbol, such a grotesque twist of ordinary bodily signals, is very rare. Perhaps the closest parallels are provided by two related moments in the Doloneia episode of Book 10. In the first, Odysseus gives a sinister smile in the course of interrogating Dolon, the doomed Trojan spy he and Diomedes have captured (10.400). In the second, just after telling Nestor of the killing spree he and Diomedes have returned from, Odysseus laughs raucously (καγχαλόων, 10.565) as he elatedly drives the captured horses of Rhesus back into the Greek camp. In this last passage, the seemingly onomatopoeic verb καγχαλάω represents an eruption of visceral delight, a noisy cachinnation. The word occurs elsewhere in the depiction of the stallion-like exuberance of Paris as he rushes back to the battlefield at 6.514, in Hector's image of how the Greek soldiers supposedly roar with laughter at the ironic thought of a warrior (Paris) who has good looks but no prowess (3.43), and in the *Odyssey*'s description of Eurycleia's euphoria at the slaughter of the suitors.[15] The Paris passage in Book 6 shows how laughter can be regarded as a combination of affective surge and 'animal' bodily energy: though Paris is alone, he is swept along by an excitement he cannot contain without a release of vigorous exhilaration. In the case of Odysseus' laugh at the end of Book 10, and Eurycleia's in *Odyssey* 23, this kind of elation is associated with celebrating the death of one's enemies, even the very sight of their gore.[16] The difference at *Iliad*

496–9)? On madness and laughter see 92–6 below. The ancient derivation from an actor's vocalisation in a play by Carcinus jun. (see *TGrF* 1 211, Arnott (1979–2000) 11 496–7) is implausible; cf. Grossmann (1968) 65, speculating that the laughter of Ajax in Sophocles was prefigured in the *Little Iliad*. The attempt of Miralles (1993) 29, 44 to make Ajax's smile at *Il.* 7.212 characteristic of Iliadic heroism erases its special narrative status. Equally, one should not translate the common χάρμη by specific body language: e.g. Lombardo (1997) 150 (at *Il.* 8.252: 'The Greeks smiled . . .').

[14] Diomedes' scornful reaction, calling Paris λωβητήρ (cf. n. 52, on Thersites), suggests that Paris' laughter smacks of cowardice. Clarke (1969) 248 locates the moment within a reading of the Iliadic Paris as a comic character. On laughter and physical crowing, see ch. 1, 34–5.

[15] For the last passages, see *Od.* 23.1, 59; cf. n. 88 below. *À propos* Paris at 6.514 (perhaps Odysseus too, subliminally, at 10.565), cf. the later association between laughter and equine neighing (ch. 1 n. 7) and the use of καγχαλάω of other animals (ch. 1 n. 5). καγχαλάω is possibly cognate with κα(γ)χάζω/κα(γ)κάζω, 'guffaw': on both words see Chantraine (1968) 478, 507, Frisk (1960–70) 1 751, 804, Tichy (1983) 222–5, 245–6, Arnould (1990) 161–3, with my Appendix 1 n. 17; on the forms cf. Jebb (1896) 42, with Mallory and Adams (2006) 359–60 for the IE root.

[16] Eurycleia's joy goes back to 22.401–8 and the spectacle of Odysseus covered in the suitors' blood. Miralles (1993) 30–1 struggles to square Odysseus' laughter at *Il.* 10.565 with his thesis that laughter does not befit Iliadic heroism (28–31); cf. n. 13 above. For a tragic perversion of visceral joy in bloodshed, see Aesch. *Agam.* 1388–92.

7.212, and likewise with Odysseus' smile at 10.400, is that the gratification of killing is prospective, not yet actual. But the grimly paradoxical coupling of ostensible mirth with thoughts of bloodshed is fundamentally the same.[17]

The *Iliad*'s conjunctions of laughter/smiles and merciless killing, not least on the gruesome face of Ajax at 7.212, are addressed to the same audience as the intimate encounter between Hector and his wife and child in Book 6. And since Hector and Astyanax are themselves destined to be butchered in war, such an audience has to be able to do more than identify vicariously with the bloodlust of a Greek hero. The proximity of Ajax's smile to the meeting of Hector and Andromache, in which smiles and laughter play such a different part, reinforces and heightens the point. Anyone who hears or reads Book 7 directly after Book 6 needs to grasp, if only subliminally, how the look on Ajax's face is a world apart from Hector's smiles and laughter at his own baby, yet at the same time how a single character, Hector, can move between these two worlds, playing an intelligible role in each of them and even linking them in his hope that Andromache herself will one day rejoice at the sight of Astyanax's 'bloody spoils'. The laughter of Book 6 is a reflex of life-nurturing love, however shadowed it may be by Hector and Andromache's prescience of doom. The smile on Ajax's face in Book 7, by contrast, is an almost supernatural, Gorgon-like look of self-confidently destructive violence. The relationship between the two draws attention to the *Iliad*'s perpetual concern with the stark polarities of experience created by war, but it also exposes some of the disturbing undercurrents which run beneath such disparate images of life and death. Among much else, then, Homer's audience needs to face the challenge of contemplating and making sense of laughter both in its simplest expressiveness and at the extremes of what can be humanly imagined.

DIVINE CONFLICT AND PLEASURE IN THE *ILIAD*

The very first laughter heard in the *Iliad* is of a different order again. It is divine laughter, heard resoundingly and with a kind of programmatic force in the final scene of Book 1. A confrontation between Hera and Zeus over the latter's meeting with Thetis has left a heavy air of tension among the gods; they are described as 'weighed down' or oppressed with anxiety

---

[17] Levine (1982b) 101 is surely wrong to treat 10.400 as a smile of reassurance; the context makes the gesture grimly ironic (cf. n. 89 below). For smiling in anticipation of killing, cf. Heracles at ps.-Hes. *Scutum* 115 (half battle-lust, half acknowledgement of Iolaus' promise of support).

(ὤχθησαν, 1.570).[18] Hephaestus takes it upon himself to reconcile his parents and thereby change the mood on Olympus. To do so he invokes, and combines, two pairs of opposites: gods and mortals; quarrelling and feasting. Humans, he seems to imply, are not worth divine 'strife' (574). But it is important to notice that he stops short of the idea, which I shall explore in Chapter 7, of the 'cosmic' insignificance of human existence. The attitudes of Homeric gods to the lives of mortals are, in fact, laden with ambiguity. The deities of the *Iliad* invest great concern in, and seek to exercise real influence over, the human scene; that is precisely why the current crisis on Olympus has arisen. Accordingly, and crucially, Homeric gods never laugh at the conditions of mortality *per se*. They find the world of men and women emotionally too absorbing for that – hence their fluctuating pity, anger, and affection towards individuals and communities. Homeric eternity, it is at least partially justifiable to say, 'is in love with the productions of time'.[19] Even so, the status of human life can ultimately be of only transient significance from the viewpoint of Olympus; divine withdrawal and detachment are always, in principle, an available option. Later in the poem, matching Hephaestus' sentiment in Book 1, Apollo tells Poseidon, less than ingenuously, that human beings are too wretched to justify fighting between gods (21.462–7): but 'wretched' (*deilos*) not 'ridiculous' is what he says, and the difference matters. This ambiguity – which seems to open up a glimpse, and yet to decline the possibility, of a sense of the 'absurdity' of human life from a god's-eye perspective[20] – lends enriched irony to the contrast which unfolds in *Iliad* 1 between the divine gathering and the episode of human strife (*eris*, 1.8) that has dominated recent events in the Greek camp, events which themselves have led to the current tensions on Olympus. Earlier in the book, Achilles was enjoined by Athena to 'cease from strife' (210, cf. 319), but his decision to withdraw from the fighting has guaranteed that his quarrel with Agamemon will have far-reaching, lethal consequences. Seeking a rapprochement between Zeus and Hera, on the other hand, Hephaestus implies, with due sensitivity to both parents, that

---

[18] Sikes (1940) 122 makes a bad misjudgement in calling the quarrel between Zeus and Hera, before Hephaestus' intervention, 'frankly comic'. On 'the comic' more generally in Homer, I have not been able to see Zervou (1990). Butler (1913) is a stupefying mixture of whimsy and crassness.

[19] Blake, 'Proverbs of Hell', *The Marriage of Heaven and Hell*, in Keynes (1969) 151. Woodbury (1944) 115 notes that Homeric gods never deride heroes.

[20] For a 'god's-eye' view of the world and the possibility of treating human existence as 'absurd', see ch. 7 *passim*; cf. ch. 10, 511–12. Even the scornful Dionysus of Eur. *Bacchae* does not laugh at human existence as such; on the contrary, human worship *matters* to him; his malicious-yet-serene laughter reflects intense engagement with the human world: ch. 3, 133–9. Nietzsche *Human, All Too Human* 1 16 (Nietzsche (1988) II 38) uses 'Homeric laughter' to echo the ultimate insignificance of reality, but such existential laughter is never actually sounded, by gods or men, in Homer.

it is *easy* for gods to step back from their wranglings (κολῳός, 575) and quarrels (νεῖκος, cf. 579). Easy enough, at any rate, provided Hera can do what Achilles could not do: that is, accept an aristocratic hierarchy within which one person ultimately carries unquestionable supremacy.[21]

The immediate desirability of Hera's yielding to Zeus's power and assuaging his feelings with 'soft words' (582) rests on the need, as Hephaestus sees it, to prevent the feast being spoilt (575–6, 579), in itself a consideration that betokens the gap between divine and human strife. To reinforce his advice Hephaestus employs a gesture that enacts the contrast between feasting and quarrelling. The gesture is at the same time visual, verbal and psychological: Hephaestus places a cup in his mother's hand (584–5), inviting her to initiate a feast of reconciliation (one cannot drink with one's enemies); he supports his own deference to Zeus by telling how the latter once hurled him from Olympus; and as Hera's response intimates (she smiles and accepts the cup), his anecdote contains an element which gods, from the safety of their immortality, can perceive as somehow ridiculous. But how exactly are we to decode Hera's smile? A mythologically informed and alert hearer might relish the irony that Hera herself, Hephaestus' mother, had once thrown her child from Olympus in disgust at his disability – a 'canonical' episode referred to later in the poem as well as in the *Homeric Hymn to Apollo*.[22] The normal scholarly assumption that the two stories of Hephaestus' ejection from Olympus are mythological 'variants', providing alternative explanations of the god's lameness, is unsatisfactory. It is preferable to take 1.590–4 as an ironic witticism on Hephaestus' part, an *ad hoc* invention, though one which shrewdly plays on a recognisable type of divine violence. Anyone who finds this too radical an interpretation of the passage should remember that the *Iliad* contains at least one indisputable piece of mythological 'fiction' from the mouth of a god, in Hera's speech of deception to Aphrodite at 14.201–4.[23] The hypothesis of Hephaestean irony best explains why Hera smiles at 1.595. On this reading, Hera knowingly appreciates her son's point: his apparent erasure of her maternal violence fuses with a pragmatic reminder of Zeus's capacity to wield his authority with irresistible force.[24]

---

[21] Cf. Taplin (1992) 133 on ironic echoes of the Achilles–Agamemnon conflict in Hephaestus' diplomacy.

[22] See *Il.* 18.395–7, with *Hom. Hymn* 3.316–18; further details in Gantz (1993) 74–6.

[23] See the full discussion of that passage in Janko (1992) 180–3; cf. 66 below.

[24] On my ironic reading, we can still find an allusion to the kind of episode recalled by Zeus himself at 15.21–4 (65 below; cf. 14.257, 19.130–1, with West (1997) 390), as do scholars who take 1.590–4 at face value: thus e.g. Pulleyn (2000) 270–1 (but finding Hera's smile enigmatic/dissimulatory, 272), Kirk (1985) 113 (but contrast 'may have been designed . . . to provide light relief', 114). Lang (1983) 147–62

From the point of view of the human audience of the poem, there is a further layer of significance. Whether or not Hephaestus' anecdote is taken to be contextually 'true', it discloses something about the different conditions of divine and human antagonism, and thus about the different possibilities of divine laughter. Whether Zeus or Hera (or both) once threw Hephaestus from Olympus, and even though Zeus has physically constrained his wife in the past (as he has just threatened to do again), neither the violence nor the conflict is terminal, unlike the all-too-deadly consequences of much human strife. Even if one Olympian feast is spoilt, there will be future feasts to restore the divine community. From a human point of view, Hephaestus' emphasis on the need for harmony betrays, as it were, the ultimate immunity of the gods. So too, paradoxically, does his account of how, in falling from Olympus, he took a 'whole day' to reach the earth, how he fell (in effect) almost 'lifeless' on Lemnos, and yet, after all, how the Sintians were waiting to care for him (592–4). As she accepts the cup from her craftily persuasive son, Hera, it seems, has more than one reason to smile. And as she does so, she is giving her approval for the whole feast to proceed. Albeit temporarily (a point to which I shall return), the gods have agreed to avert their thoughts from the human scene. They have stepped back into their own world of feasting, a world where everything other than the self-contained pleasure of the moment is, so to speak, bracketed. The Olympians can live out what human symposiasts (the subject of my next chapter) can only fantasise about.[25]

Hephaestus' conflict-resolving strategy goes beyond words. He assumes the role of 'wine-butler' at the feast, pouring sweet nectar for all the gods in order. His bustling gait, as he serves them, makes the others break out into a surge of 'unquenchable laughter' (ἄσβεστος . . . γέλως, 599), described in a line that will recur exactly and only at *Odyssey* 8.326, where Hephaestus is once again, though in radically different circumstances, the cause of divine laughter.[26] The adjective 'unquenchable', *asbestos*, which carries extra weight from its predicative position (in effect, 'laughter swelled up with unquenchable force . . .'), conveys an intensity of sound and resonance, as

---

rationalises 1.590–4, 14.257, 15.21–4 in relation to a lost story-pattern (about Heracles); this is too intricate to be convincing: see Scodel (2002) 147–9 for doubts. Latacz (2000) 181, Collobert (2000) 135–6 both detect humour in Hephaestus' tale (cf. ΣT on 588), but neither takes the further step of seeing it as fictive. Plato's Socrates, *Rep.* 2.378d, makes no allowance for comedy in this passage, while seeming to imply that allegorical interpretations of it already existed (cf. n. 27 below).

[25] For the human symposium as a fantasy of immortality, see ch. 3, esp. 104–5, 113.

[26] The verb ἐνόρνυμι (ἐνῶρτο), *Il.* 1.599 = *Od.* 8.326 (cf. the simplex at *Od.* 20.346), is elsewhere in Homer used only (transitively) of strong feelings of grief or fear: *Il.* 6.499, 15.62, 366. The detail underlines laughter's psychosomatic strength. On collective laughter, cf. ch. 1, 30–3.

we gather from its application on six occasions in the *Iliad* to the frenzied shouting of troops in battle.[27] But it also intimates an irresistible, collective urge to laugh; hence Socrates' citation of this passage in Plato's *Republic* as an example of the unacceptability of depicting good people, let alone gods, being *overcome* by laughter.[28] As Socrates' qualms indicate, 'unquenchable' suggests a loud, impulsive manifestation of the bodily and emotional energy of laughter. Indeed, the phrase underlines that the gods who succumb to it are here imagined in their most robustly corporeal form. Laughter – like feasting, fighting and sex – contributes to an image of the divine that is anything but spiritually ethereal. The only group other than the gods to exhibit 'inquenchable' laughter in Homer are the Ithacan suitors (*Od.* 20.346). And in their case, to which we will come in due course, it forms part of a macabre physical seizure inflicted on them by Athena.

Just what is it, though, about Hephaestus' bustling movement that sparks such hilarity among the Olympians? The verb ποιπνύειν (600) seems peculiarly suitable for the busy, assiduous movements of servants: it is used in this way in two other passages of the *Iliad* and twice in the *Odyssey* as well.[29] Although occasionally found in other contexts too, being applied even to Agamemnon (*Il.* 8.219) and Poseidon (14.155), its use in the present setting sharpens the image of Hephaestus as a diligent 'wine'-server. Two points converge here: the eruption of laughter is a signal of the lifting of tension from the gods (who were collectively oppressed at 570), but it is also specifically triggered by the sight of a half-lame god engaging industriously in a

---

[27] 11.50, 500, 530, 13.169, 540, 16.267. This is one of several points which undercut the claim of Stanford (1936) 117 n. 1 that '*gelōs* was primarily a *visual* not an *auditory* thing to the Greeks' (see Appendix 1, 520–4); likewise Lopez Eire (2000) 36, who cites the Homeric idea of an 'unquenchable flame' but ignores the six applications of *asbestos* to shouting. Simon (1961) 646–7 connects *asbestos* as used of divine laughter with its Homeric application (connoting 'undying') to fame, *kleos* (*Od.* 4.584, 7.333), and infers that divine laughter itself symbolises immortality. But the argument, which again neglects other Homeric uses of *asbestos*, strikes me as tenuous. Cf. Clarke (1999) 94 n. 85, who stresses the application of *asbestos* to things manifesting 'vigorous vital movement'. The adj. is translated by Procl. *In Remp.* 1 127–8 (Kroll), within an allegorical reading of *Iliad* 1.599–600, into a symbol of the eternally abundant, beneficent force of divine providence; cf. *iden In Tim.* 11 98.12–13 (Diehl). See Sheppard (1980) 81–2, Arnould (1990) 265–6, Lamberton (1986) 205–6, with n. 80 below for a further allegorisation of the laughter of Homeric gods; cf. n. 24 above. But Homeric epic itself never directly links divine laughter with cosmic creativity in the way found in some esoteric ancient thought: cf. ch. 1 n. 32.

[28] κρατουμένους ὑπὸ γέλωτος: *Rep.* 3.388e–389a. Later, at 390c, Socrates also expresses disapproval of Hephaestus' shackling of Ares and Aphrodite in *Od.* 8; cf. n. 75 below. Yet Plato expects his readers to enjoy a subtly humorous manipulation of that episode at *Symp.* 192d.

[29] *Il.* 18.421, Hephaestus' servants, 24.475, two heroes serving Achilles; *Od.* 3.430, 20.149. Probably cognate with πνέω, 'breathe' (though linked by ancient scholars with πονῶ, 'toil'), the verb denotes bustling or scurrying; it does not mean 'hobble' (e.g. Kirk [1985] 113), even though we might picture Hephaestus in those terms (like Lucian's Hermes at *Charon* 1: ch. 9, 445). Bremer (1987) 39 ('clumsy efforts') imports a nuance not in the text; Buckley (2003) 61 paraphrases wildly.

menial task. One possibility, then, is that Hephaestus' very lameness is an object of laughter here, highlighted by his servile movements round the circle of divine banqueters: if so, this strikes a note that will soon recur, with a different twist, in the Thersites scene of Book 2. But there is an alternative, more subtle way to interpret the situation. It makes better sense (especially if we adopt my earlier suggestion about the god's smile-inducing anecdote at 590–4) to follow the ancient view, found in the scholia, that Hephaestus' busy butlering movements are deliberately mimetic, an ostentatious piece of play-acting which makes the (ugly) god into a parodic substitute for the beautiful young figures, Hebe or Ganymede, who elsewhere serve the Olympians. The laughter of the gods, on this premise, is positively appreciative of Hephaestus' intentions, not aimed at his lameness as such.[30] If that is right (and, after all, Hephaestus' lameness is nothing *new*), we have the act of a self-conscious *gelōtopoios*, a 'laughter-maker' or jester, using his own body to 'perform' for others' pleasure. Certainly there is no better framework for such behaviour than a feast at which all cares are put aside in the heady sensuality (food, drink and music) of the self-sufficient present. The gods, to this extent, are a magnified image of a kind of commensal laughter that humans too can experience. But only gods are capable of using such conviviality to dispel dark clouds of divisive rancour.[31]

The Homeric depiction of the gods holds up a kind of oblique mirror to the human scene that takes place below them. Significantly, then, the laughter which Hephaestus stage-manages at the end of Book 1 leaves us, for all its ethos of divine carefreeness and ease, with a sense of unfinished business. Even the gods put aside their conflicts only temporarily. When they return to their separate palaces at the end of the banquet, Zeus lies awake in the dead of night, brooding on how to fulfil his promise to Thetis

---

[30] See ΣbTA on 584, ΣT on 588, with Griffin (1978) 7 ('clowning'), Burkert (1985) 168, Kirk (1985) 113–14, Slater (1990) 216 ('parody'), Lateiner (1995) 220 ('clowning antics'), Pulleyn (2000) 274 ('prepared to make himself the butt of laughter'). Garland (1994) 77, (1995) 79–80 (cf. 61–3 on Hephaestus' lameness) is doubtful (but the claim, Garland (1995) 86, that no Greek ever questioned the risibility of physical defects overlooks Plut. *Mor.* 35a–c, specifically denying that Homer thought lameness laughable). Hedreen (2004) 39 ('struggling to walk and feebly [*sic*] imitating . . . Ganymede') seems caught between readings; Rinon (2006) 17 (cf. 3, 6), on Hephaestus' 'tragic lot as an object of derision', overreads the scene. (I note in passing Galen's image of a buffoon aping a cripple for laughs, *Usu part.* 3.16: III 264 Kühn, I 194 Helmreich.) Fehr (1990) 186–7 less aptly sees reference to an 'uninvited' (*aklētos*) symposiac guest debasing himself to entertain the company (cf. ch. 3, 143–4). Shorey (1927) 223 compares Eur. *Ion* 1172–3 (the old man's deliberate assiduity, concealing his nefarious purposes); a better comparison still is Xen. *Cyr.* 1.3.9, where young Cyrus plays the role (cf. *mimeisthai*, 1.3.10) of cup-bearer Sacas so zealously that Astyages and Mandane burst out laughing (as, then, does Cyrus himself). Cognate is Philippus' advice to the wine-pourers at Xen. *Symp.* 2.27 to rush round like charioteers.

[31] For laughter-makers at the symposium, see ch. 3, esp. 143–9.

by honouring Achilles and causing mass casualties to the Greeks. The cause of his dispute with Hera has anything but evaporated, and when the motif of divine feasting reappears at the start of Book 4, we find that Zeus now takes the opportunity to taunt his wife openly. In fact, his behaviour there is a premeditated provocation (though with a concealed tactical purpose) that disrupts the harmony of the feast with jeering sarcasm.[32] Shared, celebratory laughter cannot, it seems, be a permanent condition even for the gods – and the crucial reason for this lies in their emotional investment in the affairs of the human world. Olympian laughter marks a degree of detachment from care that is a prerogative of divine existence but beyond the reach of human beings. Paradoxically, however, the exercise of that divine prerogative in the *Iliad* is always provisional and temporary for the very reason that the gods are unable to disentangle themselves from involvement with the human realm. Laughter is a feature of Homeric godhead that is far from being a pure reflection of immortality. It cannot help being influenced by the gods' unending pursuit of power, honour and self-interest.[33]

The inseparability of divine laughter from divine conflicts of value in the *Iliad* is reinforced by an echo of Book 1 (a long-range echo, but one well within the scope of associative memory) much later in the *Iliad*. After Zeus has woken to discover the trick played by Hera's seduction of him in Book 14, he recollects how he once punished his wife for persecuting Heracles by hanging her upside down and throwing from Olympus any god who took her side. After menacing his wife with this reminder, Zeus smiles enigmatically (15.47) at her attempt to assuage him (with a lie, as it happens) and Hera rushes off to relay his instructions to Iris and Apollo. Finding the other gods feasting in Zeus's palace, she accepts the offer of a cup from Themis (15.88), as she had done with Hephaestus in Book 1, but proceeds to berate the malevolence of Zeus's plans. After her initial outburst, which plunges the gods into the same gloom as the quarrel between Hera and Zeus had done in Book 1 (15.101, largely and uniquely repeated from 1.570), she sits down. As she does so, 'she laughed with her lips [sc. alone]' (ἡ δ' ἐγέλασσε | χείλεσιν, 101–2, a unique phrase), while her brow remains furrowed – an oxymoronic combination that wonderfully projects the image of a face on which there is the merest, ironic hint of the mouth movements of laughter

---

[32] His attempt to 'provoke' (ἐρεθίζειν, 4.5) by taunts might be compared to the suitors at *Od.* 20.374 (94, 96 below). Although *Il.* 4.6 is verbally similar to *Hom. Hymn* 4.56, the latter involves consensual, ritualised badinage; see ch. 3, 101–3.

[33] Friedländer (1969) stresses that the comic and the sublime are equally integral to Homer's conception of the gods. Somewhat differently, Reinhardt (1960) 23–6 speaks of the gods' 'as if' earnestness and their existence 'beyond good and evil' (25); note the quotation from Wilhelm von Humboldt in Friedländer (1969) 4 for a pre-Nietzschean version of this last formulation. Cf. n. 43 below.

(and perhaps the merest suggestion of forced vocalisation). The bitterness of Hera's look is then voiced in a further, if somewhat sly, complaint about the situation (104–12).[34] The configuration of reminiscences of the episode in Book 1 – the confrontation between Zeus and Hera, with Zeus's specific reference, at 15.76–7, to his original supplication by Thetis; the motif of expulsion from Olympus (15.23 matching 1.591); the gods' general gloom; Hera's acceptance of a cup from another god; the involvement of (true or false) smiling and laughter – sets into relief the very different shape of events in the later situation. Zeus now stays away from the feast of the gods. Hera is overtly unreconciled. While accepting a cup of conviviality, she directly refers to the threat that Zeus's plans pose to the feasting of both men and gods (15.97–9).

Zeus's enigmatic smile at 15.47 and Hera's strange half-laugh at 15.101–2 are both signs of the gap that separates the wills of the divine couple. Correspondingly, there is no shared laughter here to break the oppressive air of anxiety that besets the other gods. This is a good juncture, therefore, at which to register that Zeus (three times) and Hera (four times) are the only gods who smile in the *Iliad*. Even Aphrodite *philommeidēs*, 'lover of smiles', is never specifically said to do so in the poem: her defining smile – symbolic of seductive sensuality – is, so to speak, temporarily suspended in a world, both divine and human, where the upheavals of war (albeit a war caused in part by Aphrodite herself) make fully positive, unproblematic sexuality apparently impossible.[35] The smiles of Zeus and Hera in the *Iliad* are emblems of their deeply manipulative power. While Zeus is capable

---

[34] Hera's laughter on the lips, which *pace* Levine (1982b) 97 hardly shows 'self-confidence', was classed as 'sardonic' in antiquity (cf. n. 100 below): ΣbTA *ad loc.*, Phot. *Lex. s.v.* σαρδόνιος γέλως, Eustath. *Comm. Il.* III 707 (van der Valk). Cf. Appendix 1, 525–6. The lips may obliquely connote abusiveness; cf. ps.-Arist. *Physiogn.* 3.808a32–3, 6.811a26–7; note that *chleu-* terms for mockery may be etymologically related to χεῖλος, 'lip', Chantraine (1968) 1262–3. Different is the suitors' rage-suppressing lip-biting at Hom. *Od.* 1.381, 18.410, 20.268. Though brief, Darwin (1965) 212 on forced laughter is worth consulting.

[35] Aphrodite *philo(m)meidēs*: *Il.* 3.424, 4.10, 5.375, 14.211, 20.40, *Od.* 8.362 (see 84 below), Hes. *Theog.* 989, *Hom. Hymn* 5.17, 49 (combined with laughter), 56 etc., cf. *Hom. Hymn* 10.3; the specious etymology at Hes. *Theog.* 200 is unique. The adj. should not be translated 'laughter-loving': LSJ 1937, *s.v.* φιλομμειδής, and e.g. Garvie (1994) 310, O'Higgins (2003) 46. Further analysis in Boedeker (1974) 23–6, 32–5; Gentili (1988) 89 gratuitously pictures a 'fixed, immobile smile'. In the famous Sappho 1.14 *PLF*, the goddess is both cause and (putative) reliever of erotic sufferings: so the smile is inscrutable; mere amusement (Page (1955) 15) is a flat interpretation. Deception is sometimes involved (Hes. *Theog.* 205, with 547 for deceptive smiles more generally), hence the ironic reverse at *Il.* 14.211 (cf. Hera's smile, 14.222–3, with 66 below); modern research on smiles and deception in Ekman *et al.* (1997), cf. Schmidt and Cohn (2001) 17. For a *laughing* Aphrodite, cf. Maccius, *Anth. Pal.* 5.133.2, Leonidas, *Anth. Pal.* 9.320.3, anon. *Anth. Pal.* 16.174.3; a Hermetic Aphrodite bestows laughter on humans at Stob. 1.49.44.201 (= Scott (1924) 472, with Scott (1926) 521–5 for context). Deceptive erotic laughter is visualised at Theoc. 1.36–7 (cf. the resonance of *ibid.* 90–1); Aphrodite's laughter in the same poem (1.95–6), while associated with deception, is more complex: n. 95 below.

of something like an affectionate smile (to Athena, 8.38, and perhaps less straightforwardly at 5.426, where he seems caught between amusement and conciliation at the clash between Athena and Aphrodite), his smile at 15.47 is to some degree inscrutable: a veiled expression of his authority and an oblique signal of his confidence that he has Hera cornered. Elsewhere, at 14.222–3 Hera smiles with cynical but also erotically coloured satisfaction at outwitting Aphrodite, the 'lover of smiles' herself (see 14.211). The psychological intricacies of this last gesture are multiple. Hera has just deceived the goddess of sexual desire with a story of ostensible sexual intentions (to reconcile the supposedly sexless marriage of Ocean and Tethys) that is cunningly designed to conceal her *real* sexual strategy (the seduction of Zeus) and its further ends. Her smile, emphasised by parataxis (222–3) as in Book 1, is itself erotically charged but devious: it encapsulates her sense of triumph at having appropriated the resources of Aphrodite (embodied in the goddess's mysterious 'love-band', 214–17) for her own special purposes. It is similarly with a malicious superiority that Hera smiles at 21.434, where she has just encouraged Athena to knock Aphrodite and Ares to the ground (and has listened to her crowing over them), and again soon afterwards at 21.491, where she thrashes Artemis with the huntress's own arrows and reduces her to tears.[36] I shall shortly return to the theomachy to which these last two passage belong.

It seems apt, then, that Zeus's enigmatic smile at 15.47 (how far does does he see through his wife's guile? cf. 15.53)[37] and the peculiar half-laughter of Hera 'with the lips' which seems to echo it (how far does she admit to the failure of her ruse? cf. 15.104) are reserved for the pivotal clash of wills between them in Books 14–15. Within the larger Iliadic setting, the hidden depths that may lie behind a smile befit the supreme divine couple especially well, helping to evoke the interplay between their intense but unharmonious concern for the course of the war and their networks of self-interested dealings. When Zeus and Hera smile, they do so not with transparent affability but in ways that express the complex workings of major divine agency. On the faces of the two most assertive gods, nominally complementary yet mostly at odds with one another, smiles function as a language of calculating but (from a human point of view) incompletely intelligible power: a language that partly discloses, partly masks their motivations and attitudes.

---

[36] The complex 'physiognomy' of Hera's Iliadic smiles/laughter is ignored in the claim of Gilhus (1997) 33 that Homeric laughter 'exists in a context of cunning skill and *male* power' (my itals.).

[37] Gods certainly laugh/smile in reaction to attempted deception at *Hom. Hymn* 4.281 (Apollo at Hermes; cf. Philostr. maj. *Imag.* 1.26.5, a different moment from the story), 389 (Zeus at Hermes), Hom. *Od.* 13.287 (Athena at Odysseus; cf. n. 89 below).

In terms of the unfolding drama of divine machinations, Zeus's smile at 15.47 can be read as a motivic counterpart to, and a kind of reversal of, Hera's at 14.222–3. Hera had smiled with erotically charged but wily expectations at the power she knew she could wield over her husband. He, in turn, having discovered the plot and induced a terrified Hera to profess total allegiance to his will, smiles as he instructs her to carry out his orders. Zeus, as it were, has the last smile, as the irony of Hera's laughter 'with the lips' subsequently, though still inconclusively, appears to acknowledge.

The combination of resemblances and differences between the Olympian episodes in Books 1 and 15 underlines, in retrospect, just how special the divine laughter of Book 1 is. It transpires that while such communal pleasure, like supplies of nectar, ought to be available to the gods at all times, it requires exceptional circumstances – i.e. both an initial tension and a means of dissolving it – to tap its availability. The gods laugh in this way only once in the *Iliad*, and the same will turn out to be true in the *Odyssey* as well (though for rather different reasons). It is the cumulative impression of both epics that the scarcity of shared divine laughter is itself a symptom of the state of the world. The Olympians are too emotionally entrammelled in the lives of humans to take full advantage of the privileged conditions of their own pleasures. In Homeric epic, human suffering can impede, but never causes, divine laughter. This is one reason why the 'theology' of the Homeric poems can still resonate so powerfully in the imagination of audiences that do not actively worship such gods. All deities, after all, 'reside in the human breast'.[38]

One other cluster of divine laughter and smiling in the *Iliad* calls for mention here. It is found in the stretch of the theomachy at 21.383–513 where several confrontations between individual Olympians take place. This section of the scene is framed by two contrasting moments of laughter from Zeus himself. First we hear how as he sat on Olympus watching the other gods fight (to the accompaniment of the resounding earth and the 'trumpeting' of the sky), 'his very heart laughed with joy' (ἐγέλασσε δέ οἱ φίλον ἦτορ | γηθοσύνῃ, 389–90), a reaction which seems to bespeak an elemental joy in the spectacle of divine conflict.[39] Later, at 508, Zeus 'laughs with pleasure/relish' (ἡδὺ γελάσσας, the same phraseology used of human laughter at 2.270, 11.378, 23.784, and several times in the *Odyssey*),

---

[38] Blake, *The Marriage of Heaven and Hell*: Keynes (1969) 153.

[39] Zeus's laughter at 389 is not 'internal' in the same sense as Odysseus' at *Od.* 9.413 (n. 95 below). The phrasing denotes 'heartfelt' emotion; it may imply, at root, a heightened rhythm of breathing: Miralles (1993) 54. Note (erotic) laughter 'from the very heart' (ἐξ αὐτῆς κραδίης) in Rufin. *Anth. Pal.* 5.61.2.

as he speaks with apparent sympathy to his wounded daughter Artemis, a moment reminiscent of the way he had smiled at his injured daughter Aphrodite at 5.426.[40] The three human parallels of pleasurable laughter just cited, where in every case the agent is openly enjoying another's discomfort, alert us to a nuance of uncertainty in Zeus's laughter at 21.508. The adverbial ἡδύ ('with pleasure') refers in the first instance to his own feelings, not to the effect of his laughter on Artemis; there is therefore at least a hint of amusement on Zeus's part at his daughter's discomfiture (as perhaps also to some extent with Aphrodite in Book 5), even though the rest of the context (he holds her and addresses her with affection) conveys a sympathetic tone.[41] This makes the framing effect of Zeus's laughter at 389 and 508 on the theomachy as a whole interestingly ambivalent, especially when we add to the picture, from this same portion of the work, the abusive laughter of Athena after she has floored Ares with a boulder (408), and the two malicious smiles of Hera (434, 491) already noted.[42] Something in the 'heart' of Zeus thrills at the general sight of divine violence, at any rate when it poses no direct threat to his own supremacy. At the same time, he remains capable of a more paternal response to the injuries incurred by his daughters. And in both those ways he finds reason to laugh.

Many critics have seen the battle of the Olympian gods as essentially frivolous, even comic, though thereby setting in grimmer relief the tragic character of the surrounding human warfare.[43] But the significance of the theomachy is more problematic than this. The fighting of the gods is protected from the risk of death that mortal warriors perpetually face; to that extent it acts as a foil to the human events at Troy. Furthermore, the Olympian section of the theomachy serves only a limited, subordinate kind

[40] Cf. Eur. *IT* 1274, where Zeus laughs at baby Apollo's request for help in establishing lucrative worship at Delphi. More straightforwardly, Callim. *Hymn* 3.28 has Zeus laugh benignly at young Artemis' effusive requests.
[41] See related phraseology, combining ἡδύ with γελᾶν, at Hom. *Od.* 18.35, 111, 20.358, 21.376 (97 below); cf. *Hom. Hymn* 5.49 and, later, e.g. Soph. fr. 171 *TrGF*, Ar. *Eccl.* 1156, Theoc. 7.42, 128, Meleager, *Anth. Pal.* 12.137.4, Rufin. *Anth. Pal.* 5.61.2. Both Crane (1987) 164–6 and Cameron (1995) 412–15 obscure the basic point that the phrasing denotes the pleasure of the one who laughs (rightly Arnould (1990) 164), leaving the impact open to context; cf. Miralles (1993) 66, Beck (1991) 125. Cf. the adj. ἡδύγελως, 'laughter-enjoying', of Pan at *Hom. Hymn* 19.37, of comedy in *CEG* 550.3, 773 (ii).
[42] The Iliadic Zeus never laughs with the malign triumph of Hes. *WD* 59 (retaliating against Prometheus by sending Pandora to earth), *à propos* which Miralles (1993) 13–14 strains to connect smiling with the idea of the feminine.
[43] See Taplin (1992) 229–30, Richardson (1993) 87, 95, Seidensticker (1982) 55–9, Bremer (1987) 39–40 for various perceptions of the theomachy as comic. Graziosi and Haubold (2005) 65–75 provide a partial critique of views of Homeric gods as 'frivolous'; further reflections in Burkert (2003) 107–18. Cf. n. 33 above.

of causation – to ward off Achilles' premature conquest of Troy (20.26–30) – and, beyond that postponement, offers no prospect of a decisive change to the course of events. Yet for *both* those reasons it appears all the more 'pure' an exhibition of divine power and violence (defining attributes of the gods) in free flow. Watching these forces at work fills Zeus's heart with joyous laughter because Zeus himself is their ultimate possessor; and even seeing Artemis suffering (temporarily) from the effects of the violence might make such a supreme god laugh, since Artemis is just as much part of this system of power as any other Olympian. Laughter in the *Iliad* (and elsewhere) is, for sure, too variable to be reduced to a single formula.[44] Indeed, part of the point of Zeus's laughter, as of his smiles, is the elusiveness of meaning which plays around it. But it is legitimate to see one facet of Zeus's laughter (and Athena's and Hera's in the same book) as an externalisation of divine pleasure in its own exercise of strength and domination. If so, the laughter of the gods in *Iliad* 21, though contextually far removed from that in Book 1, is equally representative of the divine at a moment of self-sufficiency in its own eternal conditions of existence. Like that earlier scene, however, it is also shadowed by the connection between those conditions and the inevitability of conflict.

THERSITES AND THE VOLATILITY OF LAUGHTER

The laughter of the gods at the end of *Iliad* 1 draws its immediate significance, as we saw, from being embedded in the delicate negotiation of divisions within the Olympian community. But it also carries its thematic implications forwards, preparing the poem's audience in part for the very different gelastic dynamics of the incident at Troy, shortly afterwards, involving Thersites. It is no accident that these two outbreaks of laughter, one divine and one human, come so close together. As soon as Thersites is introduced, his elaborate description brings into play a dense cluster of ideas and motifs, several of which reflect back on the Hephaestus episode and, beyond it, on the disastrous rupture between Achilles and Agamemnon to which that episode had itself been both a counterpart and a contrast. Like both Achilles and Hephaestus, Thersites chooses to step into the limelight

---

[44] Redfield (1994) 286 n. 77 seems to suggest that Iliadic laughter always involves 'release of social tension': I fail to see what this explains about such cases as Athena at 21.408 or Hera at 15.101 (both adduced by Redfield). Griffin (1978) 5–6, (1980) 183–4, Levine (1982b) 97 explain Zeus's laughter at 21.389, and much other Iliadic laughter, in terms of 'superiority'; but this is not an adequate model for 21.389, where pleasure in violence for its own sake seems essential. Jäkel (1994) offers a mechanical classification.

at a juncture of acute discord. He is given one of the most remarkable portraits anywhere in Homer.

Θερσίτης δ' ἔτι μοῦνος ἀμετροεπὴς ἐκολῴα,
ὃς ἔπεα φρεσὶν ᾗσιν ἄκοσμά τε πολλά τε ᾔδη
μάψ, ἀτὰρ οὐ κατὰ κόσμον, ἐριζέμεναι βασιλεῦσιν,
ἀλλ' ὅ τι οἱ εἴσαιτο γελοίιον Ἀργείοισιν   215
ἔμμεναι· αἴσχιστος δὲ ἀνὴρ ὑπὸ Ἴλιον ἦλθε·
φολκὸς ἔην, χωλὸς δ' ἕτερον πόδα· τὼ δέ οἱ ὤμω
κυρτὼ ἐπὶ στῆθος συνοχωκότε· αὐτὰρ ὕπερθε
φοξὸς ἔην κεφαλήν, ψεδνὴ δ' ἐπενήνοθε λάχνη.
ἔχθιστος δ' Ἀχιλῆϊ μάλιστ' ἦν ἠδ' Ὀδυσῆϊ·   220
τὼ γὰρ νεικείεσκε· τότ' αὖτ' Ἀγαμέμνονι δίῳ
ὀξέα κεκλήγων λέγ' ὀνείδεα· τῷ δ' ἄρ' Ἀχαιοὶ
ἐκπάγλως κοτέοντο νεμέσσηθέν τ' ἐνὶ θυμῷ.

(2.212–23)

Thersites alone, unruly in speech, continued to wrangle,
A man whose mind abounded with disruptive words.
He was given, so rashly and with no sense of order, to quarrelling with kings
And to saying whatever he thought would arouse the Argives' laughter.   215
He was the ugliest man who went to Ilion:
He was bandy-legged and lame in one foot, and his shoulders
Were hunched, bent towards his chest, while up above
He had a pointed head, with thin straggly hair on top.
He was particularly hated by Achilles and Odysseus   220
Since he regularly abused the pair of them. And on this occasion in turn
He shrieked reproaches at godlike Agamemnon, so that the Achaeans
Felt terrible anger and resentment against him in their hearts.

Thersites' name ('man of boldness [*thersos = tharsos*]'), in itself ambiguous, is reinterpreted by the doubly unique Homeric description of him as 'unruly in speech' and as knowing many 'disruptive' or 'disorderly' words.[45] There is a direct match between these details and his impulse to wrangle (κολῳᾶν, 212, which probably implies a shrill voice: cf. 222) in a situation where the other troops submit to the intimidating authority of Odysseus. Shrill 'wrangling' is exactly how Hephaestus had described the quarrel between

---

[45] *Thars-/thras-* terms in the *Iliad* normally lack connotations of shamelessness; they are standardly applied to military courage, e.g. 5.2, 124, 254, 602, 639; cf. n. 46 below. The name may therefore have been originally positive: see Chantraine (1963), but he ignores the pejorative sense of the word-group glimpsed in Poltherseïdes (?mock patronymic of the jeering suitor Ctesippus at *Od.* 22.287) and in *tharsaleos* at *Od.* 17.449, 18.330, 390, 19.91; cf. Nagy (1999) 260–1. Compare, much later, the proximity of laughter and *thrasos* at Isoc. 1.15, and cf. ch. 5, 232. Details of Thersites' description are fully discussed in Kirk (1985) 138–40, Latacz *et al.* (2003) 69–74. For his linguistic characterisation, see Beta (2004) 7–14.

Zeus and Hera at 1.575 (60 above); these are the only two occurrences of this word-group in the entire poem (and there are no occurrences at all in the *Odyssey*). That link is supplemented by the verb ἐρίζειν, 'quarrel' (2.214, cf. 247), which recalls Hephaestus' ἐριδαίνειν (1.574) while also glancing back at the strife (*eris*) between Achilles and Agamemnon themselves. These verbal points draw out something of the problematic status of Thersites. His description stamps him as provocatively insubordinate, but his love of verbal conflict gives him an ironic affinity with some of his betters, not least, as often noted (especially in connection with the speech which Thersites goes on to deliver at 2.225–42), with Achilles himself. Both figures have a kind of boldness (*tharsos*) that relates to speaking out in a public setting;[46] both step forward when others just accept the situation; both confront Agamemnon. We cannot distinguish between Thersites and Achilles by saying that the former is characterised as foul-mouthed, since in his dispute with Agamemnon Achilles gives one of the supreme exhibitions of foul-mouthed abuse in Homeric epic.[47] Despite all this, there is one fundamental factor which does distinguish Thersites' way of speaking from Achilles', but which at the same time sustains a curious parallelism between Thersites and the Hephaestus of Book 1. Thersites' unruly, disorderly speech is generally motivated, we are told, by a desire to make his audience *laugh* (215), something very far from the dark, violent passions that drove Achilles' outburst in the previous book. Achilles, indeed, lives further from the possibility of laughter than arguably any other Iliadic character.[48]

Thersites' habitual interest in arousing laughter makes him something rather different from the disgruntled plebeian he is usually taken to be.[49] In the myth of Er at the end of Plato's *Republic*, Thersites, observed on the point of becoming reincarnated as an ape or monkey, is called a *gelōtopoios* (10.620c), a 'laughter-maker' or buffoon, even a 'professional' comedian (it is no coincidence that Plato applies the cognate verb to Aristophanes in the *Symposium*).[50] Wrangling and laughter form a plausible pairing, since

---

[46] Although *thars*- words are not used of Achilles himself in Book 1, he encourages Calchas to speak out with boldness/courage (*tharsēsas*, 1.85, cf. 92).

[47] On Achilles' *aischrologia*, cf. ch. 5, 216–17. For Thersites' relationship to Achilles see Thalmann (1988) 19–21, Meltzer (1990) 267–72.

[48] Achilles does smile, once, at 23.555, within the context of Patroclus' funeral games; see 99 below.

[49] Standard views of Thersites are documented and challenged in Thalmann (1988), a sophisticated discussion which sets Thersites' quasi-comic status (esp. 16–17) in a larger context, and Rose (1988).

[50] *Symp.* 189a8; cf. how at *Rep.* 10.606c the impulse to rouse laughter (*gelōtopoiein*), if indulged, turns one into a 'comic poet' (*kōmōidopoios*) in one's own life (see ch. 6, 300–1). Thersites' habitual interest in making others laugh anticipates Aristotle's model of the *bōmolochos* at *EN* 4.8, 1128a33–5: cf. ch. 6, 311. Thersites as 'ape': ch. 6 n. 94.

abuse, whether real or stylised, so easily shades into mockery. Even the mockery of kings, in which Thersites is said to specialise, can readily be imagined as laughable in the right circumstances: a military camp during a long siege presents its own opportunities for jokers or jesters. Equally, as Lessing partly appreciated in his remarks on Thersites in *Laocoon*, laughter and ugliness can well operate in tandem, since ugliness, in Greek terms, is a species of 'shame(fulness)' that can itself be an object of ridicule and/or a badge of the grotesque antics of those who, like the later padded actors of Athenian Old Comedy, put on a gelastic performance for an audience.[51] Ugliness carries an intrinsic complexity *vis-à-vis* laughter. It may be viewed as an apt target of derision in its own right; it may somehow legitimise (by marking as socially licensed) the performers whose business it is to generate laughter; but it may also be regarded, by moralists at least, as a signal that laughter itself is an ugly, 'shameful' thing which disfigures those who yield to it. In Thersites' case, his lameness might additionally remind us of Hephaestus in Book 1, who had elicited the other gods' laughter by mimetically bustling round Zeus's palace as cup-bearer. Thersites, in short, is both verbally and physically equipped to be a 'laughter-maker', a sort of soldiers' jester-cum-satirist. But the equipment of laughter is dangerously double-edged. It needs adroit handling, especially if it is not to cause a resentment that will rebound against itself.

Far from making anyone laugh (immediately), Thersites is resented by the other Greeks (2.223). In this respect he seems the polar opposite of Hephaestus, exacerbating strife and tension where the lame god had dispelled them with subtly deployed play-acting, both verbal and visual. It is hard to see how Thersites could expect anyone to laugh *with* him in such circumstances, since he is surrounded by exhausted troops who were deflected from mass desertion only by Odysseus' timely intervention. The immediate narrative context threatens to make Thersites' behaviour opaque. He relentlessly denigrates Agamemnon, unmistakably echoing Achilles' outburst against the general in Book 1. A vocabulary of aggressive recrimination is employed by both narrator and characters to describe this behaviour (νεῖκος, ὄνειδος, κερτομεῖν: 221–4, 251, 256), including the term λωβητήρ (275), literally 'maimer' and thus denoting an almost physical

---

[51] On laughter and shame(fulness), see esp. ch. 5. Note the (legendary) ugliness of the iambic satirist Hipponax at Pliny, *HN* 36.12 (= Hipponax test., *IEG* 1 109). Cf. the physical deformities often associated with licensed 'fools' in various cultures: Welsford (1935) 55–75, with my Appendix 2 n. 81 on dwarfs. Was Descartes subliminally influenced by such traditions in *Les passions de l'âme* (1649) when claiming that the physically deformed are particularly inclined to derision? See Adam and Tannery (1996) 465, with English translation (by Stoothoff) in Cottingham *et al.* (1985) 393. For Lessing's discussion of Thersites, see *Laocoon* §§23–4.

viciousness.[52] Are we to imagine Thersites trying to take advantage of a situation in which the army's chief commander has lost control? But given the soldiers' disillusionment, this hardly seems a platform for the art of the 'laughter-maker'. Perhaps, then, Thersites' downfall is precisely a demonstration of the misguidedness of laughter 'out of place'. Odysseus, before lashing him across the back and shoulders, calls him ἀκριτόμυθε (246), a term that could mean either a 'speaker without judgement (sc. of what to say)' or a 'speaker of senseless things'.[53] Either way, Odysseus' reproof reinforces the initial image of Thersites as someone deficient in a sense of orderliness, *kosmos*, and 'measure', *metron*. But can we get any closer to seeing the connection between this disorderliness and an addiction to laughter?

The key to a cogent interpretation of Thersites lies, I believe, in a recognition of him as a problematically ambiguous figure. This ambiguity is implied in the very terms of his initial portrait. Since Agamemnon and the other leaders possess the military power to deal with individual insubordination, why should they be imagined as ever tolerating an inveterate wrangler and abuser? It cannot be that they do not care, since Thersites is especially hateful to both Achilles and Odysseus as a result of his biting criticism of them (2.220–1). Yet Thersites' habitual desire to make the Greeks laugh seems to point to the status of a partially sanctioned figure with a recognised function in the Greek camp. At the same time, it is clear from the trenchantly negative description of his unruliness that Thersites is not *simply* tolerated. His position looks uncertain and precarious. Might it, indeed, embody instabilities that inhere in laughter itself – the laughter, at any rate, of scathing ridicule?[54]

The preliminary signals of ambiguity are concretely dramatised by the manner in which Thersites becomes caught between two very different types of context and their possible dynamics: on the one hand, face-to-face

[52] The noun λωβητήρ indicates habitual behaviour on Thersites' part; cf. Schubert (2000) 64–5, 76–7. In the very last word of his speech (242) Thersites, repeating the words of Achilles (1.232), uses the verb λωβάομαι of Agamemnon's dishonouring of Achilles. On Homeric usage of *kertom-* terms, see Lloyd (2004) 82–7; cf. Miralles (1993) 63–5.

[53] The second sense fits better with the use of the word of 'indecipherable' dreams at *Od.* 19.560. Cf. Martin (1989) 110–13.

[54] Cf. Nagy (1999) 259–64, for whom Thersites is a (negative representation of the) 'blame poet', polar opposite of the epic poet – a suggestive reading, though the implications of Thersites as laughter-maker are broader: see Rosen (2007) 67–116 for analysis of this issue. Lowry (1991) rightly senses licensed abuse behind Thersites' status, but the details of his argument are flawed. Postlethwaite (1988), stressing the parallels between Thersites' and Achilles' attacks on Agamemnon, resists a reading of Thersites as quasi-comic. In antiquity, Lucian, *Ver. Hist.* 2.20 wittily made Thersites accuse Homer himself of mocking him (*skōptein*).

encounters between members of the heroic élite, including their rhetorical exchanges in councils and assemblies; on the other, settings in which he might perform as laughter-maker to an audience of rank-and-file troops, tapping into the pent-up frustrations and the 'lower orders' mentality of the ordinary soldier. The averted rout in Book 2 that provides the backdrop to Thersites' vilification of Agamemnon does not fall straightforwardly into *either* of these classes of occasion, yet it shares some features with each of them.

It matters in this connection that Thersites' ancestry and social status are themselves indeterminate. In a later tradition whose sources are obscure, Thersites is at least semi-aristocratic, a kinsman of Diomedes. In one account, Diomedes becomes involved in conflict with Achilles after the latter's killing of Thersites for having taunted Achilles for his supposed love of the Amazon Penthesileia. The killing of Thersites was recounted in the Cyclic epic *Aethiopis*, as was the resulting discord (*stasis*) among the Greeks (leading to Achilles' blood-purification, with Odysseus' help, on Lesbos), though Diomedes' kinship with Thersites is not attested for this version.[55] It is possible that the story of Thersites' later death at Achilles' hands already existed at the time when the *Iliad* was composed, especially given the reference at *Iliad* 2.220 to a particular enmity between Thersites and Achilles. If such a story was known to early audiences of the *Iliad*, it would deepen the complexity of Thersites' depiction as a figure who can simultaneously echo Achilles' abuse of Agamemnon yet deliver a sideswipe at Achilles himself too (2.241–2). It would also add depth, regardless of the putative kinship with Diomedes, to the problem of Thersites' status: why would the latter's killing lead to an outbreak of *stasis* among the Greeks unless his standing was more than that of an ugly plebeian at the margins of the army?

In fact, the Iliadic scene itself points to Thersites' peculiar position in other ways too. Above all, he is acknowledged by Odysseus to be a vocally penetrating public speaker (λιγύς ... ἀγορητής, 246, a phrase also applied to the great orator Nestor),[56] albeit one lacking in judgement or sense. The

---

[55] Thersites' taunting of Achilles is mentioned in Proclus' summary of the *Aethiopis* (*EGF* p. 47); cf. Σ to Soph. *Phil.* 445, with Gantz (1993) 333, 621–2 for other sources, including Pherecydes fr. 123 (Fowler). On this mythological tradition, including Chaeremon's play *Achilles Thersites-Killer* (*TrGF* 1 217–18), see Morelli (2001), Rosen (2007) 104–16. The relationship of the *Iliad* to other stories about Thersites is discussed speculatively by Rankin (1972) 44–51.

[56] *Il.* 1.248, 4.293 (cf. Telemachus at *Od.* 20.274); see the generalisation at 19.82 and the adverb λιγέως in the description of Menelaus' oratory at 3.214. λιγύς and cognates imply sounds of penetrating clarity; they are used in Homer of birds, lyres, winds and the wailing sounds of mourning. It is unjustified to treat Odysseus' description of Thersites' vocal ability, with e.g. Latacz *et al.* (2003)

role of such a speaker is elsewhere in the *Iliad* the preserve of leading warriors and princes, the political counterpart to their battlefield prowess. One may even discern irony in the fact that oratorical forcefulness is a particular asset of Odysseus himself.[57] On the other hand, as Odysseus implies in his brutal silencing of Thersites, a strong voice, together with the boldness required to face a large audience, does not guarantee authority; Thersites' vocal ability might be merely parallel to that of heralds (called λιγύφθογγοι, 'clear-toned', 2.50, 442 etc.). Thersites has the voice to *perform* as a public speaker, and his rhetorical assault on Agamemnon leaves no doubt about his ability to *mimic* the invective of Achilles (with its economic, military and sexual gibes against the commander). Everything Thersites says could be said by a sufficiently eminent warrior in a different context. This is obviously true of his echo (at 2.231, surely a ludicrous piece of mock boasting coming from someone lame in one foot) of Achilles' complaint that he labours to win booty which Agamemnon then appropriates (1.158–68); and it is even true of his general mockery of the Greeks as 'Achaean women, no longer Achaean men' (235), a taunt flung by Menelaus later in the poem against his colleagues (7.96). Thersites' desperately ill-chosen timing in the present situation, together with his addiction to seeking the rewards of laughter from his audience, shows that he lacks the mentality and influence to contribute to the deliberations of the army's leaders. Yet his boldness of speech empowers him to offend the reputation of individual warriors, exploiting the intense sensitivity to honour, shame and insult that characterises their world.[58] Thersites even alienates his general army audience (2.223), who are too caught up in the confusion of the immediate crisis to be disposed to laughter at Agamemnon.

On one level, then, Thersites speaks and acts like an individual warrior of hero status capable of upbraiding Agamemnon or Odysseus fearlessly in front of the whole army. But on another level he is nothing more than a vocally shrill laughter-maker, a camp entertainer, who, while equipped on the right occasion to reenact the quarrel between Achilles and Agamemnon for the gratification of other soldiers, has badly mistimed his present performance of military 'satire'. He is, in every sense, a mock orator, a parodist

---

[80], as merely sarcastic; Thersites' rhetorical self-confidence rebuts that: cf. Martin (1989) 109. See ps.-Dion. Hal. *Ars Rhet.* 11.8 for an interesting ancient perception of Thersites as orator; cf., more artificially, Liban. *Progym.* 8.4.17.

[57] Such irony was, in effect, appreciated by Sophocles: see the momentary misunderstanding between Philoctetes and Neoptolemus over the identity of the base but clever speaker at Soph. *Phil.* 438–45; cf. Worman (2002) 94.

[58] Insults between Iliadic warriors involve an 'art of battle mockery' that complements the fighting itself: Vermeule (1979) 99–105, Martin (1989) 65–77, Parks (1990) esp. 56–67.

of the discourse of army councils. His case accordingly demonstrates the potential ambiguity of laughter itself and its intricate interplay with factors of context, identity and expectation. It does this in two basic ways. First, because behaviour that might be effectively gelotopoeic in an appropriate framework such as an 'off-duty' gathering of soldiers[59] is an overtly dangerous act, a threat to military order and hierarchy, that brings Thersites a violent beating from Odysseus. Secondly, because that beating paradoxically succeeds in producing the laughter that Thersites otherwise so craved (and for which others might, in the right circumstances, value him). When the army laughs from *Schadenfreude* at the sight of his pain and humiliation, while he himself weeps (268–70), the scene reaches a double-edged resolution. The sadism of this mass reaction underlines Thersites' reduction to a physical victim of his betters but also suggests a kind of psychological *displacement* on the part of the troops. Fearful of the sceptre-wielding figure of Odysseus, the men are able to direct against Thersites' debasement the laughter they had withheld from his outburst against Agamemnon. There may even be a subtextual hint of the sort of mock beating that could form part of a buffoon's routine in other contexts: what might belong to Thersites' gelastic repertoire on an appropriate occasion is here converted into a merciless punishment.[60] We are left, at any rate, with a feeling that it is precisely because Thersites was an established focus for the laughter of the troops that they can now deride him as a scapegoat for the emotional upheaval caused by the abortive defection. The significance of line 270, in particular ('for all their demoralisation, they laughed at him with delight', οἳ δὲ καὶ ἀχνύμενοί περ ἐπ' αὐτῷ ἡδὺ γέλασσαν), is not just that the soldiers relish the sight of physical suffering, but, more subtly, that Thersites is a *familiar* arouser of laughter who can therefore readily, if here involuntarily, channel a discharge of the tensions built up by recent events.[61]

The proximity of the Thersites and Hephaestus episodes in *Iliad* 1–2 draws attention to some striking but conflicting permutations of laughter.

---

[59] *Il.* 3.43 (57 above) imagines Greek soldiers laughing raucously in an 'off-duty' setting. Compare, somewhat differently, the army's collective laughter during Patroclus' funeral games, *Il.* 23.786, 840. Other instances of soldiers' mockery: ch. 10 n. 4.

[60] Beatings are a stock element in Greek comic drama; cf. Kaimio (1990) for some material. In late antiquity, ps.-John Chrys. *De paen.* 2 (59.760 *PG*) mentions a kind of jester (*gelōtopoios*) whose act revolves round being beaten: cf. Nicoll (1931) 87–8.

[61] Thalmann (1988) 21–6 presents a full-blown view of Thersites as scapegoat. For the soldiers' laughter as 'displacement', cf. Rankin (1972) 43 n. 25, but taking no account of Thersites' addiction to laughter. Rose (1988) 20–1 strains in taking Odysseus as the 'latent' object of the army's laughter. Parks (1990) 89 sees Thersites as 'fool and braggart'. Spina (2001) explores the history of creative reinterpretation of the figure.

Hephaestus had used three different means – diplomatic speech, a (perhaps 'fictional') story of his own physical punishment, and a piece of visual play-acting – to create an atmosphere in which laughter could be superficially directed against himself while serving to heal (or hide) wounds and create (temporary) harmony. Thersites, on the other hand, uses shrill denunciation in a way that could well, in another time and place, have elicited the laughter of the troops against their commanders; yet he succeeds only in making himself the isolated object of mass derision and physical punishment. In both cases there is a taut counterpoint between the possibilities of laughter and a moment of social crisis.[62] Hephaestus takes it upon himself, by deftly managed role-playing and mock self-abasement, to negotiate a transition from acrimony to mirth. Thersites, carried away by his addiction to scathingly 'satirical' speech, disastrously misjudges the moment (acting in a way which, in later Greek, would be called *akairos*, 'untimely'), and becomes the victim of his own public performance: his impulse to laughter makes him succumb to a kind of self-ignorance.[63] The contrast between the two scenes reveals something important about the complex potential of laughter, as well as about the disparity between the existences of gods and men. Where laughter itself is concerned, however, that disparity is not absolute. We can see that by turning now to a further episode of divine mirth, this one in the *Odyssey*. It happens once again to revolve around Hephaestus, but in a very different role from his intervention in the first book of the *Iliad*.

SEX AND HILARITY ON OLYMPUS

The songs performed in *Odyssey* 8 by the blind bard Demodocus at the Phaeacian court, and in the presence of Odysseus himself (still at this stage anonymous to his hosts), constitute an elaborately unfolding triptych. The first (8.73–82) recounts a verbally ferocious quarrel between Odysseus and Achilles at a feast, a quarrel that gladdened Agamemnon's heart (since he took it as a good-omened fulfilment of an oracle) but which now, by strange contrast, reduces the listening Odysseus to tears and groaning. The second (266–366) – sung out of doors after athletic competitions, possibly

---

[62] Powell (2004) 69 suggests that the stampede which leads up to the Thersites episode 'is a joke and meant to spark laughter'; this is unfounded, as well as unintegrated with his perception of Thersites as himself 'an object of laughter' (70).

[63] For Thersites as symbol of self-ignorance see ps.-Hippoc. *Epist.* 17.5, with ch. 7, 362; cf. ch. 6, 300–2, for a Platonic view of self-ignorance as the key to 'the laughable'. On untimely laughter and the principle of the 'right moment', *kairos*, see ch. 1 n. 99, ch. 3 n. 38.

accompanied by young male dancers,[64] and enjoyed by Odysseus as much as by the Phaeacians – concerns the adulterous liaison between Aphrodite and Ares, the revenge taken by Aphrodite's husband, Hephaestus, and the laughter of the other gods at the spectacle of sexual exposure involved in that revenge. The third song, performed after another interval (for dancing, gift-giving and further feasting), is on a theme of Odysseus' own choosing: the story of the Wooden Horse and the events surrounding the Greeks' final storming of Troy. Like the first song, this one reduces Odysseus himself to weeping and groaning, behaviour compared, in a searing simile, to the grief of a woman slumped over the body of her dying warrior husband. So Demodocus' triptych enacts a set of thematic variations – humans/gods/humans, war/sex/war, tears/laughter/tears (perhaps even tragedy/comedy/tragedy) – though the configurations involved are complicated by the varying reactions of different audiences both within and outside the songs, not least the reactions of Odysseus himself. Why Odysseus should regard the (memory of the) Trojan War and his own part in it as quasi-tragic (at the start of Book 9 he will summarise his life as being one of 'grievous sorrows') stretches beyond my present concerns. But his reactions to the first and third of Demodocus' songs need nonetheless to be kept in view as we examine the details of the middle song on the adultery between the goddess of love and the god of war, with the reverberating laughter of the divine audience summoned to witness the cuckolded Hephaestus' revenge. The whole triad of songs raises questions about what makes the difference, and for *whom*, between sombre and ridiculous story-patterns. And the framing of the middle song by the two episodes of human war and sorrow lends it an elusive ethos: are we to hear it as set in fictitious relief against the 'historicity' of the narratives that flank it, or as an account that sheds a real if unusual light on the divine powers that rule the world? Furthermore, we should observe that while the song is enjoyed by the audience, including Odysseus, we are not told that they laugh at it (8.367–9). Laughter is at work *within* the song, though juxtaposed with other, very different elements. Whether or how far it is the right response *to* the song – that is something that neither the Homeric narrator nor the song itself directly discloses.

The scenario of the adultery song is entirely divine, yet it has something, as often noticed, of the character of a transposed folktale – as it were: the

---

[64] This depends on whether we think the circular dance at 8.262–4 accompanies the song which starts at 266: assumed by e.g. Friedländer (1969) 3, 5, denied by Hainsworth in Heubeck *et al.* (1988–92) 1 362. See *Il.* 18.590–606 for the song-dance nexus. The adultery story later lent itself to 'ballet': witness the pantomime at Lucian, *Salt.* 63.

lame blacksmith, his beautiful (perhaps bored) wife, and her dashing military seducer.[65] But it is unclear that the superimposition of such categories onto the gods makes the setting immediately comic. It is true that a marriage of Hephaestus and Aphrodite appears nowhere else in Homer or in other early sources; it may have been invented for the sake of this story ('just imagine if the ugly blacksmith god found himself married to Aphrodite, of all deities . . .'), conceivably as an ironic foil to the separate tradition of a marriage between Ares and Aphrodite.[66] Equally, however, the incongruity of the match might be felt to heighten the pathos of Hephaestus' torments, on which emphasis is laid, and to bring out the real cost of the situation to the injured husband. Ares makes love to Aphrodite in Hephaestus' own marriage-bed (a marked detail: 8.269, 277, 314). When Hephaestus is informed by the Sun, the revelation plunges him into bitter heartache (272, 303), malevolent brooding (273), and fierce anger (276, 304, 314). Yet a crucial twist in the tale shifts it from the realms of the humanly intelligible into a different mode of imagination: the lovers are trapped, during their post-coital sleep, by the invisibly thin yet unbreakable metal fetters which Hephaestus has contrived to hang round the bed and which clasp Ares and Aphrodite in an inescapable imprisonment. How does this divinely exquisite ingenuity, which occurs in other stories about Hephaestus as well, affect the tone of the story for a human audience?[67] Simple answers are suspect. The capture of human lovers *in flagrante* might well, if given appropriate treatment, make material for comedy – which is to say that even so socially and ethically fraught a subject can be viewed, for certain purposes, in a morally relativised light. It is also true in more general terms that public knowledge of adultery might be a cue for laughter, even

---

[65] To call the song a glimpse of 'the daily life of Olympus', with Hainsworth in Heubeck *et al.* (1988–92) I 363, is naïve: quasi-bourgeois humanisation (364) is nearer the mark. On Ovid's treatment of the story (*Met.* 4.169–89, *Ars Am.* 2.561–92), including Venus' mockery and mimicry of Vulcan's disfigured body (*Ars Am.* 2.567–70), cf. Janka (1997) 404–20, with nn. 77, 81 below. For the depiction of the story in Renaissance and later art, see Reid (1993) I 195–203, 505–10, Arbury (1998) 495.

[66] *Pace* the speculative readings of particular artefacts in e.g. Schefold (1992) 10, Burkert (1960) 134 and n. 9, Gantz (1993) 76, there is no secure early artistic evidence for the story: see the survey in Delivorrias (1984) 125–7. On the possible roots of an Aphrodite–Hephaestus link, cf. Hermary and Jacquemin (1988) 628–9. Rinon (2006) 15–16 takes a different angle on Hephaestus' marriage(s). For an Ares–Aphrodite marriage see Hainsworth in Heubeck *et al.* (1988–92) I 364.

[67] Especially pertinent is the story of how Hephaestus crafted a throne which trapped his mother Hera; the adultery song may ironically invert the idea that Ares initially promised to capture Hephaestus on this occasion: cf. Alc. 349(b) *PLF*, and the fragmentary *Hymn to Dionysus* in *P. Oxy.* 670 (with West (2001)). Alcaeus' account may have included divine laughter, Page (1955) 260–1. But *contra* e.g. Friedländer (1969) 5 there is no early evidence for a version in which Hephaestus won Aphrodite by freeing Hera; cf. West (2001) 7. Note the Sun's winged bed, made by Hephaestus, in Mimnermus 12 *IEG*, with Allen (1993) 95–9.

for open mockery of the cuckolded husband (if he could be regarded as ineffectual), by those sufficiently detached or pleased to be immune to sympathy.[68] But how transfer such possibilities to a divine scenario as peculiar as that of Demodocus' song? The broader evidence of Greek mythological tradition leaves the matter wide open. Sexual adventures on the part of male gods can certainly be regarded on occasion in a comic light: Zeus's many adulterous affairs receive this treatment in, for example, the mythological burlesques of Attic Middle and New Comedy. But it is equally true that the same themes can furnish material, at the extreme, even for tragedy.[69]

Perhaps, then, the audience of the *Odyssey* itself is placed in an ambivalent position *vis-à-vis* Demodocus' theme, finding itself suspended between a sense of the extravagantly comic-burlesque and an awareness of the dark undertow of a story of sexual betrayal and revenge. If such ambivalence is in order, it is a nice irony that the Homeric text confronts us with a rare textual puzzle. There was already disagreement in antiquity over whether, after catching the guilty couple in his trap, Hephaestus summons the other gods to witness things that are 'laughable' (γελαστά) or the very opposite, '*no* laughing matter' (ἀγέλαστα).[70] The difference depends entirely on word-division (which would not have been marked in early texts), not on changing anything in the sequence of letters. Yet it matters greatly to the interpretation of the scene. Either way, as it happens, we are faced with a word that occurs nowhere else in Homer. In view of the tonal and functional ambiguities of laughter itself (as well as the textual nicety), the choice is not straightforward; modern editors have been divided. On the first reading, Hephaestus is calling for humiliating, punitive ridicule against Ares and Aphrodite. On the second, he is presupposing but *deprecating* the laughter

---

[68] Some sort of recognisable social reality lies behind Eur. fr. 1063.15–16 *TrGF*, where a woman describes the circumstances of a weak ('useless', *achreios*) cuckold as causing 'great laughter'; Hdas. 1.77 implies public ridicule of cuckolds. Cf. general derision of neighbours etc., ch. 1, 30–2.

[69] One strikingly comic angle on the subject, complete with obscene cynicism, is Ar. *Birds* 556–60. Comedies and satyr-plays on the theme included Aesch. *Diktyoulkoi*, (probably) Soph. *Danae*, and the (lost) Greek model of Plautus' *Amphitryo*. But there were tragedies too, including Eur. *Alope*, *Alcmene* and *Danae*.

[70] 8.307: van Thiel (1991) 105 (γελαστά), von der Mühll (1962) 140 (ἀγέλαστα) display the division in modern editions. For various positions, ancient and modern, see Nuchelmans in *LfgrE* I 59 (*s.v.* ἀγέλαστος), Hainsworth in Heubeck *et al.* (1988–92) I 367, Brown (1989) 285 with n. 7, Garvie (1994) 301–2 (printing ἀγέλαστα), Frisk (1960–70) I 294 (implicitly accepting ἀγέλαστα), de Jong (2001) 208: given pitch accent, the latter wrongly claims that in performance the difference would be 'barely discernible'. Miralles (1993) 20–1, 35 ignores the point (as well as Hephaestus' pathos), as do Schmidt (1876–86) IV 191, Garland (1995) 76, Collobert (2000) 137–8, all taking for granted γελαστά; *DGE* I 19 s.v. ἀγέλαστα inexcusably omits the line. (For the active sense of ἀγέλαστος at Hom. *Hymn* 2.200, see ch. 4, 162). Lucian, *Dial. D.* 21.2, with typical mischief, makes Hephaestus himself laugh.

of something like ribaldry, titillation, or frivolous insouciance (the very kind he himself encourages in *Iliad* 1), a lighthearted attitude that could only exacerbate his distress and dishonour (309). What tilts the argument, I think, in favour of the second reading is that there is no hint of any gelastic tone in Hephaestus' speech, which is delivered at a raucous pitch of wild outrage (304–5): he laments the contrast between his own physical shortcomings and Ares' attractiveness; wishes he had never been born (a strange sentiment in the mouth of an immortal god: see below); speaks openly of his anguish; and promises to keep the lovers trapped until Zeus returns the bride-price that had been part of the original marriage pact. If an audience can *find* laughter in this situation, it must be at the expense of all the well-founded emotions with which Hephaestus' indignation is charged. Such an audience would surely have to treat Hephaestus not as a gravely injured victim with genuine feelings, but as a mere if ingeniously vengeful cuckold. It would have to disregard the underlying issues of betrayal and dishonour, and focus on the titillating sexual embarrassment of the trapped lovers. It would have to enjoy a laughter beyond morality. Is this what the *Odyssey*, whose own plot hinges round the threat to Odysseus' marriage, invites its own audience to do? Importantly, Odysseus himself takes deep pleasure in the song (8.368). But as I have stressed, neither he nor any of the Phaeacians is said to laugh at it. It is otherwise, however, with the divine audience inside the story.

In response to Hephaestus' summons, the female deities stay at home out of sexual bashfulness (*aidōs*, 8.324), a factor which complicates the narrative but should not be translated into a general archaic conception of the conduct of goddesses.[71] But several male gods arrive with alacrity, stand in the entrance of the house, and roar with a laughter that is described by the same line as *Iliad* 1.599: ἄσβεστος δ' ἄρ' ἐνῶρτο γέλως μακάρεσσι θεοῖσι ('and laughter swelled up, with unquenchable force, among the happy gods', 8.326). In addition to the possibility that the line actively alludes to the Iliadic scene itself, this irrepressible laughter carries a contextually rich force.[72] It simultaneously expresses surprised admiration for

---

[71] As by e.g. O'Higgins (2003) 45. Goddesses are well capable of risqué mockery. It is often observed that on the François vase the return of Hephaestus to Olympus (n. 83 below) seems to be accompanied gesturally by Athena's, possibly also Aphrodite's, (indirectly sexual) mockery of Ares; ill. in e.g. Boardman (1974) pl. 46.7. As for the male gods in *Od.* 8, note that Zeus, though invited (306), apparently absents himself (322–3).

[72] That Demodocus' song presupposes the *Iliad* 1 scene (and other Iliadic passages) is argued most fully by Burkert (1960). But his reading of *Odyssey* 8 blurs important distinctions: stressing (136–7) how the song helps to smooth out earlier tensions between Odysseus and Euryalus, he ignores the tension associated with laughter *within* the song; to say the adultery causes 'only laughter' ('nur Gelächter',

Hephaestus' cunning (a sprung trap is, in one respect, like a good joke), release of the psychic charge associated with sexual exposure, and an element of *Schadenfreude* at the humiliation of Aphrodite and Ares. But it is difficult to accept the view that this laughter represents righteous public chastisement of the illicit lovers, even if the spectating gods pay lip service to Hephaestus' feelings by agreeing with one another that 'wicked deeds do not prosper' (329).[73] The gods' laughter is prompted directly by the spectacle of Hephaestus' artful capture of the adulterous pair (327). Their response has the look of an instantaneous outburst of mirth, not a reflective act of condemnation; it contrasts pointedly with Hephaestus' own state of mind ('I am distraught as I look at them', 314), as though they simply ignore his torment. When, moreover, Apollo asks Hermes (a deity multiply associated with laughter elsewhere)[74] whether he would willingly suffer such painful confinement as the price of sex with Aphrodite, Hermes answers lasciviously that he would endure even greater pain and humiliation for the chance – and the gods' laughter is renewed (343), indicating that they share a sexual frisson at the sight of Aphrodite's body. No wonder the scene proved objectionable to ancient moralists, both pagan and Christian.[75] Finally, the fact that Poseidon alone abstains from laughter (at least the second time), urgently interceding on Ares' behalf by promising to stand as guarantor of compensation, cements the impression that the other gods' reaction is no show of ethical reproof but a burst of laughter beyond morality: the very phrasing at 8.344, 'laughter took no hold of Poseidon' (οὐδὲ Ποσειδάωνα γέλως ἔχε), clinches the implication that the other gods laugh involuntarily and unreflectively.[76] If Ares' and Aphrodite's adultery can be heard on one

---

140) bypasses Hephaestus' grief-stricken response (as well as Poseidon's refusal to laugh and the absence of the goddesses), as does Seidensticker (1982) 59–60. Braswell (1982) discusses parallels between the Hephaestus/Ares and Odysseus/Euryalus relationships, but stays strangely silent about the gods' laughter.

[73] Garvie (1994) 306 rightly notes that the story as a whole undermines the surface moralism of 329–32; cf. n. 77 below.

[74] For laughter in *Hom. Hymn Hermes*, see ch. 3, 100–3. Even in the *Iliad* Hermes is capable of a kind of wittiness: see his mock deference to Leto at 21.497–501; cf. Richardson (1993) 95. The Odyssean conversation between Hermes and Apollo is taken further by Lucian, *Dial. D.* 17, 21 (cf. ch. 9 n. 28). The Hermes–Aphrodite liaison which produced Hermaphroditus is a mythological invention later than the *Odyssey*.

[75] Xenophan. 11.3 *IEG*/DK probably has this passage, among others, in mind; cf. ch. 6, 269. Zoïlus (*apud* ΣT *Od.* 8.332 = *FGrH* 71 F18) complained about it, as does Socrates at Pl. *Rep.* 3.390c (cf. n. 28 above). Some ancient copies of the poem excised the exchange between Apollo and Hermes at 333–42 (ΣH *Od.* 8.333). Christian authors often refer to this episode with outrage or contempt: e.g. Clem. *Protr.* 4.58 (the 'godless' comedy of pagan mythology), Athanas. *Ctr. gentes* 12 (cf. ch. 10 n. 9), Evagrius schol. *Hist. Eccl.* 1.11 (with a broader swipe at pagan phallicism: cf. ch. 4 n. 88), the last two 'laughing' reprovingly at the mythological scenario itself.

[76] On Poseidon and abstention from laughter, cf. the Tirynthian story cited in ch. 4, 155–7.

level as a tale of the amoral workings of 'divine' forces of sexual allure and physical prowess, the hilarity of their fellow deities, particularly as encapsulated in Hermes' lustful admission (induced by Apollo's salaciously leading question), leaves a sense of laughter itself as a sign of instinctive complicity in the excitement of such forces.[77]

At the same time, the episode as a whole offers a powerful image, in the figure of the anguished Hephaestus, of the pain of adultery to its victim. After all (a prime consideration as regards the wording of 307, noted above), there is no trace of laughter on the injured husband's own part, even when his trap is sprung. Remarkably, he goes so far as to echo what was probably already, and was certainly to become, a formula of *human* pessimism, 'best never to have been born'.[78] The unbridgeable gap between these two perspectives – the crippled husband's anger at betrayal and the titillation of the male gods who form the audience for the sexual dénouement – gives Demodocus' song the thematic and psychological piquancy which makes it irreducible to a neat antithesis between adultery as a 'game' for the gods and a grave problem for humans.[79] On my account, Hephaestus' own description of the situation as *agelasta*, 'no laughing matter' (307), proves dramatically ironic, paving the way for the jolt of uncontrollable ribaldry among the other gods. Even if we were to keep the reading γελαστά, 'laughable', at 307, we would still be left with an emotional incompatibility between the expectation of self-righteous derision and the lubricious hilarity which the gods actually display. However we turn the story round, divine laughter in this scene is far from the unifying force it appears to be in *Iliad* 1, especially when we remember the absence of the female deities and the agelastic stance of Poseidon. This is itself a sufficient refutation of one ancient attempt to allegorise the episode as an account of the harmonisation of cosmic forces.[80] If the gods of Homer were to be interpreted as

[77] Garland (1995) 81–2 sees how the gods' laughter ironically undercuts Hephaestus' revenge. Brown (1989) insists that the laughter of 8.326 is a matter of moral shame, but he struggles (290–1) to integrate the second outburst into this reading; Rudhardt (1992) 401–2 overreads the gods' laughter as reestablishing 'the sacred order of things'; Rinon (2006) 16–18, though right to stress Hephaestus' seriousness, is one-sided in seeing him as 'humiliated' by the gods' laughter. Alden (1997) 517, 528–9, and Scodel (2002) 86–7 take Hephaestus himself, without sufficient reason, as the object of ridicule. Ovid, *Met.* 4.187–9, *Ars Am.* 2.585–6 captures the ribaldry of the gods' laughter.

[78] *Od.* 8.312, 'my two parents, who should never have begotten me' (τὼ μὴ γείνασθαι ὄφελλον). The human motif already occurs at *Il.* 22.481 (6.345–8 is related but slightly different): cf. ch. 7, 339–40, for the embedding of the motif in the Silenus–Midas story. That Hephaestus himself does not laugh is noted (as a reason for Poseidon's abstention from laughter) in ΣE on line 344. Hart (1943) 265, calling the whole song 'mere farce', is (like many) blind to the darker side of the story.

[79] De Jong (2001) 207 is a token instance of this oversimplified contrast.

[80] Heraclitus, *Qu. Hom.* 69 (esp. 69.11, laughter as symbolic of concord); see the notes of Buffière (1962) 125–6, with Buffière (1956) 168–72, Russell (2003) 222–3. Heraclitus' reading depends in part

impersonal cosmic forces, their laughter in Hephaestus' palace would have
to count as symbolic of volatile, unstable energies rather than of integration
or concord.

The implications of Demodocus' song for the possibilities of *human*
laughter can only be complex. The song is performed for an audience,
including Odysseus, which takes deep pleasure in it but is not described as
actually laughing either with or at the gods. The *Odyssey* as a whole treats
the subject of adultery – committed with such dire consequences by the
sisters Helen and Clytemnestra – as an issue of potentially life-destroying
significance. Nothing matters more to Odysseus than the faithfulness of
his own wife, and critics have often drawn attention to the oblique connection between the Ares–Aphrodite song and the human hero's own circumstances. Yet Demodocus' song, with its contrast between Hephaestus'
outrage and the mirth of the other gods, seems to offer its audiences, both
inside and outside the poem, a choice between judging adultery with real
censure or occupying the vantage point of a Hermes and relishing the sexual content of the story without inhibition. For (some of) the gods, such
amoral laughter is possible in part because the condition of immortality
exempts them from the terminal nature of human pains. Even Hephaestus, having emerged the victor in a contest of deception, will survive the
trauma of the episode, just as the divine adulterers themselves survive it
with only temporary discomfiture – a swift departure to Thrace for Ares
(with a mere 'fine' as his penalty), and a restorative bath in her native Cyprus
for Aphrodite, who is significantly given her (Iliadic) epithet of 'lover of
smiles' at *only* this one point in the *Odyssey* (362): surely a wry marker of
how, as it were, her eroticism remains intact.[81] In human reality, on the
other hand, such events could be expected to cast, at the least, a permanent
shadow (as with Helen and Menelaus),[82] and might generate a far worse
outcome than that (as with Clytemnestra and Agamemnon). Two circumstances, however, leave open the option of human laughter at Demodocus'
song. The first is that the story is not, after all, *about* humans but about the
gods themselves. In that respect it is the psychological equivalent to turning
the tables on the gods: if they can (sometimes) laugh among themselves

---

on the tradition that Harmonia was the offspring of Ares and Aphrodite (Hes. *Theog.* 933–7). Cf.
Proclus' Neoplatonic allegorisation of the gods' laughter in this scene at *In Tim.* II 27.16–27 (Diehl),
with n. 27 above.

[81] At 318–20 Hephaestus appears to envisage 'divorce', but no further reference is made to this. Garvie
(1994) 294 overstates the point when claiming the story ends 'happily'. Ovid, *Ars Am.* 2.589–90
wickedly allows the affair to continue even after its exposure.

[82] This holds for the *Odyssey*'s own treatment of the couple in Book 4: happily reunited on one level, but
unable to recover exactly what they once had (note the symbolic lack of further children, 4.12–13).

with eternal carefreeness, we can surely sometimes laugh back at them – not 'to their faces', for sure, but in echoing response to divine laughter itself. The second circumstance is that the shape of Demodocus' song, for all its asymmetries between the reactions of the various gods (Hephaestus himself, Poseidon, the other male gods, the absent female deities), is redolent of an artful comic plot: a comedy in which sexual misdemeanours are committed, unmasked, punished – but also finally resolved without lasting harm. On this comic model, laughter dissolves seriousness in a (temporary) regression to pleasures more basic than those of morality.

The combination of Iliadic and Odyssean scenes in which Hephaestus is associated with outbursts of divine laughter suggests that the blacksmith god, with his physical disfigurement and his craftiness, lent himself to burlesque fables. Particularly well attested elsewhere is the story of how he schemed revenge against his mother for throwing him from Olympus in vexation at his disability but was eventually compelled to return to Olympus under the control of Dionysus (who had made him drunk) and, in the commonest version, seated on a donkey – a story which gave visual artists in the archaic and early classical periods an opportunity to embed Hephaestus in a situation populated by a cast of sileni or satyrs.[83] The poet of *Odyssey* 8 (like that of *Iliad* 1) is likely to have been drawing on a familiarity with burlesque associations such as these. Even so, I have tried to argue that his representation of (and, more equivocally, his encouragement to) laughter is far from *simply* burlesque, above all because it makes so much of the pathos of the cuckold's anguish, a pathos frequently neglected in modern readings of the scene.[84] The result is a delicately serio-comic uncertainty of tone. This uncertainty is compounded by the way in which the story dramatises how laughter itself can easily slide from the domain of the

---

[83] On visual representations see Hermary and Jacquemin (1988) 637–45, 653–4 (with *LIMC* iv.2, 390–401, for images), Carpenter (1991) 13–17, with ills. 1–19 (on 22–8), Schefold (1992) 28–33, Lissarrague (1990) 40–4, Hedreen (2004), Green (1994) 43–4; on the blurring of sileni and satyrs, Padgett (2003) 29–30. A possible link with Lemnian ritual is noted by Burkert (1983) 195–6 (cf. ch. 4 n. 95); one might even moot an allusion to the kind of 'folk justice' later characteristic of charivari, in which the 'donkey ride' was a known type: see Alford (1959) 507–9, 511–13, cf. ch. 4 n. 73, and note a general affinity between donkeys and Dionysiac revelling, with Lada-Richards (1999) 132–5. The return to Olympus was dramatised in comedy and satyr-plays: Epicharmus' *Komastai/Hephaestus* treated the theme (*PCG* 1 51), as did Achaeus' satyr-play *Hephaestus* (*TrGF* 1 120); cf. Carpenter (1991) 27, ill. 14. Hephaestus (as cup-bearer, surmises Nesselrath (1990) 209 n. 96) is threatened by Zeus in Alcaeus com. fr. 3 *PCG*. As a folk curio, note the saying recorded by Arist. *Meteor.* 2.9, 369a31–2, that in the noise of a flame one could hear 'Hephaestus laughing'.

[84] Lesky (1961) 40, Kerényi (1962) 196 are unusual in denying that the Homeric scenes of divine laughter are burlesque: but Kerényi's account (192–200) suffers from a surfeit of schematised abstractions, while Lesky's appeal to an Ionian spirit or sensibility ('Ionischer Geist') explains little; on this last point cf. Friedländer (1969) 4.

ethical, where it might be imagined as working with the grain of social control and censure, into a more psychologically fluid zone where its impulsiveness (its 'unquenchability') seems antipathetic to a steady grip on moral values or purposes. And to complicate things further, Demodocus' song sets up this divinely magnified image within an epic that makes laughter a significant marker of character at several important junctures. It is to this bigger Odyssean picture that I now want to turn.

FROM DEBAUCHERY TO MADNESS: THE STORY OF THE SUITORS

The thematic contours of laughter's place in the *Odyssey* start to stand out as soon as one registers its basic coordinates. The poem's twenty-two separate references to laughter[85] are found in the following settings: one in a generalisation (spoken, not without guile, by Odysseus) about the symptoms of inebriation; two, already considered, in Demodocus' song of divine adultery; twelve in the behaviour of the suitors (twice specifically that of Antinous, most prominent of the group and most detested by Penelope); two in the actions of the palace maidservants who fornicate and collude with the suitors; two in moments of partly involuntary behaviour on Penelope's part; one, self-ascribed, in a speech of dissimulation by Telemachus; one in Eurycleia's exhilaration at the death of the suitors; and, finally, just one (and hidden from exterior view) in the conduct of Odysseus himself. This pattern of distribution is sharpened when we notice in addition that all but three of the fourteen cases of laughter involving the suitors and maidservants are concentrated in two stretches of the poem, in Book 18 and in Book 20.

The human laughter of the *Odyssey* centres, for sure, around the suitors' tainted milieu of aggression and licentiousness. No unmodified laughter is to be found within Odysseus' own family. In all five cases relating to Odysseus, Penelope and Telemachus, a special factor is active – whether concealment, subconscious significance, or an element of mystery. By focusing predominantly on laughter's association with rampant sensual drives, the *Odyssey* turns the motif into a two-sided reflection of the poem's opposing groups: its conspicuous presence among the suitors marks debauched indiscipline, while its near absence on the part of Odysseus and his family corroborates their psychologically and socially fractured existence. The resonance of this contrast can be heard, as a complex subtext, in the reference Odysseus himself makes at 14.463–6 to 'soft' laughter as one element in

---

[85] I count each occurrence of *gelōs/gelan* as a separate reference, except for the paratactically linked occurrences at 8.343–4, 20.346–7; I also count καγχαλόωσα at 23.1, 59 as a single reference. Miralles (1993) 34–52 offers an overview of Odyssean laughter; Miralles (1994) is closely related.

an ensemble with intoxication, singing, dancing, and unguarded speech. In the close confines of Eumaeus' hut, Odysseus intimates – though with calculated dissimulation, delivered in his 'Cretan' guise – that the wine he has just drunk is loosening his tongue and will lead him to speak boastfully. The imagery he uses stands in ironic contrast to the immediate setting in the hut; indeed, it conjures up, for an audience familiar with the rest of the poem, something like the inebriated, hedonistic milieu of the suitors in the palace.[86] In particular, the idea of laughing 'softly' or 'sensually' (ἁπαλόν), a phrase paralleled only in the *Homeric Hymn to Hermes* 281 (where it is used of Apollo's amused reaction to Hermes' lies), here evokes a state that is both self-indulgent and untroubled, in both respects the very reverse of Odysseus' condition as a hardbitten figure to whom everything 'soft', one might say, has become alien.[87] Such laughter seems unthinkable for someone who has suffered so much and has learnt to take constant precautions against the risk of self-revelation. While early Greek culture recognises an acceptable place for wine, song, laughter, and dance within well-ordered festivity, the ironic force of Odysseus' words sets in stark relief the absence of celebration which blights the hero's own deferred restoration to his rightful kingdom.

The *Odyssey* as a whole suggests that while the dissipated lives of the suitors are characterised by reckless laughter, the predicament of Odysseus and his family is too fraught to allow more than a marginal place for it. The point is strikingly emphasised by the interdict placed by Odysseus on overt rejoicing even after the killing of the suitors, an interdict which Eurycleia's instinctive relief finds it hard to obey.[88] The more controlled and discreet act of smiling, on the other hand, is something denied to the suitors, whereas Odysseus smiles three times (once inwardly, and not openly until he has killed the suitors) and is twice benignly smiled at by deities (Calypso and Athena), while Telemachus smiles once, unobtrusively, to his father

[86] Cf. the suitors' dancing: *Od.* 1.152, 421, 17.605, 18.304. Dancing is apt for good feasting (cf. Phaeacia, 8.248) but is tainted by the suitors' illicit excess. The only dancing associated with Odysseus is the fake wedding-party at 23.134, 145, 298. Dancing and laughter are both forms of 'play' (ch. 1 n. 45) which combine exuberantly in komastic celebrations (ch. 3, esp. 105–6); but when physically excessive or contemptuous, both tip over into *hubris* (ch. 1 nn. 89, 91).

[87] 'Soft', ἁπαλός, is a rare word in the *Odyssey*; elsewhere it describes the bodies of the young suitors (21.151, 22.16) or their like (13.223). Some ancient critics took soft laughter to be effeminate: see Athen. 5.180a, Clem. *Paed.* 2.5.48 (a Christian slant: ch. 10, 493), with Plut. *Mor.* 503e–f, 645a for further reflections on *Od.* 14.463–6; cf. ch. 3, 107–8. Stanford (1965) II 235 suggests 'feebly' for ἁπαλόν; that cannot be right. See Appendix 1 n. 17; cf. Arnould (1990) 165–6.

[88] The interdict, at 22.411–12 (cf. ch. 1, 29), significantly permits rejoicing 'in the heart' (θυμῷ), in keeping with Odysseus' own behaviour at 20.301–2 (see 90–1); cf. ch. 1 n. 65. Even so, Eurycleia cannot inhibit noisy jubilation (καγχαλάω: n. 15 above) as she runs to tell Penelope the news (23.1, 59).

and is also smiled at with affectionate admiration (for his quasi-Odyssean shrewdness) by his surrogate father Menelaus.[89] In all these cases, smiling is laden with oblique, knowing significance. There is thus a recurrent contrast between the insolent, coarse laughter of the usurping suitors and the largely suppressed laughter, but also the subtle smiles, of the king, his family and his divine helpers.

The laughter of the suitors merits closer scrutiny. While functioning in general as an extrovert trademark of their contemptuous occupation of the palace, it also develops, in the later parts of the epic, into a sign of the increasingly light-headed and (at a supremely eerie moment) *crazed* way in which their arrogant feasting carries them unseeing towards a violent death. Most of the suitors' laughter is heard in the build-up to their downfall, from Book 16 onwards, but an early occurrence alerts us to some of the subject's thematic potential. In Book 2, after the assembly at which he has denounced the suitors and announced his intention to sail to Pylos and Sparta, Telemachus returns to the palace, distressed at heart (2.298), to find the usual feast being prepared in the great hall. Antinous approaches him directly, with a laugh and a handshake (301–2), and invites him to join them in eating and drinking. The invitation is doubly ironic: the suitors are illicitly appropriating Odysseus' goods (and, by extension, Telemachus', 313), and there has already been a prominent indication of their self-engrossed disregard for the customs of hospitality (1.119–20). Furthermore, Antinous' words leave no doubt that he is belittling Telemachus' plan to sail off in search of news of his father. In this respect, Antinous gives a cue to the group as a whole. In the passage that follows, the suitors – whose youthfulness is mentioned twice in this context (324, 331) – collectively sneer and jeer at the purpose and possible outcome of the voyage. The language describing their behaviour (ἐπελώβευον καὶ ἐκερτόμεον, 323) is related to that used of Thersites; but it also insinuates a corruption of permissible conventions of banter at a feast.[90] Throughout the *Odyssey* the suitors' laughter expresses

[89] Odysseus' smiles: 20.301–2 (inwardly sardonic; see 90–1), 22.371 (sparing Medon's life), 23.111 (at Penelope's caution). All three are discussed, as a rising sequence, by Levine (1984). Others' smiles *at* Odysseus: 5.180 (Calypso, reacting to his fear of her), 13.287 (Athena, in response to his deceit; cf. n. 37 above), 16.476 (Telemachus, unobtrusively, at news of the suitors' ship's return); Arist. *Hom. Probl.* fr. 399 Gigon (176 Rose) apparently used the last passage to exemplify Telemachus' emotional self-control. Menelaus' smile at Telemachus: 4.609 (with allusion to Odysseus at 611); why Lateiner (1995) 193 pictures Menelaus as 'condescending' baffles me. Cf. Camps (1980) 20, 91–2 on the range of Homeric smiles/laughter. The suitors' *lack* of smiles, stressed by Levine (1982b) 103–4 (though *Il.* 10.400 is a counterinstance to his claim that Homeric smiles are never ironic: cf. n. 17 above), should not be compromised by translating γελᾶν as 'smile', e.g. de Jong (2001) 62 (on *Od.* 2.301), 445 (on *Od.* 18.163: n. 104 below).
[90] See *Il.* 2.256, 275, for the relevant descriptions of Thersites, with 72–3 above. The youthfulness of the suitors, stressed at *Od.* 2.324, 331 (note 20.374–5 for the same formula in conjunction with

the dynamics of an aggressive group-identity, an identity which stands in a polarised relationship to 'outsiders', especially Telemachus and Odysseus himself. Antilochus' laugh at 2.301, therefore, when Telemachus reenters the hall, is a travesty of an amicable gesture. On the surface it suggests an offer of goodwill after the tense confrontation in the assembly, but it is simultaneously and hypocritically a continuation of that conflict by different means: it attempts to turn Telemachus into a target of derision. It also takes on, however, an unintended irony in the context of feasting. Feasting is the setting *par excellence* for reciprocal laughter, yet here, because of the overweening and antagonistic traits of the participants, it counts as the very reverse of a propitious opportunity for any shared good cheer – hence Telemachus' explicit repudiation of the idea of enjoying relaxed or carefree conviviality (εὐφραίνεσθαι ἕκηλον, 311).[91] The encounter shows the impossibility, within the dystopic state of Ithaca, of a socially benign use of laughter. Telemachus answers Antinous' laugh with a grim threat of death (316), just as he spurns the handshake (321). The passage activates an association between mockery and perverted feasting which recurs with growing intensity in later books of the poem.

The first of the *Odyssey*'s two most concentrated dramatisations of the suitors' laughter takes place in Book 18.[92] The sequence starts at line 35, where Antinous laughs out loud with pleasure at the prospect of a fight between two beggars, Irus and (the disguised) Odysseus. Irus himself has already, with braggadocio, appealed to the suitors as an audience keen for a spectacle of violence (18.11–12, 30–1); and he has hurled coarse abuse at his rival (26–7) in response to the latter's offer of peaceful coexistence. Antinous' excitement is patent at 36–9: the fight will be a 'god-sent delight' for the suitors; the noun τερπωλή, 37, denoting a strong thrill of pleasure, occurs nowhere else in the *Odyssey*.[93] The suitors' sensuality is attuned to a 'show' that promises the spilling of blood, and, as in Book 2, Antinous' individual laughter is echoed by the response of the group as a whole (40). While boxing is a standard sport in the world of Homeric epic, as we see from the funeral games for Patroclus at *Iliad* 23.653–99 and repeated references in

laughter), helps explain their recklessness; cf. de Jong (2001) 63. But it has particular resonance *vis-à-vis* feasting and mockery; cf. Hom. *Hymn* 4.55–6, with ch. 3, 101–3, for a pertinent image of banter at the feast, of which the suitors' behaviour at 2.323–36 (and elsewhere) is a perversion. On laughter and youthfulness, see ch. 1, 22–4.

[91] See ch. 3 n. 24 for *euphrosunē* and feasting.

[92] Before that, Amphinomus' laughter at 16.354 is exceptional among the laughter of the suitors, a burst of relieved surprise at the sight of the returning ship; cf. his reservations about killing Telemachus, 16.394–405, with Hewitt (1928) 442–3. 'Self-mockery', Levine (1982b) 99, is hardly the point.

[93] Theog. 1068 uses the noun with reference to the youthfully sensual pleasures of symposium and *kōmos*; similar connotations at Archil. 11.2 *IEG* (cf. 215 *IEG*). The cognate verb is linked to feasting at *Od.* 1.369, 8.542, 15.399, 18.305–6 (cf. e.g. Theog. 1047).

the Phaeacian episode of the *Odyssey* itself (8.103, 130, 206, 246), the present instance, like everything sponsored by the suitors, is a corrupted distortion of it. A crudely unnecessary intrusion into a feast (as well as a divergence from the norms of hospitality), it is grossly out of place here; it is, indeed, more of a bare-knuckle brawl than a boxing-match, lacking the latter's recognised trappings (not least its leather fist-straps, *Iliad* 23.684). In these circumstances the suitors' flippant enjoyment of a fight they could easily have prevented betokens the larger depravity that infects their behaviour. What's more, Antinous augments the air of sadistic pleasure with gratuitous cruelty: he threatens Irus, should he lose, with slavery and the mutilation of his nose, ears and genitals (18.84–7).

That the suitors' laughter effortlessly slips into raw bloodthirstiness, and one whose dramatic ironies (given the prospect of their own gory end) are impossible to miss, is underlined in what follows. When Odysseus easily floors Irus with a single blow, we hear that the suitors 'threw up their hands and died with laughter' (18.100, χεῖρας ἀνασχόμενοι γέλῳ ἔκθανον), an idiom which enacts a grim pun on the fate awaiting the suitors.[94] Their laughter is iterated a few lines later (111) when, still oblivious to what his prowess presages for themselves, they toast the victor with a prayer that Zeus may fulfil his dearest wish. Although Odysseus himself rubs in Irus' defeat with harsh words, he has no reason to enjoy his victory in the terms in which the suitors perceive it – not because he is sentimental (he considers hitting Irus hard enough to *kill* him, 91) but because defeating Irus (and winning a blood sausage, 118–19!) can matter little to him. He does, however, inwardly exult over the blindness manifested by the suitors' congratulatory prayer (117), just as his 'heart laughed' at his success in tricking the Cyclops into believing his false name (9.413, in sharp contrast to the Cyclops' own groans, 415), and just as we shall later be told how he 'gave a very sardonic smile in his heart (*thumos*)' when he avoided the cow's foot thrown at him by Ctesippus (20.301–2).[95] The cautious *internalisation*

---

[94] See Arnould (1990) 222–3, with my ch. 1 n. 21 for related metaphorical expressions; cf. Levine (1982a) 203 for the thematic subtext in the suitors' case. As for the raised hands, Eustath. *Comm. Od.* II 170 (Stallbaum) takes it as a reflex of hilarity, but it was sometimes interpreted as mockery (see Kassel and Austin on Cratinus fr. 301) – perhaps, conceivably, a parody of the boxers' own gestures (*Od.* 18.89, 95, cf. *Il.* 23.686)?

[95] Odysseus' inner laugh at 9.413 (cf. n. 39 above) involves suppressed triumph, his heart's laugh at 18.117 proleptic satisfaction at the suitors' ignorance, and his inner smile at 20.301–2 a combination of grim bitterness with anticipated revenge (on 'sardonic', see n. 100 below). Concealed laughter/smiling occurs later at Theog. 59/1113 (ch. 3 n. 52), Aesch. *Cho.* 738 (Clytemnestra's hypocrisy, detected by the nurse: Garvie (1986) 245–6), Theoc. 1.95–6 (a vexed case: divergent construals in Gow (1952) II 21–2, Zuntz (1960), Crane (1987), Hunter (1999) 94–5), Epict. *Ench.* 48.2 (ch. 6 n. 107); Soph. *Aj.* 955–9 seems to slide from inner to outer exultation (imagined). (Note also Genesis 18.13,

of pleasure, as highlighted by the paradoxical imagery of inward laugh-ter/smiling, is an index of Odyssean cunning and forbearance. It forms a telling contrast to the raucous laughter of the suitors. But that contrast raises a larger question about the interpretation of the whole Odysseus–Irus scene. Some critics have seen an element of burlesque or even comedy in this episode.[96] I think it is hard to sustain this reading. What blocks it is precisely the suitors' own laughter. To find the scene comic would be to connive in some degree at the suitors' self-ignorance, at their callous delight in a sordid, unequal fist-fight between two beggars (one of whom they had previously found useful, 18.6–7). Sophisticated hearers/readers of the epic, aware of Odysseus' mounting revenge-plot, cannot afford to align themselves with the mentality of such characters. The passage restricts its audience to the knowing, 'inward' laughter practised by the hero himself: it requires us to track the suitors' gelastic group-dynamic from a wary distance.[97]

Later in this same evening, Odysseus tells the palace maidservants to go and wait on Penelope, leaving him to look after the braziers in the hall. They laugh spontaneously at the beggar's instructions, and the tone of their response is coloured by the verbal assault on Odysseus which Melan-tho proceeds to deliver.[98] The maidservants function here as a secondary echo of the suitors themselves, whose own laughter is sounded one last time in this scene shortly afterwards (350). This time it is Eurymachus (appropriately, given his relationship to Melantho, 325) who picks up the mood of abusiveness towards the nameless beggar in order to elicit further hilarity from the carousing group. His ironic suggestion that Odysseus' bald head is magnifying the firelight in the hall leads into an exchange of taunts with the beggar. But Eurymachus' jeering is weakly derivative. He

---

where Sarah laughs to herself: ch. 10 n. 26.) Cf. Odysseus' endurance of mockery as a model for the Cynic Diogenes' superiority at Dio Chrys. 9.9 (ch. 7 n. 116). A more cheerful (but still metaphorical) laughter is located in the *thumos* by Pindar's adj. γελανής at *Pyth.* 4.181: Bowra (1964) 235 translates 'with laughing heart' and is wrongly criticised by Braswell (1988) 263; cf. Pind. *Pyth.* 5.2, Bacchyl. *Epinic.* 5.80 (the verb, γελανόω, hapax). Demeter's smile in her *thumos* in *Orphica* fr. 52.4 Kern, *apud* Clem. *Protr.* 2.21.1 (cf. ch. 4 n. 25), denotes a transformed mood, not a concealed impulse.

[96] See e.g. de Jong (2001) 437 ('burlesque', but qualified on 438), Richardson (1993) 241 ('somewhat comic'). Levine (1982a) more aptly stresses Irus–Antinous resemblances and the scene's premonition of the suitors' deaths. Eustath. *Comm. Od.* II 167 (Stallbaum) discerns a comic dimension, despite his reasons (*ibid.* 166) for regarding the suitors' laughter as reprehensible.

[97] Lateiner (1995) 28 appositely speaks of the suitors' 'gang-laughter'. Cf. n. 102 below, with ch. 1, 30–3, on group laughter.

[98] The adverb αἰσχρῶς, 'shamefully', at 321 is unique in the *Odyssey*; it occurs in similar phrasing only once in the *Iliad*, at 23.473: cf. ch. 5 n. 3. For a general reference to the maidservants' ridicule of the beggar, see Eurycleia's words at 19.372, with ch. 1 n. 68 on the verb καθεψιάομαι.

repeats some of his mistress Melantho's own lines (390–3 = 330–3) as well as one of the goatherd Melanthius' gibes from earlier in the day (362–4 echo 17.226–8); and even his physical aggression, in throwing a footstool, repeats the earlier action of Antinous at 17.462–5 (a gesture the others had deprecated, 17.483–7). There are many important strands in the scene of rising tension and menace which develops in the course of Book 18, engineered by Athena to increase Odysseus' anger (18.346–8) and brought to an end only by Telemachus' decisive intervention, backed up by Amphinomus, at 405–21. Laughter adds a thematically distinctive dimension to the atmosphere. In the first part of the book it is associated with the suitors' perversion of feasting by the pleasure they take in a gory brawl, including a kind of grudging admiration for the victor's strength. By the end of the book, taking its cue from the maidservants, it has been redirected into derision for this same beggar and a renewed threat of violence against him. At both stages, their mirth exhibits the unruly excesses of a group blinded by its self-ignorance but watched by the secret smiles of the disguised figure in their midst.

The motif of the suitors' laughter is restated and brought to an extraordinary climax in Book 20. Before we reach that climax, there is an incident which casts a lurid light back on the preceding day's events. Near the start of Book 20, the sound of laughter is caught in passing, as it were, when Odysseus, lying awake brooding on revenge, hears the mirth of the maidservants ('sharing laughter and merriment [*euphrosunē*] with one another', 20.8) as they make their way to sexual assignations with the suitors. The note struck by this line, while harking back to the conduct of both suitors and maids in Book 18, gives a sudden provocation to Odysseus. It leads into a wonderfully vigorous description of the 'barking' of his dog-like heart of anger and the impulse he feels to kill the maids there and then. The connection between the noise of the passing servants and the surge of anger it causes vividly evokes the instant at which the overheard laughter cuts to the roots of Odysseus' vexed and restless consciousness. What makes this so psychologically penetrating is the way in which Odysseus is, in a sense, caught off his guard. The paradox is that in Books 17–18 Odysseus was calculatingly resolute and self-controlled in response to the various taunts and laughter directed against him. Now, for a brief but intense moment, he is on the point of lashing out against the maids, even though the right time for revenge has not yet arrived. It is precisely the difference between overt goading and accidentally overheard hilarity – between mockery to his face and mockery, so to speak, behind his back – with which even long-suffering Odysseus finds it momentarily hard to cope. This remarkable passage dramatises how the sheer sound of laughter can become an almost unbearable provocation to one who hears it as insulting him in his absence. It is all the more compelling because the maidservants are not described as actually laughing at Odysseus, only as being in the high spirits of sexual excitement. Yet this glimpse of their light-heartedness, and the licentious disorder in his own palace that it bespeaks, pierces Odysseus' uneasy, wakeful mind.[99]

It is during the next day's feasting in the palace that the *Odyssey*'s sub-theme of laughter reaches its symbolic climax. The background is a continuation of the earlier pattern of Odysseus' abuse by the suitors, this time led by Ctesippus. When the latter ironically offers the beggar a 'guest-gift' by throwing a cow's foot at him, Odysseus leans out of the way of the missile and is described as 'smiling in his heart very sardonically' (μείδησε δὲ θυμῷ | σαρδάνιον μάλα τοῖον, 301–2), a hidden gesture, it seems, of bitterness and disdain.[100] But this corroboration of the opposition between the suitors' crude brashness and Odysseus' inwardly monitored command of the situation does not prepare us for the *coup de théâtre* which follows. After Telemachus has exchanged further words with the suitors, blending true and false feelings with a dissimulation worthy of his father, an episode of disorientating strangeness intervenes.

> ὣς φάτο Τηλέμαχος· μνηστῆρσι δὲ Παλλὰς Ἀθήνη
> ἄσβεστον γέλω ὦρσε, παρέπλαγξεν δὲ νόημα.
> οἱ δ' ἤδη γναθμοῖσι γελώων ἀλλοτρίοισιν,

[99] The moment of overheard laughter stands in dramatic counterpoint with Odysseus' overhearing, in a strange half-comatose state (Russo in Heubeck *et al.* (1988–92) III 114), of Penelope's prayer for death (20.56–90). On the maids' sexual laughter as the polar opposite of Penelope's demeanour, cf. Levine (1987).

[100] I interpret the phrase as an inward, metonymic smile; likewise e.g. West (1997) 434, de Jong (2001) 500. See Stanford (1965) II 352–3, Russo in Heubeck *et al.* (1988–92) III 121 for the alternative; Lateiner (1995) 193–5 posits a visible smile but 'privately experienced'. Zuntz (1960) 38 (while right about the sense of *gelan* at Theoc. 1.95–6) is confused in suggesting that one can 'laugh' but not 'smile' inwardly in Greek. A 'sardonic' laugh/smile can cover either a pained grimace (e.g. Meleager, *Anth. Pal.* 5.179.4, with Gow and Page (1965) II 612, anon. *Anth. Pal.* 16.86.6; Plut. *Mor.* 1097f signifies 'forced' laughter in pain) or a look/sound of bitter derision (e.g. Pl. *Rep.* 1.337a, with ch. 6, 286, Polybius 18.7.6, Plut. *Mor.* 169d, Lucian, *Iup. Trag.* 16, with Coenen (1977) cxxvii): Odysseus' inner smile is a special variation on the latter, befitting his general concealment of emotion. See Stanford and Russo *locc. citt.*, together with Pearson (1917) I 112–13 on Soph. fr. 160 (*TrGF* IV 171–2), Arnould (1990) 223–6, LSJ *s.v.* σαρδάνιος, Chantraine (1968) 988, 996–7, and Frisk (1960–70) II 678 for the two main ancient etymologies of *sardanios/sardonios* as applied to laughter, one from Sardinia (ch. 1 n. 21), the other from σαίρειν/σεσηρέναι, 'bare the teeth' in a grin/grimace (e.g. Ar. *Wasps* 901 of a dog, and Alexis fr. 103.26 of prostitutes; cf. n. 12 above, Appendix 2 n. 12). For an alternative laughter-related etymology cf. Mallory and Adams (2006) 362. Kretschmer (1955), Miralles (1987) offer various interpretations of the epithet. Cf. Renaissance discussions at Erasmus, *Adages* 3.5.1, Joubert (1980) 88–9, with Barasch (1997) 194–9 for a link with depictions of Death. *Risus sardonicus* has become a medical term (ch. 6 n. 141).

αἱμοφόρυκτα δὲ δὴ κρέα ἤσθιον· ὄσσε δ' ἄρα σφέων
δακρυόφιν πίμπλαντο, γόον δ' ὠΐετο θυμός.

(20.345–9)

So spoke Telemachus. But among the suitors Pallas Athena
Roused up unquenchable laughter and deranged their minds.
They started to laugh with jaws that were not their own,
And the meat they were eating was sodden with blood. Their eyes
Filled up with tears, their hearts were obsessed with thoughts of wailing.

Several earlier narrative ideas are distilled and transformed here into a
moment of uniquely disquieting power. We have seen how laughter was
established in Book 18 as a leitmotif of the suitors' behaviour, and in
that same book Telemachus had called the suitors mad (18.406). Twice
Athena had earlier helped to goad individuals, Antinous and Ctesippus,
into laughter-seeking mockery of Odysseus (18.346–64, 20.284–302). Now
she sends the whole group temporarily insane, mixing together the body
language of their own mental recklessness (laughter) with portents of the
death that is slowly encircling them (blood-soaked meat, tears and grief).[101]
The effect is enhanced by the vision of Theoclymenus, the seer (and fugitive killer) whom Telemachus had brought back with him from the Peloponnese. Theoclymenus speaks of seeing the suitors' bodies swathed in
darkness, their cheeks drenched with tears, the walls and rafters spattered
with blood, the palace swarming with ghosts of the dead, and the sun's
light blocked out by thick mist (351–7). But the suitors, already emerging
from their insanity, laugh heartily at Theoclymenus' words; Eurymachus
accuses *him* of being mad (360). Soon after, they laugh twice more, but
now once again in their old familiar ways and with the gelastic dynamic of
the group restored:[102] first, in sarcastic expression of mock sympathy with
Telemachus for the oddity of his guests (374), and then in the general spirit
of heady feasting that envelops them (390).

The impact of the extraordinary scene at 20.345–58 is made all the greater
by its peculiar evanescence and its mysterious suspension between the real
and the hallucinatory.[103] It is unclear how to demarcate the boundaries
between the suitors' subjective delirium, Theoclymenus' prophetic vision

---

[101] The meat, in a gruesome prolepsis, is suggestive of their own bodies. The same idea is intimated by
the contrast between 'meals' at 20.390–4; cf. Odysseus' ironic equation of the suitors' death with
their dinner at 21.428–30.

[102] Notice how group laughter is reinforced by the looks they exchange, 20.373–4; the same detail
occurs with the maidservants' laughter at 18.320.

[103] Treatments of this much-discussed passage can be found in Russo's notes in Heubeck *et al.* (1988–
92) III 124–7, Rutherford (1992) 231–7, Fenik (1974) 233–44, Levine (1983b), Hershkowitz (1998)
149–50, 158–9, de Jong (2001) 501–3, and Guidorizzi (1997), the latter arguing for overtones of
Dionysiac possession and *ōmophagia*.

of them, and the 'objective' impression pictured by the narrator. This uncertainty lends the outburst of uncontrollable yet 'alienated' laughter ('with jaws that were not their own') a marked uncanniness – a factor found also, though to more delicate effect, in the 'pointless' laughter of Penelope prompted by an earlier intervention of Athena's in Book 18.[104] The suitors are, it appears, simultaneously laughing (346–7) and weeping (349, 353); alternatively, we can imagine their faces bursting into manic laughter *before* (348–9) turning to tears at the sight of the blood-sodden meat they are eating. Either way, the combination presents a pathology for which there are parallels in ancient (and modern) medical literature.[105] Drastically different from the sympathetically nuanced 'laughter through tears' of Andromache at *Iliad* 6.484 (54–5 above), the duality of features displayed by the suitors forms a crazed superimposition of conflicting states of mind which nonetheless point dramatically in the same direction: a madness portending death. The suitors' laughter at 346–7, 'unquenchable' in its sudden frenzy, is a weirdly twisted version of the excesses of their feasting. This is brought out by the arresting phrasing of 347, 'they started to laugh with jaws that were not their own'. The precise but surprising reference to 'jaws' perhaps implies that the suitors' mouths are wide open, their teeth bared in a kind of hysterical grin as they eat their bloody meat. However we construe this visual cue, the adjective *allotrios* – literally 'belonging to someone else' – is a startling detail.[106] The suitors' very faces, as well as their minds, are 'possessed' from outside and alienated from themselves; their facial muscles are unhinged from conscious control: the connection between mind and body has snapped. The suitors become, as it were, psychologically convulsed marionettes under Athena's control, allowing us,

---

[104] In 'she laughed a pointless laugh' (ἀχρεῖον δ᾽ ἐγέλασσεν), 18.163, I take the adj. to imply uncanny light-headedness: under Athena's influence, Penelope cannot fully comprehend her own mood and motivation. Cf. Russo in Heubeck *et al.* (1988–92) III 59, Levine (1983a). In later texts, 'pointless' (ἀχρεῖος) laughter becomes more straightforwardly pejorative: see Cratinus fr. 360 (though in *comic* criticism of the audience), anon. *Anth. Pal.* 16.86.5. Penelope's other laugh in the *Odyssey*, at 17.542 (in response to Telemachus' sneeze, which she takes as an auspicious omen in relation to her speech at 529–40), also has a touch of the uncanny: it represents a quasi-intuitive sense of the direction events are taking. (For its instinctiveness, cf. the similar wording of *Hom. Hymn* 4.420, with ch. 1 n. 35.) On both Penelope's laughs cf. Colakis (1986) 140–1, invoking a Freudian unconscious.

[105] Laughter and tears are conjoined symptoms of mental disturbance in the case of the Thasian woman at Hippoc. *Epidem.* 3, 2nd series case 15 (cf. ch. 1 n. 40). For modern documentation of PLC, pathological laughing and crying resulting from neural impairment, see McCullagh *et al.* (1999), Parvizi *et al.* (2001); more briefly, Damasio (2004) 77–9. The modern term 'gelasmus' is sometimes used to denote hysterical involuntary laughter: Winn (2001) 425.

[106] It is reasonable (only a narrow conception of 'oral' poetic diction denies such possibilities) to detect an ironic overtone of the suitors' consumption of property 'not their own', ἀλλότριος: cf. e.g. 1.160, 18.280, 20.171. Hor. *Sat.* 2.3.72 adapts Homer's image of the suitors' laughing jaws, but with altered implications.

with Theoclymenus' help, to perceive them as unwittingly enacting both their folly and their doom in a paradoxically unified image. For this instant, their laughter is a form of manic seizure, all the more tellingly so for the manner in which it is converted abruptly back into their habitual laughter of disorderly hilarity and derision (358, 374, 390). This is the earliest and most haunting but by no means the only passage in Greek literature where laughter is explicitly imprinted with the symptoms of madness.[107]

Having used the fluid expressiveness of laughter at the end of Book 20 to create a macabre vision of the suitors' fate lurking beneath the surface of their perpetual mirth, the *Odyssey* contains two further references to the theme during the final stage of preparations for the hero's revenge, the archery contest of Book 21. The passages in question spotlight Telemachus' relationship to the suitors; they form a contrasting but complementary pair. In the first, at 21.105, Telemachus tells the suitors that at the (supposed) prospect of his mother's remarriage 'I laugh and take pleasure in my foolish heart' (γελόω καὶ τέρπομαι ἄφρονι θυμῷ). Several critics have mistakenly tried to explain Telemachus' laughter as though it were a narrative datum. But to say 'I laugh' is not the same as actually to laugh, and Telemachus' initial exclamation, at 102, reinforces doubt in the present case.[108] Telemachus is in fact the only character in Homer to speak of his own 'laughter'. The point needs to be taken together with his self-description as 'foolish' (stressed by repetition: 102, 105), which purports to convey a sort of giddy excitement at Penelope's intentions but is actually disingenuous, a calculated move to advance the archery contest (by attempting to string the bow himself) in a way which will prepare the ground for the vengeance Odysseus has planned with him. It is certainly legitimate to regard Telemachus as responding at the same time to Antinous' preceding words (91–5), where he anticipated the archery contest and recalled his childhood memories of Odysseus in total ignorance of the latter's presence in the hall. The pregnancy of the dramatic moment invests Telemachus' words with more than one layer of meaning as he observes the various agents' motives from the privileged position of his pact with his father. But what adds most depth to Telemachus' words, for my purposes, is his professed association between laughter and 'folly'. For the poem's audience, the attachment of this thought to the mention of Penelope's remarriage implies a knowing awareness of the self-blinding celebrations of the suitors. Telemachus adopts a laughing guise that shows,

---

[107] See ch. 1, 17–18.

[108] More often than not, ὢ πόποι (102) expresses dismay or shock; its only Homeric coupling with laughter is in the army's response to Thersites' beating, *Il.* 2.272.

with psychological subtlety, how much he has learnt from what he has endured for so long.[109]

The suitors' trademark behaviour is exhibited for the last time a little later in the archery scene. In response to Telemachus' seemingly despairing wish for their expulsion from the palace, 'they all laughed wholeheartedly at him and relaxed their harsh anger against him' (21.376–7, 376 being a repetition of their reaction to Theoclymenus at 20.358). Whereas at 21.105 Telemachus used the idea of his own 'laughing' excitement to lure the suitors into a complacent belief in his ineffectualness, he now achieves the same end (as well as overcoming their resistance to Odysseus' attempt to string the bow) by reverting to a menacing tone towards them, but a menace which feigns its own futility. On the very threshold of their slaughter, the suitors laugh for the last time with supreme heedlessness. The scornful insolence which had started with their mockery of Telemachus in Book 2 thus comes full circle. As throughout, the suitors' laughter is laden with psychological and ethical flaws that are only thinly masked by aggressive bravado. Theirs is a brittle laughter of profound self-ignorance which only death can silence.

EPILOGUE: ACHILLES' ONLY SMILE

This chapter has explored the rich symbolism and semantics of laughter's occurrences in the *Iliad* and *Odyssey*. The results are anything but simple, and I hope at least to have established why it would be misguided to claim a univocal significance for 'Homeric' laughter. In the *Odyssey*, laughter is predominantly associated with the overweening, licentious behaviour of the suitors. But precisely because that behaviour represents a corrupted form of life, laughter itself outruns the suitors' perverted use of it. This is confirmed, with emblematic irony, by the way in which Athena turns laughter against the suitors, trapping them as its manic victims, in the ominous moment of gelastic seizure at 20.345–9. It is also underlined by the poem's intermittent indications (in particular, the internalised laughter and smiles of Odysseus' own heart) that there is a very different, prospective laughter that awaits a future when the palace of Odysseus will have been restored to its inherited state. There is a further level, however, at which the *Odyssey* can be felt

---

[109] Hoffer (1995) 515–17 rightly stresses that Telemachus only *speaks* of laughing (though he overlooks that this could in itself involve ironic enactment of mirth); he reads a complex rhetoric of deceit, as does Lateiner (1995) 160 (cf. 141, 'sham'); cf. also Beck (1991) 125 (under 2b). Other interpretations of the scene, treating the laughter as 'objective', include Stanford (1965) II 360, Colakis (1986) 138, Olson (1994), Miralles (1993) 38–9, Fernández-Galiano in Heubeck *et al.* (1988–92) III 158 (apparently perpetrating the documentary fallacy in suggesting, *à propos* 21.102, that 'perhaps Telemachus has inadvertently let fall a smile of joy' and 'now tries to divert his listeners' attention from the slip').

to leave its audience with an unresolved tension between different kinds of laughter. The laughter of the gods in Demodocus' song of the adultery of Aphrodite and Ares is not (or so I argued) a moral laughter. In part, at least, it is a form of sexual titillation, mixed with the collective hilarity of the group at the humiliation of two of its members. The scene assigns to laughter an energy or pleasure-flow of its own which seems to ignore the distress and pathos of Hephaestus emphasised by the narrator/singer. But in that respect the story might be thought to assimilate the *gelōs* of the gods to that of the suitors themselves (or *vice versa*). While the *Odyssey* as a whole situates the suitors' laughter within a steady perspective of moral condemnation, the gods' unquenchable laughter in Book 8 detaches itself from morality. In this way, gelastic themes become part of the larger fabric of the poem's treatment of the complex relationship between the worlds (and values) of gods and humans. Homeric gods are ultimate embodiments of both the plenitude and the conflict-ridden nature of existence. Far from being the *sources* of morality, they are in part the agents of a perpetual tension between morality and power.

In the *Iliad* too laughter is irreducible to a uniform significance. No two of its occurrences are quite the same. Its ascription to gods is more frequent than in the *Odyssey*, since in addition to the collective outburst at the end of Book 1 (in itself, an instance more freighted with suppressed meaning than appears at first glance) it crops up in several encounters between individual deities. But its divine manifestations are unstable: from Hera's lips (15.101–2) to Zeus's very heart (21.389), the *gelōs* of gods, whether forced or explosive, is never entirely without an element of the inscrutable. In the human scenes of the *Iliad*, laughter finds its way into the representation of sharply contrasting contexts, from the poignant intimacy of Andromache and Hector in Book 6 to the rasping cackle of Odysseus as he celebrates the exploits of a nocturnal killing-spree in Book 10. In keeping with the poem's gelastic variations and ironies, the only context of (relative) social tranquillity and harmony in which laughter is heard is also a context of competition, as well as one shadowed by death: the funeral games of Patroclus in Book 23. The cluster of laughter and smiles which we meet in that passage seems at first sight simple and 'natural', but here too there are modulations. The Greeks *en masse* laugh at Ajax son of Oileus, just defeated in the footrace by Odysseus, not merely, as often implied, because he slips and falls into a pile of dung, but also because he gets up and complains that Odysseus always receives help from Athena ('like his mother', he gibes) – itself an irreverent side-view, so to speak, of the epic world's nexus between select heroes and their divine champions. The sight of the dung-spattered figure is of course a *sine qua non* of the army's laughter, but the latter breaks out only (23.784) after Ajax has made his spluttering complaint, which is itself a kind of emotional compensation for losing. We should not reduce the spectators' laughter to a sense of 'superiority', and while (unlike the laughter at Thersites' suffering in Book 2) there is no animus to it, as Antilochus' smile at 786 helps to confirm, it is a surge of collective freedom which the conventional translation 'sweet laughter' fails to capture.[110] Similarly, the laughter of the troops at 840 can be partially understood as an amused response to Epeius' incompetence at shot-putting, but the chance to laugh at such things takes on its full significance only against the still overhanging backdrop of the poem's traumas and tragedies.[111]

This last point is borne out by a moment, earlier in the games, whose paradoxical strangeness makes it a fitting image with which to close this chapter. For what could be stranger, in the darkness of the *Iliad*, than a 'natural' yet unique smile on the face of Achilles? Even he, it seems, is touched by the special mood of the games, the opportunity they provide for a socially celebrated competitiveness that lacks the deadly outcomes of war. After all that has gone before (and that has fixed the nearness of his own death), Achilles proves finally capable of affectionate admiration, as well as a gesture of prompt reconciliation, in response to Antilochus' complaint about the distribution of prizes in the horse race (23.555). The smile of spontaneous warmth on the part of a hero whom the *Iliad* elsewhere compels us to imagine weeping but never laughing is a fleeting hint of a set of possibilities remote from those which have played themselves out in the poem. It is, for a split second, the smile of a different Achilles and a different world.

---

[110] This inadequate translation is adopted by e.g. Kirk (1985) 144, Griffin (1980) 183; cf. Garland (1995) 80, translating *Il.* 2.270, where it is even less apt: on the interpretation of ἡδὺ γελᾶν etc., see n. 41 above. The troops' laughter is (inappropriately) traced to a sense of 'superiority' by e.g. Griffin *loc. cit.*, Levine (1982b) 97.

[111] Taplin (1992) 251–60 offers insightful remarks on the mood of the funeral games. On the specific implication of laughter at 23.840, cf. Howland (1954–5) 16; contrast the earlier *silent* respect for Epeius' boxing challenge at 676.

CHAPTER 3

Sympotic elation and resistance to death

πλεῖ καὶ Διόνυσος ἐπὶ κῶμον τῆς Ἄνδρου . . . τὸν Γέλωτά τε ἄγει
καὶ τὸν Κῶμον ἱλαρωτάτω καὶ ξυμποτικωτάτω δαίμονε . . .

([In the picture] Dionysus himself is coming by sea to take part in a
kōmos on Andros . . . He is bringing with him Laughter and Kōmos,
the most exuberant of deities and the most fitting for a symposium . . .)

Philostratus major, *Imagines*[1]

DREAMING OF IMMORTALITY

Hermes, son of Zeus and Maia, is a deity who has many affinities, even
an intimate familiarity, with laughter. In Book 8 of the *Odyssey*, as we saw
in the previous chapter, it was Hermes who told Apollo, amidst the gods'
general mirth at the sight of adulterous Ares and Aphrodite ensnared in
Hephaestus' trap, that he would consider such a price, and more, well
worth paying for the chance to have sex with the goddess of love herself.
His remark reignited the laughter of the Olympians, the sullen Poseidon
excepted. Hermes' connections with the scope of laughter were of interest
also to the poet of the *Homeric Hymn to Hermes*, a work generally assigned
to the late sixth century. Twice in this poem Hermes' persona as a sly
trickster, the trademark he shows practically from birth, elicits laughter
from other gods: first from Apollo (281), whose cattle Hermes has stolen,
then from Zeus himself (389), who bursts into loud laughter when his son
lies to him shamelessly but with expert guile about the theft of the cattle.
Both Apollo and Zeus laugh partly (it seems) in their confidence to see
through the 'infant' Hermes' falsehoods, partly in knowing appreciation of
his precocious guile. Theft and mendacity, like adultery, can in the right

---

[1] *Imag.* 1.25.3. For the personifications, cf. nn. 6, 14 below. This section of Philostratus was later the basis for Titian's painting 'The Andrians', but without Dionysus and Laughter: cf. Saxl (1970) 89–97, Puttfarken (2005) 133–4.

circumstances somehow cheer the minds even of the greatest gods – and the minds of humans too: Hermes was always a suitable inhabitant of the more comic versions of the Olympians' world.[2] But the Homeric hymn does not restrict Hermes to arousing mirth in others. He laughs himself as well; and as with his lying, he does so precociously. No sooner does he leap from his cradle and leave the cave where he had been born than he finds a tortoise grazing on the grass outside. 'And the moment he set eyes on it, he laughed.'[3] The tortoise's shell is about to become the body of the first lyre, Hermes' great invention. Laughter externalises the delight of a deity who will draw music from a mute object of nature, just as, later in the hymn, it will externalise the leap of joy felt by Apollo (subsequently the supreme exponent of the lyre himself) when he hears the sounds produced by Hermes' new instrument (420).

When Hermes first constructs his lyre by stretching sheep-gut strings across the sound-box of the tortoise shell, he immediately starts to experiment with his invention, attempting to coax from it a suitable accompaniment for his beautiful singing.

θεὸς δ' ὑπὸ καλὸν ἄειδεν
ἐξ αὐτοσχεδίης πειρώμενος, ἠΰτε κοῦροι
ἡβηταὶ θαλίῃσι παραιβόλα κερτομέουσιν, . . .

(54–6)

And the god began to sing beautifully,
Testing the lyre with improvisations, just as young men
Swap matching insults with one another at banquets.

The simile is *prima facie* rather odd, but actually rather subtle, in bringing together beautiful song and the trading of insults. The tenor of the comparison is the practice of improvisatory musical 'snatches': Hermes is engaged in a kind of exchange with his instrument, testing it with fragments of song and adapting his performance, as musicians do, to what he finds his new lyre capable of. Equally, the 'vehicle' of the comparison pictures

---

[2] In addition to Ar. *Peace* and *Wealth*, Hermes figured in Old comedies by Phrynichus (fr. 61) and Plato com. (fr. 204). For parodic versions of Hermes' persona in Lucian, see ch. 9, esp. 443–55.
[3] ἀθρήσας ἐγέλασσε, 29. Lucian makes Hermes a smiling/laughing baby at *Dial. D.* 11.3 (on the verb προσγελᾶν, see Appendix 1, 524–5). Cf. the infancy laughter/smiles of various gods and semi-divine humans: Pan at *Hom. Hymn* 19.37, Perseus in Aesch. fr. 47a.786 *TrGF* (cf. his faint smile, on the day of birth, at Lucian, *Dial. Mar.* 12.2), Heracles (strangling Hera's snakes) in Philostr. min. *Imag.* 5.1, Beroe daughter of Aphrodite and Adonis at Nonnus, *Dion.* 41.212, Dionysus in Soph. fr. 171 *TrGF*, Nonnus, *Dion.* 9.36, Dionys. Perieg. *Orb.* 949. Pliny, *HN* 7.72 claims Zoroaster was the only human to laugh on the day of birth; see Herrenschmidt (2000) on the Iranian background. Cf. Stuart (1921) 216–21, Norden (1924) 65–7, *à propos* Verg. *Ecl.* 4.60–3. On the laughter of real infants, see ch. 6 n. 142.

the young men in question pursuing a custom that converts insults into a quasi-musical activity, something with its own antiphonal or amoebean rules of form, each utterance (perhaps even in the *form* of song) prompting the next, which in turn responds to its cue – a principle of exchange which reflects the wider practices of mutuality and reciprocity in the symposium.[4] The association between the god's actual music and the young men's improvised yet formalised badinage is strengthened by the lyre's own suitability for the 'banquets' at which the banter occurs. Hermes has already called his lyre 'companion of the feast' (31); later, Apollo will refer to music that belongs at 'banquets of the young' (though he thinks this inferior to the new music), and Hermes will associate the lyre afresh with feasting, dancing, the 'glory-loving *kōmos*' (480–2) and the spirit of heady elation, *euphrosunē* (a term to which I shall return). There is, at several points in the hymn, a clear chain of associations between commensality, music and celebratory (komastic) exhilaration. It is even possible, if uncertain, that lines 54–6 allude to jocular jousting typical of feasts specifically in honour of Hermes.[5]

Part of the interest of the simile at lines 55–6 of the hymn is that it locates one kind of formalised repartee ('flyting') within a perceived framework of shared pleasures of body and mind. This laughter-related practice is attached, furthermore, to the young, and is accordingly redolent of their vigorous life-force.[6] It thus functions as a symbolic enactment of human energies within an accepted space of festive play. At the same time, the verb used of the young men, κερτομεῖν, is a word undoubtedly apt for socially

---

[4] On amoebean 'flyting', Greek and otherwise, see ch. 4 n. 116. Compare the musical/verbal competition of young aristocrats at the famous symposium at Hdt. 6.129; on general sympotic exchanges of poetry, reflected comically at Ar. *Wasps* 1224–49, see Collins (2004) 63–163, and cf. Ferrari (1988) 187–8, Zanetto (1996) 261–2. Stylised exchanges of insults might themselves be in song-form: Barker (1984) 43 n. 19. West (1974) 16–18 detects traces of sympotic badinage in surviving elegy. Nagy (1999) 245 n. 5 misreads the syntax of *Hom. Hymn* 4.56–9 by making the young men, not Hermes himself, sing of the strife between Zeus and Maia; contrast Monaco (1963) 24. Neither Pind. *Ol.* 1.14–17 nor Hdt. 6.127, both cited by Allen *et al.* (1936) 289, seems to picture quite the same practice as the hymn. Reitzenstein (1893) 26 n. 2 erases an essential distinction between ritualised badinage and disruptive abuse. 'Improvised poems' are sympotically coupled with 'jokes' (*skōmmata*), in a sort of hendiadys, at Athen. 2.39d. Finally, the phrase 'by improvisation' in the Homeric hymn (ἐξ αὐτοσχεδίης, 55), applying to both parts of the simile, marks the spirit of spontaneity which Aristotle ascribed to phallic songs as precursors of comedy, *Poet.* 4.1449a9–13; cf. ch. 4, 181.

[5] See Eitrem (1906) 252–3, Allen *et al.* (1936) 289, Cassola (1981) 520–1; but Hesych. *s.v.* τετραδισταί ('[young men] who meet on the fourth of the month', to honour Hermes or other gods: cf. Arnott (1996) 728) lends flimsy support to this possibility.

[6] Cf. the young Argonauts' quasi-symposiac badinage at Ap. Rhod. *Argon.* 1.457–9, where lack of *hubris* is noted but the verb ἐψιάομαι is used (with Caggia (1972) 25–8 for two senses of the word; cf. ch. 1 n. 68) – while what follows degenerates into near-violence (492–4); cf. n. 61 below. On laughter and the young more generally, see ch. 1, 19–25. *Kōmos* is personified as young at Philostr. maj. *Imag.* 1.2.2; cf. n. 14 below.

abrasive and aggressive abuse (as well as having a resonance with Hermes' own sharp speech habits: 338). In the *Iliad*, its cognate adjective describes, for instance, Hera's verbal assault on Zeus at 1.539, while the verb itself is applied to Zeus's own sarcastic provocation of Hera at 4.6 (partly, however, under cover of the banter of feasting) and to Thersites' denigration of Agamemnon at 2.256.[7] In the *Odyssey*, moreover, the jeering abusiveness denoted by κερτομεῖν is not only conspicuously associated with the youthful suitors but, as I argued in the last chapter, marks their perversion of the ideally consensual, reciprocal badinage of feasting: in their hands, what ought to entail shared enjoyment is corrupted into a reckless weapon of insult.[8] The verb's connotations of wounding abuse make *Hymn to Hermes* 55–6 pointedly paradoxical. The young men use ostensibly offensive speech, yet because of the recognised procedures of the banquet's social rules this counts as a special 'language-game' which is (partly) exempted from the normal consequences of confrontational exchanges of abuse. Compressed into the image of their behaviour is a sense of paradox, ambiguity and risk.

Even as a compact simile, the *Hymn to Hermes'* evocation of laughter-inducing practices against a quasi-sympotic backdrop alerts us to a set of cultural problems. These problems are the basis of the present chapter. The aim of what follows is to explore the distinctive role of laughter within the protocols, ethics and psychology of the symposium (and closely related activities) in archaic and classical Greece. Because the symposium was a highly formalised, post-prandial[9] drinking-party for a small group of companions, it created an intimate, psychologically intense type of commensality that was usually framed by the close space of a 'men's dining room' (*andrōn*). Crucial is the activity of drinking as a medium of face-to-face

[7] There is both verbal similarity and significant difference between *Iliad* 4.6 and *Hom. Hymn* 4.56; cf. ch. 2 n. 32. In the former, Zeus is as it were taking advantage of a sympotic convention to goad Hera. In line 56 of the hymn, I take παραιβόλα to imply a provocative tone and tit-for-tat form (senses consistent with other uses of *paraball-* words).

[8] κερτομεῖν and the suitors: *Od.* 2.323, 16.87, 18.350 (directly causing laughter), 20.263, 22.287, with ch. 2, 86–97. Cf. the adj. κέρτομος of the young men's raucous *kōmos* in adesp. lyr. 1037.16 *PMG*, with n. 15 below.

[9] A symposium typically followed a meal (e.g. Theog. 999–1001, Lycoph. fr. 3 *TrGF*, Pl. *Symp.* 176a, Plato com. fr. 71, Xen. *Symp.* 2.1). But the whole occasion could still be called a 'shared meal' (Pl. *Symp.* 172b, σύνδειπνον); cf. meal/symposium, interchangeably, at Xen. *Symp.* 6.5, 6.10. The vocabulary of 'dining together' overlaps with 'drinking together': see Cic. *Ad fam.* 9.24.3 for one reflection of this; the term σύσσιτοι, usually designating 'mess-mates', probably denotes symposiasts at Theog. 309. Cf. compound Aristophanic images of eating and drinking at *Ach.* 1088–93, *Eccl.* 837–52. The food consumed with wine, from so-called 'second tables' (Arist. fr. 675 Gigon, 104 Rose), was sometimes termed 'nibbles', τραγήματα (Ar. *Ach.* 1091, *Eccl.* 844, Alexis fr. 190, cf. fr. 168), but could be substantial: Xenophan. 1.9–10 *IEG*/DK, Alcm. 19 *PMG*; cf. the Homeric antecedents at *Od.* 9.8–10, 15.333–4. Olson and Sens (1999) 24–6 provide an overview of Greek dining protocols.

interaction and bonding, as opposed to merely functional refreshment. Many variables (size, location, occasion, specific *raison d'être*, status and identities of participants, etc.) will have shaped the form and mood of individual symposia. But the nature of these variables will be considered here only where they intersect with my main topic, which is how Greek poets (and others) imagined the workings of laughter within the context of the symposium. As a culturally sophisticated institution, the symposium lent itself to self-reflection in a double sense: reflection on the (social-cum-ethical) lives and values of the participants; and reflection on the needs and priorities of the sympotic occasion itself. Much archaic Greek poetry was not only designed for performance at actual drinking-parties, it was pre-occupied with the dramatisation of *imaginary* symposia, a literary practice subsequently adapted by many prose writers from the classical to imperial periods. The horizons of Greek sympotic literature existed in a delicate relationship with the experiences of real symposiasts, both (partly) deter-mining and (partly) being determined by the heightened mentality that such occasions promoted.[10] My focus here is on how those horizons were constructed and contemplated in their own imaginative terms, but as a setting for the expression of important and complex cultural concerns.

Against that background, it is apposite to recall that the only outburst of shared laughter among the gods of the *Iliad* occurs at an Olympian drinking-party, even though the term *sumposion* itself is absent from Homer, as are some of the conventions of the symposium proper (especially the custom of reclining on couches). The surge of laughter at the end of *Iliad* 1 marks a scene in which divine exemption from the most piercing kinds of sorrow underpins a collective (if temporary) willingness by the gods to leave aside their emotional engagement in human affairs and immerse themselves in what Hephaestus, self-appointed 'wine'-pourer, calls 'the delight of the fine banquet' (1.575–6). Part of the case I will present in this chapter revolves round the thought that the thematic place of laughter in *human* symposia is connected at least subliminally to a simulation of immortality: a simulation that, for the duration of the symposium, tacitly renders the participants god-like, suspended in the hoped-for perfection of the moment and able to float temporarily free of the downward drag of pessimism.[11] It was, I

---

[10] On the symposium (and *kōmos*) as prime performance context of much archaic Greek poetry, see Bowie (1986) 15–21. Imperio (2004b) discusses the performance of comic poetry at the symposium. For the Hellenistic period cf. Cameron (1995) 71–103.

[11] 'Am ehesten noch wird das Symposion, und was daran hing, eine Abwehr des Pessimismus gewesen sein' ('It is most likely that the symposium and its customs were a means of warding off pessimism'): Burckhardt (1977) II 363; translation from Burckhardt (1998) 98. The paradox of 'temporary

think, this psychological and 'existential' resonance of the occasion which gave rise to the trope of death itself as the act of 'leaving the symposium', a figure of speech which poignantly exposes the illusory immortality of the party (and life) itself.[12] From this perspective, it is no accident that the greatest of all literary expressions of a sympotic state of mind, Plato's *Symposium*, is preoccupied at its 'centre' (in the vision of Diotima-Socrates) with an aspiration to immortality and transcendence of the human – but an aspiration ecstatically dramatised within a context replete with possibilities of laughter. At one extreme, the spirit of sympotic laughter can turn minds implicitly towards a dream of the divine, of gods whose own banquets echo with laughter. But at the same time, the precariousness of the sympotic moment of pleasure makes laughter both possible and necessary in other, less lofty ways too.[13]

Before pursuing these considerations further, we need to bracket the symposium together with the *kōmos*, which, as we have already glimpsed, is an element in the *Homeric Hymn to Hermes'* imagery of celebration (480–2, with 102 above). Symposium and *kōmos*, though technically separable, are frequently linked events. They constitute kindred reflections of a unitary Dionysiac sensibility. The *kōmos* – usually a 'revel-band' and its energetically processional activities[14] – can easily be thought of as a mobile or transitional symposium. Sometimes it is the direct sequel (less commonly, the prelude) to a drinking-party, as the guests' high levels of intoxication and exuberance carry them out from the *andrōn* in the direction of (or search for) a new locus of celebration. While participants in a symposium typically recline on couches, their komastic counterparts are paradigmatically on the move, revelling and dancing through the streets or other public spaces. But the context and character of *kōmoi* could vary greatly, from a handful of people to massed crowds. At one end of the spectrum, a *kōmos* might signify a

immortality' through intense celebration is applied to a wider festive context at *Hom. Hymn* 3.151–3, but by an observer not a participant.

[12] The figure of speech is attested from the late Hellenistic period onwards and associated with various philosophical schools; but its origins are surely older: Kindstrand (1976) 281–2, on Bion Bor. F68 (= Teles fr. 11 Hense), cites copious references.

[13] Pl. *Symp.* 212c, the end of the Diotima-Socrates section, is a Platonic masterstroke in this respect: drunken Alcibiades banging on Agathon's door reasserts inebriated laughter against the (philosophical) dream of immortality.

[14] The term *kōmos* could describe many kinds of animated celebration; its use of a funerary group at Eur. *Tro.* 1184 is extreme. On personified Kōmos as a deity at Philostr. maj. *Imag.* 1.25.3 (epigraph, 100; cf. *Imag.* 1.2), and Komos as a satyr's name on vases (e.g. the Attic RF cup London (BM) 1847.9–9.6: cf. Carpenter (1995) 145–8), see Kossatz-Deissmann (1992); for other occurrences of Komos as personal name, note Osborne and Byrne (1994) 277 (with *ibid.* 92 for Gelos too). Visual representations of Hephaestus' return to Olympus (ch. 2, 85) as a quasi-Dionysiac *kōmos* are discussed by Hedreen (2004) 48–50.

self-contained private entertainment by hired musicians and dancers (as at Xenophon *Symp.* 2.1). Its commonest forms, however, were more exposed and roving than this: an anonymous lyric of uncertain date depicts 'all the young men' of a city engaging in a high-spirited revel of shouted insults, music and laughter, while Pindar's epinician odes frequently present the celebration of athletic victory as a *kōmos*, sometimes linked directly to a symposium.[15] With revel as with symposium, my discussion will largely bypass the detailed reconstruction of practical circumstances in order to concentrate on the expectations and values that inform the representation of laughter as a symbolic component of such behaviour.

In sympotic and komastic settings laughter is regarded as part of a larger configuration of mutually influencing factors. It interacts with substantial consumption of wine, the performance of poetry and/or music, intimacy between friends, a mood of heady exhilaration (often called *euphrosunē*), the wish-fulfilling desire for escape from sorrow (and even from death), and, last but not least, an inclination to sensuality that makes the symposium a prime site for erotic words and deeds.[16] Psychologically, the drinking-party's elaborate armature of protocols (including garlands, incense, perfume, physical contact, music, games and stylised exchanges of speech) creates a set of choreographed conditions for immersion in a mood of 'ecstatic' celebration: a kind of temporarily induced protection against the most pressing burdens of life. In a hauntingly beautiful Pindaric image, symposiasts sailing on a metaphorical sea of luxury ('gold-rich opulence') lose their heavy cares and 'swim' (or float) 'towards an imaginary shore'.[17]

---

[15] See adesp. lyr. 1037.15–21 *PMG* for a mass *kōmos* of young men, possibly at a wedding (ch. 4 n. 125); compare ps.-Hes. *Scutum* 272–85, Sappho 44.24–34 *PLF* (with mixing-bowls, 29, and a probable reference to laughter, 27), and note Bacchyl. *Paeans* fr. 4.79 Maehler, where *symposia* take place in the streets (cf. *kōmoi, ibid.* 68). On the Pindaric *kōmos* see Heath (1988), Lefkowitz (1991) 181–3, 198–201, with *Nem.* 9.48–52 for a sympotic link. Pl. *Symp.* 212c–e is one obvious instance of a small-scale, private *kōmos*. Vierneisel and Kaiser (1992) 289–302 illustrate the visual imagery of *kōmoi*. Eubul. fr. 93.8 makes *kōmoi* a more degenerate stage of a symposium even than *hubris*!

[16] For sympotic eroticism see e.g. Theog. 1063–4, Solon 26 *IEG*, Anac. 357–8, 376, 396, carm. conv. 902 *PMG*, Bacchyl. fr. 20B.5–9 Maehler, Panyas. 12.15, 13.3–4, 14.3 *EGF*, Eur. *Cyc.* 495–502 (with the broader hint at *Bacch.* 773–4), Critias 6.18 *IEG*, Pl. *Rep.* 1.329a, Eubul. fr. 93.4, as well as the testimony of vase-paintings (cf. Lissarrague (1990), esp. 56–61, 80–6) and the central themes of both Plato's and Xenophon's *Symposium*. Cf. Pl. *Symp.* 177e, referring to comedy, for Aphrodite and Dionysus combined, with ps.-Arist. *Probl.* 30.1, 953b30–954a6, for a 'physiology' of the link. Horace's famous ascription to Mimnermus of 'love and jokes' as life's prime pleasures ('amore iocisque', *Epist.* 1.6.65–6) reflects a symposiac mentality in the Greek poet. Bowie E. (1993) 362–4 places erotic topics on a sketch map of sympotic discourse. Note the highly coloured laughter ('grinning roses', ῥόδα προσσεσηρώς, and 'laughing horse-celery', γελῶν ἱπποσέλινα, i.e. lewdly) of a decadent symposiast in Pherecrates fr. 138.

[17] ψευδῆ πρὸς ἀκτάν, Pind. fr. 124b Snell–Maehler: see van Groningen (1960) 84–103, esp. 93–5. Nautical imagery (positive/negative) is applied to sympotic experience at e.g. Bacchyl. fr. 20B.14–16

Given the goal of such a transfigured state of mind, laughter can serve as a solvent of oppressive sombreness and an agency of mutually pleasurable intimacy. But it also comes to be perceived as a potent symbol of the ambiguities and possible tensions of the symposium. Like alcohol, laughter is a substance that needs to be enjoyed in the right mixture, and with sensitivity to the harmony of the group, if it is not to prove dangerously disruptive.

The anxieties that often surface in this area of Greek cultural self-awareness are hinted at subtly as early as *Odyssey* 14.463–6, where Odysseus (testing the swineherd Eumaeus) purports to feel impelled to boast by the wine he has drunk:

εὐξάμενός τι ἔπος ἐρέω· οἶνος γὰρ ἀνώγει
ἠλεός, ὅς τ᾿ ἐφέηκε πολύφρονά περ μάλ᾿ ἀεῖσαι
καί θ᾿ ἁπαλὸν γελάσαι καί τ᾿ ὀρχήσασθαι ἀνῆκε,
καί τι ἔπος προέηκεν ὅ πέρ τ᾿ ἄρρητον ἄμεινον.

I'll speak a word in boastfulness. The wine encourages me,
Befuddling wine that impels even a sensible man to sing
And prompts him to laugh sensually and start to dance,
And makes him say things that would better be left unsaid.

This passage is all the more telling, as a vignette of wine-fuelled high spirits, for being heavy with implications for the situation of the suitors in Odysseus' own palace, while at the same time coming disingenuously from the mouth of a character paradigmatic in his wariness of ever being caught off guard.[18] Odysseus evokes a relaxed but impulsive state of inebriation that threatens to tilt over into loss of self-control. The heady liberation of wine may encourage lapses into bodily indulgence, while sensual laughter (with overtones, perhaps, of both verbal and erotic loosening) appears here as a symptom of how the process of excess can deteriorate from mere exuberance into offensive confrontation, the saying of things that would better be left

Maehler (cited at Athen. 2.39e *à propos* symposiac fiction/illusion, *pseudes*: cf. Pindar *loc. cit.*), Dion. Chalc. 4–5 *IEG*, Critias 6.19 *IEG*, carm. conv. 917(c) *PMG* (= Lyr. adesp. 20 *CA*), Timaeus *FGrH* 566 F149 (*apud* Athen. 2.37b–e); see Slater (1976), Lissarrague (1990) 107–22, Nünlist (1998) 317–25, Maehler (2004) 248–50; cf. Dionysus' self-revelation through a kind of nautical symposium, *Hom. Hymn* 7.34–42. The diver on the ceiling of the famous painted tomb at Paestum may allude to this trope: good illustration in Pontrandolfo (1996) 460–1, with *ibid.* 458–9 for a different reading; cf. n. 33 below. Modern scholars have emphasised the special mentality of the symposium: 'simulated experience', Lissarrague (1990) 9; 'transition to a different state of existence', Rösler (1995a) 108; 'organised and regulated alterity', Frontisi Ducroux and Lissarrague (1990) 229–32. Cf. Athen. 2.39e, where sympotic *euthumia* (n. 24 below) 'alters the mind and turns it towards the imaginary/illusory' (ἀλλοιούσης τὴν γνώμην καὶ πρὸς τὸ ψευδὲς τρεπούσης).

18 See ch. 2 n. 87 for ancient texts that distinguish good/bad drinking on the basis of this passage, with 86–7 for its larger thematic resonance in the poem.

unsaid. Laughter, like the symposium as a whole, has the capacity to unite or, if the balance slips, to divide.[19]

Two underlying issues will gradually emerge in what follows. First, what role can laughter play *vis-à-vis* the 'serious' dimensions of the symposium (its opportunities for friendship, love, political and ethical reflection, education, and so forth)? Secondly, what *kind* of laughter is appropriate for the symposium, and how are the wrong kinds to be excluded? The face-to-face intimacy of the event calls for the laughter of affectionate familiarity, but its competitive exchanges can readily generate strain and derision. What's more, while the 'model' symposium might presuppose drinkers who already enjoy close friendship, this condition is not always met in practice, a point with ramifications for the mood of the occasion.[20] In his book of prose memoirs, *Epidemiai* ('Visits'), Ion of Chios recorded an eyewitness account of a drinking-party at which the poet Sophocles, 'a man playful and urbane in his cups' (ἀνδρὶ παιδιώδει παρ' οἶνον καὶ δεξιῷ), was entertained by his Chian friend Hermesilas. When Sophocles took a fancy to the slave-boy serving the wine and, seeing him blush, quoted a poetic phrase about 'purple cheeks', an Eretrian schoolteacher who was one of the other guests challenged him, insisting that 'purple' could never denote facial beauty. Sophocles laughed at the teacher with disdain, commenting that various other poetic uses of colour, including the Homeric epithet 'rosy-fingered', would presumably also merit his literal-minded criticism. At this put-down, the other guests all laughed, leaving the Eretrian feeling 'crushed by the rebuke', in Ion's emphatic language (γελασάντων δέ, ὁ μὲν Ἐρετριεὺς ἐνωπήθη τῇ ἐπιρραπίξει . . .). Sophocles then turned back to the boy, lured him into leaning over his couch, and kissed him (on the lips, we should assume); the others again broke into laughter and applause, and the moment was capped by a punning joke on the poet's part.[21] The anecdote provides a sharply focused glimpse of two sides of sympotic laughter: its shared pleasures in sophisticated self-display, and its potentially antagonistic edge. By both word and action, Sophocles controls the merriment of

---

[19] On sympotic violence, see n. 22 below. The symposium's emblematic status as a setting for exuberant laughter is long-lasting: see e.g. laughter and *thorubos* in Argentarius, *Anth. Pal.* 9.246, or such (hostile) Christian texts as Athanas. *Ctr Ar.* 1.4 (26.20 *PG*), condemning the scurrilous songs of Arius (Reich (1903) 135–6); cf. ch. 1 n. 20.

[20] Cf. the initially uneasy relations between the different guests in Xen. *Symp.*: 142–4 below.

[21] Ion Chi. *FGrH* 392 F6, *apud* Athen. 13.603e–604d: text and annotation in Leurini (1992) 144–8; cf. Jouanna (1998) 166–8 (blurring laughter/smiles), with Dover (1986) 32–5 on the *Epidemiai*. Compare the 'play' motif in Ion's own poems, n. 36 below. Sophocles' behaviour may reflect a sympotic custom of kissing: cf. the 'prize' of kisses at Xen. *Symp.* 5.9, 6.1, and applause for the dancers' kisses, *ibid.* 9.4. For a sympotic gibe with graver (long-term) consequences, see Anaxarchus' story at Diog. Laert. 9.58–9: ch. 7, 356.

the group to his own advantage, while turning it against the schoolteacher who ineptly challenges him. The great dramatist commands the occasion by deploying both verbal and erotic deftness. His 'playful' mastery of the games of the drinking-party can reveal an agonistic streak when required, though it is part of his social dexterity to dismiss his challenger with cultured wit, not crude abuse. The Eretrian pedant, misjudging the moment, finds himself pained by the amusement of the group. In other sympotic company his fate could have been worse.

FACE-TO-FACE TENSIONS: INTIMACY AND ANTAGONISM

Much archaic and classical thinking about the symposium moves along a spectrum of ideas which extends from images of quasi-divine bliss to fears of destructive violence.[22] Laughter is a key motif in defining the different parts of this spectrum and the tensions between them. The normative image of the symposium in archaic and classical Greek literature pictures the flourishing of *euphrosunē* (elation or exhilaration) and *philophrosunē* (warm companionship) in an atmosphere of wine, poetry, laughter and sensuality. The idea of 'atmosphere' applies semi-literally here: symposiasts breathe a special air, made aromatic by the fragrances of incense, flowers (including garlands), unguents and the wine itself.[23] Both *euphrosunē* and *philophrosunē* connote the happiness of immediate, subjective well-being, as opposed to the more objectively well-blessed, stable prosperity of *eudaimonia*. With sympotic encouragement, they can become states or moods of intense delight and hedonistic intimacy, reciprocally expressed in small

---

[22] Symposiac/komastic violence and *hubris* are abundantly thematised: Pratinas 708 *PMG*, Panyas. 13.8–13 *EGF* (with Matthews (1974) 76–7; cf. West (2003) 207 n. 21), Epicharm. fr. 146 *PCG* (148 Kaibel), Eur. *Cyc.* 534, Ar. *Ach.* 979–85 (metaphor), *Wasps* 1299–1325, Antiph. *Tetr.* 1.1.4 (hypothetical murder), Lysias 3.23 (referring back to 3.6), Pl. *Rep.* 6.500b (metaphor), Eubul. fr. 93 *PCG* (with Hunter (1983) 185–9 = fr. 94), Isae. 3.13, Aeschin. 1.65, Alexis fr. 160 (stemming from 'painful' gibes, *skōpsis*; cf. Arnott (1996) 471–2), adesp. com. 101.11 *PCG*, Anacharsis fr. 27A (with Kindstrand (1981) 141–2), Arist. fr. 566 Gigon (558 Rose), *apud* Athen. 7.348a–c (an insulting *kōmos* leads to civil strife then tyranny on Naxos; possibly *iambos*-influenced fiction: West (1974) 27). Other quarrels at feasts include Hom. *Od.* 8.75–8 (Odysseus and Achilles), Solon 4.9–10 *IEG* (metaphor for political disruption: Irwin (2005) 207–9); cf. Centaurs/Lapiths at the wedding of Pirithous and Hippodamia (*Od.* 21.293–304), the gods at the wedding of Peleus and Thetis, as well as the Odyssean suitors, with Seaford (1994) 53–65 and my ch. 2, 88–92. Cf. the Hellenised Judaic exhortations at Ecclesiasticus 31.25–31. Murray (1990b) 142–5, Fisher (1992) 201–47 discuss symposiac/komastic *hubris*. Belfiore (1992) ch. 1, esp. 12–14, treats Gorgon heads in drinking-cups as a symbol of *aidōs* (shame-fearing restraint) needed to avert sympotic violence. On a wider laughter–violence nexus, cf. ch. 1, 25–30.

[23] Xenophan. 1.3–7 *IEG*/DK triply emphasises the scented air (from perfume, wine, incense), as well as mentioning garlands and (11) flowers.

groups that enjoy the gifts of Aphrodite, Dionysus and the Muses.[24] An ideal symposium calls for close, mutually gratifying company (symbolised by the drinking of a 'cup of friendship', κύλιξ φιλοτησία), a condition in which laughter can play its part as an embodiment of genial camaraderie. Such a symposiac ethos serves as the basis for a self-sufficient absorption in the present, a time to transcend past sufferings and leave worries for the future on one side.[25] The cultural affirmation of this ideal in elegiac and lyric poetry (as well as in the images of visual art) smoothes over the contingencies of mood at actual drinking-parties. While much archaic elegy and lyric was produced with symposiac performance in mind, the internal 'world' of such poetry is characteristically a matter of *imaginary occasions*, occasions enacted in song itself, even where they incorporate reflections of the actual.[26] The concrete circumstance of performance and the imaginary occasion evoked in the poem may or may not converge. Whether or not they do, the imaginary occasion retains an emblematic power of its own, an idealising capacity to transform the significance of the present moment.

With these preliminaries in mind, let us turn to Theognis 757–64, a text which economically sketches the desirable mood of a symposium. It is itself a sympotic prayer/hymn which starts by calling on Zeus and other gods to protect the speaker's city and on Apollo to keep the participants' tongues and minds 'straight' (a hint of risk which will soon interest us further), then

---

[24] Sympotic and kindred *euphrosunē* (including the verb εὐφραίνειν/-εσθαι): Hom. *Il.* 15.99 (gods and men), *Od.* 2.311, 9.6, *Hom. Hymn* 4.482 (*kōmos*; cf. 449), Theog. 765–6, 776 (festivals), 1068, Solon 4.10 (with Mülke (2002) 115–16), 26.2 *IEG*, Anac. 2.4 *IEG*, Xenophan. 1.4, 1.13 DK/*IEG* (cf. ch. 6 n. 12), Simonid. 519 fr. 1 ii.2 *PMG* (*kōmos*), Bacchyl. 11.12 (*kōmoi*), Panyas. 12.17–19 *EGF*, 13.1 (characterising the Horai, honoured at the symposium), carm. conv. 887.4 *PMG* (skolion), Eur. *Alc.* 788, *Cyc.* 507, *Bacch.* 377 (cf. 133 below), Ar. *Eccl.* 1123, Xen. *Hieron* 6.2, *Symp.* (e.g.) 1.15, 8.2, 8.5, *Cyr.* 2.2.5 (accompanying laughter), 2.2.13, Theophr. *Char.* 20.10 (with a vulgar twist), Lucian, *De par.* 53, *Ver. Hist.* 2.16. Germane is the hendiadys 'laughter and *euphrosunē*' at Hom. *Od.* 20.8 (the giddy maidservants; see ch. 2, 92–3), the conjunction of laughter, *euphrosunē* and 'just *hubris*' in *SEG* 1 248 (fourth-century Thessalian inscription, cited by Fisher (1992) 91 n. 41), and several cases of *euphrosunē* in the Septuagint (laughter/wine-loving hedonism, Ecclesiastes 2.1–10, 10.19, cf. 7.4; three times in the Hellenised sympotic advice at Ecclesiasticus 31.27–31, though a more spiritual nuance prevails at 1.11–12, 4.12, 30.23); cf. the general conjunction of laughter and *euphrosunē* at Hippoc. *Morb. Sacr.* 17. Wine itself is *euphrōn* at *Iliad* 3.246; one of the Charites is Euphrosune at Hes. *Theog.* 909. (On the similar use of *euthum-* terms see ch. 7 n. 42; cf. n. 17 above.) Sympotic and related *philophrosunē*: e.g. Ion Chi. 26.11, 27.8 *IEG*, Critias 6.16 *IEG*, Pind. *Ol.* 6.98 (epinician *kōmos*), Xen. *Symp.* 2.24 (cf. 1.10), Plut. *Per.* 7.4–5; for a Christian adaptation, see ch. 10, 494.

[25] Suspension of concern about the future is explicit at Theog. 1047–8. Cf. Greenfield (2000) 153–7 for modern reflections, from a neurological perspective, on laughter and immersion in the here and now. *Kulix philotēsia*: e.g. Ar. *Ach.* 983, *Lys.* 203; further references in Olson (2002) 314–15.

[26] The idea of 'imaginary occasions' is a corrective to schematic correlation of song-types with material performance contexts: Halliwell (2003a) 184. It does not deny the predominance of sympotic performance of elegiac and lyric poetry: n. 10 above.

proceeds to delineate a scenario of lyre and *aulos* music, libations to the gods, and an ambience in which laughter, alcohol and an escape from the future blend together:

πίνωμεν χαρίεντα μετ᾽ ἀλλήλοισι λέγοντες,
μηδὲν τὸν Μήδων δειδιότες πόλεμον.

(763–4)

Let's drink and exchange sparkling speech with one another,
But holding no fear about war with the Medes.

The exact historical allusion is unsure (it *may* be the Persian invasion of 480–79) but also unimportant for my argument. So too is the question of authorship within the Theognidean collection. My concern is not with (auto)biographical particulars of the real Theognis (if there ever was such a person), or with the ways in which a collection bearing his name evolved, but with patterns of feeling and types of mentality expressed in the elegies. What is vividly clear at 757–64 is that in stepping inside the symposium the imagined participants hope to enter a kind of divinely protected haven from the future and become engrossed in the pleasures of the present. These pleasures are mediated by a reciprocal charm or wit – 'sparkling speech' (χαρίεντα) – which lends itself to shared laughter.[27]

In the immediately following lines, 765–8 (whether or not they belong to the 'same poem' as 757–64: a rather artificial question in the circumstances), the psychology involved is even more marked. What is desired is captivation in a mood of heightened contentment and elation (*euphrosunē*, 765–6) that puts aside 'evil cares, wretched old age and the finality of death' (767–8).[28] As such phrasing intimates, there is something paradoxical about the symposiac aspiration to 'forget' the darker realities of existence in general

[27] *Charis* covers many kinds of radiant grace, charm, beauty, wit: cf. lyre music at *Hom. Hymn* 4.484, a feast at *Od.* 9.5–11, and other sympotic instances at Alc. 395.3 *PLF* (by implication), 368, Anac. 402(a), (c) *PMG*, Dion. Chalc. 1.3 *IEG*, Ar. *Lys.* 1226, Xen. *Symp.* 7.5; cf. Slater (1990). The context at Theog. 763 suggests laughter-rousing 'wit' or repartee: for this sense of *charis* see Simonid. 33.2–4 *IEG*, Anac. 402(c) *PLF* (again), Pind. *Pyth.* 8.85–6, Epicharm. fr. 32 *PCG* (35 Kaibel), Eur. fr. 492.2 *TrGF* (n. 84 below), Ar. *Wasps* 1400, fr. 171, Eup. fr. 172.12, Diod. com. fr. 2.33 *PCG* (the last two involving parasites: cf. n. 101 below), Pl. *Apol.* 24c, 27a, 27d (all ironic), *Rep.* 5.452b, 8.563a, *Tht.* 168d, 174a, Xen. *Cyr.* 2.2.12 (Persian symposium), Dem. 18.138, Plut. *Mor.* 632e–633a, Cic. 38.2, Lucian, *Symp.* 12, *Dial. mort.* 2.3 (ironic), Athen. 4.162f. Cf. Demetr. *Eloc.* 128, 136, 161, with Grant (1924) 35, 103–6. See ch. 1 n. 42 for pejorative laughter-related *charis*.

[28] Hdt. 2.78 projects onto Egyptian culture a mentality in which a 'memento mori' awareness underpins sympotic celebration; cf. Plut. *Mor.* 148a–b, with Lloyd (1975–88) II 335–7, Grottanelli (1995), esp. 62–6. Death is symbolically pictured as loss of symposiac pleasures in a drinking-song, adesp. lyr. 1009 *PMG*. Reworking traditional sensibilities, Epictetus later compared life itself to a symposium, from whose 'playfulness' one can always exit (by suicide): *Diss.* 2.16.37; cf. n. 12 above. Differently, a symposium may *celebrate* an enemy's death: Alc. 332 *PLF*. Cf. n. 33 below.

or the anxieties of specific predicaments, since those burdens of thought must always be acknowledged in the very expression of willing their erasure from the mind. Alcaeus, for instance, astutely dramatises this attitude as a moment of *willed* forgetting. In some songs he draws attention to the paradox by showing how an impulse to 'forget' can even end up feeding its own pains. In others the paradox is partially displaced by the use of laughter itself as a means of converting oppressive feelings into fuel for temporary exhilaration: this is one function of aggressive gibes at the great enemy, Pittacus (called 'stuffed-sausage-belly', 'splay-foot' and the like).[29] In one variant of the sympotic 'will to forget', the longing to escape from sorrow cannot prevent itself from generating the very reverse of laughter – a kind of melancholy conveyed, for example, by the imagistically poignant movement of thought in Theognis 983–8 from relaxed hedonism to an awareness of transience, and then to thoughts of warfare (hence, by implication, of mortality itself).[30] The downward drag of such melancholy gives a fraught urgency to the sympotic aspiration to hide from the besetting problems of the world outside.

A passage such as Theognis 757–64 therefore implies a conception of symposiac identity which ideally suspends the passage of time: 'holding no fear about war with the Medes' is not a statement of military resolve but, as a counterpart to the enjoyment of alcohol, music and laughter, a way of drawing a protective barrier round the imaginations of the guests in the exclusive delight of the here-and-now. An illuminating parallel for such a state of mind occurs in Xenophon's *Hieron*, where the Syracusan tyrant, unable to trust anyone, recalls nostalgically the elations (*euphrosunai*, 6.1) of his younger days, when in the company of his closest friends he 'spent time at symposia, often achieving oblivion of all the difficulties of human existence' (6.2, πολλάκις μὲν μέχρι τοῦ ἐπιλαθέσθαι πάντων εἴ τι χαλεπὸν ἐν ἀνθρωπίνῳ βίῳ ἦν) and 'immersing my soul in songs, banquets and dances'. 'Immersing' here translates συγκαταμείγνυμι, literally 'mix in

---

[29] Willed forgetting: Alc. 70.9–10 *PLF* (but looping back on itself), 73.8–10; cf. 346.3, with Eur. *Cyc.* 172 (see 128 below); Alc. 335 is germane. Other instances of symposiac escape from sorrow include Panyas. 12.13, 14.4 *EGF*, Pind. fr. 248 Snell–Maehler, Pl. *Laws* 2.666c, Xen. *Symp.* 2.24; cf. Critias fr. 1.4 DK, describing Anacreon, *qua* sympotic poet, as *alupos*, 'without pain'. Laughter itself, as gift of laughter-loving (*philogelōs*) Dionysus, is later generalised as escape from sorrow in Choric. *Apol. Mim.* 31–2; a Renaissance parallel in Castiglione's *Courtier* 2.45 (Castiglione (1998) 184, Castiglione (2002) 105). Derisive sympotic laughter against enemies: note the catalogue of abusive terms at Diog. Laert. 1.81 (= Alc. 429 *PLF*); Alc. 129 *PLF* illustrates a dark side of this.

[30] The contrast between symposiac relaxation and the 'toil' of warfare is heightened by καταθώμεθα θυμόν, 'let's put aside our passion/anger' (983); the phrase is probably a metaphor from laying down weapons (cf. Ar. *Birds* 401, with Dunbar (1995) 290) and is associated directly with laughter at Ar. *Wasps* 567.

together with', a verb which has at least overtones of wine-mixing: the symposiast's 'soul' itself becomes part of the Dionysiac liquid of the occasion. Where such an intense drive to 'forget' life's problems is active, it is no surprise that texts of various sorts link the symposiac ethos with the idea of men in their youthful prime. It is not, of course, that all or even most actual symposiasts were young, but rather that the state of youthful energy and vigour (*hēbē*, which starts with puberty) is emblematic of the life-affirming, sensuous companionship that the symposium ideally embodies and commemorates.[31] Within the dream of perpetual or temporarily renewed *hēbē*, we can sometimes detect the ultimate gesture of sympotic wish-fulfilment, an aspiration (precariously poised over the equally sympotic awareness of death) to immortality. This aspiration may tap the roots of a sort of cultural nostalgia for the perpetual feasting of the lost Golden Age, as well as reflecting the idea of the Olympians themselves as gods of drinking (sometimes served their nectar, as at *Iliad* 4.2–3, by none other than Hebe, goddess of eternal youth).[32] The imagery of the symposium clearly recommended itself, in more than one quarter of Greek culture, as a way of picturing the conditions of a blissful afterlife. Whether psychologically, metaphorically or symbolically, the symposium can be thought of as a suspension of or reprieve from mortality. No wonder, then, that in one of the surviving drinking-songs (*skolia*) from classical Athens, the tyrannicide Harmodius is addressed as someone who has not really died but has merely been transported to live with other heroes in the 'isles of the blest'.[33]

---

[31] For emphasis on symposiac/komastic 'youthfulness'/*hēbē* (chronologically imprecise, but for 'puberty' see e.g. Solon 27.4 *IEG*), including the verb συνηβᾶν, see *Hom. Hymn* 4.56 (101–3 above), Theog. 241–2, 567 (with *paizein*, 'play'), 877, 985, 1063, Alc. 38A.11(?), 73.9(?) *PLF*, Anac. 374–5, 402(a) *PMG*, adesp. lyr. 1037.15 *PMG*, carm. conv. 890.4, 902.1 *PMG*, Pind. *Pyth.* 4.294–5, Bacchyl. 11.11, frs. 4.67–8, 20B.5–6 Maehler, Eur. *Bacch.* 190 (with 135 below), *Cyc.* 504, Pl. *Rep.* 1.329a. The Unjust Argument's list of sympotically coloured pleasures at Ar. *Clouds* 1073 (where καχασμῶν, 'guffaws', not κιχλισμῶν, 'giggles', should be read: Del Corno (1996) 314 wrongly adduces *Clouds* 983; cf. Dover (1968) 226, with ch. 1 n. 53) is targeted at *young* Pheidippides (1071). On the general nexus of laughter and youth: ch. 1, 22–4.

[32] But Pindar's version of Tantalus' tale at *Ol.* 1.60–4 ironically illustrates the unbridgeable gulf between real and sympotic immortality: Tantalus is undone, and loses immortality, by stealing the gods' nectar and trying to serve it at a human symposium.

[33] 894 *PMG*. Slater (1991) 4 speaks of the symposiast 'defying death in celebrating life'. In Hesiod's Golden Age men live like gods, enjoying perpetual banquets (ἐν θαλίῃσι: cf. Theog. 983 for a symposiac parallel) before falling into sleep-like death (*WD* 111–16). Cf. Hdt. 4.95 for the doctrine of immortality propounded in a sympotic context by the Thracian Salmoxis, supposedly reflecting his experience of Ionian culture and Pythagorean philosophy (though Herodotus is sceptical, 4.96). Some Greek funerary art, including the 'tomb of the diver' at Paestum (n. 17 above), uses sympotic imagery; interpretation is vexed: Murray (1988) 241–9, Boardman (1990) 127–9, Garland (1985) 70–1. A symposiac afterlife of 'eternal intoxication' is satirically noted as Orphic at Pl. *Rep.* 2.363c–d; it is apparently present in the text of a funerary gold lamella from Thessaly and may also have Eleusinian

It is not hard to see why laughter – the laughter of life-affirming (and death-denying) happiness, of close-knit friendship and of youthful well-being – might figure prominently in such a context. But the sympotic function of laughter is always a variable quantity that interacts with other factors. If at Theognis 763–4 it seems to express surrender to the pleasure of the immediate 'now', its significance can be complicated by other considerations. We can unpick some of that complication by looking at an anonymous elegy (probably of late classical date, just possibly earlier) which pictures the symposium emphatically as a serio-comic institution.

χαίρετε συμπόται ἄνδρες ὁμ[. . . . . . ἐ]ξ ἀγαθοῦ γὰρ
  ἀρξάμενος τελέω τὸν λόγον εἰς ἀγαθόν.
χρὴ δ', ὅταν εἰς τοιοῦτο συνέλθωμεν φίλοι ἄνδρες
  πρᾶγμα, γελᾶν παίζειν χρησαμένους ἀρετῇ,
ἥδεσθαί τε συνόντας, ἐς ἀλλήλους τε φλυαρεῖν   5
  καὶ σκώπτειν τοιαῦθ' οἷα γέλωτα φέρειν.
ἡ δὲ σπουδὴ ἐπέσθω, ἀκούωμέν τε λεγόντων
  ἐν μέρει· ἥδ' ἀρετὴ συμποσίου πέλεται.
τοῦ δὲ ποταρχοῦντος πειθώμεθα· ταῦτα γάρ ἐστιν
  ἔργ' ἀνδρῶν ἀγαθῶν, εὐλογίαν τε φέρειν.[34]   10

Greetings, fellow drinkers [. . .]! I'll give my speech a good beginning
  And carry it through to a good conclusion too.
Whenever we gather together as friends for such an occasion,
  We should laugh and play (while still upholding excellence)
And take pleasure in each other's company, and send up each other   5
  With mockery of a kind that yields laughter.
But seriousness must be maintained as well. Let's listen to each other
  Speaking in turn: that's a symposium's mark of excellence.
And let's follow the instructions of our drinking-master. This way of behaving
  Belongs to good men, and is apt to yield good repute.   10

Like so much sympotic elegy, the poem is a 'mimetic' dramatisation of a symposium in action. The voice is that of the host (though not, line 9 seems to imply, the symposiarch), who welcomes the guests and frames the occasion as an opportunity for good men to exercise and display their goodness. Because the guests are friends (3), they can afford to engage in

and/or Pythagorean connections: Graf (1974) 98–103, (1993) 241, 246, Edmonds (2004) 84, Murray (1988) 253–4, West (1983) 23–4. Are there symposiac overtones to the tomb of the 'scrutineers', with their parallel stone couches, at Pl. *Laws* 12.947d–e?

[34] Adesp. el. 27 *IEG* (with reduced editorial markings), from a papyrus of c. 300 BC: commentary in Ferrari (1988) 219–25; cf. *CA* 192 (lyr. adesp. 21). Gentili and Prato (*PETF* II 130) suggest a late-fifth-century date, West (1974) 15 calls it 'probably fourth-century', Ford (2002) 33 'late classical'; Page (1941) 445, (1981) 443 thinks it contemporary with the papyrus; cf. Cameron (1995) 74–5.

a mixture of 'laughter' and 'play' (4), mutual pleasure (5), and even good-natured exchanges of ridicule (5–6).[35] The idea of 'play' is often used to (attempt to) bracket symposiac experience from the consequential business of political and social life in general.[36] The speaker qualifies the note of hedonistic lightheartedness, however, in two ways: first, with a reminder of the need to uphold excellence or virtue, *aretē* (4), in other words to avoid demeaning themselves;[37] secondly, with the injunction that laughter should be counterbalanced or accompanied by 'seriousness' (7), a seriousness allowing for mutual respect, orderly proceedings and the preservation of good reputation. We see here the common Greek values of 'measure', *metron*, and 'the right time', *kairos*, translated into a protocol of sympotic psychology and ethics. There is, after all, 'a time (*kairos*) to weep and a time to laugh'.[38]

The poem's own form mirrors its statement of harmonious balance of conduct. A two-line announcement of the host's good intentions is followed by a quatrain each on the themes of laughter and seriousness; there is a verbal echo between the ends of these quatrains (γέλωτα φέρειν, 6, 'to yield laughter', and εὐλογίαν φέρειν, 10, 'to yield good repute').[39] But this balance partially betrays the precariousness of the ideal at issue. The combination of infinitives in asyndeton in line 4 creates a forceful hendiadys (i.e. 'to engage in playful laughter') which was probably quasi-proverbial: a comparable effect occurs in an elegy by Ion of Chios, where the sympotic speaker urges his companions 'let's drink, let's play' (πίνωμεν, παίζωμεν), a combination which became practically formulaic for 'drink-and-be-merry'

---

[35] Line 6 is paralleled by Xen. *Cyr.* 5.2.18 (Gobryas observing Persian habits), where joking, *skōptein*, affords mutual pleasure: for instances of such good-natured sympotic joking, cf. *Cyr.* 8.4.12, 18–23, with Gera (1993) 132–91 for all the sympotic scenes in this work. For its symbolic (not biographical) value, compare Socrates' remark at ps.-Plut. *Lib. educ.*10d that the performance of Aristophanes' *Clouds* was like 'a big symposium' (ὡς ... ἐν συμποσίῳ μεγάλῳ), with Heath (1987) 26.

[36] 'Play' and symposia: e.g. Pind. *Ol.* 1.16, Hdt. 2.173–4, Ion Chi. *FGrH* 392 F6 (with 108–9 above), 26.16, 27.7 *IEG*, Thuc. 6.28.1 (but spilling over into vandalism: ch. 1 n. 95), Pl. *Phdr.* 276d–e, Xen. *Symp.* 1.1 (with 141 below), Plut. *Alex.* 38.1; cf. Alc. 70.3 *PLF* (the verb ἀθύρειν, belittling music/dance of Pittacus' symposium). See Collins (2004) 63–6; cf. n. 97 below. Theog. 1211 deprecates the laughter of a woman who is 'playing' (παίζουσα) with the speaker (cf. ch. 1 n. 51): the scenario is probably sympotic; for women in sympotic exchanges, see West (1974) 17 n. 26.

[37] The translation of Page (1941) 445, 'behaving bravely', is misjudged. Cf. the collocation of lightheartedness with 'justice' in Ion Chi. 26.16 *IEG*.

[38] Ecclesiastes 3.4 (Septuagint), καιρὸς τοῦ κλαῦσαι καὶ καιρὸς τοῦ γελάσαι. See ch. 10, 480–2, 513–14, for various Christian reinterpretations of this thought. For an (ironical) reflection of the criterion of *kairos* (the right time/moment) for laughter, see Ar. *Frogs* 358. Sympotic laughter is aligned with *kairos* at Demetr. *Eloc.* 170 (n. 50 below), Callim. *Epig.* 35 Pfeiffer (*Anth. Pal.* 7.415), Plut. *Mor.* 631c, *Lyc.* 25.2 (Sparta); cf. Index, *s.v. kairos*. On sympotic 'measure', see n. 67 below.

[39] *Eulogia* may also mean the 'good speech' of the symposiasts: Ferrari (1988) 224; cf. Pl. *Rep.* 3.400d11, with *eu mutheisthai* in a sympotic context at Theog. 493. The two senses could converge in symposiasts' mutual praise.

hedonism.[40] In the anonymous elegy this mood of playful immersion in the present is intensified by a further hendiadys of terms for laughter-inducing repartee in 5–6. Here the verb *phluarein* is notable, since it is sometimes associated with denigration, more commonly (and pejoratively) with empty nonsense or bluster; but it is also pertinent that one of its cognates lent its name to a genre of earthy comedy, the *phlyax* play, characteristic of Magna Graecia. In the anonymous elegy, the modern connotations of 'nonsense humour' can almost certainly be left out of the equation. The coupling of *phluarein* with *skōptein* is best taken to designate an exaggerated, stylised tone that all parties can appreciate as a signal of simulated ridicule.[41]

The accumulated weight of four verbs for the practice of symposiac laughter makes the following stress on the accompanying need for 'serious-ness' appear guarded. If so much laughter and mockery are to be released under the influence of wine, it will require a finely tuned agreement between the guests to keep such gelastic liberties within the ambit of friendship and mutual pleasure. Moroeover, it is not just a matter of keeping laughter within acceptable limits, important though that is; there is also a need to know when to *abstain* from laughter, allowing space for the activities of 'seriousness' (which might include prayers, political bonding, philosoph-ical discussion, memorialisation of ancestors). Everything in the last four lines of the poem should therefore be read as a counterweight to what has gone before: 'seriousness' must prevent the force of laughter from getting out of control and insist on its own right to be heard; the guests must listen to one another 'in turn' (as opposed to the unruliness of cross-talk);[42] they must defer to the authority of the symposiarch, the one 'leading the drinking' (9), tempering consumption and conduct to a common purpose; and they must sustain their standing as 'good men' (avoiding the shameful extremes with which laughter is readily associated). Like most other elegiac poetry, the anonymous poem does not document the perceptions of any

---

[40] Ion Chi. 27.7 *IEG*; cf. the 'drink, play . . .' combination (πῖνε, παῖζε . . .) in Amphis fr. 8, Aristob. Cass. *FGrH* 139 F9 (Sardanapalus: ch. 6 n. 116), with Ameling (1985), Lattimore (1962) 260–2 on 'eat, drink and be merry' topoi. Laughter is implicitly a (sweet) wine to assuage life's bitter taste in anon. *Anth. Pal.* 7.155.1–2

[41] Φλυαρεῖν is associated with denigration/mockery at Xen. *Hell.* 6.3.12 (διαβάλλειν: cf. Chadwick (1996) 87–94 on this verb) and Isoc. 5.79 (*blasphēmein*); cf. LSJ *s.v.* φλυαρέω II, adding Hesych. *s.v.* κατακερτομεῖ, with ch. 7 n. 76. One should treat φλυαρεῖν καὶ σκώπτειν as hendiadys (differently, Gerber (1999a) 489); Nisbet (2003) 26 n. 16 justifiably translates as 'horseplay', 'messing about'; Calder, *apud* Huß (1999b) 397, translates *phluarein* as 'tease'. Compare Ar. *Frogs* 524 ('fool around'), and the hendiadys παιδιὰ καὶ φλυαρία, 'playful bluster', at Pl. *Crito* 46d (complicated by Socratic irony). On *phluaria* in Socrates' reference to comedy at Pl. *Apol.* 19c, see ch. 5 n. 94. *Phlyax* plays: Taplin (1993) 48–54, Trendall (1967) 9–18.

[42] Contrast the drunken Median symposium at Xen. *Cyr.* 1.3.10, or the drunken abusiveness of Philo-cleon at Ar. *Wasps* 1319–21 (though at 1314 still *partly* within the spirit of the symposium).

particular person or persons. But it expresses a set of standards which fit well with the patchwork of our evidence as a whole. It attests centrally to a sympotic ideal of equilibrium between the psychological needs of laughter and seriousness.

The ideal symposium is a dream, even hallucination, of perfection. Sympotic texts recognise the risk of a gap between ideal and reality into which ambiguous manifestations of laughter can insidiously find their way. Some lines in the collection of Theognis point us towards the resulting problems.

ἐν μὲν συσσίτοισιν ἀνὴρ πεπνυμένος εἶναι,
   πάντα δέ μιν λήθειν ὡς ἀπεόντα δοκοῖ,
εἰς δὲ φέροι τὰ γελοῖα· θύρηφι δὲ καρτερὸς εἴη,
   γινώσκων ὀργὴν ἥντιν' ἕκαστος ἔχει.
                    (Theognis 309–12)

Among dining companions a man should be shrewdly sagacious
   Seeming not to notice all that happens – as though he weren't present.
He should contribute material for laughter. Then once outside let him be tough,
   Using his knowledge of the temperament of each individual.

Interpretation (including punctuation) of these lines has proved vexed. But one thing is clear enough, that the poet draws a distinction between demeanour (and state of mind) inside and outside a sympotic framework.[43] The pivotal contrast (311) is between what the symposiast should 'contribute' to the party – namely, material for laughter (here implicitly treated as a symposiac commodity alongside food and drink) – and what he should take away for use in life 'outside'. Before probing that contrast further, however, we need to register the complicated movement of thought that precedes and sets it up.

The poet's advice unfolds in an intricately balanced set of stages. I take the second clause subtly to modify the first, just as the third will in turn modify the second – and the fourth will put the whole configuration of attitudes in perspective. The first couplet begins with the need to retain self-awareness and a sense of standards of behaviour. The verb πέπνυμαι (309), stamped by common Homeric usage, denotes both sagacity and an ethical capacity for good judgement (cf. Theognis 29, its only other occurrence in the corpus). Its frequent application to Telemachus in the *Odyssey* may be pertinent to Theognis' sympotic scenario, since it picks out an ability to

---

[43] My text follows *IEG*; cf. West (1974) 152–3 on text and interpretation. Van Groningen (1966) 124–6 offers a different reading, but ignores the implications of δοκεῖν; his punctuation of 311, like that of Young (1961) 21, isolates the second half of the line from what follows. Cf. Levine (1985) 189. Other views: Harrison (1902) 325, Hudson-Williams (1910) 197.

develop and retain good sense in severely testing circumstances. There is, indeed, a fuller Odyssean feel to the whole quatrain: Theognis counsels a skilful use of *seemingly* inebriated sociability not unlike the manipulative behaviour of Odysseus at *Od.* 14.463–6 (107 above); and his general principle of 'knowing the temperament' of every man resonates with the opening of the *Odyssey* itself (1.3). The symposiast, on this view, needs to protect his prudence in a situation where dropping one's guard is all too tempting. The subtext, in keeping with some of the hints already detected in the anonymous elegy discussed above, is a recognition that the conjunction of wine, intimacy and mirth may easily prompt lapses in self-discipline. What follows reinforces the point obliquely. While maintaining his own scruples, the symposiast should not *show* any scruples about what others say or do. Now, if it is advisable to seem not to notice what is said and done within the confines of the drinking-party, that presupposes that participants might find it convenient (and, given intoxication, easy) to apply a kind of 'amnesty', an agreed forgetting, of events. There is some expectation, in other words, that what takes place within the framework of the symposium should be bracketed from the normal conditions of social life. The alcoholic atmosphere of the occasion allows experience to pass through a symposiac memory filter. 'I hate a fellow drinker who has a memory' (μισέω μνάμονα συμπόταν), as the fragment of one drinking-song puts it – though admittedly one with which not all Greeks would have automatically concurred.[44]

But the author of Theognis 309–12 enjoins only ostensible adherence to this sentiment. The third line is crucial here. It recommends contributing to the shared laughter of the party, with a pun, in εἰσφέρειν (lit. 'bring along'), on the idea of contributing food or drink.[45] The object of that verb (τὰ γελοῖα) standardly refers to the materials of comedy and humour; in the present context it could clearly embrace joke-telling, banter and even – especially given the surrounding advice – self-consciously amusing role-playing. But the implications are ambivalent: overt engagement in laughter is a requisite of a good symposium, yet it is also a means of seeming outwardly engaged in the spirit of the occasion while remaining inwardly watchful. The point is underlined by the contrast with what

---

[44] Adesp. lyr. 1002 *PMG*, embedded in Plut. *Mor.* 612c–d (which attests the subsequently traditional character of the theme). The seeming inattention recommended at Theog. 310 is a positive reversal of the 'absentmindedness' faulted at e.g. Heraclitus fr. 34 DK, Ar. *Kn.* 1119–20. Differently, memory loss is criticised as an effect of intoxication at Critias 6.11 *IEG* (with 125–7 below); Xenophan. 1.20 *IEG*/DK urges symposiasts to be sober enough to recall edifying deeds for discussion.

[45] Compare Philippus' joke at Xen. *Symp.* 1.11. For sympotic uses of εἰσφέρειν, cf. Pl. *Symp.* 177c, Hegesander frs. 31–2 *FHG*.

should happen 'outside', when one steps back out across the threshold of the *andrōn* into the harsher, less free-and-easy world of consequential social dealings.[46] The spatial imagery of inside and outside, whose function is both literal and symbolic, creates the impression that shared laughter can be actively pursued only within the controlled conditions of a special locus: social life in general is too dangerous an arena to leave space for exuberant mirth.

The psychology of the quatrain is intrinsically problematic. Outside the symposium, one needs assiduously to read the minds of others – to know who one's friends and enemies are, who can be trusted and who cannot (a recurrent Theognidean anxiety). But the speaker's implicit advice is that such knowledge can be valuably acquired at symposia themselves, since they provide opportunities to observe others in a state of relaxed intimacy where 'in vino veritas' (lurking in the background of the poem) is operative. Yet the advice presupposes that others will enter wholeheartedly into the mood of good cheer and openness:[47] if *everyone* acted on the injunctions of this poem, the symposium would collapse into an exercise in mutually hypocritical scrutiny of each other. The lines posit a symposiast who is only outwardly immersed in the occasion while inwardly assessing it for his own purposes – someone who trades on, while cannily undercutting, the normative sympotic commitment to truthfulness and jocular self-exposure.[48] And the ironies of the poem only deepen if we imagine it, like much other paraenetic elegy, being itself delivered within the setting of a symposium. What kind of shadow would such a poem cast on the circumstances of its own performance?

An authentically sympotic atmosphere depends on a preselection of suitable partners who will make intimacy rewarding (and safe), as well as on a common understanding of the special rules of the game. As a traditional saying, ascribed to the Socratic philosopher Antisthenes, puts it: 'no symposium that lacks a meeting of minds (*homonoia*) is

---

[46] Cf. Theog. 468, 1001 for similar spatial markers *à propos* the symposium, with the essays in part II of Murray (1990a) for the cultural *Realien* of dining-rooms etc.

[47] One *leitmotif* of sympotic openness is speaking 'in(to) the middle' (*es meson* etc.), i.e. both candidly and for all to share: see Theog. 495, Hdt. 6.129.2, cf. 130 (involving musical/verbal competition), Xen. *Symp.* 3.3 (round-robin discussion). The idea is ironically applied to the position of the mixing-bowl at Eur. *Cyc.* 547 (cf. 129 below).

[48] On Greek versions of 'in vino veritas' see Rösler (1995a). Cf. Pericles' motive for shunning symposia at Plut. *Per.* 7.4–5, alluding to his supposed aversion to laughter (*ibid.* 5.1; see ch. 6, 270–1). Another allegedly anti-symposiac politician was Epaminondas: e.g. Plut. *Mor.* 192d–e, 1099c, Themistius *Orat.* 7.88c; cf. his status as quasi-proverbial agelast at Choric. *Laud. Arat.* 63–4 (Foerster), with ch. I n. 101.

pleasurable'.[49] Only on the premise of truly mutual commensality can laughter serve as a medium of shared pleasure and temporary refuge from the grimmer realities of the world 'outside'. 'Even sensible people', as one ancient author puts it with a slight defensiveness, 'will use humour at the appropriate time, on occasions such as festivals and symposia'.[50] But for the kind of symposiast modelled at Theognis 309–12, laughter becomes a *cloak* of amiability. The lines conjure up a world (or mentality) in which the trust of friendship is never fully reliable, never fully beyond doubt – an anxiety that must have been familiar to many symposiasts, judging at any rate by its appearance in more than one standard drinking-song from the classical period (*skolion*).[51] Theognis' quatrain attests to the cultural perception that laughter is a necessary lubricant for the gratifications of the symposium. But it also exploits this viewpoint to hint at the social tensions that might lie just beneath the surface of a seemingly harmonious drinking-party. By doing so the poem indicates indirectly something about the instability of laughter itself as an expression of both friendship and enmity. Theognis' preoccupation with the uncertain trustworthiness of others – a preoccupation which paradoxically combines suspicion of duplicity with *advocacy* of duplicity ('possess the mentality of the cunning octopus', 213, as his most pungent formulation puts it) – forms an apposite backcloth to a keen awareness of the ambiguity and potential deceptiveness of laughter.[52]

---

[49] Stob. 3.1.28 (= Antisth. fr. 93 Decleva Caizzi = v A 125 *SSR*), reading ὁμονοίας for ὁμιλίας. On Antisthenes' own attitude to laughter, however, see ch. 6 n. 81, with 146–7, 150, 153 below for his depiction in Xen. *Symp.*

[50] χρήσονται δέ ποτε καὶ οἱ φρόνιμοι γελοίοις πρός τε τοὺς καιρούς, οἷον ἐν ἑορταῖς καὶ ἐν συμποσίοις . . .: Demetr. *Eloc.* 170 (cf. n. 38 above). The symposium as locus of mocking banter is marked in Alex. Aet. fr. 7.2 *CA*: see ch. 4, 168.

[51] See carm. conv. 889 *PMG* (if only one could 'see into' others' minds . . .), 892 *PMG* (the crab[!] tells the snake[!]: a companion should be 'straight' and shun crooked thoughts); cf. 903, 908, 912(a) *PMG*, and the skolion ascribed to Solon in Diog. Laert. 1.61. Such fear of deception is in counterpoint to 'in vino veritas' (n. 48 above). Cf. abhorrence of one who deceives with 'soft' words, Theog. 851–2. A related concern, that sympotic friendship may not stand the test of 'serious action' outside, is voiced at Theog. 115–16, 641–4,

[52] See Theog. 59/1113 for the laughter of those who deceive one another; *epi* + dative here denotes hostile intent: cf. Hom. *Il.* 2.270, *Od.* 20.374, Pl. *Rep.* 7.518b, Xen. *Symp.* 2.17, Men. *Perik.* 293–4, Chilon *apud* Diog. Laert. 1.70; contrast the jester's/parasite's chosen role as butt of jokes, Xen. *Symp.* 1.14, 2.23, Nicolaus fr. 1.31 *PCG*. So Theog. 59 looks like a semi-metaphorical description of inward gloating, not face-to-face laughter as implied by Van Groningen (1966) 33 ('accompagne'), Hedreen (2004) 48. Cf. Kurke (1989) 540, positing an aristocratic slur on retail traders; and see ch. 2 n. 95 for the Odyssean paradigm of inner laughter/smiles. The evocation of inward gloating also counts against the suggestion of Forsdyke (2005) 82, adducing Edwards (1993) 99 (whose view, however, seems more oblique), that ritual/festive insults are involved. Even if overt laughter *were* meant by Theognis, it would not follow that *gelan* itself means 'cheat', *pace* Fränkel (1975) 404. Other associations between laughter and deception: Eur. *Hipp.* 1000–1, Pl. *Symp.* 181d6, Xen. *Anab.* 2.6.26 (unscrupulous Menon), ps.-Polemon, *Physiogn.* 20 Foerster; cf. ch. 2 n. 35 on deceptive

A number of poems in the Theognidean collection help to broaden this perspective on the mindset of the symposium, including its potentially darker side. Of these, 467–96 (sometimes attributed to the fifth-century poet Euenus; but authorship, once again, is not crucial here) is the fullest and richest specimen. In this passage the elegiac voice addresses a companion, Simonides (addressee of two other poems in the corpus, but unidentifiable), surveying the scene at a symposium that has stretched far into the night. He mentions the possibility (but not the need) for guests to leave if they wish to do so, observes that some have fallen into inebriated sleep, but recommends that others should be left free to continue drinking: 'for it is not every night one may enjoy such sensuality' (474). The speaker then emphatically announces his own departure. He is ready for sleep and content to have imbibed enough wine to be neither drunk nor sober. This leads him into some reflections on the ethics of symposiac drinking.

> ὃς δ' ἂν ὑπερβάλλῃ πόσιος μέτρον, οὐκέτι κεῖνος
> τῆς αὐτοῦ γλώσσης καρτερὸς οὐδὲ νόου,
> μυθεῖται δ' ἀπάλαμνα, τὰ νήφοσι γίνεται αἰσχρά,
> αἰδεῖται δ' ἔρδων οὐδὲν ὅταν μεθύῃ,
> τὸ πρὶν ἐὼν σώφρων, τότε νήπιος.
>
> (Theognis 479–83)[53]

Whoever oversteps the measure of drinking, that man loses
    Control over not only tongue but even his mind.
His utterances are reckless, things that are shameful for the sober,
    And he shows no compunction about doing anything once drunk:
A man who previously had self-mastery is now a puerile fool.

In defining a yardstick of acceptable drinking, the speaker employs the same adjective to mean 'in control of' or 'with strength over' tongue and mind (*karteros*, 480) as was used at 311 to denote the tough realism called for *outside*

---

smiles. For the Theognidean ethic of suspicion (people are untrustworthy; only feign friendship with them) see esp. 59–70, 73–6, 119–28, 213–18 (including the octopus image), 221–6, 1071–4; even close associates cannot always be trusted (254). Lane Fox (2000) 44, van Wees (2000) 54–57, discuss possible historical backgrounds to these themes.

53 On ἀπάλαμνα, 'reckless' (481), cf. Page (1955) 315, Campbell (1967) 248; *aischra*, 'shameful', in the same line, implies a notion of aischrology: see ch. 5 n. 3, cf. Critias 6.9 *IEG*. Giangrande (1968) 98–100 documents Theognidean concerns about aberrant sympotic behaviour; cf. Bielohlawek (1940) 24–6. For the special importance of controlling the 'tongue' at a symposium, note Chilon *apud* Diog. Laert. 1.69 (cf. ch. 6, 266), Soph. fr. 929 *TrGF* (referring, like Theognis, to both *nous* and tongue), Critias 6.8–9, 6.16 *IEG* (with 125–6), and Anacharsis *apud* Diog. Laert. 1.104–5 (alongside reservations about drinking, 103–4): on Anacharsis see Kindstrand (1981) 136–9 (tongue), 139–45 (drinking), and Martin (1996) 145–6. Epicureans, among others, upheld this concern: Epicurus warned against drunken 'drivelling' (accepting the emendation ληρήσειν at Diog. Laert. 10.119; cf. Marcovich (1999) 788, Long (1964) ii 119; a different text in Epic. *Symp.* fr. 63 Usener); cf. Philod. *De bono rege* xix–xx (criticising sympotic obscenity and scurrility).

the symposium. Whether or not the two passages are the work of the same poet, the relationship between them exposes a tension in the sympotic code of conduct. If 311 implied that the *typical* symposiast relaxes self-control, and allows himself to be 'softened' (cf. the 'soft' sensuality, ἁβρός, of drinking at 474), the second poem puts limits on this psychological loosening.[54] On this view, the companionable intimacy of the drinking-party requires its participants to remain conscious of what they do and say, and thus in control of their relations to others. Wine threatens this by impairing mastery of thoughts and words (recall the prayer to Apollo at Theognis 759–60, cited on 110 above): what comes out under the influence of alcohol may break the boundaries of shame (the 'sober' at 481 could in principle include fellow symposiasts) and reduce the individual to a babbling, childish state.[55] After berating Simonides himself for never being able to say 'no' to more wine (491), the speaker concludes by expressing the wish that those who stay behind will accompany their drinking with agreeable exchanges of words, avoiding the disruption of 'strife' (*eris*) and maintaining the ambience of *charis*, 'graceful' reciprocity (496, cf. 477), a concept whose importance we have already encountered. Although there is no direct reference to laughter in 467–96, the contrast of *charis* and *eris* strongly implies the conflicting gelastic poles of mutually pleasing wit and disruptively aggressive mockery.[56]

The opposing possibilities of sympotic laughter are encapsulated with startling clarity in a pair of Theognidean couplets that are inversions of each other. Both have an air of gesturing vividly towards particular circumstances yet lack precise social contextualisation. It would be a mistake to try to reconstruct a documentary 'script'; we are dealing here, once again, with imaginative projections which symposiac performers could interpret in more than one way. The first passage, at 1041–2, reads:

[54] The lexicon of 'soft(ness)' (ἁβρός, μαλακός, ἁπαλός), highly pertinent to the sensuality of symposium/*kōmos* (e.g. Anac. 373 *PMG*, Pl. *Rep.* 3.398e), can attach itself to laughter: Meleager, *Anth. Pal.* 12.125.1, the erotic dream of a boy who 'laughs softly', ἁβρὰ γελῶντος; the same phrasing of a male beloved at anon. *Anth. Pal.* 12.156.4 ('in the eyes') and of drunken symposiasts at *Anacreontea* 43.3, 44.5 (West). Cf. Appendix 1 n. 17. For wider debates about sympotic 'softness', see Hammer (2004) 493–9.

[55] The literal sense of *nēpios* (483), 'incapable of [sc. intelligible/sensible] speech' (cf. Heraclitus fr. 79 DK, with ch. 7, 350, 356), is in play here, evoking the slurring/incoherence of intoxication. At Theog. 1039 the word applies to the folly of those who do *not* drink wine (in summer). Other reflections on the regulation of sympotic drinking: Xenophan. 1.5–6, 17–20 *IEG*/DK, Panyas. 13–14 *EGF* (with Matthews (1974) 78–81), adesp. com. 101.9–13 *PCG*; cf. the moralistic advice of Isoc. 1.32 to 'leave early' before drunkenness takes hold.

[56] For symposiac *eris* cf. Dion. Chalc. 2.2 *IEG*, Hdt. 6.129 (but legitimate 'competition'); on sympotic violence, see n. 22 above.

δεῦρο σὺν αὐλητῆρι· παρὰ κλαίοντι γελῶντες
πίνωμεν, κείνου κήδεσι τερπόμενοι.

This way, with the piper! Reclining by one who weeps, let's laugh
And drink – taking his griefs as our pleasure!

The second, at 1217–18, runs:

μήποτε πὰρ κλαίοντα καθεζόμενοι γελάσωμεν
τοῖς αὐτῶν ἀγαθοῖς Κύρν᾽ ἐπιτερπόμενοι.[57]

Let's never sit and laugh next to one who weeps,
Taking pleasure, Cyrnus, in our own good fortune.

Both couplets assume laughter to be a primary ingredient of sympotic (and, in the first case, komastic) behaviour; they cohere with the injunction of 311 to 'bring' material for laughter to the party. The second couplet clearly invokes the sympotic norm of a gathering of like-minded friends, among whom any marked disparity of mood would spoil the animating spirit of the occasion. What it repudiates might bring to mind the Odyssean suitors, who persistently revel in the teeth of Telemachus' sorrows and in defiance of the protocols of hospitality.[58] Equally, however, the speaker of 1217–18 might be urging the avoidance of a companion who could not be expected to share the high spirits of the group. The grieving individual need not be imagined as an outsider, just one whose present melancholy would mar the desired *euphrosunē* of the party – a thought which illuminates the point of another Theognidean couplet (989–90), where a downcast symposiast is advised to *conceal* his distress from his companions.[59] Either way, 1217–18 contemplates the possibility of what it negates; there is no point in rejecting what is inconceivable. So the couplet pictures, even as it deprecates, a symposium at which laughter expresses a mood in which, one way or another, not everyone present is caught up.

Yet Theognis 1041–2 appears to encourage the enjoyment of such a state of affairs. It anticipates (in fact, seeks out) with relish a situation in which the unhappiness of an individual guest is visible to the rest of the drinkers. Is this a call to sheer *Schadenfreude*? But why would anyone enduring real grief even consent to take part in an exuberant party? A key to the

---

[57] West (1974) 69–70 believes 1217–18 have been doctored from a sentiment like that of 1041–2; he accordingly brackets the negative in the text of *IEG*. This is possible but far from certain.

[58] See esp. the suitors' laughter at *Od.* 20.373–83, with ch. 2, 94, 96. Contrast Alcinous' behaviour at *Od.* 8.536–43, aptly cited by Cerri (1976) 25–6 *à propos* Theog. 1217–18.

[59] Cf. the Christian Greg. Naz. *Orat.* 27.4, where 'tears at a drinking-party' (πότῳ δάκρυον) exemplifies jarring incongruity (as does 'laughter-rousing during grief', πένθει γελωτοποιΐα, if an emendation is accepted: Norris (1991) 91–2; cf. ch. 6 n. 41).

couplet's mentality is its evocation not of a voluntary symposium but a *kōmos* (processing through the streets with a piper) which sets out to impose itself on, indeed 'invade' the house of, the unhappy person.[60] Numerous scenarios involving discrepant states of mind on the part of symposiasts might be imagined.[61] But the language of the present couplet – particularly the strong term *kēdos*, 'grief' or 'mourning' – is not compatible with just any discrepancy of this kind. It does not fit a lovesick companion, for instance, even though a contrast between fretful lover and cheerful sympotic group is sometimes a theme in other texts.[62] Nor does Theognis 1041–2 simply suggest a sentiment of malice towards an enemy, since that seems hard to square with the idea of reclining (implied by the preposition *para*) alongside the grieving other. The compression of the lines invites but resists psychological decoding. At their heart lies the anomaly of *forcing* someone in the wrong frame of mind to participate in a celebratory symposium. But that anomaly draws additional piquancy from the idea, which we saw earlier, that the symposium is a way of *overcoming* (or suspending) the troubles of life. We can trace elsewhere in sympotic writing a sense of tension between the aim of transcending or escaping from suffering and an awareness that sorrows may block the pleasures of shared drinking.[63] Theognis 1041–2 implies a high-spirited impulse to test this difference at someone else's expense. The motif of laughter marks a privileged freedom from care on the part of the addressees ('us'), but it leaves uncertain their

[60] For the idea of an invasive *kōmos*, see e.g. Theog. 1045–6, Ar. *Ach.* 980, Plut. *Mor.* 128d–e (invading a house of *mourning*); further references in Headlam (1922) 82–3, Olson (2002) 314; cf. ch. 8 n. 33. See 131–3 below on the ironic shadowing of such a situation in Eur. *Alc.*; cf. Cassandra's macabre vision of the Furies as invasive *kōmos* at Aesch. *Agam.* 1186–90. Cerri (1976) ingeniously takes Theog. 1041–2 to allude to the 'mournful' sounds of the *aulos*, not the sorrows of a person; but I am unconvinced, especially given the use of *para* + dative for reclining symposiasts.

[61] In Alc. 368 *PLF* the speaker, perhaps for erotic reasons, will enjoy a symposium only if Menon is present. Panyas. 12.18–19 *EGF* pictures someone who, after overeating, sits out the drinking-party as grim as a vulture. Cf. Xen. *Symp.* 6.1–2 (with 151–2 below), where Socrates rebukes Hermogenes (ironically) for surly taciturnity towards his fellow symposiasts. In myth, Ap. Rhod. *Argon.* 1.457–71 sets Jason's brooding at odds with the mood of the feast (cf. n. 6 above). The speaker of Archil. 11 *IEG* contemplates suppressing his sorrows to take part in a feast. Cf. Ammianus, *Anth. Pal.* 9.573 for criticism of the (?parasite) guest who weeps hypocritically with others' tears, laughs with their laughter.

[62] Van Groningen (1966) 388 moots an erotic subtext for the Theognis couplet. Asclepiades, *Anth. Pal.* 12.50, 12.135 are images of erotic discontent surfacing at symposia; cf., more discreetly, Callim. *Epig.* 43 Pfeiffer (*Anth. Pal.* 12.134), with Giangrande (1968) 120–2. By contrast, a disconsolate lover seeks quasi-symposiac *escape* at Men. *Perik.* 174–7: cf. *Epitr.* fr. 3 Sandbach, and see ch. 8, 411–12.

[63] Theog. 825–9 asks others how they can bring themselves to revel at a time of suffering. Archil. 13.1–2 *IEG* seems to picture bereavement bringing a halt to feasting; but see Burnett (1983) 47 n. 39 for disputed interpretation. Archil. 11 *IEG* (n. 61 above) suggests, by contrast, that grief changes nothing – so feasting should continue; cf. n. 79 below.

exact relationship to the individual on whose grief they will komastically intrude.

Theognis 1041–2 and 1217–18, though very elliptical (as they stand), both rest on the recognition that the laughter of sympotic elation may equally unite or divide a human group.[64] Everything depends on the extent to which individual participants share an inclination – and ability – to enjoy the spirit of heady mirth and badinage. At worst, the symposium's mix of alcohol, intimacy and hedonism may become a disastrous recipe for the laughter of derision, with all the possibilities of violence, verbal and/or physical, that can flow from that. We saw that Theognis 494 alludes to such a collapse of commensality into 'strife', and many other texts voice a fear that laughter can fracture the concord of a drinking group.[65] The function of laughter in the ideal symposium involves a delicate poise of relationships and values; if the balance slips, intimacy can rapidly degenerate into face-to-face hostility – something that would test to breaking point the capacity of symposiasts to 'overlook' what is said and done between them (cf. Theognis 310, above). The result would then be the very reverse of the divine paradigm narrated in *Iliad* 1, where strife gives way to sympotic reconciliation.

To end this section it will be helpful to glance at an elegy by Critias, uncle of Plato and one of the ruthless leaders of the oligarchic regime of Thirty Tyrants at Athens in 404–3.[66] Despite some textual uncertainties, what survives of the elegy is built round an opposition between the Spartans' habits of drinking and those of other Greeks, including the Athenians. On the negative side, the poem brands the paraphernalia of elaborate drinking vessels an 'Asiatic' invention of the Lydians (5), and thus by implication the creation of a 'soft', unmanly culture; complains about the conventions of toasts and 'rounds' whose excesses degenerate into shameful speech and bodily dissipation (8–9); and dwells on both the physical effects of inebriation (glazed eyes, memory loss, impaired judgement) and the damage done to household order and resources by habitual partying (10–13). By contrast, young Spartans are said to drink only as much as is conducive to a cheerful state of mind, a spirit of friendly companionship (*philophrosunē*) in conversation, and 'moderate' or 'measured' laughter (μέτριον . . . γέλωτα, 14–16). Such controlled drinking benefits body and mind, is compatible

---

[64] A step further is to imagine the symposia of one's enemies, as in Alc. 70.3–5 *PLF*, assuaging the bitterness of the thought by condemning their decadence. This is a scenario, once again, with Odyssean overtones.

[65] For various instances, see n. 22 above.

[66] Critias 6 *IEG*, fr. 6 DK. For Critias' laconising position, cf. frs. 32–7 DK from his prose *Constitution of the Spartans*. Nails (2002) 108–11 summarises what is known of Critias' career.

with good experience of sex and sleep, and accords with both health and self-discipline, *sōphrosunē* ('neighbour of piety', 21). In the other surviving lines of the poem the key note of sympotic 'measure', *metron*, rings out: while others drink 'over the measure' (22) and set aside designated days to stupefy themselves with 'immoderate' (*ametros*) amounts, the Spartan way of life (*diaita*) involves eating and drinking in balanced measure (*summetra*) for the needs of both thought and work.[67]

Critias' uncompromisingly antithetical argument is deliberately provocative. It attests to the accumulated weight of a tradition of discourse about the ideal symposium and its ethical (as well as alcoholically calibrated) prerequisites which most Greeks would have found familiar. Yet it presents us with an Athenian poet whose (partial) alienation from his own city's culture leads him to project the fulfilment of that ideal exclusively onto the 'alternative' lifestyle of Sparta. Within this hyper-laconising framework, laughter itself takes on the status, alongside wine, of a sort of quantifiable commodity, a form of bodily as well as psychological expression which must be subjected to the principle of 'measure' (hence 'moderate laughter', 16). In keeping with the broader evidence for Sparta which I summarised in Chapter 1, Critias depicts the Spartans not as puritanical agelasts but as people who practise laughter within a matrix of carefully balanced forces of body, speech and companionship, allowing it a controlled outlet while avoiding such decadent practices as, say, the public scurrility of Dionysiac festivals (a point alluded to in the last lines of the elegy).[68] Critias vicariously accommodates Spartan fears of dissent or subversion by positioning laughter in a perspective which is simultaneously social (good for friendship), ethical (maintaining the respect and restraint that belong to *sōphrosunē*),[69] and political (conforming to a tightly regulated system of public order). To laugh to excess, the elegy leaves us to infer, belongs with all the other symptoms of instability – of language, vision, memory, thought, and bodily conduct – which the poem catalogues. The poem is an ideological speech-act, not a factual document; it may not tell us the whole story of Critias'

---

[67] Sympotic 'measure' or moderation: Panyas. 13.5–10 *EGF* (punning on moderation/limit), 14.5, Euenus 2.1 *IEG* (= *Anth. Pal.* 11.49, punning on wine/water mixtures: cf. Wilson (2003) 115–16), Lycophron fr. 3.2 *TrGF*. Cf. the description of Thersites as ἀμετροεπής, lacking measure/moderation in speech: *Iliad* 2.212–13 (ch. 2, 69–73).

[68] On Spartan laughter, see ch. 1, 44–50, with n. 123 there for Spartan drinking. Note the affinity between lines 26–7 of the poem and Pl. *Laws* 1.637a–b (see ch. 4, 177–8), where the Spartan Megillus claims that his city excludes scurrilous Dionysiac festivities.

[69] Hippolytus, at Eur. *Hipp.* 1000, regards avoidance of mockery (associated with duplicity to 'friends': cf. n. 47 above) as an aspect of *sōphrosunē* (*ibid.* 995). For symposiac *sōphrosunē* (of speech), combined with measure/moderation, cf. Lycophron fr. 3 *TrGF*.

own attitudes.[70] But it does corroborate, with peculiar trenchancy, the intricate network of ideas and values which bound together the normative aspirations of the symposium. And it confirms that laughter, as a juncture between virtues of body and mind, forms a nodal point in that network.

SATYRIC AND TRAGIC VERSIONS OF SYMPOTIC LAUGHTER

The poetic expression of sympotic ideals exercised such a strong influence on Greek cultural sensibilities that the imagery of the 'good' and 'bad' symposium, together with the problems involved in attempts to define the differences between them, produced a repertoire of themes and motifs that could be used for symbolic effect in many contexts, not just in cod-ifying the drinking-party in its own right. With its double-sided gelastic associations, the symposium became a metaphor for a whole range of psy-chological and social experience.[71] To explore the expanded availability of this fund of imagery and figurative vocabulary, I turn in this section to some Euripidean material which dramatises notions of sympotic laugh-ter in far-reaching ways. My argument will proceed from the extravagant travesties of the satyric mode, via a scenario that floats strangely between the satyric/comic and the tragic, to a remarkable encroachment of the lan-guage of laughter into the realm of tragedy. As we follow this sequence, the relationship between laughter inside the dramatic world and (possible) laughter on the part of an audience will become increasingly difficult to decipher.

I start with selective observations on the sympotic-komastic nuances which colour parts of the fabric of Euripides' *Cyclops*. The ambiguities of the symposium (and *kōmos*) as an embodiment of Dionysiac liberation, or, on its dark side, a setting for the eruption of violent instincts, are important to the play's giddy treatment of the basic Greek values at stake in a familiar myth. The *Odyssey* had already established the figure of Polyphemus as a kind of grotesquely perverted symposiast – the monster who dines and, with Odysseus' encouragement, drinks *alone*, not only denying hospitality to others but inverting hospitality into cannibalism.[72] Euripides' *Cyclops*

---

[70] Contrast Critias fr. 1 DK, a hexameter poem which effusively praises the sensual sympotic lyrics of Anacreon and relishes the rounds of 'toasts' (10) which are deprecated in the elegy, 6.3–4, 6–7 *IEG*; cf. also the praise of *kottabos* and luxury vessels in Critias 2 *IEG*.

[71] Old Comedy – itself in some way an offshoot of the *kōmos* – is a prime place where symposiac imagery/thematics can be seen at work: Bowie (1997), Pütz (2007).

[72] This point is not undermined by the absence in Homer of the fully institutionalised protocols of the symposium: it is enough that the epics recognise quasi-sympotic norms of formalised drinking. For some germane reflections, see Slater (1990).

gives a more explicitly Dionysiac, but also burlesque, twist to these motifs
by entangling Polyphemus in interaction between the wine-bringing 'guest'
Odysseus and the satyric entourage of Dionysus. The satyrs' captivity in
service to the Cyclops is, as Silenus explains, a separation from their god (25–
6). When the chorus enters, it tries to recapture the spirit of a Bacchic *kōmos*
by dancing the vigorous and probably indecent *sikin(n)is*.[73] The play's own
parodos thus evokes the tone of a possible revel, yet inconclusively, since the
satyrs' current existence has exiled them from the resources for a sustained
kōmos: they are living, as Silenus later states, in a land 'without dances'
(124). Hence the wine Odysseus brings with him forges a fresh Dionysiac
rapport with the satyrs (139–40), reactivating their desire to dance (156)
as well as their blatantly erotic impulses (169–71, 179–87). Silenus and the
chorus want a liberation from captivity that characterises itself as a sort of
enlarged version of the psychological release of the symposium, including
the 'oblivion from suffering' (172) which is a sympotic topos in archaic
poetry. With a comically heightened crudity, the satyrs represent a longing
for the shared ecstasy of drinking and revelling – the polar opposite of
Polyphemus' self-worshipping egotism (334–5).

But the play proceeds to complicate that contrast between sympotic-
komastic choral yearnings and Polyphemus as a solipsistic anti-image of
the symposium. The latter is himself a creature of sensual appetites not
unlike those of the satyrs; Odysseus finds it easy to undermine him by
means of the 'belly' which he worships. In doing so, Odysseus ironically
converts Polyphemus into a kind of symposiast, albeit a solitary one. He
gives him cups of wine to drink after his meal (of the flesh of Odysseus'
own companions, 409–12), eliciting praise of the liquid from the Cyclops
(418–19), who then starts to sing as a symposiast might, even if in an unmusical manner (426) and to the grotesque counterpoint of the weeping of
Odysseus' surviving men. This last detail (425–6; cf. 488–90) underlines the
(parodic) perversion of a sympotic template, though it might also remind
some hearers of less extreme contrasts between happy and unhappy drinkers
found in earlier poetry (122–5 above). As it happens, *Cyclops* 425 ('he sings
alongside my weeping shipmates') displays a verbal resemblance to Theognis 1041 ('reclining by one who weeps'), discussed earlier: both cases sketch
a situation in which one party celebrates while another is compelled, despite
grief, to participate. Polyphemus' conversion into a (gruesome) symposiast
even overcomes his solitary, egotistic disposition. Under the influence of

[73] 37–40: see Seaford (1984) 103–6 for discussion; indecency, as he notes, is signalled by σαυλούμενοι,
implying salacious body movements. On the *sikinnis*, cf. ch. 1 n. 91.

inebriation, he expresses a desire to go on a *kōmos* with others (445–6, 451, 503–10). Odysseus has to find a way of blocking this dangerous prospect and in doing so create an acceptable, positive *kōmos* for the true followers of Dionysus. In keeping with this, the chorus anticipates its own authentic revel (492–502), drunken but reliant on the support of real friends (498).

Yet the relationship between the two sympotic-komastic frames of reference becomes somewhat blurred. Euripides builds multiple layers of paradox into the scenario. Not only are the revels partly performed alongside one another at 495–510, but both inescapably involve violence. Polyphemus eats his fellow 'guests', while the satyrs intend to participate in a revel whose purpose is to blind the Cyclops in turn (492–4). What's more, it is by manipulating symposiac practice (reclining, the mixing-bowl, wearing garlands, Odysseus as 'wine-pourer', etc.: 542–89) that Odysseus and Silenus lure Polyphemus into the intoxication which renders him defenceless against the firebrand that blinds him. Odysseus tells Polyphemus that Dionysus never harms anyone (524) yet warns him, in a familiar though here ironic observation, that komastic celebrations readily produce quarrelling and violence (534). Polyphemus himself is induced by drinking to reveal his cannibalistic self all the more unequivocally, yet he is also inspired to want to share his wine with his brothers (531–3): in his own gross way, even he attests to the contrasting possibilities of sympotic consumption. It might be misguided to moralise these motifs too earnestly in the present case, though they do carry a rich resonance of cultural experience.[74] Euripides toys with the ambivalences of sympotic/komastic drinking, but the expectations of satyr-play surely demand an opportunity for unimpeded laughter on the audience's part. But what sort of laughter, exactly? One kind seems prompted by the lusty exuberance of the satyrs, another by the caricatured bestiality of Polyphemus. And yet another kind is assimilated into the action of the play itself: in a moment of quizzically burlesque pathos, the blinded Cyclops finds that his final humiliation is to be mocked and ridiculed – 'How I'm laughed at! You jeer at me in my suffering!' (687, cf. 675). Although this reflects the Odyssean prototype of the story, it gives it a more theatrical twist, staging the moment with shades of something like a game of blind man's buff (675–89). In this detail above all, it is hard to escape a sense of lingering indeterminacy in the tone of the laughter depicted and/or invited. Has Euripides deflated an originally horrifying

---

[74] Rossi (1971) take the theme of the *kōmos*, and a (failed) education in sympotic drinking, to be a key to the construction of *Cyclops*.

myth to the status of a blindfold children's game, or followed through the logic of the taunting laughter of victimisation?[75] Either way, Polyphemus has been turned into the giant butt of his own symposium and *kōmos*. And to reach that climax in the thematic design of his play, Euripides has had repeated recourse to a powerful contrast between positive and negative, life-enhancing and life-destroying, versions of Dionysiac celebration. We shall see later how he returns to such contrasts, but in an unmistakably deadly form, in his final play, the *Bacchae*.

If *Cyclops*, for all its teasing fusion of cannibalism and laughter, is an unequivocal representative of the satyric genre, *Alcestis*, which is formally a tragedy yet was performed as the fourth play in its set and therefore in the normal position of a satyr-play, offers (for my purposes) a strange mixture of tragic and comic/satyric elements. It is against a backdrop of generic uncertainty that the potency of symposiac symbolism, including the instabilities of laughter itself, comes into its own.[76] That symbolism is activated emphatically in the passage where Admetus explains to his wife, as she prepares to die in his place, that not only will he never remarry but he will honour her with perpetual mourning:

> παύσω δὲ κώμους συμποτῶν θ' ὁμιλίας
> στεφάνους τε μοῦσάν θ' ἣ κατεῖχ' ἐμοὺς δόμους.
> οὐ γάρ ποτ' οὔτ' ἂν βαρβίτου θίγοιμ' ἔτι
> οὔτ' ἂν φρέν' ἐξάραιμι πρὸς Λίβυν λακεῖν
> αὐλόν· σὺ γάρ μου τέρψιν ἐξείλου βίου.
>
> (343–7)

> I will end the revels, the gatherings of symposiasts,
> The garlands and music that used to fill my palace.
> I could never again touch the strings of a lyre
> Nor rouse my spirits to sing to Libyan pipes:
> You have taken with you all pleasure from my life.

Given the implicit 'denial' or suspension of death which can sometimes be discerned at work within the traditional mentality of the symposium, Admetus' renunciation of all previously enjoyed revels takes on a subtle irony. The real death of his wife, despite its aim of saving Admetus himself from the grave, strips his life of all the value that used to find expression precisely in sympotic-cum-komastic festivity, and ensures that the sounds of

---

[75] A Greek form of blind man's buff (peculiarly called 'bronze fly') is attested at e.g. Hdas. *Mim.* 12.1, Suet. *Lud.* 17, Pollux, *Onom.* 9.123 (cf. carm. pop. 876(a) *PMG*), Hesych. *s.v.* μυῖα χαλκῆ. Seaford (1984) 222 notes the game's relevance to the present scene; cf. Garland (1990) 126–7, (1995) 84, and see ch. 10 n. 2.

[76] For readings of the play's generic uncertainty, see Seidensticker (1982) 129–52, Slater (2005).

the drinking-party will never again be heard in the palace. But the starkness of Admetus' contrast between life before and after Alcestis' death prepares the way for an even more ironic thematisation of symposiac values later in the play, a thematisation that revolves round the arrival of the conspicuously ambiguous figure of Heracles.

Heracles is a double-faced figure in Greek mythology, especially in the versions of myth developed in poetry and drama. His life-threatening labours align him with the ordeals and extreme sufferings of other heroes. But this is offset by his burlesque persona as a magnified embodiment of sensual appetites (both gastronomic and sexual), as well as a figure readily imaginable as breaking into hearty laughter.[77] Unlike some heroes, therefore, he moves equally easily in the worlds of tragedy and comedy. His arrival in *Alcestis* brings hints of both roles with it. He is in the course of his third labour (fetching the man-eating horses of Diomedes, 481–506), but he comes also as a guest in need of hospitality (538–50). When Heracles hears of the death of a woman in the palace (but not Alcestis, he is persuaded), both he and Admetus voice sentiments that might remind us of Theognis 1217–18, discussed earlier. Heracles states that it is shameful for guests to be feasted in the house of those who mourn (542), while Admetus, insisting that Heracles nonetheless be taken to the separate guest-quarters, adds that it is wrong for visitors, while feasting, to be troubled by the sounds of others' grief (549–50). The motif of hospitality has important ramifications in the play, as the following stasimon, 568–605, underscores. Hospitality was the cause of Apollo's gratitude to Admetus (and therefore of the god's deferral of the latter's death), and it will be the cause of Heracles' gratitude too. But in the exchange between Admetus and Heracles the motif exposes the incongruous place that feasting now occupies in Admetus' home. The king himself has forsworn such things for ever, yet he wants to protect a place for them that will allow him to uphold guest-friendship by playing the generous host. This commitment turns out to prefigure his salvation – a salvation enacted partly, and paradoxically, through the force of laughter.

In the servant's subsequent account of how Heracles, confined to separate quarters, enjoyed Admetus' hospitality while the latter mourned, we

---

[77] For Heracles' own laughter, see e.g. Ar. *Frogs* 42–6 (with ch. 6 n. 138), Callim. *Aitia* fr. 24.3 Pfeiffer (with ch. 4, 187); late sources (ps.-Nonnus, *Narr.* 39, p. 375 Westermann, *Suda s.v.* Μελαμπύγου τύχοις) depict him overcome by laughter while carrying the Cercopes, probably an old element in the story: see Gantz (1993) 441–2, with my Appendix 2 n. 31, and now Rosen (2007) 57–66. On Heracles as comic glutton, see Wilkins (2000) 90–7, with Galinsky (1972) 81–100 for his general comic/satyric status. Cf. ch. 1 n. 105 for the Athenian jesters' club which met at the precinct of Diomeian Heracles.

encounter an anomalous situation parallel to the case of Polyphemus in
Cyclops – that is, a *solitary* symposium (756–60).[78] The anomaly extends
into a solitary *kōmos* at 773 (the language of revelry is salient: 804, 815, 831),
where the drunken Heracles enters complaining bitterly about the servant's
scowls and thus implicitly calling for laughter, as the servant's response
at 804 acknowledges ('our present situation has no place for *kōmos* and
laughter').[79] Heracles' avowal of the principle of living hedonistically for
the present, in a spirit of *euphrosunē* (cf. 788) and fuelled by drink (788,
795), exhibits a symposiac-komastic mentality that seems to exist in temporary disregard of death. While the servant considers Heracles insensitive
to the family's grief, the visitor's ignorance blocks this charge for the play's
audience. In any case, his feasting assumes a larger-than-life, quasi-satyric
dimension as the embodiment of a kind of resilient defiance of death, an
affirmation of temporary human cheerfulness in the face of the inevitable.
What gives this characterisation dramatic depth is its counterpoint with the
larger situation of the play. Heracles is no empty comic foil to the tragedy
taking place in the palace. He is a flesh-and-blood instantiation of a would-
be anti-tragic philosophy of life, delivered with a sententiousness which
though intoxicated is also redolent of much Greek folk wisdom (779–802).
As the voice of this mentality Heracles both engages in and invites a degree
of laughter. But he simultaneously poses questions that would have struck
many Athenians as apt material for sympotic reflections on the relationship
between life and death.

Euripides engineers the possibility of laughing at/with Heracles only to
cancel this laughter abruptly. When Heracles learns the truth about Alcestis,
he channels his komastic energies into an active defiance of death, rushing
off to wrestle with Thanatos himself and thereby decisively translating
his *kōmos* into something which, while sustaining its life-affirming force,
is no longer a laughing matter. During his absence, there is a scene of
mourning during which Admetus hauntingly recalls the sounds of a distant
kōmos, the procession of his original wedding to Alcestis (918). But when
Heracles returns at 1008, it is precisely to restore what seemed irreversibly
lost. He brings with him the veiled Alcestis and in a dramatically profound
sense is now able finally to convert tears to laughter, echoing and inverting
Admetus' earlier deception about his wife's death and allowing the king to

---

[78] The parallelism is heightened by the often noticed verbal resemblance between the two characters'
'unmusical' singing, *Alc.* 760 and *Cyc.* 425; cf. Seaford (1984) 185.

[79] At 805–6, 'do not grieve to excess', Heracles has shifted (from his initial reaction at 542) to a quasi-
sympotic sentiment: cf. Archil. 11 *IEG* (n. 63 above). But his shift depends on a perception that the
dead woman is a stranger to him (778, 805, 810).

announce a renewal of dancing in the city (1154–5). I cannot pursue here all the critical questions raised by Euripides' interweaving of tragic and satyric/burlesque material in this play. All I have tried to do is draw out how the symbolism of sympotic and komastic *euphrosunē* serves a much more sophisticated purpose than the mere depiction of Heracles in his persona as a drunken gourmand. Heracles' revelry turns out to be the hinge of the entire play: it looks back to Admetus' insistence on providing hospitality, and it triggers the moment at which he feels obliged to repay that hospitality by going to confront death itself. What starts as Heracles' escape from toil and his overcoming of mortality in the *mind* (two fundamental sympotic motifs, as we have seen) is transmuted into a more literal confrontation with death than any symposium as such could bring about, yet a confrontation that seems to retain something of the sympotic outlook that immediately precedes it. As many critics have realised, Euripides has made *Alcestis* a deeply ambiguous surrogate for a satyr-play, and Heracles a figure who fuses together comic and tragic perspectives. As a result, the work places its audience, like Heracles himself, in a position where the possibilities of laughter and tears begin by clashing but end up intermingling – through the dialectic of Heracles' two forms of resistance to death – in a harmonised response to the return of Alcestis.

If the *Alcestis* sets sympotic laughter against death before bringing them to a tragicomic resolution, the dark vein of sympotic imagery that runs through Euripides' *Bacchae* is of an altogether different order of significance. In the play's first stasimon the chorus calls upon Reverence (*Hosia*) to witness the aggressive attitudes (*hubris*, a term whose overtones of symposiac disorder are activated here) which Pentheus has shown towards Dionysus through his treatment of Cadmus and Teiresias. They characterise Dionysus as prime deity of *euphrosunē*, the archetypal mood of the symposium ('first of the gods in the elated celebrations where beautiful garlands are worn', παρὰ καλλιστεφάνοις εὐφροσύναις: 376–8), and describe his sphere of action in the following terms:

> θιασεύειν τε χοροῖς
> μετά τ᾽ αὐλοῦ γελάσαι
> ἀποπαῦσαί τε μερίμνας,
> ὁπόταν βότρυος ἔλθῃ
> γάνος ἐν δαιτὶ θεῶν, κισ-
> σοφόροις δ᾽ ἐν θαλίαις ἀν-
> δράσι κρατὴρ ὕπνον ἀμ-
> φιβάλλῃ.
>
> (379–86)

> . . . to bring the band of worshippers together in dance,
> to laugh to the accompaniment of the pipes,
> to bring an end to anxieties,
> when the glory of the grape
> comes into the feast in honour of the gods
> and at the banquets where men wear ivy
> the mixing-bowl of wine bestows sleep.

The chorus imagistically conjures up a synthesis of Dionysiac worship, one that embraces the spirit of various forms of festival, revel and symposium, and brings together a cluster of motifs we have already encountered in archaic texts: the *euphrosunē* of a closely bonded group, dancing, music, laughter, wine, sleep, and the desire for escape from sorrow which is such a typical psychological inflection of the sympotic frame of mind. Euripides uses these ideas and their associations to add a complex dimension – part literal, part metaphorical – to his treatment of Pentheus' character and story. The double-sided place of laughter in this treatment is worth tracing in a little detail.[80]

The first stasimon of *Bacchae* pits a violently mocking Pentheus against a god who offers his followers the experience of laughter within an ecstatic form of worship. The scene that precedes this ode ensures that the *hubris* of 375 has unmistakable connotations of antagonistic ridicule.[81] At line 250 Pentheus had scornfully exclaimed that the sight of Teiresias and Cadmus in bacchic garb, including ivy (253), struck him as ludicrous: suitable for out-right laughter (πολὺν γέλων). That moment epitomises the malevolently jeering tone that stamps the whole of Pentheus' tirade against Dionysus and his impact on Thebes, a tone it is not difficult to imagine an actor conveying with some gelastic vocalisation. Teiresias draws attention to this jeering in his rebuttal of Pentheus' charges: three times he refers to the attitude of blatant derision (διαγελᾶν, καταγελᾶν: 272, 286, 322) that the king has shown towards both Dionysus and his elderly adherents.[82] Two of these references frame the famous passage where Teiresias discourses on the blessings given to humanity by Demeter and Dionysus, in the latter's case dwelling on benefits of wine-drinking – erasure of sorrowful memories, the

---

[80] The gelastic dimension of Pentheus' story is partly captured by Philippus Thess. *Anth. Pal.* 9.253.3 ('the rites of Dionysus which Pentheus first laughed at, then lamented').

[81] On laughter and *hubris* see ch. 1 n. 60. On the theme of mocking rejection of a deity, cf. Versnel (1998) 161–2, 170–1, 200.

[82] I cannot follow Seidensticker (1978) 314–15 in taking Pentheus' laughter at the old men as 'the reaction the author intended to produce [sc. from his audience]'. Contrast now Donzelli (2006). Cf. Dillon (1991) 345, 352, 'there is nothing funny about laughter in Greek tragedy', with *ibid.* 351 on Pentheus; for possibilities of audience laughter at tragedy, see also Jouanna (1998), Goldhill (2006).

'drug' of sleep – which reappear in the following stasimon. The confrontation between Pentheus and Teiresias, together with the lyric commentary on it that the chorus then supplies, thus sets up a situation in which laughter takes on symbolic as well as practical significance. When the chorus sings of Pentheus' *hubris* against the Dionysus who inspires the elated, life-enhancing laughter of the symposium (and related forms of celebratory worship), the audience can perceive the Pentheus of the preceding scene as, literally and metaphorically, a figure both hostile to the ideals of the symposium and an embodiment of the aggressive, alienating laughter that is incompatible with sympotic concord.[83]

That Pentheus, like Dionysus himself, is a young man (274, a clue to the character's theatre mask) and therefore a paradigmatic age for the youthful vigour (*hēbē*) which I earlier documented as a topos of sympotic texts, adds a further irony to the king's refusal of, and self-exclusion from, the world of the symposium. The positive qualities of *hēbē* are displaced onto Teiresias and Cadmus, as the former expressly indicates at 190. Literal age-differences are symbolically obliterated, as Teiresias also explains (206–9), by the transformative psychological energies that give a specifically Dionysiac twist to the old motif of the agelessness of symposiasts. That Pentheus' violent rejection of Dionysus can be understood metonymically as a repudiation of sympotic laughter, and its replacement by the laughter of vicious enmity (all the more disturbing for being directed against his own kin), is underlined in the first antistrophe of the first stasimon. Immediately after their depiction of Dionysiac elation at 379–85, quoted above, the chorus anticipates Pentheus' doom by singing of 'unbridled mouths and lawless folly' (ἀχαλίνων στομάτων | ἀνόμου τ' ἀφροσύνας, 386–7). We can detect here a subtle allusion to the kinds of excess with which a certain sort of laughter belongs. Not only do we find the same phrase (with a difference only of word order) for 'unbridled mouths' in an anonymous lyric description of the abusiveness of a *kōmos* of young men who move through the streets to an accompaniment of music and laughter, but Euripides himself in an earlier play had used the same expression in explicit association with laughter, in a passage of *Melanippe Desmotis* where a speaker deprecates those who deliberately practise mockery of others (probably at symposia).[84] There is an interesting subtextual relationship

---

[83] In the first stasimon itself, the notion of *rejecting* the symposium is sounded at 424: the god 'hates' those who spurn his gift of wine.

[84] Adesp. lyr. 1037.17 *PMG* (with nn. 8, 15 above), Eur. fr. 492 *TrGF* (ἀχάλινα . . . στόματα), with Cropp's notes in Collard *et al.* (1995) 244, 271 (but with unsatisfactory translations of the second line on 255, 271; for the term *charis* see n. 27 above); for the 'biographical' influence of fr. 492, cf.

of ideas between this last passage and the same phrase in the *Bacchae*. In one case we have the point of view of the bacchants who contrast benign symposiac laughter with the malicious mockery of their cult's opponents. In the other, though the precise situation is unknown, we are faced with the attitudes of someone who criticises symposiasts, seemingly from a somewhat 'puritanical' angle, for (excessive) indulgence in laughter for its own sake. Despite their differences, the two contexts complement each other in illuminating how laughter can be perceived as marking inclusion in or exclusion from a social group. Where the speaker in *Melanippe* distances himself cynically from symposiac jokers, aligning himself with a view of life too sober to accommodate such mirthfulness, the chorus of *Bacchae* present an ideal vision of a Dionysiac laughter quasi-musical in its operations (μετά τ' αὐλοῦ γελάσαι, 'to laugh to the accompaniment of the pipes', 380), against which the violent anti-Dionysiac scoffing of Pentheus, as displayed in the preceding scene, stands out all the more starkly.[85]

The thematic significance of laughter in the *Bacchae* turns out, however, to be more problematic than the chorus's initial contrast between hubristic mockery and the inclusive pleasures of Dionysiac celebration. Although this contrast echoes prevailing Greek ideas about socially integrative and divisive forms of laughter, Euripides complicates the polarity by connecting it with two other salient factors in the play, Dionysus' own laughing apparition and the god's vindictive use of ridicule in his revenge against Pentheus. In theatrical terms, several critics have supported the hypothesis that Dionysus is to be taken as wearing a mask that incorporates a symbolically enigmatic smile, perhaps reminiscent of those found on the faces of many late-archaic Greek statues. This hypothesis is an inference from two lines of the text: 439, where a servant describes how Dionysus allowed himself to be captured like a tame animal and while 'laughing'; and 1021, where the chorus chillingly invoke the god to come 'with laughter on your face' (προσώπῳ γελῶντι) to place a deadly noose round Pentheus' neck. But to translate these powerful images of laughter into a 'smiling' mask may confuse specific moments of highly charged significance with the fixture of an unchanging, albeit potentially ambiguous, look.[86] What matters for my purposes, however, is not the theatrical hypothesis itself but the

---

ch. 6 n. 18. Lucian allows the 'unbridled mouths' of *Bacch.* 387 to be used against his satirical alter ego, Parrhesiades, at *Pisc.* 3, though he also turns the phrase against the ignorant (though certainly *mocking*) critic at *Pseudol.* 32.

[85] For the conjunction of laughter and music, cf. the *kōmos* in adesp. lyr. 1037.20–1 *PMG*.

[86] The 'smiling' mask advocated by e.g. Dodds (1960) 131, Foley (1980), esp. 127 ('smiling as we *know* . . .', my itals.), Segal (1982) 249, previously attracted me: Halliwell (1993b) 206 and n. 35. But it is rightly challenged by Radke (2003) 174–80, though I do not share her concern to

revealing symbolism of the two passages in question. In the first, Dionysus is a docile animal; in the second he is imagined as a wild beast (bull, snake or lion) turning on the hunter who tries to ensnare him. Laughter, we can say, is equally emblematic of the two sides, the two faces, of Dionysus – his gentleness and his savagery.[87] The implications are unsettling. The expressiveness of a laughing face (and voice) is equally capable of encompassing ostensible amiability or destructive hostility, yet there is no guaranteed way of reading the difference between the two from the face alone. As the play progresses, we move away from the clear-cut antithesis that structured the chorus's perspective in the first stasimon, and are forced to contemplate the disturbing presence of *both* kinds of laughter within the realm of the Dionysiac itself.

This thematic intricacy is developed in Dionysus' active pursuit of vindictive laughter, a familiar behaviour of Greek deities, in his revenge against Pentheus. The god *replicates* his own enemy's derisive disposition in the act of punishing it.[88] Like his followers, Dionysus is motivated by his resentment of Pentheus' mockery. He admits as much at 1080–1, where the messenger describes how Dionysus' voice shouted to the bacchants, 'I bring you the one who hurls laughter at you, me and my sacred rites – punish him!' On the way to luring the king into this fatal trap Dionysus makes a point of wanting to humiliate him:

> χρήζω δέ νιν γέλωτα Θηβαίοις ὀφλεῖν
> γυναικόμορφον ἀγόμενον δι' ἄστεως
> ἐκ τῶν ἀπειλῶν τῶν πρίν, αἶσι δεινὸς ἦν.
>
> (854–6)

> I want him to incur laughter among the Thebans
> By being led in woman's form through the city's streets,
> To pay him back for his own violent threats against me.

---

escape the ambiguities of laughter. Cf. Marshall (1999) 196 for milder scepticism. Seaford (1996) 186 correctly resists translating γελῶν (*Bacch.* 439, 1021) as 'smiling'. At *Hom. Hymn* 7.14 Dionysus smiles enigmatically/ominously when captured by pirates; his smile at Dionys. Perieg. *Orb.* 949 (n. 3 above) is that of a precocious child; in a third-century AD hymn inscribed at Dura-Europos he is invoked to approach his worshippers 'laughing': see Porter (1948), but again inadvisedly modifying γελῶν to 'smiling', 32 n. 8 (where the reference to Orphic Hymns is also mistaken); cf. Gilliam (1952) 122. 'Laughing' (γελόωντα) and 'lover of smiles' (φιλομειδέα) are among Dionysus' epithets at anon. *Anth. Pal.* 9.524.4, 22; Dionysus is 'laughter-loving', *philogelōs*, at Lucian, *Pisc.* 25. On the 'archaic smile' in Greek art, a putative model for Dionysus' mask, see Appendix 2, 536–9.

[87] See e.g. Dodds (1960) 131; Segal (1982) 199, 290–1 notes the play's broader thematics of laughter.

[88] Dionysus' retaliation for Pentheus' mockery in *Bacchae* was later adduced as a pagan paradigm of divinity (and thus a reason to doubt the godhead of Jesus, who *allowed* himself to be mocked): see ch. 10 n. 10. Cf. the vengefully laughing deity (*daimōn*) of Aesch. *Eum.* 560. But Greek gods do not mock human existence *per se*: ch. 2, 59.

This psychologically crucial moment picks up the fears Pentheus himself had expressed just a few lines earlier. At 840–2, Pentheus asked Dionysus how he would be able to avoid being seen by the Thebans on his way, disguised in female dress, to spy on the bacchants; 'anything is better', he declared, 'than letting the bacchants laugh at me' (ἐγγελᾶν, in the emended text now standardly printed). It is as though Pentheus' mind jumps from the risk of being jeered at as he is led through the streets (the point of his question in 840) to the thought of being ridiculed by the bacchants themselves.[89] It matters less whether we can identify exactly the imagined scenarios which fuel Pentheus' anxieties than that we should recognise the dramatic irony of his obsessive fear of mockery. The hubristic scoffer knows all too well (and therefore fears for himself) the power of public ridicule. But Dionysus, himself both object and subject of laughter in the course of the play, knows it even better, and knows how to intensify that power to the point of unsparing cruelty by harnessing it to anticipation of his enemy's death – something Athenian law allowed to the relatives of murder victims and which might well therefore have had special, if troubling, resonance for an Athenian audience of Euripides' play.[90] When combined with the chorus's viewpoint in the first stasimon, this justifies us in saying that the Dionysiac has the power to tap both the positive and the negative energies of laughter, just as it seems more generally to be implicated in both benign and sadistic aspects of (human) nature. Such doubleness fills the religious horizons of the entire work.[91]

From my own particular angle, a final facet of this doubleness is worth highlighting. In the real social world of classical Greek cities, especially Athens, there was one readily recognisable context in which certain men might move through the streets in female or feminised dress. This was precisely a (Dionysiac) *kōmos*. Even the god himself, especially in scenes of revelling, is sometimes depicted on Greek vases wearing a type of long robe (a saffron *krokōtos*) which was chiefly associated with women and could therefore be perceived as feminine.[92] So Dionysus' plan to lead Pentheus

---

[89] Stevens (1988) takes line 842 to mean: 'anything (even dressing as a woman) is better than letting the bacchants triumph over (i.e. defy) me'. But ἐγγελᾶν should not be denied its powerful gelastic force: Eur. *Medea* 1355, 1362, cited by Stevens, do not warrant eliminating the *idea* of laughter from the verb (Medea is obsessed with that idea; cf. Mastronarde (2002) 20, with ch. 1 n. 63). Neuburg (1987) argues, not without reason, that line 842 may be corrupt; though his emendation is unconvincing, he is right to emphasise Pentheus' fear of ridicule as the key to the passage.

[90] See ch. 1 n. 64 for the Athenian practice in question, with 24–33 for the dynamics of public ridicule more generally.

[91] For interpretations of the doubleness of Dionysus, see Henrichs (1984) 234–40.

[92] Philostr. maj. *Imag.* 1.2.5 (with a verbal echo of *Bacch.* 836) specifies the *kōmos* as an opportunity for transvestism; Schönberger (1968) 277–8 cites (with misprinted Greek) ps.-Plut. *Vitae or.* 847e

through Thebes in this manner carries pervertedly komastic connotations. It is part of Pentheus' blindness that he is an unwitting participant in a cryptic 'revel' choreographed by Dionysus, a revel that ironically forms the prelude to a tragic dénouement. The force of this suggestion is both vindicated and amplified by the play's finale. When the crazed Agave enters carrying the severed head of her son, the chorus macabrely perceives the spectacle as nothing less than a *kōmos* (1167, 1172), an ecstatic revel-procession in which they too half wish to join, but from which they gradually recoil in horror. This is the climax of Euripides' working of sympotic-komastic elements into the fabric of the drama, and it is not far-fetched to imagine it filled out with sounds of grotesque laughter on Agave's part, to match her lyric exclamations and deluded dance steps. Laughter is only one strand, of course, in the play's tightly woven texture of imagery, but it complements and strengthens the ambiguity of other strands too. Just as, for example, Pentheus is both a hunter and the quasi-animal victim of a hunt, so he is both a mocker of the god and the target of that god's sadistic ridicule. The *Bacchae* not only exhibits the ambiguities of laughter, its involvement in both celebration and cruelty; it transmutes them into the material, the motivations and the disastrous consequences of tragic conflict. One of the supreme, perpetually challenging paradoxes of the play is that Euripides has superimposed the body language of laughter, divine as well as human, onto the bleakest face of tragedy.[93]

SOCRATIC COMPLICATIONS: XENOPHON'S *SYMPOSIUM*

Having looked at some of the ways in which the values of the good symposium, and the fears of its contrary, acquired a symbolic significance extending beyond the bounds of the drinking-party proper, I now return to representations of the symposium itself. If the ideal atmosphere of sympotic pleasure is often characterised, as we saw earlier, in terms of a serio-comic equilibrium, this can be understood on one level as a means of controlling

for the same idea. Visual depictions of komasts in (quasi/semi-)female garb, including the so-called Anacreon vases, are variously interpreted by Kurtz and Boardman (1986), Frontisi Ducroux and Lissarrague (1990), Price (1990), Vierneisel and Kaeser (1992) 276–9, Parker (2005) 321–3. On the *krokōtos* as both female and Dionysiac, see Lada-Richards (1999) 17–19, Austin and Olson (2004) 102, with Ar. *Thesm.* 136–8, 941–2, and *Frogs* 46 for 'gendered' perception of such garments. For vases showing Dionysus himself in quasi-female dress (not always the *krokōtos*), see e.g. Carpenter (1991) ill. 15, 48, *LIMC* III.1 figs 84, 87, III. On Dionysiac ritual transvestism, see Seaford (1994) 271–4, Csapo (1997) 261–4. That Pentheus' transvestism is (partly) 'comic' is argued by Seidensticker (1978) 316–19, (1982) 123–7.

[93] Cf. Foley (1980), esp. 117–21, for the contribution of the *kōmos* motif to the play's mixing of tragic and 'comic' structures.

the instabilities of laughter itself. The tensions that can arise between the quest for sympotic elation and the danger of excessive inebriation, between deep intimacy and abrasive confrontation, between sensuality and decadence, between play and aggression – all these can be either resolved or exacerbated by laughter. But how can a harmony of seriousness and play be calculated? Can symposiasts consciously aim to achieve it, or is it a Dionysiac gift of ecstatic *euphrosunē*?

We can find an instructive test of the serio-comic or serio-ludic ideal in Xenophon's *Symposium*. Less philosophically intense than its Platonic counterpart, Xenophon's work allows us more direct access to the personal relationships and exchanges that structure the drinking-party on which it is based. At the same time, it shares with the Platonic dialogue, which I take to have preceded and influenced it (though that hypothesis is immaterial to my analysis of Xenophon's text), a representation of sympotic aspirations which is intertwined with a portrait of an extraordinary yet elusive individual, Socrates.[94] Because Socrates is pivotal to Xenophon's *Symposium* as to Plato's, it is impossible to examine the work's serio-ludic dynamics without considering Socrates' distinctive status in this regard. I shall have more to say in a later chapter about the subtle presence of laughter within the Socratic persona(e) in Plato. I will argue there that Socrates became, perhaps even during his lifetime and certainly soon afterwards, a figure whose relationship to laughter was perceived (by both his disciples and others) in heavily contested ways which Plato obliquely acknowledges in his characterisation of the man. In this respect as in others, part of the perplexing, paradoxical and disputed character of Socrates seems to have been his capacity to be regarded in contradictory ways: as someone who distanced himself from the derisive tactics of other public intellectuals (the sophists) or who, on the other hand, redeployed those tactics in more covert form; someone who never laughed at others or who was constantly laughing surreptitiously at them; someone who displaced laughter with irony or, on the contrary, used the latter to elicit the former; someone who was always deadly serious or always merely playful.

If the chances of reconstructing the 'real' Socrates practically vanish behind such contradictions, we can nonetheless learn something by focusing on the ways in which his persona became available as a vehicle of the serio-comic mode. There is no doubt that Xenophon was aware of this aspect (or conception) of Socrates. In both the first and last books of his

---

[94] The orthodox view that Plato's *Symposium* is earlier than Xenophon's is challenged by Danzig (2005), a work marred by confusion between authors and characters (e.g. 334 n. 12, with the circular argument on 356). Cf. Carrière (1998) 271.

Memorabilia he draws attention to the ability of Socrates to fuse together seriousness and play, even though one may feel that this feature is less visible in the body of the 'memoir' than the author's general remarks might lead one to expect.[95] But this same trait, much more captivatingly depicted, lies at the heart of Xenophon's *Symposium*. It opens up a simultaneous perspective on the double-sided character of both Socrates himself and the cultural priorities of the symposium. The programmatic force of the serio-ludic in Xenophon's *Symposium* is hard to miss. The author announces at the very start that it is worth recording not only the serious deeds of distinguished men (καλοὶ κἀγαθοί, a term the work itself will expose to complicated treatment),[96] but also the things they do in their 'playfulness' (*paidiai*). Xenophon could count on his readers to recognise the symposium as a form of 'play' in virtue of its self-contained relaxation from the rigours of life and its ritualisation of social intimacies in which joking and laughter have a practically obligatory role.[97] But the phrasing of that first sentence also leaves open the possibility that the events narrated in the work will themselves straddle the distinction between seriousness and play.

The possibility of a hybrid, complex sympotic ethos is broached as soon as the circumstances of the party, which takes place during Athens' greatest festival, the Panathenaea (of 422), are recounted. Callias, the immensely wealthy 'socialite' but also patron of sophists, is already set on giving dinner to Autolycus (a beautiful young athlete to whom Callias is sexually attracted, 1.2), Autolycus' father Lycon (later one of Socrates' prosecutors), and Niceratus (son of the general Nicias), when he encounters Socrates and four of his associates.[98] In inviting the Socratic group as well to dinner, Callias calls them (probably with an allusion to Pythagoreanism) 'men

---

[95] See *Mem.* 1.3.8 (note the theme of eating/drinking), 4.1.1–2, with ch. 6, 295–6, and *ibid.* 290–95 for the gelastic ambiguities of the Platonic Socrates. Vlastos (1991) 30–1 contrasts the 'gray' hues of the *Memorabilia* with the 'bright, even garish, colours' of Xen. *Symp.*, and detects only in the latter something akin to the 'complex irony' of Plato's Socrates.

[96] This term (often jarringly translated as 'gentleman(ly)') carries no automatic connotations of social elitism; that is only one possible nuance: cf. the incisive remarks of Dover (1974) 43. At Xen. *Symp.* 1.1, its reference is immediately complicated by the diversity of guests (they can hardly all be *kaloi kagathoi* in the same sense), and its later appearances in the work pull it away from social towards 'Socratic' values (though not without irony): nine of the fourteen occurrences are in Socrates' mouth (2.4, 4.50, 63, 8.3 [n.b. the flourish of doubt], 8.11, 8.12, 8.17, 26, 35, the last referring to Sparta), one is predicated *of* Socrates (9.1), two are effectively determined by Antisthenes (3.4), and the last comes from the Socratic Critobulus (4.10).

[97] On sympotic play, see n. 36 above. Cf. the idea of drinking as 'play', *paidia*, at Arist. *Pol.* 8.5, 1339a16–20 (cf. 1339b15–17), reflecting generally held views (and note Aristotle's allusion to Eur. *Bacch.* 381, with 133–4 above). Hunter (2004) 9–13 characterises the symposium in terms of the 'serio-comic', *spoudaiogeloion* (cf. ch. 7, 372–4).

[98] Prosopographical information on the named guests can be found in Nails (2002): the host is catalogued as Callias III of Alopece, Antisthenes as Antisthenes II, Niceratus as Niceratus II. Like

whose souls have been purified',[99] and states, with obvious paradox, that the occasion will be more sparkling if adorned by them than by figures of prominent public standing such as generals (like Niceratus' father) and cavalry commanders. Socrates treats Callias' supposed preference for the former over the latter as covert derision. 'You always mock and despise us (ἐπισκώπτεις ἡμᾶς καταφρονῶν)', he responds, 'because you yourself have paid large sums of money for wisdom (*sophia*) to Protagoras, Gorgias, Prodicus and many others, while you can see that *we* are like mere smallholders (αὐτουργοί) of philosophy' (1.5). A reader might suppose, however, that Callias' compliment was genuine; we are told, after all, that he was badly disappointed by the Socratics' initial refusal of his invitation (and that, in fact, it was this disappointment which persuaded them to change their minds, 1.7). Equally, anyone familiar with Socrates' reputation might wonder whether his first response, with its teasing confusion between economic and intellectual values, is tinged with irony. But might the exchange – a kind of pre-sympotic banter – involve sly humour on both sides? Could it be that Callias and Socrates (members of the same Athenian deme yet diametrical opposites in their lifestyles) *both* need to couch their social dealings in serio-comic form? Such a reading makes good sense of Callias' wry rejoinder to Socrates: 'In the past I concealed from you my great fund of wisdom, but now, if you'll visit my house, I'll show you that I'm worth taking very seriously' (1.6, where the noun *spoudē* echoes the work's opening sentence). Xenophon's text leaves the nuances of the scene open to further interpretation. But an underlying sense comes through that relations between Callias and the Socratics are ambivalent: there is some social awkwardness between them, but enough familiarity to allow for semi-friendly ironies. Those relations may therefore need to be mediated, in the intimacy of a dinner and drinking-party, by a mixture of gestures and feelings – in short, by a compromise between earnestness and play.

The scene-setting of Xenophon's *Symposium*, then, depicts Callias and Socrates facing up to one another with a coy disingenousness that reflects the host's two very different personae, that of the rich socialite and that of the would-be intellectual. The encounter strikes a note of both social and gelastic ambiguity. Is laughter something that can enable such contrasting figures to find a way of talking to one another, at least in 'play'? Or is there

---

others, Nails (2002) 72–3 notes the probable indebtedness of Xen. *Symp.* to comic precedents, esp. Eup. *Autolycus*, on which see Storey (2003) 81–94.

[99] For Pythagoreans and (musical) *katharsis* of the soul, see Aristox. fr. 26 Wehrli. Bowen (1998) 89 mentions the possible Pythagorean resonance of Callias' words; Huß (1999a) 80–1 ignores the point.

the risk of that 'mockery' and contempt between them of which Socrates purports to accuse Callias? Having hinted at such questions, Xenophon introduces a further, blatant dimension of 'play' into the work. As the symposiasts recline in a hushed atmosphere, overcome (Xenophon suggests) by a quasi-religious awe for young Autolycus' dazzling beauty, the silence is shattered by a sudden banging at the door – an obvious reprise of Alcibiades' entry in Plato's *Symposium*, and one of the work's many reminiscences of Platonic texts. In comes Philippus the 'laughter-maker' (*gelōtopoios*) or jester. Philippus acts a self-advertisingly comic role: he has come, he lets it be known, 'fully equipped with all provisions for dining – at another's expense!'; and he describes his slave as 'completely worn out by carrying – nothing!', thereby exploiting twice over a standard joke-form. Similar, though with a slightly more subtle implication, is his statement that because he is a well-known *gelōtopoios* he thought it would be funnier to turn up uninvited than invited. A jester, like a 'parasite' or professional 'flatterer', might indeed manage to gain entrance to a dinner/symposium on the basis of ability to provide a desirable commodity for such an occasion, laughter itself. This distinguishes him from the 'standard' invited guests – even if, rather ironically, we have seen that more than half of Callias' guests on this occasion were present as a result of an accidental encounter. Yet it also, as it were, legitimises Philippus' presence, so that he ceases to count merely as 'uninvited'. In fact, the situation is more convoluted. Because we do not have a perfect grasp of the social conventions of Callias' milieu, we cannot be sure whether Philippus is really to be understood as 'uninvited' at all. The game is at least partly given away by the narrator's subsequent statement that he was in fact regularly invited to dinner (1.14, cf. 1.15) specifically to provide entertainment. We are encouraged to imagine Philippus turning up frequently at Callias' house. And this in turn makes it more plausible that Callias himself – who at first, tongue in cheek, purports to be showing Philippus a kind of charity ('it would be shameful to deny him *shelter*', 1.12) but then tells him to recline (1.13), immediately putting him on the same footing as the other guests – is to be taken as knowingly participating in a playful routine and social pretence, rather than being actually taken by surprise.[100] Philippus' status as jester-cum-guest is inherently, teasingly ambiguous – something that fits with the sentiment attested in Epicharmus

---

[100] On this reading, *skōmma* at 1.12 covers Callias' as well as Philippus' behaviour; cf. Huß (1999a) 109–11. That Philippus is 'actually' uninvited is taken for granted by e.g. Danzig (2004) 25. Whatever we make of him, Philippus is not an outsider; poles apart is the *aklētos* who turns up at a wedding feast in Asius 14 *IEG*. Gilula (2002) 208 unjustifiably infers from Xen. *Symp.* 4.55 that Philippus heard about the party from the Syracusan.

that a certain kind of guest (the sort later called 'parasite') will turn up any time he is invited, but *also* even if he is not.[101]

The ambiguities of a figure like Philippus are not, however, simply a matter of amusement. They harbour potential problems of social interaction. In the present setting, anyone familiar with the inclinations of the Socratic circle might wonder whether they would welcome the presence of an ostentatious 'professional' of hilarity, one who says 'I could no more be serious (*spoudazein*) than become immortal' (1.15). Xenophon highlights the tensions of the situation by making Callias invite Philippus to recline with the observation, 'the guests are full, as you can see, of seriousness (*spoudē*), but perhaps a little lacking in laughter' (1.13). Given the work's programmatic opening, there is dramatic irony here: bringing together some of his usual acquaintances with a group of Socratics, Callias has so far failed to generate anything like an ambience of sympotic play. Furthermore, and despite the encouragement of the host, Philippus' initial attempts to arouse laughter fall decidely flat (1.14). But Xenophon does not seem to want his readers to think that the problem lies wholly in the disparity between the Socratics and the rest. It seems rather to be a matter of finding the psychological secret to create the special mood of intimacy and relaxation called for by the symposium (or, at this stage, the pre-sympotic dinner). That secret is shown to be contained within laughter itself.

Philippus finds his own solution to the problem by making a paradoxical routine out of the conflict between producing and denying laughter. He displays extravagant dismay at his failure to arouse laughter – covering his head and groaning (with parodic overtones of the Odysseus of *Odyssey* 8),[102] lamenting with delicious melodrama that 'laughter has been lost from mankind' (1.15), and then purporting to sniffle and weep. This last detail reminds us of other texts, considered earlier in the chapter, which deal with anomalous situations in which guests are imagined weeping at symposia.[103]

---

[101] Epicharm. fr. 32.1–2 *PCG* (35 Kaibel). On the history of the flatterer/parasite as comic/social type, see Nesselrath (1985) 92–111, Fisher (2000) 371–8, Wilkins (2000) 71–86, Arnott (1996) 553–5, 542–5, Andreassi (2004) 19–25, Olson and Sens (1999) 80. Note esp. Eup. fr. 172.12–13, with Storey (2003) 188–92, and Antiphanes fr. 142 for the laughter-making (and -sharing) expectations of such figures; cf. Theophr. *Char.* 2.4, with the symbolic *ne plus ultra* of the parasite who laughs without even hearing what he is laughing at: Hegesander fr. 6 *FHG, apud* Athen. 6.249e. Lucian, *Dial. mort.* 17, discussed in ch. 9, 441–3, gives the parasite's addiction to laughter an ironic twist. See Appendix 2, 543, for a possible image of a laughing/smiling parasite, and note the density of laughter-related terms in Pollux's description of the 'flatterer', *kolax, Onom.* 6.122–3 (cf. ch. 5, 220).
[102] The Odyssean allusion (to the head-covering at *Od.* 8.83–4, 92) perhaps yields a pun in Callias' question (1.15), 'has pain (*odunē*) taken hold of you?' The Odyssean parody is supplemented at 1.16, where Philippus tells his soul to have courage (overtones of *Od.* 20.17–18). Xenophon makes it clear that Philippus only *seems* to weep (κλαίειν ἐφαίνετο, 1.16); Gera (1993) 163 misses the point.
[103] See 122–5 on Theog. 1041–2, 1217–18, 128 on Eur. *Cyc.* 425–6.

But Philippus is professionally equipped to use such an anomaly, which would normally constitute a fracture in the unity of the symposium, to unlock the resources of sympotic mirth. At his show of grief, the guests all enter the spirit of the act. 'Everyone' purports to console him, reassuring him they *will* laugh the next time, and one of the Socratics, Critobulus, guffaws (ἐκκαγχάζειν, 1.16) at his self-pitying antics. Since, by his own definition, Philippus is incapable of seriousness, the whole scene is a tissue of laughter-rousing pretence: mimetic play-acting was a speciality of *gelōtopoioi*.[104] Even if the company's initial resistance to him was 'serious', Philippus has the repertoire to win them over and make them complicit in his performance; to contribute laughter to sympotic *euphrosunē* (cf. 1.15) is his métier. On his own premises, he dramatises the thought that a symposium without laughter is a contradiction in terms. But does his brand of laughter suit all the present company equally well?

Part of what Xenophon explores in the first part of the *Symposium* is the gradual emergence of a gelastic atmosphere, an atmosphere compatible with 'play', among a less than wholly integrated sympotic group. The ostensibly unexpected arrival of the laughter-maker, followed by the mini-drama or mime of his assimilation into the occasion, vividly enacts a question of sympotic priorities. Philippus' main role in the work turns out to be the initiation of playful laughter. How that playfulness might be sustained or developed is another matter. The jester's own involvement in the subsequent stages of the party becomes relatively minor, finding its place as just one piece of a larger mosaic of contributions. A suspicion lingers that Socrates and his companions might not want to depend on a 'hired' *gelōtopoios* for their commensal pleasures. Admittedly, Xenophon's *Symposium* presents a Socrates who does not consistently hold to the position he adopts in Plato's *Protagoras*, where he disparages the idea of symposiasts who rely on professional entertainers such as female musicians (sometimes purveyors of *more* than just music to the male guests) and who are incapable of gratifying each other's company from the resources of their own minds.[105] In the present work, by contrast, Socrates praises as 'highly enjoyable' (2.2)

---

[104] Philippus' parodic dancing at 2.21–2 is explicitly marked as mimetic. Mimetic jesters are cited at e.g. Athen. 1.19f (= Aristox. fr. 135 Wehrli), Diod. Sic. 37.12.2, Galen, *Usu part.* 3.16 (ch. 2 n. 30). Cf. Hephaestus' role-playing as cupbearer in *Iliad* 1 (ch. 2, 61–3); as it happens, Philippus' instructions at Xen. *Symp.* 2.27 make that comparison interesting.

[105] Pl. *Prot.* 347c–d; cf. *Symp.* 176e. Ideas about more/less reputable forms of symposiac entertainment formed a wider issue. Compare the anti-Macedonian traditions about Philip II's low-grade companions: Dem. 2.19, Theopomp. *FGrH* 115 F81, 162, 236; but note the revisionist, 'pro-gelastic' interpretation of Choric. *Apol. Mim.* 60–7 (Foerster). Cf. ch. 5 n. 33, ch. 6 n. 116. A group of jesters, *gelōtopoioi*, appear at a Thracian drinking-party at Xen. *Anab.* 7.3.33; cf. the imaginary dinner in Lucian, *Gallus* 11.

the musical and choreographic performances of the Syracusan troupe laid on by the host, and he requests their continuation (2.7) instead of pursuing a debate about whether true distinction (*kalokagathia*) is teachable. Later, Socrates will even speak of learning to dance such steps himself (2.16), an ambition which makes the others laugh but should not be read in context as entirely disingenuous (see below). On the other hand, Socrates does bluntly reject Callias' proposal that perfume be used by the guests (2.3); by spurning (the wrong kind of) hedonism in this way he gives a glimpse of a very different set of values from those of Callias himself and indeed of most Greek symposiasts (for whom perfume was an expected component of the occasion).[106] Moreover, he subsequently draws an explicit contrast between enjoying the performances of the musicians and providing each other with a superior pleasure from their own conversations (3.2), a contrast which coincides with the sentiments cited above from Plato's *Protagoras*.

If the Xenophontic Socrates seems to fluctuate in his sympotic preferences, we might continue to wonder what kind of laughter he thinks suitable for himself and his associates in such a setting. A partial answer starts to emerge at 2.10. Antisthenes responds to Socrates' comment that women's nature makes them as good as men where learning skilled activities is concerned by asking: 'how come then, Socrates, if you think this, that you don't yourself educate your wife Xanthippe but endure a woman who is the most difficult not only of all who now exist but of all women past and future?' To make a derogatory remark about another's wife by name is a highly unusual act for an Athenian; even in comedy and oratory such things are extremely rare. Yet in the present instance it comes from one of Socrates' inner circle and is taken without offence as a piece of sympotic repartee. Antisthenes has countered a quasi-philosophical thesis with an *ad hominem* objection. Socrates in turn responds by implicitly accepting the premise of the objection but turning it to his own argumentational advantage by explaining that, like an expert horse trainer (itself both a typically Socratic comparison *and*, here, a patently gelastic move), if he can master the most recalcitrant human material, he will be able to deal with *anybody* after that. The exchange is a mock philosophical version of the convention of sympotic games of amoebean banter which I cited at the very start of this chapter.[107] What this means is that the Socratics at the party have by now entered fully into the gelastic spirit of the occasion. In fact, the work hinges around the fact that Socrates and his friends will increasingly

---

[106] Socrates here flirts with attitudes that some might think 'boorish' (*agroikos*) or unrefined: see Theophr. *Char.* 4.3; on *agroikia*, cf. ch. 6, 293, 311–12.

[107] See 101–3 above.

redefine and dominate that spirit, throwing into the shade the rather naive Niceratus and the quiet Lycon (whose son, Autolycus, is limited by his age to a demure presence in the background), largely subordinating the jester Philippus to their agenda, doing the most to interact (on their own terms) with the host Callias, and even engaging the interest of the Syracusan mime-master.

The impression of Socrates' and Antisthenes' first exchange is cemented by a repetition of the pattern shortly afterwards. When the Syracusan's girl has executed a dangerous sword-dance with consummate skill, Socrates 'hails' Antisthenes (2.12, itself a gesture inviting further repartee) with the observation that the display they have just watched proves that courage (*andreia*, literally 'manliness') is teachable, when even a woman can so conspicuously be trained in it. There is some independent reason to believe that the historical Antisthenes followed Socrates in asserting the teachability of 'virtue' (*aretē*), and that he may have applied this thesis equally to men and women.[108] Whether or not Xenophon expects his readers to catch a genuine philosophical subtext to this moment in the work, Antisthenes' response to Socrates is markedly droll: he wonders whether the Syracusan should hire himself to the Athenian democracy as a trainer of *soldiers* (who like the girl, but in a different sense, have to face up to sharp weapons). Antisthenes' irony gives Philippus a cue to interject, rather like a bomolochic character in Old Comedy, with a gibe at the allegedly cowardly Athenian politician Peisander. So it is indeed the Socratics who are now creating the agenda for exchanges of sympotic humour by playing with (or putting into serio-ludic form) subjects which elsewhere they take extremely seriously. The hired jester can only tag along behind them.

We can go further. A process is underway whereby Socrates himself displaces (and improves on) Philippus in the role of *gelōtopoios*, the agent of laughter-making. That way of looking at the evolving tone of the symposium is corroborated by the very next episode of the party (Xenophon's whole work, unlike Plato's *Symposium*, is a concatenation of miniature episodes). This is the juncture at which Socrates' admiration for the Syracusan troupe induces him to voice a desire to learn such dance movements for himself (2.16). When the Syracusan asks what use he would have for them, Socrates answers, 'I'll dance them by Zeus!' This brings a peal of laughter from everyone present. The response of collective mirth at which Philippus himself had originally aimed in vain (despite the promise at 1.16

---

[108] Virtue as teachable: Antisth. frs. 23, 69 Decleva Caizzi (V A 99, 134 *SSR*), *apud.* Diog. Laert. 6.105, 6.10; virtue the same for men and women: Antisth. fr. 72 (V A 134 *SSR*), Diog. Laert. 6.12. On Antisthenes in Xen. *Symp.*, cf. Rankin (1986) 13–23.

that they would all laugh 'next time') is now achieved, inadvertently (it might seem), by Socrates himself. The second event ironically plays on the components of the first. Philippus, having lamented the absence of laughter, had been reduced to trying to arouse it by an elaborate show of mock anguish. Socrates, on the other hand, purports to be surprised and pained at the laughter he has *already* caused. With a very serious look on his face (2.17: his own equivalent to part of Philippus' gelotopoeic act), he asks 'Are you laughing at me?', before posing a series of questions that ostensibly rebuke his audience for mistaken mirth and imply a series of good reasons (relating to balanced bodily health and exercise) for wanting to dance.[109] A further exchange with Charmides confirms (within the work's own frame of reference) that Socrates already uses *some* dance steps for private exercise, but also shows that this fact is *prima facie* startling (Charmides himself had worried at first that Socrates was 'mad'): beyond the immediate humour of the moment, Xenophon's text is ambiguous on whether, or in what circumstances, the physically unprepossessing philosopher would 'really' dance.[110] The topic is then wrenched into a more boisterous style of amusement by Philippus, who first makes a joke at the expense of Charmides' own physical shortcomings (2.20), then (with his own glance back at Socrates' remarks on gymnastic efficacy) proceeds to perform a parodic version of the Syracusan dances. What Socrates had started as a serio-comic reflection on how to live one's life is exaggerated by the jester into a physical reductio ad absurdum.

That whole stretch, at 2.16–22, reinforces the gelastic ambiguity of Socrates which had started to emerge in his earlier exchanges with Antisthenes. He prompts laughter without appearing to intend to; he responds to that laughter with a pointedly straight face (a Xenophontic parallel to the

---

[109] Hobden (2004) 130 misconstrues Socrates' contrast with runners and boxers (not wrestlers) at 2.17.

[110] Huß (1999b) 387–9, (1999a) 155 distorts the passage by ignoring the difference between private exercise and learning 'professional' dance steps; his reading of Charmides' testimony (2.19) as pretence, followed by Hobden (2004) 131, is tendentious. Contrast Wohl (2004) 344–5. Pl. *Menex.* 236c–d treats (impromptu) Socratic dancing as hard to imagine. But dancing *per se* is not infra dig for respectable Athenians. Theophr. *Char.* 15.10 (misused by Diggle (2004) 252) pictures the surly man refusing to dance in an implicitly symposiac setting; someone in Alexis fr. 224 wryly suggests that dancing is universal at Athenian symposia; cf. Alexis fr. 102, with Arnott (1996) 271, and, more broadly, Panyas. 12.15 *EGF*, Ion Chi. 27.8 *IEG*. Sympotic dancing might vary, of course, in respectability: Theopomp. *FGrH* 115 F81 depicts a dancing flatterer-cum-jester (at the court of Philip II: cf. n. 105 above), and dancing the obscene *kordax* is a standard slur against the intoxicated, e.g. Dem. 2.18, Mnesimachus fr. 4.18 *PCG*, Theophr. *Char.* 6.3, with ch. 5 n. 61; cf., in an earlier context, *Odyssey* 14.463–5, with 107 above. Military dances, by Greeks and others, at Xen. *Anab.* 6.1.5–13 involve no indignity; cf. Athen. 4.155b–c. Note the Persian dancing (mocked by young Cyrus) at Xen. *Cyr.* 1.3.10.

striking facial gestures ascribed to Socrates in Plato);[111] he uses the moment of amusement to smuggle in, as it were, some reflective thoughts (about bodily health and balance), implicitly deflecting the laughter back at others and challenging them to see through the surface absurdity to an underlying puzzle. In all these respects he leaves an impression that he both is and is not playing a part, thereby matching Philippus' routines while at the same time seeming to be motivated by something more than the jester's desire for instant mirth. This Socratic configuration of serio-ludic behaviour is consistent with, but gradually complicates, older sympotic ideals. When he offers the company his advice on how much they should drink at 2.24–6, Socrates echoes the mainstream of a tradition which we examined earlier in this chapter: his formula that they should drink enough to 'lull cares to sleep' and encourage intimate friendliness (*philophrosunē*), to avoid physical and mental deterioration and promote a 'rather playful' spirit (παιγ-νιωδέστερον, 2.26), is familiar in all respects, though it is humorously undercut by Philippus' request for the faster circulation of cups which follows it. But as Xenophon's *Symposium* unfolds further, the sense of a peculiarly Socratic manipulation of the 'playfulness' of the occasion accumulates weight.

An important juncture in this respect occurs at 3.10, where Socrates' answer to the question of his 'chief pride' (which all the guests have to declare in their sympotic round robin) is 'pimping' or 'procuring'. Like his desire to learn to dance, but with a more blatant turn of wit, this avowal sets up an ironically serio-comic incongruity: Socrates gives the answer with a deliberately posed look of solemnity (involving raised eyebrows);[112] the reaction is again a general outburst of laughter; Socrates adds to his irony by stating that he could make a lot of money from such activity if he chose to; and there is once more an interplay with the gelotopoeic status of Philippus, to which Lycon draws attention in the immediate aftermath of this moment of laughter (3.11). The explanation of this latest Socratic paradox has to wait a while. When we return to it at 4.56–64, we are given a miniature parody of Socratic dialectic, as the other guests answer Socrates' series of questions in a collective chorus. While managing to gloss his earlier self-description with a veneer of respectability, by extending the idea of 'pimping' to the aim

---

[111] See ch. 6, 282, for Socrates' 'facialised irony' in Plato.

[112] The verb ἀνασπᾶν (to draw or pull up) is elsewhere used with eyebrows as object (e.g. Ar. *Ach.* 1069, Alexis fr. 16.1–2; cf. Olson (2002) 331, Arnott (1996) 99, with Appendix 1, 527); cf. *metōpon*, 'brow' at Ar. *Kn.* 631. The present passage is the only one where the object is the whole 'face', *prosōpon*, but it is reasonable to infer reference (in part) to the eyebrows. More than one Platonic passage suggests Socrates' use of his face, including eyebrows, to convey irony: see ch. 6, 281–2. Cf. n. 115 below.

of making people pleasing to one another for virtuous reasons, Socrates also turns this exchange into a sort of joke-form. He uses it to switch attention at the last minute to Antisthenes, who practises, he suggests, the cognate art of a 'go-between' (4.61). When Antisthenes appears to treat this seriously by taking offence, Socrates saves the spirit of the symposium by showing that the 'insult' can be easily translated into a compliment: Antisthenes is an *intellectual* match-maker, negotiating meetings of minds between various parties, including Socrates himself. Antisthenes is not only appeased; like a good disciple of Socrates, he can learn from him in the realm of philosophical irony. He makes a joke of his own on Socrates' model (4.64), but he does more than that by storing up the theme for use in further repartee. When at 8.4 Socrates asks him if he is the only person who does not feel erotic desire for anyone else, Antisthenes is ready with the answer, 'But I *do* – for you!' And when Socrates then assumes the role of a hard-to-get young man (in an overtly 'camp' manner that mocks [*episkōptein*] his lover), Antisthenes says: 'you self-pimper (σὺ μαστροπὲ σαυτοῦ), it's so blatant how you always behave like this!' (8.5).[113] This exchange of pseudo-sexual banter (modelled on the Socrates–Alcibiades confrontation in Plato's *Symposium*) brings to a climax the sympotic repartee between Antisthenes and Socrates which has developed since the former's reference to Xanthippe at 2.10. But even here it is part of a Socratic ploy (elaborated by his discourse in chapter 8 as a whole) to interfuse seriousness with play. He uses the time-honoured eroticism of the symposium to broach questions about what different people mean to, and what they desire from, one another; yet his manner appears to be that of someone pursuing nothing more than a lighthearted party game.

My analysis, though very selective, has now proceeded far enough to establish that one of Xenophon's literary-philosophical objectives in the *Symposium* is to show how the traditional protocols of sympotic laughter and exhilaration can be given a new Socratic twist, a distinctive (and quizzical) variation on an old form. Socrates oscillates between 'seriousness' and 'play' – in itself an axiomatic sympotic desideratum – in ways which lack complete transparency and pose a challenge of interpretation both to his hearers and to Xenophon's readers. The Xenophontic Socrates may lack the philosophical depth of his Platonic counterpart, but

[113] The vocative μαστροπέ in this sentence is unique in surviving Greek; unfortunately it has slipped through the net of Dickey (1996). Callias will squeeze one further joke out of the pimping theme, at 8.42.

in the *Symposium* he shares with him a fundamental tendency not to one-dimensional irony or simple switches of tone, but to a teasing instability of manner, an instability of which the shifting possibilities of laughter (by him and/or towards him) are a constitutive element. Socrates imposes his intriguing yet elusive character on the pursuit of self-understanding even in the midst of friendly sympotic banter. He discreetly *displaces* Philippus, I have argued, in the role of 'laughter-maker'. But in the process of doing so he partly transforms the function of laughter itself, turning it from a self-sufficient goal (which the 'hired' jester will do anything to achieve) into a defter, more delicate mediating factor in relations between the guests at the party. Even so, and despite an idealising strain in Xenophon's representation of his serio-ludic personality, Socrates does not and cannot master laughter altogether. I would like to end this section, and the chapter, by glancing at one final passage – a sequence of two contrasting but interlocked episodes – which illustrates the implications of this claim.

The sequence starts at 6.1–2 and arises from an accidental conjunction of comedy and seriousness in the mood of the party. Socrates has just lost a mock 'beauty contest' with Critobulus. This is an example of the kind of games real symposiasts played, but it is given a distinctively Socratic slant by being used to toss lightly into the conversation some thought-provoking questions about the concept of beauty itself. The contest has been a sort of cross between, and double parody of, Socratic interrogation, *elenchos*, and legal examination (*anakrisis*, 5.2). Socrates, one might feel, has won the argument but lost the vote, just as at his trial. The absurdity is that the only judges in the beauty contest are the Syracusan's boy and girl, and the announcement of Critobulus' victory has caused a general air of hilarity to erupt: joking (*skōptein*) of various kinds is being swapped. One guest, however, Hermogenes (close associate of Socrates, but also, as it happens, half-brother of Callias, and therefore a sort of hybrid in the present company), stays silent. Sympotic 'silence' has already been given a certain thematic charge in this work. Most of the guests (in awe of Autolycus' beauty, but also, we are led to infer, because of social awkwardness between the two groups Callias had brought together) were originally rather silent during dinner (1.9, 1.11) – until, that is, Philippus' banging at the door. We might think of the initial failure to laugh at Philippus' jokes too as a sort of silence, a potentially embarrassing failure to ignite the symposiac spark of good cheer. At least some kinds of silence pose an obvious threat to the intimacy and harmony of the symposium, and the narrative implies that this is not the first time Hermogenes (who has come across as an earnestly pious character) has failed to join in the mirth of the occasion. Socrates now seizes on his silence.[114]

Socrates asks Hermogenes for a definition of *paroinia*, drunken row-diness or abusiveness, in itself the quintessential breakdown of sympotic sociability. Hermogenes, evidently attuned to Socratic habits, distinguishes between objective and subjective definition before suggesting that *paroinia* is a matter of causing pain to one's fellow symposiasts. This allows Socrates to suggest, at least half-ironically, that Hermogenes' own silence, *qua* fail-ure to contribute to the shared pleasure of the occasion, fits the definition. But Hermogenes argues back; Socrates (as though *he* were the victim of interrogation, *elenchos*: 6.3) appeals to Callias for help, and the conversation unwinds in a flippant exchange about dialogue, music and theatrical per-formance, reaching its conclusion in Antisthenes' proposal that the victims of his own interrogation deserve catcalls (6.5). On one level, Socrates has reintegrated Hermogenes into the spirit of the party by chaffing him and giving him an opportunity to 'outargue' Socrates himself. On the other hand, Hermogenes' taciturnity was clearly not meant to be offensive, and Socrates does not actually succeed in changing his manner of behaviour. Later on, at 8.3–4, Socrates will tease Hermogenes again, this time for his moral and religious earnestness, and for a demeanour (including 'serious eyebrows') which embodies it.[115] But the young man's only further utter-ance in the work, at 8.12, is a rather solemn one, and we are left with the impression that he remains resistant even to the gelastically inflected ges-tures of the Socrates to whom he is so devoted. One way, at any rate, of reading the exchange between them at 6.1–4 is as an indication that not all Socrates' intimate companions can perfectly match the serio-ludic poise of the man himself.

After that exchange, there is a segue into a sharply contrasting moment of dialogue which provides the most piquant paradoxes of laughter (heard or implied) in the entire work. It stems from the Syracusan's irritation

---

[114] Hobden (2004) 128 overreads Socrates' chaffing of Hermogenes: the narrative does not bear out the idea that Hermogenes' silence troubles anyone. On the ambiguities of sympotic silence, cf. Kindstrand (1976) 293–4 *ad* Bion Bor. F77, Gray (1992) 62–71 (rather solemn on Xenophon), adding the anecdotes at Plut. *Mor.* 503f–504a. Different is Critobulus' boast, during the beauty contest (4.18), that even in silence he could outdo clever but ugly Socrates in persuading the dancers to kiss him.

[115] 8.3–4 alludes to Hermogenes' previous formulation of his relationship to the gods at 4.46–9. It also, surprisingly, calls Hermogenes' character *hilaros*, which normally denotes cheerfulness (ch. 10 n. 106): if not ironic (the preferable interpretation), the word here probably suggests calmness. For expressive eyebrows, cf. n. 112 above, with Appendix 1, 526–7. On Xenophon's and Plato's different depictions of Hermogenes, see Nails (2002) 162–4.

that the guests are taking too much pleasure in one another (6.6: an echo, ironically, of Socrates' view at 3.2: see 146 above) and not enough interest in the dances he is supplying. He feels resentment specifically towards Socrates, recognising that the latter has himself become the centre of attention, the main 'performance' on the bill.[116] To rile him, he invokes the figure of Socrates in Aristophanes' *Clouds*, asking pointedly: 'Are you the one whose nickname is "the thinker" (*phrontistēs*)?' To Socrates' riposte that this is better than being called 'thoughtless', the Syracusan follows up first with a further allusion to *Clouds*, this time to the motif of studying things 'up in the air' (*meteōra*), and then with a gibe about intellectual 'uselessness'. Having just a moment ago played the role of tongue-in-cheek, well-meaning provoker of Hermogenes, Socrates now finds himself the object of cruder provocation. He is reduced to some frivolous word-play to deal with the Syracusan's insults, apparently admitting that he has been nettled: 'If my jokes are rather flat (ψυχρά), that's your fault for annoying me' (6.7). When the Syracusan threatens to descend into even coarser goading (asking him, with yet another reference to *Clouds*, about measuring the distance a flea could jump), Antisthenes tries to come to Socrates' aid – and, with dramatic irony, by trying to enlist the services of Philippus to retaliate against the Syracusan's abusive mockery. The latter really has blurred the line between acceptable (mutually pleasurable) and unacceptable (insulting) uses of sympotic laughter. Antisthenes' idea is that the jester has the licence to make the Syracusan take some of his own medicine: an idea which, if implemented, could change the whole ethos of the occasion.

But Socrates takes control again, preventing Philippus from engaging in a game of comparisons (*eikazein*) intended here to serve as tit-for-tat abuse.[117] Despite a problem in the text, it becomes clear that Socrates (unlike the more aggressive Antisthenes) wants to ensure that full-blown exchanges of insults (*loidoreisthai*) do not mar the party. Furthermore, when Philippus asks him how in that case he can stay silent yet still earn his place at the dinner, Socrates' rejoinder, 'very easily, if your silence means not saying things that *shouldn't* be said', we are brought back round, but with an overt note of ambiguity, to the theme of silence which Socrates had shortly before employed to have his fun with Hermogenes. Xenophon adds a narrator's

---

116 The Syracusan's resentment involves *phthonos*, 6.6: for its association with laughter, cf. ch. 6 nn. 90, 93. The entrepreneur is not himself a 'guest', *pace* Davidson (2000) 52.

117 On the sympotic game of *eikazein* (framing comic likenesses), including this passage itself, see Monaco (1963) 59–69. It could obviously be played with reciprocal pleasure but might degenerate, as threatened here, into insults. A comically magnified image of the latter is Ar. *Wasps* 1308–21 (n. 42 above); cf. Pütz (2007) 98–9.

comment, 'This then is how the drunken rowdiness (*paroinia*) was quelled' (6.10), which completes the ring-composition that binds together the Hermogenes and Syracusan episodes in the work's sixth chapter. This section has set up a thematic interplay between mock and real *paroinia*, good and bad sympotic silence, shared and one-sided laughter. In addition, it has shown Socrates as both an agent and (in contrast to earlier) an *unwilling* object of ridicule, and it has thereby made him an intensified symbol of the gelastic ambiguities of the symposium itself. With the other symposiasts, Socrates has a dominant but still not completely commanding relationship; he needs hints of laughter, it seems, to smooth out the personal twists and turns he encounters in his dealings with them. But the Syracusan has no established social relationship with Socrates; he is not part of the symposium proper (he is not a reclining guest but a paid purveyor of entertainment) and is on a different footing in every way. When the Syracusan sees Socrates as an obstacle to the attention he needs for his own performers, he resorts to an 'Aristophanic' mode of derision which has its place in the theatre, not in the symposium. Socrates eventually triumphs over this, but not before being a little unsettled.

The tension created by the exchange is not immediately dissipated. A dispute continues at 7.1, amidst an atmosphere of some uproar (*thorubos*), about whether a slanging match between Philippus and the Syracusan should after all be encouraged. As well as underlining how different a symposium might have developed if Socrates were *not* present, this requires further Socratic steps to restore harmony and *charis* (7.5), graceful reciprocity – including even a gesture to assuage the Syracusan (7.2).[118] In the end, a *rapprochement* prevails. But Xenophon has done enough to let his readers sense that the dynamics of Socratic conversation and the dynamics of the symposium have been held together, from the outset in fact, in a very delicate balance. Laughter of more than one kind has played a vital part in making that balance possible, as well as in threatening to destroy it.

---

[118] On sympotic *charis*, cf. n. 27 above.

CHAPTER 4

Ritual laughter and the renewal of life

φιλοπαίσμονες γὰρ καὶ οἱ θεοί.
(The gods too are lovers of play.)

Plato

Gods take delight in mockery: it seems they cannot suppress laughter
even during sacred rites.

Nietzsche[1]

WORSHIPPING THE GODS WITH LAUGHTER

In a bizarre anecdote related by Theophrastus in his lost work *On Comedy*
and preserved in paraphrase by Athenaeus, we are told that the people of
Tiryns in the north-east Peloponnese once suffered from a pathological
addiction to laughter which incapacitated them for the serious business of
life. They consulted the Delphic oracle, which told them they could escape
their affliction by throwing a bull into the sea as a sacrifice to Poseidon, but
on one strict condition: that they did so in an atmosphere free from laughter
(ἀγελαστί). Anxious to adhere to Apollo's instructions, the Tirynthians
took the precaution of excluding children from the sacrificial ritual. But one
child infiltrated the crowd. When caught and rebuked, he asked: 'What's
the matter? Are you afraid I'll upset your bull/bowl?' The Tirynthians burst
into laughter, apparently at an (accidental) pun on two senses of 'upsetting',
i.e. enraging the sacrificial victim and overturning the bowl – a play on the
imagery of wine and animal sacrifice that may also allude to the Tirynthians'
reputation for intoxication. The episode taught the city just how hard if
not impossible it was to be 'cured' of an inveterate habit.[2]

---

[1] Epigraphs: Pl. *Crat.* 406c (for φιλοπαίσμων/-γμων, 'play-loving', see Pl. *Rep.* 5.452e; cf. Ar. *Frogs*
333, 211 below); Nietzsche, *Beyond Good and Evil* 294, Nietzsche (1988) v 236 ('Götter sind spottlustig:
es scheint, sie können selbst bei heiligen Handlungen das Lachen nicht lassen').

[2] Athen. 6.261d–e = Theophr. fr. 124 Wimmer, fr. 709 Fortenbaugh (1992) II 554; the latter notes
the pun on σφάγιον (victim), σφαγεῖον (bowl), but not on ἀνατρέπειν. Cf. Fortenbaugh (2005)

We do not know precisely why Theophrastus recorded this far-fetched fiction, itself a sort of joke with its own 'punchline' (involving the inversion of initial expectations). But for my purposes it has several interesting facets. For one thing, it might be read against the views of laughter espoused by Theophrastus' teacher Aristotle (to be discussed in Chapter 6), who holds appropriate indulgence in laughter to be a context-relative virtue for which, as with all virtues, there are cognate faults of deficiency and excess. The Tirynthians are a paradigm of hypergelotic excess. Their laughter is out of control and interfering with the conduct of their lives: a social magnification, in part, of the familiar experience of being incapacitated by bodily convulsions of laughter. Moreover, that excess amounts to a sort of communal disease (the Tirynthians seek a 'cure' or therapy from Apollo), and we are made aware by other sources, in a tradition as old as Homer, that uncontrollable impulses to laughter can assume pathological proportions, even those of mania.[3] This aspect of the Tirynthians' predicament is, however, only half the story. There seems also to be something (ultimately) affirmative about the role of laughter in the episode. The connection with children is obvious but nevertheless important; it resonates with a long-established nexus between laughter and 'play' in the Greek cultural lexicon. If laughter *qua* play is a healthy element of adult life, the Tirynthians seem unsuccessfully to be trying to stifle the instinctive child in themselves. Perhaps, then, Apollo is showing them that spontaneous laughter is something they need to come to terms with, not simply extirpate. The Tirynthians, in a sense, fail the test set them by Delphi: Apollo's own oracle plays a joke on them, as well as teaching them a lesson. Maybe their 'disease' is not so bad after all.

This inference becomes firmer when we take account of a religious ambiguity that is overlaid on the psychological ambiguity of the narrative. Theophrastus' story poses a religious dilemma: to laugh or not to laugh? It is Delphi, ironically, which lures the Tirynthians into a situation where the second option turns involuntarily into the first. Apollo recommends a laughterless sacrifice, and there is no doubt that some Greek cult activities called for heightened solemnity and ritualised dignity. Laughter, it might

---

364–75, who rightly treats the story as fiction (368), a point on which Parke and Wormell (1956) 1 412 equivocate. The version in Eustath. *Comm. Od.* 11 170 (Stallbaum), paraphrased from Athenaeus, makes the Tirynthians' hypergelotic affliction itself the butt of jokes. The Tirynthians' reputation for inebriation is attested at Ephip. fr. 2 *PCG*, *apud* Athen. 10.442d, Ael. *VH* 3.15; cf. the pun on blood/wine in Ar. *Thesm.* 689–759 (with σφαγεῖον, 754), *Lys.* 188–205. Various links between Poseidon and bulls: ps.-Hes. *Scutum* 104, Eur. *Hipp.* 1214–48, Athen. 10.425c.

[3] Laughter and disease/madness: ch. 1, 16–18, ch. 2, 93–6. The physical convulsiveness of laughter: ch. 1, 8–10.

be thought, is too disruptive, too hard to control, and too irreverent to be admitted to such settings, not least where a god as stern as Poseidon is concerned.[4] Yet the Tirynthian boy's (seemingly innocent) question can be decoded as asking whether it could really be such a bad thing to laugh when worshipping a god. And the question is pertinent. There was in fact no general incompatibility between religion and laughter for pagan Greeks. On the contrary, festivity (the enactment of *heortai*) is the prime framework of Greek cult and is regularly pictured as a suitable occasion for laughter, both as accompaniment to the enjoyment of life-enhancing goods (such as wine, meat, music, sex) and as emblem of the communal well-being which worship of the gods was designed to solicit and celebrate.[5]

But we can go further than this. If laughter was a general characteristic of Greek festivity (though also, apparently, a threat to some kinds of religious solemnity), it could also be turned into an active feature of ritual practice. 'Ritual laughter', in this more concrete sense, can be provisionally described as a family of practices in which laughter not only arises inside a context of religious ceremonial but appears to be invited and expected at certain junctures, thus becoming a constitutive component of the prescribed

---

[4] See laughter's incompatibility with ritual solemnity at Ar. *Clouds* 296–7 (*euphēmia*: n. 133 below), *Frogs* 357–8 (212 below); cf. the repulsive man's laughter, Theophr. *Char.* 19.9, and the paradox at Callim. *Aitia* fr. 7.19–20 Pfeiffer (**F8** in my text). Poseidon's aptness for laughterless worship might echo Homer *Od.* 8.344, where he declines to laugh (ch. 2, 82–5). Was he generally thought a 'severe' deity? Cf. the skit on his aloofness at Ar. *Birds* 1565–1693. For a different laughterless ritual (descent into Trophonius' subterranean oracle), see Paus. 9.39.13, with ch. 7 n. 89; Propp (1984) 128–31 adduces interdictions on laughter in death-like initiation rituals in other cultures. At the opposite extreme, some Greeks had no qualms about mocking religious practices themselves: *IG* IV² i.121.24–5 (ὑποδιασύρειν, 'sneer slyly': hapax), 34–7, 74–6 (reading ἐγέλαν at 74? cf. Buck (1955) 293) depicts sceptical derision of healing claims at Epidaurus (in the late fourth century) even within Asclepius' shrine; cf. Herzog (1931) 125–6 on the motifs involved, with Rhodes and Osborne (2003) 532–42 for recent text and commentary. Cf. the 'manic laughter' of atheists at Plut. *Mor.* 169d.

As regards laughter's ambiguity *vis-à-vis* religion, note Burkert (1996) 7 ('Religion is serious; hence it is vulnerable to laughter and derision'), with 189 n. 27 ('This does not exclude laughter . . .from . . . a place within a religious system'). Cf. Burkert (1985) 105, Parker (1983) 78–9 on contrasts of ritual tone; Radermacher (1947) 61 sees serio-comic tension at the core of Greek cult. Ar. *Clouds* 623 ('you pour libations and laugh', σπένδεθ' ὑμεῖς καὶ γελᾶτε) expresses a fusion of worship and mirth; Plut. *Mor.* 369e (n. 130 below) implicitly confirms the point. Festivity (*heortē* etc.) is a nodal point in this area: cf. nn. 5, 138 below, with Mikalson (1982), esp. 215–18; note the verb παίζειν, 'play', of celebrating a festival at Hdt. 9.11. Generalised polarities between religion and laughter, e.g. Kundera (1995) 9, (2007) 107–8, Saroglou (2002), are *a priori* and historically uninformed; a partial corrective is Gilhus (1997). Hesych. *s.v.* Σαρδόνιος γέλως pictures primeval Sardinians requiring laughter during sacrifices to Cronus. Even clubs of jesters could meet at a temple: see ch. 1 n. 105.

[5] Festive worship may please the gods themselves even to the point of laughter: see e.g. Hom. *Hymn* 2.202–5 (with 162–4 below), Pind. *Pyth.* 10.36 (with Fisher (1992) 232–3), Ar. *Thesm.* 977–80, Callim. *Hymn Delos* 323–4 (with 169 below), Theoc. 7.156–7, Archias, *Anth. Pal.* 9.91, Philostr. maj. *Imag.* 2.24.4 (cf. n. 101 below), Lucian, *Bis Acc.* 10. Cf. Connor (1996) 84–7 on the shared 'happiness' of gods and men in Athenian festival culture.

proceedings, a ritual event or item in its own right.[6] The attested practices
which fit this description involve not just a broad ambience of public merriment (though that may be a typical backdrop) but 'scheduled' opportunities
for *performances* of ridicule by/of individuals or groups, and usually ridicule
marked by obtrusively 'shameful' language, aischrology (*aischrologia*), or by
equivalently indecent actions and objects. Since a strong sense of taboo-
flouting or shame-breaking behaviour attaches to such performances, it is
justifiable to speak cautiously of licensed 'obscenity' in this connection. In
using this term, however, one's point of reference must always be the standards of discursive propriety belonging to the communities in question,
not a sensibility borrowed from other times or places.[7]

Comparative anthropological evidence suggests that many pre-modern
cultures possessed opportunities for ritualised laughter that are generically
analogous to those attested for ancient Greece. This evidence has often
encouraged the production of totalising theories of the motivations for
such behaviour.[8] But stimulating though comparative perspectives can be,
they will remain at the margins of the present enterprise; I shall say just
a little more about them at a later stage of my argument. My approach
here will emphasise cultural specificity; I shall contextualise the relevant
material closely in relation to the schemata of Greek religion and society.
Everything about the interpretation of ritual laughter calls for analysis of
'locally' defined expectations and sensitivities. A thought-provoking illustration of this – a paradox from the *outside* – is the fact that while the
Eleusinian Mysteries in classical Athens made provision for multiple 'official' moments of ritualised scurrility (see **F1** below) and associated these with
Demeter's own delight at being (sexually) mocked by an old slave woman
(Iambe), parodies of the Mysteries carried out by private drinking-clubs
could be judged not only scandalously irreligious but politically subversive and could lead, at least in the highly charged circumstances of 415, to
judicial sentences of execution and exile.[9] How, when and where laughter can become acceptably ritualised is always a delicate matter of cultural
negotiation and potential conflict.

---

[6] Ancient Greek lacks a unitary term for 'ritual'; cf. Calame (1991), esp. 196–204, Parker (2005) 369–79.
   But several Greek words (including *hiera*, *orgia*, and *teletē*) are pertinent. Hdt. 5.83 twice applies
   hirourgia to one of my cases of 'ritual laughter' (**F7** below).
[7] See ch. 5, esp. 219–25, for 'obscenity' in relation to Greek *aischrologia*.
[8] Apte (1985) 151–76 offers a cross-cultural overview of religious laughter: stressing social structures and
   functions, he passes over older fertility and apotropaic models of explanation (see 196–202 below).
[9] Thuc. 6.28 reports the denouncers of the parodied Mysteries in 415 as alleging acts of scandalous,
   mocking offensiveness, *hubris*: see ch. 1 n. 95.

Because much of the evidence for ritual laughter remains vexingly skimpy (though fortunately there is a sufficient concentration from classical Athens to anchor the enquiry), I will set it out systematically before attempting to identify salient patterns and values that may help to clarify the functions of laughter within ritual settings. As a preliminary to the catalogue of evidence, however, I want to ask whether Greek culture itself possessed anything like a *concept* of ritual laughter. I submit that it did, and in support of this claim I adduce five primary witnesses, all of whose testimonies will recur in the course of the chapter. The first is Plato *Laws* 1.637a–b (see **F6a** below), which attests to a sense of institutionalised aischrology within Dionysiac festivals. The passage draws attention to variations in tolerance of such practices in different areas of the Greek world, but it leaves no doubt that a connection between certain festivities and stylised exhibitions of scurrility could be actively perceived in the classical period. A similar inference is warranted by a passage of Aristotle's *Politics* Book 7 where the philosopher expects his hearers to recognise a class of religious occasions ('in the worship of certain gods') which make special provision for 'mockery' or 'raillery', *tōthasmos*, a term which here carries clear connotations of (sexual) indecency.[10] Not only does Aristotle himself grant a privileged status to these occasions, exempting them from the full force of his strictures against indecent words and images. He also links this exemption to an existing cultural tradition or unwritten law (*nomos*). Much patchier is the evidence of Callimachus, *Aitia* fr. 21.9–10 Pfeiffer (23 Massimilla); see **F1c**, with **F8** and **F9** below. But despite the considerable textual obscurity of these fragments we can make out that the poet juxtaposes three cults from different locations, and in honour of three different gods, in which mockery or scurrility of some kind played an acknowledged role: whatever else Callimachus is doing here, the spotlighting of a shared or cognate religious feature is an inescapable inference. In the imperial period, we find two passages of Plutarch (but drawing on the early Academic philosopher Xenocrates) which indicate awareness of a 'family resemblance' between certain ritual and cultic practices. In one there is reference to festivals which contain 'foul utterances or shameful speech' (δυσφημίας ἢ αἰσχρολογίαν), in the other to an idea of 'aischrology in sacred places' (αἰσχρολογίαι πρὸς ἱεροῖς), which is said to occur 'in many places' though some doubt remains about

---

[10] *Pol.* 7.17, 1336b16–19; see further under **F1b** below. Aristotle apparently supposes that only *males* will take part in such rituals (1336b19); he disregards various rites of Demeter (**F1–5** in my text) in which women participated: the focus of his larger argument is on the education of males. Simpson (1998) 249 mistakenly connects Aristotle's views on such practices to religious 'awe'.

exactly which cults are encompassed by these remarks.[11] Finally, a section of the Neoplatonist Iamblichus' treatise *On Mysteries*, from the third or early fourth century AD, speaks of the (otherwise) shameful things which it may be beneficial to see or hear within 'protected' religious contexts, including phallic rites. He offers a pair of explanations for such rituals: one involves symbolism (the phallus as emblem of fertility), the other a psychological *katharsis* of desires and emotions that might lead to harmfully equivalent behaviour in real life.[12] Leaving aside for now the dynamics of Iamblichus' own theory, what matters for my immediate purposes is the continuing recognition of a type of ritual setting within which markedly laughter-related behaviour – especially obscenity and/or mockery – can be engaged in and (somehow) *celebrated* on different terms from those which normally apply elsewhere.

The five texts cited above cover a span of more than six centuries. Their authors' vantage points stretch from classical Athens, via Callimachus' Hellenistic Alexandria and Plutarch's Greece under Roman rule, to the eastern Mediterranean of late antiquity in which Iamblichus moved. More could (and will) be said about the standpoints of the individual texts. But their wide separation in time and place lends weight to my contention that Greek culture was consistently familiar with configurations of ritual behaviour in which laughter had a charged significance in its own right. How much more than that one can legitimately claim for ancient perceptions or under-standing(s) of 'ritual laughter' will emerge only from the detailed scrutiny of evidence to which I now proceed.

A MAP OF RITUAL LAUGHTER

The following catalogue is organised according to individual festivals or cults. In each case, material is ordered for the most part in chronological sequence. Other evidence that does not specify particular occasions is incorporated where most appropriate.[13] I have not included a number of

---

[11] Plut. *Mor.* 361b, 417c, with 199–201 below.

[12] *De myst.* 1.11 (incorporating Heraclitus fr. 68 DK, of doubtful status), which some think reflects an Aristotelian concept of *katharsis*: see Arist. *Poet.* fr. V in Kassel (1965) 52, with Sorabji (2000) 286–7, Adoménas (1999) 91–2; cf. ch. 6 n. 169. On Iamblichus' explanations cf. 197–8 below; note Dillon (2002) 324 n. 5 for a modern assumption that aischrology is kathartic. For male genitals as a religious 'symbol' (*xumbolon*), cf. Aretaeus, *De causis* 2.12.1 (on priapic depictions of satyrs).

[13] This is preferable to lumping together many cases under the heading of *tōthasmos* (cf. 167–8 below), as does Fluck (1931) 11–33; cf. criticism in Deubner (1932) 267. I have benefited from Fluck's spadework, but his analysis is now dated.

cults for which a claim of ritual laughter is circumstantial or tenuous.[14] Readers may find it useful to refer to the chart on 192 for orientation.

F1 The Eleusinian Mysteries

It is beyond doubt that elements of ritual laughter were embedded in the Eleusinian Mysteries, held annually in honour of Demeter and Kore (Persephone) and under the control (from around 600) of Athens.[15] Five main pieces of evidence call for consideration in this section; between them, they support the thesis that ritual laughter was integrated into more than one segment of the festival. I leave on one side for now what appears to be a diffuse reflection of this aspect of the Mysteries in the initiates' parodos of Aristophanes' *Frogs*. The dramatic intricacy of that passage is best addressed within a wider perspective, which I shall present later in the chapter, on Old Comedy's internalisation of ritual laughter.

F1a

A famous episode in the *Homeric Hymn to Demeter* (dating from around 600), and retold in several later texts, provides a mythological *aition* for ritual ribaldry within the Mysteries. After Demeter, disguised as an old woman, has wandered the earth in self-imposed exile from the other gods,

---

[14] I have not included the following festivals/cults.

(1) The Adonia. See Winkler (1990) 189–93; cf. McClure (1999) 216, O'Higgins (2003) 31–2, 161–2. Despite *paidia*, 'play', at Men. *Sam.* 41, and the sexual joking in Diphil. fr. 49, female mirth here looks circumstantial, not religiously formalised; compare all-night female festivities at the Tauropolia, Men. *Epitr.* 473–7. *Contra* Burton (1995) 200–1 n. 51, there is no link between Theoc. 15.87–8, set during the Adonia in Alexandria, and ritual laughter. Cf. n. 117 below.

(2) The Argive Hubristika, said by Plut. *Mor.* 245e–f (= Socrates Arg. *FGrH* 310 F6) to involve transvestism, but for which no ritual mockery is attested. Halliday (1909–10) links transvestism with *rites de passage*; cf. Graf (1984) 246–54 for more caution. The festival's name need not evoke mocking abusiveness; cf. Fisher (1992) 118 with n. 232. The claims of Stehle (1997) 113, O'Higgins (2003) 15–16 outrun the evidence.

(3) The Kronia. It involved merrymaking by slaves (Plut. *Mor.* 1098b, Lucian, *Sat.* 13), but there is no evidence for ritually formalised scurrility. Julian *Symposium* (in which Silenus repeatedly makes jokes at emperors) is largely coloured by sympotic humour; cf. Sardiello (2000) 84–6 on the opening of the work. Versnel (1993) 89–135 reviews the festival, esp. 115–21 on 'the festival of reversal'.

(4) The mystery cults of the Kabeiroi at Lemnos and Thebes. See e.g. Guthrie (1952) 123–5, Burkert (1985) 281–2. There are various but elusive hints of ritual 'play' in this context: cf. n. 95 below, with Appendix 2 n. 52; see ch. 1 n. 45 for a restored inscription.

(5) The Boeotian Daedala, in honour of Hera goddess of marriage. It is unclear, *pace* Reinach (1911) 586–7, whether a priestess symbolically reenacted Hera's laughter (at discovering Zeus's deception of her) in the aetiological myth at Plut. fr. 157.6 in Sandbach (1969) 282–95; cf. Morris (1992) 54–8.

[15] The claim of Henderson (1991) 16 that 'the Eleusinian mysteries included no obscenity or ritual abuse' is misleading; it refers only to the core moments of initiation (about which, in any case, we know little).

mourning the loss of her daughter Persephone, her state of mind is eventually transformed at Eleusis (shortly after she has given her hosts a first glimpse of her divinity) by the scurrility of Celeus' old servant Iambe:

ἀλλ᾿ ἀγέλαστος ἄπαστος ἐδητύος ἠδὲ ποτῆτος
ἧστο πόθῳ μινύθουσα βαθυζώνοιο θυγατρός,
πρίν γ᾿ ὅτε δὴ χλεύῃς μιν Ἰάμβη κέδν᾿ εἰδυῖα
πολλὰ παρὰ σκώπτουσ᾿ ἐτρέψατο πότνιαν ἁγνὴν
μειδῆσαι γελάσαι τε καὶ ἵλαον σχεῖν θυμόν·
ἡ δή οἱ καὶ ἔπειτα μεθύστερον εὔαδεν ὀργαῖς. (200–5)[16]

Averse to laughter, and refusing food and drink,
Demeter sat wasting with longing for her deep-girded daughter –
Until the moment when shrewd Iambe resorted to mocking her
And with many jests moved the sacred mistress
To smile, to laugh and to lift her spirits in benevolence.
Thereafter, indeed, Iambe was pleasing to the goddess in spirit.

The direct link to Demeter's cult signalled by line 205 has been taken by some scholars to refer not to Eleusinian scurrility but to ritual mockery by women in another Demeter festival, the Thesmophoria.[17] It is true that Iambe is sometimes elsewhere linked to the Thesmophoria (see **F3**), and her quasi-personificatory identity may, for sure, have a larger resonance for ritual laughter within Demeter cults. But it is no objection to the *prima facie* Eleusinian reading that Iambe makes Demeter laugh at a point in the story which has no precise correlate (so far as we know) within the sequence of ritual events adumbrated by the larger narrative of the hymn. The myth as told here need not have a one-to-one match with the Mysteries at every point; the hymn is a creative reworking of Demeter's story and an oblique view of elements in her cult, not a simple programme of the Mysteries. In any case, the Eleusinian Mysteries seem to have involved multiple opportunities for scurrility, as items **F1b–e** will demonstrate. As some of these

[16] See Richardson (1974) 219–24, Foley (1994) 45–6, Brown (1997) 16–21 for details; cf n. 19 below. Other versions of the Iambe story include Philochorus *FGrH* 328 F103 (see Jacoby's comm. *ad loc.*), Philicus, *Hymn Cer.* 54–62 (*SH* no. 680; transl. in Page (1941) 402–7), Nicander, *Alex.* 128–32, ps.-Apollod. *Bibl.* 1.5.1 (cf. **F3** in text), Σ on Eur. *Or.* 964; cf. Brown (1997) 21–4. For the male figure Ascalabus or Ambas, a mythological warning against *mistimed* Eleusinian laughter, see Richardson (1974) 215.

[17] The Thesmophorian reading is developed by Clinton (1992) 28–37, 96–9, superseding Clinton (1986); Foley (1994) 172–5 puts some objections. Clinton wrongly claims that *gephurismos* was the only Eleusinian form of aischrology: he ignores *Wasps* 1362–3 (**F1b**) and the implications (for multiple scurrility) of the parodos of *Frogs* (which he does take to reflect the Mysteries); he also places too much weight on ps.-Apollod. 1.5.1 (**F3a**). Clinton is followed by O'Higgins (2003) 57 (cf. 42), whose claim (53) that Iambe was invented by the author(s) of the Hymn is unsupported, and Suter (2002) 6–7, 146. Cf. Parker (2005) 274 n. 19.

occurred at junctures, including the procession from Athens to Eleusis, preliminary to the main procedures of initiation (a 'chronological' point at least compatible with the hymn's narrative), there is no need to treat Iambe's behaviour as anomalous or in the wrong place. See **F1b** below for a further possibility.

Iambe is a lowly yet shrewd figure, seemingly marginal to the situation yet capable of intervening decisively. It is as though she intuitively knows how to tap the hidden spring of Demeter's life-force. Her narrative profile makes her symbolise an instinctive, 'earthy' but transformative power of laughter. Her name renders her an implicit personification of the activity of *iambizein*, to hurl/exchange coarse abuse (in a festive custom or competition).[18] In other contexts she is explicitly the eponym of iambic poetry, *iambos*, and her description in the hymn is redolent of the performative freedom of the genre, as well as its life-affirming energies: consider here the sentiment of a grieving voice, 'I have no care for *iamboi* or for joys', in Archilochus 215 *IEG*. The hymn's combination of the noun *chleuē* (202, cf. **F1c** below) and the verb *skōptein* (203) suggests vigorous jeering, though both words are compatible with a range of intentions from the aggressive to the spiritedly jocular (as here, given the demands of the situation and Demeter's response).[19] Furthermore, while the goddess herself is ostensibly targeted by the servant's mockery, which is probably to be understood as sexual in character (though it is left, intrinsically, to the imagination),[20] it does not follow that Demeter is thought of as an object of mockery within her own cult, nor that the all-female situation in the story must match a specific cultic context: once again, narrative and ritual need not be in step-for-step correspondence in every respect.

The passage associates laughter emphatically with one side of a great polarity between life-promoting and life-denying forces, linking it with the

---

[18] Does Iambe's (later) genealogy as daughter of Echo (Σ^B Eur. *Or.* 964, *Etym. Magn. s.v.* Ἰάμβη) encode a link with amoebean, tit-for-tat (games of) abuse (cf. n. 116 below)? Mockery is associated with Echo herself at Ar. *Thesm.* 1059: cf. Austin and Olson (2004) 322, who miss the force of 'crowing' (ch. 1 n. 89).

[19] On *skōptein* (and cognates) see ch. 1 n. 41. At 203, it is uncertain whether we should read παρασκώπτειν or treat παρά as a preverb with ἐτρέψατο: see Richardson (1974) 222, but his claim that the compound first occurs in Plutarch is wrong; cf. Men. *Phasma* 90 (Arnott), with ch. 8 n. 31. Foley (1994) 45 is inconsistent with her Greek text (13).

[20] That Iambe makes Demeter herself a target is inferred by e.g. Brown (1997) 20–1, O'Higgins (2003) 44. On the sexual subtext see Arthur (1977) 21–2 (= Foley (1994) 229–30), Clay (1989) 234–5, O'Higgins (2003) 43–5; Lincoln (1991) 80–1 focuses on sexual initiation, but the context hardly encourages this. Given the lack of direct speech, one cannot detect 'euphemism' on Iambe's part, Foley (1994) 46. The *chleu-* wordgroup is compatible with sexually coarse laughter; cf. e.g. Aeschrion, *Anth. Pal.* 7.345.4 (with Gow and Page (1965) II 3–5), ch. 1 n. 86. Rosen (2007) 47–57 reads the Iambe episode as emblematic of 'poeticised' mockery.

idea of both bodily and mental well-being.[21] Before Iambe acts, Demeter's agelastic state is placed on a par with her refusal of food and drink (200), as though laughter itself is an indispensable need of life. Lines 203–4 are shaped so as to convey a sense of laughter welling or surging up involuntarily from Demeter. Her mood starts to turn, she smiles, and then laughter itself breaks out with full pleasure; Iambe has overcome the goddess's death-centred resistance. The moment transmits an impression of the *body's* restorative powers, previously blocked by Demeter's grief, with which, in normal circumstances, an attempt to make jokes would be jarringly incompatible.[22] Iambe activates a laughter of reinvigoration and renewal, a laughter related to the polarity (and cycle) of life and death, both human and agricultural, which underpins experience of the Mysteries. The power of this allegory is strengthened by the fact that Iambe arouses a gelastic response which exceeds her own powers of jesting. Expressive of divine beneficence, the goddess's reaction is evocative of a more-than-human restorative strength and therefore aptly perpetuates itself in the subsequent history of her cult (205).[23] But there is an important rider. It is Iambe's mirth which triggers Demeter's laughter: a human act instigates the process, impinges on the divine, and is answered with a propitiousness that will translate itself into benefits for humankind in general. In other words, laughter *binds* the human (*qua* worshipper) and the divine (*qua* bestower of fertility and prosperity), but it is not itself a gift from the gods. Divine laughter, on this religious model, is intelligible from, and even mirrors, a human perspective. This stands in contrast to various 'esoteric' ideas and images encountered later in antiquity (in gnostic, Hermetic, and some Neoplatonic texts) of divine *gelōs* as a primordial, world-creating force whose workings transcend the human plane.[24]

---

[21] Cf. the 'laughter' of sky, earth and sea (13–14), a positive life-force suffusing the world (though about to be shattered): see ch. 1, 13–16. In some versions, Demeter sat at the 'Laughterless Rock', Ἀγέλαστος πέτρα: see Richardson (1974) 219–21, Clinton (1992) 14–27; cf. ch. 7 n. 89. Even where Iambe is left out of the story, Demeter's life-restoring laughter survives: Eur. *Helen* 1349. Later references include Julianus, *Anth. Pal.* 7.58 (ch. 7, 370). Cf. Demeter's laughter (*not* 'smiling', e.g. Crane (1987) 166) as harvest goddess, Theoc. 7.156. For cross-cultural parallels, see Fehrle (1930) 1–2, di Nola (1974) 68–90, Richardson (1974) 216–17, Gilhus (1997) 19, 35, with Karle (1932/3) 868–74, Propp (1984) 131–46 for laughter's life-creating powers.

[22] Cf. the proverb 'to jest among mourners' at Demetr. *Eloc.* 28 (ch. 6 n. 41). Iambe promises release from grief in Philicus, *Hymn Cer.* 62 (*SH* no. 680), where laughter is also a 'benefit', *kerdos* (*ibid.* 58, cf. 55, the latter misconstrued by Page (1941) 404). Usener (1913) thinks the Iambe episode reflects ritual joking at funerals; for Roman examples cf. Versnel (1970) 99–100.

[23] But one should not call Iambe's joking 'magic(al)', O'Higgins (2003) 43, 52, 64 (eliding the jesting with Demeter's later treatment of Demophon, cf. 50). For beneficent divine smiles, see the adj. *eumeidēs* at Callim. *Hymn Art.* 129, Ap. Rhod. *Argon.* 4.715.

[24] See ch. 1, 12–13. Note esp. Procl. *In Remp.* 1 128 (Kroll), interpreting mystery religion through a Neoplatonic symbolism of divine laughter.

Sometimes interchangeable with Iambe, so to speak, is Baubo, a figure with a tangled presence in both mythology and cult. Baubo does not appear in any known telling of the Eleusinian story of Demeter before the fourth century BC, but we cannot rule out older versions. Vexed questions can be circumvented here. My only concern is with the genital self-exposure (*anasurmos*, lit. 'lifting the dress') by which, in some accounts of Baubo's Eleusinian entertainment of Demeter, she has the same effect on the goddess as Iambe does with mockery and jesting.[25] Here it may be legitimate to see a primary aetiological connection with the Haloa (**F2** below) and/or, as several scholars have proposed (following an ancient lead), the Thesmophoria (**F3**), since in both those festivals models of the vulva are said to have played a ritual role, something not attested for Eleusinian practice. Baubo's obscene gesture, which recurs in other contexts (see **F13**) and in some sources is also ascribed to Iambe herself, has frequently been interpreted as either apotropaic or fertility-promoting in function, categories of explanation to which I shall return at a later stage. It should be noticed, however, that other ancient occurrences of the gesture seem primarily to denote an insult or an attempt to shame the beholder; that indeed is the motive ascribed to Baubo in Clement's summary of the story, even though the *result* is delight on Demeter's part.[26] Just how far we can trust the report or interpretation of a hostile Christian like Clement is debatable. But it is at least of interest that his version foregrounds an incongruity – between ostensible offensiveness and the recipient's pleasure – which may capture the paradoxical spirit of 'ritual laughter' as a form of licensed indecency incorporated in acts of worship. It looks as though different tellings of the Iambe/Baubo narrative might inflect the psychological intentions of the woman involved in more than one way. Yet the consequence was always the same: the jolting of Demeter out of grief into life-affirming joy. Some versions gave that jolt a more overtly sexual significance than others. But

---

[25] The main references to Baubo's *anasurmos* (not *anasurma*, a non-existent form) are Clem. *Protr.* 2.20.2–21.2 (cf. Euseb. *Praep. Ev.* 2.3.30–5), Arnobius, *Adv. Nat.* 5.25–6, giving discrepant versions of *Orphica* fr. 52 Kern; cf. Marcovich (1988) 20–7. Other references in Guthrie (1952) 136–7, Headlam (1922) 288–9; discussion in Olender (1990), Graf (1974) 166–71, 194–9, di Nola (1974) 19–53, Richardson (1974) 80–2, Furth (1975), Rosen (2007) 49–51. Cf. O'Higgins (2003) 51–3, with Karaghiorga-Stathacopoulou (1986) for Baubo(-related) images, and Johns (1982) 72–5 for the vulva as apotropaic symbol. Cf. Appendix 2 n. 5.

[26] For Clement, see n. 25 above. Apart from the Egyptian *anasurmos* at Hdt. 2.60.2 (**F13** below), combined with verbal mockery (*tōthazein*), see the gesture at Plut. *Mor.* 241b, 246a (cf. 248b), where Spartan/Persian women wish to shame their cowardly menfolk; cf. its use (as insult, in a dream) at Artemid. *Oneir.* 4.44 and, possibly, Ar. *Eccl.* 890 (n. 115 below). We have no context for ἀνασυρτόλις, 'a woman who lifts her dress', in Hipponax 135a *IEG*. Cf. Eibl-Eibesfeldt (1989) 316–17 for a modern example (from a Kalahari tribe) of female genital self-exposure as mockery. See King (1986) 60–8 for further discussion.

all relied on the implicit power of laughter, welling up from the body (both human and divine) and transforming the mood of the situation.

F1b

At Aristophanes *Wasps* 1360, the old but comically rejuvenated Philocleon, who has been trying (with some phallic byplay) to convince a pipe-girl he abducted from a symposium that he has the youthful sexual energy to keep her as his mistress (*pallakē*), sees his son Bdelucleon approaching. He hurriedly gives the girl the following instructions:

> ἀλλ᾽ ὡς τάχιστα στῆθι τάσδε τὰς δετὰς
> λαβοῦσ᾽, ἵν᾽ αὐτὸν τωθάσω νεανικῶς,
> οἵοις ποθ᾽ οὗτος ἐμὲ πρὸ τῶν μυστηρίων.
>
> (1361–3)

Quickly, hold this torch. Stand over here
So I can give him some filthy abuse, in a young man's style,
The way he once did to me before the Mysteries.

The passage not only fixes an Eleusinian reference point. It also appears to entail a (distorted) case of a 'joking relationship' (*parenté à plaisanteries*) between kinsmen, a phenomenon quite widely found in other cultures but rarely attested in ancient Greece.[27] The only other clear intra-familial case I know of is part of Dicaeopolis' phallic procession, prior to his phallic song, at Aristophanes, *Acharnians* 254–6 (cf. **F6c** below): since it could be doubted whether an Athenian father would engage in risqué teasing of his daughter in the midst of a public procession, we might wonder whether *Acharnians* echoes the kind of banter that might take place *within* family gatherings at the Rural Dionysia. The comic inversions (and confusions) of father/son roles in Philocleon's speech at *Wasps* 1341–63 make it hard to be sure whether in the sort of Eleusinian context to which 1362–3 alludes it would be father mocking son or *vice versa* (or, conceivably, both). But the former is more plausible on the general grounds that mockery would be more likely aimed at *new* initiands (and a father would be more likely, though not certain, to be initiated before his son).[28]

---

[27] On the anthropological category of 'joking relationships', see Apte (1985) 29–66 (cf. Apte (1996) 619–20): interestingly for the *Wasps* passage, he points out that close family members are not normally involved, *except* in rites of passage (37–8, 162). Cf. Radcliffe-Brown (1952) 90–116, Palmer (1994) 11–23. On Philocleon acting *neanikōs*, 'like a headstrong young man', see ch. 1, 23–4.

[28] See MacDowell (1971) 309; the reference to 'frightening' initiands in Σ on *Wasps* 1363 is misplaced. The familial specificity envisaged by Philocleon is more than a 'general reference' to Eleusinian aischrology, Richardson (1974) 215. How and Wells (1928) II 47 bizarrely cite the passage for 'choruses of men at the feasts of Dionysus'! See further at 208–11 below.

In trying to narrow down the context further, we have little to go on other than the chronological marker (and the suggestion, probably, of preparation for initiation) in the phrase 'before the Mysteries'. This could denote an event either prior to the festival proper or at some point after arrival at Eleusis (perhaps during the all-night celebration, *pannuchis*) but before the epoptic rites as such. We cannot even altogether rule out a link with the Lesser Mysteries, held at Agrai and serving (by the early fifth century) as a preparatory stage for the Greater Mysteries themselves. It is unlikely, however, that *Wasps* 1363 is an allusion to *gephurismos*; the mention of a prostitute in one of Hesychius' references to the latter (**F1d** below) provides an insecure basis for the link.[29] Although we cannot discount the idea of a privately organised family occasion within, or related to, the celebration of the Mysteries, an alternative is to posit a link to the purificatory ceremony of ritual 'enthronement', *thronōsis*. One consideration here is that the scurrility of Iambe at *Hom. Hymn Dem.* 202–5 (**F1a** above) follows immediately on from, and breaks the solemnity of, the silent, veiled seating of Demeter (192–201), which is itself a mythological *aition* for the ceremonial *thronōsis* or *thronismos* of the initiand.[30] *Thronōsis*, moreover, sometimes involved torches, and the torch at *Wasps* 1361 is a further visual signal of Eleusinian proceedings, though, again, not one that suits *gephurismos*.[31] We shall see later on (**F11**) that *thronōsis* in other cults than the Mysteries certainly sometimes involved ritual mockery. As it happens, anthropologists have noted an association between joking rituals and rites of purification in a number of cultures.[32]

Whatever its exact force, the ritual allusion in this passage of *Wasps* is reinforced by the verb *tōthazein*, which Herodotus 2.60.2 (**F13**) uses to describe the jeering and obscene gestures of Egyptian women during the festival of 'Artemis' (Bastet). Aristotle *Pol.* 7.17, 1336b17, already mentioned (159 above), similarly employs the noun *tōthasmos* in mentioning the types of scurrility allowed by law and tradition (*nomos*) in the worship of certain

---

[29] Rusten (1977) 159–60 connects *Wasps* 1363 with *gephurismos*; cf. scepticism in Parker (2005) 349 n. 96. Rusten follows Burkert (1972) 314–15 [= Burkert (1983) 278, a jumble of ideas] in stressing the 'prostitute' link. He also claims (161), wrongly, that nudity was part of all cultic *tōthasmos*.

[30] For *thronōsis* in various initiatory contexts, including Eleusis, see Burkert (1983) 266–8 (including the suggestion, 268 with n. 16, of parody at Ar. *Clouds* 254–73), with Pl. *Euthd.* 277d–e (**F11** below), Dio Chrys. 12.33. But Edmonds (2006) maintains a sharp distinction between Eleusinian and Corybantic practices; cf. n. 103 below.

[31] Torches and Eleusis: e.g. Richardson (1974) 215, with 165–8; Demeter is often depicted holding a torch, of course, as in the E frieze of the Parthenon; so too sometimes is Persephone. Is the pipe-girl, *abducted* from the symposium (*Wasps* 1369), a kind of ersatz Persephone?

[32] See Douglas (1975) 107–8, citing further literature.

deities; the context in the *Politics* carries connotations of sexual indecency.[33] While *tōthazein* and cognates have more general applications, their classical usage normally refers to at least semi-ritualised taunting: at *Wasps* 1362 the word denotes a crude speech-act, rather than a deceptive ploy, as confirmed by the sequel at lines 1364–70 (to which I shall return in the last section of the chapter).[34] A vital nuance of the *tōthasmos* word-group is conveyed by Aristotle *Rhet.* 2.4, 1381a34, which states that people desire as friends those who have a witty facility for both giving and taking *tōthasmos* (οἱ ἐπιδέξιοι καὶ τῷ τωθάσαι καὶ τῷ ὑπομεῖναι).[35] In other words, *tōthazein* is a kind of mockery and teasing recognisable as something other than aggressive abuse; it has a culturally demarcated *raison d'être* – whether within social friendship or religious ritual – that requires participants (both 'subjects' and 'objects') to accept its privileged character. This explains how Aristotle can speak of widespread approval for people who know the rightful place of *tōthasmos*; he could never have made the same point about a term such as *loidoria* (wrangling abusiveness), whose force is always pejorative. In tune with this mentality is the fragment of the early Hellenistic poet Alexander Aetolus in which Euripides is described as 'laughter-hating' (*misogelōs*) and 'someone who has not learnt how to engage in banter (*tōthazein*) even at a drinking-party'.[36]

F1c

Part of the first book of Callimachus' *Aitia* was devoted to the origins of two specimens of ritual laughter, one in the cult of Apollo Aigletes on the island of Anaphe (**F8** below), the other in that of Heracles at Lindos on Rhodes (**F9**). In tracing the former back to an incident between the Argonauts and the Scherian maidservants of Medea, Callimachus apparently compared the mockery on that occasion with a feature of the Eleusinian worship of Demeter ('Deo [i.e. Demeter] Rarias', named after the plain of Rarion at Eleusis).[37] Two significant details can be picked out with confidence from

---

[33] Cf. Semus of Delos *FGrH* 396 F24 (under **F6c**), with reference to the *phallophoroi*.

[34] MacDowell (1971), on Ar. *Wasps* 1362–3, Henderson (1998a) 393 (translating *Wasps* 1362, 1368) take *tōthazein* here to denote trickery or 'leg-pulling', not ridicule; cf. Rusten (1977) 157 n. 1 for criticism, with n. 149 below. The two things may easily blend (cf. n. 106 below), but usage shows that the sense of verbal mockery is basic; see Cope (1877) II 49–50. Cf. the combination of *tōthasmos* and laughter in Troglodyte burial ritual at Agatharch. *Mar. Eryth.* 63 (*apud* Phot. *Bibl.* 250; cf. Diod. Sic. 33.3, Strabo 16.4.17). Passages like Theoc. 16.9, Hdas. 7.103 suggest *tōthazein* could cover malicious denigration; but the link with (ritualised) joking is more common.

[35] See ch. 6, 308.

[36] Alex. Aet. *Mousai* fr. 7.2 *CA*; but cf. ch. 6 n. 16 for authorship.

[37] Callim. *Aitia* fr. 21.9–10 Pfeiffer (23.9–10 Massimilla); on 'Rarian' Demeter see Massimilla (1996) 284, Richardson (1974) 297–8.

the Eleusinian reference. One is the noun *chleuē* ('jeering' or 'taunting') or one of its cognates, i.e. the same vocabulary found in *Hom. Hymn Dem.* 202 (**F1a**), as well as in the quasi-Eleusinian scenario at Aristophanes *Frogs* 375 (see 212 below). The other is a mention of fasting as part of the Demetrian cult (cf., again, the *Homeric Hymn*, line 200), though the state of the fragment does not disclose the relationship posited between fasting and laughter. It is just possible that in Callimachus' verb ἀπεκρύψαντο (fr. 21.9 Pfeiffer), 'they concealed (themselves)', there is a reference to veiling of the head, which may have played some part in the Mysteries and is a component of one account of *gephurismos* (**F1d** below).[38] As already noted (159 above), it is culturally significant that Callimachus is conscious of an affinity between a number of festivals which incorporate moments of ritual laughter, indeed ostensibly 'shameful' and 'ill-omened' speech (*Aitia* fr. 7.19–20 Pfeiffer; **F8–9** below). Given his keen eye for the phenomenon, as attested by two different sections of the *Aitia*, it is worth mentioning another possible instance. Callimachus' *Hymn to Delos* ends with a vignette of a mysterious cult of Apollo on that island which is described as a 'game and source of laughter' (παίγνια . . . καί . . . γελαστύν, 324) for the young god. Though the immediate point is the god's own pleasure in what is done in his honour, it is hard to resist the suspicion that the (initiatory) rites in question, apparently including dancing and flagellation, involved laughter on the part of the participants themselves, possibly in a form similar to the Corybantic initiation documented in **F11** below.[39]

F1d

Several sources, all post-classical, refer to a practice or group of practices known as *gephurismos*, denoting mockery delivered from or beside a bridge (or bridges: which one(s) being a purely antiquarian question).[40] Earliest is Strabo 9.1.24, who merely notes the connection of the practice with a

---

[38] On veiling in the Mysteries, see Richardson (1974) 212, with *Hom. Hymn* 2.197. On veiling *vis-à-vis* aischrology, cf. the (metaphorical) adverb, ἀπαρακαλύπτως, 'bare-facedly' (lit. 'unveiled'), *Suda s.v.* τὰ ἐκ τῶν ἁμαξῶν σκώμματα, and see Dem. 19.287 (180 below) on masking for performers of ritualised scurrility.

[39] On the end of the Hymn, cf. Mineur (1984) 247–50.

[40] The two main possibilities are: a bridge (if not more than one) over the Cephisus between Athens and Eleusis, some 3.5 kilometres NW of the city, as at Strabo 9.1.24 (see my text); or one over the Eleusinian Cephisus, just east of Eleusis itself. Xenokles of Sphettus built a stone bridge over one of the two around 320: *IG* II² 1191, Antagoras, *Anth. Pal.* 9.147. Various views: Frazer (1898) II 492, Gow and Page (1965) II 30–1, Parke (1977) 66, 194 n. 63, Parker (2005) 346, 350 n. 96. At least one other bridge might have been crossed between Athens and Eleusis, over the Eridanus, just NW of the city. For the decree of 422/1 (*IG* I³ 79) concerning a footbridge over the Rheita/Rheitoi near Eleusis (not the site of *gephurismos*, despite Burkert (1985) 105; contrast Burkert (1983) 278 n. 19), see Robertson (1998) 555–6. The bridge crossed by initiates in *Etym. Magn.* s.v. Γεφυρεῖς is uncertain,

bridge over the river Cephisus, several kilometres north-west of Athens, a bridge that would be crossed en route from the city to Eleusis. Leaving aside some extended uses of the word-group to signify strong mockery or abuse in non-Eleusinian settings,[41] all other occurrences of the relevant terminology, mostly from late lexica, give slender scraps of putative information. Hesychius' entry on the feminine noun γεφυρίς cites a certain Heracleon (conceivably the late-Hellenistic grammarian from Ephesus) for the sense of 'a prostitute on a bridge'; it is perhaps implied, though far from unambiguous, that Heracleon linked such a person to ritual mockery. The same entry then records disagreements over whether a woman or a man, perhaps with his head covered (a kind of masking? cf. under **F6b**),[42] sat on a bridge to deliver insults by name at 'well-known citizens' as the initiates passed by on their way to Eleusis. A second Hesychian entry defines the plural noun γεφυρισταί ('practitioners of *gephurismos*') as jokers who mocked passers-by 'on the bridge at Eleusis'. We can probably leave out of the reckoning an entry found in more than one Byzantine version of a dictionary of lexical differences (possibly going back to the second-century AD grammarian Herennius Philo) which defines *gephurismos* (or perhaps γεφυριασμός) as abuse *inscribed* on Athenian bridges, an idea that surely collapses a distinctive custom during the procession to Eleusis with something more like the production of pasquinades or the carving of graffiti.[43]

The paltriness of the ancient evidence has allowed modern speculation free rein.[44] We remain largely in the dark. Given the existence of the terminology and its (partial) connection with Eleusis, it is reasonable to accept that a specifically ritualised practice of mockery did exist, occurring where

as too is the origin of Demeter's epithet Γεφυραία (not peculiar to her; cf. Apollo in *IG* ii² 4813): Parker (1996) 288 n. 11.

[41] See esp. Plut. *Sulla* 2.1, 6.12, 13.1; cf. *Suda s.v.* γεφυρίζων. The first of these, quoting a trochaic tetrameter (itself a generically 'iambic' metre), refers to a class of lampooners (*gephuristai*) but no Eleusinian link is visible. Ael. *NA* 4.43 lists *gephurismoi* alongside Dionysiac festivals as occasions of idleness, as though a class of festivities were meant.

[42] συγκαλυπτόμενον. Reckford (1987) 464, Rusten (1977) 160 posit a man *dressed* as a woman; Hesychius' masculine participle need not imply this. Cf. n. 38 above.

[43] See the similar entries in Ammonius, *Vocab. diff.* 443 (Nickau), Herennius Philo σ 167, Ptolem. Asc. *De diff. voc.* p. 400 – all three works in far from their original form. Cf. Thom. Mag. *Ecl. s.v.* σκῶμμα.

[44] Burkert (1985) 105 imagines *gephuristai* 'terroriz[ing]' the initiates (contrast 287, 'grotesque buffoonery'). We do not know that a woman 'mimed Baubo or Iambe', Adrados (1975) 300, or that initiates themselves engaged in exchanges of insults: Brumfield (1981) 195, O'Higgins (2003) 20. Segal (1961) 235 n. 40 misattributes *gephurismos* to the Dionysia. No source counts *gephurismos* part of comedy's prehistory, *pace* Del Corno (1994) 177. It is unhelpful to extend the term to other forms of ritual abuse, e.g. Fisher (2001) 178. General discussion in Fluck (1931) 52–9, De Martino (1934), both of them incautious with some of the evidence.

the procession of initiates en route from Athens to Eleusis crossed one or more bridges over one or other river Cephisus.[45] The ritual was probably performed by designated individuals or groups, whether male or female, whose heads may have been conventionally veiled or masked. A snatch of popular song of uncertain date, in which Persephone herself is apparently addressed and urged to (?)approach a bridge, sheds no direct light, but it does reinforce the suspicion that bridges figured in Eleusinian symbolism.[46] This is hardly surprising, especially given the length of the journey made by the procession from Athens to Demeter's sanctuary: as marked points of transition, bridges are associated in many cultures with ritually significant moments or settings, including the passage between life and death. Moreover, if the story of Iambe and Demeter (**F1a**) represented or echoed a psychological pattern that meant something to the worshippers themselves, then various forms of ritual laughter, including *gephurismos*, may have conveyed a subliminal sense of a religious journey in which earthily affirmative life-forces would triumph over the power of grief, sterility and even death, though that hardly entitles us to treat *gephurismos* as a 'repetition' of the Iambe episode itself.[47] Whatever its origins, *gephurismos* could have developed into a ribald custom that was only loosely integrated into the experience of the Mysteries.[48] But what militates against that view is the larger range of evidence for multiple moments of ritual laughter within the Eleusinian programme. Whether *gephurismos* as such is echoed or adapted at Aristophanes *Frogs* 416–30 will be discussed in the final section of the chapter.

F1e

The *Suda*'s entry under the heading 'jests from the wagons' (τὰ ἐκ τῶν ἁμαξῶν σκώμματα) states that women rode to Eleusis on wagons and 'abused one another in the street [or 'on the road']'. This passage (as well as Photius' *Lexicon* under the same heading) also refers to 'jests from the wagons' in other contexts, especially the Choes (Anthesteria) and the Lenaea at Athens: see **F6b** below. The wording of the *Suda*'s entry, and of a scholion to Aristophanes *Wealth* 1014 which overlaps with it, might be taken to imply that the women's abuse took place during the journey to Eleusis;

---

[45] Robertson (1998) argues for *two* processions to Eleusis, one for new initiates, the other (the Iacchus procession) for the already initiated. He does not mention *gephurismos*.
[46] See 877 *PMG*: LSJ 346, *s.v.* γέφυρα, takes the reference, without good reason, to be to a 'causeway' between Athens and Eleusis.
[47] As does Lincoln (1991) 86, without argument; cf. the views cited in Olender (1990) 95 n. 63.
[48] Cf. Fluck (1931) 55.

but to accept this as evidence for a link with *gephurismos* (**F1d**) requires a leap of faith.[49] Aristophanes *Wealth* 1013–14 itself refers to a woman riding on a wagon on the occasion of the Great Mysteries, but whether there is an allusion to 'jests from the wagon', as the source of the scholia believed, remains moot. It was presumably not uncommon for women to travel on wagons for longer journeys; Demosthenes 21.158 refers to a rather different case where an ostentatious vehicle (a *zeugos* pulled by two white Sicyonian horses) was put into service.[50] This, then, is the weakest of the testimonies to ritualised Eleusinian laughter, though it probably preserves a grain of authentic awareness of connections between women and laughter in Demetrian rituals.

F2

The Athenian mid-winter festival Haloa has significant affinities with Eleusis. It was celebrated there in a special form, in honour of Demeter and Persephone (and Dionysus?), and is described by our main ancient source, the scholia to Lucian, as 'containing mysteries'.[51] According to this source, a secret rite took place at Eleusis for women alone, accompanied by 'a great deal of playful and jesting talk' (παιδιαὶ λέγονται πολλαὶ καὶ σκώμματα). They were permitted to abuse one another with reciprocal indecency; they handled model genitalia, both male and female; priestesses whispered encouragement to adultery into their ears; and they feasted lavishly on both wine and food (excepting certain items prohibited under a

---

[49] Brumfield (1981) 218 n. 16 misleadingly cites the scholion as testimony for *gephurismos*; Usher (1993) 212 muddles the women's wagons with *gephurismos* and conflates them with Dionysiac wagons; Fluck (1931) 59 dismisses the scholion as sheer 'Ideenassoziation', Calame (1997) 139 accepts it rather breezily. Kerényi (1960) 11–16 confusingly maintains that *Wealth* 1014 itself refers to *gephurismos* and Baubo-like exposure.

[50] Van Leeuwen (1904), van Daele (1930) on Ar. *Wealth* 1013 are misleading: Dem. 21.158 spotlights a deluxe vehicle; it does not imply that only the rich travelled to Eleusis on *hamaxai*, a term that could denote ordinary wagons (on whose religious use cf. Krauskopf, *ThesCRA* v 286–92). Cf. Robertson (1998) 553 n. 19, with 556 n. 28 on the spurious claim at ps.-Plut. *Vit. Orat.* 842a.

[51] ἑορτή . . . μυστήρια περιέχουσα: the opening of Σ to Lucian, *Dial. Meret.* 7.4 (279–81 Rabe), using the same phrase as for the Thesmophoria. Text and translation of the whole passage in Lowe (1998) 167–8, with an important analysis; text and Lowe's translation (both with misprints) also in O'Higgins (2003) 18–19; cf. Brumfield (1981) 108–9, 128–9, and translation alone in Winkler (1990) 194–5. Parker (2005) 199–201 gives a synopsis of the festival; cf. Skov (1975), Brumfield (1981) 104–31, though Brumfield misconstrues the end of the Lucianic scholia by making the archons show model genitalia outside the shrine (113). Parker (1983) 83 contrasts the Haloa's licentiousness (cf. 'deliberately outrageous obscenity', 78) with abstinence at the Thesmophoria; but he neglects the fact that both festivals reportedly contained female aischrology and model genitalia (though Robertson (1996) 370–1 is sceptical about genital 'pastries'). On the dietary point cf. Parker (1983) 358. There is no evidence, *contra* McClure (1999) 48, for men participating in obscene exchanges at the Haloa. Patera and Zografou (2001) question whether obscenity was central to the festival.

restriction relating to the Mysteries), including genital-shaped cakes. The scholia look like a curious combination of precise detail, especially the long list of prohibited foods, and dubious speculation; caution needs to be exercised.[52] Not least, it looks suspicious that information should be available about what priestesses whispered in women's ears during a secret rite. That suspicion grows if we recognise a resemblance to the stereotype of women (as alcoholic and sex-crazed) found in Old Comedy: could comedy itself have contributed to the ideas that have found their way into the scholia?[53] We need at any rate to separate the text's *prima facie* claim that priestesses recommended illicit love from the more complex possibilities of a ritualised sexual 'freedom of speech'. Where women-only rituals are concerned, the risk of distortion by male fantasy is always to be reckoned with. But it is hard to doubt the basic testimony that female joking, heavily coloured by the themes of Demetrian fertility rites, was integral to some stage of the Haloa. If, furthermore, the imagery or symbolism of female genitalia was actively employed, a parallel with both the Thesmophoria (**F3**) and the motif of Baubo's self-exposure (**F1a**) readily suggests itself.[54]

Scholars have disputed how far courtesans were involved in the Haloa, a question which has some bearing on the ethos of sexual joking at the festival. The only reference to the Haloa in a classical literary source is pseudo-Demosthenes 59.116 (*Against Neaira*), dating from the late 340s and probably written by Apollodorus, the main prosecution speaker. We learn from this that *hetairai* could certainly attend parts of the festival, though as it happens the same text indicates that the parts in question were ones at which even a man could be present.[55] When, in one of Alciphron's *Letters* (written in the second century AD but set fictionally in classical Athens), the courtesan Thais expresses annoyance and surprise at the way in which she was sexually mocked by two other *hetairai* during the Haloa, the point has ironic overtones. The (male) reader can be expected to appreciate that

---

[52] The mid-winter date of the festival (late Poseideon: Philochorus *FGrH* 328 F83) was close to the Rural Dionysia, with which some conflation may have occurred in the scholia's sources: Deubner (1932) 63–4, Winkler (1990) 195.

[53] Ar. *Lys.* 107, 212–16, *Eccl.* 225 (cf. *Thesm.* 398: a Freudian slip, following 395–7?), are paradigmatic of Old Comedy's 'adulterous' wives; see the almost self-parodic extreme at *Thesm.* 476–501. Cf. Stehle (1997) 118, 'fantasy', but without mention of comedy. Winkler (1990) 195–6, by contrast, posits an authentic 'phenomenology . . . of playful sexual liberation' within women-only rites; cf. O'Higgins (2003) *passim*, with n. 113 below. Parker (2005) 279 poses but sidesteps the question of how women's secret 'whisperings' would be known to men.

[54] Skov (1975) 142 conjectures that model genitalia were used for 'a mimetic performance of the sexual act'. Σ on Lucian, *Dial. Meret.* 2.1 (275 Rabe) call the model snakes and phalli at the Thesmophoria *mimēmata*.

[55] Ps.-Dem. 59.116 cites a charge of impiety brought against Archias, but the latter's presence at the Haloa is not depicted as an offence in itself, *pace* Carey (1992) 145; cf. Kapparis (1999) 411–12.

the context is one in which ritual laughter was permitted and called for. The attitude of Thais, who swears revenge, might therefore be seen as naively misjudged; alternatively, there is a general piquancy in the blurring and confusion between permissible ritual laughter and a catty 'professional' rivalry (carried beyond a joke) between courtesans.[56] Finally, the possibility has been mooted that certain vase-paintings illustrating women with giant phalloi and/or 'phallos-plants' may be connected to the Haloa; but the link is speculative and remains unestablished.[57]

F3

Elements indicative of ritual laughter are attested in two different forms for the Thesmophoria, another women-only festival of Demeter and Kore but this one not peculiar to Athens.[58]

(a) Two late sources refer to women's laughter and obscene talk within the festival. Pseudo-Apollodorus, *Bibl.* 1.5.1 states, rather vaguely, that 'they say that the women engage in joking/mockery (*skōptein*) at the Thesmophoria', and he derives the practice aetiologically from the manner in which old Iambe made Demeter 'smile' (**F1a** above); Cleomedes, *Cael.* 2.1.498–500 (Todd) compares Epicurus' alleged penchant for crude language both to the speech of brothels and to 'the things said in the worship of Demeter by women celebrating the Thesmophoria'.[59] Neither text refers expressly to Athens, and no further details are forthcoming. A passage of Diodorus Siculus, possibly deriving from Timaeus, refers to a ten-day autumn festival of Demeter in Sicily which is standardly identified as a version of the Thesmophoria: 'it is their practice during this period', he writes, 'to exchange indecent speech (*aischrologein*) in their encounters with

---

[56] Alciph. *Epist.* 4.6.3–4, including *kichlizein*, 'giggle' (ch. 10 n. 52), and the singing of ribald songs (cf. Ar. *Eccl.* 884–923); cf. Parker (2005) 488–9 for Alciphron's knowledge of Athenian festivals. *Hetairai*, with their sexual-cum-sympotic lifestyles, were easily associated with laughter: see the collection of courtesans' witticisms in Athen. 13, with McClure (2003), and cf. ch. 6 n. 41, ch. 10 n. 52, Appendix 1 n. 39, Appendix 2 nn. 19, 48.

[57] See e.g. Kilmer (1993) 192–3 (with an incorrect claim about the literary sources), 197–8, Deubner (1932) 65–6, Johns (1982) 42 (with colour ill. facing 48); Parke (1977) 99 overstates the match between vase-paintings and Lucianic scholia. Brumfield (1981) 112, Winkler (1990) 206 (with his frontispiece) doubt the Haloa link; Winkler discerns 'humorous fantasy' in the images, as does Kilmer (1993) 198 and n. 24; cf. Lewis (2002) 83 ('the joke of women raising phalloi', but on 128 she accepts a religious background), Parker (2005) 288–9.

[58] On the festival programme, see Parker (2005) 271–83, Versnel (1993) 235–60, Austin and Olson (2004) xlv–li. Fluck (1931) confines female scurrility to the preceding Stenia (**F4** below).

[59] For fuller translation of the context, see Bowen and Todd (2004) 125. Richardson (1974) 214 thinks ps.-Apollodorus may refer to the preliminary Thesmophoria (10 Pyanepsion) in the deme of Halimous. Bremmer (1994) 77 surmises that Herodotus' reticence about the Thesmophoria at 2.171.2 may relate to female aischrology. With the language of 'brothels', cf. ch. 5 n. 21. On Iambe and the Thesmophoria, cf. Graf (1974) 168–71.

one another, because it was indecent speech which made the goddess laugh when she was grieving over the snatching away of Kore'.[60] If this *is* the Thesmophoria, however, we need to register that Diodorus is describing obscene mockery either by men alone or by both sexes (and apparently in general social contexts); his use of masculine pronouns rules out exclusively female behaviour.[61] Involvement of both sexes in ritualised ribaldry within a festival of Demeter is not intrinsically implausible (cf. **F5** below).

(b) The scholia on Lucian *Dial. Meretr.* 2.1 (275–6 Rabe), which contain an important statement about interpretative approaches to ritual (see 197–9 below), mention women's handling of phallus-shaped cakes in the part of the Thesmophoria known as the *arrhētophoria* ('the carrying of unnameable things').[62] Athenaeus 14.647a,[63] citing an otherwise unknown Heracleides of Syracuse, describes cakes in the shape of female genitalia as being consumed during the Syracusan Thesmophoria. A symmetry with the Haloa (**F2**) is obvious both in this detail and in the broader combination of obscene words and deeds by the women. According to the Christian bishop Theodoretus of Cyrrhus, *Graec. Aff.* 3.84 (written in the fifth century AD, but mostly well informed about pagan practices, despite the author's disgust for them), the female genitalia were thought 'worthy of religious honour' within the Thesmophoria.

The most likely setting for the *eating* of cakes is the final day of the festival, Kalligeneia or 'Fair Offspring' (13 Pyanepsion), i.e. the day after the Nesteia or 'Fasting' and the one on which the idea of new, abundant fertility appears to have been celebrated. But it remains unclear whether the genital-shaped cakes were always eaten; if not, they could have occupied a place earlier in the festival. In any case, we cannot be confident that the actions involving

[60] Diod. Sic. 5.4.7 = Timaeus *FGrH* 566 F164.77–81. For the Thesmophoria in Syracuse, cf. under **F3b**.

[61] This elementary point, correctly observed by Fluck (1931) 20, McClure (1999) 51, is often overlooked: e.g. Winkler (1990) 197, n. † [*sic*] (gratuitously extending the reference to the Athenian Thesmophoria), Olender (1990) 94–5, O'Higgins (2003) 23–4, Collins (2004) 228 n. 9. Burkert (1985) 244, asserting *a priori* that the Thesmophoria 'must' have contained derision of women by men as well, nonetheless cites the Diodorus passage (443 n. 33) as though applying to women. For banter between the sexes in an (imaginary) social context, cf. the encounter between Archilochus and (disguised) Muses in the Mnesiepes inscription, *SEG* 15.517, A col. II.29–31, now available in Clay (2004) 104–10: a legendary setting, symbolic of *iambos*, but suggestive of how laughter might mediate dealings between young men and women.

[62] The full context is quoted and translated in Lowe (1998) 165–6, O'Higgins (2003) 21–2, Brumfield (1981) 73–4, 98, Austin and Olson (2004) xlviii–l; translation alone in Winkler (1990) 196–7, Parker (2005) 273. Robertson (1996) 365–74 argues that the scholion in part describes the Proerosia, the pre-ploughing festival held at Eleusis and elsewhere a few days prior to the Thesmophoria. For the term *arrhētos*, literally 'not to be spoken of', see ch. 5 n. 28.

[63] Brumfield (1981) 130 n. 38 needs correcting. Burkert (1985) 244 asserts, without reason, that such cakes were 'obviously' eaten outside the Thesmophoria too.

them were the (only) time during which the women might have engaged in aischrology. Callimachus, *Aitia* fr. 21.8–10 Pfeiffer (see **F1c** above) connects fasting and rituals of derision in the Eleusinian Mysteries, though we cannot say exactly how; but the Iambe episode of the *Homeric Hymn to Demeter* (**F1a** above) points aetiologically to the emotional-cum-symbolic sequence of fasting (and mourning) followed by restorative laughter. Plutarch characterises the middle day of the Thesmophoria as σκυθρωποτάτη, 'the grimmest-faced'. *Skuthrōpos* is a term which implies absence or denial of laughter, though Plutarch elsewhere links aischrologic or obscene rituals precisely with contexts to which he applies this same word.[64] There are larger issues of interpretation at stake here, to which I shall return. Where the Thesmophoria is concerned, the balance of probabilities is that activities that might be described as 'joking' (*skōptein*) belonged to the final day; but (other) elements that could have been called aischrologic (i.e. involving explicit sexual references), and their physical counterparts (the handling of sexual symbols), may have been involved at earlier stages. Aristophanes' *Thesmophoria*, notionally set on the day of fasting, unfortunately sheds no clear light on the question.[65]

F4

The Stenia was an Athenian festival in honour of Demeter which took place two days before, or perhaps as a preliminary part of, the Thesmophoria. Like the latter it was exclusively for women (cf. Ar. *Thesm.* 834–5). The lexicographers record exchanges of jesting and abuse between participants on this occasion too.[66] Hesychius even attests a verb στηνιῶσαι, 'to use Stenia abuse': though certainly a rarity, it adds to the evidence of *gephurizein* (**F1d**), *pompeuein* (**F6b**), and expressions like 'from the wagon(s)' (**F6b**) for the fact that perceptions of ritual scurrility (as recognisable forms/contexts of behaviour) could be encapsulated in linguistic usage. Photius locates the occurrence of female abuse (*loidoreisthai*) within the nocturnal part of the

---

[64] *Skuthrōpotatē*: Plut. *Dem.* 30.5. See further at 200–1 and n. 130 below.
[65] The setting of *Thesm.* on Nesteia is indicated at line 80. McClure (1999) 230–1 thinks the play is free of traces of ritual aischrology (cf. ch. 5 n. 69). The significance (if any) of *Thesm.* 962–4 in this respect is unclear: see Austin and Olson (1994) 301. But Bowie A. (1993) 210–12 (cf. 208) hears echoes of the festival's 'obscenity' in the play, including the 'handling of sexual objects' at *Thesm.* 643–8, while Rösler (1993) 77–80 (closely followed in Rösler (1995b) 119–23) finds aischrology comically echoed in the play's motif of 'speaking ill' (by both Euripides and the women); Harrison (1922) 136 oddly adduces *Thesm.* 533 (a misprint?). Parke (1977) 86–7, Bremmer (1994) 77 speculatively locate Thesmophorian aischrology at the *end* of Nesteia.
[66] Hesych. *s.v.* στήνια, στηνιῶσαι (aorist infin., suggesting a specific, perhaps unique, literary occurrence), Phot. *Lex. s.v.* στήνια (= Eubul. fr. 146). There is no evidence, *contra* McClure (1999) 48, that men participated in obscene exchanges at the Stenia.

Stenia, citing the comic poet Eubulus as a witness – reassuringly classical anchorage for the phenomenon, one might suppose, after the dismayingly late sources for the equivalent features of the Haloa and Thesmophoria. Claims based on comic poets' depictions of women, however, must always be treated with circumspection. But if we can rely on the nocturnal context projected by Eubulus, we are likely to be dealing with a *pannuchis*, an all-night celebration of the kind found in various festivals (including the Eleusinian Mysteries; cf. under **F1b**) and predominantly marked by an atmosphere of exhilarated revelling.[67]

F5

Pausanias 7.27.9–10 refers to the Mysaion or sanctuary of Mysian Demeter some distance outside Pellene in the northern Peloponnese. The shrine was the location for a seven-day festival of Demeter on the third day of which all males withdrew in order to allow the women to carry out nocturnal rites. When the men came back on the following day, exchanges of 'laughter and jokes' (γέλωτι . . . καὶ σκώμμασιν) took place between the sexes, though the women, according to Pausanias, were responsible for more of this than the men.[68] Altogether, the evidence surveyed in **F1–5** shows that ritual laughter in festivals of Demeter (and Kore/Persephone) was sometimes confined to groups of women on their own, sometimes shared between the sexes.

F6

Dionysiac festivals, at Athens (the primary source of our evidence) and elsewhere, furnished a major category of opportunities for the performance of laughter-inducing rituals.

F6a

At Plato *Laws* 1.637a–b, the Spartan Megillus praises his city's laws for prohibiting the types of revelling in which people 'succumb to the greatest pleasures, to acts of outrageous offensiveness (*hubris*) and to every kind of derangement' (καὶ μεγίσταις προσπίπτουσιν ἡδοναῖς καὶ ὕβρεσι καὶ ἀνοίᾳ πάσῃ). Neither in the countryside nor in the urban centres under Sparta's control, he says, would you find symposia or kindred phenomena. Intoxicated komastic behaviour would be punished severely, and no Dionysiac festivals are allowed to provide a pretext (*prophasis*) for the kind

---

[67] Cf. Parker (2005) 166; Foxhall (1995) 104, referring to the Haloa, speaks of 'bonfire parties'. Compare the *pannuchis* mood of *Frogs* 371, 446, with 211–14 below. For a comic 'pre-nuptial' *pannuchis*, see Men. *Dysc.* 857–8, with ch. 8, 400.

[68] O'Higgins (2003) 16 refers to 'choruses' of men and women, conflating the case with **F7** below.

of inebriated antics 'on wagons' which Megillus was scandalised to see both
at Athens and during communal celebrations in the Spartan colony of Taras
(Tarentum) on the south coast of Italy. The phrase 'on wagons' or 'on carts'
(ἐν ἁμάξαις) refers to the floats or mobile stages on which ritualised joking
was enacted; see **F6b**. It is evidently sufficient to evoke for Plato's readers
vivid images of Dionysiac licentiousness in full flow.

This is an important passage in several respects. The 'puritanical' slant
of Megillus' remarks fits with other evidence for a distinctively Laconian
anxiety about socially uncontrolled laughter, though these remarks should
neither be treated as factually straightforward nor automatically equated
with Plato's authorial endorsement.[69] By dramatising Spartan disapproval,
and setting it in counterpoint to the Athenian's (qualified) approval for
Dionysiac celebrations, Plato provides pointed evidence for conflicting perceptions of a particular kind of festive revelling. Megillus picks out three
related features of such revelling which he sees as tending towards shameless
excess: one, its (supposedly) wild abandon (to the point of 'derangement');
two, its proclivity for drunkenness; three, its public staging of scurrility
'on wagons'. It is striking, moreover, that Megillus' train of thought moves
from symposia to *kōmoi* to Dionysia: he traces an expansion of the 'spaces'
of Dionysiac revelry from private indoor gatherings, via mobile eruptions
into the streets, to civically organised festivals (he speaks of seeing 'the
whole city' drunk at Taras). In his evaluation of such behaviour Megillus
is explicitly going against the grain of widely held cultural attitudes in the
Greek world. What he sets his face against is rampant *pleasure* (cf. 636e:
Spartan law forbids 'the pursuit of pleasures'), which his Athenian interlocutor maintains should be moderated but not totally shunned. Megillus
is presented, therefore, as a more extreme spokesman for anti-hedonistic
Spartan values than Plato's uncle Critias, whose elegiac poem on the symposium, discussed in my last chapter, alludes to Sparta's avoidance of drunken
festivities while specifically allowing room for 'moderate laughter' within
the carefully regulated confines of the drinking-party.[70]

F6b

The Dionysiac festive practice of conspicuously indecent displays 'on wagons' is confirmed by a number of other sources. As mentioned under **F1e**
above, the entries in Photius' *Lexicon* and the *Suda* under 'jests from the

---

[69] Megillus is silent about Sparta's own brand of ritual-cum-comic performers: see **F12b** below. (Limited) support for licensed Dionysiac festivity is voiced by the Athenian in this passage of *Laws*, and
appears elsewhere in Plato too: see Halliwell (1991b) 67–8.
[70] Critias 6 *IEG*, with ch. 3, 125–7.

wagons' (τὰ ἐκ τῶν ἁμαξῶν σκώμματα) cite the Choes (second day of the Anthesteria)[71] and, 'later', the Lenaea as occasions for such ritualised scurrility. The Lenaea is also adduced by the *Suda* under ἐξ ἁμάξης (ε 1530) and by the scholia to Aristophanes *Knights* 547 (which mention Demosthenes 18.122, cited below, in this connection). The sources fluctuate between describing the performers on wagons as engaging in mockery of one another or of separate targets such as politicians.

It is also reasonable to attach to Dionysiac occasions those classical sources which, without specifying particular festivities, refer to insults delivered 'on/from wagons' (ἐν ἁμάξαις, ἐπὶ/ἐκ τῶν ἁμαξῶν, *vel sim.*) and link this custom to 'processional abuse' (πομπεία, πομπεύειν).[72] Demosthenes 18.122–4, contrasting formal judicial accusation with foul-mouthed abuse (*loidoria*), lambasts Aeschines for having shouted indecencies 'as if from a wagon'; he uses the verb *pompeuein* as synonymous with the latter (harking back to the noun *pompeia* at 18.11). One intriguing possibility here, given the accusation/abuse distinction, is that some processional scurrility might be perceived as a form of 'folk justice', picking out victims for popular denunciation, somewhat like the medieval and early modern practices known generically as 'charivari': but if so, the last thing Demosthenes wants to suggest is any respectability or reliability for such customs.[73] Our sources in general stress the coarseness of men 'on wagons'. In a fragment of Menander's *Perinthia* someone refers to 'very abusive processional lampoonings on the wagons'.[74] A fragment of Philemon involves a version of what was to become the proverbial expression '[to abuse] from the wagon(s)'

---

[71] Ar. *Ach.* 1198–1234 may echo phallic scurrility at the Choes. Bekker (1814–21) 1 316 refers to licensed scurrility against 'politicians and others' on the third day (Chutroi) of the Anthesteria; cf. Hamilton (1992) 38 (T45). Burkert (1983) 229, followed by Reckford (1987) 455–6, strains to establish a connection between mockery 'from wagons' and quasi-demonic 'spirit'-mummers at the Anthesteria.

[72] *Pace* Leutsch and Schneidewin (1839) 453, Burkert (1983) 229 n. 18, Ar. *Kn.* 464 is no allusion to jests 'from wagons'. Harpocration, Photius and *Suda s.v.* πομπείας refer to Dionysiac processions without further specification (though citing Men. *Perinthia*, n. 74 below); Σ on Lucian, *Iup. Trag.* 44 likewise. For possible non-Dionysiac instances see F1e above, F10 below; at a later date, cf. the indecent 'wagon-song' (ἁμαξῶν ᾆσμα) at Philostr. *Vita Ap.* 4.20.

[73] See further in ch. 5, 228–31. On charivari, see the overview in Alford (1959), with Davis (1975) 97–123, Le Goff and Schmitt (1981) for more penetrating historical analysis; cf. Welsford (1935) 203–6, Gray (1984) 24–6, Minois (2000) 148–52. Possible ancient precursors of the 'donkey-ride' charivari type (in particular, for the shaming of adulterers) are attested in Nicolaus Damasc. *FGrH* 90 F103, Plut. *Mor.* 291e–f, Hesych. *s.v.* ὀνοβάτιδες: discussion in Schmitt-Pantel (1981); cf. Alford (1959) 507, Mellinkoff (1973) 154 (expressing caution). F10 in my text is somewhat redolent of the charivari model. See ch. 2 n. 83 for a more speculative analogue.

[74] ἐπὶ τῶν ἁμαξῶν εἰσι πομπεῖαί τινες | σφόδρα λοίδοροι: fr. 8 Sandbach (1990), fr. 5 Arnott (1979–2000). Arnott moots a link with a wedding procession; cf. n. 125 below. On the laughter of wedding finales in Menander's plays, cf. ch. 8, 400.

(ἐκ τῶν ἁμαξῶν, ἐξ ἁμάξης).[75] Some three centuries later, Dionysius of Halicarnassus, when claiming affinities between Roman and Greek customs of ribaldry, mentions the ridicule of prominent public targets by men 'in procession on wagons' at Athens, a practice he ostensibly takes to be still alive.[76]

Processions and wagons (*qua* floats or mobile stages) go happily together, especially in the parades or pageants of Dionysiac festivals. The evidence suggests that such performances belonged to the City Dionysia, the Lenaea, the Anthesteria and the Rural Dionysia at Athens; a link with phallic processions (**F6c** below) is also possible.[77] Moreover, a case can be made for linking wagons with the anecdotal tradition that Thespis, founder of tragedy, took a troupe of travelling players around Attica on wagons.[78] The historicity of the tradition may be tenuous (and Thespis, of course, is the wrong genre for our purposes), but the image of wagons as mobile performance platforms points towards a plausible *idea* of emergent drama; to that extent it chimes with images of ritual laughter as a 'staged' event within Dionysiac processions.

Demosthenes 19.287 should be added here. Demosthenes describes Epicrates (dubbed 'the accursed Curebion'), brother-in-law of Aeschines, as someone 'who revels in the processions without the mask' (ὃς ἐν ταῖς πομπαῖς ἄνευ τοῦ προσώπου κωμάζει). This probably refers to a performance in front of onlookers, a *kōmos* as festive spectacle; that makes best sense of the slur 'without the mask', which implies that traditionally

---

[75] Philemon fr. 44. Variations on proverbial usage are exemplified by Lucian, *Eun.* 2, *Iup. Trag.* 44, *Pseudol.* 32. Cf. Philod. *De bono rege* xx.15–16 (metaphorical use, with reference to sympotic joking: cf. ch. 3 n. 53). In modern Greek the expression τα εξ αμάξης still signifies coarse mockery.

[76] *Antiq. Rom.* 7.72.11, which follows a description (10) of Greek/Roman scurrilous dances by men in silenus and satyr costumes; see Versnel (1970) 96–8. Cf. nn. 79, 118 below.

[77] The law quoted at Dem. 21.10 refers to a *pompē* in the Piraeus Dionysia, the Lenaea and the City Dionysia (as well as the Apolline Thargelia): see MacDowell (1990) 230–35, with Dem. 22.68 (colourfully) for dancing on such occasions; cf. Wilson (2000) 97–8, Hoffman (1989) 93–6. Fluck (1931) 47–8 makes the lack of (literary evidence for) a formal procession at the Anthesteria seem more significant for 'wagon abuse' than it need be. For the link between wagons and phallic processions, see the third-century evidence of *IG* i³ 673.7–18, with Krentz (1993) 13, 15. Hedreen (2004) 51–8 argues for interwoven verbal/visual obscenity in Dionysiac processions; Cole (1993) offers an overview. Such conduct contrasted with the solemnity of many religious processions; cf. the general image at ps.-Pl. *Alcib.* 2.148e, with *ThesCRA* 1 1–8 for a conspectus. Clem. *Paed.* 2.3.35, 2.5.45 (c. AD 200) still recognises processions with costumed/masked figures (including women) as a setting for licentious antics: perhaps another Dionysiac reference, but Marrou (1965) 78 n. 4 suggests Isis; cf. ch. 10, 488.

[78] Thespis' wagons: Hor. *Ars Po.* 276 (Thespis test. 14 *TrGF*). Pickard-Cambridge (1927) 112–16 (with vase-paintings of processions with the god himself on a wagon with musical satyrs: cf. Pickard-Cambridge (1968) 13 and facing 14) is understandably sceptical, but I would rather posit inherited awareness of folk practices than 'confusion' on Horace's part; cf. Brink (1971) 312. Σ^Ald Ar. *Clouds* 296 claims comic poets themselves (?originally) performed from wagons. Cf. Hamilton (1992) 26–7.

sanctioned scurrility needs markers of its special nature and should be engaged in (if it all) only by those whose normal social identities are disguised (and, in effect, suspended).[79] The broad thrust of the phrase 'the processions' confirms that there were multiple contexts of this kind. Were such customs officially supervised by the magistrates responsible for the organisation of festivals or left to *ad hoc* groups? The phrasing of Demosthenes' text, together with other evidence for Dionysiac scurrility, supports the speculation that (masked) revelling 'on wagons' must have been accommodated within official processional programmes but nonetheless possessed a performative licence which could not have been closely controlled in all respects.[80]

F6c

Various kinds of highly ritualised scurrility are associated with phallic processions in the Greek world. Since symbolic phalluses were themselves sometimes transported on wagons, a convergence or overlap with **F6a–b** is to be reckoned with.[81] Aristotle famously states that comedy itself originated from improvisations by 'the leaders of the phallic songs which remain even now a custom in many cities' (*Poetics* 4.1449a10–13).[82] For present purposes, two points are worth making concisely about this much-discussed passage: first, while not all Greeks would have agreed with Aristotle's claim (*Poetics* 3.1448a29–38 shows that the Megarians, for one thing, told an alternative history of comedy), it is made in a manner which assumes *prima facie* credibility; secondly, whether or not his thesis about comedy's origins would have been widely accepted, Aristotle takes it as self-explanatory that laughter-inciting activity was expected of the leaders of phallic songs.

[79] Jebb (1870) 227 shrewdly stresses the definite article at Dem. 19.287: '*the* (indispensable) mask'. See Σ *ad loc.*, treating masks as avoiding shame (compare Σ^Ald Ar. *Clouds* 296, referring to face-paint); cf. the Christian reminiscence at Greg. Nyss. *Contra Eun.* 1.1.32. Theophr. *Char.* 6.3 may make a similar point, but the text is uncertain: ch. 5 n. 61. Dem. 21.180 implicitly recognises processions as legitimising *some degree* of licensed drunkenness etc.: the scholia here posit revellers costumed as satyrs, bacchants and sileni; cf. n. 118 below. For comparison, the *phallophoroi* described by Semus of Delos (see **F6c**) do not wear masks but some sort of floral headdress. Plut. *Mor.* 527d considers masks in the Rural Dionysia a 'modern' practice.

[80] Sourvinou-Inwood (2003) 70 (in a detailed reconstruction of the City Dionysia programme, 69–100) argues that Demosthenes means Cyrebion had wrongly transferred behaviour from the *kōmos* (*and* without a mask) into the solemn procession: but (a) the phrasing (including the dative plural) does not support such an exclusive reading, (b) metaphorical usage of *pompeuein* etc. (ignored by Sourvinou-Inwood) establishes a strong association between Dionysiac processions and mockery, and (c) if the whole festival could be referred to as *kōmoi* in *IG* ii² 2318, as Sourvinou-Inwood concedes (79), Demosthenes can hardly be exploiting a rigorous separation between procession and *kōmos*.

[81] See n. 77 above.

[82] For a connection between improvisation and ritualised abuse, see ch. 3, 101–3 with n. 4 there.

Approximately a century and a half earlier, in a punning remark which presumably reflects non-Athenian (or not exclusively Athenian) practices, Heraclitus (fr. 15 DK) had observed that Dionysiac cult provided a framework in which phallic processions and songs that would otherwise constitute grossly shameful behaviour have a special licence (and validate a special *mentality*). He sees them as forming culturally recognised instances of what can be termed ritually institutionalised shamelessness: 'if it were not Dionysus in whose honour they process and chant a song to genitals (lit. 'parts that induce shame'), their behaviour would have been most shameful'.[83] When describing the worship of 'Dionysus' (Osiris) in Egypt, Herodotus makes it clear that iconic phalli and phallic processions are standard elements in the Greeks' Dionysiac festivals.[84] Fifth-century Athens could officially require a colony to send a phallus (together with a delegation equipped to parade it) for the celebration of the Great Dionysia.[85] Our most evocative 'evidence' for phallic processions and songs in the classical period is Aristophanes *Acharnians* 241–79, a 'private' enactment of the Rural Dionysia, where Dicaeopolis, accompanied by a slave carrying a phallic pole, sings in praise of the personification Phales (the ritual phallus is in some sense an embodiment of the divine)[86] in terms that mix the language of intoxication, revelry, rampant sexual desire, and escape from war. Dicaeopolis' song is likely enough to reflect the spirit of such occasions, though it is hard to gauge the historical authenticity of details (see my comments on intra-familial obscenity under **F1b** above). I shall have a little more to say about this Aristophanic scene later in the chapter.

Phallic processions are attested in various post-classical sources as well. Two merit mention here. A Lindian figure called Antheas, of uncertain date, is reported by Athenaeus to have been a lifelong devotee of Dionysiac practices: he wore Dionysiac dress, supported a large group of 'fellow

---

[83] εἰ μὴ γὰρ Διονύσῳ πομπὴν ἐποιοῦντο καὶ ὕμνεον ᾆσμα αἰδοίοισιν, ἀναιδέστατα εἴργαστ' ἄν. Interpretation in e.g. Adoménas (1999) 92–4, Marcovich (1967) 252–5, Kahn (1979) 264–6, Babut (1975) 40–51; on the rest of the fragment (identifying Hades and Dionysus), see Seaford (1994) 321–2. Cf. ch. 7, 346–51, for laughter in Heraclitus' own mentality. Extensive discussion of phallic processions in Csapo (1997), esp. 265–79, Bierl (2001) 300–61; for phalloi and Dionysus at Athens, cf. Parker (2005) 317–21. On phallic ritual more generally see Burkert (1983) 69–72, though his biologico-psychological explanation is far from perspicuous. Eibl-Eibesfeldt (1972) 305–7 (with ills., 307–10) advances a cross-cultural theory of phallic symbolism derived from aggressive genital display in pre-human primates; see the editorial reservations on 314. Fehling (1974) 7–27 pursues a related line for antiquity; cf. Dover (1989) 105. Hartland (1917), though conceptually dated, provides a conspectus of phallic symbolism/rites in many cultures. Cf. n. 131 below.

[84] 2.48–9: see Lloyd (1975–88) II 220–1.

[85] *IG* I³ 46.16–17, foundation of a colony at Brea (c. 445); translation in Fornara (1983) 110–11.

[86] See esp. the hymn of the *ithuphalloi*, carm. pop. 851 *PMG*, at Athen. 14.622c, where the phallus is treated as the god himself, 'swollen erect' (ὀρθὸς ἐσφυδωμένος).

bacchants', led komastic revels by day and night, and wrote poetry (including comedies) which he performed 'at the head of his *phallophoroi* (phallus-carriers)'.[87] Semus of Delos, a Hellenistic antiquarian, referred in his work *On Paeans* to two different groups of theatrical performers, one called *ithuphalloi* ('erect phalli'), who wore masks and chanted a phallic song, the others *phallophoroi*, who (without masks but wearing an elaborate headdress) sang a Dionysiac hymn before running up to their audience and hurling ribald abuse (*tōthazein*) at individual spectators.[88] Here the configuration of Dionysiac celebration, theatrical setting, phallic symbolism and verbal mockery fits with a larger picture of convergence (or overlap) between ritualised phallic indecency and comic drama. I shall return to this point.

F7

Herodotus 5.83 recounts the Aeginetans' assertion of independence, at some point in the seventh century, from their mother-city, Epidaurus. One of their acts of aggression was to steal statues of the female deities Damia and Auxesia (made from Athenian olive-wood and previously erected at Epidaurus, on Delphi's instructions, to promote the city's agricultural fertility: Hdt. 5.82), which they then made the object of cult at Oa. This cult included not only sacrifices but also female choruses (supervised by male *chorēgoi*) who engaged in jeering and abuse (χοροῖσι γυναικηίοισι κερτόμοισι . . . κακῶς δὲ ἠγόρευον οἱ χοροί) but only of other women, not men. Herodotus states that comparable practices existed at Epidaurus itself, and he explicitly categorises the choral performances as one kind of sacred or ritual action, *hirourgia*. He indicates that further rituals, these others 'secret' or 'unnameable' (ἄρρητοι ἱρουργίαι – for the epithet cf. **F3b** above), existed alongside them, and presumably in what he took to be a significant relationship to them, at Epidaurus. Damia and Auxesia were also worshipped at Troezen; their names (meaning, approximately, 'Homeland' and 'Fruitfulness') suggest an intrinsic link with fertility. Pausanias records that he sacrificed to them in the same way as was customary

---

[87] Athen. 10.445a: Antheas is included as a comic poet in *PCG* II 307.

[88] *FGrH* 396 F24 (containing carm. pop. 851 *PMG*: n. 86 above) *apud* Athen. 14.622a–d; translated in Csapo and Slater (1995) 98. Pickard-Cambridge (1927) 231–7 is perhaps too sceptical about affinities between *phallophoroi* and (Attic) comedy: cf. Pütz (2007) 125–8, Sourvinou-Inwood (2003) 78, 172–6, Cole (1993) 32–3, Brown (1997) 31–5. Note the name *ithuphalloi* for young men's clubs at Dem. 54.14, with ch. 1 n. 93: such clubs had a mock ritual character (Dem. 54.17); they were hardly transferring fertility ritual 'into everyday life', *pace* Carey and Reid (1985) 86. For a (derisive) Christian depiction of rampant phallicism in pagan religion, see Evagrius schol. *Hist. Eccl.* 1.11; cf. ch. 2 n. 75.

at Eleusis, and scholars have discerned a general affinity with the cult of Demeter.[89]

A salient detail of the Herodotean passage is the historian's statement that the women constituted formal choruses organised by twenty male *chorēgoi* (ten for each deity) appointed expressly for the purpose. Herodotus nowhere else uses the term *chorēgos*; it is hard to be sure just what he means by it here. Conceivably it carries its literal sense of 'chorus leader'. But more likely it signifies something akin to the role of dramatic and dithyrambic *chorēgoi* or (financial) 'sponsors' familiar to us from classical Athens.[90] In that case, the implication is that organisation of the choruses called for substantial expenditure; it may also suggest an element of competition between the groups. Either way, what we have here is not impromptu or formless scurrility but a carefully planned and (perhaps literally) choreographed event – one, moreover, which seems to treat ritual as a highly prepared *display*, to be watched and appreciated as spectacular performance by an audience.[91]

F8

In Apollonius' *Argonautica*, the Argonauts' penultimate land stop before reaching home is a small island to the north of Crete. It is miraculously revealed to them by Apollo in response to Jason's prayer for rescue from the perils of a preternaturally pitch-dark atmosphere in which the heroes find themselves engulfed.[92] In gratitude, the Argonauts create a sanctuary for Apollo Aigletes, named (on this etymologising account: but see below) after the 'gleam' (*aiglē*) of the newly manifested island, which they duly name Anaphe (etymologised speciously as meaning 'revelation'). When Medea's Phaeacian maids, a gift from queen Arete (4.1221–2), see the men pouring libations over firewood (for they have nothing else to sacrifice), they burst into laughter. The heroes 'hit back' with foul language and uninhibited ridicule (αἰσχροῖς . . . ἔπεσσι and χλεύῃ), and both groups *enjoy* the

[89] For Troezen see Paus. 2.32.2, and 2.30.4–5 for the Eleusinian connection, with Frazer (1898) III 266–7, How and Wells (1928) II 46, Lambrinudakis (1986); Figueira (1993) 35–60 analyses the larger contexts of the story. De Martino (1934) 73–4 n. 6, 79, is unwarranted in taking the choruses of Hdt. 5.83 to be transvestite males and in treating choruses and *chorēgoi* as identical. Jeffery (1976) 150, Figueira (1993) 27–9 place Aeginetan independence at different points in the seventh century.

[90] See Wilson (2000) 281–2 (supporting the 'sponsor' interpretation), 385 nn. 78–80; cf. Nagy (1990) 364–5 (but misunderstanding the verb ἀποδείκνυσθαι in this context). For various senses/functions of *chorēgoi*, see Calame (1997) 43–73.

[91] Cf. Stehle (1997) 112, who sees scope for 'serious shaming' of unpopular or deviant women; that may be too strong an inference. Collins (2004) 228 unjustifiably speaks of 'an exclusively female *audience*' (my itals.).

[92] *Argon.* 4.1694–1730, with Livrea (1973), esp. 472–3, Green (1997) 356–8. *Pace* Fluck (1931) 60, 62, the Phaeacian identity of Medea's maidservants is not proof we are dealing with a pre-Greek cult.

ensuing exchange of raillery or flyting, a crucial detail which Apollonius highlights by the oxymoron γλυκερή . . . κερτομίη, 'delicious slanging' (1726–7).[93] In the psychology of the narrative, two things are pertinent: the recent escape from grave danger, and the overtones of a sexual frisson between the slave women and the men (a challenge to the latter's *virility* is a plausible subtext of the situation). Both groups employ uninhibited, even obscene, laughter as an instinctive means of negotiating their relationship, while at the same time celebrating the potency of their saviour Apollo. The competition in mockery, Apollonius records, was the origin of ritual repartee between men and women which still (i.e., in the third century) forms part of the worship of Apollo Aigletes on the island.

This same episode was also treated by Callimachus in his *Aitia*, in a passage probably but not certainly written earlier than the *Argonautica*.[94] Fr. 21 Pfeiffer (23 Massimilla), already cited in **F1c** above, compared the ritual laughter of the occasion – which the poet had picked out as a *paradoxical* phenomenon, requiring an explanation from the Muses (fr. 7.19–20 Pfeiffer, 9.19–20 Massimilla) – with that which occurs in an Eleusinian context. The details of the Callimachean treatment can hardly be reconstructed, but they included coarse jeering (χλεύη or a cognate, fr. 21.9 Pfeiffer) as well as an indication of the women's (original) pleasure in the badinage (fr. 21.8).[95] Both these points match the version of Apollonius (4.1726–7), who enriches their implications by using the noun *molpē* (1728), a term which may combine nuances of 'song' (the badinage is quasi-antiphonal) and 'game' or 'sport' (the abuse is playfully stylised); suggestions of dance-like enactment are perhaps additionally present.[96] There is a clear affinity here with the choruses of ritual mockery on Aegina in **F7** above. We should

---

[93] The verb ἐπιστοβέω, 1725 (cf. the women at 3.663: callous jeering, not ritualised banter), seems to signify 'hitting out' with abuse, perhaps also, here, with boastful self-assertion: cf. Livrea (1973) 472, Chantraine (1968) *s.v.* στέμβω, Campbell (1983) 109. On flyting, see n. 116 below.

[94] Callimachus' priority to Apollonius is a standard view, e.g. Fraser (1972) 1 638, 722, though the broader relationship between them remains vexed: see e.g. Hutchinson (1988) 85–9, Cameron (1995) 247–62. But relative chronology has no bearing on my present concerns.

[95] See Massimilla (1996) 280–1, 283–4 for further details, with *idem* 255–7 and Fantuzzi and Hunter (2004) 45 on the earlier request to the Muses. It is sometimes conjectured that *Aitia* frs. 603, 656 Pfeiffer (128, 132 Massimilla), both of which refer to exchanges of abuse, might have belonged to this episode; but see Massimilla (1996) 457, 460. Note also Callim. fr. 668 (134 Massimilla), of unknown context, mentioning the victory of the Argonaut Erginus in a race on Lemnos: Σ on Pind. *Ol.* 4.32, cited by Pfeiffer and Massimilla *ad loc.*, tell how before his victory the prematurely greying Erginus was mocked (noun *chleuē*) by the Lemnian women; Burkert (1983) 195 speculatively links this with ritual laughter for Hephaestus (and the Kabeiroi) on Lemnos (cf. n. 14 above).

[96] Apollonius uses μολπή also at 1.28 (Orpheus' singing), 3.897, 949–50 (flower-picking as pastime), 4.894 (the Sirens' song); cf. Livrea (1973) 259. Homeric usage of noun and verb covers various combinations of song, dance and play; cf. Garvie (1994) 106–7, Pulleyn (2000) 241. Compare Italian *canzonare*, 'tease', from *canzone*, song. On antiphonal form, see 194–5 below.

also register an oblique thematic interplay between the Anaphe myth as told in Apollonius and the Lindian story of Heracles in Callimachus (**F9**): in the former the women laugh because the improvised 'sacrifice' is a pale imitation of the sacrifices of *bulls* they had seen on Scheria (*Argon.* 4.1723–4). It is possible that Callimachus is creating an ironic counterpoint between the laughter/sacrifice themes in the two narratives.

Ritual scurrility between the sexes in the cult of Apollo Aigletes at Anaphe is also attested by later mythographers: Conon *Dieg.* ch. 49 (*FGrH* 26 F1, *apud* Phot. *Bibl.* 186), refers to Medea's maids getting drunk and teasing the heroes at a nocturnal celebration, and pseudo-Apollodorus *Bibl.* 1.9.26 has a similar version. Slightly different from the Callimachean/Apollonian accounts, these sources nonetheless share an emphasis on the role of the women as *initiating* the badinage, though Conon stresses the reciprocity of the resulting flyting by using the unique verb, ἀντιτωθάζειν (to answer mockery with mockery). This makes it likely that involvement of female groups was (thought) a prominent feature of the Anaphaean cult. Finally, Conon's account calls the maids a 'wedding present' to Medea, which perhaps hints at a connection with the sexual scurrility that was sometimes ritualised at weddings.[97]

Inscriptional evidence from Anaphe shows that the earliest form of Apollo's cult title on the island was Asgelatas and the cult itself was called the Asgelaia. Walter Burkert has suggested that this is a version of the Akkadian *azugallatu*, 'the great healer', a title of the goddess Gula.[98] Whether or not that is right, it is striking that the non-Greek form, Asg*el*atas, would lend itself to a pseudo-etymological connection with *gelōs*, laughter. Is this coincidence, or did it at some stage encourage a custom of ritual laughter which was in due course explained by an *aition* relating to the Argonauts' return?

F9

Juxtaposed with the Anaphaean rites of Apollo Aigletes (**F8**) in Callimachus, *Aitia* fr. 7.19–21 Pfeiffer (9.19–21 Massimilla) is the incorporation of foul language or 'curses' (*dusphēma*) in sacrifices to Heracles at Lindos. The poem went on to tell the story of how a Lindian farmer originally cursed Heracles after the hero had stolen an ox from him; the curses washed over Heracles (who had enjoyed his meal so much), a piquant case of mockery insouciantly disregarded as well as of Heracles' fluctuating persona (which

---

[97] Cf. n. 125 below.
[98] Burkert (1992) 78–9; cf. West (1997) 55. The forms Ἀσγελάτας and Ἀσγελαῖα are found in *IG* XII 3.248–9.

moves, as discussed in Chapter 3, between heroic ruthlessness and comic buffoonery). The incident subsequently gave rise to an obligatory element in the Lindian cult of *Bouthoina*, 'Bull Sacrifice', dedicated to Heracles. The paradoxical combination of sacrifice with cursing led to the proverbial expression, 'the Lindians and sacrifice', applied to those who carry out rituals with foul language.[99]

In a second Heraclean theft of an ox (this time from the Thessalian Theiodamas) related by Callimachus in this same stretch of the *Aitia*, we meet a double reference to laughter: first, the mixed laughter and discomfort of Heracles as he carries his hungry baby son, Hyllus (*Aitia* fr. 24.3 Pfeiffer, 26.3 Massimilla: a wry adaptation of the mixed parental emotions in the famous episode of Hector and Andromache at *Iliad* 6.466–93);[100] second, the spiteful roar of laughter from Theiodamas as he refuses Heracles' request for food (fr. 24.13). In what followed it seems that Theiodamas reviled Heracles in language Callimachus counts as unrepeatable ('may none of it slip through my teeth . . .', fr. 24.20). It looks, therefore, as though the pair of Heraclean stories complemented the Anaphaian narrative (**F8**) by developing an interwoven, paradoxical pattern of laughter and abuse. In the first story, Heracles is the object of abuse but is capable, because of his preoccupation with food, of brushing it aside – though it then attaches to him perpetually in the resulting cult. In the second story, he laughs himself with paternal gentleness but is also laughed at and viciously abused again: this time his reactions are both similar (the theft of another ox) and different (great anger, triggering a chain of events that will involve, among much else, the death of Theiodamas). The shifting significance of laughter and insults is dramatically foregrounded, and Heracles stands at the centre of a complex thematic web which is in keeping with the ambiguities of his traditional persona as well as with the ironies that are sometimes embedded in the aetiologies of Greek cultic practice.[101]

---

[99] Callim. *Aitia* frs. 22–3 Pfeiffer (24–5 Massimilla) is what remains of the story; cf. Hutchinson (1988) 43–7 for some aspects of its telling. The proverb, Λίνδιοι καὶ θυσίαν, is attested at e.g. Zenob. *Epit. paroem.* 4.95, Lactantius, *Div. Inst.* 1.21.31–7; cf. ps.-Apollod. *Bibl.* 2.5.11. Cf. Fluck (1931) 63–5, Burkert (1970) 364–5.

[100] See ch. 2, 53–5.

[101] Pfeiffer (1922) 78–102 sifts the sources for both Heracles' thefts of oxen in the *Aitia*; cf. Fraser (1972) I 722–3, II 1008–9, with Massimilla (1996) 285–99 for commentary. On other aspects of the Lindian story, see Durand (1986) 149–59, and Barigazzi (1976) on the Theiodamas story in Callimachus and Apollonius (*Argon.* 1.1211–20). In the version followed in the (imaginary) painting at Philostr. maj. *Imag.* 2.24, where Theiodamas is the name of the Lindian farmer himself, Heracles' smiles (Appendix 2 n. 2) at the curses hurled at him are the aetiology of the pleasure he now takes in his cult. On Heraclean ambiguities *vis-à-vis* laughter, see ch. 3, 131–3.

F10

The *Suda*'s entry *s.v.* τὰ ἐκ τῶν ἁμαξῶν σκώμματα (cf. **F1e**, **F6b** above)
refers to occasions ('specified days') when the people of Alexandria carried
out a 'purification of souls' (καθαρμὸν ἐποιοῦντο ψυχῶν).[102] 'Men on
wagons' went through the streets, stopped outside any house they wished,
and abused the inhabitants – but only, we are assured, with *true* reproaches.
The stated purpose of this allegedly charivari-type practice of folk justice,
which seems not to be attested anywhere else, was to make people 'shun
wickedness'. But the entry as a whole seems to amalgamate two models of
explanation for such blatant verbal assaults, one quasi-apotropaic and the
other a matter of social control through public shaming (as, e.g., in **F12a**
below).

F11

At Plato, *Euthydemus* 277d–278e, against a background of gelastically
charged antagonism (discussed fully in Chapter 6), Socrates offers young
Cleinias reassurance and help in the face of two sophists' bewildering arguments. He tells Cleinias that Dionysodorus and Euthydemus are behaving
'like people in the Corybantic rites, when they carry out the ritual enthronement (*thronōsis*) of the person they are about to initiate': the sophists, he
explains, are 'dancing playfully' (ὀρχεῖσθον παίζοντε) round Cleinias in a
way comparable to the 'dancing and play' (χορεία . . .καὶ παιδιά) which
takes place round the initiate in the Corybantic setting.[103] Ritual enthronement was an element in more than one religious context, including certain
mystery cults; I suggested earlier that the *tōthasmos* at Aristophanes *Wasps*
1362–3 may comically refract events belonging immediately after the rite
of *thronōsis* for Eleusinian initiands (see **F1b** above). But we have no other
source which refers to precisely what Plato has in mind in the present passage. The language of 'dance' and 'play' often overlaps in Greek.[104] But
Socrates' ironic imagery evokes a special kind of dancing, and evidently
ascribes to the sophists an intention to mock their would-be 'initiate'. The

---

[102] The purification posited here looks quasi-apotropaic and therefore different from the psychological
katharsis at Iambl. *De myst.* 1.11 (160 above).

[103] At 277d9 the mss. mostly have χορηγία (cf. on **F7** above) for χορεία. On the dramatic context,
see ch. 6, 288–9. Dodds (1951) 79, with n. 104, takes at face value the implication that Cleinias,
and perhaps Socrates himself, might have been a Corybantic initiate; cf. Morgan (1990) 27. But we
should not rule out the possibility of some irony in this respect. Cf. Edmonds (2006), though he
neglects the emphasis on ritual play. The most recent discussion of Plato and Corybantic ritual in
general is Velardi (1989) 73–98. For another possible combination of ritual laughter with dance in
an initiatory context, see Callim. *Hymn Delos* 321–4, with 169 above.

[104] See ch. 1, 20.

passage should therefore be treated as an allusion to a type of ritual laughter. There are two main possibilities: one, that the dancing is imagined as accompanied by verbal play or teasing; the other, that the dancing itself is meant to convey and/or cause mirth.[105] A combination of verbal and choreographic ridicule seems most plausible. This reading of *Euthd.* 277d produces a parallelism to the pattern of behaviour posited at Aristophanes *Wasps* (**F1b** above). In both cases, ritualised mockery or teasing is a prelude to initiation. Although Socrates goes on at *Euthd.* 278b to refer to making fun of people by tripping them up or pulling a stool from under them, and while practical jokes do sometimes figure in ritual settings in other cultures, it does not look as though there is a direct connection here with the 'play' of *thronōsis*.[106]

F12a

Plutarch's life of *Lycurgus* 14.3 describes (unnamed) festivals at Sparta when choruses of girls aim jokes or gibes (*skōmmata*) at individual young Spartiates in an audience consisting of kings, elders and the rest of the citizens. The passage is part of a larger description of the singing and dancing of Spartan girls: the gibes in question could themselves be embedded in choral song (like the encomia which complement them on the same occasions) or might perhaps be just spoken (Plutarch uses the verb λέγειν, though that is not a decisive consideration). Either way, we have here another case of female group performance, conceivably with choreographic accompaniment. Plutarch explains the performance as a manifestation of 'play' (*paidia*) that was nonetheless targeted against young men who exhibited faults of some kind; it was therefore meant to carry a certain 'bite' (δήξεις) and to serve as a social corrective (cf. **F10** above). This moralised account is of a piece with Plutarch's overall presentation of laughter in Spartan society; this may or may not reinforce its reliability as evidence for a much earlier period of Spartan history.

F12b

As noted in Chapter 1, a number of Spartan traditions of scurrility are attested for the archaic period and later. Since the evidence, though skimpy, includes special terminology for the performers (especially δ(ε)ικηλίκται,

---

[105] For mocking dances, see ch. 1 n. 91. Lucian, *Salt.* 15 asserts that there is no initiation ritual (*teletē*) without dance.

[106] The lack of a connection seems marked by Socrates' use of a different word for 'stool' (σκολύθριον) in the second passage. Douglas (1975) 109 mentions practical jokes during initiation rituals; cf. n. 34 above.

'exhibitors', and βρυλλιχισταί, a word of unknown meaning) and goes back in part to the early Hellenistic Spartan antiquarian Sosibius, it can be trusted in outline at least.[107] Some of the performers in question have the look, from a later perspective, of 'regular' comic actors. Sosibius apparently classed the acting of the 'exhibitors' as a species of 'comic play' (κωμικὴ παιδιά), and their miniature scenarios sound like free-standing shows, though we have no idea of the occasions of their performances. At the same time, we should notice that among the other groups with whom Athenaeus compared these Spartan mummers are the 'phallus-carriers', *phallophoroi* (**F6** above). It is prudent, therefore, not prematurely to disengage 'comedy' from 'ritual' in this area; the relationship between the two is complex for the understanding of ritual laughter in general and will require further thought below. Hesychius' description of the murky βρυλλιχισταί – they 'put on ugly female masks and sing hymns' – underlines the need to reserve judgement on the appropriate categories with which to interpret such phenomena. One other intriguing but elusive consideration is a possible connection between this second group and the seemingly 'grinning' (in some cases possibly female) terracotta masks found among archaic deposits of votives in the shrine of the goddess Ortheia at Sparta. Exactly which of these masks, if any, signify expressions of laughter, as opposed to scared/scaring grimaces or the like, is a question fraught with difficulties. The most elaborate attempt to explain the origins and use of the masks (or their presumed originals) focuses on a hypothetical fertility cult borrowed from Phoenician models but does not accept the *brullichistai* connection.[108] No decisive conclusion can be reached here. But the possibility remains open that the masked hymn-singers and the masks on which the Ortheia votives were modelled belonged independently (or conceivably in conjunction) to frameworks of performance involving elements of ritual laughter.

F13

Finally, as oblique evidence for Greek perceptions of ritual laughter, I catalogue here the Egyptian case already cited from Herodotus 2.60 (cf. **F1b**). This describes the celebration of the festival of 'Artemis' (Bastet) at Bubastis. En route to Bubastis, crowded barges of Egyptian men and women sail along the coast in a heady atmosphere of music (for *aulos* and castanets), singing and clapping. Whenever they pass a city, the barges approach the shore and

---

[107] See ch. 1, 46.   [108] Carter (1987): see ch. 1 n. 122, Appendix 2, 546.

some of the women shout obscene taunts (*tōthazein*) at the women of the place, while others dance or lift their dresses to expose themselves, a gesture we have already encountered in connection with Baubo/Iambe (**F1a**) but which there is reason to believe is an authentically Egyptian detail.[109] To a Greek mind, the mood of the journey as depicted is unmistakably komastic, though unlike a normal Greek *kōmos* in the free mixing of men and women: it is not surprising that Herodotus comments directly on the exceptional amount of wine consumed in the festival at Bubastis itself. Against that background, both the *tōthasmos* and the act of genital exposure look like modes of ritualised derision which also embody temporary liberation from the shame-regulated norms of ordinary life. But as with all the material catalogued above, the question of just what is being expressed in ritual conduct of this kind raises knotty issues of cultural interpretation. And it is to those issues that I now turn.

PATTERNS AND EXPLANATIONS

The sources surveyed in the previous section are so disparate – in date, character and quality of information – that it would be foolhardy to erect a monolithic theory of ritual laughter on the basis of them. But as I argued near the start of the chapter, Greek culture generated an awareness of affinity between various cultic contexts in which ridicule and obscenity (whether verbal or visual) played a constitutive part. The catalogue of individual festivals has borne out that claim, as well as demonstrating a heavy concentration of relevant phenomena within the worship of Demeter and Kore (**F1–5**) and Dionysus (**F6**).[110] With these deities, ritual laughter seems well embedded by (at least) the later archaic period and occurs in multiple festivals (and in more than one city), whereas in the cases of Apollo (**F8**) and Heracles (**F9**), for example, we are dealing with what may have been unique instances. In addition to individual details already broached above, we can construct a basic typology of Greek ritual laughter in terms of the permutations of (a) the cult (deity and location) to which it belongs, (b) the status of the participants, (c) the objects or targets of laughter (where known), (d) the timing and precise context (especially whether public or private). The results can be seen from the Table.

---

[109] On Hdt. 2.60 see Lloyd (1975–88) II 272–6, esp. 275 for independent evidence of genital self-exposure by Egyptian women.

[110] Cole (1993) 33, Robson (2006) 74 are wrong, however, to make ritual obscenity *exclusive* to Demeter and Dionysus.

	LOCATION	DEITY	PARTICIPANTS	TARGETS	OTHER DETAILS
F1	Eleusinian Mysteries	Demeter, Kore (and Iacchos)	men and women, according to context	passers-by etc. (*gephurismos*); family (**F1b**)	various locations and contexts; aetiology: Iambe's (or Baubo's) amusement of Demeter
F2	Haloa (Eleusis)	Demeter, Kore (and Dionysus?)	women	members of group	held in secret; fertility symbols
F3	Thesmophoria (Athens and Sicily)	Demeter, Kore	mostly women (but some men, **F3a**)	members of group (and others?)	held in secret; fertility symbols
F4	Stenia (Athens)	Demeter, Kore	women	members of group	prelude to Thesmophoria
F5	Mysaion, near Pellene	Demeter	men and women	members of other sex	follows nocturnal women-only rites
F6	Dionysia (various), Athens and elsewhere (incl. Taras, cf. **F6a**)	Dionysus	(masked) jesters 'on wagons'; singers of phallic songs; komasts	general	use of wagons as mobile stages in processions
F7	Oa (Aegina) and Epidaurus	Damia and Auxesia	'choruses' of women	other women	choruses led/organised by male *chorēgoi*
F8	Anaphe	Apollo Aigletes	women	men?	aetiology: Medea's Phaeacian maids
F9	Lindos	Heracles	worshippers at sacrifice	not known	paradox of 'foul-mouthed' sacrifice
F10	Alexandria	not known	'men on wagons'	local inhabitants	for 'purification of souls'
F11	Corybantic ritual (Athens)	Kybele? Dionysus?	those present at ritual *thronōsis*	initiands	mockery enacted in dancing
F12	Sparta	Ortheia? Artemis? (and others?)	(a) choruses of Spartan girls; (b) masked mummers	young Spartiate males (in some cases)	general citizen body present at (some) performances
F13	Bubastis (Egypt)	Bastet ('Artemis')	local women on boats	women of other towns	song, dance; female exposure

Rarest, it seems, is the combination of male participants and a 'secret' (or private) setting: only **F1b** conceivably falls into this class. The conjunction of female participants with a secret setting, on the other hand, is common: this is chiefly a reflection of the number of cases relating to Demetrian cults which count, more or less strictly, as 'mysteries'.[111] It is not to be underestimated, however, that mystery cults can admit public ritual laughter too; the Eleusinian Mysteries undoubtedly included at least one such phenomenon (*gephurismos*), however sketchy the evidence. Furthermore, public and concealed rituals could obviously intersect in a number of ways: in **F5** nocturnal women-only rites are *followed*, the next day, by public exchanges of jokes between men and women; and in the Epidaurian (though not the Aeginetan) case in **F7** Herodotus speaks of a coupling of secret rites with the public mocking songs of organised choruses. Ritual laughter, it appears, can turn up anywhere in a Greek festival (*heortē*), from its core rites (*teletai*) to the wider social celebrations that surround them.

It is difficult to make much headway with the interpretation of cases where women are said to have engaged in ritual laughter in secret. Even if secrecy was not preserved in all respects, our ancient sources transmit little knowledge of what went on. Not a single text indicates anything like a plausibly fleshed-out familiarity with the mockery or jesting that took place on these occasions. Revealingly, when Aristotle generalises about cults in which religious tradition permitted *tōthasmos*, he does not even acknowledge that women themselves participate in some of these; he speaks, in fact, of adult males worshipping on behalf of their wives or female relatives.[112] I have already suggested (under **F2**) that some of our sources in this area may have been influenced by ultimately *comic* stereotypes (found in such works as Aristophanes' *Thesmophoriazusae*, as well as perhaps circulating in humorous gossip) of how women would be likely to behave in secret, especially if fuelled by alcohol (as, for instance, at the Haloa) and occupied with rituals relating (in part) to sexual fertility. Some of what comes down to us concerning women-only rites may be little more than a tissue of male fantasy and prejudice. Modern speculations about a distinctive female 'subculture' within the secrecy of such festivals carry some plausibility, though

---

[111] The evidence for ritual scurrility in another Demeter festival, the Skira, is practically non-existent. For what is known of the festival see Parker (2005) 173–7, Parke (1977) 156–62, Burkert (1983) 143–9. *Contra* O'Higgins (2003) 20 (wrongly citing Rosen (1988) 30 n. 73, where the same claim is not made), Ar. *Eccl.* 877–937 has no bearing on the Skira. Both Burkert (1985) 230 and, more blatantly, Keuls (1985) 357 use Ar. *Eccl.* naively in drawing large inferences about the festival.

[112] See n. 10 above.

we cannot afford to forget that the framework of such events remained under the control of civic magistrates.[113] It makes attractive sense, but cannot be more than an imaginative reconstruction, to suppose that female ribaldry on these occasions reflected in part an atmosphere of religously sanctioned sexual self-awareness (in keeping with the sexual symbols sometimes employed: **F2**, **F3b**, and the possible allegory of Baubo's story, **F1a**), and in part a temporary independence from male surveillance.

Where the settings of ritual laughter were fully public, we seem to be on safer ground. One thing which stands out here is a strong tendency towards the dynamics of quasi-theatrical performance, i.e. the provision of a 'staged' spectacle for an audience (sometimes literally a theatre audience: **F6c**). That basic schema does not exclude the possibility of interaction (and to that extent a blurring of the distinction) between performers and audience, especially where the latter becomes itself an object of ridicule (**F1d**, **F13**), but it does draw attention to a notable type of arrangement. A conspicuous case of ritual laughter as staged performance is the Aeginetan and Epidaurian choruses in **F7**, where the role of *chorēgoi*, however exactly we understand the term, presupposes elaborate organisation of groups for public and probably competitive display. Two related implications of this situation are that the groups were selected (as singer-dancers) and that they *rehearsed*, rather than indulging in wholly improvised derision.[114] It is unclear from Herodotus' words ('they denigrated no male but the local women') whether the choruses in question mocked each other or only third parties. In the circumstances mentioned in both **F5** and **F8**, however, reciprocal or amoebean exchanges of badinage are certain, though between groups of opposite sex. Agonistic traditions of this kind may have influenced Aristophanes' handling of his double chorus in *Lysistrata*, in which the antagonistic groups of old men and old women engage – in both lyric (sung) and recitative (chanted) metres – in markedly tit-for-tat, competitive abuse, some of it evidently reinforced with obscene gestures.[115] That play's

---

[113] The fullest case for such a subculture is made by O'Higgins (2003), esp. 15–36, stressing women's assertion of control over their own fertility; cf. Brumfield (1996) 71–4, though she sees ambiguity in the incorporation of 'secret' female fertility within (male-organised) religious structures. Forsdyke (2005) 81 overstates in claiming that at the Thesmophoria and elsewhere 'women took control . . . by excluding men'. Cf. n. 53 above. Comedy (perhaps reliably) hints that genuine secrecy surrounded (some) elements of the Thesmophoria: see esp. Ar. *Eccl.* 442–3, with Austin and Olson (2004) xlv. For imagined moments of non-ritual sexual banter between women in private, see Ar. *Lys.* 81 (*double entendre*), Hdas. 1.18–21, 6.78–80.

[114] It is risky, however, to claim that ritual abuse was 'usually' rehearsed rather than 'spontaneous or free-form': Henderson (1991) 14 n. 34. For improvised insults, cf. 181 with n. 82 above.

[115] See Henderson (1987a) 98 (but wrongly claiming *men* were involved in exchanges of insults at the Stenia: see **F4**); cf. Henderson (1991) 17, Winkler (1990) 198 n. * (*sic*), with Wallochny (1992) 13–21

antiphonal stylisation of insults, which also occurs between individuals elsewhere in Aristophanes (for example, between the Paphlagonian and the Sausage-Seller in *Knights*, or the two Arguments in *Clouds*), surely echoes to some extent the conventions of game-like abuse or 'flyting' that are at any rate one dimension of the ritual laughter reported in **F5, F7, F8**, and possibly in **F3b** and **F4** too.[116] Where the occasions of ritual laughter were shaped by 'choruses', allowance has always to be made for specifically choreographic, including gestural, elements of ridicule or mirth (see under **F8, F11, F13**). This is one of several ways in which ritual laughter could enlist the resources of the whole body, not just the voice.

It is undeniable, then, that many cases of ritual laughter took the form of a 'stage-managed' event presented by designated groups for the gratification of spectators; such a factor might even have entered into some of the rituals held away from the public gaze.[117] Despite doubts about its details, this may have been true of *gephurismos* (**F1d**) as well, especially if some sort of masking was involved. The mask (allegedly) *not* worn by Epicrates in the scene deplored at Demosthenes 19.287 (**F6b**) bears out the same principle in reverse, as it were. Because 'Curebion' dispenses with the mask (and perhaps a more extensive costume) which would conceal his identity and transform him into a participant in an officially sanctioned *kōmos*, his behaviour can no longer count as 'framed' by ritual convention and becomes vulnerable to a charge of shamelessness.[118] This is not to

on tit-for-tat abuse in Aristophanes. Adrados (1975) 293–7 discusses 'fighting' choruses, but very freely. Note Ar. *Lys.* 824–8 for a hint of Baubo-like genital exposure (with **F1a** and n. 26 above); cf. *Eccl.* 890, with Σ[R] *ad loc.*, for a probably cognate gesture, conveying contempt: see Ussher (1973) 197–8 for hypotheses. *Eccl.* 97 gives the motif a different comic twist.

[116] See esp. *Lys.* 354–86, *Kn.* 284–302, 367–81, 694–711, *Clouds* 908–48; cf. Collins (2004) 30–43, 48–50, Hesk (2007). Sympotic exchanges are glimpsed at e.g. *Hom. Hymn* 4.55–6 (with ch. 3, 101–3), Ar. *Wasps* 1308–13 (*eikasmos*: see MacDowell (1971) 304); cf. Halliwell (1991a) 291, and note the idea of comic tit-for-tat (ἀνταποδιδόναι) at Pl. *Phdr.* 236c. There may be (ironic) hints of stylised badinage at Theoc. 1.33–5 (reflected in the girl's laughter, 36?). Comparative material for amoebean insults/jokes can be found in numerous cultures, including Rome (fescennine verses: Hor. *Epist.* 2.1.145–6): in addition to the cases adduced by Parks (1990) 42–3, Hesk (2007) 126 n.9, see Elliott (1960) 70–4, Steblin-Kamenskij (1978–9) 161–2 on Iceland, van Gelder (1988) on Arabia (cf. Geertz (1993) 116–17 on Moroccan–Islamic song); cf. Finnegan (1977) 158, Huizinga (1949) 66–71, Cochran (1979). On the term 'flyting' itself, see Gray (1984). Auden (1963) 383 diagnoses tension between hostility and artistry in such exchanges.

[117] In the Iambe story (**F1a**) the seated goddess is herself the audience (as well as target) of the old woman's 'performance'. Some festivals might fall between public and private: the Adonia (n. 14 above), held by women alone but partly on rooftops, sometimes allowed observation by men (Ar. *Lys.* 389–98, Diphil. fr. 42.38–41, Men. *Sam.* 42–3; Theoc. 15.96–144 is a special case).

[118] Frontisi-Ducroux (1992) maintains that whole satyr costumes were normally worn by performers in such processions; cf. Σ *Dem.* 21.180 (n. 79 above), with ch. 5 n. 31 and Wilson (2000) 345–6 n. 213. For masks to conceal identity, note Chrysippus' claim (*SVF* III 196, XVII fr. 3), *apud* Origen, *Cels.* 4.63, that prostitutes formerly wore them.

suggest that in such settings a quasi-theatrical performance simply *displaces* or takes over from 'ritual'; the strands of spectacle and religiously prescribed protocols are interwoven. Nonetheless, it is important to recognise that in some instances the prominence of a kind of street-theatre provides a *raison d'être* in its own right. This is perhaps most obvious with Dionysiac 'men on wagons', parading through the streets in festive processions or pageants (**F6**). In stark contrast to the enclosure and concealment accompanying several Demetrian occurrences of ritual laughter (**F2, 3, 4**), Dionysiac processions invite open attention as mobile displays. The wagons themselves serve as stages, comparable to the floats of late-medieval carnivals and other similar events. In one sense, then, some types of ritual laughter constitute their own form of 'theatre'.[119]

Yet it is not those rituals which centre on public display and quasi-theatrical performance, but those whose secrecy makes them intrinsically arcane, which have dominated modern attempts to conceptualise and even 'explain' ritual laughter. More specifically, it is the esoteric phenomena of concealed rites which have done much to encourage the two most widely favoured explanatory models of ritual laughter, those hinging round ideas of 'fertility magic' and of 'the apotropaic'. Theories of fertility magic are particularly associated with nineteenth-century comparative religion and anthropology, but their influence has been long lasting. Fertility magic rests on the principle that certain rituals are believed by their agents to activate or stimulate the natural forces of fertility, whether agricultural, animal or human, and thereby to conduce to the continuation and well-being of the community.[120] There are, for sure, some ancient traces of an explicit belief in the efficacy of obscenity upon fertility. Theophrastus, *Historia Plantarum* 7.3.3 reports a folk belief that 'cursing and using foul language'

[119] Schechner (1994) distinguishes between ritual, *qua* 'efficacy', and theatre, *qua* 'entertainment'. Although allowing for some overlap (622–3), he overstates the contrast between 'rule-bound' and 'freely creative' behaviour. Huizinga (1949) 14–26 discusses ritual, partly *qua* 'dramatic performances' (15), as a form of social play. On carnival floats (in Reformation Germany), see Scribner (1978) 303–9.

[120] Fertility magic: see, with varying nuances, e.g. Frazer (1911–36) vii 62–3 ('homoeopathic'/'imitative' magic), Reinach (1911), esp. 593, 596, Harrison (1922) 136, Propp (1984) 124–46 (with a Marxist-materialist theory of human evolution), Lloyd (1975–88) ii 275–6, Reckford (1987) 457, 461, 466–7, the last two combining fertility magic with an apotropaic model; cf. di Nola (1974) 75–7. Brumfield (1981) 93–4, 121–2 posits a 'mimic combat' between fertility and sterility, and a ritual of 'invigoration'; at 122–6 her position is hybrid, accepting a 'magical purpose' for sexual symbols at the Haloa but arguing that obscene joking 'simply arises out of the situation' (wine, absence of men, uninhibited concern with fertility) and need not be seen as 'magical' by the participants themselves. Olender (1990) 90–7 surveys modern apotropaic-cum-fertility models of explanation; his own preferred approach towards Baubo (97–106) posits a complex psychological counterpoint of fear and attraction. Cf. Adams (1982) 4–6 from a Roman angle. Note here, tangentially, a classic (but flawed) attempt to trace all 'satire' back to magic and ritual: Elliott (1960).

(καταρᾶσθαί τε καὶ βλασφημεῖν) while sowing cumin will assist the plant's growth; later in the same work (9.8.8), drawing an explicit analogy with the cumin passage, he mentions the idea of using explicit sexual language (and a dance) when cutting mandrake, presumably to increase the plant's efficacy as (in this instance) an aphrodisiac.[121] It is not out of the question that a belief of this kind lies behind the depiction on a mid-fifth-century Athenian red-figure vase of a woman sprinkling something over a group of phalli planted in the ground. There is here, at least, an association between phalli, fertility and the symbolic actions of women, though the precise significance of the image remains a matter of conjecture.[122] Because of the uneven survival of evidence, we cannot estimate how widespread was belief in some kind of 'fertility magic' in Greek antiquity. More importantly, there is little direct reason to connect any of the specific ritual contexts considered earlier in the chapter to such beliefs.

A preoccupation with fertility can be separated, however, from the hypothesis of 'magic', and once we make that move we can and should accept that much of the material with which we are concerned involves sexual-cum-procreative *symbolism*. This is most patent with the model genitalia, whether male or female, used in the relevant contexts of the Haloa (**F2**), Thesmophoria (**F3**) and Dionysiac phallic processions (**F6c**). The idea of such symbolism is expressly formulated in some ancient sources. The résumé of an ancient exegesis of Athenian festivals found in the scholia on Lucian's *Dialogues of Courtesans*, and already cited under **F2** and **F3b** above, calls phalli in the (supposed) context of the Haloa a 'symbol' or 'agreed sign', *sunthēma*, of human fertility, and likewise with the piglets thrown into pits at the Thesmophoria.[123] The Neoplatonist Iamblichus (cf. 160), *De mysteriis* 1.11, uses the same term in designating phallic rites a symbol (*sunthēma*) of sexual fertility, while also advancing a psychological justification for such occasions with the principle that certain emotions and/or desires – obviously sexual in the case of phallic rites – will be 'moderately' and 'briefly' aroused but will then harmlessly subside, thus producing the end result of *katharsis* or psychic cleansing. We must, of course, exercise great caution in using intellectual texts of this kind (the Lucianic scholia may ultimately

---

[121] Theophr. *ibid*. 9.9.1, lists several applications of mandrake/mandragora; cf. Arnott (1996) 419 for its use in Greek culture. Ariston of Chios *SVF* 1 387 (= Stob. 2.215.20) attests the same folklore about cumin-sowing and obscenity; cf. Graf, in *ThesCRA* 111 297–8, on botanical magic.

[122] B. Mus. E819, ill. in e.g. Deubner (1932) plate 3.3, Kilmer (1993) R940, Winkler (1990) frontispiece, Lewis (2002) 85: see n. 57 above.

[123] Σ on Lucian, *Dial. Meret.* 7.4 (280 Rabe), 2.1 (275 Rabe). The text distinguishes between 'physical'/'natural' (*phusikos*) and 'mythic' principles of explanation: see Lowe (1998) 153–6; cf. Parker (2005) 277 on 'instrumentalist' *versus* 'expressive' concepts of ritual.

derive from Hellenistic scholarship) in trying to reconstruct rationales of ritual that could have had a purchase on the minds of communities at large. There need not be a complete gap, however, between the two levels of thinking. Whatever his own special philosophical commitments,[124] Iamblichus refers uncontroversially to the notion of sexual symbolism *à propos* some major contexts of ritual laughter, both Demetrian and Dionysiac; he appears to presuppose an existing sense that such contexts were in part an expression of their communities' needs and hopes for fertility. Moreover, his text purports to characterise a participant 'phenomenology' in which a heightened state of sexual feeling was regarded as a legitimate part of the experience (though the *katharsis* theory added to this is an intellectualist construal of the matter). To jump back from this to a much earlier and totally different kind of text, we ought to notice that in Dicaeopolis' phallic song in *Acharnians* (**F6c** above, with 207–8 below) the ribald remarks he makes about his daughter are focused on the thought of her marriage and fertility. To that extent, and however much Aristophanes may have adapted the phallic setting to his own comic agenda, Dicaeopolis' sentiments may echo at any rate a subliminal concern of phallic rituals. Since sexual scurrility and mockery were also found in (some) wedding customs, a correlation between ritual laughter and a desire/hope for fertility forms a culturally well-embedded pattern.[125]

The most sophisticated analysis of the Lucianic scholia has stressed that a principle of fertility 'magic' as such is not present in their discussion (though we have seen traces of it in some ancient horticultural folk beliefs). Instead, great weight is placed on the idea that Demeter and Dionysus gave and give humans crops which are the basis of *civilisation*, i.e. life in agriculturally and socially settled communities: the relevant rituals, on this account, constitute 'commemorative symbols'.[126] If that is right, the element of laughter *per se* in such rituals might best be understood – as seems to be prefigured in Iambe's resistance to the death-related negativity

---

[124] Struck (2004) 218–24 discusses the terminology of *sumbola* and *sunthēmata* in Iamblichus' philosophy. Note that Iamblichus' cathartic model is an exception to the common principle that (e.g. obscene) words lead to equivalent deeds: cf. ch. 5 n. 19.

[125] Sexual scurrility in wedding songs is comically reflected at Ar. *Peace* 1340–1, 1359–60. The aischrologic *kōmos* of young men in adesp. lyr. 1037.15–17 *PMG* (ch. 3 n. 15) possibly pictures a wedding. John Chrys. *Prop. forn.* 1–3 (51.210–12 *PG*) attacks the 'ancient custom' (a description he disputes on a Judaeo-Christian timescale) of wedding processions with 'obscene songs' (πορνικὰ ᾄσματα, 210, cf. *Hom. in Mt.* 37.5, 57.425 *PG*, with 68.4, 58.644, and *Prop. forn.* 1, 51.209, for an association with the theatre), dissolute dances, unrestrained laughter, etc, including agonistic exchanges between groups (51.212 *PG*); see the related passage, *In ep. 1 Cor.* 12.5–7 (61.102–5 *PG*), with ch. 10 n. 68. Cf. n. 74 above.

[126] Lowe (1998) 153–6.

of Demeter's grief – as life-affirming exuberance, a vivacious accompaniment to festive celebration (or anticipation) of the fecundity of humans, animals and earth. It seems hermeneutically prudent, at any rate, to avoid projecting 'magical' properties onto laughter itself in this context, and to regard its concurrence with fertility rituals as more a matter of communal psychology and symbolism than the activation of covert processes or agencies. But this provisional conclusion will call for further refinement later on.

The second commonest explanation of ritual laughter in modern scholarship appeals to the notion of the apotropaic, i.e. the use of ritual acts to avert or ward off harm. This was undoubtedly a Greek concept of one function of ritual, but how closely can we associate it with ritual laughter? As with the 'fertility magic' model, this category of explanation can be further subdivided into symbolic cases, where no strong conviction about causation need be involved, and quasi-magical cases, where the ritual is taken (or hoped) to carry causal efficacy.[127] Of the specific testimonies catalogued earlier in this chapter, only one appears to involve an apotropaic assumption: that, at least, is likely to be the meaning of the 'purification of souls' (i.e. the warding off of evil spirits) in the *Suda*'s sketchy account of Alexandrian ritual mockery (**F10** above). However, an ancient theory of apotropaic aischrology is attested in two passages of Plutarch's *Moralia* that paraphrase the views of Xenocrates, third head of the Academy.[128] In the first of these, Xenocrates is named as the source of the principle that no true gods but only the worst sort of 'spirits' or 'demons', *daimones*, take pleasure in ritual aischrology (δυσφημίας ἢ αἰσχρολογίαν), and that 'when they receive it [sc. such worship] they turn to nothing worse' (καὶ τυγχάνουσαι πρὸς οὐδὲν ἄλλο χεῖρον τρέπονται): obscene language deflects the capacity of such spirits to do something 'worse'. The second passage, without mentioning Xenocrates, uses very similar terms to characterise rites performed 'for the sake of warding off (*apotropē*) such spirits' and calculated

---

[127] The apotropaic is the fundamental explanation of Fluck (1931) 31–3, 49, though like others (n. 120 above) he combines this with a fertility model (esp. 25–6, 32); he also allows for cultural evolution (esp. 50). Crawley (1917) explains ritual abuse as apotropaic gestures of *contempt*, deriving from the idea of sexual power (cf. n. 83 above). Zeitlin (1982) 145 denies apotropaic status for secret female obscenity.

[128] Plut. *Mor.* 361b, 417c (= Xenocrates frs. 229–30 Isnardi Parente); cf. 159–60 above. Plut. *Mor.* 587f describes abuse/curses as apotropaic, but this seems to refer to deflecting another's foul language with insults of one's own. Fluck (1931) 30–1 cites Philostr. *Vita Ap.* 2.4, where Apollonius abuses the bogey Empousa to scare her apparition away: this illustrates apotropaic use of foul speech, but its relevance to the phenomena of ritual laughter is dubious. For what it's worth, Pollux, *Onom.* 7.108 (citing Ar. fr. 607) calls objects designed to ward off the evil eye (ch. 8 n. 18) 'risible' (*geloios*), which may imply that they are apotropaic (partly) in virtue of the laughter they arouse.

to appease them. These texts leave no doubt about the basic notion of apotropaic rituals. However, their explanation of ritual indecency has little entitlement to be treated as a clue to a widely held mentality. Not only are its terms of reference those of a peculiarly philosophical theory of religion (Xenocrates'), but its main premise, that 'real' gods could take no pleasure in such things, is incompatible with the prominence of ritual laughter in the popular cults of Demeter and Dionysus. (In the *Homeric Hymn to Demeter*, we remember (**F1a**), the laughter originally instigated by Iambe becomes a permanent part of Demeter's gratified reaction to her cult.) Indeed, it is quite possible that Xenocrates intended his own position to involve a denial of orthodox views of such religious phenomena, translating their overtly celebratory features into evidence for a darker 'underside' to Greek religion.[129]

On the other hand, there is uncertainty about just what range of rituals Xenocrates' explanatory model was intended to embrace. Plutarch's paraphrase seems to connect the use of aischrology with cult contexts that count as gravely solemn or sombre, *skuthrōpos* (lit. 'grim-faced'), a term which unequivocally excludes laughter. Elsewhere, Plutarch himself uses a classification of religious practices which identifies the apotropaic with the sombre (*skuthrōpos*) and directly equates the latter with the 'laughterless'.[130] Two possible hypotheses suggest themselves here. The first is that the Plutarchan-Xenocratean texts in question have a restricted focus on types of aischrology that were not accompanied by any kind/idea of laughter (a focus that would exclude most of the material investigated in this chapter). The second, as already mooted, is that they represent a revisionist standpoint which ignores the ostensibly positive, celebratory traits of much ritual laughter in order to posit an alternative, 'demonological' account of apotropaic aischrology. Either way, the upshot for my purposes is a lack of strong support for any standard alignment in Greek religion between apotropaic explanations and the practices of ritual scurrility. While apotropaic customs and symbols may have been not uncommon

[129] Xenocrates may have had Demetrian rites in mind, especially the Thesmophoria, since Plut. *Mor.* 361b, 417c both refer to fastings in this same connection. On the larger issues of philosophical 'demonology', see Soury (1942) 50–3, Gwyn Griffiths (1970) 383–7, Brenk (1977) 85–112, Dillon (1996) 31–2, 216–19, Isnardi Parente (1982) 414–18.

[130] Plut. *Mor.* 361b, 417c use *skuthrōpos* (as well as ἀποφράς, '[day] of ill omen': for the combination cf. *Mor.* 518b) in connection with aischrologic rituals. At *Mor.* 369e, referring to Zoroastrianism but using a contrast evidently intelligible to Greek readers (cf. 370c), Plutarch sets up a dichotomy between ἀποτρόπαια/σκυθρωπά and rituals of prayer/thanksgiving. Cf. 378d for the equation of *skuthrōpos* with 'laughterless' (ἀγέλαστος: ch. 1 n. 100), and *Mor.* 517c for general usage. On the 'grimmest-faced' middle day of the Thesmophoria, see 176 and n. 64 above.

in antiquity,[131] there is scant reason to suppose that the apotropaic principle, especially in a form involving causal influence on supernatural powers, played much recognised part in the traditions of ritual mockery and obscenity.

This is an apt juncture, in fact, at which to temper the desire for 'explanations' altogether, or at any rate to lower our expectations of what they can do for us. Ritual laughter, *qua* prescribed provision for indecent mirth or mockery within a religious setting, is always *prima facie* incongruous – a highly paradoxical 'language game'. In Greek terms this can be seen most easily from the fact that ritual in general is associated with values of purity, shame, reverence and careful speech, whereas the immediate operations of ritual laughter are described by a vocabulary that stresses the opposite of all this. Ritual standardly calls for the careful filtering of utterances and the silencing of potentially inappropriate speech; hence the term, *euphēmia*, literally 'auspicious speech', often actually denotes 'silence'. Ritual laughter, by sharp contrast, is fuelled by unrestrained, shocking and 'unholy' speech, sometimes directly designated by *dusphēm-* terms (cf. **F9** above), i.e. as obtrusively 'foul-mouthed' or 'of ill omen', and frequently evaluated as 'shameful' (*aischros*). This deep-rooted tension was not lost on some ancient observers, though they responded to it with varying degrees of insight. Aelius Aristides, in second-century AD Smyrna, insisting that religious custom proclaims or requires *euphēmia* as a central value, vehemently deprecates the 'contradiction' of this principle in the grossly abusive, shameful language of various (especially Dionysiac) festivities, including comedy. He can see that the second phenomenon itself appeals to a religious justification ('we make the gods to whom we are sacrificing the pretext [*prophasis*] for hearing and saying the most shameful things'), but he struggles, indeed fails, to see that it is just as firmly embedded in religious tradition as the euphemic principle which it so pointedly infringes.[132] Another imperial author, Plutarch, goes so far as to characterise *most* (Greek) religion as embodying a conflict between euphemic theory and dusphemic practice, though he is thinking in part of the general atmosphere of public celebration which was typical of Greek festivals.[133] In Callimachus, *Aitia* fr. 7.19–20

---

[131] On apotropaic phallic images (including Herms and Priapus), see Johns (1982) 50–2, 62–75, Slane and Dickie (1993) 486–94; cf. Wace (1903–4), esp. 110, Garland (1995) 108–9. For phallus-birds on vases, see Kilmer (1993) 195, Lewis (2002) 89, 127–8; cf. Dover (1989) 133.

[132] Ael. Arist. *Orat.* 29.4–11 Keil (40.505–7 Dindorf).

[133] Plut. *Mor.* 378d (where γελοῖα, 'ludicrous things', is pejorative but reflects actual laughter-related conduct), associating dusphemic practice with the realm of 'processions and festivals'. On the contrast between *euphēmia* and aischrology, cf. Burkert (1985) 73, 248, Stehle (2004) 126–30, 154–5, with n. 4 above.

Pfeiffer (**F8, F9** above), the paradox is flaunted by the poet's request to the muse Calliope for an explanation of how the Anaphaean ritual, with its *aischra* ('shameful words'), and the Lindian ritual with its (?)*dusphēma* ('foul words'), could have come into being. Because of the aetiological poetics of his project, Callimachus' narrative voice seeks an explanation in terms of origins. But that is only one way of explaining or interpreting a ritual. One might equally seek its significance in relation to its religious context (a city's festival calendar, for example), its overt symbolism, its attached myths (if any), its implicit or even 'secret' doctrine, its social dynamics, and no doubt other things besides – all of which may be grasped with varying degrees of clarity in the minds of different participants. On top of all this, laughter itself (whether as corporeal actuality or in the cultural resonances of what it betokens) is an exceptionally supple, volatile form of expression whose Greek meanings, as every part of this book attempts to demonstrate, are open to shifting construal.

Neither fertility magic nor the apotropaic will furnish a monolithic, let alone a neatly functionalist, explanation of ritual laughter. And nothing else will do so either. It makes best sense, indeed, to think of the very idea of explanation in this context as irreducible to a single origin or reference point. As Wittgenstein said of Frazer's *Golden Bough*, it is a mistake to assume a single motive or reason beneath every ritual action.[134] Cultural practices as complex as rituals need have no unitary origins at all, as opposed to an accumulation of layers that may not be separable in the minds of participants but were never designed in their totality by anyone. 'Ritual, every ritual', wrote Primo Levi, 'is condensed history and pre-history,' a condensation which defies transparent analysis: as a result, in the formulation of one distinguished anthropologist of religion, rituals are extremely plastic.[135] What's more, even if we could reach back to earlier phases of a ritual's evolution, it would not follow that it would provide the key to later phases.[136] Since the phenomena that can be bracketed together as 'ritual laughter' are, whatever else may be said about them, forms of complex social behaviour (and always only one element in a larger religious ensemble) for which our evidence is inescapably selective, it is preferable to put on one side the pursuit of their long-range historical development and concentrate instead

---

[134] See the report of Wittgenstein's lectures in Moore (1959) 315–16, with Cioffi (1998) 155–81 for discussion of Wittgenstein's views in this area.

[135] Quotations from Levi (1985) 184 ('il rito, ogni rito, è un condensato di storia e di preistoria'), (1991) 199, Douglas (1975) 61. Cf. O'Higgins (2003) 17, Collins (2004) 230.

[136] Rösler (1993) 80 (cf. Rösler (1995b) 123) makes the strangely inflated claim that the roots of ritual aischrology 'lie at the origins of Greek culture'. Parker (2005) 157–9, 201 is sceptical about explaining Athenian festivals/rituals in terms of explicit functions or goals.

on producing the most carefully attuned, 'thick' descriptions of them that we can achieve.[137] That is why I have given priority to an account of culturally visible patterns over conjectural 'deep structures' and have tried to anchor the discussion in categories and ideas that we know were articulated by Greek experience. I do not thereby take for granted, however, that the workings of ritual were always or entirely perspicuous to those who took part in them.

If we apply to the material in my earlier catalogue the (unstable) distinction between 'consequential' and 'playful' laughter which I explained in Chapter 1, there is no reason to expect a uniform judgement to cover all cases. Nonetheless, there are grounds for maintaining that ritual laughter is paradigmatically not just framed but confined and controlled by inclusion within highly organised festive structures. Here it is important to register that Greek festivals in general provided a recognised setting and justification for behaviour that was exempted from some of the pressures and inhibitions of ordinary social life and which can count to that extent as 'playful' (meeting my three criteria of immunity from harm, self-conscious role-playing, and shared pleasure). Some of the texts catalogued earlier in the chapter foreground the keen if paradoxical pleasure taken by participants in ritual laughter: see, for instance, **F8**, where the ostensible hurling of insults is described (in the aetiological myth) as a source of mutual enjoyment, a kind of verbal and psychological game, for the groups involved. The gods created festivals, according to the Athenian in Plato's *Laws* (2.653c–d), as 'respite from toil' for human beings; to celebrate festivals (*heortazein*) is associated with pleasure and 'playing' (*paizein*) in the same text.[138] 'Even sensible people', as one Hellenistic writer puts it, 'will employ mirth (*geloia*) at the appropriate time, on occasions such as festivals and symposia'.[139]

Yet precisely because festivity in general legitimises the place of laughter in Greek religion, this factor on its own lacks the specificity to illuminate the occurrence of formalised joking and obscenity in particular cultic contexts. It needs therefore to be 'thickened' by being situated within individual festive-cum-ritual patterns, such as the contrasts between death and life, grieving and restoration, loss and recovery, which lie at the heart of the

---

[137] For 'thick' descriptions (originally Gilbert Ryle's usage), i.e. culturally nuanced and contextually rich accounts of behaviour, see Geertz (2000) 3–30.

[138] Pl. *Laws* 2.653c–d, 657d–e. Associations between festivity and laughter, play and release: e.g. Ar. *Birds* 729–34 (ch. 1, 22), Arist. *Rhet.* 2.3, 1380b3 ('play, laughter, festivity [*heortē*]'), Men. *Sam.* 41–2, Demetr. *Eloc.* 170, Strabo 10.3.9, Plut. *Mor.* 466e (with ch. 7 n. 44), 477d, 1101e.

[139] Demetr. *Eloc.* 170; cf. ch. 3 n. 50.

Demeter–Persephone story, or the distinctively Dionysiac parading of sexual disinhibition which seems to characterise such practices as the scurrility of 'men on wagons' or the performance of phallic songs. The enjoyment of aischrology and obscene antics within ritual settings, in other words, can be elucidated (though not, to repeat, fully 'explained') as typically bound up with symbolic (re)enactments of social affirmation in relation to fundamental parameters of communal experience. The overcoming of loss and grief; expectation of renewed life or increased fertility; awareness (or hope) of divine beneficence and protection; relief from tension in the face of the powerful forces of the gods and nature: glimpses of these and related possibilities can be found in the evidence already surveyed. We cannot, of course, rule out an element of 'consequential', goal-directed shaming of the targets of ritual laughter in some circumstances; that perception was always available, at any rate, as a rationalisation for those who needed it (cf. under **F10**, **F12**). But a spectrum of phenomena encompassing aischrology in the Thesmophoria, *gephurismos* on the way to Eleusis, the competing female choruses at Oa and Epidaurus, and various displays of demonstratively phallic ribaldry seems held together far more by a sense of 'worshippers at play' than by the consequential hostilities of laughter that were all too familiar in the normal flow of social life.

As a coda to this section, I would like to ask briefly how one might position Greek ritual laughter *vis-à-vis* the theory of carnival (and its attendant 'culture of laughter') elaborated in the writings of Mikhail Bakhtin. Bakhtin's model of 'the carnivalesque', both as a sociological phenomenon in late-medieval and early-modern Europe and as a literary mode (with some ancient antecedents) developed by Rabelais and others, has proved widely influential over the past half-century. But it has also prompted keen debate among historians about the definition of 'popular' culture, the social dynamics of carnival, and much besides.[140] Among classicists, Bakhtin's work has mostly received attention on the literary side, particularly in relation to Aristophanic comedy, but less so for the light it might shed on ritual laughter.[141] The main components of the Bakhtinian theory

---

[140] See esp. Bakhtin (1968) 1–58. Brief but trenchant criticisms of Bakhtin, including remarks on traditional Russian attitudes to laughter, in Averintsev (1993). Klaniczay (1990) 10–27 presents a balance-sheet *pro* and *con* Bakhtin's model of carnival; further appraisals in Gurevich (1988) 176–83, (1997), Morson and Emerson (1990) 433–70, Humphrey (2001) 28–36, Liberman (1995) 144–5. Renfrew (1997) 187–90, citing passages omitted from the English translation of Bakhtin's *Rabelais*, argues that Bakhtin himself was aware of instabilities in the concept of carnival.

[141] Bakhtin (1968) 28 n. 10 cites Old Comedy for 'grotesque realism', *ibid.* 98 n. 42 downplays resemblances between Aristophanes and Rabelais; cf. Edwards (1993) 94–7. Bakhtin has been discussed in relation to Old Comedy by Goldhill (1991) 176–88 (good on the tension between conservative

are, first, a somewhat problematic distinction between 'official' (political, ecclesiastical) and 'unofficial' (popular, anti-authoriarian) cultural forces; secondly, a centring of the latter on the expressive mode of 'grotesque realism' (conveyed above all by the imagery of the 'lower body' and its orifices); and, thirdly, an explication of the social function of carnival in terms of the renewal and revival of the community through the celebration of festive freedom.

Greek ritual laughter is hard to square with the first of these components. Although an element of 'unofficial' folk culture may sometimes have been present in the practices documented in this chapter, the dominant impression we receive is of integration into highly organised state festivals. Even a custom such as the scurrility of 'men on wagons' (**F6** above), however uninhibited its contents may have been, was probably a planned, scheduled part of festival processions. What's more, the deficiencies of our evidence cannot obscure the fact that in many cases (see the table on 192 above) the *targets* of ritual laughter were themselves (willing) participants in the event, not (simply) authority figures viewed with animosity. By the same token, the association of carnival on occasions, though by no means always, with outbreaks of active social protest or resistance, even sometimes with the violent overthrow of authority, is something hard to parallel on the Greek side, where ritual laughter took place under the auspices of politico-religious authority and was rarely if ever at odds with it.[142] As for Bakhtin's second carnivalesque feature, 'grotesque realism', there is good reason to accept that something of this sort was indeed a conspicuous factor in many forms of Greek ritual laughter: in the texts surveyed we have seen recurrent evidence for 'obscene' language and gesture, phallic and other sexual symbols, and some use of masked costumes. Finally, Bakhtin's view of the 'regenerative' power of carnival-type celebrations provides some comparative reinforcement for the line of argument I have taken above. Bakhtin posits what can be thought of as a culturally psychologised alternative to older anthropological concepts of fertility magic. To that extent, his account of carnival as figuring 'the death of the old and birth of the new'

and subversive factors), Edwards (1993), von Möllendorff (1995); Silk (2000) 299 denies that Old Comedy is carnivalesque in Bakhtin's sense. On Bakhtin's broader relevance to antiquity, see Rösler (1986), (1993) 86–91, and the essays in Branham (2002); cf. ch. 9 nn. 23, 53.

[142] Forsdyke (2005) interestingly but speculatively contends that social unrest in archaic Megara may have emerged from festive revelry. Rösler (1993) 90–1 reads a (supposed) outbreak of fighting between the sexes at the Dionysia on Chios (Harpoc., *Suda s.v.* Ὁμηρίδαι) as an 'escalation of (ritual) aischrology'; the story is too flimsy to sustain the thesis. On the various forms and effects of the early-modern carnival, see the classic case study of Le Roy Ladurie (1981), allowing for multiple social functions (283–99), Scribner (1978) 314–29 (carnival in Reformation Germany varying from 'youthful high spirits' to revolutionary ferment), Burke (1978) 178–204.

is one which, in its outlines at least, could be adapted to some forms of Greek ritual laughter. On such a reading, 'rebirth' or regeneration, as I have contended, becomes less a matter of actual (reproductive) fertility, important though that might be in certain contexts – the Thesmophoria being one – than a metaphor for and symbolic enactment of communal revivification through the bodily energies and psychological release of laughter. And the cogency of this conclusion is underpinned by the fact that most Greeks, unlike most (medieval) Christians, had reason to think of laughter as a suitable vehicle for the worship of the divine.

IS OLD COMEDY A FORM OF RITUAL LAUGHTER?

If one returns to my provisional definition of ritual laughter as not only arising inside a framework of religious ritual but constituting an expected component of the occasion, the question prompts itself: might not comic theatre at Athens, and especially Old Comedy, itself be classed as a case of 'ritual laughter'? Four immediate considerations could be cited in *prima facie* support of believing that it was. First, Old Comedy is embedded in Dionysiac festivities, one of the prime settings for other occurrences of ritual laughter; Aristophanes can even apply the specific vocabulary of 'secret rites' (*orgia*) directly to his genre, albeit within the fabric of verbally blatant parody.[143] Secondly and relatedly, Old Comedy was perceived by some Greeks as deriving genetically from phallic rituals (Aristotle, *Poetics* 4.1449a10–13, with **F6c** above), a circumstance arguably reflected in the wearing of the phallus by its actors.[144] Thirdly, Old Comedy exhibits strong parallelisms and affinities with the characteristic indecency of other practices discussed above, especially in its habits of extreme aischrology/obscenity and uninhibited personal mockery: like them, it is a manifestation of culturally institutionalised shamelessness. Finally, in the work of Aristophanes at any rate, Old Comedy displays an inclination to incorporate echoes and adaptations of ritual laughter into its own performances, as we have already had occasion to notice.[145] It is on a selection of these echoes and adaptations,

---

[143] See *Frogs* 356–7, treating comedy (with heavy irony, *pace* Lada-Richards (1999) 224–5) as a solemn initiation ritual; the point gets lost in Del Corno (1994) 176. For the term *orgia*, see the comic euphemism at Ar. *Lys.* 832 (cf. 898), and *Frogs* 384 (212 below), with n. 6 above.

[144] At *Pol.* 7.17, 1336b20 (cf. 159 above), Aristotle implicitly brackets comedy (and iambos) with obscene religious rituals: the words 'from the stage', gratuitously interpolated into the Oxford translation at 1336b13–4 (and kept in Barnes (1984) ii 2120), spoil the logic of the argument. Cf., more cautiously (but preserving the parallelism), Kraut (1997) 164–5.

[145] See esp. under **F1a–b**, **F1d**, **F6b–c**, **F11** and n. 116 above. For other traces of ritual themes in Old Comedy, see Bowie (2000) 327–31.

rather than the well rehearsed (but ultimately indecipherable) subject of Attic comedy's origins, that I now want to focus.[146]

Let us return first to the phallic procession and song at *Acharnians* 237–79 (cf. under **F6c, F1b**). Legitimate doubts can be raised about how authentically Aristophanes depicts this prototype of Dionysiac worship. And what, in any case, should count as the 'prototype' – a standard form (if there was such a thing) of phallic processions, or a markedly 'rustic' variety appropriate to the Rural Dionysia (as opposed to the grander, centrally organised version of the City Dionysia), or even an individual, family-oriented contribution to a larger pageant?[147] Such questions are essentially unanswerable. But it is at least possible to identify on a dramatic level the main ingredients of the imagined (or fantasised) ritual action. However solipsistically (in terms of the plot), Dicaeopolis is motivated to hold the Rural Dionysia by a desire to celebrate his escape from war and his recovery of the freedoms of peace (195–202). The taste (but also symbolism) of wine, which even carries a heady delusion of *divine* pleasure ('ambrosia and nectar', 196), arouses impulses of intoxicated joy at the renewal of his old life. These impulses carry over into the phallic procession and song, whose themes make a striking chain of associations, as well as some paradoxical juxtapositions: escape from (death-shadowed) war (251, 269–70, 279), the (re-)integration of the household, including slaves (249), the prospect of his daughter's marriage and therefore of reproductive continuity (253–8), the riotous sexual pursuits of a nocturnal revel (*kōmos*, 264–5), a return to the land (267), mockery of the city's official leaders (270), a fantasy of rural rape (271–5), and, hanging over the whole event, the spirit of deep intoxication (277–9).[148] Alcohol, sex, obscenity, scurrility and the mood of a return to 'the earth' are all bundled together, as it were, in the Dionysiac-phallic affirmation of the ritual. It is difficult to disentangle the depiction of ritual *per se* (with procession, prayers, sacred objects, sacrifice, etc., all alluded to in the text) from the activation of those pleasures which drive the whole comic plot forwards. In other words, the shamelessness, freedom and inebriated excesses of Dicaeopolis' Dionysia constitute not just an isolated

---

[146] As regards origins, a subject on which speculation has abounded, Pütz (2007) 123–8 cites a range of literature; Rusten (2006) provides a useful overview and composite model; cf. the more heterodox Stark (1995). Del Corno (1994) 177 says vaguely that *gephurismos* was considered (by whom?) part of the prehistory of comedy. I can find no trace of pre-comic antecedents in the Attic festival of Pyanopsia (or Pyanepsia), as suggested by Zanfino (2001), with sources on 67–71. More plausibly, Henderson (1991) 17 thinks obscenity in cult 'prepared the way' for similar comic freedom.

[147] Scholars have doubted that Dicaeopolis' song is an 'authentic' *phallikon*: e.g. Henderson (1991) 16 ('a humorous takeoff'), Thiercy (2000) 54 ('parodie'); cf. Kugelmeier (1996) 153–4.

[148] Cf. Halliwell (2002a) 120–4; detailed commentary in Olson (2002) 141–52.

theatrical episode but also a staged metaphor for the hedonistic licence of the comic genre to which it belongs.

If that is right, two alternative inferences suggest themselves. One is that Aristophanes has appropriated and distorted the customs of phallic processions for his own purposes, in the same way, for instance, that the Assembly scene earlier in the play is put at the service of an escapist political fantasy. The other is that he is dramatising, with whatever degree of inventiveness, a sort of *(con)fusion* of ritual laughter and Old Comedy which his audience could have felt as rooted in the underlying structures of cultural experience. Credibility is lent to this second possibility not only by the affinity on which Aristotle's view of comedy's evolution depends, but also by the Platonic vignette in the *Laws* (**F6a** above) of Dionysiac festivities in which intoxication, hedonism and exuberant scurrility come together in the entire social spirit of the event – a vignette which, notwithstanding the hostile slant put on it by the Spartan, must have at least some surface plausibility. Further corroboration can be drawn from Heraclitus' general observation on phallic processions (182 above), which attests a perception that such events carried a justification for saying and doing things which in other settings would count as 'most shameful'. And it is worth recalling, finally, that for those who attach basic importance to a 'fertility model' of the phenomena of ritual laughter, Dicaeopolis' procession includes a risqué anticipation of his own daughter's childbearing in marriage (254–6: cf. 166, 198 above). This looks like a comic encoding of one component of 'real' phallic ritual – all the more comic (but also conceivably true to latent tensions in the social organisation of such rituals) because of Dicaeopolis' preceding insistence that his daughter must not *smile* at any onlookers (254).

If the phallic procession and song of *Acharnians* allows Aristophanes to provide a 'domesticated', family-centred view of a larger context of ritual laughter, something comparable is also partly true at *Wasps* 1361–79 (**F1b** above), where Philocleon seems to evoke an Eleusinian setting (possibly that of 'enthronement', *thronōsis*, as I suggested earlier) by telling the abducted pipe-girl to stand with a torch while he prepares to engage in adolescent 'ribbing' or 'raillery', *tōthasmos*, of Bdelycleon, 'the way he once did to me before the Mysteries'. After Bdelycleon appears, there is indeed an exchange of abuse between father and son. But who exactly says what? Jeffrey Rusten, modifying the line attributions indicated in the manuscripts, assigns 1364–5 to Philocleon himself rather than his son, thus making him instantly fulfil his promise of *tōthasmos*:

ὦ οὗτος οὗτος, τυφεδανὲ καὶ χοιρόθλιψ,
ποθεῖν ἐρᾶν τ' ἔοικας ὡραίας σοροῦ.

You there! You there! You lunatic, you pussy-stroker!
You seem to long and lust for a lovely – coffin!

Rusten's proposal is attractive. It produces a scurrilous exchange that needs to be understood, in keeping with the preceding passage, as a spicily ironic inversion of the relationship between father and son. Philocleon abuses Bdelycleon as though he were a son retaliating for his father's teasing of him before initiation into the Mysteries; he does this by treating Bdelycleon as the old man (ready for his 'coffin', or even already dead, 1370) that he actually is himself.[149] But it is immaterial for my purposes which line attribution we adopt: one way, we get the inverted *tōthasmos* just indicated; the other, we get the comic surprise that just when he thinks he can take revenge on his son (or his 'father', in the terms of his fantasy) Philocleon suddenly *receives* foul abuse.

Philocleon's position in this whole scene is that of a solo, perverted komast whose alcoholic celebrations have run out of control. He also nicely reverses the force of Aristotle's definition of wittiness as 'educated *hubris*':[150] Bdelycleon's catastrophic attempt to 'educate' his father ends up creating new environments for his *hubris* to rampage through. Philocleon returns so drunk that he keeps falling over (1324); he has 'stolen' the naked pipe-girl from his fellow guests at the symposium (1369); he has engaged in verbal and physical *hubris*, both at the symposium and since leaving it (1303, 1319–23, 1388–1441); and he daydreams the role of a sexually rampant young man with an importunate phallus, though the 'reality' of sexual decrepitude is all too evident in the visible wilting of the latter (1341–50). Laughter is *part* of this state of inebriated, hubristic over-indulgence and hyper-egotism: on the one hand a laughter so thrustingly physical as to be palpably animal in character ('he jumped up, leapt around, farted and scoffed at everyone as though he were a donkey full-feasted on barley', 1305–6);[151] on the other, the laughter of boorish, abusive disregard for the interests of others (1319–20, 1406). This is laughter that starts at a symposium but

---

[149] See Rusten (1977), whose view fits best with *tōthazein* at 1368, which must otherwise be taken to mean 'play a practical joke' (cf. n. 34 above). Sommerstein (1983) 238 misses the possible irony of the passage. On the age-reversal theme in *Wasps* cf. Bowie A. (1993) 93–6.

[150] Arist. *Rhet.* 2.12, 1389b11–12, with ch. 6, 322–5.

[151] Cf. laughter and 'leaping' (σκιρτᾶν) at *Clouds* 1078, an association with 'natural' (i.e., in a sense, animal) shamelessness; Dover (1968) 227 cites Pl. *Rep.* 9.571c for the metaphorical σκιρτᾶν of the 'bestial' part of the soul. See ch. 1 n. 91, with 1–3 on animals and laughter.

becomes disastrously at odds with the canons of symposiac 'good cheer' or companionship, and then spills over into random violence in the streets. The possibilities of a disrupted symposium or a violent *kōmos* are threats which, as we saw in Chapter 3, the traditions of symposiac moralising had always recognised.[152] But Philocleon's 'solo' *kōmos* is a contradiction in terms, a one-man fantasy on a hyperbolical trajectory. It is in line with this that when he sees Bdelycleon approaching at 1360, his instinct is to resort to filthy abuse, *tōthasmos*, of a kind that had its accepted ritual place at some point in the preliminaries to the Mysteries, but which makes no sense at all in the 'real' social situation depicted at this point in the play.

With the themes of symposium/*kōmos* and Eleusinian *tōthasmos*, then, Aristophanes creates an extreme comic scenario illustrating behaviour that spills recklessly over the bounds of accepted 'play' (the solo *kōmos*) and imports a special practice (ritual laughter) into a context where it makes no sense. In both cases Philocleon ludicrously, but also *laughingly* (i.e. for his own pleasure), perverts special cultural customs. Yet he does so as a character in a performance that is itself not only a part of Dionysiac festivities but one which lays claim to special cultural status in terms of its licensed obscenity, a fact exhibited by this scene in its own right. The point is perfectly epitomised by Philocleon's phallus: on the one hand, the badge of Old Comedy itself; on the other, a dramatic sign of the character's sexual shamelessness. All this makes Aristophanes' image of Philocleon into a paradoxical exploitation of (ritual) laughter. If one were to regard the old man's behaviour, as Bdelycleon does (not to mention Philocleon's irate victims), in terms of 'real' social transgression, it would be a matter for outright condemnation: on that level, we could say, Philocleon turns social and religious ritual into *crime*, and in that light his own laughter, as an expression of *hubris*, would only compound his offence. But on the comic stage Philocleon's wild behaviour is unquestionably offered as a pleasurably laughable spectacle for the theatre audience. This means that Aristophanes is exploiting a (perverted) image of ritual laughter in a way that enacts Old Comedy's own status as a civically sanctioned performance in which, among other things, spectators can enjoy watching characters who infringe legal, cultural and ethical codes basic to the city's social fabric. Whether or not Dionysiac festivals at large were the occasions of hubristic hedonism and scurrility which the puritanical Spartan Megillus took them to be (**F6a** above), this picture fits remarkably well the

---

[152] On sympotic violence, see esp. ch. 3 n. 22.

behaviour exhibited *inside* the world of Old Comedy by a protagonist like Philocleon.

As with the phallic song in *Acharnians*, then, the rampant behaviour of Philocleon in *Wasps* raises the question of what kind of pleasure Old Comedy might afford its audience in such scenes. The basic choice is between an 'escapist' pleasure that at least subliminally identifies with the character on stage and laughs vicariously *with* him, or a more mixed, semi-detached pleasure that sees through the character's extreme absurdity and laughs *at* him, while nonetheless deriving enjoyment from the festive fantasy of the play. If the question does not admit of a definitive answer, we can at any rate see that in *Wasps* as in *Acharnians* Aristophanes has, so to speak, internalised ritual laughter within Old Comedy. Adapting ritual practices at one remove, and enclosing them within anomalous situations (perhaps more so in *Wasps* than in *Acharnians*) that hardly conform to real observance of the rituals in question, Aristophanes produces a kind of blurring of ritual and comedy. By showing his protagonists reaching, as it were, for ritual paradigms to give scurrilous shape to their impulsive celebrations, Aristophanes turns them into zanily magnified instances of the recognised need for ritual laughter, but at the same time embodiments of comedy's own gelastic priorities.

The last of my triad of Aristophanic reworkings of ritual laughter, the initiates' parodos in *Frogs* (316–459), has received close attention from historians of Greek religion; it is often cited as (indirect) evidence for the Eleusinian practice of *gephurismos* (**F1d** above). My observations on this fascinating scene will be strictly selective.[153] However particular details are interpreted, the parodos as a whole bears out the impression that ritualised laughter formed an element of more than one stage of the celebration of the Mysteries during the long procession from Athens to Eleusis. At the same time, because of the way in which Eleusinian motifs are woven into the texture of the work, we should be cautious about treating the parodos as 'testimony' for the real festival. What I want to highlight here is how Aristophanes allows a sort of fluctuating assimilation between the festive spirit of the Eleusinian procession and the Dionysiac ethos of his own comedies.

The key-note of the parodos in this respect is struck at an early stage, when the chorus appeal to Iacchus, god of the procession, to join in dancing they call 'unbridled', ἀκόλαστος, and 'fond of play', φιλοπαίγμων (332–3). The first of these adjectives is associated (disapprovingly) with circumstances

---

[153] Further interpretations of the parodos can be pursued through Graf (1974) 40–51, Dover (1993) 57–69, 232–53, Rosen (2007) 29–32; Parker (2005) 348–50 provides a compendium of the evidence, including *Frogs*, for the procession from Athens to Eleusis.

of uninhibited laughter in a fragment of Euripides and in a substantial number of later texts as well.[154] Since the word is standardly pejorative, its occurrence in *Frogs* draws attention to a festive licentiousness (enacted with the energy of an exuberant dance)[155] that is also evidently appropriate for a chorus of Old Comedy. Soon afterwards, in fact, in the initiates' version of a ritual proclamation at 354–71 (which is also a version of the conventional comic parabasis, here displaced from its usual position in the play), the idea of comedy as itself a ritual is turned into a comic paradox. When the chorus speak of those who have not been 'initiated into the bacchic rites of the tongue of bull-eating Cratinus', and of anyone 'who takes pleasure in buffoonish [*bōmolochos*] utterances when these are not in place' (357–8), they appear to convert Dionysiac comedy into a mystery religion in its own right, and then in the next breath to suspend laughter in the interests of religious solemnity. Later in the same section they will refer to comedy again as the 'ancestral rites (*teletai*) of Dionysus' (368). To treat these passages as somehow transmitting a lofty Aristophanic vision of his own genre or its religio-civic importance is to miss the comic text's multiple ironies (including the patently ludicrous image of Cratinus) and to lose all sense of the spirit of scurrility which runs through the parodos.[156] Precisely because the chorus of initiates is here also (indeed, primarily) a comic chorus, its mixed identity is a teasing, unstable hybrid.

That last point is borne out by the remainder of the parodos. After its mock proclamation, the chorus returns to the imagery of dancing and laughter intertwined. The verb ἐγκρούειν (374), to 'stamp the feet', recalls the earlier invitation to Iacchus and is emphatically combined with a triad of verbs denoting the mockery (*episkōptein*), play (*paizein*) and jeering (*chleuazein*) in which all the initiates are invited to engage. These motifs are reinforced by the iambic song to Demeter at 384–93, in the second stanza of which the chorus characterise themselves as speaking 'many ridiculous things, and many serious ones too' (πολλὰ μὲν γέλοιά μ' εἰ-|πεῖν, πολλὰ δὲ σπουδαῖα, 389–90). This last remark has been almost universally understood by modern critics as a pronouncement on the supposedly serio-comic

[154] Eur. fr. 362.22 *TrGF* (ch. 1 n. 56); later texts include Dio Chrys. 32.29, Plut. *Cato min.* 7 (Archilochus), Iambl. *Babyl.* fr. 98 (cf. Stephens and Winkler (1995) 242), Porph. *Qu. Hom.* on *Od.* 8.267 (the gods' laughter), Basil, *Hom.* 1 (31.177 *PG*), John Chrys. *In ep. Col.* 1.6 (62.307 *PG*), Phot. *Lex. s.v.* κιχλισμός. Cf. ch. 8 n. 13.
[155] On the motif of *paizein*, to play/dance, see Dover (1993) 57–9; cf. ch. 1 n. 45.
[156] Lada-Richards (1999) 224–5, Baier (2002) 202–3 succumb to Aristophanes' (comic) rhetoric and lose the gelastic thrust. Riu (1999) 136 n. 38 misses the irony in Cratinus' description at 357. In performance, Dionysus and Xanthias are still visible on stage, watching the dancing with growing excitement.

nature of Aristophanes' own work, the playwright's 'view of his function and duty as a comic dramatist'.[157] But it occurs in a song resoundingly focused on Demeter (addressed at the outset, 384) by the initiates, who muse on 'playing and dancing safely *all day*' (387–8) and 'playing and joking worthily *of your festival*' (391), these last two phrases both marking the Eleusinian frame inside the comedy and not the performance frame of the Aristophanic play. It is true that in the final clause of the song the chorus voice the idea of receiving a victor's ribbons (393), which suits the theatrical chorus rather than the Eleusinian. But that is precisely a concluding shift or blurring of perspective, after the song as a whole has pictured the mood of the initiates' journey to Eleusis. I submit, therefore, that the immediate and primary force of the serio-ludic formulation at *Frogs* 389–90 is to characterise the compound nature – part playful, part solemn – which made up the long Iacchus procession to Eleusis. If that is right, it complements the evidence gathered in **F1** earlier (161–72) that the Eleusinian proceedings provided multiple opportunities for ritual laughter, opportunities interspersed, it would seem, among more solemn prayers and actions. The parodos of *Frogs* adds weight to that thesis not by any details we can treat as 'documentary' but by its recurrent emphasis on the mood of choreographed 'play' and scurrility that accompanies much of the festival, not least on the journey to Eleusis.

In the later portions of the parodos Aristophanes adds to that thematic emphasis by making the chorus once more invoke Iacchus in a spirit of light-hearted joy that specifically finds its outlet in *gelōs*. Here they sing of the hilarity produced by the torn clothing they wore as initiates, and the idea spills over into a risqué anecdote of (male participants) getting a glimpse of a young girl's breast as she dances alongside them. This is the juncture, however, at which the convergence or blurring of Eleusinian and Dionysiac perspectives again becomes prominent. In theatrical terms it is precisely the reference to a glimpse of a young female breast that brings Xanthias and Dionysus out of hiding to join in the dance of the initiate/Aristophanic chorus. The iambic rhythms which have predominated since 384 now coalesce into a song of punchy iambic stanzas, a song which draws together all the earlier hints of mockery and 'unbridled' exuberance into a burst of obscene derision of three contemporary characters. It is not the personal details of the song which matter here but its gelastically unabashed ethos and its climactic function within the parodos. Partly because of the excited

---

[157] Sommerstein (1996) 191; similarly Stanford (1958) 108, Del Corno (1994) 178. Even as scrupulous a reader as Silk (2000) shows the grip of orthodoxy in translating the choral persona of the lines into the 'he' of 'the author' (46–7; cf. 53, 203). For partial resistance, see Dover (1993) 58.

intervention of Dionysus and Xanthias, this song is probably the most vivid evocation of *improvised scurrility*, and its embodiment in a dance of irrepressible energy (in which sex and mockery blend together), to be found anywhere in Aristophanes.

But do we have here a reflection of the (possibly) improvised style of mockery practised in Eleusinian *gephurismos* (**F1d**) or simply an example of 'iambic' traditions of abuse which were typical of comedy itself? Opinions are divided, but the dull truth is that we can hardly decide, since we know so little of the form(s) which *gephurismos* took.[158] There is some chance that Aristophanes is drawing on symptomatic features of Eleusinian scurrility. Grounds for inferring this are not only the heavy stress placed on the Eleusinian connection throughout the parodos, but also, more concretely, the vigorous dramatisation of improvised song and dance in the lines following 413. Xanthias and Dionysus impulsively step forward to join in the revels, and there is clearly some physical interaction before, at 416–17, the chorus-leader invites a spontaneous lampoon: 'well then, would you like us all to join together in mocking Archedemus . . .?' (βούλεσθε δῆτα κοινῇ | σκώψωμεν Ἀρχέδημον . . . ;). One putative model for such a scene would be the behaviour of processional crowds or of practised 'performers' among them. On the other hand, there is nothing in Aristophanes' text which fixes the concluding song at a scheduled moment or determinate location during the procession to Eleusis, so that any allusion of that kind must be entirely tacit. But if the issue remains undecidable on this level, we have seen that the parodos as a whole has certainly attached both Eleusinian and Dionysiac resonance to the idea of festive mockery. In the end, Aristophanes has produced an elaborate fusion of two frameworks (one imagined, one taking place in the theatre itself) for the celebration of laughter as a defining component in acts of religious and social unity. Whether we take this as confirmation that Old Comedy should indeed count as a form of ritual laughter, or alternatively that the latter embraced a set of practices which had all along aspired to the condition of comedy itself, is a question that can perhaps best be left as the gelastic conundrum which Aristophanes has made of it.

---

[158] Favourable to a *gephurismos* reading: Lada-Richards (1999) 98, 158, Richardson (1974) 214, Graf (1974) 45–6, Macleod (1983) 50, Sommerstein (1996) 193, Bowie A. (1993) 239–40, Parker (1997) 29. Against: Fluck (1931) 55–8, Dover (1993) 247–8, Henderson (1991) 16 n. 49, Storey (2003) 142–3, Edmonds (2004) 126 n. 36. Parker (2005) 350 n. 96 reserves judgement.

CHAPTER 5

Aischrology, shame and Old Comedy

VLADIMIR Ceremonious ape!
ESTRAGON Punctilious pig!
VLADIMIR Finish your phrase, I tell you!
ESTRAGON Finish your own!
    [*Silence. They draw closer, halt.*]
VLADIMIR Moron!
ESTRAGON That's the idea, let's abuse each other.

Samuel Beckett, Waiting for Godot[1]

WHO IS SHAMED BY SHAMEFUL SPEECH?

The ritualised performances investigated in the previous chapter are characterised not only by a general association with the symbolic arousal of
laughter, but also by a marked tendency towards the use of *aischrologia*,
'shameful' or offensive speech. In sacred contexts, such aischrology is a
pointedly paradoxical transgression of the normal religious requirement of
euphēmia (auspicious, pure speech, often equated with 'silence'). But at the
same time it is observably framed and protected by the ritual setting itself,
and thereby converted into a function of the worship and celebration of a
deity. However difficult it may be for us to recover the authentic mentality
of those who participated in such events, we can see that ritual aischrology,
together with the laughter which typically accompanies it, is controlled
and made somehow acceptable by its inclusion within a culturally codified set of protocols. Outside such frameworks, by contrast, aischrologic
behaviour takes on the appearance of an intrinsically shameful, aggressive and destabilising phenomenon, a threat to communal necessities of
restraint, cooperation and order. In the common flow of social life, moreover, aischrology seems to possess a sort of doubleness in relation to the

---

[1] Beckett (1986) 70.

workings of shame. Aischrologic speech-acts are, in the first place, shameful in the sense that they are deemed by hearers or observers to reflect shame back on the speaker; hence the vocabulary of *aischrologia* and its cognates is always *prima facie* pejorative. But they can also be perceived, not least by their users, as directing or projecting shame onto others. The potentially problematic nature of this doubleness can be immediately grasped by noticing that in certain conditions the very same utterances can belong, according to one's evaluative viewpoint, in either of these categories (or even, conceivably, in *both*). In the very earliest exemplification of this point in extant Greek, it is a matter of profound ambiguity whether the force of shame which is activated by Achilles' ferocious tirade against Agamemnon at *Iliad* 1.149–71 (a tirade that starts with a vivid accusation of *shamelessness*: 'you who are cloaked in shamelessness', ἀναιδείην ἐπιειμένε, 1.149) should count as reflecting more on the speaker or on his target. Extremes of language are here one aspect of the acutely strained psychology and tangled ethics of intense conflict.

The purpose of the present chapter is to explore some of the cultural complexity that surrounds Greek ideas of *aischrologia*, and above all the implications of that complexity for the possibilities of laughter. Laughter itself, as we have already had multiple occasions to recognise in this book, stands in an oscillating relationship to shame, and therefore to 'shameful' speech. It can focus shame on others, operating as a powerful medium of public ridicule and humiliation. If ill-judged, however, it can bring shame on the one who laughs (or, at a further remove, the one who enjoys such laughter). Where particular kinds of speech are concerned, then, how is aischrology to be defined or identified? Who judges this, and for what purpose? And how can the perception or use of aischrology activate (or block) laughter? Furthermore, what are we to make of the widespread use of aischrologic speech in Old Comedy? Can that genre's distinctive recourse to various kinds of transgressive language be judged by the same criteria as aischrology in general social contexts, or do we need a special frame of reference to make sense of it? I argued in the last chapter that in certain respects Old Comedy can be regarded as akin to, perhaps even a sort of offshoot from, ritual laughter. In the final section of the present chapter I shall attempt to reinforce that position by considering the cultural status of the genre in the specific light of canons of decent and indecent speech.

One way of constructing an illuminating cultural perspective on these matters is to situate the phenomena of aischrology in relation to notions of freedom of speech. Against a Greek background, freedom of speech can be conceptualised not only at the level of explicit legal regulation and formal political provision but also in terms of the expectations embodied in what came to be known as 'unwritten law', νόμος ἄγραφος. Over and above questions about the overt entitlement (of individuals or groups) to speak in particular contexts, we can also take account of the social values and pressures that in a more diffuse, less easily demarcated way help to determine what people feel free, or not free, to say. One important dimension of this second class of issues in relation to Greek culture of, for my purposes, principally the archaic and classical periods is precisely what Greeks themselves denoted by the name of αἰσχρολογία, 'shameful speech', as well as by a cluster of closely associated terminology (including κακολογία, κακηγορία, λοιδορία, βλασφημία and their cognates). *Aischrologia* or aischrology, as I shall standardly call it (while permitting myself, in ways which should be transparent, to refer to it more or less synonymously as shameful, indecent or foul speech), is a locus of social, educational, psychological, ethical, political and religious concern throughout the whole of Greek antiquity. It occupies a notable space within the realm of 'unwritten law', a realm heavily influenced by the operations of shame, as attested by the remark of the Thucydidean Pericles that unwritten laws carry with them 'agreed shame', or, to interpret his phrase a little more incisively, 'a social contract of shame'.[2] Some manifestations of (arguably) aischrologic behaviour, though not the *aischrolog-* wordgroup itself, first appear, dramatised in emblematic fashion, in the Homeric epics: above all, as already mentioned, in the Achilles–Agamemnon quarrel of *Iliad* 1, as well as in the Thersites episode of Book 2 and the recurrent behaviour of the suitors in the *Odyssey*.[3] The apprehensions attaching to aischrology thereafter crop up repeatedly in a range of oratorical, historical and philosophical sources, and their deep-rootedness is later reflected in the new lease of life which they acquire in the ethical discourse of Christianity, where aischrology appears in the writings of Paul, Clement of Alexandria, John Chrysostom (and others) partly as an object of moral condemnation in its own right but also as a target of attempts to depict aischrologic speech as a fundamentally pagan

---

[2] αἰσχύνην ὁμολογουμένην: Thuc. 2.37.3.

[3] In addition to the scenes mentioned, note the phrases αἰσχροῖς ἐπέεσσιν (Hom. *Il.* 3.38, 6.325, 13.768) and ἔπεσσ'αἰσχροῖσιν (24.238), plus the adverb αἰσχρῶς at *Il.* 23.473, and *Od.* 18.321. While the basic force of *aischros* in these cases seems to be 'insulting', it may also imply that such speech reflects badly on the speakers – or that it would *normally* be shameful: see Nagy (1999) 255–6, Cairns (1993) 58–9, Cairns (2001) 206–8. The attempt of Lowry (1991) 17–57 to link the description of αἴσχιστος at *Il.* 2.216 to what Thersites says is unconvincing. For one ancient recognition of Homer as the first exponent of a lexicon of abuse, see Suet. *Blasph.* pref., Taillardat (1967) 48. Koster (1980) 41–55 surveys Homeric scenes of abuse rather superficially.

vice.[4] What's more, this whole tradition of thought, from archaic pagan moralising to early Christian polemics, frequently connects the problem of aischrology with questions of laughter. Foul speech, as we shall see, is a subject fraught with gelastic implications. Does it, might it, should it make anyone laugh? And why, or why not? And if laughter is ever aroused by aischrology, at what or whom is that laughter directed?

The extent of the issues just sketched would lend itself to study from various angles. In the present context I want to limit myself to a pair of aims. The first is to explore the basic psychological-cum-ethical dynamics of certain Greek anxieties about shameful speech and the way these attitudes impinge on the domains of sex, politics and religion, but concentrating in particular on the relevance of ideas of aischrology to the workings of public abuse and insult. The second is to say something about the distinctive (and problematic) status of Old Comedy – arguably the most aischrologic of all literary genres – *vis-à-vis* this wider nexus of cultural values. Because of my eventual focus on Old Comedy, it is with classical Athenian perceptions of *aischrologia* that I want primarily to engage, and therefore with the relationship between aischrology and explicitly democratic ideology. I can anticipate one of my key concerns by saying that if democratic 'frank speech', *parrhēsia*, includes (some) freedom to say what is unpopular or even offensive, it thereby generates acute problems about both the definition and the regulation of aischrology, not least where frank speech intersects with the arousal of laughter. Classical Athens, in both its laws and its general political self-image, was caught between a democratic impulse towards freedom of speech and, on the other hand, an inclination (embodied, for instance, in laws against slander, *kakēgoria*, but also against *hubris*, which encompassed verbal as well as physical offensiveness) to provide protection and redress against abusiveness. Athens certainly did not recognise the principle, articulated by one modern philosopher of jurisprudence, that 'in a democracy no one . . . can have a right not to be insulted or offended'.[5] It is consequently no accident that Athenian texts contain evidence of a climate

---

[4] The *aischrolog-* wordgroup is not found before the fourth century: the earliest occurences are Pl. *Rep.* 3.395e, Xen. *Lac. resp.* 5.6, Arist. *Rhet.* 3.2, 1405b10, *Pol.* 7.17, 1336b4. But the root concept is clearly older (n. 3 above). Cf. e.g. Theog. 479–84 (ch. 3, 121–2) on inebriated utterances that would be *aischra* to the sober. The verb αἰσχροεπεῖν appears in Hippoc. *De arte* 1 (fifth century?), applied to the writer's intellectual opponents, and Ephip. fr. 23 (240 below). The verb αἰσχρομυθεῖν occurs twice in Hippoc. *Epid.* 3, case 11, and 4.15, of obscene speech as a symptom of mental disorder; cf. Lloyd (1987) 22–4. For Christian polemics against aischrology and related speech-acts, see e.g. Paul I Cor. 5.11, 6.10–11, Eph. 5.3–5, Col. 3.8, Clem. *Paed.* 2.5.45–8, 2.6.49–52, 2.10.98, John Chrys. *In ep. Eph.* 17.2–3 (62.118–121 *PG*); see ch. 10 for fuller discussion of such views.

[5] Dworkin (2006), defending 'the right to ridicule' (a defence prompted by a controversy over Danish newspaper cartoons of Mohammad). On laws against *kakēgoria*, see n. 65 below, with n. 32 on verbal

of unease about the nature and desirability of *parrhēsia*.[6] Symptomatic here, though in a complex way, is the Theophrastean slanderer (*kakologos*), who is depicted as defending his penchant for defamation by (mis)describing it, for his own convenience, as 'frank speech (*parrhēsia*) and democracy and freedom'.[7] I shall return to this arrestingly (but laughably?) foul-mouthed character. My interest here is not in the entire ideology of *parrhēsia* as such but specifically in the risk of aischrology to which it gives rise, as well as in the intricate, unstable relationship between shame and laughter that underlies this risk. In attempting to track the shifting configurations of frank speech, aischrology and laughter, I shall pursue an argument that spans a whole spectrum of texts, moving broadly from philosophy, which scrutinises aischrology from a moral distance, via oratory and Theophrastus' *Characters* (both of which, in somewhat different ways, reflect and appeal to norms of acceptable speech while adapting for their own purposes some of the ways in which those norms can be breached), to my final destination of Old Comedy, whose generic existence seems to depend on the unabashed celebration of aischrology.

THE SOCIOLINGUISTICS OF AISCHROLOGY

It is not difficult to identify in general terms the semantic and evaluative field of *aischrologia*. The concept covers language that causes (or could reasonably be expected to cause) individual or social offence by obtrusively breaching norms of acceptable speech, especially in one or more of the following ways: by explicit, non-technical reference to sexually sensitive topics (a form of offensiveness that at any rate overlaps with later classifications of

---

hubris. Note also the possibility of religious restrictions on Athenian freedom of speech, with Todd (1993) 310–12.

[6] A positive democratic value is assigned to *parrhēsia* at e.g. Eur. *Hipp.* 422, Aeschin. 3.6, Dem. 7.1, 15.1, 60.25–6, Dinarchus 5.1, Isoc. 6.97; cf., more equivocally, ps.-Xen. *Ath. pol.* 1.12. The term appears as the name of an Athenian trireme (*IG* II^2 1624.81, with Hansen (1991) 83)! Anxieties over risks/abuses of *parrhēsia*: e.g. Eur. *Or.* 905, Isoc. 7.20, 12.218, 16.22, Dem. 6.31–2, Theophr. *Char.* 28.6 (with 238–9 below); cf. n. 45 below on *parrhēsia* and shamelessness. Aeschin. 1.80 applies the concept to the behaviour (viz. obscene jeering) of democratic *audiences*; Eur. *Or.* 905 (above) possibly hints at the same extension; cf. n. 48 below. Outside Athens, ambivalence towards *parrhēsia* is glimpsed in Democ. fr. 226 DK, maybe the word's earliest occurrence: cf. ch. 7, 357. Monoson (2000) 51–63 examines *parrhēsia* in democratic ideology; Foucault (2001) offers a stimulating overview, but needs some historical caution; Saxonhouse (2006), esp. 85–99, emphasises differences between Athenian *parrhēsia* and modern, rights-based notions of 'free speech'. Ahl (1984) studies the other side of the coin, ancient ideas about oblique 'figured speech'.

[7] Theophr. *Char.* 28.6. I take the verb ἀποκαλεῖν, which often means to 'disparage' *vel sim.*, to imply that the man *misdescribes* his slander in terms of democratic ideals (which he thereby tarnishes). Cf. 239 below.

obscenity);[8] by personal, *ad hominem* vilification; or by direct mention of religiously protected and normally 'unspeakable' or 'unnameable' subjects (ἄρρητα, ἀπόρρητα), though these Greek terms can also embrace the two preceding categories as well.[9] Some of this territory is charted schematically, but in a manner that serves to broach issues which will later prove important, by the lexicographer Pollux. Despite Pollux's imperial date, parts of his work can still be usefully brought to bear, with due caution, on classical contexts, since his compilation of linguistic data preserves traces of much older habits of language and thought. This is pertinently illustrated for my purposes by the fact that one of the two lexical notes of most immediate interest here shows the influence of a Demosthenic text. In an entry of the *Onomasticon* which catalogues the vocabulary appropriate to describing the flatterer (*kolax*) and his activities, and in the process echoes the terms in which Demosthenes had stigmatised the dissolute figures with whom Philip II of Macedon supposedly surrounded himself at court, Pollux includes the adjective/noun *aischrologos* alongside (among others) the 'jester' or 'buffoon' (γελωτοποιός), 'the poet of foul [i.e. sexually obscene] songs' (ποιητὴς αἰσχρῶν ᾀσμάτων), 'the person who dances the [sc. sexually indecent] *kordax*', 'the teller of jokes' (σκωμμάτων συνθέτης), and the parasite.[10] *Aischrologia* here has the stamp of a self-consciously comic or scurrilous activity, the dedicated arousal of laughter for its own sake, and thus something that can even be practised 'professionally'. In a later entry from the *Onomasticon*, however, Pollux links the *aischrologia* word-group with the practice of slander or defamation (*kakologia*) and abusiveness (*loidoria*, *blasphēmia*, etc.): here, by contrast, the dominant connotations seem to be of socially dangerous insults, wrangling and so forth, including

---

[8] Henderson (1991) 6 is right to say that αἰσχρολογεῖν is wider than 'obscenity', but wrong that it is 'very different'. Sexually and scatologically indecent language, Henderson's own sense of obscenity (2), is central to aischrology; cf. n. 18 below. Reckford (1987) 22, 68, 461, Stewart (1994) 33, Rösler (1993) 76, 83 readily count (some) *aischrologia* as 'obscene'; Barnes (1984) II 2482 indexes Arist. *Rhet.* 3.2, 1405b9 under 'obscenity'; cf. Adams (1982) 1–2, Richlin (1992) 1–31, 273–5, for a Roman comparison. The distinction in Henderson (1991) 2–12, followed by O'Higgins (2003) 7–8, between ancient obscenity (involving 'shame of exposure') and modern (involving ideas of dirt and disgust), is overstated. Disgust is not part of all modern understandings of obscenity: see Hughes (1991) 246–8 for the history of the concept in English, Feinberg (1985) 97–248 for interesting jurisprudential considerations; Nussbaum (2004) 134–47 challenges notions of obscenity that depend on disgust. Equally, feelings of dirt/disgust are not entirely absent from the ancient evidence: Diog. Laert. 7.187 talks of 'soiling the mouth' (μολύνειν τὸ στόμα) with certain words (the immediate subject is fellatio). Cf. Robson (2006), esp. ch. 3.

[9] For the approximate synonymity of the adjs. *arrhētos, aporrhētos*, see Dem. 18.122–3, with n. 28 below. Cf. *arrhētophoria*, 'carrying of unmentionable objects' (probably sexual models), as part of the Thesmophoria: ch. 4, 175.

[10] Pollux, *Onom.* 6.122; cf. ch. 3 n. 101. For the Demosthenic connections see Dem. 2.18–19, with ch. 3 n. 105; for the connotations of the *kordax*, cf. nn. 33, 61 below.

the exercise of political invective.[11] These two entries in Pollux's work alert us, if perhaps unwittingly (the *Onomasticon* is more a lexicological collection than an enterprise in fine lexicographical distinctions), to something central to my own enquiry – the difference, but also the possible tension, between contexts in which aischrologic behaviour may occur as a piece of 'consequential' action, embedded in social processes of cause and effect (such as confrontational derision between enemies in a public place: the Achilles of *Iliad* 1 can again stand as a paradigm), or, on the other hand, settings in which aischrology is at any rate partially detached from such consequentiality by perceived enclosure within a frame of conventionalised or even ritualised behaviour, embracing 'language games' that extend all the way from individual jokes to full-scale theatrical performances.[12]

We can start to sharpen our sense of the disquiet that usually attaches to aischrologic speech by considering a remarkable exception to the rule. The exception takes the form of a challenge to the whole concept of aischrology made in the early fourth century by a thinker called Bryson, whose views are reported by Aristotle. The point arises in a section of *Rhetoric* 3 where Aristotle is discussing metaphors, which he thinks should be chosen partly with a view to their 'fineness', 'beauty' or 'attractiveness' (κάλλος), with a corresponding avoidance of ugliness, foulness or repulsiveness (αἶσχος) – the latter, at root, a quality of being shameful.[13] Having observed that beauty and ugliness in this context can be a matter of either phonology or semantics, sound or meaning, Aristotle offers a compact refutation of what he calls the 'sophistic' argument advanced by Bryson:

ἔτι δὲ τρίτον, ὃ λύει τὸν σοφιστικὸν λόγον· οὐ γὰρ ὡς ἔφη Βρύσων οὐθένα αἰσχρολογεῖν, εἴπερ τὸ αὐτὸ σημαίνει τόδε ἀντὶ τοῦδε εἰπεῖν· τοῦτο γάρ ἐστι ψεῦδος· ἔστι γὰρ ἄλλο ἄλλου κυριώτερον καὶ ὡμοιωμένον μᾶλλον καὶ οἰκειότερον τῷ ποιεῖν τὸ πρᾶγμα πρὸ ὀμμάτων. ἔτι οὐχ ὁμοίως ἔχον σημαίνει τόδε καὶ τόδε, ὥστε καὶ οὕτως ἄλλου ἄλλο κάλλιον καὶ αἴσχιον θετέον· ἄμφω μὲν γὰρ τὸ καλὸν ἢ τὸ αἰσχρὸν σημαίνουσιν, ἀλλ᾽ οὐχ ᾗ καλὸν ἢ οὐχ ᾗ αἰσχρόν· ἢ ταῦτα μέν, ἀλλὰ μᾶλλον καὶ ἧττον.

---

[11] *Onom.* 8.80.

[12] For my use of 'consequential', see ch. 1, 20–2. The usage does not entail that (e.g.) formal comedy can never be consequential, only that its culturally recognised frames limit and inhibit this possibility: see 243–7 below.

[13] Aristotle here brackets together sensory beauty and ethical fineness. Cf. Theophrastus' definition of 'fine words' (καλὰ ὀνόματα), embracing qualities of sound and meaning, at Demetr. *Eloc.* 173 (with *ibid.* 151 for sexual innuendoes as *aischra*), = Theophr. f687 (Fortenbaugh *et al.* (1992) 534–5, with Fortenbaugh (2005) 281–6), or the correlation of 'low' words and 'low' things at Longin. *Subl.* 43. Cairns (1993) argues extensively that Greek values of shame, honour and respect were commonly conceptualised in quasi-aesthetic terms (i.e. in terms of how certain actions 'looked'); cf. n. 91 below.

There is also a third point, one that refutes the sophistic argument. Because it is not the case that, as Bryson said, no one actually does speak shamefully, on the supposed grounds that it still signifies the same thing to use one expression rather than another. This is fallacious. One expression may be more direct than another, more akin to the referent and more apt to bring the object before the mind's eye. Furthermore, different expressions signify a thing in different respects, so in this way too one should classify them as finer or more shameful. Both may signify the thing that is fine or shameful, but not *qua* fine or shameful – or they may both do so, but to a greater or lesser degree.[14]

The premise attacked by Bryson and reaffirmed by Aristotle is that ais-chrology is a distinctive kind of linguistic behaviour. If one wants to refer, say, to a political opponent's sexual proclivities, one has a choice between doing so in an aischrologic or non-aischrologic manner – or, if aischrology is a sliding scale (as Aristotle clearly proposes), a choice between doing so more or less aischrologically. This premise is readily illustrated from other Greek rhetorical writings. The *Rhetorica ad Alexandrum*, for example, when advising that orators should attack base opponents without resorting to scurrility (because gibes or jokes, *skōmmata*, 'aim at the form rather than the substance' of one's opponent's vices), warns against 'naming shameful deeds with shameful words' (τὰς αἰσχρὰς πράξεις μὴ αἰσχροῖς ὀνόμασι λέγειν), in case the speaker should thereby blacken his *own* character. It recommends that such things ought instead to be conveyed by hints or oblique suggestions (αἰνιγματωδῶς) and by referring to them with the names 'of other things', i.e. metaphorically or euphemistically – though the context makes it clear that this does not rule out rhetorical ridicule altogether.[15]

This last piece of advice, together with Aristotle's in the *Rhetoric*, crys-tallises a basic criterion of aischrology. Since certain things are considered shameful, it may count as shameful even to name them directly or to describe them explicitly; i.e., the shame of the 'thing' will adhere to its close verbal description. But it need not be shameful to 'signify' or indicate them in other ways: i.e., where these alternatives place a sort of linguistic distance or buffer between the thing and the name. In principle, it may

---

[14] *Rhet.* 3.2, 1405b8–17; good exegesis in Kraut (1997) 161–2. Most scholars identify Bryson with Bryson of Heraclea, but less than cogently: e.g. Döring (1972) 147–74 (cf. 164–5). Given the affinity between denial of aischrology and some Cynic attitudes to language (n. 21 below), it is tempting to identify him as Bryson of Achaea, teacher of Crates the Cynic (Diog. Laert. 6.85, *Suda s.vv.* Ἱππαρχία, Κράτης): see Giannantoni (1990) I 475–83, IV 107–13 for testimonia and a survey of earlier views (adding Cope (1855) 143–6).

[15] (?)Anaxim. *Rhet. Alex.* 35, 1441b20–3; 1441b21 is mistranslated in the Oxford translation, kept in Barnes (1984) II 2306. For comparable advice in later rhetoricians, see e.g. Hermog. *De inven.* 4.11, *De meth.* 8.

also be judged shameful to talk of an object, *x*, in a certain way even where *x* itself is not thought intrinsically or unqualifiedly shameful: someone may not think sexual organs/acts are shameful *per se* but may nevertheless regard as shameful/obscene certain ways of referring to them. Crates com. fr. 23, in which a speaker says that it is nice or enjoyable (ἡδύ) to perform sex but not attractive (οὐ καλόν) for it to be described, apparently adopts that very stance.[16] On the other hand, within a given speech community there may be some things for which there exists, or can be claimed to exist, *no* decent or acceptable description. This is the line deliberately taken by Aeschines in the prelude to his account of Timarchus' alleged prostitution – a line strategically useful to an orator who wants simultaneously to seem to respect social inhibitions while exploiting the salacious frisson of certain subjects for the purposes of invective.[17] But as we have already seen, this does not mean (and it would be linguistically bizarre if it did) that to speak of *anything* shameful automatically entails aischrologic transgression. Jeffrey Henderson therefore cannot be right to claim that the Greeks could not draw what he deems to be the Roman distinction (found in Cicero) between the shameful properties of things or actions and those of the language used to talk about them. 'A Greek', Henderson writes, 'would consider anything reprehensible to be αἰσχρόν and *therefore* an unfit topic for conversation' (my italics).[18] Though he does not cite any evidence in support of this claim, he presumably has in mind texts which

---

[16] This anticipates the 'Roman' view at Cic. *Off.* 1.126–8 (cf. n. 21 below). Compare the Christian Clem. *Paed.* 2.6.52 (with Σ on the passage, Marcovich (2002) 217), who contends that neither body parts nor their names are intrinsically shameful, only their wrongful use; see 2.10.92.3 for an application, with ch. 10, 483–95, on the ethics of the *Paedagogus*.

[17] Aeschin. 1.37–8 (note the idea of words 'like' their referents, τι ῥῆμα . . . ὅμοιον τοῖς ἔργοις, 37, as at Arist. *Rhet.* 3.2, 1405b12), with Fisher (2001) 166–7; cf. Aeschin. 1.45, 52 (where Fisher (2001) 184–5 sees some humour), 55, 70, 76, plus 3.174 (note the implications of 'too clearly', λίαν σαφῶς). Other oratorical passages which correlate shameful deeds with their description include Dem. 54.17 (cf. ch. 1, 36), Lys. fr. 53 Thalheim (see 246 below). Compare deprecation of aischrology at Dem. 2.19, 18.264, 21.79, 54.8–9 (cf. n. 28 below), Arist. *Rhet.* 3.7, 1408a17–18. Refusing to repeat others' foul speech compliments hearers, as well as proclaiming the speaker's decency: cf. Sandys and Paley (1910) 196–7.

[18] Henderson (1991) 6, exaggerating the scope of *aischrologein* as 'to speak of *anything* out of place' (5, my itals.); cf. his addenda, 240–1. Henderson's Roman/Greek distinction is old: see Shelley (1996) 95–6. But Cicero's concepts (n. 21 below) are just as much Greek as Roman. Henderson (1991) 2 ('an explicit expression that is itself subject to the same inhibitions as the thing it describes', defining 'obscene' in general: but see n. 8 above) wrongly makes shameful linguistic terms *replicate* the status of their referents; cf. Willi (2002) 10 (too uncritical). This claim, refuted on the Greek side by Crates fr. 23 (above) as well as by Aristotle's rebuttal of Bryson, often appears in definitions of obscenity/taboos. Crystal (1987) 8 states that taboos refer to 'acts, objects, or relationships which society wishes to avoid – and thus to the language used to talk about them. Verbal taboos are generally related to sex, the supernatural, excretion, and death . . .' But which society wishes to 'avoid' sexual acts *tout court*?

voice the moralistic sentiment that, as Isocrates puts it in his advice to the young Demonicus (immediately, it is worth noticing, after warning against excessive *laughter* and shameless talk): 'regarding things it is shameful to perform, consider it unseemly even to mention them' (ἃ ποιεῖν αἰσχρόν, ταῦτα νόμιζε μηδὲ λέγειν καλόν).[19] But this generalisation alludes only to certain types of behaviour, especially sexual acts, and to certain ways of talking about them. It cannot mean that it is shameful ever to mention, say, cowardice or political treachery, even though they are unquestionably 'shameful' actions within Greek communities. Our collective evidence for Greek attitudes leaves no doubt that aischrologic speech is correlated with, but not reducible to, the light in which its subject-matter is perceived. While linked to underlying evaluations of non-linguistic acts, *aischrologia* is a phenomenon of language as such and in part a matter of sociolinguistic register.[20]

Yet Bryson's paradoxical attempt to nullify the concept of aischrology (an attempt which anticipates Cynic and Stoic attitudes to language)[21] depends precisely on reducing words to their referential function, stripping them of all sociolinguistic charge and differentiation. At the same time it tries to break the link between the shame attaching to certain 'objects' (which it does not purport to deny – but could this be part of Bryson's 'sophistic' agenda?) and the impact of mentioning those objects in certain verbal terms. Aristotle's rebuttal of Bryson makes two subtle points, at least the second of which effectively involves a distinction between sense and reference. First, words vary in their relationship to what they signify; some are more directly or powerfully *evocative* of their referents: in Aristotle's terms, more 'akin' to them and better able to bring them 'before the mind's eye' (as though the gap between imagination and reality were smaller in

---

[19] Isoc. 1.15; cf. Soph. *OT* 1409, with n. 17 above for oratory and Hdt. 1.138.1 for attribution of the principle to the Persians. Underlying this idea is the educational anxiety, e.g. Arist. *EN* 4.8, 1128a28–9, *Pol.* 7.17, 1336b5–6, Democ. fr. 145 DK (*apud* ps.-Plut. *Lib. educ.* 9F: 'speech is the shadow of action', λόγος ἔργου σκιή), Ael. Arist. 29.13, that words spoken (or *listened* to) pave the way to action; cf. ch. 10 n. 44 for a Christian instance, ch. 4 n. 124 for an exception. For abusiveness (*loidorein*) marking lack of education, *paideia*, see Hyp. fr. 211 (Jensen), with ch. 6 n. 158.

[20] Cf. Feinberg (1985) 207, 212, on verbal obscenity as a matter of 'word-taboos', not simply reference. Arist. *Rhet.* 2.6, 1384b17–22, correlates acts and language in terms of shame, but does not commit himself, as his later rebuttal of Bryson confirms, to a simple equivalence between the two.

[21] Cicero ascribes the same position as Bryson's to Zeno and other Stoics at *Ad fam.* 9.22, and a related view to Cynics and some Stoics at *Off.* 1.128 (both passages = *SVF* I 77): see Dyck (1996) 300–3. Note the insouciance about obscenity, including Hera's fellation of Zeus, imputed to Chrysippus at Diog. Laert. 7.187–8 (*SVF* II 1071); with the suggestion that Chrysippus' story was suitable for 'whores' not gods, cf. the anti-Epicurean complaint cited in ch. 4 n. 59. Not all Stoics discounted aischrology/obscenity: see Epict. *Ench.* 33.15–16, with ch. 6 nn. 98, 105.

such cases).[22] Secondly, words can signify the same objects in different respects, from different points of view or with different expressive force. In Aristotle's formulation, two words may both signify something shameful but not (or not to the same degree) *qua* shameful. Aristotle has the psycho-social reality of linguistic communities, Greek and otherwise, on his side. Whatever else may be said of Bryson's paradoxical argument, it is a flagrant denial of the *de facto* functioning of culture through language.

An implication of the ground I have covered above is that because the shamefulness of aischrology is a derivative of, but nonetheless distinct from, the shamefulness of its subject-matter, the shame activated by indecent speech can be expected to reflect back on the speaker – hence the *Rhetorica ad Alexandrum*'s point about blackening or damaging one's own character by referring aischrologically to others' shameful behaviour. That is why perceptions of aischrology have a bearing on issues of freedom of speech, since they involve pressures that deprecate and inhibit certain ways of speaking. But it is also, in part, why such perceptions have gelastically loaded implications, implications for whether or not to laugh, and when, and why. If, then, we ask how sensitivity to aischrology operates in practice (*whose* discourse it affects, and in what contexts), and how its gelastic implications are realised, adequate answers to such questions will need to be multi-layered.

It is appropriate, but certainly not sufficient (especially, as we shall see, where democracy is concerned), to make the general observation that con-demnation of *aischrologia* tends to be an expression of ostensibly elite discourse, whether we demarcate 'elites' here in terms of status groups, economic classes, or broader categories of ethical self-definition, though it remains an urgent and still unresolved question in the study of classical Athenian culture how far nominally elite values (in any of those senses) were distributed across the social spectrum.[23] Take, as a convenient illustration, a passage from Plato *Republic* Book 3 in which Socrates, identifying the kinds of things unsuitable for mimetic (i.e., here, dramatic) representation on the part of young members of the guardian class in the ideal city, proscribes exhibitions of 'base men . . . bad-mouthing and ridiculing one another, and using foul language, whether drunk or sober, and displaying all the other faults of speech and action that such people commit in relation both to

---

[22] See Micalella (2004) 107–9, suggesting that Aristotle has a 'mimetic' conception of language in this passage. On the phrase 'before the [mind's] eye', cf. Halliwell (2003d) 64–5.

[23] Ober (1989) 11–17 discusses elites in classical Athens but does not fully question whether ostensibly elite values could cut across socio-economic distinctions.

themselves and to others'.[24] The implications and tenor of this passage are more intricate than might appear at first sight. For one thing, the type of behaviour referred to stands as a kind of synecdoche for comic drama, just as the immediately preceding description of female characters (engaging in their own form of abuse, *loidoreisthai*, competing boastfully with the gods, or immersed in grief and lamentation, 395d) evokes scenes of tragedy, perhaps especially in the work of Euripides.[25] More specifically, Socrates focuses on what might count as paradigmatic speech-acts of comic drama – abuse, mockery, foul language – and it is a subtext of the case he is putting that future guardians could not be allowed to act out parts so heavily conducive to laughter, both (to some extent) for the characters themselves (in their use of ridicule, *kōmōdein*) and for their audiences (of fellow guardians-to-be). But if Socrates foregrounds the place of aischrology in comedy, it does not follow that his argument condemns (all) comedy *per se*, since he is preoccupied only with what it would be appropriate for prospective guardians to perform, and with the principle of mimetic 'imprinting' whereby psychological and behavioural patterns are assimilated through role-playing. This is a principle which has particularly strong purchase where the linguistic acts of 395e are concerned, since to enact the roles in question the performers must use precisely the aischrologic terms at issue – they must do exactly the same thing as such characters would do in their real speech-acts (which is not true of all details of dramatic representation). Apart from a passing concession to the possibility of 'play' (*paidia*) or make-believe at 396e, the argument leaves larger consideration of the acceptable contents, form and performance of comedy unsettled; we must look elsewhere in Plato for clues to these things.[26] But Socrates' position harbours no doubt about the ethical evaluation of the nexus of behaviour in which it situates aischrology. The sort of characters in question are 'base' people (*kakoi*), likely to be found drunk and therefore without self-control (though even when sober, Socrates indicates, their faults will emerge); their conduct is marked by publicly transgressive vice, including a general shamelessness of speech. This evaluative colouring, though overlaid on a peculiarly philosophical thesis, is consistent with much more widely attested Greek attitudes. Aischrology

---

[24] ἄνδρας κακούς . . . κακηγοροῦντάς τε καὶ κωμῳδοῦντας ἀλλήλους καὶ αἰσχρολογοῦντας . . . : *Rep.* 3.395e. Socrates' description makes no clear reference to symposia, *contra* Tecuşan (1990) 239. On comic aischrology in this passage, cf. Nesselrath (1990) 146 n. 102. For the 'even when sober' slant, cf. Hyp. *Phil.* fr. 21.3 (Jensen), Theophr. *Char.* 6.3, with nn. 31, 61 below.

[25] Female abusiveness at 395d may allude to such tragic scenes as Eur. *Medea* 465–626. Cf. Murray (1996) 176.

[26] See ch. 6, 300–2. 'Play' at *Rep.* 396e need not refer exclusively to comedy, as I implied in Halliwell (2002b) 82, though comedy seems the most obvious outlet.

can readily be thought of as the sociolinguistic manifestation of corrupt character and disreputable status, something that makes anyone engaging in it supposedly unfit to belong to a well-ordered community. Hence, in the same mould, Xenophon's portrayal of Spartiate society as a place where aischrology, alongside other obtrusive breaches of social decency, is reputedly eliminated by the weight of ideological indoctrination.[27]

Consider now, in this light, a passage from another fourth-century Athenian text, but one embedded in a very different setting from the philosophical idealism of Plato's *Republic* (or, for that matter, the idealism of Xenophon's Laconian treatise). In his vituperation of Aeschines in the *De corona* Demosthenes targets the supposedly scandalous language of his opponent, complaining in particular about what he characterises as Aeschines' 'bawling' of 'unspeakable' things and his resort to insult and abuse in place of respectable political criticism or accusation.[28] It would require lengthy analysis to tease out all the complications of Demosthenes' politico-rhetorical strategy in this part of his speech, or in an earlier passage where Demosthenes uses a whole battery of terms (λοιδορία, βλασφημεῖν, διαβάλλειν, πομπεία, ὕβρις, ἐπήρεια) to express disdain for Aeschines' foul language, relating the point to his own (putative) social superiority, but revealingly indicating that if the audience would welcome it, he will return to this side of the case later on. That earlier passage gives a hint of what does in fact materialise, namely the conversion of supposed outrage at his opponent's crudity of language into an opportunity for denigratory reprisals of a kind which is recognised to satisfy an appetite within democratic politics and which answers to a retaliatory ethic of 'manliness' commonly detectable in our sources.[29] Demosthenes' stance in this area is consequently shot through with a kind of ambivalence or double standard, a factor that becomes blatant when he goes on to say that Aeschines

---

[27] Xen. *Lac. resp.* 5.6; cf. Critias fr. 6.14–16 *IEG*. On Spartan attitudes to laughter, see ch. 1, 44–50.

[28] Dem. 18.122–4. The phrase ῥητὰ καὶ ἄρρητα κακά ('speakable and unspeakable evils') at Dem. 22.61 clearly refers in part to sexual matters. The same is probably implied at Dem. 21.79 (stressing what was said in front of *women*); Cohen (1995) 125 draws the same inference from the related expression at Dem. 54.8–9; cf. *aporrhētos* (with n. 9 above) of female genitalia at Ar. *Eccl.* 12. So it would be surprising if a sexual nuance were absent at Dem. 18.122: to gloss the phrase as 'everything' (Yunis (2001) 181) misses its frisson of outrage, for which cf. Soph. *OC* 1001 (surely mistranslated by Jebb *ad loc.*). Dem. 1.4 uses ῥητὰ καὶ ἄρρητα differently to denote both public and secret material. Lys. 10.2 uses *aporrhēta* of slanders prohibited by Athenian law.

[29] The earlier passage is 18.10–12; notice, among other details, the adv. ἀνέδην (11), 'without restraint', which while coloured, like the whole description, by Demosthenes' *hauteur* nonetheless acknowledges the cultural freedom of 'processional' scurrility. Cf. Aeschines' *blasphēmia* at 18.34 and 82, and his *loidoria* at 18.3, 15 (linked with 'jokes' or 'gibes', *skōmmata*). Compare Aeschines' own supposed deprecation of laughter at 1.135 (175, picturing Demosthenes' hypothetical gloating, is different), in a speech which itself exploits ridicule abundantly. On retaliation to insults, cf. ch. 1, 41–2.

deserves to get as good as he has given in this regard. This signal prepares the way for Demosthenes' own highly lurid vilification of his opponent in the following chapters, a vilification which simultaneously conforms to a semi-comic expectation of reciprocal, game-like swapping of insults between competing speakers: in other words, a rhetorical equivalent of the various 'flyting' practices of stylised exchanges of mockery noted elsewhere in this book.[30] What I want to draw attention to here are two interlocking features of the ethical and social slant that Demosthenes gives to this section of his counterattack against Aeschines. First, he suggests that the indecency of Aeschines' speech is socially stigmatising: it suits, as he puts it, 'you and your family background' or 'you and your breed' (*genos*, 18.122). Secondly, he stresses that indulgence in personal abuse, as opposed to measured accusation, has nothing to do with justice, nothing to do with the 'facts' of the case; it is purely a display of the *speaker*'s own 'nature', his willingness to stoop to such degrading tactics. Both these points parallel the view of (comic) aischrology we have already met in Book 3 of Plato's *Republic*, and the second of them also matches precisely the view of rhetorical invective cited earlier from the *Rhetorica ad Alexandrum*.

There is, however, a third feature of Demosthenes' posture which makes an interesting contrast with Plato's. Demosthenes describes Aeschines' insults as employing the sort of language that belongs to people shouting licentious gibes from wagons (ὥσπερ ἐξ ἁμάξης); his use of the verb πομπεύειν (literally 'to behave like someone in a procession or pageant') shortly afterwards (124, anticipated much earlier by the noun πομπεία in section 11) confirms that he is referring to traditions of festive (especially Dionysiac) mockery in which 'men on wagons', normally expected to wear masks, hurled coarse abuse either at each other or at bystanders or at other named targets.[31] The traditions assumed as familiar by Demosthenes are a case of ritual laughter, or ritualised festival laughter, which received attention in my last chapter. They involved, so far as we can judge, a quasi-comic performance protocol (the wagon or float as a mobile stage, plus the wearing of masks), together with a markedly Dionysiac indulgence not only in

[30] Readings which accept Demosthenes' quasi-comic stance include Harding (1994) 214–16, Rowe (1966), Yunis (2001) 22; Dyck (1985), 43–4 takes a different line. A historical overview in Buckler (2000). Cf. Dover (1974) 30–3 on Demosthenes' manipulation of facts, Hesk (2000) 231–9 on rhetorical strategies in the orators' exchanges, Duncan (2006) 58–89 for 'histrionic' aspects of the feud. On flyting, see 259–61 below, with ch. 4, 184–5, 194–5.
[31] That masks (even whole satyr costumes: Frontisi-Ducroux (1992)) were normal can be inferred from Dem. 19.287 (cf. Σ there and on Dem. 18.11, 19.255, with ch. 4, 180–1). Some emend Theophr. *Char.* 6.3 to produce a similar point; but uncertainty remains (n. 61 below). On the wagons in question, see ch. 4, 178–81; Usher (1993) 212 is muddled.

intoxication – by both performers and spectators – but also in the kind of behaviour that Demosthenes and other sources refer to, from a moralistic distance, as verbal *hubris*.[32] So in *De corona* Demosthenes casts Aeschines in the role of a 'vulgar' performer in a komastic street parade, and accordingly brands his style of rhetorical accusation as falling beneath acceptable standards of political debate. Demosthenes seems to take for granted that Dionysiac parades do represent a customary, permitted setting for certain kinds of aischrology – for those who like that kind of thing. His objection is that Aeschines has exposed his own social baseness and political corruption by supposedly confusing the difference between the tone of such festive contexts and the (notionally) requisite decorum of the political arena.

We know that this kind of contrast had broader rhetorical currency in this period. A comparable use of such imagery can be adduced from Hyperides' prosecution speech against Philippides (on a charge of bringing an illegal proposal to the Assembly), probably written just a few years earlier than *De corona*. In the course of his peroration, Hyperides puts it to the defendant, with colourful hyperbole: 'if you think you will get yourself acquitted by lewd prancings [lit. dancing the *kordax*] and playing the buffoon (κορδακίζων καὶ γελωτοποιῶν), as you usually do in court, you are very naive'.[33] Against a backdrop of bitter political divisions over Athenian policy towards Macedon, Hyperides finds it worthwhile to portray his opponent as a figure who even in the official setting of a courtroom cultivates a style of oratory which involves vulgar buffoonery and indecent clowning. He goes so far as to apply to him the verb κορδακίζειν, which literally means to perform an obscene comic dance, the *kordax* – a dance whose scurrilous associations were earlier touched on in my remarks on Pollux and whose significance will later recur in Theophrastus' description of a particularly crude kind of character. If there was any basis in reality for Hyperides' patently inflated gibes, it must have been a penchant for rhetorical humour and satire on Philippides' part, conceivably taken to the point of risqué mimicry. But even to speculate in such terms draws

---

[32] Dem. 18.12 refers to aischrologic *hubris*; Hyp. *Dem.* fr. b (Jensen) links *hubris* with *loidoria*. For the *hubris* of Dionysiac ribaldry, as perceived by a (fictional) Spartan, see Pl. *Laws* 2.637a–b (ch. 4, 177–8); verbal *hubris* is synonymous with aischrology in another Spartan/Athenian contrast, Xen. *Lac. resp.* 5.6 (ch. 1, 47). Cf. Fisher (1992) 91–3, 99–100.

[33] Hyp. *Phil.* fr. 21.7 (Jensen); cf. Whitehead (2000) 58–9, with n. 61 below on the *kordax*. Since Hyperides attacks Philippides as pro-Macedonian, Usher (1999) 331 shrewdly suggests an allusion to the alleged decadence of Philip II's court (ch. 6 n. 116). For shameless dancing, cf. the notorious episode of Hippocleides at Hdt. 6.129, with Scott (2005) 426–9, Nenci (1998) 308–10. On dance as a vehicle of mockery, see ch. 1, 34–5.

attention to a paradox which forms part of the instructive parallelism between the present case and Demosthenes' critique of Aeschines. Whatever may or may not have been true of Philippides, Hyperides' vignette of his supposedly habitual vulgarity and buffoonery is itself a way of exploiting the resources of laughter for his own rhetorical purposes. This is a paradox which is unlikely to have been lost on Hyperides, who himself acquired a reputation for the extensive use of jokes, sarcasm and wit.[34]

If we now return to the *De corona*, we can see all the more clearly that the contrast Demosthenes employs to depict Aeschines' scurrility in the style of 'men on wagons' represents itself a barbed trope of derision. Just as with Hyperides' evocation of a speaker doing an obscene dance in court, its piquancy lies in the sheer incongruity with which political debate in the Assembly and ritual obscenity in a masked Dionysiac procession are juxtaposed. No Athenian audience, needless to say, would take the point literally, but the orator's words, to borrow that Aristotelian phrase with which we were concerned a little earlier, are chosen to bring certain images 'before the mind's eye'. Demosthenes' and Hyperides' sarcastic use of such imagery for their own quasi-comic, laughter-inducing ends reflects the wider circumstance that all Attic orators practised a hybrid performance-art that was caught between the deadly serious dynamics of political antagonism and the potentially gelastic opportunity to exploit *parrhēsia* for the entertainment of (and, therefore, a favourable hearing from) mass audiences. The trick, or the challenge, was to find a way of harnessing supportive laughter to the pursuit of victory in debate or trial, and to avoid being regarded as demeaning the processes of politics or law by merely playing the joker and thereby being tarred as one of those whom the loftily old-fashioned Aeschylus, in the contest of tragedians in Aristophanes' *Frogs*, calls 'buffoonish monkey-politicians'.[35] To elicit your audience's laughter by mockery of your opponent yet nonetheless lose the vote would be politically or forensically pointless. Unlike those men on wagons, the orator had to face hard practical consequences.

There are, then, at least two superimposed, closely packed layers to Demosthenes' characterisation of Aeschines' foul speech. One is the

---

[34] Hyperides' repertoire of wit (*asteïsmoi*) is noted by Longin. *Subl.* 34.2: it includes *muktēr* ('nose' = sneering sarcasm: Appendix 1 n. 14), irony, jokes (though 'not vulgar'), *diasurmos* ('belittling'), 'a substantial comic element', and a 'sting' combined with 'play'; cf. Russell (1964) 161–2. Longin., *ibid.* 34.3, thinks Demosthenes, by contrast, has to 'force' himself to use laughter, and 'he does not arouse laughter so much as make himself laughable' (οὐ γέλωτα κινεῖ μᾶλλον ἢ καταγελᾶται). Did fourth-century Athenians agree?

[35] βωμολόχων δημοπιθήκων, *Frogs* 1085: the compressed semantics of this phrase suggest laughter harnessed to deceit. On the associations of 'monkey' or 'ape', cf. ch. 6 n. 94.

deployment of an ostensibly moralistic, elite disapproval of the language of those perceived as socially and ethically gross. The other is an ironic, even semi-comic, twist that accentuates the extreme disparity between normally non-adjacent cultural contexts (political/forensic debate, on the one hand, Dionysiac street parades, on the other) and appeals to the audience's ability to appreciate the game of derision that Demosthenes himself is playing. This second point is borne out by the way in which, as already noted, Demosthenes proceeds to justify himself for paying Aeschines back in his own coin with a passage which scoffs at the allegedly servile origins of his opponent's father and his mother's imagined participation in sexual debauchery of some kind.[36] This apparently blatant double standard should not be treated (or not only) as some kind of personal hypocrisy on Demosthenes' part. That, at any rate, is a historically less revealing way of looking at it than to see it, with the support of much other evidence, as a sign of ambiguity in the status of aischrology in classical Athens, particularly in relation to the city's self-proclaimed ethos of democratic *parrhēsia*. Demosthenes, I want to suggest, is working with the grain of this ambiguity, trying for his own benefit to exploit both sides of it: namely, an elite repudiation of 'low', degenerate speech, and, on the other hand, a democratically pragmatic acceptance of, even relish for, parrhesiastic freedoms exercised in an overtly agonistic and far from accidentally gelastic spirit.

Let us focus on a final, telling detail in *De corona*. One of Demosthenes' epithets for Aeschines is περίτριμμα ἀγορᾶς, an 'habitué of the agora' – or (to get closer to the pithy tone of the phrase) one who 'knocks around' the agora, an 'old hand' in its (implicitly) seedy ways.[37] The epithet is illuminated by a passage of Aristophanes' *Clouds* (447) where Strepsiades imagines, with comic irony, how people will call him a περίτριμμα δικῶν, an old hand at the legal system, if he becomes successfully trained in forensic techniques of deception. It looks, then, as though Demosthenes brandishes an existing item of colloquial vocabulary to spice up his disparagement of Aeschines. To grasp the full force of the phrase, we have to understand that the Athenian agora could be regarded, from one evaluative angle, as a sordid location, associated, in socially elite terms, with the 'crowd' or 'rabble'

---

[36] Dem. 18.127–31: even here, though, Demosthenes (like Aeschines) avoids the extreme aischrology (sexually explicit terms, in particular) found in Old Comedy; cf. n. 69 below. Dem. 22.68 is another instance of (quasi-)reciprocal accusations of servile origins.

[37] Dem. 18.127, with Wankel (1976) 678, Taillardat (1965) 229, Chantraine (1968) 1137, Beta (2004) 137. Compare the colloquial τρίβων λόγων, 'an old hand with words', at Eur. *Bacchae* 717; cf. Stevens (1976) 50–1.

(ὄχλος). Witness, for example, the pointed phrase (a kind of hendiadys) 'the rabble and the agora' found in the mouth of Theophrastus' 'oligarchic' man, or the same collocation of terms in a fragment of Menander.[38] Material and social factors combine to colour the images evoked by such passages. The actual physical conditions of parts of the Athenian agora, especially in the looser denotation of the term which included the commercial quarter around the civic agora proper, are certainly germane. The overcrowding of this district of the city is mentioned in various sources, and perceptions of the 'vulgarity' of the agora in this broader sense were probably intensified by, among other things, the concentration of brothels in that area.[39] But the overcrowding motif is also available as a code, sometimes with anti-democratic overtones, for the indiscriminate social mixing that necessarily takes place in the busiest areas of the district.

This view of the agora as a magnet for low-life brashness and vulgarity – including, as we shall shortly see, disrespectful laughter – is highlighted in Aristophanes' *Knights*, a work with far-reaching though complex implications for the whole argument of this chapter (and a text to which I shall therefore want to return). Early on in the play the Sausage-Seller is promised political greatness precisely because he is 'vile (πονηρός), straight out of the agora, and brazen (θρασύς)' (181). The theme of what I shall dub the 'ago-rafication' of Athenian public life (and discourse) is central to everything that follows in the play, mediated in great part through the stereotyped image of the market- or street-vendor's foul speech.[40] We know from the Aristotelian *Ath. pol.* (and other sources) that Cleon became the target of elite charges of having debased the tone and style of political leadership in Athens: he is said to have been the first politician to shout on the podium, to use abusive language, and to address the Assembly with his

---

[38] Theophr. *Char.* 26.3, with Ober (1998) 365–6 and 238 below; Men. fr. 871.3. Diggle (2004) 468 supplies further references.

[39] On narrower/looser denotation of *agora* in Attic, see De Ste. Croix (1972) 267–84. Brothels in the agora: Fisher (2001) 216–17; cf. the agora as a threat to morality at Isoc. 7.48, following mention of gambling-houses and female musicians.

[40] See esp. *Kn.* 218, 636–8, 1258. Associations between being *agoraios* and crude abuse etc.: e.g. Ar. *Peace* 750 (*agoraios* part literal, part metaphorical, as often), *Lys.* 457–60 (alluding to female market-traders etc.), Theophr. *Char.* 6.10 (spurious?); cf. Plut. *Mor.* 521e for a non-Athenian image. Ar. *Clouds* 991 (Just Argument speaking) treats the agora as a place to be avoided (cf. 1055); thoughts of shame and laughter follow (992), not accidentally; cf. n. 42 below on the agora and laughter. Millett (1998) 218–24 discusses elite concerns about agoraic activities; cf. Martin (1951) 298–308 for various perceptions. Wilkins (2000) 156–201 explores the comic agora in Aristophanes. Arist. *Pol.* 4.3, 1289b33, 4.4, 1291a4–6, b19–20, 6.2, 1319a28, indicates the socio-economic class, and politically low evaluation, of *agoraioi*; but cf. an Athenian law prohibiting abusive remarks about those working in the agora (Dem. 57.30). For general depreciation of persons/things *agoraios* see also Ar. *Frogs* 1015, Aeschin. 1.125.

clothes girded or hitched up.[41] Two of these three motifs – the shouting and abuse – recur in Demosthenes' attack on Aeschines' aischrology, as well as in Aristophanes' grotesque caricature of Cleon in *Knights* as a Paphlagonian slave (a caricature which may have contributed, indirectly at least, to the very slurs that eventually found their way into Aristotle's *Ath. pol.*). The third motif, unseemly dress, we shall encounter again before long. Now, it is deeply implausible in anything like literal terms that Cleon actually introduced the practice of shouting or hurling coarse abuse (*loidoria*) in the Assembly. 'Shouting', in the physical circumstances of Greek political oratory, is what you call the power of your enemy's voice projection in large, open-air meetings (to avoid admitting its formidable potency), while the ancestry of hard-hitting rhetorical invective was surely very old and is already to be glimpsed, however fictively, as early as the Homeric poems. The anti-Cleonian charges of bawling and abusiveness, as their equivalents in Demosthenes' assault on Aeschines help us to see, are clearly markers of a tendentious deployment of would-be traditional values against a supposed upstart. The same holds for the gibe about clothing. Here a further parallel is furnished by the louche (or worse) dress habits of the 'barefaced' (ἀπο-νενοημένος) and 'obnoxious' (βδελυρός) types in Theophrastus' gallery of *Characters*, about whom I shall shortly say more. So the Cleon of the *Ath. pol.*, like the monstrous travesty of him in *Knights*, is a thoroughly 'ago-rafied' politician, a man who drags political discourse in every way down to the putatively sordid level of the teeming agora of Athens.

It is important for the direction of my argument to underline that the cluster of 'agoraic' features I have sketched so far, and which are translated into such relentlessly crude hyperbole in *Knights*, is partly held together by the idea that the agora is a prime site for *laughter* itself – a place where scurrility, ridicule and abuse can thrive with little or no interference, and one whose 'demotic' atmosphere of close-packed bustle and informality allows people to sit or move about joking and mocking others. Our sources supply a wide range of images of gelastic activity in and around the agora: people gathering to joke with one another or to scoff at others; parasites (who are also semi-professional jesters) touting for trade; acts of derision arising from the 'friction' (both physical and social) of overcrowding; market-traders (especially women, according to a convenient stereotype) abusing anyone who questions their goods or gives them difficulty; crowds taking

---

[41] See Arist. *Ath. pol.* 28.3, with Rhodes (1981) 353–4; cf. Aeschin. 1.25 on the dress of orators, with Fisher (2001) 149–52. Oratorical 'shouting': e.g. Ar. *Ach.* 711, *Kn.* 137, 274–6, 285–7 (etc.), *Wasps* 596, *Peace* 314, Dem. 22.68, with Beta (2004) 62–73. Worman (2004) offers analysis of Aeschines' and Demosthenes' manipulation of vocal/oral traits in their exchanges.

delight in the discomfiture of individuals; gangs of young men showing general irreverence; even, at certain times, licentious revels (*kōmoi*) seeking the most public of spaces for their alcoholic exuberance.[42] It is tempting here to introduce an analogy with Mikhail Bakhtin's notion of the medieval and early-Renaissance market-place as a locus of 'unofficial' culture, a site of popular, 'folk' alternatives to the hierarchical world of established power and privilege. Bakhtin's larger model of the carnivalesque 'culture of laughter', which I adduced in my last chapter, has been disputed on various grounds, though it remains a stimulating and influential example of how to interpret laughter historically.[43] Certainly, some caution is called for in applying a Bakhtinian idea of the culture of the 'market-place' to classical Athens. In Athenian thinking and practice, the agora is a scene for *both* official *and* 'unofficial' activities – for magistrates' offices and public notice-boards, as well as brothels, gambling-houses and face-to-face derision. What we are dealing with in our sources is not a uniform concept of an unregulated space of demotic or folk practices, but a set of partial associations which could be exploited by orators and others for their own *ad hoc* purposes. But there is no question that those associations accumulated a weight of reproach which stamped itself on, among other things, the idea of aischrologic speech. The social fluidity and 'promiscuity' of the agora, real or imagined, was one way of symbolising the threat of foul, offensive speech in the very midst of Athenian democracy.

In sum, aischrology is evaluated by our sources in terms that are impregnated with a sense of socio-ethical distinctions and hierarchy. It can even be regarded, as it is by Aristotle, as archetypally servile speech.[44] But this perspective poses a major problem for the mores of democracy, both because of the inclusion of a large demos, an enfranchised populace, in the machinery of government and because the values of democracy include a commitment to extensive *parrhēsia*, frank and free speech. That commitment

---

[42] See e.g. Ar. *Ach.* 854–5 (implying parasites: Olson (2002) 286), *Peace* 1015 (crowds laughing at individuals), Phryn. fr. 3 (gangs of mocking youths: ch. 1 n. 55), Hyp. *Phil.* 2 (Democrates orchestrating mockery of the polis; perverted parasitism: Halliwell (1991a) 291 n. 48; cf. Whitehead (2000) 48–50), Aeschin. 1.125 (circulation of humorous gossip), Pl. *Laws* 11.935b (abusive wrangling), Plut. *Mor.* 552b (licentious *kōmoi*: Themistocles and Alcibiades). The motif of mockery in the agora finds its way into late accounts of comedy's origins: see Koster (1975) 11 = Kaibel (1899) 13².

[43] See esp. Bakhtin (1968) 153–95 for the medieval market-place, with ch. 4, 204–6, for Bakhtin's model of carnival.

[44] Arist. *Pol.* 7.17, 1336a39–b12, assumes a (practical/ethical) connection between aischrology and slaves: correctly observed by Newman (1887–1902) III 488; cf. Kraut (1997) 161, 165. Obscene slave language is evoked at e.g. Eur. *Ion* 1189, Ar. *Frogs* 746; cf. ch. 6 n. 144. Compare Aristotle's idea that only certain kinds of laughter befit the 'free', *EN* 4.8, 1128a18–32, *Rhet.* 3.18, 1419b7–9, with ch. 6, 317–18, 322; this is also implied at Pl. *Rep.* 3.395c–e (225–7 above).

consequently becomes modified, as I mentioned earlier, by a discourse of anxiety regarding the ramifications of such frankness. There is, in other words, a constant tension between the democratic aspiration for open, unrestricted speech and the fear of divisively 'shameful', ugly speech (with its practical concomitants, among them unfettered laughter). But can the (alleged) language of the agora be marginalised, we might wonder, if the agora lies at the centre of political life? (And the agora, etymologically, is the place where people gather [from the verb ἀγείρειν, to bring together] and where many transactions of public discourse [cf. ἀγορεύειν, to address an assembly] are conducted.) Can one have democratisation of discourse without a corresponding tendency to 'agorafication'? Can one have a full commitment to *parrhēsia* without accepting a risk that the aggressive assertiveness of freedom will prevail over the restraints of shame and self-control?[45] Can one, in short, have freedom of speech without tolerance of aischrology? While aischrology can be notionally excluded from respectable political dialogue, it nonetheless seems to be a temptingly popular option in many contexts of democratic rhetoric. Demosthenes himself hints at this temptation, early in *De corona*, with his promise that he will return to Aeschines' *pompeia* (his festival parade ribaldry) later on, *if the audience* wishes to hear more of a response to it (18.11).[46] The inviting gesture towards an available retribution in kind is revealing. Demosthenes, like other orators (including Aeschines himself), treads a fine line between censure of his opponent's supposedly shameless deployment of insult and his own manipulation of laughter-inducing themes of abuse. High-minded disapproval of aischrology may be partially overriden by a willingness to pander to the opportunity for tit-for-tat defamation, as we have seen proves to be the case in a later section of *De corona*. It is is probably also a subtext, or pretence, of the oration that while seeking to introduce laughter or abuse gratuitously (as Demosthenes wants his audience to believe that Aeschines does) is a crude impropriety, to *retaliate* effectively with mockery of one's own (as Demosthenes himself purports to do) carries a self-sufficient justification with it.[47]

---

[45] Excessive *parrhēsia* exhibits shamelessness at Pl. *Phdr.* 240e, Isoc. 16.22; passages such as Pl. *Grg.* 487d, Isoc. 1.34 illustrate the underlying principle in a milder form. Contrast the capacity of democratic *parrhēsia* to channel shame at ps.-Dem. 60.25–6, with n. 6 above.

[46] Dem. 18.11. See Pl. *Rep.* 8.549d for a hint that abuse (*loidoria*) is a staple in courts and Assembly; cf. Pl. *Laws* 11.935b. Bonner (1922) is a mechanical survey of 'wit' in forensic oratory. Henderson (1998b) 258 is naive in claiming that Athenian 'men of conservative, upper-class breeding were particularly loathe to resort to violent, blaming, or shameless speech'. On laughter-related rhetorical strategies, cf. Spatharas (2006).

[47] Plut. *Mor.* 803b–e, though late, is suggestive here: jokes/jibes (*skōmmata*) and laughter have a place in political oratory when, instead of gratuitous outrage and buffoonery (*hubris, bōmolochia,*

All this reflects the intricate protocols of democratic debate in classical Athens, protocols that depended on interaction between individual speakers and collective values. Very strikingly for my purposes, in a passage of Aeschines' *Against Timarchus* the concept of *parrhēsia* is actually associated with the demos's raucous jeering of speakers in the Assembly. What is pictured here is a habit of derisive heckling – often accompanied by mass hooting, whistling and the like – that is documented by numerous sources, including Thucydides (who alleges that even a speaker as forcefully persuasive as Cleon could become the victim of an outbreak of it), and which we find comically echoed, as well as exaggerated, in several passages of Aristophanes.[48] The noisy laughter of mass audiences, even in the official environment of Assembly or lawcourt, was a phenomenon that orators could choose, for their immediate purposes, either to deprecate or to exploit. But as a particularly potent version of the spotlighting laughter of crowds against individuals, which I discussed more generally in Chapter 1, it was certainly too perpetual and real a risk to be ignored, especially if we bear in mind that in classical Athens the 'official' audience of a civic gathering was often augmented by the presence of a crowd of onlookers or bystanders.[49] When Plato makes Socrates suggest in the *Theaetetus* that a public speaker who is incapable (like Socrates himself at his trial) of swapping blunt insults or crude abuse (*loidoria*) may seem *ipso facto* 'ludicrous' (*geloios*) to his audience, he provides an acerbic but credible comment on the mass psychology of political and judicial audiences, as well as on the practised repertoire of the speakers who knew how to appeal to that psychology.[50]

---

gelōtopoiein), they demonstrate an ability to retaliate opportunely. On laughter and retaliation, cf. 248 below.

[48] See Aeschin. 1.80, with n. 6 above, for mockery of speakers by audiences as one kind of *parrhēsia*; cf. Bers (1985) on heckling by jurors. Vivid vignettes of hooting, whistling etc. at Pl. *Rep.* 6.492b, ps.-Pl. *Ax.* 368d (compare the people of imperial Alexandria at Dio Chrys. 32.22, 29–30). Laughter of Assembly/dicastic audiences (sometimes deliberately aroused by speakers) is also attested at Thuc. 4.28.5 (Cleon mocked during the Pylos debate; ἐμπίπτειν denotes an outburst: cf. Plut. *Cato Min.* 13.3, *Fab.* 15.3), 6.35 (the Syracuse Assembly), Lys. 24.18, Pl. *Euphr.* 3c–e, *Prot.* 319c, Xen. *Mem.* 3.6.1, 3.7.7–8, Dem. 9.54, 10.75, 19.46, 23.206, 54.13, 20 (see ch. 1, 36–8), Men. *Sic.* 264–6 (with ch. 8 n. 26). For comic reflections, see esp. Ar. *Ach.* 38 (with Dicaeopolis' subsequent heckling), 680, *Wasps* 567 (ch. 3 n. 30), 1287, *Eccl.* 256, 399–407; and note Plut. *Phoc.* 5.1 for a striking later anecdote (with ch. 1 n. 103 for Phocion's own antipathy to laughter). Laughter in the Athenian Boule: see esp. Pl. *Grg.* 473e–474a.

[49] I take Ar. *Wasps* 1287 to be a (partly fantasised) image of how onlookers might break into laughter; for the possibility that it pictures a preliminary hearing (*anakrisis*), see Sommerstein (1983) 234, (2004b) 160–1; cf. n. 80 below. Lanni (1997) documents the presence of bystanders in Athenian courts etc.

[50] Pl. *Tht.* 174c: note the verb μελετᾶν, to practise/rehearse (expert litigants and politicians made sure they had some well-prepared gibes).

If we return now, one last time, to *De corona*, we find in it one of our most explicit and informative observations on this state of affairs. Demosthenes complains that the demos suffers from the bad habit of allowing a malicious figure like Aeschines to obliterate memories of his political treachery by indulging in laughter-rousing calumnies of loyally patriotic advisers like Demosthenes himself. The people do this, he claims, because they are happy to trade the good of the city for the pleasure and gratification they derive from slanderous abuse.[51] The passage is a tissue of rhetorically crafted sarcasm. It is designed in part to obscure Demosthenes' own willingness (as we have seen) to resort to the type of *ad hominem* denigration he depicts as a devious tactic of Aeschines', but probably also in part to counteract and blunt his opponent's real gift for ridicule. (Hyperides, in the passage I cited earlier, may have been attempting to use a comparably *preemptive* tactic, as a prosecution speaker, where Philippides was concerned.) Whatever the mixture of truth and falsehood on the two sides of this particular confrontation, Demosthenes' visibly ambivalent posture *vis-à-vis* public *loidoria* ('below the belt' invective, as it were) is both a testimony to and a way of coming to terms with practices which were ingrained in the system. So ingrained, in fact, that in a remarkable passage from another work Demosthenes even admits that Aeschines and Philocrates once managed actually to halt a speech of his by standing on either side of the rostrum, in an organised double act, and interjecting strident 'jeers' (χλευάζειν) of a kind which created an outbreak of uncontrolled *hilarity* in the Assembly.[52] Athenian orators and audiences were involved in a continuous negotiation of what could/should be permitted or tolerated in public discourse. Laughter, with its complex relationship to the workings of public exposure and shame (to which we shall have to return), was an integral but inherently unstable part of that process.

THE SPEECH HABITS OF THEOPHRASTUS' CHARACTERS

Theophrastus' *Characters* has already been cited several times in the preceding pages. It is now appropriate to expand on the work's relevance to the themes of this chapter. The *Characters* is important but also problematic for my argument because of its hybrid status as a collection that seems to embody a peculiar mixture of philosophical and at least quasi-comic

---

[51] τῆς ἐπὶ ταῖς λοιδορίαις ἡδονῆς καὶ χάριτος τὸ τῆς πόλεως συμφέρον ἀνταλλαττόμενοι: 18.138. For the (laughter-related) verb 'trip up', ὑποσκελίζειν, in this same passage, cf. ch. 6 n. 58.

[52] Dem. 19.23; for the verb, cf. ch. 4, 212.

standards. How one estimates the proportions and blending of that mixture has a major bearing on interpretation of the vignettes presented in Theophrastus' sketches. From my own vantage point, it is precisely the *Characters'* somewhat elusive fusion of ostensibly disparate elements that makes it exceptionally interesting for an enquiry into Athenian-centred perceptions of (un)acceptable speech and the intersection of those perceptions with the possibilities of laughter. However exactly one weighs the value of the *Characters* as historical evidence for specificities of social life, its judgements and nuances can be read in a way that casts a sharp sidelight on the operations of socio-ethical norms. Moreover, these judgements and nuances draw on an essentially democratic sphere of experience, despite intermittent allusions to the non-democratic forms of government that Athens went through in the years immediately after 323.[53] Several of the *Characters* elucidate individual variations of speech habits, together with the pressures of inhibition and shame in Athenian society that helped shape those habits. It is worth mentioning that some of Theophrastus' character types – notably the dissimulator (εἴρων), flatterer (κόλαξ), and obsequious man (ἄρεσκος) – react to these pressures by *overcompensation* of one kind or another, either masking their feelings or adopting an exaggerated tendency towards ingratiation. But others offend against propriety in ways that can serve to uncover some of the values bearing on 'freedom of speech', as well as on the practice or avoidance of aischrology, in the communal world of the democratic city.[54]

Most pertinent here is the *kakologos* (28), the compulsive slanderer, This is the man who, as Theophrastus puts it (in phrasing which itself betrays something like an addiction to spiteful laughter), 'enjoys nothing in life so much' as insulting and speaking ill about other people, including friends and relatives.[55] He is given, among other things, to spreading graphically malicious allegations about people's family background (casting aspersions

---

[53] Both the dramatic and compositional date of the *Characters* remain debatable: see Diggle (2004) 27–37. Lane Fox (1996) makes a good case for the multiple levels on which the *Characters* can be mined as historical evidence.

[54] The mixture of behaviour and speech types in the *Characters* can help rebut the exaggerated claims of Burckhardt (1977) II 316, IV 183 [= Burckhardt (1998) 76, 230] that in Athens ' . . . derision seems to have dominated all social relations' ('Ein . . . Hohn scheint den ganzen Verkehr beherrscht zu haben'), and that the city's outlook was 'fundamentally filled with mockery and derision' ('Die ganze Anschauung war *a priori* mit Spott und Hohn völlig angefüllt'). Burckhardt's view reflects disproportionate reliance on Old Comedy, which he thinks influenced the whole tone of Athenian social relations: Burckhardt (1977) IV 196, (1998) 234. Cf. n. 81 below.

[55] τῶν ἐν τῷ βίῳ ἥδιστα τοῦτο ποιῶν: *Char.* 28.6. The fullest treatment is in Diggle (2004) 487–98; see also Steinmetz (1960–2) II 317–33, Ussher (1993) 235–46, and cf. ch. 7 n. 110. Some aspects of Theophrastus' depiction of foul speech are examined by Worman (2008) ch. 6.

on the legitimacy of their citizen status) and the sexual behaviour of the women in certain houses: 'they snatch passers-by off the street', 'this house of theirs is like a woman with her legs in the air', 'they copulate in the street like bitches', are his lubricious remarks in the second of these cases. And he is indiscriminate in the targets of his malice, even breaking that traditional (Chilonian and Solonian) injunction against speaking ill of the dead – though he is hardly unique in that respect.[56] His speech habits manifest total disregard for personal and social restraint; in accusing others of shameless action, he displays a rank verbal shamelessness of his own. But what is most interesting for my purposes is that he justifies his penchant for scandalous insults by invoking a specifically democratic freedom of speech: as I noted earlier, he tendentiously glosses or misdescribes his *kakologia* as '*parrhēsia* and democracy and freedom' (28.6). Since the *kakologos* is shown as participating widely in social life – his slander is said to occur sometimes in response to requests for information, sometimes 'when others are engaging in slander' (28.4), sometimes in general group conversation (28.5) – this purportedly democratic dimension of his character makes a sort of pragmatic sense. This feature of his portrait is not just a swipe at the man's self-exculpation; it hints at a particular tension attaching to aischrology in democratic contexts. *Parrhēsia* does indeed, by definition, widen the scope for things to be said that would be less easy to say in more restrictive cultures (recall the Xenophontic image of Sparta, 227 above). But it also thereby opens up an 'arena of risk', both by increasing the potential for offensiveness and by creating a situation in which individuals can harm their own standing or reputation by excessive indulgence in 'bad' speech. After all, Theophrastus' *kakologos* practises in everyday discourse some of the things which democratic orators (as well as comic poets) also specialised in: his denigration of family background or ancestry and his salacious sexual slurs parallel the topoi of personal invective exchanged by Demosthenes and Aeschines.[57] Theophrastus implicitly makes the slanderer a sort of spicy street-corner equivalent to the polemical practitioners of forensic and political rhetoric.

A different kind of characteristic shamelessness is ἀπόνοια (*Characters* 6), a sort of barefaced temerity. The barefaced man also has an association with shameless speech, though the initial definition, with its direct reference to 'shameful talk', may not be authentic (as with all the definitions in this work). Textual problems also interfere with our interpretation of other

---

[56] On ambiguities in Greek attitudes to insulting the dead, see ch. 1, 26–30.
[57] Cf. *Rhet. Alex.* 35.10 for family ancestry as a topos of rhetorical *kakologia*.

parts of this character sketch. But it does seem reasonably clear that the barefaced man lacks social sensitivity, in both active and passive ways, to foul speech:[58] he is equally prepared to engage in and to tolerate abuse (*loidoria*), and this is associated with a character that makes him, literally, 'fit for the agora' (*agoraios*, a word whose social opprobrium I have already noted). He also offends against decency in visual terms, being ready to go round in public with his clothes hitched up (ἀνασεσυρμένος). Speech and dress are parallel criteria of civility. In a fragment of the fourth-century comic poet Ephippus, one character describes another's foul talk (αἰσχροεπεῖν) as a metaphorical breach of sartorial code: 'you've got your tongue improperly dressed'.[59] Improper dressing, in this connection, reminds us not only of the Cleon of the Aristotelian *Ath. pol.* (232 above) but also of Theophrastus' boorish 'rustic' (*agroikos*), who hitches his clothing above his knees when he sits down (with consequent, if unstated, indecency, 4.7) – a trait taken even further by the 'disgustingly obnoxious' or 'nauseating' man (*bdeluros*), who is prepared to expose himself deliberately in the street in front of citizen women.[60] The barefaced man is a low-life figure, at best working as a street-vendor (and thus *agoraios* in the same sense as the Sausage-Seller in Aristophanes' *Knights*), at worst indulging in criminal activity. Even so, he is presented as a functioning part of democratic society, appearing frequently in the courts (like many Theophrastean characters), and not only as a defendant. At root he lacks a grasp of the need to temper freedom of expression in the interests of social harmony and cooperation. Interestingly, therefore, he is characterised as a direct participant in coarse behaviour of a strictly *comic* kind: not only dancing the *kordax*, that lewd dance we have met before, but doing so when sober and perhaps (if we accept a desirable

[58] On the infinitive λοιδορηθῆναι at 6.2 (active or passive in sense?) see different views in Steinmetz (1960–2) II 91, Ussher (1993) 73 with n. 1, 311–12, Rusten and Cunningham (2002) 68–9. *Pace* Lane Fox (1996) 164 n. 147, the matter is not open-and-shut, since κακῶς ἀκοῦσαι at 6.2 also intimates insouciance about being denigrated by others; cf. Plut. *Alcib.* 13.5 (on Hyperbolus). But Stein (1992) 127, Diggle (2004) 251–2 (with thorough linguistic analysis) deem the whole section an interpolation. In any case, μάχεσθαι at 6.4 probably implies abusive wrangling (cf. e.g. Hom. *Il.* 1.304); 6.7 again involves *loidoria* but may be spurious.
[59] ἐπαρίστερ' ἐν τῷ στόματι τὴν γλῶτταν φορεῖς: Ephip. fr. 23.2. Ps.-Xen. *Ath. pol.* 1.10–11 implies a widely shared standard of dress among Athenian males, but one in which slaves could participate; Thuc. 1.6.3–4 takes a more complex angle. See Geddes (1987) for the cultural background (with 312 on improper dressing as such).
[60] *Char.* 11.2. On 4.7 (4.5) see Diggle (2004) 210–11, treating the last part of the sentence as an interpolated gloss. Note various connections between βδελυρία and shamelessness at Aeschin. 1.26 (cf. 31, 105, with Fisher (2001) 153–6), Ar. *Kn.* 303–4, ps.-Arist. *Physiogn.* 6.810a33; cf. Parker (1983) 4–5. For Thrasymachus' sarcastic use of the word at Pl. *Rep.* 1.338d, see ch. 6, 286.

emendation of the manuscripts) without wearing a mask.[61] An affinity with comic drama appears also in the case of the obnoxious man, whose sexual indecency was mentioned just above. The latter is actually depicted as a disruptive member of a theatre audience: constantly clapping when others have stopped, whistling at actors who are popular with the rest of the spectators, and belching ostentatiously (11.3). Editors have perhaps missed a strand of Theophrastus' own humour in this passage: the obnoxious man behaves, *qua* spectator, in a manner that would make him entirely appropriate as a certain sort of comic character on stage, which is just as true of his phallic self-exposure.[62] He is additionally in his element noisily disporting himself in a crowded agora (11.4). In both the literal and extended senses, he is another *agoraios*.[63]

So the evidence of Theophrastus can reinforce a conclusion that takes overall strength from the arguments so far advanced. In classical Athens the notion of aischrology (including the vocabulary of *kakologia* etc.) marks out anxiety over a domain of speech that the culture of democracy cannot fully regulate, precisely because this domain overlaps and interacts in complex ways with a central piece of democratic ideology. Characters such as the Theophrastean slanderer, the obnoxious man and the barefaced man all take advantage of democratic freedom or frankness of speech (and a parallel freedom of action). But they do so, as it were, accidentally: because it suits their debased, flawed characters, not because they have any kind of principled attachment to democratic values (as *Char.* 28.6 only ironically underlines). There is a sense here, I want to maintain – and I shall shortly return to this point in connection with comedy – in which democratic norms can be exploited and even undercut by impulses that are *sub*democratic, in the sense of being psychologically independent of, and more 'primitive' than, the rules and protocols of democratic institutions. At the level of formal principle, democratic freedom of speech is not and cannot be unlimited, since the total absence of limits would by definition allow the unimpeded

---

[61] *Char.* 6.3: but see Diggle (2004) 253–4 for the textual problems; cf. Stein (1992) 124 n. 3, Ussher (1993) 312. On the obscene possibilities of the *kordax*, see 220, 229 above, with Dem. 2.18–20, Pickard-Cambridge (1927) 257–9, and ch. 3 n. 110; Arist. *Rhet.* 3.8, 1408b36 (describing the trochaic tetrameter as 'more suitable for the *kordax*'), implies that it was rapid in rhythm. On masks, see n. 31 above; together with transvestism, masks are pictured in a *kōmos* at a much later date by Philostr. maj. *Imag.* 1.2.3–5.

[62] Though probably not authentic, the definition of *Char.* 11 may not be wrong, *pace* Diggle (2004) 314, to use the term *paidia* to denote the 'fooling around' of this character.

[63] Compare the middle section (8), seemingly out of place, of *Char.* 19: the person who deliberately breaches a taboo by uttering a (religious) obscenity (*blasphēmein*) as his mother is on her way to an omen-reader.

advocacy of views explicitly hostile to democracy itself.[64] The Athenians accordingly possessed both specific legal restraints on freedom of speech (including laws against slander or defamation of various kinds) and informal curbs on it (procedural rules in the Assembly, for instance).[65] But even though such measures could encompass certain aspects of aischrology, they clearly left a diffuse threat to be faced from many forms of scurrility, abusiveness and obscenity. As we have seen, that threat gives rise in surviving sources to an 'elite' unease that must have been played out again and again in social incidents that extended from individual encounters in house or street, via the more fluid interactions of the agora and other public spaces, to the major confrontations of Assembly and lawcourts which I examined earlier in the chapter.

If Theophrastus' *Characters* can at least obliquely illuminate the norms and tensions that influence speech habits in the day-to-day settings of democratic society, from another angle the work bears interesting resemblances to comic drama, albeit more the comic drama of the late fifth and early fourth centuries than of Theophrastus' own lifetime. It was Theophrastus' teacher, Aristotle, who had already pointed out in the mid-fourth century that *aischrologia* was a prime index of the difference between what he called the 'old' (*palaios*) and the 'modern' (*kainos*) comedies. The context of this remark in the *Nicomachean Ethics* makes it clear that for Aristotle the phenomenon of aischrology, and the possibilities of laughter associated with it, represented an extreme point on the socio-ethical spectrum.[66] Given the vivid crudity of some of the language of the Theophrastean *kakologos* (239 above) – language which goes beyond the conventions of rhetorical aischrology as known to us from Athenian texts[67] – this type of person can be regarded as having even more in common with the world of Old Comedy than with the democratic orators to whom I earlier compared him. It is no accident, indeed, that Aristotle in the *Rhetoric* had aligned comic poets (of the satirical variety) with the malicious gossips and slanderers of real

---

[64] My point is conceptual (not normative): democratic values cannot coherently espouse (though they may conceivably try to practise) a freedom of speech that includes the right to urge the *destruction* of democracy itself – except (see 251) in comedy!

[65] See Halliwell (1991b) 48–51, Sommerstein (2004a) 206–8 for legal restrictions on freedom of speech in Athens.

[66] Arist. *EN* 4.8, 1128a23.

[67] Praxagora is imagined heedlessly exceeding the normal bounds of political abuse at Ar. *Eccl.* 255. Did real politicians ever go so far? (One hopes so.) Published texts need not reveal the full linguistic gamut of what speakers might sometimes say while on their feet.

life.[68] Theophrastus highlights this alignment by making his own *kakologos* ostentatiously scurrilous rather than covertly malign; he flaunts his vulgarity. We have seen that some of Theophrastus' other characters, especially the more disagreeable ones, are themselves reminiscent of comic figures: that is, they display in everyday life the kinds of disreputable behaviour that would normally be watched with outright pleasure only on the comic stage itself or within comparable frameworks of cultural licence (such as the performances of 'men on wagons'). To the extent that Theophrastus expects his readers to take pleasure themselves from the depiction of these figures (as opposed to reacting with, say, stern ethical disapproval), he is laying claim to a semi-comic standpoint of his own. That is undoubtedly an element in the work's teasing elusiveness of tone. But if we compare the *Characters* to the forms of Greek theatrical comedy in which figures speaking like the slanderer or exposing their bodies like the obnoxious man (*bdeluros*) would be entirely at home, we are bound to conclude that by an Aristophanic yardstick Theophrastus' sketches are – linguistically, imaginatively and in their prevailing ethos – only partially or mildly comic. The *Characters'* snatches of some kinds of aischrologic speech, and their brief images of equivalently indecent action, can help guide us towards a crucial set of questions about the conditions under which certain kinds of shamelessness may become legitimate objects of laughter – questions, therefore, that lead ultimately to the knotty relationship between shamelessness, 'unwritten law' and comedy. But to address these questions head on we need to move inside the theatre and back a century or so before Theophrastus to the dramatic universe of Aristophanes and his contemporaries.

ARISTOPHANIC SHAMELESSNESS

In Old Comedy, 'foul speech' of almost every conceivable variety is not only permitted, it is actively expected and celebrated, with near-pervasive consequences for the genre's loidoric, sexual, political and religious *anomie* which scarcely need documenting in detail here.[69] I have maintained elsewhere, and continue to believe despite arguments to the contrary, that Old

---

[68] *Rhet.* 2.6, 1384b9–11. But in calling comic poets 'slanderers of a sort' or 'in a certain sense' (κακολό-γοι . . . πως), Aristotle hints that their abuse of individuals is not simply on a level with the slanders of social life.

[69] Henderson (1991) catalogues the lexicon of obscenity; some details are unreliable. Since Henderson stresses the *exceptional* obscenity of Old Comedy (esp. 13), his statement (242) that 'comic poets . . . were not exempt from the rules governing other kinds of public/official discourse' is baffling; cf. next note. Other perspectives on Old Comedy's aischrology: Rosen (1988), Degani (1987), (1993),

Comedy's aischrologic 'imperative' (declined by very few poets, of whom Crates was probably one) brought with it at least an implicitly recognised legal immunity or special licence (*adeia*) in relation to the Athenian law(s) of slander (*kakēgoria*). If, as seems to have been the case, there existed a specific legal prohibition against abuse in public and official settings such as temples and other state buildings, what could be more conspicuously symbolic of comedy's exceptional status than its performance, under state-sponsored conditions, in simultaneously one of the city's religious shrines and one of its largest public buildings (the Theatre of Dionysus, within the shrine of Dionysus Eleuthereus)? I do not want to discuss legal immunity itself at length here, however, though my remarks will assume its *de facto* existence.[70] My present focus will be fixed on the question of comedy's cultural status *vis-à-vis* the broader social, political and ethical issues raised by the concept of aischrology and mapped out in the preceding sections of this chapter. Although I must state my position on this question relatively concisely, I want to do so in a way that draws on the larger approach to the psychology of laughter in Greek culture developed throughout this book.

One of the main uses of laughter in Greek culture is as an agency for the projection of dishonour onto people or things perceived as shameful. 'Shameful' (*aischros*) and 'laughable' (*geloios*) are evaluations that can easily be coupled. At *Republic* 5.452c, for example, the Platonic Socrates does precisely this, stating that there was a time when male nudity used to be thought 'shameful and ludicrous' (αἰσχρά . . . καὶ γελοῖα) by the Greeks, as it still is, he adds, by barbarians. The historical basis of the claim is not my concern, only its assumption that certain kinds of (supposed) shamefulness can be equated with, or translated into, objects of risibility.[71] Of

---

Robson (2006); cf. Willi (2002) 9–11. On distinctions between male and female obscenity in the genre, see Sommerstein (1995) 78–80, McClure (1999) 205–59 (though on 227, re πόσθη, 'prick', she overlooks *Thesm.* 515); cf. Willi (2003) 188 (though *ibid.* 195, 'taboo', is too strong). McClure's suggestion (231) that Ar. *Thesm.* lacks female obscenity to avoid 'sacrilege' is highly implausible; cf. ch. 4 n. 65.

[70] A trenchant case against comedy's (*de facto*) legal immunity is put by Sommerstein (2004a), (2004b), but note his important withdrawal, (2004a) 210–11, from his earlier position on the 'decree' of Syracosius, and his telling conclusion, (2004b) 166, that attempts to restrict comic freedom 'repeatedly failed'; cf. Henderson (1998b) 260–7 for a less tightly reasoned statement on the same side of the debate. My basic position remains that of Halliwell (1991b). Cf. the arguments of Lenfant (2003) for the largely fictive status of the supposed decrees restricting comic freedom; Trevett (2000) offers an alternative (and far-fetched) interpretation of one piece of evidence. An exceptional comic freedom of speech is accepted by e.g. Heath (1987) 27, Willi (2002) 9, Parker (2005) 139.

[71] For a selection of other passages which correlate 'shameful' and 'laughable', see Pl. *Laws* 7.819d, Philo, *Mut. Nom.* 199, Dio Chrys. 32.93–4, Plut. *Aemil.* 7.1, Diog. Laert. 6.91, John Chrys. *Adv. Jud.* 6.6 (48.913 *PG*).

course, not everything shameful can automatically be regarded as 'laughable'. Aristotle famously says in the *Poetics* (5.1449a32–3) that the laughable is 'part', i.e. one species, of the shameful; and while he has his own theoretical predisposition to delimit normatively what should count as *geloios* (as emerges later on in this same chapter of the *Poetics*), he is also recording a sustainable generalisation about Greek behaviour. Reactions to what is perceived as shameful will vary according to context and viewpoint. An observer may, for example, react with angry chastisement (whether or not expressed aischrologically), as Hector does to Paris' cowardly withdrawal from Menelaus in the *Iliad*.[72] Laughter is, however, one possible reaction to some species of the shameful/shaming, and it can come from either a primary antagonist (as, for instance, the Athenian Conon, 'crowing' over his battered enemy, Ariston, according to the latter's account to the jury) or from a secondary onlooker, typically a group, as, for example, the Theban crowds in Euripides' *Bacchae* imagined laughing at Pentheus as he is taken through the city streets in women's dress.[73]

But this leads on immediately to a related point. If laughter is sometimes a culturally apt response to (and signal of) the shameful, it is also a potentially shameful thing in its own right. Greek ethical, social and educational attitudes, as attested from the Homeric poems onwards, frequently express or display reservations about inappropriate and/or excessive laughter. To laugh at the wrong time, in the wrong place, or about the wrong things, may itself reflect shame back on one who behaves in this way – or, by the same token, may betoken the *shamelessness* of one who acts this way. (The abiding test case here, although open to more than one interpretation, is the Iliadic Thersites.) Between the workings of laughter as agency and/or object of shame there is, ideally, some sort of cultural consistency and equilibrium. But it is precisely that equilibrium which becomes practically invisible in the case of (Aristophanic) Old Comedy, except fleetingly in moments of authorial irony.[74] Within the gelastically saturated world of Old Comedy, laughter is frequently used – both by individual characters and, as it were, by the dramatic flow of the comedy – to project shame and derision onto others, but at the same time there is no impediment, indeed there is a common propulsion towards, the laughter of shamelessness. Emblematic of this last point is the attitude of the Unjust Argument in *Clouds*. Having already warned Pheidippides of the sexual and symposiac pleasures,

---

[72] *Iliad* 3.38–57; cf. n. 3 above.   [73] Dem. 54.8–9, Eur. *Bacchae* 854–5: see ch. 1, 31–2, 34.

[74] Two obvious examples: the tongue-in-cheek deprecation of crude laughter at *Clouds* 537–44 (ch. 1 n. 53), and the parodic prohibition on out-of-place bomolochic laughter at *Frogs* 358 (ch. 4, 212).

including 'guffaws' (καχασμοί), which he will have to sacrifice if he follows the ways of self-control (1073), the Unjust Argument urges the young man to 'go along with nature, cavort, laugh, think nothing shameful'.[75] That sounds like a sentiment which encapsulates much of the behaviour of, say, Dicaeopolis in *Acharnians*, Philocleon in *Wasps*, or Peisetaerus in *Birds*. It is not that shameless laughter is universally practised in Old Comedy, but rather that it represents a perpetually available option, ready to be taken up and taken advantage of by any character who at the time has the momentum of comedy with him or her. What's more, the (imagined) pleasures of such laughter seem to be made available to the *audience* as well, which is invited to suspend any anxieties that may normally apply in this area and to become, so to speak, psychologically implicated in the shamelessness of what happens on stage.

If we attempt, therefore, to situate Old Comedy against the broader background of cultural attitudes I have already sketched, the question 'when, or at what, is it wrong (for the audience) to laugh?' seems to be entirely beside the point. That is because within the purview of this spectacularly uninhibited genre, the dynamics of laughter and shame are exploited for extraordinarily unruly ends. What should (by prevailing social norms) count as shameful or ugly can be laughed at freely but also 'irresponsibly', without, it seems, any fear of shamefulness on the part of the audience itself, since the objects of laughter are turned into the material of a performance framed for the collective pleasure of the spectators. Old Comedy can say and do what cannot otherwise be said or done with total impunity in public life; and the behaviour of its audience is part of that special contract. Comedy of this kind plays by different rules. The defence speaker in a fragment of Lysias (probably dating from the early years of the fourth century) tells his audience that his opponent, Cinesias (a dithyrambic poet who also had some involvement in politics and was allegedly a member of a scandalously irreligious dining-club), is guilty of acts of such impiety that 'it is shameful for everyone else even to mention them, though you hear them from comic poets every year'.[76] The particular function of this remark within its trial does not matter to us; Lysias (as speech writer), like the orators who figured earlier in this chapter, will have had an incentive to manipulate personal details to suit his case. What does matter is that Lysias can expect

---

[75] χρῶ τῇ φύσει, σκίρτα, γέλα, νόμιζε μηδὲν αἰσχρόν: *Clouds* 1078; on the imagery, cf. ch. 1 n. 91. On 'guffaws' (rather than 'giggles') at *Clouds* 1073, see ch. 3 n. 31.

[76] Lys. fr. 53 Thalheim (*apud* Athen. 12.551f); cf. Isoc. 8.14 for a similar contrast. On Cinesias, see Nails (2002) 97–8, Dunbar (1995) 660–1, with Dodds (1951) 188–9 for the scandalous dining-club (cf. ch. 1 n. 94). For the 'shameful even to mention' motif, cf. nn. 17, 19 above.

an Athenian jury to know that comedy has a singular 'freedom of speech', more specifically a freedom to override normal inhibitions of shame and to incorporate even the most 'taboo' subjects for the shared relish of its audiences. Even when, later in the fourth century, Athenian comedy had moved away from the extremes of Aristophanes and his contemporaries (though revivals of older plays also need to be reckoned with), Aristotle – who was not himself particularly fond of such humour – still feels a need to exempt comic drama, as well as performances of *iambos* and the inherited scurrilities of ritual mockery (*tōthasmos*), from his general strictures against aischrology. Provided younger children are protected, as he sees it, against the possible harmfulness of its indecencies, Aristotle accepts that comedy, like the obscenities of ritual laughter with which he brackets it, merits a culturally privileged status which it would be unreasonable to contest.[77]

The traditions of Athenian Comedy, then, most especially in the later fifth and early fourth centuries, exemplify one version of what in the last chapter I called the principle of 'institutionalised shamelessness', a principle whose clearest surviving statement is found in Heraclitus' punning comment on phallic processions and songs: 'if it were not Dionysus in whose honour they process and chant a song to genitals (literally 'parts that induce shame'), their behaviour would have been most shameful'.[78] On this model, the audience of Old Comedy is exempted from both the practical and the psychological considerations that could be expected to impinge on reactions to the shameful in many other public settings. Within this carefully demarcated framework, the pressures of shame are temporarily lifted. By cultural (and perhaps also religious) convention the theatre audience is not just permitted but encouraged to laugh at everything, including itself: Aristophanes *Clouds* 1096–1104, where the Just Argument defects to the collectively 'wide-arsed' spectators, is a classic instance of the comic loop whereby the audience is invited to greet with mirth a gibe against its own shamefulness. This, of course, presupposes consensual participation in the festive and theatrical language game of comedy, and leaves open the possibility of different responses on the part of uninvolved or resistant observers. But for such consenting participants comedy can be said to *translate* the energy of shame wholeheartedly into laughter, institutionalising and in a sense ritualising this conversion of a potentially negative force into the

---

[77] Arist. *Pol.* 7.17, 1336b16–19: cf. Kraut (1997) 164–5, with ch. 4, 159, 167, for further discussion. Unlike Aristotle, many Athenians probably took the view that even younger children should be allowed to attend aischrologic comedy: see ch. 1 n. 57.

[78] Heraclitus fr. 15 DK. See further in ch. 4, 182.

celebrations of communal enjoyment. Old Comedy thus manipulates a great polarity present in Greek attitudes to laughter – a polarity between the ideas of derisive, shame-directing antagonism, on the one hand, and reciprocal, ludic gratification, on the other – and converts the strong 'charge' associated in life with fear of the former into an intensification of theatrical pleasure in the latter.

But there is a price to be paid for the privilege of such institutionalised shamelessness, such exceptional 'freedom of speech'. This price is the blunting, even loss, of the normal efficacy of shame (including shame conveyed by ridicule) as an instrument for the regulation and control of social action. As with all forms of consensual joking, the capacity to generate shared amusement weakens, or at an extreme disables, the potential to shock.[79] To laugh derisively (*katagelan*, literally 'laugh down') is paradigmatically, in Greek culture, a hostile act, and one which therefore courts the risk of reprisals. To *be* derided is to have a compelling motive for retaliation. Thus to be derided and *incapable* of retaliation is, as Socrates observes in Plato's *Philebus* (49b), a definition of what it means to be truly laughable or comic (*geloios*). Yet the audience of Old Comedy can always laugh without danger, even when the victims of comic abuse are in reality very powerful. That is only, however, because comedy's licensed performance conditions remove it from the consequential cause and effect of real-life enmities and antagonisms, however much poets may pretend otherwise. In *Knights* for example, which I shall shortly discuss in more detail, Aristophanes' presentation (and imaginary defeat) of Cleon as a grotesque monster gives the game away: its powers of demonisation are only available because they carry no answerability to scrutiny or challenge or testing in the practical political realm.

On the other side of the coin, the unwritten rules of the genre's cultural status effectively disarm its targets, rendering them generally incapable of direct response even against the playwrights themselves. In this respect, Cleon's much-cited reaction to Aristophanes' *Babylonians* in 426 should not be treated as though it were anything other than exceptional. It seems to have revolved around a complaint about mocking the city 'in the presence of foreigners' (Ar. *Ach.* 503), which is best interpreted as reflecting specific sensitivity in a wartime setting of extremely tense relations between Athens and her allies, whose tribute-bearing ambassadors were present at the City Dionysia. We know that in the fourth century a procedure existed, called

---

[79] Douglas (1975) 106–7 has perceptive reflections on this point. Rosen and Marks (1999) provide a stimulating comparative case study in related issues.

probolē, which allowed offences allegedly committed during a festival to be put before the Boule and, if the latter did not resolve the matter, the Assembly. The law specifically covering the Dionysia did not exist in the 420s, but the (satirically garish) description of Cleon's outburst at Aristophanes, *Acharnians* 377–82 seems to picture some kind of immediate recourse to the Boule by a powerful politician who felt that the scurrilous depiction of Athenian-allied dealings in *Babylonians* was somehow embarrassing in front of visiting envoys.[80] But whatever form it took, Cleon's action against Aristophanes cannot be adduced to establish anything about the predictable or usual impact of comedy, though it no doubt illustrates that when the stakes are high enough (in a wartime crisis) even the Dionysiac freedoms of comedy, as exercised in front of visiting envoys, may come under some strain. But then again, the evidence – including the implication in *Acharnians* that the matter was not taken any further than the Council – appears to warrant the conclusion that from Aristophanes' point of view Cleon's action ended in failure.[81]

Comedy's protected 'irresponsibility', and therefore its effective immunity to reprisals, is one reason, I believe, why the dynamics of the genre, notwithstanding its *prima facie* position as an institution of democratic culture, should not be regarded as essentially democratic. Athenian comedy, contrary to what many scholars have suggested, is not a functioning 'organ' of democracy, and certainly not in anything like the sense of the Assembly or courts. In fact, it makes good sense to understand comedy as both *pre*democratic in inspiration (that is, in terms of its 'folk' roots, including such practices as phallic songs) and psychologically *sub*democratic in its appeal to impulses (whether individualist, utopian, or simply anomic) that

---

[80] For the *probolē* procedure relating to the Dionysia, including the implication that matters might sometimes go no further than the Boule, see Dem. 21.8–9, with MacDowell (1978) 194–7, (1990) 13–16; but Dem. 21.147 states that the law postdated Alcibiades' lifetime. If Ar. *Wasps* 1284–91 also refers to the clash after *Babylonians* (a disputed hypothesis, but tenable), it suggests that Aristophanes may have given some undertaking in the Boule to mollify Cleon, though such an undertaking need have had nothing to do with his comic treatment of Cleon himself (a point missed, it seems, by Sommerstein (2004b) 151).

[81] On the aftermath of *Babylonians*, Sommerstein (2004b) is the fullest treatment; see 159–60, 166 for Cleon's 'failure' (cf. n. 70 above). If Sommerstein were right (166) that it was an 'attractive' option for politicians to try to 'silence' comic poets by legal procedures, there ought to have been *endless* moves against comedy by fifth-century politicians. When Sommerstein claims that the idea of comedy's festival licence is an entirely 'modern construction' (154), he does not address all the material adduced in Halliwell (1991b) 66–70. As a historical curiosity, I note that Burckhardt (1977) II 338 translates the hyperbolic imagery of Ar. *Wasps* 1285–87 into a real beating-up of the poet in the theatre, at Cleon's behest, after the performance of *Knights*! (There are further problems with Burckhardt's sentence: the clause 'wie tadelhaft er . . .', appears to misconstrue Aristophanes' text and is additionally garbled in Stern's translation, Burckhardt (1998) 78.) Cf. nn. 49, 54 above.

run below the level of political ideology or principle. Ancient claims that Old Comedy originated in archaic, local customs of charivari-type 'folk justice' and associated popular protest – the world of the 'village' rather than the urbanised state – may not be historically authentic, and they certainly become entangled with an anachronistically moralised account of the genre's public function. But they do perhaps express some recognition of the pre-/subdemocratic spirit of 'spontaneous' (i.e. non-institutional) self-assertiveness that often drives the action of Aristophanic drama.[82] It is tempting here to invoke once again Bakhtin's concept of carnival, the realm of festive 'folk laughter', whose roots lie in an anti-authoritarianism that operates outside or beyond set political categories, including those of democracy.[83] This model requires careful handling, as I explained in the previous chapter. A Bakhtinian distinction between 'official' and 'unofficial' cultures, which may even be problematic in the late-medieval world for which it was designed, cannot be straightforwardly applied to the polis-organised festive context in which Old Comedy was staged. But the crucial point here does not concern the level of institutional organisation, which was undoubtedly 'official' (under the control of magistrates) and a fixture in the democracy's festival calendar. It concerns comedy's *internal* universe: its characters' fantasies and freedoms, and therefore the psychological level on which its audience is invited to spectate (and/or participate vicariously) in the world of those characters. On this second level, democracy is assuredly *not* in control, since nothing and no one is – not even the gods. And it is here, if anywhere, that we can locate Old Comedy's 'unofficial' voice, with the scope which it gives to the pre- and subdemocratic shamelessness of unrestrained laughter.

We can make that point a little more precise by noticing how Old Comedy dramatises and exploits a licence for mockery that is no more respectful of democratic authority than of any other kind, whatever some ancient observers may have thought to the contrary.[84] Several Aristophanic

---

[82] For theories of Attic comedy's origins in customs of public shaming *à la* charivari (ch. 4 n. 73), see Halliwell (1984) 84 (read Quintil. 10.1.65). Such views may have been influenced by the mock solemnity of a passage like Ar. *Kn.* 1274–5, but they are largely a *post hoc* assuagement of readers' moral concerns. An attempt to root comedy in the folk traditions of the 'village' (*kōmē*), i.e. outside the urban centres of power, is etymologically spurious but nonetheless old: see Arist. *Poet.* 3.1448a37–8; cf. Segal (2001) 3–9.

[83] Cf. Bakhtin (1968) 255 for carnival as outside 'all existing forms of . . . political organization': Bakhtin here has non-democratic politics in mind, but his point can be extrapolated/modified to democratic contexts. Cf. ch. 4, 204–6.

[84] Old Comedy was often regarded in antiquity as inherently democratic. The earliest evidence is from Athens itself: ps.-Xen. *Ath. pol.* 2.18 claims (falsely, given Ar. *Knights*) that comedy cannot mock the demos itself; one discussion in Mastromarco (1994). Later sources are cited in Halliwell (1991b) 66

protagonists, it needs to be emphasised, trample over democratic procedures and ideals, pitting themselves defiantly against the rule of Assembly,
magistrates and law. Their motives, of course, are not all identical, and
their actions have multiple dimensions; but the wilful circumvention of
democracy is a recurrent pattern. Dicaeopolis, in *Acharnians*, empowers
himself to suspend a meeting of the Assembly (which he regards as a corrupt sham but also a personal irritant), makes a private peace-treaty with
the city's enemies (by any 'realistic' yardstick a treasonable act), and mercilessly mocks a serving general, Lamachus. Peisetaerus in *Birds* founds his
new imperial city on a rejection of Athens: among other things, he scoffs
at the idea of making Athena the patron deity (828–31), uses physical force
to expel an Athenian 'inspector' (1021–34), and turns himself into a tyrant
(supposedly a hate-figure for Athenians). Lysistrata leads a quasi-military
occupation of the Acropolis, something reminiscent (for the male half-
chorus, 274–80) of the action of the Spartan king Cleomenes in the year
508; she defies and assaults a magistrate; and she compels the Boule to
negotiate on her own terms (with the help of a peace-treaty personified as
a naked female open to obscene examination on stage). At the extreme,
in *Ecclesiazusae*, Praxagora actually abolishes democracy, dismantling the
institutional structure of Assembly, Council and lawcourts.[85] These major
examples buttress the general thesis that comic 'freedom of speech' may
have become institutionalised and in a sense protected by democracy, but
its *imaginative* operations (in the offensive aischrology and even physical
aggression of many of its characters) are far from being intrinsically or
consistently democratic in spirit.[86] On the contrary, those operations are
frequently driven by a self-assertive, even anarchic, impulse which cannot
easily be translated into a position that would make practical sense within

---

n. 69. Modern versions occur in e.g. Reckford (1987) 68, Flashar (1994) 69–70, Sommerstein (2002)
26. For what it's worth, Old comic poets themselves do not appeal to democratic *parrhēsia* to justify
their own freedoms; the only fifth-century comic reference to *parrhēsia* is at Ar. *Thesm.* 541, where
the Kinsman is speaking as a woman in the context of the secret festival. Isoc. 8.14, but written in
355, explicitly ascribes *parrhēsia* to comic poets; later, the term is applied to the Old comic parabasis
at Plut. *Mor.* 712a (note Plut. *Mor.* 68b–c, with n. 92 below), and cf. Marcus Aur. *Med.* 11.6. Lucian,
Prom. es 6 speaks of the Dionysiac 'freedom' (*eleutheria*) of Old Comedy, Quintil. 10.1.65 of its
libertas.

[85] When the hag at *Eccl.* 945 calls the new *sexual* communism democratic, the irony does not affect
the larger political point: Praxagora has abolished Assembly, Council and lawcourts.

[86] When Goldhill (1991) 183 calls democracy 'the *very condition of possibility* for Old Comedy' (my
itals.), he fails to take sufficient account of the culturally and psychologically pre- and subdemocratic
elements in the energies of the genre. Likewise Carey (1994) 69; cf. next note. Only if one adopts a
hostile conception such as that found at Pl. *Rep.* 8.562e, where the 'democratic' psyche tends towards
bestial anarchy and shamelessness, can Aristophanic comedy count as quintessentially democratic
in spirit.

the arena of contemporary Athenian politics. This line of argument points towards bigger, thorny issues of the political interpretation of Aristophanes which I cannot fully tackle here. But it is just worth noticing that some of the most articulate modern attempts to define an Aristophanic view of Athenian democracy end up generating problematic paradoxes.[87] The relationship of Aristophanes' work to the Athenian demos and to the whole spectrum of political options in the late fifth and early fourth centuries is, notwithstanding slogans both ancient and modern, irreducibly ambiguous: a performance for democratic audiences that celebrates, as much as anything else, the (comic) possibility of 'uncrowning' democracy itself with the power of laughter.

But since the arguments of this chapter are concerned with perceptions and implications of aischrology which extend beyond the formalities of politics, it is important now to return to the general shamelessness which characterises the gelastic freedom of Old Comedy. This shamelessness, which centres on aischrologic (derisive/offensive) speech and its practical counterparts, certainly overlaps with the defiance of democratic authority which I stressed in the previous paragraph. But it has a more widespread field of play than that and is exhibited by virtually all Aristophanic protagonists. Again, there is room for only cursory examples of the point; the detailed ramifications in individual works cannot be pursued here. In *Acharnians*, Dicaeopolis does not just mock Lamachus; he brandishes his phallus at him and obscenely invites homosexual contact between them.[88] The Sausage-Seller in *Knights* is happy to boast of his activities as male prostitute and thief.[89] Strepsiades in *Clouds* wants to cheat his creditors (and

---

[87] Henderson (1998b), for instance, thinks that comic aischrology is a weapon of the demos' 'assertion of popular control' (265) *and* that comedy speaks for 'the politically excluded' (269). A related incoherence: Henderson endorses ps.-Xen. *Ath. pol*. 2.18 (n. 84 above), where the demos supposedly refuses to let itself be 'criticised' (262), yet later states that 'comic poets . . . felt free to criticize the demos' (271; variant spelling in original). Cf. Henderson (1990), with the objections of Heath (1997) 237–9 (stressing that comic poets were not in direct rivalry with politicians), Silk (2000) 306–16. MacDowell (1996) 197 states that in *Knights* 'Aristophanes . . . does not even hint . . . that democracy might be replaced . . .', but to turn this into Aristophanic 'advice' he equates a complex plot-structure with a black-and-white proposition; by the same hermeneutic, Aristophanes in *Eccl.* should be 'advising' the abolition of democracy: cf. MacDowell 323 for equivocation on this point. The most balanced survey of political readings of Aristophanes is Carey (1994), though he never quite confronts the paradox that the demos itself (esp. in *Knights*) can be both target and audience of ridicule; and he wrongly assumes that the 'carnival model' of Old Comedy is reducible to 'lighthearted' and 'goodnatured festival fun' (73). Saetta Cottone (2005) 41–58 attempts to break away from political dichotomies by reading Aristophanic abuse in terms of poetic traditions and dramatic form.

[88] *Ach*. 591–2: cf. Dover (1989) 204. Olson (2002) 226 ('excite him sexually') seems misleading.

[89] *Kn.* 1242; cf. 423–8. On the passive sense of βινεσκόμην ('I used to get fucked') in 1242, see Bain (1991) 61.

is later happy to jeer shamelessly to their face: 1236–6), while Philocleon in *Wasps* cheerfully insults his fellow-guests at a symposium and steals a pipe-girl for his private sexual gratification. Peisetaerus in *Birds* goes so far as to threaten, satyr-like, to rape a goddess, Iris (1253–6), while Lysistrata, for all her seeming solemnity, is capable of various kinds of smutty talk, as is her counterpart Praxagora in *Ecclesiazusae*.[90] Euripides' Kinsman in *Thesmophoriazusae* allows himself to be dressed as a woman (while retaining the pointedly aischrologic tendencies which marked him out from the start), and something comparable is one of the many respects in which the god Dionysus himself, ultimate emblem of comedy, parades rampant shamelessness in *Frogs*. The list could be prolonged and multiplied. And it is not just the protagonists but also many of the secondary characters – not least Pheidippides, the Unjust Argument, Euelpides, Xanthias in *Frogs*, and several of the supporting casts of women in *Lysistrata*, *Thesmophoriazusae* and *Ecclesiazusae* – who flagrantly and repeatedly disregard norms of 'respectable' speech and action.

As some of the above examples illustrate, comic aischrology (together with its visual and practical equivalents: derisive gestures, offensive actions) has particularly free scope in the domain of sex. That scope is advertised by the almost pervasive presence of the comic phallus, which on one level at least can be perceived as a generic badge of 'institutionalised shamelessness', an internalised analogue (whether or not Aristotle was right about the origins of the genre) to the large models of the male organ which, as discussed in the last chapter, were paraded in some of the processions of Dionysiac festivity. Almost all the male characters of Old Comedy, regardless of their social status within the imaginary universe of the plays, had a phallus which was permanently visible to the audience. This automatically put them at odds with the norms of Athenian society, where, as we saw earlier in Theophrastus, it is the boorish rustic who is careless about letting his genitals be glimpsed under his clothes, and the 'obnoxious' (*bdeluros*) character who uncovers his genitals deliberately in the street. If the workings of Greek shame were in general focused, in face-to-face interactions, by the manner in which people literally looked at or were seen by one another, then the blatant visibility (and, not infrequently, the gestural *use*) of the comic phallus was a constant reminder of Old Comedy's generic imperviousness to shame, even if individual characters (thereby heightening the cultural paradox) can still express sensitivities to shame which, as it

[90] See esp. *Lys.* 107–10, 124, 212–31, 1119, *Eccl.* 228, 525, 617–34.

were, are flouted by the performance to which they belong.[91] That is why Aristophanes' parabatic conceit about his supposed avoidance of the big, red-tipped phallus at *Clouds* 537–9 is not just a joke about his own work. It is a huge joke on a conspicuous presupposition of the entire genre. The matching idea of an Old Comedy with the modesty of a maiden (*Clouds* 534–7) only makes the pretence even more transparent. One would have to be culturally very misinformed to miss the palpable irony of this self-contradictory trope.[92] What's more, Old Comedy had the freedom to go a step further and represent female genitalia to its audiences, in a theatrical equivalent to the self-exposure of Baubo in one version of Demeter's laughter at Eleusis.[93] The gap between comic indecency and social taboos and inhibitions is even bolder here than with the phallus.

I have tried, then, to put a little flesh on the proposition that Old Comedy, as we know it from Aristophanes, tends strongly towards the *celebration* of shamelessness, providing its audiences with opportunities and encouragement to laugh *with* and not simply *at* its characters. One implication of this thesis, as I pointed out earlier, is that the audience of such comedy is itself at least partly implicated in, and an accomplice to, the shamelessness of the event. This was grasped acutely by the philosopher Plato, who grew up in an Athens where Old Comedy was still flourishing and where the career of Aristophanes, whom Plato is likely to have known personally, was in full flow. The testimony of Plato is all the more fascinating, though also more complex, because we know that he actively reflected on Old Comedy's satirical treatment of his philosophical hero Socrates. Contrary to what is so often asserted, however, we cannot confidently infer that Plato held comedy responsible for having created the image of Socrates which eventually led to his prosecution. In fact, in the relevant passages of the

---

[91] At Ar. *Lys.* 1095–9 the husbands are (realistically) embarrassed at the thought of being seen with erections; contrast Dicaeopolis' fantasised pride in his erection at *Ach.* 1220. On Aristophanic comedy's sexual 'shamelessness', see Halliwell (2002a). For the importance of seeing and being seen (at least in the imagination) for the workings of shame, cf. Williams (1993) 78–90 with n. 13 above; Men. *Georg.* 80–1, on not wanting 'witnesses' to a miserable existence, implies this principle.

[92] This illustrates what I take to be the status of (Aristophanes') parabases as exercises in mock authorial role-playing (with feigned personae, parodic voices and rhetorical posturings). Cf. 257–8 below on the parabasis of *Clouds*; and see Rosen (2000) for this aspect of Cratinus' work. Hubbard (1991), the fullest study of the parabasis, recognises some parabatic irony but succumbs to the temptation to construct a coherent 'autobiographical' Aristophanic self-image. An interesting perception of the parabasis in (later) antiquity is Plut. *Mor.* 68b–c, where supposedly severe political 'advice' is undermined by the admixture of scurrility (*geloion, bōmolochon*): Plutarch's viewpoint, though moralistic at base, shows awareness of how hard it is to read the parabasis within a steadily 'serious' frame of reference.

[93] For representation of female pudenda on stage (the details are clearer in some cases than others), see esp. Ar. *Ach.* 765–75, *Wasps* 1374–7, *Lys.* 824–8, 1158, *Eccl.* 890; cf. ch. 4 n. 115.

Apology – passages whose one-sided interpretation has become one of the stalest received opinions in classical scholarship – a *distinction* is indicated between the comedian Aristophanes (and by extension other comic poets too who wrote plays about Socrates) and those who over the years have maligned Socrates with real 'malice and denigration' (φθόνῳ καὶ διαβολῇ, 18d). Plato makes Socrates refer to the 'empty nonsense' (*phluaria*) of his depiction in Aristophanes' *Clouds* not in order to cast comedy as a serious causal factor in the spread of slanders about him, but in order to suggest that those slanders are no more substantial than the distorted fantasies which everyone knows are the stock-in-trade of comic drama. Notwithstanding the trauma of Socrates' trial and execution, Plato still found it possible to acknowledge the difference in status between comic absurdities and the genuine social dissemination of a damaging reputation.[94]

Given the sardonic but far from simply hostile references to comedy which the *Apology* puts into Socrates' mouth (and it goes without saying that we do not know whether Socrates actually made any such point at his trial),[95] it is intriguing that in the last book of the *Republic* Plato gives Socrates an argument, which he expects Plato's brother Glaucon to be familiar with from his own experience, that spectators in the comic theatre are invited to take strong, unabashed pleasure in the dramatic representation of laughable behaviour – behaviour of a kind they would be *ashamed to engage in directly* and would readily condemn in life. Here as elsewhere, Plato's text does not propose an outright denunciation of comedy, though it does uncover deeply disturbing questions about its audience psychology. As well as concurring with the reading of this passage from *Republic* 10 as proto-Freudian (Freud himself almost paraphrases Plato when talking of the shame sometimes felt after laughing in the theatre), I would stress how Socrates' suggestion shrewdly presupposes the sort of ambiguity in the

---

[94] A careful interpretation of Pl. *Apol.* 18b–d, 19c, distinguishing between comic 'nonsense' (*phluaria*: cf. ch. 3 n. 41) and Socrates' real maligners, was set out by Frese (1926), an article which has been almost entirely neglected (e.g. by the latest commentator, Heitsch (2002)). See also Burnet (1924) 74–5 (an important chronological detail), 79. Recent views along the same lines have been espoused by Heath (1987) 9, Stokes (1997) 105–6; cf. Halliwell (1993c) 336–7. Sommerstein (2004b) 155 does not fully consider the ironic nuances of *Apol.* 18b–d; von Möllendorff (2002) 134–5 adopts an intermediate reading. The idea that the *Apology* accuses *Clouds* of having damaged Socrates remains commonplace: e.g. Henderson (1998a) 5 ('the decisive role' [!] in Socrates' condemnation), (1998c) 21, Silk (2000) 303, Bouvier (2000) 432–4. A garish version of this idea occurs in antiquity at Eunap. *Vitae Soph.* 6.2.4–5: the success [*sic*] of *Clouds* (in the inebriated atmosphere of Dionysiac festivity) persuaded Socrates' enemies to prosecute him! Contrast Liban. *Apol. Soc.* 10, where the 'risk-free' (ἀκίνδυνος) laughter of Dionysiac comedy is distinguished from the consequentiality of the courtroom.

[95] Xen. *Apol.* contains no equivalent passage, but that tells us little, since the work admits its own selectivity (22).

relationship between laughter and shame to which I earlier drew attention.[96]
What matters for present purposes is not the implication of the argument
for Plato's own enterprise, but the way in which it exposes a tension lurking
in the culture's acceptance of (Old) comedy as a distinct, psychologically
'safe' festive experience. Whatever laughter's power to act, in appropriate
circumstances, as a medium for shaming its targets, it can also become a
mark of shamefulness on the part of those who give way to it without any
inhibitions or with any aim other than a flow of pleasure. It is this ambiguity
which allows Plato to treat audience laughter as the vehicle of a kind of
psychological complicity in the gelotopoeic atmosphere of comic theatre
(or, on a smaller scale, the practices of coarse joking between individuals
in private).[97] Socrates' argument in the *Republic* may have a moralistic
impetus which goes beyond what most Athenians would have found easy
to assimilate. But I submit that his diagnosis nonetheless tallies with the
psychological implications of Old Comedy's special cultural status and the
sway of unfettered laughter on which it thrived. Such laughter involved
not just the suspension but the obtrusively pleasure-seeking transgression
of normally prevailing principles of shame. For Athenians, that involved a
pact between masked, phallic performers and their vicariously, temporarily
shameless mass audiences. The reward of the experience was one kind of
collective self-overcoming: the laughter of both bodily and mental release,
at a level which could undercut even the values of the democracy that
sponsored the performance, but which must always have remained true to
the Dionysiac spirit of the occasion.

In order to pull together some of the strands of this chapter, it will be
worthwhile to take a final glance at the surviving Aristophanic play which
represents the *ne plus ultra* of aischrology, *Knights*. I have already cited
this work more than once for its prominent imagery of the 'agorafication'
of politics and politicians. *Knights* develops a satirical scenario according
to which the democracy has been taken over by loud-and-filthy-mouthed
figures who have supposedly transferred the physical and verbal crudities
of the backstreets round the agora onto the once dignified platforms of

---

[96] Reckford (1987) 58–61 reads *Rep.* 10.606c as proto-Freudian, but he does not cite Freud's own
comment on feeling shame after laughing in the theatre: Freud (1989) 204, Freud (1976) 283. An
interesting parallel in Cohen (1999) 81 ('do I then dislike my own laughter at the joke?'). For
complexities in Plato's references to comedy and laughter, see ch. 6, 276–8, 300–2.

[97] As the words καὶ ἰδίᾳ ἀκούων (10.606c) indicate, Plato is partly exercised by the consequences of
listening to certain sorts of humour in private; compare the Aristotelian passages cited in nn. 19,
44 above. On laughter and shamelessness in other contexts, see ch. 1, 22–5, 27–8. Cf. the shameless
man's laugh at Theophr. *Char.* 9.4, and the vignette of loud, uninhibited laughter as symbolic of
sexual shamelessness (imputed to a young male in a relationship with an older man) at *P. Oxy.* III
471 col. iv.85–8.

the democracy's Boule, Assembly and courts. Contrary, however, to the prevailing tradition of interpretation which tries to extract from the play a coherent, even earnest, critique of the state of Athenian politics in the post-Periclean 420s when Cleon rose to dominance, there is, I maintain, an inescapable set of paradoxes that adhere to Aristophanes' treatment of these themes. These paradoxes stem, *au fond*, from the fact that if aischrology (with its whole penumbra of social vulgarity) is normatively or idealistically deemed out of place in constructive political discussion and debate, it is all too obviously at home on the comic stage itself. So comedy can simultaneously feed its own (audience's) taste for scurrilous abuse and mockery, while purporting to decry its corrupting presence in the institutions of democracy. Comedy, in other words, can have it both ways. That formulation highlights the sense in which *Knights* provides a grotesquely inflated application of the psychological principle enunciated at Plato *Republic* 10.606c. The play invites its spectators to revel in what they (hypothetically) disdain, the degradation of democracy by abuse and derision. It invites them to laugh at certain forms of laughter (or laughter-inducing behaviour) itself.

Knights is a comedy of conspicuously vulgar excess, a relentless superabundance of denigration and shamelessness. Precisely this fact has repelled some critics, leading them to judge the work quasi-biographically as though it were simply vitiated by a surfeit of animus on the part of the poet.[98] But the play's excesses – the saturated atmosphere of scabrous aischrology and its physical counterparts – are a calculated feature of the dramatic fabric, not a direct sign of the playwright's (allegedly) personal motivation. When Aristophanes refers back to *Knights* in the parabasis of *Clouds* (547–50), he uses it as an instance of his ceaseless theatrical pursuit of 'novelty', 'sophistication' and 'cleverness', while at the same time boasting that it had delivered a knock-out blow to Cleon's 'belly'. Those vaunts are themselves part of a convention of parabatic self-preening, as well as transparently hyperbolic. Whatever else *Knights* achieved, it certainly did not 'floor' Cleon, in Aristophanes' wrestling metaphor, though it did contain plenty of its own

---

[98] See e.g. Ussher (1979) 15, 'the angry young playwright . . . is an unattractive figure and *Knights* is an unattractive play'; Norwood (1931) 207–8, 'Aristophanes has spoiled his play by losing his temper.' Landfester (1967) 10 n. 4 complains about the work's supposedly 'monotonous' tone (better read as its exaggerated satire of personalised political antagonism). For appreciation of the play's virtuosity of abuse, note Rosen (1988) 68–9 ('clever obscenity', 'creative invective'), with *ibid.* ch. 4 for the work's indebtedness to *iambos*. *Kn.* 510, where the chorus proclaim that the playwright 'hates the same people as us', is less clear evidence for Aristophanic animus than often thought: it is connected with comic mythologisation (as, later, at *Wasps* 1031–5) more than an authorial grudge. Note, in this connection, that the knights themselves play no real part in the play's ultimate political 'solution'.

theatrical blows to the 'belly' (the *padded* belly of the comic actor, a standard part of the genre's costuming conventions).[99] Such sentiments do not
give us unmediated access to the author's own voice. But they nonetheless
offer a clue to a more profitable angle (than personal animus) from which
to view the play, an angle which I want to adopt here in order to underline a larger thesis about Aristophanic comedy's aischrologic status. That
passage from the parabasis of *Clouds* incorporates a typically Aristophanic
double-sidedness: it presents *Knights* as simultaneously quasi-intellectual
(an exhibition of 'new' or 'modern' ideas, καινὰς ἰδέας) *and* crudely 'violent' (a blow or kick to the belly, albeit an implicitly adept wrestling blow).
From the point of view of my concerns in this chapter, we can read this
doubleness specifically *à propos* the work's dominant trait, its aischrologic
profusion. That profusion depends on a tone which is an irreducible fusion
of the gross and the comically inventive (*Knights* contains the most stylistically dense texture of writing in Aristophanes' *oeuvre*). To sense the grossness
without seeing the verbal bravura which goes into its expression as comic
poetry is to miss the throbbing heart of the play – and, equally, to miss its
exploitation of the distinctive cultural freedom which Old Comedy had at
its disposal.

The indefatigably noxious tone established in the parodos of *Knights*,
where physical aggression is coupled with verbal abuse of a histrionically
uncouth kind ('I'll thrash you like a dog . . .', 'I'll drag you through the
shit . . .', 289–95), is a comically deliberate overstatement of the possibilities of political insults (*loidoria*) and menacing defamation (*diabolē*). If we
recall the double standards displayed in the exchanges of abuse between
Demosthenes and Aeschines discussed earlier in this chapter, we can recognise that in *Knights* Aristophanes is picking up and parodying the intrinsic
ambivalence of political derision itself – its availability as a potent weapon,
where context and timing are right, but, on the other hand, its vulnerability
to charges of personal vulgarity and political 'agoraification'. At the same
time, he is pushing the register of abuse to the limits of comic exaggeration.
In doing so he requires an audience 'clever' enough to appreciate the sheer
if paradoxical virtuosity which goes into the framing of that exaggeration,
and which, by the same token, can at some level grasp the paradox of taking pleasure in the depiction of what is notionally (i.e., by the standards
of political decorum and respectability) such a shameful/-less wallowing in

---

[99] The participle κειμένῳ at *Clouds* 550 does not mean '(lying) dead' but 'floored', like a defeated
wrestler/pankratiast (cf. *Clouds* 126) – itself an allusion to the burlesque fighting in the play. See *Kn.*
274, 454 for blows to the belly, and cf. Taillardat (1965) 337 and n. 3, 353 (where n. 1 unnecessarily
concedes ambiguity). On comic violence in Aristophanes, see Kaimio (1990), esp. 58–9.

foul speech. In that respect, *Knights* calls for an audience whose cultural psychology resembles, but also takes to a more extreme degree, the attitudes implicitly ascribed to the citizen body by Demosthenes, several generations later, when he adopts the tactic of both deprecating Aeschines' (alleged) abusiveness and at the same time promising his hearers the gratification of paying his opponent back in kind. The crucial difference, however, is that what functions in the mouths of politicians themselves as a tactical weapon of debate, to be deployed with careful regard to the larger balance of issues at stake (and always subject to the delicate principle, codified by Gorgias, of destroying one's adversaries' seriousness with laughter, and their laughter with seriousness),[100] finds an uncontested, freewheeling function in comedy. There, under the banner of Dionysiac festivity, it can become for spectators a linguistically and gelastically unshackled celebration of the frisson of hubristic outrage generated by aischrologic language, though a 'safe' celebration that projects all its indecency onto the masked, padded figures of the performance.[101]

It is apposite to foreground one of the main techniques by which *Knights* activates the dynamics of shameless laughter in relation to the theme of political aischrology. This technique, which itself reinforces the comically paradoxical twin boast of cleverness and crude aggression found in *Clouds*' retrospective reference to the play, involves a verbal and dramatic 'layering' of aischrology that transmutes political discourse into a ludicrous farrago of speech genres. Three things in particular – or, better, three *ideas* – are pertinent here, all of which have figured earlier in this chapter: firstly, the 'demotic' register (Athenian Billingsgate, as it were) of backstreet and market-place ('agoraic') abuse; secondly, the formalised tit-for-tat of 'fly-ting' matches or self-consciously verbal duelling; and, lastly, the highly personalised mode of political antagonism which was known, pejoratively, as *diabolē* ('slander' or 'defamation', especially in its manifestations as a weapon of rhetorical attack). The play combines these speech genres in shifting permutations, allowing them to merge cumulatively into a com-pound of foul-mouthed insults. The tone is set from an early stage, not least by the crescendo of shrieked profanities in the *pnigos* of the paro-dos (from which I have already quoted). Here, specific references to the agora (293, 297) sit alongside explicit evocation of political *diabolē* (288), and the whole exchange is figured both as a gross *shouting* match (285–7, a parodic version of a motif discussed earlier: see 232–3) but also, in its staccato trochaic dimeter phrases, as an unmistakable game of amoebean

---

[100] See ch. 1 n. 98.   [101] For Dionysiac scurrility as collective festive *hubris*, cf. n. 32 above.

capping or flyting. That so many of the mutual insults in *Knights* are exchanged at the top of the voice is a repeated echo of one of the play's key tropes, its conversion of political rhetoric and debate into the strident vulgarity of market-traders and other denizens of the city's 'low life'. The scene is expressly set for that satirical confusion near the outset (217–18), and it is eventually brought to a climax when the defeated Paphlagonian is packed off not only to take the commercial place of the Sausage-Seller but also to swap raucous abuse with whores and bath-keepers (1400, 1403). The world of *Knights*, we could say, is an extreme and lurid premonition of that vision of 'base men . . . bad-mouthing and ridiculing one another, and using foul language . . . and displaying all the other faults of speech and action that such people commit' which Socrates was to put forward as a negative image of comedy at Plato *Republic* 3.395e (225 above).

Yet this whole play, with its overflowing discharge of aischrologic animosity on the part of the characters themselves, can still somehow be held up by Aristophanes in the parabasis of *Clouds* not as a piece of personal anger but as an exhibition of comic inventiveness and sophistication. Even allowing for parabatic rhetoric, this only makes sense if we can discern the comic virtuosity which is overlaid on and fused with the grotesque vulgarity of the world depicted in *Knights*. Consider just two small but characteristic instances of this fusion. The first comes from the *pnigos* of iambic dimeters which concludes the first half of the first agon. As with the *pnigos* of the parodos, mentioned above, we are dealing here with paired insults and threats, swapped in short, rhythmically snappy phrases, with the tit-for-tat, retaliatory venom of a flyting match:

PAPH. I'll have you tied up in the stocks!
S.-S. I'll get you indicted for cowardice!
PAPH. Your hide will be tanned on my work-bench!
S.-S. I'll flay you to make a shopping-bag – for theft!
PAPH. You'll be stretched and pinned on my tanning floor!
S.-S. I'll turn you into slices of meat!
PAPH. I'll pluck every hair of your eyebrows out!
S.-S. I'll slice your gullet out of your neck!
SLAVE Yes, by Zeus! And we'll ram a peg
   The way an expert cook would do
   Into his mouth, and then pull out
   His tongue to take a proper look
   And ascertain
   As he gapes wide open
   Whether his *anus* has measles!   (*Knights* 367–83)

Even in a plain translation, it is easy to see how the passage packages absurdly hyperbolic hostility within a rhythmical crescendo of symmetrical form.[102] It combines (and thereby in a sense tames) the language of extreme violence with the obvious imagery of the two characters' respective trades as tanner and sausage-seller, while the slave's crowning contribution supplements the Sausage-Seller's meat-dealing activities with the language of a butcher's expert examination of a pig for signs of disease. The one realistic line of possible political feuding (the threat of prosecution in 368) is swamped by an exchange of wildly burlesque bombast. Political competition is turned into a slanging match between market-traders, and yet both 'modes' or speech genres are further converted into the formality of a stylised comic agon. The rapid verbal cut and thrust may contain further layers which would be filled out in performance with gesture (not least, once more, with the help of the phallus). The word θύλακος, 'shopping-bag', in 370, for example, might easily activate echoes of θυλάκη, 'scrotum'; similarly, the verb διαπατταλεύειν in the following line, used of 'pegging out' a stretched hide for tanning, may incorporate a pun on the slang sense of πάτταλος ('peg') as 'penis' which we meet elsewhere in Aristophanes.[103] It is certainly hard to resist a sense of sexual innuendo, especially given the way that the slave's pig imagery turns from oral to anal examination. All in all, lines 367–74 show how in *Knights* Aristophanes can allow aischrology to run riot on one level (the imagined shamelessness and nastiness of the characters) while nonetheless formalising it into patterns of ingeniously crafted comic verse.

My second example occurs at the point where the two main characters come back on stage after their clash in the Boule. When the Paphlagonian starts once more to menace the Sausage-Seller with destruction, the latter replies (696–7):

> ἥσθην ἀπειλαῖς, ἐγέλασα ψολοκομπίαις,
> ἀπεπυδάρισα μόθωνα, περιεκόκκασα.

> What amusing threats! I laugh at your smoky-thunder boasts!
> I jiggle my bum with contempt, and cock-crow in circles around you!

Translation can only struggle with the extravagance of such writing, which conveys physically brazen gleefulness (accompanied by an outburst of derisive laughter) yet swathes it in a verbal texture of dense intricacy. These two

---

[102] On the form and imagery of the passage, cf. Newiger (1957) 31, Hesk (2007) 147–8; see ch. 4, 194–5, with Wallochny (1992) 13–21 on amoebean exchanges in Aristophanes.
[103] The slang sense of *pattalos* is certain at *Eccl.* 1020, and later at Automedon, *Anth. Pal.* 5.129.5. Cf. Henderson (1991) 123, but not all his examples are convincing.

lines contain no less than three compound words which occur nowhere else in the whole of surviving Greek (except in later quotations of the passage). Not everything is semantically clear about these words, but we can see that the first belittles the Paphlagonian's threats by punning on the (old poetic) idea of smoking thunderbolts; the second denotes some kind of contemptuous jig, and may here imply (and enact) a pun on an indecent gesture with the buttocks; and the third probably completes the Sausage-Seller's movements with a little cock-crowing dance round his opponent.[104] So the moment is one in which bodily and verbal exuberance unmistakably capture the vulgarity of the character while also exhibiting the comic poet's linguistic creativity.

These two examples should lend some substance to the claim that *Knights* allows us to see in particularly vivid colours how (Aristophanic) Old Comedy could celebrate its aischrologic freedom to the point of grotesque shamelessness, yet always, one way or another, translate that shamelessness into theatrical artifice. The result is a sort of blurred focus between the world inside the plays and the phallically costumed actors on display (and paid for by the polis) in the Dionysiac festival itself. As with the specific junctures (or transpositions) of 'ritual laughter' in Aristophanes which I discussed in the last section of Chapter 4, so with aischrology in general Old Comedy seems able to endow it with a subtly double role: both as material for (distorted) representation of an imaginary world, and at the same time as the fulfilment of its own Dionysiac performance. This irreducible doubleness creates, I believe, a sort of ambiguity and undecidability at the level of socio-political function. The unending (and irresolvable) modern debate about the purpose(s) of Old Comedy – a debate polarised around the difference between intelligible, committed critique and, on the other hand, a mode of drama which mocks and disaggregates the city's life without having the means to rebuild it in an achievable form – is, in the final analysis, a set of attempts to rationalise the multiple forces at work in the genre's exceptional gelastic freedoms. As we glimpsed earlier in the chapter, aischrology may always have an inbuilt tendency, in virtue of its shame-breaking/causing excesses, to outrun the

---

[104] See Neil (1901) 101 for basic details. ἀποπυδαρίζειν (697) probably plays on a folk etymology from πυγή, buttock: see Σ *ad loc.* (which also moot a possible pun on πέρδεσθαι, 'fart') and *Etym. Magnum s.v.* πυδαρίζειν. μόθων (697) is probably an indecent dance in its own right: it is invoked by the Sausage-Seller as one of his 'gods' at 635. Taillardat (1965) 176 thinks the metaphor in περικοκκύζειν (697) is unparalleled, but it probably corresponds to the crowing mockery at Dem. 54.9: see ch. 1, 34–5. For the gelastic implications of ἥσθην (696), cf. ch. 9 n. 35.

possibility of stable communal action or institutionalised judgement. Certainly, when channelled into Old Comedy's magnified, almost limitless scurrility of both language and body, the aischrologic imagination inhabits a plane from which it can return only by removing its Dionysiac costume and resubmitting to the inhibiting social pressures of shame outside the theatre.

CHAPTER 6

Greek philosophy and the ethics of ridicule

Despite that philosopher who as an authentic Englishman tried to create a bad reputation for laughter among all thinking people . . . I would even allow myself to rank philosophers in importance precisely according to the importance of their laughter.

Nietzsche[1]

ARCHAIC ANXIETIES

What (if anything) do wisdom and laughter have in common, and how (if at all) should one expect a *philosopher* to laugh, or to judge the laughter of others? Symbolically at least, Friedrich Nietzsche's intuition in the above epigraph provides an intriguing yardstick to apply to surviving testimony for the life and thought of ancient Greek philosophers. In biographical terms, that testimony, which Nietzsche knew well from his own early scholarly work on Diogenes Laertius' *Lives* of the philosophers, is predominantly anecdotal, which means that it is often of doubtful value. Such material is nonetheless potentially revealing about the mentalities and popular perceptions that lay behind the creation and dissemination of those anecdotes; it will therefore receive some attention in what follows. But for many Greek philosophers we have the direct evidence of their writings or ideas to illuminate their attitudes to laughter. It is a striking index of the significance of laughter for the values and practices of Greek culture that, unlike most of their later counterparts (Nietzsche himself being one of a handful of exceptions in this regard), many philosophers adopted an overt or at least discernible position on the subject. Equally strikingly, those

---

[1] *Beyond Good and Evil* 294, Nietzsche (1988) v 236 ('Jenem Philosophen zum Trotz, der als ächter Engländer dem Lachen bei allen denkenden Köpfen eine üble Nachrede zu schaffen suchte . . . würde ich mir sogar eine Rangordnung der Philosophen erlauben, je nach dem Range ihres Lachens . . .'). The Englishman is Hobbes: on his attitudes to laughter (simplified by Nietzsche) see Skinner (1996) 391–5, (2002) 142, 147–52, 174–6.

positions were often highly polarised – sharply divided between *pro* and *contra* stances. However paradoxical it might seem, laughter was something which many Greek intellectuals thought it worth being philosophically committed about.

In this and the following chapter I pursue two complementary, at times overlapping, approaches to Greek philosophy's dealings, both theoretical and practical, with laughter. In the present chapter I analyse certain explicit evaluations, found either in philosophical texts or in the reputations of philosophers, of laughter as an aspect of social and ethical behaviour. In the next chapter I extend my focus to consider the more diffuse possibilities of laughter (whether literal or metaphorical) as a defining response to the human condition, a response most famously though problematically encapsulated in the long-lasting legend of Democritus 'the laughing philosopher'. The difference between the two chapters is therefore thematic and perspectival, not chronological. Thus some individual Presocratics (Xenophanes, Anaxagoras and Pythagoras) will be foregrounded in the present chapter, others (Heraclitus and Democritus) in the next. Chapter 7 will also devote space to Cynics and Epicureans, the two groups of Greek philosophers whose relationship to laughter might be thought to have the broadest 'existential' implications. The present chapter will have a certain amount to say about the Stoics, who are sometimes wrongly taken to have advocated an agelastic outlook; but its two main sections will be dedicated to Plato (above all, as creator of a complex dramatisation of Socratic laughter) and to Aristotle, arguably the only ancient philosopher who saw laughter as necessary for a fully human life, and certainly the only one to have based a specific ethico-social virtue on one particular conception of laughter. Aristotle, we can be sure, would not have been at the top of Nietzsche's (imaginary) gelastic 'ranking' of philosophers. But he remains paradigmatic of one major model of an ethics of laughter.

I turn first, however, to a few remarks about the earliest figures in the traditions of Greek 'wisdom', the individuals who later constituted the canonical if somewhat fluid grouping of the 'Seven Sages'. It is telling for my purposes that Greek culture attached to these thinkers, who came to form a composite image of archaic sagacity, a dominant impression of ethical misgivings about laughter, and sometimes outright antipathy towards it. I use the word 'impression' advisedly: almost all the evidence postdates the period itself and has slender claims to historical fidelity. But impressions of this kind matter; they provide clues to the 'inherited conglomerate' of the culture and to the social tensions which Greek evaluations of laughter tried to address. Chilon of Sparta, active in the politics of his city in the mid-sixth century, was one of the sages who supposedly authored several injunctions relating to laughter. Most direct is 'do not laugh over another's misfortune' (ἀτυχοῦντι μὴ ἐπεγγελᾶν), a maxim whose psychological presuppositions cast a supplementary light on other sayings, including 'control the tongue, and especially at a symposium', 'do not denigrate (*kakologein*) your neighbours, otherwise you yourself will hear things that will cause you pain', and 'do not denigrate the dead'.[2] These apophthegms, embedded in a collection that urges self-discipline and moderation (it is no accident that Chilon was sometimes thought to be the originator of the most basic principle of Greek folk wisdom, 'nothing to excess'), assume a rather one-sided view of laughter as an instrument of antagonism. Since strict authorship is doubtful in such cases, we should not make too much of the fact that Chilon lived in a Spartan culture which, as we saw in Chapter 1, developed a heightened guardedness about the dangers of laughter. The maxims attributed to Chilon can, in fact, be easily paralleled in non-Spartan sources.[3] One of his fellow sages, Cleobulus tyrant of Lindos on Rhodes, was credited with the precept 'do not join in laughing at those who are being mocked (μὴ ἐπεγγελᾶν τοῖς σκωπτομένοις), as you will become their enemy' – an epitome of what I call 'consequential' laughter, i.e. a dynamic factor in social chains of cause and effect. To another sage, Pittacus of Mytilene, was ascribed 'do not say in advance what you intend to do – if you fail, you will be derided' (ἀποτυχὼν γὰρ καταγελασθήσῃ), which highlights the availability of laughter as a currency of communal judgement; 'do not reproach (*oneidizein*) another's misfortune – restrain yourself out of fear of resentment (*nemesis*)'; and 'do not slander (λέγειν κακῶς) a friend, nor even an enemy'. Finally, to Periander of Corinth was given the slightly cryptic utterance 'engage in abuse as one who will soon be a friend' (λοιδοροῦ ὡς ταχὺ φίλος ἐσόμενος), as well as a piece of advice which complements one of Chilon's aphorisms by seeing the situation from the other side: 'conceal your misfortunes, to avoid giving joy (*euphrainein*) to your enemies'.[4]

If the putative sayings of the Seven Sages are a repository of what many Greeks would have considered indispensable guidance for life, they seem consistently to depict laughter as an expression of gloating hostility and/or

[2] Diog. Laert. 1.69–70; cf. Stob. 3.1.172, with DK 1 61–6. On 'tongue' and symposium, cf. ch. 3, 121–2. Denigrating the dead: ch. 1, 26–30.

[3] Socrates at Pl. *Prt.* 343a–b makes *all* Seven Sages lovers of Spartan wisdom; but the claim cannot be taken at face value. Martin (1998) offers a cultural perspective on the Seven.

[4] Versions of most of these sayings are in Stob. 3.1.172 (DK 1 63–6); some occur (also) at Diog. Laert. 1.78, 93. On Cleobulus, cf. ch. 1, 41.

a cause of resentment, to be feared equally from the dual points of view of its practitioners and its targets (points of view readily reversed by the vicissitudes of fortune). The unstated backdrop to such views is a social milieu of harsh struggle, rivalry and suspicion, the kind of world conjured up trenchantly and diagnosed incisively, as we saw in Chapter 3, in the sixth-century elegiac poetry of Theognis.[5] Pertinent here is also the Athenian tradition which, accurately or otherwise, counted Solon (himself one of the Sages) as the author of legislation against public defamation of the dead and the living.[6] Though no pronouncements on laughter as such are attributed to Solon, his supposed law(s) accord with the broader sensitivity to antagonistic derision evinced by testimony on the Seven Sages. Regardless of historical uncertainties about all this material, it embodied an archetypal image of acute wariness towards laughter as a medium (and cause) of discord and strife. The only collective counterweight to this image was that strand of tradition which pictured the Seven as holding a harmonious symposium at Delphi. But this idea is not fleshed out with gelastic implications before Plutarch, even though a sympotic background is glimpsed in some of the individual maxims (such as Chilon's second above).[7]

If the Seven Sages were not typically thought of as devotees of laughter, one of them (in some lists), the rustic Myson of Chen in Laconia, was actually compared by Aristoxenus to proverbial misanthropes like Timon and Apemantus. An anecdote recounted by Aristoxenus told how Myson was once seen in Sparta laughing to himself when entirely alone. To an observer who approached and asked why he laughed with no one else present, he replied: 'for that very reason!'[8] The story (which will later merit a second mention in connection with Aristoxenus' own attitudes to laughter) portrays a somewhat unorthodox misanthrope; the usual stereotype is of the misanthrope as, by definition, an agelast. Myson's behaviour seems akin to that of 'Democritus' in the letters of pseudo-Hippocrates, where the philosopher shuns other people but is observed laughing profusely. His fellow Abderites think him mad, but it transpires that he is profoundly, wisely aware of the absurdity of (most) human existence.[9] The Myson of

---

[5] See ch. 3, 117–25. [6] See Halliwell (1991b) 49–51 for references; cf. ch. 5, 241–2, 244.

[7] The Delphic meeting is first evoked at Pl. *Prt.* 343a–b, but the only known version featuring symposiac laughter is Plutarch's *Symposium of the Seven Sages*, where most of them laugh at some point: esp. *Mor.* 146f, 149e, 151d, 152d, 154c, 156a; cf. Thales' joke at 157d.

[8] Diog. Laert. 1.108 (= Aristox. fr. 130 Wehrli). Aristoxenus himself probably did not count Myson one of the Seven: see Wehrli (1967) 86, also making the connection with Aristox. fr. 7 (n. 24 below). For an anecdote about a meeting between *two* misanthropes (Timon and Apemantus), see Plut. *Ant.* 70.2.

[9] See ch. 7, 360–3. For the standard *agelastic* misanthrope, cf. ch. 1 n. 101.

Aristoxenus' anecdote appears *contented* to escape from the company of others; his laughter evokes a positive, not a crudely misanthropic, state of mind. But it is also irreducibly paradoxical, since affirmative laughter is standardly understood to be social, not solitary behaviour: in the very act of distancing himself from society, Myson enigmatically preserves a characteristic sign of shared geniality. The only other (occasional) member of the Seven Sages associated with positive laughter is a kind of 'honorary' Greek, the sixth-century Scythian philhellene Anacharsis, who acquired a reputation for ready wit, sometimes in sympotic settings, and is credited by Aristotle with the principle that one should 'play for the sake of being serious' (παίζειν ὅπως σπουδάζῃ), that is, enjoy the laughter of relaxation in order to return with renewed vigour to the real business of life.[10]

Of the early Greek thinkers now conventionally labelled Presocratic philosophers, two call for brief mention here and one for slightly fuller treatment. (Two others, as already indicated, will be discussed in the next chapter.) To support the untypically Greek injunction 'do not be afraid of mockery' (μηδὲ δείσῃς σκωπτόμενος) – an injunction out of kilter with the wisdom ascribed to the Seven Sages – Plutarch records an anecdote about an encounter between the poet-philosopher Xenophanes and the lyric poet Lasus of Hermione. When the former refused to play dice with the poet, who then called him a 'coward', Xenophanes conceded that he was cowardly – towards *shameful* things.[11] Plutarch is here warning against an excessive susceptibility to shame that allows someone to be embarrassed into wrongdoing. His anecdote relates directly to sympotic activities ('suppose someone invites you to play dice while drinking . . .'); Xenophanes puts up principled resistance to the mockery associated with a wine-induced atmosphere of indulgence. Like Chilon, however (see above), Xenophanes is not to be thought of as an opponent of the symposium *per se*, only of the misconduct which its circumstances, including its gelastic pressures, may induce. In fact, in his poetry the historical Xenophanes, as opposed to the at least partly fictionalised figure of Plutarch's anecdote, is a prime witness to the ideal of the moderate, virtuous symposium, an ideal which subjected laughter, as well as drinking, to measured discipline. But Xenophanes' expression of this ideal appeals specifically to the

---

[10] Arist. *EN* 10.6, 1176b33–4: see 309 below, with ch. 1 n. 48, ch. 7 n. 93. The opposite view (that one should work for the sake of play), rejected by Aristotle, is also repudiated at Pl. *Laws* 7.803d, despite the conception of life as a puppet show in the same passage (ch. 10 n. 96). Anacharsis' wit: e.g. Diog. Laert. 1.101–5, with Martin (1996) on the evolution of his image and Kindstrand (1981) for his life and sayings; cf. ch. 3 n. 53.

[11] Plut. *Mor.* 530e (= Xenophan. A16 DK).

spirit of *euphrosunē*, a heady elation which undoubtedly has overtones of laughter.[12]

That is just one of several reasons for discounting any notion of Xenophanes as an agelast *tout court*. Among other things, he wrote 'lampoons' (*silloi*) which scoffed at both philosophers and poets and were later to be emulated by the early Hellenistic sceptic, Timon of Phlius. From what survives of Xenophanes' poetry, both *silloi* and other kinds, it is evident that a prominent part of his repertoire – a characteristic tone of voice – was a caustic, satirical mode which harnessed an implicit laughter against the objects of his criticism. His notorious *aperçu* (combining anthropological shrewdness with scathing religious condescension) that if cattle, horses and lions had hands they would paint gods that resembled themselves, shows this mode of invective in vivid colours. So too does his parody of Pythagorean belief in metempsychosis with an ironic claim that Pythagoras recognised the voice of an old friend in the sound of a yelping dog, or his description of the poet Simonides as a 'skinflint' (κίμβιξ, a racy colloquialism).[13] Yet Xenophanes was no advocate of unfettered laughter. His major sympotic elegy (fr. 1) presents ideals that allow scope for sympotic conviviality but impose psychological and ethical curbs on its freedom. Moreover, the satirical tone of voice in some of his poetry is not his only persona. There is also a moral sombreness discernible in the fragments. In this connection, it is likely that his condemnation of Homer and Hesiod for ascribing every kind of shameful behaviour to the gods ('stealing, adultery and deceit') was formulated partly with an eye on the story of Ares and Aphrodite's adultery in Book 8 of the *Odyssey*, the only place in Homer or Hesiod, as it happens, where the actual terminology of 'adultery' is found.[14] If (full-blown) anthropomorphism was repudiated by Xenophanes' philosophical theology, the Homeric episode of the divine adulterers, and the double outbreak of the gods' laughter at their capture and sexual exposure, must have seemed exceptionally scandalous to him.

Xenophanes can count, then, as a somewhat ambiguous figure *vis-à-vis* laughter. Capable of exploiting it himself as a scornful critic of culture,

---

[12] See Xenophan. fr. 1.4 DK/*IEG* for *euphrosunē*, symbolised in the wine itself; note the adj. *euphrōn* at 1.13, with Babut (1974) 93–4, Lesher (1992) 48. Cf. ch. 3, 109–11.

[13] See, respectively, Xenophan. frs. 15, 7, 21 DK; on the Pythagoras gibe, cf. Lesher (1992) 78–81. On the *silloi* of Xenophanes and Timon, see DK 21 A20, 22–3, B10–21A, with di Marco (1989) 17–29, Long (1978); cf. n. 82 below, ch. 7 n. 28. On Xenophanes as 'satirist', cf. Babut (1974), esp. 116–17. For the verb σιλλαίνειν ('roll the eyes' or 'squint' mockingly), cf. Appendix 2 n. 61: the genre was named after the activity, not the other way round, *contra* Cunningham (1971) 63.

[14] See Xenophan. frs. 11–12 DK; stimulating discussion in Babut (1974), esp. 84–92 (cf. the reference to Ares and Aphrodite on 87). The (unique) term μοιχάγρια, 'recompense paid by an adulterer', is at Hom. *Od.* 8.332.

not least against his 'professional' rivals (both philosophers and poets), he nonetheless harboured ethical reservations about its misuse. Quite unambiguous, by contrast, is the agelastic reputation that became attached to another Presocratic, Anaxagoras. According to Aelian, Anaxagoras 'is said never once to have been seen laughing or even smiling at all', while Plutarch ascribes directly to Anaxagoras' influence on Pericles that the latter had 'a facial composure that never broke into laughter'.[15] With Anaxagoras, a connection between the man and his philosophy is probably latent beneath the surface of the (pseudo-)biographical anecdotes. We know that this image was very much older than Plutarch or Aelian. A fragment of verse ascribed to Alexander Aetolus, third-century BC scholar-poet, but possibly from a play by Aristophanes, describes Euripides, here dubbed 'foster-child of Anaxagoras', as 'morose to speak to, a laughter-hater (*misogelōs*), and someone who hasn't learnt how to engage in mocking banter (*tōthazein*) even at a drinking-party'.[16] Embedded in this description is an enthusiastic expectation of sympotic mirth, free of the inhibitions of Chilon's 'control your tongue, and especially at a symposium' (266 above). But the tragedian and his supposed philosophical mentor are portrayed as hostile to such things.

Why Anaxagoras, we want to know, and why Euripides? In the philosopher's case, the best explanation is that the image of an agelastic temperament became affixed to someone who was believed, whether truly or otherwise, to have had no concern for personal or earthly affairs, so all-consuming was his interest in cosmic, supra-human matters. The famous story that when told of his sons' (or son's) death he responded, without emotion, 'I knew I had fathered mortals,' is emblematic of this persona; as it happens, a comparable story is told about Pericles, Anaxagoras's reputedly agelastic friend.[17] Someone so emotionally detached as to be incapable of grief might also be imagined as lacking the instincts of sociability (as well

[15] Ael. *VH* 8.13 (= Anax. A21 DK), Plut. *Per.* 5.1 (with 7.5), also mentioning avoidance of vulgar buffoonery, *bōmolochia*. See Stadter (1989) 76–8, and cf. ch. 3 n. 48. Kenner (1960) 72, endorsed by Simon (1961) 648, lacks warrant for using Pericles' aversion to laughter as evidence of a broader fifth-century 'canon' of self-control.

[16] Alex. Aet. fr. 7.1–2 *CA* = Anax. A21 DK (metre: anap. tetr. cat.): στρυφνὸς μὲν ἔμοιγε προσειπεῖν, | καὶ μισόγελως, καὶ τωθάζειν οὐδὲ παρ' οἴνῳ μεμαθηκώς. Lloyd-Jones (1994), following *Vita Eur.* 5, moots Aristophanic authorship (cf. Ar. fr. 676b2 Kock, but excluded from *PCG* III 2); di Marco (2003) posits the parabasis of a satyr-play. Euripides is also a student of Anaxagoras in Diog. Laert. 2.10, *Vita Eur.* 10, 115; cf. n. 18 below. For what it's worth, Hieron. Rhod. fr. 35 Wehrli preserved gossip about Euripides' mockery (verb *tōthazein*, as in Alex. Aet. fr. 7) of Sophocles' boy-loving escapades; cf. Wehrli (1969) 39–40.

[17] For Anaxagoras' supposed impassivity, see esp. Diog. Laert. 2.7, 10–11, 13 (= Anax. A1 DK); cf. Sorabji (2000) 197. The story of his sons' death occurs *ibid.* 2.13 and often elsewhere, e.g. A33 DK, Cic. *Tusc.* 3.30, Plut. *Mor.* 474d; but the 'I knew . . . mortals' sentiment had wider currency, e.g. ps.-Lys. 2.77.

as social rivalry) that could give rise to laughter. If so, Anaxagoras' philosophical transcendence of a human point of view was popularly pictured in terms opposite to those of the legendary Democritus, whose detachment from normal concerns supposedly produced a *proclivity* for laughter. One moral of this, as my next chapter will stress, is that (the idea of) an absolute viewpoint on the world can generate any one of a number of different judgements on the value of life, and therefore the value of laughter. As for Euripides, the idea that he was a 'student' of Anaxagoras – probably no more than a fictive extrapolation from some of the intellectualist language of his plays – may have been sufficient for the agelastic tag to be attached to him too. There remains a chance, however, that other threads of (pseudo-) biographical tradition which pictured him as a 'loner' helped to create the image of a *misogelōs*, a surly 'hater of laughter'. Nor can we discount the simple possibility (a foible of ancient biographers) that the idea was reinforced, if not invented, by foisting onto the poet the sentiments of one of his own characters. In the lost play *Melanippe Captive* someone expressed 'hatred' for those who cultivate wit and facetiousness. The 'Euripides' we are contemplating here might be, as it were, a figment of one of his own plays.[18]

The first Greek philosopher with whom it make sense to connect (though at one remove) something like an ethically principled avoidance of laughter is Pythagoras. In his case, what is at stake is a set of values more far-reaching for bodily behaviour than anything we encountered in the maxims of folk wisdom attested for the Seven Sages (though Pythagoras himself occasionally appears in their number), in Xenophanes' disapproval of sympotic excesses, or even in Anaxagoras' alleged emotional detachment. The problem, however, is that the evidence for a fundamental Pythagorean antipathy to laughter, a hardening of the agelastic into the resolutely *anti*gelastic, is mostly found in very late sources. In trying to work back from those sources to the Pythagoreanism of the classical period, as I wish tentatively to do, the greatest circumspection is required. The evolution of Pythagoreanism, in both theory and practice, was such a long-term historical process, stretching over many centuries from the shadowy founder himself to the Neopythagoreanism of the Roman Empire, that reconstruction of

---

The version at ps.-Plut. *Cons. Ap.* 118d–e is followed by a parallel story about Pericles, citing Protag. fr. 9 DK (see Plut. *Per.* 36.4–5 for a more qualified portrait). The claim that Anaxagoras committed suicide from shame, Diog. Laert. 2.13, and his request for a school holiday in his memory, 2.14, suggest a different personality: but the biographical anecdotes carry little weight either way.

[18] In addition to his supposed Anaxagorean connection (n. 16 above), Euripides is also depicted as a laughter-hater in *Vita Eur.* 65. The passage of *Melanippe* is Eur. fr. 492.2 *TrGF*; cf. ch. 3 n. 84. The poet's reputation as a loner is discussed by Lefkowitz (1981) 88–104, 163–69; cf. Stevens (1956) 88–90.

its various phases remains one of the most vexed areas in the interpretation of Greek philosophy.[19] My own interest in one particular form of behaviour will at least allow us to focus on a limited set of testimonies. And even if the conclusions reached for the earlier period can only be provisional, there is something to be learnt from following the tracks of the enquiry.

There is no doubt that at some point the idea of radical antipathy to laughter and its uses came to seem peculiarly apt for the Pythagorean movement. It is not hard to see why this should be so, given the larger philosophical 'way of life' which became associated with Pythagoreans (and which Plato could regard as already long-standing, *Rep.* 10.600b). The area of contact between aversion to laughter and a Pythagorean lifestyle is indicated concisely by Diogenes Laertius 8.19–20, where Pythagoras' own supposed prescription of dietary regulations and use of pure clothing/bedding is followed by a resounding succession of statements. 'He was never known', claims Diogenes, 'to over-indulge in food or sex or alcohol; he abstained both from laughter and from all means of seeking popularity with others, such as jokes and vulgar anecdotes (σκωμμάτων καὶ διηγημάτων φορτικῶν); he never punished slave or free man out of anger.'[20] Avoidance of laughter is situated within a mosaic of corporeal, psychological and social puritanism. Perhaps not coincidentally, it is sandwiched in Diogenes' list of details between prime instances of yielding to physical and emotional forces capable of 'overcoming' a person's self-control. Laughter, on this account, is tainted by association with the body and its unruly impulses.

The same position is attested in other late sources. In the second or early third century AD, Porphyry's *Life* of Pythagoras asserts that the philosopher 'was never visibly overcome by joy or pain; no one ever saw him either laugh or cry'. This supports the general claim that 'his soul always allowed the same character to be seen through his bodily appearance' (ἥ τε ψυχὴ τὸ ὅμοιον ἦθος ἀεὶ διὰ τῆς ὄψεως παρεδήλου).[21] As we know from other works, Porphyry, a Neoplatonist with Pythagorean leanings, treated laughter as a symptom of immersion in the corrupt pleasures of the social world,

---

[19] Huffmann (1997) gives an overview of the main issues.

[20] My translation 'abstained both from laughter ...' assumes the reading καὶ γέλωτος ... at 8.20, where most mss. have καταγέλωτος, 'mockery': cf. app. crit. in Long (1964) ΙΙ 401; the mss. are followed by Marcovich (1999) 584. The broader formulation better fits the rest of Diogenes' sentence.

[21] Porph. *Vita Pyth.* 35: with the total avoidance of laughter and tears (paralleled in historically worthless claims about Socrates, n. 40 below, and the Christian instance at Athanas. *Vita Anton.* 14 [26.865 PG]), contrast the moderation voiced at e.g. Pl. *Laws* 5.732c (n. 95 below), Epict. *Ench.* 33.4 (γέλως μὴ πολὺς ἔστω μηδὲ ἐπὶ πολλοῖς μηδὲ ἀνειμένος); cf. *ibid.* 33.10 in a theatrical context.

and thought its eschewal a hallmark of the ascetic sage; so he is unlikely to have regarded Pythagoras as anything other than paradigmatic in this respect.[22] From roughly the same period, the *Protrepticus* of another Neoplatonist, Iamblichus, records as a Pythagorean principle 'not to succumb to uncontrollable laughter' (ἀσχέτῳ γέλωτι μὴ ἔχεσθαι), which Iamblichus interprets partly as expressing an aspiration to rise above the human to the divine. Filling out the implications of that principle, Iamblichus' own *Life* of Pythagoras contains the following statements: 'he was never in the grip of anger or laughter or envy or competitiveness, or any other mental disturbance or impetuousness'; he would not agree to instruct young people in his philosophy until he had observed, among other things, 'whether they laughed when they should not' (θεωρῶν αὐτῶν τούς τε γέλωτας τοὺς ἀκαίρους); he urged his followers to lead lives free of both luxury and aggression (*hubris*), and 'to remain pure from all foul speech – vituperative, quarrelsome, abusive, vulgar, or joking'.[23] The thread running through all these assertions is an integrated puritanism of both body and soul, the implementation of an exigent need to protect the soul against the defilement of somatic desires, pleasures and emotions. Laughter is only one element in this highly coordinated ethic. But its recurrent appearance alongside larger and (we might think) more obvious anxieties suggests a consistent image of Pythagorean resistance to laughter as a form of corporeal eruption, social offensiveness and indecent pleasure.

But this picture is undeniably late, and coloured by Neoplatonism's own agenda. How early in the history of Pythagoreanism such disapprobation of laughter took hold is impossible to calculate with confidence, but there are some intriguing hints (one, for later discussion, in Plato's *Phaedo*: 279) which supply food for thought. One possible set of stepping stones back from later to earlier sources begins with another of those floating remarks of

[22] Porph. *Abst.* 4.6–7, citing the Greek-Egyptian Stoic Chaeremon (fr. 10, van der Horst (1987) 16–22 with 56–61 for notes; = *FGrH* 618 F6), describes an ascetic ideal, including scant laughter and occasional smiles, represented by Egyptian priest-philosophers. *Abst.* 1.39.4–6 refers to Pl. *Tht.* 173–4, where common laughter is symptomatic of social life (cf. the 'dinners and *kōmoi*' of Pl. *Tht.* 174c, quoted at *Abst.* 1.36); but Porphyry neglects the philosopher's own laughter in the same context, *Tht.* 174d, 175b, d (290 below). Porph. *Marc.* 2 associates laughter with hostility (jealousy, hatred, anger), *ibid.* 19 with folly. Porphyry accepts laughter as natural to humans (cf. the repeated example in *Isagoge*, esp. 12.17–22, with Barnes (2003) 208–9), but it suits him to regard it as typical of the masses: cf. *Qu. Hom.* on *Il.* 2.212 (the Thersites episode). But contrast his scornful mockery of Christianity: *Ctr. Christ.* frs. 23, 34, 49, 55 (von Harnack).

[23] δυσφημίας δὲ πάσης καθαρεύειν τῆς τε σχετλιαστικῆς καὶ τῆς μαχίμου καὶ τῆς λοιδορητικῆς καὶ τῆς φορτικῆς καὶ γελωτοποιοῦ: Iambl. *Protr.* 21 (pp. 107, 121 Pistelli), *Vita Pyth.* 10, 71; for laughter 'at the wrong time', see General index *s.v. kairos.* A vignette of Iamblichus' own laughter, contrary to his usual disposition (the wording echoes Pl. *Phd.* 64b: see 279 below), occurs at Eunap. *Vitae Soph.* 5.1.9.

Aelian's, whose reference to the reputedly agelastic Anaxagoras was quoted earlier. In that same context, Aelian tells us: 'they say that Aristoxenus was a vehement enemy of laughter'.[24] Now Aristoxenus, active in the second half of the fourth century and for part of his career a member of Aristotle's Lyceum, was undoubtedly interested in the Pythagorean movement of his own day (he wrote a book about the school) and had Pythagoreans among his first teachers. There is also evidence to suggest that Aristoxenus had a range of observations to make on the subject of laughter. He is, for one thing, the source of the anecdote already cited about the paradoxically solitary laughter of Myson (267), and we shall have to return to him later for material relating to conflicting views of Socrates' attitude to mockery. There is no strong case to be made for treating the mature Aristoxenus as himself a committed Pythagorean; anyone who wishes to give credence to Aelian's claim about him will probably have to look elsewhere for an explanation. But among the scraps of information about Aristoxenus' references to laughter there is one which allows us to make a little progress in finding within (relatively) early Pythagoreanism concerns which could have contributed to the image of the movement's (and its founder's) antigelastic stance.

In his book on Pythagoras and his followers, Aristoxenus told a story which he claimed to have heard first-hand from the former tyrant of Syracuse, Dionysius II.[25] Dionysius, himself a patron of Pythagorean and other philosophers (most famously, Plato), was goaded by some cynical courtiers into testing both the supposed freedom from emotion (*apatheia*) and the unbreakable friendship of Phintias and Damon, two Pythagoreans, by pretending to condemn the former to death. The detail of interest for my purposes is the overt scurrillity directed against the philosophers by Dionysius' courtiers. Aristoxenus' description stresses the point with forceful vocabulary: 'they frequently mentioned the Pythagoreans, rubbishing them, scoffing and calling them impostors . . .';[26] later on, the verbs *chleuazein*, 'jeer', and *skōptein*, 'mock', are also used. What the narrative brings out is the vulnerability of Pythagoreans – *qua* members of

[24] Ἀριστόξενον τῷ γέλωτι ἀνὰ κράτος πολέμιον γενέσθαι: Ael. *VH* 8.13 = Aristox. fr. 7 Wehrli. That Aristoxenus' antigelastic reputation was derived from his hostile writings on Socrates (n. 79 below) and Plato, so Wehrli (1967) 48, is unconvincing. On the laughter of the (putative) Pythagoreans Cebes and Simmias in Pl. *Phd.*, see 279 below. Alexis fr. 201.6 ascribes sullenness (στυγνότης) to Pythagorean asceticism, but the picture reflects a generalised conception of anti-social philosophers: see Arnott (1996) 582–4.
[25] Iambl. *Vita Pyth.* 233–7 (= Aristox. fr. 31 Wehrli); cf. Porph. *Vita Pyth.* 59–61. For Dionysius II's own supposed penchant for scurrility, cf. Theopomp. *FGrH* 115 F283a–b; see n. 116 below on his father.
[26] οἳ πολλάκις ἐποιοῦντο μνείαν τῶν Πυθαγορείων, διασύροντες καὶ διαμωκώμενοι καὶ ἀλαζόνας ἀποκαλοῦντες αὐτούς . . . On the (simplex) verb μωκᾶσθαι, cf. Appendix 1 n. 14.

an esoteric group that avows unusually ascetic standards of behaviour – to ridicule by outsiders. Aristoxenus' anecdote gives us a glimpse, I suggest, of how a formative element in Pythagorean attitudes to laughter might have been the experience of being simultaneously 'victimised' by it yet unable, on the grounds of self-imposed psychological discipline, to retaliate. In this connection, reference (by their critics) to the Pythagoreans' 'solemnity' or 'sombreness' (*semnotēs*) is telling.[27] Many Greek philosophers, both individually and collectively, were subject to popular derision (as well as derision by *other* philosophers). But at least some Pythagoreans put themselves at a peculiar social disadvantage because of the intersection of their public image with their defining commitments. They imposed on themselves a canon of purity which even the 'body language' of laughter would have imperilled. To suffer exposure to mockery, while renouncing the very possibility of a reply in kind, would certainly have struck most Greeks as an intolerable form of self-denial.

But even if we can identify elements in Pythagorean asceticism, with its conception of the soul 'entombed' in the body, that could have underwritten the sort of antigelastic tendency eventually attributed to the movement, we might wonder whether this could ever have been the whole story of Pythagoreanism and laughter. What of the consistent Pythagorean emphasis on close-knit friendship (exemplified in the story of Phintias and Damon) in communities of the doctrinally and ethically committed? Does such bonding, built on the proverbial principle that 'friends have everything in common', not call for at least a degree of genial interaction? True, Pythagorean 'friendship' was a special variety in several respects; an insistence, for instance, on the value of silence (conspicuous to observers as early as Isocrates, 11.29) might prompt serious doubt whether anything resembling mirthful conviviality could have thrived in Pythagorean circles. Still, a glimmer of an attitude somewhat different from the one so far hypothesised appears in a passage of Diogenes Laertius, just a little further on from the compilation of Pythagorean precepts and practices already quoted (272). In this later passage, Diogenes tells us that Pythagoras taught that 'respect (*aidōs*) and restraint (*eulabeia*) meant neither being overcome by laughter nor behaving sullenly' (8.23, μήτε γέλωτι κατέχεσθαι μήτε σκυθρωπάζειν). Here the deprecation of laughter that seizes control of the body, and thereby corrupts the mind, is tempered by disapproval for too severe a facial expression, *skuthrōpazein* (in its most pejorative uses, 'pulling

---

[27] On *semn-* terms, see Xen. *Symp.* 3.10 (n. 40 below), Eubul. fr. 25 (Dionysius dislikes the solemn; n. 116 below), Amphis fr. 13 (Plato's solemn eyebrows; n. 29 below). Cf. ch. 7 n. 76, Appendix 2 n. 16.

a long face' or 'scowling'). There is room after all, it seems, for at least an occasional smile.[28]

Despite this last passage, however, the preponderant impression conveyed by our sources is of an accentuated Pythagorean antipathy to laughter, rather than simply an inclination to moderate it. So much about the origins of Pythagoreanism, including the life of the founder, is now lost that it is hazardous to make specific psychological claims about its early stages. But we can safely conclude that the view of laughter found in later texts is at any rate compatible with what always seem to have been basic Pythagorean commitments to ethical purity, self-discipline and a general 'flight from the body'. If our evidence is at all reliable, a good Pythagorean would have considered almost any laughter, including derision of deluded opponents, to entail too much compromise with drives that welled up from the body and which, if not suppressed, would immerse one in either hedonistic indiscipline or the messy commerce of social antagonism. If that is right, it does distinguish Pythagoreans from most other Greek philosophers, many of whom were indeed aficionados of polemical mockery. It also makes them the prime pagan forerunners of those Christian moralists whose antigelastic principles, so much at odds with the mainstream traditions of paganism, will be examined in the final chapter of this book.

LAUGHTER ON (AND BEHIND) THE FACE OF SOCRATES

At first sight, there appears to be an affinity between the radical deprecation of laughter attested (however patchily) for Pythagoreanism and some of the attitudes to laughter expressed in the work of Plato. Even if we put on one side the historical fact that Plato himself (and, before him, Socrates) had direct contact with, and was to some extent influenced by, Pythagorean

[28] Permissible smiling *versus* disapproved laughter: Porph. *Abst.* 4.6 (n. 22 above); Simplic. *In Epict. Ench.* XLI Hadot (ch. 1 n. 24) limits expression to lip movements (cf. *ibid.* XLVII). There may be a Pythagorean background to the related sentiments at Sextus, *Sent.* 278–82 (late second century AD): see Chadwick (1959) 44, with 138–62 on the collection. Note the (Pythagorean-influenced?) image of young Moses at Philo, *Vita Mos.* 1.20; cf. 2.211 (with ch. 10, 481, for Philo's own conception of 'good', god-created laughter). But the basic principle is not exclusively Pythagorean: see Isoc. 1.15 (ch. 1 n. 101), the 'Hippocratic' recommendation to avoid extremes of laughter and scowling at ps.-Hippoc. *Epist.* 14 (cf. ch. 7, 361, with ch. 1 n. 101 for *skuthrōpazein*), the Stoic version (avoid downcast looks and feigned 'grinning', ἢ κατηφὲς ἢ προσσεσηρός, Marcus Aur. *Med.* 1.15; cf. Appendix 2 n. 12), and the legend of Socrates' unchanging countenance (n. 40 below). Judaeo-Christian parallels: ch. 10, 492, 516. The idea that smiling, as opposed to more overt mirth, was an 'aristocratic' badge in archaic Greece is asserted without real evidence by Yalouris (1986) 3 (cf. my Appendix 2, 537), who also (4) overstates the likelihood that the Ionian tribal name Geleontes has the same root as *gelōs*; cf. Chantraine (1968) 215, Frisk (1960–70) I 295, for caution on etymology.

circles, and even if we discard the (pseudo-)biographical traditions that Plato himself avoided laughter (at least in his youth) and established regulations against it in the Academy,[29] it is undeniable that the Platonic dialogues contain a number of passages where laughter is expressly deplored or censured, usually in the voice of Socrates. That, however, is only part of a much larger, more complex picture. With this as with other thematic features of the dialogues, we need to reckon not just with what is said but also with what is *shown*. Laughter is used by Plato as one of a whole repertoire of markers of character, tone and personal relationships. Its function within the layered texture of his writing is complicated, moreover, by the slippery and controversial concept of Socratic irony. Since I will appeal to this concept from time to time, but without reexamining it in its own right, I should declare that I treat Socratic irony for present purposes as involving a cluster of phenomena: among them, self-depreciation/deprecation (including professions of ignorance); feigned praise of others; an uncertain, fitful air of playfulness; and, more generally, an obliquity of speech that creates an impression of *arrière-pensée* and leaves Socrates' underlying feelings elusive.[30] If we take careful account of both these fundamental (and intertwined) factors – the subtlety of Plato's dramatic expressiveness, and the problematic indirectness of much Socratic speech – we should view with strong scepticism any claim to identify a one-dimensional Platonic

---

[29] Plato is depicted as sullen/scowling (*skuthrōpazein*: n. 28 above) in the (contemporary) Amphis fr. 13, but this partly reflects comic stereotypes of philosophical *hauteur*; cf. Imperio (1998) 126–7, with n. 75 below. Diog. Laert. 3.26 (= Sotion fr. 13 Wehrli) ascribes to Plato an aversion to excessive laughter in his youth; cf. Riginos (1976) 151–2, Wehrli (1978) 46. Ael. *VH* 4.9 shows him smiling quietly; *ibid.* 3.35 is the source for a supposed prohibition on laughter in the Academy, probably a fictive 'extrapolation' from *Rep.* 3.388e (300 below) and certainly not to be repeated as fact, as in Bremmer (1997) 19. Cf. n. 49 below.

[30] Two very different views of Socratic irony in Vlastos (1991) 21–44, a careful but ultimately schematic reading, and Nehamas (1998), esp. 46–69 (with notes, 201–10), (1999) 70–3, 100–3 (arguing for a richly pervasive irony but distinguishing Socratic/Platonic levels: a fascinating approach, but reservations in Halliwell (2000b)). Cf. Blondell (2002), 119–21, 125, 255–6, Rutherford (1995) 77–8, Nightingale (1995) 114–19 (ironic praise of others). Vasiliou (1999), (2002), modifying Vlastos, defines two particular techniques of Socratic irony; Wolfsdorf (2007) plays down verbal irony in early Plato, but his criteria are narrow. Narcy (2001), Lane (2006), Lane (forthcoming) insist on the pejorative, deception-centred sense of *eirōn* terminology applied to Socrates by Platonic interlocutors (an old view: e.g. Burnet (1924) 159): but (a) that need not limit the kinds of irony (*qua* serio-ludic tone, layered speech, etc.) detectable in Plato's depiction as a whole, as Lane (2006) appreciates (registering irony's 'inherent elusiveness'); (b) it is far from clear that the *eirōn*- terms at *Rep.* 1.337a, *Grg.* 489e are *reducible* to deception/evasion (a teasing, *self-advertising* manner is partly at issue), and even less clear at *Symp.* 216e, 218d, *Ap.* 38a; (c) other Platonic usage of *eirōn*- terms displays complex nuances, esp. *Crat.* 383b–384a (of Cratylus not Socrates, *contra* Diggle (2004) 166), which involves both haughtiness and quasi-'oracular' allusiveness. Cf. the semantic spectrum of *eirōn*- terms in Aristotle, 319–21 below. Opsomer (1998) 105–33 traces *eirōn* vocabulary from Plato to Plutarch; for later developments see Knox (1989). Cf. di Marco (1989) 169–70.

verdict on laughter. What I offer here will necessarily be selective. But it will reclaim for Plato's writings, above all in relation to the enigmatic persona of Socrates, a rich set of perceptions of the psychological, social and ethical possibilities of laughter.[31]

A perhaps unlikely but nonetheless revealing place from which to begin the argument is the *Phaedo*, which in itself rebuts any sweeping thesis of Platonic antipathy to laughter. The dialogue contains no fewer than nine references to the laughter (and two references to smiles) that imprints itself on the tone of Socrates' final hours in the company of his friends. Phaedo himself signals near the outset that, counterintuitively, laughter will be a leitmotif of the extraordinary story he has to tell. He explains to Echecrates the 'curious mixture' of pleasure and pain he and the others felt at Socrates' approaching death. Socrates' noble serenity set an example which tempered his friends' impulses to grief and pity, yet the thought of losing him still caused stabs of pain – with the result that they found themselves 'alternating between laughter and tears' (τοτὲ μὲν γελῶντες, ἐνίοτε δὲ δακρύοντες, 59a). Not only is this a cue to the reader to interpret the work with sensitivity to emotional ambivalence; it is also a dramatic reflection of the strangeness of Socrates, who is able, it seems, to give his friends reasons to laugh on the very last occasion they might have expected it. Laughter punctuates the dialogue in a way which communicates a peculiar quality of Socrates' character that allows him to preserve the good mirth of intimate friendship, and to sway his companions' mood accordingly, even in (outwardly) bleak circumstances. This dramatic effect matches the work's substantive suggestion, in the arguments advanced by Socrates, that death affords the true philosopher no reason to grieve. Laughter is part of the *Phaedo*'s attempt to delineate on every level a positive revaluation of Socrates' death.[32]

If we ask who actually laughs, and when, in the *Phaedo*, the answers alert us to a delicate thematic strand in the fabric of the dialogue. The Theban and perhaps Pythagorean Cebes is the first to laugh ('gently', ἠρέμα), at 62a,

---

[31] Mader (1977) deals with the 'theory' of laughter at *Phlb.* 48–50 (cf. 300–2 below), comparing Plato's own practice as 'metacomic' writer. Platonic theory/practice of laughter has attracted widespread attention: see, from various angles, Greene (1920), Vicaire (1960) 179–92, De Vries (1985), Brock (1990), Sprague (1994), Nightingale (1995) 172–92, Steiner (1995), Corrigan (1997), Rowe (1997), Jouët-Pastré (1998), Thein (2000). Murdoch (1977) 73–5 (Murdoch (1997) 450–1) is jumbled, and silent on the persona of Socrates.

[32] The total effect of the work, as 59a intimates, is complex: see Halliwell (2006) 124–8, with n. 35 below. *Phd.* 70c subtly hints that if the dialogue (partly) denies tragedy, it also thwarts simple comedy. Cf. Stella (2000) for another account of laughter in *Phd.* Together with *Apol.*, *Phd.* may have influenced ps.-Aeschines, *Socr. Epist.* 14.4–5, which claims that Socrates smiled/laughed during his trial (but see ch. 2 n. 8) and even left court laughing; cf. Max. Tyr. *Dial.* 12.10.

exclaiming in his native Boeotian dialect at Socrates' elaborate paraphrase of Cebes' own scepticism about a philosophical prohibition on suicide. It is hard to find a markedly humorous prompt in what Socrates has just said, but two things are probably germane: first, there is a trace of teasing in Socrates' hope that he may be the first person, unlike the Pythagorean Philolaus (61d–e), to give Cebes a *clear* account of the prohibition on suicide; secondly, his expectation that Cebes will be very suprised by the *simplicity* of the account is itself expressed in a convoluted sentence which hints at complications.[33] We should therefore treat Cebes' wry reaction ('may Zeus know it!', i.e. 'may Zeus be my witness that I *do* expect to be surprised') as reflecting the circuitousness of Socrates' manner of speaking and the paradox that a matter of such gravity could be thought 'simple'. If so, laughter is his knowing gesture towards the philosophical depths lurking beneath Socrates' serene poise. Something similar, but with an extra nuance, occurs at 64a–b. There Socrates has just shown casual, phlegmatic disregard for the warning, passed on by Crito from the jailer, not to allow his body to become overheated before the poison is administered: 'ignore the jailer! just let him be ready to give me the poison twice or even three times, if need be'. Ignoring the jailer's warning, Socrates insists on pursuing the idea that philosophy is a 'rehearsal for death', and observes that ordinary people do not realise that philosophers spend their whole lives practising 'to die and be dead'. Cebes' Theban companion Simmias tells Socrates: 'you made me laugh, even though I wasn't at all inclined to do so just now!' If it is correct, as the earlier reference to their association with Philolaus suggests, that Cebes and Simmias were (or could be thought to be) Pythagoreans,[34] then Simmias' self-description as 'not at all inclined to laugh' (οὐ πάνυ γε . . . γελασείοντα) may reach beyond the immediate situation and allude deftly to a supposed Pythagorean trait of the kind I discussed in the previous section. In that case, an informed reader could interpret Socrates' influence over his Theban friends as prevailing over their notional affiliation (or perhaps aspiration) to a Pythagorean way of life. Whether or not we detect that extra hint, Simmias' laughter involves the thought of popular gibes about 'deathly' philosophers. His reaction therefore fulfils the dramatic function of inviting us to notice the gulf, which subsequent phases of the argument will widen further, between a superficial and a deep understanding of the philosophical significance of the topic. Laughter, though subordinate to

---

[33] The relationship between the two clauses of the long sentence at 62a is vexed: see esp. Gallop (1975) 79–83; cf. Burnet (1911) 61–3, Rowe (1993) 126. The details do not matter here.

[34] They are associates of Philolaus, *Phd.* 61d–e. But caution is in order: cf. Rowe (1993) 7, 115–16, Nails (2002) 82–3, 260–1.

the details of the argument, is part of the *Phaedo*'s answer to the fear of death.

That point starts to stand out more boldly, in tandem with a more direct link between Socrates' own mood and the intermittent laughter of the group, at 77e. Here Socrates comments, again with gentle teasing, that Cebes and Simmias seem to have a childlike fear that if the soul, as traditional thinking has it, leaves the body as 'breath' at death (cf. 70a), it may be scattered by the wind – especially, Socrates adds, if one happens to die in windy weather! Cebes takes the quip with a laugh and asks Socrates to try to persuade 'the child inside us' not to fear death the way that real children fear 'bogey masks'.[35] The tone of the exchange reinforces the impression not only of Socratic imperturbability but also of the difficulty even his closest followers have in overcoming the fear of death felt by the 'child' in every psyche. Cebes' laughter, following on Socrates' teasing, sounds a note of some ambiguity: just how capable is he of ceasing to be the child and becoming the true Socratic?

Later on, Socrates himself laughs for the first time. Like Cebes at 62a, he does so 'gently', ἠρέμα (the laughter of bodily convulsiveness is excluded from the scene throughout), though at the same time with a colloquial exclamation of mock exasperation (βαβαί, 84d) which is commonly ascribed to him in Plato. He is responding to Simmias' admission that he and Cebes were anxious about pressing for further discussion in the present 'calamity'. Socrates' firm but good-natured insistence that he does not regard his situation as a calamity takes us back to Phaedo's scene-setting remarks on the emotional ambivalence of the group, their alternation between laughter and tears (59a). It is a reminder that only Socrates himself truly rises above the prompting to grief, but it also complements other indications, including his elaborate comparison of himself to a dying swan with a gift of prophetic song (84e–85b), that there is something abidingly inscrutable about his personality.

Of the dialogue's five further mentions of laughter or smiles, four refer to Socrates' own demeanour; the other involves Cebes' amusement at a logically teasing suggestion in the course of the discussion of 'forms' (101b).

---

[35] Late sources sometimes equate μορμολυκεῖα with tragic masks: e.g. Phot. *Lex. s.v.*, Σ on Pl. *Grg.* 473d; cf. Frontisi-Ducroux (1995) 12–14. Might that be a subtext in *Phd.* (cf. the parodic reference to tragedy at 115a, with n. 32 above)? Classical evidence for the equation is lacking. But Pl. *Grg.* 473d, *Crito* 46c make one wonder whether ironic mention of Mormo-type bogeys was a Socratic habit which Cebes is echoing; cf., differently, Charmides to Socrates at Xen. *Symp.* 4.27. For a Spartan use of the same motif, see ch. 1, 48. With Cebes' 'child in the psyche', cf. Cephalus' analogy at *Rep.* 1.330e.

At 86d Simmias' continuing scepticism about the immortality of the soul –
a scepticism whose implications for the feelings of those present needs no
spelling out – elicits from Socrates a 'wide-eyed' look (said to be characteristic of him) and a smile, together with a degree of caution about whether the
scepticism can be satisfactorily answered.[36] Socrates' reaction, physiognomically symbolised (and perhaps alluding to his notoriously bulging eyes), is,
as often in Plato, far from self-evident; irony can be transmitted by his play
of features as well as by his words. But the wide eyes and the smile leave
one thing beyond doubt: that his own cheerfulness, however mysteriously
sustained, remains undisturbed. At 102d, equally, Socrates smiles as he face-
tiously compares his precise way of speaking (in analysing how someone can
be simultaneously 'larger' and 'smaller') to 'talking like a treatise'.[37] More
tellingly, as the time to drink the hemlock approaches and Crito asks 'but
how shall we *bury* you?', Socrates laughs 'quietly' (ἡσυχῇ) and replies, 'any
way you like – that's if you can catch me and I don't escape!' (115c). He then
underlines his point by chaffing Crito for having failed to be persuaded by
the whole thrust of Socrates' position in the dialogue: namely, that it will
not *be* 'Socrates', not his soul or true self, that will be buried after death.[38]
This passage draws together the threads of the earlier ones, reminding us
of asymmetry between Socratic serenity and the emotional fluctuations of
the others, but also giving a human face, indeed a gelastic affability, to that
serenity.

The *Phaedo* contains one more reference to laughter, but this time to the
idea of the derision that Socrates would direct against himself if he thought
that he was 'clinging' to life and betraying the values he has espoused
throughout the dialogue. If he followed Crito's advice and delayed the
time for drinking the poison any longer, 'I would gain nothing', he says,
'other than to incur laughter in my own eyes' (γέλωτα ὀφλήσειν παρ'
ἐμαυτῷ).[39] This is all the more revealing in that none of the laughter
heard earlier in the *Phaedo* has been expressive of belittlement or contempt
(though some has been tinged by Socrates' unwillingness to take his followers' concerns seriously). In the present dialogue, scornful laughter belongs

---

[36] On διαβλέπειν, to open the eyes wide, see Burnet (1911) 86. Cf. n. 40 below.

[37] I borrow the translation of Dover (1997) 183 n. 66.

[38] Rowe (1993) 291 says Socrates would not have regarded failure to persuade Crito as 'a laughing matter': that presupposes that (Socrates') laughter is frivolous, rather than a complex signal of both affection for Crito and a sense of the difficulty of the issues.

[39] 116e–117a, misconstrued by De Vries (1985) 380. Such mordant self-scrutiny was later adopted by some Stoics (see 304); for a connection with the anonymous figure in *Hp. Maj.*, see 293–5. Different is the locution 'mocking oneself' (αὑτοῦ καταγελᾶν *vel sim.*) at e.g. *Prt.* 357d, *Hp. Maj.* 291e, which refers to making a fool of oneself in the eyes of others.

(hypothetically) only to Socrates' unsparing capacity for self-criticism, a fleeting point here but one with wider ramifications to which I shall return. Finally, and almost immediately after his reference to the notion of internalised ridicule, Socrates evokes yet one more note of possible laughter. This is when he takes the cup of hemlock 'very cheerfully' (μάλα ἵλεως) from the jailer and gives the latter what Phaedo calls 'a bull-like frown that was a habit of his' (ὥσπερ εἰώθει ταυρηδὸν ὑποβλέψας, 117b). Although the description is not exactly transparent, since this is (tantalisingly) the only Platonic mention of the 'habit' in question, the power of the image emerges from its piquant combination with the preceding look of cheerfulness and from its accompaniment to Socrates' request to be allowed to pour some of the hemlock as a libation to the gods. It is as if this time laughter is, as it were, both prompted and suppressed. Socrates, in his semi-inscrutable manner, is deadly serious and yet also half-playful. The language used to describe the gaze he fixes on the jailer connotes an attitude of menace and hostility, but the context subtly undercuts that. What we have here therefore, as at 86d (281 above), though there with a different cast of the features, is a look of *facialised irony*, and one which strikes an ambiguous note in relation to laughter itself.[40] Furthermore, it is a look which no really attentive reader of the *Phaedo* can fail to connect with Crito's poignant closing of the dead Socrates' eyes just a few moments later (118a). Socrates' face itself, in life and in death, becomes an emblem of the work's extraordinary conflicts of emotion.

  Plato has gone out of his way, then, to allow the sound as well as the resonant idea of laughter to be heard at several points in the *Phaedo*, yet to

---

[40] The envisaged look probably entails lowered eyebrows (see Alciph. *Epist.* 1.13.2, cf. Appendix 1 n. 30); for ὑποβλέπειν and menace see LSJ *s.v.*, adding Callim. *Hymn Dem.* 50–1. Burnet (1911) 116–17 understandably imagines 'a "mischievous look" rather than a threatening one' (LSJ *loc. cit.* wrongly *translate* as 'look mischievously'); but he misses the point of 'like a bull' (see Ar. *Frogs* 804, cf. Eur. *Medea* 92, 187–8, Callim. *Iambi* 4.101), viz. (mock) *fierceness*; Taillardat (1965) 206–7 n. 4 also loses this nuance, as does Sommerstein (1996) 226, making the look 'friendly'. Stanford (1958) 141 posits a 'quizzical' glance, also an understatement. Cf. Cairns (2005b) 136–7. *Pace* Hackforth (1955) 189 n. 1, Socrates' expression should not be equated with the wide-eyed look (and smile) at *Phd.* 86d (281 above); rightly Burnet (1911) 86, Rowe (1993) 206, 294. Cf. the ironic solemnity of Socrates' face (but with raised eyebrows) at Xen. *Symp.* 3.10 (cf. 2.17); see ch. 3, 149, noting Arist. *Hist. An.* 1.9, 491b16–17, for the mocking ironist's curved eyebrows. For laughter/smiling as 'ironic', see e.g. Ctesias, *FGrH* 688 F26.84, Dio Chrys. 15.10.1, Plut. *Cic.* 1.4, Heliod. *Aeth.* 3.7.2, 10.14.6 (note ὑποβλέπειν), cf. 10.31.4. For a later (factitious) tradition that Socrates' facial expression never changed, see e.g. Epict. *Diss.* 1.25.31, Ael. *VH* 9.7, Pliny, *HN* 7.79, Sen. *De ira* 2.7.1, *Gnom. Vat.* 573 (cf. the Lucianic joke at *Dial. mort.* 4.1); Jerome interestingly contests the claim, *Ctr. Pel.* 3.1, *Comm. in Esaiam* 12.42. The tradition was extrapolated from indifference to fortune (see Arist. *An. Post.* 2.13, 97b21–3; cf. the *megalopsuchos* at *EN* 4.3, 1124a15–16) and assimilates Socrates to the facial impassivity predicated of Pythagoreans (see 272–3); but it ignores the Platonic images of facial irony, though Aelian *loc. cit.* does use ἵλεως, 'cheerful', the same term as Pl. *Phd.* 117b (above).

do so in strange counterpoint to the natural propensity of Socrates' companions to feel profound grief at what they are witnessing. The dialogue
makes laughter play its part in conveying a Socratic defiance, an emotional
transcendence, of death. As an antidote to the sorrow that threatens to overcome the companions, it is an index (or a test) of the incomplete extent to
which they are able to celebrate their friendship with Socrates and share his
composure, while on Socrates' own part it serves as a signal of a supremely
philosophical imperturbability, especially in his amusement at the idea
that his situation is a 'calamity' (84d) and in his jest about the difficulty
the others will have in 'catching' him after death (115c). The overall effect
of the work's series of moments of laughter is irreducibly paradoxical, as
Phaedo's formulation of mixed and fluctuating emotions at 59a highlights.
The paradox might be thought of as a special Platonic variation on the
normally negative idea captured in the proverb 'jesting among mourners',
or, equally, as an intensely philosophical version of the contradictory feelings of *klausigelōs*, 'crying laughter'.[41] This dramatic aspect of the work is
all the more remarkable when we register the fact that *nowhere* else in Plato
does Socrates himself openly laugh. (The point of that 'openly' will soon be
explained.) Plato has chosen to foreground Socrates' capacity for a gentle,
philosophically positive laughter – amidst the intermittent but much less
secure laughter of his friends – at the very juncture of final preparations for
death.

That is not to say, however, that Socrates is distanced from laughter outside the *Phaedo*. On the contrary, laughter figures in a number
of important ways in many Socratic dialogues, and Socrates himself can
be seen as pivotal to its shifting, ambiguous significance. At the simplest
level, Socrates sometimes prompts others to laugh by teasing or provoking
them. He does this with young acquaintances like Charmides, Menex-
enus, Lysis and Hippocrates, with closer young friends like Glaucon, but
also, on occasion, with more formidable figures like the sophist Prodicus.[42] In such cases, he seems deliberately to invite laughter as a sort of
personal-cum-philosophical lubricant of a relationship or situation, and

---

[41] The proverb τὸ ἐν πενθοῦσι παίζειν is attested (with negative force) at Demetr. *Eloc.* 28, where it
is synonymous with the oxymoron κλαυσίγελως, here laughter inappropriately displacing grief; cf.
Rhys Roberts (1902) 288. (A similar idea, probably, at Greg. Naz. *Orat.* 27.4: see Norris (1991) 90–1
for the textual emendation; cf. ch. 3 n. 59.) κλαυσίγελως is used differently of 'crying with joy' at
Xen. *Hell.* 7.2.9, and of mixed Epicurean pleasure and pain at Plut. *Mor.* 1097f; at Athen. 13.591c it
is a courtesan's nickname (cf. ch. 4 n. 56)! Different again is Andromache's 'laughter through tears',
Hom. *Il.* 6.484: ch. 2, 54.

[42] See e.g. *Charm.* 156a, *Lys.* 207c, 208d, *Prt.* 310d, *Rep.* 3.398c, 5.451b, and the good-natured banter
which elicits Prodicus' laughter at *Prt.* 358b (cf. *Phdr.* 267b, reported).

as in *Phaedo* there is nothing aggressive or destructive about it. Much the same is true of passages where the vocabulary of *skōptein* (and cognates) is used in its playful sense of banter or jesting, rather than its harsher sense of jeering ridicule: such passages bear out that Socrates is capable of both making and taking a joke.[43] But there are many other occasions in Plato when abrasive, antagonistic derision comes into play. It is Socrates' (and Plato's) engagement with the unstable forces of such derision that now needs investigating.

The Platonic Socrates oscillates somewhat between disregard for and anxiety about the possibility of such derision. At *Rep.* 5.451a he states that to fear laughter when advancing serious but risky arguments among friends is 'childish' (*paidikon* – shades of the *Phaedo*'s 'child in the psyche' again), while in the *Euthyphro* he makes the more sweeping assertion that 'to be laughed down (sc. by the Athenian Assembly) is perhaps of no importance' (3c), before going on to suggest, with strange irony, that if his judges *were* to ridicule him, it would be enjoyable to spend time 'joking and laughing' with them in court (παίζοντας καὶ γελῶντας, 3d–e). It is also true that this ostensible insouciance about derision is virtually unprecedented in Greek culture: 'until Socrates', as one scholar has put it, 'no one . . . says "let them mock"'.[44] But the composite Platonic depiction of Socrates is more intricate than this. Insouciance sometimes gives way to apparent apprehension about 'incurring laughter': for example, when resisting Glaucon's pressure to give his view of the ultimate good at *Rep.* 6.506d, when expressing concern about allowing even more ridicule to be 'heaped onto' philosophy by allowing the wrong people to study it (*Rep.* 7.536b), or when telling Hippias that he is determined not to be mocked a second time by suffering refutation at the hands of the anonymous interlocutor (to whom we shall return) at *Hp. Maj.* 286e. Furthermore, we have already seen that in the *Phaedo* Socrates *internalises* the idea of derisive laughter, suggesting that he is prepared to turn it against himself (116e–117a). Even when we put on one side those contexts in which Socratic fear of laughter is blatantly disingenuous, as with his refusal to compete with the (falsifying) rhetoric of Phaedrus in *Symposium* or his request to the sophists in the *Euthydemus* not to mock his own 'amateur' style of dialectic, we are still left with apparent ambiguity in

---

[43] For the playful sense of *skōptein* etc., cf. ch. 1 n. 41 (contrast the harsher sense at e.g. Pl. *Euthd.* 294d, cited on 289 below). Socrates is involved in such joking at e.g. *Euphr.* 11b–c, *Meno* 80a–c (responding to the stingray comparison), *Crat.* 384c (hypothesising someone else's joke), *Phdr.* 264e, *Rep.* 6.487e.

[44] Adkins (1960) 155. But cf. the (later) anecdote about Xenophanes at 268–9 above. On insouciance to mockery as culturally aberrant, see ch. 1, 41–2.

his stance on this point.[45] The key to this ambiguity lies in the difference between the merely social shame or embarrassment of being scoffed at, a shame the Platonic Socrates seems emphatically to dismiss as 'childish' and to which he is susceptible only within the terms of irony, and, on the other hand, the real stigma of being shown to *deserve* ridicule – if only, sometimes, in his own eyes – when tested against the touchstone of truth and goodness.

A distinction between being merely laughed at and 'missing the truth' is explicit at *Rep.* 5.451a, already cited, and is elaborated later in Book 5 when Socrates and Glaucon agree that however absurd most people would find the idea of naked female athletes (as required by their blueprint for the ideal city), it would be wrong to be deterred by 'the gibes of the witty' (τὰ τῶν χαριέντων σκώμματα, 452b). It is essential, Socrates explains, to separate what is laughable only to the *eyes* (τὸ ἐν τοῖς ὀφθαλμοῖς δὴ γελοῖον) from that which is genuinely laughable because truly bad or shameful.[46] Socrates' case here depends on driving a wedge between local, mutable cultural perceptions (Greeks *used* to find male nudity 'shameful and laughable', and barbarians still do, he says: 452c) and the rational standards of good and bad which he believes should anchor all judgements of behaviour and accordingly underpin justified laughter. The person who laughs at the thought of female nudity in public gymnasia, he later asserts, 'does not *know*' what he is laughing at (457a–b). Two less than perfectly dovetailing assumptions, one social and one psychological, seem to inform the references to laughter that frame this whole stretch of argument (from 451 to 457). The first is that derision is a vehicle and channel for prevailing cultural norms and values; the other is that, in psychic terms, laughter has a kind of life of its own, able to elude or resist the control of rationality. The second of these principles appears elsewhere too in the *Republic*: earlier, in Book 3's assertion that young Guardians must not be 'lovers of laughter' (*philogelōtes*), because 'strong' laughter brings with it 'a strong change (sc. to the mind)' (ἰσχυρὰν μεταβολήν); and later, in Book 10's treatment of comic impulses as belonging to the epithumetic level of the soul – impulses that need to be held in check by reason and will destabilise

---

[45] Disingenuous fear of laughter: *Symp.* 199b, *Euthd.* 278d–e (288 below); cf. *Tht.* 161e (Socrates' maieutic as ridiculous: an ironic consequence of Protagorean subjectivism). Something more like real sensitivity to social embarrassment appears at *Euthd.* 272c (Socrates mocked by boys in music school); but there may be a subtextual allusion to comedy (Hawtrey (1981) 46) and there is certainly irony *vis-à-vis* his eristic interlocutors. Another (complex) passage that hypothetically envisages justified derision is *Phdr.* 259a.

[46] *Rep.* 5.452d: see Halliwell (1993a) 141–4 (cf. 137, 138–9), with *ibid.* 224–5 on Plato's awareness of satire of such topics in comedy (cf. n. 49 below).

behaviour if not repressed.[47] Between them, the two assumptions bolster Socrates' distinction between the spuriously and the genuinely 'laughable'. But they also arouse disquiet about the unruly irrationality of much actual ridicule.[48]

The volatility of laughter mattered greatly to Plato. This was in part because he was aware that philosophy, including his own school, was regularly exposed to public mockery both inside and outside the comic theatre.[49] But it was also, I maintain, because he perceived Socrates himself as standing in a complex relationship to the workings of ridicule. In Plato's dialogues Socrates is openly derided in conversation on a number of occasions, mostly by sophistic rivals but also (to be noted for future reference) by a dialectically impatient Diotima at *Symp.* 202b. It would be easy but superficial to suppose that Socrates never meets ridicule *with* ridicule, and that his response to Polus at *Gorgias* 473e ('are you laughing? is this an alternative form of refutation (*elenchos*), to deride what someone says rather than refuting it?') encapsulates the whole matter.[50] Certainly Socrates avoids being drawn into crudely scornful exchanges (though the tone of his response to Polus is only separated from that by a thin dividing line of irony); the swapping of mere abuse (*loidoria*) is something he expressly deplores.[51] So when, notoriously, in the first book of the *Republic* Thrasymachus bursts out with a 'highly sardonic guffaw' (ἀνεκάγχασέ τε μάλα σαρδάνιον, 337a) that accompanies a verbal assault on Socrates for talking 'rubbish' (336d), being 'nauseating' (βδελυρός, 338d), and needing his 'nurse' to wipe his runny nose (343a), Socrates replies with heavy irony but also with a refusal to trade insults directly.[52] But two qualifications

---

[47] *Rep.* 3.388e–389b (but contrast the need to 'deride' Homeric depictions of divine grief, 388d), 10.606c. *Contra* Adam (1963) I 136, *Rep.* 388e is a different principle from 8.563e (specifying a change 'to the opposite', which makes no sense in the former case). On 388e ch. 2, 62.

[48] Cf. *Rep.* 7.518a–b, making some laughter itself 'laughable' (Tarrant (1928) 58 compares *Hp. Maj.* 291e; cf. ch. 10 n. 38) and implying more and less 'rational'/justifiable forms of laughter; cf. *Tht.* 172–5, with n. 60 below. The ethological view of Lorenz (1966) 254, 'laughter . . . always remains obedient to reason', would have struck Plato (and most Greeks) as strange.

[49] For the treatment of Plato in fourth-century Attic comedy (note esp. Diog. Laert. 3.26–8) see Imperio (1998) 124–8, Webster (1970) 50–5, Düring (1941) 137–43, Olson (2007) 238–44.

[50] 473e may involve a dig at Gorgias' own principle of rhetorical laughter; see ch. 1 n. 98. At 473e–474a Socrates relates how he seemed 'ridiculous' when ignorant of the Boule's voting procedure (see Dodds (1959) 247–8): this matches the unworldly philosopher at *Tht.* 173c–175e (cf. n. 60 below).

[51] Socrates deprecates *loidoria* at e.g. *Euthd.* 288b, *Grg.* 457d, *Lach.* 195a, *Phdr.* 268d, *Rep.* 3.395d (alluding to comedy), 6.500b. Note however the resonance of self-*loidoria* within the divided soul at *Rep.* 4.440b (used by *thumos*; at *Phdr.* 254c–d it is used by the epithumetic horse). An only apparent exception to Socrates' avoidance of abuse is his use of the vocative ὦ μιαρέ: Halliwell (1995) 113–15. Diog. Laert. 2.21 preserves a tradition, from Demetrius of Byzantium, that Socrates never responded to mockery or aggression; compare Diogenes the Cynic, ch. 7, 380–1.

[52] On 'sardonic', see ch. 2 n. 100; 'guffawing', Appendix 1 n. 17; *bdeluros*, 'nauseating', ch. 5, 240–1.

should be added here. First, Socrates' narrative of the abrasive conversation with Thrasymachus includes the thought, *unspoken* at the time, that his opponent was behaving like a 'wild beast' ('intending to tear us to pieces', 336b) or a wolf (336d) – a thought which *if* voiced (and Socrates does go so far as to call Thrasymachus a lion, 341c) would strike an abusive, mocking note. Secondly, the exchange between the two men lends some vindication to Thrasymachus' complaint that Socrates resorts to derisive 'irony' (a coy pretence of ignorance, but also a means of manipulating others) in order to avoid answering questions himself (337a). In fact, Socrates' direct response to this complaint is to tell Thrasymachus how 'clever' he is to spot this, which he follows with a sarcastically parodic repudiation of the constraints that Thrasymachus wants to place on the definition of justice. Moreover, this parody involves a favourite technique of Socrates' (though hardly exclusive to him), articulating the reaction of an imaginary third party, here in a way which casts Thrasymachus in an obviously absurd light.[53] While, then, there is undoubtedly an asymmetry between the language and tone of Socrates and Thrasymachus, we should not shirk the conclusion that both of them say things that could provoke laughter in hearers suitably aligned with their point of view.[54]

We can get a fuller sense of how Socrates positions himself towards face-to-face ridicule by looking at some episodes from the *Euthydemus*. When Socrates praises the two sophists Dionysodorus and Euthydemus for being knowledgeable about many important matters, including military strategy and forensic rhetoric, he tells Crito that they laughed conspiratorially in a way which suggested that they held him in contempt (*kataphronein*), while Euthydemus proceeded to claim that they attached no weight to the sort of subjects Socrates had cited.[55] But Socrates' own attitude to the pair is, for a *reader*, so ironic from the outset (he has already described them as pancratiasts, 'all-in wrestlers', of argument, who know how to win a verbal fight regardless of whether truth is on their side, 272a–b) that within Plato's text it is far from clear how the balance-sheet of ridicule should be drawn up. There is a dramatic tension between the scornful laughter of the sophists and their supporters, on the one hand, and the 'inward', silent laughter of Socratic irony. The operations of the former

---

[53] Aristotle recommends this technique to orators at *Rhet.* 2.17, 1418b24–6.

[54] For further markers of the difference between Socratic and Thrasymachean speech, cf. Halliwell (1995) 105–6, 112–13.

[55] *Euthd.* 273c–d; this programmatic passage is ignored by De Vries (1985) 380, who attempts to divest the sophists' laughter of malice. Later, Dionysodorus tries to tempt Socrates himself into the conspiracy, smiling smugly and whispering about Cleinias' discomfiture (275e): Socrates does not respond. Cf. Branham (1989a) 69–80 on the comic/satirical strands of the work.

are so conspicuous that they have a 'choreographed' quality to them: three times the sophists' followers burst into noisy applause and laughter, at one point like a chorus on cue (276b, 276d, 303b). The agonistic atmosphere, intensified by the ambience of the gymnasium, is patent throughout (the trope of verbal 'wrestling' occurs more than once), and Socrates claims that he and Cleinias felt 'stunned' (276d).[56]

But Socrates is not so stunned as to lose his capacity to fight back with a repertoire of ironic mockery of his own. Crucial in this respect is his lengthy intervention at 277d–278e, designed to rescue Cleinias from further humiliation at the hands of the sophists. Picking up the earlier imagery of choreography, he compares Dionysodorus and Euthydemus to those who dance round an initiate in the 'enthronement' process of Corybantic ritual.[57] He refers to their antics with the language of 'play' (*paidia, paizein*), terminology which has associations with both lighthearted joking and dancing. Having explained the verbal ambiguities on which the sophists' arguments have hinged, he goes on to say that such forms of 'play' are of no more consequence than the ability to make people look silly by tripping them up or pulling a stool from underneath them.[58] He purports to believe that the pair must have intended all this as a merely ludic preface to something serious, and he invites them to move on ('let the game end; we've surely had enough', 278d) to the demonstration of wisdom and excellence which they originally professed. But before they do so, he offers to 'improvise' some of his own dialectic with Cleinias, and asks the sophists to restrain their *laughter* if he does so in a risibly unpolished manner (278d–e).

Euthydemus 277d–278e is a pivotal passage in the dialogue. From my perspective, it develops a tacit Socratic 'laughter' in counterpoint to the all-too-obvious laughter encouraged by the sophists. Socrates depicts his opponents' activity as a verbal dance-cum-ritual: their techniques are choreographed or stage-managed, prearranged rather than intellectually perceptive, and esoteric in their appeal to a clique. The implications for the supporters whose cheering and laughter have already been heard twice are

---

[56] The same verb, ἐκπλήττειν ('stun'), likewise of Thrasymachus' onslaught at *Rep.* 1.336d. Cf. Socrates' boxing imagery at *Prt.* 339d–e, against a similar background of partisan cheering. For the gymnasium setting, see ch. 1 n. 82. Agonistic laughter in debate between philosophers was common in antiquity; cf. the telling vignette at Lucian, *Iup. Trag.* 16 (ch. 7 n. 62), where the Epicurean Damis scoffs sardonically at the sweating discomfiture of the Stoic Timocles; cf. *ibid.* 5, 18, 27, 29, 41–2, 51–3, with n. 108 below.

[57] 278d. See ch. 4, 188–9 (**F11**), for the ritual itself.

[58] The verb ὑποσκελίζειν (*Euthd.* 278b), 'take the legs from under' someone, is connected metaphorically with ridicule at Dem. 18.138 (ch. 5, 237); for its literal use, but in close proximity to derisive laughter, see Dem. 54.8, with ch. 1, 34–5. The word may evoke wrestling (cf. above): Harris (1964) 207 n. 59.

clear: to be impressed by the eristic display is to take shallow entertainment in a sort of sport. But Socrates' colourful picture of this sport or game is double edged – indeed, it counts as itself an ironic piece of 'play', something he is characteristically suspected of (and occasionally seems to admit to) in Plato.[59] If the sophists could accept his challenge to drop their word games and engage seriously with the issues, they would show that what had preceded was indeed a sort of ritual foreplay, perhaps with some mildly propaedeutic value. But if, as turns out to be the case, their verbal 'wrestling' is *all* they are capable of, the language of 'play' itself becomes a dismissive gibe at their pretensions – and, implicitly, a piece of jeering in its own right. Without lapsing into overt laughter of his own, Socrates deflates the others' exhibitionist posturings but in a manner which sidesteps head-on confrontation. Furthermore, he underscores the character of his irony by requesting the others to desist from laughing at his own clumsy attempts at dialectic (using no less than four *gel-* terms in a short space at 277d–e). In thus purporting to apologise for his own 'laughable' qualities, he reinforces the subtext of his indictment of the sophists' doubly derisory 'play'.

It would be a simplification, therefore, to say that in the thematics of *Euthydemus* laughter is solely a sophistic weapon of disputation, fended off by the benignly constructive gestures of Socrates. In fact, later in the dialogue we see Socrates being drawn unmistakably into the agonistic use of mockery. To test the sophists' claims to 'omniscience', Ctesippus asks them at one point whether they each know how many teeth the other has. Socrates recounts that they were not willing to submit to the test, 'since they thought they were being made fun of' (ἡγουμένω σκώπτεσθαι, 294c–d). Far from disapproving of this method of dealing with them (which permits him, in his retrospective narrative, to compare them to wild boars: cf. 287 on his description of Thrasymachus), he says he felt 'compelled' to chip in with a question of his own, asking Dionysodorus whether he knew how to *dance* (294d–e). In the light of his earlier image of the pair's quasi-Corybantic gyrations, the sarcasm of his question (which he elaborates by alluding to dangerous professional sword-dances and the like) is patent

---

[59] See e.g. *Ap.* 20d, *Grg.* 481b–c, *Phdr.* 234d–e, *Symp.* 216e, *Tht.* 168c–d; cf. *Menex.* 235c, ps.-Pl. *Eryx.* 399c. At *Phdr.* 236b Socrates purports to think Phaedrus has taken his 'banter' (ἐρεσχηλεῖν: cf. *Rep.* 8.545e, *Laws* 10.885c, *Phlb.* 53e) too seriously. Such passages exemplify a larger lexicon of 'play' in Plato, with complex implications for his own writing: Guthrie (1975) 56–65, Rutherford (1995) 25–6, 202–5 give pointers; cf. Walter (1893) 379–85; on *Laws*, see Jouët-Pastré (2006). Huizinga (1949) 146–51 counts play (a little too loosely) as common to the sophists and Socrates/Plato; Ardley (1967) is a muddle. Note the locution πεπαίσθω, 'let the game end' or 'that's enough play', at *Phdr.* 278b, the same form as *Euthd.* 278d (cited in my text).

to an attuned reader. We are invited, however, to see Socrates' ironically understated laughter as justifiably exposing the overbearing arrogance of the sophists, whereas their own use and encouragement of ridicule are depicted as flaws symptomatic of that arrogance itself. The difference is parallel to the *Theaetetus'* famous digression on the true philosopher, whose own ineptness in worldly matters makes him a laughing-stock (like the archetypal Thales falling down a well) but who in turn is said unequivocally to deride the vanity of those obsessed with the material realm of power, wealth and ancestry.[60] In keeping with the argument earlier cited from *Republic* 3, this contrast shows that the significance and justification of laughter are only as good as the values which underlie it. In the *Euthydemus* this means that Socrates can distance himself from the noisy, conceited laughter of his sophistic opposition without thereby giving up an implicit laughter of his own. It is therefore not surprising that when actual laughter is voiced against the sophists by Ctesippus and Cleinias, Socrates effectively endorses it by asking how they can laugh at such a fine spectacle as Dionysodorus and Euthydemus are providing.[61] If, literally, 'the last laugh' in the dialogue is eventually on the side of the sophists themselves, when the gymnasium resounds to further acclaim of their eristic display (303b), that is as it were cancelled out by the satire embedded in Socrates' narrative. The supporters 'almost passed out' from laughing and cheering, he reports: a subtle echo of the Homeric passage where the suitors 'died with laughter' at the sight of Odysseus' defeat of Irus in a boxing match.[62] Over the work as a whole Plato has done more than enough to allow readers to discern that Socrates is not simply at odds with the use of ridicule. He is a figure who deflects its coarse employment by others while simultaneously refining it through irony into part of his own dialectical personality.

But a close reading of Plato might prompt one to go further than this. We ought at any rate to contemplate the hypothesis that Socrates has a probing style of dialectic which could very easily tip over into mockery of adversaries or unsympathetic interlocutors, and that irony serves specifically to keep this inclination in check. Two related considerations, both of them already touched on, lend some support to this hypothesis. The first is that Socrates sometimes reveals, by his retrospective accounts of

[60] The philosopher as laughing-stock (cf. n. 50 above): *Tht.* 172c, 174c (as public speaker: cf. ch. 5, 236), 175b; Thales' fall, 174a. The philosopher's own laughter: *Tht.* 174d (n. 86 below), 175b, d; cf. n. 22 above.

[61] *Euthd.* 300d–e; cf. Ctesippus' laugh at 298e. Ctesippus laughs more brashly than Socrates, but there is a connecting thread between them: cf. Hawtrey (1981) 12–13.

[62] *Od.* 18.100: see ch. 2, 90.

arguments or by the imaginary exchanges with which he extends his discussions, a willingness to go further in the direction of ridicule than he does in face-to-face encounters. We have seen cases of this in his unspoken thoughts on Thrasymachus in the *Republic* and his retrospective narrative of the sophists in *Euthydemus*, both involving less than flattering animal comparisons. Another revealing instance occurs in the passage of *Theaetetus* where he expresses amazement that instead of calling *man* 'the measure of all things' Protagoras did not put 'pig' or 'baboon' in that position (161c): he explains that if Protagoras had done so, 'he would have made clear that while we were admiring him like a god for his wisdom, he was in fact no superior in sagacity to a tadpole!' (161c–d). After this sneer, which might remind us of the use of animal imagery by Heraclitus,[63] Socrates proceeds to surmise that Protagoras did not actually believe his own doctrine; he must have been seeking popular éclat and merely 'playing': if his book *Truth* were itself true, it would turn all philosophy into 'nonsense', *phluaria* (161e–162a), a derisive term found in the mouth of Thrasymachus at *Rep.* 1.336b and underlined by Socrates' use of the cognate verb when imagining an absurd conversation between Thrasymachus and a startled third party (337b). These are evidently thoughts that, if spoken to Protagoras' face ('you are no wiser than a tadpole!'), would be loidoric in force. Later on, in fact, Socrates does imagine Protagoras hearing these comments and rebuking him for 'behaving like a swine' (ὑηνεῖν) in using such language (166c). He asks Socrates to refute his arguments rather than abusing them, thus treating him in just the way that Socrates himself speaks to Polus in the *Gorgias* (286 above). Yet all this, in the *Theaetetus*, comes from Socrates' own mouth in his various narrative modes, leaving us with a strangely confused sense of whether he does or does not approve of *ad hominem* mockery.

The second consideration which encourages us to see the Platonic Socrates as having a kind of (reined in) inclination to ridicule, rather than a sheer aversion to it, is the motif of his *self*-mockery.[64] This motif, *qua* 'internalised' ridicule, was mentioned fleetingly near the end of *Phaedo* (281 above), but it is glimpsed too in several passages where Socrates offers a critique of arguments he has been previously party to. One case is the end of

---

[63] Heraclitus: ch. 7, 347–8. Cf. the proverb 'every pig would know' at Pl. *Lach.* 196d, ps.-Pl. *Amat.* 134a, with 295–6 below on Socratic pig imagery in Xenophon. Germane is Socrates' analogy of 'mindless pleasure' to the life of a jellyfish or oyster, *Phlb.* 21c. For one reading of Socrates' abusive remarks about Protagoras in *Tht.*, see Lee (1973).

[64] *Symp.* 173d–e may hint that some of Socrates' followers learned this trait from him. For one perception of Socratic self-mockery, without reference to any Platonic text, cf. Nietzsche, *Beyond Good and Evil* 191, Nietzsche (1988) v 112.

Charmides, where he delivers an almost scathing verdict on the shortcomings of the preceding search for a definition of self-discipline, *sōphrosunē*. In doing so, he rebukes himself for the failure of the enquiry, calling himself bluntly a 'useless enquirer/searcher' (φαῦλον ζητητήν, 175e6, cf. 175b); he speaks of 'blaming' himself (175a10) and of being 'angry' with himself, especially for the harm he may have done young Charmides (175d–e); and he comes close to personifying the enquiry (*zētēsis*) itself, speaking of it as having 'mocked' the truth (κατεγέλασεν, 175d2) and exposed the inadequacies of the attempted definition in an aggressively taunting manner (ὑβρισ-τικῶς, 175d4). Multiple ironies can be detected in this critique.[65] What matters most for my analysis is the vehement tone of self-mockery adopted by Socrates, who belittles his own failings and depicts the (semi-personified) argument (i.e. his own work) for being itself derisive to the point of *hubris*, as though his intentions throughout had been mischievous and point-scoring.[66] On two simultaneous levels, therefore, Socrates endows himself with the self-image of a scoffer – or, at least, the image of a self-scoffer. Elsewhere too he sometimes projects such an attitude of derision onto a personified argument or an imaginary interlocutor (or both at the same time). We find this in the famous speech of the Laws in *Crito*, where Socrates is disdainfully addressed as a kind of aberrant, ungrateful child, and threatened with the prospect of looking 'contemptibly ridiculous' (*katagelastos*, 53a) if he escapes from the city.[67] We find it also in passages like *Protagoras* 361a, where in thinking back over the whole discussion (as in *Charmides*) he suggests that the argument has turned on himself and Protagoras, 'deriding' them for their inconsistencies. And I noticed earlier how in the *Symposium* Diotima – among much else, an enigmatically allegorised *alter ego* of Socrates – openly laughs at him, taunting him with his dialectical naivety and showing scorn for his failures of understanding.[68]

If the Platonic Socrates, then, scrupulously avoids overt, face-to-face mockery of his interlocutors, this restraint is modified in three important ways. First, and most commonly, by his employment of irony as a form of tacit ridicule, unmistakable in such dialogues as *Euthydemus* (discussed above), *Ion*, *Euthyphro* and *Hippias Major*. Secondly, by an inclination to allow himself a freer rein either in his unspoken thoughts (e.g. about

---

[65] Cf. Fisher (1992) 455 (but correct the nonexistent *katagelazein* to *katagelan*).

[66] Cf. e.g. *Prt.* 355c–d, where Socrates imagines objections from an aggressive mocker, *hubristēs* (a term applied to himself at Pl. *Symp.* 175e, 215b, 221e; cf. n. 86 below).

[67] The Laws' point implicitly answers Crito's earlier contention (45e) that failure to spring Socrates from jail would bring *derision* on Crito and others.

[68] Diotima's laughter, 202b; other gibes: 204b, 207c, 208c, 210a.

Thrasymachus) as retrospectively reported in a framing narrative, or in what he says about *absent* interlocutors (e.g. his parodic 'pig'/'baboon' version of Protagorean relativism in *Theaetetus*). Thirdly, by the venting of (imaginary) mockery towards *himself* or towards the arguments in which he participates. The result of these traits is an inextricable doubleness in his dialectical persona(lity), and a corresponding tension in Plato's perception of the status of laughter in relation to philosophical argument. Socrates is represented as a figure who has no truck with the purely agonistic use of laughter exhibited by, for instance, the sophists and their supporters in *Euthydemus*, even though it is a symptom of his complex persona that *others* can sometimes accuse him of simply 'wanting to win (the argument)', *philonikein*.[69] Such negative ridicule has nothing to do with either seeking the truth or engaging in rational refutation of one's opponents. Moreover, Socrates is emphatic that a cultivated person would never allow himself to be abusive towards a well-intentioned if inexperienced interlocutor.[70] At the same time, however, he permits himself not only to taunt certain opponents with his vein of irony, but also to turn a capacity for mockery against himself. He also occasionally acknowledges that his style of debate might give the impression of being 'rude' or abusive.[71] The genuinely if paradoxically Socratic rationale for his partial resort to 'tacit' ridicule can only reside in the need to target it against those who merit it through their dialectical arrogance or self-ignorance – which piquantly includes himself (in his own eyes, at any rate).

A final passage which bears out the hypothesis I have proposed is the portrait of the anonymous disputant in *Hippias Major*, a work whose authenticity I cautiously accept but whose relevance to my case would still be of great interest even if its authorship were not Platonic. The status of the disputant has been variously interpreted, but most scholars accept that the figure is an (ironic) *alter ego* for Socrates himself, as signalled more or less inescapably by the name of Socrates' father Sophroniscus at 298b–c.[72] What I want to stress here is how the persona of the disputant, introduced at 286c, tallies with my broader thesis of Socratic ambiguity in relation to ridicule. Socrates invites Hippias to address the subject of what is 'beautiful' or 'admirable' (*kalos*) by claiming that he himself was

---

[69] See esp. *Prt.* 360e, *Grg.* 515b5 (in pointed contradiction of Socrates' self-image at 457c–458b).

[70] See esp. *Hp. Min.* 364c–d, *Phdr.* 268a–269c, distinguishing 'mild' courtesy from scoffing rudeness (the verb *katagelan* is in both passages).

[71] See e.g. *Phdr.* 260d (*agroikos, loidorein*), *Rep.* 10.607b (*agroikia*); cf. n. 127 below.

[72] See e.g. Tarrant (1928) 44, Woodruff (1982) 43–4, 107–8, Tarrant (1994) 110–13. It is unsafe, with Tarrant (1927) 83–4, to make the strangeness of the anonymous disputant an argument against Platonic authorship.

recently challenged insultingly or offensively (*hubristikōs*) on the subject ('How do *you* know what is beautiful or foul . . .?'), and was 'thrown into perplexity', by an interlocutor. The experience left him 'angry'; he is determined to learn the nature of true beauty from someone 'wise' like Hippias, so that he can go and fight back against his opponent. He asks Hippias to help him avoid 'incurring ridicule' (γέλωτα ὄφλω) a second time (286e); and when Hippias expresses total confidence that he can provide enlightenment, Socrates, in a theatrical metaphor, undertakes to 'play the part' (*mimeisthai*, 287a3, cf. 292c) of the disputant himself in the present conversation.[73]

On the *alter ego* reading, which the theatrical trope of 287a pointedly legitimises, the complex irony of the scenario is arresting. Socrates, having convicted himself (fictionally) of ignorance and confusion, exposes Hippias to the same fate without the latter's recognition or self-knowledge that this is what is happening. In terms of laughter, there is a salient paradox. Socrates *internalises* mockery in facing up to his own perplexity, but he translates that mockery into ironic admiration of the sophist Hippias. As a result, Socrates' position *vis-à-vis* ridicule is intrinsically and even disturbingly double-sided: he knows how to use it openly against 'himself' (thereby expressing the unsparing candour of his self-knowledge) yet also how to disguise it (thereby directing it, conditionally, against the self-ignorance of the other). As the discussion with Hippias unfolds, it becomes abundantly clear that the anonymous disputant or *alter ego* is to be thought of as having a strong penchant for mockery. Socrates imagines him laughing directly at one reply of Hippias' (289c), subsequently as resorting to blunt vituperation (*tōthazein*) by calling Socrates (who, of course, is playing the same role *vis-à-vis* Hippias) 'you demented fool!' (ὦ τετυφωμένε σύ, 290a),[74] at a later juncture still as being likely to 'deride us now most of all' (πλεῖστον καταγελάσεται, 291e), as well as calling other arguments advanced by Socrates/Hippias 'ridiculous' (293c, 297d). To underline the issue, Hippias is presented as thinking that the other's laughter will convict the disputant himself of being absurd and laughable (288b, 290a, 291e–292a). But the double position of Socrates, as both victim and role-playing surrogate of the disputant, steers the dramatic movement of the dialogue towards the unmistakable conclusion that it is Hippias, blind to the shortcomings of his own understanding, who badly needs the (self-)

---

[73] On mimesis as theatrical impersonation see Halliwell (2002b) 51–3 (with 51 n. 35).

[74] For a connection between *tōthazein* (elsewhere in Plato only at *Rep.* 5.474a) and the vocative at 290a, compare Ar. *Wasps* 1362–4, with ch. 4, 208–9; the vocative (cf. Halliwell (1995) 113) may be particularly apt for an old man: cf. Ar. *Clouds* 908, *Lys.* 336, with Taillardat (1965) 262–3.

ridicule which Socrates intimates that he practises on himself. The reader is invited to share vicariously in the laughter of the anonymous disputant, but at the same time to appreciate how it is redirected against Hippias not Socrates.

I have tried to outline a case, then, for reading the Platonic Socrates as an ambiguous, double-sided figure where laughter is concerned. It is probable, moreover, that this ambiguity was part of Plato's conscious response to a larger, ongoing contest for the memory and posthumous image of the man himself. It is worth stepping back now from Plato for a moment to catch the echoes of that wider debate. There is evidence to suggest that Socrates was perceived in some quarters as decidedly given to mockery, insult and abuse, even to verbal *hubris*. Others were keen to defend him against such imputations. Even in his own lifetime, Socrates had lent himself to caricature on the comic stage, and while his treatment in *Clouds* is notoriously distorted by a jumble of intellectual characteristics, his deportment of mocking *hauteur* in that play takes on a curious resonance when set against the features I have drawn attention to in his Platonic persona.[75] In the generation after Socrates' death, the wholly admiring depiction of him put together in Xenophon's *Memorabilia* includes traces of more than one kind of gelastic impulse, as does the same author's *Symposium*, which I examined in the final section of Chapter 3 for its portrait of an inveterately serio-comic disposition. Early in the *Memorabilia*, Xenophon illustrates Socrates' willingness to criticise his companions. He relates how, after failing to discourage Critias' obsessive love of young Euthydemus (a different figure from the eponymous sophist of Plato's dialogue) with the remark that lovers should not act like beggars (itself a sarcastic comparison for the conduct of an aristocrat), he made a point of observing in front of many, including Euthydemus himself, that Critias' desires were 'swinish', since he wanted to 'rub himself' against Euthydemus in the way that pigs 'rub themselves against stones'.[76] Is it just coincidence that one of the most striking gestures of Socratic derision in Plato, his gibe at (the absent) Protagoras at *Tht.* 161c (291 above), also uses an image of pigs? Perhaps, but curiosity is increased only a few pages later in Xenophon's *Memorabilia*. Here the statement that Socrates cultivated a manner of 'earnest playfulness'

---

[75] Ar. *Clouds*: for mocking *hauteur* see 362–3 (cf. *Frogs* 1491–9), with derision of Strepsiades at e.g. 492, 646, 783 ('you're talking rubbish', ὑθλεῖς; cf. Thrasymachus at Pl. *Rep.* 1.336d, cited on 286). For stereotypes of philosophical *hauteur*, cf. n. 29 above. On Socrates' response to *Clouds* in Pl. *Apol.*, see ch. 5, 254–5.

[76] Xen. *Mem.* 1.2.30. On the prosopography of different Euthydemuses in Plato and Xenophon, see Nails (2002) 151; for Critias (IV), *ibid.* 108–11.

or 'playful seriousness' (ἔπαιζεν ἅμα σπουδάζων),[77] which is perhaps a partial formulation of irony (Xenophon nowhere applies *eirōn* itself or its cognates to Socrates), is linked to a vignette in which the philosopher underscores his disciplined abstemiousness over food and drink by suggesting, like an allegorising literary critic, that Circe turned Odysseus' companions into swine by tempting them into over-consumption. Unlike the Critias story, which is notable for depicting Socrates as prepared to target explicit mockery against an individual in front of friends and associates, the playful allegorising of the Circe episode in the *Odyssey* looks lighthearted in its immediate context. But even here it does not take much imagination to see the potential for abuse of others as, again, 'swinish'.

Of further passages in the *Memorabilia* which lend credibility to the notion of a gelastically inclined Socrates, I single out one in Book 4 which presents him as a figure prepared to resort to outright ridicule. As it happens, the object here is none other than the young Euthydemus of the earlier Critias anecdote. This time, we are shown how Socrates seeks out Euthydemus on several occasions, to interrogate and goad him about his intellectual pretensions. When the young man proves stand-offish, Socrates sets him up for blatantly satirical treatment in front of a group of hearers, who duly oblige by breaking into a chorus of laughter – just the kind of scenario characteristic of the sophists in Plato's *Euthydemus*. Though Xenophon wants us to believe (as the sequel bears out) that Socrates only has Euthydemus' best interests at heart, he has no qualms about showing Socrates availing himself of the social power of humiliating laughter.[78] Whatever the historicity or otherwise of such passages from the *Memorabilia*, their presence in the work confirms that there was anecdotal material in circulation which could have been seized on by those who wanted to give a less admiring account of Socrates' character. Later in the fourth century a specific accusation of derisive habits was taken up and exploited by Aristoxenus to blacken the image of Socrates. Aristoxenus is said to have called him antagonistic, abusive (*loidoros*) and offensively insulting (*hubristikos*). These are strong terms, and they are all the more trenchant coming from a person who, as was mentioned earlier, seems to have had a wider interest in the social uses of laughter but who was also himself not averse to mockery of earlier thinkers.[79] But my concern here is not to disentangle

---

[77] *Mem.* 1.3.8. Cf. *ibid.* 4.1.1–2, where the ideas of a playful/serious Socrates are juxtaposed slightly differently; see ch. 3, 140–1.
[78] The initial cornering and mockery of Euthydemus is at Xen. *Mem.* 4.2.1–5.
[79] Aristoxenus' character assassination of Socrates: fr. 54b Wehrli (where Socrates is also said to have laughed at the quarrels of his two wives). Ironically, Aristoxenus himself is said to have been offensively

the various strands in Aristoxenus' own position (and reputation), only to adduce his comment on Socrates as a testimony to one end of the spectrum of views of the philosopher which existed in the fourth century. Putting together the admiring yet revealing anecdotes of Xenophon with the severe verdict of Aristoxenus, we can get some sense of the vigorous debate about Socrates' gelastic tendencies (purely playful? mocking but well intentioned? deliberately wounding?) which developed over the generations after his death.

Another echo of that debate can be heard in an intriguing anecdote preserved by Aristotle in the *Rhetoric*. This describes an incident where Aristippus, one of Socrates' closest followers, rebuked Plato for some kind of dialectical arrogance or abrasive provocation: 'our companion [i.e. Socrates] never spoke like that', was Aristippus' put-down.[80] Though no other details are spelt out (how one would like to know what Plato was supposed to have said), the story indicates that some early Socratic circles denied that the master had any trace of aggression or offensiveness. But did Plato himself believe otherwise? Certainly, Plato was not the only disciple of Socrates open to imputations of overstepping the mark of dialectical restraint. Aeschines of Sphettus and Antisthenes both appear to have had inclinations (or to have been vulnerable to accusations) of that sort.[81] Could the difference, if it really existed, between the personalities and philosophical manners of, say, Aristippus and Aeschines have been partly a reflection of different perceptions and interpretations of the spirit in which Socrates himself conducted conversation and argument? The question is too large to be pursued in its own right here. But it is worth adding it to the other evidence I have offered for a conflict of fourth-century views about whether, or how far, Socrates had sanctioned the use of laughter or derision in philosophy. All in all, there are good grounds for believing that a dispute about Socrates' relationship to laughter came into being soon after his death if not during his lifetime. Furthermore, the stuff of this dispute was to remain part of the Socratic

derogatory (*hubrizein*) about Aristotle after the latter's death: *Suda s.v.* Ἀριστόξενος (= Aristox. fr. 1 Wehrli). As for his attitude to Plato, Riginos (1976) 167 is right to dubb him 'malicious'. For Aristoxenus' interests in laughter, see 267–8, 274–5 above.

[80] Arist. *Rhet.* 2.23, 1398b30–3; see Riginos (1976) 102, 108, with n. 129 below, cf. Antisthenes on Plato's conceitedness at Diog. Laert. 6.7 (Antisth. fr. 151 Decleva Caizzi). For Socrates as 'our companion', recall the poignant final sentence of Pl. *Phd.*

[81] Traces of Aeschines' mocking tendencies: frs. 40–2, 44, 46 Dittmar (VI A 83–5, 87, 89 *SSR*); the last involves quasi-ironic ambiguity. Antisthenes was sometimes regarded as a (proto-)Cynic 'dog', perhaps partly on grounds of a mocking tone (see ch. 7 n. 101); note his 'acrid' manner at Diog. Laert. 6.4, cf. Rankin (1986) 179–88. Theopomp. *FGrH* 115 F295, *apud* Diog. Laert. 6.14, describes him as urbane company (for the adj. *emmelēs* see n. 121 below); but cf. Flower (1994) 96–7 for caution. Xen. *Symp.* gives a mixed portrait but hints at possible abrasiveness: see ch. 3, 146–7, 150.

legacy. In the third century, for example, Timon of Phlius, writer of philosophical lampoons (*silloi*) in a parodic Homeric style, described Socrates as 'a snooty sneerer, with an orator's snoot, and an ironist of sub-Attic wit'.[82] Timon had his reasons for disparaging many different philosophers, but this is the only case in which he sets up the target as himself a practitioner of derision (by implication, both overt *and* covert). In the mid-first century, Zeno of Sidon called Socrates, in Latin, an 'Attic buffoon' (*scurra Atticus*). Zeno may have been indulging his own Epicurean penchant for ridicule, but he was also surely reflecting a long-lasting awareness of the strangely semi-comic reputation of the philosopher.[83] Seneca the younger went so far as to call Socrates 'a mocker of everyone' (*derisor omnium*), though he clearly understood the trait as ethically motivated.[84] It is beyond my scope to follow this theme through all our later sources, but it is worth registering that even on the level of legend (which is what most subsequent anecdotes about Socrates amount to) a tension between positive and negative conceptions of the philosopher's stance towards laughter continues to surface. Thus Aelian is happy to relate, in one place, how Socrates was so moralistically averse to mockery that he never went to see comedies (but was lured into doing so by his friends), while in another he claims that Socrates himself was actually amused by his ridicule on the comic stage. And the latter attitude is fleshed out in an anecdote found in pseudo-Plutarch that *Clouds* itself was taken by Socrates in the spirit of good-natured banter, 'as if at a big symposium'.[85]

To return to Plato, we can now see in a broader perspective that whatever his own temperament may have been (recall the Aristippus story, 297 above), his writings subtly acknowledge the contested and contestable nature of Socrates' disposition towards the uses of laughter. In the *Apology*, he allows Socrates to concede not only that many of his young followers specifically enjoyed hearing sciolistic individuals exposed to irreverent interrogation (and subsequently emulated this practice themselves), but that such an experience *is* indeed enjoyable. Various passages in the dialogues, as we saw earlier, follow (and complicate) the ramifications of

[82] μυκτὴρ ῥητορόμυκτος, ὑπαττικὸς εἰρωνευτής: Timon fr. 25.3 Diels/di Marco (= 799.3 *SH*), with di Marco (1989) 168–71 for detailed interpretation. On μυκτήρ, 'nostril' = sneerer, cf. Appendix 1 n. 14; the term is applied to Socrates himself (as represented in Plato, n.b.) in anon. *Anth. Pal.* 9.188.5. On the genre of *silloi*, cf. n. 13 above.

[83] 'Attic buffoon', Cic. *Nat. D.* 1.93: the point extends beyond irony; Pease (1955) 455 rightly surmises that Latin *scurra* is equivalent to *gelōtopoios* (or even *bōmolochos*). On Epicurean derision, see ch. 7, 358–9.

[84] *Benef.* 5.6.6.

[85] Contrasting images of Socrates' response to comic satire: Ael. *VH* 2.13, 5.8, ps.-Plut. *Lib. educ.* 10d (cf. ch. 3 n. 35).

such an expectation of intellectual mockery from more than one dramatic angle.[86] Socrates himself is often the butt of an arrogantly scoffing sophistic laughter, to which he never responds with explicit laughter of his own. But I have argued that his 'inside' knowledge of the philosophical value of ridicule reveals itself both through hints at how he turns the (imaginary) mockery of self-scrutiny against himself, and in his deft exposure of the self-ignorance of others to ironically veiled, understated or tacit mockery. This double-sided character is in keeping with the elusiveness of Socrates, his demeanour as a figure whom others suspect of various kinds of 'play' and dissimulation, but who always professes whole-hearted commitment to the quest for truth. The tension between overt and hidden laughter is a powerful expression of the inscrutability that others find in this figure. But it also seems related to the difference between employing laughter as a merely social statement of superiority, and subordinating it to a truth-testing exploration of the most urgent questions of ethical value. Plato's treatment of these themes across his *oeuvre*, a treatment whose layers I have probed only selectively, confronts us with an irreducibly 'serio-comic' Socrates: a man who takes the pursuit of philosophy with indefatigable seriousness, yet who never seems very far from humorous self-deprecation (even when discussing the transcendent form of 'the good');[87] a person who can emphatically put crude laughter in its place ('Are you laughing, Polus? Is this an alternative form of refutation . . .?', 286 above) and yet who is capable, as the *Phaedo* demonstrates, of laughing quietly with his friends not only in the face of, but actually *about*, death. No wonder, then, that in Alcibiades' famous speech in the *Symposium* the image of Socrates as someone with hidden depths, an inside that his (playful) exterior belies, is linked to his status as a sort of Silenus, a figure who was simultaneously the quintessence of satyric absurdity but also (according to legend) the carrier of a deep (if, unlike Socrates, a pessimistic) insight into the nature of life.[88]

---

[86] The pleasure of witnessing Socrates' interrogations: *Ap.* 23c, 33c (Socrates concedes the point; cf. *Rep.* 7.539b for related behaviour as 'play'); significantly, Plato is among those in question (*Ap.* 34a). Cf. Burckhardt (1977) II 337, Burckhardt (1998) 77. But Gottlieb (1992) ties Socratic irony too tightly to the presence of an 'in-crowd'; sometimes (e.g. *Euphr.*, *Hp. Maj.*, *Ion*) only the interlocutor is present. The idea of Socrates as (covertly) insulting is directly picked up at e.g. Pl. *Grg.* 522b, *Meno* 94e; cf. n. 66 above (*hubristēs*); note that the (Socrates-like) true philosopher at *Tht.* 174d is *seen* mocking others (cf. n. 60 above). Rossetti (2000) offers one reading of Socratic interrogation as resorting to aggressive ridicule.

[87] At the climactic passage, *Rep.* 6.509c, Glaucon's exclamation at Socrates' metaphysical language is described by the adverb γελοίως, here active ('humorously', not 'laughably'); Socrates' rejoinder is itself semi-playful ('it's *your* fault for making me say this . . .'). For other aspects of Socrates serio-comic status, see Blondell (2002) 70–3.

[88] *Symp.* 215a–b, 216c, 221d–e (compare the joke at Xen. *Symp.* 5.7); cf. the language of *hubris* in two of these passages, with n. 66 above. For Silenus' notorious pronouncement ('best never to

And yet Alcibiades' own speech is an inebriated, unintentionally 'comic' performance, which Socrates describes as *itself* 'a satyr-play' in the manner of Silenus![89] The hermeneutic loop which Plato's text creates on this point intensifies the mysterious relationship between exterior and interior, the playful and the serious, in the nature of Socrates and in others' perceptions of him.

Where, one might finally wonder, does all this leave the Platonic Socrates with regard to the discussions of the psychology of laughter in *Philebus*, *Republic* and *Laws* which are standardly used to construct an account of Plato's own supposed view, even 'theory', of laughter? At *Philebus* 48a–50b, where the subject is described as 'murky' (σκοτεινόν), Socrates argues that the pleasure of watching comedy (or, by extension, observing ludicrously deluded people in life, indeed in 'the entire tragedy and comedy of life', 50b) is actually a mixed pleasure-and-pain, fusing spite or resentment (*phthonos*) towards self-ignorant but weak characters with enjoyment of the (harmless) mishaps produced by their folly. The characters in question, however, are reckoned to fall within the category of 'friends' (*philoi*), at least in the minimal sense that they are not enemies and perhaps also in the sense that one recognises a degree of attraction to them.[90] In *Republic* 3 (388e–389a), on the other hand, Socrates holds 'strong' laughter, as we saw earlier, to be a dangerous psychic turbulence, unworthy of Guardians-to-be (let alone Olympian gods), while in Book 10 (606c) he expresses concern about the way in which theatrical comedy (or private joking) can lure people into abandoning their normal standards of shame and distaste for buffoonery (*bōmolochia*) and allowing the pleasure-seeking part of their soul to gratify itself vicariously in the indecent gelotopoeic antics of the stage figures.[91] Differently again, in the *Laws* we find both the explicit principle that the serious cannot be understood without a grasp of the ridiculous or laughable,

---

have been born'), see ch. 7, 339–40. That Socrates himself is no pessimist adds to the piquancy of Alcibiades' Silenus analogy without detracting from its strange aptness. For the later history of the Socrates–Silenus motif, cf. Nehamas (1998) 109–11.

[89] *Symp.* 222d.

[90] Laughter-inducing *phthonos* towards 'friends': *Phlb.* 49e–50a, where Taylor (1956) 170 wilfully turns laughter into smiling. For analyses of the passage see Mader (1977), esp. 13–23, Delcomminette (2006) 440–8 (struggling to understand *phthonos* as envy), Frede (1997) 285–93, (1993) lii–iii; Frede (1993) 56 wrongly introduces 'laughter' (for χαίρειν, 'enjoy') into experience of tragedy at *Phlb.* 48a (Wagner (1981) 79 misconstrues *Phlb.* 50b to similar effect). Self-ignorance recurs as a condition of the comic in Bergson (1975) 13, translated in Sypher (1980) 71. For a brief 'application' of the *Phlb.* formula to a Menandrian character, see ch. 8, 395–7.

[91] The *vicarious* quality of the pleasure involved here, unlike the 'malicious' *phthonos* of *Phlb.* 48–50, is implied by Socrates' analogy with experience of tragedy (606c), where that dimension was unmistakable (606a–b): see Halliwell (2002b) 77–83, 112–14; cf. ch. 5, 255–6.

and also a passage which dwells on the difference between laughter driven by, and laughter free of, animus (*thumos*).[92]

No simple conception of laughter emerges from this set of passages, which cannot in any case be automatically treated as pieces of a single construction (let alone 'theory'). For example, the connection between laughter and *phthonos* in the *Philebus* does not recur in any other Platonic text, though it undoubtedly picks up associations already circulating in the culture.[93] That connection posits a kind of mild *Schadenfreude* (at comically deluded characters) that is a separate matter from the psychological complicity with comic buffoonery and vulgarity on which the *Republic* 10 passage focuses. There is no contradiction here but a concentration on different aspects of comedy/laughter in different contexts, though the notion of comic characters as 'friends' in the *Philebus* perhaps points towards a sense, not wholly unlike the emphasis of *Republic* 606c, that at some level we are (partly) 'on their side', at least for the duration of the play. Equally, Socrates' statement in *Republic* 3 about the need for young Guardians to avoid 'love of laughter' follows hard on the heels of an assertion that Homeric displays of divine grief such as Zeus's for Sarpedon would harm the young if they took them seriously 'and did not deride them (*katagelan*) as unworthily spoken' (388d). Ideally, in other words, the young Guardians would know how to use ridicule against targets that deserved their scorn, but would avoid gratuitous, addictive laughter in their own behaviour. The desire to 'play the fool' and make others laugh is apparently present in every soul (*Rep.* 10.606c); if given full scope, it will ultimately turn one, like Thersites (on the point of reincarnation), not only into a buffoon but into an 'ape' (*pithēkos*), a ludicrous distortion of the human.[94] Yet, as we saw, one of the supreme paradoxes of Socrates' final hours in the *Phaedo*

---

92 *Laws* 7.816d–e, 11.934e–936a; on the latter cf. ch. 1, 24–5, with n. 95 below for another passage from *Laws*. Cf. Jouët-Pastré (2006) 83–96.

93 If one feels *phthonos* (resentment/spite) at someone's success, one will laugh at their undoing: Lys. 3.9, Arist. *Rhet.* 2.9, 1387a1–3; cf. Alexis fr. 52. Ar. *Thesm.* 146, Dem. 9.54 connect *phthonos* with *ad hominem* ridicule; cf. the Syracusan's *phthonos* towards Socrates at Xen. *Symp.* 6.6 (ch. 3, 152–3). Hubbard (1991) 3 actually translates *phthonos* (in *Phlb.*) as 'derision'; Nagy (1999) 223–32 analyses an older association between *phthonos* and mockery. Without using the term, *Phlb.* evokes notions of ἐπιχαιρεκακία (enjoying others' misfortunes, i.e. *Schadenfreude*); see 49d–50a for all its ingredients, with e.g. Soph. *Aj.* 961, Arist. *EN* 2.8, 1108b1–6, *Rhet.* 2.9, 1386b34–1387a3. Pl. *Euphr.* 3c (picked up by Socrates at 3d) implies a possible link between mockery (in the Athenian Assembly) and *phthonos*, but the latter here seems broader than in *Phlb.* Much later, Ael. Arist. *Orat.* 29.5 Keil (40.506 Dindorf) discerns *phthonos* in Dionysiac festive mockery, including comedy. See wider perspectives on *phthonos* in Konstan and Rutter (2003), Konstan (2006) 111–28, with Dunbabin and Dickie (1983) on visual depictions.

94 *Rep.* 10.620c. Apes and monkeys (but not anthropoid/great apes), sometimes kept as pets (e.g. Theophr. *Char.* 9.5, Plut. *Mor.* 64e, with Diggle (2004) 238–9), could be thought comically quasi-human: Heraclitus frs. 82–3 DK (with ch. 7, 348), Anacharsis A11a Kindstrand (1981), *apud* Athen.

is that he is able, even in the face of death, to make jokes with his closest friends and share laughter with them.

Those are just token examples of important variations on the theme of laughter in Plato's writings. There is, in short, no unqualified deprecation of laughter *per se* to be found anywhere in the Platonic dialogues. The psychological, social and ethical significance of *gelōs* is always evaluated according to cause and context.[95] The discussion of laughter and comedy as topics in their own right in *Philebus*, *Republic* and *Laws* has not been at the centre of my concerns in this section; nor have I returned to the *Apology*'s references to the satire of Socrates in Old Comedy, references which continue, as I suggested in Chapter 5, to be reductively read and misconstrued in much modern scholarship.[96] But the brief pointers given above are entirely compatible with the main task I have undertaken, which was to demonstrate that an intense Platonic awareness of the complexities of laughter can be traced in his depiction of the enigmatically ironic and gelastically doublesided character of Socrates. Trying to imagine (and interpret) laughter on the face, in the voice, but also, ultimately, inside the soul of Socrates is part of the challenge which Plato issues to readers of the dialogues in creating the profound riddle of his philosophical Silenus.

STOIC COMPROMISES: LAUGHING AT SELF AND OTHERS

Plato is the only ancient philosopher whose perceptions of laughter are extensively woven into a texture of dialogue, making it impossible to comprehend them except by following all the intricate threads of their dramatic treatment in the conduct, attitudes and interactions, as well as the direct utterances, of the characters involved. But the ethics and psychology of laughter were of interest to many other Greek philosophers from the archaic to the imperial period. The positions they occupied on the subject ranged all the way from the categorical antigelasticism of at least some

---

14.613d (interesting contrast with jesters), Arist. *Top.* 3.2, 117b17–18 (cf. *Hist. An.* 2.8, 502a16–b26), Posidon. fr. 245 Edelstein–Kidd, Galen, *Usu part.* 1.22 (1.58–9 Helmreich, 3.79–81 Kühn), 3.16 (1.194 Helmreich, 3.264–5 Kühn), with McDermott (1938) 93–100, Lloyd (1987) 325 for more on Galen and apes. Hence tropes of humans as apes/monkeys: e.g. Semonides' 'monkey-woman' (7.71–82 *IEG*: ch. 1, 31), politicians (Ar. *Frogs* 1085: ch. 5, 230), Aeschines as 'ape' of (ironically) a *tragic* actor (Dem. 18.242). See McDermott (1938) 109–46, Lilja (1980); cf. ch. 1 n. 7. *Pace* Adam (1963) 11 460, Untersteiner (1966) 322, the ape at Pl. *Rep.* 10.620c differs from the symbol of fawning servility at *Rep.* 9.590b: it purports to match Thersites' absurdity and ugliness.

95 So the late-Platonist classification of *gelōs* as intrinsically immoderate at Alcin. *Didasc.* 32.4 is not authentically Platonic, *pace* Dillon (1993) 196–7. Moderate laughter is advocated at *Laws* 5.732c (n. 21 above).

96 See ch. 5, 254–5.

Pythagoreans, as documented earlier in the chapter, to the robust willing-ness of Cynics, Epicureans and others (to be considered in the next chapter) to harness the power of laughter to their own philosophical agenda, not least the belittlement of their opponents. In between these extremes lay the possibility of a more measured attitude that saw laughter as an expressive impulse calling for control and moderation but not its expungement from personal or social behaviour.

This 'compromise' with laughter could take more than one form. Of note here is the position of Stoicism, which was more complex than the agelastic severity that some critics, understandably but erroneously, have ascribed to the school.[97] While doctrinally averse to most 'normal' emotion (especially the four passions of desire, fear, pleasure and pain), as well as to the false values underlying many bodily and social pleasures, an orthodox Stoic could still accept the right sorts of laughter both as a legitimate expression of the sage's cheerfulness and contentment, and as an appropriate component in the philosopher's dealings with others. Take Epictetus. Partly following the lead of Plato *Republic* 10.606c (300 above), he deplores the rousing of laughter by vulgar joking and 'obscenity' (*aischrologia*), the latter, however, a concept which, as we shall shortly see, not all Stoics regarded in the same way. He also disapproves of joining in the laughter of crowds in the theatre. In addition, he is perpetually aware that Stoicism itself is a common target of scurrility, though he supposes that such things cannot harm the good man, who should listen to them 'as if he were a stone'.[98] So far then, it seems, everything here belongs to an agelastic bent. Nonetheless, Epictetus can also articulate the following thought. 'Suppose I must go into exile: well, surely no one can stop me from going with laughter and tranquillity and ease of mind?'[99] Whether or not we think of this euthumic laughter (which should not be toned down into 'smiling') as literal or metaphorical,

---

[97] Joubert (1980) 101 provides a Renaissance instance: 'those who are reduced to the apathy of the Stoics, empty of all joy, are in no way tempted by laughable things'. Stoic attitudes to laughter are more complex than one would gather from Arnould (1990) 262–3, citing just one element in Epictetus' position; for a much richer account, see Nussbaum (forthcoming). A (superficial) Stoic like Aelian may occasionally approve agelastic habits (*VH* 3.35: n. 29 above), but he also endorses laughter on ethical grounds (*VH* 12.6 ~ 14.36) and shares jokes with his readers (*ibid.* 4.20).

[98] Disapproval of joking/obscenity: Epict. *Ench.* 33.15–16 (cf. a Christian equivalent at Clem. *Paed.* 2.6.49); for a different Stoic view of obscenity, see n. 105 below. Avoidance of laughter in the theatre: *Ench.* 33.10. (Different is the metaphorical theatre of life, where the good Stoic must be able to play tragic/comic roles: *Diss.* 1.29.42; cf. Long (2002) 242–3.) Popular derision of (Stoic) philosophers: *Diss.* 1.11.39, 1.22.18, 2.14.29, 3.15.11 (= *Ench.* 29.6), 3.20.18–19, *Ench.* 22; listen to mockery 'like a stone', *Diss.* 1.25.29, cf. *Ench.* 20. For other Stoic thoughts on not reacting to mockery, see Cleanth. *SVF* I 463, 599, 603, *apud* Diog. Laert. 7.170, 173, and Mus. Ruf. *Diss.* 10 (n. 104 below).

[99] γελῶντα καὶ εὐθυμοῦντα καὶ εὐροοῦντα: *Diss.* 1.1.22. Why tone down 'laugh' to 'smile', e.g. Long (2002) 63?

it is clear that the Stoic can adapt gelastic imagery to his own psychological model of virtue. In a certain frame of mind, the Roman Stoic Seneca the younger could even align himself with the pseudo-Democritean idea that the philosopher might appropriately laugh at *everything* in life, i.e. at the near-universality of human folly and delusion. In the Stoic's case, however, given his faith in the rational order of the cosmos, such dismissiveness towards life could never imply full-blown existentialist absurdity.[100]

That there is no intrinsically Stoic aversion to laughter can be discerned more concretely from three facets of Epictetus' thinking: first, the idea that a laughter of carefree dismissiveness (like that of the inhabitants of an impregnable city looking down on a besieging army) is the right Stoic response to one's enemies; secondly, the need he feels to caution (would-be) Stoics not to give way *too* readily to ridicule of the shortcomings of others; and, finally, the Socratically coloured precept that aspirant philosophers should ridicule *themselves* as part of the process of self-improvement.[101] Both internally and externally, Stoic laughter is to be brought into conformity with the ethical shaping of the self, but for Epictetus, at any rate, it is evidently to be *practised* in every sense of the word. Although the full ramifications of this point in Epictetus' writing cannot be pursued here, it may be worth proposing that details such as his use of derisive vocatives (μῶρε, 'you fool!', or, more racily, σαννίων, 'you clown!') when addressing imaginary interlocutors[102] should not only be taken as a reflection of the traditions of vivid 'diatribe' or face-to-face moral preaching, and certainly not as an unthinking endorsement of aggressive insults. It can also be construed as a subtle extension of *self*-ridicule, since throughout Epictetus' ethical reflections 'the other' is a kind of weaker self. There are connections here, albeit partly submerged, with the gelastic ambiguities and complexities which I tried to tease out of Plato's depiction of Socrates, and which I also suggested became part of the later heritage of Socratic philosophy.

Unlike Pythagoreans, Stoics had no reason to censure laughter simply on the grounds of its somatic nature. For what it's worth, there was even a story that Chrysippus had died during a burst of exceptionally hearty

---

[100] Sen. *De ira* 2.10.5, *Tranq.* 15.2–3, with ch. 7, 369.

[101] Carefree laughter, *Diss.* 4.5.24–5; caution against mockery, 1.26.12–13, 2.12.2–4, 4.4.7; self-ridicule, 4.4.20. See Diog. Laert. 7.171 (*SVF* I 602) for Cleanthes practising the last principle. Musonius Rufus, quoted by Origen, *Fragm. in Ps.* 118.161–2 (cf. Kilpatrick (1949)), also advocates the Stoic value of self-mockery; cf. 291–5 above for Socratic precedents. For a problematic case of self-ridicule, see ch. 7, 359–65; a contested case, ch. 1, 43. Skinner (2002) 164 misleadingly excludes laughing at oneself from ancient attitudes; but one voice that spoke against it was Quintil. *Inst. Or.* 6.3.82.

[102] See *Diss.* 2.16.13, 3.13.17, 3. 23.17, 4.10.33, 3.22.83 (σαννίων: on this term cf. Chantraine (1968) 984, *s.v.* σαίνω).

laughter provoked by a rather innocent little joke of his own.[103] This is legend, of course, whereas in the more reliably attested realms of doctrine we encounter a view, probably stemming from Chrysippus himself, which deprecates (as base or vulgar) both 'irony' and 'sarcasm' (σαρκάζειν), defining the latter as 'irony accompanied by an element of raillery' (ἐπισυρμός). And equally, if from a reverse angle so to speak, the Roman Stoic Musonius Rufus preached that the philosopher should himself attach no importance to the supposedly hubristic force of social derision (or even of physical violence), since he should know that such matters could not truly harm or shame him (though they were shameful for the *agent*).[104] Yet even a minimal distinction between kinds or uses of laughter is sufficient to block the inference that such attitudes bespeak a wholly antigelastic stance. As it happens, we know from a passing analogy in one of his treatises that Chrysippus was appreciative of comic drama, and untroubled even by some of its lapses into crudity. Furthermore, he himself was said to have used grossly foul language in his own treatises, which, if true, may reflect an early Stoic (and Cynic) principle that there was actually no such thing as 'obscenity' – a principle, as we have seen, that a later Stoic like Epictetus did not share.[105] Rather differently, the evidence of Cicero's *De officiis* makes it likely that Panaetius of Rhodes, leader of the Stoic school in the second century, made room in his ethical teaching (the main source of Cicero's arguments in this work) for a dichotomy between two types of laughter and joking, one crude and indecent, the other witty and refined. Panaetius' views appear to have had an Aristotelian streak to them, including a denial that human life could be properly conceived of, or reduced to, a matter of lighthearted 'play'. Like Aristotle (as we shall shortly see), Panaetius subordinated play to the serious priorities of life, but he wanted to integrate not eliminate the former. His distinction between decent and indecent styles of joking, which may have been accompanied (again in Aristotelian fashion) by a parallel with different styles of theatrical comedy, was meant to define an appropriate place for laughter – a sort of 'off duty' mode for virtue, channelled into sophisticated recreation with likeminded company – in the life of the

---

[103] Diog. Laert. 7.185: the philosopher jokes about offering wine to an ass. Other deaths from laughter: ch. 1 n. 21.

[104] The vulgarity of sarcasm: Chrysip. *SVF* III 630, *apud* Stob. 2.108.5; for the verb σαρκάζειν, cf. Appendix 1 n. 34. Musonius' insouciance about hubristic laughter: *Diss.* 10 (with the verbs ἐπεγγελᾶν, καταγελᾶν, λοιδορεῖν); cf. n. 101 above for Musonius on *self*-mockery.

[105] Chrysip. *SVF* II 1181, *apud* Plut. *Mor.* 1065d, mentions 'crude jokes' (γελοῖα . . . φαῦλα, denoting indecency of some kind) which nonetheless add charm or wit (*charis*: ch. 3 n. 27) to a play; cf. Marcus Aur. *Med.* 6.42, giving a different impression of the analogy. For Stoic/Cynic denial of 'obscenity', see ch. 5 n. 21.

good man and the true philosopher. Though Chrysippus and Panaetius elaborated somewhat different versions of Stoic ethics, there was nothing in either of them which required or recommended a sternly agelastic existence.[106]

The possibilities of Stoic laughter can be filled out a little by returning briefly to the work of Epictetus. We have already seen that Epictetus cautions against resorting too readily to ridicule of others' failings. But there is a passage where he advises that if a good Stoic ever laughs at those who do not share his beliefs, he will do so not as a flaunting gesture of antagonism (for he has no interest in 'externals' of any kind, including point-scoring) but as a private, inner affirmation of his own knowledge and virtue. His, to be precise, will be a surreptitious, concealed derision, an act Epictetus characterises with the unique and oxymoronic verb ὑποκαταγελᾶν, literally 'to laugh down covertly' – i.e., to deride someone 'up one's sleeve'.[107] So the principle here is not distaste for ridicule *per se*, nor for feelings of superiority that might motivate it, but an aversion to its socially ostentatious and potentially frictional use. If this is a counsel of self-denial where derisive laughter is concerned, it is a rather weak-sounding one. It would therefore be hardly surprising if in practice some Stoics were eager enough to indulge openly in mockery of rival schools of philosophy, not least the Epicureans.[108] But whatever degree of restraint the Stoic might show in turning laughter against others, there was nothing in his philosophical commitments to discourage him from enjoying mirth with others who shared his beliefs. Epictetus makes this last point, as well as summarising the nuances of his attitude to the whole subject, in a passage which includes the following among the principles of behaviour which the Stoic must grasp: 'what the right time is for play (*paidia*), and in whose presence; what the consequences will be, in case our companions should despise us (and we despise

---

[106] Panaetius' views are attested at Cic. *Offic.* 1.103–4. If Cicero's reference to 'ancient Attic comedy' (*Atticorum antiqua comoedia*) and the humour of Socratic literature adapts a Panaetius passage, the latter may have been akin to Arist. *EN* 4.8, 1128a22–4 (317 below); but if so, Panaetius found Old Comedy closer to his ideal than Aristotle did. See Dyck (1996) 264–8, with 17–29 for Cicero's relationship to Panaetius.

[107] ὑποκαταγελᾶν, *Diss.* 4.6.21: cf. the Stoic who 'sneers to himself' (καταγελᾷ . . . αὐτὸς ἑαυτῷ), *Ench.* 48.2; note Ar. *Ach.* 76 for a non-philosophical image of concealed derision; and cf. ch. 2 nn. 95, 100 for 'inner' laughter/smiles. Note the different force of ὑπογελᾶν, first at Pl. *Charm.* 162b (Charmides' sly dig at Critias: cf. ὑποκινεῖν, 162d), denoting an inchoate chuckle; *contra* Arnould (1990) 141, the verb is not a *hapax*: cf. e.g. ps.-Polemon, *Physiogn.* 19 (ch. 1 n. 24), (ps.-)Herodian, *Part.* 86.7 (Boissonade), Eustath. *Comm. Il. ad* 1.596. ὑπομειδιᾶν, of a sly hint of smiling (cf. Appendix 2, 532–3), also exists: a memorable instance (Philip V of Macedon) at Polyb. 18.7.6.

[108] See e.g. the Stoic denigration of Epicurus, some of it scurrilous, attested at Diog. Laert. 10.3–6. In Lucian, *Iup. Trag.* 35–53 the Stoic Timocles resorts to foul abuse of the Epicurean Damis (see esp. 52), responding to the latter's own mockery (n. 56 above).

ourselves); when to make jokes (*skōptein*) and whom to ridicule (*katage-lan*) . . . and how in one's social relations with others to preserve one's own character'.[109] In its scrupulous attention to time, place and persons, that résumé of multiple criteria for ethically judicious enjoyment of play, jokes and mockery displays a Stoic readiness to philosophise every single strand in the fabric of life. But it also reads conspicuously like an Aristotelian formulation, and therefore gives us our cue to look back to the primary source of such careful sifting of the possibilities of laughter.

HOW ARISTOTLE MAKES A VIRTUE OF LAUGHTER

Aristotle's is the most sophisticated attempt made in antiquity to reach a philosophical accommodation with laughter, indeed literally to make a virtue out of it. We can construct a picture of Aristotle's attitudes to laughter – as a phenomenon of 'anthropology', psychology, social life, comic poetry/drama and even physiology – from a number of texts. What binds the picture together is a fundamentally ethical (that is, an *ēthos*- or character-centred) perspective on those who laugh (or who fail to do so) and on the causes of their laughter. This perspective has had a long-lasting influence, which can be traced not only in antiquity itself (where it made an impact even on some Christian thinkers) but also in medieval Arabic philosophy, in Thomism, and in post-Renaissance thinking on the subject, including that of Hobbes.[110] Aristotle remains the representative *par excellence* of a philosophical position which accepts laughter as fully human and occupying a justifiable place in a good life, but nonetheless as a behaviour whose potential disruptiveness requires modification by upbringing and social constraints. Aristotle brings to bear on laughter the lucidity and reasonableness which are hallmarks of his overall cast of mind, but his treatment of it has a number of subtleties which repay close inspection. In what follows I shall take my bearings from *Nicomachean Ethics* 4.8,

---

[109] *Diss.* 4.12.17. On the right/wrong time for laughter, cf. n. 23 above.

[110] For influence on Clement of Alexandria, see ch. 10, 489, 492. Arabic philosophy: Aristotle's views are adapted (and narrowed) by the eleventh to twelfth-century Muslim mystic Al-Ghazali; cf. Goodman (1997) 1015–16, Sherif (1975) 185–6. Aquinas: see his commentary on *EN* 4.8, Aquinas (1993) 269–73, and *Summa theol.* II^a II^{ae} qu. 168 arts. 2–4, with Screech (1997) 134–40. Aristotelian attitudes in the Renaissance and beyond: cf. nn. 160, 163 below. Screech and Calder (1970) 218 underestimate the importance of Aristotle's references to laughter; they also repeat the egregious error that Aristotle 'never mentions Aristophanes'. It is confusing of Luck (1994) 762 (amend the *Metaphysics* reference to 1072b23–4; the Strabo citation is also partly misleading) to associate the highest contemplative pleasure with Aristotle's conception of laughter. For a critique of Aristotle's general contrast between seriousness and laughter (and specific contrast between tragedy and comedy), see Silk (2000) 77–83; but I disagree.

1127b33–1128b9,[111] and will configure a selection of other Aristotelian texts around that passage; readers may wish to glance ahead at the chart on 322 for guidance. Although every informative Aristotelian reference to laughter will be taken into account, my discussion will not be comprehensive; Aristotle's observations on the history of comic drama, for instance, will not be extensively analysed here.[112]

We need to start with some broad orientation. *EN* 4.8 picks up from 2.7 (1108a23–6) in developing the idea of a virtuous mean of character, *eutrapelia* ('good humour', 'urbane wittiness'), which relates specifically to the pleasures of 'play' (*paidia*) and relaxation. On this account, play and relaxation (which according to the *Politics* function as 'medicine' or therapy after the exertions of work) form the domain within which the typical activities of laughter, i.e. joking and mockery (both covered by the verb *skōptein*), find their place.[113] Aristotle's attention is directed, at heart, to the right way for laughter to be exercised within the genial rapport between friends. In the *Rhetoric*, after defining friendship in terms of *shared* pleasures and pains (2.4, 1381a3–8), Aristotle picks out as desirable friends those 'who are adroit at teasing and being teased' (οἱ ἐπιδέξιοι καὶ τωθάσαι καὶ ὑπομεῖναι) or who are able to engage in reciprocal and well judged (lit. 'harmonious') joking (ἐμμελῶς σκώπτοντες, *ibid.* 33–6).[114] A contextual contrast with competitive, aggressive behaviour (people who like quarrelling and fighting, 30–3), evoking in part the very different consequences of hostile laughter, underlines the point.

Concern with the nature and boundaries of appropriate laughter enters the *Ethics*, therefore, not as a free-standing or abstract theme for moral reflection but as a dimension of real social interaction. It is, for sure, a dimension which does not, in Aristotle's eyes, touch the most important part of life. At *EN* 10.6, 1176b27–1177a6, he explicitly denies that a happy life could consist '*in* play' (ἐν παιδιᾷ) and insists that 'serious' matters are superior to things 'that make us laugh and are done in play' (τῶν γελοίων καὶ τῶν μετὰ παιδιᾶς). That insistence is a response to a position which Aristotle clearly takes some people to hold, at least implicitly. He may even

---

[111] *EE* 3.7, 1234a4–23, offers a close but more concise parallel; cf. *Magn. Mor.* 1.30, 1193a11–19.
[112] More detail on comedy in Heath (1989), Nesselrath (1990) 102–49, Janko (1984), Micalella (2004), Halliwell (1986) 266–76. Cf. Moraitou (1994) 101–19 for Aristotle's reflections on laughter outside the *Poetics*.
[113] Aristotle links laughter and *paidia* also at *Rhet.* 1.11, 1371b33–5, 2.3, 1380b3. The rationale of play as restorative 'medicine' (*pharmakeia*) is stated at *Pol.* 8.3, 1337b33–1338a1.
[114] Uncertainty over the text of *Rhet.* 2.4, 1381a34 does not affect my argument; see Rapp (2002) II 614 for various views. Aristotle seems to have used a similar formulation to describe Spartan socialisation in laughter: ch. 1 n. 125. The use of *tōthasmos* at *Pol.* 7.17, 1336b16–19, to connote sexually licentious language (ch. 4, 167–8), means that *Rhet.* 1381a34 too might cover risqué forms of banter.

have been familiar with the sentiment ascribed to the poet Simonides, that one should 'play in life and not take anything at all seriously' (παίζειν ἐν τῷ βίῳ καὶ περὶ μηδὲν ἁπλῶς σπουδάζειν).[115] Aristotle's views are also tinged by disapproval for a lifestyle of profligate hedonism, as the preceding part of *EN* 10.6 makes clear. There, after noting that forms of play (*paidiai*) are chosen for their own sake, he proceeds to associate those who are too fond of them with the neglect of serious matters (including their health and property) and with the tastes and needs of tyrants, who are evidently assumed to relish having jesters, humorous drinking companions and such like at their courts.[116] Yet this same passage nevertheless affirms the appropriateness of an element of play in a fully human life by endorsing, as we glimpsed earlier (268), Anacharsis' principle that one should 'play for the sake of being serious' (1176b33), i.e. in order to rest and refresh one's capacity for the earnest pursuit of happiness. But if Aristotle has no room in his mature thinking for the decadence that refuses to take anything in life seriously, this needs to be distinguished from the fact that in his (probably early) *Protrepticus* he was able to adopt the platonising judgement that, *sub specie aeternitatis*, everything that supposedly matters in human life 'is a laughing-stock (*gelōs*) and worthless'.[117] From one philosophical angle of vision, in other words, Aristotle was able to see a kind of absurdity in (ordinary) human existence. But that is not a vision that appears in any of his surviving treatises, let alone in the *Ethics*.[118]

As *EN* 4.8 amply demonstrates, the laughter of relaxed 'play', while not supremely valuable in the Aristotelian scheme of things, is important enough to have its own virtue or excellence. And while a friendship based on urbane *eutrapelia* alone would not be either deep or stable, because reliant

---

[115] Simonid. 646 *PMG*: see ch. 7, 375, 385–6, for existential 'play' and the Cynics. Cf. 305–6 above on Panaetius.

[116] *EN* 10.6, 1176b9–16; *eutrapeloi* (14) seems to straddle 'witty' and 'easy-going' or 'versatile': cf. 312–13 below. Aristotle might have in mind the (semi-legendary) Assyrian king Sardanapalus (*EN* 1.5, 1095b22, *EE* 1.5, 1216a16), a byword for 'drink and be merry' hedonism: e.g. Aristob. Cass. *FGrH* 139 F9 (ch. 3 n. 40), Diod. Sic. 2.23; cf. Hesych. *s.v.* σαρδανάφαλλος, 'sardana-phallus' (an easy pun; the real name sometimes spelt Σαρδανάπαλλος), glossed as jester/buffoon, *gelōtopoios* (where Kretschmer (1955) 4 makes a forced connection with 'sardonic' laughter). Cf., differently modulated, the Egyptian Amasis at Hdt. 2.173–4. But Aristotle might also be thinking of the Macedonian court of Philip II, with his alleged penchant for vulgar performers (ch. 3 n. 105). Cf. the reputation of Dionysius I of Syracuse: Eubul. fr. 25.2–3, Theopomp. *FGrH* 115 F225b (Ael. *VH* 13.18 anomalously denies he was *philogelōs*), with n. 25 above on his son. Synesius *Regn.* 14 depicts the courtiers of monarchs as buffoons.

[117] γέλως . . . καὶ οὐδενὸς ἄξια: Arist. *Protr.* B 104 Düring (= fr. 73 Gigon, 59 Rose); for the relationship to Pl. *Phd.* see Düring (1969) 107–8, with Jaeger (1948) 54–101 on the work as a whole; cf. ch. 7, 365. The Platonic notion of human life as not worth much seriousness appears with a special slant at *Laws* 7.804b–d: see my first epigraph to ch. 7; cf. ch. 10 n. 96.

[118] For the great-souled man's conviction that *few* things are worth taking seriously, see 330–1.

purely on pleasure and not on character (as *EN* 8.3 mentions in passing),[119] nothing need stand in the way of the integration of such virtuous pleasure into a morally richer, less utilitarian form of friendship. The framework of analysis in *EN* 4 as a whole is provided by Aristotle's model of virtue as a mean between contrasting vices of excess and deficiency. His focus in chapter 8, therefore, is precisely the ethics of laughter: with when and why it is appropriate for one of good *character* (not) to laugh. But Aristotle narrows his focus at the outset by concentrating, as mentioned, on contexts of *anapausis*, 'rest' or 'relaxation',[120] i.e. contexts to some degree bracketed from active, goal-directed areas of social life. Hence the association of relaxation with 'play', seen also for example at *Pol.* 8.3, 1337b36–1338a1, where he again denies that play could be the aim (*telos*) of life but stresses that it is needed as a corrective to the toil and tension of work.

Even within the sphere of play, however, ethical standards apply; the relaxation that defines a zone of appropriate laughter is not sheer laxness but an opportunity for 'harmonious' ('well-tuned') behaviour. The term *emmelēs*, twice associated with contexts of joking in *EN* 4.8, is a musical metaphor.[121] Aristotle seems to conceptualise playfulness as a kind of mutually pleasurable interchange, somewhat like a coordinated musical performance, or perhaps (see below) a kind of dance (dance in general counting as a branch of 'music' in Greek culture). Part of the 'harmony' of well-judged playfulness involves a balancing of, so to speak, the active and passive roles which Aristotle demarcates within laughter-making, i.e. 'speaking' and 'listening' (1128a1–2, 18, etc.). This distinction is wider than another which will require further thought in due course, namely that between the maker and the *target* of a joke.[122] The kind of joking one will happily *listen* to is already marked as a factor of moral importance at Plato *Rep.* 10.606c4; this was surely a topic aired in the philosophical circles in which Aristotle had moved. What is at stake here is partly a matter of the

---

[119] *EN* 1156a12–14: but *eutrapelos* here follows general usage and falls short of the normative use at 4.8, 1128a14–15 (n. 135 below). Burnet (1900) 356 offers a different way of keeping the two passages compatible.

[120] *Anapausis*, 'rest', is close to synonymous with *anesis*, relaxation *qua* 'slackening' (as of a string: e.g. *Gen. an.* 5.7, 787b22–788a5): for the latter, cf. *EN* 7.7, 1150b17–18, *Pol.* 8.3, 1337b42, 8.7, 1341b41, *Rhet.* 1.11, 1371b34.

[121] *EN* 4.8, 1128a1, 9; for *emmelēs* of laughter, see *Rhet.* 2.4, 1381a36 (308 above), *Magn. Mor.* 1.30, 1193a18, and fr. 611 Rose (= Tit. 143,1 Gigon), the last referring to Spartans (ch. 1 n. 125). Cf. e.g. Plut. *Mor.* 629f, 632d, 633a, and ch. 10 n. 47.

[122] Cf. *Pol.* 7.17, 1336b16–23 (319 below). Burnet (1900) 197, Gauthier and Jolif (1958–9) ii.1 317 wrongly collapse the wider into the narrower distinction. *Gnom. Vat.* 327, ascribed to Theophrastus, takes the comic to comprise things a hearer will enjoy and the speaker will not be ashamed of. For reflections on the 'triangle' of joker, hearer, target, cf. Plut. *Mor.* 631c–632a; compare Freud (1989) esp. 95, 139–46, Freud (1976) 143–4, 200–9, for a modern model of the configuration.

company one keeps (the 'kind of people' one is among, 1128a2),[123] one reason why the activities of play, though bracketed from social life, still fall within the ambit of Aristotelian ethics.

EN 4.8 offers a normative appraisal of dispositions towards 'the laughable' by calibrating an excess, deficiency and mean. The excess involves blatant vulgarity or crudity (by which Aristotle understands, *au fond*, the untempered proclivities of the many)[124] and insufficient sensitivity to the effect of jokes on their human objects. The practitioner of such excess is the incorrigible buffoon, *bōmolochos*, a term which refers etymologically to some kind of beggar/scrounger who 'hangs round altars', perhaps trying to use jokes to win donations of food from a sacrifice.[125] Aristotle's description of the *bōmolochos* has some affinity with the archetypal Thersites, whose total lack of restraint involved saying *whatever* he thought would make people laugh (*Iliad* 2.213–16).[126] The only person likely to admit to such a propensity would be a 'professional' or at least habitual joker, a *gelōtopoios*, like the Philippus of Xenophon's *Symposium*, who says (in a kind of gelastic 'performative utterance') that he could no sooner be serious than become immortal (1.15). Excessive laughter, for Aristotle, carries a taint of social vulgarity and, metaphorically at least, marginality. But so, by implication, does a dour deficiency of good humour or urbane wit, since this lack is the mark of the *agroikos*, literally the 'rustic', characterised in *EN* 4.8 as 'hard' or 'harsh' (*sklēros*) and thus incapable of refinement or relaxation. The conjunction of *agroikos* and *sklēros* appears also at Plato *Rep.* 10.607b, where Socrates himself is defensively disavowing philistinism (in relation to poetry).[127] The *Republic* 10 passage is revealing: it shows that unease about seeming 'hard' and unrefined had some purchase in philosophical circles. What's more, it follows on from a section where laughter itself has been

---

[123] Cf. the noun ὁμιλία, the '(tone of) company' one keeps, at 1127b34.

[124] The social connotations of 'vulgar', *phortikos*, in Aristotle are visible at e.g. *EN* 1.5, 1095b16, *Pol.* 8.7, 1342a19–20, *Poet.* 26.1461b27–9. The term was easily applied to jokes/jokers: e.g. Ar. *Wasps* 66, *Clouds* 524, *Lys.* 1218; cf. ch. 1 n. 53.

[125] Nagy (1999) 245 n. 3 thinks the original *bōmolochos* threatened verbal abuse; but Pherec. fr. 150, which he cites, does not show this. See ch. 1, 22–4, 40–1. The term was also used of a small jackdaw, Arist. *Hist. An.* 9.24, 617b18, presumably for its intrusive squawking: cf. κολοιός, 'daw', cognate with κολῳάω ('wrangle'), the latter used of Thersites at Hom. *Il.* 2.212; see Chantraine (1968) 556, Latacz *et al.* (2000) 177.

[126] On Thersites, see ch. 2, 69–77; cf. n. 94 above on Pl. *Rep.* 10.620c.

[127] See Halliwell (1988) 154 for other instances. Note that *agroikia* can equally be linked with crude abusiveness (Ar. *Wasps* 1320, Pl. *Phdr.* 260d, 268d, *Grg.* 508d, Arist. *Rhet.* 2.17, 1418b26), the other side of the coin of boorish aversion to mutual laughter. See Cullyer (2006) 191–6, 205–9; cf. next note.

mentioned.[128] We should not overlook, therefore, that the deficiency Aristotle identifies in *EN* 4.8 might apply to the demeanour of certain philosophers as well as to that of others. The interest of this point is increased
by the possibility, discussed earlier, that an agelastic or even antigelastic
impulse featured in classical Pythagoreanism, as well as by the possibility
that Plato himself acquired a reputation for an abrasive or derisive manner.[129] Without adopting anything like a polemical tone (something for
the most part, though not totally, alien to his style), Aristotle develops an
ethics of laughter that has implications for the behaviour of philosophers
– philosophers 'at play', that is – just as much as of non-philosophers.[130]

The term *eutrapelia* which Aristotle uses for the virtuous mean in relation
to laughter, and which was to have a long history after him, means literally
'ease at turning'. It is a word which in the classical period has a broader
sense of 'flexibility', adaptability, easy-going character, etc., and a narrower
sense of 'wit(tiness)'. The connection between the two is presumably that
'wit' could readily be associated with a facility for repartee, an ability to
adapt one's humour quickly to the shifting requirements of banter.[131] The
eutrapel- wordgroup could even encompass physical behaviour. In the great
funeral speech at Thucydides 2.41.2, Pericles uses the adverb in connection with the versatility and grace (*charis*) which Athenian citizens display with their 'self-reliant bodies' (σῶμα αὔταρκες).[132] This Thucydidean

128 *Rep.* 10.606c (cf. 300–1 above) decries over-indulgence in laughter. Since *Rep.* 3.410d–411a ascribes
'harshness' and 'philistinism' to those who obsessively develop the body and the 'spirited' part of
the soul but neglect *mousikē*, a boorish aversion to laughter (as at Arist. *EN* 4.8) may also be in the
background at *Rep.* 607b.

129 I rely on the intriguing early anecdote about Plato and Aristippus at Arist. *Rhet.* 2.23, 1398b30–
3, evidently a story that circulated in the Academy: though over-assertiveness seems the primary
point of ἐπαγγελτικώτερον (related, note, to Plato's own vocabulary for sophistic pretensions), a
scoffing dialectical manner is probably implied; cf. Cope (1877) II 266, and n. 80 above. For what
it's worth, the comic vignette in Epicr. fr. 10.30–3 *PCG* pictures Plato and pupils *ignoring* ridicule
(cf. Imperio (1998) 125–6), while Plut. *Marius* 2.3 depicts him as chiding Xenocrates for being too
severe (*skuthrōpos*: cf. n. 28 above).

130 For a much later (slightly grudging) philosophical statement of the need to avoid antigelastic
extremes, see Simplic. *In Epict. Ench.* XLI Hadot; cf. n. 28 above.

131 Van der Horst (1990) 224–33 gives a chronological conspectus of the *eutrapel-* wordgroup, but the
Pindaric passages on 224 are textually uncertain and the treatment of details is unreliable. Cf. n. 132
below, with ch. 10 nn. 19, 71 for Christian usage. The late-ancient jokebook *Philogelos* has a section
(140–53) on 'wits', *eutrapeloi*: Thierfelder (1968) 78–85.

132 Gomme (1956) 125 translates 'quicker witted (more flexible)'; the parenthesis is preferable to the
first phrase; cf. Rusten (1989) 159. At Hippoc. *Dec. hab.* 7, the noun describes a doctor's easy-going
bedside manner (which need not involve wittiness). *Eutrapelos* at Ar. *Wasps* 469 seems to mean
'adept', 'to the point'. A link with wit/humour is apparent at Pl. *Rep.* 8.563a, Isoc. 7.49 (n. 135
below). The broader sense is used at Isoc. 15.296, Posidip. com. fr. 30.5 ('why do you turn amiability
[*eutrapelia*] into unpleasantness?'); *PCG*'s note on the latter fails to distinguish the broader from
the narrower sense, as does Fortenbaugh (2002) 89–90.

passage reminds us that the term *charis* too had traditionally been used of physical beauty, grace, etc., before it and its cognates became available to denote verbal 'wit' and charm (as with the adjective χαρίεις in Aristotle *EN* 4.8 itself, 1128a15; 321 below).[133] These details illuminate the quasi-sensual appeal that Aristotle discerns in the mutually pleasant, balanced laughter of *eutrapelia*; they complement the musical imagery (310 above) of his lexicon on the subject. Those whose characters are 'harmonious' in this respect have admirable qualities akin to supple, adaptable bodies, as Aristotle's own analogy between the 'movements' of character and the body confirms (1128a10–12). It may even be that, subliminally at least, Aristotle has the imagery and values of dancing in mind in *EN* 4.8. At any rate, the adjective *emmelēs* (twice at 1128a1–9), literally 'harmonious' but with an established application to urbane, suave facetiousness (it is used, for instance, if with some irony, of the spirited slave-girl who mocks Thales at Plato, *Tht.* 174a5), is cognate with *emmeleia*, a kind of dancing.[134] To be agreeably witty, on this model, would entail the stylish, elegant ability to participate in the shared laughter of a kind of verbal dance.

Having placed the virtue of *eutrapelia* between its relevant excess and deficiency, Aristotle goes on, in a typical turn of thought, to guard against too loose and indulgent an understanding of the virtue.[135] The precise way in which he makes this point is of note. 'The laughable', he says, is always 'on the surface' (ἐπιπολάζειν), i.e. casually available and easily found. Although he couples this with the observation that most people regularly engage in joking, he seems to have something more in mind. Beyond its common(place) status, Aristotle identifies laughter as a sort of constant temptation to human beings, something that lies around, as it were, on the surface of their lives and to which their natures readily give way. Though he is emphatic about the need to resist yielding indiscriminately

---

[133] Aristotle uses the adj. to mark various nuances of refinement (intellectual, social, ethical): e.g. *EN* 1.4, 1095a18, 1.5, 1095b22, 1.13, 1102a21. For the association of *charis* with laughter/humour, see ch. 3 n. 27.

[134] Cf. n. 121 above. Aspasius, *In Ar. EN* 125.5–11 (*CAG* xix) appreciates this point, using quasi-rhythmical terminology (adjs. ἄρρυθμος, εὔρυθμος) of the 'movements' of character involved; cf. Anon. *In Ar. EN* 201.14–16 (*CAG* xx), and, with wider application, Pl. *Rep.* 3.400c–401a. Other links between laughter and dancing: ch. 1, 20, 35.

[135] Van der Horst (1990) 234 misunderstands 1128a14–15 (cf. *EE* 37, 1234a13): it does not show that Aristotle was 'aware of negative connotations' of *eutrapelos* (he was, but for other reasons), but that he thinks some people *misapply* the term. Rahner (1961) 1727 makes the same mistake; even Burnet (1900) 198 surprisingly seems to miss the point. Isoc. 7.49 (children's *eutrapelia* used to be deprecated, now it is commended) is worth comparing but rests on a more niggardly evaluation; cf. ch. 1, 19–24, on the laughter of the young. Bremmer (1997) 21 gives the misleading impression that *eutrapel-* terms often had negative connotations before the fourth century; Gauthier and Jolif (1958–9) II.1 316 also go astray (with insufficient evidence) on this point.

to this temptation, Aristotle does not conceal his awareness of how real it is. Underlying this is his recognition, which now calls for attention in its own right, that laughter is deeply rooted in the *body*.

When Aristotle describes the buffoon, the incorrigible joker, *bōmolochos*, as 'under the control of the ridiculous' (ἥττων τοῦ γελοίου, 1128a34), he may think of this condition in physical as much as psychological terms. The buffoon suffers from a perpetual impulse to cause and indulge in laughter; he 'can't stop himself'. No wonder that *bōmolochia* is sometimes markedly associated with the young.[136] Elsewhere in the *Ethics* itself Aristotle uses the attempt to suppress an urge to laugh, before being defeated and 'bursting out laughing' (the verb is ἐκκαγχάζειν, the same one used of Thrasymachus by Plato at *Rep.* 1.337a, 286 above), as an illustration of resistance to an impulse that it is 'pardonable' for even a decent person to succumb to. He makes the point, characteristically, with an example (regarding a now unknown Xenophantus) which he would have filled out orally with an anecdote, showing that he observed and recalled such things with close attention.[137] The important thing here, of course, is that the person concerned really does want *not* to laugh – in complete contrast to the buffoon, who not only *never* tries to stop himself but perpetually looks for opportunities to laugh and arouse laughter in others (1128a5–6). Ethically different though the two cases are, the 'pardonable' one nonetheless brings out the sheer physical impetus that Aristotle senses behind laughter. Laughter is not just manifested on the face; it breaks out of the body, forcing its way, often compellingly, from inside to outside. Aristotle would have appreciated the Homeric phrase 'unquenchable laughter', even if he could not have believed in it literally where the gods were concerned.[138] The corporeality of laughter may have given some Greek philosophers, especially the Pythagoreans, an urgent reason to distrust it, just as in due course it would give Christian moralists grounds to condemn it. But for

---

[136] See ch. 1, 22–4.

[137] *EN* 7.7, 1150b6–12: Burnet (1900) 321 interestingly speculates that Xenophantus may have been a court musician of Alexander's, in which case Aristotle's example would be recalled from his early life.

[138] See n. 47 above for Socrates' disapproval of good people/gods being 'overcome' by laughter (Pl. *Rep.* 3.388e–389a). The physical irresistibility of laughter is often vividly registered: e.g. Heracles' lip-biting at Ar. *Frogs* 42–3, 45 (where ἀποσοβεῖν implies laughter has a 'life' of its own; Taillardat (1965) 152 misses the point, Stanford (1958) 75 is far-fetched), Hystaspas' pretended coughing fit at Xen. *Cyr.* 2.2.5, the flatterer's (feigned) mirth at Theophr. *Char.* 2.4, the Scherian maids at Ap. Rhod. *Argon.* 4.1722–3 (ch. 4, 184–5), the physiological sketch at Cic. *De or.* 2.235 (ch. 7, 345), and the chewing of bay leaves by senators faced with Commodus' lunacies at Cass. Dio 72.21.2. Cf. ch. 1, 5, 8–10.

Aristotle, laughter's rootedness in the body was a sign that it was fully, as well as uniquely, human – a peculiar property of the species, though falling short, in strict Aristotelian terms, of being a 'defining' feature.[139]

The (supposed) uniqueness of the human capacity for laughter is registered by Aristotle in a famous formulation that occurs in a physiological discussion of the diaphragm and midriff in *Parts of Animals*.[140] To illustrate the physiological proximity of these body regions to those which ground perception (*aisthēsis*) and thought (*dianoia*), Aristotle cites two kinds of involuntary laughter: the sort produced by tickling (of ribs/armpits), and the sort allegedly produced (Aristotle is cautiously inclined to believe in the phenomenon, which is also recorded in the Hippocratic corpus) by blows to the chest in battle. The explanation given explicitly for the first sort, but from which we can extrapolate to the second, is that the motion produced by tickling generates a slight heat in the midriff: the transmission of this heat, by affecting the parts of the chest involved in perceptual activity, is rapidly turned into an involuntary disturbance of the mind. Over and above its technical details, this section of *Parts of Animals* provides intriguing but oblique evidence for Aristotle's conception of laughter. In keeping with his general biological and psychological views, Aristotle regards laughter as both physical and mental, i.e. a function of the embodied psyche. Even in the case of involuntary 'laughter' which represents a muscular reflex response to a wound (an analogue to the modern classification of *risus sardonicus*) and is therefore detached from any sense of the ridiculous, Aristotle still posits a 'movement' of mind to match the movement of the physical seat of mind.[141] This points towards the important conclusion that while all laughter entails, on Aristotle's model, a body–mind interaction, this interaction can operate in either causal direction. In the military case, causation runs, involuntarily, from body to mind. The mental component,

[139] The capacity to laugh, for Aristotle (next note), is an exclusive 'property' (*idion*) of humans but is never treated as a defining characteristic: for this non-defining sense of *idion* see esp. *Top.* 1.4, 101b19–23, 1.5, 102a18–30.

[140] *Part. An.* 3.10, 673a8, with 28: Labarrière (2000) gives full analysis; cf. Hankinson (2000) 193–4, Lennox (2001) 276. For cases of 'laughter' (i.e. rictus plus staccato vocalisation) resulting from chest/diaphragm wounds, see Hippoc. *Epid.* 5.95 (= 7.121); cf. Pliny, *HN* 11.198. The tenet that humans are the only animals that laugh is Peripatetic at Lucian, *Vit. Auct.* 26 (cf. ch. 1 n. 8). It was sometimes modified into the proposition that laughter is a defining characteristic of humans: see Barnes (2003) 208 and n. 22 (adding Meletius med. *Nat. hom.* 17, 20 Cramer); cf. ch. 10, 489, for a Christian reworking. Later versions of *homo risibilis* are adduced by Adolf (1947) 251–2, Le Goff (1990), Bowen (2004) 185–90 (Rabelais), Screech and Calder (1970) 218–20, Screech (1997) 1–5, Ménager (1995) 12–17.

[141] *Risus sardonicus*, in modern medical usage (see ch. 2 n. 100 for antiquity), denotes a rictus caused by tetanus or other morbidities.

however, remains below the threshold of consciousness (the wounded soldier is unaware of any *reason* for laughter), as it does in the case of infants who, Aristotle testifies elsewhere, sometimes appear to smile (and cry) in their sleep.[142]

Since the explanation of involuntary laughter given in *Parts of Animals* applies directly to tickling, the same should hold good for that too. But there is room to suppose that in a fuller account – and the *Problemata* attests that laughter was an object of biological enquiry in the Lyceum – Aristotle might have added further factors, including a conscious element of surprise on the part of the person tickled.[143] Whatever fine-grained explication Aristotle might give of the two types of involuntary laughter mentioned, they are both produced by immediately physical causes, whereas the evidence of other works leaves no doubt that responses to the 'laughable', 'ridiculous' or 'comic' (τὸ γελοῖον) have an intentional content in the sense that they originate in consciously perceiving or judging certain things as *reasons* to laugh. Even so, Aristotle's interest in involuntary laughter corroborates his alertness to the bodily roots of *gelōs* in general. This makes it plausible to infer that in the case of the out-and-out *bōmolochos*, the man entirely under the control of (or, to adapt one of Aristotle's own metaphors, 'enslaved to') laughter, a kind of compulsiveness is at work. In this instance, however, unlike that of wholly physical involuntariness, the behaviour reflects badly on the character of the person concerned.

If we now return to the ethical schema of *EN* 4.8, we find there that a second term, *epidexiotēs* (1128a17), already noted in the *Rhetoric* (308 above), is introduced to characterise the virtuous mean. *Epidexios* literally means 'on the right'; hence 'dexterous' and 'adroit' are nice equivalents. It is clear that the adjectives *epidexios* and *eutrapelos* are semantically and ethically

---

[142] *Hist. An.* 7.10, 587b5–7 (specifying children under forty days, and noting unresponsiveness to tickling), *Gen. An.* 5.1, 779a11–12 (adducing dreams and sleep-related perception). *Gelan* in these passages may cover smiles as well as laughter/chuckles: for their appearance in infancy, see Vine (1973) 223–42, Sroufe and Waters (1976), esp. 173–80; cf. Trumble (2004) 123–32. Cf. ps.-Hippoc. *Sept. partu* 9, *Oct. partu* 1.15 (Grensemann), distinguishing instinctive (*automatos*) and responsive expression (i.e., 'reflex' and 'social' smiling, in modern terms), Pliny, *HN* 7.2 with Beagon (2005) 109, and Lydus, *De mens.* 4.26 Wünsch. At Hdt. 5.92.3 a baby's smile/chuckle arouses instinctive sympathy in a would-be killer; cf. Appendix 1, 524. Divine/legendary cases: ch. 3 n. 3.

[143] Surprise appears in the account of tickling at *Probl.* 35.6, 965a14–17 (cf. *Probl.* 35.8, 965a23–32): though blows to the midriff are again mentioned alongside it here, Aristotle himself would surely have treated tickling, *qua* pursuit of play (cf. *EN* 7.7, 1150b22, for a tickling game), as involving a different psychology of laughter from involuntary rictus. Other passages of *Probl.* attesting Peripatetic interest in laughter: 11.13, 900a20–31, 11.15, 900b7–14, 11.50, 904b22–6 (all on the sounds of laughter, though ignorant of the true vocal mechanisms, on which see Provine (2000) 75–97), 28.8, 950a17–19 (on excited laughter with friends, though the text is uncertain).

very close for Aristotle (see 1128a33). He explains *epidexiotēs* in terms that reinforce his socio-ethical standards, the standards of the decent, 'civilised' (*eleutherios*), educated man, as opposed to the 'slavish', uneducated person. *À propos* the latter, the *Politics* suggests that actual slaves can be a worrying source of indecent talk and mirth, which may help to explain why Aristotle is said to have advised, in a lost work, against exchanging laughter or smiles with one's slaves.[144] In *EN* 4.8, the dichotomy between decent and indecent wit prompts Aristotle to draw an analogy with the contrasting styles of older and newer types of comic drama (1128a22–4): the older kind, he says (thinking, no doubt, of Aristophanes and his contemporaries), was characterised by 'obscenity' (*aischrologia*), whereas 'modern' plays rely more on 'suggestiveness' or 'innuendo', *huponoia* (a term Aristotle never uses anywhere else). The analogy is only partial. Strictly speaking, Aristotle is not ascribing any kind of comic merit or failing to types of drama in this context, though it is hard not to detect his preferences in the background.[145] But there is a subtle interplay in this passage between ἐπιπολάζειν, to 'lie on the surface' (1128a12; 313 above), and *huponoia*, literally an 'under-sense'. The former, matching the idea of the *bōmolochos* as one who aims at laughter in all circumstances, conjures up blatant, uninhibited laughter, whereas *huponoia* – probably referring here principally to sexual innuendo – implies a humour that allows some things to remain unstated, just *beneath* the surface.

In the last part of *EN* 4.8 Aristotle betrays some uncertainty about just how far to moralise the sphere of humour and joking. His discussion is very compressed, but we can observe him trying to negotiate an accord between two criteria. One of these is 'decency' or 'decorum' (*euschēmosunē*), which would cover such matters as sexual explicitness. The other is the question of whether a joke 'pains' its target. (Here we might recall from *Poetics* 5.1449a35 that Aristotle regards the ideal material of comic drama as 'painless', a point to which I shall return.) As regards the second criterion, Aristotle assumes

---

[144] Slaves and indecency: *Pol.* 7.17, 1336a41–b12, with ch. 5 n. 44. Not laughing/smiling at one's slaves (προσγελᾶν: Appendix 1, 525): Arist. fr. 100 Gigon (183 Rose), mistranslated in Barnes (1984) II 2434. Cf. ch. 8 nn. 25–6. Ironically (and comically), Men. *Dysc.* 106, 515 uses *epidexios* of urbane politeness (a looser sense than Aristotle's, but related) on the part of a slave and a cook, in both cases repulsed by the agelastic Cnemon.

[145] On *huponoia* in this passage, see Micalella (2004) 130–4. If pressed, Aristotle would presumably have counted 'frigidity' (τὸ ψυχρόν) as a defect of comic drama: the adj. describes the humourless person at *EE* 3.7, 1234a31, but can also refer to 'frigid' *attempts* at humour (e.g. Xen. *Symp.* 6.7); at *Rhet.* 3.3, 1406a32–3, poetic frigidity is unintentionally comic. Aristotle's contrast between old/new plays was, alas, garbled by Aquinas: Aquinas (1993) 272.

that (much) joking, *skōptein*, involves aiming laughter specifically against another person. He also assumes that joking is paradigmatically a *sort* of 'abuse' (*loidorēma*, 1128a30), i.e. that it at least ostensibly denigrates or diminishes its target: hence his paradoxical description of it in the *Rhetoric* as a kind of 'educated *hubris*' (323 below). Now, Aristotle's two criteria are in principle quite separable. If the hearer of a joke (whether or not he is also its target) is not offended by it, then the 'pain' criterion as such will not block *indecency*. This is why Aristotle pauses to wonder (1128a27–8) whether pleasure/pain in this sphere is 'indeterminate' (ἀόριστον), 'since different people find different things distasteful or pleasant'. The decency test, on the other hand, applies standards that go beyond the immediate tolerance or pleasure of those present. Aristotle is not prepared to forgo this test, which means that he must allow it to have priority over the contingent question of whether the hearer and/or target of a joke happens to enjoy it; this is confirmed by the shorter version of the argument at *EE* 1234a21–3.[146] But the point is not simply moralistic. Aristotle appeals to the fact that some Greek lawcodes, including that of Athens, prohibited certain kinds of abuse, which implies a widely shared perception of the potential harm that abuse can cause (by, for example, damaging a reputation or leading to social friction).[147] Aristotle is not, of course, directly discussing public contexts of the kind to which such laws applied; he is drawing an analogy which implies that laughter, even in private, cannot be totally exempted from ethical standards. His remark that lawgivers 'should perhaps have prohibited certain forms of (sc. private) joking [*skōptein*] too' (1128a31)[148] is less of a strictly legislative suggestion than a way of stressing the need for canons of acceptability even in the domain of playful laughter, though Aristotle was certainly prepared, in his most idealistic moods, to argue the need for explicit regulation of both indecent speech and indecent images in the well-ordered city (see below on *Politics* 7.17, 1336b3–23). As Aristotle immediately goes on to indicate, the 'law' appropriate in this domain is one that people of good character will impose on themselves.[149]

---

[146] Aspasius, *In Ar. EN* 126.4–8 (*CAG* xix) thinks Aristotle allows that a well-judged joke might still displease some people; likewise Irwin (1999) 226. Perhaps, but the reverse emphasis (that pain might be avoided, and pleasure given, by a nonetheless improper joke) is more *à propos*. The combination of a 'decency' test (avoidance of the hubristic/shameful) with the mutual pleasure of joking (*skōptein*) appears in the description of Persian sympotic manners at Xen. *Cyr.* 5.2.18 (cf. Plut. *Mor.* 629e–f). For the general principle of not causing 'pain' in symposia, cf. Xen. *Symp.* 6.2, with ch. 3, 152.

[147] On Athenian laws against slander, see ch. 5, 242.

[148] Janko (1984) 244 seriously mistranslates this sentence, making Aristotle stress the *need* for mockery!

[149] For a modern 'ethicist' model of joking which is partly Aristotelian in spirit, compare Gaut (1998).

In typical fashion, Aristotle tries to tread a path through the subject that avoids one-sided or reductive dogmatism.[150] A final nuance that marks this approach is his observation that the buffoon, in his promiscuous desire for laughter (whether against himself or others), will say things 'that the charmingly witty person (*charieis*) would never say, and some of which he would *not even* be prepared to listen to' (1128a35–b1). Aristotle has so far asserted an apparently straightforward parallelism between the gelastic standards relevant to 'speaking' and 'listening'.[151] Now he implies some latitude as regards the latter. Why should this be so? After all, if we imagine joking between people of similar character, it makes little sense: there ought to be ethical symmetry between speaking and listening. But if Aristotle is allowing for situations of more 'mixed' company, then it seems that he can contemplate, at least at the margins, that even the decent, cultured person could tolerate listening to *some* jokes that he would never tell himself. What helps to make this reading more plausible is that in *Politics* 7.17 (1336b16–23) Aristotle explicitly qualifies his suggested regime of legal regulations against indecency (in both word and image) by permitting exceptions in the case of, first, religious contexts where obscene scurrility is a recognised cultural practice (including the festival performance of iambos and comedy), and, secondly, in the setting of sympotic inebriation, where, revealingly, he supposes that education will make people immune to the 'harm' that might otherwise be done to their characters. Both those exceptions are concessions to old, embedded cultural traditions, whose status has been analysed in earlier chapters of this book.[152] The reference to symposia is particularly pertinent to the *Ethics*' discussion of relaxation and joking, since this discussion surely presupposes the symposium as a paradigmatic framework for such 'play'.[153] Between them, then, *EN* 4.8 and *Pol.* 7.17 bear out a degree of ethical lenience, psychological flexibility and social realism in Aristotle's charting of the boundaries of 'playful' laughter.

As a supplement to the intricacies which have emerged so far from Aristotle's conception of *eutrapelia*, I now want to glance sideways, so to speak, at his remarks on irony (*eirōneia*) in a number of places. In the *Ethics* itself, he represents irony principally as a deficiency or underplaying of truthfulness about oneself, but a deficiency which, as the opposite of boastfulness,

---

[150] See Goldhill (1995) 17–19 for a harsher appraisal of Aristotle's position as tautologous. Goldhill (2006) 84–5 somewhat overstates in saying that for Aristotle laughter 'threatens the self'.

[151] But even in asserting the parallelism at 1128a28–9 Aristotle subtly implies that individuals more *obviously* limit the jokes they tell than those they listen to.

[152] See ch. 4, 159, 167, ch. 5, 247.

[153] See ch. 3, 114–16, for symposia and 'play', including adesp. el. 27 *IEG* (quoted on 114), an interesting parallel to the ethical spirit of Arist. *EN* 4.8.

is often attractive for its apparent self-deprecation.[154] Elsewhere, however, he is sometimes inclined to ascribe an explicitly laughter-related potential to 'irony'. Aristotle's usage of *eirōn-* terms shows, in fact, the semantic elasticity which belonged to them at this date. He can apply them, for one thing, to outright deception (*Rhet.* 2.5, 1382b21) – their original sense, it seems, and one still dominant in Theophrastus' *Characters*.[155] But he also recognises a (Socratic) type of irony whose problematic relationship (but not necessarily simple disjunction) between the surface and 'inner' meanings of utterances attracts attention to itself (for a suitably attuned hearer) and becomes a means of expressive subtlety, hinting at its own obliqueness and complexity of intention. The statement at *Rhet.* 2.2, 1379b31, that we sometimes get angry with those who use irony (*eirōneuesthai*) in response to our seriousness, presupposes a variant of that second type: in such instances, the irony (which Aristotle describes as 'contemptuous', *kataphronētikon*) must be intentionally discernible for the anger to make sense. It is irony *qua* subtly yet recognisably veiled expression that opens up its possible use as a means of humour and wit, as Aristotle indicates in several places in the *Politics* and *Rhetoric*.[156] In one of these passages, at *Rhet.* 3.18, it is significant that by opposing *eirōneia* and vulgar buffoonery (*bōmolochia*) Aristotle contrasts a deficiency and an excess relating to different yet 'neighbouring' virtues in the codification at *EN* 2.7 (cf. 1108a10 for the relationship). This demonstrates how Aristotelian 'irony' can move along a spectrum from a matter of pure dissimulation into a species of deliberately laughter-inducing behaviour. It expands from the sphere of truth-telling (more specifically, truthfulness about oneself) into the sphere of 'the agreeable' and of 'play'. As a result, it faces in the direction of *eutrapelia*, though without being actually equated with it.

To see a little better what the relationship between 'irony' and *eutrapelia* might amount to, we should take account of a further twist in Aristotle's interpretation of the former. Although *eirōneia* typically involves saying or implying things about oneself, its potentially gelastic form directs some degree of feeling against others: this is evident in the description of it as 'contemptuous' in *Rhet.* 2.2 (above). Yet in *Rhet.* 3.18 there is a suggestion that the *eirōn* himself somehow profits from laughter: 'irony befits a liberal

---

[154] *EN* 2.7, 1108a19–23, 4.3, 1124b30–1, 4.7, 1127a13–b32. Momigliano (1993) 65 intriguingly finds an 'indefinable touch of irony and sadness' to be 'the mark of Aristotelian genius' itself; but he does not seem to use 'irony' in Aristotle's own sense.

[155] On early usage of *eirōn* and cognates, see Diggle (2004) 166–7; but his treatment of Aristotle ignores the *Rhet.* Cf. ch. 1, 42.

[156] *Pol.* 3.2, 1275b26, *Rhet.* 3.7, 1408b20, and, above all, *Rhet.* 3.18, 1419b8–9. Cf. *Hist. An.* 1.9, 491b16–17 (n. 40 above) for the 'mocking' (μωκός) ironist.

man better than buffoonery; the ironic man arouses laughter (ποιεῖ τὸ γελοῖον) for his own sake, the buffoon for the sake of others'. That looks as though it might mean that such irony is not ideal material for the virtue of *eutrapelia*, which aims at the pleasurably reciprocal laughter of play. This is perhaps one reason why this type of irony does not figure explicitly in the *Ethics* itself, where the term is restricted to the person who understates the truth about himself. But as we have seen, irony is itself several times acknowledged as a form of wit or humour in the *Rhetoric* and *Politics*, and that prompts one to ask how, in a fuller account, Aristotle might have integrated it into the ethics of laughter set out in *EN* 4.8. The question is further justified by the fact that in categorising self-deprecating irony in *EN* 4.7 Aristotle uses the adjective *charieis* to describe the attractiveness of those who use it in moderation and discreetly (1127b31). *Charieis* ('charming', 'graceful', 'stylish', 'witty', etc.) occurs in *EN* 4.8, as we have seen (313 above), and undoubtedly has gelastic overtones. How, then, might Aristotle position irony in relation to *eutrapelia*? *Eirōneia*, for one thing, can enter into almost any kind of personal interaction and is not as closely tied to playful relaxation as Aristotle takes *eutrapelia* to be. The exact impingement of irony on the ethics of laughter will depend on variable factors of character, tone and context. Aristotle himself could scarcely have failed to notice that the Platonic Socrates exemplifies how irony operates to contrasting effect in dealings with an aggressive interlocutor such as Thrasymachus or with intimate, affectionate friends such as Glaucon. In the first case, irony might be thought of as a displaced laughter, practised in part for the advantage of the *eirōn* himself (cf. *Rhet.* 3.18, above), though that is clearly open to competing interpretations of Socratic irony in general. In the second case, it approximates more to the mutual pleasures that are served by well-judged *eutrapelia*. In short, Aristotle could have recognised ways in which moderate *eirōneia* and *eutrapelia* might converge, but he would always have needed to safeguard the latter from the scope of the former to express the very reverse of harmonious sociability.[157] Where *eutrapelia* playfully promotes shared affinities, *eirōneia* retains the capacity to place a distance (a one-sided pretence) between speaker and hearer.

It may be helpful to take stock by tabulating Aristotle's perspective on laughter in *EN* 4.8: more precisely, his evaluation of its ethical and psychological place in the domain of social relaxation. The table incorporates a selection of germane details from other treatises as well.

---

[157] For affinities between Aristotle's *eutrapelos* and (one kind of) *eirōn*, cf. Nesselrath (1990) 126–8.

	EXCESS	VIRTUOUS MEAN	DEFICIENCY
forms of behaviour	*bōmolochia* (crude buffoonery)	*eutrapelia* (urbane wit) and *epidexiotēs* (playful adroitness); perhaps moderate, low-key use of *eirōneia* (*qua* humorous self-deprecation)	*agroikia* (dour boorishness), *sklērotēs* ('hard' lack of social refinement)
standards upheld/ breached	promiscuous disregard for decency (*euschēmosunē*)	respect for *euschēmosunē*, display of *charis* (witty charm), everything done with stylish harmony (*emmelōs*)	lack of *charis* and pleasantness
(metaphorical) social traits	vulgar (*phortikos*), slavish (*andrapodōdēs*)	'educated' (*pepaideumenos*), 'free'/civilised (*eleutherios*), (physically well toned and versatile)	rustic (*agroikos*)
psychological features/ implications	(1) joker's pleasure at expense of others' pain; tendency to *hubris* (offensive abuse) (2) lack of (ethical/bodily) self-control (*EN* 1128a34–5) (3) tendency of young (*Rhet.* 1389b10–12)	(1) mutual pleasure in moderate laughter; 'educated *hubris*' (i.e. playful pretence of insults) (2) self-control prevails, in harmony with 'relaxation' (*anesis*) (3) mark of the mature (by implication)	(1) refusal to share appropriate pleasure with others (2) failure to relax (3) tendency of the old (*Rhet.* 1390a22–4)
correlates in comic drama/poetry	*aischrologia* (verbal obscenity, *EN* 1128a23), *iambikē idea* (personal denigration, *Poetics* 1449b8; cf. *psogos*, vituperation, *Poetics* 1448b37), typical of Old Comedy	moderate, generalised sense of the 'laughable' (cf. *Poetics* 1448b37); avoidance of personal satire (cf. *Poetics* 1451b11–15); *huponoia*, innuendo, typical of 'modern' comedies (*EN* 1128a24)	[the misanthropic rustic: cf. ch. 8 n. 19]

Since Aristotle recognises that it is in the nature of his mean-based model of virtue that differences of degree are of the essence, it is not surprising that there should be some tensions in his scheme. It remains to investigate these a little. The most striking admission of tension, both psychological and ethical, is the *Rhetoric*'s famously paradoxical description of *eutrapelia* as 'educated *hubris*' (πεπαιδευμένη ὕβρις, 2.12, 1389b11–12). The phrase occurs at the end of a chapter which outlines the traits of the young for the purposes of rhetorical characterisation. Aristotle describes the young as impulsively doing everything to excess: witness their tendency to wrong people 'with a view to causing offence (*hubris*) rather than for the sake of malicious harm' (1389b7–8). When he then says of them that 'they are lovers of laughter (*philogelōtes*) and accordingly witty (*eutrapeloi*), because wit is educated *hubris*', he draws on an existing Greek association between the young and (irreverent) laughter. But he also seems to be running together two partially separable points. The first is that the laughter of the young characteristically tends towards the hubristic, i.e. the aggressive and insulting, and therefore needs to be tempered by socialisation.[158] The second is that wittiness (*eutrapelia*) in general is often *prima facie* insulting (we remember his *aperçu* that jokes are 'a *sort* of abuse', *loidorēma*, *EN* 1128a30: 318 above) but is transformed into a source of mutual pleasure by the cultural protocols of play which friends assimilate into their relationships. In his own way Aristotle is perhaps here adumbrating something akin to the modern ethological interpretation of laughter as an accompaniment to mock fighting, a transmuting of aggression into play.[159]

As at *EN* 4.8, 1128a12–14, where the 'laughable' is said to be always lying freely available 'on the surface' of life, we can discern behind the *Rhetoric's* formula of 'educated *hubris*' a judgement that a propensity to laughter is intrinsic to human nature and a ready-made channel for the impulsive vitality of the young (to which the somewhat life-weary aversion to laughter of the old is later contrasted, 2.13, 1390a20–2). It is also obvious from the combined observations of the *Ethics*, *Politics* and *Rhetoric* that Aristotle deems education, *paideia*, to have an essential role in shaping that propensity into a socially positive, harmonious activity. Unlike the use made of his views on the subject in the late Renaissance, and indeed unlike the drastic simplification found in the pseudo-Aristotelian *Virtues and Vices* (where love of laughter and wit is attached exclusively to intemperance, *akrasia*), Aristotle himself does not want to denounce laughter as

---

[158] On the widespread association between laughter and the young, see ch. 1, 19–24; cf. the young and *hubris* at *Rhet.* 2.2, 1378b28. Mockery itself as a form of *hubris* is noted (as a cause of anger in its targets) at Arist. *Rhet.* 2.2, 1379a28–30. Fisher (1992) 91 n. 41 cites an interesting parallel to Aristotle's phrase 'educated *hubris*', viz. the phrase 'just/righteous *hubris*' from a fourth-century Thessalian inscription (*SEG* 1 248). Germane is Hyp. fr. 211 (Jensen), 'abuse is the most uneducated of behaviours', πάντων ἀπαιδευτότατον τὸ λοιδορεῖν. Cf. my discussion of agoraic vulgarity in Ch. 5.

[159] See van Hooff (1972) 217–19, 225–7 for evidence from non-human primates; cf. Appendix 1 n. 32.

expressive of aggression or 'contempt' *tout court*.[160] But the class of the young who form the object of his generalisations in *Rhet.* 2.12 stand, as it were, on the borderline between the crucially different types of 'play' that separate 'the educated and uneducated' (*EN* 1128a21–2). Aristotle is prepared to call them *eutrapeloi* (at least by popular standards, the yardstick of his advice to orators in the *Rhetoric*) but condenses their ambiguous relationship to laughter into that memorably pregnant phrase, 'educated *hubris*', which frames *paideia* as the modification of potentially dangerous instincts into socially acceptable forms. It is wrong to equate *eutrapelia*, *qua* 'educated *hubris*', with outright, unequivocal *hubris* (which involves a sense of superiority), and then to conclude that for Aristotle *eutrapelia* is itself an expression of superiority.[161] The ideal of *eutrapelia* sketched in the *Ethics* (as opposed to the less discriminating use of the term which Aristotle makes a point of deprecating at *EN* 1128a14–15) cannot have anything substantial in common with full-blown *hubris*, since the latter aims precisely to cause harm and *pain* to others, while, as we have seen, authentic Aristotelian *eutrapelia* avoids giving pain even to ordinary hearers of a joke, let alone to its direct targets.[162] All this reveals that Aristotle sees the 'spirit' of laughter as extending along a spectrum which his model of deficiency/virtue/excess reduces to ethical order: at one end of the spectrum, the hubristic, shaming underside of laughter runs riot, while in the virtuous middle range the impression of offensiveness (*hubris*) is 'educated' and moulded, through shared codes of play, into a medium of reciprocated friendship. Where genuine *eutrapelia* is achieved, the appearance of *hubris* will be nothing more than playful pretence. It will replace the risk of pain with the reality of pleasure, an ideal of sociable joking which finds an echo in the later

---

[160] The late Renaissance's 'Aristotelian' model of contemptuous laughter is documented by Skinner (2002), but he follows his sources in focusing on the *Rhet.* to the neglect of the *Ethics*' conception of virtuous *eutrapelia* (for whose influence cf. Ménager (1995) 86–9, Screech (1997) 132–40): as a result, his claim that Aristotle treats 'the mirth induced by jesting' as 'always an expression of contempt' (152) needs modifying; cf. Skinner (1996) 199–200. For a reductive equation of laughter with intemperate decadence, see ps.-Arist. *Virt.* 6.1251a19–20.

[161] So Sorabji (2000) 290; for *hubris* and superiority, see *Rhet.* 2.2, 1378b26–8. Partly because of his conception of comedy (326 below), Aristotle is commonly claimed as holding a 'superiority theory' of laughter/humour: e.g. Morreall (1983) 5, 16, Buckley (2003) 3. Fortenbaugh (2002) 120–6 offers necessary qualifications on this view.

[162] *Hubris* and pain: *Rhet.* 2.2, 1378b23–4. *Eutrapelia* and avoidance of pain: *EN* 4.8, 1128a7, 26; cf. Theophr. fr. 453 (Fortenbaugh (1992) II 284), with fr. 711 (*ibid.* 556), Xen. *Cyr.* 2.2.12–13. On looser usage of *eutrapelia* see nn. 119, 135 above. That joking/mockery (*skōpsis*) more often causes pain than pleasure (even at a symposium) is asserted by someone in Alexis fr. 160.3. Ar. *Kn.* 1267 ironically deprecates 'causing pain' (λυπεῖν) by means of comic satire. Cf., in a very different context, Soph. *Ant.* 551.

history of reflections on the subject, not least in the eighteenth century.[163] But virtue only exists where vice is always possible. And Aristotle remains clear that the risk of pain and offence perpetually lurks around the forces of laughter.

Aristotle's ethical reservations about the capacity of laughter, if not properly tempered, to express and/or arouse hostility do not prevent him, however, from shrewdly appreciating its social uses. We need to reckon, for instance, with his endorsement in the *Rhetoric* of Gorgias' principle that the orator should 'destroy his opponent's seriousness with laughter, and his laughter with seriousness'.[164] Since (most) oratory of the kind envisaged by Aristotle's treatise was inescapably agonistic, mockery of one's adversaries is recognised as a legitimate weapon, a means of puncturing the claims or pretensions of the opposition in the eyes of the audience, though Aristotle appends his own characteristic rider by adding, in keeping with his position in the *Ethics*, that only certain kinds of humour befit a 'free' person, deprecating buffoonery, *bōmolochia*, in particular and recommending irony (as considered above). The *Rhetoric* also contains another, rather different reference to the activation of laughter in oratorical settings. At 3.14, 1415a36–7, Aristotle touches in passing, but without disapproval, on the attempted arousal of laughter by those 'many' speakers who, for their own contingent reasons, wish to *distract* their hearers' attention from part of their case. Rather than dissolving one's opponent's seriousness, this kind is designed to dissolve one's *own* seriousness. Although the point is not certain, it seems to allude to a digressive, entertaining use of laughter, not to laughter aimed at the opposition. Even within the highly antagonistic and serious business of forensic and political oratory, therefore, Aristotle is realistically aware of different ends to which the arousal of laughter can be put.

Such passages underline the difficulty of synthesising Aristotle's psychology of laughter into a single principle. That psychology is in an important sense pluralist, a factor borne out by his references in the *Rhetoric* to the various species of 'the ridiculous' or 'the comic' (τὸ γελοῖον, τὰ γελοῖα)

---

[163] Cf. the quasi-Aristotelian terms of Adam Smith's judgement on David Hume: 'it was never the meaning of his raillery to mortify; and therefore, far from offending, it seldom failed to please and delight, even those who were the objects of it', Mossner and Ross (1977) 221. On relevant eighteenth-century attitudes to laughter, see e.g. Tave (1960), incl. 84–5 on reactions to Aristotle, Gatrell (2006) 159–77.

[164] *Rhet.* 3.18, 1419b4–6 (citing Gorg. fr. 12 DK); compare (?)Anaximenes, *Rhet. Alex.* 36, 1441b23–6. For one test case, see ch. 1, 36–8.

which he tells us he had analysed in (the lost second book of) the *Poetics*.[165] Even if Aristotle explains in the *Ethics* that the primary virtue of laughter involves its use (by friends) to promote the reciprocally pleasurable activity of 'play', this still leaves the possibility of multiple psychological *sources* of laughter. When I discussed Aristotle's remarks on the physiology of laughter, I noted that strictly involuntary laughter (as in the case of wounds to the midriff, and also, though more ambiguously, tickling) lacks a cognitive content, i.e. a perception of something as 'laughable'. But what sorts of perceptions, for Aristotle, lead people or utterances or things (the tripartite schema of *Rhet.* 1.11, 1371b35–1372a1) to be found *geloios*?

Most promising here is the definition of the 'laughable', 'ridiculous' or 'comic' at *Poetics* 5.1449a34–7: 'the laughable is constituted by a fault or mark of shame/ugliness which involves no pain or destruction' (τὸ γὰρ γελοῖόν ἐστιν ἁμάρτημά τι καὶ αἶσχος ἀνώδυνον καὶ οὐ φθαρτικόν). While it is not my purpose here to elucidate Aristotle's view of comic drama or poetry in its own right, there seems to be something more general to be learnt about Aristotle's psychology of laughter from this definition. One appropriate test, given the earlier parts of my argument, is to bring that definition to bear on the domain of conduct to which the *Ethics*' conception of *eutrapelia* applies. Does the *Poetics*' definition mean that friends, in relaxed playfulness, will tease each other for actual 'faults or marks of shame/ugliness' – and, if so, why should that give them mutual pleasure? We can readily adjust what is said in *Poetics* 5 to allow a difference of degree between the laughable material of comic drama and the playfulness of virtuous friends. In comic drama, the legitimate object of representation is 'people worse than us' (*Poetics* 2), i.e. a repertoire of 'low', inferior characters. This immediately widens the realm of theatrical laughter beyond the bounds of virtuous *eutrapelia*, and that is one reason why in the *Ethics* (4.8, 1128a22–4: 317 above) Aristotle correlates his own criteria for ethically acceptable laughter with a preference for the kind of comic drama which avoids extremes of abusive scurrility and gelastic offensiveness. That passage of the *Ethics* confirms that Aristotle's standards for acceptable laughter have some purchase on *both* the comic theatre *and* the relationships of real life. But one thing opens up a space between them. In life, there is always a risk that laughter will offend its targets and produce or intensify rancour; we have seen that Aristotle is even prepared to assimilate the power of such antagonistic laughter into his own rhetorical theory. But in the comic theatre, such a risk exists only where

---

[165] *Rhet.* 1.11, 1371b35–1372a2, 3.18, 1419b5–6. Cf. Janko (1984) 63–6, Rapp (2002) II 994–5, Fortenbaugh (2002) 121–3; see also Nesselrath (1990) 119–20, part of an extensive critique (102–49) of attempts to reconstruct the lost second book of the *Poetics* from the *Tractatus Coislinianus* (cf. ch. 8 n. 11).

real people are satirised, and the *Poetics* leaves no doubt that this mode –
the 'iambic type', as he calls it (with its ancestry in the poetry of 'blame' or
'invective', *psogos*) – is far from Aristotle's ideal or paradigm of comedy. For
most purposes, therefore, Aristotle assumes that comic drama directs its
audience's laughter towards characters who are fictional and who therefore
cannot react to it, though even in such cases the genre will presumably
retain some capacity to reflect the consequences of hostile laughter in the
relationships *between* characters in a play.[166]

Whatever the normative slant of Aristotle's reading of the history (and
the variety) of comic drama, it seems apposite, if we wish to adapt the
definition of 'the laughable' in *Poetics* 5 to the dynamics of social laughter,
to press the reservations indicated by 'no pain or destruction' very hard.
Here we must remember the *Ethics*' own emphasis on the need for virtuous joking to avoid causing pain (*lupein*). Although the vocabulary of
the two passages is not the same (the *Poetics* uses ὀδύνη not λύπη terms),
their arguments are convergent. In the *Poetics*, the example of the distorted
yet painless comic mask (*prosōpon*, 5.1449a35) makes it clear that it is the
pain of the characters which is immediately at issue (though ultimately, of
course, it is the emotions of the audience which are at stake). The point
is reinforced by the contrast with tragedy, where events involving precisely
'destruction or pain' are fundamental (11.1452b11–12). Comic drama of the
fictionalised kind Aristotle prefers allows its 'low', inferior characters to be
shown up as ridiculous, yet even they must be protected, as it were, from
the most hostile, painful kinds of derision. How much more important it
is, therefore, that in life the laughter of virtuous *eutrapelia* should cause no
pain. One thought which prompts itself here is that the safest way of keeping social joking/mocking (*skōptein*) within boundaries of mutual pleasure
would be for the 'faults' which provide the objects of laughter to be themselves imaginary, fictitious or at any rate transparently exaggerated. This
comports well with a model of 'play' (*paidia*) as dependent on pretence or
make-believe, and I pointed out in an earlier chapter that even the verb
skōptein itself sometimes effectively means 'pretend'.[167] Although Aristotle himself never quite spells out a 'fictional' model of social joking, his
treatment of the virtues and vices of playful laughter in *EN* 4.8 is certainly

---

[166] Aristotle's distinction between 'blame'-centred 'iambic' poetry (directed at real individuals) and
authentic comedy (based on generalised representations of 'the ridiculous') is sketched at *Poet.*
4.1448b24–1449a5, 5.1449a32–b9, and referred back to at 9.1451b11–15. Nagy (1999) 253–64 gives
one analysis of the distinction.

[167] *Skōptein* as 'pretend': ch. 1 n. 41. As regards such pretence, note Alcibiades' contrast between the
comic/ridiculous and 'the truth' at Pl. *Symp.* 215a (cf. 214e and, slightly differently, 212e–213a);
though swathed in dramatic irony, the contrast points to a widely held assumption.

compatible with one. In fact, when summing up at the end of that chapter (1128b4–9), he explicitly notes that the correct way of engaging in relaxation and play centres on pleasure not truth(fulness). Consistently with this, the *Rhetoric's* notion of the gelastics of friendship as involving a game-like give and take, an adroitness at 'teasing and being teased' (2.4, 1381a33–4: 308 above) and a quasi-musical harmoniousness of reciprocal banter, calls for verbal activity which it would be difficult to restrict to veridical utterances.

We need not strain, however, to remove truth altogether from Aristotle's conception of social laughter. If joking (*skōptein*) is always, for him, in some degree aimed at 'faults' (as the comic-theatrical matrix of 'the ludicrous' in *Poetics* 5 suggests), it may even be that *eutrapelia* will be promoted by a deft capacity to identify real weaknesses which nonetheless provide the right kind of material for a mirth that all parties (the makers, objects and hearers of jokes) can appreciate and share. On this level, the idea of 'relaxation' or 'release' (*anesis*), as a sort of suspension of seriousness, will depend on the relative insignificance of the faults in question, as well as on not *taking* them (too) seriously. In interaction between friends this eutrapelic deftness will allow laughter's energies to be moderate (i.e. safeguarded against extremes), held in equilibrium (through the reciprocity of playful give and take) and translated into something positively enjoyable. In the end, it will not matter whether jokes are 'true' or not, provided they activate the shared pleasures of friends who respect standards of decency and seemliness. But it is probably safe to assume that a good Aristotelian joke or witticism will always contain a thought or perception which can be cognitively appreciated for its aptness.[168] All this requires virtue or excellence of character because it is harder than it may sound; it is easy to miss the mark. The *Ethics*, with its cautious notion of a joke (*skōmma*) as a 'sort of abuse', and the *Rhetoric*, with its oxymoronic framing of wit as 'educated *hubris*', between them remind us that for Aristotle *eutrapelia* involves an emotionally, socially and ethically delicate poise from which one can readily slip into the excesses of insult and affront.

Part of the interest of Aristotle's position is that instead of treating playful and hostile laughter as quite separate entities, he sees the former as a cultural refinement and remoulding of the latter. Whether or not he believed that comic drama in the theatre involved a *katharsis* of its audiences' emotions (perhaps by aligning laughter not with hostile derision but with an

---

[168] Cf. *Rhet.* 3.11, 1412a17–b32, on ἀστεῖα (cf. ch. 9 n. 25), witty remarks or *bons mots* which spring a kind of cognitive suprise, giving hearers something new to grasp or understand.

ethically moderate response to human foibles),[169] he does seem to have regarded the virtuous enjoyment of laughter in circumstances of social relaxation as a kind of implicit 'education' of pleasures and sensibilities. This means, among other things, that Aristotle would have wanted to keep acceptable laughter, either in the theatre or in life, free of the taint of spitefulness (*phthonos*) or *Schadenfreude* with which Plato's *Philebus* 48–50 (300–1 above) had linked it.[170] Aristotle regarded *phthonos* as a troubling, 'turbulent' feeling (*Rhet.* 2.9, 1386b18–19), and also as inimical to friendship (*Pol.* 4.11, 1295b22–4). Anyone who laughed in a spirit of *phthonos* would certainly not be engaging in playful or harmonious sociability.

A final, speculative thought. How far would Aristotle's 'great-souled' person (the *megalopsuchos*) use and/or enjoy laughter? The question is worth posing because the *megalopsuchos* is a sort of pinnacle of Aristotelian virtue, the 'hero', we might say, of his ethics. He is the person who possesses 'perfect excellence' and enhances or adorns that excellence with a true, appropriately strong sense of his own worth (i.e., in concrete terms, of the honour he merits), not in a merely self-regarding sense but in relation to the values which his character embodies. Aristotle was certainly aware that more than one paradigm of *megalopsuchia* could be found in his culture; it makes a big difference whether we think here of an Achilles or Ajax, on the one hand, or a Socrates, on the other.[171] But if we limit ourselves to Aristotle's exposition of his own conception of *megalopsuchia* in *EN* 4.3 (1123a34–1125a16), we can construct an interestingly tripartite answer to the question I have posed. In the first place, since the great-souled man by definition has all the virtues (1123b30), he must possess *eutrapelia* and be inclined therefore to share playful laughter occasionally with his friends. In that respect, however, it is hard to see him as differing much from more moderately virtuous characters. If anything, in fact, his *eutrapelia* might be muted or reduced by his lack of interest in, and therefore perhaps his

---

[169] Sorabji (2000) 290–1 sketches one view of comic *katharsis*; cf. ch. 4 n. 12, Halliwell (1986) 274–5 with n. 33. Although Arist. *Pol.* 8.6–7, 1341a23–4, 1341b38, is often taken to drive a wedge between *katharsis* and 'education', the implications are not black-and-white: see Halliwell (2003c).

[170] Aristotle almost certainly knew the *Philebus* (cf. *EN* 10.2, 1172b28–9, for a probable allusion) but never mentions its section on laughter. One need not, *pace* e.g. Zanfino (2001) 15, take the definition of the comic at *Poet.* 4.1449a35 to be directly indebted to *Phlb.*; Sorabji (2000) 290, Fortenbaugh (2002) 20–1 (but modified on 120) take a different view. Aristotle's concept of *phthonos* as pain at others' good fortune makes it unequivocally an ethical fault (*Rhet.* 2.10, 1387b21–1388a28; cf. *Top.* 2.2, 109b35–8, *EN* 2.7, 1108a35–b6, *EE* 3.7, 1233b16–25). At *Rhet.* 2.9, 1386b34–1387a3, coupled with ἐπιχαιρεκακία (cf. n. 93 above), it shades into something more like the *Schadenfreude* of the *Phlb.*; cf. Taylor (2006) 120–1. However, since we feel *phthonos* for those who are like us or our rivals (*Rhet.* 2.10), Aristotle could never have made it the basis of a response to the 'inferior' characters of comedy.

[171] See Arist. *An. Post.* 2.13, 97b15–25, for these two different conceptions/kinds of *megalopsuchia*.

limited inclination to joke about, small details of social life. As Aristotle puts it, in a striking phrase, the great-souled man is not 'given to mundane talk' (*anthrōpologos*, 1125a5), a fact which makes him averse to malicious gossip.

A second, contrasting observation, however, follows on directly from that last point. After stating that the *megalopsuchos* is not given to malicious gossip (he is not a slanderer, *kakologos*), 'not even of his enemies', Aristotle adds – 'except for the sake of giving deliberate offence (*hubris*)'.[172] This is a startling admission, one which might call to mind an Achilles rather than a Socrates (though we have seen how divided opinions could be on the latter: 295–300 above). It is all the more startling given that Aristotle has already stressed (1124a11–12) that the great-souled person cares little about being dishonoured (a point which certainly distances his own model from the Achillean type) and has distinguished the *megalopsuchos*'s apparent air of arrogance from the *hubris* displayed by those who do not merit the lavish material honours they receive (1124a20–30). But we should not flinch at the brunt of Aristotle's characterisation. The great-souled man will very rarely speak derisively; in fact, he will use the false modesty of *eirōneia* to deal with ordinary people in ordinary situations (1124b30–1). But because he is frank and truth-speaking by nature (1124b26–9), he is capable, when necessary – which must mean when confronted by those who are ethically vicious and deserve to be diminished in their public status – of resorting to aggressive insults: or, in Aristotle's own terms, of stripping away the 'educated', cultured veneer of *eutrapelia* and tapping the raw power of verbal *hubris*.

But just how rarely that extreme will be reached can be gathered from the third and final component of my answer to the question of the great-souled man's relationship to laughter. When explaining what are often taken to be among the more peculiar details of his portrait of the man (a slow gait, deep voice and steady speech), Aristotle comments: 'for one who is serious about few things does not rush, nor does one who thinks nothing great become frantic' (οὐ γὰρ σπευστικὸς ὁ περὶ ὀλίγα σπουδάζων, οὐδὲ σύντονος ὁ μηδὲν μέγα οἰόμενος, 1125a14–15). This formulation of a feeling that very little in human life really matters must certainly be distinguished from the (decadent) mentality, criticised later in the *Ethics*, that supposes nothing at

---

[172] *EN* 1125a8–9. 'Haughtiness' for *hubris*, Barnes (1984) ii 1775, dilutes the point; Burnet (1900) 185 rightly glosses, 'when he wants to insult and humiliate people'. Fisher (1992) 12–13, understandably troubled by this issue, suggests that Aristotle is referring to retaliation against *others'* offensiveness; but as Fisher sees, this displaces without really solving the problem. For divided opinions on the passage, cf. Taylor (2006) 225–6.

all is to be taken seriously. On the other hand, we know that in his *Protrepticus* Aristotle himself gave voice to the superficially similar philosophical conviction that everything supposedly important in life 'is a laughing-stock (*gelōs*) and worthless'.[173] The *megalopsuchos*'s outlook is tinged, it seems, with detachment from most forms of human pursuit and value. Even the sense of 'greatness' which defines his ethical and psychological cast of mind must be qualified by the belief that 'nothing (sc. human)' is truly great. Whether or not Aristotle intended this consequence, the great-souled man has reason, at some level of consciousness, for a use of laughter that might be turned, if only silently, against the world at large – including, perhaps, himself. And in the light of what I argued in the earlier parts of this chapter, that is an inference which makes all the more intriguing the flickers of Socratic features which some readers think they detect on the face of the Aristotelian *megalopsuchos*.

---

[173] For both these views, see 308–9 above, with ch. 7 for other Greek notions of life itself as a suitable object of laughter.

CHAPTER 7

Greek laughter and the problem of the absurd

ἔστι δὴ τοίνυν τὰ τῶν ἀνθρώπων πράγματα μεγάλης μὲν σπουδ-
ῆς οὐκ ἄξια, ἀναγκαῖόν γε μὴν σπουδάζειν.
(Human affairs are really not worth much seriousness, yet all the same
we can't escape taking them seriously.)

Plato *Laws*

Nostre propre et peculiere condition est autant ridicule que risible.

Montaigne

Wipe your hand across your mouth, and laugh;
The worlds revolve like ancient women
Gathering fuel in vacant lots.

T. S. Eliot[1]

EXISTENTIAL ABSURDITY: PREDICAMENTS
ANCIENT AND MODERN

The eponymous protagonist of Samuel Beckett's early novel *Murphy* spends
most of his time in search of an escape from the burden of mundane consciousness, or from what the novel calls his 'unredeemed split self'. Murphy
survives by cultivating a sort of impassivity: in Beckett's words, a 'self-
immersed indifference to the contingencies of the contingent world which
he had chosen for himself as the only felicity'. Such impassivity is a version of Greek ataraxia, and the novel itself invites us to think of Murphy's
mental life as a whole in the terms of Greek philosophy. We learn, for one
thing, how Murphy had studied with the eccentrically Pythagorean Neary,
whose attempt to inculcate an 'attunement' and blending of 'the opposites
in Murphy's heart' had proved fruitless. An entire chapter, moreover, is

---

[1] Epigraphs: Pl. *Laws* 7.803b (cf. ch. 10 n. 96), Montaigne *Essais* 1 50 (Montaigne (1969) 360), Eliot
'Preludes' IV (Eliot (1974) 25).

devoted to the depiction of Murphy's mind as both markedly tripartite and as a kind of private Platonic Cave, divided into zones of light, half light and darkness. In the light, into which he rarely finds his way, Murphy has access to the 'forms' of a fantasised reordering of his actual existence. In the half light, he enjoys a dream-like, peaceful contemplation. But in the dark he is subject to perpetual flux, 'nothing but forms becoming and crumbling into the fragments of a new becoming, without love or hate or any intelligible principle of change': in short, a 'matrix of surds'. Murphy, one could say, is a lapsed Pythagorean and a failed Platonist who succumbs to an atomist's awareness of meaningless flux. The atomist credentials of this awareness emerge explicitly in a scene where, slumped over a chessboard in the psychiatric hospital in which he works, Murphy experiences a brief trance of negative ecstasy, 'the positive peace that comes when the somethings give way, or perhaps simply add up, to the Nothing, than which in the guffaw of the Abderite naught is more real'.[2]

The figure of the Abderite in Beckett's sentence is a creative composite in which features of the historical and the legendary Democritus (citizen of Abdera) are deliberately (con)fused. The filter of ancient ideas through which Murphy's mind is observed blurs the difference between the atomist's physical concept of empty space, on the one hand, and the putative nihilism of the proverbially laughing philosopher on the other. What's more, the image slips from a state of mind ('positive peace') that evokes Democritean tranquillity, *euthumiē* (Ionic form of *euthumia*), to a pseudo-Democritean conviction of the world's supposed pointlessness. What Beckett conjures up here, then, is an unmistakably absurdist species of existential laughter – laughter (whether literal or metaphorical) that embodies an attitude not just to specific, local circumstances but to life, even the cosmos, as a whole.[3] The task of the present chapter is to explore some of the ancient

[2] The references to *Murphy* (first publ. 1938) are from Beckett (1963a) 129–30 ('split self'), 117 ('indifference'), 6–7 etc. (Neary's Pythagoreanism), 76–80 (tripartite mind), 124 ('his cave'), 168 ('The positive peace...'). The last quotation merges the legendary Democritus with the atomist 'nothing' of Democ. fr. 156 DK, '"thing" exists no more than "nothing"': cf. Barnes (1982) 402–5 on the latter, which is also quoted by Malone (again in existentially transformed spirit), as 'Nothing is more real than nothing', in Beckett's *Malone Dies*, Beckett (1962) 22. (For ancient connections between laughter and the idea of life as 'nothing', see 360, 365 below.) Hamilton (1976), Mooney (1982) discuss the importance of Democritus (and Mooney other Presocratics) for Beckett's work. Pfister (2002b) 176–81 offers broader reflections on the significance of laughter in Beckett.

[3] I do not rule out other species of 'existential laughter', nor other varieties of absurdism. Cf. Bakhtin (1968) 7–12 for carnival (ch. 4, 204–6) viewing 'the entire world' as laughable, an idea which differs from my model of absurdism in its self-consciously temporary reversal of social norms; cf. the criticism of this theory in Silk (2000) 76, 83. Cohen (1999) 50–60 develops a further notion of absurdity, framed as a (characteristically Jewish) *acceptance* of the world's incomprehensibility, a response very different from the detached mocking of life explored in this chapter; cf. ch. 10 n. 26.

antecedents of such laughter and the problems of understanding which they raise. The question I propose to circle round, without expectations of a simple answer, is whether we can identify in antiquity itself any equivalent to modern notions of 'the absurd'.

This question will strike some as fraught with risks of anachronism (though modern absurdists have no trouble finding their own outlook prefigured in the past),[4] but it seems to me, partly for that very reason, a stimulating provocation to thought. Taking my cue from the predicament felt by Beckett's Murphy and the allegedly Democritean prototype of that predicament, I shall interpret my guiding question as amounting to this: can we give content, within the categories and sensibilities of Greek culture, to the idea of making life or existence *per se* an object of laughter? I naturally cannot dwell here in detail on alternative modern concepts, typologies or genealogies of the absurd. But I shall take as a central reference point a position which I think is essential to most versions of the absurd, and which I also count as the *problem* or paradox of absurdism. This position can be defined as a strong impulse to evaluate human life 'globally' and, as it were, from the outside (i.e., to adopt some form of what the philosopher Thomas Nagel, himself a cautious proponent of one model of existential absurdity, calls 'the view from nowhere'), but at the same time an impulse that disavows any authentically 'external' framework of value which could make sense of that goal. It is by simultaneously presuming the need for, yet denying the availability of, an externally validating vantage point that absurdists arrive at an intuition of human existence as inescapably incongruous, locked into a desire for overarching meaning (what Camus calls 'nostalgia') which the world is felt inherently incapable of satisfying. At its limits, outright absurdism ironically usurps the role of an absolute in an absolute-free universe.[5]

Now, there is an apparent difficulty in connecting the absurd with the idea of existential 'laughter' (an idea, to repeat, which needs to be understood metaphorically or metonymically, as well as sometimes literally).

---

[4] See Camus (1965) 109, translated in Camus (1955) 20, 'all literatures and all philosophies'; cf. ch. 9 n. 69 for Camus' reference to Peregrinus as an absurdist. On anthropological grounds, Douglas (1975) 110 suggests that 'a philosophy of the absurd' may even be implicit in the joking rituals of some African cultures.

[5] Sherman (2006) provides a concise philosophical genealogy of 'the absurd'. 'The view from nowhere' is the title of Nagel (1986); cf. nn. 78, 82, 84 below. When Baudelaire (1976) 527, translated in Baudelaire (1964) 149, argues (on the basis of Jesus' supposed avoidance of laughter: ch. 10 n. 83) that 'the comic vanishes from the point of view of absolute knowledge and power', in effect he excludes the possibility of absurdity as an 'absolute' view of the world (his own later talk of 'the absolute comic' is a different matter: Baudelaire (1976) 536). But Baudelaire argues from the (Judaeo-Christian) premise that laughter belongs to the 'fallen' nature of humans.

At least some modern expressions of absurdism are *prima facie* very remote from discerning anything 'laughable' about the human predicament. Indeed, the most articulate spokesman of the absurd, Albert Camus, frames his case in *The Myth of Sisyphus* in terms of the challenge of suicidal despair, while for the early Sartre experience of absurdity is notoriously associated with disgust, an association anticipated (though the connection is rarely noticed) in Nietzsche's formulation of the Dionysiac roots of the absurd at the end of Chapter 7 of *The Birth of Tragedy*. Iris Murdoch, among others, has gone so far as to equate the absurd with 'the true tragic'.[6] From such dark and angst-ridden angles of vision, it might seem appropriate to look for ancient equivalents of the absurd, if anywhere, in the traditions of Greek pessimism. That is actually a germane point, whose significance will recur more than once in the course of the chapter. It does not, however, cancel the peculiar link between absurdism and the idea of existential laughter, a link which in its modern manifestations, as my example from Beckett's *Murphy* illustrates, involves a sort of psychological counterpoint between desolation and derision, between the nihilistic and the ludicrous. Examples can readily be multiplied. Camus himself employs the vocabulary of the 'ridiculous' to reinforce that of the 'absurd'; Ionesco, with his category of 'tragic farce' and in other respects, locates only a thin dividing line between horror and laughter; and Milan Kundera presents the devil's laughter of meaninglessness as lurking just over the 'border' in whose proximity we all live.[7] But does anything comparable fall within ancient horizons of experience?

If we turn directly to the question of what it might entail to find life itself an object of 'laughter', an anonymous but well-known epigram, with a rich afterlife of translation and adaptation in the Renaissance, puts us on the tracks of one possible ancient answer – and reacquaints us, as it happens, with Beckett's 'Abderite'. The epigram, from Book 9 of the *Palatine*

---

[6] Murdoch (1997) 240, 'the true tragic, the absurd'; cf. the fleeting connection in Camus (1965) 196, Camus (1955) 97. The connection of existential absurdism with the *idea* of laughter is ineradicable from its name: cf. e.g. Kaufmann (1969) xviii ('a black laugh'). On Greek traditions of pessimism, see the old but rich treatment in Burckhardt (1977) II 348–95, partly translated in Burckhardt (1998) 85–124, with Oswyn Murray's introduction to the latter (xxxviii–xxxix). Given the special weight of modern conceptions of the absurd, one should avoid using the phrase simply to gloss ancient ideas of 'the laughable' or 'the comic', τὸ γελοῖον, as does e.g. Janko (1984) 59, *à propos* Arist. *Poet.* chs. 4–5.

[7] Camus' absurdist vocabulary includes 'rire', 'dérisoire', 'ridicule', etc. with existential inflections: Camus (1965) e.g. 101, 106, 113, 116, 145, 155–6. Esslin (1980) 128–99 provides an overview of Ionesco's absurdist blurring of the dividing line between horror/laughter, tragedy/farce. Kundera's notion of the devil's laughter and the border between meaning and absurdity: Kundera (1996), esp. 86–7, 281, 291–2. Dienstag (2006) assimilates absurdity to pessimism, but he understands the latter in a diluted sense.

Anthology and probably of mid-imperial date, apostrophises two famous, long-dead Greek philosophers from the perspective of a timeless present ('now') in which all readers are implicitly invited to situate themselves:

τὸν βίον, Ἡράκλειτε, πολὺ πλέον ἤπερ ὅτ᾽ ἔζης
δάκρυε· νῦν ὁ βίος ἔστ᾽ ἐλεεινότερος.
τὸν βίον ἄρτι γέλα, Δημόκριτε, τὸ πλέον ἢ πρίν·
νῦν ὁ βίος πάντων ἐστὶ γελοιότερος.
εἰς ὑμέας δὲ καὶ αὐτὸς ὁρῶν τὸ μεταξὺ μεριμνῶ,
πῶς ἅμα σοὶ κλαύσω, πῶς ἅμα σοὶ γελάσω.   5

Weep more profusely at life, Heraclitus, than you did
     When alive: now life is more pitiful than ever.
Laugh now at life, Democritus, even more than before:
     Now everyone's life is more ludicrous than ever.
Yet when I look at both of you, I ponder with fluctuating uncertainty   5
     How I am to weep with one of you, laugh with the other.[8]

The poem tersely poses an existential dilemma. Invoking the legendary personae of Heraclitus the weeping philosopher, Democritus the laughing philosopher, the epigram's voice employs a series of parallelisms and antitheses not simply to juxtapose the contrasting mentalities of these two figures but to convey how easily yet perplexingly reversible they are. The two standpoints curiously intersect in a feeling that the world holds no coherent meaning or hospitable anchorage for human beings: all one can do is succumb to a sense of despairing pity, or alternatively of hilarity, at the whole spectacle. The stance of the speaker (who is to be visualised, line 5 seems to suggest, gazing at images of the two thinkers) is irreducibly ambivalent. He purports to sympathise with, yet also to waver over, both the 'Heraclitean' and the 'Democritean' ways of looking at the totality of life (the life of '*everyone*', line 4). Each of the first two couplets provisionally vindicates the relevant judgement of life, asserting that the passage of time has only shown its increasing aptness. But a linguistic nicety, the lack of a connective particle between these couplets, accentuates the self-contained status of each viewpoint and therefore the clash between them: look one way, it gestures, and see things in *this* light; look the other, and the reverse is just as compelling. The choice is undecidable. Yet it ought surely to be a matter of either/or; one cannot have both. Or can one? The final couplet

---

[8] Anon. *Anth. Pal.* 9.148. The metrical licence in line 2 (*brevis in longo* at the caesura) points to a mid-imperial date; cf. West (1982) 181. Rütten (1992) 23–4 speculates on the first century AD. Beckby (1966) III 776 reports Luck's suggestion (I cannot trace the source) of Palladas' authorship. See Garcia Gomez (1984) 56–7, with 98–106, 281–6 for the poem's influence on post-Renaissance versions of the Democritus legend.

allows the thought to surface that there is only a thin, easily crossed dividing line between pessimism and absurdity, perhaps between 'tragic' and 'comic' conceptions of life. Might the speaker's oscillation guide attention, then, towards the implication that life is a hybrid 'genre', neither tragedy nor comedy but, as Socrates had suggested in Plato's *Philebus*, tragicomedy?[9] Or even more radically: that pessimism and absurdity are really alternative conceptions of the same underlying dislocation of human purposes from any larger frame of reference? Here, at any rate, is a glimpse of a partial ancient analogue to the psychological instability – the blending of anguish and 'laughter' – which I have already mentioned in some modern versions of the absurd.

The idea of surveying human life globally or in its entirety, (as if) from outside, became embedded in Greek cultural consciousness as a result of two main influences. The first was the traditional (and originally pre-Greek) picture, enshrined especially in Homeric epic, of Olympian gods who do just that, viewing human existence from a certain distance as a kind of spectacle for their own interest and consumption. The relationship between immortals and mortals is, of course, more complex and messy than this. Gods intervene in and substantially manipulate the human scene; they do not gaze passively. But a kind of divine spectatorship, salient at such momentous junctures as *Iliad* 22.166 (where the gods watch Achilles chase Hector, like competing athletes (157–64), round the walls of Troy) or *Iliad* 24.23 (where they watch Achilles drag Hector's corpse round those same walls), patently engenders a sense of human life as an object for overarching scrutiny and evaluation – in the case of the *Iliad*, a fundamentally tragic object.[10] This idea of global viewing was in turn taken up by Greek philosophy and incorporated into its notion of the human mind's own capacity for comprehensive contemplation (*theōria*, literally 'viewing') of reality: 'the contemplation of all time and all being', to cite one of the most pregnant formulations (from Plato's *Republic*).[11] The image of the gods' physically external spectatorship was converted into (or supplemented by) the spectatorship that takes place inside the philosopher's soul and places it cognitively 'above' the world. This philosophical paradigm was graphically

---

[9] Pl. *Phlb* 50b, 'the entire tragedy and comedy of life', τῆς τοῦ βίου συμπάσης τραγῳδίας καὶ κωμῳδίας: see ch. 6, 300. Plato's phrase is echoed in Porphyry's reference to life as 'tragicomedy' (*kōmōdotragōdia*) at *Ad Marc.* 2 and fr. 275 Smith (*apud* Stob. 3.21.28); cf. Halliwell (2002b) 104, with nn. 12–13 there. Note Pl. *Rep.* 10.620a: the spectacle Er witnessed was both 'pitiful' *and* 'laughable', i.e. tragicomic? There is no reason to suppose that the fourth-century comedies entitled *Kōmōdotragōdia* (see *PCG* ii 9) applied the term to life itself. On *theatrum mundi* motifs, see n. 20 below.

[10] Cf. Griffin (1980) 179–204 on the *Iliad*'s gods as spectators of the (tragic) human scene.

[11] Pl. *Rep.* 6.486a; cf. ibid. 498d, *Tht.* 174e.

conveyed (with what historical accuracy is not the issue here) by the remark conventionally attributed to Pythagoras that life is like a grand athletic 'festival' to which some come to compete strenuously, others to buy and sell, but the noblest few only to spectate.[12] To Pythagoras as well as to Anaxagoras was also ascribed the thought that the sole justification of human life is to contemplate the heavens and the whole order of nature. Such an attitude might imply a low estimation of all mundane aspects of existence, but it nonetheless opens up a vision which is incompatible with absurdism. In this connection it is symbolically apt that both Pythagoras and Anaxagoras acquired the reputation, as we remember from the previous chapter, of never having laughed. Whether or not their agelastic reputation was apocryphal, its primary point was probably to denote a detachment from ordinary human concerns and priorities. But it can also serve to highlight their implicitly 'anti-absurdist' position: they do not deny but actually proclaim an authoritative vantage point from which to survey the cosmos.[13]

In fact, both the Greek models of 'spectatorship' adduced above – the divine and the philosophical – are intrinsically resistant to anything like a notion of the absurd, since they lay claim not only to an all-encompassing 'optic' for the scrutiny of the world but also to a scheme of meaning and value which does not simply leave human lives denuded of purpose. One thing of great importance here is easily missed. While Homeric gods are depicted as laughing both collectively and individually, they never (contrary to the perception of some Christian observers) laugh at the condition of human lives *per se*.[14] The Olympians can, of course, express feelings of superiority and malice, sometimes accompanied, in post-Homeric representations, by the laughter of vengeful cruelty; and I argued more generally

---

[12] Cic. *Tusc.* 5.8–9 (= Heraclid. Pont. fr. 88 Wehrli), cf. Iambl. *Vita Pyth.* 58–9: see Gottschalk (1980) 23–35 on the origins of the story. Arist. *Protr.* B44 Düring uses a related analogy between philosophical *theōria* of the universe and festival/theatrical spectatorship. The trope became something of a commonplace: see Alexis fr. 222, with Arnott (1996) 633. But it must be distinguished from the idea, ascribed to Crates of Thebes, of life as a 'festival' for perpetual play: 375 and n. 100 below. At Dio Chrys. 9.1 the Cynic Diogenes' attends *real* festivals to observe the follies of mankind.

[13] Arist. *EE* 1216b11 (= Anax. A30 DK), *Protr.* B18–19 Düring; for the reputations of both philosophers as agelastic, see ch. 6, 270, 272–3. As it happens, the idea of an anti-absurdist Pythagoras can be detected, with some irony, in the figure of Neary in Beckett's *Murphy*; cf. n. 2 above.

[14] When Apollo reminds Diomedes and Achilles of the chasm between gods and men at Hom. *Il.* 5.440–2, 22.8–10, he asserts his own superiority and, in the second case, enjoys success in deception (hence Richardson (1993) 107 finds the tone 'lightly mocking'); but he does not deride their humanity *per se*. Nor does he at Hom. *Hymn* 3.531, where he smiles with condescension at human folly. The Christian (heretic) Tatian, *Orat.* 8.1, asserts that the whole world provides quasi-theatrical entertainment to the laughing gods of Homeric paganism, but this is a distortion driven by theological animus.

in Chapter 2 that their laughter in the Homeric epics has an ambiguous, problematic force in relation to their own psychology and the standards of (human) morality. But the gods never deride human existence in itself. When Hephaestus intimates to Zeus and Hera that the human domain is not worth quarrelling over (*Iliad* 1.573–6), he is impelled to do so by the strength of his parents' commitments to their human protégés; and the laughter that soon follows is directed at himself not at the mortals below, to whose engrossing conflicts the gods will soon (incorrigibly) return. However malevolent their aims may sometimes prove to be, the Olympians are too absorbed in the human world – implicated in it by acts of propagation, dependent on it for the honour of worship, and sharing many of its motivations – to perceive it as 'absurd'. Even when they stand back from partisan immersion in the affairs of (heroic) men and women, they do so either for only temporary withdrawal into their own privileged realm, or precisely to watch the human scene from a distance with an intensified fascination. Indeed, the gods' capacity to feel pity for human beings – selectively exercised pity, but all the more telling for that – brings them closer to seeing their lives as tragic than ridiculous. The 'view from Olympus', then, demonstrates that if a perception of human life (as if) 'from outside' is a necessary condition of the absurd, it is not a sufficient condition.

As a foil to what has just been said about the Olympians, and to clarify some of the terms in which Greek culture made it possible to conceptualise a global view of human existence, it is instructive to recall here the notorious response of Silenus (a satyr-like *daimōn* or nature spirit) to King Midas' question, 'what is the best thing for humans?'[15] When Nietzsche repeats the story in Chapter 3 of *The Birth of Tragedy*, he arrestingly makes Silenus break out into piercing laughter before uttering his irredeemably grim pronouncement, 'best never to have been born'. It is usually overlooked that this gelastic detail, which casts a grotesque air over the abyss opened up by Silenus' words, is not an invention of Nietzsche's zealous imagination. It is actually (though silently) based on Jacob Bernays' emendation of Aristotle's version of the Silenus–Midas story, as preserved by pseudo-Plutarch, an emendation which turns ἀναγκαζόμενον ('compelled [sc. to speak]') into

---

[15] See esp. Arist. *Eud.* fr. 65 Gigon (44 Rose), *apud* ps.-Plut. *Cons. Ap.* 115b–e, where the story serves a philosophical belief in something *beyond* death; see Jaeger (1948) 48–9, Hani (1972) 59–62, 182–3. Hubbard (1975) discusses literary sources of the Silenus story, Davies (2004) its character as folktale; for visual representations, see Miller M. (1997), Gantz (1993) 138, Padgett (2003) 35, 46 nn. 221–2. Further references in van Groningen (1966) 169–70, Arnott (1996) 429–30. Intriguingly, the *subjective* wish never to have been born is ascribed to a god, Hephaestus, at Hom. *Od.* 8.312: see ch. 2 n. 78.

ἀνακαγχάζοντα ('guffawing [sc. as he started to speak]').[16] The change, accepted by some earlier editors but now largely ignored, is not easy to justify, since it is textually unnecessary. But it is ingenious and, as Nietzsche shows, alluring. The nearest we come elsewhere in antiquity to an image of such existentially charged laughter is that of Tiresias in Lucian's *Menippus*. When asked like Silenus to specify the best life, Tiresias first laughs (as well as showing a Silenus-like reluctance to answer) and then, when pressed, instructs the Cynic philosopher Menippus to take nothing at all seriously – i.e., to translate the whole of life into a cause for laughter.[17] I shall return to Tiresias at the end of the chapter. But the case of Silenus is more perplexing. Even if, unlike Bernays and Nietzsche, we resist the temptation to add laughter to his pessimism, it is legitimate to wonder whether the story as a whole poses an implicitly existential riddle, creating a sort of mythological oxymoron by placing the bleakest sentiments in the mouth of a hedonistic character who in other settings could be expected to evoke (and practise) an exuberant laughter. The ironic shape of the narrative in which Silenus' 'wisdom' is encased (in the usual version, he is captured by the simple bait of wine) at least suggests something radically different from an Olympian viewpoint on human existence. Though he is sometimes cast as the 'teacher' of Dionysus, Silenus' words come from too obscure a source to be securely intelligible. Through the voice of its strangely hybrid character (half-animal, half-deity; half-buffoon, half-sage), his story may perhaps hint at something akin to a darkly ambiguous version of absurdity lying beneath the surface of pessimism. And yet, it cannot do more than hint, since Silenus, like the Olympians in this respect at any rate, lacks one indispensable requirement for an absurdist mentality: he is not himself human, and the absurd, on my construal, is a (dubious) prerogative of human beings.

---

[16] Ps.-Plut. *Cons. Ap.* 115d (= Arist. fr. 65 Gigon, 44 Rose), with Bernays (1861) 238–9. Bernays (n. 2) cites Julian, *Symp.* 36, 335b, for a guffawing Silenus, but in a very different context (Verg. *Ecl.* 6.23, *ille dolum ridens*, is different again); cf. (probably) guffawing satyrs in Soph. fr. 314.357 *TrGF*, with Appendix 2 n. 62. Bernays' emendation was accepted by Rose (1886) 49 (fr. 44) but ignored by Ross (1955) 19 (fr. 6), Gigon (1987) 295 (fr. 65); it is not mentioned by Davies (2004), who would certainly reject it (see 688) but is clearly unaware (682 n. 2) of Nietzsche's silent adoption of Bernays' suggestion. The influence of the emendation on ch. 3 of the *Birth of Tragedy* is documented in von Reibnitz (1992) 127–31; Aristotle is cited as the source of the Silenus story in Nietzsche's earlier draft, 'Die Geburt des tragischen Gedankens', Nietzsche (1988) I 586. Cf. here Bernays' rumoured remark (mentioned in a letter of Nietzsche's) that he saw his *own* views, though exaggerated, in the *Birth of Tragedy*. The remark is usually interpreted in relation to Bernays' theory of Aristotelian *katharsis*, but the treatment of the Silenus story is pertinent: for remark and context see Momigliano (1994) 162–3; cf. Silk and Stern (1981) 398 n. 60, 415 n. 97, for caution on the *katharsis* issue, with Halliwell (2003b) 113–17 for Nietzsche's ambivalence on that. Porter (2000) 134–5 suggests a link between Silenus and Democritus in Nietzsche's mind.

[17] Lucian, *Menip.* 21; see 386–7 below.

It was not Greek gods or nature spirits who opened up vistas of the absurd in antiquity, but one peculiar application of the philosophical aspiration to an impersonal, all-inclusive, yet still somehow human perspective on the world. To develop this claim carefully, I need to introduce an important distinction between what I shall call contextual or relative absurdity and, on the other hand, global or absolute absurdity. Contextual absurdity can be perceived in most areas of human behaviour, but it is always construed as a failing or incongruity in relation to particular standards of sense and value and is judged from a position that takes *itself* to be non-absurd. Global absurdity, by contrast, involves the human condition as such; it implicates *everyone* (cf. the anonymous epigram, 336 above), not least the person who feels or observes it, and therefore cannot be transcended – though, if one listens (in different ways) to Nietzsche, Camus or Beckett, it can somehow be lived with. Once we adopt a distinction between contextual and global, relative and absolute, absurdity, it becomes easier to see why full-blown absurdism is absent from one part of the ancient cultural landscape where many would instinctively look for it, in Aristophanic comedy (or Attic Old Comedy more generally). Aristophanes admittedly employs techniques of distortion and discontinuity that can be paralleled in much absurdist literature; but literary techniques alone do not generate an existential mentality. Aristophanes can treat just about anyone or anything, in isolation, as absurd, but he never allows the *totality* of existence to appear meaningless. Indeed, his characteristic blend of satire and fantasy, with its shifting modes of daydream, escape and utopianism, is intrinsically resistant to the absurd: one way or another, his comedy remakes or saves the world, while absolute absurdity permits no redemption (no 'leap', as Camus likes to call it). Even when Aristophanes sets up a quasi-external perspective on life, by taking his protagonists into the sky (even to Olympus) or down to Hades, he does not project an impression of an ineliminably ludicrous human condition. Far from it: such journeys lead somewhere and achieve something, however far-fetched that something may be. Yet we need to register carefully the vividness which Old Comedy lends to the idea and imagery of an external perspective on life. Combined with other influences, that imagery could and did move closer to the absurd than Aristophanes himself had brought it. So, at any rate, I shall argue in my discussion of some of Lucian's works in Chapter 9.

It is hard in fact (as well as problematic) to be a global absurdist. For most Greek philosophers (we shall consider the exceptions later), it was out of the question, since they posited a cosmic order which, while it might reduce earthly life in its own terms to something ephemeral and insignificant, expressly allowed the mind to find its home in a larger source of truth and value. Such thinkers might diagnose 'absurdity' in most human pursuits and preoccupations, but this could only be a comparative, not an absolute absurdity; it was always contextualised in relation to a more-than-human framework of meaning. Despite first appearances, that claim is actually corroborated not undermined by the tenacity of the *theatrum mundi* and related topoi in antiquity. Conceptions of human life – from Plato to Plotinus, and beyond – as a theatre of shadow puppets, a stage-play, mime, or game, employ a trope which can certainly in principle serve as the vehicle for feelings of absurdity, as they do indeed for some modern absurdists: witness, for example, Camus' talk of the collapsing 'stage-set', the 'meaningless pantomime' of life, 'the great mime' of human existence.[18] The reappropriation of such imagery by a twentieth-century absurdist, however, sets in relief its different use in most ancient philosophical settings. When we read in *The Myth of Sisyphus* that 'the whole of existence for a person who has turned his back on the eternal is simply a huge mime under the mask of the absurd', we see how for Camus it is precisely the lack or loss of a larger framework of meaning (the turn away from 'the eternal') which defines the absurdist mentality.[19] But in antiquity the *theatrum mundi* motif often contradicts a sense of existential meaninglessness precisely by positing something more important *outside* the 'theatre' or beyond the 'game'. This is evidently true of the famous puppet imagery of the Cave in Plato *Republic* Book 7 or the puppet simile of *Laws* 1.644d, as well as later analogues such as Plotinus' vision of human life as a stage-play at *Ennead* 3.2.15–17 and numerous other ancient versions of the *theatrum mundi* topos.[20] Plotinus, for instance, is able to describe human beings and their lives as παίγνια, 'playthings', precisely because he avows a system of value whose sphere lies 'outside' and beyond the stage-play. Not only does his philosophy not give rise to absolute absurdity; it emphatically blocks it. The point is underlined by the occurrence of such motifs in Christian writers. When John Chrysostom, for example, writes that 'life is not a mime/game (*paignion*) – or rather, our present life *is*, but not the life to come', his emphatically two-world model of reality does not depart far from the spirit in which many pagan philosophers had exploited such figures to distinguish between the mortal and the eternal.[21]

[18] Camus (1965) 106 ('les décors s'écroulent'), 108 ('pantomime privée de sens'), 174 ('le grand mime').
[19] 'L'existence tout entière . . . n'est qu'un mime démesuré sous le masque de l'absurde': Camus (1965) 174. On the theatrical sensibility of Camus' absurdism, cf. Barish (1981) 365–9.
[20] On this much discussed topic see e.g. Curtius (1953) 138–44, Kokolakis (1960a), Dodds (1965) 8–13, Schildknecht and Konersmann (1998), Radke (2003) 324–40, Puchner (2006) 93–105. Cf. n. 9 above, ch. 10 n. 96.
[21] John Chrys. *In Mt.* 23.9 (57.318 *PG*); for *paignion* as 'mime', see ch. 10 n. 96.

The *theatrum mundi* topos, therefore, by no means automatically takes one down a road to full-blown absurdity. However, we shall later need to consider some further ancient uses of it which may point more compellingly in that direction. But first we must return to our starting-point and try to unpick some of the knotted threads that come together in the legend of the laughing 'Abderite' which echoed in the mind of Beckett's Murphy.

LAUGHING DEMOCRITUS (AND WEEPING HERACLITUS)

If most Greek philosophy left room for existential absurdity only in relative or comparative terms, there is one apparently striking exception, namely atomism, whose reductively materialist cosmos seems to make nonsense of any human need for meaning and value. It looks as though we should not be surprised, then, to find that it is Democritus who became the proverbially laughing philosopher of antiquity, the person who (on some reports of the legend) laughed at all human life, not just parts of it. Actually, we *should* still be surprised, for two reasons: first, because the historical as opposed to the legendary Democritus does not at all seem to have been an absurdist, as I shall shortly explain; secondly (a point I have already made *à propos* modern absurdism), because imagining an infinite but morally 'cold' cosmos does not seem to give one unequivocal grounds for laughter. Or does it? Much depends on how one conceives of laughter itself, a subject on which Greek culture contained polarised but unstable attitudes. If laughter is thought of as a life-affirming symptom of exuberant health and well-being, a medium of shared pleasure and an embodiment of 'play', then it seems a contradiction in terms to suppose that one could laugh at the *whole* of human existence. As well as requiring a positive context of friendship or something similar, 'playful' laughter seems to require a suspension not a permanent abolition of seriousness: on what basis could it become an entire way of life? If, on the other hand, we think of *gelōs* as *katagelōs* – laughter as derision and belittlement – how could such a stance take the human condition as its target without succumbing to self-implicating paradox? Just as Epicurus objected that no one could seriously believe Silenus' pessimism of 'best never to have been born, and second best to depart life as soon as possible' without implementing the second part of the proposition, so equally the person who purported to laugh derisively at existence in its entirety ought surely to choose suicide (which was the challenge that prompted Camus' defence of absurdism in *The Myth of*

Sisyphus).[22] Might it even be that truly global absurdity is an impossibility for humans, whether ancient or modern? We need to bear this conundrum in mind as we attempt to track down the laughter that ancient folk wisdom ascribed to Democritus.

Democritus' laughter, as we saw earlier, was one half of a diptych with the tears of Heraclitus. These legendary personae, whose rich Renaissance *Nachleben* in literature (and, to a lesser degree, visual art) draws in such important figures as Ficino, Rabelais, Erasmus, Montaigne and Robert Burton (the latter self-dubbed as 'Democritus Junior'),[23] count for almost nothing within rigorous modern historical scholarship on the two thinkers in question. And understandably so. My purpose here is not to claim that they should be taken as reliable clues to Heraclitean and Democritean philosophy; far from it. I want, though, to treat them, and especially that of Democritus, as a stimulus to reflection on some possible relationships between laughter and (philosophical) interpretations of 'the meaning of life', in Carlyle's now trite but indispensable phrase. As my argument progresses, positioning the legends *vis-à-vis* the 'reality', I shall attempt to elucidate three main varieties of laughter *qua* existentially charged behaviour: first, the manifestation of ease of mind or good spirits (*euthumiē*, in Democritus' own vocabulary); secondly, the expression of a sage's superior wisdom and the mockery of (but also, perhaps, the offer of 'therapy' to) those who subscribe to false or deluded values; thirdly, a response of ostensibly global 'absurdism' to existence *per se*.

The origins of the personae of the 'weeping' and the 'laughing' philosopher cannot be identified with confidence and were probably rather tangled. The notion of Heraclitus as a somewhat 'melancholic' individual was at least as old as Theophrastus, but it looks as though this was a biographical

---

[22] Epicurus' eloquent rebuttal of Silenus' 'wisdom' is at *Epist. Men.* 126–7. Cf. Metrodorus, *Anth. Pal.* 9.360, answering 9.359: on these epigrams see respectively Page (1981) 71–3, Gow and Page (1965) II 501–2. Plotinus rebuts the 'best never to have been born' dictum, when dealing with the problem of evil/suffering, at *Enn.* 3.2.15.

[23] Burton (1989) 32–7 paraphrases the ps.-Hippoc. letters at length; he also (115, cf. 37) adapts *Anth. Pal.* 9.148 (336 above). See Rütten (1992), esp. 27–32, 144–213, for the general influence of the letters; cf. Garcia Gomez (1984). Renaissance treatments of the two philosophical personae are adduced in Wind (1968) 48–9, Wind (1983, with plates 33–8), Buck (1963), Ménager (1995) 64–9, 84–6, Lutz (1954); on Rabelais, cf. Bakhtin (1968) 67–8, 360–1. Arbury (1998) 495 lists visual representations. (The only evidence for ancient images of the laughing/weeping philosophers seems to be Sid. Apoll. *Epist.* 9.9.14; but the paintings are imaginary. Cf. Appendix 2 n. 73.) The Cologne Rembrandt cited by Lutz (1954) 313 (cf. Cordero (2000) 229 n. 11) is no longer widely accepted as 'Democritus', though Schama (1999) 676–7 revives the view; for its identification as Zeuxis, see ch. 1 n. 21. Later creative responses to the Democritus-Heraclitus dichotomy include that of Leopardi (cf. ch. 9 n. 5); cf. Lonardi (1998). I have been unable to consult Salem (1996). Provine (2000) 171 seems to think laughing Democritus is simply historical.

speculation rather than a direct interpretation of Heraclitus' work, which, as we shall see, does not lend itself to such a reading.[24] As for Democritus, the fragments of his writings give some, though far from straightforward, support to a picture of him as refusing to take seriously many of the desires and ambitions that motivate human behaviour in general. But the explicit pairing of the laughing and weeping philosopher seems to have crystallised only at some point during the Hellenistic period. The relevant image of Democritus alone is central to the late-Hellenistic or early imperial 'epistolary novel' contained in pseudo-Hippocrates' *Epistles* 10–23 (360–4 below), while the contrasting duo had become familiar by the time of early imperial texts in both Greek and Latin. The oldest surviving trace of the gelastic Democritean persona is arguably found in a passage of Cicero's *De oratore* (written in 55) which suggests that the enigmatic nature of laughter's physical workings ('how it simultaneously takes hold of our breathing, mouth, veins, face and eyes') needs to be left to Democritus: the suggestion probably alludes ironically to the legend, though some dispute this.[25] Certainly the motif is available by the time of Hor. *Epist.* 2.1.194–200 (composed somewhere around 15), which reflects that if Democritus were alive *now* (cf., once again, the anonymous epigram, 336 above) he would laugh at the extremes of human folly. But we have no way of knowing how far back in the Hellenistic period this tradition stretched. Some scholars believe it was an invention of the Cynics, whose own complex dealings with laughter will be addressed later in this chapter; but neither this nor any other hypothesis inspires great confidence.[26] An affinity with broader Hellenistic

[24] See Theophr. fr. 233 (Fortenbaugh (1992) I 426), *apud* Diog. Laert. 9.6 (= Heraclitus A1 DK): 'melancholy' purports to explain why parts of Heraclitus' book were 'half finished'; that might but need not be a judgement on the *content* of his thought (cf. Lucian, *Vit. Auctio* 14 for a comic version of the link). 'Melancholy' is here related to Peripatetic ideas about the complex nature of exceptional minds: see ps.-Arist. *Probl.* 30.1, 953a10–955a40, with van der Eijk (2005) 139–68, Rütten (1992) 74–80, and the classic treatment in Klibansky *et al.* (1964) 15–41. On different conceptions of 'melancholy' as manic or depressive, cf. Toohey (2004) ch. 1, esp. 27–33.

[25] Cic. *De or.* 2.235, adapted in the Renaissance by Castiglione (1998) 184–5 (Castiglione (2002) 106). The passage, which denies that anyone has successfully explained the physiology of laughter, is accepted as an allusion to the 'laughing philosopher' by e.g. Guthrie (1965) 387; various other views in Viljamaa (1994) 86–7, Philippson (1928) 317–18, Leeman *et al.* (1989) 238, Rütten (1992) 8–11, Müller (1994) 45 n. 17.

[26] For the fuller version in ps.-Hippoc. *Epist.* 10–23, see 360–4 below. Sotion, *apud* Stob. 3.20.53, is probably (not definitely) the teacher of Seneca the younger; it is bold to claim he 'evidently [*sic*] introduced' the motif: Courtney (1980) 456; cf. Rütten (1992) 13–14. Further references, some discussed in my text below, include Sen. *Tranq.* 15.2–3, *De ira* 2.10.5, Juv. *Sat.* 10.28–53, Lucian, *Vit. Auctio* 13–14, *Peregr.* 7, 45 (with ch. 9, 464), *Sacrif.* 15, Julian, *Epist.* 201c (= Democ. A20 DK), Sid. Apoll. *Epist.* 9.9.14 (cf. n. 23 above), and the texts cited in n. 74 below; cf. Chitwood (2004) 129–32, 186–8 (unreliable). Stewart (1958) 186–7 conjectures a Cynic source ('circle of Menippus') for laughing Democritus; cf. Rütten (1992) 32–53, Müller (1994) 48–50, Kindstrand (1984) 155. But Stewart (1994)

ideals of emotional detachment and freedom from care (*ataraxia*) hovers in the background, but we shall see that such ideals are not sufficient in themselves to produce a strong sense of existential absurdity.

However the images of 'Democritus' and 'Heraclitus' evolved, the relationship between the popular diptych and the evidence of the philosophers' own ideas remains precarious. At first sight, indeed, one might even wonder whether the characterisation of the two figures is, on one level, the wrong way round. Heraclitus, after all, espouses a positive, totalising view of the eternal meaning and intelligibility of the cosmos, while Democritean atomism reduces the world to a 'meaningless', value-empty movement of infinitely numerous atoms in infinite void. Might not an authentic Heraclitean, therefore, have more reason to laugh (with joyful confidence in his own truth, and scorn for those who fail to grasp it), while those convinced by Democritean physics might resign themselves to nihilistic despair? There is an intricate challenge here for any project in understanding the philosophical possibilities of Greek laughter (or the Greek possibilities of philosophical laughter).

The oddity of a weeping Heraclitus can be summed up very easily. While the Heraclitean fragments convey a trenchantly low appraisal of the way in which many, probably most, people lead their lives, that appraisal – unlike the image of the proverbially weeping Heraclitus in Lucian ('I pity and grieve for them all', οἰκτείρω τε σφέας καὶ ὀδύρομαι)[27] – voices no mournful or pitying attitude towards the human condition. On the contrary; Heraclitus (like his close contemporary Xenophanes, as noted in the previous chapter) is a philosophical *satirist*: not for nothing did Timon of Phlius, a philosophical wit of very different persuasion, call Heraclitus a 'mob-abuser' (ὀχλολοίδορος).[28] A note of disparagement for

---

36, forgetting Hor. *Epist.* 2.1.194, puts the invention in the first century AD. Lutz (1954) 311–13 thinks the Heraclitean 'unity of opposites' gave rise to the contrasting philosophical pair; Herrenschmidt (2000) 509–10 speculates tenuously that Democritus' supposed dealings with Zoroastrian magi generated his gelastic image; Luria (1963) flimsily posits a link with Democritus' views on human progress (esp. fr. 5), in contrast to Heraclitus' supposed pessimism. There is no reason, *contra* Thierfelder (1968) 16, to believe that Democritean laughter itself spawned the proverbial stupidity of the Abderites.

[27] Lucian, *Vit. Auctio* 14; cf. n. 37 below. Weeping Heraclitus appears also at Lucian, *Peregr.* 7, Ael. *VH* 8.13; cf. ps.-Heraclitus, *Epist.* 7 for his 'laughterless' existence: text (including *P. Gen.* 271) of the latter, with translation, in Attridge (1976) 66–79, who discusses affinities with Cynic moralising (9–11, 25–39). Pliny, *HN* 7.79 apparently includes Heraclitus among those who neither laughed *nor* wept. Diog. Laert. 9.3 cites a reputation for reclusive misanthropy. Chitwood (2004) 66–8 is muddled on weeping Heraclitus.

[28] Timon fr. 817 *SH*, 43 Diels; contrast Timon's description of Arcesilaus as a 'mob-pleaser', ὀχλοάρεσκος (808 *SH*, 34 Diels); on Timon's *Silloi* cf. ch. 6 n. 13. Pertinent here is the perception of Heraclitus as a snarling dog in Meleager, *Anth. Pal.* 7.79, Theodoridas, *Anth. Pal.* 7.479.

(most) human minds was struck in what we know from Aristotle to have been the very first sentence of Heraclitus' book, 'though this *logos* holds good for ever, humans perpetually fail to comprehend it'. In the same passage occurred the characteristically paradoxical gibe, 'people are no more aware of what they do when awake than they are when asleep' (fr. 1 DK). This supercilious tone was a recurrent feature of Heraclitus' writing. People are said to exhibit an incomprehension which 'testifies that though present they are absent' (fr. 34); most people 'gorge themselves like cattle' (fr. 29); or, to take a more elaborate instance which scoffs at certain religious practices: 'they fatuously try to purify themselves with blood when already polluted with blood, which is the same as trying to clean oneself with mud after having stepped into mud! . . . And they pray to these statues, which is the same as trying to hold a conversation with houses!'[29] Such a mordant viewpoint implicitly creates an opportunity for scornful laughter by anyone aligned with the speaker – assuming, that is, that Heraclitus believed there *was* anyone sufficiently receptive to his views (frs. 1 and 108 seem to cast doubt on this). Elsewhere Heraclitus is prepared to ridicule prominent individuals, criticising Pythagoras' *kakotechniē* ('fake expertise' or 'fraudulence', fr. 129), mocking the supposed cleverness of Hesiod, Xenophanes and Hecataeus (frs. 40, 129) as well as the naivety of the historical Homer (fr. 56), and asserting that both Homer and Archilochus, presumably taken as representatives of different parts of the poetic spectrum, should have been 'thrashed' (an ironic echo of the treatment of Thersites in *Iliad* 2) and ejected from poetic competitions (fr. 42).[30] In such fragments we glimpse a polemical repertoire that includes insulting language, scurrilous tone and anecdotal detail, all of them features especially familiar from iambic poetry. This quasi-iambic ethos makes fr. 42 particularly striking: just as Heraclitus outrageously pictures a Homer humiliated like his own character Thersites (as well as like a disruptive participant in a festival), so, it seems, he relishes the thought of Archilochus, master of the 'stinging' art of *iambos*, being subjected to the kind of physical degradation that the iambic poetic imagination itself liked to wield.[31]

Heraclitus fr. 130 DK ('don't use laughter so much that you come to seem laughable yourself') is probably not authentic, *contra* Kullmann (1995) 82, Hügli (2001) 3.

[29] Fr. 5 DK: Adoménas (1999) 101–7 airs various interpretations, some not wholly convincing.

[30] Cf. Marcovich (1964) 41–2, (1967) 70 for divergent views of *kakotechniē* in fr. 129 DK. Heraclitus' critique of popular religion is examined by Babut (1975), Adoménas (1999), his critique of poets/intellectuals by Babut (1976).

[31] Scholars have discerned in *rhapizesthai* a pun on either 'rhapsode' (so, apparently, Most (1999) 338) or the rhapsode's staff, *rhabdos* (e.g. Kahn (1979) 111; cf. Collins (2004) 152. I doubt both suggestions. In any case, the 'thrashing' should be imagined as administered by festival stewards *vel sim.*:

We do not need to dwell on Heraclitus' often ridiculing modes of utterance in order to get the essential point in focus. Far from being the bearer of a 'weeping', tragic perspective on life, the Heraclitean view of the world, for all the uncertainty that attaches to details of its interpretation, generates not pity but a sort of scorn for those (whether prominent intellectuals or simply 'the many') who fail to grasp the universal *logos*: the hidden harmony of nature (beneath the flux of appearances), the unity of opposites, the divine wisdom steering the cosmos, the importance of an inward truth-seeking journey into the soul, and so forth. Heraclitus' fragments enunciate a mentality too affirmative (if partly mystical) to allow any kind of existential despair, no matter how many human beings may fail to hear the call of the *logos* – no matter, indeed, if *all* humans somehow inevitably fall short of the ideal ('the wisest of humans will be seen to be an ape when compared with a god', fr. 83, another piece of laughter-related imagery).[32] One precise reason why this should be so derives from Heraclitus' notion of death, which on the principle of the unity of opposites cannot be interpreted as radically different from, or a radical negation of, life itself. Whatever the unexpected, unknown things which await people after death (fr. 27), at least two fragments (62, 88) seem to confirm the eternal interchangeability of life and death, mortality and immortality, while others (including fr. 114) discern the interpenetration of the divine with the human, perhaps in keeping with the key principle that 'all things are one' (fr. 50). We have already heard Heraclitus' voice sneering at basic components of traditional religion. But he went further; he rejected any theology which by defining human limitations in contrast to divine power opened up an abyss of pessimism.

When ordinary human understanding fails, therefore, Heraclitus does not 'weep' over the spectacle of ignorance, folly and self-deception. He ridicules it. Implicitly at least, he was a practitioner of laughter, a philosophical mocker and satirist. As such, he has something important in common with many other Greek philosophers and intellectuals. A tendency to mock opponents, whether individually or as a group, can be traced in a number of the Presocratics, in many of the fifth-century sophists, even in Socrates (though in complicatedly ironic ways, as I argued in Chapter 6), in Plato (who may have had a personal weakness for abrasive argument),

cf. e.g. Hom. *Od.* 8.258–60, Ar. *Peace* 734, with Olson (1998) 217 (but misstating the comic point, which is not unlike Heraclitus': *viz.* to imagine the stewards striking a *poet*), Wilson (2000) 166. As regards Heraclitus' relationship to Archilochus, Heraclitus fr. 17 has often been thought knowingly to contradict Archil. 132 *IEG*; but cf. Marcovich (1967) 15–16.

[32] On the mocking 'ape' motif, cf. Heraclitus fr. 82 DK with ch. 6 n. 94.

and frequently in the debates of Hellenistic philosophy (not least on the part of Epicureans, to whom I shall return). No wonder that a character in Athenaeus could exclaim: 'most philosophers are by nature even more slanderous (*kakēgoroi*) than comic poets!'[33] But it is potentially misleading just to lump together philosophers in this regard. Even when they exhibit a family likeness in their readiness to use ridicule as a weapon of polemic, they do not all exhibit an inclination, or possess a motivation, to laugh *at the world*; and those of them who do may have different reasons for this attitude. This will shortly become clear in the case of Democritus/'Democritus', whose existential 'laughter' is quite distinct from anything in Heraclitus. Yet I have set out a basic case for detecting one *kind* of laughter in Heraclitus too, a laughter betokening disdain for the paradoxical failure of many human minds to realise a potential that is, as Heraclitus emphatically states, 'common' to them all (frs. 1–2). Furthermore, if Heraclitus' utterances are not just those of an individual but of the *logos* itself speaking through him (fr. 50), we might infer that the laughter sometimes heard within those utterances also belongs to the *logos* in its own right – as though reality itself were deriding human inadequacies.

As a final observation on the tone of this Heraclitean voice, we should take account of one of the most famous, but also most contentious, of his fragments, which runs as follows: αἰὼν παῖς ἐστι παίζων, πεσσεύων· παιδὸς ἡ βασιληίη ('a lifetime is a child playing games, moving pieces in a board-game; a child's is the kingship').[34] Some interpretations of this fragment, including those which choose to translate the first word as 'time' or 'eternity' rather than 'lifetime', are excessively speculative; they look for cosmological symbolism where it is more cogent to find a deflationary gesture towards the pretensions of unreflective human existence. The triple emphasis in the Greek on the motif of child (*pais*) and play (*paizein*) warrants that second reading. It implies the 'innocence' of those utterly absorbed in their

---

[33] Athen. 5.220a. On Epicureans and Cynics, see 358–9, 372–87 below. Owen (1983) offers some reflections on the traditions of philosophical invective.

[34] Fr. 52 DK: a range of interpretations in e.g. Kahn (1979) 227–9, Marcovich (1967) 493–5, Herter (1961) 81–2, Hussey (2000) 640; on the sense of *aiōn* (lifetime – some think 'eternity', but mistranslated as adj./participle in Hussey (1999) 107), cf. Degani (1961) 65–6, with Friis Johansen and Whittle (1980) II 45–6, 459–60, for crisp treatment of early usage (but not Heraclitus). Meerwaldt (1928) 162–3 overreads in taking the child to be fooling with the pieces rather than following the rules. The picture of Heraclitus actually playing with children at Diog Laert. 9.3 is maybe a 'biographical' back-projection from fr. 52. For Stoic life-as-game imagery, where the child is always free to say 'I won't play any longer', see Epict. *Diss.* 1.24.20, 1.25.7–8, 2.16.37, 4.7.30; cf. Herter (1961) 78–80, Long (2002) 202–3, and see 342 above for the metaphysically affirmative and therefore non-absurdist status of such imagery in ancient philosophy. The motif makes a modern appearance in Freud's 1927 essay 'Der Humor': n. 129 below.

own immediate consciousness, unaware of a larger world and its frame of significance. Absorption in the moves of a game, as played by the child, can be taken as a metaphor for the absence of *self*-scrutiny, a key Heraclitean prerequisite for understanding the world-binding *logos*. Whatever exactly the nature of the board game envisaged, it makes better sense to regard its limited rules and options as an image that trivialises general human ambitions (the totality of a 'lifetime' as lived by most people) than as code for lawlike cosmic processes: it is hard, otherwise, to account for the stress on a child as the person playing the game. Similarly, the second part of the fragment, which may involve a pun on 'king' as a technical term in the board game,[35] then follows more smoothly as a reinforcement of the first. Even the most powerful humans, because of their circumscribed priorities, remain in a mental childhood; and pursuit of the things most people think supremely valuable (power, wealth, prestige) is itself, from a *logos*-grounded point of view, 'childish'. Although the riddling, paradoxical, quasi-oracular cast of Heraclitus' writing always leaves doubt about his meanings, the reading of fr. 52 I have outlined certainly fits well with the use of childhood imagery in both fr. 70, which tells us that Heraclitus 'regarded human opinions as the toys of children', and fr. 79, which runs: 'a man is thought of as infantile (*nēpios*) by a god, just as a child is by a man'. Such direct use of childhood as a marker of the immaturity of (most) human thought makes it even more unlikely that the language of fr. 52 is conveying a symbolic point about the cosmos itself.

To call adults 'children' is an archetypal form of belittlement. Thus Xenophon, to take a token example, depicts the Spartans mocking their Mantinean allies for fearing light-armed peltasts in the way that children fear bogey figures.[36] Such derision implies that things could and should be otherwise. Unlike the parody of his supposedly weeping persona in Lucian ('everything changes place in the play of eternity'),[37] Heraclitus does not consider existence *per se* to be 'childish' or absurd, only the way it is irrationally conducted by most people. The laughter that can be heard through his words is aimed satirically at the gap between the unity of *logos* and the deluded fragmentation of it manifested in the lives of the

---

[35] See Σ on Theoc. 6.18, with 'king' at Pl. *Laws* 10.904a, where the world's divine overseer plays the same board game (*pettoi*, 903d) as in Heraclitus; cf. Kurke (1999) 257 n. 28 (reading board games as symbolic politics), with Pearson (1917) II 85 on the game itself.

[36] Xen. *Hell.* 4.4.17 (ch. 1, 48). For philosophical depiction of humans as 'children', cf. Pl. *Phd.* 77e (with the 'bogey' motif again: ch. 6 n. 35), 'Democritus' in ps.-Hippoc. *Epist.* 17.5, 8 (see 360–3 below), Lucr. *DRN* 2.55–8.

[37] ἀμειβόμενα ἐν τῇ τοῦ αἰῶνος παιδίῃ: Lucian, *Vit. Auctio* 14, translating the 'lifetime' (*aiōn*) of Heraclitus fr. 52 (which Lucian paraphrases) into 'eternity'; cf. n. 34 above.

'childish'. Whatever he may have thought of laughter as such,[38] the ring of his philosophical voice is not that of a despairing 'weeper' but of an exponent of its own style of existential laughter – a laughter whose sound forms a counterpoint to, but is fully harmonised with, the certainty of reason.

If the legend of 'weeping' Heraclitus is therefore out of kilter with the tone of the philosopher's own utterances, the relationship between legend and reality in the case of Democritus is also though more delicately problematic. By the early third century AD Aelian could epitomise the popular tradition of the 'laughing philosopher' by stating that 'Democritus used to ridicule all [sc. his fellow Abderites] and say they were mad, so that his townsmen called him "Laughing Mouth" (*Gelasinos*)'.[39] Here, it seems, is a figure whose face is permanently fixed in a look of derision for the lives of others; and other versions of the legend (to be cited in due course) strengthen this image. We might get a jolt, then, when we turn back to the original and find that two of the generally (though not universally) accepted fragments of Democritus' own writings say: 'it is right for humans not to laugh at the misfortunes of other humans but to lament'; 'those who derive pleasure from their neighbours' misfortunes do not grasp that all are equally vulnerable to the effects of chance'.[40] Leaving aside the knotty issue of authenticity, it is perhaps in principle conceivable that Democritus could have regarded the human condition as intrinsically laughable, while nonetheless retaining a sense of the validity of sympathetic fellow-feeling for the suffering of others. But is such an interpretation plausible?

---

[38] Leaving aside the dubious fr. 130 (n. 28 above), the only direct mention of laughter in Heraclitus is in fr. 92, where the Sibyl's utterances are described as *agelasta* (cf. ch. 1 n. 100), apparently stressing the absence of any surface charm to her deep wisdom. See Marcovich (1967) 405–6, Kahn (1979) 124–6 for further discussion; the case for seeing a parallelism between the Sibyl and Heraclitus himself is weakened by Heraclitus' own penchant for a gelastic tone of voice. Cf. also fr. 15 (with ch. 4, 182), whose wry observation on phallic rituals implies an ambiguous attitude towards the laughter of popular culture.

[39] Ael. *VH* 4.20. The nickname *Gelasinos* (cf. *Suda s.v.* Δημόκριτος = Democ. A2 DK) surely involves a pun on γελασῖνος, 'incisor tooth' (also, sometimes, 'dimple'), so called because visible when the mouth laughs/smiles (Poll. *Onom.* 2.91); cf. Appendix 1, 529. For the Abderites' diagnosis of *Democritus*' 'madness', see 360–1 below.

[40] Frs. 107a, 293 DK: with the first compare Sen. *Tranq.* 15 (where 'Democritean' laughter has just been recommended), with the second Pittacus *apud* Stob. 3.1.172 (see DK 1 64). Democ. fr. 255 acknowledges the value of pity (cf. n. 47 below). On the disputed authenticity of the sayings ascribed to Democritus (or, in some cases, 'Democrates' [*sic*]), see e.g. Guthrie (1965) 489–92, Taylor (1999) 223–7. My assumption is that while some sayings cannot be *verbatim* authentic, they collectively represent genuine Democritean material that has been excerpted and 'edited' in the course of transmission: for the possible importance of the Cynics in that process, see Stewart (1958), esp. 187–8.

To get the issues into closer focus, we should start with a (concise) reminder of the bigger picture of Democritus' *kosmos* – or, rather, his plural worlds (*kosmoi*), each of which is a local atomic agglomeration within infinite space. The only physical reality, in the Democritean scheme of things, is an infinity of atoms moving perpetually and randomly through an infinite void, in the process (which had no beginning and will have no end) unceasingly combining and separating to cause the generation, change and destruction of everything we perceive. The 'appearances' of all sensory objects are only ostensible; the hard 'truth' is exclusively that of atoms and void (fr. 9 DK). Human beings themselves are among such objects. Their senses give them a plethora of impressions of the world, but these impressions depend on interaction between the perceiver's own bodily condition and the various atomic movements of, including emissions of 'images' by, other things. The impressions are therefore in part subjective, and in any case involve only 'appearances' or phenomena; they give limited access to the hard truth of atoms 'in themselves'. Human minds, on the other hand, though themselves necessarily atomic, are capable of comprehending reality by the use of reason, authoritatively piecing together the world that lies behind, and is only flimsily apprehended by, the senses.

Though this atomist model pictures a world of randomness (i.e. lacking any kind of purpose or teleology), in another respect it makes the world intelligible as an embodiment of necessity, *anankē*. Everything about the endless movement of atoms through void simply is and must be the way it is. The question that concerns us here is how a Democritean is supposed to react, in the broadest psychological terms, to a realisation of where the materialist picture leaves the human condition. On one level, the question seems beside the point: if everything consists of physically necessitated atomic movements, then human beings cannot *deliberate* or choose how to react to anything about their world. But Democritus seems to believe in some kind or degree of human freedom. His ethical tenets, so far as they can be reconstructed, articulate normative principles for how the subscriber to atomist philosophy will try to lead his or her life. Democritean ethics looks, indeed, like a sort of reassertion of freedom in the teeth of the materialist reductionism of Democritean physics. Despite lingering doubts about the evidence in this area, the salient principles again seem clear enough. While some scholars have suspected the evidence in part because of its substantial coincidence with traditional Greek morality, this may just mean that Democritus actually had nothing ethically very original to say. For what it is worth, anyway, the emphasis of the ethical fragments and testimonies falls on the following, overlapping values: first, moderation (on the lines of 'nothing to excess', the Delphic wisdom of Apollo) and self-mastery; secondly, the avoidance of unnecessary ambition or striving, and the cultivation of satisfaction with what one already has; thirdly, a belief that the mind/soul (and its pleasures) is far more important than the body (e.g. frs. 37, 40); fourthly, a general 'cheerfulness' (which is also 'peace of mind'), *euthumiē*, in the face of what life may throw at one.

I propose to canvass, hypothetically, three distinct ways in which a philosophical place for laughter might be found within this set of attitudes. The first and perhaps most obvious – though one far from the traditional image of the laughing Democritus – is as a component, or at least manifestation, of *euthumiē*. As a concept of carefree good cheer, a sense of subjective well-being and in that sense 'happiness',[41] *euthumiē* might be thought to comport well with genial laughter. Indeed, it is notable that *euthum-* terms were sometimes associated with a specifically symposiac mentality of elation and mirth, in the same way as, though less frequently than, the language of *euphrosunē* which I documented in Chapter 3.[42] But does it make sense to place Democritus' own concept of cheerfulness at that (gelastically marked) end of the euthumic spectrum? Only, I think, if we recall that the tradition of sympotic good cheer is one which itself has different strands within it. Democritus' affinities are not with the hedonism and sensuality that dominate the more exhilarated, komastic styles of symposiac celebration, but with the steady moderation of, say, Xenophanes fr. 1 or parts of the Theognidean corpus: this is borne out by the condemnation of drunkenness and over-consumption in some of Democritus' fragments (159, 235). Our evidence for Democritean *euthumiē* stresses quietism, moderation and balance of living (esp. frs. 3, 191); part of this ethic of 'nothing to excess' is avoidance of hedonistic pleasure-seeking.[43] So if Democritus acknowledged a euthumic laughter, it would have had to be one of quiet satisfaction with modest and readily available pleasures, especially of the mind, rather than a heady, potentially destabilising laughter of physical exuberance.[44] This still

---

[41] Democritus also uses the term *euestō*, 'well-being', treated as a synonym of *eudaimonia* by Antiphon soph. fr. 22 DK; cf. Pendrick (2002) 291, and see n. 80 below. Democ. fr. 189 shows that *euthumiē* counts as happiness *qua* the 'best thing' in life (i.e. the answer to Midas' question, 339 above).

[42] For *euthum-* terms and symposiac/celebratory cheerfulness, see esp. adesp. lyr. 926(b) *PMG*, Lyr. adesp. 23 *CA* (both with dancing), Ion Chi. 26.14 *IEG* (with *paizein*, including joking, in line 16), Aesch. *Agam.* 1592 (notwithstanding the macabre context), Eur. *Cyc.* 530, Xen. *Cyr.* 1.3.12 (with laughter at *ibid.* 9); on *euphrosunē* see ch. 3, 109–10.

[43] For an anti-hedonistic note (in the standard, not philosophical, sense of 'hedonism'), see e.g. frs. 70, 178, 189, 214, 219, 234. Fr. 229 would justify *moderate* symposiac pleasures; Barnes (1982) 533 speaks of Democritean festivity as 'fairly sober and earnestly intellectual . . . a symposium rather than a pub-crawl', overlooking the komastic end of the sympotic spectrum.

[44] Plut. *Mor.* 466e cites the laughter of Crates of Thebes (see 375 with n. 100 below) to illustrate one kind of *euthumia*, while 477d contrasts this (in a heavily Platonised version) with the 'bought laughter' of

leaves self-controlled sympotic and other celebratory experiences as fully
consistent with the Democritean criterion of pleasure, a point exemplified
by fr. 230: 'a life without festivals is a long road with no inns on it' (βίος
ἀνεόρταστος μακρὴ ὁδὸς ἀπανδόκευτος). And since, we might add (with
only mild exaggeration), a festival without laughter is, in Greek terms, no
festival at all, it is reasonable to conclude that moderate, harmonious laughter has a legitimate role to play within Democritus' conception of *euthumiē*
and the deep pleasure (which he sometimes calls *terpsis*) that suffuses it.[45]
But this still leaves us a long way short of the outlook of the proverbially
'laughing philosopher' of later antiquity.

Just how far short can be brought out by glancing at the fullest fragment
on *euthumiē*, from which we learn that it is advisable 'to contemplate the
lives of the wretched, dwelling on the severity of their sufferings, so that you
may think of your own present circumstances as substantial and enviable'.
The point is reiterated later in the same fragment, where the possibility of
cheerfulness is said to be enhanced by 'comparing one's own life with the
lives of those who are faring worse than oneself', allowing one 'to deem
oneself happy when one thinks of what they suffer and of how much better one's life is going than theirs'.[46] This position presupposes, of course,
that suffering (equatable with pain, whether bodily or mental) *matters*; it
has a negative value which the atomist acknowledges, even if it remains
debatable how far he could locate it at the level of atomic reality as opposed
to that of phenomenal experience. But in keeping with frs. 107a and 293
(351 above), the position also offers something very remote from *Schadenfreude*. Democritus is not recommending laughter at the misfortunes of
others; his world (unlike Heraclitus', it seems) explicitly leaves room for
pity.[47] Democritus supposes that by contemplating vicariously how much
worse one's life could be (in a manner later famously echoed by another

mime-artists, calling life 'unsmiling' (i.e. death-like? cf. n. 89 below) for those who lack *euthumia*:
neither passage is very close to Democritean *euthumiē*. Closer, though different in certain respects
(Democritus did not consider material suffering negligible), is the Stoic laughter-plus-*euthumia* of
Epict. *Diss.* 1.1.22 (cf. ch. 6, 303). Note also the Hellenised Jewish model of the euthumically laughing
sage at Philo, *Leg. alleg.* 3.217; cf. ch. 10, 481.

[45] *Terpsis* and related terms denote a particularly fulfilling pleasure (traditionally associated with
music/poetry, feasting, sex, etc.); see esp. frs. 4, 188, 194, 200–1, 232–3, with Warren (2002)
48–52 for some discussion. On the association of festivals with laughter, cf. ch. 1, 4, 20, ch. 4
n. 138.

[46] . . . τῶν δὲ ταλαιπωρεόντων τοὺς βίους θεωρέειν, ἐννοούμενον ἃ πάσχουσι κάρτα, ὅκως ἂν τὰ
παρεόντα σοι καὶ ὑπάρχοντα μεγάλα καὶ ζηλωτὰ φαίνηται . . . παραβάλλοντα τὸν ἑαυτοῦ
βίον πρὸς τὸν τῶν φαυλότερον πρησσόντων καὶ μακαρίζειν ἑωυτὸν ἐνθυμεύμενον ἃ πάσχουσιν,
ὁκόσῳ αὐτέων βέλτιον πρήσσει τε καὶ διάγει (fr. 191).

[47] See fr. 255, where pity (οἰκτίρειν), from the powerful towards the needy, is included in a list of good
things.

atomist, Lucretius),[48] one will feel more content with existing sources of pleasure and well-being, less inclined to pursue what one does *not* have. If we were to entertain the possibility that Democritus espoused some form of the *theatrum mundi* trope (the ethical sayings happen to include the remark, 'the cosmos is a stage, life an entry in a play: you come, you watch, you depart', though this is highly unlikely to be authentic),[49] that would mean that he took the euthumic atomist to be capable of drawing psychological strength from observing the varied fortunes of others. But it would certainly not leave such a person coldly or loftily detached from the contingencies of the human condition. Since suffering is evidently a threat to the life of the atomist himself, euthumic laughter will itself always have to guard against excess and over-confidence if it is to be compatible with the calm freedom from care which is the bedrock of Democritus' thinking, as likewise of the later 'euthumist' tradition.[50] To put the point in comparative terms, the euthumic laughter of the Democritean would need to approximate to the 'smile' of serenity which appears in a later source as emblematic of the true Stoic sage (himself a practitioner, in part, of *euthumia*) as he 'sails calmly on the sea of life'.[51]

So much, then, for the possibilities of euthumic laughter. Let us now consider a second conceivable kind of 'Democritean' laughter, one which moves us closer to the legendary image and is actually incorporated in several attestations of that image, including those in the Roman satirists Horace and Juvenal. This is the kind of laughter we have already traced in Heraclitus and which also forms a major strand, as I shall later show, in Cynic practices: namely, ridicule of those who lack, or fail to grasp, the insights of true wisdom possessed and advocated by the sage. Such ridicule is very different from mocking others for misfortune over which they have no control; to that extent it would be consistent with the model of euthumic laughter I have sketched above. Presumably, however, *excessive* engagement

---

[48] See Lucr. *DRN* 2.1–13 for two images of the atomist's mind finding pleasure in contemplating the sufferings and folly of others; exhaustive analysis in Fowler (2002) 22–66. Cf. Sorabji (2000) 223–4 for several varieties of this consolatory motif.

[49] Democ. fr. 115 (*84) DK; cf. Kokolakis (1960a) 13–14. The saying itself (a) is linguistically unlikely to be fifth-century Greek (especially the extended use of *skēnē* for the theatre as a whole: cf. Palladas, *Anth. Pal.* 10.72, cited in n. 130 below), and (b) seems to confuse the roles of performer and spectator.

[50] In the later euthumist tradition, the relation to Democritus of both Seneca, *De tranquillitate animi* and Plutarch, περὶ εὐθυμίας is contentious; cf. n. 44 above. Gill (1994) offers an interesting approach.

[51] The smiling sage appears in anon. *Anth. Pal.* 9.208.1–2: ὅς κεν Ἐπικτήτοιο σοφὴν τελέσειε μενοινήν, | μειδιάει βιότοιο γαληνιόων ἐνὶ πόντῳ. On *euthumia* as one species of Stoic 'good state of feeling' (though attached to a different metaphysics from Democritus'), see Sorabji (2000) 48, with Müller (1994) 45–8. For a euthumic smile/laugh with a more easy-going Epicurean colour, see the '*lento . . . risu*' of Hor. *Odes* 2.16.26–7.

in such ridicule, like any other excess ('both deficiencies and excesses tend to come unstuck and to cause great disturbances to the soul', Democritus fr. 191), could destroy a properly euthumic balance of mind. Apart from anything else, an addiction to deriding the faults of others would increase the risk of making enemies and exposing oneself to retaliation. When the fourth-century Democritean philosopher Anaxarchus, who accompanied Alexander to India, made a symposiac gibe at Nicocreon, tyrant of Salamis, the latter subsequently had him tortured and killed (though the ultimate point of the story is that Anaxarchus preserved his tranquillity of mind to the end).[52] Just as pressing, from a euthumic point of view, is the need to avoid feeling *phthonos* or resentment (the root of derision, on the Platonic account at *Philebus* 48–50): Democritus' own fragments several times draw attention to this hostile, aggressive class of emotions and the psychological damage they inflict (frs. 88, 159, 191, 245). Furthermore, the fragments contain hints of a general aversion to personal friction and social rivalry: 'greatness of soul means tolerating error with gentleness'; 'when worthless people engage in reproaches, the good man should disregard it'; 'those who like blaming others are not well fitted for friendship'; 'competitiveness (*philonikiē*) is entirely foolish'; it is a good thing for fellow citizens to share the same values (the bond of *homonoia*).[53] Should the ideal Democritean, then, engage in the laughter of ridicule only to a cautiously restrained extent, or eschew it altogether?

In the absence of explicit statement by Democritus or reliable biographical information about him, we can only address this question in terms of the tone and thrust of the ethical fragments. As it happens, the markers of mocking, 'satirical' tone in the fragments are far less pronounced than in the case of Heraclitus. The sayings ascribed to Democritus do posit the existence of abundant folly, which is seen as a failure to recognise and work with the grain of reality ('irrationality is resistance to life's necessities', fr. 289) or to take responsibility for one's own action: 'those lacking in understanding are taught self-discipline by misfortune' (fr. 54); 'it is not reason but misfortune that teaches the infantile (*nēpioi*)' (fr. 76); 'it is better for the foolish to be ruled than to rule' (fr. 75); 'humans fashioned an image of chance as an excuse for their own fecklessness (*aboulie*)' (fr. 119). Despite an occasional detail in common with Heraclitus (such as the scornful use of *nēpios*, 'infantile': compare fr. 76 with Heraclitus fr. 79 on 350 above), there

---

[52] Anaxarchus A1 DK, *apud* Diog. Laert. 9.58–60. Anaxarchus laughs (at Alexander's divine pretensions) in Ael. *VH* 9.37 (Anaxarchus A8 DK). On Anaxarchus, see Warren (2002) 73–85; cf. nn. 54, 79 below.

[53] Frs. 46, 48, 109, 237, 255: the ideas of blame/reproach in frs. 48, 109 (μωμεομένων, φιλομεμφέες) could in principle embrace mockery.

is little sign in Democritus of the sharp edge of sarcasm often palpable in Heraclitus. In fact, Democritus seems somewhat averse, as it were, to head-on confrontation with those who fail to live according to his own standards: in addition to the precepts against rivalry and aggression noted above, we encounter the sobering maxim, 'it is better to scrutinise (*elenchein*) one's own faults than those of others' (fr. 60). We should also reckon here with the statement in fr. 177 that 'good action is not defiled by foul speech' (. . . οὔτε πρῆξις ἀγαθὴ λόγου βλασφημίῃ λυμαίνεται), where the verb expresses distaste for the quasi-polluting ethos of public insult and derision. Such a sentiment is not, of course, incompatible with the philosopher's own use of judicious ethical censure. Democritus is also credited with the saying 'frank speech (*parrhēsiē*) is proper to freedom, but judging the right occasion (*kairos*) is a source of danger', a remark whose ambivalence suitably epitomises the overall impression left by the fragments.[54]

It looks, in short, as though Democritus assigned little value to philosophically satirical ridicule, and was generally wary of the association between derisive laughter and those forces of social division and rancour that could threaten a moderate, euthumic existence. Consistent with that impression, and cementing the contrast with Heraclitus, is the fact that mockery of named individuals plays virtually no part in the evidence for the historical Democritus.[55] It is true that we might at this point introduce into the equation a distinction between two subtypes of the laughter of philosophical ridicule: one an expression of pure *superiority*, the other an instrument of the desire to challenge and *change* others. The evidence already cited for a Democritean aversion to malice, rivalry and competition decisively rules out a penchant for the first of these. But is there anything to be said in favour of the other? The fact of Democritus' production of copious writings (now mostly lost) presumably attests to a general attempt to persuade others of the truth of atomism and its consequences. But nowhere within the fragments or in respectable external testimony is there any indication of a wish to utilise the power of laughter for 'corrective' purposes.[56]

---

[54] Fr. 226; note, perhaps, the doubtful fr. 298a ('do not always allow everything to the tongue'), with the stress on *kairos* in the Democritean Anaxarchus fr. 1 DK ('one needs to know how to measure the right moment'); cf. ch. 3 n. 38. On *parrhēsia* and laughter, see ch. 5, 218–19, 234–42. Democ. fr. 104 (γέρων εὔχαρις ὁ αἱμύλος καὶ σπουδαιόμυθος, 'the wheedler who uses fine words is a charming old man'?) is interestingly interpreted by Grant (1924) 17 as alluding to the dissembling *eirōn* (cf. ch. 6, 320); but the sense remains uncertain.

[55] A possible exception is Democritus' alleged disparagement of Anaxagoras, Diog. Laert. 9.42 (A1 DK); but this is slender evidence.

[56] Contrast the pseudo-Democritean laughter at Sen. *Tranq.* 15.2–3, where a hope of changing people is one strand; cf. 369 below.

Democritus does not seem to have been disposed to exercise ridicule to undermine anyone else's convictions or convert them to his own doctrines.

If that inference is on the right lines, we can fill out its implications by noticing a marked contrast with the main later heirs of atomist physics, the Epicureans, who practised a sustained strategy of both philosophical and *ad hominem* ridicule against their opponents, even to the point of obscene abuse.[57] Epicurus himself seems to have regarded laughter *tout court* as a hallmark of his philosophy: 'we should simultaneously laugh, philosophise, look after our households . . . and never cease disseminating the utterances that arise from correct philosophy', runs one of his aphorisms.[58] The placing of the verb *gelan*, 'laugh', as the first word of this maxim gives it programmatic force, as though laughter should colour the whole of life, serving as a psychological underpinning of philosophy itself. At first sight, this could easily be supposed to be a partial Epicurean equivalent of Democritean cheerfulness and tranquillity of mind. After all, we are told that Epicurus went so far as to claim that the wise person 'often laughs at the extremes of bodily sickness', and his recurrent emphasis on freedom from fear of death would translate well into a metaphorically as well as literally laughing attitude to life.[59] But it is clear that Epicureans ascribed a further, more aggressive value to laughter, subjecting their opponents to blatant ridicule in a manner not unlike that of the Cynics. A character in Plutarch (admittedly a less than impartial witness) can refer generically to the 'ribald scoffing and laughter' (χλευασμοὺς καὶ γέλωτας) of Epicureans, not least against the religious beliefs of other thinkers; and Lucian dramatises a theological debate between a Stoic and Epicurean in which the latter's demeanour is heavily streaked with mockery.[60] Some of Epicurus' own fragments refer to vigorous laughter as an appropriate response to certain kinds of 'sophistry', and he is alleged to have directed gibes at many other philosophers,

---

[57] Philippson (1928) 319–20, after correctly noting Democritus' aversion to *Schadenfreude*, reads back from Epicurean to Democritean laughter: this is unwarranted, though a connection between the two was probably made in antiquity (Lucian, *Vit. Auctio* 19). Müller (1994) 44 likewise goes too far in claiming 'direct' Democritean influence on Epicurean laughter; he overlooks the objections stated in my text to finding a key role for laughter in the historical Democritus' outlook. Cordero (2000) 237–8 less than compellingly ascribes the origins of the laughing Democritus legend to the Epicureans; cf. n. 26 above.

[58] γελᾶν ἅμα δεῖ καὶ φιλοσοφεῖν καὶ οἰκονομεῖν . . . καὶ μηδαμῇ λήγειν τὰς ἐκ τῆς ὀρθῆς φιλοσοφίας φωνὰς ἀφιέντας: Epic. *Sent. Vat.* 41.

[59] Laughing at sickness: Plut. *Mor.* 1088b–c (cf. 1090a) = Epic. fr. 600 Usener. Hor. *Epist.* 1.4.16 famously connects relaxed laughter with his self-image as sleek Epicurean 'pig', but it is unclear whether the laughter as such is distinctively Epicurean.

[60] Plut. *Mor.* 420b (= Epic. fr. 394 Usener), Lucian, *Iup. Trag.* 35–53 (see ch. 6 n. 56); cf. Cic. *Nat. D.* 1.93 for kindred testimony. Ael. frs. 64a–g (Domingo-Forasté) supplies another apparent instance of provocative Epicurean mockery of religion.

including his own teacher Nausiphanes (whom he called, *inter alia*, a 'jellyfish' and 'whore', *pornē*), while at the same time criticising Socratic irony for (presumably) its seemingly eirenic dissimulation.[61] Metrodorus of Lampsacus, Epicurus' closest associate, wrote a number of polemical works and spoke of the need for the Epicurean 'to laugh an authentically liberated laughter' (τὸν ἐλεύθερον ὡς ἀληθῶς γέλωτα γελάσαι) at *everyone* (sc. else), but at political philosophers in particular. And there is evidence of keen awareness of the value of satirical laughter in the writings of several other members of the school, among them Colotes, Polystratus, Zeno of Sidon and the acidulous Philodemus.[62] Epicureans possessed a self-confidence in their own enlightenment which was channelled into habits of sneering at outsiders and was by no means confined to cultivation of serene cheerfulness. In this respect, they appear to have gone well beyond the example set by their atomist ancestor Democritus.

If, unlike the Epicureans, the historical Democritus shunned the socially abrasive pleasures of personal derision, and left room for only a carefully moderated mirth within his psychological ideal of 'good cheer' (*euthumiē*), that also makes him an extremely unpromising figure in relation to my third possibility of laughter – the laughter of 'absurdism', directed at the human condition *per se*. Far from being targeted only against those who deny the tenets of atomism, this third species of laughter would be turned against *everyone*, including the atomist himself.[63] There is, in truth, no hint of such global absurdism in the outlook of Democritus;[64] I shall later return to this point. But what of his legendary incarnation, so to speak – the emblematic

---

[61] Epic. frs. 29.22.3, 29.25.13, 31.14.5–19 (Arrighetti), despite lacunae, all attest relish for mockery; see Cic. *Nat. D.* 1.93, Diog. Laert. 10.7–8 for *ad hominem* gibes, with Epic. frs. 114, 231, 236 Usener, *apud* Cic. *Brutus* 292, for criticism of Socratic irony. Sedley (1976) thinks the image of Epicurus as polemical was maliciously exaggerated by Timocrates: perhaps, but the impression of a penchant for ridicule is hard to erase. On Epicurus and Nausiphanes, cf. Warren (2002) 189–92.

[62] Token instances of Epicurean mockery: Metrodorus fr. 32 Körte (*apud* Plut. *Mor.* 1127c); Colotes *apud* Procl. *In Remp.* II 105.23–106.14 Kroll (attacking Plato's myth of Er), *apud* Plut. *Mor.* 1122e (scoffing at scepticism); Polystratus, in *P. Herc.* 336/1150, col. 21a.7–14 = *De cont. irr.* xxx.7–14 Indelli (including the phrase γελᾶν ἀληθινῶς, 'to have a real laugh', which parallels Metrodorus *loc. cit.*); Zeno of Sidon *apud* Cic. *Nat. D.* 1.93; Philod. *De mus.* col. 142.14–15, 35–7 Delattre (= 4.28 Kemke), *De po.* 1.181.1–4, 186.22 Janko (cf. Janko 192: 'fierce irony, sarcasm, and ridicule'), *Rhet.* II 50.17–18 Sudhaus. Pease (1955) 449–56 documents further Epicurean derisiveness; cf. Dyck (2003) 175–7. Note the fictional scoffing Epicurean at Lucian, *Iup. Trag.* 16 (ch. 6 n. 56). Cf. Epicurus' reputation for obscene language: Cleomedes, *Cael.* 2.1.498–500 Todd, with ch. 4, 174.

[63] Laughing at 'everyone' is not *per se* absurdist: see e.g. Lucian, *Vit. Auctio* 10, where Diogenes of Sinope enjoins his would-be purchaser to 'abuse *everyone* equally [or 'continually'], both kings and ordinary individuals' (λοιδορεῖσθαι πᾶσιν ἐξ ἴσης [or ἑξῆς] καὶ βασιλεῦσι καὶ ἰδιώταις), or the similar Cynic emphasis ('everyone', 'always') at Lucian, *Dial. mort.* 1.2, 2.3. Such instances stress the irrelevance of social class to ethical censure, not the self-implicating universalism of outright absurdism.

[64] The only one, at any rate, is the highly dubious fr. 115 (*84): n. 49 above.

'laughing philosopher'? Is it such laughter for which *he* is the spokesman, as 'the guffaw of the Abderite' in Beckett's *Murphy* would have us believe? The question deserves some investigation. Of special interest here is the fullest version of the legend, found in the pseudo-Hippocratean *Epistles* 10–23 of late Hellenistic or early imperial date, perhaps first century AD. The letters dramatise, as a kind of epistolary novel, the story of how the Abderites, fearing that Democritus is mad, invite the famous doctor Hippocrates to treat him. For anyone familiar with Hippocratic medicine, the invitation might arouse ambiguous expectations, since laughter is sometimes prescribed in the corpus as a kind of 'therapy', which is how Democritus himself eventually persuades Hippocrates to regard his own laughter,[65] but it can also be taken as a symptom of derangement. In the *Epistles*, the Abderites describe the philosopher's 'sickness' as a condition in which he never sleeps but 'laughs perpetually at everything, great and small' and, in an apparent gesture of quasi-Beckettesque nihilism, 'considers the whole of life as amounting to nothing' (γελῶν ἕκαστα μικρὰ καὶ μεγάλα, καὶ μηδὲν οἰόμενος εἶναι τὸν βίον ὅλον διατελεῖ, 10.1). The configuration of insomnia, laughter and 'singing' strikingly recalls the conjunction of these three symptoms in a case study (oddly enough, involving a patient called Silenus!) in the Hippocratic *Epidemics*. A second case study too in the same work involves a combination of laughter and insomnia.[66]

While the *Epistles* go on to depict Democritus (in the voice of the internal author, Hippocrates) as turning out to be a model of self-sufficiency and freedom from care, his laughter does not simply serve as a component of this untroubled state of mind. It is not, in other words, equivalent to the first in my tripartite classification of laughter types, but assumes a much more existentially charged significance. It appears to embrace, in

---

[65] For Hippocratic laughter as therapy, see ch. 1 n. 39; this idea occurs in the *Epistles* at 17.4 (Democritus), 17.10 (Hippocrates); cf. 361 below. All references to the *Epistles* follow the edition of Smith (1990); cf. DK II 225–8 for extracts. Pigeaud (1981) 452–77, Smith (1990) 20–32, Hankinson (2000) give overviews, from different angles, of *Epistles* 10–23. (I have not seen either Hersant [1989] or Sakalis [1989].) A later idea of therapeutic laughter in a broadly 'Democritean' tradition can be traced in Laurence Sterne: see Himberg (2002).

[66] Hippoc. *Epidem.* 1, case 2, 3rd day, *Epidem.* 3, 2nd series, case 15 (cf. ch. 1, 17–18, ch. 2 n. 105); Anon. med. *Morb. acut.* 1.2 (Garofolo) echoes the second of those cases. Untimely laughter plus singing are symptoms of possession by a spirit (*daimōn*) at Philostr. *Vita Ap.* 4.20 (cf. Burkert (1996) 189 n. 27 for Christian parallels); but contrast the insouciant singing-and-laughter of certain Lucianic Cynics, n. 92 below. For the (imaginary) link between Democritus' laughter and 'nothing', cf. n. 2 above; with his *solitary* laughter compare the archaic sage Myson, ch. 6, 267. Laughter as symptom of insanity is first found in the macabre case of the suitors at Hom. *Od.* 20.345–7; see ch. 2, 93–6. Frequent, hollow laughter, sometimes accompanied by a generalised sense of absurdity, is associated with certain cases of schizophrenia: Sass (1992) 24, 112–15, 143–4, Provine (2000) 172–3; cf. Kris (1964) 234–6 (a psychoanalytic account).

the Abderites' description (not, in this respect, denied by Democritus), the whole of life *and death*.[67] It is directed equally against those who are miserable and those who are joyful in their own lives (10.1): Democritus, in other words, mocks even those who themselves laugh (for the 'wrong' reasons). But should this be classed as an example of my second or third type of laughter – as an instance of philosophical ridicule of (almost ubiquitous) human failings and self-deceptions, or rather as a sense of 'the absurd' in its full-blown form? The answer, I think, is ambiguous and repays close attention. The Abderites, as already indicated, perceive Democritus' laughter as a case of outright absurdity (there is nothing about life and death at which he does not laugh), though they consequently judge this, from their own *non*-absurdist perspective, as a case of derangement.[68] Comparably, Hippocrates too, before he has met the philosopher (and changed his mind), espouses a principle of moderation in laughter; he worries that there must be something morbidly wrong with laughing indiscriminately at *everything*. He imagines himself saying to his patient, 'when the cosmos contains both joy and pain, are you not fighting the gods by rejecting one of them?' (14, οὐ θεομαχεῖς δέ, εἰ δύο ἐόντων ἐν κόσμῳ, χαρᾶς καὶ λύπης, σὺ θάτερον αὐτῶν ἐκβέβληκας;), a question which implies that Democritus refuses to take *any* human suffering seriously. However, once he is in the philosopher's presence and has already become himself the butt of derision (see below), Hippocrates starts to worry that there may be some overwhelming *metaphysical* reason for Democritus' laughter. 'Perhaps', he starts to wonder (17.4), 'the entire cosmos has an unseen sickness and has nowhere to send for therapy – since what place could there be outside itself?' Hippocrates has a momentary inkling of a type of absolute absurdity that derives itself, in a way I earlier anticipated (343) and to which I shall shortly return, from the idea of infinity. He makes the connection explicit. 'I'm nervous', he says, 'that even in expounding infinity you may start to laugh' (17.4, εὐλαβέομαι γὰρ μή πως καὶ τὴν ἀπειρίην διεξιὼν γελᾶν ἄρξῃ). Yet, paradoxically, that last remark follows on the heels of Democritus' own insistence that infinity provides *no* grounds for a sense of existential absurdity. 'There are many infinities of worlds', he says, 'and never, my friend, disparage the richness of nature' (17.4). Democritus himself, it seems, disavows absolute absurdity. But does he do so with complete conviction?

---

[67] 10.1; cf. 14 *bis*, 17.4.

[68] Abderite diagnosis of Democritus' madness: ps.-Hippoc. *Epist.* 10.1; cf. *Epist.* 14, *Epist.* 17.2, where Democritus laughs at the Abderites' grief over his 'madness'. Müller (1994) 40–3 notes connections between the epistolary novel and Democritus' fragments, though he overstates the mockery of folly in the latter.

Democritus will eventually justify his laughter to Hippocrates as resting on an overpowering but nevertheless 'relative' sense of absurdity, an absurdity observed in the vice and folly which he finds all around him and which he ardently condemns in a tirade reminiscent of Cynic and Stoic 'diatribe' or moralising invective (17.5–9). But if that is his destination, the route by which he reaches it is far from straightforward. At the outset, he bursts into a scornful guffaw in the face of Hippocrates (μάλα ἀθρόον τι ἀνεκάγχασε καὶ ἐπετώθασε, 17.4) when he hears the doctor speak of how his own peace of mind is impeded by preoccupation with the full gamut of human experience, including children, disease, death and marriage. Hippocrates' question, 'are you laughing at the good things or the bad things I mentioned?', only elicits redoubled laughter. The initial impression, therefore, is indeed that Democritus sees the entirety of human life, without qualification, as risible. What seems to stop him (just) short of absolute absurdity is the presumption that there is at least *one* sane, wise, virtuous human being (himself) and a correspondingly privileged vantage point from which human absurdities can be derided without self-implication.[69] He starts the justification of his laughter to Hippocrates in terms that sound *prima facie* absolute: 'you think there are two causes of my laughter, good things and bad; but I laugh at just *one* – the human race' (. . . ἐγὼ δὲ ἕνα γελῶ, τὸν ἄνθρωπον, 17.5). Likewise, he later describes everyone (including, by implication, Hippocrates) as a 'Thersites of life' (Θερσῖται δ' εἰσὶ τοῦ βίου πάντες, 17.5), each individual addicted to mocking others' follies while overlooking his own. But he nonetheless purports to exclude at least himself from this charge; he narrowly avoids a self-subverting position.[70] In fact, he is subsequently prepared to exempt hypothetically from his mockery *anyone* who can attain true peace of mind (*ataraxia*) by escaping the pursuit of wealth, power and other empty desires (17.7: 'they would easily escape my laughter'). Moreover, his Thersites trope implicitly condemns laughter itself where it is not grounded in sound judgement and true values: that in itself ought to block the possibility of wholly generalised absurdity. Democritus even goes so far as to say that he does not

---

[69] That a laughing Democritus could avoid self-implication seems to be grasped by Sen. *De ira* 2.10.5 (n. 26 above), where the contrast with weeping Heraclitus includes the latter's *own* pitiable status (for taking human sufferings too seriously). The adaptation of Democritean laughter by Robert Burton accepts self-implication: Burton (1989) 37 (n. 77 below), 57.

[70] The second-century AD Cynic Demonax supposedly praised Thersites as himself 'a sort of Cynic orator' (Κυνικόν τινα δημηγόρον, Lucian, *Demonax* 61). In this respect at least it cannot be right to see the Democritus of ps.-Hippoc. *Epist.* as a Cynic *and* to count Thersites as a Cynic 'hero': thus Stewart (1958) 186, (1994) 37. For Thersiteses (plural) as designation of a human type, cf. Clem. *Paed.* 3.4.30.1 (laughing gigolos of wealthy married women!).

choose to laugh, and actually shows some inclination towards a pessimistic view of human life.[71] But that note of pessimism emerges at a juncture at which Democritus' sense of absurdity comes perilously close to swallowing even himself. Having just said that he does not choose to laugh, he suddenly exclaims to Hippocrates, 'Don't you see that I too am part of the evil? (τῆς κακίης μοῖρα) . . . Don't you see that even the cosmos is full of loathing for humans (*misanthrōpiē*)?' (17.9), before launching himself on a passage of grim vehemence which pictures the whole of human life as 'a sickness from birth'. Only after dwelling in depressing detail on human miseries and depravities does he come back round to his moralistically self-exempting stance of derision. Indeed his first-person plurals suggest that by now he expects Hippocrates to share his vision of the world (17.9): 'seeing such a profusion of unworthy and wretched pursuits, how can we fail to jeer (πῶς μὴ χλευάσωμεν) at the life that partakes of such indiscipline?' In the course of 17.9 we feel something like the tension and oscillation between tears and laughter which is formalised in *Anth. Pal.* 9.148 (336 above). And if Democritus' laughter is rooted in a disdain for others' flaws, it does not altogether lack overtones of a more far-reaching absurdity.[72]

The pseudo-Hippocratean *Epistles*, then, evoke shifting thoughts of existential laughter. Among them, as I have tried to show, there are certainly at least passing intimations of a powerfully global sense of absurdity, communicated partly through the philosopher's own half-suggestions of the near-inescapability of human folly and vanity, partly through the Abderites' (mistaken though understandable) perception of their fellow citizen's derangement, and partly through Hippocrates' (later corrected) anxiety that Democritus may have glimpsed a cosmic absurdity at the heart of infinity. That last configuration of ideas appears much less ambiguously in the philosopher's own mouth in the satirical scenario of Lucian's *Vitarum Auctio* ('Auction of Philosophers' Lives'), where Democritus explains his constant laughter by proclaiming without qualification that 'there is nothing worth taking seriously' in human affairs; 'everything is emptiness, movement of atoms and infinity' (κενεὰ δὲ πάντα καὶ ἀτόμων φορὴ καὶ ἀπειρίη).[73]

---

[71] Democritus does not choose to laugh: *Epist.* 17.9, ἐγὼ μὲν οὐδαμῶς δοκέω γελῆν. See text and app. crit. of Smith (1990) 88, but his translation 'I do not think it right to laugh' (89) is a little misleading.

[72] Temkin (1985) 461–2, using different categories from mine, briefly glimpses some of the text's unanswered questions. Pigeaud (1981) 474 is right to take the *Epistles* as thematically subtle, but smoothes out the problem of Democritus' (supposedly) self-inclusive laughter (463–4, 475–6).

[73] Lucian, *Vit. Auctio* 13: the adj. κενεός, 'empty', plays on the senses of physically 'void' and existentially 'futile'; cf. Müller (1994) 43–5, 50 for related material. Although Democritus speaks here as an exponent of a kind of existential laughter, he is understood by his interlocutor (who speaks of *hubris*), once again, to be simply mocking others.

This nexus of thoughts, inferring from cosmic infinity a sense of the vanity of all human aspirations, probably underlies other occurrences of the laughing Democritus legend in which the whole of life, without exception, is specified as the object of derision. The Roman Christian author Hippolytus, writing in Greek around the start of the third century AD, maintains that Democritus 'used to laugh at everything, on the grounds that all human affairs merited laughter' (οὗτος ἐγέλα πάντα, ὡς γέλωτος ἀξίων <ὄντων> πάντων τῶν ἐν ἀνθρώποις), and to roughly the same period belongs the similar formulation of Democritean laughter (at 'all human affairs') in Philostratus' *Vita Apollonii*.[74] By the date of such imperial sources we have left the historical Democritus far behind, but we have reached a point at which the *idea* of absurdity as an all-embracing judgement on human life has crystallised into a readily available cliché, though one whose potential implications are never again dramatised or probed in as much detail as in the pseudo-Hippocratic *Epistles*.

Now, one thing that should catch our attention here is that, taken *au pied de la lettre*, such a universalised world-view would mean that even atomism itself, or at any rate the life of its proponents, is no better than laughable. For such a 'Democritean', in other words, absurdity would be a wholly self-inclusive stance. Precisely this extrapolation is made in an anonymous epigram from the *Palatine Anthology* (7.56) which takes the form of an imaginary epitaph:

> ἦν ἄρα Δημοκρίτοιο γέλως τόδε, καὶ τάχα λέξει·
>   οὐκ ἔλεγον γελόων· πάντα πέλουσι γέλως;
> καὶ γὰρ ἐγὼ σοφίην μετ' ἀπείρονα καὶ στίχα βίβλων
>   τοσσατίων κεῖμαι νέρθε τάφοιο γέλως.

> So *that* was what Democritus' laughter was about. Perhaps he'll say:
>   'Didn't I laugh and tell you that *everything* is laughter?
> Even I, despite my limitless wisdom and a row of books
>   So numerous, lie beneath this tomb – fit just for laughter.'

The poem makes an extravagant conceit out of the superimposition of laughter on death, thereby inverting the common association of the former with fullness of life and health.[75] But it can be read as gesturing beyond the mere perception of human futility. We can see how it does so by juxtaposing

---

[74] Hippol. *Haer.* 1.13.4 (= Democ. A40 DK), Philostr. *Vita Ap.* 8.7.14; note, less decisively, Ael. *VH* 4.20 (cf. 4.29), 'Democritus derided everyone and said they were mad'. Cf. nn. 26, 39 above.

[75] Cf. the epitaph for Rhinthon, Sicilian writer of comic burlesques (*phlyakes*), in Nossis, *Anth. Pal.* 7.414, where the passer-by is urged to laugh with a 'crisp' chortle (cf. Taplin (1993) 49, 'laugh drily', with LSJ *s.v.* καπυρός II, Gow and Page (1965) II 441): laughter here offsets death, but any existential implications are muted. For ancient perceptions of a laughter-health nexus, see ch. 1, 16–17.

it with another epigram, by an otherwise unknown Glycon (*Anth. Pal.*
10.124), which is often cited as a simple parallel to it but whose own perception of futility lacks the modulation of irony:

> πάντα γέλως καὶ πάντα κόνις καὶ πάντα τὸ μηδέν·
> πάντα γὰρ ἐξ ἀλόγων ἐστὶ τὰ γινόμενα.

> Everything is laughter, everything dust, everything nothing.
> The explanation: everything comes from the meaningless.

In both poems we are confronted with laughter as a symbol or expression
of existential pointlessness.[76] But whereas 10.124 is formulated in a voice
without identity, location or viewpoint, 7.56 creates a deliberately piquant
and paradoxical setting for the thought in question. In the Democritus epigram, the triple reference to laughter in the first couplet has a quasi-auditory
effect, as though the sound of Democritus' laughter were itself *echoing* from
his grave, while the return of the motif in the very last word of the poem
appears to turn the tables on Democritus himself (as does the pun, in line 3,
on the notion of infinity). The atomist has to admit that he is just as much
an object of laughter as everyone else; he is ensnared in the ludicrous emptiness of human existence which (in his legendary persona) he notoriously
diagnosed. 'Democritean' absurdity thus becomes simultaneously self-
exemplifying *and* self-subverting: the epigram seems to pronounce a judgement on atomism's psychologically self-defeating world-view. If *nothing*
has any real value, that should be equally true of the materialist vantage
point from which Democritus (supposedly) mocked the whole world. Or,
in Burton's paraphrase of Erasmus: a Democritus is needed to laugh at Democritus.[77] A laughter which embodied such a mood or mentality would itself
appear to partake of that element of the irrational or meaningless (*alogon*)
which *Anth. Pal.* 10.124 diagnoses at the heart of reality.

   It is not difficult to see how, in principle, a materialist philosophy as
thoroughgoing as Democritean atomism *might* give rise to a sense of the

---

[76] Rutherford (1989) 128–30 cites both poems as parallels to Marcus Aurelius' reflections on the emptiness of earthly life. A similar notion of everything as 'laughter' or a 'laughing-stock' occurs in
Arist. *Protr.* B104 Düring (fr. 73 Gigon, fr. 59 Rose), in a platonising context; note *ibid.* B110 (fr. 73
Gigon, 61 Rose), everything (other than mind, *nous*) 'is empty nonsense' (φλυαρία . . . καὶ λῆρος:
for *phluaria* cf. Pl. *Rep.* 7.515d, with ch. 3 n. 41); see ch. 6, 309, 331. These passages do not voice
existential absurdity, only the worthlessness of earthly, as opposed to eternal, values. Cf. ps.-Men.
Sent. 172 Jaekel, 'the solemn things of life are laughter to the prudent' (γέλως τὰ σεμνὰ τοῦ βίου
τοῖς σώφροσιν); for Christian parallels, see ch. 10 nn. 95–7. For 'everything is dust', see the Cynic
sentiment at Lucian, *Dial. mort.* 1.3, 6.2, again with Christian parallels: e.g. Basil, *Serm. de mor.*
32.1261 *PG*, John Chrys. *Hom. de paen.* 49.346 *PG*; cf. Greg. Naz. *Anth. Pal.* 8.252.

[77] Erasmus, *Praise of Folly* ch. 48 (Miller (1979) 134), states that a thousand Democrituses would not
suffice to mock human folly – and a further Democritus would be needed for *them*. Burton (1989)
37 paraphrases and spells out Erasmus' point: '*opus Democrito qui Democritum rideat*'.

absurdity of human existence on the cosmic scale of things, i.e. as seen (or, rather, imagined) from what the philosopher Henry Sidgwick called 'the point of view of the universe'.[78] The basis of such an attitude would be twofold: first, the materialist elimination of 'value' from a reality consisting entirely of atoms and void; secondly, the contrast between the ungraspable infinity of time and space and the physically and temporally limited conditions of human life.[79] This point seems to have been taken by the author of the pseudo-Hippocratic *Epistles*, in which the Abderites' description of Democritus' manically perpetual laughter is juxtaposed with the report that he sometimes speaks of 'travelling off into infinity' (ἀποδημεῖν ἐνίοτε λέγει ἐς τὴν ἀπειρίην), an infinity where, in an eerie premonition of modern theories of 'parallel universes', he locates numberless versions of himself (10.1). The laughter that such a philosophical world-picture might generate – laughter at absolutely everything about human existence – would itself be cold and meaningless; a suitable phenomenon, perhaps, to echo from a tomb (365 above). But what is beyond doubt is that the laughter imagined as issuing from such a point of view was *not* authentically Democritean, any more than it became a feature of the comparably materialist thinking of his philosophical descendants, the Epicureans. The justification for this negative claim is that Democritus' philosophy patently does not eliminate value from the world, at any rate as that world is experienced by the mind of the atomist. On the contrary, the fragments contain explicit appeals to ideas of justice, virtue, beauty, shame and other normative concepts; cheerfulness, *euthumiē*, itself – and therefore Democritean happiness – is said to depend on leading a just life.[80] Even those scholars who discard most of the ethical sayings as spurious usually do not dispute that Democritus held

---

[78] Sidgwick (1901) 382, 420. Cf. n. 5 above on Nagel's 'view from nowhere'. Morreall (1983) 124 begs the question in saying, *à propos* a cosmic perspective, 'looked at from the right [*sic*] perspective, what is ordinarily important looks unimportant'; cf. Morreall (1989), esp. 257–63 (n. 83 below). Hepburn (1984) 171–8 offers a more subtle appraisal of cosmic viewpoints on value.

[79] The fifth-century AD Greek-Egyptian Christodorus, *Anth. Pal.* 2.134–5, makes Democritus laugh in the knowledge that time overtakes everything, i.e. *sub specie aeternitatis*; cf. Arist. *Protr.* B105 Düring (fr. 73 Gigon, with n. 76 above) on the insignificance of human timescales. There is an affinity here with Democ. fr. 285 on the short span of human life, but that fragment (whose sentiments are traditional: cf. e.g. Xerxes at Hdt. 7.46) sounds no note of laughter and argues only for moderation. Something closer to absurdity regarding finite lifetimes is sounded at Pl. *Rep.* 10.608c–d (cf. Halliwell (1988) 158–9). Note, that pseudo-Heraclitean pessimism could *equally* appeal to the crushing weight of eternity/infinity: see n. 37 above (Lucian's parody), and cf. Plut. *Mor.* 466d, where Alexander weeps over the infinity of worlds espoused by the Democritean Anaxarchus (= Anaxarchus A11 DK); cf. Ael. *VH* 4.29. Differently, Cic. *Tusc.* 5.114 ascribes to the supposedly blind Democritus the capacity to explore infinity with his mind. As regards laughing at life from a *spatially* detached perspective, see Lucian, *Icarom.* 11–19, *Charon* 6–24, with ch. 9, 429–31, 445–7.

[80] See fr. 174, with frs. 170–1 for equivalent reference to *eudaimoniē* (cf. n. 41 above).

at least some positive ethical commitments. When, therefore, Nietzsche (himself sometimes an advocate of a laughter of existential absurdity, but also of euthumic 'cheerfulness') described Democritus' view of the world as one 'without moral and aesthetic meaning', because resting on a 'pessimism of chance', he silently substituted what he thought the philosopher *should* have believed for what the evidence suggests that he did.[81] I am not concerned here to ask exactly why, given his materialist physics, Democritus seems to have continued to subscribe to many existing Greek values. Since the ethical fragments show him to have been neither a moral nihilist nor a pessimist, what I want to stress is that, contrary to the image of him generated by the later legendary tradition, his mentality unequivocally excludes a universalising sense of absurdity, as opposed to leaving a limited space for moderate euthumic laughter and for selective derision against especially self-ignorant forms of human excess and folly.

Nietzsche's mistake, it seems, was to suppose that compendious evaluations of life necessarily 'follow' from (meta)physical beliefs. But such evaluations, including notions of existential absurdity, depend on something more than consequential chains of reasoning. They entail an underlying and evolving *Weltgefühl*, an attitudinal stance or feeling that may be more or less tightly constrained by beliefs held about the larger scheme of things.[82] Consider the difficulty of translating atomist physics (or any comparable framework of thought) into an existentially practical prescription along the following lines: (a) most human beings, both individually and collectively, behave (fairly) incorrigibly as though their actions have meaning and value; (b) 'meaning and value' cannot count as components of fundamental reality, which consists exclusively of atoms and void; (c) therefore . . . But therefore *what* (i.e., what is to be done)? Several equally plausible alternatives can readily be supplied. *Prima facie*, human beings might on this basis be recommended to despair and kill themselves (the 'Silenus principle', as it were, and the challenge which Camus' *The Myth of Sisyphus* takes as its starting point). Or to regard their predicament as preposterous and to cultivate as much cheerful detachment from customary values as they can

---

[81] Nietzsche (1988) VII 555 ('Die Welt ohne moralische und aesthetische Bedeutung, Pessimismus des Zufalls'), a note of winter 1872–3. For Nietzsche's attitudes to Democritus, cf. Safranski (2002) 150–3 (though insufficiently critical of Nietzsche's interpretation), with Berry (2004) on his relationship to Democritean *euthumiē*. Nietzsche's own complex views of laughter are discussed in Lippitt (1992), (1996), (1999); cf. Branham (2004) for his self-image as Cynic mocker, and Meyer (forthcoming) for a thesis about the influence of Old Comedy on his later work.

[82] Nagel (1979) 11–23 provides rational considerations against allowing the cosmic scale of time and space to undermine human ideas of value. But such considerations may be crushed by a sheer *feeling* of human insignificance, as Nagel (1986) 214–23 comes closer to acknowledging; cf. n. 84 below.

muster (cf. the proposal ascribed to the poet Simonides that one should 'play in life and not take anything at all seriously', παίζειν ἐν τῷ βίῳ καὶ περὶ μηδὲν ἁπλῶς σπουδάζειν).[83] Or to accept (perhaps cheerfully, perhaps not) that they cannot easily escape from the grip of conventional values and should therefore just carry on roughly as normal (whatever that means, in their cultural circumstances).[84] Or to cherish – at least regard with a kind of ironic complicity – the fact that 'meaning and value' are not part of the given fabric of reality but something they themselves create.[85] Or to practise total impassivity and detachment from normal human affairs. Or, of course, to reconsider whether there is something wrong with at least one of the premises of the earlier syllogism.

Of that wide range of options (which could be extended and refined), none in fact seems perfectly to fit the evidence for the historical Democritus' psychological and ethical *Weltanschauung*. 'Cheerfulness', *euthumiē*, as we have seen, involves a degree of detachment from many of the things that humans typically believe important (power, wealth, social status, the pleasures of the body), but it leaves seemingly intact ethical ideas such as virtue and justice, as well as the basic desirability (and therefore value) of freedom from care itself. By doing so, it might be thought to try to *circumvent* 'the absurd', perhaps displacing the burden of existential futility onto the (supposedly) unthinking, deluded lives of non-atomists, while sidestepping the threat of radical incoherence posed by the apparent dislocation between Democritus' own materialist physics and the quietist but positive commitments of his ethics.

But what of the legendary, 'laughing' Democritus, whom we should now revisit one last time? Since he is connected to his historical namesake, as we have seen, by only the thinnest of threads, what exactly is *his* prescription for living? No unqualified answer seems to be possible, since the legendary Democritus is a figure whose outlook is placed at different points on the scale or spectrum of perceptions of 'absurdity' by different

[83] Simonid. 646 *PMG*, with Branham (1989b); cf. n. 130 below, with ch. 6, 309. The fragment is cited by Nietzsche, *Human, All Too Human*, I 154, to exemplify a Greek alternative to pessimism: Nietzsche (1988) I 146; cf. VIII 72, a note of 1875 for the unfinished *Wir Philologen*, translated in Arrowsmith (1990) 370. Palladas, *Anth. Pal.* 10.87 ('if we do not laugh at life the fugitive, and at chance which prostitutes herself . . .'), has a different nuance: laughter there attempts to avoid the pain of envy and injustice. Cf. Alexis fr. 222.14 (with nn. 12 above, 100 below). For a modern analogue, Morreall (1989) 257–63 advocates laughter that expresses a Zen Buddhist detachment from delusory human values; cf. Berger (1997) 41–3.

[84] This is, approximately, the position of Nagel (1979) 11–23, (1986) 214–23, taking absurdity to be an inescapable aspect of the human condition (more particularly, of the tension between 'subjective' and 'objective' viewpoints which humans can adopt towards their existence).

[85] This kind of response is a familiar postmodern move: see Rorty (1989) 73–95 for a case in point.

Greek and Roman sources. In regard to my own terms of reference, the motif of the laughing Democritus exhibits a sort of dialectic, and sometimes an instability, between construals of his laughter as a matter of relative or global absurdism. I earlier adduced some cases in which the motif is either directly associated with global absurdism (as in Lucian's version, 'there is nothing worth taking seriously', 'everything is emptiness, movement of atoms, and infinity': 363 above), or seems to stop just short of that extreme, as in the account dramatised in the pseudo-Hippocratic *Epistles*. But other variations too on the theme were possible. In invoking the legend to support a Stoically inflected stance that it is better to laugh at life than to hate (or to grieve for) other people, Seneca the younger (in his treatise *De tranquillitate*) first of all aligns Democritean laughter with a kind of wryly humane view of existence (and one which has at least a faint hope that gentle derision may help to improve people), but then changes tack to use laughter as an expression of the idea that nothing in life really matters at all, before finally pulling back and rejecting the Democritean option (as too harsh, it appears) and deciding that laughter, as well as tears, is better avoided altogether. In his tenth satire, Juvenal sets up Democritus as a figure of incessant, universal ridicule of life, a sort of patron saint of his own invective. But he suggests that this ridicule was a vehicle of moral 'censure', and at the end of the poem he implicitly exempts certain values (associated with modest self-sufficiency) from the force of Democritean laughter. If this Democritus is an absurdist, then, he is only so in relative terms, even though, like his counterpart in the pseudo-Hippocratic *Epistles*, he regards human failings as ubiquitous and *almost* incorrigible.[86]

On a quite different level, however, the legendary Democritus became available as a symbol of how humans might psychologically come to terms with their apparent lack of significance in the larger scheme of things. There was at least *one* person, it was possible to imagine, who had somehow evaded the burden of traditional pessimism ('everything is dust, everything is nothing', to recall the terms of Glycon's epigram: 365 above) and had managed to affirm something – 'everything is laughter' – which, though ambiguous (it can mean 'everything is a laughing-stock'), at any rate escaped from the prospect of undiluted misery. In concluding this section I submit that the appeal of this 'alternative' Democritus was that it carried overtones of two of the oldest Greek associations of laughter: firstly, an association with positive, life-affirming forces; secondly (and here we might recall that in the

---

[86] On Seneca (*Tranq.* 15; cf. *De ira* 2.10.5) and Juvenal (*Sat.* 10.28–53), see Anderson (1982) 174–95, Courtney (1980) 449–50, 456–7.

pseudo-Hippocratean *Epistles* Hippocrates comes to regard Democritus as 'godlike', *theoeidēs*), with the lightheartedness available to the Olympian gods, in sharp contrast to the archetypally miserable, Hades-bound destiny of human souls. An attractive expression of this more existentially assertive conception of Democritean laughter can be found in a pair of late-antique epigrams, by the sixth-century AD poet Julianus of Egypt:[87]

εἰ καὶ ἀμειδήτων νεκύων ὑπὸ γαῖαν ἀνάσσεις,
    Φερσεφόνη, ψυχὴν δέχνυσο Δημοκρίτου
εὐμενέως γελόωσαν, ἐπεὶ καὶ σεῖο τεκοῦσαν
    ἀχνυμένην ἐπὶ σοὶ μοῦνος ἔκαμψε γέλως.

(Anth. Pal. 7.58)

Even if the dead you rule beneath the earth are unsmiling,
    Persephone, welcome benignly the soul of Democritus
As it continues to laugh, since even your own mother,
    Wracked with grief, had her mind turned by laughter alone.

Πλούτων, δέξο, μάκαρ, Δημόκριτον, ὥς κεν ἀνάσσων
    αἰὲν ἀμειδήτων καὶ γελόωντα λάχοις.

(Anth. Pal. 7.59)

Blessed Pluto, welcome Democritus, so that while ruling over
    The eternally unsmiling you may obtain *one* laughing person.

If the anonymous epigram at *Palatine Anthology* 7.56 (364 above) makes Democritus' laughter echo sardonically from (beyond) the grave, Julianus goes a step further and envisages the philosopher's soul as perpetually laughing in the underworld, a pointedly exceptional condition elsewhere paralleled only by Cynics such as Diogenes, Crates and Menippus (of whom more to come shortly).[88] On this scenario, Democritus stands in contrast not only to the collectively 'unsmiling' inhabitants of Hades[89] but even

---

[87] On both epigrams see Milanezi (1995) 236–9. I take the adverb εὐμενέως in *Anth. Pal.* 7.58, by interlacing word-order, with the imperative in line 2 rather than with the adjacent γελόωσαν; likewise Beckby (1966) II 47, Desrousseaux *et al.* in Waltz (1960) 82. Contrast Paton (1916–18) II 37: but on the latter interpretation, why should Democritus' posthumous laughter be 'benign'?

[88] In anon. *Anth. Pal.* 9.145.2 (cf. Page (1981) 348), Diogenes, on arrival in Hades, mocks Croesus and paradoxically compares their 'possessions'. The Cynic symbolically 'overcomes' death, in Hades as in life, by espousing values that eliminate the difference between life and death; but his derision lacks the existential affirmativeness of Democritus' laughter in Julianus' epigrams. (As regards the latter, it is presumably coincidental that Democritus himself allegedly wrote a work called *On those in Hades*, A33, BOC DK; cf. the allusion in ps.-Hippoc. *Epist.* 10.1 = Democ. C2 DK.) For other cases of Cynics laughing in Hades, see ch. 9, 448, 460–1, and cf. 384–5 below.

[89] Cf. 'unsmiling Tartarus' in an imperial funerary epigram from Naples (*IG* XIV 769), 'unsmiling death' in Greg. Naz. *Anth. Pal.* 8.190.1, 'unsmiling Hades' in Theodoridas, *Anth. Pal.* 7.439.4, and the 'unsmiling pit' of Hades in *Argon. Orph.* 967; cf. n. 44 above, with ch. 10 n. 107 for a contrasting Christian usage. An exceptional instance of Hades smiling, but only 'with his brows', occurs at *Hom.*

to the gods of the underworld themselves, Persephone and Pluto, here imagined as desperately in need of the invigorating force of laughter to counteract the irreversible gloom of their own kingdom. Unmistakably to a Greek mind, this Democritus is also an anti-image of such figures as the dead Homeric heroes Achilles and Ajax, described in the *Odyssey* as sunk in despair over their confinement in Hades or harbouring rancour over the wrongs done them in life.[90] Against that backdrop, we might even say that this fictionalised Democritus exhibits a very different heroism of his own, the heroism of laughter itself, somehow eternally asserting the defiance of a human spirit in the face of a universe not made for it.

The idea of death-defying laughter has deep roots in Greek philosophy. We saw in the last chapter, for example, that it is no accident that the only Platonic dialogue in which Socrates is explicitly depicted as laughing is the *Phaedo*, as he spends his final hours with his friends. But it is possible to laugh in the face of death in three philosophically distinct ways: first, because nothing in life, including its ending, has any importance; secondly, because death itself, in the Epicurean motto, 'is nothing to *us*' (because in death 'we' shall have ceased to exist); or, finally and very differently, because death is a minor event, a mere staging post, in the soul's larger history. We can eliminate the third of these options as having any purchase on the case of either the legendary or the historical Democritus. For the real Democritus, the first also can be eliminated, since, as we saw earlier, whatever his physics says, his psychology and ethics accept that quite a few things still *do* matter. For his fictional homonym, however, the choice is trickier; it depends precisely on how much of an absurdist he is taken to be. And that, as I have tried to show, was an open question for those who perpetuated his reputation.

Hymn 2.357–8: see Richardson (1974) 268, Milanezi (1995) 241–5; cf. Appendix 1, 527. Theodorus, *Anth. Pal.* 7.556, where Hades laughs at the death of Tityrus the mime-artist, is an ironic take on the idea of life itself as metaphorical 'mime' (see ch. 10 n. 96); and Orpheus makes Cocytus smile in Hermesianax 7.9 *CA*. On earlier reflections of laughter's absence in death, cf. Bremmer (1983) 85–8, including suspension of the capacity to laugh on the part of those who descend into the subterranean oracle of Trophonius. For the latter, see Semus of Delos *FGrH* 396 F10 (*apud* Athen. 14.614a–b), Paus. 9.39.13, ps.-Plut. *Prov.* 1.51, *Suda s.v.* εἰς Τροφωνίου, with Frazer (1898) v 204 and n. 132 below. This feature of Trophonius' oracle is picked up by two great Christian reinterpreters of laughter: Erasmus, *Praise of Folly* 1, *Adages* 1.7.77, Kierkegaard (1959) 33. Cf. the supposed link between Attica's Laughterless Rock (Ἀγέλαστος πέτρα) and Theseus' descent to Hades (Σ Ar. *Kn.* 785, *Suda s.v.* Σαλαμῖνος); ch. 4 n. 21. Compare 'laughterless death' (θάνατος ἀγέλαστος) in the apocryphal *Acts of John* 23; see Propp (1984) 128–31 for comparative material from other cultures, with Wilfred Owen's 'dead smile' of Hell in *Strange Meeting* 9–10 (Stallworthy (1986) 125). But contrast the sardonic laughter of Renaissance depictions of the 'Dance of Death': Barasch (1997) 194–9.

[90] *Od.* 11.487–503 (though Achilles feels joy, 11.540, at the news of his son Neoptolemus), 543–65.

WHAT MADE CYNICS LAUGH?

There is one other direction in which we might look for ancient traces of the absurd, and that is towards the Cynics. I have already mentioned the (inconclusive) theory that the figure of laughing Democritus was the invention of Hellenistic Cynics, and we have also seen that the capacity to laugh in the most unpromising of locations, the underworld, is sometimes ascribed to individual Cynics as well as to Democritus himself.[91] In one of Lucian's *Dialogues of the Dead*, Menippus 'the dog' is more than a match even for the grim ferryman Charon. Menippus alone laughs (and sings) on the ferry across Acheron, while all around him weep. Having no possessions, he is able to refuse to pay Charon's two-obol fare: when told he has no choice, he responds, 'well, take me back to life, then'.[92] Charon has no hold over Menippus, whose 'freedom' makes him equally and cheerfully indifferent to both life and death. But *were* Cynics really indifferent to everything, and does this vignette, so typical of Lucian (who will be the subject in his own right of Chapter 9), illuminate what was existentially distinctive about the laughter available to these philosophers of a radically 'alternative' lifestyle?

Modern scholars have been disposed to identify the hallmark of a Cynic tradition of laughter with the idea of the 'serio-comic' or 'serio-ludic', *spoud(ai)ogeloion*, even though we have no unequivocal evidence that any Cynic ever laid claim expressly to this term as a self-description. The adjective *spoudogeloios* is rare (*spoudaiogeloios* even rarer), its status uncertain. It is an intrinsically ambiguous compound: at face value, it might denote being serious about/in laughter, or laughing about things that are supposed to be serious, or fluctuating in tone between playfulness and earnestness. The only thing we can say about it for sure is that it was sometimes applied to a recognised class of writers. Most pertinently, Strabo applies it to Menippus of Gadara, the early Hellenistic author of prosimetric 'satires' who we know influenced Lucian (as well as being fictionalised as a character by him, as in the example above) and who generated a tradition of so-called Menippean satire in Latin.[93] But some ancient readers, as Diogenes Laertius 6.99

---

[91] See nn. 26, 88 above.

[92] *Dial. mort.* 2; see ch. 9 n. 37. Singing, in part symbolically insouciant, in part mocking (n.b. the unusual sense of the verb κατᾴδειν), is again ascribed to Menippus in Lucian, *Dial. mort.* 3.1–2, and to Diogenes (lying on his back) at *Menip.* 18; cf. the carefree singing of the poor man at *Gall.* 22 (a similar image at Juv. *Sat.* 10.22). But contrast the combination of laughter and singing as symptoms of madness at ps.-Hippoc. *Epist.* 10.1, with n. 66 above.

[93] Strabo 16.2.29 (likewise Steph. Byz. *Ethn.* 193). The other occurrences of σπουδογέλοιος are Diog. Laert. 9.17 (describing a performer called Heraclitus) and Steph. Byz. *Ethn.* 357 (referring to the poet

shows, found Menippus' writings to 'contain nothing serious (*spoudaion*)' but to be 'full of sheer derision (*katagelōs*)'; and even an admirer like Marcus Aurelius (*Med.* 6.47) includes him simply in the class of 'mockers' (*chleuastai*) of human life. Given the scantiness of the evidence, we are not well placed to know how far or in just what ways Menippus was affected by his attested Cynic affiliations. Nor does the work of Lucian help to resolve the issue, since Lucian himself, as Chapter 9 will explain, handles Cynicism with some ambivalence.[94] Both Menippus and Lucian certainly targeted much ridicule, through techniques of parody, burlesque and social satire, against philosophers of various persuasions, *including* Cynicism (at any rate in Lucian's case). This is evidently one respect in which Menippean mode(s) could count as 'serio-comic', bringing an overtly 'laughing' manner to bear on beliefs and activities that normally took themselves with the utmost seriousness. It is also clear that, beyond Menippus, some Cynics used conspicuously literary means to promote their values: this is particularly notable in the case of Crates of Thebes, who authored various kinds of parodic and satirical verse, at least in some cases as an expression of a Cynic commitment to a frugal lifestyle.[95] Crates may well have been chiefly responsible for creating awareness of a distinctively 'Cynic manner' (Κυνικὸς τρόπος) in the literary and rhetorical use of mirth, a manner that was perceived as employing jesting or ridicule to convey practical ethical criticism or advice.[96] Even so, the evidence for Crates and other (quasi-) Cynic *littérateurs* does not get us far beyond the conclusion that many Cynics found mockery of others' views and behaviour a temptation they could not resist, and one to which they may have yielded in their writings just as

---

Blaesus of Capreae; see Kaibel (1899) 191). *IG* XII.8 87 (Imbros), seems to use σπουδαιογέλοιος as a profession; Leyerle (2001) 107 n. 22 erroneously claims that the word occurs in Lucian's *Bacchus*, but see Branham (1989a) 26–8 on the relevance of the concept to Lucian's work (with ch. 9 n. 12). The idea of combining seriousness and laughter/play has a broad (literary) genealogy: on some of its formulations, see Kindstrand (1976) 47–8, Gera (1993) 133–47, and the very desultory Giangrande (1972); cf. n. 109 below, ch. 1 n. 99. On Menippus and the traditions of Greco-Roman writing indebted to him, consult Relihan (1993), esp. 39–48, Hall (1981) 64–150; for the subsequent tradition, see De Smet (1996), Weinbrot (2005), with Bakhtin (1984) 106–37 for a rather free but stimulating set of reflections; cf. ch. 9, 435. Kindstrand (1981) 129 wrongly connects the saying of Anacharsis at Arist. *EN* 10.6, 1176b33–4 with *spoud(ai)ogeloion*; Aristotle is not talking about fusing the serious and laughable: see ch. 6, 268, 309. For manifestations of a distinctively serio-comic mentality in late antiquity, see Curtius (1953) 417–20.

[94] See ch. 9, esp. 448–9, 463–7.

[95] See Long (1996) 41–5 for an overview. Among others possibly influenced by Crates was Bion of Borysthenes, whose fragments contain mockery of both intellectual delusions and conventional values: see frs. 6, 10, 27, 31, 38 Kindstrand, with Kindstrand (1976) 43–8, 192.

[96] Demetr. *Eloc.* 170, 259.

much as on street-corners.[97] But since we know that a strong penchant for satire and denigration was deeply rooted in Greek philosophy, that conclusion does not shed much immediate light on the question that primarily interests me here, namely whether the Cynics developed or specialised in an existentially marked brand of laughter of their own, a laughter that somehow encapsulated their essential orientation towards life itself.

To tackle that question effectively, we need to adopt a more expansive perspective on the movement. If we do so, we can put ourselves in a position to see that the attributes and commitments of Cynics represent a peculiar challenge for Greek attitudes to, and practices of, laughter. Three points are worth highlighting in this regard; all of them involve paradox or ambiguity of some kind. The first is that Cynics are depicted as figures who make habitual use of ridicule while being themselves avowedly immune to its social force – 'But *I* do not consider myself mocked', as Diogenes is supposed to have said (in an anecdote which I shall examine later). The second is an uncertainty, which becomes entangled with larger debates about the nature of the movement, over the spirit and purpose (if any) of Cynic mockery: is it an exercise in sheer abuse and insult, the scornful renunciation of all conventional values, or a corrective instrument for changing people's lives? Finally, the Cynic is (reputedly) *kunikos*, 'dog-like', by dint of being impervious to the norms of shame.[98] Since laughter is commonly conceived of in Greek culture as a means of shaming others, while excessive or inappropriate indulgence in it is often regarded as itself a mark of shamefulness, here too Cynics seem to occupy an anomalous position in regard to laughter. But did this make them more, or less, inclined to indulge in it themselves?

Cynics are standardly portrayed as defining themselves by disengagement from the structures and networks of the social world. They live in uncompromising opposition to the views of the majority. Such a form of life seems to leave little space for the enjoyment of laughter as a shared pleasure, while setting up Cynics themselves as easy objects of ridicule from inside the consensus of collective norms and mores. Yet the ancient sources on Cynicism treat its adherents, with rare exceptions, as unusually given to laughter,[99] even if this laughter appears to vary considerably in

[97] Dio Chrys. 32.9 attests one perception of Cynics (in Alexandria) as hanging round on street-corners, near temples, etc., engaging the masses with their gibes (*skōmmata*).

[98] On Cynic shamelessness (a byword at e.g. Diog. Laert. 7.3), and the different interpretations to which it lent itself, see Krueger (1996).

[99] One possible exception is the controversial figure of Peregrinus: according to Lucian, *Demon.* 21, Peregrinus berated Demonax for not being an authentic Cynic (οὐ κυνᾷς) because he laughed

its existential implications. One image of the Cynic is of someone who by shedding all worldly attachments turns life into the practice of pure insouciance. This is the thrust, for instance, of Plutarch's description of Crates of Thebes as a person who spent his entire life 'playing and laughing as though at a festival' (παίζων καὶ γελῶν ὥσπερ ἐν ἑορτῇ τῷ βίῳ διετέλεσε), a description whose real point is the seeming erasure of any distinction between seriousness and play in the Cynic's own person.[100] On the other hand, many accounts of Cynicism emphasise compulsive mockery and belittlement of others, foregrounding the Cynic's harshly critical evaluation of people's desires and commitments. Between these two characterisations there is at least a difference of ethos, and possibly a deeper tension too – a tension, one might say, between caring about nothing and caring passionately about at least one thing (namely the need to repudiate the things that *others* care about). We need to probe this issue further if we are to discover what underlies the idea of a distinctively Cynic habit of laughter.

We can most conveniently do so by turning to the stories told about Diogenes of Sinope, whose nickname 'the dog' gives us at least a symbolic fixed point in the evolution of a Cynic way of life.[101] Diogenes is associated in the sources with a particularly vehement habit of derision, for which Diogenes Laertius 6.24 uses the rare verb κατασοβαρεύεσθαι, meaning something like 'to put people down contemptuously'. The collection of anecdotes at Diogenes Laertius 6.24–69, on which I shall concentrate, consists mostly of quips and caustic remarks ascribed to the founder of Cynicism and extracted, we can be sure, from more than one earlier source. As is often the way with *bons mots*, some of these remarks are elsewhere attributed to others; historical authenticity can never be vouched for.[102] But

---

most of the time (cf. Lucian, *Menip.* 21, with n. 130 below) and made fun of people. This is an intriguing glimpse of a division within Cynic self-conceptions; but Lucian had his reasons for depicting Peregrinus as a grim, fake-serious character: see ch. 9, 462–9.

[100] Plut. *Mor.* 466e; cf. Diogenes' remark that every day should be regarded as a festival (*ibid.* 477c), with nn. 44 above, 114 below. This use of festival imagery to symbolise carefree self-sufficiency and an inversion of the normal serious/playful hierarchy of life should be contrasted with that of the Pythagoreans (n. 12 above); Alexis fr. 222 seems to start off in the latter vein, before resolving itself into a philosophy of 'maximum laughter' (ὃς δ' ἂν πλεῖστα γελάσῃ . . . , 14).

[101] Diogenes' main contender for the title of founder of Cynicism, Antisthenes the Socratic (ch. 6 n. 81), may also have had the nickname 'dog' (Diog. Laert. 6.13); cf. Arist. *Rhet.* 3.10, 1411a24, with Goulet-Cazé (1996), Giannantoni (1990) IV 491–7, and n. 111 below. Antisthenes resembles Diogenes of Sinope in some of his apophthegms (Diog. Laert. 6.1, 3–4, 7), use of face-to-face mockery (*ibid.* 6.7, with Plato), but also insouciance about denigration (*ibid.* 6.7; n. 117 below).

[102] Goulet-Cazé (1992) is the fullest treatment of Book 6; see 3909–59 for sources, and cf. Giannantoni (1990) IV 413–19. The apparatus to the collection of Diogenes' sayings in *SSR* II 301–422 (V B 152–530) notes parallels and alternative attributions. Overwien (2005) is a richly documented study of

that hardly diminishes the usefulness of the stories for my investigation. Diogenes becomes a sort of screen onto which different possibilities of wit and derision are projected, thereby illustrating some key Greek perceptions of (and ways of imagining) laughter's uses. It is fortunate for my own focus on cultural psychology that doubts over biographical, even sociological, accuracy need not prevent us from using the heavily anecdotal traditions about Cynicism to interpret the mentalities, both *pro* and *contra*, which surrounded the movement. Values can be communicated at least as strongly by images of the thinkable or imaginable as by records of the actual.[103]

What matters for my argument, in the first place, is that Diogenes' sayings, and the narratives in which some of them are embedded, manifest a strong tension between a type of mockery that is unconstrainedly 'antinomian' (in keeping with the general Cynic rejection of social conventions) and, on the other hand, an ethically meaningful and potentially corrective style of ridicule. In the first case the effect is a characteristically *gratuitous* obnoxiousness. When an irascible man from whom he was begging says, '[I'll give you something] if you can persuade me', Diogenes retorts, 'if I could persuade you, I would have persuaded you to hang yourself' (6.59). In contravention of basic hospitality, he insults Plato to his face when a guest in the latter's house (6.26), though this is a case where Diogenes gets as good as he gives. Going further still, when warned not to spit in a luxurious house, he hawks and spits straight in the speaker's own face, telling him sarcastically that he could not find a 'worse', i.e. more suitable, place to do so.[104] Spitting is a gestural equivalent to the most demeaning, hubristic kind of laughter; in social reality, to spit in someone's face would be too grossly inflammatory to pass without retaliation, unless the victim were abjectly powerless to respond. Indeed, even if the person spitting possessed monarchical or tyrannical power, it might still be thought extraordinary to accept such treatment without response: an anecdote elsewhere in Diogenes Laertius presents it as remarkable that the Socratic philosopher Aristippus

---

all the sources (including the Arabic tradition) for Diogenes' sayings, as well as their formal and thematic characteristics.

[103] See Sluiter (2005), esp. 140, 158–60, for a recent insistence on the 'essentially literary . . . representation' of Cynicism in ancient sources.

[104] Diog. Laert. 6.32. One version of the story is commended by John Chrysostom as a pagan analogue to Christian contempt for worldly possessions: *In ep. Rom.* 11.6 (60.494 *PG*), with Downing (1992) 286–95 on John's ambivalent attitude to Cynicism. For spitting in the face, cf. Soph. *Ant.* 1232 (with murderous rage), Hdas. 5.76, Plut. *Mor.* 189a (ch. 1 n. 64), Lucian, *Catapl.* 12 (at a corpse: see ch. 9 n. 46); cf. ch. 10, 471–3, for the Roman soldiers and Jesus, and note Curtius (1953) 427 (oddly unaware of other evidence) for its use by a Christian martyr. Laughter and (metaphorical) spitting form a virtual hendiadys at Lucian, *Pisc.* 34, *Pseudol.* 29. The German verb *spotten*, 'mock', is cognate with *spucken*, 'spit': Drosdowski (1997) 695.

simply 'put up with it' when Dionysius of Syracuse spat on him, and the criticism which Aristippus receives from an observer underlines the point.[105] Yet, as often with the traditions about Diogenes the Cynic, his own act of spitting in someone's face is turned into a 'closed' story (like the comparable but even more extreme act of urinating on guests at a dinner, 6.46). Here as frequently elsewhere, predictable consequences are silently erased, even where the targets are men as powerful as Philip or Alexander. It is as if Diogenes were a 'Thersites' who somehow manages to deliver his gibes with impunity.[106] That is not invariably so; some anecdotes do show Diogenes as the victim of physical violence.[107] But when impunity is implied, the effect is starkly to isolate the Cynic's scandalous shamelessness, laying bare the dynamics of derision in a 'shocking' form. This creates a conundrum for the hearer of such stories – whether to laugh *with* Diogenes (which would involve assimilating oneself to his shamelessness) or *at* him (which seems to leave one vicariously impotent in the face of his contempt).

Other anecdotes, however, in the mould of the Cynic *chreia* or instructive parable, show mockery at work in the service of a clearly ethical or censuring purpose, rebuking hypocrisy, self-ignorance and vice of various kinds. When he is captured at the battle of Chaeronea, brought before Philip and asked who he is, Diogenes replies: 'a spy on your gluttony' (6.43).[108] To a man having his shoes put on by a slave he says, 'your happiness is not yet complete unless he also wipes your nose – which will happen when you are disabled in your hands' (6.44). As those two examples demonstrate, Diogenes' ridicule varies in register and tone from the blatantly contemptuous to the mordantly, even grimly ironic.[109] But those variations do not stand

---

[105] Diog. Laert. 2.67. An injunction precisely to ignore being spat at (and other gestures of *hubris*) is found in the Cynic-influenced Stoic Mus. Ruf. *Diss.* 10.

[106] Diogenes and Alexander/Philip: Diog. Laert. 6. 38, 43–4, 60, 68; other sources, *SSR* II 240–9; cf. Giannantoni (1990) IV 443–51. We know that Thersites came to be thought of as a model for at least some Cynics: see Lucian, *Demon.* 61 (n. 70 above). Urinating on others appears (in a dream) as an act of antisocial inebriation at Artemid. *Oneir.* 4.44; cf. the real-life use of urine in a derisive gesture (with real consequences) at Dem. 54.4. A similar act, accompanied by a social chorus of laughter, is ascribed to the treatment of a Roman ambassador by a Tarentine buffoon at Dio. Hal. *Ant. Rom.* 19.5.2–3; cf. Barnes (2005) 35–45 (historically sceptical). *Pace* Barnes *ibid.* 100, defecation may be involved in the equivalent episode at App. *Samn.* 7.5–6.

[107] See esp. Diog. Laert. 6.33, 41–2, 48; cf. a youth's smashing of the wine-jar ('barrel') in which he (supposedly) lived, 6.43, with 6.45 for his general 'baiting' by boys.

[108] The Cynic as 'spy' was a topos in its own right: Plut. *Mor.* 70c, 606b–c, Epict. *Diss.* 1.24.3–10, 3.22.24, with Giannantoni (1990) IV 507–12. The Cynic-sympathising Stoic Ariston of Chios (*SVF* I 384, 387) justifies mockery (*episkōptein*) as beneficial in both social life and education. But Ariston is not an advocate of general mirth: *SVF* I 388–9. Cf. Ioppolo (1980) III–13.

[109] Long (1999) 626 justifiably speaks of 'black humour' in Diogenes' aphorisms, though none of his examples seems to me to fit that description well. For Diogenes' manner as effectively a brand of *spoudogeloion* (cf. n. 93 above), note the wording at e.g. Dio Chrys. 9.7, 10.2; cf. Diog. Laert. 6.83,

in the way of a cumulative impression of someone whose whole personality and lifestyle are permeated by a compulsion to jeer at the folly he seems to find all around him. This trait consequently takes on the dimensions of an existential stance: not just one part of a larger repertoire of behaviour, but something more like an underlying, defining mindset. This is not, I reiterate, to treat the evidence for Diogenes as biographically authentic (in that regard, I remain methodologically sceptical) but rather as an anecdotal, imagistic projection of what an exceptionally scornful gelastic habit would do to the life of one who practised it.

Whatever its sources, the portrait of Diogenes depicts the constant exercise of a trenchant, fearless outspokenness, *parrhēsia*, which he himself calls the 'finest' or 'most beautiful' of all things.[110] The Cynic is presented as especially sharp-tongued and cutting: he refers to himself, at one point, as 'biting' others in suitably dog-like fashion, and he is called 'very acute at hitting the mark in verbal exchanges'.[111] But is Diogenes, we might wonder, interested in *laughter* as such, and, if so, whose laughter, and at what? We actually hear him laugh himself on only one occasion in Diogenes Laertius' *Lives*. This is at 6.36, which is the 'punch line' to one of a pair of quasi-practical jokes (in this case, asking a would-be disciple to carry round a fish for him) designed to expose people's attenuated sense of friendship and philosophical commitment. But throughout the collection of anecdotes there is an unmistakably high visibility of what would normally be laughter-inducing techniques (puns, wordplay, paradoxes, parodies, risqué references). Accordingly, verbs such as *skōptein* (jest, joke, scoff) and *diapaizein* (make complete fun of) are unsurprising markers of his tone.[112] Indeed, practical or visual 'jokes' seem to appeal to him. In addition to the two mentioned just above, he brings a plucked cock into Plato's school to make fun of the definition of a human as a 'featherless biped' (6.40), and

---

describing the writings of Diogenes' follower Monimus as 'trifles mixed with covert seriousness' (παίγνια σπουδῇ λεληθυίᾳ μεμιγμένα). See Döring (1993) 343–52 for this vein in early Cynicism.

[110] Diog. Laert. 6.69; cf. the enjoyment of crude *parrhēsia* by the slanderer, *kakologos*, at Theophr. *Char.* 28.6 (ch. 5, 239): but Kinney (1996) 302 n. 23 is not justified in calling this character 'probably Cynic'. Branham (1996) 97–104 discusses *parrhēsia* as a central Cynic value with implications for mockery; cf. Sluiter (2005) 154–7. For *parrhēsia* and laughter in other contexts, see ch. 5, 234–42.

[111] 'Biting': 6.60; cf. 6.45, 6.79, the latter quoting *Anth. Pal.* 7.116 (see *ibid.* 7.115 on Antisthenes for the same motif), Demetr. *Eloc.* 260 (gently 'nipping', ὑποδάκνειν); see Overwien (2005) 246–50 for Diogenes' dog-like characteristics more generally. Acuteness in repartee: Diog. Laert. 6.74 (εὐστοχώτατος ... ἐν ταῖς ἀπαντήσεσι τῶν λόγων); for εὐστοχ- terminology, cf. Athen. 8.348d on Stratonicus' witticisms.

[112] See 6.26, 72; cf. 2.68. Elsewhere, see the various markers of Diogenes' laughter, including the verbs (κατα)γελᾶν, παίζειν, σκώπτειν at e.g. Dio Chrys. 6.7, 13, 17, 20–1, 9.3, 6–7, 10.31, Plut. *Mor.* 526c, Ael. *VH* 9.34, *Pap. Vindob. gr.* 29946 col. IV.24 (= V B 143.123 *SSR*).

he walks round in daylight with a lamp, saying 'I am looking for a human being' (6.41).

Yet given his assiduously antisocial behaviour, we cannot escape the impression that in so far as Diogenes does exercise his wit with a view to arousing laughter, the latter belongs implicitly to himself (though always potentially, by extension, to a sympathetic teller or hearer of the stories concerned). He is both performer of and the prime audience for his own jests. While followers of his are occasionally referred to, and while he finds himself in a wide variety of social situations, Diogenes is pictured as essentially a Cynic *loner*, as indeed were Cynics more generally (hence the common stereotype of the rootless mendicant). Diogenes stands apart from the crowd. He is, archetypally, the person who enters the theatre when everyone else is leaving it; or, equivalently but paradoxically, in Lucian he recommends seeking out the most crowded places yet nonetheless being 'alone and unsociable (ἀκοινώνητος)' in them.[113] The corresponding notion that his particular type of serio-comic or serio-ludic manner is largely for his own benefit is found also in sources other than Diogenes Laertius. Plutarch tells us that when he was being auctioned as a slave (almost certainly part of a legendary strand in his biography), Diogenes 'lay on the ground and kept making jokes (ἔσκωπτε) at the auctioneer; when told to stand up, he refused but kept playing around and mocking the man (παίζων καὶ καταγελῶν), saying "suppose you were selling a fish . . ."'[114] On one level, the story is an obviously emblematic enactment of the Cynic's inner 'freedom'; but beyond the resulting insouciance there is a striking sense of peculiarly self-indulgent exhibitionism.[115] It is tempting to discern some resemblance to both an insolent child and a performer of street-theatre, yet the remarkable thing is the paradoxical impression that Diogenes is interested chiefly in gratifying or fulfilling himself. He may 'perform' in front of an audience, but in some strange way he shows no sign of admitting that he *needs* one.

---

[113] Entering the theatre when others are leaving: Diog. Laert. 6.64. Being antisocial in the most crowded places: Lucian, *Vit. Auctio* 10.

[114] Plut. *Mor.* 466e, juxtaposed with Crates' life-long laughter (n. 44 above). Despite Plutarch's apparent faith in the story's credentials, it appears to be an embellished variant on an episode in Menippus' *Sale of Diogenes* (Diog. Laert. 6.29). For other sources on the auction, see *SSR* II 257–66.

[115] Quasi-theatrical vulgarity is marked at Diog. Laert. 4.52, describing the ostentatiously crude Bion of Borysthenes (n. 95 above, n. 122 below) as *theatrikos*, 'exhibitionist'. The influence of comic theatre on Diogenes himself is asserted by Marcus Aur. *Med.* 11.6; see Niehues-Pröbsting (1979) 167–80, Sluiter (2005) 152–8. For an instance where Diogenes' serio-comic antics produce a laughter that supposedly influences his audience, see Dio Chrys. 9.22. Bosman (2006) now argues a general case for Diogenes as comic performer, though he is too inclined to believe in the historicity of the anecdotal tradition (cf. n. 103 above).

In all its guises, then, the distinctiveness of Diogenes' mockery of others remains linked to his persona as an individualist impregnable in his literally self-satisfied detachment from prevailing norms. But what of his mockery *by* others? Many stories identify him as an object of social reproach and scorn, but they do so by way of indicating how little this mattered to him. The issue is crystallised in a pair of telling passages. In the first, Diogenes responds to the report that 'many people mock you' (πολλοί σου καταγελῶσιν) with the riposte, 'but *I* do not consider myself mocked' (ἀλλ᾽ ἐγὼ οὐ καταγελῶμαι). In the second, he answers 'most people mock you' with: 'and perhaps asses mock *them*, but just as they take no notice of asses, so I take no notice of these people'.[116] These anecdotes, the first of which seems to have had wide currency, present Diogenes as a figure of paradox in relation to the forces of social derision – exposed to scoffing disdain from all around yet utterly self-assured of his *immunity* to the usual risks and consequences (shame, humiliation, damaged reputation) of such disdain. That immunity implies, we need to notice, a special understanding of the Cynic's self-sufficient identity: Diogenes himself, his real person, is simply not touched by ridicule.[117] However – a second layer of paradox – while deflecting mockery aimed at himself, Diogenes nonetheless exploits it abundantly against others; his remark about asses is itself a mocking rejoinder. So the Cynic, it seems, can distance himself so completely from the operations of social status and public evaluation as to become almost a separate species (consider the asses analogy, above), while at the same time reappropriating the deflationary power of laughter for his own purposes. There is, here, a complex reworking of a Socratic inheritance. But whereas the Platonic Socrates holds a subtle, somewhat ambivalent conviction that one should not fear (unthinking) laughter, Diogenes intensifies this into outright indifference towards what others think of him, leaving us with a pattern of behaviour built around a curious point of psychological tension – one aspect, perhaps, of the sense in which he was 'a Socrates gone mad', as

---

[116] Diog. Laert. 6.54, 58, with Plut. *Mor.* 460e, *Fab. Max.* 10.1–2, and Olympiod. *In Pl. Grg.* 22.2 for other reports of the first remark; cf. Glei (1998), who rightly denies a semantic difference between active/passive voices of *katagelan* but whose dogmatism about translation (with unfair criticisms of others, n. 11) obscures the paradoxical nature of Diogenes' words. Popular mockery of Cynics (and others), including Diogenes himself, is reflected at e.g. Dio Chrys. 9.8–9 (including an Odysseus comparison: cf. ch. 2 n. 95), 34.2. On imperviousness to ridicule, see ch. 1, 41–2.

[117] Cf. Epict. *Diss.* 3.22.100: the Cynic is like a 'stone' in the sense that 'no one insults him, no one strikes him, no one offends him'; see Billerbeck (1978) 159. Diog. Laert. 6.91–2 shows Crates withstanding public ridicule (for physical ugliness), though with less than perfect equanimity. The proto-Cynic Antisthenes (n. 101 above) urged caring less about denigration than about being stoned (fr. 85 Decleva Caizzi, *apud* Diog. Laert. 6.7).

Plato is said brilliantly to have dubbed him.[118] We can visualise Diogenes, standing defiantly apart from the crowd, as able to ignore the traditionally potent force of group derision of the aberrant individual, yet somehow compelled to laugh back in the faces of those whose lives he despises. Such an extreme relationship to laughter might remind us, among other things, of the legendary Democritus, not least the way in which his fellow Abderites, in the version recounted in the pseudo-Hippocratic *Epistles*, diagnosed him as mad.

The paradoxes and tensions to which I have drawn attention helped to produce some instability in the interpretation of what Cynicism could and should be. I have space here for just one revealing illustration of this point. The Stoic Epictetus, who took a strongly admiring view of a Cynic way of life but also subscribed, as we saw in my last chapter, to a conception of philosophical laughter that was cautious about face-to-face mockery, felt the need to exclude, or at any rate marginalise, the idea of a Cynic habit of denigrating and abusing others. The question is touched on several times in his main treatment of Cynicism. Twice he seeks to combat what he clearly takes to be a standard element in what others thought about the movement. Addressing one of his associates, he specifically contradicts the assumption that insulting those one meets, indeed insulting them 'inopportunely' or indiscriminately (λοιδορεῖσθαι ἀκαίρως), is integral to a Cynic existence.[119] But a little later Epictetus betrays the delicacy of the balance he wants to strike. Having just asserted that all mankind are kith and kin to the Cynic, he asks (3.22.82): 'do you think it is out of sheer rudeness that he insults those he meets? He does this as a father, as a brother, and as servant of our common father, Zeus.' The implication here is that the Cynic will employ language that may sound like abuse, but he will do so in a spirit of positive concern for the other's moral well-being, not out of mere disregard for civility and decorum (something Epictetus associates, in the same passage, with pseudo-Cynics of the present day, rather than the great figure of Diogenes himself). Anxious about the image of the scoffing Cynic, Epictetus reacts by alternatively suppressing it from his idealised portrait or transmuting it into

---

[118] Σωκράτης . . . μαινόμενος: Diog. Laert. 6.54. On Socrates' relationship to ridicule, see ch. 6, 276–300.

[119] Epict. *Diss.* 3.22.10, 51. Mocking 'inopportunely', *akairōs* (e.g. Plut. *Mor.* 803d, with *kairos* at 803c), would flout a general principle of *kairos*, the 'right time', that Epictetus commits himself to at 4.12.17: see ch. 6 n. 109, and cf. Hippocrates' (premature) concern about Democritus' 'untimely laughter' (ἀκαίρους γέλωτας) at ps.-Hippoc. *Epist.* 17.4 (360–3 above). For a Renaissance conception of Cynic ridicule as 'bastard laughter', a sneering curling of the lip, see Joubert (1980) 99.

a model of well-meaning reproof.[120] But in the end he has to leave room
for what was evidently too embedded in the traditions about Diogenes
and others to be simply written out of the story. 'The Cynic', he writes,
'needs to have a great deal of natural wit and sharpness (otherwise he will
be just a nasty sneerer), in order to have a ready, apposite response to all
eventualities.'[121] He then cites a pair of Diogenes' *bons mots* (one exchanged
with a 'nobody', the other with Alexander the Great), neither of them, it
has to be said, carrying any obvious moral weight. Epictetus has done his
best to purify the Cynic's laughter, as with the rest of his stock image (public
indecency, dirty clothes, etc.). But that image seems to cling to some of
its old associations with crude effrontery and the rejection of all norms of
social inhibition.

Epictetus gives us a convenient glimpse of a divergence within evaluations of Cynicism that had repercussions for the practice of ridicule. On
one reading, Cynic laughter could look like part-and-parcel of an unrestrained naturalism in all matters of the body, and such naturalism might
in turn be regarded as essentially a kicking over of the traces of all social
conventions. But there was an alternative conception of Cynic laughter –
the one we have seen Epictetus himself advocating – as aligned with, and
expressive of, a fully moral intention to expose vice to the benevolent influence of correction and reform. So within a larger debate about the nature
of Cynicism, a debate too large to be pursued here, an ambiguity about
laughter itself and its uses was operative. We can see an overlap in this
respect with the idea of *parrhēsia*, 'frank speech' or a general willingness
to 'say everything/anything', which we have heard Diogenes calling the
'finest of all things' (378 above). Even before the Cynics, *parrhēsia* elicited
feelings of ambivalence: it could, in principle, be admired for its honesty
and fearless truth-telling, or condemned for its shocking shamelessness.[122]
Cynic *parrhēsia* inherited this potential ambiguity. It might be thought

---

[120] Cf. his parallel uneasiness on the cognate subject of Cynic 'blaming' (μέμφεσθαι, ἐπιτιμᾶν etc.):
3.22.13, 48 suggest that it is simply *not* Cynic, while 3.22.93–6 assimilates it to the paradigm of
candid speech (*parrhēsia*) exercised for the benefit of one's 'kin'.

[121] *Diss.* 3.22.90: δεῖ δὲ καὶ χάριν πολλὴν προσεῖναι φυσικὴν τῷ Κυνικῷ καὶ ὀξύτητα (εἰ δὲ μή,
μύξα γίνεται, ἄλλο δ' οὐδέν) ἵνα ἑτοίμως δύνηται καὶ παρακειμένως πρὸς τὰ ἐμπίπτοντα
ἀπαντᾶν. See Billerbeck (1978) 150–1. On the import of 'sneerer' (lit. 'nasal mucus', perhaps
here = 'nostril') cf. Appendix 1 n. 14; an alternative interpretation of the word is 'sniveller'. On
Epictetus' attitude to Cynicism more generally, see Niehues-Pröbsting (1979) 186–95, Long (2002)
58–64.

[122] See ch. 5, 218–19, 234–42; cf. n. 21 there for Cynic denials of aischrology/obscenity. Whether Bion
of Borysthenes' alleged penchant for vulgar (*phortikos*) language, Diog. Laert. 4.52 (n. 115 above),
reflects his Cynic phase, we cannot say; but cf. Plut. *Mor.* 5c on Diogenes' verbal vulgarity, with
Kindstrand (1976) 44, 51, and my ch. 1 n. 53 on other uses of *phortikos*.

of, according to context or the observer's sympathies, as centring either on courageous censure of others, even of the powerful, or on a disgusting insensitivity to social decencies (a verbal correlate of, say, sexual acts in public, a motif which figures prominently in the mythology of Cynicism). In that respect, *parrhēsia* is the other side of the same coin as the Cynic use of ridicule. In the form in which Diogenes practises them, and when viewed from the standpoint of ordinary expectations, both these traits are irreducibly disorientating. They belong to a man who is, for instance, an exponent of extreme self-mastery yet so shameless as to masturbate (or engage in other sexual acts) publicly.[123] Laughter, stripped of its capacity to mediate shared pleasure, gets caught up in a Cynic stance of simultaneously impugning society's ingrained hypocrisy and giving outrageous offence to the scruples that underlie it.

Cynicism is an elusive phenomenon, not least because the ancient evidence for its principles is permeated by the fictionalisation of historical individuals and events. Modern scholars try to cope with this elusiveness either by stressing the different forms it could take (early/late, 'hard'/'soft', etc.) or by stressing certain strands at the expense of others. For my purposes, what matters is the recurrent impression of an instrinsic instability in the function of laughter for a Cynic mentality and way of life. Everything depends on how far Cynicism's naturalist inclinations are pushed in the direction of provocatively antisocial protest and revolt, how far they are tempered by an ethics of virtue, simplicity and self-control. It is clear enough that Cynicism in general made a habit, or was at any rate perceived from outside as making a habit, of taking up a mocking stance towards conventional preoccupations with wealth, status and power. But the tone and impetus of that mockery oscillate, in our sources, between sheer derision and constructive chastisement.

Furthermore, while it is appropriate to treat Cynics as exploiting laughter for their own quasi-existentialist brand of 'authenticity', as the expression of 'a whole view of life',[124] we are now in a position to conclude that this falls short of anything like the full-blown conception of 'the absurd' which I discussed in the earlier parts of this chapter. However eccentrically they may sometimes appear to interpret them, Cynics are generically committed to a set of values – including nature, freedom, self-sufficiency, virtue and, not least, the order of the *kosmos* (Diogenes claims to be a *kosmopolitēs*, 'citizen

---

[123] Diog. Laert. 6.46; cf. e.g. Dio Chrys. 6.17–20, Lucian, *Vit. Auctio* 10, *Peregr.* 17, Galen, *Loc. affect.* 6.15 (8.419 Kühn), and, for Christian outrage (and scepticism), Augustine, *Civ. dei* 14.20.

[124] Stewart (1994) 29, with 36–7 for the 'Democritus' link; cf. n. 26 above.

of the cosmos')[125] – which are incompatible with a sense of existential absurdity, though which undoubtedly lend themselves to ridicule of the many non-Cynics who fail to live up to those values. Even when Cynics are imagined as laughing in death, this symbolises an extreme independence from the worldly attachments that, for others, make death a matter of loss and annihilation.[126] But it does not purport to divest life of all significance or satisfaction. It only corroborates the Cynic confinement of such significance to the simplest, most 'primitivist' pursuits and pleasures.

There is, however, a problem to be noticed here, which I want to address by returning to the questions I proposed *à propos* Menippus at the start of the section (372 above). In the first of the *Dialogues of the Dead*, one of his many depictions of Cynic laughter, Lucian shows Diogenes of Sinope sending up a message to Menippus, his later follower, on earth. The message, which on one level is a coded recommendation of suicide, is in essence: 'if you grow tired of deriding the living, come and join me in Hades, where there is no end of opportunity to laugh at the lamentations of the once rich and powerful'.[127] Laughter is here marked as the perpetual condition of the Cynic, both in life and (symbolically) in death. The combined perspective of life and death is crucial to this Cynic vantage point. Indeed, Diogenes tells Menippus that mockery of this kind is always provisional or in some degree doubtful (ἐν ἀμφιβόλῳ) on earth, 'for who (sc. at that stage) is wholly sure about what follows life?' But once in the underworld, no doubt remains; 'everything is mere dust for all of us, skulls stripped of beauty', leaving those who pursued ephemeral goods in life with nothing but painful memories of what they have lost.[128] The problem that interests me here lies not so much in the surface contradiction between the idea of death as annihilation and the description of the psychological reactions of the souls of the dead: that is part of an imaginative projection, and a comic dramatisation, of contrasting views of life itself. But beneath that surface there lurks a real issue for a distinctively Cynic concept of existential laughter. For if death,

---

[125] Diog. Laert. 6.63.

[126] In addition to the Lucianic material in my text and in ch. 9, *passim*, see anon., *Anth. Pal.* 9.145, n. 88 above.

[127] *Dial. mort.* 1.1–2 (cf. ch. 9, 448); for Menippus having his fill of derision, cf. *Icarom.* 19. A (Cynic) tradition that Diogenes himself committed suicide occurs at Diog. Laert. 6.76–7, Ael. *VH* 8.14 (when already terminally ill); see his recommendation of virtual suicide at Lucian, *Vit. Auctio* 10 (alluding to the story found at e.g. Plut. *Mor.* 956b; cf. Cyniscus at Lucian, *Catapl.* 7), and his view of death as welcome at Lucian, *Dial. mort.* 21.2. But the traditions of Diogenes' death (like everything else about him) are unstable: see Giannantoni (1990) IV 437–40. The moderate Cynic Demonax starved himself cheerfully to death: Lucian, *Demon.* 65.

[128] 'Skulls stripped of beauty': 1.3; cf. 5.1, 6.2, with the fuller working of the same motif at *Menip.* 15. The torture of memory: 1.1; cf. 3.1–2, *Menip.* 12.

by rendering their values ephemeral, makes pointless the lives of those who pursue earthly goals (especially the rich, the powerful, the beautiful, and 'professional' philosophers), why does the same not hold for Cynics themselves? If death is the same for everyone, then the relationship between life and death – between whatever one has or does now and will lose or cease to do then – must also be the same. If the Cynic's critique of futility, the formula of his laughter, depends on, so to speak, the view from Hades, then he is surely snared by his own perception of the vanity of human wishes. *If* temporal finitude, if death as loss and annihilation, robs life of all meaning, the Cynic may try to circumscribe what he will lose in death by stripping down his worldly allegiances to the bare minimum, but he is inescapably left with no basis on which to claim more validity for his own way of life than for any other. He possesses no vantage point from which to deliver his existentially charged mockery of others – nowhere, that is, other than the imaginary space of death. So the Cynic should either stop laughing, or laugh at himself as much as at anyone else. On this reading, Diogenes' pretence of impregnability – 'But *I* do not consider myself mocked' – may turn out to be hollow.

The Cynic ought, then, either to recognise that human values are not entirely undermined by temporal (or any other kind of) finitude, *or* to subscribe to a sense of 'the absurd', of the intrinsically laughable emptiness of every form of finite human existence, including his own. But is the second option viable at all? Can it really be translated into a form of life, or can it only be imagined and fictionalised from the point of view of death itself? These are questions I shall ponder further in Chapter 9, but for now I use them to adumbrate the thought that an absurdism which makes no exceptions – which admits, like the legendary Democritus of *Palatine Anthology* 7.56 (364 above), that it is included in the object of its own laughter – propounds an existential logic which may permit no sustainable form of life. The same may well be true of absurdism's seemingly opposed yet curiously similar sibling, unmitigated pessimism. To laugh at everything or to grieve over everything: each reaches a global verdict on human existence by reaching for an absolute viewpoint to which it does not have access. It appeals to me, therefore, that in Lucian's *Vitarum Auctio* Democritus and Heraclitus, in their *legendary* personae (laughing and weeping, respectively, over life), are the only figures who do not attract a single bidder in the auction of philosophies. Nobody wants them, because nobody could truly live with them.

We cannot, however, quite let the matter rest there. What is livable is determined as much by feeling as by logic, and the idea that life itself is a suitable object of laughter can evidently survive as an intermittent mood, even a *Weltgefühl*, as well as, perhaps (if we follow Freud's short 1927 essay on humour), the ultimate joke-form.[129] In a passage of Lucian's *Menippus* which I touched on earlier in the chapter (340), Tiresias, asked (like Silenus) to name the best life for humans, first *laughs* at the question and then, when pressed, tells Menippus to spend his life 'laughing at most things and taking nothing seriously'.[130] This is a piece of advice with some Cynic resonance, and therefore apt for its addressee; but it also has an older, wider presence in antiquity. Aristotle, for instance, is evidently aware of its proponents when, in the *Nicomachean Ethics* (10.6, 1176b30–1177a5), he criticises as childish (and 'absurd', *atopon*) the view that the end of life is 'play', *paidia*, a view which he sees as a recipe for mere ethical decadence. In the context of Lucian's *Menippus*, the idea of taking nothing seriously is complicated firstly by Tiresias' own enigmatic laughter (which hints at a more-than-human perspective that it cannot divulge), and secondly by the recommendation to choose the life of an ordinary person and give up all philosophical aspirations to understand either the first or last principles of existence. Menippus' response is, therefore, revealing: he cannot wait to get back to life – not, as sometimes said, in order to continue his Cynic preaching, but rather, it seems, to savour an existence that will now be somehow at ease with itself.[131] Menippus has been given more reason than ever to laugh, yet he can do so only from inside a life of his own. What's more, in what I think is a nicely ironic touch, Tiresias shows him a short cut through the Boeotian cave of Trophonius, a cave whose rituals, as we gather from Pausanias and other sources, were specifically reputed to *incapacitate* laughter – a circumstance that conspicuously fails to apply in Menippus'

[129] Freud's essay takes humour to be the superego's way of temporarily dismissing the ego's concerns by treating life as a children's game, fit only to be the subject of jokes ('ein Kinderspiel, gerade gut, einen Scherz darüber zu machen!'): Freud (1989) 282, translated in Freud (1961) 166. Ancient imagery of life as a (children's) 'game': n. 34 above.

[130] γελῶν τὰ πολλὰ καὶ περὶ μηδὲν ἐσπουδακώς, *Menip.* 21. See Branham (1989a) 25 (but τὰ πολλά is more than 'a great deal'), Branham (1989b), who compares Simonid. 646 *PMG* (n. 83 above) but goes too far in claiming 'no parallel in Cynic teachings' (159); for Lucian, at any rate, finding *everything* in life laughable is precisely a Cynic option: e.g. *Icarom.* 4, 17 (cf. 19 *ad fin.*), *Demon.* 21 (cf. n. 99 above), *Dial. mort.* 1.1, with ch. 9, esp. 448–9. Branham (2004) 177–8 now accepts the Cynic connection. As regards seeing the *whole* of life as ridiculous, cf. Democritus at e.g. Sen. *Tranq.* 15, *De ira* 2.10.5, Lucian, *Vit. Auctio* 13, with 363–5, 368–9 above. Compare Palladas, *Anth. Pal.* 10.72, on the 'theatre' (*skēnē*) and 'mime' (*paignion*: ch. 10 n. 96) of life, with a choice between 'play' and 'seriousness'.

[131] Cf. Lucian, *Dial. mort.* 8.2, where Menippus, while appreciating the absurdity of a desire for immortality, rejects Chiron's *choice* of death (thereby questioning one possible version of Cynicism: n. 127 above) and advises instead an uncomplaining acceptance of whatever life presents. This is a different Menippus from Lucian, *Dial. mort.* 20, where he is eager to die. See ch. 9 for other examples of Lucian's teasing manipulation of his repertoire of (Cynic) figures and ideas.

case.[132] Like many things in Lucian, the episode leaves a faintly quizzical impression. But it lends some plausibility to the thought that if absurdism's impulses find a metaphorical or symbolic outlet in Hades, its ambiguities keep it securely anchored to the land of the living. As with much of the other testimony I have explored in this chapter, Lucian's *Menippus* points us towards the conclusion that the strongest sense of the absurd can be experienced only by minds, whether ancient or modern, which contradict it in the very act of believing that they are embracing it.

---

[132] The agelastic effects of Trophonius' cave are mentioned at Paus. 9.39.13: n. 89 above. In Lucian, *Dial. mort.* 10, Menippus scoffs at Trophonius' own pretensions as cult-hero, including the ridiculous requirements imposed on visitors to his oracle.

CHAPTER 8

The intermittencies of laughter in Menander's social world

> What if everything in the world were a misunderstanding, what if
> laughter were really tears?
>
> Kierkegaard, Either/Or [1]

THE CONFUSIONS OF LAUGHTER AND TEARS

Early in Act III of Menander's *Dis Exapaton*, the young Athenian Sostratus,
recently returned from a trip to Ephesus during which he had fallen in love
with the hetaira Bacchis (of Samos), comes unexpectedly face to face with
his friend Moschus. While still in Ephesus, Sostratus had sent a letter to
Moschus asking him to track down Bacchis after she had been brought
to Athens by a rival lover; but at this stage he wrongly believes his friend
betrayed him by starting an affair of his own with her. Moschus, who has
in fact fallen for Bacchis' twin sister (also called Bacchis) and has no reason
not to anticipate a happy reunion with his friend, realises as soon as he
sets eyes on Sostratus that something is amiss. What confronts him is the
reverse of the laughter or smiles that should be normal in such an encounter:
Sostratus strikes him as being on the verge of tears. He asks immediately
for an explanation:

> τί κατηφὴς καὶ σκυθρωπός, εἰπέ μοι;
> καὶ βλέμμα τοῦθ᾽ ὑπόδακρυ; [2]

> Why are you so downcast and sullen, tell me?
> And what's this tearful look about?

The fragmentary papyrus text breaks off soon after this, just as the misunderstanding between the two young men is on the point of being cleared

---

[1] Kierkegaard (1959) 21.

[2] *Dis Ex.* 104–5. Unless otherwise indicated, all Greek quotations from Menander (including line
numbers) correspond to the three-volume edition of Arnott (1979–2000); Sandbach (1990), whose
line numbers Arnott very largely follows, should also be consulted. (Smaller fragments, as always, are
cited from *PCG*.) For full details of the text of the first scene of *Dis Exapaton*, see Handley (1997).

up. But I choose this brief moment in the play because, with its evanescent image of a face whose scowl (projected onto the mask of the actor playing Sostratus) contradicts Moschus' expectations of laughter, it neatly crystallises some of the social and psychological issues I want to explore in this chapter. The audience, of course, knows the truth: that Sostratus is mistaken in thinking he has been double-crossed by Moschus and cheated by his own Bacchis. But does this mean that the spectators should find the misunderstanding purely 'comic'? Do they themselves have any reason to laugh at this agelastic moment in the drama?

Menander seems to go out of his way to highlight Sostratus' distress, which the actor's whole body language (his 'forms' or 'postures', *schēmata*, as the Greeks called them) would have reinforced. In particular, the term ὑπόδακρυς, 'on the verge of tears' or 'starting to cry', is extremely rare; it is unique in what survives of Menander (as too is κατηφής, 'downcast', in the preceding line) and conveys a nuance of emotional vulnerability, especially as applied to a young man whose attitude towards his supposedly treacherous friend is coloured by an uncertain degree of anger (as we gathered in the preceding scene, at line 99; see below). Since the prefix *hupo-* often has the force of 'secretly' or 'surreptitiously' or the like, Moschus' remark probably also indicates that he can see Sostratus is trying to *hide* his (incipient) tears from his friend.[3] The concentrated vocabulary of lines 104–5 suggests, at any rate, an emotionally fragile Sostratus. When Plautus adapted this section of *Dis Exapaton* at *Bacchides* 534–8, he converted the tone of the encounter into one of heightened sarcasm, irony and comically exaggerated cross-purposes. To achieve that effect he chose to excise the careful psychological hints of the two Menandrian lines I have quoted.[4] The change helps, in retrospect, to draw attention to the way in which Menander himself seems to want to test his audience's alertness to the awkward tension between the two characters. The audience has heard Sostratus, just a moment ago, expressing his judgements of Moschus and Bacchis (91–102): outright condemnation in the woman's case, but (with a typically Greek double standard) a mixture of pity, anger and partial

[3] Cf. the verb ὑποδακρύειν at Heliod. *Aeth.* 10.8.1 (not cited by LSJ), where the character's attempt to conceal her tears is made explicit. Note also that the adj. κατηφής is coupled with 'being not far from tears' at ps.-Hippoc. *Epist.* 17.2; the word is more generally associated with weeping: e.g. Eur. *Med.* 1012, Plut. *Caes.* 16.7, Philo, *Flac.* 9, Heliod. *Aeth.* 7.11.9, 22.3. Cf. the combination of 'downcast' and 'grim-faced' (*skuthrōpos*: n. 5 below) at ps.-Hippoc. *Epist.* 10.1 (where Democritus laughs at those who do not laugh themselves: see ch. 7, 361). On Menandrian weeping, cf. 411–13 below.
[4] The details of Plautus' changes have been much discussed: e.g. Bain (1979) 27–9, Hunter (1985) 16–18, Damen (1992), Handley (1997) 13, 29–31, 38–42, (2002) 183–5. On Sostratus' 'body language' at *Dis Ex.* 103–6, and its connections to other images of unhappy lovers, cf. Handley (1997) 41.

exculpation towards Moschus. So it would expect Sostratus to react coolly
to his friend, and perhaps to employ some dissimulation to work out the
latter's motives. But would they foresee what actually happens? At the sudden meeting with Moschus, Sostratus starts with a bare attempt to preserve
civility by returning his friend's greeting (at the start of 103); but, as Moschus
at once detects, he rapidly threatens to be overcome by his feelings. For the
audience, then, any prospect of laughter is unexpectedly thwarted by the
character's impulse to tears. Comic release is deferred, for a few lines at
least, by the tension of pathos. But for Moschus himself, there is a further
aspect to the situation. He is not alone among Menandrian characters in
trying to read the emotions of other people from the flickering signals of
their faces. Despite (or perhaps, in part, because of) the theatrical presence
of masks, Menander depicts, and invites his audience to follow, a social
world in which attentiveness to such facial signals is of importance. And
several of the clearest cases of this attentiveness involve, as in Moschus'
case, observations of the striking absence of smiles or laughter, an absence
readily denoted by the term *skuthrōpos*, 'sullen', 'glum' or even 'scowling'.[5]
Noticing when others are averse to mirth or geniality can be a crucial piece
of information about their state of mind. It is also one marker of a broader
Menandrian representation of the erratic ways in which laughter appears
and disappears in his characters' dealings with one another.

The notion voiced in Plutarch's *Quaestiones Convivales* that Menander's plays mix ludicrous and serious material, playfulness and earnestness
(παιδιά and σπουδή), is common ground for most modern critics.[6] But
the phenomena covered by this diffuse perception of a serio-comic or serio-
ludic dimension to Menander's work remain rather intangible. How exactly
can we hope to tell when or how far (or for whom) Menandrian drama is
designed to elicit or to inhibit laughter? To ask what makes *any* comic text
'laughable' (in Greek terms, *geloios*) can be a slippery exercise, given both
the historical relativity of humour and the notorious recalcitrance of laughter's 'semantics' to critical analysis. In Menander's case, the problem of what
constitutes 'the comic' or 'the ridiculous' is exceptionally testing; it ramifies
into all areas of his delicately poised writing and dramaturgy. No one, I take
it, would dispute that much Menandrian humour, in the broadest sense of
the term, is resistant to confident diagnosis. But the hardest questions are

---

[5] See esp. *Sam.* 129, a moment of greeting but thwarted smiles/laughter very similar to that at *Dis Ex.*
104–5 (though Demeas' sullenness is not directed at Moschion), *Epitr.* 260 (the absence of expected
geniality in a social friendship), *Sic.* 124. For Men. fr. 226, see ch. 1 n. 10. On the term *skuthrōpos* as
the negation of laughter, see more generally ch. 1 n. 101.
[6] Plut. *Mor.* 712b (= Men. test. 104 *PCG*).

also the most interesting; we can learn much from addressing them, even if final answers escape us. Of course, there is more than one possible approach to the 'serio-comic' tendencies and variations that critics ancient and modern have detected in Menander. Pertinent considerations could be, and have been, formulated in terms of the historical evolution of Greek comedy, the generic interplay between Menander's plays and the plots/conventions of tragedy, his relationship to certain ethical, even philosophical, values current in his time, or his adherence to some kind of mimetic 'realism'. My own central aim is compatible with such familiar approaches, and even presupposes them at certain points. But it is also distinct from them. I am less concerned here with the comic principles as such of Menandrian drama than with the ways in which the 'atmosphere' of the social world *within* the plays is influenced by the fluctuating presence or absence of laughter.

I should stress at once, therefore, that I do not intend to scrutinise individual techniques of humour (verbal, visual, or otherwise) that can be identified – somewhat like joke-forms – and discussed in their own right.[7] I shall concentrate not on such comic 'mechanics' but instead on more oblique but nonetheless vital aspects of dramatic register, tone and effect, and above all on the contribution made to these things by the shifting gelastic implications (positive or negative) of the characters' own attitudes and behaviour. Among the main claims I shall advance are, first, that in Menander's work laughter is sometimes deliberately *blocked* or even contradicted within the social world of the plays (as, emblematically, in the meeting of Moschus and Sostratus from which I started); secondly, and partly in consequence, that the appropriateness of laughter for the audience is sometimes rendered indeterminate or problematic by a subtle shading of mood and feeling, a tonal *chiaroscuro*, in the handling of characters and contexts; thirdly, that the workings of 'the comic' in Menander depend to a considerable extent on the multiple perspectives from which he invites (or makes it feasible for) his audiences to interpret the action and direction of his plots, not least the possibilities of and impediments to laughter itself which arise within their social situations. Whereas in Aristophanes (and Old Comedy more widely, it is safe to say) 'laughter' typically runs riot, finding irresistibly ludicrous features in virtually every domain of human behaviour, exposing those features with the resources of uninhibited mockery and even obscenity (as discussed in Chapter 5), and in the process using its gelastic impetus to knock over every kind of social protocol, Menander constrains 'the ridiculous' much more tightly by creating a sense of how it

---

[7] See Arnott (1997) for a well-documented exercise of this kind.

appears intermittently and sometimes uncertainly in the dealings between his characters, *emerging* from but also *disappearing* back beneath the surface of their relationships and interactions. Even if the larger picture of Attic comedy's evolution in the classical period must have been more complex than the contrast between Aristophanes and Menander can convey,[8] that complexity forms no obstacle to (and might even reinforce) my contention that a dialectic between the disclosure and the concealment of grounds for laughter is an apt formula for the comic poetics, as well as the social and psychological dynamics, embedded in Menandrian drama. If that contention is valid, furthermore, it is legitimate to read the plays as not simply 'instruments' or providers of laughter, but actually in part *about* laughter – about its conditions, its instabilities, its elusiveness and the social negotiation of its limits in the *comédie humaine* which Menander composes and frames through his carefully filtered lenses. Such is the thrust of my argument in the present chapter.

The canonical traditions of tragedy and comedy have, it goes without saying, conventionally been defined by reference (in part) to the audience responses each genre is thought to seek and require. But there is a notable asymmetry between these two foundational categories of drama and narrative art. If tragedy paradigmatically arouses 'pity and fear' or comparable emotions, the putatively defining response to comedy, i.e. laughter, is not itself an emotion with a specific 'content' (it may be the *expression* of more than one emotion) and it is peculiarly difficult to explain or legislate for.[9] Even so, an intrinsic connection between comic drama and some idea of 'the laughable' seems self-evident. One of the anonymous, late-antique treatises now grouped together under the heading of *Prolegomena de comoedia* encapsulates the point by saying that comedy 'begins from and ends with laughter' (ἀπὸ γέλωτος εἰς γέλωτα). Similarly, whatever the source(s) of the *Tractatus Coislinianus*, which I do not regard as a reliable guide to the lost second book of Aristotle's *Poetics*, its pithy aphorism that laughter is 'the mother' of comedy seems to capture an indisputable principle of the

---

[8] Csapo (2000) diagnoses some problems with the traditional (and in origin, he thinks, Peripatetic) evolutionary model of Old, Middle and New Comedy. Nothing in the core of my argument in this chapter depends on a strong version of that model.

[9] Ancient texts occasionally appear to call laughter itself an emotion. Longin. *Subl.* 38.6 says laughter is a pleasurable *pathos*. But he has a peculiarly wide understanding of *pathos* (at 22.1 he interestingly says there is an indefinitely large number of *pathē*), so he is best understood as claiming that laughter is associated with an agreeable emotional charge, rather than constituting a definite emotion in its own right. *Tract. Coisl.* 4 (see next note) makes 'pleasure and laughter' a pair of comic *pathēmata*, but its naive duplication of the Aristotelian definition of tragedy carries little weight: cf. Janko (1984) 156–7, but he obscures the fact that Aristotle himself never calls laughter a *pathos/pathēma*.

genre.[10] Yet it is an important dimension of the work of Menander (and perhaps of other poets of New Comedy, though that larger subject lies outside my scope here) that it renders the ostensibly necessary link between comedy and laughter rather problematic. It is far from simply true, for one thing, that Menandrian plays always 'begin from' laughter; sometimes, quite the reverse is the case. Works like *Aspis, Misoumenos* and *Perikeiromene* challenge their audiences, as I shall explain in more detail below, precisely by starting from situations that for the most part exclude or prevent the possibility of laughter. It may be revealing that the ancient critical tradition – so far as we can reconstruct it from mostly late sources – observed the far from straightforward relationship between Menander (or, sometimes, New Comedy as a whole) and 'the laughable' or 'the ridiculous'; Plutarch's remark, already cited, is not an isolated case. While Old Comedy is standardly taken as the benchmark of 'the ridiculous' in an outright (even, for some, an excessive) form, Menandrian comedy is judged to lean much more towards some kind of 'seriousness' or 'gravity' (τὸ σεμνόν or the like).[11] In surviving ancient criticism there is very little talk of τὸ γελοῖον as such, or the arousal of laughter more generally, in connection with Menander. Even references to his verbal wit tend to be overshadowed by stylistic, thematic and moral(istic) observations that converge on the playwright's supposed mastery of 'every situation, character and emotion' (*'omnibus rebus, personis, adfectibus'*, as Quintilian put it) – in other words, the material of 'all life', in the ancient cliché.[12]

Whatever stance we adopt on the issue of Menander's supposed mimetic *verismo*, the remains of ancient criticism bear traces of a realisation that the function of 'the laughable' in his plays is far from obvious. In keeping with this, the only extended surviving discussion of Menander, Plutarch's (epitomised) *Comparison of Aristophanes and Menander*, offers a view of this aspect of his work almost entirely through the implications of negative statements about Aristophanes, such as how the latter's sense of the comic 'is not playful but scurrilously mocking' and how he writes 'shameful and lewd things' to please 'licentious' people, and 'slanderous' things to please the

---

[10]   *Proleg. de com.* xiia (Koster (1975) 50), perhaps by Tzetzes; *Tract. Coisl.* 4 (Koster (1975) 64.12; Janko (1984) 24–5).

[11]   See e.g. *Tract. Coisl.* 18 (Koster (1975) 67.55–9), which defines Old Comedy in terms of an excess of the ridiculous (τὸ γελοῖον), New as a movement away from this and a leaning towards earnestness (τὸ σεμνόν), and Middle as a mixture of the two. Janko (1984) 244–50 gives references to other sources, though I dissent from his larger thesis on the Aristotelian credentials of the *Tractatus*; cf. Nesselrath (1990) 56, 102–5 (noting 333 for his own judgement of Menander as deliberately less 'comic' than many other playwrights in the genre).

[12]   My generalisations rest on testimonia 83–170 to Menander in *PCG* vi.2, 25–45; see Quintil. 10.1.69.

malicious.[13] What Menander avoided or excluded, by comparison to earlier Attic comedy, is certainly a factor worth noting (see below). But an understanding of where this leaves his interest in laughter will have to progress beyond that point. If we ask historically, 'how much are Menander's original Athenian audiences likely to have laughed at his work?', we inevitably come up against a lack of concrete evidence of the kind that would allow us to reconstruct the comic tastes or standards (the 'sense of humour', if you like) of his contemporaries in any detail. Variations of response between both individuals and socio-cultural classes of spectator can be posited with vague plausibility but cannot be charted with any precision. But this lack of hard evidence does not incapacitate the interpretation of Menandrian comedy: dramatic meaning is not positivistically *reducible* to contingent audience response. It is in a more general critical spirit, rather than on the basis of speculation about the putative behaviour of actual audiences, that we need to pose questions about the functions of 'the laughable' in Menander.

We are, in any case, far from entirely in the dark about the broad contours of fourth-century Athenian cultural psychology where laughter and comedy were concerned. There are important clues to help us in several near-contemporary sources – clues, in particular, to various ways (not necessarily identical to Menander's, but forming interesting comparanda to them) in which laughter rises and falls, so to speak, with the movements and exchanges of social life. Prominent among these sources is, of course, Aristotle's *Poetics*, particularly his definition of τὸ γελοῖον, 'the laughable' or 'the ludicrous', as that which is shameful/ugly (*aischron*) but 'without pain and destruction', ἀνώδυνον καὶ οὐ φθαρτικόν, as well as his distinction in the *Nicomachean Ethics* between the 'old' plays which revolved around *aischrologia* (obscenity and indecency) and the 'modern' plays whose humour depends on *huponoia*, a term Aristotle uses nowhere else but which could embrace innuendo and 'understatement' of various kinds (including irony) and which fits the idea of a laughter that lies not (entirely) on, but *under*, the surface of the comedy.[14] Though pre-Menandrian (the playwright's career began very close to the date of the philosopher's death), Aristotle's views seem attuned to comic trends that are borne out by what we now know of Menander's work. Moreover, the general evidence of Aristotle's attitudes

---

[13] Plut. *Mor.* 854d, καὶ τὸ γελοῖον οὐ παιγνιῶδες ἀλλὰ καταγέλαστον . . . ὁ ἄνθρωπος ἔοικε . . . γεγραφέναι . . . τὰ μὲν αἰσχρὰ καὶ ἀσελγῆ τοῖς ἀκολάστοις, τὰ βλάσφημα δὲ καὶ πικρὰ τοῖς βασκάνοις καὶ κακοήθεσιν. For the adj. ἀκόλαστος, and its associations with excessive/disreputable laughter, see ch. 4 n. 154.

[14] See *Po.* 5.1449a32–7, *EN* 4.8, 1128a22–5, with ch. 6, 317, 326–8 for further discussion of these passages.

to laughter is pertinent here. As my discussion in Chapter 6 tried to draw out, Aristotle has a wide-ranging, if philosophically normative, sense of the psychological and social inflections of laughter. This includes an alertness to the interplay between the various parties (agents, targets and hearers) involved in joke-making and related situations, as well as to the thin dividing line between different kinds of gelastic behaviour. We may or may not wish to put some faith in the biographical tradition (quite a slender one, in truth) that Menander was educated by Aristotle's successor Theophrastus, and therefore perhaps exposed to specifically Peripatetic views on comedy and laughter. But either way we can accept that Menandrian comedy exploits an awareness of the fine gradations of laughter, and their correlation with the forces at work in social life, in ways which at least match up well to the spirit of Aristotle's perception of laughter as something of which one can have (psychologically, ethically and socially) too much or too little.[15]

More obliquely relevant, perhaps, but still thought-provoking is the treatment of comedy in Plato's *Philebus* (48–50), a work which, in its reference to 'the entire tragedy and comedy of life' (50b), happens to voice the idea of life itself as moving in and out of the reach of laughter. Specially useful here is the notion of laughable characters as those who are self-ignorant yet lacking the capacity to take revenge against their enemies (49b–c).[16] This is a formulation that can help us to judge, for example, when and how far an audience might be inclined to laugh at Smicrines the antisocial miser in Menander's *Aspis*, or, on a very different dramatic plane, at the deluded Moschion of *Perikeiromene* (who will receive attention later in the chapter). The case of Smicrines is worth a little reflection here.[17] Once they have heard Tuche's prologue to *Aspis*, spectators are left in no doubt about the framework that has been put in place for their emotional and evaluative responses towards the oldest of the family's three brothers. The goddess's emphatic description of Smicrines as avaricious, as well as thoroughly bad (*ponēros*), sets the scene for the comic-cum-dramatic irony of his desire – the first thing he mentions on reentering – *not* to be thought 'avaricious' (149). This desire is itself a piece of duplicity, a pretence of humane decency (*philanthrōpia*), which he will later abandon at the

---

[15] Menander's Peripatetic education is claimed by Diog. Laert. 5.36 (= Men. test. 8 *PCG*), following the female scholar Pamphile of Epidaurus (first century AD). For Theophrastus and laughter, cf. ch. 4, 155–7, ch. 5, 237–43. Other sources (Men. test. 7 *PCG*) claim that in his late adolescence Menander knew Epicurus, but it would be utterly tenuous to connect Menandrian comedy with (later) Epicurean views on laughter (for which see ch. 6, 358–9).

[16] Cf. further in ch. 6, 300–1.

[17] Smicrines' self-ignorance is ironically signalled by Daos' remark at *Aspis* 191.

first opportunity (391–6). Furthermore, Smicrines admits (to himself) that others curse and denigrate him. He uses, uniquely in surviving Menander, the verb βασκαίνειν, whose original sense is to 'put the evil eye' on someone but which becomes metaphorically extended to the sense of 'denigrate'.[18] This idea amplifies the implicit scope for an audience to align its own feelings with the general resentment felt towards Smicrines within his own family circles, and to translate those feelings into the laughter of derision against him, a derision he proves unable to ward off.

What's more, Tuche describes Smicrines as an antisocial 'loner', *monotro-pos* (121), though one, it soon emerges, who tries to dissimulate his real nature even in this respect as well (184–5). It is apposite here to compare the deeply agelastic cast of another Menandrian loner, Cnemon in *Dyscolus*. Cnemon is a figure scarred by an inveterate incapacity to share any sort of mirth or amiability with others ('an inhuman human, and surly to everyone', *Dysc.* 6–7); but in his case, unlike that of the two-faced Smicrines, the absence of sociable laughter is accompanied by an almost manic penchant for sarcastic abusiveness (*loidoria*) – a combination which eventually sets him up as the butt of group mockery, meriting him a physical ragging by a slave and a cook.[19] Cnemon rejects laughter and has to be both punished and, in some (very uncertain) degree, reclaimed by it. In constructing such characters, Menander was drawing on an old seam of Greek folklore. To take just one convenient example, in Phrynichus' *Monotropos*, an Old comedy which came third behind Aristophanes' *Birds* at the Dionysia of 414, the legendary misanthrope Timon was the play's eponymous loner. He portrayed his own existence as one without (among other things) marriage, company, laughter and conversation – a collocation which not only provides a general indication of some Greek perceptions of laughter but makes a particularly apt reference point for the isolated status of Smicrines in *Aspis*, and only slightly less apt for Cnemon.[20] But the firm clues to Smicrines' nature supplied in the prologue of *Aspis*, and reinforced in its immediate

---

[18] The 'evil eye' is literally a quasi-magical curse (on the general subject see Plut. *Mor.* 680c–683b), hence the need to ward it off with a symbolic object, a *(pro)baskanion*: see Ar. fr. 607; cf. Dunbabin and Dickie (1983) 11, Wace (1903–4) 103–14, with ch. 4, 200–1, for such apotropaic practices. Herodian, *Philet.* 143 associates metaphorical *baskainein* with mockery and laughter. Smicrines' use of the verb at *Aspis* 153 draws attention to the ways in which he merits both resentment and mockery.

[19] Cnemon is specifically marked as 'loidoric' at *Dysc.* 355, 487, 623; for his sarcasm/irony, see esp. 153–78; for his punishment through laughter, cf. n. 29 below. Note how Chaireas connects the report of Cnemon's aggressive unfriendliness with a stereotype of harsh rustics, *Dysc.* 129–31; beyond its immediate dramatic point, this reflects a wider association between *agroikia* and aversion to sociable laughter: cf. Men. fr. 14, and see ch. 6, 311.

[20] Phryn. fr. 19: cf. ch. 1, 39. Contrast Myson of Chen, one of the Seven Sages – a loner who paradoxically laughs to himself: ch. 6, 267. *À propos* Smicrines, note that the idea of a *miser* as specifically incapable of laughter is found at Dio Chrys. 4.91–2 (cf. ch. 1, 19), where the speaker is Diogenes the Cynic (see ch. 7, 375–81).

aftermath, set in relief the earlier challenge which Menander poses for his audience (to laugh or not to laugh?) during the first scene of the play. There, Smicrines appears lurking around the margins of a scene of proleptically funereal, quasi-tragic lamentation for the supposedly dead Cleostratus. It is arguable that in this first scene, despite one glaring forewarning (at 33) of how money matters to Smicrines more than anything else, the situation – including Smicrines' power to influence it – is too uncertain to allow more than awkward or hesitant laughter. It is only when Tuche's prologue has given the audience an unequivocal ethical orientation, but also only when the serious threat posed by Smicrines to the interests of the family as a whole has been put into reverse (with the conceiving of Daos' plans in Act II), that the scope for derision of the miser comes into its own.[21] Like Cnemon (though for subtly different reasons), Smicrines is an agelast who must be made to pay the price of laughter. And the *Philebus'* formulation of the powerlessness or ineffectualness of the objects of ridicule can help us see how Menander plots a trajectory for his character which only gradually releases the laughable potential of his behaviour.

The last of the fourth-century sources for attitudes to laughter which we might bring to bear in a comparative spirit on Menander's work, and the one closest in date to Menander himself, is Theophrastus' *Characters*, which illustrates how various kinds of excess, deficiency and incongruity can make people socially risible, especially where their faults involve unco-operative, indecent or unrefined habits. But as I tried to show in Chapter 5, the *Characters* also implicitly illustrates some of the ambiguities and variable perspectives of laughter, since its own apparently 'comic' slant is complicated by the fact that several of its gallery of types are themselves exponents of (excessive or inappropriate) laughter. Who exactly laughs at whom, and how different figures become agents or objects of laughter, is therefore a tangled question within Theophrastus' images of the quirks and idiosyncrasies of the Athenian social world. The point here includes but goes beyond the old question of supposed parallels between Menander's and Theophrastus' character-types as such;[22] it involves a wider sense of the workings and the fluctuating propriety of laughter. As with the other fourth-century sources cited above, I adduce Theophrastus not for the purposes of a detailed comparison but as a revealing segment of the cultural

---

[21] A somewhat different slant on the opening scene of *Aspis* is taken by Handley (1970) 24–5, who seems to feel a need to discover traces of 'comic effect' at this stage of the play. My own (larger) thesis is that Menander stretches the genre by testing how far the *blocking* of laughter can be structurally integrated into its resources.

[22] For basic guidance on that issue, see Hunter (1985) 148–9 (plus 173–4 nn. 19–21), Diggle (2004) 8 (with further literature cited in n. 26 there).

hinterland of Menander's theatre. Menander wrote plays at a time when there existed a widespread recognition of laughter not as a static or uniform aspect of conduct but something more like a social currency that could change hands in multiple ways. Thus Theophrastus' *Characters* might assist us, for instance, in grasping how certain figures in Menander can simultaneously be gelastically inclined themselves (in their scornful treatment of others) and yet also, for that very reason, legitimate objects of an audience laughter which presupposes more refined standards of behaviour. Equally, however, the *Characters'* partial affinities with *Old* Comedy (affinities which, again, I commented on in Chapter 5) underline, in a manner parallel to Aristotle's distinction between older (indecent) and 'modern' (more restrained) comedies, some of the forms (and/or causes) of laughter which Menander seems to take pains to *eliminate* from his work.

Those last two points can both be integrated into a larger generalisation about Menander's *oeuvre*. We know that Greek culture was familiar with a spectrum of 'laughters' that ran from vindictive, hostile mockery (*katagelōs*) to the banter and amusement of shared, mutual play (*paidia*), or, on a different though matching level, from crude obscenity (breaching verbal or visual restraints of shame) to mild, urbane wit. Now, the prevailing ethos of Menandrian *philanthrōpia* (humane sensitivity, friendliness and sociability) means, among other things, that the more aggressive, hubristic end of this spectrum is substantially excluded from view, just as is the language of outright aischrology and its visual counterparts (such as the exposed phallus and indecent dances like the *kordax* – both things, we may remember, which appear in Theophrastus' *Characters* as well as being rampant in Old Comedy).[23] Where vindictive mockery (or verbal obscenity) does occur, as in the treatment of Cnemon in Act V of *Dyscolus* or the probably similar treatment of Smicrines towards the end of *Aspis*, it is mostly perpetrated by slaves and cooks and usually coordinated with an impulse to correct social and ethical imbalances that promotes the eventual triumph of *philanthrōpia*. We might tentatively infer from this that even where Menandrian 'loners' (see above) fully deserve the ridicule they receive, the playwright is still careful to hold back his main citizen characters from direct involvement in laughter's most raucous varieties of revenge.[24]

---

[23] For the exposed phallus see Theophr. *Char.* 11.2, with ch. 5, 240; for the *kordax*, *Char.* 6.3, with ch. 5, 240–1.

[24] Note *Dysc.* 900–1, where Sicon is concerned about what will happen if (the ethically scrupulous) Gorgias finds out about the ragging of Cnemon. On the other hand, it is presupposed that the *audience* will vicariously enjoy the ragging of Cnemon: see συνήδεσθαι at *Dysc.* 965, just before the closing appeal to Nike *philogelōs*; for the verb as a marker of laughter, cf. ch. 1 n. 7, ch. 9 n. 35.

Likewise, on its rare appearances in Menander's text, crudely insulting language is predominantly addressed by and/or to slaves or other 'low' characters. In broad terms, it is displaced from the mouths of free citizens into those of slaves in order to preserve the impression of respectability on the part of the former.[25] There is a general avoidance of such overt abuse, as of other kinds of head-on antagonism, between citizens. A rare instance like *Sicyonius* 266, where the young, 'pale-skinned' Moschion is contemptuously called λάσταυρε ('pervert'?), is distanced by being placed in the mouth of an anonymous figure and reported at second hand, as too is the insult ἱππόπορνε ('you great big whore', literally 'horse-whore') at *Theoph.* 19.[26]

But the case I want to make goes beyond this undoubted preference for understated styles of humour over aggressive, contemptuous styles. My further claim is that Menander deliberately controls the stimulation of laughter *tout court* so as to produce a kind of dramatic counterpoint between its presence and absence and thereby open up a correspondingly shifting psychological experience for his audiences. The view I take here is somewhat distinct from a position like that of Armando Plebe, who argued that because of Menander's 'moderate' or 'tempered' realism ('realismo moderato'), his comedy does not involve 'authentic laughter' but rather 'a smile streaked with subtle humour, which only rarely reaches a full and authentic sense of the ludicrous'.[27] Plebe posits a near-pervasive

---

[25] We will never know whether the language of real slaves in Athens typically made more use of *aischrologia* than the speech of the free, but some of the latter could at any rate *believe* that it did: see ch. 6 n. 144 for Aristotelian testimony, and Ar. *Frogs* 743–53, Pl. *Lys.* 223a for two (different) hints of how slaves might be thought to 'lapse' into less respectable speech when talking among themselves. Cf. 417–18, 419–21 below.

[26] On the term λάσταυρος at *Sic.* 266, see Gomme and Sandbach (1973) 658, Belardinelli (1994) 184–5, Lape (2004) 226–9, and Meleager, *Anth. Pal.* 12.41.4, with Gow and Page (1965) II 658. This passage of *Sic.* is the only known Menandrian vignette of crude heckling in the Assembly, a phenomenon reflected more frequently in Aristophanes: see ch. 5 n. 48. On Men. *Theoph.* 19, where the identity of the reported speaker is unknown, see Gomme and Sandbach (1973) 402 (though the inference in the final sentence of their note is naive). For another reported insult, see *Kolax* fr. 6, with Arnott (1997–2000) II 193. Linguistic abuse/crudity occurs in the mouth of slaves/cooks at e.g. *Aspis* 242, *Dysc.* 462, 488 (reading the adverb, σκατοφάγως, lit. 'like a shit-eater'), 640, 892 (with Gomme and Sandbach (1973) 270; cf. n. 60 below), *Epitr.* fr. 12 (speaker uncertain), *Perik.* 366, 373–8, 394 (with n. 56 below), 485 (with 419 and n. 62 below), fr. 351.11. *Sam.* 69 is exceptional abuse of a master by his slave, but Parmenon is a trusted confidant and well intentioned. Abuse addressed *to* slaves by non-slaves: e.g. *Dysc.* 481, *Carch.* 35 (cf. *Aspis* 398), *Perik.* 268, 324, *Sam.* 105, 678. Attribution at *Dysc.* 441 remains uncertain; I strongly prefer giving Getas the abusive vocative (probably addressed to another slave): see Gomme and Sandbach (1973) 202–3.

[27] Plebe (1956) 135–6: 'il comico [sc. Menandreo] . . . non è . . . un autentico riso, ma piuttosto un sorriso venato di sottile umorismo, che solo raramente raggiunge autentica e piena comicità.' Cf. Arnott (1997) 69 for the idea of smiles rather than laughter as the appropriate response to much of Menander's work.

gentleness of humour which almost never arouses full-blown laughter. This is, I think, a half-truth. My own thesis, by contrast, is that the plays involve a more complex, sometimes indeterminate, fluctuation in the level and tone of comedy, providing a perpetual dialectic between (possible) reasons for laughter and (possible) reasons for its suppression.

The challenge posed for its audiences by this Menandrian dialectic is heightened by the paucity of laughter or its direct provocation *within* the social world of the plays. Its most diffuse presence, as it were, can be felt in the atmosphere of the quasi-komastic, wedding-centred finales of some of the plays, where the familiar laughter of group celebrations can be imagined as thriving. Exhilarated anticipation of drinking and all-night revels marks Sostratus' and his father's expectations of the pre-nuptial festivities at *Dysc.* 855–9;[28] and even amid the fragmentary tatters that survive from the start of Act V of *Aspis* there are unmistakable hints of the scene of exuberantly festive partying (εὐωχία, 535) projected onto the double marriage taking place off-stage. Such scenes, furthermore, accentuate the defining contrast between the celebrating groups and the markedly agelastic individuals (Cnemon in *Dyscolus*, Smicrines in *Aspis*) whose opposition or obstruction has had to be overcome and who are now 'punished' (though also perhaps socially reintegrated) with the assistance of outright derision.[29] Once we look beyond these comically decisive *dénouements*, however, an overt role for laughter within the action of the plays is far more uncertain. Explicit Menandrian references to laughter are in fact few and far between; significantly, the playwright's gelastic vocabulary is much smaller than that of Aristophanes.[30] When they do occur, those references belong mostly to localised exchanges in which characters either laugh, or are perceived by others as laughing, for

---

[28] For the gelastic associations of an all-night revel, *pannuchis*, cf. ch. 4 n. 67. Note also *Dysc.* 901 for Getas' reference to the 'hubbub' of the drinking-party atmosphere indoors: θόρυβος here evokes a laughter-filled atmosphere; for this connotation of the word cf. Pl. *Euthd.* 276b–d, ps.-Dem. *Exord.* 53.4, Aeschin. *Tim.* 83, ps.-Arist. *Mir.* 101, 839a1, Marcus Arg. *Anth. Pal.* 9.246.5–6. On specifically nuptial settings for (ritualised) laughter, cf. ch. 4 n. 125.

[29] In advance of his punishment, the self-imposed agelastic isolation of Cnemon is made conspicuous by his refusal to attend the party: *Dysc.* 874–8. The play's *kōmos*-like finale (n. 33 below) uses a dialectic of laughter, both aggressive and inclusive, first to punish Cnemon but then also to integrate him (compulsorily) into the celebrations and the 'dance' (953–7). It makes little sense to ask whether Cnemon will 'really' be reformed: laughter is both a theatrical and a would-be social solvent of the situation, but like any *kōmos* its present use postpones (or suppresses) some hard questions. For a reading of the play's final scene, see Schäfer (1965) 66–74.

[30] Words found in Aristophanes but not Menander include ἐγχάσκω, ἐπιγελάω, καγχάζω, κιχλίζω, προσγελάω, though this situation could obviously be changed by further Menandrian finds. As things stand, there is not a single reference to smiling in Menander (but only one in Aristophanes: *Thesm.* 513).

psychologically contingent reasons – one slave's (probably lewd) smirking at another's expense at *Heros* 38–9, for instance; Chaireas' ironic mockery of the love-sick Sostratus at *Dyscolus* 50–4 ('Had you decided, when you left the house, to fall in love with someone . . . ?'); the false doctor's pretence that Smicrines is mocking his judgement (when, dramatically, quite the reverse is taking place) at *Aspis* 460; Demeas' suspicion that Moschion is making fun of his distress at *Sam.* 138–9; vignettes of joy (such as *Mis.* 971 or fr. 881) or gloating (*Perik.* 293); or occasionally, in a reflection of ordinary conversational protocols, one character's appreciation of a joke or witty remark made by another.[31] But the sprinkling of such material found in the plays (and leaving aside the problem of whether an audience's laughter can be aligned with that of the characters in all these instances) is greatly out-weighed by the seriousness with which many Menandrian characters take themselves and their lives. Accordingly, where direct references to laughter or its symptoms are exiguous, references to anxiety, anger, grief, pain and tears are commonplace. This seriousness, for sure, can *itself* be a source of comedy. When the Sostratus of *Dyscolus* describes the manifestation of his own lovesick impatience as 'lamentation' (θρηνεῖν, 214), and later uses the verb παραποθανεῖν, 'practically die' (379, apparently *hapax legomenon* in extant Greek), for his perilous prospects if he does not get the girl he is besot-ted with, the hyperbolic self-dramatisation is comically pointed: this is a blatant though light-headed species of self-ignorance (in the terms of Plato's *Philebus*). But that is by no means true of all characters' self-dramatising emotions. In this and other respects, the demarcation of 'the ridiculous' in Menander remains an extremely tricky matter. Menandrian humour, though it certainly displays stock elements, cuts across and complicates the recurring patterns of the genre's conventions. There is no formulaic way of judging character-types. Some lovers, for instance, are more obviously ludicrous than others (as we shall shortly have a chance to observe in more detail); it is easier to laugh at some deceived fathers than at others; and so forth.

As the last paragraph indicates, the relationship between what Menan-drian characters themselves find (or fail to find) laughable and what the audiences of the plays might be induced to regard in that light is not

---

[31] See *Kolax* fr. 3, where Strouthias, the ingratiating flatterer, purports to laugh at the thought of an earlier joke (cf. the note in Arnott (1979–2000) II 191, with Theophr. *Char.* 2.4 for an analogue); *Sam.* 110–12, where Niceratus enjoys Demeas' witty remark: cf. Lamagna (1998) 221–2. Note the rare verb παρασκώπτειν, 'mock sarcastically', at *Phasma* 90, where the conversation is hard to interpret; cf. ch. 4 n. 19.

mechanical. Before looking in detail at some particular cases of the dialectic of laughter's presence and absence, a few further general observations are in place. Especially germane here is Menander's modulation of what one might call the tonal range of different phases of a play.[32] The (admittedly restricted) evidence of what survives suggests that Menander has a liking for shaping his works in such a way as to enable a full-bloodedly comic ethos to suffuse the fabric of the plot (even if some of its implications may remain hidden from certain characters) in at least one substantial block of action. In *Dyscolus*, this means above all those parts of Acts III (the pair of mirror scenes at 456–521) and V (880–969) where Getas and Sicon are pitted against Cnemon, first being worsted by him and then taking their komastic revenge.[33] In *Aspis* it is the elaborately staged tragedy of Chairestratus' feigned death in Act III which stands out in this respect: its blatantly metatheatrical playacting (from the audience's point of view) makes a kind of comedy inside a comedy serve dramatically as a 'tragedy' and thereby ensnare the misanthropic Smicrines into revealing his self-ignorance as well as being fooled by the situation. In *Perikeiromene*, as we shall shortly see in more detail, the most explicitly comic material is concentrated in the main scenes involving slaves in Acts II and III. In *Samia* it is found principally in the section of Act IV where Nicostratus remains the only person in the dark (several steps, as it were, behind the inferential disclosures of the plot, and stranded in a paratragic delusion of his own) once earlier misunderstandings have been cleared up. But if such highlighted stretches of action, marked by acute asymmetries between the knowledge or intentions of the different parties, provide audiences with opportunities to enjoy the eruption of unrestrained laughter, they do so in part precisely because of what they gain from juxtaposition with sharply contrasting dramatic material. The fake tragedy in *Aspis* Act III, for instance, is set against (and is, indeed, a comic transfiguration of) Chairestratus' genuine collapse in the preceding act, as well as against the 'real' family mourning for Cleostratus' imagined death: there is simply nothing for a sophisticated audience to laugh at in

---

[32] See e.g. Goldberg (1980) 22–8, Hunter (1985) 53–5, Zagagi (1994) 46–59 on Menandrian juxtaposition of different types/modes of comedy (or 'polyphony' in Zagagi's term); but cf. n. 46 below.

[33] The revenge is given an ironically *kōmos*-like twist (cf. ch. 3, 122–5) not only by the noisy invasion of Cnemon's house (see 59–60 for an extravagant image of a violently komastic 'forced entry'; cf. ch. 3 n. 60) but more pointedly by Getas and Sicon's pretence that they want to borrow *symposiac* paraphernalia (cf. 940): twelve tables (916), a woven hanging (922; cf. Ar. *Wasps* 1215), and a *kratēr* (928). See the komastic imagery of 963–4 (with *Sam.* 731, a wedding *kōmos*, and fr. 903.13); cf. Fantuzzi and Hunter (2004) 416–17, with Lape (2006) 95–105 on associations of the *kōmos* more generally in Menander. On the mixture of *kōmos* and 'war' in *Perik.* Act III (467–80), see 419–20 below.

those strands of the play. Moreover, in some works there may never have been an eruption of the unambiguously ridiculous at any juncture in the play. In the present state of our knowledge (very incomplete, for sure), we cannot locate this kind of upsurge of τὸ γελοῖον anywhere, for example, in *Misoumenos*. This impression is unlikely to be wholly misleading, since we do know that the play specifically sustained its rather dark themes, albeit relieved by smaller touches of comedy (such as Getas' servile coarseness), until the start of Act V. Crateia's belief, and later her father's, that Thrasonides has killed her brother is not exposed as false until the final act, so that even the father–daughter reunion in Act III feeds into a fresh period of grief; concomitantly, Thrasonides' despairing, potentially suicidal angst over Crateia's alienation continues for a full four acts. *Epitrepontes* is another case where laughter seems not to have been given free rein, as opposed to a kind of wavering intermittency, until Onesimus' twitting of Smicrines in the final Act.

Oscillations between thematically 'dark' and 'light' patches are an undeniable feature of Menandrian dramaturgy. What I want to explore further are the intricate correlations between this phenomenon (as a matter of laughter's appearance and disappearance within the social world of the plays) and the kinds of experience – the possibilities but also the 'denials' of laughter – made available to the audience of the plays. Tonal variations of the sort already noted clearly put the audience itself in a shifting position. If, for instance, it is obvious that the outwitting of Smicrines in *Aspis* Act III places the audience in the position of bystanders 'in the know', who can therefore relish the conspiratorial humour of the situation, it is equally obvious that the audience itself was 'deceived', though with the reverse of humorous effect, in the play's opening scene. That example illustrates a wider point I want to develop. By creating multiple perspectives in the course of a play Menander makes it difficult for an audience to occupy a fixed stance towards the action; he also thereby makes the appropriateness of laughter on their part both unpredictable and unstable. He does this, I contend, by fostering a constant interplay between 'internal' (character-centred) and 'external' (audience-centred) viewpoints. Much of Menander's dramatic subtlety hinges on the mobile ways in which he allows 'external' perspectives, whereby spectators watch events like independent witnesses (the position in which prologues usually position them: see below), to converge with and diverge from those of the agents themselves at different points in the flow of the plot. The intricacy of this process is enriched by the fact that character-centred perspectives are themselves multiple, not only because attached to different characters but also because the same characters can be seen even within their own social settings from *both* the dramatic 'inside', especially through monologue, *and* the dramatic 'outside', through others' observations of them. Thrasonides' behaviour at the start of *Misoumenos* (1–23), presented first through an impassioned soliloquy and then through Getas' cynically detached remarks about him, is a striking example of this further duality. For the soldier, the night is erotically charged and heavy with dark anxiety. For his slave, it is just filthy weather ('not even fit to let a dog outside', 15–16) and his master is a fool to be out in it. Can or should an audience adopt Getas' down-to-earth perspective and find Thrasonides' melodramatic feelings laughable? Can it shift positions (or even adopt a confident detachment) and laugh at *both* characters? Or is it part and parcel of Menander's gelastic dialectic to create initial uncertainty in this regard? To have much chance of making headway with such difficult questions, we need to look with close attention at a fuller sample of the kind of writing which gives rise to them.

MENANDRIAN PERSPECTIVISM

The combined permutations of 'external' and 'internal' viewpoints available to an audience, together with changes between first- and third-person points of view within the plays, constitute what can be called Menander's dramatic perspectivism. This perspectivism greatly affects the possibilities of laughter, including its deferral and contradiction, for the spectators of the plays. To pursue this argument in more detail I shall take parts of *Perikeiromene* (*The Woman with Shorn Hair*) as the main framework of my case, but will incorporate supplementary points with reference to other works as I proceed. In particular, I want to analyse how *Perikeiromene* places its audience, as its plot unfolds, in a fluid position *vis-à-vis* interpretation and judgement of the action, first exposing them to the 'raw' emotions displayed in (and aroused by) Polemon's rift with Glycera, then creating for them a privileged vantage point from which to observe the whole dramatic landscape, but a vantage point which does not preclude continuing engagement with a more character-centred, 'internal' perspective on the action.

Although we cannot piece together every element of the pre-prologue scene(s) of *Perikeiromene*, we can be confident that the confrontation between Polemon and Glycera, the flaring up of Polemon's jealous anger, and his violent cropping of Glycera's hair in a drunken rage – whether shown on stage or only reported – formed a disturbing, even shocking, sequence.[34] This is one of a number of known Menandrian cases (others are *Aspis* and *Misoumenos*) in which the audience is faced with, and emotionally tested by, a deliberately *anti*-comic opening, an opening at which it would be out of place (by the standards of 'normal' Greek cultural attitudes) to laugh.[35] Agnoia's prologue provides a retrospective textual clue to what is at stake on this level of the play. She voices the thought that spectators might have reacted to the preceding scene(s) with strong displeasure and a sense of disgracefulness. But all will turn out for the best, she reassures them:

> ὥστ' εἰ τοῦτ' ἐδυσχέραινέ τις
> ἀτιμίαν τ' ἐνόμισε, μεταθέσθω πάλιν.
>
> (167–8)

> So if anyone felt displeased by what preceded
> And thought it disgraceful, let him change his mind.

We need not deduce from this, over-literally, that Athenian spectators are likely to have been unhappy with the play as such. We should infer, rather, that the mood of the drama had so far *blocked* any space for laughter: to be 'displeased' or resentful (δυσχεραίνειν) is a state of mind incompatible with laughter.[36] This impression is corroborated by the fact that on more than one subsequent occasion ethically severe language is used to refer back to the initial incident. Glycera herself calls what Polemon had done to her *hubris*, i.e. aggressively offensive, and 'impious', ἀνόσιον (723–4), as well as a matter of 'drunken outrage' (παροινεῖν, 1022); Pataecus, while pleading Polemon's case, concedes that the latter's behaviour had been 'terrible' or 'appalling' (τὸ δεινόν, 724; cf. 492, 1017); and Polemon himself comes to repent what he did (which, according to Agnoia, was out of character:

---

[34] Konstan (2003) 23 cites Polemon's behaviour in his interesting discussion of Greek ideas of jealousy, but when he says the soldier 'does not articulate it as such [sc. jealousy]' he overlooks the (retrospective) term ζηλότυπος at line 987; see now Konstan (2006) 235 for a fuller (but slightly awkward) position on this point. As for anger, Blanchard (1998) sketches one approach to its shifting relationship to laughter in Menandrian theatre.

[35] Very like *Misoumenos* in terms of the night-time opening and the male speaker's distress is adesp. com. 1084 *PCG* (= *P. Ant.* 1.15), possibly by Menander himself; see most recently Handley (2006).

[36] Lamagna (1994) 178 draws too empirical an inference about audience reactions from Agnoia's words; their importance is as a pointer to the prevailing mood of the opening scene(s). For the verb δυσχεραίνειν, cf. Aristotle's reference to harsh characters who do not make jokes themselves and 'resent' it, or take it badly, when others make them, *EN* 4.8, 1128a8 (with ch. 6, 311–12 for context). Other cases where the verb denotes a negative response to laughter include Plut. *Alex.* 50.8–9, *Dion* 5.9, *Mor.* 634a. Note a parallelism with *Aspis* 97 (reflecting the larger tonal parallelism between the first scenes of *Aspis* and *Perik.*), where Tuche's prologue starts by seeking to squash the preceding impression of something 'untoward' (δυσχερές, cognate with δυσχεραίνειν).

164–5) as an act of drunken outrage (παροινεῖν again, 988): he needs Glycera's forgiveness at the end (1023). In the opening scene, as the prologue confirms, the audience had actually witnessed Glycera's distress (127), as well as seeing or hearing about Polemon's violent anger (162–4); Agnoia also emphasises Glycera's unhappiness at Moschion's previous approach to her (160–1). In short, the initial dramatic situation is dominated by a strongly anti-comic, 'agelastic' ambience, which must have been shot through with emotional agitation on all sides. And this is reinforced not just by the tone of Agnoia's specific back-references to the preceding scene but by the absence of any overt humour throughout the prologue itself, which depicts a larger world of precarious fortunes and multiple risks.[37]

If spectators have been given little choice but to experience the opening scenario of *Perikeiromene* on its own sombrely anti-comic terms, the prologue rapidly reorientates them, exactly as in *Aspis*, into a privileged position. This is a dramatic move which, by carrying a promise that a destination 'without pain and destruction' (to recall Aristotle's phrase) will eventually be reached (divine agency can make the scales tilt from evil to good, as Agnoia puts it at 169), is conducive to the emergence of some form of the comic. Yet it would be a mistake to suppose that such reorientation instantly transposes everything into the register of 'the laughable' or annuls the pain already exhibited. Since the information divulged by the prologue comes from a more-than-human source, we can usefully think of the audience's own resulting perspective as quasi-divine. It can be assimilated, that is, to the traditional image of Olympian deities who observe the human world with privileged knowledge but also, crucially, with (some) emotional involvement.[38] The psychological implications of this analogy for Menandrian audiences are suitably ambiguous. Just as Olympian gods can move between detachment from and absorption in human affairs, so the informed Menandrian audience is capable of seeing beyond the immediate foreground to a predicted outcome – Agnoia's metaphorically tilting scales[39] – but also continuing to sympathise with the agents' own concerns and feelings. Scholars often notice only half of this psychological model, stressing the 'superior' vantage point of an informed audience. My contention is that

---

[37] In addition to the circumstances of Polemon's jealousy/rage, the prologue mentions human problems and risks of various kinds at 125–6, 131–3, 137, 140–2, 144, 148–50. There is no reason to think the innuendo of 142–4 comic: incest between children of the same mother (*homomētrioi*), even in a Corinthian setting, is unlikely to have struck most Athenians as amusing.

[38] For further comments on this double-sided conception of the gods, see ch. 7, 337–9.

[39] Gomme and Sandbach (1973) 474 suggest that, given Agnoia's identity, a spectator might not take what she says here altogether seriously: 'he may half believe it, half enjoy the paradox'. Such an interpretation, though debatable, would only strengthen my case for seeing the prologue as opening a duality of perspectives for the audience.

such a vantage point does not cancel the serious human interest of a dramatic situation. If it did, it would be very hard to make sense of, say, the early part of *Aspis* Act II, where we see Chairestratus collapsed in despair (a motif redolent of tragedy)[40] before the comic scales start to tilt the other way. An audience which laughed at such a scene simply because it knew that Cleostratus is not really dead and that Chairestratus' troubles will not last indefinitely would be poorly attuned to Menander's dramatic artistry. For similar reasons, an audience of *Perikeiromene*, even after it has heard the prologue, must follow the predicament of characters whose own pains and misunderstandings will actually *deepen* before they are resolved. Accordingly, such an audience is set a challenge by what Agnoia tells them: they are required not simply to replace the internal perspective of the opening scene(s) with their own knowing, external perspective, but rather to hold the two in a sort of twin focus, remaining alert to, while also savouring, the differences between them. A further consideration which needs to be borne in mind throughout, but whose 'weight' is very hard to calculate, is that for an Athenian audience (though at least some of Menander's plays may have had first performances outside his own city) the Corinthian setting of *Perikeiromene* might add an extra dimension to their perspective, allowing them perhaps to feel at one remove from the society of the play though also stimulating them to wonder whether it is really very different from their own.

The dramatic convention of a divine prologue, particularly familiar in Euripides, started its theatrical life as a tragic device (itself echoing Homeric precedents) to confront the audience with a sense of the gulf between a compendious 'god's-eye' view of things and an incomplete, partially obscured human standpoint. By its very nature, the divine prologue is always something more than a channel for supplying information; it is also a way of obliging an audience to reflect on the different angles from which a human story can be seen (and told). In keeping with this, Menander employs the convention as a means of affording theatre-audiences a double perspective that permits (alternately or simultaneously) both emotional involvement and emotional distance. It goes without saying that by retaining the choice between divine (or quasi-divine) and human prologue-speakers, and even by varying the precise content of divine disclosures, Menander always has scope to tailor his audience-viewpoint to the circumstances of the individual play. What matters above all, for my purposes, is that the information an audience possesses from its 'external' perspective does not automatically

---

[40] Cf. e.g. the collapse of Hecabe at Eur. *Hec.* 438–502. The staging of *Aspis* 299–387 is uncertain; Cleostratus seems to collapse just offstage and is then revealed through the open doors: if the *ekkyklema* was used, as first proposed by Jacques (1978) 51–2, this would amplify the (initially) tragic resonances of the scene.

simplify its psychological options (though it may sometimes do that, as we have seen with the Smicrines of *Aspis*) but can actually complicate its relationship to the internal perspectives of the characters themselves. And that means, not least, that it can complicate the availability of laughter as a response to what happens on stage.

In *Perikeiromene*, Menander invites his audience to check, adjust and modify its emotional reactions at various junctures during the play. He does this immediately after the prologue, when Sosias enters and starts to grumble cynically about his master Polemon's current unhappiness. The cropping of Glycera's hair had symbolically assimilated her to servile status; it may also have triggered associations with the conventions of female ritual mourning, as though Polemon were imposing on the woman responsibility for the 'death' of their relationship.[41] In these and other respects, Polemon's action must have carried the disturbing frisson to which Agnoia had then referred back in the prologue. Yet with Sosias' entry this same action now becomes the subject for a slave's ironic reflections on his soldier-master's 'warlike' character. I have already adduced the first scene of *Misoumenos* as a comparable instance where a character or situation is presented from both the inside and the outside. The sudden and potentially disorientating shift of tone is a standard Menandrian technique: a further parallel, but marked by a more blatant form of 'bathos', is the grumbling Cook's entry in Act I of *Aspis* (216–20), where the (believed) death in the family is distanced and reinterpreted through the utilitarian filter of the Cook's self-interested concerns.[42] But such abrupt shifts of viewpoint and tone should not be regarded as always or purely comic. They offer the opportunity for a kind of split perspective, enabling an audience to see a context from two or more sides in close conjunction. In Sosias' description of Polemon at *Perikeiromene* 172–80, the result is spiced with an irony that could surely only take an audience by surprise: the furious Polemon, after causing so much distress to Glycera, is now himself, of all things, weeping (174).[43] What Sosias observes from his own position with sarcasm is at the same time a blurred, even confusing, cue for the audience. It is, indeed, highly pertinent to a study of the intermittencies and elusiveness of laughter in Menander, as well as in line with the passage of *Dis Exapaton* from which this

---

[41] We cannot work out the exact circumstances in which Anacreon mentioned the cropping of (the slave boy) Smerdies' hair in his poetry: the act of a jealous lover (supposedly Polycrates) is one ancient theory, but the combination of Anac. 347 *PMG* with the testimonia in Anac. 414 leaves some uncertainty. It is not impossible, however, that Menander wanted to evoke this Anacreontic episode, at least subliminally, in the minds of his audience.

[42] See Handley (1970) 14–16 (reading 'Kleostratos' for 'Kleainetos' on 16).

[43] Cf. 412–13 below, with n. 50, for Glycera's own various moments of crying in the play.

chapter started, to notice that his plays have plenty of scope for characters (both male and female) who shed 'serious' tears – a point to which I shall return shortly.[44] The alternation of tears and laughter seems, appropriately, to have been a formula for the vicissitudes of Menandrian 'life' in the conclusion to one of his lost plays.[45]

Another salient instance of the effect of split perspective can be found in *Misoumenos* Act IV, where Cleinias' protracted attempt to gain Getas' attention (including some evidently stylised stage-humour as the former 'follows' the latter's pacing movements) is superimposed on the psychologically dark qualities of the scene between Thrasonides, Crateia and Demeas that Getas is recounting. Menander here builds up what one might think of as an exceptionally dense 'layering' of perspectives. Cleinias, half piecing together what he hears, is an immediate, though unintended, 'audience' to Getas' account. Getas himself was a silent witness to what has recently happened in Thrasonides' house, but now, in reconstructing it, he supplies his own commentary (which reveals his somewhat blind allegiance to his master's point of view). Within the situation described by Getas, Thrasonides has a double audience, Demeas and Crateia. But while Demeas answers the soldier's tearful pleadings with gruff refusals, Crateia responds to his protestations of love (and threat of suicide) by simply turning away (706) and keeping a (for Thrasonides and Getas) baffling silence (711). The beauty of such a scene is that the spectators can understand each of the conflicting perspectives of the characters, yet cannot simply align themselves with any of them. As a result, they do not have to choose between laughing at the stage-humour of Cleinias' frustrated attempts to interrupt, or, on the other hand, taking seriously Getas' description of the psychologically fraught scene that has recently occurred indoors. To do justice to the whole ensemble, they need to take in both these things at once. Like watching gods, they can sympathise with each of the incomplete human perspectives on show yet simultaneously adopt a standpoint that discerns the total pattern to which they belong. If that is right, then in such contexts, so characteristic of Menander's dramatic art in general, 'the comic' can be only one dimension of a larger configuration of tonal elements, and

---

[44] Cf. 388–9 above, 411–13 below, for further instances. By contrast, weeping by Aristophanic characters/choruses is almost always blatantly comic (e.g. *Kn.* 9–10, *Wasps* 983, cf. 881, *Birds* 540, *Lys.* 127, 1034, *Frogs* 654).

[45] See Men. fr. 903.5 (κλάειν, γελᾶν), with the term *metabolē* ('change' of fortune, 'vicissitude') in line 7 (cf. e.g. *Dysc.* 279, 769, fr. 602.11); authorship of the fragment is not, however, certain. For piquant juxtaposition of weeping and laughing as the opposing poles of life, compare the very different contexts at Theog. 1041, 1217 (with ch. 3, 122–5) and the beatitudes of Jesus at Luke 6.21, 25 (with ch. 10, 475–6).

a dimension likely to be perceived as moving in and out of view. Laughter itself can be no more than one component in a sophisticated response to this part of the play.

Perhaps the most sustained case of this kind, which has received much attention from critics and need only be noted in passing here, is the wonderful Act III of *Samia*. This stretch of the play seesaws, one might say, between Demeas' severely wounded emotions (he starts the act as a man hit, as he puts it, by a sudden storm, 207) and the variously uncomprehending reactions of those he assails (Parmenon, the Cook and the sorely distressed Chrysis). It is a critical commonplace that passages of this kind use figures like the Cook to introduce humorous 'relief' into what might otherwise stray too far from the domain of the comic. But that is, I think, too limited and schematic a judgement. Passages of this type epitomise, I would prefer to say, the fluid and uncertain relevance of laughter to what Menander offers his audiences. When, for example, after Demeas' exceptionally long and emotionally raw monologue (206–82), Parmenon and the Cook enter at 283, engaged in familiar kinds of servile banter, the switch from one mood to another is not entirely straightforward. Demeas stays on stage, making the audience visually aware of the gap between his (so far) private angst and the bustle of wedding preparations he himself had initiated in the previous act. Menander is demonstrating, as he often likes to, how radically different emotions and viewpoints can coexist side by side within the same social space. The whole act is dominated by tonal contrasts and juxtapositions, which pose a sort of emotional challenge to the audience – take Demeas' feelings seriously on their own terms (and how could one not, up to a point, given his intimate, vehement expression of them?) or laugh at the disparities between the perceptions of the various agents in the tangled scenario? There is a recurrent dramatic dichotomy between Demeas' inner torment, to which the audience has privileged access, and his physically overwrought behaviour towards others, which allows an element of traditional 'comic' stage-violence to enter his dealings with the Cook and Parmenon. Menander twists together the different strands of the situation so effectively that an audience is left unable, I suggest, to occupy a clear-cut position and is encouraged to hold the conflicting viewpoints of the characters in a sort of equipoise.[46] The result is a theatrical

---

[46] I disagree here with the view of Zagagi (1994) 57 that the conversation between Demeas and Parmenon at *Sam.* 304–25 is 'purely comic' (could *anything* involving Demeas be 'purely comic' at this stage?), though her general treatment of Menandrian 'polyphony' is admirably sensitive to tonal complexities. On tonal contrasts in *Samia*, cf. Handley (2002) 176–82. Casanova (2004) offers a one-sided reading of the tone of *Samia* overall.

experience that makes it seem somehow justifiable both to laugh and to restrain laughter. By the end of *Samia* Act III, where Chrysis' own weeping is foregrounded at both the start and finish of the scene involving her (370–1, cf. 406, then 426, 440–4), and where it is no longer possible to distinguish the 'inner' and 'outer' features of Demeas' distress, we might legitimately imagine an audience suspended or caught between laughter and tears.

To reinforce the idea that the entry of, say, a grumbling slave or cook into a situation independently defined and coloured (for the audience) by the sufferings of other characters may complicate the atmosphere of a play rather than simply switching it into a blatantly laughable mode, let us now return to Act I of *Perikeiromene*. Sosias' arrival at 172, immediately after the prologue, ostensibly introduces a drastic change of mood. The violent cropping of Glycera's hair, which Agnoia had referred to as potentially disgusting just a few moments earlier, is now the subject for a slave's caustically ironic reflections on his soldier-master's character (172–3, 'the one who was recently swaggering and ready for war, the one who won't let women keep their *hair*! . . .'). But Sosias' irony, which of course involves no sympathy for Glycera herself, only partly undercuts the gravity of the situation. His remarks actually impart the crucial information, which supplements and modifies Agnoia's reference to Polemon's anger, that the latter is now as distressed as we have recently heard/seen that Glycera is: like Glycera, he has been reduced to tears (174, cf. 160, 189). Sosias' blunt cynicism does nothing, in other words, to blot out a sense of the emotional ordeal of the main characters. In fact, part of what makes his mentality semi-comic is precisely its unwillingness to take the strength of Polemon's feelings seriously (though we shall see that things will later change). In this respect, Sosias puts the audience in a special, somewhat ambiguous position. They can enjoy his wry detachment up to a point but they cannot simply see things with his eyes, since they know details that he does not. The prologue has informed them of the basis of the prevailing misunderstanding, as well as its prospective resolution. But they have also (as the prologue itself revealed: 405 above) been drawn into feeling the powerful emotions at work in the situation. Sosias' information about Polemon's tears belongs, despite the slave's own intentions, to that deeper level of the plot and so cannot simply be written off. That leaves an audience room for various justifiable reactions to Polemon himself, but sharing Sosias' sheer cynicism hardly seems to be one of them. Even if the image of the tearfully distressed lover having a consolatory meal (and perhaps even, paradoxically, a symposium)[47] with his friends need not arouse sympathy, which might any-way have been already alienated by Polemon's violent treatment of Glycera (or so Agnoia's prologue presupposed), at any rate the audience has in some sense to take Polemon seriously in a way in which Sosias himself (at this stage) does not. So far from simply cashing out the situation into sheer laughter for the spectators, Polemon's slave, by his very sarcasm, draws attention to the psychological knottedness of his master's predicament. At least part of the upshot, then, of Sosias' entry monologue at 172–80 is a sort of gelastic uncertainty.

Sosias' cynically grumbling attitude is, in any case, only one element in a complex, rapidly changing set of circumstances. Although most of the remainder of Act I is lost in the lacuna after 190, we are able at least to make out that this section incorporated a threefold 'slave's-eye' reading of the situation, each component of which could help shape an audience's own sentiments but none of which can be taken over without modification. Sosias' behaviour is set in the first instance against Doris' tender commiser-ation with her mistress (185–8). That tenderness is the reverse in every way of Sosias' viewpoint, but it is also accompanied by a blanket condemnation of professional soldiers ('they're all lawless, totally unreliable', 186–7) which an alert audience, prepared for an ultimate reconciliation between Polemon and Glycera, might hesitate over.[48] The contrast between Sosias and Doris, which is heightened by the interweaving of their stage movements (Doris comes out of Polemon's house, where Glycera still is, just before Sosias goes into it: 181/4), is spotlighted at 188–90. There has been disagreement about the attribution of these lines, which read:

> εὐφρανθήσεται
> κλάουσαν αὐτὴν πυθόμενος νῦν. τοῦτο γὰρ
> ἐβούλετ' αὐτός.

> He'll be delighted
> When he now learns she's crying. That's the result
> He wanted himself.

---

[47] That Polemon is reclining (174) is double-edged: it might underline his distress (Gomme and Sandbach (1973) 475), but could also signal that the meal (175) will turn into a symposium. For the paradox of an unhappy symposiast (lover), see ch. 3, 122–5, with n. 61 there; cf. n. 65 below. Note Polemon's later statement (471–3) that in his misery he deliberately avoided drinking too much; see n. 59 below, with 422–3 for a comparison/contrast with Moschion's behaviour.

[48] Doris' words 'totally unreliable' (οὐδὲν πιστόν, 187) recall in spirit Agnoia's statement that Glycera's 'foster' mother had regarded Polemon as 'not to be relied on' (βέβαιον . . . οὐθέν, 144). These are among the ways in which the play tarnishes Polemon's character before it finally 'redeems' him; they lay a set of evaluative challenges which spectators might negotiate in different ways.

It is possible these lines are spoken by Doris herself, while she waits for someone to answer the door of Myrrhine's house (on which she has just knocked); this may be the attribution found in the one papyrus of the passage, though some doubt remains.[49] If so, the words will be uttered in bitter contempt for Polemon's supposed callousness, but they will also generate the dramatic irony that Doris is unaware that, as the audience knows from Sosias, Polemon himself is weeping with self-pity in another house. It makes better sense, however, to give the lines to Sosias himself, since they seem to presuppose that he will presently report back Glycera's distress to Polemon. On that hypothesis, we should imagine that Sosias delivers the words as soon as he comes back out of the house, to indicate (a gesture could underline the point) that he has himself *just* seen Glycera weeping indoors.[50] Moreover, in Sosias' mouth the lines tell us more about the speaker himself than about Polemon; they seem suitable to be spoken with a chuckle of mirth or glee on the slave's own part. Sosias knows only too well of Polemon's current tearfulness: why should he assume that news of Glycera's weeping will give the soldier great pleasure? In context, this surely tells a sensitive audience nothing at all about Polemon, but corroborates the impression already gained of Sosias' emotional crudity. Yet it also adds a subtle thematic nuance to Menander's treatment of the whole situation. Sosias uses a term with strong gelastic overtones to anticipate Polemon's delight.[51] In effect, he imagines laughter breaking out at the very point at which both the main characters, Glycera and Polemon, are to be pictured in tears by the audience. Sosias, we might say, is gelastically at loggerheads with the circumstances in which he finds himself.

After the events which take place during the textual lacuna (between 191 and 260), including the transfer of Glycera from Polemon's to Myrrhine's house (where her brother Moschion also lives), a third slave's views are briefly added to the mixture with those of Sosias and Doris. Just before the act ends, Daos, who knows of Moschion's feelings for Glycera but is ignorant (as is Moschion himself) that the pair are in reality siblings,

---

[49] For this point, and further views on the attribution of the lines, see Gomme and Sandbach (1973) 478, Lamagna (1994) 186, Arnott (1979–2000) II 384–5.

[50] Arnott (1979–2000) II 385 brings Sosias back on stage somewhere between 185 and 188, allowing him to overhear Doris' words of sympathy for Glycera; he thus takes Sosias' reference to tears as a reaction to what the female slave has just said. But that connection appears too loose to make good sense of 189. Note additionally that, whoever the speaker, 189 implies that Glycera was not seen (or reported as) crying when Polemon originally cropped her hair, though we have already heard of her crying on another occasion (160). When she appears again in Act IV, Glycera is notably strong and poised (cf. n. 69 below), and even rebukes Doris for crying, 758, where the reason for the slave's tears is textually uncertain: cf. Bain (1977) 122.

[51] On the connection of εὐφραίνεσθαι and cognates with laughter, see ch. 3 n. 24.

approves of Glycera's move into Myrrhine's house and rushes off to give
Moschion the news he expects to please him. Unlike Sosias, Daos has
reasonable grounds for the reaction he expects his message to elicit. Yet he
is inescapably blind to the direction in which his action is leading, in part
because he is unaware (as later emerges, but was probably clear in the fuller
context now lost) of the recent crisis between Glycera and Polemon. So
each of the three slaves we see in what remains of Act I represents a partial
and partially (un)informed viewpoint. All are constrained, what's more,
by subservience to the interests of their respective masters/mistresses. Only
the audience, from its 'godlike' though hardly all-knowing position, can see
how these multiple viewpoints (and, behind them, the shifting positions of
the characters whose interests the slaves serve) intersect and interact beyond
the intentions of the agents themselves.

But the result of all this is much more than unqualified amusement
at the ramifications of misunderstanding. It is no accident that Agnoia's
prologue was free, as we saw, of overt humour or promptings to laughter.
Misunderstanding is not intrinsically comic (it can even, as we know, be
tragic); and an audience's superior knowledge, as I have suggested, complicates the scope for sympathy with the characters, rather than simply
reducing it. What Menander achieves, through and beyond the characters' own criss-crossing viewpoints, is a vivid sense (his 'perspectivism') that
human actions are interpreted by agents and victims from *limited* angles of
vision, and that 'the same' circumstances look very different (and therefore,
among much else, can be regarded as more or less suitable for laughter) from
those various angles. Menander's audience are given a chance to appreciate
this complexity from the 'inside'. Their witnessing of events before the prologue of *Perikeiromene* left them in the dark about the underlying truth –
Agnoia had to ask them to change their minds (168), i.e. their judgements
not just their factual beliefs, about what had so far occurred. From the
position of privileged observers which they occupy after the prologue, they
can to some extent distance themselves from the individual emotions felt
by the parties to the action, but not completely so. Superior knowledge can
enhance as well as muting sympathy; after all, if that were not so, much of
the experience of *tragedy* would be unintelligible.[52] The initially anti-comic

[52] Gomme and Sandbach (1973) 25, speaking of Menander's work in general, say, 'The characters feel
deeply . . . , but *because* the spectator has a superior viewpoint the sympathy that he must entertain
for them is tinged with amusement' (my itals.); similarly, Goldberg (1980) 54. I see no reason to posit
a necessary causal principle of this kind: in addition to the case of tragedy, the analogy with divine
spectatorship of human affairs has some purchase here. Sandbach (1970) 126 is nonetheless right
to stress that an audience may be simultaneously 'amused and moved' by Menandrian characters,
finding them both 'ridiculous and sympathetic'; cf. *ibid.* 128, Hunter (1985) 134.

situation of *Perikeiromene* gives way to an interplay of conflicting dramatic viewpoints and sentiments in which the audience's own reactions become entangled and in which 'the laughable' becomes an unpredictable, far from determinate factor. In the next section I shall pursue this theme of tonal ambiguity, and its implications for the intermittencies of laughter (both inside the play and from the point of view of its audience), by examining some of the fluctuations of mood which ensue in Acts II and III of *Perikeiromene*.

LAUGHTER BLOCKED AND RELEASED

Act II of *Perikeiromene* exhibits a number of indisputably comic credentials that were conspicuous by their absence in the first act. Having endowed his scenario at the outset with potentially disturbing emotional depth, Menander now takes special steps to achieve a lightening or relaxing of the dramatic atmosphere. He does this principally by decentring the *mise en scène* from the distressed characters, Glycera and Polemon, and turning attention towards what will turn out to be the more lightweight figure of Moschion, here almost certainly appearing on stage for the first time but described in Agnoia's prologue as 'wealthy and always drunk' (142) as well as 'rather impulsive' (151). This shift of focus, which also forms a bridge across the act-division (see Daos' hasty exit at 264–6), is given a strongly comic colour (enriched by the change of metre to trochaic tetrameters) in the vigorous banter between Moschion and Daos which opens the act. The exchanges between a suspicious but also excited master and a boastful but crafty slave start off in a familiar mould of attack *versus* defence; Moschion's accusations of unreliability and threats of punishment are answered by reassurances and (false) claims of achievement ('*I'*m the one who persuaded Glycera to move in . . .') on the part of Daos. This then develops over some thirty lines into a hyperbolic fantasy about the possible roles that Daos could fill in life, strung along with a series of verbally artificial jokes (275–91). This is a very different style of dialogue from anything (that survives) in Act I. It is virtually free-standing repartee, with a patently digressive relationship to the forward movement of the plot – in fact, for Menander, an unusually blatant specimen of this kind of writing.[53] What follows, too, while reconnecting with the dramatic situation, opens up fresh scope for laughter in several ways: first, Moschion's obvious nervousness about

---

[53] The comically expansive nature of this scene prompts Zagagi (1994) 179 n. 61 to cite Plautine parallels. Equally one might look back to numerous Aristophanic antecedents: a token instance is the opening of *Frogs*.

going inside (295–8; ironically accompanied by a premature *desire* to 'laugh' exultantly over his perceived rival Polemon, 293), yet combined with his inability to suppress a touch of vanity and self-ignorance about his supposed attractiveness to women (302–4, 308–9);[54] secondly, the 'to-and-fro' humour of Daos' repeated and less than meticulous 'reconnaissance' of the situation in the house (306–10, contradicting Moschion's expectations of Daos' efficiency at 298); thirdly, and following on from both the preceding points, the comic surprise and (for Moschion) disappointment of discovering that the *last* person his mother wants to see at this critical juncture is her (foster) son (317–24).[55] Daos' report of Myrrhine's annoyance accentuates the gap between the continuing offstage crisis of Glycera (a figure associated, in the audience's mind, with weeping) and the poorly informed position and misdirected intentions of the two characters on stage, who as a result can be perceived as somewhat ludicrous. Daos' bad news also brings the Moschion–Daos relationship back round full circle to where things stood at the start of the act: Moschion turns on Daos with abuse (324), forcing him to resort, with transparent disingenuousness, to denying his earlier boasts (327–8, cf. 271–5). Further exchanges of comic 'attack and defence' now pass between them, including stage-movements of pursuit and evasion (334–5, cf. 345), until Moschion eventually awards his slave 'victory' in the conflict between them (ὁμολογῶ νικᾶν σε, 352). The metaphor is telling. The entire scene has had something of the quality of a diversionary game or theatrical routine. In terms of the progress of the action, it has achieved nothing more than a temporary delay of Moschion's entry into the house, as well as intensifying the uncertain state of mind in which he makes that entry. From the audience's standpoint, however, it has provided for the first time in the play (so far as we can make out) an unequivocal cue for the release of laughter.

This whole stretch of Act II, then, allows the tone to drop from the level of emotional turbulence, even trauma, represented by both Glycera and Polemon to that of a more traditionally comic repertoire of witty interplay, physical as well as verbal, between a master and slave both of whom are made to look somewhat peripheral to the heart of the action, and certainly more peripheral than they realise. Crucial here is the difference of characterisation between Moschion, whose mixture of vanity and immaturity makes

---

[54] 301–2 refer to the same event as Agnoia related at 154–62: an alert audience would realise that Moschion, in putting a favourable gloss on the episode, is suppressing the discouraging signals of Glycera's described at 159–62.

[55] Here and below, I use 'foster' son/mother for the relationship between Moschion and Myrrhine in a non-technical sense; for the uncertainty of the legal relationship posited, see Gomme and Sandbach (1973) 473, 502.

him emotionally rather frivolous, and Polemon, who, whatever else may be true of him, is someone who takes his own feelings extremely seriously. Menander can afford, indeed he needs, to handle Moschion as a much lighter character than Polemon; this is because the plot has built into it the impossibility that the former could actually be a successful lover of a woman who, unbeknownst to him, is his twin sister. Moreover, whereas both 'rivals' suffer from ignorance about Glycera's circumstances, Moschion's ignorance is partly transformed into a kind of comic *self*-ignorance, the symptoms of which are his vanity and his nervousness about facing up to his mother and admitting his desire for Glycera. Polemon's misunderstanding, by contrast, is channelled into a much darker, more disturbing course of behaviour: whether or not this makes an audience *like* him, it leaves them little room to laugh at him (as yet). Both figures are young men, and both have a streak of rashness (cf. 128, 151). What distinguishes them, *au fond*, is the difference between a weak, ineffectual and therefore in some degree ridiculous character and, on the other hand, a threateningly impetuous (though ultimately 'redeemed') figure. Here, and not for the only time (see 395–6 above), we can see how the conditions under which self-ignorance enters the sphere of Menandrian comedy are compatible with the discussion of that connection in Plato's *Philebus*.

Having, in the first part of Act II, manoeuvred *Perikeiromene* (and its audience) much closer to the realm of 'the laughable', Menander sustains and broadens this ethos in the aggressive confrontation that soon follows between Sosias and Daos (373–97), a confrontation marked by mostly mild *bōmolochia* (though σκατοφάγος, literally 'shit-eater', 394, strikes an earthier note) but also by a strain of military imagery that paves the way for Act III's mock siege. It is unnecessary for my present purposes to scrutinise in great detail the comic features of the sarcastic slanging match that takes place between the two major slave roles of the play. It is worth noticing, however, that the exchanges between them have gelastic implications on two (partly correlated) levels: first, in so much as Daos (who knows more than Sosias does about Glycera's whereabouts) exploits the situation to aim provocative insults and even overt jokes at Sosias and those he represents;[56] and secondly, because the overall air of scorn and abusiveness between the

---

[56] Daos cracks a joke at Sosias' expense (371–2) even before the conversation starts; he then sets at least a mildly abusive tone with his opening vocative, ἄνθρωπε κακόδαιμον, at 373 (cf. Dickey (1996) 168 for the register), followed by further gibes at 377–8 and a jeering remark at 380–2 (which Sosias deems ἀσελγές, 'outrageous': cf. ch. 1 n. 85). By 390 the exchange is insulting on both sides, and the climax is Daos' ironic apology for 'joking' (*paizein*, echoing Sosias at 388), followed immediately by his 'shit-eater' taunt (which Sosias purports to find shocking, 394–5).

slaves (as Sosias is gradually drawn into trading insults in return) provides a pleasurable spectacle, in the tradition of comic 'shamelessness' (the tradition of what the Platonic Socrates called 'base men . . . bad-mouthing and ridiculing one another'), for the audience to enjoy with impunity.[57]

Before the slaves square up to one another, there is a moment of a rather different kind which calls for comment in relation to my argument as a whole. Sosias enters grumbling at 354 in a manner reminiscent of his earlier entry at 172. The effect is a kind of dramatic reprise, and, just like the first time round, we learn something important about Polemon's state of mind: he is desperate to know what state Glycera is in (355). Sosias toys sardonically with the idea of going back and lying to Polemon, in order to startle him out of his depressed state (356–7), by saying that he has found Moschion with Glycera (a dramatically ironic idea, of course, in view of what has recently taken place). But he then interrupts this train of thought with an expression of *pity* for his master (εἰ μή γε παντάπασιν αὐτὸν ἠλέουν, 'if only I didn't feel so *sorry* for him', 357) and a reflection on the depth of Polemon's unhappiness (359–60). The jolt of hearing such sentiments in the mouth of a slave who has so far been nothing but cynical about his master's plight produces one of those distinctively Menandrian moments (not unlike the meeting between Sostratus and Moschus in *Dis Exapaton*, 388 above) where laughter is occluded by, so to speak, a cloud that passes over the scene. After the semi-farcical encounter between Moschion and Daos, we are abruptly, if only briefly, transported back to the emotionally darker atmosphere of Act I and reminded that nothing at all has yet changed for Polemon. Menander is making sure that his audience maintains that double perspective – from 'inside' the characters' own troubles, and simultaneously from the external viewpoint of privileged information – which he had previously opened up for them. He does so in part by staging a kind of contest between the prompting and the negation of laughter within the texture of the characters' psychological and social frustrations.

If we move ahead now to Act III of *Perikeiromene*, we find here a more elaborate case of counterpoint between laughter and seriousness, between τὸ γελοῖον and τὸ σπουδαῖον. This occurs at the point where the uproar of the pseudo-military 'siege' on the house of Myrrhine undertaken by Polemon, Sosias and a few others (probably all slaves) is replaced by an earnest, taut conversation between Pataecus and Polemon (486–525). In one germane sense, the opening of the act (after a further lacuna) takes us

---

[57] For the Platonic reference, see *Rep.* 3.395e with ch. 5, 225–7, and *ibid.* 243–63 for the shamelessness of comic abuse more generally.

into quintessentially comic territory, since the siege – with its inebriated confusion between warfare and erotic pursuit – is unmistakably redolent of a rather ramshackle *kōmos*, a point no doubt heightened by the presence of a pipe-girl, Habrotonon, in the group (476).[58] Even here, though, there is a discernible tension between the behaviour of Sosias (ludicrously, drunkenly bellicose) and that of Polemon, who seems pathetically aware of his own need for guidance from someone more responsible than his disorderly slave. Polemon tells Pataecus that, in his misery, he has deliberately avoided too much alcohol,[59] and he declares himself ready to listen to the older man's advice (471–4). Precisely how we should read the resulting inflections of the scene is uncertain; but this uncertainty is arguably part of Menander's dramatic design. In performance, as with everything else in the text, such issues could of course be affected by the actors' choices of tone and gesture, though it is important to remember that actors do not have totally free rein – they too are textual interpreters. Rather than reading the siege scene as unequivocally or one-sidedly comic, as though Sosias' rampant behaviour were unquestioned (as it might be in the more free-flowing scurrility of Old Comedy), it seems to me preferable to treat it as a tonally complex continuation of that 'contest' between laughter and its negation to which I referred above and which is a hallmark of much Menandrian dramatic writing. On this view, the drunken wildness of the action, crystallised in the antics of Sosias, does indeed draw on the genre's komastic traditions to give an audience *some* overt grounds for laughter. But this dramatic layer is superimposed on, and only partly masks, the underlying anguish of Polemon, who must retain enough credibility of character to make his ensuing conversation with Pataecus psychologically persuasive.

However one calibrates the tone of the siege scene as a whole, there is a palpably sharp disparity of dramatic register between what precedes and follows the departure of Sosias. The latter's final lines are highly striking. As he turns to leave the stage (disgruntled after his repeated dismissal by Pataecus), he makes a pair of thinly disguised puns on the sexual prowess of Habrotonon. Then, when she responds to the innuendo, he feigns surprise at her embarrassment but makes matters irredeemably worse by calling her λαικάστρια, which in sense and force is close to 'cocksucker' and served

---

[58] For two rather different cases of the comic merging of imagery of war and *kōmos*, cf. Ar. *Ach.* 524–9, 978–87. On the parodic *kōmos* of the end of *Dysc.*, cf. 402 with n. 33 above.

[59] In the surviving text, we gather only at 988, 1022 that Polemon was drunk when he cropped Glycera's hair, but it is quite likely this was mentioned somewhere in the lost first scene of the play. If so, Polemon's deliberate control of his drinking (471–3) would carry an extra nuance. In the larger connection, I think it is misleading of Zagagi (1994) 150 to describe Pataecus as 'one of Polemon's drinking mates'.

as a more emotive synonym of *pornē*, 'prostitute'.[60] Even 'veiled' sexual puns, or *doubles entendres*, of the sort Sosias perpetrates are unusual in Menander; and outright obscenities, of the kind he then resorts to, are extremely scarce. But over and above that linguistic observation there is an intriguing question to pose about this passage in its own right. From one point of view, it is as though Sosias slips back along the scale demarcated by Aristotle's (pre-Menandrian) contrast between innuendo (*huponoia*) and obscenity (*aischrologia*).[61] But precisely because his linguistic behaviour stands out, by Menandrian canons, as quite exceptional, its comic weight is not easy to judge. After all, we are given (again, visually as well as textually) a pointed indication of Sosias' contravention of standards of verbal seemliness: Habrotonon herself turns away in shame and/or disgust (484–5), though that only incites Sosias to add further offence by purporting to see no reason for her reaction (485). This is not the dramatic world of Aristophanes, in which obscenity is often part and parcel of the celebration of comic freedom and is so widely distributed that that it can be found even in the mouth of a Lysistrata or Praxagora.[62] Menander, as I earlier mentioned (399 above), seems to 'protect' his respectable citizen characters from obscenity as well as from excessive scurrility of other kinds. So is Sosias' vulgarity 'comic' only because it is in the mouth of a slave? That cannot be the whole story. His drunkenness too is conspicuously at work, as Pataecus had been quick to realise (469–71). Indeed the presence of Pataecus himself, as well as Polemon, adds a further twist to Sosias' speech-act. Menander quite often gives (reciprocal) crudity of speech to (male) slaves

[60] The relationship of λαικάστρια to *pornē* is nicely visible at Ar. *Ach.* 524–9, where two uses of the second term are supplemented with a climactic application of the first. On the verb λαικάζειν and cognates, see Jocelyn (1980), esp. 12–16, Dover (1989) 204–5, (2002) 95, Bain (1991) 74–7, Olson (2002) 96, 211; Silk (2000) 154 n. 117 strangely dismisses the solid philological case for the meaning 'fellate'. The other Menandrian use (of the verb) is in the Cook's mouth at *Dysc.* 892, probably meant as a response to a perceived sexual slur: see Gomme and Sandbach (1973) 270, Jocelyn (1980) 40–1, Bain (1991) 76 n. 202; cf. n. 26 above, with Arnott (1995) 153–5 on Sicon's language in general. The speech register and function of *laikaz-* terms (i.e., as foul-mouthed expletives) are readily glimpsed both from the comic characters who use them and from the vehemence with which they do so: in Aristophanes see Dicaeopolis at *Ach.* 79, 529, 537, the slave at *Kn.* 167, and the provocative Inlaw at *Thesm.* 57; Cephisodorus fr. 3.5 *PCG* is spoken by a self-consciously uncouth slave; and Strato fr. 1.36 *PCG* is spoken to a cook of servile origin (*ibid.* 49) by an exasperated character who describes himself as down-to-earth (*agroikos*) in speech habits (25).

[61] For the Aristotelian contrast, see n. 14 above. The rarity of Menandrian sexual puns is noted by Gomme and Sandbach (1973) 505, *ad* 485, though they overlook Ar. *Wasps* 1341 as the best parallel for the *double entendre* on ἀναβαίνειν, 'mount' (their Aristophanic references involve other terms).

[62] On Lysistrata's (sometimes denied) use of obscenity, see ch. 5, 253. It is instructive to compare Sosias' 'joke' about sexual positions in *Perik.* 484 with Aristophanic jokes on the same subject at (e.g.) *Wasps* 500–2, 1341–50 (see n. 61 above), *Lys.* 59–60, *Thesm.* 123: although the Aristophanic cases vary in their relation between character, utterance and context, nowhere is there anything like the explicit sense of social offence/shame which Menander makes a point of foregrounding at *Perik.* 485.

when they are alone, as in the sparring between Daos and Sosias in Act II of this play. In doing so, he is probably conforming to a standard sociolinguistic assumption on the part of Athenians,[63] as well as preserving an old comic convention. But Sosias here insults Habrotonon gratuitously in the hearing of 'citizens', which makes his behaviour more blatantly shameless. All these considerations, which would of course impinge on an audience (an audience attuned, that is, to Menandrian standards) without conscious analysis, complicate the question of whether or how to laugh at Sosias – something that Pataecus, for one, surely does not do.

Whatever one's precise take on this sudden intrusion of obscenity, Sosias' parting lines exemplify two larger aspects of my argument in this chapter. In the first place, they fit with a Menandrian tendency to allow certain kinds of gelastically charged signals (in Sosias' case, his inebriated gibes at Habrotonon) to emerge from and disappear beneath the surfaces of the social world with a sort of mercurial rapidity. In the second place, they throw starkly into relief the problem of discrepant positions and divergent perspectives in relation to the possibility of laughter – and they do so twice over, both by opening a gap between Sosias and the other characters on stage, and by facing the audience with a somewhat unstable choice of responses (to laugh indulgently with Sosias? to laugh with superiority *at* his crudity? or not to laugh at all?), rather than furnishing them with an unequivocal cue for hilarity. Certainly, the shift of dramatic tone is immediate and drastic once Sosias has exited; however an audience has reacted to what went before, it must now adjust to a far more sombre, introspective register. Polemon, left alone with Pataecus, at once betrays his emotionally sensitive state. He is ready to flare up in anger (see 489), while his remaining sense of betrayal makes him feel 'pain' (494) at Pataecus' suggestion that he had failed to treat Glycera well. Pataecus is left in no doubt about the force of the passion which is driving him (494–5). Polemon, as critics have often observed, is far from being a stereotypically vain, blustering (and therefore simply laughable) soldier-lover. In fact, his loss of 'military' strength during the siege-scene (see a hint of this at 479–80, though division of the text is uncertain) might even be interpreted as symbolic of his deeper erotic wound as a (seemingly) rejected 'husband', which he emphatically considers himself (489). Polemon is remarkable for a highly strung combination of impetuosity (cf. 128, with his later undertaking at 1018–19) and emotional vulnerability. The latter is seen at its most naked in 506–7, lines which (following a gesture towards suicide, 505, cf. 976, 988) project emotional

---

[63] See n. 25 above.

helplessness, patterned in a sort of sobbing chiasmus, with as pure a pathos as one can find anywhere in Menander:[64]

> Γλυκέρα με καταλέλοιπε, καταλέλοιπέ με
> Γλυκέρα . . .
>
> Glycera has left me, she's left me
> Glycera . . .

Immediately after this, Polemon confirms his dependency on Pataecus by begging him to act as intermediary and proceeding to insist that Pataecus come to inspect the finery he had lavished on Glycera. When he reveals that he thinks himself deserving of pity (518), we are reminded of how even Sosias came round to feeling strong sympathy for his master's troubles (357). With the possible exception of Pataecus' exasperation at being pressed to inspect Glycera's clothes and jewellery (516–18, a gesture that inadvertently prepares the way for a dénouement), and perhaps also the soldier's self-deprecation of his own crazed infatuation at 523, it is hard to detect any trace of even oblique humour in the entire stretch of conversation from 486 to 525. That is not to rule out altogether a more diffuse sense in which Polemon might be perceived as (faintly) ludicrous in his self-consuming obsession with Glycera. But, once again, the presence of any such uncertainty is itself a feature of the often elusive 'pitch' of Menander's comic tone or (a different formulation of the same phenomenon) the ambiguous social light in which he places some of his characters.

Admittedly, some of Polemon's traits – self-pity, emotional extravagance, even suicidal inclinations – are generically shared with other despairing comic lovers, to some extent even with Moschion. But I have already contended that Menander invites his audience to take Polemon much more seriously than Moschion, partly, I suggested, because the latter exhibits a greater degree of *self*-ignorance. The two characters' different emotional profiles correspond to their relative positions in the plot: Polemon's centrality and Moschion's secondary role are converted by the playwright into qualitatively distinct treatments of their emotional lives. Even when, in Moschion's appearance at the end of Act III, we hear of him 'lying down' in self-pitying distress (541, 547), just as Polemon was earlier reported as doing (172),[65] his predicament continues to be handled more lightheartedly than

---

[64] Cf. Goldberg (1980) 47–9 for this and other features of Polemon's 'despairing' character; Handley (2002) 175 notes *Perik.* 506–7 as a kind of patterning which poetically enhances 'real' emotion. To call Polemon a 'figure of fun' *tout court*, as does Green (1990) 74, is remarkably insensitive to Menandrian characterisation.

[65] See n. 47 above. Cf. *Epitr.* fr. 3, which possibly describes Charisius' distraught state.

Polemon's. His self-dramatisation, for one thing, is articulated in a familiar, obtrusive kind of comic rhetoric. Take, for instance, his parenthesis on the current 'crop' of misery all over Greece (533–4), which he uses to bolster his claim to be the most wretched person of all: in context, this lends his words an air of absurd hyperbole, rather than the kind of impetuous desperation that marked Polemon's words in the preceding scene. But the key factor in the difference between the two men's characters is Moschion's continuing nervousness towards, but also dependency on, his *mother*, evinced by his description of how he both avoided her in the house (trying, once more, to use Daos as go-between) and yet lay on his bed fantasising how she would soon bring news of Glycera's readiness to accept him (537–50).

We witnessed earlier in the play how Moschion saw his mother as pivotal to his further pursuit of Glycera (296–8, 312–15). It is not that a young Greek male's emotional or even practical dependence on his mother is intrinsically unthinkable. Far from it: Moschion's state of mind economically evokes an intriguing type of craving for maternal approval which must have made some sort of sense to Menander's audience, and which may even match up with the apparently 'absent (foster) father' role of Myrrhine's husband in *Perikeiromene* (though textual gaps make judgement on this point inconclusive).[66] It does, however, make Moschion appear emotionally more of a fantasiser, more naive and more immature than Polemon (though the latter too is just as young, 129), and therefore a more suitable object for some kind of (gentle) laughter. It is one thing for Polemon to need an older male acquaintance (of both parties) to act as go-between with his alienated 'wife' (507–13),[67] but quite another for Moschion to anticipate a mother's assistance (547–50) in promoting a sexual relationship with a woman he regards as a courtesan and at whom he has so far only made a brief, abortive pass in the street (152–60, 300–3). When Glycera later defends herself to Pataecus against the suspicion of having moved in with Myrrhine in order to become Moschion's hetaira, she expresses incredulity at the thought of

---

[66] On the problem of whether/when Myrrhine's husband may have shown up, cf. Gomme and Sandbach (1973) 515 (with 502 for rejection of the theory that Pataecus himself is Myrrhine's husband). Relationships between (adult) sons and their mothers in classical Athens form a dimension of life to which we have hardly any historical access. The present case is all the harder to judge because of the foster relationship involved (n. 55 above). Menander seems to go out of his way to stress Moschion's over-dependence on maternal approval and help. For a peculiar case in which a mother was apparently involved in promoting the sexual relationships of her son, see the tantalising allegation at Lys. 1.20 that Eratosthenes' mother was party to his seduction of Euphiletus' wife (befriending the latter, at least, after the affair had begun).

[67] The play's presentation of the legally fuzzy relationship which Polemon regards as 'marriage' to Glycera has attracted much attention: see Konstan (1995) 110–11, Rosivach (1998) 53–5, Omitowoju (2002) 215–18, Fantuzzi and Hunter (2004) 410–12.

such a tactic. 'Don't you think that I, *as well as he*, would have been eager to keep his family in the dark?', she asks (711–12); and, in the same spirit, 'Do you think I would have been such a fool as to create enmity between his mother and me?' (714–15). Glycera never had the motivation, of course; but if she had, she knows that involving Moschion's mother is the last thing it would have been prudent to do. Her point is presented as self-evident. But somehow the force of it seems to have eluded young Moschion's own mind. It is as if Moschion, unlike the soldier Polemon – volatile and far from straightforwardly admirable, but with an established stake in the adult world – is still struggling to leave his adolescence behind.

If the differences I have highlighted between Moschion and Polemon are justified, it is nonetheless worth adding that Menander's juxtaposition of the two lovers can productively be interpreted as showing how *thin* a dividing line separates the serious (i.e., psychologically complex) from the comic (i.e., psychologically schematic) where young male lovers, like other human types, are concerned. This way of looking at the matter complements and extends my earlier argument that it is a Menandrian hallmark to juxtapose passages, or sometimes fleeting moments, in which 'the laughable' or 'the comic' and its occlusion run in a sort of dramatic counterpoint to one another. What I am now proposing is not that Moschion and Polemon can be unambiguously equated with the two sides of that contrast, but that the significant differences between them – differences that stand out against the background of their superficially parallel situations as distressed lovers of Glycera – convey a cumulative sense of just how precariously balanced the conditions of 'the comic' may be in relation to psychological and social behaviour. Both men are emotionally fixated on the same woman, yet Moschion's unknown kinship to her creates, for the audience, a basic asymmetry of possibilities and expectations that Menander works into the emotional fabric of the play. Perhaps the neatest way of summarising this asymmetry is to say that the audience is encouraged to feel that while Glycera is uniquely, indispensably important to Polemon, for Moschion she is an erotic object that can relatively easily be replaced (as indeed she is, in the dénouement) by another woman. It is an implication of this psychological difference that it seems appropriate to be amused by Moschion's foibles – his naive vanity, his nervousness, his incongruous dependence on his mother, his self-deception – for much of the play (even, up to a point at least, during the *anagnōrisis* of Act IV), whereas Polemon is too intense and troubled (as well as troubling) a character to be a cause of laughter at more than the margins of his behaviour – at any rate until his deliriously recovered happiness in the final act, when the restoration of harmony all round brings with it the obligatory exuberance of comic celebration.[68] At the same time, what distinguishes the two figures is apparently more to do with circumstance and contingency, more a matter of the positions they find themselves in, than with anything Menander requires us to think of as intrinsic to them as individuals. Modify the details of circumstance, redistribute the 'ignorance' which Agnoia personifies in the prologue and which casts its shadow over all the action before Act IV's recognition, and the possibilities of laughter would change as well. Fundamental to Menandrian comic perspectivism is the tacit awareness that people move in and out of the range of risibility according to configurations of social factors over which they have only a small degree of control.

The preceding pages have, of course, not offered a comprehensive reading of *Perikeiromene*, only a selection of remarks on the fluctuations, intricacies and indeterminacies of tone that can be traced in parts of the comedy. My aim has been to use *Perikeiromene* to explore a characteristically Menandrian fluidity both in depicting the possibilities of laughter within the social world of the plays and, correspondingly (though not identically), in varying the possibilities of laughter which the plays make available to their audiences. Material which has had to be left on one side but which would, I believe, strengthen the case I have made, includes the entire recognition scene of Act IV, as well as the tense passage immediately before it (708–54) in which Glycera, with vehement eloquence, defends her integrity to Pataecus (cf. 423 above) and reactivates, for anyone who might have forgotten it, the frisson of outrage (*hubris*) attaching to Polemon's earlier treatment of her (722–5; cf. 405 above). It is ironic that in the midst of that exchange Pataecus should try to protest that Glycera's behaviour is 'ridiculous' (*geloion*, 748) – in terms, he means, of its resistance to his mediation – when in fact her stance clearly emerges from the scene as the very reverse of laughable: dignified, strong-willed and ethically resolute.[69] The climactic recognition scene

---

[68] Before he allows himself to believe that Glycera is coming back to him, Polemon needs reassuring (by Doris) that she is not *mocking* his feelings (990). Fear of mockery is a potent motif for the Greek imagination: see Men. *Epitr.* fr. 10 (Arnott/Sandbach), with ch. 1, 25–6, for general discussion. Polemon's anxiety is at this point such a sign of erotic dependency, but also so superfluous, that an audience must surely find it comic in its own right; cf. 427 below.

[69] In a short space Glycera shows herself, by implication, to possess robust powers of reasoning (708–19), standards of good sense (713–16), sensitivity to shame (717), pride in her good reputation (718–19), determination (722), and ethical self-confidence (722–4), as well as an ability to dominate Pataecus in argument (749). Menander seems here deliberately to distance Glycera from any earlier show of emotional weakness (cf. n. 50 above). On the general importance of her 'proud and independent' character for the nature of the play, see Konstan (1995), esp. 110–13; but the later pages of his argument (115–19) are skewed by the exaggerated view, followed also by Rosivach (1998) 55, that Glycera is reduced to 'a silently obedient wife' in the last part of the play: see Lamagna (1994) 298–9

itself has been extensively analysed by others; its semi-tragic tension and pointed (but evidently not comic) sentimentality only augment the emotional complications of the play as a whole. Furthermore, the *anagnōrisis* offers another, somewhat different example of the Menandrian perspectivism which I defined earlier in the chapter, this time neatly internalised in the drama. Recognition of identity is combined with a *peripeteia*, a 'reversal' or twist of direction, which transforms Pataecus' position from that of observer and go-between into a centrally implicated agent, thus heightening our overall impression of the mutable character of human interests and fortunes.

Taking a compendious glance back over the play from the vantage point I have adopted, one could maintain that the only (known) scenes which aim to arouse unproblematic laughter occur in Act II, involving first Moschion and Daos (in a largely digressive hold-up to the advance of the plot), then Daos and Sosias (in a traditionally comic exchange of 'low' abuse). Even the quasi-komastic siege scene in Act III seems to counterbalance the unrestrained antics of the drunken Sosias with the anguished and far from ridiculous state of mind of Polemon himself. Although I have argued that all of Moschion's appearances are coloured, despite (or in part because of) his own melodramatic self-presentation, by a degree of absurdity that grows from his naive immaturity, he too is less of an outright comic figure than an ambiguous counterfoil to the darker mentality of Polemon. And in the recognition scene, it is arguable that Moschion, an observer from the sidelines, is even granted a little pathos of his own (before his eventual 'reward'), as he seems to see his emotional needs collapsing around him – though this is a reading which goes against the grain of scholarly consensus on the passage.[70] Helping to round out the work's serio-comic dynamics, it should be added, is a consistent treatment of both Pataecus and Glycera – a matching father–daughter pair, so it transpires – as characters of notable psychological sobriety and weight who are never compromised, it seems, by anything like a lapse into 'comic' weakness. Only Polemon himself is

---

(cf. 294–5), Arnott (1979–2000) II 464–6, for the assignation of a speaking part to Glycera at 1021–3, *contra* Sandbach (1990) 221.

[70] There is nothing indubitably comic about Moschion's self-pitying asides at *Perik.* 778, 783–4, 793; I take the view that they cannot afford to strike too overtly a ludicrous note (a range of tonal shadings would be available to actors) if they are not to detract from the sustained seriousness of Glycera and Pataecus' conversation. Bain (1977) 115 n. 6 cites several scholars who feel strongly otherwise; add e.g. Goldberg (1980) 53–5, Hunter (1985) 134 ('element of farce'), Zagagi (1994) 178 n. 37, Lamagna (1994) 51–2. Bain's own position, 115–17, is somewhat equivocal, as is that of Gomme and Sandbach (1973) 520; cf. Fantuzzi and Hunter (2004) 428. At (and from) *Perik.* 819, the mood changes: Moschion himself now starts to see the situation in a new light, i.e. as the discovery of a father rather than the loss of a woman he loves, and the surprise he feels seems to call for laughter.

allowed to veer from one end of the scale to the other. For most of the work, he is a disturbing mixture of violent self-assertion and emotionally confused remorse. In Act V, we are given a final glimpse of the 'suicidal' impulses which this mixture brings into being (976–8; cf. 421 above), before the release switch of reconciliation converts him into an increasingly, though now at last a benignly, comic figure. As a lover, he now becomes overwhelmingly lightheaded (982–9); his previous angst is reduced to worrying (absurdly) that Glycera may be making fun of him (990); and, in an ultimate betrayal of his soldierly prowess (which, in any case, he will never need again: 1016), all he can do is run away and hide (1004) at the sight of Glycera's father (Pataecus). But Menander has kept his audience waiting a long time for admitting this bathos of laughter into his play. And even then he does not permit the joyful comic *rapprochement* to be signed and sealed without a delicate reminder, in the mouths of all three characters on stage, of just how unpleasant a crisis between Polemon and Glycera has been survived (1016–22).

Agnoia's prologue in *Perikeiromene* enables us to construct an 'ideal' trajectory of audience response that starts from emotional shock and ends with vicarious pleasure in the celebrations of a double wedding. Menander orchestrates the psychological movement from the first to the second of those things not (entirely) by dramatic sleight of hand but by a subtly managed progression through which the comic theatre's inherited right to laughter has to be 'earned', as it were, in competition with some of the forces – anger, violence, alienation, grief, despair, even pity – that threaten to nullify it. Menandrian comedy, I hope to have shown, allows its audience no automatic outlet for laughter but something more like an appreciation of the unstable, unpredictable relevance of laughter to a social world destabilised by strange intersections of knowledge and ignorance, purpose and chance, deception and self-deception. To achieve maximum satisfaction from the spectacle of such a world, Menander's audience is encouraged to adopt shifting perspectives – both 'internal' and 'external' – on the agents of the plays, thereby alternating between close sympathy for (some of) their concerns and a more knowing, 'godlike' overview of the total pattern made by the lives of the characters. What stamps this experience as authentically 'comic', in Greek terms, is an indomitable expectation that the potential for celebration will ultimately be assured and that the problems of life will turn out to be soluble in a laughter of psychological and social unity. But before it can be rewarded with final fulfilment, that expectation must negotiate its winding, serio-comic path through a web of dramatic tensions that link together the anticipation, the obstruction and the release of laughter. If the goddess Nike (Victory – emblem of success in the theatre, but also of difficulties defeated in the world of the plays) was well disposed to Menander in the end, she must have learnt to expect from him something other than instant gratification of her 'laughter-loving' nature.[71]

---

[71] Nike φιλόγελως ('laughter-loving') is formulaically invoked at *Dysc.* 968, *Mis.* 995, *Sic.* 422–3, and (probably) fr. 903.20; cf. Posidip. com. fr. 6.12–13.

CHAPTER 9

Lucian and the laughter of life and death

τί τοῦτο ἀνεκάγχασας, ὦ Μῶμε; καὶ μὴν οὐ γελοῖα τὰ ἐν ποσίν·
παῦσαι κακόδαιμον, ἀποπνιγήσῃ ὑπὸ τοῦ γέλωτος.

(Zeus: 'Why did you guffaw like that, Momus? What we're dealing
with *really* isn't funny at all. Stop it, you wretch! You'll choke yourself
laughing.')

Lucian, *Iuppiter Tragoedus*

Der Tod is gross.
Wir sind die Seinen
lachenden Munds.

(Death is great.
We belong to him
with our laughing mouths.)
Rilke, 'Schlussstück'[1]

THE VIEW FROM THE MOON

In one of his many Lucianic incarnations, Menippus of Gadara – supposed
Cynic, inventor of a genre of satirical burlesque that amalgamated the
traditions of comedy and philosophy, and a literary influence on Lucian's
own writing – explains to a friend how a realisation that human affairs are
ludicrous helped throw him into a state of existential aporia. Having lifted
his vision to the totality of the cosmos, he was utterly perplexed. 'I could
not discover', he confides, 'how it came into being, who made it, what its
beginning or end was.' The philosophers he consulted were of no use to him.

---

[1] Epigraphs: (1) Lucian, *Iup. Trag.* 31 (cf. n. 24 below); all quotations from and references to Lucian
follow the edition of Macleod (1972–87). Momus is the personification of carping fault-finding (see
the ordinary concept at e.g. Hom. *Od.* 2.86, Bacchyl. 13.202–3, Pind. *Ol.* 6.74), which is usually
thought too darkly spiteful (cf. Momus' birth from Night, Hes. *Theog.* 214) to involve laughter. But
Lucian, *Iup. Trag.* 31 makes him a quasi-Cynic mocker; cf. esp. *Deor. Conc.* for his persona. (2) Rilke
'Schlussstück', in *Das Buch der Bilder*, II 2.

All equally doctrinaire, they nonetheless disagreed utterly about such vast concepts as time and space, infinity, the plurality of worlds and the existence of gods. Taking matters into his own hands like an Aristophanic Trygaeus or Peisetaerus, Menippus strapped on wings and flew up to the moon. Unlike Aristophanic protagonists, however, who are always too preoccupied with some particular goal or ambition to contemplate the world with wry detachment, Menippus found that the human show looked even more risible from his cosmic vantage point.[2] He could see it, in its paltry smallness (like the scurrying of ants), as no more than a chaotic dance in the theatre of life. 'When I'd had my fill of looking and laughing at everything [sc. on earth]' (ἐπειδὴ δ' οὖν πάντα ἱκανῶς ἑώρατο καὶ κατεγεγέλαστό μοι), his account continues, he proceeded to the outer heavens which the gods themselves inhabit. There he encountered a rather weary, neglected and irritable Zeus (a figure closely akin to the one Lucian dramatises in the early chapters of *Bis Accusatus*), who shares with Menippus a sense of the derisory vanities of philosophers in particular. Each of them, the god expostulates, is like a tragic actor – 'take away his mask and gold-sequinned costume, and all you're left with is an absurd homunculus (γελοῖον ἀνθρώπιον)!' After threatening rather unconvincingly (why has he waited till now?) to annihilate mankind in the near future, Zeus politely strips Menippus of his wings and has him returned to earth.[3]

As the mythologically loaded title of Lucian's work, *Icaromenippus* ('Icarus-Menippus'), implicitly makes clear (with its evocation of a fateful fall back to earth), the person who tries to laugh at the whole of life cannot really transcend the human viewpoint for long. But Lucian, who himself tries to encompass the whole of life in his comico-satirical writing, can at least invite his audience to imagine a spatial detachment from the domain of anthropocentric concerns and to find laughter the most appropriate response to this symbolic 'thought experiment'. And yet, a niggling doubt might strike anyone who pauses to reflect on this strategy. It is so much easier to laugh at others than at oneself. If Menippus was right that (almost) all human affairs are absurd, how can he himself (how can Lucian, how can we?) avoid becoming an object of (self-)ridicule? How, shorn of his wings yet having had a glimpse of what life looks like 'from the outside', is Menippus supposed to continue with normal existence? Has his experience

---

[2] For my denial that Aristophanic comedy is itself fully absurdist, see ch. 7, 341. Lucian's work, reflecting Menippean tradition as well as the whole intervening history of Greek philosophy, echoes Aristophanic motifs while modulating them into a more overtly absurdist mode.

[3] See Lucian, *Icarom.* 4 (the absurdity of life and Menippus' existenial aporia), 11–12 (the winged journey), 16 (the chaotic dance of life), 19 (having his fill of laughter), 29 (Zeus's tragic actor analogy).

been nothing more than a temporary, playful fantasy, or has it formulated a truly existential dilemma – how to come to terms with absurdity?[4]

The writings of Lucian abound with both direct references and indirect promptings to laughter, though these two sets of things, we should notice, do not always correspond to one another. While that laughter turns its focus sequentially on numerous phenomena – historical, fictional, generic, mythological – there is an important sense in which life and death themselves compete for, and perhaps ultimately share, the status of serving as its supreme subject-matter. This crucial dimension of Lucian's literary mentality has been better appreciated by some of his creative emulators, including Erasmus (a great Christian ironist) and Giacomo Leopardi (a great romantic pessimist and proto-existentialist), than by his scholarly critics, many of whom have mistaken a lightness of touch for a lack of real substance.[5] But Lucian's attachment of laughter to 'life and death' themselves is a trait I intend to place at the centre of my argument in the present chapter. That argument will attempt to reappraise the gelastic principles of Lucian's essays and dialogues against the background of some of the larger traditions of writing and thought examined elsewhere in this book. Threaded through much of the fabric of Lucian's work, and contributing to its characteristically satirical-cum-absurdist ethos, is a constant generation and evocation of the 'existential laughter' which I discussed in Chapter 7: laughter, that is, which reaches beyond specific targets to open a perspective on the conditions of human life (and, by extension, death) *in toto*. But can we afford to say that life as such, in its entirety, is made a risible object from a Lucianic perspective? Or is it only parts of life – the flawed, deluded lives of power-crazed tyrants, the greedy rich, or conceited philosophers, for instance – that are presented as laughable. Is Lucian, in the terms defined in that earlier chapter, an absolute or only a comparative absurdist? And how can *death*, of all things, be laughable? Is it because its finality and inevitability somehow make life itself ludicrous? Is it because the rare but genuine philosopher is not afraid of it (we recall Socrates' laughter in Plato's *Phaedo*, spotlighted in Chapter 6)? Or is there some other sense in which Lucian's work broaches

---

[4] *One* aspect of Lucian's (use of) Menippus, as suggested in Chapter 7, is to hint at the overcoming of Cynic severity and its replacement with a more relaxed acceptance of life 'as it is': see esp. *Dial. mort.* 8.2, with ch. 7, 386.

[5] Leopardi's extensive interests in Lucian have been largely neglected by anglophone writers on Lucian: they go unmentioned, for instance, in Robinson (1979); Branham (1989a) has only an allusion (212); see Highet (1949) 432 for a brief mention. Leopardi reworks Lucianic material/modes into his own (arguably darker) perspective of comico-satirical 'existentialism', for example in *Dialogue between Earth and Moon*, *Wager of Prometheus*, and *Dialogue between a Physicist and Metaphysician*: for a bilingual edition of all the *Operette Morali*, see Leopardi (1982). Discussion can be found in e.g. Mattioli (1982), Sacco Messineo (1982), Sangirardi (1998). Cf. vii, ch. 7 n. 23.

the imagined possibility of laughing not just at but *in* death, thereby inverting the traditional Greek paradigm of Hades as the dark, 'unsmiling' realm, the place where souls have lost laughter for ever?

These are questions which I hope to show can provide a revealing angle of approach to a number of Lucian's dialogues and narratives. They are questions, however, which have to be interpreted simultaneously on two levels: that of the human (or, sometimes, non-human) agents pictured in the world of the works; and that of the comic/satirical point of view, the (quasi-)authorial eye, that observes and plots their actions. In the kinds of contexts with which I shall be primarily concerned, the question of laughter, as well as what in Chapter 7 I called the problem of the absurd, is always in some sense both inside and outside the dramatic or narrative framework – always an issue lurking around the satirical optic that the works turn on human behaviour, but also, therefore, an issue that can creep up on *anyone*, author and audience included. The minuscule, nugatory yet frantically ant-like scurryings on earth that Menippus watches from the moon in *Icaromenippus* are his world as well as ours. As we laugh (if we do) with Menippus (and/or Lucian), we may be left unsure whether we do so because we imagine ourselves equipped with his bird's-eye vision from above, with all the 'superiority' that position supposedly entails, or simply because we recognise so clearly what life is like on the ant-hills themselves.

Lucian is not only alert to, but revels in, the potentially self-subverting paradoxes of laughter which his work toys with. His *oeuvre* presents itself as an incongruous, ambiguous hybrid, a literary equivalent to the legendarily anomalous 'goat-stag' (*tragelaphos*), as well as, perhaps, a quasi-Promethean act of deceptively wrapping (comic) bones in (philosophical) fat.[6] It is a hybrid purportedly created from the coupling of philosophical dialogue with comic drama: a cross, if you like, between Plato and Aristophanes. In *Prometheus es* (6) the authorial voice personifies Dialogue as a private, intimate, sombre (male) figure, Comedy as a female with a penchant for wildly public Dionysiac celebration involving dancing, laughter and mockery – not least (the allusion to Aristophanes' *Clouds* is evident), mockery of the philosophers who are 'companions of dialogue' (τοὺς τοῦ διαλόγου ἑταίρους). Related imagery is used, though somewhat differently slanted, in *Bis Accusatus*. There, the aged figure of (philosophical) Dialogue indicts the author for having compelled him to share his life with jokes, *iambos*,

---

[6] Both analogies occur at *Prom. es* 7. At *Bis Acc.* 33 (cited in my text) Lucian's hybrid writing is called a 'centaur'.

Old Comedy, Cynicism and Menippus (a dog who laughs while he 'bites'); this new life-style has turned him, Dialogue protests, into a sheer buffoon. In defence and self-justification, the Syrian persona of Lucian's own work pleads that he has revitalised old Dialogue by sprucing him up and forcing him to '*smile*' (ἀποπλύνας καὶ μειδιᾶν καταναγκάσας), in order to make him attractive to a wider public than the supposedly dry dialogues of philosophical argument.[7] Prior to the appearance of Dialogue as plaintiff, however, 'the Syrian' defends himself against a charge from Rhetoric (his former 'wife', the love of his early life) of having abandoned her precisely for a shameless liaison with the elderly Dialogue. He defends himself on *that* accusation by claiming to have wanted to escape to the sobriety of a philosophical life from Rhetoric's wild existence of komastic decadence, a decadence in which she herself was constantly 'laughing' (31). So in *Bis Accusatus* Lucian allegorises his work, not least its gelastic component, as capable of being seen and judged from various angles. He creates a multiple personality for himself which playfully eludes simple definition. Both Rhetoric and Dialogue have some claim on him, but both also believe they have been betrayed by him. He in turn accuses Rhetoric of having slipped into a life of promiscuous debauchery, and accuses Dialogue, by contrast, of badly needing some mirth to rejuvenate his dull habits. However one looks at it, laughter itself comes out of the story as an ambiguous, shifting force which Lucian's own writing can manipulate for all it is worth.

Despite the litigious ambience of *Bis Accusatus*, Lucian has some fondness for the idea, glimpsed in the relationship between the Syrian and Dialogue in that work, of reconciling those who are not thought naturally disposed to seek out or enjoy each other's company. In *Piscator*, which again puts Lucian's own work 'on trial', this time in the personified form of the outspoken satirist Parrhesiades ('Frank Speaker'), he makes Philosophy herself protect the good name of her 'friend' Comedy. 'You know that despite the things said about me by Comedy at the Dionysia', proclaims Philosophy, 'I've continued to count her a friend and never brought legal action or confronted her with any criticism. Instead, I let her play in the ways that were only right and proper for the festival (παίζειν τὰ εἰκότα καὶ τὰ συνήθη τῇ ἑορτῇ), because I know that nothing can be made worse by a joke (ὑπὸ σκώμματος) . . .'[8] If Old Comedy is indeed a

---

[7] *Bis Acc.* 33–4.

[8] *Pisc.* 14; see 25–6, with my text, for Diogenes' later reference to the connection between comedy and festivity (and cf. ch. 5, 243–63, for the cultural importance of this point). The association between 'play' and festivity occurs as a trope in Plutarch's description of the life of the Cynic Crates of Thebes: see ch. 7 nn. 12, 100.

vital precedent for Lucian's work, then the latter can claim to exist, like its ancestor, within the protection of a (metaphorical) domain of festivity, a domain, in Philosophy's words, of 'play' and 'jokes'. But this analogy hardly offers a transparent rationale for Lucianic satire. In *Piscator* itself, the prosecution spokesman, the Cynic Diogenes of Sinope, goes on to deny that Dionysiac festive licence (which he accepts as valid in the historical context of classical Athens) can justify Parrhesiades' denigration of philosophers en masse (25–6). Furthermore, Parrhesiades himself does not defend those attacks in terms of 'play'. On the contrary, he presents himself as a 'lover of truth' and a lover of true philosophy, but a scourge of the impostors who masquerade as philosophers. Far from igniting a feud between Comedy and Philosophy, Lucian's surrogate has enlisted the help of the former against the latter's counterfeiters and thus cemented the friendship between them. He even manages to persuade the jury of canonical (dead) philosophers who hear his case that this is, on considered reflection, a justified defence.

But is this itself too convenient, even disingenuous, a piece of 'self'-exculpation' by the (personified) author? After all, he writes his own works to suit himself; and all satirists like to claim Truth on their side (they stand 'for Truth's defence', in Pope's phrase). The great philosophers accept Parrhesiades' case, we cannot help noticing, despite the fact that in *Vitarum Auctio* ('Auction of Philosophers' Lives'), the dialogue which originally caused their anger against him and brought them up out of Hades – itself a comic twist on the old theme of (avoiding) ridicule of the dead – no distinction at all is drawn between old and new, or true and false, philosophers. Yet surely it cannot be that Parrhesiades hoodwinks his distinguished judges?[9] *Piscator* offers a slyly teasing self-image of Lucianic priorities, not only by positing an ostensible yet fictitiously distanced equation between the author and Parrhesiades (an equation which many critics are too quick to translate into straightforward 'autobiography'), but also by presenting itself as both comedy and philosophy – Dionysiac in its wild freedom yet constrained by its truth-telling duties – while leaving behind a quietly bemusing sense of unresolved business between the 'friendship' of the two identities. The nature of that bemusement and that unresolved business is partly advertised by the multiple ironies of Diogenes' complaint, at *Piscator* 26, that Parrhesiades has not only appropriated philosophy's 'servant',

---

[9] For a hint of this inference, but coming from a somewhat different angle from mine, see Elliott (1960) 272–3; Branham (1989a) 32–4 comments on some of *Piscator*'s self-dramatising ambiguities. On (not) slandering the dead, see ch. 1, 26–30, with 462–70 below for a further, darker Lucianic take on the subject.

Dialogue, as his own 'actor' or theatrical mouthpiece, but has also suborned Menippus, himself a supposedly Cynic satirist and therefore 'a companion of ours', to betray philosophy and join in mocking it or making it comic (συγκωμῳδεῖν, a unique term, surprisingly, in surviving Greek literature). Whatever the implications of this passage for Lucian's relationship to so-called Menippean satire – and I see no way of distilling a clean historical residue from Diogenes' sarcasm – its dramatic (and comic) force, replete as it is with the imagery of theatrical role-playing, complicates the whole idea of a fusion or 'friendship' between philosophy and comedy. Where masks come into play, how can one be sure of discriminating between serio-comic philosophical satire (a partly Cynic tradition), satire *of* philosophy, and, finally, a kind of constant, provocative crisscrossing between philosophical and comic mentalities?[10]

No sophisticated interpretation of Lucianic texts – texts which are them-selves quintessentially sophistic(ated) – can afford to ignore their hybrid yet ultimately elusive character. The remarks of the previous paragraphs are therefore necessarily cautionary prolegomena to the argument I want to develop in this chapter. They are not, however, the prelude to a synoptic reading of Lucian's writing. It would take a very different enterprise from mine to come wholly to terms with the pervasively quizzical tone of that writing, whose perpetually shifting mixture of parody, burlesque, pastiche and satire opens up a spectrum of tones that runs from, at one end, an air-ily frivolous, even 'rococo' ethos (the chasing of what Nietzsche called the faded, wind-scattered blossoms of ancient mythology), to the deployment, at the opposite extreme, of what we shall find to be some extremely disturb-ing, 'black' ridicule.[11] The aim of this chapter is not to address the many intricate ways in which Lucian invites, exploits and manipulates some kind of laughing response to the materials of his work (of how, as Eunapius put it, he was 'serious about being ridiculous', σπουδαῖος ἐς τὸ γελασθῆναι – one variant on the ancient notion of the *spoud(ai)ogeloion*, the serio-comic or serio-ludic), but to investigate how he throws a spotlight on the

---

[10] The theatrical language of *Pisc.* 26 includes the verb ὑποδύεσθαι (which can mean to put on a costume/mask), the phrase συναγωνιστὴς καὶ ὑποκριτής (fellow actor), and the unique συγκ-ωμῳδεῖν, which Kokolakis (1960b) 78–80 thinks implies the role of a subordinate actor. For another example of Lucian's teasingly self-deprecating use of the imagery of masks, acting, etc., see *Nigr.* 11; cf. *Salt.* 82–4 for a subtle suggestion of how good acting/mimesis needs to *differ* from the plain 'truth'. On the play of authorial and/or narrative voices in Lucian, see Whitmarsh (2004).

[11] 'Nach diesem letzten Aufglänzen fällt er [der Mythus] zusammen, seine Blätter werden welk, und bald haschen die spöttischen Luciane des Alterthums nach den von allen Winden fortgetragnen, entfärbten und verwüsteten Blumen.' ('Myth crumbles, its leaves wither, and soon the satirical Lucians of antiquity are trying to catch its faded, shrivelled blossoms as they are carried away by all the winds.') *Birth of Tragedy* 10, in Nietzsche (1988) I 74.

existential laughter of 'life and death', actively thematising its possibilities through a whole gamut of references, images and episodes.[12] It is laughter not (principally) as a response to reading Lucian but as a Lucianic leitmotif in its own right which I want to explore.

OTHER AERIAL PERSPECTIVES (OR HEAD IN THE CLOUDS?)

Laughter has an almost pervasive presence in Lucian. His work rarely escapes from a sense that human life itself is in some degree fit only for ridicule. But that generalisation encompasses and simplifies an often complex counter-point between at least three different ways of perceiving absurdity: first, as the aberrations of folly, with its gallery of character-types and their mostly stereotyped traits; second, as the collective ephemerality of human needs and goals, when judged by some 'higher' standard of value; and last, but hardest to pin down, as a flickering conviction that existence *per se* – when observed 'from outside' – is an intrinsically, irredeemably absurd predicament. These three points of view, which in practice are by no means always easy to disentangle within the burlesque texture of Lucian's writing, can be thought of as lying along a scale of increasing distance and/or detachment from life. The argument of this chapter represents one attempt to chart some of the points on that scale, but also to do justice to the imaginative facility with which Lucian can slide along it.

A useful first step towards recognising the gradations and nuances of absurdity in Lucian is to take some orientation from the dialogue *Nigrinus*. This is a work which provides at first sight a relatively stable alignment of (satirical) laughter with a viewpoint that allows certain forms of human life to be held up as risible while exempting other possible lives from this ver-dict. That viewpoint is identified and fixed by reference to the Platonism of the (possibly fictional) philosopher Nigrinus, whose ideas are summarised by the anonymous main speaker of the dialogue. This speaker should not be automatically equated with Lucian; I shall call him 'the convert', since he explains to his companion that his encounter with Nigrinus converted him

---

[12] Eunapius' remark, at *Vitae soph.* 2.1.9 (where, as Branham (1989a) 228 n. 34 rightly points out, Eunapius also claims that Lucian was sometimes simply 'serious'), certainly evokes the notion of being *spoud(ai)ogeloios*, on which see ch. 7, 372–4. Note, however, the similar but pejorative phrasing (ἡ σπουδὴ γελασθῆναι, 'keenness for being laughed at') in Libanius' description of Limenius (as someone who did not *deserve* to be taken seriously) at *Orat.* 1.45. Synoptic accounts of Lucian's comic and/or serio-comic modes are available in Robinson (1979) 1–63, Branham (1989a), esp. ch. 1, Hall (1981), Angeli Bernardini (1994). Relihan (1993) 46–8, 103–14 has suggestive remarks on Lucian's satirical thematics of death. Korus (1984) and Husson (1994) collect Lucianic references to laughter/humour.

from a materialistic lifestyle to philosophy (4). Nigrinus, like a good Platonist (concerned with 'the contemplation of all time and all being'),[13] sees
the world from an implicitly 'cosmic' or god's-eye observation point. When
the convert (supposedly, and symbolically, in search of an 'eye doctor', 2;
cf. 4) visits Nigrinus in the teeming metropolis of Rome, he finds him in
possession of, among other philosophical paraphernalia, a sphere (made of
reeds) that appears to represent the whole universe (2). But in terms of his
studied inspection of human behaviour, Nigrinus later prefers to present
his vantage point not as wholly removed from life but as 'theatrically' raised
above it, albeit in a way whose description carries possible overtones of
having one's head 'in the clouds'. 'Seating myself in a very elevated spot
(σφόδρα που μετέωρος) in, as it were, a massively packed theatre', he
explains, 'I gaze down on what takes place – things which can at the same
time provide much enthralment and laughter (πολλὴν ψυχαγωγίαν καὶ
γέλωτα) but which also make an authentic test of a man's resoluteness.'[14]
So, in what was by Lucian's day an old cliché, stretching all the way back
to Plato's reference in *Philebus* to 'the entire tragedy and comedy of life',
Nigrinus positions himself to scrutinise (and enjoy scrutinising) life as a
sort of stage-show, and a piece of predominantly *comic* drama at that, it
seems.[15] The real theatre is a dangerous place for a Platonist to find himself,
given the articulation in Plato's own writings of various criticisms of its psychologically subversive allure. Furthermore, real *Roman* theatres, together
with hippodromes, are themselves an explicit target of Nigrinus' critique of
the crazily crowded, frantic social world of the city (29). But 'the theatre of
life' or 'theatre of the world' (*theatrum mundi*) is a metaphorical location
where the Platonist can occupy his rightful place as a detached, critical,
knowing spectator. The person who can occupy an 'elevated' seat in this
theatre is, indeed, somewhat akin to the philosopher who has escaped from
the *Republic*'s allegorical cave. It is therefore appropriate that the convert in
Nigrinus speaks of the liberation which philosophy afforded him in terms
unmistakably reminiscent of that allegory. 'I felt a pleasure as if I was looking up from the murky air of my previous life into the clear open sky and

[13] Pl. *Rep.* 6.486a; cf. ch. 7, 337.
[14] *Nigr.* 18; for the concept of 'enthralment', *psuchagōgia*, in this context, cf. *ibid.* 21. The word *meteōros* that describes Nigrinus' 'high' seat has obvious overtones of philosophical elevation above the earthly or mundane: it is used at the very beginning of the work (1) and again in 5 to describe the effect of inspiring uplift which Nigrinus had on the convert. But Lucian would expect his ideal readers to recall its emphatically parodic use in Ar. *Clouds*, esp. 228, 360, 490, 1284, for the 'airy', head-in-the-clouds realm which Socrates' mind there inhabits, echoed at *Prom. es* 6. Cf. the ambivalent, semi-satirical use of the term at Lucian, *Icarom.* 1, 3, 5, 11, 23, *Menip.* 21.
[15] The life-as-theatre or *theatrum mundi* motif recurs in sections 20, 25, 30. On 'the tragedy and comedy of life' at Pl. *Phlb.* 50a, see ch. 7, 337.

a great light' (4, ἔχαιρον δ' αὖ ὥσπερ ἐκ ζοφεροῦ τινος ἀέρος τοῦ βίου τοῦ πρόσθεν ἐς αἰθρίαν τε καὶ μέγα φῶς ἀναβλέπων).

The convert's escape from the 'Cave', with the help of Nigrinus' shining example, involves coming to see that the things most people value (wealth, reputation, power, status), including his own previous self, deserve to be treated as laughably contemptible, *katagelasta* (4, together with the cognate verb).[16] So the work's 'Platonism' seems securely tied to a transcendent framework of value that rises above the bustling, competitive, deluded world of social hierarchy and materialism. But there is something more Lucianic than authentically Platonist about the way in which the work turns this two-world model into a source of so much laughter. Nigrinus invites the convert to join him in looking down on the sordid realm of false goods, and the convert's report, eagerly received at one remove by his companion, apparently invites Lucian's readers in turn to share their perspective. Nigrinus specifically picks out as 'laughable', in increasing degrees, the rich (21, γελοῖοι), their flatterers (22, γελοιότεροι), and, worse still, philosophers-turned-flatterers (24–5, ἔτι . . . γελοιότερα). As so often with Lucian, philosophy, under different guises, supplies both the means to criticise life and one of the main objects of that critique. But in effect the whole of Nigrinus' scornful survey of life at Rome is an exercise in moral derision. Later on, the convert cannot stop himself laughing (Lucian, as will repeatedly emerge, likes making something of the *compulsion* to laugh) when he listens to Nigrinus' account of Roman obsessions with funerals and wills (30), and Nigrinus is said also to have 'ridiculed heartily' (*diagelan*) those with an exorbitant addiction to the pleasures of the palate (33).[17] Centre stage in the drama of folly which the Platonist Nigrinus enjoys watching with such lofty yet cheerful disdain are clearly all the corrupt, body-tethered desires that impel human lives.

But what does that leave the Platonists themselves to value? Not much is said on this. At the outset of his discourse to the convert, Nigrinus praises the 'poverty', freedom and simplicity of the lives supposedly led by Athenians, providing the work with a basic contrast between philosophical poverty-with-contentment, on the one hand, and all the crazy, materialist

[16] The friend's initial description of him, at 1, pictures the convert as displaying a newly found *loftiness* (cf. μετέωρος), anticipating what we will later hear about Nigrinus himself (n. 14 above); cf. the adj. ὑπεροπτικός (1), a term which has at least overtones of 'looking down on' (as well as 'overlooking', i.e. ignoring).

[17] How far *Nigrinus* offers a distinctively anti-Roman view is a moot point; cf. Swain (1996) 315–17, 323, in the context of a larger treatment of Lucian's cultural identity/allegiances. For Lucianic references to the compulsion to laugh, compare e.g. *Menip.* 17 (*bis*), *Peregr.* 7, 8, 37, *Dial. mort.* 1.1, with 448, 465 below.

cravings of social life on the other: between Athens (here a quaintly idealised symbol of provincial tranquillity) and Rome (the wicked metropolis whose streets are like an open sewer of vice, 16). But if we ask what it is that makes the pursuit of wealth, power and sensual gratification laughable or absurd, the dialogue itself does not expressly tell us. It seems, for sure, to presuppose certain philosophical standards – truth, (inner) freedom, detachment from worldly ambition and bodily desires – but apart from noting the vulnerability of material goods to chance, *tuchē* (20), it does not pause to explain what is so ludicrous about living by this-worldly values. What exactly is it that Nigrinus can see from that high, 'airy' seat of his? The work is not without ambiguities and paradoxes that bear on this question. For one thing, the convert prefaces his account of Nigrinus' thoughts by describing himself self-consciously as a (bad) actor (8–12), an idea which sets up a somewhat ironic interplay with the work's later life-as-drama imagery: are we being given authentic philosophy at all, or just a poor *impersonation* of it, a lofty tragedy rendered comic by the actor's incompetence?[18] For another, the convert starts out by oscillating between practically weeping for the loss of his erstwhile earthly goals and, on the other hand, learning from Nigrinus to *scoff* at their worthlessness (4); eventually he will end up shedding a new kind of tears (35) and wavering between pleasure and tears (37). Where exactly in all this does the psychology of philosophical 'laughter' belong, especially when, as I have already noted, Platonism is not a school of thought traditionally associated with habits of mockery? Here we might recall that while Plato's own writings contain many subtle reflections on laughter, including a sense of its elusive presence within the personality of Socrates, the *Republic* suggests that the benighted condition of life in the human cave is, if anything, an object more suitable for pity than laughter.[19] The *echt*-Platonic Platonist may attach small significance to the terrestrial realm of existence, but he cannot afford to relegate it to the level of the irredeemably laughable. To adapt the theatrical imagery of *Nigrinus*, we might say that the present world cannot be viewed by such a person as a merely absurd spectacle in its own right, since he needs to understand it as a 'rehearsal' for another, higher world. This does not, of course, mean in itself that Lucian (or his contemporaries) could not

---

[18] Whitmarsh (2001) 265–79 offers one reading of this and other paradoxes of 'theatricality' in the work.

[19] See esp. *Rep.* 7.518b (cf. ch. 6 n. 48), which offers a guarded judgement and strictly speaking applies to those having trouble adjusting to life outside the cave; but it certainly comes nowhere near Nigrinus' lofty derision: Adam (1963) II 97, 'more of pity than of malice', hits the mark, though his reference to a 'philosophical smile' unnecessarily waters down the force of the verb *gelan*.

have conceived of a Platonism of Nigrinus-like derision. But it adds to the reasons for hesitating before taking the Platonist colouring of the work as a wholly cogent explanation for its gelastic thrust.

There is a further detail worth highlighting here. Lucian's convert speaks of the overwhelming effect on him of Nigrinus' words as a (temporary) 'bewitchment' (the verb κηλεῖν), a powerfully physical faintness or dizziness, a strong 'blow' and deep 'wound', and a drug-induced 'possession' or 'madness' (35–8). This cluster of images carries a rich history of usage in earlier literature, but a history partly related to things other than philosophy: erotic desire, the experience of song/poetry, and the spellbinding impact of persuasive speech in general could be characterised in such vocabulary.[20] In this context, the imagery depicts a supposedly passionate, life-transforming conversion to philosophy, but it makes the convert sound more stricken or stunned than rationally enlightened, as one might perhaps expect a true Platonist to be. Indeed, *Nigrinus* ends with the convert's friend admitting that he too has been infected, like someone bitten by a person himself previously the victim of a mad dog's bite, an obvious allusion to Alcibiades' image, in Plato's *Symposium* (217e), of the 'snake bite' of philosophy he had received from Socrates. Bewitchment, tears, blows, wounds, drugs, madness and even dog bites! In the final sections of *Nigrinus* we seem to come perilously close to a parody of the lexicon of philosophical possession.[21] Whatever its strange blend of mockery and seriousness may add up to, *Nigrinus* purports to assert the ridiculous status of many but not all nonphilosophical lives. In doing so, it dramatises one kind of philosophical laughter without making it entirely clear where that laughter might start or finish. We are left far from sure where Nigrinus goes, or what he does, when not occupying his elevated seat in the theatre of life – or why, when 'Athens' is so unequivocally superior to 'Rome', he bothers to spend any time at all in the latter. It surely cannot be simply because Rome provides such ample material for the pleasure of 'laughter' (21). Is it his equivalent of the *Republic*'s return to the cave? Or is Lucian's version of the Platonist just a thinly disguised surrogate for the laughter-impulse in his own writing, an impulse that may be clearer about how to target others than to be explicit

---

[20] *Nigr.* 35 specifically recalls the impact of Odysseus' (quasi-poetic) narratives on the Phaeacians at *Od.* 11.333–4, 13.1–2, but its language is also reminiscent of the list of erotic(?) symptoms in Sappho 31 *PLF*. With Nigrinus' 'dizziness', *iliggos* (35), compare Socrates' reaction to Protagoras at Pl. *Prot.* 339e (as though hit by a boxer!). Gorg. *Helen* 14 (fr. 11.14 DK) is the *locus classicus* for the imagery of *logos*-administered drugs found in *Nigr.* 37.

[21] Cf. Robinson (1979) 53–4 for related observations. Hall (1981) 157–64 (cf. 242–51) surveys various readings of *Nigrinus*; she is reluctant to detect irony in the work, but also refuses to treat Lucian as a real 'convert' to philosophy. Cf. Anderson (1978) for further views.

about its self-motivations? After all, Lucian's authorial voice in the preface to the work expresses the fear of seeming 'ridiculous' by taking 'an owl to Athens', that is, offering Nigrinus a superfluous echo of his own philosophical voice. But if Nigrinus is no more than a Lucianic character, where does that leave the dialogue's enthusiastic idea of 'conversion'? And if the very idea of philosophical/Platonic dialogue has been appropriated by Lucian for his own hybrid and layered purposes (see above on *Prometheus es*), then the preface to *Nigrinus* starts to look less like an authentic expression of philosophical respect than a case of Lucian laughing at himself, as it were, in the mirror.

From the point of view of my concerns in this chapter, *Nigrinus* remains a work that resists a conclusive reading. Apparently simple on the surface (if, at any rate, one chooses to treat Nigrinus as a real figure), it contains just enough hints of uncertainty to leave us wondering who exactly is laughing at whom – and just which seat they occupy in the 'theatre of life' that enables them to do so. But to enlarge and enrich the interpretation of existential laughter in Lucian, we need to seek clarification of what makes the difference between being 'inside' and 'outside' the theatre, between being a spectator and an actor in that theatre, and, indeed, between laughing at life and death themselves. It is a remarkable fact about Lucian's comic-cum-satirical repertoire that the perspective on life 'from death' is almost an obsession of his. For him, death is the very reverse of a taboo subject: it is, in a peculiar way, both a mediator and an object of laughter. It supplies, most obviously, the setting for a number of his works, not least the collection of thirty *Dialogues of the Dead* (*Dialogi mortuorum*), in which a whole host of figures – human, divine, mythological and fictional – meet in Hades and enact a burlesque life-in-death existence.[22] The world of Hades is, of course, one of the oldest features of the Greek mythological imagination, and Lucian had precedents in Old Comedy, Menippean satire and elsewhere for his wry take on the twilight zone of the afterlife. But he nonetheless makes something distinctive out of it, turning it into a 'carnivalised nether world', as Bakhtin called it. That distinctiveness has much to do with the overt thematisation of laughter as, so to speak, a life-and-death phenomenon.[23]

One small vignette out of many to illustrate this point in a preliminary way can be found in *Dialogues of the Dead* 17, where the recently

[22] See ch. 7, 384, for one example.
[23] Bakhtin (1984) 142 refers to Lucian's 'carnivalised nether world' in immediate reference to *Menippus*. Cf. n. 53 below.

deceased character Callidemides is accosted in the underworld by Zenophantus, a former parasite. The latter asks Callidemides how he died; while waiting for the answer, he recalls that he himself had choked to death by over-eating at his patron's table. Since parasites are specialists in laughter-making, and since one can (literally and metaphorically) 'choke' when laughing, Lucian is playing allusively here on a suitably overdetermined death for Zenophantus.[24] In answer to the latter's enquiry, Callidemides proceeds to narrate how he mistakenly drank the poison he had intended for Ptoeodorus, a rich, childless man who had promised to leave his property to Callidemides. Zenophantus, in (ironic) keeping with his parasite's credentials, finds Callidemides' story hilarious, as he explains when the latter asks him, 'why are you laughing? you shouldn't laugh at a *friend*' (2). He calls Callidemides' account 'droll' or 'witty', as though it were not accidentally amusing but actually a well-formed joke.[25] In response to the question of how Ptoeodorus himself reacted to the incident, Callidemides (who observed what ensued with the post-mortem vision sometimes allowed the dead in Lucian) recounts that the old man too, once he had grasped the situation, broke out into laughter – an expression, clearly enough, of relief and moral satisfaction. But what about Zenophantus? Is his amusement spontaneously amoral, does it savour the twist of poetic justice, or does it dramatically betoken a larger sense of existential absurdity, implying that all reports of death can be quickly converted into jokes? A simple decision seems impossible, since Lucian's text contains no direct judgement on its own anomalous profusion of laughter in the land of the dead.

However interpreted, this miniature scenario yields a fable of poetic justice that nonetheless functions, for some of those involved, as a sort of comedy of errors. In its small way it draws attention to something about Lucian's thematisation of laughter that should not be taken for granted, namely its capacity to transmute what ordinarily counts as horrific – choking, attempted murder, death by poison at the dinner table – into an occasion for somebody's unabashed mirth, thus setting up an internal incongruity of values and mentalities. This Lucianic collapse of the potentially ghastly into the obtrusively ludicrous contradicts a traditional

---

[24] The same verb, ἀποπνίγεσθαι, is used (quasi-metaphorically) of choking from laughter at Lucian, *Iup. Trag.* 31 (first epigraph to this chapter), and literally for the supposed death from laughter of the comic poet Philemon at Lucian, *Macrob.* 25 (= Philemon test. 5 *PCG*), on which see ch. 1 n. 21. On parasites and laughter, see ch. 3 n. 101.

[25] The adj. *asteios* and its cognates are often associated with deliberate witticisms and amusing anecdotes: see e.g. Ar. *Frogs* 5, Xen. *Cyr.* 2.2.12, 8.4.23, Arist. *Rhet.* 3.11, 1412a17–b32 (with ch. 6 n. 168), Theophr. *Char.* 19.9; cf. ch. 10 n. 35 for a carefully adapted Christian use of the term. Lucian, *Charon* 6 (446 below) provides another instance of laughter at sudden death.

conception of 'the comic' or 'the ridiculous' like Aristotle's which tethers laughter to mistakes or faults that are free from 'pain or destruction'.[26] The effect is compounded by the impression which runs through the *Dialogues of the Dead* as a whole that there is no real difference between life and death. For comico-satirical purposes at least, one can use the (fictive) perspective of death to rerun life and lay bare its absurdities for all to see.

To probe this aspect of Lucian's work, I want to consider the dialogue *Charon*, which is simultaneously a divine burlesque (displaying, in certain respects, a farcically anthropomorphised conception of the gods) and a story of the absurd appearance that human life as a whole can assume when observed from a god's-eye view of the world (a god's-eye view as *imagined*, of course, by humans themselves). Complicating and spicing this combination, however, is a further element, the laughter of a figure who is neither god nor mortal: the grim infernal ferryman Charon himself. Lucian organises these various possibilities of laughter into a dialectical exercise or dramatised essay in gelastics. Weaving together threads of mythology, epic poetry, drama, Herodotean history and philosophy, he produces a fabric which manages to be ingeniously facetious and teasingly thought-provoking at the same time.

A salient, immediately puzzling note of laughter is sounded right at the start of the piece. 'Why are you laughing, Charon?' are the dialogue's very first words, introducing what will turn out to be something of a leitmotif in the work. The question (whose precise answer gets deferred for a little while) is posed by Hermes when he comes across Charon paying an unprecedented visit to earth. Charon's usual job is one that would hardly be thought to provide much opportunity for laughter. Merriness of any kind is nowhere ascribed to him in any of the other eight works of Lucian's (including three *Dialogues of the Dead*) in which he appears, and his traditional persona in both literature and art is unremittingly bleak (or worse).[27] He is employed, after all, in the land of the proverbially 'unsmiling' dead, where, as he proceeds to tell Hermes, all his previous experience of human beings has been of their tearful lamentations when they descend to Hades. So Charon has obtained permission to spend a day in the land of the living, in order to find out just what it is about life that makes humans consider death such a traumatic event. Hermes, on the other hand, is a deity with some good

---

[26] Though made in passing, the judgement of Barasch (1997) 188 that 'the transformation of gruesome details into risible images is perhaps the core of Lucian's satirical literature' makes a shrewd point which is highly pertinent to my argument in this chapter. Aristotle's definition of 'the comic' (τὸ γελοῖον) is at *Poet.* 5.1449a34–7: see ch. 6, 326–8.

[27] Sourvinou-Inwood (1986) surveys both visual and literary representations.

credentials for laughter: he is prominent among the Olympians who laugh at the sexual exposure of Ares and Aphrodite at the hands of Hephaestus in *Odyssey* 8 (and Lucian himself elsewhere highlights Hermes' position in that notorious episode); the *Homeric Hymn to Hermes* pictures him chuckling as a precocious child on the very first day of his existence; and he has associations with theft and deception which, not surprisingly, had proved attractive to comic poets.[28] Moreover, Hermes' composite mythological persona is too enterprising and inventive to make him a whole-hearted devotee of Charon's morose devaluation of earthly pleasures – a point nicely picked up in Lucian's *Cataplus* 1–2 (to which I shall return), where Charon crabbily conjectures that Hermes' habitual tardiness in bringing down souls to Hades reflects the god's addiction to pleasure (wrestling, music, discussion . . . and *theft*) and his aversion to the stygian gloom of the lower world. What, then, should we expect from an encounter between these two very different figures from opposite reaches of the mythological universe, when they meet on the intermediate territory of earth? And what exactly *was* Charon laughing about?

The two of them are, as it happens, old acquaintances, since one of Hermes' regular duties is that of the 'escort of souls', *psuchopompos*, on the journey down to Hades (as, most famously, at *Odyssey* 24.9–14). In that capacity, which will be mentioned again near the end of the dialogue (22, 24), he has often been on Charon's ferry (where he appears in Lucian's own *Dialogi mortuorum* and elsewhere).[29] Charon reminds him how well he is always treated there, being allowed to sleep or chat to passengers instead of made to help with the rowing. Through this and other considerations Charon persuades Hermes to act as his 'tourist guide' for the day, an image drolly underlined by Lucian's vocabulary: human life will be encapsulated in a brief spell of divine sightseeing, though Charon's difficulties with the unwonted daylight make him 'blink' like a figure emerging from the cave in Plato's *Republic*.[30] Hermes is not only well travelled but by 'profession' a

---

[28] Lucian's use of the Ares–Aphrodite story (see ch. 2, 77–86) is at *Dial D.* 21.1, which starts with Hermes being *asked* (by Apollo) 'why are you laughing?' (Note two further occurrences of this question in Lucian: *Dial. mort.* 13.2–3, where Diogenes the Cynic laughs at the folly of the Greeks and Alexander the Great; and *Vit. Auctio* 13, where Democritus laughs at the vanity of all human endeavours: see ch. 7, 363–4.) On the *Homeric Hymn to Hermes*, see ch. 3, 100–3. The comic potential of Hermes' association with theft and wiliness is reflected at e.g. Ar. *Peace* 362–728, *Wealth* 1139–58; at Lucian, *Catapl.* 4 Aeacus refers to Hermes' penchant for theft as a matter of 'games' or 'tricks' (*paidiai*).

[29] Lucian, *Dial. mort.* 2, 14, 20; cf. *Catapl.* 1–3 etc., with 454–5 below.

[30] ξεναγεῖν (1), περιηγεῖσθαι/περιήγησις (1–2), connote 'tourism': compare their ironic use in Hades at *Dial. mort.* 5.1, 6.1. Charon's blinking is described by the verb ἀμβλυώττειν, which occurs also at Pl. *Rep.* 7.516e, 517d (but with reference to one *returning* to the cave's darkness from the light outside); cf. 6.508c–d. See 437–8 above for a different Lucianic reminiscence of the cave.

guide and escort, so an ideal companion for Charon. He will also be taking the day off, without permission, from his service to Zeus, which fits with his image as a sly deceiver and malingerer.[31] But this also makes him afraid of possible punishment. He recalls Hephaestus' account of being thrown from Olympus by Zeus (at *Iliad* 1.590–4), an account which had made Hera smile and had immediately preceded the gods' collective laughter at the sight of the bustling god of fire playing the role of divine butler.[32] Lucian uses this reminiscence, very near the outset, to position his dialogue concisely in relation to a paradigm of divine burlesque, but a burlesque set within and against a context of Olympian gravity. Yet the Homeric echo does not so much provide a clue to the register of the Lucianic text as create a quizzical effect of uncertainty. Is Homer's own epic world being 'sent up', or is Lucian implicitly recuperating a possibility of tonal depth and subtlety for which the *Iliad* itself, no less, supplies the ultimate model?

To make Charon's sightseeing as extensive as possible, Hermes himself takes specific inspiration from, but also outdoes, a Homeric precedent. Extrapolating from the story of how Otus and Ephialtes piled Pelion on Ossa (ironically, a story of an assault on the gods), he adds two more mountains, Oeta and Parnassus, for good measure. He does this to produce a suitably towering viewing station, a quasi-theatrical stageset, and a piece of geographical 'architecture':[33] Homer is here spoken of as the great masterbuilder, *architektōn* (4), in keeping with his traditional standing in Greek culture and education as an expert in all fields of knowledge. Authorially, the moment is a nicely oblique exercise in literary self-imaging: Parnassus, sacred to Apollo and the Muses, is a mountain of poetic inspiration, so its placing at the pinnacle of Hermes' geological construction makes a witty claim for Lucian's own creative ambition. Dramatically and thematically, the extended mountain mass enables Charon and Hermes to watch the human world from a supremely aerial vantage point, making people themselves look vanishingly small and turning whole cities into marks on the earth (their 'dens' or lairs, 6). Spatial remoteness is here figurative of detached, compendious contemplation of the object under inspection, just as with Menippus' scrutiny of earth from the moon in *Icaromenippus*,

---

[31] Two partial precedents for this image are Ar. *Peace* 376–81, *Wealth* 1099–1170.

[32] Lucian's Hermes (*Charon* 1) recalls and connects both parts of the scene: the story of the expulsion and the laughter aroused by the god's bustling wine-service. See ch. 2, 58–64.

[33] The story of Otus and Ephialtes is at Hom. *Od.* 11.305–20. Theatrical overtones of Lucian's scene: the noun *mēchanē* in 5 perhaps suggests a theatrical 'machine' (of the *deus ex machina* type); Hermes and Charon 'trundle' the mountains around (the verb ἐπικυλίνδειν, 3 and 5), a term which may have theatrical resonance (cf. the *simplex* at Ar. *Kn.* 1249).

a scrutiny that gave him an enlarged sense of human absurdity.[34] Unlike
Menippus, however, Charon lacks the 'inside' understanding of the human
scene that would allow him to take advantage of the grandly external perspective. He is dissatisfied with the synoptic but distant view offered him
by Hermes: 'I didn't just want to look at cities and mountains the way they
appear in paintings' (6), he protests. He needs to get closer to the human
scale itself, to know more precisely what people actually do and say. Only
with this more intimate scrutiny can he find out their real mode of existence
and the values that motivate it. And to reinforce his request, he belatedly
explains to Hermes what was making him laugh when they first met.

He was laughing, he says (6), because he had just overheard an encounter
between two friends. One had invited the other to dinner on the following day, but the guest, immediately after accepting the invitation with
eagerness, was killed by a falling roof-tile. Rather as with Zenophantus'
response to Callidemides' fatality at *Dial. mort.* 17 (442 above), Charon had
found the thought of this 'broken promise' hilarious, enjoying it, despite
its 'deadly' seriousness, just like someone hearing a good (or perhaps a bad)
joke: he reacts, for instance, just like Strepsiades in Aristophanes' *Clouds*
when hearing about a lizzard that defecates on Socrates from a roof.[35] The
question posed at the start of Lucian's *Charon* receives its answer, but it
is an answer with a curious twist. When Charon starts to discover the
conditions of human life, he begins to see death itself in a new light, as
an unpredictable impingement or contingency. But far from sympathising
with human reactions to death (all those tears and lamentations), he finds
the relationship instantly amusing. Observing from outside the interplay
of (self-)ignorance, chance and ephemerality, he is struck, it seems, by the
absurdity of human existence. But his quasi-Democritean laughter is possible precisely because his viewpoint is *only* external. He wants to discover
what matters to human beings, but he seems utterly incapable of sharing
their perspective and seeing why they react to certain things the way they
typically do. He cannot combine an inside with an external understanding
of their existence. When he complains to Hermes that the view from the

---

[34] *Icarom.* 11–12: see 429–31 above. The idea of spatially comprehensive contemplation of human life
is already anticipated at Pl. *Tht.* 174e, *Phd.* 109a–b (the famous 'frogs round a pond' image); on the
correlative of temporally extended contemplation, see ch. 7 n. 79, with Dodds (1965) 7–8 for further
instances of both points.

[35] With Charon's words ἥσθην εἰς ὑπερβολήν, 'I find that incredibly amusing', compare Ar. *Clouds*
174, 1240 (with 1238, 1241), *Peace* 1066, all of which use the same expression (ἥσθην) to explain a
speaker's laughter at something (supposedly serious) he has just heard; cf. *Kn.* 696 (with ch. 5 n.
104), Men. *Dysc.* 965 (ch. 8 n. 24), and the hendiadys ἥσθη . . . καὶ ἐπεγέλασεν, 'laughed with
pleasure', at ps.-Pl. *Amat.* 134b.

mountaintop is too remote, Hermes responds (in another ironic gesture of Homeric emulation) by removing the 'mist' from his eyes and allowing him, as Athena had done with Diomedes at *Iliad* 5.127–8, to see the difference between gods and men (7). What Hermes cannot do, however, is give Charon an authentically anthropic sensibility. The ferryman is permitted to *watch* life close-up, but his sense of its absurdity remains entirely bloodless.

Charon's position intensifies as the work unfolds. He and Hermes, yet again in obviously but hyperbolically reworked Homeric fashion, look down on earth in a sort of *teichoskopia*, like the Trojan elders surveying the battlefield from the city walls in *Iliad* 3 (which supplies a cue at the start of section 8). What they witness turns out to be a succession of individuals from the archaic world of the sixth century. First is the athlete Milon, fêted for his victories and in particular for the feat of carrying a whole bull: 'he'll soon provide us with something to laugh about, when he's on my boat and unable to lift a gnat, never mind a bull!', exclaims Charon. Then they observe Cyrus the Great, founder of the Achaemenid Persian Empire, followed by the Lydian Croesus, on whose conversations with the Athenian sage Solon, partly modelled on Herodotus, they eavesdrop, noting how Solon 'laughs with contempt' (*katagelan*) at Croesus' infatuation with wealth. When the spectacle of Croesus' folly has been duly noted, attention returns to Cyrus. Hermes tells Charon that he has heard from Clotho, one of the Moirae (Fates), that Cyrus will die a grisly death at the hands of a woman, Tomyris, from the central Asian tribe of the Massagetae. Informed that she will behead Cyrus and put the head in a wineskin full of blood (after which Cyrus' son Cambyses will rule, before eventually going mad), Charon exclaims, 'how hilarious!' (ὢ πολλοῦ γέλωτος, 13). Lucian has too often been treated as a merely lighthearted writer, but the clash of tone here is patently and challengingly grotesque. Charon, it begins to transpire, may resemble the Olympians in his capacity to observe human life with detachment, but he entirely lacks the compensating factors of personal interest and even pity that can complicate, and sometimes soften, divine attitudes to events on earth.

Charon not only speaks, then, with the voice of death. He *laughs* on behalf of death. He is what we might call a personification of death by mythological proxy. But he has only discovered laughter by leaving his usual domain in Hades and acquiring some (superficial) familiarity with human life up above. We are given no encouragement to suppose that Charon ever laughs in his normal role down under: on the contrary, his usual image in Lucian, as elsewhere, is that of an incorrigibly mirthless figure. His glee at what he learns on his day-trip to earth consequently assumes the character of an eruption of amoral satisfaction at the sheer incongruity between life and death. The incident which caused him to laugh just before his encounter with Hermes depends on nothing more than the extreme contingency and the accidental mechanism of the individual's death, not on any personal insight into the situation. Likewise, he enjoys the thought of Milon's death for the pure disparity between physical strength during life and physical insubstantiality in Hades. And his mirth at the prediction of Cyrus' death seems to involve a thrill at the raw corporeal details of the beheading, as his behaviour a little later in the work will confirm.

As we follow the pattern of Charon's laughter further, one important reference point to keep in mind is the mockery targeted by the Cynics against conventional human values. In Lucian's own writings this is a prominent motif, especially in *Dialogi mortuorum*. In Chapter 7 I quoted from the first of these dialogues, where Diogenes sends a message to Menippus that when he has had his fill of laughter at earthly folly and delusions, not least those of wrangling philosophers, he should come down to Hades, where he will find even more to laugh at in the spectacle of former tyrants and such like lamenting their lost power and wealth.[36] It soon emerges in this passage, however, that it is not just the privileged few but practically all human beings whose (false) values are the target of Cynic derision. Even so, as I argued in that earlier chapter, such images of the existential stance of Diogenes and his followers do not encode a pure sense of 'the absurd', since they focus on (near-ubiquitously) erroneous human values but still do not empty human life of all meaning or value. Cynic laughter, which Lucian frequently assimilates into his work but never definitively makes his own, is a contemptuous matter of *katagelan* (literally 'laughing down') and combines two related strands: it mocks others, both in life and in death, for the hollowness and self-deception of their aspirations, and it scoffs with a completely carefree spirit of 'freedom' at death itself.[37] But this Cynic

---

[36] *Dial. mort.* 1.1; cf. ch. 7, 384. With the idea of having one's fill of laughter (ἱκανῶς . . . καταγεγέλασ-ται), note the similar wording at Lucian, *Icarom.* 19 (quoted on 430 above).

[37] For Lucian's liking for this last theme see *Dial. mort.* 1.2 (Menippus always laughs, and mocks charlatan philosophers), 2.3 and 3.1–2 (Menippus the only person who laughs, jokes and even sings (cf. ch. 7 n. 92), while others grieve, in Hades), 4.2 (Diogenes and Menippus the only people who laugh when entering Hades), 6.6 (Menippus mocking tyrants in Hades), 11.5 (Diogenes mocking the dead), 13.2–3 (Diogenes laughing at the Greeks' belief in Alexander's divinity and at dead Alexander's own conceit), 20.9 (Menippus the only person laughing among the newly dead), 22.1, 5 (Diogenes and Crates laughing at behaviour of dead), 29.3 (Diogenes laughing in Hades). Cf. Micyllus, the quasi-Cynic cobbler, at *Catapl.* 3, 20, with 459–60 below, and *Menip.* 17–18, with its repeated reference to laughter (Menippus' and Diogenes') at the sight of death's treatment of former rulers etc. But for Lucian's ambivalence towards (some) Cynics, see esp. *Peregrinus* (462–70 below), and e.g. *Pisc.*

stance retains some recognisably human options, however radically modified, since it allows for adherence to such values as virtuous self-discipline, freedom and living in accordance with 'nature'. Charon's outlook, on the other hand, is (imagined as being) an amorally death-*relishing* point of view. Admittedly, the two positions converge to some extent on amusement at the disproportion between the seriousness with which people take themselves and the sheer nullity to which death (supposedly) reduces them. But in the case of the Cynics what is involved is an uncompromisingly ethical evaluation of this disproportion; hence their targeting, in particular, of the rich, powerful, or intellectually conceited, i.e. those who succumb most spectacularly to self-deception or self-ignorance about their earthly assets. Charon, by contrast, comes closer to laughing at the brute fact of death's impingement on life: the figure killed by the roof-tile is too anonymous to be anything other than a kind of 'everyman', the circumstances of his death as meaninglessly accidental as they could be.[38] Charon takes conspicuously callous delight in the thought of gruesome physical sufferings. Hearing of the fate (betrayal and crucifixion) that awaits the Samian tyrant Polycrates, he urges Clotho, 'Burn them, cut off their heads and crucify them, so they can learn they are human!', gleefully running together the destinies of Cyrus and Polycrates.[39] 'Meanwhile,' he adds, 'let them be raised up all the higher, so that their fall will be all the greater and more painful! *I* will then laugh when I recognise each of them naked on my little skiff.' While Hermes shows at least a flicker of sympathy in this passage (he speaks of Polycrates' 'wretched fall from prosperity [ἄθλιος ἐκπεσὼν τῆς εὐδαιμονίας . . .] in a mere instant of time', 14), Charon continues to treat the whole matter like a huge joke, a joke that implicates *all* human existence and yet is enjoyed by someone who patently lacks any (human) values at all.

   We need to tread cautiously, however, in assessing the sadistic force of Charon's pleasure in imagining extremes of bodily torment and the death that follows them. While it is tempting to regard this aspect of his mentality as heightening his non-human (and inhuman) status, there is wider

---

45, 48, *Menip.* 4 (where Cynic-type figures are condemned together with other philosophers, yet Menippus himself, and Diogenes [18], are treated approvingly), with Goulet-Cazet (1990) 2763–8, Nesselrath (1998), (2001) 147–9 for various assessments and Relihan (1996) 277–80 on the shifting status of Lucian's Menippus figure(s). Cf. Niehues-Pröbsting (1979) 195–201, 211–13, Hall (1981) 171–2, Kullmann (1995) 91–5.

[38] The falling roof-tile recurs as a motif in one of Montaigne's remarkable meditations on death, *Essais* I 20: see Montaigne (1969) 132, with translation in Screech (1991) 96.

[39] *Charon* 14. 'Burn' may allude to torture; cf. burning out the eyes at Hdt. 7.18, Pl. *Grg.* 473c, *Rep.* 2.361e, 10.613e. Hdt. 3.125 regards the method by which Polycrates was killed as too gruesome to describe. On the tone of *Charon*, cf. Relihan (1993) 114–16.

Lucianic evidence for the sardonic appeal of such nakedly gloating *Schaden-freude*. This whole seam in Lucian's writing connects with a much older Greek awareness of the disturbing but psychologically deep-seated connections between certain kinds of laughter and cruelty.[40] I shall return to this subject later in the chapter when I consider the strikingly sadistic laughter manifested, and authorially endorsed, in the *Death of Peregrinus*. But staying for the moment with *Charon*, it is important to watch how the eponymous ferryman's laughter subsequently becomes attached to, but also modulates into, a more contextualised, quasi-Cynic evaluation of the mistaken values that underwrite (most) human lives. In the later sections of *Charon* (15–21), Hermes turns his visitor's attention to the human masses. The two figures observe the frantic, troubled existence of people perpetually surrounded by hopes and fears, their lives suspended by the delicate, soon-to-snap threads spun for them by the Moirae. Charon finds the spectacle 'totally ridiculous' (παγγέλοια, 16), and Hermes now agrees. Human aspirations and hopes, if harboured with all seriousness, are contemptibly laughable beyond words (καταγέλαστα, 17), he remarks, especially given the ubiquitous failure to heed the warnings brought by the 'messengers of death' in the form of diseases and mortal dangers of many kinds. Charon is puzzled how people attach any value at all to life: if even tyrants live amidst constant threats, what hope for the rest (18)? Everyone's existence, he remarks, is a 'bubble', bound sooner or later to burst (19). But Charon's tone has started to change in a curious way. He now suggests shouting out a warning (like a street-corner philosopher, but on a cosmic scale) to the whole species, telling people to give up their futile strivings and to live with a self-control (*sōphrosunē*, following Hermes' cue in 17) that accepts the final certainty of death (20). Hermes tells him that self-ignorance and self-deception are so rife that such a warning would be ineffectual, while it would be superfluous in the case of those very few individuals who already know the truth and contemptuously deride (*katagelan*) the worthlessness of life (20–1). The work concludes (22–4) with further observations in the same vein, this time on the pointlessness of funerary practices (as if the dry bones of the dead could drink libations, exclaims Charon) and on the ephemeral nature even of supposedly great cities (they too 'die', says Hermes), a topic which forms an element of ring composition with the aerial perspective of section 6. When the two figures slip quietly away at the end to resume their normal responsibilities (with a promise from Hermes that he will soon be down to Hades with his next batch of the dead), the subtext is

---

[40] See ch. 1, 11–12, 25–30.

clear. Nothing is about to change; the nature of human life will continue on the same lines as before.

Although, then, a sense of generalised absurdity continues to surface when the dialogue's focus shifts from supposedly successful individuals to the great mass of human beings, there is no doubt that the tone of the conversation becomes more sober and moralistic from section 15 onwards. Charon, in particular, no longer shows any signs of wanting to *enjoy* seeing the price that many people pay for their folly and vanity; and, as I mentioned, he follows Hermes in identifying at least one positive virtue – *sōphrosunē*, here an existentially extended modesty of aims – which a human life might in principle put into practice. Charon's description of the 'bubble' of life reminds Hermes of the famous Homeric comparison of the generations of mankind to the annual growth of leaves on trees, and Charon himself seems to become at least a little sympathetic to their plight: hence his idea (comic though its 'literal' resonance is) of shouting out a warning. Similarly with Hermes, whose lengthy speech in section 17 contains a rich interplay of imagery in the sustained metaphor of death's unheeded 'messengers' and 'assistants' (ἄγγελοι . . . καὶ ὑπηρέται) and the accompanying cameos of human blindness. The latter include the man who builds a new house but does not even live to have dinner in it (a variant on the anecdote Charon had told, and been so amused by, at 6), and the person who has such high but empty hopes for his newborn son ('he notices the man, father of an Olympic-winning athlete, who enjoys his son's success, but he fails to notice the neighbour who is burying a young child'). All in all, a degree of pathos seems to displace laughter in the later pages of the work. After the blatantly burlesque features of the original, mountain-stacking scenario, and the gloating in which Charon indulges for much of the dialogue, there are only a few, restricted touches of obvious humour towards the end, none of them with much thematic weight. It is as though the longer Charon and Hermes survey the scene, the less easy they find it to laugh and the more inclined they become to regard humans as victims of a miserable predicament. Hermes calls both Cyrus (14) and the anonymous house-builder (17) 'wretched' (ἄθλιος), and Charon's closing verdict on the species is that they are κακοδαίμονες (24), doomed to misfortune and unhappiness.

Taken as a whole, therefore, the dialogue leaves us with a somewhat unstable tone, shifting from humans' apparently intrinsic risibility to their somewhat 'pathetic' inability to grasp the true conditions of their existence. Existential laughter, projected onto a representative of Hades and onto a god (but also attributed to those few enlightened individuals who recognise the truth, 21), is set in counterpoint with a moralising, quasi-philosophical seriousness grounded in the principle (originally Pythagorean-cum-Platonic in cast) that human life should be lived 'with death always before the eyes' (20). By the end, then, a residual question for readers is whether, or how far, their own laughter has been aroused by the dialogue, and, if so, what kind of laughter it is – 'light' amusement at the burlesque frame of the whole piece, or something more congruent with the existentially trenchant laughter both practised and recommended by Charon (and, somewhat less so, Hermes)?

Several factors make the response of a shrewd, observant reader inevitably complex. One is the sheer seductiveness of Lucian's own urbane, allusive and colourful writing, with the rewards it offers those who bring with them a knowledge of Homer, Herodotus, Plato, history and myth, as well as other items of traditional Greek *paideia*. To some extent it is hard to avoid feeling that such suavely styled erudition, with its own implicit attachment to a certain sophistication of cultural attainments and pleasures, undercuts any hope of taking Charon's view of things at face value. After all, even from an orthodox Cynic viewpoint, let alone one as extreme as that of an infernal ferryman obsessed with the ineluctability of death, knowledge of Greek literature, or of *paideia* more generally, is as utterly redundant as wealth or power or social influence. To appreciate the niceties and nuances of Lucianic satire is already to be engaged in an activity that is as vulnerable as any other to a Charonesque critique of human vanity. More specifically, enjoyment of the texture of Lucian's dialogue means taking pleasure in a mythological burlesque whose extravagances (Charon and Hermes taking time off from normal duties, sitting on a pile of mountains with magnified vision of the earth below, and spouting bits of Homer to one another) are manipulated with a transparent relish that is in tension with the idea of internalising the critique of life articulated by these same figures. Finally, because Charon is the work's central embodiment of that critique, and Charon is paradigmatically morose (and, even when he laughs, either a macabre or a preposterous figure), who would *want* to identify with his way of perceiving things?

But there is a further and deeper consideration to reckon with. The external point of view adopted by Charon and Hermes is by definition not a truly human option. It is 'available' only in the imagination, whether comic or otherwise. Psychologically and cognitively, no human evaluation of life can be made from outside life. The impossibility for humans of finding an archimedean position from which to inspect their own condition is, however, a positive as well as a negative constituent of their natures. If human minds are incapable, except in very restricted respects, of appraising the 'meaning of life' from a truly external viewpoint, it is equally the case that they are capable of finding genuine value in spatio-temporally finite existences. Lucian's presentation of Charon's perspective on the human world actually helps to draw out a subtle point which we also encountered in Chapter 7. Brute contrasts between the dimensions of the human and more-than-human worlds – the 'smallness' of the former's social geography in comparison with an 'extra-terrrestrial' space, and the difference between finite lifetimes and an eternity of death – do not in themselves nullify the value of the first element in each of those contrasts. Things do not lose their value simply because those who recognise their value will die.[41] It is important to grasp the difference between more and less extreme positions on this point; differences of degree matter. When Solon is described by Hermes as 'laughing with contempt' at Croesus' wealth (11), this (metonymic) laughter represents a suspicion of great riches and overweening ambition that many could acknowledge as falling within their horizon of moral attitudes. But when Hermes uses the same verb (καταγελᾶν) later on (21) to describe those very few people who have putatively detached themselves from the common delusions of life, what is involved here is a *total* negativity towards earthly values, an unmodified desire to 'escape' to death. Part of the challenge that Lucian's dialogue poses for its readers is that it confronts them with the disequilibrium between these two types of view and between the two kinds of laughter associated with them.

So, in the end, Lucian's work toys with ideas (of human folly, contingency and self-ignorance) that could certainly have some purchase on a reflective reader's view of life, but it does so in a form that presupposes a richer commitment to human pleasures and satisfactions than is compatible with the extreme version of those ideas espoused by Charon and Hermes. One way of summing up this argument is to say that Lucian has too much use for laughter, and too much need to make it available to his sophisticated audience, to let it be reduced to an expression of a dehumanised sense (whether 'infernal' or 'divine') of the worthlessness of all worldly aspirations. Lucianic laughter itself, in all its multiplicity, finally reasserts itself over the Charonian laughter that is only *one* of its voices. Furthermore, I have tried to explain how the characterisation of Charon itself captures something about the strangeness of the absurd. My claim is that while Charon finds human beings 'totally ridiculous', or good for nothing but laughter (παγγέλοιος, 16, see above), he fails the test of full-blown absurdism as a world-view.

---

[41] Cf. ch. 7, 367–8.

He is shown as able to react to the human predicament in the way that he does precisely because he is so unencumbered with a capacity to see human experience from the inside. Absurdity, we might say, is not *his* problem. This does not leave us with an easy view of how to read the dialogue as a whole, or Lucian's work more generally. But it does, I think, block the simple conclusion that *Charon* is designed to guide readers to unqualified acceptance of the case for a Hades-based condemnation of earthly goals and goods. If Charon adumbrates an absolute, uncompromising version of 'the absurd' which devalues human existence *per se*, his oxymoronically grim laughter ends up being put in its place within the more diffuse absurdity of the work's parodic mythology. Paradoxically, Lucian's own writing can be thought of as a comic protection against, even a redemption from, the existential derision of Charon, death's burlesque representative: not for nothing did David Hume, a great lover of laughter, turn to Lucian during what he knew to be the final weeks of his life, finding in his work, and in the self-mocking encounter with Charon which it stimulated in his own imagination ('Get into the boat this instant, you lazy loitering rogue!'), a means of coming cheerfully to terms with the prospect of his own end.[42] Seen in this light, Lucian might be said to stage a contest between the laughter of life and the laughter of death. Ostensibly – that is, inside the world of the work – victory appears to belong to the second of these. But we know that Lucian has a vested authorial interest (an interest invested in the world of his readers) to stage-manage an ultimate victory for the laughter of life.

THE VIEW FROM HADES

One illuminating comparandum for some of the issues I have highlighted in *Charon* is provided by *Cataplus* (*Descent to Hades*), another of Lucian's encounters between the underworld ferryman and Hermes *nekropompos*, 'escort of corpses'.[43] The scenario of *Cataplus* finds Charon back in his own domain. Hermes brings down a batch of souls to Charon's ferry and a

---

[42] See the famous letter of Adam Smith to William Strahan of 9 November 1776, in Mossner and Ross (1977) 217–21, at 219 (where the reference to *Dialogues of the Dead* might include, from the sound of things, Lucian's *Cataplus*). Hume cites Lucian occasionally in his own writings: see e.g. the reference to *Menippus* in his essay 'The Sceptic': Hume (1993) 109.

[43] The very rare term *nekropompos* (*Catapl.* 1), in the mouth of Charon, is an ironic echo of Eur. *Alc.* 441 – ironic, because it is there applied to Charon himself. The impatience of Charon at the start of *Cataplus*, and again later in section 5, involves another (and bathetic) Lucianic reworking of Euripides' text: compare esp. 'what are we still waiting for?' (5, τί οὖν ἔτι διαμέλλομεν . . .;) with Eur. *Alc.* 255–6.

number of the newly arrived dead are held up to scrutiny. Charon himself is here restored to (a comically reductive version of) his traditional persona as an *un*laughing curmudgeon. The work begins with him grumbling about Hermes' lateness and fretting that *he* will get the blame from Pluto. For Charon, indeed, transporting the souls across Acheron is nothing more than his busy day's work; here he has no interest in the narratives, let alone the internal motivations, of their (former) lives. To him, the dead are mere cargo; the work goes on to describe how they have to be numbered and checked on arrival, like so many animals.[44] But if Charon in *Cataplus* is simply a peevish, overworked ferryman, with Hermes alongside him as, initially at least, a flustered drover (sweaty, dusty, out of breath) who has been struggling with a particularly recalcitrant member of his batch (4), that in itself sets up a typically Lucianic ambiguity of tone. If all this is, as it were, a *reductio ad absurdum* of the idea (and the inherited imagery) of death, what exactly constitutes the absurdity? Is it just a matter of frivolous mythological pastiche (how could one possibly believe in, let alone fear, such patently parodic agents of death?), or is there a darker effect that arises from a sardonic refashioning of the traditional notion that death really does amount to a desolate cancellation of all life's meaning and value? It seems clear enough that laughter must play some part in our response to Lucian, but what form and object is it supposed to take where the burlesquing of death itself is concerned? Let us see what pointers can be found in the work's own fabric.

One evident point of connection between the techniques of *Charon* and *Cataplus* is precisely the thematic but incomplete signalling of laughter at an early stage. Just as Hermes' opening question in *Charon*, 'why are you laughing?', has to wait a little while for an answer and thereby stimulates (and symbolises) the reader's or hearer's gelastic choices, so too in *Cataplus* Clotho's description of the approaching Hermes and his herd of souls includes an indeterminate expectation of laughter. 'But what's this?', she asks (3); 'I can see one of them is tied up, while another is laughing, and there's an individual . . . with a bitter look on his face who's hustling the others along.' This trio of characters – who turn out to be Megapenthes the desperate tyrant, Micyllus the contented cobbler, and Cyniscus the Cynic – become the central cast of the work, foregrounded against the more formulaically catalogued sequence (a sort of *danse macabre*) of the general categories of the dead: exposed infants, the old, war casualties, suicidal

---

[44] *Catapl.* 3–4; cf. 21 for the ferrying of animals themselves. The characterisation of Charon as curmudgeonly recurs in *Dial. mort.* 2.

lovers, political rivals, the executed, and so forth (5–6). It is the triangular relationship between the three highlighted individuals, including the permutations of laughter which their destinies bring into view, that will orientate but also complicate the work's perspective on human attitudes to life and death.

Megapenthes (whose 'speaking' name, 'Great-griever', sets up a direct and piquant counterpoint to the sound of laughter) is a stereotypically evil tyrant whose persona is built round two interlocked components, a corrupt lust for life and a pathetic desire to cheat death. He tries more than once to escape from Hermes. Even when recaptured, with the help of Cyniscus (who thereby enacts a Cynic insistence on facing up to death), he persists in begging for a reprieve and is prepared to offer bribery to that end, or even, Admetus-like, the substitution of a loved one in his place. Megapenthes, we learn, had murdered others to obtain his wealth and power (8–9); in his megalomania he wants to return to life in order not only to conquer foreign peoples but to leave the grandest of monuments inscribed with a record of all he has accomplished (9). If Megapenthes' exorbitant vices and shameless self-pity make him a typecast player in the scene, Lucian gives his case an edge by turning him into an object not only for the reader's easy contempt (encouraged, in part, by Clotho's exclamation, 'o you ridiculous fool!', ὦ γελοῖε)[45] but also for colourful derision by those who had known, and have survived, him.

Two moments stand out in this last respect. The first is when, as Clotho explains to him, 'the painting and statues which your city long ago erected in your honour will be destroyed and will provide a hilarious spectacle for onlookers' (γέλωτα παρέχουσι τοῖς θεωμένοις, 11). The discrepancy between Megapenthes' grandiose self-image and the view others have of him could not be starker: if he laments in quasi-tragic fashion over his own death, others find the termination of his life and regime a subject for uproarious celebration. The ridicule of his fate is made more personal and coarse by his slave Carion, who, we are told, copulated with Megapenthes' mistress Glycerium in the very room where the tyrant's body was laid out, before turning to the corpse to insult it verbally, pluck out its hair, punch its head, and spit on it (12). The pronounced crudity of Carion's behaviour is conveyed with details reminiscent of Old Comedy,[46] making it

---

[45] *Catapl.* 9; this vocative is rarer than one might have expected: it occurs elsewhere only at Lucian, *Demon.* 25, where it likewise conveys ridicule for a misconceived evaluation of life; cf. Dickey (1996) 172 (with 288), where the reference to Men. *Georg.* fr. 4 should be deleted.

[46] See esp. the sexual slang σποδεῖν ('bang'), with Henderson (1991) 172, and the vivid description of spitting at Ar. *Peace* 814–15. On spitting and mockery, compare Menippus' behaviour in Hades at

perhaps a vigorous invitation to relish the mocking humiliation of the dead ruler, but at the same time leaving it inherently sordid. Moreover, Carion's actions form an ensemble that could hardly go further in disregarding the traditional prohibition (more honoured, perhaps, in the breach than the observance) against abusing the dead. Notwithstanding the fictional story which frames it, the vignette is evocative of a kind of impulsive exultation that in practice no doubt often overrode moral or religious scruples of the 'de mortuis . . .' variety; as early as Homer, after all, we encounter the image of dancing on someone's tomb.[47] The only person, it seems, who did not need to wait for Megapenthes to die before expressing contempt for him openly was none other than Cyniscus. When the latter helps Hermes bundle the resisting tyrant onto Charon's boat and even threatens to strike him with his Cynic staff, Megapenthes says to him (13): 'will Cyniscus dare to brandish his stick at me? Wasn't it only the other day that I practically crucified you for being too outspoken, harsh and censorious?' The Cynic's contempt for worldly power was fearless in life and is apparently vindicated in death.

The reverse of Megapenthes in every way is the cobbler Micyllus, who after witnessing the former's discomfiture steps forward to try to ensure his own place on Charon's boat (14). Micyllus, a figure who makes an extended appearance in another of Lucian's works (*The Cock*), explains that while Megapenthes' prosperity served as 'birdlime' to ensnare his soul, turning his attachment to material possessions into a kind of sickness, the cobbler himself was too poor to place any 'surety' on life and can therefore depart from it with equanimity. Far from looking back with any nostalgia at what he has left behind, he is eager to enter a realm where 'equal rights' (*isotimia*), the permanent egalitarianism of death, obtain for all. But the satirical bite of Lucian's work requires something more than a conception of death the great leveller. It needs the dramatic psychology of role reversal, and with it the release of one kind of laughter. Micyllus articulates this point of view by speaking on behalf of his whole social class in Hades: 'we poor men are laughing, while the rich are distressed and lament' (15). Death, on this reading, is a sort of tragicomedy which inverts the positions occupied in life: it stages the downfall of one group of characters for the pleasure of the

---

Lucian, *Dial. mort.* 6.2; cf. also ch. 7 n. 104. For a more banal version of the idea of a slave abusing a dead master, see Men. *Aspis* 385–6, with ch. 5 n. 44 on slaves abusing their living masters behind their backs.

[47] Other Lucianic cases of mockery of the dead include *Dial. mort.* 12.5 (derision of Alexander the Great's divine pretensions in the presence of his corpse), 16.3, 20.12 (celebration at a tyrant's death, including stoning his young children to death). For the complex feelings attaching to abuse of the dead, see ch. 1, 26–30.

rest, who become a mass audience for the spectacle. The 'theatre of life' has, so to speak, been superseded by the theatre of death – a trope, as we shall soon see, which Lucian will elaborate more fully in the *Death of Peregrinus*. And Micyllus' enjoyment of the elimination of worldly differences is made all the more trenchant by its contrast with Megapenthes' earlier, quasi-Achillean request to be allowed to return to life if only 'as one of the poor, or even as a slave', a request whose Homeric prototype forms the subject of one of Lucian's own *Dialogues of the Dead*.[48]

But there is an underlying anomaly here, and one embedded in the very old eschatological imagery and mythology of Greek culture. Death cannot be both a remover *and* a reverser of social inequalities: it cannot simultaneously reduce everyone to the same pile of bones and yet, as in the analogous scenario of the *Menippus* (17), turn former rulers into posthumous fish-sellers, elementary schoolteachers, cobblers and beggars. When Micyllus proclaims that in Hades 'all is peace' (i.e., freedom from suffering) and then proceeds to his statement that 'we poor men are laughing, while the rich are distressed and lament', he perpetrates a blatant non-sequitur. Lucian's story makes sense only in terms of how it reflects back on the psychology and evaluation of different forms of *life*. Even then its sense is partial. On the most fundamental Greek premise about death – that it is an annihilation of everything that seems to humans to matter on earth – no Micyllus will get a chance in the underworld to mock the fate of the evil tyrant or of other unjust figures. But Lucian's *readers* can enjoy the thought that those who seem to have everything in the world of the living (wealth, power, sexual satisfaction and the rest) will soon lose it all for ever. That pleasure can be imaginatively enhanced, in the form of a malicious wish-fulfilment, by positing a moment at which the former tyrants and their like will have to contemplate their losses with a misery that will match or even outweigh their previous prosperity. So Micyllus' own laughter is a sort of satirical echo-effect, a projection into the land of the dead of (our) gratification at the thought that the wicked will not benefit from their crimes for long. But unless this thought translates itself into a hope of post-mortem justice (as, indeed, happens in the last part of the present work, with proceedings at the underworld court of Rhadamanthys: see below), it runs the risk of supplying a contradiction of its own grounds for laughter. If the only calculus needed to assess the desirability of life is that of temporary

---

[48] See *Catapl.* 13 for Megapenthes as an Achilles figure (echoing, of course, Hom. *Od.* 11.488–91, the subject of *Dial. mort.* 26); by contrast, Micyllus speaks as a kind of Odysseus at 14 ('I get no pleasure from that famous gift of the Cyclops, the promise that "I shall eat you last" . . .', echoing Hom. *Od.* 9.369). For the *isotimia* of death (15, 22), cf. *Dial. mort.* 1.4, 8.2, 29.3, 30.2, *Navig.* 40.

possession and eternal loss, then no life can be more desirable than any other. If all that death will do is annihilate, it will obliterate *everything* of value – including laughter itself.

In this connection it is worth glancing sideways to notice a detail from Lucian's *Death of Peregrinus*, a work I shall return to in its own right later. The unflattering treatment of Christianity in *Peregrinus*, a treatment which earned the work a place on the Council of Trent's index of banned books in 1564, includes the sneering observation that its 'wretched' (κακοδαίμονες) followers 'have persuaded themselves that they will be immortal and will live for ever, which allows them to despise death and willingly give themselves up to it'.[49] The belief and attitude in question here are intrinsically alien to a 'mainstream' Greek-pagan mentality, a mentality unaffected, that is, by the special promises of mystery religion. Such a mindset offers no basis on which to 'despise death' or treat it as insignificant, unless it be the idea, taken up in different ways by the Cynics and Epicureans, that precisely because it is a state of nullity death need hold no fear for us. But simply to abandon fear of death, to count it as a state of true nothingness, does not get us to the point which Lucian's imagination reaches, where laughter itself – however metaphorically or symbolically – can somehow survive and overcome death. Furthermore, if death is nothing, there is a sense in which life becomes *everything*, and it looks correspondingly harder to refute the rationale of those who seek to maximise their selfish gains and pleasures. The successful tyrant, after all, will have no more to fear in death than anyone else.[50]

If Micyllus' laughter is not to end up sounding rather hollow, then, we certainly need to know more about its presuppositions. At the point where he voices the laughter of the poor, Clotho recalls how she had noticed him laughing at the outset, when the group of souls being led by Hermes had first come into view. She asks him to explain his mirth (16). Micyllus now admits, in keeping with a very old strand in popular Greek thought, that during life he had been convinced that the tyrant really *was* the happiest of men, indeed superhuman (ὑπεράνθρωπός τις), a godlike figure in his possessions, pomp and power. It was only when he saw the man after death, now stripped of all his finery (and therefore, by implication, reduced to a

---

[49] *Peregr.* 13. On Lucian's treatment of Peregrinus as a Christian, see n. 54 below. For the Council of Trent, see Screech (1997) 143–7; cf. Baumbach in Pilhofer *et al.* (2005) 207. But see Goldhill (2002) 43–54 for trenchant remarks on the complexities of sixteenth-century attitudes to Lucian, especially those of Erasmus.

[50] *Peregr.* 23 makes this point: if Peregrinus teaches others to be fearless of death, then wicked people will become even bolder in pursuit of their own gains.

mere naked 'body'), that he found him 'totally ridiculous', the same word that Charon used for *all* humans.[51] But what exactly has Micyllus come to realise? 'I laughed even more at *myself*', he adds, 'for having gazed in admiration at a piece of scum, inferring his happiness from the mere smell of a feast...' The cobbler has seen the 'naked emperor' and realised, it seems, that his envied happiness was a mere shell: material goods are a matter of pure exteriority. Micyllus laughs equally, however, at Gniphon the money-lender (17), who spent his life amid perpetually anxiety-ridden parsimony ('wealthy only in his fingers') and never allowed himself the pleasure of his money; now, in Hades, he groans and laments with regret. Here, by contrast, the cause of laughter appears to be at least as much the failure to *use* and thereby enjoy material goods as the implicit delusion of permanence which underlies the money-lender's obsessive hoarding. The story of Gniphon, in the terms in which it is pictured here (he died without having ever 'tasted' his wealth), might at least be interpreted as a parable of missed opportunity, a failure to live life to the full in the circumstances available, rather than a demonstration of the futility of seeking *any* fulfilment in life. Before trying to get on Charon's boat, Micyllus reiterates his enjoyment at the sight of others' grief: 'we'll laugh as we watch them lamenting' (γελασόμεθα οἰμώζοντας αὐτοὺς ὁρῶντες, 17). *Prima facie*, the cobbler laughs only at those who have been brought face-to-face in death with the delusions of their previous existence. Yet the impression lingers that he has reached the point of supposing he has no reason not to laugh at everyone (his former self included) who has ever believed in the material possibility of human happiness. When Micyllus later tells Hermes that he himself can find nothing at all to lament or grieve over (20), he shows that he has become a kind of Cynic, utterly detached from all normal human attachments and aspirations; no surprise, then, that on the other side of Acheron he and Cyniscus advance hand-in-hand (22). His laughter escapes hollowness by becoming an unqualified acceptance of death, an acceptance which is given a blatantly comic twist when he decides to start *swimming* across Acheron after initially being denied room on Charon's ferry (18).

Even so, Micyllus' laughter, like the censorious mockery of Cyniscus, could claim no permanent vindication if it were not for the post-mortem justice enacted in the courtroom of Rhadamanthys in the last section of the dialogue. There the great judge inspects the souls (in the manner adumbrated at Plato, *Gorgias* 524d–525a) for 'marks' that betray how they lived

---

[51] *Charon* 16, with 450 above. Forms of παγγέλοιος occur thirteen times in Lucian, far more often than in any other Greek author.

their lives. This enables him to establish the essential purity of both Micyllus and Cyniscus, though even the latter has some faint traces of his own pre-philosophical vices (24); he sends both of them off to the Isles of the Blest. In the same way, Rhadamanthys discerns the full horror of Megapenthes' depravity and punishes the tyrant, on Cyniscus' suggestion, by condemning him to eternal torture of the mind: forbidden to drink the water of forgetting (Lethe), he will have to endure perpetual, ineradicable awareness of all his lost power (28–9). So it turns out, after all, that Micyllus' quasi-Cynic laughter can itself triumph for eternity, but only on a premise that clashes with the work's own images of death the great leveller.

Where does all this leave Lucian's own thematics of laughter? Because the dialogue has taken rich advantage of a composite eschatology, in which death is a permanent nullity for almost everyone while a very few souls are singled out for special rewards or torments, it is able to evoke two different ways of laughing at (life and) death without any need to reconcile them. On the one hand, there is the laughter of satirical satisfaction at the downfall and chastisement of evil, paradigmatically incarnated in the unlimited viciousness of the tyrant; on the other, a quasi-Cynic laughter, as in *Charon*, at the emptiness and ultimate senselessness of *all* human hopes and desires for happiness. The first is a laughter activated from a position of moral superiority (combined, for sure, with some *Schadenfreude*); the second is, as it were, a laughter 'from nowhere', nowhere, at any rate, other than the incongruously dramatised nullity of death itself.[52] Any attempt to negotiate some kind of final *rapprochement* between these two kinds of laughter within Lucian's work is made all the more difficult by the pervasively burlesque ethos of the operations of Hades and the non-human agencies in charge of them. If part of what consitutes that ethos is a self-consciously playful reduction of Charon, Hermes, Clotho and even Rhadamanthys to the level of preposterous functionaries, that in turn reduces the feasibility of detaching the potentially serious (i.e., life-influencing) attitudes of Micyllus and Cyniscus from their setting in a ramshackle underworld organisation that is more than faintly redolent of a cattle-market. Where, in short, death itself is held up in so patently absurd a light, how can it provide a perspective from which to reach a true verdict on life? There is too much scope for gelastic ingenuity and sophistication in the very fabric of Lucian's writing to allow any definitive force to a quasi-philosophical devaluation of life as a whole. If Lucian constantly invokes the possibility of existential laughter – laughter at the intrinsic (self-)delusions of human existence – he does so in

---

[52] For Nagel's phrase, 'the view from nowhere', see ch. 7 n. 5.

a spirit which readily dissolves into the all-encompassing wittiness, parody and irony of his own imagination.[53]

THE ABSURD SUICIDE OF PEREGRINUS

I want now to extend the range of my argument, and to put the (tentative) conclusions reached about works such as *Charon* and *Cataplus* to a stiffer test, by examining the most sustained and complex Lucianic thematisation of the laughter of 'life and death'. This occurs in his remarkable work *De morte Peregrini* (*On the Death of Peregrinus*), which sets itself the task of conjuring ostentatious hilarity out of nothing less than the gruesome suicide, by self-immolation, of the itinerant Cynic-cum-Christian guru Peregrinus, a historical event that took place at (more precisely, immediately after) the Olympic Games of AD 165.[54] Right at the start of *Peregrinus* the suicide is given something like the form of a pair of 'jokes'. In the first place, Peregrinus is said to have lived up to his other name, 'Proteus', by transmuting himself into fire. In the second, he was 'reduced to cinders' *à la* Empedocles, who, as legend had it, threw himself into volcanic Etna, though whereas the Sicilian philosopher had done so to deceive people (by supposedly vanishing from earth like a god), Peregrinus, being the great publicity-seeker he was, had advertised the event in advance![55] As if these remarks were not sufficient to set up the conspicuous paradox of finding a cause of huge mirth in an exceptionally painful and grisly suicide, Lucian underlines the point with a flourish of callous glee. He expressly pictures the addressee of his work, Cronius, 'laughing at the old man's snivelling stupidity' (γελῶντα ἐπὶ τῇ κορύζῃ τοῦ γέροντος, 2).[56] This Cronius is

[53] Bakhtin (1968) 387 compares Lucian's underworld laughter unfavourably (as 'abstract, ironical, devoid of true gaiety') with that of Rabelais; but this seems too brisk a judgement. Contrast the remark of Bakhtin's cited in n. 23 above. Cf. Branham (1989a) 247 n. 60 on the limitations of Bakhtin's treatment of Lucian.

[54] Among the latest treatments of Lucian's work, Pilhofer *et al.* (2005) contains a wide-ranging commentary and a set of essays; Schwartz (1951) is an older commentary. Clay (1992) sets the work against the background of other sources; on one *admirer* of Peregrinus, Aulus Gellius, note Holford-Strevens (2004) 145–7. Dudley (1937) 170–82 (with the older calculation of 167 for the date) and Jones (1986) 117–32 attempt a general reconstruction of Peregrinus' career; Edwards (1989) tackles the Christian dimension, as does Pilhofer in Pilhofer *et al.* (2005) 97–110. König (2006) offers a subtle reading of the work's partly parodic manipulation of the conventions of (auto)biographical writing, including some of its echoes of Christian motifs. Other angles on *Peregrinus* can be found in Branham (1989a) 186–94, Niehues-Pröbsting (1979) 201–13, Hall (1981) 176–81, Overwien (2006).

[55] At Lucian, *Dial. mort.* 6.4 Menippus accuses Empedocles of having committed suicide from vanity and stupidity (including the term κόρυζα: cf. the next note).

[56] κόρυζα literally denotes nasal mucus: it can easily function as synecdoche for the decrepitude of the old, as here (cf. Lucian, *Iup. Trag.* 15, *Dial. mort.* 9.2, verb), or equally the immaturity of children;

sometimes identified with an attested Platonist of that name. Since we know of the latter that he was interested in both reincarnation and the properties of *fire*, it deserves mention that the identification would bring into play the possibility of a subtextual (or private) joke on Lucian's part.[57] The idea of laughing at Peregrinus' death is taken a notch further, and authorially reinforced, when Lucian recounts how he himself was an eyewitness to the self-immolation (though it would be prudent to reserve judgement on the autobiographical veracity of this)[58] and was joined by a number of other people who shared his *laughter* while standing by the pyre, much to the chagrin of other Cynic philosophers present. When that episode is later elaborated in more detail, a marked association between derisive laughter and violence emerges. As Peregrinus' Cynic friends stare silently (and without tears) into the flames, Lucian goads them by expostulating: 'let's go, you fools! It's unpleasant, in the thick of this nasty stench, looking at a roasted old man' (37), an image paralleled by Zeus's complaint about the fumes from the burning body at the start of *Fugitivi*. Lucian adds an ironic comparison to the death of Socrates surrounded by his friends, and when the Cynics seem ready for a brawl, he grabs some of them and threatens to throw them too into the flames. What can justify such flagrant *Schadenfreude*, gleefully aggressive in its disregard for the traditional wisdom ('de mortuis . . .') of eschewing denigration of the dead? Or is Lucian simply acting on the equally old Greek impulse to celebrate, no matter how maliciously, the death of one's enemies?[59]

In embarking on his full account of what he claims to have witnessed near Olympia, Lucian sets up an explicit contest – a kind of head-on existentialist clash – between 'tragedy' and 'comedy'. The clash had already been anticipated by his previous description of Peregrinus as someone who 'played the tragedian throughout his life' (ἐτραγῴδει παρ' ὅλον τὸν βίον, 3), in other words, a portentously theatrical self-dramatiser.[60] 'Tragedy' is

---

for the latter, cf. Thrasymachus' sarcastic gibe at Socrates, Pl. *Rep.* 1.343a (with ch. 6, 286), with Lucian's echo of that passage at *Nav.* 45.

[57] On the Platonist Cronius, see Dillon (1996) 362, 379–80. On Platonists and laughter, cf. 438–40 above. The suggestion of Macleod (1991) 270–1 that Lucian's work might have been intended to persuade Cronius to abandon sympathy for Peregrinus makes no sense at all of the addressee's pictured laughter at both start and finish. For another case of a writer imagining his addressee laughing, see the Christian Iren. *Haer.* 1.9.3 Harvey (cf. Epiphan. *Pan.* II 26 Holl), with reference to what he considers the absurdities of gnostic doctrines.

[58] See n. 64 below.

[59] See ch. 1, 26–30, with 456–7 above.

[60] Lucianic references to tragic theatre are abundant: they are catalogued by Kokolakis (1960b) and Karavas (2005), though neither engages with the sustained thematic significance of tragic motifs in *De morte Peregrini*.

here equated, in a very old trope, with inflated, bombastic melodrama. Lucian's own work will counteract the bogus stage-show of Peregrinus' life with the antidote of derision, thereby piquantly reducing (fake) 'tragedy' to the subject-matter of comic debunking – itself a dramatic strategy with an origin in Lucian's ancestor-genre Old Comedy. Prior to the occasion of the suicide itself, Lucian hears another Cynic, Theagenes, advertising the event at the nearby town of Elis. Theagenes delivers a rantingly hyperbolic speech, comparing Peregrinus to various tragic heroes and to Zeus himself, before apparently dissolving into tears and quasi-tragic gestures (4–6).[61] 'He wept really ludicrously and tore at his hair (but being careful not to pull too hard!).' And as Theagenes is led away sobbing by other Cynics, a further speaker (taken by some to be an authorial self-portrait) mounts the platform to indulge in a very different vocalisation, and in triplicate: he starts with what is described as a vigorous 'belly laugh' (ἐπὶ πολὺ ἐγέλα καὶ δῆλος ἦν νειόθεν αὐτὸ δρῶν), then undertakes to pit 'the laughter of Democritus' against 'the tears of Heraclitus' (the latter here involving a nice pun on the fiery means of Peregrinus' impending suicide), and finally bursts out again into laughter, this time drawing most of his audience into an infectiously matching response (7).[62] Since all these motifs, as we shall see, are repeated or mirrored in the later parts of the piece, they come to form a symmetrical frame of derision for the narrative of Peregrinus' life and death.

The Democritus–Heraclitus contrast crystallises our options. Are we to consider Peregrinus' story as a solemn, heroic tragedy, with something profound to tell us about the human condition, or as the ludicrous tale of a posturing charlatan? The work leaves, in reality, no choice at all. At any rate, to try to maintain the first option in the face of Lucian's account would be inescapably to choose to identify with a mercilessly exposed laughing-stock. The piece is such an emphatic exercise in biting derision, gloatingly constructed from the materials of self-heroising pretensions, that there is no room for an alternative response (short of denouncing the totality of *Peregrinus* – a real option, as we have seen). Lucian makes sure of that,

---

[61] As it happens, Galen, *Meth. med.* 10.914–15 Kühn preserves an account of Theagenes' own death, at Rome, from liver disease: it describes how Theagenes' companions followed their Cynic convictions by refusing to indulge in grief. This matches Lucian's almost inadvertent reference to the Cynics' lack of tears at *Peregr.* 37 (see my text above). But *Peregr.* as a whole succumbs to the temptation to depict (sham) Cynic 'tragedy', not least on Theagenes' own part. Cf. Bernays (1879) 14–19, Dudley (1937) 183.

[62] Other Lucianic references to the legendary Democritean/Heraclitean personae occur at *Sacr.* 15, *Vit. Auctio* 13–14; cf. ch. 7, 346, 363. On the idea of a 'belly laugh', note Lucian, *Eun.* 12 (the stomach 'sore' from heaving with laughter), and cf. ch. 1 n. 24. For the uncertain status of the anonymous platform speaker, see Pilhofer in Pilhofer *et al.* (2005) 54.

with an insidious technique of satirical intensification, by swathing the story in nothing less than a quadruple layering of laughter: first, his own as author and eyewitness narrator ('I couldn't contain my laughter', uttered at the very point when Peregrinus has just jumped into the flames, 37; cf. 34); secondly, the pitiless ridicule projected by his anonymous speaker (and seeming alter ego), who lambasts Peregrinus in a blow-by-blow exposé of his career and laughs emblematically both when mounting (7, see above) and when leaving (31) the platform; thirdly, the reaction of the speaker's auditors in the preliminary gathering at Elis (7, cf. 31, with the counterpart in some of the same people's laughter in response to Peregrinus himself, 2); and, finally, the expected response of the addressee of Lucian's own work, Cronius, who is imagined as laughing at the author's account at both start and finish (2, 37, cf. 43, 45), and as being primed by the work to scoff at any admiring account of Peregrinus he may hear from others (45). We have here, in other words, a matching pair of narrator–audience relationships, one internal and one external. Their superimposed, mutually reinforcing laughter comes as close as any satirical narrative could to compelling a third audience – the (unresisting) reader – to repeat and reaffirm the contemptuous mockery of Peregrinus, both alive and dead.[63]

The force of all this, as I have already mentioned, is heightened by the pungently 'anti-tragic' cast of the narrative. The initial description of Peregrinus, quoted earlier, as one who 'played the tragedian throughout his life' introduces what will turn out to be a recurrent thematic device. That description is expanded by the ironic addition, 'outdoing Sophocles and Aeschylus'; and if we wonder why not Euripides too, at least part of the answer is supplied later. When Peregrinus, though still some kind of Christian, first appears in Cynic garb ('he grew his hair long, wore a dirty little cloak, carried a pouch, and had a stick in his hand', 15), he is said to have 'costumed himself in a thoroughly tragic fashion' (ὅλως μάλα τραγικῶς ἐσκεύαστο), with a sort of pun on the idea of Euripides' tragic beggars (as parodied by Aristophanes, at any rate) and on the conceited attention-seeking allegedly involved in all his behaviour. His grandiose suicide plan is later dismissed as involving 'this paraphernalia from tragedy' (τοῖς ἀπὸ τῆς τραγῳδίας τούτοις, 21), and scornful reference is made to

---

[63] The only chink, as it were, through which one glimpses the possibility of an alternative reading is the description of the Cynics' dignified response at 37 ('they did not weep but silently showed some grief by staring into the fire') – but it is closed off at once by Lucian's scurrilous outburst against them (see 463 above). On the laughter of *Peregrinus* as a way of creating a 'satirical community', note the brief remarks of Whitmarsh (2004) 472. For another case where Lucian imagines his own work successfully arousing laughter, see *Apol.* 1.

the pseudo-parallelism with the death of Heracles in Sophocles' *Trachiniae* (already invoked by Theagenes (4), one of Peregrinus' Cynic friends, who is now (21) cast in the role of the helping Philoctetes). Whereas Heracles was immolated in a remote spot, Peregrinus has chosen a public gathering – 'he'll roast himself virtually on a stage-set!' (μόνον οὐκ ἐπὶ σκηνῆς ὀπτήσει ἑαυτόν). The Heracles and Philoctetes motifs return at 33, in Peregrinus' own self-dramatising mouth, and the suicide scene itself is given strong theatrical presentation. Under moonlight, Peregrinus 'comes on stage in his usual costume', Theagenes is 'not a bad deuteragonist' (i.e. a secondary actor), the Cynic stick or staff is now ironically called 'Heraclean', the whole situation is referred to as 'the tragedy', and the climactic act of self-immolation is 'the *dénouement*' or the 'dramatic finale' of the play (τὴν καταστροφὴν τοῦ δράματος).[64] But it is precisely at that climax that Lucian blocks any frisson of horror that might attach to the event by emphatically summoning up again the sound of laughter, both Cronius' and his own (37). The latter is prompted in particular by the reflection of how incongruous it was that the final words of Peregrinus should be an invocation of the 'gods of his father', when he had strangled his own father to death some years earlier (cf. 10)!

The timing of this gesture of authorial derision in section 37 could not be more incisive. It rings out at the very moment at which we are asked to imagine Peregrinus swallowed up by the flames. This is not laughter in the face of death so much as laughter that relishes the thought – or, in Lucian's own dramatisation, the actual sight – of another's revolting end. It is therefore symbolic of the whole work's incongruous (some might think self-deceiving) combination of, on the one hand, an insistence that Peregrinus' suicide was nothing more than a melodramatic publicity stunt with, on the other, the claim that it was only what he *deserved* (21, 39, cf. 31). Standing back from the work's animus, we ought to wonder whether laughter is being employed to suppress or camouflage some of the darker questions that might be raised about the event. But within the satire's own perspective there is no doubt that this is *Schadenfreude* of an unflinchingly malevolent kind. Lucian's narrative has explained that Peregrinus rationalised and justified his suicide as a model demonstration, in Cynic fashion, of how to treat death with contempt (θανάτου καταφρονεῖν: 23, 33). But that model is rejected on several grounds: first, because it was actually a sham (Lucian *saw* Peregrinus' fear, 33, which made him laugh directly, 34; and he had witnessed

---

[64] *Peregr.* 36–7. I agree with Kokolakis (1960b) 77, against Pickard-Cambridge (1968) 133, that *deuteragōnistēs* (36) has inescapably theatrical force; cf. Karavas (2005) 212.

the man's true cowardice previously too, which he offers to Cronius as a further reason for laughter, 43–4); secondly, because it was (allegedly) self-dramatising and self-promoting; thirdly, because to abandon fear of death would only provide encouragement to evil people to be all the bolder in pursuit of vice (23); and, finally, because the visible fact of Peregrinus' painful death is, as I have noted, precisely what allows the work to translate it from an imposingly self-chosen destiny into a richly deserved punishment for a lifetime of crime and imposture.

Laughter ties these various strands together not by mocking death as such but by displacing contempt from death onto Peregrinus himself, just as it turns the latter's own 'art' of Cynic denigration, *loidoria*, back against him.[65] In the process it reasserts the claims of the living to a pleasure that patently includes that of physically uninhibited exultation, and it wins a triumph for a ruthless version of 'the comic' over the stage-managed fraudulence of 'the tragic'. Unlike the impression created by some other Lucianic writings, *Peregrinus* refuses to align itself with the Cynic principle of escaping from the absurdity of life as soon as possible. Indeed, it specifically and 'authorially' repudiates that idea (21) by glossing it as an act of slave-like cowardice, 'running away from life' (δραπετεύειν ἐκ τοῦ βίου) no less. It does so, in part at least, because it needs to reserve all its resources of vindictive laughter for Peregrinus himself (and his followers). To allow the notion of life as inherently absurd to dominate the picture would negate the work's central vituperative impetus, which is to *destroy* Peregrinus' reputation with laughter. By mockingly depicting and reinterpreting its target's death, the work enacts its own symbolic annihilation of him.

Lucian keeps one last use of the comic/tragic polarity up his sleeve to complete his exhibition of the former's superiority, its victory over the fake tragedy of Peregrinus' departure from life. As he makes his way back from Harpina, where the suicide had taken place, to Olympia itself, he encounters various people coming in the other direction in the hope of still managing to see Peregrinus' self-immolation. To anyone sane he told 'the events plain and simple', just as he supposedly has to Cronius (a transparent case of the satirist's pose of disinterested veracity). For the gullible, on the other hand, it was appropriate to deploy his own version of the 'tragic' mode of magniloquence. To them, he peddled 'some highfalutin nonsense of my own' (ἐτραγῴδουν τι παρ' ἐμαυτοῦ, 39) by elaborating

---

[65] Peregrinus' Cynic *loidoria* is stressed at 18–19 (cf. Philostr. *Vitae Soph.* 2.1, 563); the same feature belongs to Theagenes at 3, and to other Cynics at 37: on Cynic denigration see ch. 7, 372–87. According to Lucian, *Demon.* 21, however, Peregrinus himself was not an exponent of Cynic *laughter* in its more taunting style: ch. 7 nn. 99, 130.

a fictitious account of great portents, namely an earthquake and a vulture that rose from the flames to speak (in tragic quotation) with the voice of a deified Peregrinus on his way to Olympus – another gibe, of course, at the pseudo-Heraclean resonance (or pretensions) of the event. Lucian later hears the story of the vulture solemnly repeated to a crowd by an old man: the vulture, as he puts it, which he himself had sent into flight 'to deride the fools and idiots' (καταγελῶντα τῶν ἀνοήτων καὶ βλακικῶν, 40). The irony is far-reaching. Even the wild exaggerations of satire can be believed by those credulous enough. The work's central thrust is directed against the religious credulity of large numbers of people in a world hungry with an insatiable appetite for new cults, prophets and legends. Lucian purports to show how pathetically easy it is to satisfy and make fun of this appetite in the same breath; in doing so, he may even have obliquely in his sights the sort of Christian narratives found at, for example, Matthew 27.51–4.[66] He also indirectly draws attention, however, to the sheer inventiveness of his own imagination. The point has wider ramifications; it is something no reading of the work *as a whole* can afford to forget. Historians rely on Lucian's *Peregrinus* for the fullest account available of the circumstances of the self-immolation, but we will never know whether the author's claim to have been an eyewitness is true (Lucian could easily have used information from others). Even if it is, there is much about the luridly tinted satirical filter through which the event is seen that it would be prudent not to take on trust.[67] Anyone who does so without caution may unknowingly become just another victim of Lucianic laughter.

Where, then, does all this leave the evaluation of life and death in *De morte Peregrini*? In the contest, as it were, between Democritean and Heraclitean viewpoints, there is no doubt about the answer. 'Don't you think Democritus would deservedly have laughed at the man?', Lucian asks Cronius at the end. 'Yet where would he have found *so much* laughter? You at any rate, dearest of friends, should laugh yourself . . .'.[68] But there is perhaps a lingering question in the background, since (the legendary) Democritus

---

[66] This is not, however, the only resonance of the narrative; in addition to pseudo-Heraclean overtones, the apotheosis of emperors is also somewhere in the satirical picture. For a range of points on the portents, see Schwartz (1951) 110, Karavas (2005) 167–8, Pilhofer (2005) 81, 87–8, König (2006) 241–3.

[67] Historians often underplay, or even ignore, features of the work which are actually fundamental to its slant. See e.g. Bowersock (1994) 71–2: 'an element of mockery' is considerable understatement, while his description of Peregrinus' attitude to death ignores Lucian's *parti pris* in section 33 and elsewhere. Lucian's manipulation of his own readers is well brought out by König (2006), esp. 243–7; cf. Whitmarsh (2004) 467. Anderson (1976) 52–6, 72–6 is rightly sceptical about many details of *Peregrinus*.

[68] *Peregr.* 45. The idea of what Democritus *would* have laughed at, if he had been present, occurs earlier at both Hor. *Epist.* 2.1.194 and Juv. *Sat.* 10.36; the motif is later echoed in Petrarch, *Fam.* 11.9.

was associated not so much with selective laughter at egregious human targets as with the idea of the intrinsic risibility of life in its (near) entirety. As I have already stressed, however, *Peregrinus* itself hardly occupies such a standpoint. It cannot afford to do so. If it did, Peregrinus' suicide might look like a magnificent statement of a Cynic's imperturbable sense of existential absurdity, as even Albert Camus, modern spokesman *par excellence* of 'the absurd', seems to have taken it to be (at any rate on the plane of legend).[69] Instead of allowing this Cynic paradigm, which we have seen him else-where exploiting for his own burlesque repertoire, to get in the way of his profusely dramatised gloating, Lucian coopts 'Democritus' for his highly partial purposes. Having occluded any idea of existential absurdity as the motivator of a controlled exit from life, Lucian is free to clothe Peregrinus' life and death in the garb of the *faux*-tragic and thus to expose it to all his techniques of parodic deflation and vitriolic character assassination. The work's sixteen references (and encouragements) to laughter are carefully organised into a sort of gelastic fugue whose repetitions and variations are wound around the remorselessly spiteful account of Peregrinus' immola-tion. But this means, to return to the conclusion reached in my reading of *Charon*, that Lucian himself, *qua* satirist, is necessarily committed to being on the side of the real 'laughter of life' (in all its varieties, from the blithe to the venomous) against the imaginary 'laughter of death'. In so far as he incorporates the latter too in his writing, he does so only on his own terms, extracting from it always a play of contextual absurdity which holds the ultimately self-confounding problems of absolute absurdity at arm's length.

Lucian, for sure, is a great lover of literary masks. It is as dangerous to try to relate his work to a fixed centre (whether of philosophical or comic principles) as it is, I believe, to read Aristophanic comedy through the rhetoric of authorial self-imaging performed in the parabases of his plays. What I have attempted in this chapter is not a diagnosis of stable authorial intentions, but an exploration of just some of the ways in which Lucian orchestrates the voices of laughter (as well as the whole scale of its tones, from the amiable to the venomous) within the texture and narrative pat-terns of his writing. I hope it has become clear, even from a discussion of only a selection of works, that the relationship between laughter in life and in death is, for Lucian, a flexible, indeed a reversible perspective: one can stand, as it were, at either end, and find things to mock as one gazes

---

[69] Camus (1965) 102, translated in Camus (1955) 14, refers to Peregrinus in passing as an apparently authentic illustration of the absurd: see Camus (1965) 1431 for the editors' notes on Camus' likely French source.

towards the other. Perhaps, in a work like *Cataplus* (or, equally, the *Dialogi mortuorum*), one can even do both simultaneously – at any rate, in the gelastic imagination. It is almost as if, in the end, laughter is itself the prime source of energy in the Lucianic universe – an energy greater than the gods (who are among its victims), capable of echoing beyond death (but only for the benefit of the living), and fashioning a multiplicity of forms through which to relive and revalue, albeit at the price of a ubiquitous irony, much of what had been fundamental to the history of Greek culture.

CHAPTER 10

Laughter denied, laughter deferred: the antigelastic tendencies of early Christianity

Τοῦ κυρίου τοὺς νῦν γελῶντας κατακρίνοντος, εὔδηλον ὅτι οὐδέπ-
οτε καιρὸς γέλωτός ἐστι τῷ πιστῷ.

(Since our master condemns those who laugh in this life, it is patent
that for the believer there is never a right time for laughter.)

Basil of Caesarea

Καὶ γὰρ καὶ αὐτὸς ἐδάκρυσεν. καὶ τοῦτο μὲν πολλάκις ἔστιν ἰδεῖν
αὐτὸν ποιοῦντα, γελῶντα δὲ οὐδαμοῦ· ἀλλ᾽ οὐδὲ μειδιῶντα ἠρέ-
μα· οὐκοῦν τῶν εὐαγγελιστῶν οὐδεὶς εἴρηκε.

(Christ himself wept . . . We can often observe him doing so, but never
laughing – nor even smiling gently: none of the evangelists states that
he did so.)

John Chrysostom[1]

MOCKING 'THE KING OF THE JEWS'

It is a fact with deep, long-lasting repercussions that laughter plays a disturbing part in the founding narrative of Christianity. In the account of
Jesus' arrest presented in the gospel of Mark, probably the earliest of the
synoptics, we are told that after Pilate had released Barabbas and handed
over 'the king of the Jews' for crucifixion, the governor's soldiers took
Jesus inside the praetorium and organised their own humiliation of the
supposedly regal prisoner.

. . . καὶ συγκαλοῦσιν ὅλην τὴν σπεῖραν. καὶ ἐνδιδύσκουσιν αὐτὸν πορφύραν καὶ
περιτιθέασιν αὐτῷ πλέξαντες ἀκάνθινον στέφανον· καὶ ἤρξαντο ἀσπάζεσθαι
αὐτόν· χαῖρε, βασιλεῦ τῶν Ἰουδαίων· καὶ ἔτυπτον αὐτοῦ τὴν κεφαλὴν καλάμῳ
καὶ ἐνέπτυον αὐτῷ καὶ τιθέντες τὰ γόνατα προσεκύνουν αὐτῷ. καὶ ὅτε ἐνέ-
παιξαν αὐτῷ, ἐξέδυσαν αὐτὸν τὴν πορφύραν καὶ ἐνέδυσαν αὐτὸν τὰ ἱμάτια
αὐτοῦ. καὶ ἐξάγουσιν αὐτὸν ἵνα σταυρώσωσιν αὐτόν.

---

[1] Epigraphs: (1) Basil, *Reg. brev.* 31 (31.1104 *PG*): see 514–15 below; (2) John Chrys. *In Mt.* 6.6. (57.69
PG), mistakenly ascribed to ps.-Chrysostom by Screech (1997) 48; see n. 83 below.

And they summoned the whole company of troops, draped Jesus in a purple robe, and placed on his head a crown which they had twisted together from thorns. And they began to salute him: 'Hail, King of the Jews!' And they struck him about the head with a stick, spat on him, and falling to their knees made obeisance to him. And when they had toyed with him, they removed the purple cloak and put his own garments back on him. And they led him off to crucify him.[2]

This narrative, closely matched by the accounts found in Matthew and John, is a notorious instance (shocking to most modern readers, whether Christians or not) of the laughter of degradingly spiteful derision, embedded in a framework of cruelly fantasised role-playing. While the setting in Jesus' passion makes this episode part of a momentous chain of events, the form taken by the act of mockery is of a kind recognisable in various respects from other ancient testimony. At the most basic level the situation manifests the aggressive ridicule of an individual by a crowd, a 'classic' pattern of the social focusing of laughter on a spotlighted victim. We are told that the soldiers gathered their whole group together, to maximise the audience for the event. Their behaviour acquires an additional edge from its sadistic timing, the gleeful humiliation of a man about to be executed – though we have seen earlier in this book that such conduct was by no means unprecedented in antiquity.[3] It can also be read as a display of distinctively military 'humour', providing the soldiers with a temporary escape from the rigours of obedient discipline and allowing them to give vent to pent-up anti-authoritarian (if also, perhaps, all-too-habitually brutal) feelings.[4]

---

[2] Mark 15.16–20; text from Aland and Aland (1979). Cf. Matthew 27.27–31, where the soldiers put the staff in Jesus' hand before beating him with it, and John 19.2–3. Luke lacks the episode with crown, cloak and mock sceptre; but at Luke 22.63–5, before Pilate's verdict (paralleling Matthew 26.67–8, Mark 14.65, where the agents are Jews and their slaves), the soldiers blindfold Jesus and challenge him to use 'prophetic' powers to say which of them has struck him: describing this sadistic perversion of blind man's buff (for such ancient games see ch. 3 n. 75), Luke uses ἐμπαίζειν (toy with, mock) and βλασφημεῖν (abuse); cf. n. 11 below. For Jesus' anticipation of mockery, see Matthew 20.19, Mark 10.34, Luke 18.32. Bauer (1979) 767, *s.v.* στέφανος 1, lists older literature on the mocking scene. Screech (1997) 19–20, 24–7 offers an important perspective (but neglects Luke 22.63–5). Vermes (2005) 48–9, 65–6, 116 accepts the soldiers' mockery, but not that of the Jews, as historically authentic. For jeering at Jesus on the cross, see n. 11 below.

[3] See ch. 1, 27, for a legal entitlement to jeer at condemned criminals before execution at Athens. For a striking Roman case of mockery before death, see the humiliating treatment of Vitellius at Cass. Dio 65.21.

[4] Crowds and individuals: ch. 1, 31–3. Military humour: note sadistic mockery of the Syrian Baetis by Alexander's troops ('soldiers' *hubris*') at Gaza in Hegesias *FGrH* 142 F3 (*apud* Dion. Hal. *Comp. verb.* 18); cf. ch. 2 n. 59. Notably Roman, as an outlet for soldiers' irreverence, were the satirical songs sung at triumphs: Suet. *Div. Iul.* 49.4, 51.1; but that practice lacked the freedom for violence that could surface in treatment of a condemned prisoner. The soldiers' sarcasm in the gospels would be heightened if the robe in which they drape Jesus is a military cloak, as seems to be so in Matthew's version (27.28). Delbrueck (1942) analyses other possible associations of the regalia mentioned.

What better outlet for such feelings than an opportunity to victimise a supposed 'king' with an outburst of *Schadenfreude* reinforced by casual violence?

Yet these soldiers do not simply use Jesus as a convenient target. They compel him to be a mute character in a miniature 'comedy' which they stage for their own perverted entertainment, just as, in a near-contemporary incident reported by the Jewish historian Philo, a group of Alexandrian Greeks dress up a lunatic as a mock king in a political charade which they consciously model on theatrical mimes.[5] Maliciously vindictive though the behaviour of Pilate's soldiers appears in its immediate surroundings, it is a grotesque adaptation of the kind of play-acting that in other circumstances might be celebratory and innocent – most obviously, in a children's game of 'being royalty', like the one illustrated in Herodotus' narrative of the boy Cyrus (the Great) and his friends.[6] Even the motif of contemptuous spitting which occurs in both Mark and Matthew contributes ambiguously to this scenario: since the soldiers are enacting mock deference, their spitting, like their kneeling, serves as a parodic distortion of the kiss of homage which belonged to traditional rituals of obeisance (*proskunēsis*) in the Near East.[7] More pointedly, perhaps, the scene might call to mind the antics of the Roman Saturnalia, in which a mock king was established during the period of 'misrule' that marked the midwinter festival. Other rituals too involving pretend kings have been adduced by historians. But specific parallels matter less than the overall impression that, in the mockery of Christ, deadly violence has been superimposed on gestures of a type familiar from exuberant festivity or children's play. The result is a macabre melding

---

[5] Philo, *In Flaccum* 36–9, cited by Radermacher (1930) 32 (cf. Lane Fox (1991) 292): note the similarly 'theatrical' improvisation of costume/props; Philo's reference to mime reflects the agents' own intentions. Various episodes in the mockery of Jesus are ironically called 'comedy' (*kōmōdia*) *vel sim.* by John Chrys., e.g. *In Mt.* 85.1–2 (58.757–77 *PG*), *Epist. ad Olymp.* 7.4 (both 'tragedy' *and* 'comedy'), *Scand.* 8.7, 14.8, 14.10. κωμῳδεῖν refers to derision of the resurrection at ps.-Ignat. *Epist. Smyrn.* 7.7; cf. n. 95 below.

[6] Hdt. 1.114–15 (cf. 120), where the game goes wrong (when a boy is actually beaten) with momentous consequences. We know there was a Greek children's game called βασιλίνδα, 'playing king': Pollux, *Onom.* 9.110, Ael. Dion. *Att. s.v.*, Suet. *Lud.* 18 (Taillardat); for what it's worth, Hesych. *s.v.* βασιλίνδα describes it as a game of 'kings and soldiers'; *Suda s.v.* Κῦρος (κ 2777 Adler) applies the term to the Persian game played by Cyrus. For an echo of children's games in adult cruelty, cf. ch. 3, 129–30.

[7] Mark 15.19 actually has the verb προσκυνεῖν, used both of obeisance to rulers and worship of deities: see Bauer (1979) 716–17, Neil (1901) 28, Diggle (2004) 358 for pagan/Christian usage. For *proskunēsis* on knees cf. Matthew 4.9 (devil speaking), Paul, 1 Cor. 14.25. Spitting in gross contempt: cf. Matthew 26.67, Mark 10.34, 14.65, Luke 18.32, with ch. 9 n. 46.

together of the hilarity of make-believe travesty with vicious gloating over a doomed enemy.[8]

The image of Jesus derisively costumed in ersatz regalia, and surrounded by a malevolently scoffing mob, would readily have elicited contrasting reactions from believers and non-believers in antiquity. Far from being shocked by the mockery of Jesus before his crucifixion, many pagans were in effect to perpetuate this mockery by treating the crucifixion itself (of a supposed god) as a subject fit for ridicule. 'Greeks denigrate and deride our faith, they laugh in our faces', wrote Athanasius in the fourth century, 'directing their gibes precisely at the crucifixion of Christ'.[9] To a pagan mind, accustomed to the idea of cruel laughter as an appropriate behaviour for the gods themselves, Jesus' meek submission to jeering humiliation was bound to seem utterly unintelligible: to some, indeed, a refutation of claims to divinity. 'What great action did Jesus perform of the kind that a *god* would do – despising men, laughing openly at them, and belittling what was happening?', asked the pagan Celsus, with scornful disbelief, in the later second century. And we do not need to speculate whether Celsus' question was underpinned by recollection of a paradigm such as Dionysus' vengeful laughter against the taunting Pentheus in Euripides' *Bacchae*, since the reminiscence is explicitly attested.[10] But on the minds of Christians themselves, with the striking exception of certain gnostic sects who took the crucifixion to be a stage-managed illusion not a real event, that same image of their derided god was bound to stamp an indelibly negative conception of the force of laughter, especially since the episode

---

[8] Saturnalian mock kings are attested at Sen. *Apocol.* 8.2, Lucian, *Saturn.* 2, 4, Epict. *Diss.* 1.25.8; cf. Versnel (1993) 205–11. Some scholars have seen a connection with the Babylonian festival Sacaea, in which a slave/criminal was treated as mock king (Athen. 14.639c = Berosus *FGrH* 680 F2, Ctesias *FGrH* 688 F4) before being killed: see Dio Chrys. *Orat.* 4.66–8 (counting the festival as Persian, as does Strabo 11.8.4–5 and, presumably, Ctesias *loc. cit.*). Radermacher (1930) 32 dismisses parallels with both Saturnalia and Sacaea; but it is unwise to be restrictive where possible parodic affinities are concerned. For mockery of condemned criminals, see n. 3 above.

[9] ὁποῖα διαβάλλοντες Ἕλληνες χλευάζουσι, καὶ πλατὺ γελῶσι καθ' ἡμῶν, οὐδὲν ἕτερον ἢ τὸν σταυρὸν τοῦ Χριστοῦ προφέροντες: Athanas. *Ctr. gentes* 1; cf. Meijering (1984) 11. Athanasius pays back pagans in kind with his own mockery of anthropomorphic polytheism (cf. the language of laughter and mockery at 10, 12, 22): see ch. 2 n. 75.

[10] Τί δέ . . . καὶ γενναῖον ἔδρασεν οἷον θεός, καταφρονῶν ἀνθρώπων καὶ διαγελῶν καὶ παίζων τὸ συμβαῖνον ὁ Ἰησοῦς; (Celsus *apud* Origen, *Cels.* 2.33). The question is put in the mouth of a Jew (see 1.28) who makes specific reference, as Origen twice mentions (2.34), to Eur. *Bacchae*: Chadwick (1965) 94–5 has translation and notes, with xvi–xxix for the nature of Celsus' work. In reply to Celsus' mockery (γελᾶν, παίζειν: 2.34), Origen claims Jesus' behaviour as a model of how to 'despise' (καταφρονεῖν) those who laugh at one: a Christian parallel to certain Cynic and Stoic attitudes to laughter (ch. 6, 303, ch. 7, 380–1). Cf. the same paradigm later at e.g. John Chrys. *David* 3.4 (54.700 *PG*), citing Matthew 5.11 ('blessed are you when people insult you . . . because of me'). Cf. nn. 16–17 below.

in Pilate's palace has a sequel on Golgotha when Jesus is again mocked and reviled mercilessly, this time by both soldiers and others.[11] If this is the company that laughter keeps, or the extremes of contumely to which it can run, who (one might wonder) would want any part of it?

We should therefore not be surprised that the evidence of the New Testament as a whole suggests the activation of a general suspicion of laughter in the development of early Christianity, and on more than one level. Even if we leave on one side, as historically elusive (though we shall later encounter strong views on the subject), the question of Jesus' own disposition in this regard, we cannot ignore the fact that nowhere in the New Testament is anyone depicted as smiling or laughing benignly. Nor is there much trace of laughter-related states of mind in either its narratives or its doctrinal content, despite the attempts of some scholars to highlight elements of irony and wit in certain passages.[12] In the gospels themselves the only occurrence of laughter as such, apart from the episodes of the passion already cited, is the ridicule of Jesus by some bystanders on the occasion when, as recounted in all the synoptics, he declares the daughter of Jairus to be asleep not dead.[13] Elsewhere laughter is mentioned directly in the gospels only as a generalised symbol of joyfulness. In Luke's version of the beatitudes Jesus states 'happy are you who now weep, since you shall laugh' (μακάριοι οἱ κλαίοντες νῦν, ὅτι γελάσετε), but conversely 'woe to you who now laugh, since you shall grieve and weep' (οὐαί, οἱ γελῶντες νῦν, ὅτι πενθήσετε καὶ κλαύσετε).[14] These schematic contrasts echo a number of passages in the Old Testament which I shall shortly adduce.

---

[11] Matthew 27.39–44, Mark 15.29–32, Luke 23.35–7, 39. All three use ἐμπαίζειν and βλασφημεῖν (cf. n. 2 above). Luke also has ἐκμυκτηρίζειν (cf. 16.14: n. 13 below), lit. 'snort down the nostrils', used of god's derision in the Septuagint at Psalms 2.4 (n. 25 below), but of the enemies of the righteous at Psalms 34.16 [= 35.16]; it recurs in numerous later Christian authors but is rare in pagan texts, where the simplex μυκτηρίζειν (and cognates) is more usual. Cf. Screech (1997) 17–18, 24–7, with my Appendix 1 n. 14. Gnostic reversal of Jesus' mockery: n. 110 below.

[12] See Luck (1994) 765–7 for bibliography and debate on humour in the New Testament; Embry (1976) 433–5 provides a catalogue of examples, not all of them convincing; cf. Berger (1997) 198 ('rather labored interpretations'). Douglas (1975) 99–100 is happy to discern joke forms in some of Christ's parables; contrast Murdoch (1977) 73 = Murdoch (1997) 450, 'Christ makes witty remarks but not jokes,' Eco (1984) 81, 130. For a defence of Jesus against the charge of aversion to laughter, see Murray (1908); cf. n. 110 below. Morreall (1983) 126 runs together history and theology in maintaining that Christ *could* not have had a sense of humour. Saroglou (2002) makes too sweeping a psychological case for relative incompatibility between humour and 'religion' (largely Christianity; cf. ch. 4 n. 4); an opposing perspective in Berger (1997), esp. 205–15.

[13] Matthew 9.24, Mark 5.40, Luke 8.53: the verb is *katagelan* in every case. Cf. the mockery (ἐκμυκτηρίζειν: n. 11 above) of Jesus by the Pharisees at Luke 16.14.

[14] Luke 6.21, 25; cf. Epistle of James 4.9 (with Dion. Hal. *Ant. Rom.* 19.5.4 for a vivid pagan parallel to the second sentiment). Rengstorf (1964) 660 thinks these passages link laughter with worldly attachments; the beatitudes are not explicit on this point.

But we can immediately notice how they lend themselves to an image of Christians as suffering in the present – and suffering, among other things, the scoffing of their exultant enemies – for the sake of much greater rewards (including heavenly laughter) in the future.[15] Laughter, as a metonym for the soul's elation, is here displaced from the current life of the body onto the spiritualised joy of an eternal afterlife. This disjunction will prove a leitmotif in the materials to be discussed in this chapter.

Beyond the passages already noted, the presence of laughter in the New Testament is otherwise confined to its possible implication in, or association with, disapproved forms of verbal behaviour: abusiveness or insults (for which *loidoria* and *blasphēmia* are the commonest descriptions), foul or obscene speech (*aischrologein*) more generally, and joke-telling or facetious mirth (*eutrapelia*). The blind man who claims he was healed by Jesus is the object of abuse from the Pharisees at John 9.28, and Paul is accused of using abuse against the High Priest Ananias at Acts 23.4: the context in both cases is a tense dispute where the speaker wishes to expose an opponent to public belittlement. But it is in Paul's own ethical preaching that the themes of mockery, indecent language and joking figure most prominently. In the Pauline epistles such behaviour can represent either of two negative phenomena: the world's contempt for Christians, or an immoral temptation which Christians themselves must resist. At 1 Corinthians 4.12 Paul characterises Christian believers as being the object of an abusiveness to which they (should) respond only with pure speech: 'when we are insulted (λοιδορούμενοι) by others, we speak well of them (εὐλογοῦμεν)'. This characterisation no doubt implicitly alludes to the model of Jesus himself, a model explicitly invoked by the early Christian author of 1 Peter 2.23 ('when he was reviled, he did not revile in return').[16] The ethic adumbrated

---

[15] See e.g. the invocation of the beatitudes, with comments on the 'promise' of laughter, at Origen, *In Jer.* 20.6 (cf. n. 26 below), *Fragm. in Lam.* 10 (mentioning a patriarch called Gelos, cf. *Fragm. in Lucam* 110). Notoriously, Tertullian, *Spect.* 30 anticipates the Christian's revenge, laughing in heaven at pagans burning in Hell; cf. Screech (1997) 18. Some later Christians ascribe mockery of the damned directly to god: Verberckmoes (1997) 81. Note, by contrast, the rabbinical refusal to make claims about such future laughter: Rengstorf (1964) 662, Embry (1976) 433. Some Christians denied that future laughter would be bodily: see quotation from Gregory the Great in Resnick (1987) 92; cf., more obliquely, Basil, *Hom. de grat. act.* 31.228 *PG*, cited on 516 below.

[16] ὃς λοιδορούμενος οὐκ ἀντελοιδόρει. Cf. 1 Peter 3.9 for the same ideal in didactic form; later formulations include Greg. Naz. *Fun. Or.* 35.1033 *PG*, Cyrillus, *In Johan.* 2.454 *PG*, John Chrys. *In ep. 2 Cor.* 61.480 *PG*, Ephraem Syr. *Serm. mon. Eg.* 31 (Appendix 1 n. 26); for impassive endurance of laughter more generally, see e.g. Basil, *Epist.* 18.1, 169.1. In contrast, Greg. Nys. *Eun.* 1.1.612 (45.440 *PG*) considers 'turning laughter back' against the neo-Arian Eunomius (using the unique verb ἀντιγελᾶν), while Gregory of Nazianzus and others experimented with traditional 'iambic' modes of mockery: see Agosti (2001). For a remarkable case of combative Christian laughter in action, see Conybeare (2002), esp. 188–98, on Prudentius' depiction of the martyr Laurence.

in these texts pointedly overturns an inveterate tendency towards the justification of retaliatory, agonistic ridicule in many contexts of pagan Greek
culture, though it involves a form of self-denial which does have some
precedents in Greek philosophy.[17] Christians need not, however, actively
invite defamation or derision. In 1 Timothy 5.14 Paul expressly urges that
young widows should remarry and avoid giving their enemies 'any opening
for abuse/slander (*loidoria*)' on the grounds, we are left to infer, of suspected
sexual impropriety.

On the other hand, insulting language itself can be regarded as a vice
to which Christians themselves may yield, and one to be avoided as much
as any other form of sinfulness. Paul's first letter to the Corinthians twice
urges his readers to exclude from their group anyone who is given to abusiveness or slander: such people are bracketed by him in the same rank
of immorality as various sexual wrongdoers (including adulterers and perhaps male prostitutes), usurers, idolaters, drunkards and thieves.[18] Given
the vehemence and scope of Paul's denunciations in this setting, the epithet λοίδορος may well denote not just a propensity to rancour but also a
more diffuse habit of foul, unseemly language. If that is right, an emphasis
of this kind would align the Corinthians passages with two other Pauline
texts. The first is Ephesians 5.3–5. The authorship of this epistle has been
strenuously contested, but for my purposes this debate can be passed over,
since on any account the work represents views which the early church
accepted as Pauline. In this section of the letter certain speech habits are
again denounced in immediate proximity to sexual sins. This time, however, there is a more transparent association of thought between immorality
in word and action. The trio of nouns here applied to unacceptable language – *aischrotēs* (literally 'shamefulness'), *mōrologia* ('foolish speech'), and
eutrapelia (originally denoting elegant 'wittiness' but transformed in Christian usage to characterise deplorable frivolity or facetiousness) – makes it
clear that the author has in his sights a whole cluster of things that includes
lewd talk, sexual innuendo (or worse) and probably joking *tout court*.[19] The
other relevant Pauline passage is Colossians 3.8, which unquestionably refers

---

[17] John Chrys. *Virg.* 44 claims avoidance of retaliatory abuse as a new Christian ethic, missing from
Judaic morality. For pagan precedents, see ch. 6, 268, 275, 284, 303; but cf. ch. 1, 41–2, for the standard
Greek conviction that it was unmanly *vel sim.* not to retaliate to insults.
[18] 1 Cor. 5.11, 6.10–11; cf. Boswell (1980) 106–7, 335–53 on problems of sexual terminology in the second
passage.
[19] With this passage (expanding the stricture against 'rotten (σαπρός) talk', 4.29), compare ps.-Ignat.
Epist. Tars. 4.8, including *aischrologia* and *eutrapelia* in a long list of vices. On Christian *eutrapelia*,
see Rahner (1961), Screech (1997) 132–40 (unconvincing in his attempt, 134–5, to limit the damage
of Paul's denunciation), van der Horst (1990), O'Brien (1999) 360–1; cf. n. 71 below, with ch. 6,
312–13, on classical usage. Despite the conjunction of sexual acts with obscene talk, Paul, Ephes.

to impure, indecent speech (yet again alongside other sins, among them anger and lust) under the dual description of *blasphēmia* and *aischrologia*. The term *aischrologia* in particular, like *aischrotēs* in the preceding case, is likely to embrace both sexual obscenity and religious profanity, whether in situations of abusive quarrelling (which *blasphēmia* too, like *loidoria*, readily suggests) or in the carefree use of expletives. It is tempting to detect in these passages of Ephesians and Colossians a strong impulse towards a general (self-)censorship of Christian speech habits, a will to purge them not just of crude offensiveness but also of anything that might smack of the pursuit of mirth for its own sake. This means, among other things, that when in a later passage of Colossians Paul recommends his addressees to cultivate speech that is 'seasoned with salt', he has in mind something much closer to the savour of piety than the spirit of wittiness.[20]

Even if we give full weight to Paul's concern in the three letters I have cited with extremes of mockery, insults and swearing (the devil himself, *diabolos*, after all, was a 'slanderer'),[21] and even after we have taken account of the respects in which his strictures can be paralleled in the pagan traditions of moralising examined earlier in this book, it remains hard to see any worthwhile place at all for laughter in his austere moral outlook. Certainly that is an interpretation to which his words are open – in fact, the interpretation that was subsequently put on them by John Chrysostom, whose own antigelastic proclivities will bulk large later in this chapter.[22] Over and above, or perhaps in part because of, his awareness of the role that derision and public insults might play in the victimisation of Christians (having met with mockery himself for preaching the resurrection at Athens, he couples vilification, ὀνειδισμός, with physical violence among the tribulations of the early church),[23] Paul enunciates an aversion to abuse, indecency and

---

5.3–5 does not state the old principle (ch. 5 n. 19) that words conduce to equivalent deeds. But John Chrys. *In ep. Eph.* 17.2 (62.118–19 *PG*) does so (see 496 below); cf. Clem. *Paed.* 3.4.29 on the laughter of effeminate men as 'precursor of debauchery' (πορνείας πρόδρομον), with n. 52 below, and e.g. ps.-John Chrys. *Ascet. fac.* 48.1056 *PG* ('as you are in your speech, so in every way will you be – and far worse in your inner person').

[20] Coloss. 4.6: ὁ λόγος ὑμῶν πάντοτε ἐν χάριτι, ἅλατι ἠρτυμένος. 'Salt' can hardly mean laughter-inducing spiciness here; together with *charis* (here 'grace', not wit; cf. n. 45 below), it denotes the 'savour' of Christian wisdom.

[21] Or perhaps better, 'deceiver': see Chadwick (1996) 91–2, and for alternative derivations and associations cf. *PGL* 344–5, *s.v.* διάβολος. Paul condemns 'slanderers' at 1 Timothy 3.11, 2 Timothy 3.3. On the devil and laughter, cf. 498–9, 508 below.

[22] For John's treatment of Ephes. 5.3–5, see *In ep. Eph.* 17.2 (62.118–19 *PG*), with 496–503 below. Cf. Origen's commentary, *Fragm. in ep. Eph.* 24.

[23] See Hebrews 10.33: notice the verb θεατρίζεσθαι (to be 'put on show' etc.), which suggests intense public exposure; cf. Bauer (1979) 353, *PGL* 616, *s.v.* θεατρίζω. Athenian mockery (χλευάζειν) of Paul's preaching of the resurrection: Acts 17.32. Ridicule of Christians is attested in numerous later

ribaldry which has an ethical momentum of its own. Under the influence of this aversion, orthodox Christian views of laughter developed in a direction which not only represented a marked divergence from prevailing pagan practices and mores, but also opened up some distance from the codified Judaic sensibilities of the Old Testament.

Though it would stretch my brief to examine the latter in detail here, we do need to register that the Old Testament exhibits a wider, less filtered range of attitudes to laughter than can be found in the New.[24] Most fundamentally, even if some exegetes have tried to escape the point, Jahweh himself is thought of as a god capable (in whatever theological sense) of laughing, albeit predominantly with menacing scorn for evildoers, while a further layer in the divine endorsement of laughter is contributed by the motif of god's gift of laughter (the 'filling of mouths' with it) to those whom he favours.[25] Human characters can even laugh in response to Jahweh's own actions. Both Abraham and Sarah memorably do so in light-headed disbelief at the promise of a son in their old age (the eventual Isaac, whose name piquantly means 'may (god) laugh'). Sarah then falsely denies it when challenged by god, though she later proclaims, in regard to Isaac's birth, that 'the lord created laughter for me' (γέλωτά μοι ἐποίησεν κύριος), the latter a joyous laughter that others will share with her.[26] It is true that the Old Testament equates laughter chiefly with aggressive mockery. This is an

sources: e.g. Origen, *Cels.* 1.7, 46, 2.34 (cf. n. 10 above), 36, 4.23, 30, etc., Athanas. *Incarn.* 1.1–2, 33.2, 41.1–4, *Ctr. gentes* 1 (n. 9 above), Basil, *Reg. fus.* 8 (31.937 *PG*), *Hex.* 1.4, 8.6, John Chrys. *Oppugn.* 1.2–3 (47.322–3 *PG*), *Adv. Jud.* 8.8 (48.941 *PG*; n. 85 below), *In Mt.* 23.3 (57.311 *PG*), *Lud.* 4 (56.269 *PG*), ps.-Ignat. *Epist. Smyrn.* 7.6–7, ps.-Clem. *Hom.* 1.10–11; cf. nn. 40, 98 below on theatrical mockery of Christianity.

[24] See Baconsky (1996) 31–53 for a survey of Old Testament references to laughter, with Brenner (1990) for the Hebrew semantics (stressing the derisive end of the spectrum); cf. Embry (1976) 431–2, Kuschel (1992) 109–16.

[25] Jahweh's own laughter: esp. Psalms 2.4 (n. 11 above), 37.13, 59.8 (in all of which the Septuagint [nos. 2, 36, 58] has non-standard usage of ἐκγελᾶν as transitive, i.e. 'dismiss with laughter'), with Wisdom's laughter at Proverbs 1.26 (n. 27 below); god's mockery of the just at Job 9.23 is, of course, only putative. The attempt of Rengstorf (1964) 661 to deny that the Old Testament ascribes laughter to god is casuistry. Laughter bestowed on the virtuous: e.g. Genesis 21.6 (Sarah's verdict: n. 26 below), Psalms 126.2 ('mouths filled with laughter', where the Septuagint (125) has χαρά), Job 8.21 ('will fill their mouths with laughter', where the Septuagint does have γέλως). On Septuagint translations of Hebrew terms for 'laughter', consult Rengstorf (1964) 659, 661–2, Embry (1976) 430–1, with Brenner (1990) 45–58 for further information. At Amos 7.9 the Septuagint translates 'Isaac' (n. 26 below), here metonymic for Israel, by γέλως.

[26] Genesis 17.17, 18.12–15, 21.6: see Gilhus (1997) 24–5 for one interpretation, including an erotic subtext; cf. the shrewd remarks of Cohen (1999) 52–60 (though his statement on 53 about the Septuagint version of Genesis 18.13 is wrong: Sarah 'laughed to herself', ἐγέλασεν . . . ἐν ἑαυτῇ), arguing for laughter as a human response to incomprehensibility (cf. ch. 7 n. 3). On Isaac's name, see Sarna (1971) 4, Brenner (1990) 51–2. Origen, *In Jer.* 20.6 (n. 15 above) reads the episode in relation to Jesus' beatitudes. For Clement's and Philo's rather different allegorical emphases, see my text below.

especially common theme in Proverbs, where laughing is associated with folly, evil, pride and strife, and set in contrast to the ways of Wisdom – though Wisdom, like Jahweh himself, can in turn be imagined as laughing at the calamities of those who rejected her, while mockery *qua* religiously grounded satire of human failings is present in the authorial voice of more than one book of the Old Testament itself.[27] The association of laughter with folly also appears in a non-canonical text, Ecclesiasticus, which has much in common with Proverbs: in a passage whose Christian influence will be noted later, it states that 'a fool raises his voice in laughter, but a shrewd man will barely and quietly smile'.[28] Occasionally elsewhere in the Old Testament, however, we do encounter a positive acceptance of laughter as the appropriate expression of life-affirming well-being. This is most straightforwardly so in the laconic principle of Ecclesiastes that 'for every thing under the sky there is a right time . . . a time to weep and a time to laugh' – a principle which makes laughter emblematic of, as well as subject to, the shifting but ultimately balanced (and divinely ordained) cycles of existence.[29] As we shall see, this text is a frequent presence in the Greek patristic writings I shall shortly be scrutinising. But their understanding of it is heavily modified by the theological presupposition that the 'right time' for laughter is not in this world at all.

Even from the short collection of references just supplied it is possible to discern an uncertain but somewhat less constricting or anxious evaluation of the place of laughter in human life than the writings of Paul envisage. Judaic traditions clearly recognised the power of laughter as a weapon of religious and social enmity, but they also left room for a sense that laughter was part of the variegated totality of god's world (and therefore an image of god himself): to be guarded against, certainly, in its more foolish manifestations,

---

[27] The insulting laughter of folly: e.g. Proverbs 1.22, 9.7–8, 13.1–3, 14.6–9, 21.24, 22.10. Wisdom's own laughter: Proverbs 1.26. Cf. the non-canonical Wisdom 5.4: on judgement day the foolish/godless will recall with remorse their mockery of the virtuous. But the Old Testament also contains traces of 'mocking songs' in its own composition: Eissfeldt (1965) 92–4.

[28] 21.20, with 490 below. Cf. Ecclesiasticus 27.13 on fools' laughter (at 20.17 the fool himself is mocked), with 7.11 for a warning against derision of the unfortunate. *Ibid.* 19.30 is more subtle: one can learn everything about a person from dress, walk and 'the laughter of his teeth'. Ecclesiasticus 8.4, 'don't joke with an uneducated person, lest your ancestors be dishonoured', allows for a gentler as well as coarser kind of laughter but stresses the danger that the latter will overrun the former. Ecclesiasticus 30.9–10 warns against indulging the laughter of the young.

[29] Ecclesiastes 3.1–4 (cf. 8.6), where the Septuagint version uses *kairos* (cf. n. 65 below). The same book also speaks of laughter as a mark of folly or madness (περιφορά, Septuagint) and the vanity of earthly pleasures (2.2, 7.3–4, 7.6); it glances disapprovingly at the laughter of hedonistic feasting (10.19). See Greg. Nys. *Hom. in Eccl.* 2 (44.645–6 *PG*), with ch. 1 n. 23, for a vehement endorsement of this negative view; like his brother Basil (513–14 below), Gregory circumvents the worldly implications of Ecclesiastes 3.4 by equating its laughter with the deferred laughter of the beatitudes: see *Hom. in Eccl.* 6.

but appreciated in its rightful contexts, accepted as natural, and not stifled as inherently suspect or dangerous. It is worth noticing in passing here, as a special variant on those traditions, the position of the hellenised Jew Philo of Alexandria, who returns repeatedly in his philosophical reflections on the Old Testament (which, importantly, he read only in the Septuagint) to the story of Isaac's birth to Sarah and Abraham. Philo interprets this episode of Genesis in semi-allegorical terms, treating Isaac as figurative of god's gift of spiritual joy (*chara*) to the world of fallen humanity and a reward for those who lead lives of virtue. Philo reads the passage, in fact, as a narrative of the birth not so much of an individual as of laughter itself, the 'good laughter', as he sometimes calls it, which only god could create – god, as he spells out, himself the begetter of laughter. There is no doubt that Philo, partly under the influence of the Greek philosophy (Platonic, Pythagorean and Stoic) in which he was intensively educated and which left such an imprint on his mind, harboured some reservations about the most worldly forms of mirth, though that does not stop him going so far as to endorse even the hilarity involved in the good-natured inebriation of the wise. Certainly Philo does not drive a wedge between actual laughter and its spiritual symbolism; indeed, he defines laughter in one place precisely as 'a visible somatic sign of the invisible joy of the mind' (σημεῖον ἐπὶ τοῦ σώματος φανερὸν ἀφανοῦς τῆς κατὰ διάνοιαν χαρᾶς). Body and soul may belong to different realms, but there are values which can unite them. Philo has theological convictions to support his advocacy of a wisdom which displays itself in the laughter of a joyful countenance and which knows, in a renewal of an old Greek motif, how to mix 'play' and 'seriousness' in harmonious proportions.[30]

By contrast with Philo in particular and Judaic thought in general, early Christianity generated the conditions for a newly accentuated suspicion and principled avoidance of laughter. It did so with the ostensible warrant of the beatitudes at Luke 6.21 and 25 (475 above), together with the

---

[30] Philo's thoughts on the story of Isaac occur at e.g. *Praem.* 31–5, *Deter.* 124 (with god's creation/fatherhood of 'good laughter'), *Plant.* 168–9, *Leg. alleg.* 3.87, 217–19, *Mut. Nom.* 130–1, 137, 154–69, 175–6 (with 157, 166 for the birth of laughter); cf. Goodenough (1935) 153–5, Baconsky (1996) 38–42, with Dillon (1996) 139–83 for an overview of Philo's relationship to Greek philosophy. For Philo's (balanced) reservations about worldly laughter, see e.g. *Vita Mos.* 1.20 (Moses' avoidance of excessive childhood frivolity), 2.211 (disapproval of the laughter of games, mimes, dancing shows, *à propos* the celebration of the sabbath), *Congr. erud.* 61 (the foolish life 'full of laughter and comic jeering'). But set against this is the symbolism of the detestable life 'without laughter', *Quis rer. div.* 47–8, or the endorsement even of inebriated hilarity, *Plant.* 165–70 (cf. the laughter of the good symposium, *Somn.* 2.167–8), the latter possibly indebted to Aristotle's lost *Symposium* (fr. 677 Gigon, 102 Rose). The laughter of virtue and wisdom (e.g. *Leg. alleg.* 3.217) harmoniously mixes play and seriousness, *Plant.* 167–8; for Greek parallels, cf. ch. 3, 114–17, ch. 6, 295–6 (Socrates), 308–11 (Aristotle). Contrast the Pauline separation between 'joy', χαρά, and laughter: n. 82 below.

uncompromising impetus of that streak in Pauline ethics which I have already sketched. The tension that was created in this area between Judaic tradition and Christian innovation might be succinctly (if contestably) pictured as revolving around the difference between a laughing Jahweh and a laughterless Christ, but also, more broadly, between the divinely endorsed validity of human laughter in the right context ('a time to weep and a time to laugh') and the divinely enjoined *deferral* of laughter from earthly existence to the afterlife. In this regard, as the first epigraph to this chapter indicates, it became imperative for some Christians to relocate Ecclesiastes' 'right time' (*kairos*, in the Septuagint version) in another world and on another plane of existence altogether.

If Christian attitudes to laughter could find themselves in tension with Judaic traditions, they were in more pronounced conflict with the mores of the pagan environment which encircled them. The pagan culture of the Greek world had long been familiar with the idea of exceptionally agelastic, even antigelastic, individuals, and Greek philosophy had sometimes found reasons to cultivate deep wariness of the impulses that might feed laughter. But such reasons related to laughter's (arguably) symptomatic connections with purely worldly forms of folly (even, at the extreme, madness), lack of self-control, and social antagonism. Paganism as a whole, which ascribed a capacity for 'unquenchable laughter' to the gods themselves and which regarded human laughter as (among much else) finding an exemplary, life-enhancing setting in the festive worship of those gods, could never have grounded a systematic repudiation of laughter. Yet that was at any rate a path that was to be opened up for Christianity, and one which some of its adherents were to take. It is not the main purpose of this chapter to make sociological generalisations about entire groups or communities of Christians in this domain of behaviour. The extent to which hostility to laughter was translated into stable practice must have varied considerably. We shall glimpse frictions between principle and practice (as well as between discrepant principles) at several junctures in what follows. But my concern is not to gauge such variations in any detail, nor to grapple with such complicating factors as the existence of non-orthodox Christian sects which may have occupied divergent positions on some of the issues raised in this chapter.[31] I want, instead, to examine a series of bold and psychologically far-reaching attempts to use a negative evaluation of laughter as one element in the formulation of a new spiritual mentality, a religious *Lebensphilosophie*. My case will be built around an analysis of writings by three major church

---

[31] For one striking divergence, the laughing Jesus of some 'gnostic' gospels, see n. 110 below.

fathers, Clement of Alexandria, John Chrysostom and Basil of Caesarea, all of whom are important for my project in part because of their high level of education in Greek literature and philosophy and their corresponding ability to shape arguments about laughter that intersected with older issues in the traditions of Greek pagan thought.[32] I have chosen these three figures in particular, and taken in this order (even though Basil was actually an older contemporary of Chrysostom's), so as to construct a sequence of increasingly severe existential standpoints. If 'present mirth hath present laughter' is a sentiment that might serve to encapsulate a central tenet of Greek paganism, and even one strand in Judaic morality, the development of Christian ethics was gradually to bring into being its polar opposite: the conviction that 'true' laughter could only follow the death of the body and an escape from everything embedded in the world of the present.

CLEMENT OF ALEXANDRIA: THE PROTOCOLS OF THE CHRISTIAN BODY

Clement of Alexandria, writing in the late second and early third centuries, represents in his ethical outlook a concerted effort to synthesise elements of Christian and pagan thought. He works, in this respect, from the premise that Greek philosophy, in which he was fully educated, was a partial prefiguration of the true doctrines of Christianity. His *Paedagogus*, 'Tutor' (whose identity is that of Christ, the Logos, himself, *vis-à-vis* the 'children' who are his followers), offers practical instruction for Christians moving in a world of non-believers. Its subject-matter delineates the profile of an authentically Christian existence in relation to such fundamental areas of life as eating and drinking, sleeping, procreation, dress and bodily adornment, exercise and bathing. To some extent Clement is operating here in the traditions of Judaic wisdom literature which early Christianity had inherited. It is therefore no accident that the essay on laughter which occurs in the second book of *Paedagogus* quotes Ecclesiasticus 21.20, 'a fool raises his voice in laughter, but a shrewd man will barely and quietly smile'.[33] Nonetheless, Clement's exhortations have pointedly contemporary application. He writes with his

---

[32] Compact treatments of early Christianity's suspicions of laughter in Adkin (1985), who underestimates the amount of relevant material in John Chrysostom, and Gilhus (1997) 60–9 (largely neglecting the influence of Paul). A useful range of references in *PGL* 309, *s.v.* γέλως. The fullest account is Baconsky (1996).

[33] *Paed.* 2.5.46.4; for a later citation of the same passage of Ecclesiasticus, also drawing on Clement himself, see John Damasc. *Sacr. Par.* 96.77 *PG*. Clement's essay on laughter occupies *Paed.* 2.5.45–8: my references follow the edition of Marcovich (2002); there is light annotation in Marrou (1965), brief discussion in Baconsky (1996) 184–9.

gaze fixed pragmatically on the possibilities of a style of life suitable for relatively well-to-do Christians in economically and socially advanced urban centres such as Alexandria itself. One of his concerns, indeed (he wrote a separate work on the topic), is precisely with the route to salvation for the rich. Moreover, part of Clement's engagement with the sophistication of hellenised cultural life lies in the intellectual cast of his own writing, a form of writing permeated by knowledge of Greek philosophy and literature. Clement, himself a convert from a pagan milieu in which he had received an extensive grounding in literary-cum-philosophical *paideia*, works within a conceptual and cultural framework in which Greek mores provide simultaneously an object for criticism and a source of ideas that can be revised so as to help mould a new model of Christian ethics. How Clement negotiates between the two sides of this enterprise is a key aspect of his mentality.[34]

Laughter figures prominently as a subject in its own right in Book 2 of *Paedagogus*, where Clement turns to substantive issues of how to live a Christian life – and above all how to maintain a strict regime of discipline over the body (2.1.1) – in the culturally hellenised, politically Roman, present of Alexandria. After discussing questions of diet (where plain food, frugality and little or no wine-drinking are enjoined) and household luxury (gold, silver, glass and other costly materials are to be shunned), he treats the theme of 'how one should relax at feasts' (2.4). From there he moves directly to a disquisition on laughter (2.5), which is followed in turn by a section on obscenity, *aischrologia* (2.6), and another on 'what is to be guarded against by those who share refined companionship' (τοὺς ἀστείως συμβιοῦντας, 2.7), the last dealing essentially with rules and procedures of conviviality.[35] The chain of associations between this series of topics is significant. Clement focuses on issues of lifestyle and personal conduct that arise for those existing at a social level where customs of conspicuous consumption in dining, feasting and domestic luxury have a strong hold (or temptation). But he is far less interested in the socio-economic entailments of these phenomena than in their implications for the physical demeanour and ethical formation of the Christian individual. Paganism is here principally conceived as an arena of material, psychological and moral forces.

---

[34] Brown (1988) 122–39 appraises Clement's spiritual protocols for body and mind, including the influence on him of Stoic ideas; cf. Osborn (1976) 50–83. On Clement's relationship to Greek philosophy see Lilla (1971), esp. 9–59; for some Cynic affinities (though hardly concerning laughter: cf. ch. 7, 372–87) see Downing (1992) 241–8.

[35] The adverb ἀστείως in the title of 2.7 refers to refined standards of conduct at dinners/feasts; but Clement knew that *asteios* had associations with wit (ch. 9 n. 25) – hence his emphatic opening: 'let us steer entirely clear also of jokes that pave the way to offensiveness . . .' (ἀπέστω δέ, ἀπέστω ἡμῶν καὶ τὸ σκώπτειν ὕβρεως προκατάρχον).

Yet this fact itself exhibits the ambiguity of intellectual stance to which I have already referred, since it allows Clement to deploy ethical concepts and arguments that had been produced within earlier Greek culture, from whose philosophy and literature he frequently quotes alongside his scriptural sources. Indeed, given the emphasis on feasting in this stretch of the treatise, Clement is here engaged in rewriting the protocols of Greek pagan sympotic behaviour (which I examined in Chapter 3) in order to design a new Christian template of commensality.

The essay on laughter frames its subject as a matter of practical ethics, treating the propensity to laugh as symptomatic of bad character, a corruption of the 'inner person', an enemy of reason, and a step on the path to active immorality – all of which confirms how remote from corporeal literalism was the spiritual, indeed 'mystic', laughter and play of which, in a passage based on part of the story of Isaac in Genesis, Clement had spoken at one point in Book 1.[36] Right at the start of *Paedagogus* 2.5 Clement echoes and adapts the treatment of laughter in Books 3 and 10 of Plato's *Republic*. He borrows the Platonic motif of banishing dramatic poets and performers from the community, *politeia*, reapplying the latter term to '*our* community', i.e. the new Christian 'city of god' or 'heavenly state'.[37] In these terms Clement declares that 'people who act out comic (γελοῖα) or, rather, derisible (καταγελάστων) experiences must be expelled from our community'. The contrast between Clement's two adjectives, both of which etymologically imply 'meriting laughter', involves self-conscious moral nicety, as well as a further Platonic resonance. The theatrical performers in question naturally intend their words and actions to produce laughter, but Clement implies that the whole ethos of their performance deserves a different 'laughter', the reproachful dismissal of the (Christian) moralist. There is no doubt that Clement is conscious here of a passage from Plato's *Republic* where laughter itself (in certain contexts) is described as 'derisible' or 'contemptible' (*katagelastos*); he will quote this very passage later in his essay.[38] But there is something more than verbal paradox for Clement in calling laughter itself laughable. It is essential for

---

[36] See *Paed.* 1.5.21–3, where Clement translates the erotic 'play' (*paidia*) between Isaac and Rebecca at Genesis 21.8 (where the Septuagint's παίζειν translates a Hebrew verb for 'laugh') into a symbol of the 'divine play' which befits true believers; for Isaac's own outburst of 'mystic laughter', see 1.5.23.2. Cf. Philo's allegorical reading of Isaac (481 above), where there is less of a gap between the spiritual and bodily.

[37] *Paed.* 2.5.45.1. See Clement's 'heavenly state' at *Paed.* 1.12.98, with *PGL* 1113 for other Christian usage of *politeia*.

[38] καταγέλαστος . . . γέλως: Pl. *Rep.* 7.518b (ch. 6 n. 48), quoted at Clem. *Paed.* 2.5.47.1. Similar paradoxes: anon. *Comp. Men. Phil.* II 157–8 Jaekel, 'making mockery of laughter' (γέλωτος κατάγελως), Greg. Naz. *Orat.* 11.5 (35.837 *PG*), 'let us deride excess of laughter' (γέλωτος ἀμετρίας

the coherence of his case that the 'laughter' of contempt or condemnation is metaphorical or symbolic, since that case, as we shall see, depends
precisely on excluding ostentatious laughter from a Christian life.[39] What,
though, is so fundamentally objectionable about – so it seems – all forms of
(pagan) comedy? All language, Clement explains, flows from 'thought and
character' (ἀπὸ διανοίας καὶ ἤθους), and, in the language of Jesus at Luke
6.43, rotten fruit comes only from rotten trees. The subtext is evidently that
there is no comedy without polluted speech. In concrete terms Clement
is here condemning 'low' theatrical performers (μιμηλοί, 'impersonators',
as he calls them) of comic mimes and related public shows. In so doing
he is pronouncing a standard Christian judgement (which we shall meet
again), a judgement reflected in the church's refusal to baptise practising
mime-artists and one that is all the more intelligible if we take into account
that Christianity itself could be a target of parody in some kinds of mime.[40]

But Clement is also treating stage performers as agents of a corruption
that must be excluded from the soul of the individual, a tacit reworking of
the position expressed in Plato, *Republic* 10.606c. In that passage, Socrates
had warned against the danger of taking enjoyment in the theatre (but
also in listening to conversational jokes) from comic material one would
be ashamed to voice in one's own person: by relishing such performances
a spectator is insidiously exposed to influences that corrode his sense of
shame and turn him eventually into a 'comedian in his own life'. But this is
not offered in Plato's text as a clinching argument against either all comic
performances or all personal laughter. Comparison with *Republic* 3.396e,
where Socrates prohibits the young Guardians from acting out (or reciting)
comic scenes involving foul-mouthed, scurrilous figures, is pertinent here.
In both cases the concern is not with comedy *per se* but with comedy
whose contents might lead its audience to enjoy and feel indulgent towards
disreputable patterns of behaviour. Consistent with this are two passages of

καταγελάσωμεν), *Carm.* 933.15 *PG* (γέλως γέλωτος εὖ φρονοῦσιν ἄξιος, 'to the wise, laughter
deserves to be laughed at'); cf., with different force, 'the laugh laughing at the laugh' in Beckett's
Watt, Beckett (1963b) 47. Even antigelastic Christians use *katagel-* vocabulary liberally: e.g. John
Chrys. (twice) on Plato's *Republic* as 'derisible', *In Mt.* 1.4–5 (57.18–19 *PG*), or his injunction to
'deride' the present world (*ibid.* 4.12, 57.54 *PG*). Metonymic Christian derision of pagan laughter
itself appears in e.g. the passages of Athanasius and Evagrius schol. cited in ch. 2 n. 75; cf. n. 9 above,
and a fictional reflection in Eco (1984) 133.

[39] But it is hard to draw a line between metaphor and literalism at e.g. *Paed.* 2.3.39.2: extravagances
like silver/glass chamber-pots merit 'jeering and outright laughter' (χλεύη δὲ καὶ γέλως πλατύς).

[40] For anti-Christian mimes, see John Chrys. *In Mt.* 6.7 (57.71 *PG*), with 505–7 below, Greg. Naz.'s
references to theatrical mockery of Christians, *Orat.* 2.84 (35.489 *PG*), 22.8 (35.1140 *PG*), and the
parody of baptism at *Chron. Pasch.* p. 513 Dindorf. Cf. Reich (1903) 80–109, Baconsky (1996) 221–6,
Leyerle (2001) 25–6.

the *Laws*: 7.816d–817a, where the Athenian states that 'without laughable things it is not possible to understand serious things' and thus justifies the performance of suitable comic plays (though only by slaves and foreign professionals), and 11.935d–936b, where comedy and laughter of a playful kind (*paizein*) are deemed acceptable and restrictions are placed only on comic material that involves *thumos*, aggressive malice, including personal mockery of individuals.[41]

Clement's position on laughter is actually more radical than any of those adopted in Plato's texts. He contends, with some manipulation of the nuances of the adjective *geloios*, that because comic or amusing speech cannot but be the product of a 'risible' (and, by implication, flawed) character, not only must professional comic performers of comedy be 'expelled' but all the more so must 'we ourselves' eradicate laughter-making or joking (*gelōtopoiein*) from our lives.[42] Where Plato had made Socrates (and the Athenian in *Laws*) propose the selective 'censorship' of comedy/laughter on ethical and social grounds, while leaving room for engagement of humorous 'play' (*paizein*), Clement regards not only comic performances but *any* attempt to produce laughter, to create an effect of the 'laughable', as intrinsically undesirable. Even Plato, as the passage from *Laws* 7.816d–817a cited above indicates, had been prepared to contemplate an argument that some (though certainly not all) forms of laughter could be safely enjoyed at a distance, so to speak: the distance provided by professional stagings. Clement turns around such reasoning: if professional laughter-makers are intolerable, Christians will simply be making themselves into *surrogates* for them (which is even worse) if they laugh and joke in their own lives. If it is forbidden to be audiences of mime-artists etc., how, asks Clement, can we be 'emulators' or 'imitators' (*mimētai*, half-punning on the preceding use of *mimēloi*) of them? Nothing is further from Clement's intentions than the possibility of allowing a psychological or ethical 'safety margin' to be interposed between the mind of one who laughs and the things that prompt that laughter. Indeed, he repeats his equation between being deliberately 'comic' (*geloios*) and being actually 'derisible' or 'contemptible' (*katagelastos*). Anyone who tries to make others laugh can only do so, it seems, by making himself 'grossly shameful and contemptible' (ἐφυβριστὸν καὶ καταγέλαστον).

---

[41] Cf. ch. 6, 300–2, for Plato's treatment of comedy.

[42] The idea of a link between character and behaviour in the case of comic performers is not specifically Christian; it appears at Arist. *Poet.* 4.1448b24–7 (referring to early invective or 'blame-poetry') and is implicit in the restriction of comic acting to slaves and non-citizens at Pl. *Laws* 7.816–17, cited in my text above.

The spiritual core of Clement's view is vividly revealed when, referring to long-lasting pagan traditions of festive-cum-ritual revelry, he reasons that 'if we would never allow ourselves to take on a comic pose/form, as some people are seen to do in the processions, how could we endure having the *inner* person changed to a laughable form? And if we would never choose to twist our face into a laughable shape, how could we practise both being and appearing laughable in our words, making a mockery of that which is more precious than all other human attributes, the capacity for speech?'[43] Clement uses the image of pagan festival processions, in which masked performers traditionally indulged in obscene scurrility, to insinuate that there is something intrinsically debauched about the pursuit of laughter. But such festivities produce their immediate effect through the comedy of outward forms – masks, costumes and the bodily antics of the performers (the verb *schēmatizesthai* here echoing the established terminology of actorial gestures and poses, *schēmata*, including dance movements). That does not redeem them, of course; but how much worse, Clement stresses, to allow laughter to mould the 'inner person' (which ought, we must understand, to be an image of the divine) or to disfigure the nature of our speech-acts, 'accustoming us through the very words to shameful deeds'. The tightness of the causal chain of consequences in which laughter is implicated stands complete. One will not say certain laughter-making words (and Clement obviously has sexual obscenity firmly in mind) unless one has a correspondingly debased mind and character. And if one does say them, one is not far from *doing* them – a traditional anxiety.[44] It starts to look, then, as though the emphatic denunciation of comic performances is not only literally applicable to Christian avoidance of pagan festivities but is also and more potently a metaphor, in Platonic spirit, for what must be eradicated from the individual soul.

Clement's position is not exactly, however, a recipe for sheer puritanical dourness. As in other areas of conduct he eschews extreme asceticism or social withdrawal. But his position is finely balanced. This starts to emerge with a striking juxtaposition of statements: first, that 'one should be affable

---

[43] εἰ γὰρ γελοίως σχηματισθῆναι, καθάπερ ἐν ταῖς πομπαῖς ὁρῶνταί τινες, οὐκ ἂν ὑπομείναιμεν, πῶς ἂν εἰκότως τὸν ἐντὸς ἄνθρωπον ἐπὶ τὸ γελοιότερον σχηματιζόμενον ἀνασχοίμεθα; καὶ εἰ τὸ πρόσωπον οὐκ ἂν ἑκόντες ἐπὶ τὸ γελοιότερον μετασρέψαιμέν ποτε, πῶς ἂν κατὰ τοὺς λόγους ἐπιτηδεύσαιμεν εἶναί τε καὶ φαίνεσθαι γελοῖοι, τὸ τιμιώτερον πάντων τῶν ἐν ἀνθρώποις κτημάτων καταμωκώμενοι, τὸν λόγον; (*Paed.* 2.5.45.3–4). Cf. 2.3.35.4 (a slightly different point), with ch. 4, 177–83, for the kind of processions in question.

[44] The causal link between indecent words and actions is emphasised at 2.6, on *aischrologia*; cf. 2.7.54.1, 2.10.98. On the words–deeds nexus, see n. 19 above. The 'inner person' (a Pauline motif: Romans 7.22, Ephes. 3.16): *Paed.* 2.12.121.2, *Strom.* 3.4.34.2, with *Protr.* 10.98.4 for its status as 'in god's image'. On the latter motif, cf. Osborn (1957) 84–94.

but not make outright jokes' (χαριεντιστέον, οὐ γελωτοποιητέον, where the first Greek verb often itself means to be witty);[45] secondly, that 'laughter itself must be bridled' (αὐτὸν τὸν γέλωτα ἐπιστομιστέον). The notion of 'bridling' (literally, in Greek, 'to curb in the mouth') is ambiguous; when used later of obscene speech (2.6.49) and of loud-mouthed people (2.7.59), it denotes the imposition of total censorship or silence. But in the case of laughter, it becomes clear that Clement's goal is restriction not elimination. If he gave the impression at the start of the essay that laughter *per se* was to be deprecated, that was because his use of the terms *geloios* (comic, ludicrous) and *gelōtopoiein* (joke, play the buffoon) were stamped with the ribald excesses of mime actors and carnivalesque street performers. But he now explains that *how* one laughs matters, since it can express differences of moral character: it can display either orderly self-discipline (*kosmiotēs*) or rank indiscipline (*akolasia*). Throughout this passage there are overtones of the famous equestrian model of the soul in Plato's *Phaedrus*: laughter itself is to be 'bridled'; humans should no more laugh at everything than a horse neighs or snorts at everything (Clement is evidently thinking of the whinnying sound of loud laughter);[46] and the ideal is to give controlled relaxation (χαλᾶν, the verb used of slackening reins) to the 'severe' (αὐστηρόν) and 'highly tensed' (ὑπέρτονον) tendencies of a serious demeanour. Entwined with Platonic imagery, moreover, is a robustly Aristotelian principle, and one which would often create tension with antigelastic impulses in Christian thought. 'Put simply, whatever belongs by nature to human beings should not be extirpated from them; instead, one should impose measure (*metron*) and a sense of the appropriate time (*kairos*) on them: it does not follow from the fact that humans are animals capable of laughter that they should laugh at everything.'[47]

---

[45] Clement had used χαριεντίζεσθαι at 2.2.22 when allowing pleasantries at feasts to older men while implicitly denying them to younger people, whose tendency to become sexually 'inflamed', physically and psychologically, was foregrounded in discussion of drinking (2.2.20–1). See also 2.5.47, 2.7.57, with 494 below. For *charis* terms and laughter, see ch. 3 n. 27.

[46] Various Greek texts assimilate laughter (esp. κιχλίζειν, 'giggle', 'cackle': n. 52 below) to equine whinnying, usually against an erotic background: e.g. Hdas. *Mim.* 7.123, Macedonius, *Anth. Pal.* 5.245, with Headlam (1922) 366; cf. ch. 1 nn. 7–8.

[47] *Paed.* 2.5.46.1–2: for the Aristotelian tradition behind this, see Clem. *Strom.* 8.6.21, with ch. 6, 307–31. Christian tensions between antigelasticism and Aristotelian acceptance of laughter are observed by Le Goff (1990), (1992b) 161–2, (1997), Resnick (1987). On laughter and the 'right time', see General index *s.v. kairos*. Sextus, *Sent.* 279–80a (Chadwick (1959) 44) applies criteria of both *kairos* and *metron* to laughter. A further Aristotelian strand in Clement's position is his use of musical metaphors for (un)harmonious laughter at 2.5.46.2–3: see esp. χαλῶντας ἐμμελῶς, 'relaxing [sc. our seriousness] in a harmoniously balanced manner', with ch. 6 n. 121. But laughter as relaxation could be grounds for Christian suspicion: see Basil, *Epist.* 2.2.

Fortified with these philosophical tenets, alongside his conception of the sanctity of the 'inner person', Clement can offer a concise but revealing evaluation of the body language of laughter. 'The harmonious and orderly relaxation of the face . . . is called a smile . . . this is the laughter of the self-controlled. But the discordant dissolution of the face is called giggling in the case of women, which is the laughter of prostitutes, and guffawing in the case of men, which is a laughter like that of the suitors [sc. in the *Odyssey*], a laughter of wanton offensiveness.'[48] It is at this point that Clement quotes Ecclesiasticus 21.20 ('a fool raises his voice in laughter, but a shrewd man will barely and quietly smile'), characteristically allowing biblical and classical perspectives to converge; the folly of the Odyssean suitors is seen to exemplify a larger moral. But his attempt to exploit a further classical exemplum is much less effective. To reinforce his advice that avoidance of unruly laughter should not induce the Christian to be seen scowling (*skuthrōpos*), he adduces the case of Ajax at *Iliad* 7.212, entering battle 'with a smile on his gruesome face', μειδιόων βλοσυροῖσι προσώπασι.[49] It seems bizarre to appeal to what is (so I argued in Chapter 2) a startling image of Homeric blood-lust as a model for the Christian's sober yet smiling countenance; no other Christian writer in Greek, so far as I know, ever cites the Homeric line for such a purpose. In Clement's defence, he was probably influenced by ancient traditions of interpretation which misguidedly took the passage to describe a look of something like noble courage on Ajax's face.

Ajax apart, Clement's sensitivity to nuances of the body language of laughter shows traces of a Pauline wariness of sexuality. A crucial premise here is that excessive mirth involves a loosening of bodily control and decorum, and therefore tends to be both a symptom and sometimes even a cause of lasciviousness.[50] In this regard the laughter of women is considered especially disturbing, since it enacts a breakdown of the bashfulness and modesty paradigmatically expected of them. If the sight of a woman's neck, as she leans back her head to drink, can be erotically arousing (because,

---

[48] *Paed.* 2.5.46.3: ἡ μὲν γὰρ καθ' ἁρμονίαν τοῦ προσώπου . . . κόσμιος ἄνεσις μειδίαμα κέκληται . . .· σωφρονούντων ὁ γέλως <οὗτος>· ἡ δὲ ἐκμελὴς τοῦ προσώπου ἔκλυσις, εἰ μὲν ἐπὶ γυναικῶν γίνοιτο, κιχλισμὸς προσαγορεύεται, γέλως δέ ἐστι πορνικός, εἰ δὲ ἐπὶ ἀνδρῶν, καγχασμός· γέλως ἐστὶν οὗτος μνηστηριώδης κἀξυβρίζων. As regards smiling, it is misleading to say, with Baconsky (1996) 188, that Clement 'cites' Sextus, *Sent.* 280b ('don't allow yourself to relax beyond a smile', σεαυτῷ διαχεῖσθαι πέρα τοῦ μειδιᾶν μὴ ἐπιτρέψῃς: Chadwick (1959) 44; cf. ch. 6 n. 28). For guffawing, see 2.7.56.3 (after quotation from Pl. *Laws* 5.732c); cf. n. 104 below.

[49] See ch. 2, 55–8, for interpretation of the Iliadic passage. On attitudes to scowling, cf. n. 67 below.

[50] For other Christian descriptions of laughter as bodily 'loosening', see ch. 1 nn. 23–4.

for Clement, a kind of symbolic nakedness), how much more inviting might her suggestive giggling or tittering be?[51] 'It is above all adolescents and women', the *Paedagogus* tells us, 'whom laughter causes to slip into disrepute' (μάλιστα γὰρ μειρακίοις καὶ γυναιξὶν ὄλισθος εἰς διαβολὰς ὁ γέλως ἐστίν, 2.5.47.3). Concern with the dangers of (excessive) laughter on the part of the young had a long pedigree in pagan moralising. But Clement's reference to women in this connection represents a distinctively Christian unease. The connotations of his description of female giggling in this context as prostitutes' or whores' laughter, γέλως πορνικός (above), should not be diluted, even though the terminology of *porneia* is diffusely employed in Christian Greek for sexual lustfulness and depravity of every kind. Clement's phrase alerts us to a real fear of sexual temptresses: laughter, unless carefully monitored, is an instrument of erotic seduction.[52] Later in Book 2, Clement goes so far as to maintain that tickling or scratching the ears and making oneself sneeze are 'swinish itchings, rehearsals for unrestrained debauchery' (2.7.60, ὑώδεις εἰσὶ κνησμοί, πορνείας ἀκολάστου μελετητικοί). If such incidental movements can carry so much significance, it is no surprise that Clement perceives laughter, one of the most socially active and communicative forms of somatic expression, as worth so much attention by Christians who need to match their deportment with the spiritual demands of the 'inner person'.

---

[51] A woman's neck: *Paed.* 2.2.33.1; cf. the neck of the (allegorical) prostitute (also 'giggling': next note) at Philo, *Sacr. Ab.* 21, and Clement's general disapproval, endorsing the Stoic Zeno of Citium, of a 'neck thrown back' (*Paed.* 3.11.74.4 = Zeno *SVF* I 246), with 2.7.60.5 for a related point. See *Paed.* 2.7.54.2 for appropriate female dress in dining contexts. Clement thinks even a woman's foot should ideally not be seen: 2.11.117, 2.10.114.3; cf. 2.6.51.1 for a general prohibition on improper bodily exposure, with 2.10.107.5 against diaphanous garments.

[52] A definition of giggling as 'prostitutes' laughter' is also found in an anonymous glossary, Bekker (1814–21) I 271. The verb κιχλίζειν refers to girls at Theoc. 11.78, courtesans in Alciph. *Epist.* 2.24, 4.6 (cf. ch. 4 n. 56), prostitutes at Philo, *Sacr. Ab.* 21 (allegorical), and erotically active women at Hdas. *Mim.* 7.123, Macedonius, *Anth. Pal.* 5.245, Irenaeus epig. *Anth. Pal.* 5.251; cf. Perpillou (1982) 249–51. Clement himself uses it of feminised men (*Paed.* 3.4.29; cf. n. 19 above); cf. its use of young boys (implying high-pitched voices) at Ar. *Clouds* 983 (ch. 1 n. 53). Laughter and the female are often linked in Christian texts. John Chrys. *In Mt.* 4.7 (57.48 *PG*) compares perpetual guffawing (ἀνακαγχάζειν: n. 104 below) to a smirking courtesan (cf. ch. 4 n. 56); he links the laughter of immodest virgins with that of prostitutes, *Quod reg. fem.* 1, and treats laughter as a sort of proleptic loss of virginity, *ibid.* 11 (cf. Leyerle (2001) 176–7). More luridly, *Ad pop. Ant.* 14.4 (49.149 *PG*) describes how prostitutes first 'drink their victims' blood', then scoff mercilessly. Greg. Naz. contrasts bashful women's avoidance of laughter with others' sexually licentious mirth, *Carm.* 37.569.9, 586.1, 637.1, 646.3–4, 909.9 *PG*; like Clement and John, he also calls some laughter *pornikos*, *Carm.* 37.934.1 *PG*, *Orat.* 27.7; contrast his praise of his own mother, Nonna, for having *never* laughed (*Anth. Pal.* 8.25.3, with allusions to pagan profanities). Basil, *In ebr.* 14 (31.445–8 *PG*) describes the laughter and lewdness of female dancers during Easter festivities. Methodius, *Symp.* 5.6.17 (Debidour-Musurillo) connects laughter with other female vices.

Clement's reflections on laughter proceed by a conspicuously cautious dialectic. To seek out laughter is wrong, but gentle humour is permissible. One cannot extirpate something so natural, yet one need not give it free rein either. Smiling relaxation from excessive austerity is in order, but giggling and guffawing open the door to lasciviousness. Only a fool laughs loudly, but the Christian should avoid a scowling face; one can avoid the latter by use of smiling, yet 'even smiling needs to be tutored' (2.5.47.2, χρὴ δὲ καὶ τὸ μειδίαμα παιδαγωγεῖσθαι). That last remark allows Clement to circle back round to sexual concerns. If one is reacting to 'shameful' remarks, one should be seen to blush, not smile with complicit pleasure; and if one is reacting to 'painful' remarks (i.e. cruel jokes against others), one should look stern rather than pleased. As these qualifications indicate, two of Clement's prime concerns are with sexual jokes (which he condemns out of hand in section 2.6)[53] and aggressive, potentially wounding derision, the kind designed to cause pain to its targets and likely, as 2.7 explains, to lead to conflict and even violence (though that no doubt leaves scope even for a Christian to mock others behind their backs).[54] In both respects Clement is touching on ancient pressure points in moral attitudes to laughter; parallels with Aristotle, for instance, are obvious.[55] A quasi-Aristotelian dimension to Clement's case is also visible in his compendious formulation of the variables that affect an ethics of laughter: 'one should not always laugh (for that is immoderate), nor in the presence of older people or of others who deserve our deference (unless, at any rate, they themselves use pleasantries to relax us); nor should one laugh in front of just anybody or in every place or with everyone or at everything' (2.5.47). But there is a largely negative slant to all this, and a corresponding lack of much positive recognition of the value of laughter – in short, a very *un*aristotelian one-sidedness. Chief among the reasons for that difference is Clement's spiritual preoccupation with the snares of temptation that lurk inside and all around the Christian's body.

That preoccupation is again foregrounded in the final part of the essay on laughter, where the ideal of gravitas (*semnotēs*) is recommended as a social-cum-ethical prophylactic: 'to seem censorious, even from afar, is a way of scaring off those who would tempt you; for the mere look of gravitas

---

[53] Note there, however, Clement's insistence that parts of the body and their names are not *intrinsically* shameful: see ch. 5 n. 16.

[54] For an example of Clement's own gelastic vocabulary, see n. 39 above. For Christians' use of laughter, cf. e.g. the scoffing at gnostic heretics, partly stemming from Irenaeus, in Epiphan. *Pan.*, e.g. I 277 Holl, II 26 (but with emotional ambivalence: cf. II 42, 312), 314, III 476.

[55] See ch. 6, 317 (sexual jokes) and 317–18, 324 (causing/avoiding 'pain'); the latter issue is touched on again at Clem. *Paed.* 2.7.53.

can ward off the assaults of indecency'.[56] Clement has a highly developed
but apprehensive sense of the ethical expressiveness of the face, a sense
which may owe something, once more, to Ecclesiasticus, a book he knew
well.[57] The proleptic *refusal* of laughter, it seems, is not only a crucial badge
of inner character but also a beneficial strategy that can keep the insidious
dangers of others' giggles, sniggers and guffaws, with all the attendant
temptations of the flesh, at bay. When he goes on here, in typical fashion,
to quote Homer for his own purposes, the citation of *Odyssey* 14.465, with
its reference to 'laughing softly' (under the influence of wine),[58] brings to
the surface a worry about the *feminising* effects of bodily pleasure which
Clement voices elsewhere too. Here he speaks of wine, with its incitement
to laughter and dancing, as 'turning the *androgynous* character to softness'.
In the previous chapter, in a context dealing with the dangers of 'soft' music
at feasts, he had characterised the pleasure of the eyes and ears in general as
'effeminising' (2.4, ἀποθηλύνουσαν ἡδονήν). Together with intoxication,
music (excepting religious hymns), dancing, gluttony and, above all, sexual
indulgence, laughter is part of a nexus of feminised hedonism against which
Clement defines the scrupulous care of the self which the Christian must
cultivate.[59]

This makes it all the more notable, therefore, that Clement nonetheless
possesses a conception of Christian commensality framed in terms of the
'symposium' – the 'sober symposium', as he calls it (νηφαλίου συμποσίου,
2.4.41; cf. 'sober cups of friendship', 2.2.32.1), despite some allowance for
moderate wine-drinking. He assumes that eating and drinking at organised 'feasts' (εὐωχίαι, a term with some eucharistic resonance) is an integral
component of his community's social life, though attendance needs to be
regulated by mostly excluding the young of both sexes, as well as women of
all ages (2.7).[60] While the licentious pagan configuration of 'revel (*kōmos*),
sex and drunkenness' must of course be banished (2.4.40.1), together, as we

---

[56] 2.5.48.1: τὸ δὲ καὶ φαίνεσθαι καταπληκτικὸν πόρρωθεν τῶν πειρώντων ἐστὶ φυγαδευτικόν·
δυνατὴ γὰρ ἀποκρούσασθαι τῆς ἀσελγείας τὰς προσβολὰς καὶ ἐκ μόνης τῆς προσόψεως ἡ
σεμνότης. For the antigelastic connotations of *semnotēs*, cf. ch. 6 n. 27.

[57] Ecclesiasticus 19.29–30: despite the possibility of dissimulation, a man's appearance, including the
look on his face, displays his moral character. Clement quotes this passage for a different purpose at
Paed. 3.3.23; Chrysostom quotes it more than once, e.g. *Hom. in Mart.* 50.666 *PG*, *In Isaiam* 3.8.

[58] For the line in its context, see ch. 2, 86–7.

[59] Clement's derogatory language of the feminine, ingrained in Greek, can coexist with his assertion of
the ethical/spiritual equality of the sexes (*Paed.* 1.4.10–11). For later Christian equations of hedonism
(including laughter) with feminisation, see Greg. Nys. *Hom. in Eccl.* 2 (44.645–6 *PG*), Basil, *Reg.
fus.* 17 (31.964 *PG*).

[60] Clement's advice that 'women must not be allowed to reveal any part of their body' at 2.2.33.4, in
the course of attacking female shamelessness at feasts (cf. n. 51 above), implies that their attendance
is sometimes permissible. Few of his recommendations are black-and-white.

have just seen, with the effeminising allure of music and related pleasures, this still leaves room for an ideal of 'friendly companionship in drinking' (ἡ παρὰ πότον φιλοφροσύνη, 2.4.43; cf. ἡ πρὸς τοὺς συνόντας φιλο-φροσύνη, 2.7.53), and even, in a kind of Christianised oxymoron, 'the revel of thanksgiving', 'the eucharistic revel' (ὁ κῶμος ὁ εὐχάριστος, 2.4.43).[61] If Clement is prepared to appropriate and adapt in this way pagan conceptions of *kōmos* and *philophrosunē*, he can also be said to specify a determinate role for laughter within this commensal space. But it is an extremely attenuated role. Once a general aversion to full-blown laughter as a corporeally unseemly, distorted form of behaviour has been overlaid by the elimination of any trace of either sexual humour or *ad hominem* ridicule, what remains is reduced to the possibility that older men may occasionally use the gentlest kind of playfulness (*paizein*) and pleasantries (*charientizesthai*), not to poke fun at younger males but to educate them by drawing delicate attention to their virtues (2.7.57). Clement's two examples are hardly encouraging: a father may say of his bashful, taciturn son, 'my son never stops talking', thereby drawing attention to his good qualities by ironic reference to the vice that he lacks; and the same principle is instantiated by calling a disciplined teetotaller a rowdy drunkard. Moreover, only a very little of such banter is in place; those who like jokes (φιλοσκώμμονες) should be silenced (2.7.57.3). Odysseus was right to thrash Thersites (2.7.59.2), representative of the 'loud-mouths' of whom Clement says, as he did of laughter itself, that they must be 'bridled'.

Although, then, Clement's chapter on laughter, together with his remarks on the subject in the nearby sections of Book 2, ascribes some validity to laughter (or, more strictly, smiling) as a means of occasional relaxation from the strain of self-discipline, the balance of his views comes down ultimately on the antigelastic side. Anxieties about the unruliness, insidiousness and seductiveness of laughter prevail over acknowledgement of its naturalness or its associations with friendship and the shared pleasures of congenial company. This is because laughter is rooted in the easily 'effeminised' body, entangled in a cluster of desires and appetites that converge on the most seductive of pleasures: sex. Even so, Clement does to some extent grapple with the moral, psychological and social implications of laughter. It is an issue on which we can see him striving, partly under the influence of the Aristotelian naturalism in his Greek philosophical background, to negotiate

---

[61] Clement's positive appropriation of the term *kōmos* in just this one passage is remarkable. See *Paed.* 2.2.25 for another pejorative use (a detailed image of sympotic dissipation), and cf. the word's negative associations at Paul, Romans 13.13, Galatians 5.21, with ch. 3, 105–6, for the pagan practices involved. On the concept of sympotic *philophrosunē* see ch. 3 n. 24.

between considerations of *pro* and *contra*. He stops well short, for sure, of the uncompromisingly hostile approach to the subject which we meet in the next figure I want to examine – a figure prepared to state unequivocally that laughter belongs to the realm of the devil.

JOHN CHRYSOSTOM AND THE DANCE OF THE DEVIL

Two centuries after Clement and his learnedly formulated morality for the mostly well-to-do Christians of Alexandria, we find John Chrysostom preaching on the acute perils of laughter to a socially mixed Christian audience both in his home town of Antioch (from 386, the year of his ordination, to 397) and then, as its patriarch, in the imperial capital Constantinople (398–403/4). Although John himself received a substantially pagan education in classicising rhetoric, partly under Libanius, and writes (and/or speaks) in a carefully honed style that draws, though to a lesser extent than Clement's, on a heritage of pre-Christian Greek literature, his perspective on laughter is much more scathing and inflexible than Clement's. He raises the subject, at times obsessively, in numerous passages of his prolific output of sermons, many of which are couched in the form of commentaries on biblical works. I will concentrate on just three main examples from this homiletic corpus, the first two from his Antioch years, and the third from Constantinople.[62] In contrast to the rather urbane, somewhat impersonally protreptic manner of Clement, John fashions a vigorous, personalised technique of preaching that makes much use of one kind of rhetorical 'apostrophe', namely questions and exhortations addressed to the individual members of his congregation. The result is often a sense of attempting to get inside the souls of ordinary Christians, to tackle their most basic urges and temptations. Chrysostom's impassioned homiletic rhetoric, incorporating a 'confrontational' element that has roots in older traditions of pagan oratory, matches up spiritual guidance with trenchant observation of his congregations' real lives, or at any rate with an acerbic view of the life of the city around them. On his own testimony, his combative style sometimes won him passionate devotion, sometimes provoked resistance, among his hearers. Against the backdrop of this relationship, laughter, as we shall see, acquires complex significance. For the preacher himself, it comes to signify a faultline in human nature: its almost incorrigible attachment to the body, its immersion in the present, and its addiction to the thrills of gratification.

---

[62] The sermons on which I concentrate date from 390 (Matthew), c. 395–7 (Ephesians), and 402–3 (Hebrews): see Kelly (1995) 90–2, 133. I discuss the first two in reverse order for purely presentational reasons.

While John's own stance is clearly aligned with a sort of Pauline puritanism, his audience as a whole is assumed to be drawn to the powerful, indeed 'diabolical', appeal of mirth and scurrility. Where laughter is concerned, John is by no means preaching to the converted.[63]

I turn first to a portion of his discussion of the Epistle to the Ephesians, whose warnings against indecent and foolish speech habits I cited earlier (477 above). John starts by underlining, indeed strengthening, the Pauline association between lewd speech and sexual deeds ('words are paths that lead to deeds': οἱ γὰρ λόγοι τῶν πραγμάτων εἰσὶν ὁδοί – a sentiment with pagan antecedents), but he also makes a gesture in the direction of defending Paul against the charge of being excessively severe by wanting to expunge wit or facetiousness (*eutrapelia*) altogether.[64] He even implies, quite against the grain of Ephesians 5.4, that the apostle was keen on his own part to avoid the appearance of such harshness. It is telling that John himself occasionally displays some sensitivity to potential complaints about antigelastic harshness, but it has to be said that this sensitivity counts for extremely little, as will become clear, in the overall economy of his moralising critique of laughter. Having introduced his text from Ephesians 5.4, John frames a seemingly simple question: 'What good does it do to say something witty (*asteion*)? Laughter is all that you arouse.' Anyone who found that question and its answer, or the following analogy with craftsmen (who do not waste their time with useless tools), somewhat low key would be startled by the abruptness with which John then turns the whole subject of laughter into a momentously existential issue. 'The present time is not one for relaxation but for grief, afflictions, and lamentations – and yet *you*', he continues (with the second-person singular that singles out the individual auditor), 'are engaging in facetiousness!'[65] A reference to

---

[63] Kelly (1995) 55–103, 130–7 describes the context of John's sermons in Antioch and Constantinople; he rejects (92–3) the theory that John did not compose all the sermons for actual delivery; note the use of stenographic records in compiling the texts (*ibid.* 57–8, 93–4). Mayer and Allen (2000) 26–40, Hartney (2004a) 33–51, argue for diversity in the social composition of the congregations; cf. Baur (1959) I 206–30, II 82–93, an impressionistic treatment. On preaching as rhetorical performance art, see Leyerle (2001) 62–7; D'Alton (1940) 33–6 observes points of contact between John's preaching style and classical rhetoric. For the larger picture of John's ethical and social views, see Osborn (1976) 114–42, Chadwick (2001) 479–98, Frend (1984) 749–52, Hartney (2004a).

[64] *In ep. Eph.* 17.1 (62.118 *PG*); this use of φορτικός (harsh, severe: cf. e.g. *Prop. form.* 2, 51.210 *PG*) is very different from its application to joking etc. in pagan texts (ch. 1 n. 53). All subsequent references in my discussion of the sermon are to 17.2–3 (62.118–21 *PG*). On the words–deeds nexus, see nn. 19, 44 above. On John's own denials that he wishes to extirpate laughter altogether, see *In Mt.* 6.6 (57.69 *PG*), *In ep. Hebr.* 15.4 (63.122 *PG*), with my text below.

[65] οὐ διαχύσεως ὁ παρὼν καιρός, ἀλλὰ πένθους, θλίψεων καὶ ὀδυρμῶν· σὺ δὲ εὐτραπελεύῃ; On the 'right time' (*kairos*) motif, several times in this context (62.118–19 *PG*), cf. nn. 29, 47 above; but here it refers to the *whole* of the present life.

athletes, who do not make jokes when entering the stadium, both appeals to a conspicuous area of contemporary pagan culture (Antioch itself was a centre for athletic competition) and also hints at the (Pauline) trope of the Christian as competitor in the existential contest for eternal life.[66] But the nature of that contest is made all the more hazardous by the fact that the real antagonist is immensely powerful yet visible only to the spiritual imagination. John evokes the figure of the devil in characteristically incisive terms. 'He is prowling around, roaring with threats to snatch you . . . He is scheming to eject you from your shelter(?), he grinds his teeth, he bellows, he breathes fire that imperils your salvation. And *you* sit there making witty remarks and foolish conversation . . . !' Enacting his opposition to laughter through the vividly fearsome gestures of his own rhetoric, John is demanding that each of his hearers make a radical revaluation of seemingly trivial, everyday behaviour. They must shun all forms of casual banter and joking, because the flames of damnation are being stoked beneath them all. In this way laughter is transmuted from an ostensibly inconsequential, quotidian habit into a sign of disastrous self-ignorance, a foolish blindness to impending disaster – a dropping of one's guard against a literally diabolic menace.

Christians are, in fact, 'at war' with the (devil's) world. They are soldiers of god, and soldiers demonstrate on their very faces ('grim, tense, with fearful looks', σκυθρωπά . . . συνηγμένα . . . φοβερά) their concentrated readiness for the battles ahead.[67] Using a militant strain of imagery different from anything in Clement's reflections on laughter, John nonetheless converges on the latter's preoccupation with the suitability of a stern bodily exterior (sterner, in truth, than Clement had thought desirable) to express the moral dedication of the true believer. Not only do soldiers on campaign avoid shameful language, he claims (with great implausibility, though he is thinking of those on the brink of battle); they avoid speaking altogether. Silence befits the Christian warrior: language, the extended simile suggests, is both the principal ground on which the battle must be fought and a kind of flank that must not be left exposed. And laughter, John insists,

[66] John makes comparisons with athletes also at e.g. *In ep. Eph.* 13.3 (62.98 *PG*), 22.5 (62.162); cf. the wrestling imagery of *In Mt.* 6.7 (57.71 *PG*), echoing Paul, Ephes. 6.12, with 505 below. Paul as major source of such tropes: 1 Cor. 9.24–7 is a *locus classicus*; cf. e.g. Philippians 3.14, 2 Timothy 4.7–8, with Pfitzner (1967). For other such imagery in Christian texts, see esp. 1 Clement 5, 2 Clement 20, with *PGL* 46 (*s.vv.* ἀθλέω etc.). On Antioch as an athletic centre, see e.g. Downey (1939), Millon and Schouler (1988).

[67] For the adj. *skuthrōpos*, 'grim-faced', 'scowling', as agelastic or antigelastic signal, see 490 above, n. 108 below, with ch. 1 n. 101. In keeping with Jesus' words at Matthew 6.16, John does not always advocate a grim countenance: see esp. *In Mt.* 20.1 (57.285–7 *PG*), 30.3–4 (57.366–7), *In ep. Rom.* 21.2 (60.603 *PG*).

is a polluter of both language and action: it is both fed by and a feeder of shameless immorality. In the career of spiritual militarism, accordingly, 'the time for laughter could have no place' (οὐδένα τόπον ἐνταῦθα ὁ τοῦ γέλωτος ἂν ἔχοι καιρός).

Translating the danger of mirth into literal terms, and revealingly acknowledging that some of his hearers may fail to see why all this matters so much ('do you play and live amid dissipation, tell jokes, raise laughter, and think it doesn't matter?'), Chrysostom spells out the hard consequences of supposedly amusing speech: perjury, injury, obscenity. Yet the hearer is imagined as being still resistant: 'but our jokes (*asteia*) are not like that', he will counter. This is important in itself as an indication of a psychological gap between the mentality of 'ordinary' Christians and their preachers; laughter was more readily extirpated in sermonising theory than in practice.[68] John has to work hard to close the gap; as we shall see, it can open up even inside the church itself. The Pauline position of expelling *every* form of flippancy or facetiousness (*eutrapelia*) is now reasserted without the earlier gesture of defensiveness. It is reinforced by Christ's words, in the context of his prediction of his own death in the fourth gospel (John 16.20), that 'the world will rejoice, but you shall grieve'. This gives Chrysostom's dialectic a deadly thrust at this point – 'Christ was crucified on account of your sins, and do you laugh?' (a guilt-inducing rhetoric we shall encounter again) – and one which implicitly trades on the emotional charge, discussed at the start of this chapter, of the mockery of Jesus himself both in Pilate's palace and on the cross. It is as if laughter as such was irredeemably tainted by those acts of mockery, and thus made forever unavailable to a Christian life. It becomes progressively harder at this point to hear John's imaginary interlocutor daring to respond, 'but our jokes are not like that'.

Yet the next stage in John's argument does in fact return to the residual risk that his wholesale condemnation of mirth and wit will seem unsustainable and overdone. 'Since some people think the matter unimportant (*adiaphoron*)', he offers to explain the magnitude of its evil more fully. It is precisely part of the devil's own work, he suggests, to make us negligent about seemingly insignificant things; so that even if laughter *were* unimportant in itself, we would need to maintain an awareness of how 'great evils are generated and increased by it', frequently culminating in debauchery

---

[68] The same disjunction appears also in e.g. John's defensiveness about his prohibitions on dissolute wedding processions (cf. ch. 4 n. 125), *Prop. forn.* 2 (51.210 *PG*), *In ep. 1 Cor.* 12.5 (61.103 *PG*). On the relation of those remarks to John's preaching on marriage, cf. Brown (1988) 313–14.

(*porneia*).[69] This is, of course, an iteration of the Pauline linkage between laughter and sexual sin, a linkage we have also seen perpetually lurking in Clement's thoughts on the subject. John supplements it with an appeal to 'pagan' values, suggesting that everyone regards inappropriate or indecent indulgence in laughter as socially degrading (even going so far, he notes in later passages, as to try to control the behaviour of their *slaves* and *women* in this regard). Having asserted that no one who uses flippant witticisms (*eutrapela*) can be saintly, he adds, 'even if he is a Greek, such a person is contemptible (*katagelastos*, an almost incongruous term in this context); these things are permitted only to those on the stage'. Even pagans, John is claiming, condemn the person who indulges in (vulgar or excessive) laughter, though they permit the alliance of laughter and obscenity (*aischrotēs*) free rein in their theatres.[70] In the last part of the sermon, in fact, Chrysostom picks and chooses rather indiscriminately from a repertoire of arguments that at any rate educated pagans would have found familiar. He stresses that those who engage in mockery are likely to incur personal enmities; he portrays a taste for crude jesting as unworthy of the 'free', even of their slaves, befitting rather such socially low types as the buffoon (see below) and parasite; he even introduces an etymological argument that plays on a double sense of *eutrapelos* (on the one hand 'witty', on the other 'shifty' and unreliable).[71] At the same time he combats any thought that laughter could be related to virtue, or be something socially amiable, charming, or graceful (ἐπίχαρι): nothing, he insists, is more *ungraceful* (ἄχαρι). Patently he wants no truck with anything like an Aristotelian outlook that can locate certain forms of laughter within a scheme of excellences of character. On the contrary, John cannot resist insinuating that joking is the beginning of every other kind of vice: 'the one who practises wit will soon become a

---

[69] Cf. *Prop. forn.* 1 (51.209 *PG*): laughing at shameful jokes arouses evil desires. Laughter specifically opens the soul to the devil at ps.-John Chrys. *Ascet. fac.* 48.1056 *PG*. The devil himself proclaims laughter, along with drunkenness, lewdness and other pleasures, as a means of ensnaring souls in *Ev. Barth.* 4.44 (with 4.38). Cf. e.g. Greg. Nys. *Epist.* 17.3, and the demons who try to make the unsmiling abbot Pambo laugh at *Apophth. Patr.* 65.372 *PG*, with Baconsky (1996) 160–8 on the 'demonology' of laughter. For later versions of diabolic/demonic laughter, see Barasch (1991) 100–11, (1997) 185–6, 199–201, Ménager (1995) 126–9, Sauerländer (2006) 7, Karle (1932/3) 881–3. Modern formulations include Baudelaire (1976) 528–33 (cf. n. 83 below), translated in Baudelaire (1964) 150–4, Eco (1984) 474–7 (fictional), Kundera (1996) 85–7, 292; cf. Averintsev (1993) 13–14 on the Russian sobriquet of 'joker' for the devil.

[70] For pagan texts that stress the exceptional nature of theatrical contexts of laughter, see Pl. *Rep.* 10.606c, Lys. fr. 53 Thalheim, Arist. *Pol.* 7.17, 1336b20–3, with ch. 5, 246–7, 255–6.

[71] On Christian ideas of *eutrapelia*, cf. n. 19 above. John's pejorative conception of *eutrapelia* emerges not only in the Pauline terms of reference of the sermons on Ephesians – esp. 14.2 (62.103 *PG*), 17.1 (62.118), 17.2 (62.119) – but also in e.g. the image of laughter-soaked debauchery at *In ep. Col.* 1.6 (62.307 *PG*).

slanderer, and the slanderer will heap up myriad other evils on himself'. Equally, he condemns facetiousness (*eutrapelia*) for making the soul 'soft, lazy and slack', but also for 'giving birth' to acts of violence (*hubreis*) and even, with hyperbole, for 'causing wars'. This juxtaposition of two older themes in Greek moralising about laughter – its capacity to aggravate verbal derision into physical conflict, and its associations with the 'softness' of a luxurious, dissipated lifestyle – leaves a tension that John makes no attempt to resolve. Part of the price that he (no doubt willingly) pays for the unremittingly high-minded tone of his whole argument is an inability to distinguish between disparate kinds (and psychologies) of laughter.

John condemns the modes of laughter without nicety or compromise because, *au fond*, he is preaching to a society which he perceives as saturated with indecent mirth. Indeed, in the last part of the present sermon he inveighs against the invasion of churches themselves by the 'sickness' of jesting and humour. He even goes on to voice an expectation that by quoting examples of the type of witticisms he deprecates he will make (some of) his own congregation laugh. John finds himself in the paradoxical situation of being unable to condemn laughter without thereby arousing it with his own words. This section of the sermon thus leaves us with the unmistakable impression that its message is anything but congenial to all its hearers. It represents, rather, an elaborately antigelastic harangue of a community seemingly addicted to laughter, a society whose psychological 'horses' of passion and desire, as the concluding flourish of an allusion to Plato's *Phaedrus* indicates, are anything but under the firm control of the 'charioteer' reason. We shall see in more detail below just how concretely the indiscipline of laughter could infiltrate contexts of Christian worship itself.

We have already had a glimpse of how John's perception of the power of laughter was shaped in part by an awareness of the huge cultural presence of the theatre and its penumbra of public performances. In Antioch, we know that one of the churches where he preached was adjacent to a theatre, and both there and in Constantinople he complains that the theatre could draw away some of his congregation.[72] 'The stage', as the sermons on Ephesians emphasise, is the place *par excellence* to find shameless obscenity (*aischrotēs*), untimely laughter (γέλως ἄκαιρος), and general facetiousness (*eutrapelia*).[73] The public shows teem with a mass of comic performers – 'the so-called buffoons, the obscene dancers (τοὺς λεγομένους γελωτοποιούς,

---

[72] *Ad pop. Ant.* 15.1 (49.153 *PG*), *Lud.* 4 (56.268 *PG*).
[73] In addition to *In ep. Eph.* 17.2 (62.119 *PG*), Chrysostom speaks of 'untimely laughter' at e.g. *Ad pop. Ant.* 6.1 (49.82 *PG*), referring to the closing of the theatres at Antioch in 387, *In ep. 1 Cor.* 27.5 (61.231

τοὺς κόρδακας) . . . mime-artists, dancers and prostituted women' (μίμων, ὀρχηστῶν, γυναικῶν πορνῶν)'. What John has in his sights in this context, and in many equivalent passages elsewhere in his work, is principally the performance of 'mimes', a capacious genre with several sub-varieties but chiefly comprising short dramatic sketches with 'lowlife', often sexual, scenarios, and readily admitting elements of music, song, dance, juggling, and other assorted activities.[74] A mixture of male and female performers was involved; John, like most Christian authors, standardly denigrates the women in question as 'prostitutes', in part because female nudity was a regular ingredient (see below), in part because prostitution probably flourished in the vicinity of, even inside, the theatres.[75] Shows of mime type were not only put on in a variety of venues (amphitheatres, stadia, hippodromes, public squares, as well as theatres proper) but also spawned troupes of artists who could be hired for smaller gatherings such as private banquets, weddings (about whose bawdy customs John more than once expostulates: n. 68 above), or local festivals.

There are many threads to John's abundant references to theatre and associated performances. He has understandably been called 'one of the most remorseless of antitheatrical crusaders', but he is also clearly obsessed with the captivating power of theatre and is even prepared to speak for his own purposes of heaven as 'the theatre above'.[76] My focus here is on the manner in which parts of Chrysostom's confrontation with the culture and morality of theatre cluster around the phenomenon of laughter. In such passages the theatre is picked out as a prime symbol of, influence on, and mirror to, the immoral levity – the frivolous 'prostitution' and degeneracy of life itself – which John senses all around him and castigates unsparingly. It is where the sinful lusts of the time are most conspicuously dramatised for all to see. But it is also, in a Platonising twist of his case, a magnified image

---

PG), one of many tirades against luxury, and *In ep. Eph.* 17.2 (62.119 *PG*). On John's association of the theatre with obscene laughter, see also ch. 4 n. 125.

[74] Cunningham (1971) 3–11 supplies a concise overview of the varieties of mime; texts and translations of the fragments of mimes are in Rusten and Cunningham (2002) 355–421. Reich (1903), though dated, remains the fullest account of the genre's history; he discusses Chrysostom and other Christian views at 109–30. Cf. Wiemken (1972). Leyerle (2001) 13–41 surveys late-imperial theatrical performance practices, including mime.

[75] For a cultural perspective on John's and others' attitudes to female performers, see Webb (2002). John refers to 'prostitution' in the theatre also at e.g. *In Mt.* 10.5 (57.189 *PG*), *Lud.* 2–3 (56.266–7 *PG*).

[76] The first quotation comes from Barish (1981) 52; see 38–65 for his sketch of early Christianity's anti-theatrical polemics. 'The theatre above' (τὸ ἄνω θέατρον): John Chrys. *In Ep. ad Titum* 2.3 (62.674 *PG*). See Miles (2003) for this and other complexities in John's attitude to theatre, with Hartney (2004a) 140, 189, (2004b) 83–98 for the 'microcosmic theatre' of John's own preaching. Leyerle (2001) 42–74 finds hostility to theatre entwined with John's whole moral and social outlook.

of what individuals and social groups are in danger of becoming themselves if they do not follow the antigelastic principles which John urges on them: 'you are becoming a mime-actor, and yet are you not ashamed?'[77] The consequences of laughter overflow from the stage into the souls of those who gaze at its lascivious, buffoonish spectacles. In these terms John regards the performances of mime-actors, jesters, obscene dancers and the rest, not just as vulgar entertainment for the masses, but as a source of depraved feelings which are constantly, sinfully replenished in their eager audiences. It is this connection which allows him, when preaching on Paul's censure of *eutrapelia*, to treat as intertwined the private jokes of individuals and the sexually lubricious farces enacted in public venues.

The same preoccupations with both the spiritual and social evils stimulated by laughter appear in my second case study, a selection of passages from the long series of sermons on the gospel of Matthew which Chrysostom had delivered a few years earlier than those on Ephesians. In the first of the series John stresses how Christian ethics have been worked out 'down to the smallest details' of behaviour, regulating not only desire but also such things as 'intemperate use of the eyes, offensive language, and unruly laughter' (ὄψιν ἀκόλαστον καὶ ῥήματα ὑβριστικὰ καὶ γέλωτα ἄτακτον), as well as every aspect of physical and vocal deportment.[78] The restriction of laughter is part of a meticulous protocol for the Christian body, and while the adjective 'unruly' or 'disorderly' (ἄτακτος) – a recurrent favourite of John's – might be thought to leave open the possibility of a more judicious kind of laughter, there is no real sign of it in the reflections that John develops at various points during these homilies (and one has to look hard for such signs anywhere else either).[79] This can be explained in large part by his polemical engagement with what he takes to be the ingrained sinfulness of his hearers. In a world where (almost) everyone laughs too much, the need to elucidate any positive use for laughter is scarcely an urgent task. His congregation, evoked by means of inclusive first-person plurals, is collectively characterised as one that neglects speaking in ways pleasing to god, preferring instead to give voice to whatever the devil

---

[77] *In ep. Eph.* 17.3 (62.119 *PG*). This is a variant on the argument of Pl. *Rep.* 10.606c that enjoyment of comic theatre makes one 'a comic poet in one's own life'; cf. 486 above on Clement.

[78] *In Mt.* 1.5 (57.19 *PG*). John also calls laughter 'unruly' at e.g. *Laz.* 1.11 (48.978 *PG*), *Ad pop. Ant.* 15.1 (49.155 *PG*), 15.4 (49.199), *Pelag.* 4 (50.583 *PG*), *Expos. Psalm.* 41[42].2 (55.157 *PG*); cf. Greg. Naz. *Carm.* 934.2 *PG*.

[79] At *Ad pop. Ant.* 14.4 (49.158 *PG*) John concedes that 'laughing and telling jokes' are not *per se* sinful, but he does so to stress that they lead inexorably to sin, either by a slide from words to deeds (n. 19 above) or in the escalation from laughter to physical conflict. They should therefore be shunned as much as the sins themselves. Cf. *In ep. Hebr.* 15.4 (63.122 *PG*), with 509 below.

prompts – 'laughing, telling jokes, cursing aggressively, swearing, lying, perjuring', and more besides.[80] As if this accumulation were not enough to depict a thoroughly contaminated fabric of speech habits, John goes on to describe a scandalous perversion of priorities. 'Which of you standing here, tell me,' he challenges them, 'could recite a single psalm, or any other part of holy scripture, if asked to do so? None of you! And to compound this terrible state of affairs, you have become so slack towards matters of the spirit that you are all the more eager for the things that belong to satan's fires. If someone wants to test you on slanderous ditties or lewd and debauched songs (ᾠδάς . . . διαβολικάς, καὶ πορνικὰ καὶ κατακεκλασμένα μέλη), he'll find that you know these word for word and pass them on with great relish.'[81] Crude and obscene songs here form a telling link between casual ribaldry and the public performances of the theatre, which John will later address head-on. The transmission of such songs represents the laughter-imbued depravity of the theatre spilling over into the channels of daily social circulation. The laughter aroused by these songs is, for John, part of the common currency of sexual sinfulness.

John's fullest thoughts on laughter in the homilies on Matthew occur at 6.6–8 (57.69–72 *PG*), where he broaches the subject by way of elucidating the paradox of true Christian joy. Working in the Pauline tradition of Christians as 'grieving yet always rejoicing' (λυπούμενοι ἀεὶ δὲ χαίροντες), John holds that spiritual joy must be incessantly mediated through the sinner's tears of self-abasement and repentance.[82] To weep, in the right spirit, is to be an authentic 'imitator' of Christ, who, we are told in the passage printed as my second epigraph to this chapter, frequently wept himself but never laughed or smiled (though that does not stop Chrysostom, later in these sermons, from speaking of Jesus' quasi-gelastic derision, *kōmōdein*, of the Pharisees).[83] Rather as in his homily on Ephesians 5.4,

---

[80] *In Mt.* 2.5 (57.30 *PG*): γελῶντες . . . ἀστεῖα λέγοντες . . . καταρώμενοι καὶ ὑβρίζοντες . . . ὀμνύοντες καὶ ψευδόμενοι καὶ ἐπιορκοῦντες.

[81] *Ibid.* Cf. the similar complaints about knowledge of theatre and horse racing, but ignorance of scripture, at *Hom. in Rom. 16:3* 1.1 (51.188 *PG*), *Hom. in Joan.* 58.4 (59.320 *PG*); for lewd songs etc. cf. e.g. *Lud.* 2 (56.266 *PG*). John pictures members of his congregation leaving church to attend horse races, in an atmosphere of laughter, at *Lud.* 1 (56.263 *PG*): this dates from mid 399; see Kelly (1995) 131. Horse races, theatres and (popular) songs are catalogued together as pagan frivolities at Greg. Naz. *Orat.* 27.3. On Antioch's theatre and horse races, cf. Liebeschuetz (1972) 144–8.

[82] See Paul, 2 Cor. 6.10, with *ibid.* 7.4, Romans 5.3, 1 Thessalonians 1.6 for other conjunctions of joy and sorrow. (Note that at *In ep. Col.* 12 [62.383 *PG*] John suggests contemplating the sufferings of Paul himself as an antidote to the impulse to laugh.) Rudhardt (1992) 393–6 rightly observes that in the New Testament joy (χαρά etc.) is kept separate from laughter and subsumed into praise of god; differently Kuschel (1992) 120–6. Contrast the Jewish philosopher Philo, 481 above.

[83] Jesus never laughed or smiled: *In Mt.* 6.6. (57.69 *PG*), duplicating the claim for Paul; for the phrasing, cf. *Virg.* 63. Jesus' mockery (*kōmōdein*) of the Pharisees, *ibid.* 19.1–2 (57.275 *PG*), with n. 85 below;

where he showed some nervousness about the image of Paul as an enemy of every kind of humour, John here disavows any intention of eradicating laughter *tout court* (οὐ τὸν γέλωτα ἐκκόπτων) before proceeding to deem it as out of the question for Christians in the light of the last judgement. 'When you will have to render your accounts for so many things, are you sitting there laughing and joking and besotted with decadence?'[84] After reminding his congregation of Christ's beatitudes – 'woe to you who now laugh . . .', 'happy are you who now weep . . .' – John condenses his severe message into a characteristic trope (to which I will return): 'this is not the theatre of laughter; we have come together not to burst out into guffaws but to groan with grief' (οὐ γάρ ἐστι τὸ θέατρον τοῦτο γέλωτος, οὐδὲ διὰ τοῦτο συνήλθομεν, ἵνα ἀνακαγχάζωμεν, ἀλλ' ἵνα στενάζωμεν). Yet the person who would not even dare to smile in front of a king or emperor, he complains, laughs repeatedly without fear of the god who 'dwells within him'. As in the previous sermon I discussed, John hears laughter all around him and considers it a kind of echo of existential blindness and sinfulness.

But, again as in his remarks on Ephesians, Chrysostom confronts the possibility of resistance. This time, it comes not in the form of the objection that 'our jokes are not like that' but in a much stronger version, namely adherence to the hope that god will actually grant one a life of 'laughter and play' (γελᾶν καὶ παίζειν) rather than one of tears. We cannot identify specific dissenters here, but it is clear that they include those who see no reason to banish laughter from a Christian life; some of them may even

In Mt. 15.2 (57.224 PG) uses the same verb of Jahweh. The agelastic Christ recurs in John Chrys. In ep. Hebr. 15.4 (63.122 PG), and, a little earlier (overlooked by Resnick (1987) 96), in Basil, Reg. fus. 17 (31.961 PG); see 514–15 below; the reference to Ephraem Syrus in Barasch (1997) 184 appears to be an error. The idea is subsequently found in the pseudonymous *Epistle of Lentulus*, a medieval forgery: see Suchomski (1975) 12, Ménager (1995) 123–5, Frenschkowski (2002); Latin text in Aufhauser (1925) 43; English extracts in James (1924) 477–8, Elliott (1993) 542–3, Cartlidge and Elliott (2001) 47, Baxandall (1988) 57, 165–6 (wrongly calling it a 'Greek' forgery). Sarrazin (1994) 218 errs badly in claiming that Chrysostom cites the Lentulus letter; nor do we have reason to suppose John was 'repeating' an older apocryphal tradition, *pace* Innes (2002) 147 and (somewhat ambiguously) Le Goff (1990) 93 (mistiling the Lentulus epistle). Medieval versions of a non-laughing Christ can be traced through Curtius (1953) 420–1, Suchomski (1975) 11–13 (with 258 n. 26 for an important correction of Curtius), Le Goff (1990) 93, (1992a), Resnick (1987) 96–7, Barish (1981) 68, Kolve (1966) 126 (despite his misunderstanding at 297 n. 6), Verberckmoes (1997) 80, Ménager (1995) 121–6. Baudelaire (1976) 527–8 (with editor's note, 1346–7), translated in Baudelaire (1964) 150, recalls this tradition in making laughter a 'Satanic' symptom of the Fall; see n. 69 above, Sarrazin (1994) 218–19, and the fictional treatment in Eco (1984) 95, 130–1, 133. For pagan precedents of agelasticism, cf. ch. 1, 38–40. For non-canonical images of a laughing Jesus, see n. 110 below.

[84] τοσούτων τοίνυν μέλλων διδόναι εὐθύνας, κάθη γελῶν καὶ ἀστεῖα λέγων καὶ τρυφῇ προσέχων; Cf. Ephraem Syrus' notion that laughter *forgets* (the meaning of) death (οὐκ ἔχει μνήμην θανάτου), though it *is* a form of 'death': *Non rid.* 199–200 Phrantzoles. I have not seen Heffening (1927).

have regarded this, on their own terms, as a matter of principle. But if that was so, it made it all the more imperative for John to deal with them uncompromisingly. 'What could be more childish (παιδικώτερον) than this mentality?', he asks, punning on the etymology of *paizein* ('play'). But that dismissal is only a prelude to a much more devastating judgement. Together with its paradigmatic expression in laughter, 'play', *qua* frivolous immersion in the world, is the work of the devil. The fate of those who give themselves up to play is demonstrated by the doom of Sodom and by the degenerate humanity of Noah's time who were swept away by the flood. In contrast to the attitude we saw earlier in Clement, John's perspective excludes any possibility of 'play' as a temporary relief from the harsh demands of life. He offers a mutually exclusive choice between Christian values of humility, sobriety, repentance and, on the other side, the paganising pursuit of fleshly pleasure in the service of the devil (6.7). The starkness of the choice allows John to reintroduce his favoured imagery of contest, 'wrestling', and, above all, battle between 'the soldiers of Christ' (those who 'wield spiritual weapons') and the army of the devil, as well as to emblematise the latter by associating them with, so to speak, the professionals of laughter – 'those on the stage, the whoring women . . . the parasites, the flatterers'.

The devil is here presented as the ultimate patron of diseased culture. It is he who has 'built theatres in the cities, trained those jokers (*gelōtopoioi*), and used their harmfulness (*lumē*) to inflict such a pestilence (*loimos*) on the whole city'. And laughter itself is the root of the matter, since it is this response of the crowd to the foul-mouthed performances of 'the mime-actors of those comedies' (οἱ μῖμοι τῶν γελοίων ἐκείνων) which keeps the whole show going. 'If there were no one to watch such things, there wouldn't be anyone to perform them either,' as John remarks with a logic designed to block any self-exculpation: the devil's patronage of theatres and actors would count for nothing if the spectators did not themselves succumb to the invitation. John makes it clear here that he is aiming at the mass audiences of mimes (in a flexible application, as I earlier explained) on festival days. He addresses those who abandon their 'workshops and crafts' to spend the whole day watching such things. By doing so they expose to ridicule 'the solemn business of marriage' (John evidently has mimes on adultery themes, a common type, in mind), and, worst of all, they even allow mockery of 'the great mystery' of Christian ritual itself.[85] The idea

---

[85] *In Mt* 6.7 (57.71 *PG*). The verb ἐκπομπεύειν, 'put on parade', is used often by Chrysostom, both positively and negatively; cf. e.g. *In Mt.* 3.2 (57.33 *PG*), 4.3 (57.42). Here it signifies 'expose to

of Christianity itself being mocked – a repetition of the Roman soldiers' sadistic humiliation of Jesus himself – is always lurking in the shadows of John's tirades.

John is preaching, then, in the very teeth of the theatrical culture of his era, openly admitting that he is attacking forms of experience to which many of his hearers are addicted. He is frank about the mass appeal of the cultural institutions against which he directs his spiritual invective. During the performance of 'adultery' mimes, the theatre rings with the sound of 'applause, clamour, and peals of laughter' (κρότοι καὶ κραυγὴ καὶ γέλως πολύς, 6.8). To try to undercut the popularity of such shows, John sketches two further, and subtly related, lines of argument. One (6.7) is that after enjoying adultery on stage spectators should be unable to look their own wives in the eye (the eye, as he later stresses, being the very organ of corruption in the theatre), an interesting attempt to associate guilt with the idea of taking pleasure in the degradation (he uses the verb *hubrizein*) of women *per se*. The other (6.8) is a riposte to the imagined objection that 'what takes place [sc. in the theatre] is just play-acting' (ὑπόκρισις τὰ γινόμενα). That riposte involves a reworking of two old Platonic arguments. Firstly, if it is wrong to do something, it must be wrong to encourage the mimesis – the representation or artistic enactment – of this same behaviour (unless at any rate, as a Platonist would say, there is a corrective element of censure built into the very terms of the depiction). Secondly, such dramatic performances actually infect people's lives: 'adultery plays' produce real-life adulterers.[86] But in both respects John knows that he is battling against the ingrained assumption that there *is* a difference between life and theatre. He complains that people who would never tolerate female nudity in the agora go to the theatre precisely to see and enjoy it, and he tries to block the excuse that 'the one stripped naked is a whore' by insisting that what is debased in either case is 'the same nature and the same body'. When John reminds his congregation that (self-awareness of) 'nakedness' is a mark of original sin, the obviousness of his biblical reference disguises a subtle subtext, since nakedness was precisely that to which

---

ridicule'; cf. ch. 4, 179, for the simplex verb, with John's use of it for Jesus' own derision of the Pharisees at *In Mt.* 19.1 (57.275 *PG*), cf. n. 83 above. For mimes that mocked Christianity itself see n. 40 above. As regards John's sensitivity to derision of Christians by other groups, note *Adv. Jud.* 8.8 (48.941 *PG*) for supposed mockery of Antiochene Christians by Jews, with Meeks and Wilken (1978) 25–36, Liebeschuetz (1972) 34–5 on the context of John's antisemitic attitudes. For adultery as a mime theme, see e.g. Choric. *Apol. Mim.* 26, 33, 35, 54–5, 75 (Foerster), with Reynolds (1946), esp. 80–1.

[86] See Halliwell (2000b) 37–117 for the Platonic texts that bear on these two lines of argument. Cf. John's tirade at *Lud.* 2–3 (56.266–7 *PG*), where watching 'prostitutes' on stage (cf. n. 75 above) makes men take home (an image, *eidōlon*, of) the prostitute in their souls.

Adam and Eve's *eyes were opened* when they ate the forbidden fruit (Genesis 3.7), while it is 'licentious' or 'unrestrained' viewing (ἀκόλαστος ὄψις) of theatrical nudity that is the central target of this part of his argument. And we might add that by concluding the sermon with a critique of sexual shamelessness in both actors and audiences, Chrysostom does not lose sight of his earlier case against laughter: the disobedience of Adam and Eve was the beginning of human sin and grief, the very conditions which require the tears of repentance and the avoidance of laughter which he had earlier driven home at some length.

I move now (more briefly) to my third example of John's antigelasticism, which belongs to the sermons he delivered in Constantinople on Paul's letter to the Hebrews. This final selection of material both reinforces and, in some respects, clarifies the texts I have already examined. Revealingly, John gets onto the subject of laughter by an abrupt, oblique movement, as though looking for any chance to introduce it. After commenting on Paul's condemnation of the love of money, he shifts, via an image of the covetous man standing around laughing like an actress (a stock motif, as we have seen, in the lexicon of John's invective), to a diatribe against laughter itself. The boundaries between different forms of vice are blurred; there is a sense, rather Pauline in its elasticity, that any form of sin will create openings for others – a sense which the fluidity of laughter suits well. But there is also an authentic immediacy here, a vehement confrontation with the bodily unruliness that John perceives all around him. The sound of laughter echoes behind Chrysostom's very words.

All our affairs have turned into laughter, mirth, and facetiousness … I am saying this not only to worldly men; I know those I am alluding to – the church itself has been filled with laughter. If somebody says something facetious, laughter immediately spreads among those seated nearby. And what is most shocking is that many people do not desist from laughter even during the actual time of prayers.[87]

This is perhaps John's most vivid evocation of laughter as a contagious behaviour so compulsive that it pollutes even the inside of his church, where ordinary habits of socialising are clearly present and defy the demand for a special atmosphere of unbroken piety.

But precisely because what he is trying to counteract is, on one level, so ordinary and commonplace, John resorts to his ultimate diagnosis of

---

[87] γέλως γέγονε τὰ ἡμέτερα καὶ πολιτισμὸς καὶ ἀστειότης· . . . οὐ πρὸς τοὺς βιωτικοὺς ἄνδρας μόνον λέγω ταῦτα, ἀλλ' οἶδα οὓς αἰνίττομαι· γέλωτος γὰρ ἐμπέπλησται ἡ ἐκκλησία. ἂν ὁ δεῖνα ἀστεῖον εἴπῃ, γέλως εὐθέως ἐν τοῖς καθημένοις γίνεται· καὶ τὸ θαυμαστόν, ἐν αὐτῷ τῷ καιρῷ τῆς εὐχῆς οὐ παύονται πολλοὶ τοῦ γελᾶν. (*In ep. Hebr.* 15.4: 63.121 *PG*.) All following citations are from this same section (63.121–4 *PG*).

its perniciousness. 'The devil is dancing everywhere, he has got inside everyone, he is controlling everyone,' he expostulates, with a rhetorically intense vision (we should hardly think of it as metaphor) of laughter as a diabolical *incarnation*.[88] To complement this vision, which trades on but greatly amplifies an established association between the physical exuberance of laughter and dancing, John not only reminds his audience of Paul's attack (in Ephesians, not Hebrews) on shameful speech and facetiousness, he also returns to the image of the agelastic Christ which he had promoted in his sermons on Matthew. He now challenges each of his hearers to look that image in the face. 'Do *you* laugh?', he asks them with almost incantatory repetition (no less than eight times, in fact, in a short space). 'You who have been crucified, you who are in mourning – do *you* laugh, tell me? Where did you hear Christ doing this? Nowhere, though he was often downcast . . . and wept . . . and was troubled . . . And do *you* laugh?'[89] This is spiritual interrogation delivered at the highest pitch of accusatory fervour. John's congregation must choose between having a body inhabited by the dancing devil, or living a life of 'grief and tribulation, mortification and subjection of the flesh' that is, ideally, a sort of reenactment of the crucifixion of the god-man who never laughed. By comparison, the references which follow, to god's rebuke of Sarah for laughing (in Genesis 18.13–15) and to the familiar beatitude, 'woe to those who laugh, for they will weep' (a paraphrase of Luke 6.25), seem homiletic gestures of a by now much more routine kind.

As in his sermons on Matthew, John is aware that however forceful his own antigelasticism, it may nonetheless meet a barrier of insouciance. How can something as natural as laughter really be the work of the devil? Indeed, he imagines his own sermon being *rebutted* by laughter: 'Perhaps there are some of you so dissipated and frivolous as actually to laugh in the face of this rebuke, at the very fact that laughter is the subject of this discussion.' In part he is no doubt aiming this challenge at those on the fringes, as it were, of his audience, those least open to his message and least afraid, as he says, of the consequences of their behaviour. But he is also attempting to combat

[88] πανταχοῦ χορεύει ὁ διάβολος, πάντας ἐνεδύσατο, πάντων κρατεῖ. The verb ἐνδύεσθαι, which can mean 'put on' garments/costume, is sometimes used to express the doctrine of incarnation: see John himself in the same sermons, *In ep. Hebr.* 4.3 (63.41 *PG*), with *PGL* 469–70 for further references; cf. Paul, *Ephes.* 4.24, where it describes assuming a new (spiritual) identity, with Pl. *Rep.* 10.620c for its application to a soul's entry into a body. The devil also 'dances' (as he did 'through Salome') at *In Mt.* 48.5 (58.493 *PG*), *In ep. Col.* 8.5 (62.358 *PG*). John associates laughter and dancing pejoratively at *Ad pop. Ant.* 18.4 (49.187 *PG*); cf. ch. 1 nn. 45, 91 for pagan antecedents. Like laughter, true Christian dancing is deferred to the next world, *In ep. Hebr.* 29.7 (63.201 *PG*), cf. e.g. *In Mt.* 1.5 (57.20 *PG*); but at *Ad pop. Ant.* 19.1 (49.187) John appropriates the imagery of dance and festivity for the cult of martyrs.
[89] The metaphor of the Christian 'crucified' with Christ depends especially on Paul, Romans 6.6.

instincts that many if not most of his congregation might find it difficult to consider sinful.[90] This is clear, for one thing, from the way in which he moves on to address respectable married women, women who, he says, would hesitate to laugh openly in the presence of their husbands but who are 'always' doing so in the church, despite the seeming piety of their veiled heads and their intention of confessing their sins. Chrysostom is evidently not describing deliberately irreverent scurrility. He is speaking of the low-level laughter that accompanies social interactions between women inside the church building, yet his words make such things sound inescapably offensive to god ('how, then, will you be able to appease him?'). What this brings out is that the preacher's severity runs the risk of making extreme demands on the habits, the psychological reflexes, of the laity.[91]

Knowing this, John makes a very rare gesture of compromise on the subject.

> And what is wrong with laughter, it will be said. There is nothing wrong with laughter as such; what is wrong is to practise it excessively and at the wrong time. Laughter has been planted in our nature, so that when we see friends after a long interval we may behave this way, or when we see people distraught and afraid, we may soothe them with a smile – but *not* so that we should guffaw and always be laughing! Laughter has been planted in our soul so that our soul may sometimes be relaxed, but not dissipated.[92]

Taken in isolation, this stance looks measured. But we know from what precedes and follows it, as well as from the kind of material already adduced from other sermons, that the ostensible moderateness is a hook with which to fix the hearer's concentration on John's more far-reaching advice. Two points about the final section of the present sermon will be sufficient to cement that claim. Having made his apparent concession to human nature, John makes a pair of moves which reestablish his priorities. The first is a comparison between the instinctive roots of laughter and the instinctive nature of sexual desire: in both cases, the presence of the instinct, he insists,

---

[90] Another indication of John's awareness of being mocked (*kōmōdein*) for his views is *In ep. Col.* 7.5 (62.349 *PG*), where he is attacking decadent luxury (including silver chamber-pots: cf. n. 39 above) but feels the need, given his sarcasm, to *deny* that he himself is 'speaking in mirth' (γελῶντά με λέγειν, 62.350).

[91] On the presence of wealthy women in John's congregations, see Hartney (2004a) 133–42, with 85–105 for his attitudes to women in general.

[92] καὶ τί κακὸν ὁ γέλως, φησίν; οὐ κακὸν ὁ γέλως, ἀλλὰ κακὸν τὸ παρὰ μέτρον, τὸ ἄκαιρον. ὁ γέλως ἔγκειται ἐν ἡμῖν, ἵνα ὅταν φίλους ἴδωμεν διὰ μακροῦ χρόνου, τοῦτο ποιῶμεν, ὅταν τινὰς καταπεπληγμένους καὶ δεδοικότας, ἀνῶμεν αὐτοὺς τῷ μειδιάματι, οὐχ ἵνα ἀνακαγχάζωμεν καὶ ἀεὶ γελῶμεν· ὁ γέλως ἔγκειται τῇ ψυχῇ τῇ ἡμετέρᾳ ἵνα ἀνῇταί ποτε ἡ ψυχή, οὐχ ἵνα διαχέηται. (*In ep. Hebr.* 15.4: 63.122 *PG*.) The attempt of Leyerle (2001) 100–42 (cf. 6) to trace Aristophanic/comic strands in some of John's own work is overstated (and faulty in detail).

is not an argument for simply yielding to it. The comparison is more than formal. The subtext, Pauline in spirit, is that laughter has an affinity with sexual desire: both are ways of seeking the gratifications of a bodily existence in the present. John's second gesture is to reassert his protreptic pressure towards a life of 'tears', not laughter. 'Serve god with tears, so that you may be able to wash away your sins.' Yet here at once he anticipates not only scepticism but actual mockery (he uses the rare verb διαμωκᾶσθαι, to 'pour scorn on') on the part of the 'many' Christians who are familiar with his preaching but are themselves, as he sees it, wedded to the philosophy of 'let us eat and drink, since tomorrow we die', a biblical quotation but one which matches the real opposition to asceticism that we heard about also in the sermons on Matthew.[93] To counter this worldly viewpoint, Chrysostom can only reiterate the biblical backing for his puritanism in Ecclesiastes' critique of hedonism, though without finding space to integrate the counterbalancing motif of 'a time to weep and a time to laugh' from that same book. Rather, and as we shall shortly see in Basil as well, the contrast between those two 'times' is remapped onto the difference between the temporary life of the present and the future of eternity. There is, in the end, no real balance to be struck in this world. 'Let us grieve, my beloved, let us grieve', intones John, 'in order that we may truly laugh, in order that we may truly take pleasure in the time of pure joy.' For anyone who has followed the path of his thoughts, the conclusion is unquestionable. The only authentic Christian laughter must be postponed to another realm.

From the selection of evidence I have assembled, we can be left in no doubt that John Chrysostom's attitude to laughter grows out of an uncompromising ethical code of both corporeal and psychological self-surveillance. Holding a standard Christian 'two-world' model which construes the present life as a kind of grief-ridden exile, John defers the experience of true rejoicing to the 'kingdom' to come.[94] Laughter in the present becomes an indicator of sinfully perverted values: a contradiction of Christ's own example as well as the message of the beatitudes, a refusal of repentance, a shameless celebration of the fallen state itself (especially as symbolised in human nakedness), a yielding to the impulsive gratifications of the

[93] 'Let us eat . . .', from Isaiah 22.13 (quoted at Paul, 1 Cor. 15.32), is a commonplace in both Greco-Roman and Near Eastern literature: Pfeiffer (1960) 63–4, Ameling (1985); cf. ch. 3 n. 40. John also uses διαμωκᾶσθαι, of his Christian critics, at *In Acta* 16.3 (60.131 *PG*), a context where he tells his audience that 'relaxation is always wrong' (πανταχοῦ γὰρ ἡ ἄνεσις . . . κακόν). On μωκ- terms, cf. Appendix 1 n. 14.
[94] Note the idea of laughter (at death) on the day of resurrection in ps.-John Chrys. *Serm. pasch.* 5–6, Baur (1953) 108.

present – in these and other respects, the work of the devil. To reinforce this standpoint, not only does John often focus on the theatre as a culturally paradigmatic and intrinsically pagan venue for the release of collective laughter (through the alliance between enacted shamelessness on stage and in the gazing eyes of the audience), but he gives a new twist to the old life-as-drama topos which allows him to place his evaluation of laughter in a spiritually stark perspective. I have already cited his statement that life is not 'the theatre of laughter' (504 above). Later in the set of homilies on Matthew than the passages previously discussed, he develops the same trope in a complex form. 'Life', he declares, 'is no playful farce (*paignion*) – or, rather, our present life *is* a farce, but not the life to come. And perhaps indeed our present life is something worse than farce – it doesn't end in laughter . . .'[95] The term *paignion* can denote anything playfully trivial, a game or toy (including a puppet). It was also the name of one particularly vulgar type of 'mime' (501 above), and the clause 'it doesn't end in laughter' shows that the second of these senses is operative here.[96] So, in self-consciously piquant fashion, John measures his Christian conception of life against the 'generic' scale of pagan dramatic traditions. Caustically, he speaks the language of theatre in order to condemn a mentality fed on such experience.

The self-correcting nature of what John says in this passage reflects an inescapable paradox. From a Christian vantage point, present existence has no intrinsic value (it cannot be an end in itself), and to that extent might

---

[95] οὐκ ἔστι παίγνιον ὁ βίος· μᾶλλον δὲ ὁ μὲν παρὼν βίος παίγνιον, τὰ δὲ μέλλοντα οὐ παίγνια. τάχα δὲ οὐδὲ παίγνιον μόνον ὁ βίος, ἀλλὰ καὶ τούτου χεῖρον. οὐ γὰρ εἰς γέλωτα τελευτᾷ . . . : *In Mt.* 23.9 (57.318 *PG*). Cf. John's question, 'surely our [sc. Christian] existence is not a stage-show and performance?' (μὴ γὰρ σκηνή τίς ἐστι τὰ ἡμέτερα καὶ ὑπόκρισις;), *In Mt.* 79.3 (58.721 *PG*). Note his grim description of the mockery of Christ by certain Jews as a 'comedy', n. 83 above; the same term is applied to the risible life of vice at *Epist. ad Olymp.* 11.2. For John's own ability to evoke typical mime-scenes, see e.g. his introduction of the old female seller of amulets and incantations at *In ep. Col.* 8.5 (62.359 *PG*).

[96] *Paignion* is attested as a type of mime ('full of buffoonery and nonsense') at Plut. *Mor.* 712e and this sense is surely alluded to in the famous epigram of Palladas, *Anth. Pal.* 10.72, 'the whole of life is theatre (σκηνή) and a *paignion* . . .'; see ch. 7 nn. 49, 130, with *paignion* in *Anth. Pal.* 10.80, also Palladas (cf. Bowra (1960) 121–2, but missing the allusion to mime). In the sixth century AD, Choric. *Apol. Mim.* 23, 25, 33, 35, 108 (Foerster), uses the term of mime-scenes; cf. the diminutive παιγνίδιον in a theatrical context, cited in *PGL* 995, *s.v.* 2. See Reich (1903) 417–22, Wiemken (1972) 197–9, with Davidson (2000), esp. 42–52, on the history of *paignion* as a generic designation (but note the justified reservations in Prauscello (2006) 54–9). Other Christian descriptions of life on earth as a *paignion*: Greg. Naz. *Anth. Pal.* 8.157, *Orat.* 7.19 (35.777 *PG*), 33.12 (36.229 *PG*), *Epist.* 178.10 (with clear theatrical imagery in the last two cases); cf. Curtius (1953) 138–40. Kokolakis (1960a) 63, 80 cites a similarly metaphorical use of *paignion* in the astrologer Vettius Valens, *Anthol.* p. 246 Kroll (1908). The puppet simile at Pl. *Laws* 1.644d–e, reiterated at 7.803b–d (cf. ch. 6 n. 10), was a strong influence on such imagery; see the extensive reworking at Plotin. *Enn.* 3.2.15–17 (including *paignion* several times, 3.2.15, surely with theatrical overtones), with ch. 7, 342.

count as a sort of absurdity. Thus, for example, Gregory of Nazianzen was able to echo a pagan formulation in saying that everything in the present life is 'absurdity' or 'a laughing-stock'.[97] At the same time the present world cannot merely be disparaged as meaningless; if it were, god's creation would be mocked and the incarnation would lose all significance. But it has to be reinterpreted as, so to speak, the prelude to a drama whose true unfolding and moral dénouement lie in the next world. Yet the ironic turn of Chrysostom's dramatic imagery is its implication that while we must take full responsibility for the role we play in life, the 'genre' in which we find ourselves acting is determined by the divine dramaturge. If present laughter prevails, then life will be a misdirected 'farce' – one, however, which will not 'end in laughter' but rebound against the sinner. If, on the other hand, life is full of the tears of sincere repentance, it will lead on, as the beatitudes promise, to the redeemed laughter of eternal joy. Thus Christian eschatology transcends the possibilities of tragic, comic and even tragicomic lives that the horizons of paganism had encompassed. The 'generic' map of existence has been not just reorientated but redrawn.[98]

ASCETIC DISCIPLINES FOR THE FACE AND THE SOUL

The reservations about laughter manifested by Clement of Alexandria and John Chrysostom differ in both degree and precise motivation. Where Clement's nervousness on the subject belongs to a larger project of subjecting the pressures of the body to a spiritual monitoring that will allow a safer coexistence with pagan society, John's deeper anxieties centre on the dark, unwavering conviction that most forms of earthly laughter are an echo of the voice of the devil and therefore call for the utmost resistance. If both thinkers share a desire to convert their concerns into practical principles for their respective, though culturally somewhat different, Christian communities, the vehemence of John Chrysostom's teaching (a vehemence he acknowledges himself)[99] betrays the tension of which he was acutely aware

---

[97] Greg. Naz. *Carm.* 37.780.3 *PG*: πάντα μόγος θνητοῖς τἀνθάδε· πάντα γέλως ('everything in this world is toil for humans, everything is absurdity [lit. 'laughter']'). Cf. ch. 7 n. 76, with the next note for the other side of the coin.

[98] See ch. 7, 336–7, for examples of pagan imagery of life as tragic, comic and tragicomic. Cf. Greg. Naz. *Orat.* 22.8 (35.1140 *PG*), the Christian's 'tragedy' (by implication including the killing of Jesus) is turned into 'comedy' (partly literally, i.e. on the stage) by its scoffers, who belong to a city that is 'zealous about mocking religion, like everything else' (ἣ σπουδάζει τὸ τὰ θεῖα παίζειν, ὥσπερ τι ἕτερον); cf. nn. 5, 40 above.

[99] See e.g. *In Mt.* 6.8 (57.72 *PG*), where he calls his preceding discourse '[all the] more vehement' (σφοδρότερον).

between a spiritual aversion to mirth and the multiple impulses to bodily expression of pleasure and joviality in the lives of his congregation. The resolution of that tension could only be achieved by radical means.

Truly to rid life of laughter, one of the most basic of affective urges, requires an extreme form of asceticism. It should come as no surprise, therefore, that Christian suspicion of laughter was readily channelled into the religion's most highly organised type of ascetic life, monasticism. We can see this most clearly by taking a short step back in time, approximately a generation before the great period of Chrysostom's preaching. To this period belongs the *Asceticon* or so-called 'Rules' (*Regulae*) of Basil of Caesarea (c. 330–79), a work probably compiled in the course of the 360s and 370s and which became the basis of subsequent monastic regulations in both eastern and, via Benedict, western Christianity.[100] Even though Basil's rules represent a template of piety designed to have some applicability outside the confines of institutionalised monasticism, they crystallised a set of spiritual and ethical demands that could only have been contemplated, let alone met, by those aspiring to a strenuously exacting standard of self-discipline. In a section of the shorter version of the Rules from which I have taken the first epigraph to this chapter (471 above), Basil answers the question 'whether it is not permissible to laugh at all' (εἰ καθόλου γελᾶν οὐκ ἔξεστι) with an emphatic 'never', which he then fills out with the severe rider, 'especially among such a throng of those who by contravention of the law dishonour god and die in sin, for whom one should feel sadness and grief'.[101] The inflection of the question is doubly revealing: first, because of its inbuilt leaning towards agelastic habits; secondly, because at the same time it hints at just how rigorous a challenge to deep-seated instincts the cultivation of such habits poses. But Basil offers more than an injunction. He gives a reason for it ('since god condemns those who laugh in this life'), and one whose edge is sharpened by its ostensible contradiction, or at any rate radical reinterpretation, of Ecclesiastes 3.4 ('for every thing there is a right time . . . : a time to weep and a time to laugh'). While the Ecclesiastes passage affirms, *prima facie*, a proper place for laughter within the oscillating circumstances and fluctuating moods of life, Basil implicitly reconfigures it in the light of the beatitude, 'woe to you who now laugh, since you shall grieve and weep' (475 above), thereby constructing, like John Chrysostom, an unequivocal

---

[100] On the date of the *Asceticon* see Silvas (2005) 140–5, with 19–37, 51–101, and Brown (1988) 287–91, on Basil's relationship to the development of monasticism. Osborn (1976) 87–101 summarises Basil's rigoristic asceticism.
[101] Basil, *Reg. brev.* 31 (31.1104 *PG*); cf. Silvas (2005) 292.

contrast between the laughter of sinners in the present and the prospective joy of true believers in the eternal hereafter.

Basil's attitudes in this domain are set out most fully in the seventeenth of his longer version of the Rules, which expounds the proposition 'that self-control must extend to laughter as well', or 'even laughter' (ὅτι δεῖ καὶ γέλωτος ἐγκρατῶς ἔχειν).[102] After the treatment in his preceding rule of self-control or continence as standardly understood, i.e. disciplined abstinence from fleshly and worldly desires, Basil's transition to the subject of laughter locates it at once within the pull of appetitive and therefore potentially sinful corporeal impulses, implicitly denying it any right to be regarded as a mere, insignificant reflex. He has already insisted that self-control prescribes limits for many forms of behaviour, inhibiting 'the tongue, the eyes, the ears'. But his initial indication that the extension of this virtue to cover laughter is 'overlooked by most people' highlights the insidiousness of an urge which might easily escape the grave censure attaching to greed, lust and other excesses. Basil recognises, in other words, that laughter is so threaded through ordinary, everyday life that its extirpation will seem counterintuitive to many. To give weight to his antigelastic case he lays immediate stress on uncontrolled laughter, the kind by which one can be physically 'gripped' or 'overcome'.[103] Such laughter is an outward sign of inward indiscipline (*akrasia*), a failure 'to repress the soul's slackness with strict principle' (τοῦ μὴ ἀκριβεῖ λόγῳ τῆς ψυχῆς τὸ χαῦνον καταπιέζεσθαι). Smiling, he concedes, is permissible as a way of intimating cheerfulness, but the mirth of noisy vocalisation and heaving patterns of breathing – Basil dwells puritanically on the physical symptoms[104] – is prohibited, and associated in the process with the fool's noisy laughter of Ecclesiastes 7.6 ('like the sound of thorns under the cooking-pot'). The clinching consideration, shared with John Chrysostom (see 503 above), is

---

[102] Basil, *Reg. fus.* 17 (31.961–5 *PG*); cf. Silvas (2005) 208–11. Compare Basil, *Epist.* 22.1, including prohibitions on profanity (*blasphēmein*), telling jokes (εὐτράπελα φθέγγεσθαι), laughter *tout court*, and tolerating others' jokes/laughter.

[103] κατέχεσθαι: cf. Diog. Laert. 8.23 (Pythagoras' avoidance of laughter), with ch. 6, 275. With Basil's description of laughter as 'uncontrollable' (ἄσχετος), compare Iambl. *Protr.* 21 (pp. 107, 121 Pistelli), with ch. 6, 273.

[104] He uses the verbs ἐγκαγχάζειν ('guffaw') and ἀναβράζεσθαι ('heave' and/or 'overheat' with laughter). The first, a very rare compound, is parallel to the old forms ἀνακαγχάζειν, ἐκκαγχάζειν (see ch. 6, 286, ch. 7, 362); for other Christian deprecation of guffawing see 490, 492 above, with John Chrys. *Oppugn.* 1.2 (47.322 *PG*), *Hom. in Rom. 16:3* 2.1 (51.197 *PG*), *Hom. in Acta* 24.4 (60.190 *PG*), *In ep. Col.* 12 (62.383 *PG*). The second verb, lit. 'boil' or 'bubble up', is used of laughter only in texts of the Christian period (see *PGL* 96 *s.v.* ἀναβράζω 2, 304 *s.v.* βράσμα 2a, βρασματώδης, the latter citing Greg. Naz. *Orat.* 5.23 (35.692 *PG*), part of a fascinating description of mantic ecstasy). Basil, *Hom. de grat. act.* 31.228 *PG*, quoted on 516 below, links laughter with heating (ἀναβρασμός, 'boiling') of the blood. Cf. ch. 1 n. 23.

that Christ himself clearly underwent all 'the necessary experiences of the flesh' (τὰ ἀναγκαῖα πάθη τῆς σαρκός), including feelings of tiredness and pity, yet is never said in the gospels to have laughed.[105] Moreover, in the beatitudes, as we know, he pronounced woe on those who laugh in the here and now.

Basil's position thus combines a psychologico-ethical diagnosis (laughter as a bodily sign of moral dissolution) with scriptural testimony (the non-laughing Christ of the gospels and the negative verdict on 'present laughter' in the beatitudes). To buttress his case he adds one more line of argument, that the Christian must be careful to distinguish between 'homonymous' uses of the term *gelōs* in scripture. On the one hand this word can designate the believer's legitimate joyfulness of soul, as in Sarah's 'the lord created laughter for me' (Genesis 21.6), the promise that god 'will fill a true mouth with laughter' found in the book of Job (8.21), or Christ's other beatitude, 'happy are you who now weep, since you shall laugh'. On the other hand there is the laughter of what Basil calls *hilarotēs*, which here (notwithstanding the positive associations of this word-group in some Christian texts, including other places in Basil's own writings) must mean frivolous, foolish merriment, as already exemplified by his quotations from Ecclesiastes.[106] Despite the apparent balance in the distinction between good and bad emblems of laughter, the negative totally outweighs the positive in practical terms. Apart from his earlier endorsement of smiling, Basil offers no clear pointers to how approved laughter might enter a Christian life. This is because there is, as the short version of the Rules spells out, no place at all for actual laughter *in* life, only beyond it.

The implications of this standpoint are subtly reinforced by the second half of the section on laughter in the longer Rules, even though Basil here says no more specifically on the subject and instead returns to broader thoughts on self-discipline. This virtue is now characterised as the 'death' or mortification (*nekrōsis*) of the body, a vocabulary whose force is directed away from the metaphorical towards the literal by the

---

[105] Sorabji (2000) 344–56 documents Christian discussion of the human emotions/impulses to which Jesus *was* susceptible.

[106] ἱλαρός etc. characterises Christian/heavenly joy at e.g. Origen, *Fragm. in Lam.* 10 (cf. n. 15 above), Basil, *Epist.* 2.2, *Hom.* 2 (31.196 *PG*: cf. n. 108 below), *Hom. de grat. act.* 31.228 *PG* (see 516 below); it has a looser reference to cheerfulness at Basil, *Hexaem.* 5.2; note Clem. *Paed.* 2.2.22.3, in connection with wine-drinking (and humour: n. 45 above); Paul, Romans 12.8 is somewhat different. For pagan usage in relation to laughter/smiles, see e.g. Hippoc. *De medico* 1 (a doctor who laughs too much), Antiphanes fr. 80.9–10 *PCG* (a parasite), Apollod. Car. fr. 5.12 *PCG* (sympotic play), Cornut. *ND* 45 (erotic smiles), Palladas, *Anth. Pal.* 10.56.13 (contrasting with *ibid.* 9–10), (?) Hermocles, *Ithyphalli* 7–8 (*CA* 173–4: Demetrius Poliorcetes *qua* epiphanic god); cf. ch. 3 n. 115.

The antigelastic tendencies of early Christianity

statement that whereas a normal athlete (the paradigm of physical manliness) will be conspicuous by the healthy tone and colour of his skin, the Christian 'athlete' should be equally conspicuous for withered flesh and an oxymoronically 'blooming pallor' (ἐπανθοῦσα ὠχρία). It is particularly striking that Basil should choose to complement his reflections on laughter with remarks on the corpse-like face of the ascetic, the athlete of the soul. This is a countenance on which it is impossible to imagine laughter of any familiar kind – a facial advertisement for an antigelastic mentality.[107]

There is no space here to refine this picture by documenting every normative remark, in Basil's writings as a whole, on the relationship between spiritual states and physical expression. A painstaking trawl of all the evidence would for sure bring to light some fluctuations of emphasis, since Basil, like many other Christian moralists, is sometimes exercised to reconcile the principle that believers should weep and grieve at what they find in this world of sin, as Jesus himself did, with the Pauline injunction to 'rejoice always' in god (Philippians 4.4, 1 Thessalonians 5.16). In one of his sermons Basil specifically poses the question how tears and joy can both be essential to the Christian frame of mind. His answer – a commentary, yet again, on 'happy are you who now weep, since you shall laugh' – is that they are two sides of the same coin, equally reflecting the genuine joy that is rooted in the values of eternity. But in this same passage he adds a revealing gloss on the form that 'laughter' will (not) take even in the hereafter: by using this word (*gelōs*), he explains, Christ 'does not mean the noise emitted from the cheeks when our blood is warmed, but the pure joyfulness that is unmixed with any trace of scowling looks'.[108] Basil here encapsulates his deprecation of ordinary laughter as mired in the workings of the body: it is, in a rather

---

[107] Cf. Basil's brother, Greg. Nyss. *Hom. in Eccl.* 2 (44.645 *PG*), on an ascetic temperament as 'unsmiling' (ἀμειδές: cf. pagan associations with death, ch. 7 n. 89). John Chrys. *In ep. 1 Tim.* 14.3 (62.575 *PG*) describes monasteries as places where 'no laughter' is heard. The contemporary exhortation of Ephraem Syrus to Syriac monks to avoid laughter and engage in constant grief is ostensibly tempered (in the Pauline tradition) by the principle that true sorrow is internal to the heart: 'let us have shining countenances (φαιδροὶ τῷ προσώπῳ) . . . but weep and grieve in our thoughts' (*Non rid.* 199–200 Phrantzoles). For further monastic prohibitions on laughter, see e.g. Antiochus mon. *Hom.* 95 (89.1721–6 *PG*), *Apophth. Patr.* 65.308 *PG*, *Apophth. Coisl.* 54 (Nau), with Steidle (1986), Schmitz (1980), Le Goff (1990), (1997) 45–6, Resnick (1987), Baconsky (1996) 125–79 for elements of the bigger picture in both western and eastern monasticism.

[108] γέλωτα δὲ λέγει οὐ τὸν διὰ τῶν παρειῶν ἐκπίπτοντα ψόφον ἐν τῷ αἵματος ἀναβρασμῷ, ἀλλὰ τὴν ἄκρατον καὶ ἀμιγῆ παντὸς σκυθρωποῦ ἱλαρότητα: *Hom. de grat. act.* 31.228 *PG*. There is an allusion here to Christ's injunction (cited directly at *Hom.* 2 [31.196 *PG*]: n. 106 above) that those who fast should not be like 'scowling hypocrites' (ὑποκριταὶ σκυθρωποί), whose looks are disingenuous (Matthew 6.16). But there is also an echo of more general precepts, pagan as much as Christian, to avoid *both* laughter and scowling: cf. ch. 6 n. 28, Athanas. *Vita Anton.* 14 (26.865 *PG*), and n. 67 above.

literal sense, the noise produced by flesh and blood. Yet he is also anxious, in a way which has implications for the Christian's present life, to maintain compatibility between a countenance that never succumbs to quotidian laughter and the expression of truly spiritual joy. On the surface at least, he is in this respect more closely aligned with Clement than with John Chrysostom, who, as we saw, was prepared to recommend a sternly scowling look to the battle-ready 'soldiers' of god. But Basil, unlike Clement, is not defining a moderation of bodily deportment or a general standard of affability that will allow integration into a largely pagan society. He is imagining a future jubilation which will be an asomatic 'laughter' of the soul and will accordingly transcend the paganism of the body altogether.[109]

EPILOGUE: A DISPUTED LEGACY

Early Christian attitudes to laughter, as the argument of this chapter has tried to demonstrate, were caught up in a dialectic between the conflicting demands of the present and the future, the body and the soul. I do not, of course, purport to have offered a comprehensive account of the full range of those attitudes. There were alternative possibilities which appealed to some Christian groups but which have had to remain outside my scope here, including the fact that in some so-called gnostic gospels Jesus himself was depicted explicitly, even emphatically, as resorting to laughter.[110] My overriding aim has been to examine the strongly antigelastic current that runs through much of the ethical and psychological thinking of some of the most important and eloquent Greek church fathers. As we have glimpsed along the way, the forces that generated that current undoubtedly owed something to pagan intellectual traditions, especially those of Platonism and Pythagoreanism. But the new religion's momentum, both spiritual and communal, steadily built up a distinctive perspective on the body,

[109] Cf. the conception of internal, spiritualised laughter (as well as condemnation of ordinary mirth) in the seventh-century Byzantine monk John Climacus: see Baconsky (1996) 176–9 for references.

[110] In the Greek version of the *Infancy Gospel of Thomas* (A) 8.1, the child Jesus laughs loudly at his teacher's frustration and when working a miracle; at (B) 6.2 he laughs at the idea of being taught by anyone: translations in Elliott (1993) 77–8, 81. Of Coptic gnostic texts, see the recently published *Gospel of Judas*, in which Jesus laughs more than once, partly at the spiritual ignorance of his disciples: Kasser *et al.* (2006) 21, 24, 31, 42. Cf. the gnostic idea that the true Jesus laughed at his persecutors' delusions while another was crucified in his place. This is attested as the view of Basilides by Iren. *Haer.* 1.24.4 (Latin version; cf. Epiphan. *Pan.* 1 260 Holl) and found in the Coptic *Apocalypse of Peter* 81–3, *Second Treatise of Great Seth* 56 (cf. 53, 60 for other ridicule): English translations in Robinson (1977) 332, 344; Havelaar (1999) 46–9 has text and translation, with some analysis on 101–2, 188–9. Pagels (1980) 70–101, esp. 72–3, 82–3, sets the wider context; cf. Dart (1988) 93–101, Gilhus (1997) 69–77 (with 109–12 for modern attempts to reconstitute a 'laughing' Christ). For another dimension of gnostic laughter, see ch. 1 n. 32.

on personal and social relationships, on women, on the theatre and other elements in the cultural environment of paganism, and, ultimately, on the meaning of life *sub specie aeternitatis*. By reading between the lines of the exhortations of Clement, John Chrysostom and Basil, it is easy to discern that for many Christians, much of the time, there must have been an awkward discrepany between condemnations of (most) laughter and the lived actuality of their ordinary social lives. Except for a very few individuals or in a small number of carefully controlled 'pockets', early Christianity certainly did not succeed in excising laughter from the life of the body. But what it did do was to bring the subject, with startling clarity, to the surface of ethical and existential self-consciousness: to make it – in more senses than one – a moral, social and religious crux.

The later history of Christianity proves that the ways in which the problem of laughter might be faced and wrestled with cannot easily be delimited. The antigelastic tendencies traced in this chapter contributed to a long medieval inheritance in which laughter continued to count from a theological point of view as a deeply troubling feature of mankind's fallen state, both a symptom and a cause of sinfulness. At the same time, markedly countervailing tendencies emerged in the course of the Middle Ages, as communities found ways of not only accepting the need for habits and rituals of mirthfulness but even moulding them into a distinctive 'culture of laughter' that stood in a complex relationship to the institutional authority of religion.[111] The results of this resistance to agelastic severity were diverse. They included making room for specifically scheduled opportunities for laughter within the Christian calendar (the New Year Feast of Fools, the pre-Lenten traditions of Carnival, and 'Easter laughter' or *risus paschalis* being the best-known types); the creation of a role for laughter even within religiously based forms of drama; the depiction of laughter or smiles in visual art as no longer (from the late-twelfth century) the exclusive preserve of demons, but imaginable even on the faces of angels; and, on a different level of discourse, Aquinas' revival of an Aristotelian virtue of measured indulgence in sociable humour.[112] A major, complex turning-point is

---

[111] For various strands in medieval (Christian) attitudes to laughter, see Curtius (1939) 6–26 (= Curtius (1953) 420–35), Kolve (1966), esp. 124–44, Le Goff (1990), (1992a), (1992b), Gilhus (1997) 78–101, Innes (2002), the contributions of Kries and Johnston to Pfister (2002a), several chapters in Röcke and Velten (2005), and the stimulating if one-sided theory of medieval carnivalesque in Bakhtin (1968), esp. 1–29, 73–96, 286–99. I have not seen Horowitz and Menache (1994).

[112] The Feast of Fools: Chambers (1903) I 274–335, Welsford (1935) 199–203, Burke (1978) 192. Carnival: ch. 4, 204–6, with nn. 140–1 there. *Risus paschalis*, including comic sermons and other Easter celebrations: Fluck (1934), concentrating on the early modern period, Screech (1997) 226–7. Visual art: most recently, Sauerländer (2006) 7–10. Aquinas: see ch. 6 n. 110, with Rahner (1961) 1728–9.

later reached with the revaluation of laughter, and its reincorporation into the possibilities of a religious stance towards the world, in the Christian-humanist writings of Erasmus, who was even able to find inspiration in the pagan mockeries of Lucian and, in the same vein, to appropriate the legendary 'laughing Democritus' as a symbol of his own mentality. Erasmus did not set the whole agenda for Christianity's later dealings with laughter, since in the same period we also witness the rise of a new agelastic impetus in the shape of Calvinistic Puritanism and its return to the severest suspicion of the depraved promptings of the body.[113] But these mere signposts are sufficient to indicate that by the early modern period Christianity was destined to live with an unending struggle over the peculiarly elusive phenomenology of laughter, with its palpable rootedness in the body's own surges of feeling yet its capacity to function as a currency of personal and social exchanges of value. Though filtered through the religion's own long history of doctrines and divisions, many of the fundamental terms of this unresolved debate find their ultimate ancestry in the older pagan traditions of reflection on laughter which have been explored throughout this book. And when we later find the greatest of all post-Erasmian Christian advocates of laughter, Kierkegaard, not only refashioning the idea of Socratic irony for his own purposes but also appealing to the ancient cult site of Trophonius' cave (where laughter can be lost and found again) to symbolise his personal discovery of a laughter of religious existentialism, we are made freshly aware that highly charged echoes of the past can still reverberate even across an immense cultural distance.[114]

---

[113] Erasmus' revaluation of laughter is fruitfully explored in Screech (1997), esp. 154–204; cf. Screech (1980), esp. 128–33, 184–5; see Goldhill (2002) 43–54 for a vigorous reading of Erasmus' relationship to Lucian. The Christianised figure of Democritus is discussed by Wind (1983); cf. Arbury (1998) 493. But Wind's reference (83) to Erasmus' *Praise of Folly* contains a misstatement; and note the correction of Wind's position in Buck (1963) 170 n. 14. Calvinist and other puritanical attitudes to laughter are noted in e.g. Thomas (1977) 79–81.

[114] Kierkegaard's use of the Trophonius motif is in *Either/Or.* Kierkegaard (1959) 33 (cf. 'the ambiguity which lies at the root of laughter', *ibid.* 21). For the ancient motif itself, see ch. 7 n. 89. Lippitt (1996) 66–71, more extensively Lippitt (2000), discusses Kierkegaard's concept of laughter.

The Greek (body) language of laughter and smiles

Ancient Greek, like modern English, possesses separate word-groups, from different roots, for laughter and smiling. This is not true of all languages: some (such as Latin and its Romance descendants) use closely related word-groups, while others make no lexical distinction at all.[1] Whether linguistically or corporeally, the relationship between laughter and smiles is intricate. Distinguishable in principle, the two can overlap or shade into one another. In physiological terms, laughter paradigmatically involves staccato vocalisation and a tautening of facial musculature (with mouth opened to facilitate intensified breathing), while smiling is a facial but not vocal form of expression. Although such details are not always made explicit, there is no doubt that they form the basis of the distinction between γελᾶν (laugh) and μειδ(ι)ᾶν (smile).[2] It is possible to hear without seeing someone laugh, as the insomniac Odysseus overhears the maidservants' indecent mirth in a scene of thrilling psychological tension at *Odyssey* 20.5–8. But one can only *see* (or imagine one sees) a smile – or at any rate, by poetic extension, picture one on a symbolic 'inner' face, as Homer does.[3] Despite the difference between laughter as facio-vocal and smiling as purely facial, there are varieties and gradations of both behaviours, and these complicate classification.[4] In particular, the *visual* impressions of laughing and smiling can be thought of as forming a (blurred) continuum.

---

[1] Buck (1949) 1106–8 summarises the position in Indo-European languages. On modern Greek, cf. n. 7 below.

[2] For, as it were, the minimal conditions of a smile, see the lovers at Heliod. *Aeth.* 3.5.5: 'a brief, furtive [lit. stolen] smile detectable only in the relaxation of their glance' (ἐμειδίασαν βραχύ τι καὶ κλεπτόμενον καὶ μόνῃ τῇ διαχύσει τοῦ βλέμματος ἐλεγχόμενον). Furiani (2000) surveys laughter and smiles in the Greek novel.

[3] Homer, in fact, internalises both smiles *and* laughter: see ch. 2 nn. 95, 100.

[4] On varieties of smiles, see van Hooff (1972) 218–27, 231–5, Ekman (2003) 204–12, with Frank *et al.* (1997) for more detail; Schmidt and Cohn (2001) review relevant facial expression research (without any interest in historical evidence). Trumble (2004) offers a cultural conspectus. Le Goff (1997) 48 strangely proposes that smiling may have been 'one of the creations of the Middle Ages'. On vocal variations in laughter see Bachorowski and Owren (2001), Ruch and Ekman (2001); cf. n. 12 below.

Greek writers presuppose a basic distinction, as well as expressive affinities (but not identity), between γελᾶν and μειδ(ι)ᾶν. This is easiest to observe where the two are juxtaposed and combined. At *Homeric Hymn to Demeter* 204, Iambe's scurrilous antics induce the grieving goddess 'to smile, to laugh and to lift her spirits in benevolence' (μειδῆσαι γελάσαι τε καὶ ἵλαον σχεῖν θυμόν). At Theocritus 7.19–20, the goatherd Lycidas has a smile in his 'eyes' and laughter 'hanging on his lips' (σεσαρὼς | ὄμματι μειδιόωντι, γέλως δέ οἱ εἴχετο χείλευς). In the case of the Hymn, the impression is of an expanding process of physical-cum-psychological transformation, as a new mood surges through the divine body (and mind). In Theocritus' image, there is a quizzical aura, a sort of suspension *between* smiling and laughing, with a corresponding uncertainty about the psychology 'behind' the face.[5] It would not help the interpretation of either passage (indeed, it would blunt the force of both) to deny a semantically clear *background* distinction.[6] That distinction gives significance to Demeter's progression from smiles to laughter, and the goatherd's enigmatic wavering between the two.[7]

Although a wide range of ancient texts can be consistently correlated with modern typologies of facial signals, cultural variation in the emphasis and nuances of body language, as well as in broader presuppositions about how to read the mind through the body, is a factor of demonstrable importance.[8] In Greek antiquity, we have to reckon, for instance, with habits of perceiving character physiognomically (though we have no way

[5] On *Hom. Hymn Dem.*, see ch. 4, 161–4; for smiles expanding into laughter, cf. the miraculously animated statue of Hecate at Eunap. *Vitae soph.* 7.2.9–10 Giangrande. At Theoc. 7.19–20, the participle σεσαρώς (see 524 below) reinforces the idea of both smiling and (half-)laughing; Hunter (1999) 157, 'with . . . mockery', may be too strong: cf. Gow (1952) II 137, Puelma (1960) 148–50; note Dionysus' enigmatic/ominous smiling eyes at *Hom. Hymn* 7.14–15. For 'eyes' and 'lips' in laughter/smiles, see 522, 525 below. Cf. διαμυλλαίνειν, Ar. *Wasps* 1315, 'twist the mouth' into a condescending smirk: see MacDowell (1971) 305, adding the entries of Hesychius and Photius *s.v.* to his evidence.

[6] Even Ach. Tat. 2.6.2, where Leucippe 'smiles sweetly and reveals by her laughter . . .' (μειδιάσασα γλυκὺ καὶ ἐμφανίσασα διὰ τοῦ γέλωτος) does not make smiling and laughing synonymous but depicts their subtle co-presence (cf. 2.6.3).

[7] The distinction between laughter and smiles is rightly insisted on by Zuntz (1960) 38 (though his claim that γελᾶν 'denotes a smile' is muddled), Simon (1961) 644–5; cf. Arnould (1990) 140–1 (with some equivocation), Schmidt (1876–86) IV 188–97. Lopez Eire (2000) 14 confusingly treats γελᾶν as both a species of (French) 'rire' and the generic designator of 'rire'; his distinction between γελᾶν as 'completed' action and μειδιᾶν as incomplete/adumbrated (e.g. 16, 43) is artificial. Clarke (2005a) 39 oddly asserts that 'γελάω is, of course, the standard word for smiling and laughter', yet his addition 'including the hostile laughter discussed above' refers back to passages (Hom. *Il.* 7.212, *Od.* 20.301) in which μειδ(ι)ᾶν not γελᾶν is used. Milanezi (1995) 244 rightly sees γελᾶν as encompassing both visual and vocal expression. In modern Greek, γελῶ remains 'laugh'; χαμογελῶ (etymologically suggesting 'low', subdued laughter) is standard demotic for 'smile', while μειδιῶ ('smile') is confined to katharevousa.

[8] The fullest survey of Greek references to facial expression, with emphasis on physiognomics, is Evans (1969). For a larger perspective on ancient body language, see Cairns (2005a).

of telling just how widely such habits were practised). When we are told by one physiognomonic text that various kinds of laughing eyes are a sign of deceit and malice, we might ask not only what is meant by laughing eyes, but also what it might mean to observe such eyes as an index of unreliable character.[9] The first of those questions is somewhat easier than the second. Laughter can affect the whole face, including the musculature round the eyes and the appearance (brightness, moistness, etc.) of the eyes themselves; by a sort of metonymy, therefore, the eyes themselves can be said to exhibit 'laughter'. But clearly the statement about laughing eyes cannot mean that everyone who laughs betrays deceit and malice. It must imply, rather, that the eyes themselves can possess a gelastic 'look' which may be observed and interpreted independently of individual acts of laughing. Nor should we simply equate laughing eyes with smiling eyes. As it happens, the text just cited actually distinguishes between the two. It thereby illustrates the complexity of cultural categories.

While the terminology of γελᾶν may sometimes understandably shade into smiling (see below), lexicographers have no warrant for making 'smile' a primary sense of the verb.[10] Nor is it justifiable to infer from the relative rarity of μειδιᾶν and cognates in classical Attic that Athenians normally used γελᾶν etc. equally for both laughing and smiling.[11] It does not follow from the fact that many texts (unsurprisingly) refer to the face when describing laughter and smiling that Greeks did not principally think of *gelōs* as possessing an audible element. Although vocalisation is not always spelt out (but then neither is any specific facial expression), it often enough is – for example, by adverbial modifiers ('loudly' etc.) or by the compound ἐκγελᾶν, 'burst out laughing'.[12] Vocalisation can in any case be implied by other factors, e.g. the physical difficulty of repressing a (respiratory-cum-muscular) urge to laugh, something that, in the Greek imagination, may

---

[9] For the text in question, ps.-Polemon, *Physiogn.* 20 (Foerster), see ch. 1 n. 24.

[10] As do LSJ, Supplement, 75, and *DGE* IV 791, both *s.v.* γελάω.

[11] As claimed by Arnould (1990) 141, Sommerstein (2000) 66. But μειδιᾶν, though not common, is patently available in Attic ('presque complètement tombé en désuétude', Furiani (2000) 78, is a gross misstatement): Ar. *Thesm.* 513; five times in Plato; Xen. *Cyr.* 2.2.16 (marked: ch. 1 n. 103); Arist. *Hom. Prob.* fr. 399 Gigon (176 Rose), Theophr. *Char.* 8.2. The relative rarity of μειδ- terms in Attic should be treated as purely contingent.

[12] Modifiers: see n. 17 below. ἐκγελᾶν, 'burst out laughing' (see LSJ 503, *s.v.*): note the bold metaphor at Eur. *Tro.* 1178, describing the crushed head of young Astyanax; LSJ translates, '[the blood] rushes out with a *gurgling* sound' [their itals.]; likewise *DGE* VI 1342, *s.v.* Stanford (1936) 115 belittles LSJ's translation, which is followed by Barlow (1971) 117 (Barlow (1986) 221 changes her mind); but Stanford's own discussion is flawed (n. 16 below); Arnould (1990) 139 sees light and (metonymic) sound combined in this passage; cf. Clarke (2005a) 42–3, with 50 n. 22 (where the objection is not decisive). For the Greek vocalisation of laughter, see ch. 1 n. 20.

afflict a god's body just as much as a child's.[13] The Aristotelian *Problemata* pronounces that people laugh 'with' the diaphragm, and makes several direct remarks on vocal features of laughter; other texts refer to the physically spasmodic patterns of laughter.[14] Not for nothing is the collective mirth of Homeric gods called 'unquenchable' (ἄσβεστος), a word several times used of the clamour of armies in the *Iliad*. The claim that *gelōs* 'was primarily a *visual* not an *auditory* thing to the Greeks' is utterly factitious.[15] It stems from the etymological fallacy that because the *gel-* root is (probably) related to ideas of brightness, γελᾶν itself essentially *means* 'shine'.[16]

Greek can mark gradations or degrees of both laughter and smiles. It can do so by (e.g.) attaching the prefix *hupo-* (denoting understated, even furtive action) to either verb; by describing laughter as 'gentle' or 'soft'; or, at the opposite end of the scale, by marking laughter as 'vehement' *vel sim.*, evoking a 'belly laugh', or using the vocabulary of (ἀνα)κα(γ)χάζειν and cognates ('guffaw') to accentuate explosive, raucous hilarity.[17] In visual terms distinctions can be drawn between, for instance, retracting or parting

---

[13] On the difficulty of stifling an urge to laugh (of holding it 'in the chest', Ap. Rhod. *Argon.* 4.1723), see ch. 6 n. 138. Cf. ch. 1 nn. 23–4 for ancient descriptions of the muscular spasms of laughter.

[14] Laughing 'with' the diaphragm (φρένες): ps.-Arist. *Probl.* 35.6, 965a15–16; cf. ch. 6 n. 143 for other references. Arnould (1990) 158–68 documents 'sonorities' of laughter, including 'giggling' (κιχλίζειν: ch. 10 n. 52); add the Boeotian verb κριδδέμεν = γελᾶν (Strattis fr. 49.7 *PCG*), i.e. κρίζειν, 'shriek', with Perpillou (1982) 242–3. Clem. *Paed.* 3.4.29.1 condemns *snorting* laughter ('through the nose') as the body language of debauchery. (For some modern reactions to the sound of laughter, see Miller W. (1997) 83–4.) Note the lexicon of μυκτήρ ('nostril' = sneerer), μυκτηρίζειν, etc., for derision and sarcasm; the implication may sometimes be of 'snorting' rather than (or in addition to) 'turning up' the nose: see e.g. Men. fr. 607.4, 615, adesp. com. 1059.14 *PCG*, with ch. 5 n. 34, ch. 6 n. 82, ch. 7 n. 121, ch. 10 n. 11; cf. Gow (1951) 81, 84, Sittl (1890) 87–8, Russell (1964) 161, di Marco (1989) 168–9, Knox (1989) 151–6. On the sonic side, cf. finally the ancient claim that μωκᾶσθαι (scoff) was derived from the sound made by camels! See LSJ *s.v.*, Chantraine (1968) 729, with Allen (1987) 75 n. 36 for the phonology.

[15] Stanford (1936) 117 n. 1 (his itals.); cf. 116. Contrast Schmidt (1876–86) IV 188.

[16] Stanford (1936) 115–17: 'the basic meaning of γελᾶν is *to be bright* [his itals.] *and nothing more* [my itals.]' (115), '*laughter* [his itals.] is only an incidental [*sic*] meaning, although a common one [!]' (*ibid.*), and 'γελᾶν does not essentially [*sic*] mean *to laugh* [!]' (117 n. 1). By this yardstick, laugh is only an incidental meaning of English 'laugh'. That γελᾶν is predominantly visual is claimed in less extreme form by Lopez Eire (2000), esp. 23–5, ignoring widespread usage which suggests no separation between visual and auditory *gelōs*. Cf. ch. 1 n. 33.

[17] ὑπογελᾶν, ὑπομειδιᾶν: ch. 6 n. 107. Laughing 'gently', 'softly', etc.: Hom. *Od.* 14.465, Hom. *Hymn* 4.281 (ἁπαλός: ch. 2, 86–7), Pl. *Phdo* 62a, 84d (ἠρέμα: ch. 6, 278, 280), Meleager, *Anth. Pal.* 12.125.1 (ἀβρός: cf. ch. 3 n. 54), Philostr. maj. *Imag.* 2.2.2 (ἁπαλός). Laughing 'vehemently', 'powerfully': in addition to the obvious μέγα, 'loudly' (*Hom. Hymn* 4.389, Pl. *Euthd.* 276d, Plut. *Nic.* 7.6), see σοβαρόν, perhaps 'haughtily' but implying forceful expiration (note the explosive wind at Ar. *Clouds* 406), ps.-Theoc. 20.15, ps.-Pl. *Anth. Pal.* 6.1, Galen, *Diff. puls.* 8.572.7 (Kühn), cf. Plut. *Lys.* 5.1, with Page (1978) 44–6; ἁδρόν, 'vehemently', Antiphan. fr. 142.9 (the flatterer at a drinking-party); and καπυρόν, with a crisp cackle, Nossis, *Anth. Pal.* 7.414 (ch. 7 n. 75). A 'belly laugh': ch. 9, 464. ἀνακαγχάζειν etc.: ch. 2 n. 15, ch. 6, 286, ch. 10 n. 104; cf. e.g. ps-Hippoc. *Epist.* 17.4, Galen, *Diff. respir.* 7.834 Kühn.

the lips (σεσηρέναι < σαίρειν) in a smile, smirk or sometimes bared-teeth grimace, and, on the other hand, opening the mouth to full stretch (χάσκειν, ἐγχάσκειν, καταχάσκειν) when roaring with laughter: the first of these verbs implies nothing audible (though vocalisation may occasionally be anyway present), whereas the second group denotes a gaping mouth that maximises a vocal outburst (though that does not preclude symbolic, non-literal usage, as with the gelastic lexicon in general).[18]

If laughter and smiles both have a range of intensities and can overlap facially, are the two Greek vocabularies ever interchangeable? It is impossible, I believe, to show that *meid-* terms ever imply vocalisation, and to that extent it is never warranted to translate them by 'laugh'.[19] Aphrodite φιλομ(μ)ειδής, for example, should not be called 'laughter-loving', even though the goddess is capable of laughing as well as smiling.[20] A case can be made for treating the *gelōs* word-group as sometimes generically encompassing smiles as well as laughter, though nowhere near as often as the practice of translators would lead one to believe. A more specific question arises about the compound verb προσγελᾶν, but interpretation is complicated by figurative usage. As it happens, the earliest surviving occurrence, in the mouth of the Furies at Aesch. *Eum.* 253 (as they follow the tracks of the matricide Orestes), is densely figurative: 'the smell of human blood leers invitingly at me' (ὀσμὴ βροτείων αἱμάτων με προσγελᾷ). The trope is not only macabrely oxymoronic (the allure of blood) but also synaesthetic (an odour functioning visually); a 'literal' choice between laughter/smiles is impossible to decode. Another figurative case, Soph. *Ichn.* fr. 314.298 *TrGF*, where the subject of the verb is 'the reliable words of a goddess', is easier to analyse (as a metaphorically reassuring look) but no easier to reduce to a clear-cut semantic choice. It is usual to settle on 'smile' in non-figurative passages such as Eur. *Medea* 1041 (τί προσγελᾶτε τὸν πανύστατον γέλων;), describing the children's innocent look at their mother, or *Medea* 1162, where Glauke enjoys her own beauty in a mirror. But neither of these cases is decisive: the children, blithely ignorant of what Medea is contemplating, can be as easily pictured chuckling as smiling, and the same goes for Glauke, whose physically excited joy is emphasised (esp. 1165). At Hdt. 5.92.3 a new-born baby is the subject of the verb. Realistically a neonate

---

[18] On σεσηρέναι see Appendix 2 n. 12. On χάσκειν and compounds, see Sommerstein (2000) 68–9, with e.g. ps.-Arist. *Probl.* 11.15, 900b12, Soph. fr. 314.353, 370 *TrGF* (Appendix 2 n. 62); these verbs have no implications for the tongue: Appendix 2 n. 36.

[19] Anon. med. *Physiogn.* 25 (Foerster) imagines a person who 'smiles in laughter' (μειδιῶν ἐν γέλωτι), a compromise between guffawing and aversion to laughter: but this does not make μειδιᾶν *mean* 'laugh'.

[20] Cf. ch. 2 n. 35.

can neither laugh nor smile, so once again the special nature of the story does not lend itself to a simple verdict.[21]

Uncertainty attaches, in fact, to many uses of προσγελᾶν. Another case in point is an interesting fragment of Aristotle which uses the verb when advising against sharing too close a friendliness with one's slaves.[22] What seems clear, however, is that unlike both (the simplex) γελᾶν and μειδιᾶν, προσγελᾶν always signifies a *perceived* affability or warmth (though ulterior motives may be present).[23] It may well be, therefore, that the semantics of the verb foreground an affective impression rather than physical particulars of laughter/smiles. This would help to explain the verb's aptness for elaborately figurative applications: in addition to the examples from Aeschylus and Sophocles above, see Ar. *Peace* 600 (the crops and flora of Attica welcome back the goddess Peace with gestures of delight), Eubul. fr. 109.1 (both the sparkling appearance and the exciting noise of a boiling cooking-pot), and Diphilus fr. 32.5 (an expensive fish on a market stall tempts a customer with a gleaming, quasi-erotic look).[24] If, then, προσγελᾶν is fluid enough to encompass (literally or metaphorically) smiles as well as laughter, its expressiveness is often more a matter of mood or feeling than of precise body language.

The possibility of overlap and/or interplay between laughter and smiles can be pursued further by considering some special cases. Recall the image of Hera at *Iliad* 15.101–2 (ch. 2, 64–7), where the goddess ends a reproachful outburst against (absent) Zeus by 'laugh[ing] with her lips [sc. alone]', ἣ δ' ἐγέλασσε | χείλεσιν (a unique Homeric phrase), while her brow remains furrowed. This passage has been used to argue that μειδ(ι)άω and γελάω are interchangeable in Homer.[25] But this contention (which

---

[21] Griffiths (1995) 40 n. 26 translates the verb here as 'laugh', but 'smile' is more often preferred. προσγελᾶν of a baby (Hermes) also at Lucian, *Dial. D.* 11.3. On infants, cf. ch. 3 n. 3, ch. 6 n. 142.

[22] See ch. 6 n. 144.

[23] See e.g. Pl. *Rep.* 566d, Aeschin. 3.87 for welcoming gestures. On the emotional force of the verb, cf. Pearson (1917) I 259–60. But see Fronto, *Epist.* 2.15.3 (van den Hout) for deceptive (feminine) προσγελᾶν, with (?)closed lips (certainly not lip-biting, as van den Hout (1999) 89 implies by citing Eur. *Bacchae* 621) contrasting with the bared-teeth openness of 'guileless laughter'.

[24] On Ar. *Peace* 600, see Olson (1998) 195, who reads 'a laugh of delight' like that of children. Cf. Taillardat (1965) 41 (where the references in n. 2 confuse matters), who prefers 'smile'; but the imagery projects physical animation. In Eubul. fr. 109, 'smile' (Wilkins (2000) 32) fits the *noise* of the boiling food less well than 'laugh'. On erotic overtones in Diphilus fr. 32 (the fish like a seductive woman), see Davidson (1997) 10 (cf. e.g. the women touting for business in Men. fr. 1025.1). Among later figurative usage, Plut. *Mor.* 663f is a good illustration of semantic/imagistic complexity: *erōs* (representing actual lovers), when responding favourably to jokes, is like the enhanced glow of a fanned fire. It is easier to think of a fire laughing than smiling (cf. ch. 2 n. 83); but the trope is too elaborate to be reduced to a simple choice. For a case where vocalisation is present, ruling out 'smile', see the neighing horse at Eutecnius, *Para. Opp.* 12.28 Tüselmann (cf. ch. 1 n. 7).

[25] Miralles (1993) 19.

falls foul of other evidence) misses the point. The description of Hera is paradoxical; to translate the verb as 'smiled' dilutes its force. In ordinary visual terms it might be difficult to distinguish Hera's 'laughter' from a false smile, and Greek can for sure depict certain kinds of smiles by reference to the lips.[26] But the unique Homeric phrase goes beyond the ordinary; it is an ironic symbol of Hera's highly charged feelings. (The paradox was recognised by a later poet in the epic tradition, Nonnus, who speaks of Hera's 'laughing anger', γελόωντι χόλῳ, *Dion.* 1.325.) Furthermore, the idea of laughter on the 'lips' made sense to later Greek writers and readers as a subtly concentrated form of body language.[27] I have already cited the quizzical (half-)laughter that hangs on Lycidas' lips at Theocritus 7.20. Related, if somewhat different in feeling, are pseudo-Theocritus 20.13, where a scornful woman 'sneers with her lips' (χείλεσι μυχθίζοισα) at the cowherd whose advances she spurns, and then bursts into a loud, sarcastic laugh (14–15); and Aristaenetus, *Epist.* 1.17, where a grudging courtesan allows only occasional laughter to 'sit on the edge of her lips'. The Homeric description of Hera's ironic laughter depends, then, not on stretching the semantics of γελᾶν to accommodate ordinary smiles, but on complicating the idea of laughter by setting it in tension with the goddess's manipulation of her facial features.

An expressively different use of a comparably paradoxical image of 'laughter' can be found at Pindar, *Pyth.* 9.38, where Chiron 'laughs brightly(?) with his gentle eyebrows', ἀγανᾷ | χλοαρὸν γελάσσαις ὀφρύι. The verb is commonly translated here as 'smile'.[28] But this blunts the piquancy of the image: the vocabulary of laughter does not automatically signify smiling when connected to the eyes, even though eyes can 'smile' too (see Theoc. 7.20, above).[29] We should think, rather, in terms of a teasing metonymy, something comparable (obviously not identical) to 'internal' laughter. Chiron's laughter – a response to a remarkable scenario (Apollo's coyly phrased but eagerly felt sexual desire for Cyrene, who is wrestling a lion

---

[26] Lucian, *Calumn.* 24 depicts a false smile 'with the edge of the lips' which conceals grinding teeth of rage. Heliod. *Aeth.* 2.19.2 describes a 'brief, forced smile which ran across their lips' (ἐμειδίασαν ὀλίγον καὶ βεβιασμένον καὶ μόνοις τοῖς χείλεσιν ἐπιτρέχον), where the point is *muted* not fake pleasure (cf. *ibid.* 2.8.1 for similarly 'forced' laughter). The fourth-century AD Ephraem Syr. *Serm. mon. Eg.* 31 enjoins the Christian monk to respond to abuse with a smile on the lips that is also, paradoxically, a kind of 'solemn' laughter (μειδιάσας τὰ χείλη ἐν σεμνῷ γέλωτι); cf. ch. 10 n. 16, with Appendix 2 n. 16 for the term *semnos*.

[27] The physiognomist Adamantius, *Physiogn.* 1.17 Foerster (cf. ps.-Polemon, *Physiogn.* 20), lists the lips, alongside other features, as a location of laughter; cf. ch. 1 n. 24.

[28] E.g. Fowler (1983) 159, 167–8, whose discussion of the passage as a whole is useful, Burton (1962) 43, Bowra (1964) 247, Richardson (1974) 268.

[29] For laughter in the eyes see e.g. Meleager, *Anth. Pal.* 5.180.2, anon. *Anth. Pal.* 12.156.4. Note two striking verbs: (ἐγ)κατιλλώπτειν, 'leer' etc., with Gow and Page (1965) ii 578, Sommerstein (1989) 104–5, Appendix 2 n. 15; (δια/κατα)σιλλαίνειν, 'roll the eyes' mockingly, with Appendix 2 n. 61.

in the background!) – is as it were intimated or betrayed not by normal reflexes but a more finely controlled reaction of the face. A fuller interpretation of the passage might show that Pindar shapes this notable image to match, and prepare for, the knowing, allusive speech which Chiron proceeds to deliver. But it is enough here to register that, like Homer, Pindar can exploit the physiognomy of laughter to inventive effect, employing it to hint at more than it tells (a visual counterpart to his pregnant narrative technique). Raising or moving the eyebrows in Greek literature is mostly associated with severity of some kind, as indeed in Hera's case (above) at *Iliad* 15.102.[30] Pindar, however, makes it convey Chiron's gentle astuteness. One can usefully compare and contrast (Pindar may, of course, have had it in mind) the way in which Hades *smiles* 'with his brows' in *Hom. Hymn* 2.357–8 when informed of Zeus's order to return Persephone to her mother. There the resonance of the facial image is more ambiguous: Hades appears to accept the order without demur, but the smile (always more unstable in meaning than laughter) is not only incongruous for the god of the underworld but bespeaks the complexity of how Persephone's fate will turn out.[31] Further cases of the involvement of eyebrows in laughter/smiles will be noted in Appendix 2, in relation to (descriptions of) visual works of art. But the passages cited above underscore the need to do justice to the intricacies of individual texts and avoid flattening out γελᾶν and μειδιᾶν into a homogenised semantics.

I would now like to consider briefly a different kind of linguistic evidence for Greek understanding of laughter and smiles. Modern ethological research suggests the likelihood of separate evolutionary origins for the two behaviours. Laughter probably developed from the 'play face' or relaxed open-mouth display of some primates, bringing with it the kind of vocalisations (such as the panting of chimpanzees) which often accompany or complement such displays within the setting of playful activity (and to which analogues have been claimed among non-primates such as dogs and even rats). Smiling, on the other hand, is more likely to be the legacy of the (silent) bared-teeth display found in many mammals but especially certain primates, among whom it appears to have evolved from an original threat signal into a sign of submission, reassurance etc.[32] If these hypotheses are on the right lines, they prompt a number of points worth pursuing within

[30] Note the contrast between arched eyebrows and laughter in Diphilus fr. 86.4 (cf. Ar. *Lys.* 7–8), knitted eyebrows and laughter at Palladas, *Anth. Pal.* 10.56.9–10. Further references in Pearson (1917) III 86–7, Gomme and Sandbach (1973) 649, Olson (1999); cf. ch. 3 nn. 112, 115, ch. 6 n. 40.

[31] See ch. 7 n. 89.

[32] Modern ethological investigations begin with Darwin (1965) esp. 131–2; note his hypothesis (208–9) of a continuum between laughter and smiling. Cf. Apte (1985) 240–5 for a survey of ethological approaches. The best synthesis in van Hooff (1972), (1981) 171–3, positing different evolutionary

the cultural materials of Greek antiquity, some of which have already been tracked in the arguments of the preceding chapters. The ancient world lacked, of course, anything like the modern science of ethology (or, occasional speculations aside, anything like the theory of evolution on which ethology is founded). But we can arguably find traces of a sort of 'folk ethology' in antiquity.

I noted at the start of this book that the Aristotelian view that humans are the only animals capable of laughter did not go unchallenged. Although that challenge is articulated directly in just one text (from the African-Roman Christian Lactantius), the personification of animals in the Greek traditions of fable literature, a personification which encompasses both laughter and smiles, indirectly reflects a more general willingness to see resemblances and affinities between human and non-human expressive capacities.[33] But there is another oblique and intriguing layer of evidence, embedded in language, which bears on this point. The Greek verb σαρκάζειν seems originally to have meant to 'tear flesh [sc. with the teeth]' on the part of animals, but it came to be used of bared-teeth grimacing or grinning.[34] In the Greek concept of 'sarcasm', therefore, may lurk a (partly subconscious) perception of how certain kinds of laughter/smiling, at the more hostile end of their expressive spectrum, betray a connection with the violence of animal nature. But such a perception contains a possible ambiguity. The (implicitly) bared teeeth of 'sarcasm' may signal potential aggression; but equally they may represent the *displacement* of violence, its muted conversion into ritualised social symbolism.[35]

---

origins for laughter and smiles; more technical data in van Hooff (1973) 119–24; see Lockard *et al.* (1977) for supporting evidence from humans. Provine (2000), esp. 75–97, emphasises links (but also differences) between chimpanzee 'ritualized panting' (in play) and human laughter. For dogs' 'laughter' see the qualified acceptance of Douglas (1975) 84–5 (cf. ch. 1, 2, for an ancient allusion), but the doubts of Glenn (2003) 172 n. 2; on rats' vigorous chirping (during play and also in response to tickling by humans), Panksepp *et al.* (2001). Ramachandran *et al.* (1996) 52–4, Ramachandran (1998a), (1998b) 203–7, 291–2 uses ethological evidence to ground a 'false alarm' theory of laughter's origins: laughter-like sounds signal the relief which follows a false alarm of attack. He seems unaware that this theory is older: see Hayworth (1928), esp. 368–70, 383–4; as Hayworth 381 hints, the theory is an evolutionary analogue to Kant's conception of laughter, in the *Critique of Judgement*, as 'an affect resulting from the sudden transformation of a heightened expectation into nothing', Kant (2000) 209.

[33] See ch. 1, 1–3.

[34] See e.g. Ar. *Peace* 482, (?)Eup. fr. 192.172, Chrysip. *SVF* III 630 (ch. 6 n. 104), Philo, *Legat.* 353, Galen, *Ling. Hippoc.* 19.136 Kühn, Hesych. *s.vv.* σαρκάζει, σαρκάζων, σαρκάσας. On the noun *sarkasmos*, see esp. Herodian, *Fig.* 92, where it is classified as a species of *eirōneia*, alongside mockery (*katagelōs*) and others.

[35] One modern ethologist, Eibl-Eibesfeldt (1989) 137–8, speculates (indecisively) on a 'common root' to laughter and smiling in a 'biting intention'. Cf. n. 4 above for different perspectives.

These observations can be reinforced by noticing that ancient texts some-times assimilate σαρκάζειν and σαίρειν, the latter (in its perfect tense, σέσηρα) usually denoting, as mentioned earlier, the open mouth and/or bared teeth of a smirk, grin or grimace. The force of σέσηρα varies consider-ably. It can be employed of laughter or smiling that is wholly unthreatening, as well as of more menacing looks; it can evoke anything from slight part-ing of the lips to prominent exposure of the teeth.[36] This tends to confirm the underlying ambiguity of Greek perceptions of the bared teeth of (some kinds of) laughter and smiles. If the sight of the teeth might function as a (latent) reminder of aggression, it can also be cited as evidence of the open 'guilelessness' of benign laughter.[37] The ambiguity in question also crops up in places which do not involve either of the verbs adduced above. When someone invented the nickname Gelasinos for the philosopher Democritus, the name compressed into a pun the fact that the ordinary noun γελασῖνος meant 'incisor tooth' (because visible in a laughing mouth).[38] Democritus, in his legendary persona, embodied the strange (and puzzling) notion of laughing at life itself: did that make him a threat, or simply harmless, to others? Differently, but equally piquantly, the 'sharp-toothed smile' (κάρ-χαρόν τι μειδήσας) which the wolf gives the heron in a fable by Babrius (94.6) nicely encapsulates (and allegorises) a double-edged request for help: the smile makes a show of friendliness or submissiveness, yet inadvertently discloses the danger lying behind it. Finally, and at the other end of the scale, a courtesan can be pictured in comedy as laughing ostentatiously in order to show off her 'lovely teeth' to potential clients.[39] Here (surely?) is a gelastic promise of only the most pleasurable kind of biting.

But where does that leave the most notoriously menacing teeth in the Greek imagination, those on the face of the Gorgon(s)? Are Gorgons the *ne plus ultra* of a 'bared-teeth grin', or do they represent a visage that lies beyond the bounds of anything interpretable as laughter and smiles? To address this question requires us to examine the visual evidence of Greek culture – the task of the next appendix.

---

[36] On σαίρειν, see 521, 524 above.   [37] See the passage of Fronto cited in n. 23 above.

[38] See ch. 7 n. 39.

[39] Alexis fr. 103.20–1. A less transparent instance is *Vita Aesopi (W)* 24 (Perry): Aesop's laughter involves bared teeth, but the rest of his face looks stern; this may be akin to Hera's laughter 'on the lips', 525–6 above.

APPENDIX 2

Gelastic faces in visual art

The presence and/or significant absence of laughter and smiles in ancient Greek visual art prompts some intriguing questions. This appendix will broach these questions without attempting a comprehensive art-historical enquiry.[1] My orientation will be towards themes and arguments developed elsewhere in the book.

An immediate caveat. In dealing with single images, it is often intrinsically difficult to distinguish between facial configurations of laughing and smiling. Both can involve an open and/or retracted mouth, with the muscles of the cheeks and around the eyes contracted and sometimes (more so with laughter than smiles) the upper teeth, less frequently the lower, exposed.[2] Since, moreover, real laughter and smiles can succeed one another in rapid, blurred sequence, a 'frozen' image of a face (even in a photograph) may make a definitive choice between the two expressions impossible. In the most explosive kind of laughter the mouth 'gapes' (the force of the Greek verb χάσκειν) in a way which is never the case with smiling. But depicting such laughter seems not to have appealed to ancient Greek artists: we know nothing from antiquity to match, say, the wide open mouth of uproarious laughter portrayed in a remarkable ink drawing of Leonardo's, or the features of extreme mirth found in some of Hogarth's works.[3] An alternative

---

[1] The fullest discussion of the subject is Kenner (1960), esp. 62–95; I cite details from her treatment below, with some reservations. See Simon (1961) for an intelligent critique.

[2] On the lips and (descriptions of) laughter, see Appendix 1, 525–6; cf. the (painted) Democritus at Sid. Apoll. *Epist.* 9.9.14, n. 73 below. For a case of the cheeks (in art) being read as smiling, see Philostr. maj. *Imag.* 2.24.3: Heracles, indifferent to Theiodamas' curses (ch. 4, 187), 'relaxes his cheek(s)' (τὴν παρειὰν ἀνεῖσθαι), an anatomically inaccurate phrase of nonetheless obvious import. Cf. 'soft laughter' on young Achilles' cheeks at Philostr. maj. *Imag.* 2.2.2; see also n. 12 below.

[3] Leonardo's ink drawing 'A man tricked by gypsies' is reproduced in Clayton (2002) 97 (plus 75: detail): one figure throws back his head, mouth wide open, in an unmistakable guffaw, another has a toothy grin. Clayton *ibid.* 74, 116 comments on Leonardo's interest in such faces, including his reasons for excluding them from his formal paintings. Hogarth: see e.g. his print 'The Laughing Audience' or his painting 'An Election Entertainment', Paulson (1975) plates 58, 106, 112, Arbury (1998) 490. Arbury 494–5 lists other visual depictions of laughter; von Graevenitz (1997) offers one approach to their relative rarity.

might be to show an overall bodily 'profile' of laughter, with (say) head thrown back and perhaps arms raised. (The suitors' uncontrolled hilarity at Hom. *Od.* 18.100 is a striking literary vignette of such whole-body convulsion.) In certain ancient images, it is arguable that this kind of profile is a surrogate for facial depiction of laughter.[4] This is most notably so with images of satyrs' wild 'dancing' and/or bodily (including sexual) excitement, which is not matched, as we shall see, by very frequent attempts to give them explicitly gelastic faces. This last point holds good, incidentally, for representations of ordinary human sex-acts on Athenian ceramics.[5]

In contrast to literary texts, which describe innumerable gradations and variations on the spectrum of laughter and smiles (from inscrutable laughter 'hanging on the lips', Theoc. 7.20, to the unforgettably manic laughter of the suitors, 'with jaws not their own', at Hom. *Od.* 20.345–9), Greek visual artists can rarely be said, on existing evidence, to have been interested in fine shadings of such bodily expression. One must add, however, a problematic qualification to that generalisation. Some of the strongest 'evidence' for gelastic expression in ancient artworks comes from descriptions in ancient *texts*. What exactly does this tell us? Do such descriptions record 'objective' details of those works, i.e. details any observer could have pointed to? Or do they deliberately display the visualising powers of language itself (powers enshrined in the whole ancient tradition of ecphrasis), supplementing what stone, metal or paint could do with an imaginative process more properly literary than ocular (especially where 'fictional' artworks are concerned)? Or is that distinction between language and vision too sharp? Can verbal descriptions of the faces of visual artworks reveal how ancient viewers processed and articulated what they saw in statues or

---

[4] Cf. e.g. the antics of the 'padded dancers' on archaic Corinthian vases: Wannagat (2007), which I have not seen, is the latest treatment.

[5] Kilmer (1993) 20 and n. 19, 62 n. 9, hesitantly detects smiles on the faces of, respectively, a young male having his genitals petted (RF cup by the Brygos painter, Oxford 1967.304) and a (?)prostitute holding a young man's erect penis and preparing for fellatio (RF cup by Phintias: Malibu 80.AE.31): I think he imagines both. Different again is the likelihood that the posture of the Scythian (not Persian) on the so-called Eurymedon vase (Hamburg 1981.173) signals sexual derision, reinforced by hand gestures mimicking ass's ears (see Persius, *Sat.* 1.59 and Σ *ad loc.* for a Roman version) and equivalent to a modern 'nose thumb' (Morris *et al.* (1979) 25–42): for the comic nature of the vase, and against a political interpretation, see Pinney (1984), with plates VIIIc, d, though she offers a different explanation of the hands (181–2). Cf. Davidson (1997) 170–1 (with ill. two pages before 167). Smith (1999) largely loses the comic features of the depiction (140–1 seems somewhat belated); her interpretation of the Scythian's hands as a gesture of weakness/terror (137–8) is unconvincing. As regards sex and laughter in other visual registers, Kerényi (1960) 15 claims that the so-called Baubo figurines from Priene (a woman's head above a vulva and pair of legs) show a 'laughing face'. This is not true of all and may not be true of any; the figures are too hard to read with precision: see ills. in Olender (1990) 110–13, where fig. 3.5 is the likeliest case; cf. *LIMC* III.2, 67–8.

paintings?[6] These questions cannot be examined systematically here, but they require some thought before we proceed to the material evidence in its own right.

ANCIENT PERCEPTIONS OF SMILING/LAUGHING FACES IN ART

The *idea* of incorporating laughter or smiles in a visual artwork was not foreign to Greek antiquity. In Theocritus' first idyll, for instance, the goatherd's bowl depicts a beautiful woman who laughs (deceptively) at one of the young lovers who compete for her affections.[7] Lucian's account of Zeuxis' painting of a centaur family refers to laughter on the wild face of the male as he leans over his suckling wife.[8] The ecphrastic descriptions by the two Philostrati of (imaginary) collections of paintings refer frequently to laughter/smiles. Notable instances include Philostr. maj. *Imag.* 1.2.5 (a *kōmos*, where the context evokes the *sound* of laughter, a synaesthetic paradox typical of Philostratus' work), 1.6.5 (frolicking Erotes), 1.19.6 (Dionysus, after turning pirates into dolphins), 1.24.4 (Zephyrus jeering at Apollo over the death of Hyacinth), 2.2.2, 2.2.5 ('soft laughter', later guffaws, from young Achilles); Philostr. min. *Imag.* 2.2 (the bloodthirsty grin of the barbarian sharpening his knife to flay Marsyas), 2.3 (Apollo's nonchalant smile of sadistic satisfaction), 10.21 (blood-crazed Pyrrhus, with an echo of *Iliad* 7.212).[9] Other pertinent descriptions include Longus, *Daphnis* 1.4.2, where the statues of nymphs disclose 'a smile around the eyebrows' (μειδίαμα περὶ τὴν ὀφρύν),[10] and Ach. Tat. 1.1.13, where Eros, in a painting of the abduction of Europa, is turning towards Zeus 'with a sly [or 'incipient'] smile, as though mocking him . . .' (ὑπεμειδία, ὥσπερ αὐτοῦ καταγελῶν . . .). In

---

[6] Although recent writing on ancient art has addressed the question of ways/frames of viewing (e.g. Stewart (1997), Elsner (1995), Goldhill and Osborne (1994)), little attention has been specifically paid to treatment of the face in this regard. Compare Baxandall (1988) for a probing attempt (based on a portfolio of sources not available for antiquity) to reconstruct the visual habits/culture of the fifteenth-century Renaissance as brought to bear on the viewing of art. While arguing for extensive differences between those habits and modern visual practices, Baxandall nonetheless concludes that 'we probably miss very little through not reading faces in a fifteenth-century way' (58).

[7] Theoc. 1.36. For a hint that the contest is quasi-poetic, see Hunter (1999) 80; cf. ch. 3 n. 4 for song contests. Theocritus' description is compatible with laughter that is *both* a response to the contest and erotically deceptive.

[8] Lucian, *Zeuxis* 4–5.

[9] On the last passage, cf. ch. 2, 55–8 (but contrast the smiles of the Ethiopians at Philostr. maj. *Imag.* 1.29.3). Further instances: Philostr. maj. 1.26.5 (Apollo, at Hermes' theft of his bow; cf. Schönberger (1968) 359–60), 2.22.4 (Heracles, scornful of the pygmies), 2.24.3 (n. 2 above); see also Callistratus, *Stat.* 3.2 (Eros).

[10] Cf. the 'laughing Nymphs' of a (supposed) statue by Praxiteles, anon. *Anth. Pal.* 16.262. On eyebrows, see 545 below.

this last case, the verb καταγελᾶν so commonly denotes a state of mind (metonymically) that there is no necessary suggestion of laughter *per se* in addition to the 'sly smile'. At the same time, it is typical of ecphrasis to treat visual artworks as though they somehow captured *multiple* moments in time. Achilles Tatius' words may therefore evoke a sequence of expression, inviting the viewer to superimpose mocking laughter over the visible smile. Such 'blurring' of facial moments may certainly help explain the complex visual clues contained in some other passages of the same type.

One test case worth tackling here is a pair of descriptions of the face of Praxiteles' statue of Cnidian Aphrodite, one of the most famous and widely copied of all statues in antiquity. Since some copies (though of uncertain fidelity and value) survive, a comparison between the textual descriptions and modern readings of the goddess's face might be thought feasible. But the issues are complex, and not only because of the dubious status of the copies.[11] One of the ancient descriptions, in pseudo-Lucian, *Amores* 13, seems to claim that the goddess 'has a delicate, slight smile, with her lips parted in laughter' (σεσηρότι γέλωτι μικρὸν ὑπομειδιῶσα). Since Aphrodite also has an 'arrogant' or proud look (ὑπερήφανον), and given the evidence of the copies (which, at the very least, are incompatible with anything like a grin), we must assume that σεσηρότι, which originally denoted retracted lips and exposed teeth, here conveys a more muted expression.[12] The same must be true when the word is again combined with ὑπομειδιᾶν (of an inchoate smile: the same word in Ach. Tat. 1.1.13, cited above) in two passages of Heliodorus and in another pseudo-Lucianic text.[13] Modern translators sometimes simplify the effect of *Amores* 13 by omitting reference to laughter, producing e.g. 'a slight smile which just reveals her teeth', 'a disdainful smile plays gently over her parted lips', or 'smiling just a little

---

[11] On the statue and the problems of its 'copies', see Robertson (1975) I 390–4, with II pl. 127, Stewart (1990) I 177–8, with II pls. 503–7, Delivorrias *et al.* (1984) 49–52.

[12] On σέσηρα (> σαίρειν), cf. Appendix I, 521. LSJ 1580, *s.v.* σαίρειν (A), distinguishes benign grinning and pained/hostile grimacing, but misses the problem about *Amores* 13; cf. Gow (1952) II 137, with ch. 2 n. 100. For a selection of uses of σέσηρα see ps.-Arist. *Physiogn.* 3.808a17 (a bitter sneer: Evans (1969) 38 n. 93, 'sly grin . . . of a silly disposition', is erroneous; Hippoc. *Gland.* 12 (the rictus of those hallucinating with brain disease: ch. 1, 17), Plut. *Mor.* 223c (Cleomenes' manic laughter), Philostr. maj. *Imag.* 1.20.2 (a painting of satyrs leering with lust), Philo, *Sacr. Ab.* 21 (a smirking, giggling prostitute as allegory of pleasure; the verb of real prostitutes at Clem. *Paed.* 3.11.71, John Chrys. *In Mt.* 4.7, 57.48 *PG*), Marcus Aur. *Med.* 1.15, 11.18.9 (feigned grins: see Farquharson (1944) 465, 873), Cass. Dio 72.21.2 (Commodus' deranged grinning), Ach. Tat. 1.1.7 (another painting, cf. 532 above; the girls' *cheeks* apparently denote fearful tautness), Pollux, *Onom.* 3.131–2 (malign scowling), 4.145 (a sneer? see 545 below), 6.123 (compound προσσαίρειν, a fawning dog: cf. Ar. *Wasps* 901). A somewhat different emphasis in Schmidt (1876–86) IV 194–5. See next note.

[13] Heliod. *Aeth.* 4.5.4, 7.10.5 (cf., with varying tone, 5.22.2, 7.21.1, 10.31.4), ps.-Lucian, *Philopatr.* 26. σαίρειν is also used of Marsyas' bloodthirsty slayer at Philostr. min. *Imag.* 2.2 (532 above).

haughty smile'; if a translator follows the Greek more closely, as with 'arrogantly smiling a little as a grin parts her lips', the results can be puzzling.[14] As
I argued in Appendix 1, we should not lightly elide the semantic distinction
between laughter and smiles. A Greek text which uses both vocabularies
should be assumed to be putting both to work, not merely interchanging
them. It is best to understand the whole phrase quoted above as a case of
semantic-cum-visual *telescoping*, implying an inchoate smile which carries
a suggestion of laughter (to follow). One might translate, then: 'with her
mouth open for laughter, and just faintly smiling . . .' Such writing points
towards a kind of viewing (at the very least as idealised in literature) which
'sees beyond' the fixity of the physical image and builds up a more layered
reading of the figure's expression.

When we turn to the Lucianic description of the same statue at *Imagines*
6, we find an ironically tinged version of the close, detailed interpretation
connoisseurs might practise. The goddess's eyes are said to have 'a melting
look that blends with a bright, joyful expression' (τὸ ὑγρὸν ἅμα τῷ φαιδρῷ
καὶ κεχαρισμένῳ). Here there are connotations, but no direct observation,
of smiles; and erotic overtones are unmissable: φαιδρός, 'bright', is sometimes elsewhere linked to smiling, while ὑγρός, 'melting', suggests soft
voluptuousness.[15] The speaker Lycinus, who is trying to evoke a stunningly
beautiful woman through an imagined synthesis of several famous works of
art, proceeds to add to the composite face a 'serious, furtive smile' (μειδίαμα
σεμνὸν καὶ λεληθός: at least a partial oxymoron) which he claims can be
seen on the face of a statue of 'Sosandra', probably another Aphrodite, by
the sculptor Kalamis.[16] Lycinus intends the face of his imaginary statue to
be expressively coherent, so the melting, bright eyes and the furtive smile
must complement, even reinforce, one another. There is some overlap with
the passage of pseudo-Lucian already considered. Crucially, both texts intimate a 'smile' that is not straightforwardly *there*, but has somehow to be
detected or projected by the absorbed viewer.[17]

Because the passages of (pseudo-)Lucian adduced above are embedded
in literary traditions of ecphrasis, their relationship to 'real' ancient viewing

---

[14] Translations, in order: Pollitt (1965) 131, Stuart Jones (1966) 155, Stewart (1990) I 280, Macleod (1967)
169. Lopez Eire (2000) 24 combines 'sourire' and 'rire'.

[15] See ch. 1 n. 33, with 545 below, for φαιδρός; for ὑγρός of the eyes, see LSJ *s.v.*, II 5. Another
voluptuous smile in a statue's eyes: Priapus in Hedylus, *Anth. Pal.* 5.200 (cf. Appendix 1 n. 29 on
κατιλλώπτειν). On Lucian's *Imagines*, cf. Steiner (2001) 295–306.

[16] Lucian, *Imag.* 6: see Pollitt (1965) 60 (who translates 'holy and inscrutable smile') with n. 16, Stuart
Jones (1966) 61–2 (who translates 'noble, unconscious smile') for identification of the statue. The
adj. σεμνός is normally *contrasted* with laughter; but cf. ch. 6 n. 27, Appendix 1 n. 26.

[17] For the viewer of a visual artwork 'mimetically' *projecting* things onto it, see Philostr. *Vita Ap.* 2.22,
with Halliwell (2002b) 309–10.

of faces in visual art must remain uncertain. But we can at least infer that Greek culture possessed the idea of looking closely and imaginatively for delicate shades of facial expression in visual images. This has implications for the possibilities of 'smiling' in ancient art, less so for outright laughter (though the passage of pseudo-Lucian, as we saw, plays with the notion of visually 'subtextual' laughter in an image). In so far as we can form an impression, from surviving copies, of what Praxiteles' Cnidian Aphrodite looked like, we might be inclined to posit a rather 'neutral' set of features, perhaps with lips just parted but not markedly retracted, and without the tightened cheeks of an unmistakable smile.[18] The texts cited do not claim that Aphrodite's smile is 'unmistakable', only that it might be discerned by a suitably equipped 'critic' or enthusiast.[19] Modern art historians have in fact paid scant attention to the face of Praxiteles' statue; they have been preoccupied with arguments over its depiction of the goddess's nudity.[20] But ancient viewers are likely to have needed to *coordinate* the statue's nudity with a reading of Aphrodite's face. This is, after all, the goddess poetically famed as 'lover of smiles' (*philommeidēs*), and it is no accident that Lucian's Lycinus later imagines Homer himself completing his composite statue by poetically 'colouring' its face with that very feature (*Imagines* 8). Aphrodite, not only divinely beautiful but also cause of the intertwined pleasures and pains of erotic experience, is an apt figure for the ambiguity, even inscrutability, of some kinds of smiles (a fact exploited by poets as well).[21] As a token instance of how one might follow this thread elsewhere in ancient art, see the faintly smiling Aphrodite, protecting herself with a raised slipper against Pan's evidently lustful approach, in a late Hellenistic sculptural group from Delos: the small winged Eros in the same group, pushing away Pan's horns, echoes the goddess's smile.[22] Here the faces betray recognition but also a blithe rebuff of Pan's sexual intention. They wryly adapt the tradition of Aphrodite's smiles to hint at her knowing command even of another deity's desires.[23]

---

[18] See the ills. cited in n. 11 above. One might compare another famous (and surviving) statue traditionally if uncertainly assigned to Praxiteles: Hermes with infant Dionysus at Olympia. Hermes' face is a candidate for the kind of reading Lucian and ps.-Lucian attest for Cnidian Aphrodite; see ills. in e.g. Lullies (1960) pls. 228–31, Stewart (1990) II pls. 607–8, with Robertson (1975) I 386–8 for disputed authorship.

[19] Another statue of Praxiteles' supposedly displayed a more explicit smile/laughter: see his 'joyous courtesan', *meretrix gaudens*, at Pliny, *HN* 34.70.

[20] An exception is Pollitt (1972) 157–9, who suggests 'we can perhaps still appreciate' the facial expression posited in literary descriptions of the statue.

[21] E.g. Sappho 1.14 *PLF*, Theoc. 1.95–6; cf. Crane (1987), with ch. 2 n. 35.

[22] See ill. 138, Pollitt (1986) 131.

[23] Hellenistic *erōtes* accompanying Aphrodite are quite often given a smiling look. This can be seen as subtly (and paradoxically, given their ostensible child-status) displacing the signals of erotic awareness from the goddess onto her symbolic attendants. Some other examples in e.g. Stewart (1997) 222.

While there are no easy generalisations to be drawn from the literary descriptions of Praxiteles' Cnidian Aphrodite, there is plenty of food for thought. When we add into the equation the other texts cited above for descriptions of laughter and smiles in art, we might provisionally conclude that there was more inclination in antiquity to perceive or read such features in visual artworks than a positivist set of criteria for facial expression can now give us access to. As we proceed to consider particular categories of images, we need at the very least to bear in mind that we cannot automatically intuit the predispositions of ancient viewers.

THE 'ARCHAIC SMILE' IN SCULPTURE

Many late-archaic Greek sculptures (preponderantly from the mid-sixth to the early fifth century) depict facial features – gently curved lips, correspondingly highlighted cheeks, and sometimes vertical indentations at the mouth ends to emphasise retraction – which give the appearance of smiling. This practice (arguably paralleled in some vase-painting too, though there the scale of features makes judgement harder) becomes so common as to constitute a stylistic paradigm, albeit one which permits many subtle variations and gradations. It is associated especially with the life-size (or larger) statues of males generically known to art historians as *kouroi* ('young men', though their identity as humans, heroes, or gods is mostly undecidable), and with their female counterparts, *korai* ('maidens'); but it is not invariable with either of those types.[24] It is also found on a range of other figures, some of which are securely identifiable as gods, heroes, ordinary humans or hybrid categories (centaurs etc.).[25] In origin, the phenomenon

---

[24] Examples are widely illustrated: in addition to Richter (1968), (1970), see e.g. Robertson (1975) II pls. 10–26, Robertson (1981) 25–31, Lullies (1960) pls. III (colour), 14–15, 21–3, 34–47, 70, Boardman (1978) pls. 101–46.

[25] Token examples of categories other than *kouroi/korai*. (a) (i) The late-archaic Olympian terracotta statue of Zeus abducting Ganymede: Boardman (1985) XX (pl. 33), Lullies (1960) 21 (pl. V), Carpenter (1991) 55 (pl. 59). (ii) The colossal head of a goddess (Cybele?) from Cyprus, c. 510, with a Dionysiac headdress perhaps symbolising ecstatic celebration of (divinised) fertility: Worcester Mass. 1941.49, ill. in Vermeule (1981) 73 (and colourplate 7). (b) Theseus and Antiope, from the Eretrian temple of Apollo (Chalkis no. 4): Robertson (1975) II pl. 50b, Robertson (1981) 45 (pl. 65), Lullies (1960) pls. 66–8. (c) The mid-sixth century Acropolis horseman (Louvre 3104): Lullies (1960) pls. 30–1, Robertson (1975) II pl. 25c (cf. 27b). (d) (i) The Attic bronze centaur of c. 530 (Princeton Art Museum, 1997–36), illustrated in Padgett (2003) 158–61 and discussed by Conrad Stibbe, who interprets the 'archaic smile' in terms of youth, energy and beauty (161); but cf. *ibid.* 14 for Padgett's suggestion that it evokes something alien to the human. (ii) The mid-to-late-sixth century triple-bodied monster/daimon from a pediment found on the Acropolis (Acr. 35): Boardman (1978) 176, fig. 193, Robertson (1975) II pl. 27e, Robertson (1981) 28 (pl. 36). (iii) The Acropolis Sphinx (Acr. 632): Lullies (1960) pl. 56.

may owe something to Egyptian and near-Eastern traditions, where possible antecedents can be found. This factor cannot be pursued here. But it will not in any case answer the question of the evolved functions of such faces within Greek art itself.

Interpretation of the 'archaic smile' sometimes lures scholars into floundering confusion. One, for instance, starts by denying (rightly) that the expression (always) represents 'a momentary feeling of joy', since it is found even on the faces of figures for whom joy would be unintelligible. He then proposes, first, that it is part of an archaic tendency 'to concentrate on the universal and typical' (but why, of all things 'universal and typical', a *smile*? – and 'typical' of what?), and, secondly, that it reflects the ethos of an epoch 'whose interest was focused upon earthly beauty and joy' – so that 'joy', having initially been excluded, makes a perplexing reappearance in the explanation.[26] Other attempts to account for the phenomenon have fore-grounded such things as an (allegedly) aristocratic outlook or *Lebensgefühl* of smiling at life, the idea of the 'blissful fate' of heroes beyond death, a sign of belief in the (Daedalic) 'magic' of representing living bodies in a material medium, a symptom of the divine/immortal associations of laughter and smiling, or, most commonly, a fundamental sense of (psychic) animation and life.[27] All these approaches open up worthwhile lines of thought. But none succeeds in accounting for all the relevant evidence. It will not do to *reduce* the archaic smile to a matter of technique, as though makers and viewers of images could simply have screened out the look of such faces.[28]

---

[26] Lullies (1960) 23. Lullies is, after all, prepared to see 'momentary joy' in particular cases, e.g. 65 on Theseus (pls. 66–8). General interpretative perspectives on *kouroi* in Stewart (1997) 63–70, Osborne (1998) 75–85.

[27] An aristocratic outlook: Yalouris (1986), very speculatively (cf. ch. 6 n. 28). The 'blissful fate' of heroes beyond death: Pollitt (1972) 7–9, but taking the 'smile' as a 'symbol . . . beyond emotion'. (Daedalic) magic, combined with the apotropaic: Kenner (1960) 63–8 (with a survey of earlier explanations). Reflection of the 'immortality' of (divine) laughter/smiling: Simon (1961) 646–8 (with the dubious claim that smiling was 'originally' or 'primarily' part of the divine world); cf. Charbonneaux *et al.* (1971) 126 ('symbolizing man's likeness to the gods'). (Psychic) animation *vel sim.*: Robertson (1975) I 101–2 ('sense of life', 'expression of the joy of living' – though the convention can become 'tiresome'!), Ridgway (1993) 14–15, Kris (1964) 228–9, Trumble (2004) 11–18, Boardman (1978) 66 ('features look more alive', but denying 'good cheer'), Gombrich (1982) 118 (making a larger point; cf. n. 75 below), Fowler (1983) 167 ('animate existence', with intimations of 'joy'); cf. Stibbe, cited in n. 25 above, Carpenter (1959) 64–7, Stewart (1990) 111–15. I am not sure what Jenkins (1994) 157 implies by 'artificial smile'; Osborne (1998) 81 oddly talks of a 'smiling but stony gaze' (supposedly characteristic of the 'impassivity' of *kouroi*). See ch. 1 n. 119 for Jacoby's speculation that the supposed Spartan divinity Gelos was merely a statue with a smile: implausible, given the commonness of the convention.

[28] Biers (1996) 166 regards the 'smile' as by-product of an attempt to show the anatomy of the lower face. This obscures what is at stake, and will hardly account for the range of pertinent material.

A conclusive interpretation of the archaic smile may now indeed be beyond our reach, especially since we have no ancient exegesis to work with: I cannot locate a single reference to the phenomenon in an ancient text.[29] A type of facial pattern attached to such a wide variety of figures (gods, heroes, wounded warriors, funerary memorials, sphinxes, centaurs, etc.) is unlikely to fit a single, neat template of explanation. Moreover, not all the faces in question are exactly the same; they differ in emphasis and nuance of (apparent) expression even to modern eyes, and may have done so even more to archaic Greek viewers. In so far as these faces do suggest smiles (more true of some than others), it is important that smiling is recognised in archaic Greek sources to be variable and often uncertain or enigmatic in significance. The smiles of Zeus and Hera in the *Iliad*, for instance, or of Odysseus in the *Odyssey* belong to an extended spectrum of contextually charged meanings (see Chapter 2). The distance between, say, the seductive but easily duplicitous eroticism of smiling (cf. again, archetypally, Aphrodite 'lover of smiles') and the ghastly look of bloodlust on Ajax's face at *Iliad* 7.212 shows how far we may need to stretch the connotations of a smile in order to be sensitive to perceptions available to archaic artists and viewers.[30] While there is probably a degree of stylisation in late-archaic sculpture which militates against clear particularity of expression in each and every 'archaic smile', we should not rule out the scope for individual works to exploit the convention for their own effect – arguably even (in rare cases) for comic impact.[31] In an archaic Greek frame of reference, smiling (and often laughter too) is subject to fluctuations and indeterminacies which make it peculiarly intriguing yet frequently resistant to interpretation. We should regard this as a resource implicitly activated by many sculpted faces: such images attract scrutiny by seeming to open up the mind or soul through the face, but they withhold any significance that can be exhausted by an act of viewing.[32]

---

[29] Sittl (1890) 344 n. 5 thinks Longus, *Daphnis* 1.4 (532 above) alludes to the archaic smile: conceivably, but it is not a reference to the stylistic phenomenon as such.

[30] Arnould (1990) 90 asserts, without argument, the influence of the idea of Aphrodite *philommeidēs* on the archaic smile; Lopez Eire (2000) 32 hints at something similar. But this on its own can hardly provide a general explanation.

[31] Some art historians see laughter on the faces of the Cercopes (suspended upside down from a pole carried by Heracles) on a mid-sixth century metope (Palermo 3920C) from Temple C at Selinous: ills. in e.g. Robertson (1975) II pl. 32d, Robertson (1981) 19 (pl. 23), Carpenter (1991) 153 (pl. 217). Gantz (1993) 442 diagnoses broad grins, pointing out (441–2) that (late) literary versions of the story ascribe laughter to both the Cercopes and Heracles (see ch. 3 n. 77); cf. Schefold (1992) 145–6 ('cheeky Kerkopes . . . hilarious tale . . . burlesque'), and Giuliani (1979) 22, detecting a comic undertone without reference to the faces. Robertson (1981) 19 ('as though smiling at the camera') makes a different point. Woodford (1992) provides an overview of the story in art.

[32] The idea of an artwork expressing the mind/soul through the face appears explicitly at Xen. *Mem.* 3.10.1–8: see Halliwell (2002b) 122–4, with further bibliography. Broader reflections on the inside/outside of statues in Steiner (2001) 125–34.

The conviction of many art historians that the archaic smile involves a sort of psychic mimesis, conveying 'animation' on the face, is justifiable. But it does not go far enough. We should think in terms of not only the visual simulation of life, but a subtle impression of expressiveness which by its nature invites but also (without further contextual clues) eludes a simple or complete reading. The appearance of a smile beautifully connects, but also *complicates*, the relationship between inner and outer, visible and invisible.

GORGONS

Do Gorgons laugh? Once again, it is a precarious task to align modern hypotheses with ancient evidence. The characteristic Gorgon face or Gorgoneion of the archaic and early classical period has a widely retracted mouth, usually both sets of teeth bared (sometimes with fangs or tusks exposed), and the tongue often extruded or hanging out.[33] Although nobody disputes that this configuration signifies terrifying ferocity, some scholars allow themselves, with varying degrees of qualification, to describe its appearance with terms like 'grin', 'smile', even 'laughter' itself.[34] But if the Gorgon's mouth is shaped to advertise demonic cruelty, does that not erase the facial semantics of laughter/smiles? Or could the two kinds of expression somehow be co-present?

The teeth of Gorgons are often clamped shut. This is not only *not* indicative of smiling/laughter (whose muscle movements typically part the teeth) but has its own menace. One conceivable implication is of teeth-*grinding*; as it happens, not the Gorgons themselves but their head-snakes do just that at pseudo-Hesiod, *Scutum* 235. Another is of readiness to bite (fangs obviously reinforce this), a readiness enlarged to monstrous proportions.

---

[33] See Krauskopf (1988) for a detailed survey of Gorgon images, with numerous ills.; Howe (1954), Napier (1986) 83–134 (to be used with caution) offer speculations on origins and significance. Cf. Padgett (2003) 84–9, 304–29 for various interpretations; Padgett's own view, following Frontisi-Ducroux (1989) 159, (1995) 11, that Gorgon images convey 'the idea of a terrifying roar' (90), hardly suits the closed teeth (or protruding tongue) of many images; but this is an old idea with some ancient antecedents: Howe (1954) 210–12. Cf. Stewart (1997) 182–7 for further reflections; but is it apt to call the Gorgon type a 'stare of sheer nothingness' (183)?

[34] Kenner (1960) 68–70 speaks of a laughing, grinning or grimacing face (German 'lachen', 'grinsen', 'grimassieren'); Stibbe, in Padgett (2003) 318, hesitantly moots a 'sarcastic', 'jeering' smile; Vernant (1991) 113 sees a 'gaping, grinning mouth' and 'hideous smile' (149), Jenkins (1994) 151 a 'manic grin'; Simon (1961) 648 uses 'Grinsen' (grin, sneer) but insists on a distinction from laughter; Arnould (1990) 228 (cf., somewhat differently, 49–50) compares the Gorgon face to the suitors' demented laughter at *Odyssey* 20.347; Clarke (2005) 37–8, adducing *Iliad* 7.212 (see ch. 2, 55–8), reads a savagely 'toothy grin'. Frontisi-Ducroux (1989) 159–60 finds the Gorgon 'grimace' ambivalent, seeing some images as more laughable than others. Cixous (1981) 255 uses the idea of Medusa's laughter as an ironic feminist symbol ('she's beautiful and she's laughing').

But I pointed out in Appendix 1 that the verb σαρκάζειν, which originally denoted 'tearing flesh' with the teeth, came to be used of various kinds of bared-teeth laughter and/or grimacing (producing the term 'sarcasm' in the process).[35] Might Greek viewers have seen Gorgoneia as suspended between a bestial readiness to bite and a look of sinister mockery, the ambiguity perhaps heightened by the commonly protruding tongue, which is compatible with mockery but not an exclusively gelastic gesture (and may, in the Gorgon's case, denote bloodthirstiness)?[36] Precisely because the extremes of Gorgon imagery part company with the inflections of human facial expression, the question is hard to weigh. For one thing, no ancient text actually applies the vocabulary of σαρκάζειν to Gorgons. Furthermore, although literary references to the horrific look of Gorgons, starting with the epithet βλοσυρῶπις ('fierce-eyed', 'grim-faced') at *Iliad* 11.36, are reasonably common, the language of laughter or smiles (however malign) is never used of them. One fascinating, though more oblique, connection might be traced through the association of the adjective βλοσυρός with the gruesome smile of Ajax at *Iliad* 7.212 (discussed in Chapter 2). It is legitimate to discern here a latent perception of the fierceness of Gorgons as akin to a cruel or bloodthirsty smile; but the Homeric passage is brilliantly special in what it conjures up, and not to be taken as evidence for a standard mindset.[37] Equally, Greeks could in principle have described a Gorgon's facial expression by the verb σαίρειν (perf. σέσηρα), which we saw earlier can denote the mouth of a laugh, smirk, etc., but also a horrible grimace: it is found, we might note, in the description of the grisly Achlus (personified 'mist'

---

[35] See Appendix 1, 528–9. Gorgons and teeth-grinding: cf. Frontisi-Ducroux (1989) 159.

[36] Gorgon's tongue as bloodthirsty: Sittl (1890) 90. But some images suggest a tongue extruded in mockery (certainly a Roman gesture, Persius, *Sat.* 1.60, and later too: Knox (1989) 59–61). See *ARV²* 396.20, with Kenner (1960) 99 pl. 11, for a lyre-playing satyr with tongue apparently hanging out: Kenner 75 interprets the figure as laughing, though her apotropaic reading and direct connection with the Gorgon are dubious. A satyr-head antefix from the archaic temple of Apollo at Thermon has a tongue at least half hanging out; the open mouth was a water spout, but this does not cancel gelastic design: Winter (1993) 131 with pl. 55; good ill. in Durando (2005) 126. Bieber (1961) 42, pl. 180, shows *kordax* dancers two of whom have lolling tongues. I take Dionysus with protruding tongue and clamped teeth on an Athenian BF lekythos of around 500 (*LIMC* III.2, 298, ill. 27) to be deliberately assimilated to a Gorgon. (Bizarrely, Cornut. *ND* 37 allegorises the Gorgon's tongue as a sign of *logos*!) Carden (1974) 23, following the unsubstantiated assertion of Starkie (1897) 185, claims that (ἐγ)χάσκω (cf. Appendix 1, 524) can 'denote' sticking out the tongue; but that is not shown by Callim. *Iambi* 1.82–3, even if (as is unclear) the second line pictures a rude tongue gesture. Different is the projecting tongue in depictions of the grimacing, self-strangling envy (e.g. a bronze statuette, Athens Arch. Mus. 447): see Dunbabin and Dickie (1983), esp. 12, 22, with pls. 3a–b, Slane and Dickie (1993) 494–6. For cross-cultural comparison, note the protruding tongue of a devil in a fifteenth-century drawing cited by Barasch (1997) 193–4.

[37] See ch. 2, 55–8. The connection in Vernant (1991) 113–14 between Gorgons and the laughable genital exposure of Iambe/Baubo (ch. 4, 165) involves tenuous 'free association'.

of death) at pseudo-Hesiod, *Scutum* 268. But, again, there is no surviving text which actually uses this verb of a Gorgon's visage.

Finally, the status of the Gorgoneion as an apotropaic, evil-averting symbol is not in dispute. The point is built into the mythology of the Gorgon's (literally) petrifying gaze; it is also reflected in the long-standing use of the emblem on military shields (including, sometimes, Athena's, as well as her breastplate). But this in itself only intensifies, rather than solving, the interpretative problem I have formulated. The idea of apotropaic laughter has some grounding in ancient evidence but is not secure enough to settle whether it ever makes sense to perceive Gorgon images as smiling or laughing.[38] Once we move beyond the core association between Gorgons and terror, we have very little access to the nuances which might have coloured Greek perceptions of particular representations. It is worth noticing, however, that in contingent circumstances a Gorgoneion might even be imagined as *causing* laughter: witness Lysistrata's reaction to the sight of a man with a Gorgon-shield buying fish in the market.[39] The main point here seems to be that a banal context deflates the character of the blazon. But is this just Aristophanic absurdity or an echo of a wider cultural possibility of 'subverting' the primordial horror of the Gorgon? Unfortunately, this comic chink does not really get us any closer to sensing whether a (paradoxically) gelastic factor was ever discerned in such images themselves. That question remains ultimately unanswerable. It belongs at an inarticulate level of cultural psychology to which we can hardly hope to penetrate.[40]

MASKS

One of the most obvious places to look for visual representations of laughter/smiling is the evidence (principally figurines, vase-paintings and ceramic

[38] Apotropaic laughter: ch. 4, 199–201. On Gorgons as apotropaic, see e.g. Dahlinger in Krauskopf (1988) 287, Belfiore (1992) 11–30.

[39] Ar. *Lys.* 559–60 (cf. *Ach.* 1124–6). It is of course true that *any* image of a Gorgon is intrinsically paradoxical, asking one to look at that which (in myth) cannot be looked at and therefore somehow transforming the primal experience of terror; cf. Osborne (1998) 72 ('Medusa is herself frozen by the artist and her evil power is both seen and contained'). This is anticipated in myth itself by Perseus' use of a mirror when killing Medusa.

[40] The only possible glimpse of a Greek etymologising link between Gorgons and smiles appears in Latin at Fulgentius, *Myth.* 1.21, where 'Medusam' is glossed as 'quasi meidusam'. But it is preferable to understand 'meidusam' as μὴ ἰδοῦσαν (with Muncker's emendation to 'quod videre non possit': Helm (1898) 33) rather than μειδῶσαν; a reference to smiles makes no sense of Fulgentius' (admittedly rambling) argument, *pace* Whitbread (1971) 62 (translation and note both dubious) and, apparently, Ziegler (1912) 1644–5. For a *contrast* between Medusa and smiling, cf. Eutecnius, *Para. Opp.* 33.17–18 Tüselmann.

model masks) for the actors' masks of Greek comedy (Old, Middle and New), including *phlyax* plays.[41] Or so one might think. Even here, however, such representations turn out to be relatively scarce, all the more strikingly so given the frequency of frowns, scowls and assorted looks of anxiety or severity found on comic masks. Several difficulties bedevil interpretation of these artefacts. First, many are small and/or of mediocre quality; reading their facial expressions with confidence is often not feasible. Secondly, the images relating especially to Old and Middle Comedy, as well as to certain categories of New Comedy masks, exhibit a degree of grotesque distortion which is important in its own right (in Old Comedy, it is fair to speculate, probably *everybody* was grotesque)[42] but also makes the decoding of expression insecure, not least where miniature figurines are concerned. Finally, the evidence for New Comic masks in particular is spread over half a millennium or more; it turns into a Greco-Roman amalgam that blocks accurate correlation with the theatre of specific times and places. These difficulties ramify far beyond my present scope. I limit myself to a few remarks on possible perceptions of laughter/smiles in the facial repertoire of the material.

I have mentioned the distortion and exaggeration stylistically typical of Old and Middle (as well as *phlyax*) masks. Although this factor, which applies also to certain mask-types (especially slaves) of New Comedy, throws the idea of determinate, univocal expression into doubt, it may by the same token open up an art of multiple, shifting comic expressiveness. In actual performance, the actor's head and body movements might draw out (or induce an audience to see) different facets of a mask at particular junctures of a play. This helps to explain why many representations of masks possess at least one feature (above all, a markedly widened and/or sharply curving mouth, and/or rounded cheeks) *compatible* with laughter (or smiles), while at the same time having other features (say, a furrowed brow and/or depressed, v-shaped eyebrows) which appear to send contrasting signals. Comic masks, in other words, may blur the differences between facial

---

[41] A broad range of ills. in Bieber (1961) 36–50, 87–107, 129–46, whose discussions are lively but sometimes tendentious; more specialised publications are cited below. Note Bieber's general caution (106), *à propos* facial expression, about the relationship between 'imitated' masks and real masks. For an overview of the material evidence, see Green (1994), esp. 34–8, 69–78, 99–104, 108–41, 145–69, and the same author's contributions to Webster (1995) I 53–76; cf. Pickard-Cambridge (1968) 210–31. On *phlyax* plays, or *phlyakes*, cf. ch. 3 n. 41.

[42] I suspect that in Aristophanes, at any rate, even supposedly attractive figures like Diallage in *Lysistrata* would be physically distorted and overblown; cf. Halliwell (2002a) 125, 137 n. 16. See now Revermann (2006) 145–59 for one approach to the 'grotesque corporality' of Old Comedy, though I am less confident than he is about possible exceptions.

possibilities, making themselves available for variable effects in the performances of mobile actors.[43]

Nevertheless, the quantity of visual evidence for Middle and New Comedy (less so for Old), as well as fourth-century *phlyax* plays, suggests that it was the exception not the rule for comic masks to show unequivocal laughter or smiling. The following is a small selection of some of the likelier cases (all dates BC).

(1) An early-fourth century figurine depicts a male slave with hands tied behind his back but his mouth pronouncedly curving into a seeming grin, with upper teeth exposed.[44] (When teeth are visible in depictions of masked actors, we cannot be sure whether they would be included in the mask itself or imagined/glimpsed through its open mouth.) The gelastic symbolism suits a slave-type involved in wilfully mischievous behaviour.

(2) A figurine-type of which several good examples survive, some from the second quarter of the fourth century, shows a clean-shaven, fat-bellied figure wearing a wreath and holding his phallus in his left hand. In the clearest cases, the face is animated by a relatively naturalistic grin, i.e. less schematically mask-like than many figurines (though the presence of tights makes the depiction of a comic actor explicit). One conjecture is that the type represents a parasite, a figure 'professionally' associated, both inside and outside drama, with laughter as a social lubricant, not least at symposia.[45] But the combination of beardless face (marking youth and/or effeminacy), gelastic mouth and hand on phallus nudges the viewer towards the salacious end of the comic spectrum; a male prostitute is an alternative guess. A 'smile of ecstasy' is a fanciful description.[46]

(3) A mid-fourth century figurine of an old man (one hand stroking his beard, the other on his hip) has a mirthful-looking open mouth and visible teeth; the hands reinforce that impression (perhaps evoking a scheming relish).[47]

---

[43] Cf. the discussion of Kenner (1960) 85–8, interestingly stressing the ambiguity of some masks' features (but lapsing, as ever, into an apotropaic-cum-magical conception of laughter). Wiles (1991) 95–6 (cf. 98) thinks the mouth of a slave-mask could represent mischievous 'grinning' or pained grimacing in different postures.

[44] Webster (1978) 60 (AT24a), with pl. XIb, Bieber (1961) 40 (pl. 149).

[45] On parasites and laughter, see ch. 3 n. 101.

[46] The last suggested by Robinson (1931) 86–7 (no. 404, with pl. 46). Robinson also toys with the idea of a hermaphrodite, citing the fullish breasts; Bieber (1961) 280 n. 49 (cf. 47, with poor-quality ill. 195) disputes this, though her own suggestion of an 'older man' ignores the clean-shaven face. For the parasite identification see Webster (1978) 20 (Q), 54–5 (AT19); cf. ill. in Webster (1969) pl. IX (Q), with *ibid.* 26–7 (AT18c). Other ills. in Himmelmann (1994) 129 (pls. 63, 64A–D), who identifies a male prostitute (126), and Pickard-Cambridge (1968) fig. 99 (with text on 215).

[47] Webster (1978) 77 (AT44c, with plate 1b).

(4) A mid-fourth century figurine of a female, probably a *hetaira*, apparently in the act of unveiling her face, wears something like a broad smile.[48] We might think in terms of a connection between *hetairai* and symposiac/komastic hedonism: the woman's face (to which the withdrawn veil adds piquancy) is a promise of sensual, including sexual, pleasure. In roughly this same period, the Athenian sculptor Praxiteles produced a statue which became known as 'the laughing courtesan' (n. 19 above).

(5) A mid-fourth century terracotta miniature shows a pair of characters, one of whom raises a leg in what is surely a dance step, while the other (with visible phallus) supports him with a mask-face that looks decidely merry.[49] The latter figure at least has the marks of a slave, accentuating the (grotesquely heightened) spirit of drunken disinhibition.

Although these examples could be added to,[50] I reiterate the thesis that it was generally exceptional for a comic mask to display, as opposed to invite, laughter. Perhaps that is not, after all, surprising. It is in line, for one thing, with the testimony of Aristotle, who famously regards the typical comic mask (of roughly Middle and early New Comedy) as 'ugly and distorted': an *object* not an expression of laughter.[51] Only a small amount of the laughter of Greek comedy, taken as a whole, is 'inside' the plays themselves. Laughter is the prerogative of comedy's audience; it is only an intermittent act within comedy's own world. It is most conspicuous, for sure, in the shameless scurrility of Old Comedy (see Chapter 5), but that is where the surviving evidence for masks is thinnest; and what evidence there is for this phase of the genre points to strong conventions of bodily grotesqueness, rendering characters objects of laughter in their own right.[52] In Middle and New Comedy, gelastically explicit masks probably belong largely to non-citizen (or, at the very least, socially dubious) characters: slaves, parasites, *hetairai*, 'cooks', etc.[53] Most New roles would not encode

---

[48] Webster (1978) 90 (AT78a), Bieber (1961) 41 (pl. 160): Bieber speaks of a 'laughing girl'. Identification of female figurines etc. as courtesans *vel sim.* is often precarious: see e.g. Bieber (1961) 97, on pl. 357 (a probably smiling face: Bieber 105, 'boisterous laughter', is an over-reading), where multiple uncertainties are glossed over.

[49] Webster (1978) 91 (AT84), Bieber (1961) 39 (pl. 134): Bieber sees both faces as 'grotesque[ly] grinning'; her characteristic cross-reference to 'Peloponnesian goblins' should be discarded.

[50] Among the Lipari finds, see esp. the female masks in Bernabò Brea (1981) 53–5 (with colour ill. 3 facing 56), 213 fig. 353; cf. Webster (1995) II 28 (1AT64e), 77–8 (1ST62) for the supposed types.

[51] Arist. *Poet.* 5.1449a35–7.

[52] The generalisation could be extended to the mythological burlesques or caricatures on vases from the Theban sanctuary of the Kabeiroi (cf. ch. 4 n. 95), as well as the grotesque statuettes from the same location: for selected details, see Webster (1978) 61–4 (cf. 4), Bieber (1961) 48–9, Boardman (1998) 258, 260–2, Vierneisel and Kaeser (1992) 448–9 (Pfisterer-Haas), Himmelmann (1994) 89–122.

[53] Bieber (1961) 101, with pl. 379, argues plausibly for one particular case of a 'grinning' cook; cf. Webster (1995) II 203 (3DT37).

the characters' own (possible) laughter/smiles in their masks: with notable exceptions – some (but not all) slaves, and the most irascible old men – masking seems to have supported the broad (though stylised) ethos of a sort of social realism.

That last conclusion is borne out by the list of New Comedy mask-types in the second-century AD lexicographer Pollux, a list which has received a great deal of attention from theatre historians but whose status remains controversial.[54] Though Pollux's list mentions numerous facial features and expressions, only three cases have any connection with laughter or smiles. One of the 'grandfather' masks is said to look 'very gentle round the eyebrows' (ἡμερώτατος τὰς ὀφρῦς) – in contrast to the raised or contracted eyebrows of several other masks – and to display 'a degree of cheerfulness above the eyes' or 'on the forehead' (τὸ μέτωπον ὑπόφαιδρος, 4.144).[55] A parasite (cf. the previous paragraph) is said to be 'rather cheerful' (φαιδρότερος, 4.148).[56] In both those cases we have the same adjective, 'cheerful' = literally 'bright', which is found in Lucian's description of Praxiteles' Aphrodite (534 above) and is sometimes used elsewhere to convey a smiling countenance. Finally, the mask of the pimp or brothel-keeper in Pollux is said to have 'a slight curl of the lips' (τὰ χείλη ὑποσέσηρε, 4.145). We have seen that σαίρειν, here in a compound, can mean to (bare the teeth in a) 'grin' or 'grimace'. Since the pimp's mask is said to have contracted eyebrows (i.e. a frown?), the reference to the lips seems to describe a sneer rather than a smile.[57]

These are slim pickings from the quantity of detail in Pollux's list. For all the uncertainties regarding its sources and reliability, the catalogue is notable for the rarity of its allusions to any kind of overtly mirthful features.

---

[54] Pollux, *Onom.* 4.143–54; see Wiles (1991) 75–7, Csapo and Slater (1995) 400–2 for translations. On this section of Pollux, including translation, see Webster (1995) I 6–51 (with important revisions by Green and Seeberg), Pickard-Cambridge (1968) 177–9. Cf. Nesselrath (1990) 79–102 on Pollux's relationship to the classification of Greek comedy more generally, Handley (1965) 33–9 for some thoughts on matching masks with characters in Menander. Bernabò Brea (1981) 143–234 uses Pollux to classify the New Comic masks from Lipari, but not always convincingly; cf. n. 56 below.

[55] Laughter and eyebrows: Appendix I, 526–7. τὴν ὄψιν κατηφής in the same description, if the passage is not garbled, must mean 'dim-sighted' *vel sim.* rather than the usual 'downcast' (cf. ch. 8, 388–9), *pace* Wiles (1991) 75: Csapo and Slater (1995) 400 have 'with . . . lowered gaze', Webster (1995) I 9 'downcast glance', Krien (1955) 91 and Bernabò Brea (1981) 143 similarly; the point is missed by Evans (1969) 38. Cf. the contrast with the second 'grandfather' type, said to have 'keener vision', ἐντονώτερος τὸ βλέμμα. The ill. in Webster (1978) 16 (E), contrary to what is mooted there, makes a misleading match for Pollux's first 'grandfather'; likewise Bernabò Brea (1981) 146–7.

[56] The Lipari parasite masks in Bernabò Brea (1981) 192–4 are hard to square with Pollux's use of this adj., despite the editor's general reliance on Pollux's classification.

[57] For putative examples from Lipari, see Bernabò Brea (1981) 152–3.

To that extent it corroborates my contention that comic masks only very occasionally embodied explicit expressions of laughter.

Away from Attic comedy, we find one group of Greek masks (or, rather, votive models of masks) which might appear to be concerned to depict laughter. These are some of the images found in the archaic sanctuary of the Spartan goddess Ortheia: in particular, masks whose *prima facie* expression is a toothy grin. As noted in Chapters 1 and 4, the function and meaning of these artefacts, which also include gorgon and satyr masks, remain obscure. A connection with ritual, quasi-comic performances is possible, but it cannot be discounted that they represent fierce demons of some sort: without knowing the context of use, we lack the framework of perception that would unlock the semantics of these weird faces.[58]

Finally, and paradoxically, from comic to tragic masks. Although, *a priori*, we would scarcely expect tragic masks to allow for smiling/laughing expressions, there is at least one case where this is conceivable: the mask originally and/or implicitly envisaged for Dionysus in Euripides' *Bacchae*. There are two textual references to Dionysus as 'laughing' in the play (439, 1021), and on this basis several modern scholars have posited a 'smiling' (*sic*) mask. But it may be significant that neither of those lines refers directly to the god's appearance as seen on stage. Both conjure up an image in the mind's eye, but neither need correspond to what the audience in the theatre can (expect to) see. I argued in Chapter 3 that despite the temptation to posit a mask encoding the god's polarities in a sinisterly ambiguous gelastic symbolism, it is doubtful whether the lines in question do provide clues to the intended masking.[59] It is worth adding that despite the frequency with which Dionysus is depicted in late-archaic and classical Greek art, there is no special propensity to depict him with a smiling or laughing face. The more obvious instances involve the 'archaic smile' (536–9 above) and do not distinguish Dionysus from other figures.[60] It remains thinkable, of course, that Euripides intended a mask with an 'archaic smile' to be used for the god in *Bacchae*, but the textual evidence falls short of a cogent case for this.

---

[58] See ch. 1, 46, ch. 4, 189–90; illustrations in Dickins (1929), Pickard-Cambridge (1927) between 254 and 256.

[59] See ch. 3, 136–7.

[60] See e.g. *LIMC* iii.2, 296 (ill. 11). Gasparri (1986) makes no comments on facial expression. Seaford (1996) 186, claiming a smiling mask of Dionysus on a BF amphora (*ABV* 275.8 = Berlin F3997), has confused the god with the satyr on the other side of the vase (n. 64 below). But a BF cup (Boulogne F559) does sketch a smiling, lyre-playing Dionysus: see Frontisi-Ducroux (1989) 152.

SATYRS

Dionysus leads us to his companions, satyrs (and/or sileni: the difference, whatever it amounts to, I leave on one side). There was an ancient belief that the word 'satyr' was derived from the verb σεσηρέναι, 'grin' (see above). The etymology is false, as is the derivation of 'silenus' from σιλλαίνειν, to 'roll the eyes' or 'squint' mockingly.[61] But such connections tell us something. Satyrs are readily thought of as betraying a gelastic addiction on their faces – indeed, capable of hearty guffawing, not least while engaging in phallic 'play'.[62] The frequency with which satyrs feature on Athenian vases might have made one expect to find depictions of their laughter or smiles, especially since kindred symptoms of exhilaration (dancing, running, sexual excitement, etc.) are explicitly shown. The standard convention of a half-profile face in Greek vase-painting limits the possibilities of showing signs of laughter, but it does not rule it out: an open mouth with curving lips is entirely feasible. What's more, satyrs account for a fair proportion of the frontal faces on Attic vases.[63] But even in the latter group, few indubitable depictions of laughter or smiles can be identified. One instance has a satyr mask-face with a schematically curved mouth, contrasting with the unsmiling god's mask on the other side.[64] Korshak finds a 'bold, gleeful, toothy grin' on the frontal-faced satyr (part of a scene of satyrs, maenads and donkeys) on a red-figure cup in Laon;[65] although the draughtsmanship is poor, this is a likely reading of the expression. Two other possible but not conclusive cases involve frontal-faced satyrs on black-figure amphorae: one, a figure (following Dionysus, as he is led to Zeus by Hermes) with lips retracted and teeth showing, the other a running satyr (part of a vintage-scene) with a small curved mouth.[66] But parted lips and/or visible teeth are not alone sufficient to suggest a smile. We should probably not see one

---

[61] Etymologies: Cornut. *ND* 59, Ael. *VH* 3.40; cf. Philostr. maj. *Imag.* 1.20.2 (n. 12 above). On σιλλαίνειν see Headlam (1922) 20–1; cf. ch. 6 n. 13. Note the invocation of a laughing satyr (alongside Dionysus) in a graffito third-century AD hymn from Dura-Europos: Porter (1948) 29–31, Gilliam (1952) 122; cf. ch. 3 n. 86.

[62] See Soph. *Ichn.* fr. 314.353, 370, where (ἐγ)χάσκειν (Appendix 1, 524) describes the satyr chorus; cf. *ibid.* 357, (probably) καχάζειν, 'guffaw', with 'stupid' childishness (354, 366, 369) and phallic antics (368). For a possibly guffawing Silenus, see ch. 7 n. 16. Simon (1997) gives an overview of satyrs/sileni in Greek art.

[63] Korshak (1987) 5–11.

[64] Berlin F3997: cf. n. 60 above.

[65] Korshak (1987) 10 (with 89, ills. 12–13): Laon 37.1054 (*ARV²* 150.23, 1628).

[66] (1) Boston 01.8053 (*ABV* 246.72), side A (Korshak (1987) 46 no. 16). The other side shows a satyr (again behind Dionysus) with clenched teeth and less curved mouth (Korshak (1987) 85, ill. 7): if this too denotes a grin, it is less convincingly so. (2) Boston 01.8052 (*ABV* 242.35 + 259.26); Korshak (1987) 84, ill. 6.

on the face of the moulded satyr-head on an Athenian red-figure kantharos of c. 470, nor the black-faced satyr on the other side of the same vessel:[67] in these instances, the parted lips reveal teeth that look clenched, making expression hard to read but not obviously gelastic. More unambiguous is the satyr-mask on a black-figure lekythos in Munich, where the curvature of the mouth (with grapes(?) hanging from the lips) is so extreme ('grinning from ear to ear') as to impose this reading.[68] Clearest of all is the face modelled in relief on the outside of a red-figure kantharos in the Getty Museum, showing a satyr with sharply retracted lips, both sets of teeth exposed, and a strong sense of gay animation in the cheeks.[69] Examination of further cases is unnecessary here. It would not do much to unsettle the significant conclusion that depictions of satyrs on classical vases (as opposed to the later type of the 'laughing satyr' in Hellenistic and Imperial sculpture) only rarely make a special effort to depict mirth on the face. Instead, they let the satyr's whole-body demeanour (what Greeks called *schēma*: 'form', 'bearing') do the work of evoking pleasure, hilarity and surges of (sexual and/or alcoholic) excitement.[70]

It remains conceivable, however, that ancient viewers were culturally primed to detect the flaring of mirth and glee on practically any satyr face or profile. We should register here that satyrs are paradigmatically snub-nosed (σιμός), and there was clearly a kind of sneering laugh associated with this feature in antiquity: Meleager three times uses phrasing of this kind of the mischievously cruel Eros.[71] It is perhaps surprising that such a look is never directly ascribed to Socrates, snub-nosed and satyr-like figure that he was (taken to be), as well as someone open to the suspicion of being, at

---

[67] Cleveland 1979.69, ill. in Padgett (2003) 249–50 and discussed there by Jenifer Neils.

[68] Munich 1874: see Vierneisel and Kaeser (1992) 421 (pl. 75.11), Kenner (1960) 99 pl. 9, Haspels (1936) II, pl. 31.1a–b; cf. Carpenter (1997) 95.

[69] Getty Museum, Malibu, 85.AE.263: ill. in Towne-Markus (1997) 42. Dionysus, on the other side (88.AE.150), is a little less obviously gelastic: see Carpenter (1997) pl. 39B.

[70] Lissarrague (2000) 111 mentions the rarity of laughing satyrs on Attic vases but cites only one case (the Getty vase in my previous note, on which he seems non-committal); he suggests that satyrs are objects more than agents of laughter, '. . . plus que rieurs, ridicules' (112). Close inspection suggests that Frontisi-Ducroux (1989) 156, on fig. 215, is unwarranted to see the satyr in the tondo of Louvre F130 as 'grimacing'. Kenner (1960) 74–6 (ills. on 99) cites further cases of possibly gelastic satyrs on classical vases, though her interpretation is far from secure in all instances (and caution should be exercised, as always, over her theory of the 'originally magical' significance of laughter). Cf. *ibid.* 76–82 for the evolution of 'laughing' satyrs (and, less so, centaurs) in Hellenistic sculpture; for good ills. of two examples, see Vermeule (1981) 165, Pollitt (1986) 136. Note the early third-century smiling satyr-mask from Lipari in Bernabò Brea (1981) 127 (H1, with colour ill. facing 128), though uncertainty remains over the type: Webster (1995) I 19.

[71] *Anth. Pal.* 5.177.4, 178.3 (with laughter in the following line), 179.3–4; cf. Gow and Page (1965) II 629.

least covertly, a sneerer.[72] But the idea of 'snub-nosed' contempt is nowhere directly ascribed to satyrs themselves. Yet ancient viewers of painted and sculptured satyrs may not have needed to be told such things for their eyes to be aware of them.

PORTRAITS

The mainstream Greek tradition of 'portraiture' (i.e. the depiction of name-able individuals), from the late classical era onwards, has virtually no place for smiles, let alone laughter.[73] In contrast to so many modern uses of por-trait photography, the figures suitable for ancient portraits – politicians, orators, poets, philosophers, athletes, etc. – were almost always required to display a poise and gravitas that would have been subverted by the presence of any gesture of instinctual bodily behaviour. The canonical avoidance of 'mobile' facial expression in portraits applies even to figures – such as Socrates, the Cynics Diogenes, Menippus and Crates, and comic poets (including Aristophanes) – who might have been expected, on other grounds, to show traces of their (partially) gelastic reputations.[74] My earlier caveat that ancient viewers may sometimes have 'read' expressions which now elude us in visual works of art applies here too, especially as there is independent reason to suppose that portraits lend themselves to projective interpretation.[75] With Socrates, for instance, his (often) snub nose, thick lips and puffy cheeks might for some evoke the 'Silenus' of Alcibiades' speech in Plato's *Symposium*, in which case the viewer of a portrait would by definition be looking at a sort of mask which *concealed* a different inte-rior. But the same features might remind others of the haughty, remote and absurd protagonist of Aristophanes' *Clouds*. Readers of Plato in gen-eral might look for quizzical uncertainty (even tinges of irony) in images of Socrates' face; others (less favourably) for signals of mockery. Then again, we know that some ancients supposed, probably quite fictitiously, that Socrates had exemplified an unchanging (perhaps genial) countenance

---

[72] Socrates as satyr: Plato *Symp.* 175e, 215b, 216c. Socrates as sneerer: e.g. Ar. *Clouds* 362–3, with ch. 6 n. 75.

[73] Sid. Apoll. *Epist.* 9.9.14 mentions the 'open lips' of an (imaginary) painting of laughing Democritus: cf. Richter (1965) I 120 (correcting her reference), with my ch. 7 n. 23.

[74] See Richter (1965) I 109–19 (Socrates; cf. n. 77 below), 140–1 (Aristophanes), II 181–6 (the Cynics).

[75] Gombrich (1982), esp. 116–36, has a stimulating approach to this question; note his comment (118) on the ambiguous, multi-valent potential of depictions of an 'arrested smile' (cf. n. 27 above). Brilliant (1971) ponders the historically variable schemata which have influenced the making and recognition of portraits. Wardman (1967) is a case study in the differences between two individual ancient viewers.

of self-control.[76] Such presuppositions could dispose individual viewers towards corresponding readings of portraits. They might even still do so.[77]

To be sure, among the huge number of surviving Greek portrait sculptures (most of them Roman copies) it is feasible to distinguish some faces as more severe, others as more 'relaxed'. A complex physiognomic typology might even be worked out, though this has never, to my knowledge, been attempted. But given the quantity of material it is nonetheless hard to deny the ostensible narrowness or faintness (if also, perhaps, subtlety) of the available range of facial expression. This does not eliminate a variety of other respects in which portraits could evoke or symbolise certain ideas and values, especially where a whole body was depicted.[78] But it does mean that anything resembling laughter was deliberately excluded from the repertoire.

FINAL REFLECTIONS

The material considered in the previous sections yields multiple uncertainty, ambiguity and paradox. Descriptions of artworks in literary texts suggest a close, subtle interest in reading gelastic expression on a wide range of faces (gods, heroes, ordinary humans and other groups), sometimes in ways which defy (or see beyond) the fixity of the single image. Yet finding actual examples to match such texts in *modern* eyes is hard work. Even comic masks and satyrs/sileni (at least before the Hellenistic period) produce slimmer pickings than might have been anticipated, though both open perspectives whose general promptings to laughter are not in doubt. On the other hand, where we are confronted by the apparent lineaments of laughter or smiles in whole clusters of images, it is uncertain what we are dealing with. If the 'archaic smile' in Greek sculpture is a smile at all, it can only be interpreted as a fluid not a univocal signifier (perhaps in itself an invitation to read 'beyond the face'). If some of the masks dedicated to the Spartan Ortheia are to count as 'grinning', we do not know why. And if Gorgons smile or laugh, they do so in an extreme manner so fused with, or overlaid by, horror as to be profoundly oxymoronic, yet even so without ever attracting comment in this respect from any surviving text (other than a single, brilliant *sub*text at *Iliad* 7.212).

[76] For this last view of Socrates' face, see ch. 6 n. 40. Socrates as Silenus: ch. 6 n. 88; Socrates' face in Plato: *ibid.* 281–2.

[77] After citing various intellectual, moral and psychological qualities ascribed to Socrates (including eyes 'keen on learning' and 'full of passion, *erōs*'), Richter (1965) I 109 claims: 'All these qualities, as well as his . . . sense of humour . . . are evident in the best of Sokrates' portraits' – a rather hopeful claim. Cf. Lapatin (2006) 110–20 for an informative recent overview.

[78] Zanker (1995) develops a rich thesis on this whole subject.

It goes without saying that the enquiry could be extended in other directions which would complement the arguments of this book. Take the case of children. Several uncontroversial cases of smiling children can be found in Greek art. This reflects a general, unsurprising association between childhood and laughter/smiles; but it can also bring to light some scope for ambivalence of feeling. A smile, marked by retracted lips and highlighted cheeks, is evident on two fourth-century Attic grave stelai for female children. The first is the profile face of Melisto on her gravestone of c. 340; the second, a generation later, is the frontal face of Demainete.[79] Both images involve children who hold toys or pets. The monuments use smiles to evoke childhood innocence, but at the same time they contextually deepen the expression with a pathos that relies, I suggest, on an unspoken contrast with the idea of Hades as the land of 'the unsmiling'.[80] There is a sort of visual dialectic here between the affirmation of life and the acknowledgement of death: themes which have appeared in numerous guises throughout this book. Very different, and less complex, is a Boeotian figurine of late fourth-century date which shows a seated girl holding a tambourine and wreath.[81] Here death is out of sight; the connotations are entirely of a nexus of festivity, music and dance (we might think of an affinity with, for example, the girl dancer belonging to the Syracusan impresario in Xenophon's *Symposium*): the figure is not an individual but a symbol of pleasurable activities. The gap between the gravestones and the figurine neatly encapsulates the distance between exuberantly life-affirming and ambiguously death-fearing expressions of laughter.[82]

Even after we have made allowance for modifications and refinements of the arguments sketched in this appendix, it is hard to doubt that gelastic expression was not a common or prominent element in Greek art. This is only one aspect of a larger phenomenon, the tendency of much Greek art to deny itself the resources of overt facial communication. 'Greek artists in general . . . were normally reluctant to represent the more obvious

---

[79] Melisto (Harvard 1961.86): see Neils and Oakley (2003) 307, no. 124 (a 'broad, happy smile'), with xviii (colour ill.). Demainete (Getty 75.AA.63): Neils and Oakley (2003) 307–8, no. 125, with 183 for further ill. For general Greek associations between childhood and laughter, see ch. 1, 19–24.

[80] See ch. 7 n. 89.

[81] Boston 10.230: Neils and Oakley (1993) 295, no. 109, with 78 for further ill. Cognate in gelastic spirit is the small late-Hellenistic bronze of a female dwarf, her semi-naked body in torsion (probably dancing) and her tilted head unmistakably grinning: Pollitt (1986) 138, no. 149 (left). For further possible evidence of dwarfs as entertainers in Greece, cf. Dasen (1993) 240–2. On the nexus of laughter, festivity, dance, etc., see esp. ch. 1, 4, 20, 22. Some New Comedy masks of smiling female children can be found in Bernabò Brea (1981) 236; but age/status can be debated to some extent: cf. Webster (1995) I 50–1, II 78–9.

[82] Further gelastic images of children are cited by Kenner (1960) 89–91.

expressions of emotional variability', as one scholar has put it – and he starts his (negative) list with 'howls of laughter'.[83] Another scholar has gone much further than this, however, by claiming that 'nuances of facial expression played little part' in either the visual arts *or* the literature of the Greeks.[84] This is a dangerous overstatement. 'Nuances' are a different matter from 'obvious expressions'. They are, by their very nature, subject to delicacy of perception (or projection) and judgement, as some of my earlier analysis has explained. (The 'archaic smile', whatever else it is, is certainly a facial 'nuance'.) So we should not exclude the scope for discernment of facial nuances, including those with gelastic inflections, on the part of ancient viewers of art. What remains true, though, is that easily readable facial expression was largely filtered out from most archaic and classical Greek art (less so from Hellenistic styles), as well as from later classicising trends in the Greco-Roman tradition.[85] The rarity of depictions of laughter, less so of subtle smiles, is in part a reflection of this larger pattern of artistic choices and cultural preferences. It is possible, however, that further factors were at work in limiting the visual representation of laughter, in particular its potential association, in ways this whole book has explored, with ideas of bodily excess, indecency and shamefulness – associations which would have been in tension with the elevated subject-matter and idealising modes characteristic of much Greek art.[86] But to pursue such speculation further would stretch the boundaries of this already lengthy appendix.

[83] Pollitt (1972) 6. Cf. Kilmer (1993) 131 n. 5 (on late-archaic ceramics), Halliwell (1993b) 203–6, with Brophy (1945) 74–9 on the larger legacy of the 'classic face'.

[84] Stanford (1983) 82: his statement is exaggerated on the literary side. See Evans (1969) for a survey of references to the face in ancient texts, though not always reliable on details.

[85] Those trends stretch, in fact, beyond antiquity. See Barasch (1997), esp. 193–4, for the rarity of laughing faces in Renaissance art (smiling is a different matter: 201–6); cf. n. 3 above. On other periods/types of Western art, note Barasch (1997) 184, 'early Christian art shows no laughing face', and Barasch (1991) 100–11 (arguing for the influence of ancient comic masks) on the mostly grotesque laughter, especially that of demons, in medieval art. Cf. the general remarks, and the lists, of Arbury (1998) 493–5, noting the salience of the laughing Democritus (with ch. 7 n. 23). One case study of the larger function of laughter in painting (not just its depiction on the face) is Gibson (2006) on Pieter Bruegel. One could make a case for saying that much Western art has intuitively followed the sentiment articulated by the early experimental psychologist William McDougall that 'the smile is beautiful, the laugh is ugly': McDougall (1923) 167.

[86] As regards gelastic *scenes*, I note that no artistic depiction survives from antiquity of either of the Homeric episodes involving Hephaestus and the laughter of the gods, nor of Thersites as agent or object of laughter. Zimmermann (1997) 1208–9 identifies a mid-fifth century Attic RF hydria (British Museum, E196) as the only possible depiction of an *ugly* Thersites; cf. *LIMC* 1.1, 270 (no. 81*), with 1.2, 200 (ill. 81). But the scene shown does not correspond closely to anything in *Iliad* 2.

Bibliography

(Abbreviations of journal titles follow *L'Année philologique*. For other abbreviations, see xii–xiii.)

Adam, C. and Tannery, P. (1996) *Oeuvres de Descartes*, rev. edn, vol. XI. Paris.
Adam, J. (1899) 'On the word βλοσυρός', *CR* 13: 10–11.
   (1963) *The Republic of Plato*, 2nd edn (2 vols.). Cambridge.
Adams, J. N. (1982) *The Latin Sexual Vocabulary*. London.
Adkin, N. (1985) 'The Fathers on laughter', *Orpheus* 6: 149–52.
Adkins, A. W. H. (1960) *Merit and Responsibility: a Study in Greek Values*. Oxford.
Adolf, H. (1947) 'On mediaeval laughter', *Speculum* 22: 251–3.
Adoménas, M. (1999) 'Heraclitus on religion', *Phronesis* 44: 87–113.
Adrados, F. R. (1975) *Festival, Comedy and Tragedy*, Eng. tr. C. Holme. Leiden.
Agosti, G. (2001) 'Late antique iambics and *iambikè idéa*', in *Iambic Ideas: Essays on a Poetic Tradition from Archaic Greece to the Late Roman Empire*, eds. A. Cavarzere *et al.* Lanham: 219–55.
Ahl, F. (1984) 'The art of safe criticism in Greece and Rome', *AJPh* 105: 174–208.
Aland, K. and Aland, B. (1979) *Novum Testamentum Graece*, 26th edn. Stuttgart.
Alden, M. J. (1997) 'The resonances of the song of Ares and Aphrodite', *Mnemosyne* 50: 513–29.
Alford, V. (1959) 'Rough music or charivari', *Folklore* 70: 505–18.
Allen, A. (1993) *The Fragments of Mimnermus*. Stuttgart.
Allen, D. S. (2000) *The World of Prometheus: the Politics of Punishing in Democratic Athens*. Princeton.
Allen, T. W., Halliday, W. R. and Sikes, E. E. (1936) *The Homeric Hymns*, 2nd edn. Oxford.
Allen, W. S. (1987) *Vox Graeca: the Pronunciation of Classical Greek*, 3rd edn. Cambridge.
Ameling, W. (1985) 'ΦΑΓΩΜΕΝ ΚΑΙ ΠΙΝΩΜΕΝ. Griechische Parallelen zu zwei Stellen aus dem Neuen Testament', *ZPE* 60: 35–43.
Anderson, G. (1976) *Lucian: Theme and Variation in the Second Sophistic*. Leiden.
   (1978) 'Lucian's *Nigrinus*: the problem of form', *GRBS* 19: 367–74.
Anderson, W. S. (1982) *Essays on Roman Satire*. Princeton.
Andreassi, M. (2004) *Le facezie del Philogelos*. Lecce.

Andrisano, A. (2003) 'Les performances du *Symposion* de Xénophon', *Pallas* 61: 287–302.

Angeli Bernardini, P. (1994) 'Umorismo e serio-comico nell' opera di Luciano', in Jäkel *et al.* (1994–7) vol. i, 113–20.

Apte, M. L. (1985) *Humor and Laughter: an Anthropological Approach*. Ithaca.

(1996) 'Humor', in *Encyclopedia of Cultural Anthropology*, eds. D. Levinson and M. Ember, vol. ii. New York: 618–22.

Aquinas, Saint Thomas (1993) *Commentary on Aristotle's Nicomachean Ethics*, Eng. tr. C. I. Litzinger, rev. edn. Indiana.

Arbury, A. S. (1998) 'Laughter', in *Encyclopedia of Comparative Iconography*, ed. H. E. Roberts, vol. i. Chicago: 489–96.

Ardley, G. (1967) 'The role of play in the philosophy of Plato', *Philosophy* 42: 226–44.

Arnott, W. G. (1979–2000) *Menander* (3 vols.). Cambridge Mass.

(1995) 'Menander's manipulation of language for the individualisation of character', in *Lo spettacolo delle voci*, eds. F. de Martino and A. H. Sommerstein. Bari: 147–64 (parte seconda).

(1996) *Alexis: the Fragments*. Cambridge.

(1997) 'Humour in Menander', in Jäkel *et al.* (1994–7) vol. iii, 65–79.

Arnould, D. (1990) *Le rire et les larmes dans la littérature grecque d'Homère à Platon*. Paris.

(1998) 'Le ridicule dans la littérature grecque archaïque et classique', in Trédé and Hoffmann (1998) 13–20.

Arrighetti, G. (1973) *Epicuro Opere*, 2nd edn. Turin.

(2000) 'Le rire chez Hésiode', in Desclos (2000) 143–53.

(2006) *Poesia, poetiche e storia nella riflessione dei Greci*. Pisa.

Arrowsmith, W. tr. (1990) *Friedrich Nietzsche: Unmodern Observations*. New Haven.

Arroyo, S. *et al.* (1993) 'Mirth, laughter and gelastic seizures', *Brain* 116: 757–80.

Arthur, M. (1977) 'Politics and pomegranates: an interpretation of the Homeric *Hymn to Demeter*', *Arethusa* 10: 7–47. [Rpr., with abridged notes, in Foley (1994) 214–42.]

Attridge, H. W. (1976) *First-Century Cynicism in the Epistles of Heraclitus*. Missoula.

Auden, W. H. (1963) *The Dyer's Hand and Other Essays*. London.

Aufhauser, J. B. (1925) *Antike Jesus-Zeugnisse*. Bonn.

Austin, C. and Olson, S. D. (2004) *Aristophanes Thesmophoriazusae*. Oxford.

Averintsev, S. S. (1993) 'Bakhtin and the Russian attitude to laughter', in *Bakhtin: Carnival and Other Subjects*, ed. D. Shepherd. Amsterdam: 13–19. [= *Critical Studies* vol. 3.2–4.1/2]

Babut, D. (1974) 'Xénophane critique des poètes', *AC* 43: 83–117.

(1975) 'Héraclite et la religion populaire', *REA* 77: 27–62.

(1976) 'Héraclite critique des poètes et des savants', *AC* 45: 464–96.

Bachorowski, J.-A. and Owren, M. J. (2001) 'Not all laughs are alike', *Psychological Science* 12.3: 252–7.

Baconsky, T. (1996) *Le rire des Pères. Essai sur le rire dans la patristique grecque*. Paris.

Baier, T. (2002) 'Zur Funktion der Chorpartien in den *Fröschen*', in Ercolani (2002) 189–204.

Bain, D. (1977) *Actors and Audience: a Study of Asides and Related Conventions in Greek Drama*. Oxford.

(1979) '*Plautus vortit barbare*: Plautus, *Bacchides* 526–61 and Menander, *Dis exapaton* 102–12', in *Creative Imitation and Latin Literature*, eds. D. West and T. Woodman. Cambridge: 17–34.

(1985) 'ΛΗΚΥΘΙΟΝ ΑΠΩΛΕΣΕΝ: some reservations', *CQ* 35: 31–7.

(1991) 'Six Greek verbs of sexual congress (βινῶ, κινῶ, πυγίζω, ληκῶ, οἴφω, λαικάζω)', *CQ* 41: 51–77.

Bakhtin, M. (1968) *Rabelais and his World*, Eng. tr. H. Iswolsky. Cambridge Mass.

(1984) *Problems of Dostoevsky's Poetics*, tr. and C. Emerson. Minneapolis.

(1986) *Speech Genres and Other Late Essays*, Eng. tr. V. W. McGee, eds. C. Emerson and M. Holquist. Austin.

Barasch, M. (1991) *Imago Hominis: Studies in the Language of Art*. New York.

(1997) 'De risu: laughter in renaissance psychology, literature, and art', in *The Language of Art*. New York: 172–206.

Barigazzi, A. (1976) 'Eracle e Tiodamante in Callimaco e Apollonio Rodio', *Prometheus* 2: 227–38.

Barish, J. (1981) *The Antitheatrical Prejudice*. Berkeley.

Barker, A. (1984) *Greek Musical Writings I: the Musician and his Art*. Cambridge.

Barlow, S. A. (1971) *The Imagery of Euripides*. London.

(1986) *Euripides Trojan Women*. Warminster.

Barnes, C. L. H. (2005) *Images and Insults: Ancient Historiography and the Outbreak of the Tarentine War*. Stuttgart.

Barnes, J. (1982) *The Presocratic Philosophers*, rev. edn. London.

ed. (1984) *The Complete Works of Aristotle* (2 vols.). Princeton.

(2003) *Porphyry Introduction*. Oxford.

Baudelaire, C. (1976) 'De l'essence du rire' [publ. 1855], in *Oeuvres complètes*, ed. C. Pichois, vol. ii. Paris: 525–43 (with editor's notes, 1342–52).

(1964) 'On the essence of laughter', in *The Painter of Modern Life and Other Essays*, Eng. tr. J. Mayne. London: 147–65.

Bauer, W. (1979) *A Greek–English Lexicon of the New Testament*, Eng. tr. W. F. Arndt and F. W. Gingrich, 2nd edn. Chicago.

Baur, P. C. (1953) 'Drei unedierte Festpredigten aus der Zeit der Nestorianischen Streitigkeiten', *Traditio* 9: 101–26.

(1959) *John Chrysostom and his Time* (2 vols.). Vaduz.

Bausinger, H. (1992) 'Lachkultur', in *Vom Lachen. Einem Phänomen auf der Spur*, ed. T. Vogel. Tübingen: 9–23.

Baxandall, M. (1988) *Painting and Experience in Fifteenth Century Italy*, 2nd edn. Oxford.

Beagon, M. (2005) *The Elder Pliny on the Human Animal: Natural History Book 7*. Oxford.

Beck, W. (1991) 'γελάω-γέλως', *LfgrE* ii 124–6.

(1993) 'μειδήματα-μειδιάω', *LfgrE* 15. Lieferung, 84–5.

Beckby, H. (1966) *Anthologia Graeca* (4 vols.), 2nd edn. Munich.
Beckett, Samuel (1962) *Malone Dies*. Harmondsworth. [Orig. French version 1951, English version 1958.]
  (1963a) *Murphy*. London. [1st publ. 1938.]
  (1963b) *Watt*. London. [1st publ. Paris, 1953.]
  (1986) *The Complete Dramatic Works*. London.
Bekker, I. (1814–21) *Anecdota Graeca* (3 vols.). Berlin.
Belardinelli, A. M. (1994) *Menandro Sicioni*. Bari.
Belfiore, E. S. (1992) *Tragic Pleasures: Aristotle on Plot and Emotion*. Princeton.
Berger, P. L. (1997) *Redeeming Laughter: the Comic Dimension of Human Experience*. Berlin.
Bergson, H. (1975) *Le rire. Essai sur la signification du comique*. Paris. [1st publ. 1900.]
Bernabò Brea, L. (1981) *Menandro e il teatro greco nelle terracotte liparesi*. Genoa.
Bernays, J. (1861) 'Aus dem Aristotelischen Dialog *Eudemos*', *RhM* 16: 236–46. [Rpr. in *idem, Gesammelte Abhandlungen*, ed. H. Usener, 2 vols. Berlin, 1885: I, 130–40.]
  (1879) *Lucian und die Kyniker*. Berlin.
Berry, J. N. (2004) 'Nietzsche and Democritus: the origins of ethical eudaimonism', in *Nietzsche and Antiquity*, ed. P. Bishop. Rochester: 98–113.
Bers, V. (1985) 'Dikastic *thorubos*', in *CRUX: Essays Presented to G. E. M. de Ste. Croix*, eds. P. A. Cartledge and F. D. Harvey. Exeter: 1–15.
Beta, S. (2004) *Il linguaggio nelle commedie di Aristofane*. Rome.
Betz, H. D. (1992) *The Greek Magical Papyri in Translation*, 2nd edn. Chicago.
Bieber, M. (1961) *The History of the Greek and Roman Theater*, 2nd edn. Princeton.
Bielohlawek, K. (1940) 'Gastmahls- und Symposionslehren bei griechischen Dichtern', *WS* 58: 11–30.
Bierl, A. (2001) *Der Chor in der Alten Komödie: Ritual und Performativität*. Munich.
Biers, W. R. (1996) *The Archaeology of Greece*, 2nd edn. Ithaca.
Billerbeck, M. (1978) *Epiktet vom Kynismus*. Leiden.
Blanchard, A. (1998) 'Colère et comédie: les conditions du rire dans le théâtre de Ménandre', in Trédé and Hoffmann (1998) 91–100.
Blankert, A. (1973) 'Rembrandt, Zeuxis and ideal beauty', *Album Amicorum J. G. van Gelder*, eds. J. Bruyn *et al*. The Hague: 32–9.
  (1997) 'Looking at Rembrandt, past and present', in *Rembrandt: a Genius and his Impact*, ed. A. Blankert. Melbourne: 32–57.
Blondell, R. (2002) *The Play of Character in Plato's Dialogues*. Cambridge.
Bloom, P. (2004) *Descartes' Baby: How the Science of Child Development Explains What Makes Us Human*. New York.
Blundell, M. W. (1989) *Helping Friends and Harming Enemies: a Study in Sophocles and Greek Ethics*. Cambridge.
Blurton Jones, N. G. (1972) 'Non-verbal communication in children', in *Non-verbal Communication*, ed. R. A. Hinde. Cambridge: 271–96.
Boardman, J. (1974) *Athenian Black Figure Vases*. London.
  (1978) *Greek Sculpture: the Archaic Period*. London.

(1985) *Greek Sculpture: the Classical Period.* London.

(1990) '*Symposion* furniture', in Murray (1990a) 122–31.

(1998) *Early Greek Vase Painting.* London.

Boedeker, D. D. (1974) *Aphrodite's Entry into Greek Epic.* Leiden.

Boissonade, J. F. (1819) *Herodiani Partitiones.* London. [Rpr. Amsterdam, 1963.]

Bond, G. W. (1981) *Euripides Heracles.* Oxford.

Bonner, R. J. (1922) 'Wit and humor in Athenian courts', *CPh* 17: 97–103.

Borthwick, E. K. (1993) '*Autolekythos* and *lekythion* in Demosthenes and Aristophanes', *LCM* 18: 34–7.

Bosman, P. (2006) 'Selling Cynicism: the pragmatics of Diogenes' comic performances', *CQ* 56: 93–104.

Boswell, J. (1980) *Christianity, Social Tolerance, and Homosexuality.* Chicago.

Bouvier, D. (2000) 'Platon et les poètes comiques: peut-on rire de la mort de Socrate?', in Desclos (2000) 425–40.

Bowen, A. (1998) *Xenophon Symposium.* Warminster.

Bowen, A. C. and Todd, R. B. (2004) *Cleomedes' Lectures on Astronomy.* Berkeley.

Bowen, B. C. (2004) *Humour and Humanism in the Renaissance.* Aldershot.

Bowersock, G. W. (1994) *Fiction as History: Nero to Julian.* Berkeley.

Bowie, A. M. (1993) *Aristophanes: Myth, Ritual and Comedy.* Cambridge.

(1997) 'Thinking with drinking: wine and the symposium in Aristophanes', *JHS* 117: 1–21.

(2000) 'Myth and ritual in the rivals of Aristophanes', in Harvey and Wilkins (2000) 317–39.

Bowie, E. (1986) 'Early Greek elegy, symposium, and public festival', *JHS* 106: 13–35.

(1993) 'Greek table-talk before Plato', *Rhetorica* 11: 355–73.

Bowra, C. M. (1964) *Pindar.* Oxford.

Brady, F. and Wimsatt, W. K. (1977) *Samuel Johnson: Selected Poetry and Prose.* Berkeley.

Branham, R. B. (1989a) *Unruly Eloquence: Lucian and the Comedy of Traditions.* Cambridge Mass.

(1989b) 'The wisdom of Lucian's Teiresias', *JHS* 109: 159–60.

(1996) 'Defacing the currency: Diogenes' rhetoric and the invention of Cynicism', in Branham and Goulet-Cazé (1996) 81–104.

(2002) *Bakhtin and the Classics.* Evanston.

(2004) 'Nietzsche's Cynicism: uppercase or lowercase?', in *Nietzsche and Antiquity*, ed. P. Bishop. New York: 170–81.

Branham, R. B. and Goulet-Cazé, M.-O. eds. (1996) *The Cynics: the Cynic Movement in Antiquity and its Legacy.* Berkeley.

Braswell, B. K. (1982) 'The song of Ares and Aphrodite: theme and relevance to *Odyssey* 8', *Hermes* 110: 129–37.

(1988) *A Commentary on the Fourth Pythian Ode of Pindar.* Berlin.

Brecht, F. J. (1930) *Motiv- und Typengeschichte des griechischen Spottepigramms. Philologus Suppl.* XXII.II. Leipzig.

Bremer, J. M. (1987) 'The so-called "*Götterapparat*" in *Iliad* xx–xxii', in *Homer: Beyond Oral Poetry*, eds. J. M. Bremer *et al.* Amsterdam: 31–46.

Bremmer, J. N. (1983) *The Early Greek Concept of the Soul*. Princeton.

(1994) *Greek Religion*. Oxford.

(1997) 'Jokes, jokers and jokebooks in ancient Greek culture', in Bremmer and Roodenburg (1997) 11–28.

Bremmer, J. and Roodenburg, H. eds. (1977) *A Cultural History of Humour*. Cambridge.

Brenk, F. (1977) *In Mist Apparelled: Religious Themes in Plutarch's Moralia and Lives*. Leiden.

Brenner, A. (1990) 'On the semantic field of humour, laughter and the comic in the Old Testament', in Radday and Brenner (1990) 39–58.

Brilliant, R. (1971) 'On portraits', *Zeitschrift für Ästhetik und allgemeine Kunstwissenschaft* 16: 11–26.

Brink, C. O. (1971) *Horace on Poetry: the 'Ars Poetica'*. Cambridge.

Brock, R. (1990) 'Plato and comedy', in *'Owls to Athens'. Essays on Classical Subjects Presented to Sir Kenneth Dover*, ed. E. M. Craik. Oxford: 39–49.

Brockmann, C. (2003) *Aristophanes und die Freiheit der Komödie*. Munich.

Brophy, J. (1945) *The Human Face*. London.

Brown, C. G. (1989) 'Ares, Aphrodite, and the laughter of the gods', *Phoenix* 43: 283–93.

(1997) 'Iambos', in *A Companion to the Greek Lyric Poets*, ed. D. E. Gerber. Leiden: 13–42.

Brown, P. (1988) *The Body and Society. Men, Women, and Sexual Renunciation in Early Christianity*. New York.

Brumfield, A. C. (1981) *The Attic Festivals of Demeter and their Relation to the Agricultural Year*. Salem.

(1996) 'Aporreta: verbal and ritual obscenity in the cults of ancient women', in *The Role of Religion in the Early Greek Polis*, ed. R. Hägg. Stockholm: 67–74.

Buchheim, T. (1989) *Gorgias von Leontinoi: Reden, Fragmente und Testimonien*. Hamburg.

Buck, A. (1963) 'Democritus ridens et Heraclitus flens', in *Wort und Text. Festschrift für Fritz Schalk*, eds. H. Meier and H. Sckommodau. Frankfurt: 167–86.

Buck, C. D. (1949) *A Dictionary of Selected Synonyms in the Principal Indo-European Languages*. Chicago.

(1955) *The Greek Dialects*. Chicago.

Buckler, J. (2000) 'Demosthenes and Aeschines', in *Demosthenes: Statesman and Orator*, ed. I. Worthington. London: 114–58.

Buckley, F. H. (2003) *The Morality of Laughter*. Ann Arbor.

Buffière, F. (1956) *Les mythes d'Homère et la pensée grecque*. Paris.

(1962) *Héraclite: allégories d'Homère*. Paris.

Burckhardt, J. (1977) *Griechische Kulturgeschichte* (4 vols.). Darmstadt. [Orig. publ. posth., ed. J. Oeri, 1898–1902.]

(1998) *The Greeks and Greek Civilization*, Eng. tr. S. Stern, ed. O. Murray. New York.

Burke, P. (1978) *Popular Culture in Early Modern Europe*. New York.
Burkert, W. (1960) 'Das Lied von Ares und Aphrodite', *RhM* 103 (1960) 130–44.
[Rpr. in id., *Kleine Schriften I. Homerica* (Göttingen, 2001) 105–16.]
   (1970) 'Buzyge und Palladion', *ZRGG* 22: 356–68.
   (1972) *Homo Necans*. Berlin.
   (1983) *Homo Necans*, Eng. tr. P. Bing. Berkeley.
   (1985) *Greek Religion*, Eng. tr. J. Raffan. Cambridge Mass.
   (1992) *The Orientalizing Revolution*, Eng. tr. M. E. Pinder and W. Burkert. Cambridge Mass.
   (1996) *Creation of the Sacred*. Cambridge Mass.
   (2003) 'Götterspiel und Götterburleske in altorientalischen und griechischen Mythen', in *Kleine Schriften II. Orientalia*, eds. L. M. Gemelli Marciano *et al.* Göttingen: 96–118. [Orig. publ. in *Eranos-Jb* 51 (1982) 335–67.]
Burnet, J. (1900) *The Ethics of Aristotle*. London.
   (1911) *Plato's Phaedo*. Oxford.
   (1924) *Plato's Euthyphro, Apology of Socrates, and Crito*. Oxford.
Burnett, A. P. (1983) *Three Archaic Poets: Archilochus, Alcaeus, Sappho*. London.
Burton, J. B. (1985) *Theocritus's Urban Mimes*. Berkeley.
Burton, Robert (1989) *The Anatomy of Melancholy*, eds. T. C. Faulkner *et al.*, vol. 1. Oxford. [1st edn 1621.]
Burton, R. W. B. (1962) *Pindar's Pythian Odes*. Oxford.
Butler, S. (1913) 'The humour of Homer', in *The Humour of Homer and Other Essays*. London: 59–98.
Caggia, G. (1972) 'Due parole omeriche in Apollonio Rodio', *RFIC* 100: 23–31.
Cairns, D. L. (1993) *Aidōs: the Psychology and Ethics of Honour and Shame in Ancient Greek Literature*. Oxford.
   (2001) 'Affronts and quarrels in the *Iliad*', in *Oxford Readings in Homer's Iliad*, ed. D. Cairns. Oxford: 203–19. [Orig. publ. in *Papers of the Leeds International Latin Seminar* 7 (1993) 155–67.]
   ed. (2005a) *Body Language in the Greek & Roman Worlds*. Swansea.
   (2005b) 'Bullish looks and sidelong glances: social interaction and the gaze in Greek antiquity', in Cairns (2005a) 123–55.
Calame, C. (1991) '"Mythe" et "rite" en Grèce: des catégories indigènes?', *Kernos* 4: 179–204.
   (1997) *Choruses of Young Women in Ancient Greece*. Eng. tr. D. Collins and J. Orion. Lanham.
Cameron, A. (1995) *Callimachus and his Critics*. Princeton.
Campagner, R. (2001) *Lessico agonistico di Aristofane*. Rome.
Campbell, D. A. (1967) *Greek Lyric Poetry*. London.
Campbell, M. (1983) *Studies in the Third Book of Apollonius Rhodius' Argonautica*. Hildesheim.
Camps, W. A. (1980) *An Introduction to Homer*. Oxford.
Camus, A. (1965) '*Le mythe de Sisyphe*', in *Essais*, eds. R. Quilliot and L. Faucon. Paris: 89–211, with editorial material, 1410–55. [Orig. publ. 1942.]
   (1955) *The Myth of Sisyphus*, Eng. tr. J. O'Brien. London.

Carden, R. (1974) *The Papyrus Fragments of Sophocles*. Berlin.
Carey, C. (1992) *Apollodoros Against Neaira*. Warminster.
　(1994) 'Comic ridicule and democracy', in *Ritual, Finance, Politics*, eds. R. Osborne and S. Hornblower. Oxford: 69–83.
Carey, C. and Reid, R. A. (1985) *Demosthenes Selected Private Speeches*. Cambridge.
Carpenter, R. (1959) *The Esthetic Basis of Greek Art*. Bloomington.
Carpenter, T. H. (1991) *Art and Myth in Ancient Greece*. London.
　(1995) 'A *symposion* of gods?', in *In Vino Veritas*, eds. O. Murray and M. Tecuşan. London: 145–63.
　(1997) *Dionysian Imagery in Fifth-Century Athens*. Oxford.
Carrière, J.-C. (1979) *Le carnaval et la politique: une introduction à la comédie grecque*. Paris.
　(1998) 'Socratisme, platonisme et comédie dans le *Banquet* de Xénophon', in Trédé and Hoffmann (1998) 243–71.
Carter, J. B. (1987) 'The masks of Ortheia', *AJA* 91: 355–83.
　(1988) 'Masks and poetry in early Sparta', in *Early Greek Cult Practice*, eds. R. Hägg *et al.* Stockholm: 89–98.
Cartledge, P. (1995) *Aristophanes and his Theatre of the Absurd*, 2nd edn. London.
Cartlidge, D. R. and Elliott, J. K. (2001) *Art and the Christian Apocrypha*. London.
Casanova, A. (2004) 'Il comico nella *Samia* di Menandro', in *La cultura ellenistica: l'opera letteraria e l'esegesi antica*, eds. R. Pretagostini and E. Dettori. Rome: 1–17.
Cassola, F. (1981) *Inni Omerici*, 2nd edn. Milan.
Castiglione, B. (1998) *Il libro del cortegiano*, ed. W. Barberis. Turin.
　(2002) *The Book of the Courtier*, Eng. tr. C. Singleton, ed. D. Javitch. New York.
Cerri, G. (1976) 'Frammento di teoria musicale e di ideologia simposiale in un distico di Teognide', *QUCC* 22: 25–38.
Chadwick, H. (1959) *The Sentences of Sextus*. Cambridge.
　(1965) *Origen: Contra Celsum*, corr. edn. Cambridge.
　(2001) *The Church in Ancient Society*. Oxford.
Chadwick, J. (1996) *Lexicographica Graeca: Contributions to the Lexicography of Ancient Greek*. Oxford.
Chambers, E. K. (1903) *The Mediaeval Stage* (2 vols.). Oxford.
Chantraine, P. (1963) 'A propos de Thersite', *AC* 32: 18–27.
　(1968) *Dictionnaire étymologique de la langue grecque*. Paris.
Charbonneaux, J. *et al.* (1971) *Archaic Greek Art 620–480 BC*, Eng. tr. London.
Chitwood, A. (2004) *Death by Philosophy: the Biographical Tradition in the Life and Death of the Archaic Philosophers Empedocles, Heraclitus, and Democritus*. Ann Arbor.
Chryssavgis, J. (2004) *John Climacus: from the Egyptian Desert to the Sinaite Mountain*. Aldershot.
Cioffi, F. (1998) *Wittgenstein on Freud and Frazer*. Cambridge.
Cixous, H. (1981) 'The laugh of the Medusa', Eng. tr. K. and P. Cohen, in *New French Feminisms*, eds. E. Marks and I. de Courtivron. Brighton: 245–64.

Clarke, H. W. (1969) 'The humor of Homer', *CJ* 64: 246–52.

Clarke, M. (1999) *Flesh and Spirit in the Songs of Homer*. Oxford.

(2005a) 'On the semantics of ancient Greek smiles', in Cairns (2005a) 37–53.

(2005b) 'Etymology in the semantic reconstruction of early Greek words: the case of ἄνθος', *Hermathena* 179: 13–37.

Clay, D. (1992) 'Lucian of Samosata: four philosophical lives', *ANRW* II.36.5: 3406–50.

(2004) *Archilochos Heros: the Cult of Poets in the Greek Polis*. Washington.

Clay, J. S. (1989) *The Politics of Olympus. Form and Meaning in the Major Homeric Hymns*. Princeton.

Clayton, M. (2002) *Leonardo da Vinci: the Divine and the Grotesque*. London.

Clinton, K. (1986) 'The author of the Homeric *Hymn to Demeter*', *OAth* 16: 43–9.

(1992) *Myth and Cult. The Iconography of the Eleusinian Mysteries*. Stockholm.

Cochran, C. M. (1979) 'Flyting in the mystery plays', *Theatre Journal* 31: 186–97.

Coenen, J. (1977) *Lukian: Zeus Tragodos*. Meisenheim.

Cohen, D. (1995) *Law, Violence and Community in Classical Athens*. Cambridge.

Cohen, T. (1999) *Jokes: Philosophical Thoughts on Joking Matters*. Chicago.

(2001) 'Humor', in *Routledge Companion to Aesthetics*, eds. B. Gaut and D. McIver Lopes. London: 375–81.

Colakis, M. (1986) 'The laughter of the suitors in *Odyssey* 20', *CW* 79: 137–41.

Cole, S. G. (1993) 'Procession and celebration at the Dionysia', in *Theater and Society in the Classical World*, ed. R. Scodel. Ann Arbor: 25–38.

Collard, C., Cropp, M. J. and Lee, K. H. (1995) *Euripides: Selected Fragmentary Plays*, vol. 1. Warminster.

Collins, D. (2004) *Master of the Game: Competition and Performance in Greek Poetry*. Cambridge Mass.

Collobert, C. (2000) 'Héphaïstos, l'artisan du rire inextinguible des dieux', in Desclos (2000) 133–41.

Connor, W. R. (1996) 'Festival and democracy', in *Colloque international: démocratie Athénienne et culture*, ed. M. Sakellariou. Athens: 79–89.

Conybeare, C. (2002) 'The ambiguous laughter of Saint Laurence', *JECS* 10: 175–202.

Cope, E. M. (1855) 'On the sophistical rhetoric', *Journal of Classical and Sacred Philology* 2: 129–69.

(1877) *The Rhetoric of Aristotle* (3 vols.). Cambridge.

Copenhaver, B. P. (1992) *Hermetica*. Cambridge.

Cordero, N.-L. (2000) 'Démocrite riait-il?', in Desclos (2000) 227–39.

Corrigan, K. (1997) 'The comic-serious figure in Plato's middle dialogues: the *Symposium* as philosophical art', in Jäkel *et al.* (1994–7) vol. III, 55–64.

Cottingham, J. *et al.* (1985) *The Philosophical Writings of Descartes*, vol. 1. Cambridge.

Courtney, E. (1980) *A Commentary on the Satires of Juvenal*. London.

Courtonne, Y. (1957–66) *Saint Basile: Lettres* (3 vols.). Paris.

Cousin, V. (1864) *Procli Philosophi Platonici Opera Inedita, Pars Tertia Continens Procli Commentarium in Platonis Parmenidem*. Paris. [Rpr. Hildesheim, 1961.]

Cramer, J. A. (1836) *Anecdota Graeca*, vol. III. Oxford.

Crane, G. (1987) 'The laughter of Aphrodite in Theocritus, *Idyll* 1', *HSPh* 91: 161–84.

Crawley, A. E. (1917) 'Obscenity', in *Encyclopaedia of Religion and Ethics*, ed. J. Hastings, vol. IX. Edinburgh: 441–2.

Critchley, S. (2002) *On Humour*. London.

Cropp, M. J. (1988) *Euripides Electra*. Warminster.

Crystal, D. (1987) *The Cambridge Encyclopedia of Language*. Cambridge.

Csapo, E. (1993) 'Deep ambivalence: notes on a Greek cockfight', *Phoenix* 47: 1–28, 115–24.

    (1997) 'Riding the phallus for Dionysus: iconology, ritual, and gender-role de/construction', *Phoenix* 51: 253–95.

    (2000) 'From Aristophanes to Menander? Genre transformation in Greek comedy', in *Matrices of Genre: Authors, Canons, and Society*, eds. M. Depew and D. Obbink. Cambridge Mass.: 115–33.

Csapo, E. and Slater, W. J. (1995) *The Context of Ancient Drama*. Ann Arbor.

Cullyer, H. (2006) '*Agroikia* and pleasure in Aristotle', in *City, Countryside, and the Spatial Organization of Value in Classical Antiquity*, eds. R. M. Rosen and I. Sluiter. Leiden: 181–217.

Cunningham, I. C. (1971) *Herodas Mimiambi*. Oxford.

Curtius, E. (1939) 'Scherz und Ernst in mittelalterlicher Dichtung', *RomForsch* 53: 1–26. [Revised version in Curtius (1953) 417–35.]

    (1953) *European Literature and the Latin Middle Ages*, Eng. tr. W. R. Trask. London.

Dale, A. M. (1954) *Euripides Alcestis*. Oxford.

D'Alton, J. F. (1940) *Selections from St John Chrysostom*. London.

Damasio, A. (2004) *Looking for Spinoza: Joy, Sorrow and the Feeling Brain*. London.

Damen, M. L. (1992) 'Translating scenes: Plautus' adaptation of Menander's *Dis Exapaton*', *Phoenix* 46: 205–31.

Danzig, G. (2004) 'Apologetic elements in Xenophon's *Symposium*', *C&M* 55: 17–47.

    (2005) 'Intra-Socratic polemics: the *Symposia* of Plato and Xenophon', *GRBS* 45: 331–57.

Dart, J. (1988) *The Jesus of Heresy and History*. San Francisco.

Darwin, C. (1965) *The Expression of the Emotions in Man and Animals*. Chicago. [1st publ. 1872.]

Dasen, V. (1993) *Dwarfs in Ancient Egypt and Greece*. Oxford.

David, E. (1989) 'Laughter in Spartan society', in *Classical Sparta*, ed. A. Powell. London: 1–25.

Davidson, J. N. (1997) *Courtesans and Fishcakes: the Consuming Passions of Classical Athens*. London.

    (2000) '*Gnesippus paigniagraphos*: the comic poets and the erotic mime', in Harvey and Wilkins (2000) 41–64.

Davies, M. (2004) 'Aristotle fr. 44 Rose: Midas and Silenus', *Mnemosyne* 57: 682–97.

Davis, N. Z. (1975) *Society and Culture in Early Modern France*. London.
Davis, P. (1996) 'In defence of Hobbes against Lippitt', *Cogito* 10: 225–8.
Davison, J. A. (1968) *From Archilochus to Pindar*. London.
Debidour, V.-H. and Musurillo, H. (1963) *Méthode d'Olympe. Le banquet*. Paris.
Decleva Caizzi, F. (1966) *Antisthenis Fragmenta*. Milan.
Degani, E. (1961) *Αἰών da Omero ad Aristotele*. Padua.
    (1987) 'Insulto ed escrologia in Aristofane', *Dioniso* 57: 31–47.
    (1993) 'Aristofane e la tradizione dell'invettiva personale in Grecia', in *Aristophane*, eds. J. M. Bremer and E. W. Handley. Fondation Hardt Entretiens XXXVIII Geneva: 1–49.
De Jong, I. J. F. (2001) *A Narratological Commentary on the Odyssey*. Cambridge.
Delattre, D. (2007) *Philodème de Gadara: Sur la musique*. Paris.
Delbrueck, R. (1942) 'Antiquarisches zu den Verspottungen Jesu', *ZNTW* 41: 124–45.
Delcomminette, S. (2006) *Le Philèbe de Platon*. Leiden.
Del Corno, D. (1994) *Aristofane: le Rane*, 3rd edn. Milan.
    (1996) *Aristofane: le Nuvole*. Milan.
Delivorrias, A. *et al.* (1984) 'Aphrodite', *LIMC* II.1: 2–151 (with ills., II.2: 6–153).
De Martino, E. (1934) 'I gephyrismi', *SMSR* 10: 64–79.
Desclos, M.-L. ed. (2000) *Le rire des Grecs. Anthropologie du rire en Grèce ancienne*. Grenoble.
De Smet, I. A. R. (1996) *Menippean Satire and the Republic of Letters 1581–1655*. Geneva.
De Sousa, R. (1987) *The Rationality of Emotion*. Cambridge Mass.
De Ste. Croix, G. E. M. (1972) *The Origins of the Peloponnesian War*. London.
Deubner, L. (1932) *Attische Feste*. Berlin.
De Vries, G. J. (1985) 'Laughter in Plato's writings', *Mnemosyne* 38: 378–81.
Dickey, E. (1996) *Greek Forms of Address from Herodotus to Lucian*. Oxford.
Dickins, G. (1929) 'The masks', in *The Sanctuary of Artemis Orthia at Sparta*, ed. R. M. Dawkins. London: 163–86 (with pls. XLVII–LXII).
Diehl, E. (1903–6) *Procli Diadochi in Platonis Timaeum Commentarii* (3 vols.). Leipzig.
Diels, H. (1901) *Poetarum Philosophorum Fragmenta*. Berlin.
Dienstag, J. F. (2006) *Pessimism: Philosophy, Ethic, Spirit*. Princeton.
Diggle, J. (2004) *Theophrastus: Characters*. Cambridge.
Dillon, J. (1993) *Alcinous: The Handbook of Platonism*. Oxford.
    (1996) *The Middle Platonists*, rev. edn. London.
Dillon, M. (1991) 'Tragic laughter', *CW* 84: 345–55.
    (2002) *Girls and Women in Classical Greek Religion*. London.
Dillon, S. (2006) *Ancient Greek Portrait Sculpture*. New York.
Di Marco, M. (1989) *Timone di Fliunte: Silli*. Rome.
    (2003) 'Euripide in Alessandro Etolo (fr. 7 Magnelli): una nuova ipotesi', *SemRom* 6.1: 65–70.
Dindorf, L. (1832) *Chronicon Paschale*, vol. 1. Bonn.
Dindorf, W. (1829) *Aristides ex recensione Guilielmi Dindorfii* (3 vols.). Leipzig.

Di Nola, A. M. (1974) *Antropologia Religiosa*. Florence.

Dittmar, H. (1912) *Aischines von Sphettos*. Berlin.

Dodds, E. R. (1951) *The Greeks and the Irrational*. Berkeley.

(1959) *Plato Gorgias*. Oxford.

(1960) *Euripides Bacchae*, 2nd edn. Oxford.

(1965) *Pagan and Christian in an Age of Anxiety*. Cambridge.

Domingo-Forasté, D. (1994) *Claudius Aelianus: Epistulae et Fragmenta*. Stuttgart.

Donald, M. (1991) *Origins of the Modern Mind*. Cambridge Mass.

Donlan, W. (1985) 'Pistos philos hetairos', in *Theognis of Megara*, eds. T. J. Figueira and G. Nagy. Baltimore: 223–44.

Donzelli, G. B. (2006) 'Il riso amaro di Dioniso. Euripide, *Baccanti*, 170–369', in *ΚΩΜΩΙΔΟΤΡΑΓΩΙΔΙΑ: intersezioni del tragico e del comico nel teatro del V secolo a.C.*, eds. E. Medda *et al.* Pisa: 1–17.

Döring, K. (1972) *Die Megariker*. Amsterdam.

(1993) '"Spielereien, mit verdecktem Ernst vermischt"', in *Vermittlung und Tradierung von Wissen in der griechischen Kultur*, ed. W. Kullmann. Tübingen: 337–52.

Douglas, M. (1975) *Implicit Meanings. Essays in Anthropology*. London.

Dover, K. J. (1968) *Aristophanes Clouds*. Oxford.

(1974) *Greek Popular Morality in the Time of Plato and Aristotle*. Oxford.

(1986) 'Ion of Chios: his place in the history of Greek literature', in *Chios*, eds. J. Boardman and C. E. Vaphopoulou-Richardson. Oxford: 27–37.

(1989) *Greek Homosexuality*, 2nd edn. Cambridge Mass.

(1993) *Aristophanes Frogs*. Oxford.

(1997) *The Evolution of Greek Prose Style*. Oxford.

(2002) 'Some evaluative terms in Aristophanes', in *The Language of Greek Comedy*, ed. A. Willi. Oxford: 85–97.

Downey, G. (1939) 'The Olympic Games of Antioch in the fourth century AD', *TAPhA* 70: 428–38.

Downing, F. G. (1992) *Cynics and Christian Origins*. Edinburgh.

Driessen, H. (1997) 'Humour, laughter and the field: reflections from anthropology', in Bremmer and Roodenburg (1997) 222–41.

Drosdowski, G. (1997) *Herkunftswörterbuch der deutschen Sprache*, 2nd edn. Mannheim.

Du Boulay, J. (1974) *Portrait of a Greek Mountain Village*. Oxford.

Dudley, D. R. (1937) *A History of Cynicism*. London.

Dunbabin, K. M. D. and Dickie, M. W. (1983) 'Invida rumpantur pectora. The iconography of phthonos/invidia in Graeco-Roman art', *JbAC* 26: 7–37.

Dunbar, N. (1995) *Aristophanes Birds*. Oxford.

Dunbar, R. (2004) *The Human Story: a New History of Mankind's Evolution*. London.

Duncan, A. (2006) *Performance and Identity in the Classical World*. Cambridge.

Durand, J.-L. (1986) *Sacrifice et labour en Grèce ancienne*. Paris.

Durando, F. (2005) *Greece: Splendours of an Ancient Civilization*, new edn. London.

Düring, I. (1941) *Herodicus the Cratetean*. Stockholm.

(1969) *Aristoteles Protreptikos*. Frankfurt on Main.

Dworkin, R. (2006) 'The right to ridicule', *NYRB* 53.5: 44.

Dyck, A. R. (1985) 'The function and persuasive power of Demosthenes' portrait of Aeschines in the speech *On the Crown*', *G&R* 32: 42–8.

(1996) *A Commentary on Cicero De Officiis*. Ann Arbor.

(2003) *Cicero De Natura Deorum Liber I*. Cambridge.

Eco, U. (1984) *The Name of the Rose*, Eng. tr. W. Weaver. London.

(1986) 'The comic and the rule', in *Faith in Fakes*, Eng. tr. W. Weaver. London.

Edelstein, L. and Kidd, I. G. (1989) *Posidonius. Vol. I. The Fragments*, 2nd edn. Cambridge.

Edmonds (III), Radcliffe G. (2004) *Myths of the Underworld Journey: Plato, Aristophanes, and the 'Orphic' Gold Tablets*. Cambridge.

(2006) 'To sit in solemn silence? *Thronosis* in ritual, myth, and iconography', *AJPh* 127: 347–66.

Edwards, A. T. (1991) 'Aristophanes' comic poetics: τρύξ, scatology, σκῶμμα', *TAPhA* 121: 157–79.

(1993) 'Historicizing the popular grotesque: Bakhtin's *Rabelais* and Attic Old Comedy', in *Theater and Society in the Classical World*, ed. R. Scodel. Ann Arbor: 89–117.

Edwards, M. J. (1989) 'Satire and verisimilitude: Christianity in Lucian's *Peregrinus*', *Historia* 38: 89–98.

Ehrenberg, V. (1951) *The People of Aristophanes: a Sociology of Old Attic Comedy*, 2nd edn. Oxford.

Eibl-Eibesfeldt, I. (1970) *Ethology*, Eng. tr. E. Klinghammer. New York.

(1972) 'Similarities and differences between cultures in expressive movements', in *Non-verbal Communication*, ed. R. A. Hinde. Cambridge: 297–314.

(1989) *Human Ethology*. New York.

Eissfeldt, O. (1965) *The Old Testament*, Eng. tr. P. R. Ackroyd. Oxford.

Eitrem, S. (1906) 'Der homerische Hymnus an Hermes', *Philologus* 19: 248–82.

Ekman, P. *et al.* (1997) 'Smiles when lying', in *What the Face Reveals*, eds. P. Ekman and E. L. Rosenberg. New York: 201–14.

(2003) *Emotions Revealed: Understanding Faces and Feelings*. London.

Elias, N. (1978) *The Civilizing Process: the History of Manners*, Eng. tr. E. Jephcott. Oxford.

Eliot, T. S. (1974) *Collected Poems 1909–1962*. London.

Elliott, J. K. (1993) *The Apocryphal New Testament*. Oxford.

Elliott, R. C. (1960) *The Power of Satire: Magic, Ritual, Art*. Princeton.

Elsner, J. (1995) *Art and the Roman Viewer*. Cambridge.

Embry, E. M. (1976) 'Laugh: γελάω', in *The New International Dictionary of New Testament Theology*, ed. C. Brown, vol. II. Exeter: 429–36.

Ercolani, A. ed. (2002) *Spoudaiogeloion: Form und Funktion der Verspottung in der aristophanischen Komödie*. Stuttgart.

Ermerins, F. Z. (1840) *Anecdota Medica Graeca*. Leiden. [Rpr. Amsterdam, 1963.]

Esslin, M. (1980) *The Theatre of the Absurd*, 3rd edn. Harmondsworth.

Evans, E. C. (1969) *Physiognomics in the Ancient World*. Philadelphia. (*TAPhS* 59.5.)

Exum, J. C. and Whedbee, J. W. (1990) 'Isaac, Samson, and Saul: reflections on the comic and tragic visions', in Radday and Brenner (1990) 123–34.

Fantuzzi, M. and Hunter, R. (2004) *Tradition and Innovation in Hellenistic Poetry*. Cambridge.

Farquharson, A. S. L. (1944) *The Meditations of the Emperor Marcus Antoninus*, vol. II. Oxford.

Fehling, D. (1974) *Ethologische Überlegungen auf dem Gebiet der Altertumskunde*. Munich.

Fehr, B. (1990) 'Entertainers at the *symposion*: the *akletoi* in the archaic period', in Murray (1990a) 185–95.

Fehrle, E. (1930) 'Das Lachen im Glauben der Völker', *ZV* 2: 1–5.

Feinberg, J. (1985) *Offense to Others*. New York.

Fenik, B. (1974) *Studies in the Odyssey*. Wiesbaden.

Ferrari, F. (1988) '*P. Berol*. Inv. 13270: i Canti di Elefantina', *SCO* 38: 181–227.

Figueira, T. J. (1993) *Excursions in Epichoric History. Aiginetan Essays*. Lanham.

Finnegan, R. (1977) *Oral Poetry: its Nature, Significance and Social Context*. Cambridge.

Fisher, N. R. E. (1989) 'Drink, *hybris* and the promotion of harmony in Sparta', in *Classical Sparta*, ed. A. Powell. London: 26–50.

  (1992) *Hybris: a Study in the Values of Honour and Shame in Ancient Greece*. Warminster.

  (2000) 'Symposiasts, fish-eaters and flatterers', in Harvey and Wilkins (2000) 355–96.

  (2001) *Aeschines Against Timarchos*. Oxford.

  (2004) 'The perils of Pittalakos: settings of cock fighting and dicing in classical Athens', in *Games and Festivals in Classical Antiquity*, eds. S. Bell and G. Davies. Oxford: 65–78.

Flashar, H. (1994) 'Aristoteles, das Lachen und die Alte Komödie', in Jäkel *et al.* (1994–7) vol. I, 59–70.

Flower, M. A. (1994) *Theopompus of Chios. History and Rhetoric in the Fourth Century B.C.* Oxford.

Fluck, H. (1934) 'Der Risus paschalis', *Archiv für Religionswissenschaft* 31: 188–212.

  (1931) *Skurrile Riten in griechischen Kulten*. Endingen.

Foerster, R. (1893) *Scriptores Physiognomonici Graeci et Latini* (2 vols.). Leipzig.

  (1929) *Choricii Gazaei Opera*. Leipzig.

Foley, H. P. (1980) 'The masque of Dionysus', *TAPhA* 110: 107–33.

  (1994) *The Homeric Hymn to Demeter*. Princeton.

Follet, S. (1974) 'Deux vocables religieux rares attestés épigraphiquement', *RPh* 48: 30–4.

Ford, A. (2002) *The Origins of Criticism: Literary Culture and Poetic Theory in Classical Greece*. Princeton.

Fornara, C. W. (1983) *Archaic Times to the End of the Peloponnesian War*, 2nd edn. Cambridge.

Forsdyke, S. (2005) 'Revelry and riot in archaic Megara: democratic disorder or ritual reversal?', *JHS* 125: 73–92.

Fortenbaugh, W. W. (2000) 'Une analyse du rire chez Aristote et Théophraste', in Desclos (2000) 333–54.

(2002) *Aristotle on Emotion*, 2nd edn. London.

(2005) *Theophrastus of Eresus: Sources on Rhetoric and Poetics*. Leiden.

Fortenbaugh, W. W. *et al.* (1992) *Theophrastus of Eresus. Sources for his Life, Writings, Thought and Influence* (2 vols.). Leiden.

Foucault, M. (2001) *Fearless Speech*, ed. J. Pearson. Los Angeles.

Fowler, B. (1983) 'The centaur's smile: Pindar and the archaic aesthetic', in *Ancient Greek Art and Iconography*, ed. W. G. Moon. Madison: 159–70.

Fowler, D. P. (2002) *Lucretius on Atomic Motion: a Commentary on De rerum natura 2.1–332*. Oxford.

Fowler, R. L. (2000) *Early Greek Mythography*, vol. 1. Oxford.

Foxhall, L. (1995) 'Women's ritual and men's work in ancient Athens', in *Women in Antiquity: New Assessments*, eds. R. Hawley and B. Levick. London: 97–110.

Fraenkel, E. (1950) *Aeschylus Agamemnon* (3 vols.). Oxford.

Frank, M. G. *et al.* (1997) 'Behavioral markers and recognizability of the smile of enjoyment', in *What the Face Reveals*, eds. P. Ekman and E. L. Rosenberg. New York: 217–38.

Fränkel, H. (1975) *Early Greek Poetry and Philosophy*, Eng. tr. M. Hadas and J. Willis. Oxford.

Fraser, P. M. (1972) *Ptolemaic Alexandria* (3 vols.). Oxford.

Frazer, J. G. (1898) *Pausanias's Description of Greece* (6 vols.). London.

(1911–36) *The Golden Bough*, 3rd edn (12 vols.). London.

Frede, D. (1993) *Plato Philebus*. Indianapolis.

(1997) *Platon Philebos*. Göttingen.

Frend, W. (1984) *The Rise of Christianity*. London.

Frenschkowski, M. (2002) 'Lentulusbrief', in *Religion in Geschichte und Gegenwart*, eds. H. D. Betz *et al.*, vol. v. Tübingen: 263.

Frese, R. (1926) 'Die "aristophanische Anklage" in *Platons Apologie*', *Philologus* 81: 377–90.

Freud, S. (1961) *The Standard Edition of the Complete Psychological Works*, ed. J. Strachey, vol. xxi. London.

(1976) *Jokes and their Relation to the Unconscious*, Eng. tr. J. Strachey, rev. A. Richards. Harmondsworth.

(1989) *Studienausgabe*, eds. A. Mitscherlich *et al.*, vol. iv. Frankfurt.

Friedländer, P. (1969) 'Lachende Götter', in *Studien zur antiken Literatur und Kunst*. Berlin: 3–18. [Orig. publ. in *Die Antike* 10 (1934) 209–26.]

Friedrich, R. (1983) 'Drama and ritual', in *Drama & Religion*, ed. J. Redmond. Cambridge: 159–223.

Friis Johansen, H. and Whittle, E. W. (1980) *Aeschylus: the Suppliants* (3 vols.). Copenhagen.

Frisk, H. (1960–70) *Griechisches Etymologisches Wörterbuch* (2 vols.). Heidelberg.

Frontisi-Ducroux, F. (1989) 'In the mirror of the mask', in *A City of Images: Iconography and Society in Ancient Greece*, eds. C. Bérard *et al.*, Eng. tr. D. Lyons. Princeton: 150–65.

  (1992) 'Un scandale à Athènes: faire le *comos* sans masque', *DHA* 18: 245–56.

  (1995) *Du masque au visage: aspects de l'identité en Grèce ancienne*. Paris.

Frontisi-Ducroux, F. and Lissarrague, F. (1990) 'From ambiguity to ambivalence: a Dionysiac excursion through the "Anakreontic" vases', in Halperin *et al.* (1990) 211–56.

Furiani, P. L. (2000) 'Le rire comme élément de communication non verbale dans les romans grecs d'amour', in Desclos (2000) 77–94.

Furley, W. D. and Bremer, J. M. (2001) *Greek Hymns* (2 vols.). Tübingen.

Furth, W. (1975) 'Baubo', in *Der Kleine Pauly*, eds. K. Ziegler and W. Sontheimer, vol. I. Munich: 843–5.

Gage, J. (1993) *Colour and Culture: Practice and Meaning from Antiquity to Abstraction*. London.

Galinsky, G. K. (1972) *The Herakles Theme*. Oxford.

Gallop, D. (1975) *Plato Phaedo*. Oxford.

Gantz, T. (1993) *Early Greek Myth*. Baltimore.

Garcia Gomez, A. M. (1984) *The Legend of the Laughing Philosopher and its Presence in Spanish Literature (1500–1700)*, 2nd edn. Cordoba.

Garland, R. (1985) *The Greek Way of Death*. London.

  (1990) *The Greek Way of Life from Conception to Old Age*. Ithaca.

  (1994) 'The mockery of the deformed and disabled in Graeco-Roman culture', in Jäkel *et al.* (1994–7) vol. I, 71–84.

  (1995) *The Eye of the Beholder. Deformity and Disability in the Graeco-Roman World*. London.

Garofalo, I. (1997) *Anonymi medici de morbis acutis et chroniis*. Leiden.

Garvie, A. F. (1986) *Aeschylus Choephori*. Oxford.

  (1994) *Homer Odyssey Books VI–VIII*. Cambridge.

  (1998) *Sophocles Ajax*. Warminster.

Gasparri, C. (1986) 'Dionysus', *LIMC* III.1: 420–514 (with ills., III.2: 296–406).

Gatrell, V. (2006) *City of Laughter: Sex and Satire in Eighteenth-Century London*. London.

Gaut, B. (1998) 'Just joking: the ethics and aesthetics of humor', *Philosophy and Literature* 22: 51–68.

Gauthier, R. A. and Jolif, J. Y. (1958–9) *L'Éthique à Nicomaque* (2 vols. in 3). Louvain.

Geddes, A. G. (1987) 'Rags and riches: the costume of Athenian men in the fifth century', *CQ* 37: 307–31.

Geertz, C. (1993) *Local Knowledge: Further Essays in Interpretive Anthropology*. London.

  (2000) *The Interpretation of Cultures*, 2nd edn. New York.

Gentili, B. (1988) *Poetry and its Public in Ancient Greece*, Eng. tr. A. T. Cole. Baltimore.

Gera, D. L. (1993) *Xenophon's Cyropaedia*. Oxford.

Gerber, D. E. (1999a) *Greek Elegiac Poetry*. Cambridge Mass.
  (1999b) *Greek Iambic Poetry*. Cambridge Mass.
Gernet, L. (1968) *Anthropologie de la grèce antique*. Paris.
Giangrande, G. (1968) 'Sympotic literature and epigram', in *L'Épigramme grecque*, ed. O. Reverdin. Geneva: 93–174.
Giangrande, J. (1956) *Eunapii Vitae Sophistarum*. Rome.
Giangrande, L. (1972) *The Use of Spoudaiogeloion in Greek and Roman Literature*. The Hague.
Giannantoni, G. (1990) *Socratis et Socraticorum Reliquiae* (4 vols.). Naples.
Gibson, W. S. (2006) *Pieter Bruegel and the Art of Laughter*. Berkeley.
Gigon, O. (1987) *Aristotelis Opera III, Librorum Deperditorum Fragmenta*. Berlin.
Gilhus, I. S. (1997) *Laughing Gods, Weeping Virgins: Laughter in the History of Religion*. London.
Gill, C. (1994) 'Peace of mind and being yourself: Panaetius to Plutarch', *ANRW* 11.36.7: 4599–4640.
Gilliam, J. F. (1952) 'The Dolicheneum: the inscriptions', in *The Excavations at Dura-Europos: Preliminary Report of the Ninth Season of Work, 1935–1936, Part III*, eds. M. I. Rostovtzeff *et al.* New Haven: 107–24.
Gilula, D. (2002) 'Entertainment at Xenophon's *Symposium*', *Athenaeum* 90: 207–13.
Giuliani, L. (1979) *Die archaischen Metopen von Selinunt*. Mainz.
Glare, P. G. W. (1982) *Oxford Latin Dictionary*. Oxford.
Glei, R. F. (1998) 'Passiv in der Tonne (zu Diog. Laert. 6.54)', *Hermes* 126: 256–8.
Glenn, P. (2003) *Laughter in Interaction*. Cambridge.
Goethe, J. W. (1998) *Werke*, Jubiläumsausgabe, eds. F. Apel *et al.* (6 vols.). Frankfurt.
Goldberg, S. M. (1980) *The Making of Menander's Comedy*. London.
Golden, L. (1990) 'τὸ γελοῖον', *HSPh* 93: 47–57.
Goldhill, S. (1991) *The Poet's Voice*. Cambridge.
  (1995) *Foucault's Virginity. Ancient Erotic Fiction and the History of Sexuality*. Cambridge.
  (2002) *Who Needs Greek? Contests in the Cultural History of Hellenism*. Cambridge.
  (2006) 'The thrill of misplaced laughter', in *ΚΩΜΩΙΔΟΤΡΑΓΩΙΔΙΑ: intersezioni del tragico e del comico nel teatro del V secolo a.C.*, eds. E. Medda *et al.* Pisa: 83–102.
Goldhill, S. and Osborne, R. eds. (1994) *Art and Text in Ancient Greek Culture*. Cambridge.
Gombrich, E. H. (1982) 'The mask and the face: the perception of physiognomic likeness in life and in art', in *The Image and the Eye. Further Studies in the Psychology of Pictorial Representation*. Oxford: 105–36.
Gómez, P. and Jufresa, M. (1999) 'La risa y el vino en los escritos simposíacos de Plutarco', in *Plutarco, Dioniso y el vino*, eds. J. G. Montes *et al.* Madrid: 255–67.
Gomme, A. W. (1956) *A Historical Commentary on Thucydides*, vol. II. Oxford.

Gomme, A. W. and Sandbach, F. H. (1973) *Menander: a Commentary*. Oxford.

Goodenough, E. R. (1935) *By Light, Light: the Mystic Gospel of Hellenistic Judaism*. New Haven.

Goodman, L. E. (1997) 'Morals and society in Islamic philosophy', in *Companion Encyclopedia of Asian Philosophy*, eds. B. Carr and I. Mahalingam. London: 1000–24.

Gottlieb, P. (1992) 'The complexity of Socratic irony: a note on Professor Vlastos's account', *CQ* 42: 278–9.

Gottschalk, H. B. (1980) *Heraclides of Pontus*. Oxford.

Goulet-Cazé, M.-O. (1990) 'Le Cynisme à l'époque impériale', *ANRW* ii.36.4: 2720–2833.

　(1992) 'Le livre vi de Diogène Laërce', *ANRW* ii.36.6: 3880–4048.

　(1996) 'Who was the first dog?', in Branham and Goulet-Cazé (1996) 414–15.

Gow, A. S. F. (1951) 'Notes on noses', *JHS* 71: 81–4.

　(1952) *Theocritus* (2 vols.). Cambridge.

Gow, A. S. F. and Page, D. L. (1965) *The Greek Anthology: Hellenistic Epigrams* (2 vols.). Cambridge.

　(1968) *The Greek Anthology: the Garland of Philip* (2 vols.). Cambridge.

Graf, F. (1974) *Eleusis und die orphische Dichtung Athens in vorhellenistischer Zeit*. Berlin.

　(1984) 'Women, war and warlike divinities', *ZPE* 55: 245–54.

　(1993) 'Dionysian and Orphic eschatology: new texts and old questions', in *Masks of Dionysus*, eds. T. H. Carpenter and C. A. Faraone. Ithaca: 239–58.

Grant, M. A. (1924) *The Ancient Rhetorical Theories of the Laughable*. Madison.

Gray, D. (1984) 'Rough music: some early invective and flytings', *Yearbook of English Studies* 14: 21–43.

Gray, V. (1992) 'Xenophon's *Symposion*: the display of wisdom', *Hermes* 120: 58–75.

Graziosi, B. and Haubold, J. (2005) *Homer: the Resonance of Epic*. London.

Green, J. R. (1994) *Theatre in Ancient Greek Society*. London.

Green, P. (1990) *Alexander to Actium: the Historical Evolution of the Hellenistic Age*. Berkeley.

　(1997) *The Argonautika by Apollonios Rhodios*. Berkeley.

Greene, W. C. (1920) 'The spirit of comedy in Plato', *HSPh* 31: 63–123.

Greenfield, S. A. (2000) *The Private Life of the Brain*. London.

Grensemann, H. (1968) *Hippokrates: über Achtmonatskinder, über das Sieben-monatskind*. Berlin.

Griffin, J. (1978) 'The divine audience and the religion of the *Iliad*', *CQ* 28: 1–22.

　(1980) *Homer on Life and Death* Oxford.

Griffiths, A. (1995) 'Latent and blatant: two perspectives on humour in Herodotus', in Jäkel *et al.* (1994–7) vol. ii, 31–44.

Grossmann, G. (1968) 'Das Lachen des Aias', *MH* 25: 65–85.

Grottanelli, C. (1995) 'Wine and death – east and west', in *In Vino Veritas*, eds. O. Murray and M. Tecusan. London: 62–89.

Gruner, C. R. (1997) *The Game of Humor: a Comprehensive Theory of Why We Laugh*. New Brunswick.

Guidorizzi, G. (1997) 'The laughter of the suitors: a case of collective madness in the *Odyssey*', in *Poet, Public, and Performance in Ancient Greece*, eds. L. Edmunds and R. W. Wallace. Baltimore: 1–7.

Gurevich, A. (1988) *Medieval Popular Culture*, Eng. tr. J. M. Bak and P. A. Hollingsworth. Cambridge.

    (1997) 'Bakhtin and his theory of Carnival', in Bremmer and Roodenburg (1997) 54–60.

Guthrie, W. K. C. (1952) *Orpheus and Greek Religion*, 2nd edn. London.

    (1965) *A History of Greek Philosophy II. The Presocratic Tradition from Parmenides to Democritus*. Cambridge.

    (1975) *A History of Greek Philosophy IV. Plato. The Man and his Dialogues: Earlier Period*. Cambridge.

Gwyn Griffiths, J. (1970) *Plutarch's De Iside et Osiride*. Cardiff.

Hackforth, R. (1955) *Plato's Phaedo*. Cambridge.

Hadot, I. (1996) *Simplicius: commentaire sur le Manuel d'Épictète*. Leiden.

Hainsworth, B. (1993) *The Iliad: a Commentary. Volume III: Books 9–12*. Cambridge.

Hall, J. (1981) *Lucian's Satire*. New York.

Halliday, W. R. (1909–10) 'The Hybristika', *ABSA* 16: 212–19.

Halliwell, S. (1984) 'Ancient interpretations of ὀνομαστὶ κωμῳδεῖν in Aristophanes', *CQ* 34: 83–8.

    (1986) *Aristotle's Poetics*. London. [Rpr., with new intro., 1998.]

    (1988) *Plato Republic 10*. Warminster.

    (1991a) 'The uses of laughter in Greek culture', *CQ* 41: 279–96.

    (1991b) 'Comic satire and freedom of speech in classical Athens', *JHS* 111: 48–70.

    (1993a) *Plato Republic 5*. Warminster.

    (1993b) 'The function and aesthetics of the Greek tragic mask', *Drama* 2: 195–211.

    (1993c) 'Comedy and publicity in the society of the polis', in *Tragedy, Comedy and the Polis*, eds. A. H. Sommerstein *et al.* Bari: 321–40.

    (1995) 'Forms of address: Socratic vocatives in Plato', in *Lo spettacolo delle voci*, eds. F. de Martino and A. H. Sommerstein. Bari: 87–121 (parte seconda).

    (2000a) 'Le rire rituel et la nature de l'Ancienne Comédie attique', in Desclos (2000) 155–68.

    (2000b) Review of Nehamas (1998), *AncPhil* 20: 492–500.

    (2002a) 'Aristophanic sex: the erotics of shamelessness', in *The Sleep of Reason: Erotic Experience and Sexual Ethics in Ancient Greece and Rome*, eds. M. C. Nussbaum and J. Sihvola. Chicago: 120–42.

    (2002b) *The Aesthetics of Mimesis: Ancient Texts and Modern Problems*. Princeton.

    (2003a) 'From functionalism to formalism, or Did the Greeks invent literary criticism?', *Arion* 10.3: 171–85.

    (2003b) 'Nietzsche's "daimonic force" of tragedy and its ancient traces', *Arion* 11.1: 103–23. [Italian version, 'La "forza demonica" della tragedia e le sue tracce antiche nel pensiero di Nietzsche', in *Arte e Daimon*, ed. D. Angelucci (Macerata, 2002) 189–205.]

    (2003c) 'La psychologie morale de la catharsis: un essai de reconstruction', *EPh* 4: 499–517.

(2003d) 'Aristotelianism and anti-Aristotelianism in attitudes to theatre', in *Attitudes to Theatre from Plato to Milton*, ed. E. Theodorakopoulos. Bari: 57–75.

(2004) 'Aischrology, shame, and comedy', in *Free Speech in Classical Antiquity*, eds. I. Sluiter and R. M. Rosen. Leiden: 116–44.

(2005) 'Greek laughter and the problem of the absurd', *Arion* 13: 121–46.

(2006) 'Plato and Aristotle on the denial of tragedy', in *Oxford Readings in Ancient Literary Criticism*, ed. A. Laird. Oxford: 115–41. [Revised version: orig. publ. in *PCPhS* 30 (1984) 49–71.]

Halperin, D. *et al.* eds. (1990) *Before Sexuality: the Construction of Erotic Experience in the Ancient Greek World*. Princeton.

Hamilton, A. and K. (1976) 'The guffaw of the Abderite: Samuel Beckett's use of Democritus', *Mosaic* 9: 1–13.

Hamilton, R. (1992) *Choes and Anthesteria. Athenian Iconography and Ritual*. Ann Arbor.

Hammer, D. (2004) 'Ideology, the symposium, and archaic politics', *AJPh* 125: 479–512.

Handley, E. W. (1965) *The Dyskolos of Menander*. London.

(1970) 'The conventions of the comic stage and their exploitation by Menander', in *Ménandre*, ed. E. W. Turner. Geneva: 3–26.

(1997) 'Menander, *Dis Exapaton*', in *The Oxyrhynchus Papyri*, vol. LXIV. London: 14–42.

(2002) 'Acting, action and words in New Comedy', in *Greek and Roman Actors*, eds. P. Easterling and E. Hall. Cambridge: 165–88.

(2006) 'Dialogue with the night (PAnt 1.15 = *PCG* VIII 1084)', *ZPE* 155: 23–5.

Hani, J. (1972) *Plutarque Consolation à Apollonios*. Paris.

Hankinson, J. (2000) 'La pathologie du rire: réflexions sur le rôle du rire chez les médecins grecs', in Desclos (2000) 191–200.

Hansen, M. H. (1991) *The Athenian Democracy in the Age of Demosthenes*, Eng. tr. J. A. Crook. Oxford.

Harding, P. (1994) 'Comedy and rhetoric', in *Persuasion: Greek Rhetoric in Action*, ed. I. Worthington. London: 196–221.

Harris, H. A. (1964) *Greek Athletes and Athletics*. London.

Harrison, E. (1902) *Studies in Theocritus*. Cambridge.

Harrison, J. E. (1922) *Prolegomena to the Study of Greek Religion*, 3rd edn. Cambridge.

Hart, W. M. (1943) 'High comedy in the *Odyssey*', *UCPPH* 12: 263–78.

Hartland, E. S. (1917) 'Phallism', in *Encyclopaedia of Religion and Ethics*, ed. J. Hastings, vol. IX. Edinburgh: 815–31.

Hartney, A. M. (2004a) *John Chrysostom and the Transformation of the City*. London.

(2004b) 'Transformation of the city: John Chrysostom's oratory in the homiletic form', in *Oratory in Action*, eds. M. Edwards and C. Reid. Manchester: 83–98.

Harvey, D. and Wilkins, J. eds. (2000) *The Rivals of Aristophanes: Studies in Athenian Old Comedy*. London.

Harvey, W. W. (1857) *Sancti Irenaei episcopi Lugdunensis libri quinque adversus haereses*, vol. I. Cambridge.

Haspels, C. H. E. (1936) *Attic Black-Figured Lekythoi* (2 vols.). Paris.

Havelaar, H. W. (1999) *The Coptic Apocalypse of Peter.* Berlin.

Hawtrey, R. S. W. (1981) *Commentary on Plato's Euthydemus.* Philadelphia.

Hayworth, D. (1928) 'The social origin and function of laughter', *Psychological Review* 35: 367–84.

Headlam, W. (1922) *Herodas. The Mimes and Fragments.* Cambridge.

Heath, M. (1987) *Political Comedy in Aristophanes.* Göttingen.

  (1988) 'Receiving the κῶμος: the context and performance of epinician', *AJPh* 109: 180–95.

  (1989) 'Aristotelian comedy', *CQ* 39: 344–54.

  (1997) 'Aristophanes and the discourse of politics', in *The City as Comedy: Society & Representation in Athenian Drama*, ed. G. Dobrov. Chapel Hill: 230–49.

Hedreen, G. (2004) 'The return of Hephaistos, Dionysiac processional ritual and the creation of a visual narrative', *JHS* 124: 38–64.

Heffening, W. (1927) *Die griechische Ephraem-Paraenesis gegen das Lachen.* Leipzig.

Hegel, G. W. F. (1975) *Aesthetics*, Eng. tr. T. M. Knox (2 vols.). Oxford.

Heitsch, E. (2002) *Platon: Apologie des Sokrates.* Göttingen.

Helm, R. (1898) *Fabii Planciadis Fulgentii Opera.* Leipzig.

Helmreich, G. (1907–9) *Galenus De Usu Partium* (2 vols.). Leipzig.

Henderson, J. (1987) *Aristophanes Lysistrata.* Oxford.

  (1990) 'The *dēmos* and the comic competition', in *Nothing to Do with Dionysus? Athenian Drama in its Social Context*, eds. J. J. Winkler and F. I. Zeitlin. Princeton: 271–313.

  (1991) *The Maculate Muse: Obscene Language in Attic Comedy*, rpr. with addenda. New York.

  (1998a) *Aristophanes: Clouds, Wasps, Peace.* Cambridge Mass.

  (1998b) 'Attic Old Comedy, frank speech, and democracy', in *Democracy, Empire, and the Arts in Fifth-Century Athens*, eds. D. Boedeker and K. A. Raaflaub. Berkeley: 255–73 (notes, 405–10).

  (1998c) *Aristophanes: Acharnians, Knights.* Cambridge Mass.

Henrichs, A. (1984) 'Loss of self, suffering, violence: the modern view of Dionysus from Nietzsche to Girard', *HSPh* 88: 205–40.

Hense, O. (1905) *Musonii Reliquiae.* Leipzig.

  (1909) *Teletis Reliquiae*, 2nd edn. Tübingen.

Hepburn, R. W. (1984) *'Wonder' and Other Essays: Eight Studies in Aesthetics and Neighbouring Fields.* Edinburgh.

Hercher, R. (1866) *Claudii Aeliani de natura animalium libri xvii, varia historia, epistolae, fragmenta*, vol. II. Leipzig.

Herman, G. (2006) *Morality and Behaviour in Democratic Athens.* Cambridge.

Hermary, A. and Jacquemin, A. (1988) 'Hephaistos', *LIMC* IV.1: 627–54 (with ills., IV.2: 386–404).

Herrenschmidt, C. (2000) 'Le rire de Zarathustra, l'Iranien', in Desclos (2000) 497–511.

Hersant, Y. (1989) *Hippocrate sur le rire et la folie.* Paris.

Hershkowitz, D. (1998) *The Madness of Epic*. Oxford.

Herter, H. (1961) 'Das Leben ein Kinderspiel', *BJ* 161: 73–84.

Herzog, R. (1931) *Die Wunderheilungen von Epidauros (Philologus* Supplementband XXII.3). Leipzig.

Hesk, J. (2000) *Deception and Democracy in Classical Athens*. Cambridge.

(2007) 'Combative capping in Aristophanic comedy', *Cambridge Classical Journal* 53: 124–60.

Heubeck, A. *et al.* (1988–92) *A Commentary on Homer's Odyssey* (3 vols.). Oxford.

Hewitt, J. W. (1928) 'Homeric laughter', *CJ* 22: 436–47.

Highet, G. (1949) *The Classical Tradition*. Oxford.

Himberg, K. (2002) '"Against the spleen": Sterne and the tradition of remedial laughter', in *A History of English Laughter: Laughter from Beowulf to Beckett and Beyond*, ed. M. Pfister. Amsterdam: 69–82.

Himmelmann, N. (1994) *Realistische Themen in der griechischen Kunst*. Berlin.

Hinchliffe, A. P. (1969) *The Absurd*. London.

Hobbes, T. (1994) *Leviathan*, ed. E. Curley. Indianapolis.

Hobden, F. (2004) 'How to be a good symposiast and other lessons from Xenophon's *Symposium*', *PCPhS* 30: 121–40.

Hoffer, S. E. (1995) 'Telemachus' "laugh" (*Odyssey* 21.105)', *AJPh* 116: 515–31.

Hoffman, R. J. (1989) 'Ritual license and the cult of Dionysus', *Athenaeum* 67: 91–115.

Holford-Strevens, L. (2004) *Aulus Gellius*, rev. edn. Oxford.

Holl, K. (1915–33) *Epiphanius* (3 vols.). Leipzig.

Hornblower, S. (1991) *A Commentary on Thucydides, Volume I: Books I–III*. Oxford.

Horowitz, J. and Menache, S. (1994) *L'humour en chaire: le rire dans l'Église médiévale*. Paris.

How, W. W. and Wells, J. (1928) *A Commentary on Herodotus*, corr. edn (2 vols.). Oxford.

Howe, T. P. (1954) 'The origin and function of the gorgon-head', *AJA* 58: 209–21.

Howland, R. L. (1954–5) 'Epeius, carpenter and athlete (or what made the Achaeans laugh at *Iliad* xxiii.840', *PCPhS* 3: 15–16.

Hubbard, M. (1975) 'The capture of Silenus', *PCPhS* 21: 53–62.

Hubbard, T. (1991) *The Mask of Comedy: Aristophanes and the Intertextual Parabasis*. Ithaca.

Hudson-Williams, T. (1910) *The Elegies of Theognis*. London.

Huffmann, C. (1997) 'Pythagoras and Pythagoreanism', in *Encyclopedia of Classical Philosophy*, ed. D. Zeyl. Westport Conn.: 465–71.

Hughes, G. (1991) *Swearing: a Social History of Foul Language, Oaths and Profanity in English*. Oxford.

Hügli, A. (1980) 'Lächerliche (das)', in *Historisches Wörterbuch der Philosophie*, eds. J. Ritter and K. Gründer, vol. v. Basle: 1–8.

(2001) 'Lachen, das Lächerliche', in *Historisches Wörterbuch der Rhetorik*, ed. G. Ueding, vol. v. Tübingen: 1–17.

Huizinga, J. (1949) *Homo Ludens: a Study of the Play-Element in Culture*, Eng. tr. R. Hull. London.

Hume, David (1993) *Selected Essays*, eds. S. Copley and A. Edgar. Oxford.

Humphrey, C. (2001) *The Politics of Carnival: Festive Misrule in Medieval England.* Manchester.

Hunter, R. L. (1983) *Eubulus: the Fragments.* Cambridge.

(1985) *The New Comedy of Greece and Rome.* Cambridge.

(1999) *Theocritus: a Selection.* Cambridge.

(2004) *Plato's Symposium.* Cambridge.

Huß, B. (1999a) *Xenophons Symposion: Ein Kommentar.* Stuttgart.

(1999b) 'The dancing Sokrates and the laughing Xenophon, or the other *Symposium*', *AJPh* 120: 381–409.

Hussey, E. (1999) 'Heraclitus', in *The Cambridge Companion to Early Greek Philosophy*, ed. A. A. Long. Cambridge: 88–112.

(2000) 'Heraclitus', in *Greek Thought: a Guide to Classical Knowledge*, eds. J. Brunschwig and G. E. R. Lloyd. Cambridge Mass.: 631–41.

Husson, G. (1994) 'Lucien philosophe du rire, ou "pour ce que rire est le propre de l'homme"', in *Lucien de Samosate: actes du colloque international de Lyon 1993*, ed. A. Billault. Lyon: 177–84.

Hutcheson, F. (1997) 'Reflections upon laughter' [publ. 1725–6], in *The Scottish Enlightenment: an Anthology*, ed. A. Broadie. Edinburgh: 226–42.

Hutchinson, G. O. (1988) *Hellenistic Poetry.* Oxford.

Huys, M. (1991) *Le poème élégiaque hellénistique, P. Brux. inv. E 8934 et P. Sorb. inv. 2254.* Papyri Bruxellenses Graecae 11.22. Brussels.

Hvidberg, F. F. (1962) *Weeping and Laughter in the Old Testament.* Leiden.

Ideler, J. L. (1841) *Physici et Medici Graeci Minores*, vol. 1. Berlin.

Imperio, O. (1998) 'La figura dell'intellettuale nella commedia greca', in *Tessere. Frammenti della commedia greca: studi e commenti*, eds. A. M. Belardinelli *et al.* Bari: 43–130.

(2004a) *Parabasi di Aristofane: Acarnesi, Cavalieri, Vespe, Uccelli.* Bari.

(2004b) 'I comici a simposio: le *Quaestiones Convivales* e la *Aristophanis et Menandri Comparatio* di Plutarco', in *La biblioteca di Plutarco*, ed. I. Gallo. Naples: 185–96.

Indelli, G. (1978) *Polistrato: sul disprezzo irrazionale delle opinioni popolari.* Naples.

Innes, M. (2002) '"He never even allowed his white teeth to be bared in laughter": the politics of humour in the Carolingian renaissance', in *Humour, History and Politics in Late Antiquity and the Early Middle Ages*, ed. G. Halsall. Cambridge: 131–56.

Ionesco, E. (1964) *Notes and Counter Notes*, Eng. tr. D. Watson. New York.

Ioppolo, A. M. (1980) *Aristone di Chio e lo stoicismo antico.* Naples.

Irwin, E. (2005) *Solon and Early Greek Poetry.* Cambridge.

Irwin, T. (1999) *Aristotle Nicomachean Ethics*, 2nd edn. Indianapolis.

Isnardi Parente, M. (1982) *Senocrate, Ermodoro: Frammenti.* Naples.

Jacques, J. M. (1978) 'Mouvement des acteurs et conventions scéniques dans l'acte 11 du *Bouclier* de Ménandre', *GB* 7: 37–56.

Jaeger, W. (1948) *Aristotle. Fundamentals of the History of his Development*, Eng. tr. R. Robinson, 2nd edn. Oxford.

Jaekel, S. (1964) *Menandri Sententiae. Comparatio Menandri et Philistionis.* Leipzig.

Jäkel, S. (1994) 'The phenomenon of laughter in the *Iliad*', in Jäkel *et al.* (1994–7) vol. I, 23–7.

Jäkel, S. *et al.* eds. (1994, 1995, 1997), *Laughter Down the Centuries* (3 vols.). Turku.

James, M. R. (1924) *The Apocryphal New Testament.* Oxford.

Janka, M. (1997) *Ovid Ars Amatoria Buch 2.* Heidelberg.

Janko, R. (1984) *Aristotle on Comedy: Towards a Reconstruction of Poetics II.* London.
  (1992) *The Iliad: a Commentary. Volume IV: Books 13–16.* Cambridge.
  (2000) *Philodemus On Poems Book 1.* Oxford.

Jebb, R. C. (1870) *The Characters of Theophrastus.* London.
  (1896) *Sophocles the Plays and Fragments: Part VII, the Ajax.* Cambridge.
  (1905) *Bacchylides: the Poems and Fragments.* Cambridge.

Jeffery, L. H. (1976) *Archaic Greece.* London.

Jenkins, I. (1994) 'Face value: the mask in Greece and Rome', in *Masks: the Art of Expression*, ed. J. Mack. London: 151–67.

Jensen, C. (1917) *Hyperides Orationes Sex cum Ceterarum Fragmenta.* Stuttgart.

Jocelyn, H. D. (1980) 'A Greek indecency and its students: ΛΑΙΚΑΖΕΙΝ', *PCPhS* 26: 12–66.

Johns, C. (1982) *Sex or Symbol. Erotic Images of Greece and Rome.* London.

Jones, C. P. (1986) *Culture and Society in Lucian.* Cambridge Mass.

Jouanna, J. (1998) 'Le sourire des Tragiques grecs', in Trédé and Hoffmann (1998) 161–76.

Joubert, L. (1980) *Treatise on Laughter*, Eng. tr. G. D. de Rocher. Alabama. [Orig. French edn, *Traité du ris*: Paris, 1579.]

Jouët-Pastré, E. (1998) 'Le rire chez Platon: un détour sur la voie de la vérité', in Trédé and Hoffmann (1998) 273–79.
  (2006) *Le jeu et le sérieux dans les Lois de Platon.* Sankt Augustin.

Kahn, C. H. (1979) *The Art and Thought of Heraclitus.* Cambridge.

Kaibel, G. (1899) *Comicorum Graecorum Fragmenta.* Berlin.

Kaimio, M. (1990) 'Comic violence in Aristophanes', *Arctos* 24: 47–72.

Kant, I. (2000) *Critique of the Power of Judgment*, ed. P. Guyer, Eng. tr. P. Guyer and E. Matthews. Cambridge.

Kapparis, K. A. (1999) *Apollodoros 'Against Neaira'.* Berlin.

Karaghiorga-Stathacopoulou, T. (1986) 'Baubo', *LIMC* III.1: 87–90 (with ills., III.2: 67–8).

Karavas, O. (2005) *Lucien et la tragédie.* Berlin.

Karle, B. (1932/3) 'Lachen', in *Handwörterbuch des deutschen Aberglaubens*, eds. E. Hoffmann-Krayer and H. Bächtold-Stäubli, vol. VI. Berlin: 868–84.

Kassel, R. (1965) *Aristotelis Ars Poetica.* Oxford.

Kasser, R. *et al.* (2006) *The Gospel of Judas from Codex Tchacos.* Washington.

Kaufmann, W. (1969) *Tragedy and Philosophy.* New York.

Keil, B. (1898) *Aelii Aristidis quae supersunt omnia*, vol. ii. Berlin.
Kelly, J. N. D. (1995) *Golden Mouth: the Story of John Chrysostom*. London.
Kemke, J. (1884) *Philodemi De Musica librorum quae exstant*. Leipzig.
Kenner, H. (1960) *Weinen und Lachen in der griechischen Kunst*. Vienna.
Kerényi, K./C. (1960) 'Parva realia', *SO* 36: 5–16.
  (1962) *The Religion of the Greeks and Romans*, Eng. tr. C. Holme. Westport.
Kern, O. (1922) *Orphicorum Fragmenta*. Berlin.
Keuls, E. C. (1985) *The Reign of the Phallus. Sexual Politics in Ancient Athens*. Berkeley.
Keynes, G. (1969) *Blake: Complete Writings*, rev. edn. Oxford.
Kierkegaard, Søren (1959) *Either/Or*, Eng. tr. D. F. and L. M. Swenson, rev. H. A. Johnson, vol. i. Princeton.
Kilmer, M. (1993) *Greek Erotica on Attic Red-Figure Vases*. London.
Kilpatrick, G. D. (1949) 'A fragment of Musonius', *CR* 63: 94.
Kindstrand, J. F. (1976) *Bion of Borysthenes*. Uppsala.
  (1981) *Anacharsis. The Legend and the Apophthegmata*. Uppsala.
  (1984) 'The Cynics and Heraclitus', *Eranos* 82: 149–78.
King, H. (1986) 'Agnodike and the profession of medicine', *PCPhS* 32: 53–75.
Kinney, D. (1996) 'Heirs of the dog: Cynic selfhood in medieval and renaissance culture', in Branham and Goulet-Cazé (1996) 294–328.
Kirk, G. S. (1985) *The Iliad: a Commentary. Vol. I: Books 1–4*. Cambridge.
  (1990) *The Iliad: a Commentary. Vol. II: Books 5–8*. Cambridge.
Klaniczay, G. (1990) *The Uses of Supernatural Power: the Transformation of Popular Religion in Medieval and Early-Modern Europe*, Eng. tr. S. Singerman. Cambridge.
Klibansky, R. *et al.* (1964) *Saturn and Melancholy: Studies in the History of Natural Philosophy, Religion, and Art*. London.
Knox, D. (1989) *Ironia: Medieval and Renaissance Ideas on Irony*. Leiden.
Kock, T. (1880–8) *Comicorum Atticorum Fragmenta* (3 vols.). Leipzig.
Koestler, A. (1975) *The Act of Creation*, 2nd edn. London.
Kokolakis, M. M. (1960a) *The Dramatic Simile of Life*. Athens.
  (1960b) 'Lucian and the tragic performances in his time', *Platon* 12: 67–109.
Kolve, V. A. (1966) *The Play Called Corpus Christi*. London.
König, J. (2005) *Athletics and Literature in the Roman Empire*. Cambridge.
  (2006) 'The Cynic and Christian lives of Lucian's *Peregrinus*', in *Biographical Limits*, eds. B. McGing and J. Mossman. Swansea: 227–54.
Konstan, D. (1995) *Greek Comedy and Ideology*. New York.
  (2003) 'Before jealousy', in Konstan and Rutter (2003) 7–27.
  (2006) *The Emotions of the Ancient Greeks*. Toronto.
Konstan, D. and Rutter, N. K. eds. (2003) *Envy, Spite and Jealousy: the Rivalrous Emotions in Ancient Greece*. Edinburgh.
Korshak, Y. (1987) *Frontal Faces in Attic Vase Painting of the Archaic Period*. Chicago.
Körte, A. (1890) *Metrodori Epicurei Fragmenta*. Leipzig.
Korus, K. (1984) 'The theory of humour in Lucian of Samosata', *Eos* 72: 295–313.
Kossatz-Deissmann, A. (1992) 'Komos', *LIMC* vi.1: 94–8 (with ills., vi.2: 43–4).

(1994) 'Paidia', *LIMC* VII.I: 141–3 (with ills., VII.2: 94–6).

Koster, S. (1980) *Die Invektive in der griechischen und römischen Literatur*. Meisenheim.

Koster, W. J. W. (1975) *Scholia in Aristophanem Pars I, Fasc. 1A: Prolegomena de Comoedia*. Groningen.

Krauskopf, I. with Dahlinger, S.-C. (1988) 'Gorgo, Gorgones', *LIMC* IV.I: 285–330 (with ills., IV.2: 163–88).

Kraut, R. (1997) *Aristotle Politics Books VII and VIII*. Oxford.

Krentz, P. (1993) 'Athens' allies and the phallophoria', *AHB* 7: 12–16.

Kretschmer, P. (1955) 'Das sardonische Lachen', *Glotta* 34: 1–9.

Krien, G. (1955) 'Der Ausdruck der antiken Theatermasken nach Angaben im Polluxkatalog und in der pseudoaristotelischen "Physiognomik"', *JÖAI* 42: 84–117.

Kris, E. (1964) *Psychoanalytic Explorations in Art*. New York.

Kroll, W. (1899–1901) *Procli Diadochi in Platonis Rem Publicam Commentarii* (2 vols.). Leipzig.

(1908) *Anthologiarum Libri Vettii Valentis*. Berlin.

Krueger, D. (1996) 'The bawdy and society: the shamelessness of Diogenes in Roman imperial culture', in Branham and Goulet-Cazé (1996) 222–39.

Kugelmeier, C. (1996) *Reflexe früher und zeitgenössischer Lyrik in der alten Attischen Komödie*. Stuttgart.

Kühn, C. G. (1821–33) *Opera Omnia Claudii Galeni* (22 vols.). Leipzig.

Kullmann, W. (1995) 'Die antiken Philosophen und das Lachen', in Jäkel *et al.* (1994–7) vol. II, 79–98.

Kundera, M. (1995) *Testaments Betrayed*, Eng. tr. L. Asher. London.

(1996) *The Book of Laughter and Forgetting*, Eng. tr. A. Asher. London.

(2000) *The Art of the Novel*, Eng. tr. L. Asher, rev. edn. New York.

(2007) *The Curtain*, Eng. tr. L. Asher. London.

Kurke, L. (1989) 'ΚΑΠΗΛΕΙΑ and deceit: Theognis 59–60', *AJPh* 110: 535–44.

(1999) 'Ancient Greek board games and how to play them', *CPh* 94: 247–67.

Kurtz, D. and Boardman, J. (1986) 'Booners', *Greek Vases in the J. Paul Getty Museum* 3: 35–70.

Kuschel, K.-J. (1992) '"Christus hat nie gelacht"? Überlegungen zu einer Theologie des Lachens', in *Vom Lachen. Einem Phänomen auf der Spur*, ed. T. Vogel. Tübingen: 106–28.

Labarrière, J.-L. (2000) 'Comment et pourquoi la célèbre formule d'Aristote: "Le rire est le propre de l'homme", se trouve-t-elle dans un traité de physiologie (*Partie des Animaux*, III, 10, 673a8)?', in Desclos (2000) 181–9.

Lada-Richards, I. (1999) *Initiating Dionysus. Ritual and Theatre in Aristophanes' Frogs*. Oxford.

Lamagna, M. (1994) *Menandro: la fanciulla tosata*. Naples.

(1998) *La donna di Samo*. Naples.

Lamberton, R. (1986) *Homer the Theologian: Neoplatonist Allegorical Reading and the Growth of the Epic Tradition*. Berkeley.

Lambrinudakis, W. (1986) 'Damia et Auxesia', *LIMC* III.1: 323–4.

Landfester, M. (1967) *Die Ritter des Aristophanes*. Amsterdam.

Lane, M. (2006) 'The evolution of *eirôneia* in classical Greek texts: why Socratic *eirôneia* is not Socratic irony', *OSAPh* 31: 49–83.

(forthcoming) 'Reconsidering Socratic irony', in *Cambridge Companion to Socrates*, ed. D. Morrison. Cambridge.

Lane Fox, R. (1991) *The Unauthorized Version: Truth and Fiction in the Bible*. London.

(1996) 'Theophrastus' *Characters* and the historian', *PCPhS* 42: 127–70.

(2000) 'Theognis: an alternative to democracy', in *Alternatives to Athens*, eds. R. Brock and S. Hodkinson. Oxford: 35–51.

Lang, M. L. (1983) 'Reverberation and mythology in the *Iliad*', in *Approaches to Homer*, eds. C. A. Rubino and C. W. Shelmerdine. Austin: 140–64.

Lanni, A. M. (1997) 'Spectator sport or serious politics? οἱ περιεστηκότες and the Athenian lawcourts', *JHS* 117: 183–9.

Lapatin, K. (2006) 'Picturing Socrates', in *A Companion to Socrates*, eds. S. Ahbel-Rappe and R. Kamtekar. Oxford: 110–55.

Lape, S. (2004) *Reproducing Athens: Menander's Comedy, Democratic Culture, and the Hellenistic City*. Princeton.

(2006) 'The poetics of the *kōmos*-chorus in Menander's comedy', *AJPh* 127: 89–109.

Latacz, J. *et al.* (2000) *Homers Ilias. Gesamtkommentar*, vol. 1.2. Leipzig.

(2003) *Homers Ilias. Gesamtkommentar*, vol. II.2. Munich.

Lateiner, D. (1977) 'No laughing matter: a literary tactic in Herodotus', *TAPhA* 107: 173–82.

(1992) Review of Arnould (1990), *AJPh* 113: 448–52.

(1995) *Sardonic Smile: Nonverbal Behavior in Homeric Epic*. Ann Arbor.

Lattimore, R. (1962) *Themes in Greek and Latin Epitaphs*. Urbana.

Lee, E. N. (1973) '"Hoist with his own petard": ironic and comic elements in Plato's critique of Protagoras (Tht. 161–171)', in *Exegesis and Argument: Studies in Greek Philosophy Presented to Gregory Vlastos*, eds. E. N. Lee *et al.* Assen: 225–61.

Leeman, A. D. *et al.* (1989) *M. Tullius Cicero De Oratore Libri III*, vol. III. Heidelberg.

Lefkowitz, M. R. (1981) *The Lives of the Greek Poets*. London.

(1991) *First-Person Fictions: Pindar's Poetic 'I'*. Oxford.

Le Goff, J. (1990) 'Le rire dans les règles monastiques du haut Moyen Age', in *Haut Moyen-Age: Culture, Éducation et Société*, ed. M. Sot. La Garennes-Colombe: 93–103.

(1992a) 'Jésus a-t-il ri?', *L'Histoire* 158: 72–4.

(1992b) 'Laughter in *Brennu-Njáls saga*', in *From Sagas to Society: Comparative Approaches to Early Iceland*, ed. G. Pálsson. Enfield Lock: 161–5.

(1997) 'Laughter in the Middle Ages', in Bremmer and Roodenburg (1997) 40–53.

Le Goff, J. and Schmitt, J.-C. eds. (1981) *Le charivari*. Paris.

Lenfant, D. (2003) 'Des décrets contre la satire: une invention de scholiaste? (Pseudo-Xén. II, 18, *schol. Ach.* 67, *schol. Av.* 1297)', *Ktema* 28: 5–31.

Lennox, J. G. (2001) *Aristotle on the Parts of Animals I–IV*. Oxford.

Lenormant, F. (1896) 'Gephyrismoi', in *Dictionnaire des Antiquités Grecques et Romaines*, eds. C. Daremberg and E. Saglio, vol. II. Paris: 1548–9.

Leopardi, G. (1982) *Operette Morali: Essays and Dialogues*, ed. and tr. G. Cecchetti. Berkeley.

Le Roy Ladurie, E. (1981) *Carnival in Romans: a People's Uprising at Romans 1579–1580*, Eng. tr. M. Feeney. Harmondsworth.

Lesher, J. H. (1992) *Xenophanes of Colophon*. Toronto.

Lesky, A. (1961) 'Griechen lachen über ihre Götter', *WHB* 4: 30–40.

Leumann, M. (1950) *Homerische Wörter*. Basle.

Leurini, A. (1992) *Ionis Chii Testimonia et Fragmenta*. Amsterdam.

Leutsch, E. L. von and Schneidewin, F. G. (1839) *Corpus Paroemiographorum Graecorum*, vol. I. Göttingen. [Rpr. Hildesheim, 1958.]

Levi, Primo (1985) *L'altrui mestiere*. Turin.
  (1991) *Other People's Trades*, Eng. tr. R. Rosenthal. London.

Levine, D. B. (1982a) '*Odyssey* 18: Iros as paradigm for the suitors', *CJ* 77: 200–4.
  (1982b) 'Homeric laughter and the unsmiling suitors', *CJ* 78: 97–104.
  (1983a) 'Penelope's laugh: *Odyssey* 18.163', *AJPh* 104: 172–8.
  (1983b) 'Theoklymenos and the apocalypse', *CJ* 79: 1–7.
  (1984) 'Odysseus' smiles: *Odyssey* 20.301, 22.371, 23.111', *TAPhA* 114: 1–9.
  (1985) 'Symposium and the *polis*', in *Theognis of Megara*, eds. T. J. Figueira and G. Nagy. Baltimore: 176–96.
  (1987) 'Flens matrona et meretrices gaudentes: Penelope and her maids', *CW* 81: 23–7.

Levinson, J. (1998) 'Humour', in *Routledge Encyclopedia of Philosophy*, ed. E. Craig, vol. IV. London: 562–7. (Also at http://www.rep.routledge.com/article/M027)

Lewis, S. (2002) *The Athenian Woman: an Iconographic Handbook*. London.

Leyerle, B. (2001) *Theatrical Shows and Ascetic Lives. John Chrysostom's Attack on Spiritual Marriage*. Berkeley.

Liberman, A. (1995) 'A laughing Teuton', in *Across the Oceans: Studies from East to West in Honor of Richard K. Seymour*, eds. I. Rauch and C. Moore. Honolulu: 133–50.

Liebeschuetz, J. H. (1972) *Antioch: City and Imperial Administration in the Later Roman Empire*. Oxford.

Lilja, S. (1980) 'The ape in ancient comedy', *Arctos* 14: 31–8.

Lilla, S. R. C. (1971) *Clement of Alexandria: a Study in Christian Platonism and Gnosticism*. Oxford.

Lincoln, B. (1991) *Emerging from the Chrysalis: Studies in Rituals of Women's Initiation*, 2nd edn. New York.

Lipka, M. (2002) *Xenophon's Spartan Constitution*. Berlin.

Lippitt, J. (1992) 'Nietzsche, Zarathustra and the status of laughter', *British Journal of Aesthetics* 32: 39–49.

(1994) 'Humour and incongruity', *Cogito* 8: 147–53.

(1995a) 'Humour and superiority', *Cogito* 9: 54–61.

(1995b) 'Humour and release', *Cogito* 9: 169–76.

(1996) 'Existential laughter', *Cogito* 10: 63–72.

(1999) 'Laughter: a tool in moral perfectionism?', in *Nietzsche's Futures*, ed. J. Lippitt. Basingstoke: 99–125.

(2000) *Humour and Irony in Kierkegaard's Thought*. Basingstoke.

Lissarrague, F. (1990) *The Aesthetics of the Greek Banquet*, Eng. tr. A. Szegedy-Maszak. Princeton.

(2000) 'Satyres, sérieux s'abstenir', in Desclos (2000) 109–19.

Livrea, E. (1973) *Apollonii Rhodii Argonauticon Liber Quartus*. Florence.

Lloyd, A. B. (1975–88) *Herodotus Book II* (3 vols.). Leiden.

Lloyd, G. E. R. (1987) *The Revolutions of Wisdom. Studies in the Claims and Practice of Ancient Greek Science*. Berkeley.

Lloyd, M. (2004) 'The politeness of Achilles: off-record conversation strategies in Homer and the meaning of *kertomia*', *JHS* 124: 75–89.

Lloyd-Jones, H. (1975) *Females of the Species: Semonides on Women*. London.

(1994) 'Alexander Aetolus, Aristophanes and the life of Euripides', in (no editor) *Storia poesia e pensiero nel mondo antico*. Naples: 371–9.

(2005) *Supplementum Supplementi Hellenistici*. Berlin.

Lloyd Morgan, C. (1914) 'Laughter', in *Encyclopaedia of Religion and Ethics*, ed. J. Hastings, vol. VII. Edinburgh: 803–5.

Lockard, J. S. *et al.* (1977) 'Smiling and laughter: different phyletic origins?', *Bulletin of the Psychonomic Society* 10: 183–6.

Lombardo, S. trans. (1997) *Homer Iliad*. Indianapolis.

Lonardi, G. (1998) '"Alter ridebat . . . flebat alter": a proposito di Democrito/Eraclito in Leopardi', in *Il riso leopardiano: comico, satira, parodia. Atti del IX convegno internazionale di studi leopardini*, ed. R. Garbuglia. Florence: 97–105.

Long, A. A. (1978) 'Timon of Phlius: Pyrrhonist and satirist', *PCPhS* 24: 68–91.

(1996) 'The Socratic tradition: Diogenes, Crates, and Hellenistic ethics', in Branham and Goulet-Cazé (1996) 28–46.

(1999) 'The Socratic legacy', in *Cambridge History of Hellenistic Philosophy*, eds. K. Algra *et al.* Cambridge: 617–41.

(2002) *Epictetus. A Stoic and Socratic Guide to Life*. Oxford.

Long, H. S. (1964) *Diogenis Laertii Vitae Philosophorum* (2 vols.). Oxford.

Lonsdale, S. H. (1993) *Dance and Ritual Play in Greek Religion*. Baltimore.

Lopez Eire, A. (2000) 'À propos des mots pour exprimer l'idée de "rire" en grec ancien', in Desclos (2000) 13–43.

Lorenz, K. (1966) *On Aggression*, Eng. tr. M. Latzke. London.

Lowe, N. J. (1998) 'Thesmophoria and Haloa: myth, physics, and mysteries', in *The Sacred and the Feminine in Ancient Greece*, eds. S. Blundell and M. Williamson. London: 149–73.

(2000) *The Classical Plot and the Invention of Western Narrative*. Cambridge.

Lowry, E. R. (1991) *Thersites: a Study in Comic Shame*. New York.

Luck, G. (1958) 'Palladas, Christian or pagan?', *HSPh* 63: 455–71.

(1994) 'Humor', in *Reallexikon für Antike und Christentum*, ed. E. Dassmann, vol. XVI. Stuttgart: 753–73.

Lullies, R. (1960) *Greek Sculpture*, rev. edn. New York.

Luria, S. (1963) 'Heraklit und Demokrit', *Altertum* 9: 195–200.

Lutz, C. E. (1954) 'Democritus and Heraclitus', *CJ* 49: 309–14.

MacDowell, D. M. (1971) *Aristophanes Wasps*. Oxford.

(1978) *The Law in Classical Athens*. London.

(1990) *Demosthenes Against Meidias*. Oxford.

(1996) 'Aristophanes and democracy', in *Colloque international: démocratie Athénienne et culture*, ed. M. Sakellariou. Athens: 189–97.

Macleod, C.(1983) *Collected Essays*. Oxford.

Macleod, M. D. (1967) *Lucian*, vol. VIII. Cambridge Mass.

(1972–87) *Luciani Opera* (4 vols.). Oxford.

(1991) *Lucian: a Selection*. Warminster.

Mader, M. (1977) *Das Problem des Lachens und der Komödie bei Platon*. Stuttgart.

Maehler, H. (1970) *Bacchylidis Carmina cum Fragmentis*. Leipzig.

(2004) *Bacchylides: a Selection*. Cambridge.

Magdalino, P. (2007) 'Tourner en dérision à Byzance', in *La dérision au Moyen Age*, eds. E. Crouzet-Pavan and J. Verger. Paris: 55–72.

Mallory, J. P. and Adams, D. Q. (2006) *The Oxford Introduction to Proto-Indo-European and the Proto-Indo-European World*. Oxford.

Malten, L. (1961) *Die Sprache des menschlichen Antlitzes im frühen Griechentum*. Berlin.

Marcovich, M. (1964) 'Pythagorica', *Philologus* 108: 29–44.

(1967) *Heraclitus: Greek Text with a Short Commentary*. Merida.

(1988) *Studies in Graeco-Roman Religions and Gnosticism*. Leiden.

(1999) *Diogenes Laertius: Vitae Philosophorum*, vol. I. Stuttgart.

(2002) *Clementis Alexandrini Paedagogus*. Leiden.

Marrou, H.-I. (1965) *Clément d'Alexandrie: le Pédagogue livre II*. Paris.

Marshall, C. W. (1999) 'Some fifth-century masking conventions', *G&R* 46: 188–202.

Martin, R. (1951) *Recherches sur l'agora grecque*. Paris.

Martin, R. P. (1989) *The Language of Heroes: Speech and Performance in the Iliad*. Ithaca.

(1996) 'The Scythian accent: Anacharsis and the Cynics', in Branham and Goulet-Cazé (1996) 136–55.

(1998) 'The seven sages as performers of wisdom', in *Cultural Poetics in Archaic Greece*, eds. C. Dougherty and L. Kurke. Cambridge: 108–28.

Massimilla, G. (1996) *Callimaco Aitia libri primo e secondo*. Pisa.

Mastromarco, G. (1994) 'Teatro comico e potere politico nell'Atene del V secolo (Pseudo-Senofonte, *Costituzione degli Ateniesi*, II 18)', in *Storia poesia e pensiero nel mondo antico* (no editor). Naples: 451–8.

Mastronarde, D. J. (2002) *Euripides Medea*. Cambridge.

Matthews, V. J. (1974) *Panyassis of Halikarnassos*. Leiden.

Mattioli, E. (1982) 'Leopardi e Luciano', in *Leopardi e il mondo antico: atti del V convegno internazionale di studi leopardini* (no editor). Florence: 75–98.

Mayer, W. and Allen P. (2000) *John Chrysostom.* London.

McClure, L. (1999) *Spoken Like a Woman: Speech and Gender in Athenian Drama.* Princeton.

(2003) 'Subversive laughter: the sayings of courtesans in book 13 of Athenaeus' *Deipnosophistae*', *AJPh* 124: 259–94.

McCullagh, S. *et al.* (1999) 'Pathological laughing and crying in amyotrophic lateral sclerosis', *Journal of the Neurological Sciences* 169: 43–8.

McDermott, W. C. (1938) *The Ape in Antiquity.* Baltimore.

McDonough, J. and Alexander, P. (1962) *Gregorii Nysseni Opera*, vol. v. Leiden.

McDougall, W. (1923) *An Outline of Psychology.* London.

Meeks, W. A. and Wilken, R. L. (1978) *Jews and Christians in Antioch.* Missoula.

Meerwaldt, J. D. (1928) 'De verborum quae vulgo dicuntur imitativa natura et origine', *Mnemosyne* 56: 159–68.

Meijering, E. P. (1984) *Athanasius: Contra Gentes.* Leiden.

Mellinkoff, R. (1973) 'Riding backwards: theme of humiliation and symbol of evil', *Viator* 4: 153–76.

Meltzer, G. S. (1990) 'The role of comic perspectives in shaping Homer's tragic vision', *CW* 83: 265–80.

Ménager, D. (1995) *La Renaissance et le rire.* Paris.

Merkelbach, R. and West, M. L. (1970) *Hesiodi Fragmenta Selecta.* Oxford.

Meyer, M. (forthcoming) 'The comic nature of *Ecce Homo*', *International Studies in Philosophy.*

Micalella, D. (2004) *I giovani amano il riso: aspetti della riflessione aristotelica sul comico.* Lecce.

Mikalson, J. D. (1982) 'The *heorte* of heortology', *GRBS* 23: 213–21.

Milanezi, S. (1992) 'Outres enflées de rire. À propos de la fête du dieu Risus dans les *Métamorphoses* d'Apulée', *RHR* 209: 125–47.

(1995) 'Le rire d'Hadès', *DHA* 21: 231–45.

Miles, R. (2003) 'Unmasking the self: church and theatre in the homilies of John Chrysostom', in *Attitudes to Theatre from Plato to Milton*, ed. E. Theodorakopoulos. Bari: 103–15.

Miller, C. H. (1979) *Opera Omnia Desiderii Erasmi Roterodami*, vol. iv.3. Amsterdam.

Miller, M. C. (1997) 'Midas', *LIMC* viii.1: 846–51 (with ills., viii.2: 569–72).

Miller, W. I. (1997) *The Anatomy of Disgust.* Cambridge Mass.

Millett, P. (1998) 'Encounters in the agora', in *Kosmos: Essays in Order, Conflict, and Community in Classical Athens*, eds. P. Millett *et al.* Cambridge: 203–28.

Millon, C. and Schouler, B. (1988) 'Les jeux olympiques d'Antioche', *Pallas* 34: 61–76.

Milner, G. B. (1972) 'Homo ridens. Towards a semiotic theory of humour and laughter', *Semiotica* 5: 1–30.

Mineur, W. H. (1984) *Callimachus Hymn to Delos.* Leiden.

Minois, G. (2000) *Histoire du rire et de la dérision.* Paris.

Miralles, C. (1987) 'Le rire sardonique', *Métis* 2: 31–43.

　(1993) *Ridere in Omero*. Pisa.

　(1994) 'Laughter in the *Odyssey*', in Jäkel *et al.* (1994–7) vol. I, 15–22.

Momigliano, A. (1993) *The Development of Greek Biography*, expanded edn. Cambridge Mass.

　(1994) *Essays on Ancient and Modern Judaism*, ed. S. Berti. Chicago.

Monaco, G. (1963) *Paragoni burleschi degli antichi*. Palermo.

Monoson, S. S. (2000) *Plato's Democratic Entanglements*. Princeton.

Montaigne, M. de (1969) *Essais. Livre I*, ed. A. Micha. Paris.

Mooney, M. E. (1982) 'Presocratic scepticism: Samuel Beckett's *Murphy* reconsidered', *English Literary History* 49: 214–34.

Moore, G. E. (1959) *Philosophical Papers*. London.

Moraitou, D. (1994) *Die Äußerungen des Aristoteles über Dichter und Dichtung außerhalb der Poetik*. Stuttgart.

Morelli, G. (2001) *Teatro attico e pittura vascolare: una tragedia di Cheremone nella ceramica italiota*. Zurich.

Morgan, M. (1990) *Platonic Piety: Philosophy and Ritual in Fourth-Century Athens*. New Haven.

Morreall, J. (1983) *Taking Laughter Seriously*. Albany.

　(1989) 'The rejection of humor in Western thought', *Philosophy East and West* 39: 243–65.

Morris, D. *et al.* (1979) *Gestures: their Origins and Distribution*. London.

Morris, S. P. (1992) *Daidalos and the Origins of Greek Art*. Princeton.

Morrow, G. (1993) *Plato's Cretan City*, 2nd edn. Princeton.

Morson, G. S. and Emerson, C. (1990) *Mikhail Bakhtin. Creation of a Prosaics*. Stanford.

Mossner, E. C. and Ross, I. S. (1977) *The Correspondence of Adam Smith*. Oxford.

Most, G. W. (1999) 'The poetics of early Greek philosophy', in *Cambridge Companion to Early Greek Philosophy*, ed. A. A. Long. Cambridge: 332–62.

Mulkay, M. (1988) *On Humour: its Nature and its Place in Modern Society*. Oxford.

Mülke, C. (2002) *Solons politische Elegien und Iamben*. Munich.

Müller, R. (1994) 'Demokrit – der "lachende Philosoph"', in Jäkel *et al.* (1994–7) vol. I, 39–51.

Murdoch, I. (1977) *The Fire and the Sun: Why Plato Banished the Artists*. Oxford.

　(1997) *Existentialists and Mystics. Writings on Philosophy and Literature*, ed. P. Conradi. London.

Murray, J. R. (1908) 'Laughter', in *A Dictionary of Christ and the Gospels*, ed. J. Hastings, vol. II. Edinburgh: 9–11.

Murray, O. (1988) 'Death and the symposion', *Aion* (Archeol.) 10: 239–57.

　ed. (1990a) *Sympotica. A Symposium on the Symposion*. Oxford.

　(1990b) 'The Solonian law of *hybris*', in *Nomos: Essays in Athenian Law, Politics and Society*, eds. P. Cartledge *et al.* Cambridge: 139–45.

　(1991) 'War and the symposium', in *Dining in a Classical Context*, ed. W. J. Slater. Ann Arbor: 83–103.

Murray, P. (1996) *Plato on Poetry*. Cambridge.

Nagel, T.(1979) *Mortal Questions*. Cambridge.

(1986) *The View from Nowhere*. New York.

Nagy, G. (1990) *Pindar's Homer*. Baltimore.

(1999) *The Best of the Achaeans*, 2nd edn. Baltimore.

Nails, D. (2002) *The People of Plato: a Prosopography of Plato and Other Socratics*. Indianapolis.

Napier, A. D. (1986) *Masks, Transformation, and Paradox*. Berkeley.

Narcy, M. (2001) 'Qu'est-ce que l'ironie socratique?', *Journal of the International Plato Society* 1: online at http://www.nd.edu/plato/narcy.htm

Nau, F. (1907) 'Histoires des solitaires égyptiens', *Revue de l'Orient Chrétien* 12: 48–68.

Nehamas, A. (1998) *The Art of Living: Socratic Reflections from Plato to Foucault*. Berkeley.

(1999) *Virtues of Authenticity: Essays on Plato and Socrates*. Princeton.

Neil, R. A. (1901) *The Knights of Aristophanes*. Cambridge.

Neils, J. and Oakley, J. H. eds. (2003) *Coming of Age in Ancient Greece: Images of Childhood from the Classical Past*. New Haven.

Nenci, G. (1998) *Erodoto le storie: libro VI*. Milan.

Nesselrath, H.-G. (1985) *Lukians Parasitendialog*. Berlin.

(1990) *Die attische Mittlere Komödie*. Berlin.

(1998) 'Lucien et le Cynisme', *AC* 67: 121–35.

(2001) 'Lukian und die antike Philosophie', in *Lukian: Die Lügenfreunde*, eds. M. Eber *et al.* Darmstadt: 135–52.

Neuburg, M. (1987) 'Whose laughter does Pentheus fear? (EUR. *BA.* 842)', *CQ* 37: 227–30.

Newiger, H.-J. (1957) *Metapher und Allegorie: Studien zu Aristophanes*. Munich.

Newman, W. L. (1887–1902) *The Politics of Aristotle* (4 vols.). Oxford.

Nickau, K. (1966) *Ammonii qui dicitur liber de adfinium vocabulorum differentia*. Leipzig.

Nicoll, A. (1931) *Masks Mimes and Miracles*. London.

Niehues-Pröbsting, H. (1979) *Der Kynismus des Diogenes und der Begriff des Zynismus*. Munich.

Nietzsche, F. (1988) *Sämtliche Werke: Kritische Studienausgabe*, eds. G. Colli and M. Montanari, 2nd edn (15 vols.). Munich.

Nightingale, A. W. (1995) *Genres in Dialogue: Plato and the Construct of Philosophy*. Cambridge.

Nisbet, G. (2003) *Greek Epigram in the Roman Empire*. Oxford.

Norden, E. (1924) *Die Geburt des Kindes: Geschichte einer religiösen Idee*. Leipzig.

Norris, F. W. (1991) *Faith Gives Fullness to Reasoning. The Five Theological Orations of Gregory Nazianzen*. Leiden.

Norwood, G. (1931) *Greek Comedy*. London.

Nuchelmans, J. (1955) 'ἀγέλαστος', *LfgrE* I, 59.

Nünlist, R. (1998) *Poetologische Bildersprache in der frühgriechischen Dichtung*. Stuttgart.

Nussbaum, M. C. (2004) *Hiding from Humanity: Disgust, Shame, and the Law.* Princeton.

(forthcoming) 'Stoic laughter: a reading of Seneca's *Apocolocyntosis*', in *Seneca and the Self,* ed. S. Bartsch and D. Wray. Cambridge.

Ober, J. (1989) *Mass and Elite in Democratic Athens.* Princeton.

(1998) *Political Dissent in Classical Athens.* Princeton.

O'Brien, P. T. (1999) *The Letter to the Ephesians.* Leicester.

O'Higgins, L. (2003) *Women and Humor in Classical Greece.* Cambridge.

Olender, M. (1990) 'Aspects of Baubo', in Halperin *et al.* (1990) 83–113. [French version: 'Aspects de Baubo', *RHR* 202 (1985) 3–55.]

Olson, S. D. (1994) 'Telemachos' laugh (*Od.* 21.101–105)', *CJ* 89: 369–72.

(1998) *Aristophanes Peace.* Oxford.

(1999) 'Kleon's eyebrows (Cratin. fr. 228 K–A) and late 5th-century comic portrait-masks', *CQ* 49: 320–1.

(2002) *Aristophanes Acharnians.* Oxford.

(2007) *Broken Laughter: Select Fragments of Greek Comedy.* Oxford.

Olson, S. D. and Sens, A. (1999) *Matro of Pitane and the Tradition of Epic Parody in the Fourth Century BCE.* Atlanta.

Omitowoju, R. (2002) *Rape and the Politics of Consent in Classical Athens.* Cambridge.

Opsomer, J. (1998) *In Search of the Truth: Academic Tendencies in Middle Platonism.* Brussels.

Osborn, E. F. (1957) *The Philosophy of Clement of Alexandria.* Cambridge.

(1976) *Ethical Patterns in Early Christian Thought.* Cambridge.

Osborne, M. J. and Byrne, S. G. eds. (1994) *A Lexicon of Greek Personal Names, Volume II: Attica.* Oxford.

Osborne, R. (1998) *Archaic and Classical Greek Art.* Oxford.

Overing, J. (2000) 'The efficacy of laughter: the ludic side of magic within Amazonian sociality', in *The Anthropology of Love and Anger: the Aesthetics of Conviviality in Native Amazonia,* eds. J. Overing and A. Passes. London: 64–81.

Overwien, O. (2005) *Die Sprüche des Kynikers Diogenes in der griechischen und arabischen Überlieferung. Hermes* Einzelschriften 92. Stuttgart

(2006) 'Lukian als Literat, Lukian als Feind: das Beispiel des Peregrinos Proteus', *RhM* 149: 185–213.

Owen, G. E. L. (1983) 'Philosophical invective', *OSAPh* 1: 1–25. [Rpr. in *idem, Logic, Science and Dialectic* (London, 1986) 347–74.]

Padgett, J. M. ed. (2003) *The Centaur's Smile: the Human Animal in Early Greek Art.* New Haven.

Page, D. L. (1941) *Select Papyri III: Literary Papyri.* Cambridge Mass.

(1955) *Sappho and Alcaeus.* Oxford.

(1978) *The Epigrams of Rufinus.* Cambridge.

(1981) *Further Greek Epigrams.* Cambridge.

Pagels, E. (1980) *The Gnostic Gospels.* London.

Palmer, J. (1994) *Taking Humour Seriously.* London.

Panksepp, J. *et al.* (2001) 'Towards a genetics of joy: breeding rats for "laughter"', in *Emotions, Qualia, and Consciousness*, ed. A. Kaszniak. Singapore: 124–36.

Parke, H. W. (1977) *Festivals of the Athenians*. London.

Parke, H. W. and Wormell, D. E. W. (1956) *The Delphic Oracle* (2 vols.). Oxford.

Parker, L. P. E. (1997) *The Songs of Aristophanes*. Oxford.

Parker, R. (1983) *Miasma. Pollution and Purification in Early Greek Religion*. Oxford.

(1996) *Athenian Religion: a History*. Oxford.

(2005) *Polytheism and Society at Athens*. Oxford.

Parks, W. (1990) *Verbal Dueling in Heroic Narrative: the Homeric and Old English Traditions*. Princeton.

Parvizi, J. *et al.* (2001) 'Pathological laughter and crying', *Brain* 124: 1708–19.

Pasquali, G. (1908) *Proclus Diadochus: in Platonis Cratylum Commentaria*. Stuttgart.

Passow, F. (1841) *Handwörterbuch des griechischen Sprace*, rev. V. C. F. Rost and F. Palm, 5th edn (4 vols.). Leipzig. [Rpr. Darmstadt, 1993.]

Patera, I. and Zografou, A. (2001) 'Femmes à la fête des Halôa: le secret de l'imaginaire', *Clio*: at http://clio.revues.org/document102.html

Paton, W. R. (1916–18) *The Greek Anthology* (5 vols.). London.

Paulson, R. (1975) *The Art of Hogarth*. London.

Peachin, M. (2001) 'Friendship and abuse at the dinner table', in *Aspects of Friendship in the Graeco-Roman World*, ed. M. Peachin. Portsmouth RI: 135–44.

Pearson, A. C. (1917) *The Fragments of Sophocles* (3 vols.). Cambridge.

Pease, A. S. (1955) *M. Tulli Ciceronis De Natura Deorum Liber Primus*. Cambridge Mass.

Pelling, C. (2000) *Greek Literature and the Historian*. London.

Pendrick, G. J. (2002) *Antiphon the Sophist: the Fragments*. Cambridge.

Perpillou, J.-L. (1982) 'Verbes de sonorité à vocalisme expressif en Grec ancien', *REG* 95: 233–74.

Perry, B. E. (1952) *Aesopica*, vol. I. Urbana.

(1965) *Babrius and Phaedrus*. London.

Pfeiffer, R. (1922) *Kallimachosstudien*. Munich.

(1965) *Callimachus*, corr. edn (2 vols.). Oxford.

Pfeiffer, R. H. (1960) 'Hebrew and Greek sense of tragedy', in *The Joshua Bloch Memorial Volume*, eds. A. Berger *et al.* New York: 54–64.

Pfister, M. (2002a) 'Introduction: a history of English laughter?', in *A History of English Laughter: Laughter from Beowulf to Beckett and Beyond*, ed. M. Pfister. Amsterdam: v–x.

(2002b) 'Beckett, Barker, and other grim laughers', *ibid.*, 175–89.

Pfitzner, V. C. (1967) *Paul and the Agon Motif. Traditional Athletic Imagery in the Pauline Literature*. Leiden.

Philippson, R. (1928) 'Verfasser und Abfassungszeit der sogenannten Hippokratesbriefe', *RhM* 77: 293–328.

Phrantzoles, K. G. (1989) Ὁσίου Ἐφραίμ τοῦ Σύρου ἔργα, vol. II. Thessalonica.

Pickard-Cambridge, A. W. (1927) *Dithyramb Tragedy and Comedy*. Oxford. [Preferred to 2nd edn (Oxford, 1962).]

(1968) *The Dramatic Festivals of Athens*, 2nd edn. Oxford. [Rpr. with select addenda, 1988.]

Pigeaud, J. (1981) *La maladie de l'âme: étude sur la relation de l'âme et du corps dans la tradition médico-philosophique antique.* Paris.

Pilhofer, P. *et al.* (2005) *Lukian: der Tod des Peregrinos.* Darmstadt.

Pinker, S. (1998) *How the Mind Works.* London.

Pinney, G. F. (1984) 'For the heroes are at hand', *JHS* 104: 181–3.

Pistelli, H. (1888) *Iamblichi Protrepticus.* Leipzig.

Plebe, A. (1952) *La teoria del comico da Aristotele a Plutarco.* Turin.

(1956) *La nascita del comico nella vita e nell'arte degli antichi Greci.* Bari.

Plessner, H. (1941) *Lachen und Weinen: eine Untersuchung nach den Grenzen menschlichen Verhaltens.* Arnhem.

(1970) *Laughing and Crying: a Study of the Limits of Human Behavior*, Eng. tr. J. S. Churchill and M. Grene. Evanston.

Pollitt, J. J. (1965) *The Art of Greece 1400–31 BC.* Englewood Cliffs.

(1972) *Art and Experience in Classical Greece.* Cambridge.

(1986) *Art in the Hellenistic Age.* Cambridge.

Pontrandolfo, A. (1996) 'Wall-painting in Magna Graecia', in *The Greek World: Art and Civilization in Magna Graecia and Sicily*, ed. G. P. Carratelli. New York: 457–70.

Porter, J. I. (2000) *The Invention of Dionysus: an Essay on the Birth of Tragedy.* Stanford.

Porter, H. N. (1948) 'A Bacchic graffito from the Dolicheneum at Dura', *AJPh* 69: 27–41.

Postlethwaite, N. (1988) 'Thersites in the *Iliad*', *G&R* 35: 123–36.

Powell, B. B. (2004) *Homer.* Oxford.

Praechter, K. (1912) 'Der Topos ΠΕΡΙ ΣΠΟΥΔΗΣ ΚΑΙ ΠΑΙΔΙΑΣ', *Hermes* 47: 471–6.

Prauscello, L. (2006) 'Looking for the "other" Gnesippus: some notes on Eupolis fragment 148 K–A', *CPh* 101: 52–66.

Preisendanz, W. (1976) 'Komische (das), Lachen (das)', in *Historisches Wörterbuch der Philosophie*, eds. J. Ritter and K. Gründer, vol. iv. Basle: 889–93.

Price, S. D. (1990) 'Anacreontic vases reconsidered', *GRBS* 31: 133–75.

Propp, V. (1984) *Theory and History of Folklore*, Eng. tr. A. Y. Martin and R. P. Martin. Manchester.

Provine, R. R. (1996) 'Contagious yawning and laughter', in *Social Learning in Animals: the Roots of Culture*, eds. C. M. Heyes and B. G. Galef. San Diego: 179–208.

(2000) *Laughter: a Scientific Investigation.* London.

Prusak, B. G. (2004) '*Le rire* à nouveau: rereading Bergson', *Journal of Aesthetics and Art Criticism* 62: 377–88.

Puchner, W. (2006) 'Zur Geschichte der antiken Theaterterminologie im nachantiken Griechisch', *WS* 119: 77–113.

Puelma, M. (1960) 'Die Dichterbegegnung in Theokrits "Thalysien"', *MH* 17: 144–64.

Pulleyn, S. (2000) *Homer Iliad Book One*. Oxford.

Puttfarken, T. (2005) *Titian and Tragic Painting*. New Haven.

Pütz, B. (2007) *The Symposium and Komos in Aristophanes*, 2nd edn. Oxford.

Rabe, H. (1906) *Scholia in Lucianum*. Leipzig.

Rabelais, F. (1994) *Oeuvres complètes*, eds. M. Huchon and F. Moreau. Paris.

Radcliffe-Brown, A. R. (1952) *Structure and Function in Primitive Society*. London.

Radday, Y. T. and Brenner, A. eds. (1990) *On Humour and the Comic in the Hebrew Bible*. Sheffield.

Radermacher, L. (1930) 'Zur Charakteristik neutestamentlicher Erzählungen', *Archiv für Religionswissenschaft* 28: 31–41.

    (1947) *Weinen und Lachen: Studien über antikes Lebensgefühl*. Vienna.

Radke, G. (2003) *Tragik und Metatragik: Euripides' Bakchen und die moderne Literaturwissenschaft*. Berlin.

    (2006) *Das Lächeln des Parmenides: Proklos' Interpretationen zur Platonischen Dialogform*. Berlin.

Rahner, H. (1961) 'Eutrapélie', in *Dictionnaire de Spiritualité*, vol. xxv. Paris: 1726–9.

Ramachandran, V. S. (1998a) 'The neurology and evolution of humor, laughter, and smiling: the false alarm theory', *Medical Hypotheses* 51: 351–4.

    (1998b), with Blakeslee, S., *Phantoms in the Brain: Human Nature and the Architecture of the Mind*. London.

Ramachandran, V. S. *et al.* (1996) 'Illusions of body image: what they reveal about human nature', in *The Mind-Brain Continuum*, eds. R. Llinás and P. S. Churchland. Cambridge Mass: 29–60.

Rankin, H. D. (1967) 'Laughter, humour and related topics in Plato', *C&M* 28: 186–213.

    (1972) 'Thersites the malcontent, a discussion', *SO* 47: 36–60.

    (1986) *Antisthenes Sokratikos*. Amsterdam.

Rapp, A. (1947–8) 'The dawn of humor: the transition from ridicule to true humor seen in Homer', *CJ* 43: 275–80.

Rapp, C. (2002) *Aristoteles Rhetorik* (2 vols.). Berlin.

Rawson, E. (1969) *The Spartan Tradition in European Thought*. Oxford.

Rebenich, S. (1998) *Xenophon: die Verfassung der Spartaner*. Darmstadt.

Reckford, K. J. (1987) *Aristophanes' Old-and-New Comedy*. Chapel Hill.

Redfield, J. M. (1994) *Nature and Culture in the* Iliad, expanded edn. London.

Reich, H. (1903) *Der Mimus: ein Litterar-Entwicklungsgeschichtlicher Versuch*. Berlin.

Reid, J. D. (1993) *Oxford Guide to Classical Mythology in the Arts 1300–1990s* (2 vols.). New York.

Reinach, A. (1921) *Textes Grecs et Latins relatifs à l'histoire de la peinture ancienne*. Paris. [Rpr. Chicago, 1981.]

Reinach, S. (1911) 'Le rire rituel', *RUB* (May): 585–602. [Rpr. in *Cultes, mythes et religions*, vol. iv (Paris, 1912) 109–29.]

Reinhardt, K. (1960) *Tradition und Geist: Gesammelte Essays zur Dichtung*. Göttingen.

Reitzenstein, G. (1893) *Epigramm und Skolion*. Giessen.

Relihan, J. C. (1993) *Ancient Menippean Satire*. Baltimore.

(1996) 'Menippus in antiquity and the Renaissance', in Branham and Goulet-Cazé (1996) 265–93.

Renfrew, A. (1997) 'The carnival without laughter', in *Face to Face: Bakhtin in Russia and the West*, eds. C. Adlam *et al.* Sheffield: 185–95.

Rengstorf, K. H. (1964) 'γελάω, καταγελάω, γέλως', in *Theological Dictionary of the New Testament*, ed. G. Kittel, Eng. tr. G. W. Bromiley, vol. 1. Grand Rapids Mich.: 658–62.

Resnick, I. M. (1987) '"Risus monasticus"', *RBen* 97: 90–100.

Revermann, M. (2006) *Comic Business: Theatricality, Dramatic Technique, and Performance Contexts of Aristophanic Comedy*. Oxford.

Reynolds, R. W. (1946) 'The adultery mime', *CQ* 40: 77–84.

Rhodes, P. J. (1981) *A Commentary on the Aristotelian* Athenaion Politeia. Oxford.

Rhodes, P. J. and Osborne, R. (2003) *Greek Historical Inscriptions 404–323 BC*. Oxford.

Rhys Roberts, W. (1902) *Demetrius on Style*. Cambridge.

Richardson, N. (1974) *The Homeric Hymn to Demeter*. Oxford.

(1993) *The Iliad: a Commentary. Volume VI: Books 21–24*. Cambridge.

Richer, N. (1999) '*Aidōs* at Sparta', in *Sparta: New Perspectives*, eds. S. Hodkinson and A. Powell. London: 91–115.

(2005) 'Personified abstractions in Laconia: suggestions on the origin of Phobos', in *Personification in the Greek World*, eds. E. Stafford and J. Herrin. Aldershot: 111–22.

Richlin, A. (1992) *The Garden of Priapus: Sexuality and Aggression in Roman Humor*, 2nd edn. New York.

Richter, G. M. A. (1965) *The Portraits of the Greeks* (3 vols.). London.

(1968) *Korai: Archaic Greek Maidens*. London.

(1970) *Kouroi: Archaic Greek Youths*, 3rd edn. London.

Ridgway, B. (1993) *The Archaic Style in Greek Sculpture*, 2nd edn. Chicago.

Riginos, A. S. (1976) *Platonica. The Anecdotes Concerning the Life and Writings of Plato*. Leiden.

Rinon, Y. (2006) 'Tragic Hephaestus: the humanized god in the *Iliad* and the *Odyssey*', *Phoenix* 60: 1–20.

Riu, X. (1999) *Dionysism and Comedy*. Lanham.

Robertson, M. (1975) *A History of Greek Art* (2 vols.). Cambridge.

(1981) *A Shorter History of Greek Art*. Cambridge.

Robertson, N. (1992) *Festivals and Legends: the Formation of Greek Cities in the Light of Public Ritual*. Toronto.

(1996) 'New light on Demeter's Mysteries', *GRBS* 37: 319–79.

(1998) 'The two processions to Eleusis and the program of the Mysteries', *AJPh* 119: 547–75.

Robinson, C. (1979) *Lucian and his Influence in Europe*. London.

Robinson, D. M. (1931) *Excavations at Olynthus, Part IV: the Terra-Cottas*. Baltimore.

Robinson, J. M. ed. (1977) *The Nag Hammadi Library in English*. Leiden.

Robson, J. (2006) *Humour, Obscenity and Aristophanes*. Tübingen.

Röcke, W. and Velten, H. R. eds. (2005) *Lachgemeinschaften: kulturelle Inszenierungen und soziale Wirkungen von Gelächter im Mittelalter und in der Frühen Neuzeit*. Berlin.

Rorty, R. (1989) *Contingency, Irony, and Solidarity*. Cambridge.

Rose, P. W. (1988) 'Thersites and the plural voices of Homer', *Arethusa* 21: 5–26.

Rose, V. (1886) *Aristotelis Fragmenta*, 3rd edn. Leipzig.

Rosen, R. M. (1984) 'The Ionian at Aristophanes *Peace* 46', *GRBS* 25: 389–96.

(1988) *Old Comedy and the Iambographic Tradition*. Atlanta.

(2000) 'Cratinus' *Pytine* and the construction of the comic self', in Harvey and Wilkins (2000) 23–39.

(2006) 'Comic aischrology and the urbanization of *agroikia*', in *City, Countryside, and the Spatial Organization of Value in Classical Antiquity*, eds. R. M. Rosen and I. Sluiter. Leiden: 219–38.

(2007) *Making Mockery: the Poetics of Ancient Satire*. New York.

Rosen, R. M. and Marks, D. R. (1999) 'Comedies of transgression in gangsta rap and ancient classical poetry', *New Literary History* 30: 897–928.

Rosivach, V. J. (1998) *When a Young Man Falls in Love: the Sexual Exploitation of Women in New Comedy*. London.

Rösler, W. (1986) 'Michail Bachtin und die Karnevalskultur im antiken Griechenland', *QUCC* 23: 25–44.

(1993) 'Über Aischrologie im archaischen und klassischen Griechenland', in *Karnevaleske Phänomene in antiken und nachantiken Kulturen und Literaturen*, ed. S. Döpp. Trier: 75–97.

(1995a) 'Wine and truth in the Greek *symposion*', in *In Vino Veritas*, eds. O. Murray and M. Tecuşan. London: 106–12.

(1995b) 'Escrologia e intertestualità', *Lexis* 13: 117–28.

Ross, W. D. (1955) *Aristotelis Fragmenta Selecta*. Oxford.

Rossetti, L. (2000) 'Le ridicule comme arme entre les mains de Socrate et de ses élèves', in Desclos (2000) 253–68.

Rossi, L. (1971) 'Il *Ciclope* di Euripide come κῶμος "mancato"', *Maia* 23: 10–38.

Rowe, C. J. (1993) *Plato Phaedo*. Cambridge.

(1997) 'The good, the reasonable and the laughable in Plato's *Republic*', in Jäkel *et al.* (1994–7) vol. III, 45–54.

Rowe, C. (tr.) and Broadie, S. (2002) *Aristotle Nicomachean Ethics*. Oxford.

Rowe, G. O. (1966) 'The portrait of Aeschines in the *Oration on the Crown*', *TAPhA* 97: 397–406.

Ruch, W. and Ekman, P. (2001) 'The expressive pattern of laughter', in *Emotions, Qualia, and Consciousness*, ed. A. Kaszniak. Singapore: 426–43.

Rudhardt, J. (1992) 'Rires et sourires divins. Essai sur la sensibilité religieuse des Grecs et des premiers Chrétiens', *RThPh* 124: 389–405.

Russell, D. A. (1964) *'Longinus' On the Sublime*. Oxford.

(2003) 'The rhetoric of the *Homeric Problems*', in *Metaphor, Allegory, and the Classical Tradition*, ed. G. Boys-Stones. Oxford: 217–34.

Rusten, J. S. (1977) 'Wasps 1360–1369: Philokleon's ΤΩΘΑΣΜΟΣ', *HSPh* 81: 157–61.

(1989) *Thucydides: the Peloponnesian War Book II*. Cambridge.

(2006) 'Who "invented" comedy? The ancient candidates for the origins of comedy and the visual evidence', *AJPh* 127: 37–66.

Rusten, J. and Cunningham, I. C. (2002) *Theophrastus Characters, Herodas Mimes, Sophron and Other Mime Fragments*, 3rd edn. Cambridge Mass.

Rutherford, R. B. (1989) *The Meditations of Marcus Aurelius: a Study*. Oxford.

(1992) *Homer Odyssey Books XIX and XX*. Cambridge.

(1995) *The Art of Plato*. London.

Rütten, T. (1992) *Demokrit – lachender Philosoph und sanguinischer Melancholiker. Eine pseudohippokratische Geschichte*. Leiden.

Sacco Messineo, M. (1982) 'Menippo ed Eleandro (il "riso" in Luciano e Leopardi)', in *Leopardi e il mondo antico: atti del V convegno internazionale di studi leopardini*, no editor. Florence: 529–39.

Saetta Cottone, R. (2005) *Aristofane e la poetica dell'ingiuria: per una introduzione alla λοιδορία comica*. Rome.

Safranski, R. (2002) *Nietzsche: a Philosophical Biography*, Eng. tr. S. Frisch. London.

Sakalis, D. T. (1989) Ἱπποκράτους Ἐπιστολαί. Ioannina.

Salem, J. (1996) *La légende de Démocrite*. Paris.

Sandbach, F. H. (1969) *Plutarch's Moralia, XV: Fragments*. London.

(1970) 'Menander's manipulation of language for dramatic purposes', in *Ménandre*, ed. E. G. Turner. Fondation Hardt Entretiens XVI. Geneva: 113–36.

(1990) *Menandri Reliquiae Selectae*, 2nd edn. Oxford.

Sandys, J. E. and Paley, F. A. (1910) *Demosthenes: Select Private Orations. Part II*, 4th edn. Cambridge.

Sangirardi, G. (1998) 'Luciano dalle "prosette satiriche" alle *Operette Morali*', in *Il riso leopardiano: comico, satira, parodia. Atti del IX convegno internazionale di studi leopardini*, ed. R. Garbuglia. Florence: 305–73.

Sardiello, R. (2000) *Giuliano Imperatore: Simposio – i Cesari*. Galatina.

Sarna, N. M. (1971) 'Isaac', *Encyclopaedia Judaica*, vol. IX. Jerusalem: 1–4.

Saroglou, V. (2002) 'Religion and sense of humor: an a priori incompatibility?', *Humor* 15: 191–214.

Sarrazin, B. (1994) 'Jésus n'a jamais ri. Histoire d'un lieu commun', *RecSR* 82: 217–22.

Sass, L. A. (1992) *Madness and Modernism*. New York.

Sauerländer, W. (2006) 'The fate of the face in medieval art', in *Set in Stone: the Face in Medieval Sculpture*, ed. C. T. Little. New Haven: 3–17.

Saunders, T. J. (1972) *Notes on the Laws of Plato. BICS* Supplement 28. London.

Saxl, F. (1970) *A Heritage of Images*. Harmondsworth.

Saxonhouse, A. W. (2006) *Free Speech and Democracy in Ancient Athens*. New York.

Schäfer, A. (1965) *Menanders Dyskolos: Untersuchungen zur dramatischen Technik*. Meisenheim.

Schama, S. (1999) *Rembrandt's Eyes*. London.

Schechner, R. (1994) 'Ritual and performance', in *Companion Encyclopedia of Anthropology*, ed. T. Ingold. London: 613–47.

Schefold, K. (1992) *Gods and Heroes in Late Archaic Greek Art*, Eng. tr. A. Griffiths. Cambridge.

Schildknecht, C. and Konersmann, R. (1998) 'Theatrum mundi', in *Historisches Wörterbuch der Philosophie*, eds. J. Ritter and K. Gründer, vol. x. Basle: 1051–4.

Schmidt, J. H. H. (1876–86) *Synonymik der griechischen Sprache* (4 vols.). Stuttgart. [Rpr. Hildesheim, 1969.]

Schmidt, K. L. and Cohn, J. F. (2001) 'Human facial expressions as adaptations: evolutionary questions in facial expression research', *Yearbook of Physical Anthropology* 44: 3–24.

Schmitt-Pantel, P. (1981) 'L'âne, l'adultère et la cité', in Le Goff and Schmitt (1981) 117–22.

Schmitz, G. (1980) '. . . quod rident homines, plorandum est. Der "Unwert" des Lachens in monastisch geprägten Vorstellungen der Spätantike und des frühen Mittelalters', in *Stadtverfassung, Verfassungsstaat, Pressepolitik*, eds. F. Quarthal and W. Setzler. Sigmaringen: 3–15.

Schönberger, O. (1968) *Philostratos: die Bilder*. Munich.

Schubert, P. (2000) *Noms d'agent et invective*. Göttingen.

Schwartz, G. (1985) *Rembrandt: His Life, His Paintings*. London.

Schwartz, J. (1951) *Lucien de Samosate: Philopseudès et De Morte Peregrini*. Paris.

Scodel, R. (2002) *Listening to Homer: Tradition, Narrative, and Audience*. Ann Arbor.

Scott, L. (2005) *Historical Commentary on Herodotus Book 6*. Leiden.

Scott, W. (1924) *Hermetica*, vol. I. Oxford.

(1926) *Hermetica*, vol. III. Oxford.

Screech, M. A. (1979) *Rabelais*. London.

(1980) *Ecstasy and the Praise of Folly*. London.

(1991) *The Essays of Michel de Montaigne*. London.

(1997) *Laughter at the Foot of the Cross*. London.

Screech, M. A. and Calder, R. (1970) 'Some renaissance attitudes to laughter', in *Humanism in France at the End of the Middle Ages & in the Early Renaissance*, ed. A. H. T. Levi. Manchester: 216–28.

Scribner, B. (1978) 'Reformation, carnival and the world turned upside-down', *Social History* 3: 303–29.

Scruton, R. (1983) *The Aesthetic Understanding*. London.

Seaford, R. (1984) *Euripides Cyclops*. Oxford.

(1994) *Reciprocity and Ritual*. Oxford.

(1996) *Euripides Bacchae*. Warminster.

Sedley, D. (1976) 'Epicurus and his professional rivals', in *Études sur l'Épicurisme antique*, eds. J. Bollack and A. Laks. Lille: 121–59.

Seeberg, A. (1995) 'From padded dancers to comedy', in *Stage Directions: Essays in Ancient Drama in Honour of E. W. Handley*, ed. A. Griffiths. London: 1–12.

Segal, C. (1961) 'The character and cults of Dionysus and the unity of the *Frogs*', *HSPh* 65: 207–42.

(1982) *Dionysiac Poetics and Euripides' Bacchae*. Princeton.

Segal, E. (2001) *The Death of Comedy*. Cambridge Mass.

Seidensticker, B. (1978) 'Comic elements in Euripides' *Bacchae*', *AJPh* 99: 303–20.

(1982) *Palintonos Harmonia: Studien zu komischen Elementen in der griechischen Tragödie*. Göttingen.

Shapiro, H. A. (1993) *Personifications in Greek Art*. Zurich.

Shelley, P. B. (1996) 'A discourse on the manners of the ancient Greeks relative to the subject of love' [publ. 1818], in *Shelley on Love: Selected Writings*, ed. R. Holmes, 2nd edn. London: 85–96.

Sheppard, A. D. R. (1980) *Studies on the 5th and 6th Essays of Proclus' Commentary on the Republic*. Göttingen.

Sherif, M. A. (1975) *Ghazali's Theory of Virtue*. Albany.

Sherman, D. (2006) 'Absurdity', in *A Companion to Phenomenology and Existentialism*, eds. H. L. Dreyfus and M. A. Wrathall. Oxford: 271–9.

Shorey, P. (1927) 'Homeric laughter', *CPh* 22: 222–3.

Sidgwick, H. (1901) *The Methods of Ethics*, 6th edn. London.

Sikes, E. E. (1940) 'The humour of Homer', *CR* 54: 121–7.

Silk, M. S. (2000) *Aristophanes and the Definition of Comedy*. Oxford.

Silk, M. S. and Stern, J. P. (1981) *Nietzsche on Tragedy*. Cambridge.

Silvas, A. M. (2005) *The Asketikon of St Basil the Great*. Oxford.

Simon, E. (1961) Review of Kenner (1960), *Gnomon* 33: 644–50.

(1997) 'Silenoi', *LIMC* VIII.1: 108–33 (with ills., VIII.2: 746–83).

Simpson, P. (1998) *A Philosophical Commentary on the Politics of Aristotle*. Chapel Hill.

Sittl, C. (1890) *Die Gebärden der Griechen und Römer*. Leipzig. [Rpr. Hildesheim, 1970.]

Skinner, Q. (1996) *Reason and Rhetoric in the Philosophy of Hobbes*. Cambridge.

(2002) 'Hobbes and the classical theory of laughter', in *Visions of Politics. Volume 3: Hobbes and Civil Science*. Cambridge: 142–76.

Skov, G. (1975) 'The priestess of Demeter and Kore and her role in the initiation of women at the festival of the Haloa at Eleusis', *Temenos* 11: 136–47.

Slane, K. W. and Dickie, M. W. (1993) 'A Knidian phallic vase from Corinth', *Hesperia* 62: 483–505.

Slater, N. W. (2005) 'Nothing to do with satyrs? *Alcestis* and the concept of prosatyric drama', in *Satyr Drama: Tragedy at Play*, ed. G. W. M. Harrison. Swansea: 83–101.

Slater, W. J. (1976) 'Symposium at sea', *HSPh* 80: 161–70.

(1990) 'Sympotic ethics in the *Odyssey*', in Murray (1990a) 213–20.

(1991) 'Introduction', in *Dining in a Classical Context*, ed. W. J. Slater. Ann Arbor: 1–5.

Slings, S. R. (1990) 'The I in personal archaic lyric', in *The Poet's I in Archaic Greek Lyric*, ed. S. R. Slings. Amsterdam: 1–30.

Sluiter, I. (2005) 'Communicating Cynicism: Diogenes' gangsta rap', in *Language and Learning: Philosophy of Language in the Hellenistic Age*, eds. D. Frede and B. Inwood. Cambridge: 139–63.

Smith, A. (1993) *Porphyrii Philosophi Fragmenta.* Stuttgart.

Smith, A. C. (1999) 'Eurymedon and the evolution of political personification in the early classical period', *JHS* 119: 128–41.

Smith, M. (1986) 'P Leid J 395 (*PGM* XIII) and its creation legend', in *Hellenica et Judaica: Hommage à Valentin Nikiprowetzky*, eds. A. Caquot *et al.* Leuven: 491–8.

Smith, W. D. (1990) *Hippocrates: Pseudepigraphic Writings.* Leiden.

Snell, B. (1960) *The Discovery of the Mind*, Eng. tr. T. Rosenmeyer. New York.

Snell, B. and Maehler, H. (1989) *Pindari Carmina cum Fragmentis: II, Fragmenta.* Leipzig.

Sommerstein, A. H. (1983) *The Comedies of Aristophanes. Vol. 4: Wasps.* Warminster.

(1989) *Aeschylus Eumenides.* Cambridge.

(1995) 'The language of Athenian women', in *Lo spettacolo delle voci*, eds. F. de Martino and A. H. Sommerstein. Bari: 61–85 (parte seconda).

(1996) *The Comedies of Aristophanes. Vol. 9: Frogs.* Warminster.

(2000) 'Parler du rire chez Aristophane', in Desclos (2000) 65–75.

(2002) *Greek Drama and Dramatists.* London.

(2004a) 'Comedy and the unspeakable', in *Law, Rhetoric and Comedy in Classical Athens*, ed. D. Cairns. London: 205–22. [German version, 'Die Komödie und das "Unsagbare"', in Ercolani (2002) 125–45.]

(2004b) 'Harassing the satirist: the alleged attempts to prosecute Aristophanes', in *Free Speech in Classical Antiquity*, eds. I. Sluiter and R. M. Rosen. Leiden: 145–74.

Sorabji, R. (2000) *Emotion and Peace of Mind: from Stoic Agitation to Christian Temptation.* Oxford.

Sourvinou-Inwood, C. (1986) 'Charon I', *LIMC* III.1: 210–25 (with ills., III.2: 168–74).

(2003) *Tragedy and Athenian Religion.* Lanham.

Soury, G. (1942) *La démonologie de Plutarque.* Paris.

Spatharas, D. (2006) 'Persuasive ΓΕΛΩΣ: public speaking and the use of laughter', *Mnemosyne* 59: 374–87.

Spina, L. (2001) *L'oratore scriteriato: per una storia letteraria e politica di Tersite.* Naples.

Sprague, R. K. (1994) 'Platonic jokes with philosophical points', in Jäkel *et al.* (1994–7) vol. 1, 53–8.

Sroufe, L. A. and Waters, E. (1976) 'The ontogenesis of smiling and laughter: a perspective on the organization of development in infancy', *Psychological Review* 83: 173–89.

Stadter, P. A. (1989) *A Commentary on Plutarch's Pericles.* Chapel Hill.

Stallbaum, G. (1825–6) *Eustathii Archiepiscopi Thessalonicensis Commentarii ad Homeri Odysseam* (2 vols.). Leipzig.

Stallworthy, J. (1986) *The Poems of Wilfred Owen.* New York.

Stanford, W. B. (1936) *Greek Metaphor.* Oxford.

(1958) *Aristophanes the Frogs.* London.

(1965) *The Odyssey of Homer*, 2nd edn, rpr. with addn. (2 vols.). London.

(1983) *Greek Tragedy and the Emotions*. London.

Stark, I. (1995) 'Who laughs at whom in Greek comedy<?>', in Jäkel *et al.* (1994–7) vol. II, 99–116.

(2004) *Die hämische Muse: Spott als soziale und mentale Kontrolle in der griechischen Komödie*. Munich.

Starkie, W. J. M. (1897) *The Wasps of Aristophanes*. London.

Steblin-Kamenskij, M. I. (1978–9) 'On the history of laughter', *Mediaeval Scandinavia* 11: 154–62.

Stehle, E. (1997) *Performance and Gender in Ancient Greece*. Princeton.

(2004) 'Choral prayer in Greek tragedy: euphemia or aischrologia?', in *Music and the Muses: the Culture of 'Mousikē' in the Classical Athenian City*, eds. P. Murray and P. Wilson. Oxford: 121–55.

Steidle, B. (1986) 'Das Lachen im alten Mönchtum', in *Beiträge zum alten Mönchtum und zur Benediktusregel*. Sigmaringen: 30–9. [Orig. publ. in *Benediktinische Monatschrift zur Pflege religiösen und geistigen Leben* 20 (1938) 271–80.]

Stein, M. (1992) *Definition und Schilderung in Theophrasts Charakteren*. Stuttgart.

Steiner, D. T. (2001) *Images in Mind: Statues in Archaic and Classical Greek Literature and Thought*. Princeton.

Steiner, P. M. (1995) 'Das Lachen als sozialer Kitt. Über die Theorie des Lachens und des Lächerlichen bei Platon', in Jäkel *et al.* (1994–7) vol. II, 65–78.

Steinmetz, P. (1960–2) *Theophrast Charaktere* (2 vols.). Munich.

Stella, M. (2000) 'Rire de la mort. Le philosophe, la cité, le savoir', in Desclos (2000) 459–67.

Stephens, S. A. and Winkler, J. J. (1995) *Ancient Greek Novels: the Fragments*. Berkeley.

Stevens, P. T. (1956) 'Euripides and the Athenians', *JHS* 76: 87–94.

(1976) *Colloquial Expressions in Euripides. Hermes Einzelschriften 38*. Wiesbaden.

(1988) 'Whose laughter does Pentheus fear? (EUR. *BA.* 842)', *CQ* 38: 246–7.

Stewart, A. (1990) *Greek Sculpture: an Exploration* (2 vols.). New Haven.

(1997) *Art, Desire, and the Body in Ancient Greece*. Cambridge.

Stewart, Z. (1958) 'Democritus and the Cynics', *HSPh* 63: 179–91.

(1994) 'Laughter and the Greek philosophers: a sketch', in Jäkel *et al.* (1994–7) vol. I, 29–38.

Stokes, M. (1997) *Plato Apology*. Warminster.

Storey, I. C. (1995) 'Philoxenos . . . of Doubtful Gender', *JHS* 115: 182–4.

(2003) *Eupolis Poet of Old Comedy*. Oxford.

Struck, P. T. (2004) *Birth of the Symbol: Ancient Readers at the Limits of their Texts*. Princeton.

Stuart, D. R. (1921) 'On Vergil *Eclogue* iv. 60–63', *CPh* 16: 209–30.

Stuart Jones, H. (1966) *Select Passages from Ancient Writers Illustrative of the History of Greek Sculpture*, 2nd edn, ed. A. N. Oikonomides. Chicago.

Suchomski, J. (1975) *'Delectatio' und 'Utilitas': ein Beitrag zum Verständnis mittelalterlicher komischer Literatur*. Bern.

Sudhaus, S. (1892–6) *Philodemi Volumina Rhetorica* (2 vols.). Leipzig.

Susemihl, F. and Hicks, R. D. (1894) *The Politics of Aristotle: Books I–V.* London.

Süss, W. (1920) 'Das Problem des Komischen im Altertum', *Neue Jahrbücher für das Klassische Altertum* 23: 28–45.

Suter, A. (2002) *The Narcissus and the Pomegranate: an Archaeology of the Homeric Hymn to Demeter.* Ann Arbor.

Swain, S. (1996) *Hellenism and Empire.* Oxford.

ed. (2007) *Seeing the Face, Seeing the Soul: Polemon's Physiognomy from Classical Antiquity to Medieval Islam.* Oxford.

Sypher, W. (1980) *Comedy.* Baltimore. [Includes, pp. 61–190, Eng. tr. of Bergson (1900) by C. Brereton and F. Rothwell, first publ. 1911.]

Taillardat, J. (1965) *Les images d'Aristophane.* Paris.

(1967) *Suétone ΠΕΡΙ ΒΛΑΣΦΗΜΙΩΝ, ΠΕΡΙ ΠΑΙΔΙΩΝ.* Paris.

Taplin, O. (1992) *Homeric Soundings.* Oxford.

(1993) *Comic Angels and Other Approaches to Greek Drama through Vase-Paintings.* Oxford.

Tarrant, D. (1927) 'The authorship of the *Hippias Major*', *CQ* 21: 82–7.

(1928) *The Hippias Major Attributed to Plato.* Cambridge.

Tarrant, H. A. S. (1994) 'The *Hippias Major* and Socratic theories of pleasure', in *The Socratic Movement*, ed. P. A. Vander Waerdt. Ithaca: 107–26.

Tave, S. M. (1960) *The Amiable Humorist: a Study in the Comic Theory and Criticism of the Eighteenth and Early Nineteenth Centuries.* Chicago.

Taylor, A. E. (1956) *Plato Philebus and Epinomis.* London.

Taylor, C. C. W. (1999) *The Atomists: Leucippus and Democritus.* Toronto.

(2006) *Aristotle Nicomachean Ethics Books II–IV.* Oxford.

Tecuşan, M. (1990) '*Logos sympotikos*: patterns of the irrational in philosophical drinking: Plato outside the *Symposium*', in Murray (1990a) 238–60.

Temkin, O. (1985) 'Hippocrates as the physician of Democritus', *Gesnerus* 42: 455–64.

Teodorsson, S.-T. (1989–96) *A Commentary on Plutarch's Table Talks* (3 vols.). Gothenburg.

Thalheim, T. (1913) *Lysiae Orationes*, 2nd edn. Leipzig.

Thalmann, W. G. (1988) 'Thersites: comedy, scapegoats, and heroic ideology in the *Iliad*', *TAPhA* 118: 1–28.

Thein, K. (2000) 'Entre ἄνοια et ἄγνοια. La nature humaine et la comédie dans les dialogues de Platon', in Desclos (2000) 169–80.

Theocharidis, G. C. (1940) *Beiträge zur Geschichte des byzantinischen Profantheaters im IV. und V. Jahrhundert.* Munich.

Thiercy, P. (2000) 'Le vocabulaire des chants et danses religieux dans le théâtre d'Aristophane', in *La lengua científica griega II*, ed. J. A. López Férez. Madrid: 47–60.

Thierfelder, A. (1968) *Philogelos der Lachfreund.* Munich.

Thomas, K. (1977) 'The place of laughter in Tudor and Stuart England', *TLS*, 21 Jan.: 77–81.

Tichy, E. (1983) *Onomatopoetische Verbalbildungen des Griechischen.* Vienna.

Timonen, A. (1995) '*Ridens res humanas*. Marcus Aurelius' derision for the concerns of men (the *Historia Augusta* and the *Meditations*)', in Jäkel *et al.* (1994–7) vol. II, 161–70.

Todd, R. (1990) *Cleomedis Caelestia.* Leipzig.

Todd, S. C. (1993) *The Shape of Athenian Law.* Oxford.

Toohey, P. (2004) *Melancholy, Love, and Time. Boundaries of the Self in Ancient Literature.* Ann Arbor.

Towne-Markus, E. (1997) *Masterpieces of the J. Paul Getty Museum: Antiquities.* London.

Travlos, J. (1971) *Pictorial Dictionary of Ancient Athens.* London.

Trédé, M. and Hoffmann, P. eds. (1998) *Le rire des anciens.* Paris.

Trendall, A. D. (1967) *Phlyax Vases*, 2nd edn. *BICS* Supplement 19. London.

Trevett, J. (2000) 'Was there a decree of Syrakosios?', *CQ* 50: 598–600.

Trumble, A. (2004) *A Brief History of the Smile.* New York.

Turk, H. (1995) 'Kulturgeschichtliche und anthropologische Bedingungen des Lachens', in *Differente Lachkulturen? Fremde Komik und ihre Übersetzung*, eds. T. Unger *et al.* Tübingen: 299–317.

Tüselmann, O. (1900) *Die Paraphrase des Euteknios zu Oppians Kynegetika.* Berlin.

Untersteiner, M. (1966) *Platone Repubblica Libro X*, 3rd edn. Naples.

Usener, H. (1887) *Epicurea.* Leipzig.

   (1913) 'Klagen und Lachen', *Kleine Schriften* IV. Leipzig: 469–70.

Usher, S. (1993) *Demosthenes: On the Crown.* Warminster.

   (1999) *Greek Oratory: Tradition and Originality.* Oxford.

Ussher, R. G. (1973) *Aristophanes Ecclesiazusae.* Oxford.

   (1979) *Aristophanes. Greece & Rome* New Surveys 13. Oxford.

   (1993) *The Characters of Theophrastus*, rev. edn. London.

Van Daele, H. tr. (1930) *Aristophane, Tome V*, ed. V. Coulon. Paris.

Van den Hout, M. P. J. (1988) *M. Cornelii Frontonis Epistulae.* Leipzig.

   (1999) *A Commentary on the Letters of M. Cornelius Fronto.* Leiden.

Van der Eijk, P. J. (2005) *Medicine and Philosophy in Classical Antiquity.* Cambridge.

Van der Horst, P. W. (1987) *Chaeremon. Egyptian Priest and Stoic Philosopher*, 2nd edn. Leiden.

   (1990) 'Is wittiness unchristian?', in *Studies on the Hellenistic Background of the New Testament*, eds. P. W. van der Horst and G. Mussies. Utrecht: 223–37. [Orig. publ. in *Miscellanea Neotestamentica II*, eds. T. Baarda *et al.* (Leiden 1978) 163–77.]

Van der Valk, M. (1971–87) *Eustathii Archiepiscopi Thessalonicensis Commentarii ad Homeri Iliadem Pertinentes* (4 vols.). Leiden.

Van Gelder, G. (1988) *The Bad and the Ugly. Attitudes towards Invective Poetry (hija) in Classical Arabic Tradition.* Leiden.

Van Groningen, B. A. (1960) *Pindare au banquet: les fragments des scolies édités avec un commentaire critique et explicatif.* Leiden.

   (1966) *Theognis.* Amsterdam.

Van Hooff, J. A. (1972) 'A comparative approach to the phylogeny of laughter and smiling', in *Non-verbal Communication*, ed. R. A. Hinde. Cambridge: 209–41.

(1973) 'A structural analysis of the social behaviour of a semi-captive group of chimpanzees', in *Social Communication and Movement*, eds. M. von Cranach and I. Vine. London: 75–162.

(1981) 'Facial expressions', in *The Oxford Companion to Animal Behaviour*, ed. D. McFarland. Oxford: 165–76.

Van Leeuwen, J. (1904) *Aristophanes Plutus*. Leiden.

Van Thiel, H. (1991) *Homeri Odyssea*. Hildesheim.

Van Wees, H. (2000) 'Megara's mafiosi: timocracy and violence in Theognis', in *Alternatives to Athens*, eds. R. Brock and S. Hodkinson. Oxford: 52–67.

Vasiliou, I. (1999) 'Conditional irony in the Socratic dialogues', *CQ* 49: 457–62.

(2002) 'Socrates' reverse irony', *CQ* 52: 220–30.

Velardi, R. (1989) *Enthousiasmos. Possessione rituale e teoria della communicazione poetica in Platone*. Rome.

Verberckmoes, J. (1999) *Laughter, Jestbooks and Society in the Spanish Netherlands*. London.

(1997) 'The comic and the Counter-Reformation in the Spanish Netherlands', in Bremmer and Roodenburg (1997) 76–89.

Verdenius, W. J. (1972) 'Notes on the proem of Hesiod's *Theogony*', *Mnemosyne* 25: 225–60.

Vermes, G. (2005) *The Passion*. Harmondsworth.

Vermeule, C. C. (1981) *Greek and Roman Sculpture in America*. Berkeley.

Vermeule, E. (1979) *Aspects of Death in Early Greek Art and Poetry*. Berkeley.

Vernant, J.-P. (1991) *Mortals and Immortals: Collected Essays*, Eng. tr. ed. F. I. Zeitlin. Princeton.

Versnel, H. S. (1970) *Triumphus: an Enquiry into the Origin, Development and Meaning of the Roman Triumph*. Leiden.

(1993) *Transition and Reversal in Myth and Ritual*. Leiden.

(1998) *Ter Unus: Isis, Dionysos, Hermes*. Leiden.

Vicaire, P. (1960) *Platon critique littéraire*. Paris.

Vierneisel, K. and Kaeser, B. eds. (1992) *Kunst der Schale: Kultur des Trinkens*, 2nd edn. Munich.

Viljamaa, T. (1994) 'Quintilian's theory of wit', in Jäkel *et al.* (1994–7) vol. i, 85–93.

Vine, I. (1973) 'The role of facial-visual signalling in early social development', in *Social Communication and Movement*, eds. M. von Cranach and I. Vine. London: 195–298.

Vlastos, G. (1991) *Socrates: Ironist and Moral Philosopher*. Cambridge.

Von der Mühll, P. (1962) *Homeri Odyssea*, 3rd edn. Stuttgart.

Von Graevenitz, A. (1997) 'Das Lachverbot in der bildenden Kunst', in Jäkel *et al.* (1994–7) vol. iii, 141–53.

Von Harnack, A. (1916) *Porphyrius: Gegen die Christen*. Berlin.

Von Möllendorff, P. (1995) *Grundlagen einer Ästhetik der Alten Komödie. Untersuchungen zu Aristophanes und Michail Bachtin*. Tübingen.

(2002) *Aristophanes*. Hildesheim.

Von Reibnitz, B. (1992) *Ein Kommentar zu Friedrich Nietzsche, 'Die Geburt der Tragödie aus dem Geiste der Musik' (Kap. 1–12)*. Stuttgart.

Wace, A. J. B. (1903–4) 'Grotesques and the evil eye', *ABSA* 10: 103–14.

Wagner, C. (1981) 'Geloion bei Sophokles und Platon (zu Soph., *Aias* 132f.)', *GB* 10: 77–81.

Wallace, R. (1994) 'The Athenian laws on slander', in *Symposion 1993: Vorträge zur griechischen und hellenistischen Rechtsgeschichte*, ed. G. Thür. Cologne: 109–24.

Wallochny, B. (1992) *Streitszenen in der griechischen und römischen Komödie*. Tübingen.

Walter, J. (1893) *Die Geschichte der Ästhetik im Altertum*. Leipzig. [Rpr. Hildesheim, 1967.]

Waltz, P. (1960) *Anthologie grecque, première partie, anthologie Palatine*, vol. IV, with transl. by A. Desrousseaux *et al.*, 2nd edn. Paris.

Wankel, H. (1976) *Demosthenes: Rede für Ktesiphon über den Kranz* (2 vols.). Heidelberg.

Wannagat, D. (2007) *Archaisches Lachen*. Berlin.

Wardman, A. E. (1967) 'Description of personal appearance in Plutarch and Suetonius: the use of statues as evidence', *CQ* 17: 414–20.

Warren, J. (2002) *Epicurus and Democritean Ethics*. Cambridge.

Webb, R. (2002) 'Female performers in late antiquity', in *Greek and Roman Actors*, eds. P. E. Easterling and E. Hall. Cambridge: 282–303.

Webster, T. B. L. (1969) *Monuments Illustrating Old and Middle Comedy*, 2nd edn. *BICS* Supplement 23. London.

(1970) *Studies in Later Greek Comedy*, 2nd edn. Manchester.

(1978) *Monuments Illustrating Old and Middle Comedy*, 3rd edn rev. J. R. Green. *BICS* Supplement 39. London.

(1995) *Monuments Illustrating New Comedy*, 3rd edn rev. J. R. Green and A. Seeberg (2 vols.). *BICS* Supplement 50. London.

Wehrli, F. (1967) *Die Schule des Aristoteles: Aristoxenos*, 2nd edn. Basle.

(1969) *Die Schule des Aristoteles: Hieronymos von Rhodos*, 2nd edn. Basle.

(1978) *Die Schule des Aristoteles: Sotion*. Basle.

Weinbrot, H. D. (2005) *Menippean Satire Reconsidered: From Antiquity to the Eighteenth Century*. Baltimore.

Welsford, E. (1935) *The Fool: his Social and Literary History*. London.

West, M. L. (1966) *Hesiod Theogony*. Oxford.

(1974) *Studies in Greek Elegy and Iambus*. Berlin.

(1978) *Hesiod Works and Days*. Oxford.

(1982) *Greek Metre*. Oxford.

(1983) *The Orphic Poems*. Oxford.

(1984) *Carmina Anacreontea*. Leipzig.

(1997) *The East Face of Helicon: West Asiatic Elements in Greek Poetry and Myth*. Oxford.

(2001) 'The fragmentary Homeric hymn to Dionysus', *ZPE* 134: 1–11.

(2003) *Greek Epic Fragments*. Cambridge Mass.

Westermann, A. (1843) Μυθογράφοι: *Scriptores Poeticae Historiae Graeci*. Brunswick.

Whitbread, L. G. (1971) *Fulgentius the Mythographer*. Ohio.

Whitehead, D. (2000) *Hypereides: the Forensic Speeches*. Oxford.

Whitmarsh, T. (2001) *Greek Literature and the Roman Empire: the Politics of Imitation*. Oxford.

(2004) 'Lucian', in *Narrators, Narratees, and Narratives in Ancient Greek Literature*, eds. I. de Jong *et al*. Leiden: 465–76.

Wiemken, H. (1972) *Der griechische Mimus*. Bremen.

Wild, B. *et al*. (2003) 'Neural correlates of laughter and humour', *Brain* 126: 2121–38.

Wiles, D. (1991) *The Masks of Menander: Sign and Meaning in Greek and Roman Performance*. Cambridge.

Wilkins, J. (2000) *The Boastful Chef: the Discourse of Food in Ancient Greek Comedy*. Oxford.

Willi, A. (2002) 'The language of Greek comedy: introduction and bibliographical sketch', in *The Language of Greek Comedy*, ed. A. Willi. Oxford: 1–32.

(2003) *The Languages of Aristophanes: Aspects of Linguistic Variation in Classical Attic Greek*. Oxford.

Williams, B. (1993) *Shame and Necessity*. Berkeley.

Wilson, H. (2003) *Wine and Words in Classical Antiquity and the Middle Ages*. London.

Wilson, P. (2000) *The Athenian Institution of the Khoregia*. Cambridge.

Wimmer, F. (1866) *Theophrasti Eresii Opera*. Paris.

Wind, E. (1983) 'The Christian Democritus', in *The Eloquence of Symbols: Studies in Humanist Art*. Oxford: 83–5. [Orig. publ. in *JWI* 1 (1937) 180–2.]

(1968) *Pagan Mysteries in the Renaissance*, rev. edn. London.

Winkler, J. J. (1990) *The Constraints of Desire: the Anthropology of Sex and Gender in Ancient Greece*. New York.

Winkler, M. (1998) 'Komik, das Komische', in *Historisches Wörterbuch der Rhetorik*, ed. G. Ueding, vol. iv. Tübingen: 1166–76.

Winn, P. (2001) 'Laughter', in *Dictionary of Biological Psychology*, ed. P. Winn. London: 424–5.

Winter, N. A. (1993) *Greek Architectural Terracottas*. Oxford.

Wohl, V. (2004) 'Dirty dancing: Xenophon's *Symposium*', in *Music and the Muses: the Culture of 'Mousikē' in the Classical Athenian City*, eds. P. Murray and P. Wilson. Oxford: 337–63.

Wolfsdorf, D. (2007) 'The irony of Socrates', *Journal of Aesthetics and Art Criticism* 65: 175–87.

Woodbury, L. (1944) '*Quomodo risu ridiculoque Graeci usi sint*', *HSPh* 55: 114–17. [Summary of Harvard dissertation.]

Woodford, S. (1992) 'Kerkopes', *LIMC* vi.1: 32–5 (with ills., vi.2: 16–18).

Woodruff, P. (1982) *Plato Hippias Major*. Oxford.

Worman, N. (2002) *The Cast of Character: Style in Greek Literature*. Austin.

(2004) 'Insult and oral excess in the disputes between Aeschines and Demosthenes', *AJPh* 125: 1–25.

(2008) *Abusive Mouths in Classical Athens*. Cambridge.

Wünsch, R. (1898) *Ioannis Lydi liber de mensibus*. Leipzig.

Yalouris, N. (1986) 'Das archaische "Lächeln" und die Geleontes', *AK* 29: 3–5.

Young, D. (1961) *Theognis*. Leipzig.

Yunis, H. (2001) *Demosthenes On the Crown*. Cambridge.

Zagagi, N. (1994) *The Comedy of Menander*. London.

Zajonz, S. (2002) *Isokrates' Enkomion auf Helena*. Göttingen.

Zanetto, G. (1996) *Inni Omerici*. Milan.

Zanfino, A. (2001) *Sul comico e sulla commedia dei Greci*. Naples.

Zanker, P. (1995) *The Mask of Socrates: the Image of the Intellectual in Antiquity*, Eng. tr. A. Shapiro. Berkeley.

Zeitlin, F. (1982) 'Cultic models of the female: rites of Dionysus and Demeter', *Arethusa* 15: 129–57.

Zervou, A. K. (1990) *Ironie et Parodie: le comique chez Homère*. Athens.

Ziegler, K. (1912) 'Gorgo 1', *RE* VII.2: 1630–55.

Zijderveld, A. C. (1983) 'The sociology and humour of laughter', *Current Sociology* 31: 1–103.

(1996) 'A sociological theory of humor and laughter', in *Semiotik, Rhetorik und Soziologie des Lachens*, eds. L. Fietz *et al.* Tübingen: 37–45.

Zimmermann, K. Z. (1997) 'Thersites', *LIMC* VIII.1: 1207–9.

Zuntz, G. (1960) 'Theocritus 1.95 f.', *CQ* 10: 37–40.

Index of selected authors and works

(Abbreviations of authors and titles generally follow the *Oxford Classical Dictionary*; those for works are indicated below only where uncertainty might arise. A few authors appear also, for biographical points, in the *General index*.)

GREEK TEXTS

Achilles Tatius (Ach. Tat.), *Leucippe and Clitophon* 521 n.6, 532

Adamantius, *Physiognomonica* 9 n.24, 526 n.27

adespota elegiaca *IEG* (adesp. el.) 114–17

adespota lyrica *PMG* (adesp. lyr.) 106 n.15, 118

adespota tragica *TrGF* (adesp. trag.) 15 n.36

Aelian (Ael.)
De natura animalium 2
Varia Historia 270, 274, 303 n.97, 351
fragments 358 n.60

Aelius Aristides (Ael. Arist.) 201

Aeschines (Aeschin.)
Against Timarchus (1) 43, 223, 236
On the Embassy (2) 27

Aeschines (Socraticus) 297 n.81

pseudo-Aeschines, *Socratic Epistles* 55 n.8, 278 n.32

Aeschylus (Aesch.)
Agamemnon 57 n.16, 124 n.60
Choephori 39 n.101, 39 n.102, 90 n.95
Eumenides 56 n.10, 137 n.88, 524
fragments 18 n.40

pseudo-Aeschylus (ps.-Aesch.), *Prometheus Vinctus* 15 n.36

Aesop, *Fables* 3

Agatharchides (Agatharch.), *De mari Erythraeo* 168 n.34

Alcaeus (Alc.) 79 n.67, 112

Alcaeus comicus (Alcaeus com.) (*PCG*) 85 n.83

Alcinous (Alcin.), *Didascalicus* 302 n.95

Alciphron (Alciph.), *Epistles* 173

Alexander Aetolus (Alex. Aet.) 6 n.15, 168, 270

pseudo-Alexander of Aphrodisias (ps.-Alex. Aphr.), *Problemata* 54 n.5

Alexis (*PCG*) 148 n.110, 274 n.24, 324 n.162, 375 n.100

Ammianus (*Anth. Pal.*) 124 n.61

(pseudo-)Ammonius, *De adfinium vocabulorum differentia* 18 n.41

Amphis (*PCG*) 21, 277 n.29

Anacreon (Anac.) 408 n.41

Anaximenes (Anaxim.), *see Rhetorica ad Alexandrum*

Anonymus medicus (Anon. med.)
De morbis acutis 18 n.40
De natura hominis 10 n.24
Physiognomonica 524 n.19

Anthologia Palatina (*Anth. Pal.*), anonymous epigrams from 335–7, 355 n.51, 364

pseudo-Apollodorus (ps.-Apollod.), *Bibliotheca* 174, 186

Apollonius Rhodius (Ap. Rhod.), *Argonautica* 102 n.6, 124 n.61, 184–6

Archilochus (Archil.) 29, 31, 163

Aretaeus, *De causis acutorum morborum* 160 n.12

Argonautica Orphica 54 n.5

Aristaenetus, *Epistles* 526

Ariston of Chios 197 n.121, 377 n.108

Aristophanes (Ar.)
Acharnians 182, 198, 207–8, 249, 252
Babylonians 248–9
Birds 22, 157 n.4
Clouds 22, 153, 231, 245, 247, 254, 257, 295
Ecclesiazusae 253
Frogs 32 n.82, 211–14, 230, 314 n.138, 399 n.25
Knights 24 n.56, 232–3, 256–62
Lysistrata 194, 253, 541
Peace 30, 525

LATIN TEXTS

Index of selected Greek terms

(Standard terms, including those which appear transliterated in the *General index*, are not included here except where special points of usage arise. Unless otherwise indicated, individual entries implicitly subsume related parts of speech.)

ἁβρός 122 n.54, 523 n.17
ἀγέλαστος 18 n.40, 19, 38 n.100, 39 n.102, 80 n.70
  see also General index, s.v. agelastos
αἰσχροεπεῖν 218 n.4
αἰσχρός 217 n.3
ἀκόλαστος 211, 394 n.13, 491, 502, 507
ἀναβράζεσθαι 514 n.104, 516 n.108
ἀνακαγχάζειν 286, 340, 362, 429, 491 n.52, 504, 509 n.92, 523, 523 n.17
ἀνασυρμός 165
ἀνταποδιδόναι 195 n.116
ἀντιγελᾶν 6 n.15, 476 n.16
ἁπαλός 87 n.87, 122 n.54, 523 n.17
ἀπασκαρίζειν 35 n.91
ἀποπνίγεσθαι 442 n.24
ἀπόρρητος 220, 227 n.28
ἄρρητος 175, 220, 227 n.28
ἄσβεστος, *see General index s.v.* laughter, 'unquenchable'
ἀσέλγεια 33 n.85, 394 n.13, 417 n.56, 493 n.56
ἀστεῖος 484 n.35

βασκαίνειν 394 n.13, 396
βδελυρία 240 n.60, 286
βλασφημεῖν 24, 197, 227, 241 n.63, 394 n.13, 472 n.2, 475 n.11, 478
βλοσυρός 55 n.8, 56 n.10, 490, 540
βρασμός 9 n.23, 514 n.104
βρυλλιχισταί 46 n.122, 190

γάνυμαι 14 n.33
γελᾶν 13 n.33, 137 n.86, 520–3
γελανής 91 n.95
γελασῖνος 351 n.39, 529

δ(ε)ικηλίκται (δεικηλισταί) 46 n.122, 189

δεννάζειν 21 n.51
διαγελᾶν 15 n.38, 134, 474 n.10
διαμυλλαίνειν 521 n.5
(δια/κατα)μωκᾶσθαι 274 n.26, 320 n.156, 488 n.43, 510, 510 n.93, 523 n.14
(δια/κατα)σιλλαίνειν 269 n.13, 526 n.29, 547

ἐγγελᾶν 138 n.89
ἐγκαγχάζειν 514–15 n.104
(ἐγ)κατιλλώπτειν 526 n.29, 534 n.15
ἐκγελᾶν 15 n.36, 479 n.25, 522
ἐκκαγχάζειν 145, 314
ἐκμυκτηρίζειν 475 n.11, 475 n.13
ἐκπομπεύειν 505 n.85
ἐμμειδιᾶν 2 n.5
ἐμμελής 47 n.125, 308, 310 n.121, 489 n.47
ἐξορχεῖσθαι 35 n.91
ἐπεγγελᾶν 27, 30, 41 n.108, 266, 305 n.104
ἐπιγελᾶν 15 n.38
ἐπιστοβεῖν 185 n.93
ἐρεσχηλεῖν 289 n.59
ἐψιάομαι 28 n.68

ἡδύγελως 68 n.41

ἱλαρός 152 n.115, 515 n.106, 516 n.108

κα(γ)χάζειν 25 n.60, 57 n.15, 113 n.31, 246, 490 n.48, 547 n.62
καγχαλάω 2 n.5, 57, 57 n.15
καθυβρίζειν 28
κατασοβαρεύεσθαι 375
κερτομεῖν 29, 72, 88, 185
κιχλίζειν 23 n.53, 113 n.31, 174 n.56, 179 n.74, 489 n.46, 490 n.48, 491 n.52
κλαυσίγελως 283 n.41
κλώζειν 35 n.89

General index

Authors are normally included here only where (pseudo-)biographical issues independent of their works are involved. Consult the separate *Index of selected authors and works.*

77030701R00349

Made in the USA
Middletown, DE
16 June 2018